Distribution of Export Markets for U.S. Firms (in billions of $)

Source: *Survey of Current Business*, 1993. Numbers are rounded to the nearest billion.

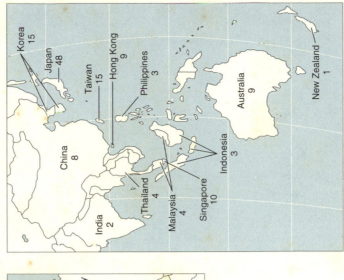

Korea 15
Japan 48
Taiwan 15
Hong Kong 9
Philippines 3
New Zealand 1
Australia 9
China 8
Indonesia 3
Thailand 4
Malaysia 4
Singapore 10
India 2

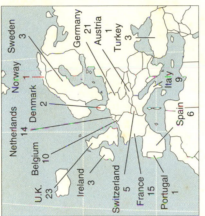

Sweden 3
Germany 21
Austria 1
Turkey 3
Norway 1
Italy 9
Netherlands 14
Denmark 2
Spain 6
U.K. 23
Belgium 10
Ireland 3
Switzerland 5
France 15
Portugal 1

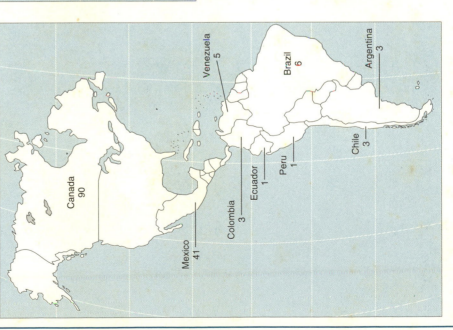

Venezuela 5
Brazil 6
Argentina 3
Canada 90
Chile 3
Colombia 3
Ecuador 1
Peru 1
Mexico 41

FOURTH EDITION

INTERNATIONAL FINANCIAL MANAGEMENT

FOURTH EDITION

INTERNATIONAL FINANCIAL MANAGEMENT

JEFF MADURA

Florida Atlantic University

WEST PUBLISHING COMPANY
ST. PAUL   NEW YORK   LOS ANGELES   SAN FRANCISCO

WEST'S COMMITMENT TO THE ENVIRONMENT

In 1906, West Publishing Company began recycling materials left over from the production of books. This began a tradition of efficient and responsible use of resources. Today, up to 95 percent of our legal books and 70 percent of our college and school texts are printed on recycled, acid-free stock. West also recycles nearly 22 million pounds of scrap paper annually—the equivalent of 181,717 trees. Since the 1960s, West has devised ways to capture and recycle waste inks, solvents, oils, and vapors created in the writing process. We also recycle plastics of all kinds, wood, glass, corrugated cardboard, and batteries, and have eliminated the use of Styrofoam book packaging. We at West are proud of the longevity and the scope of our commitment to the environment.

Production, Prepress, Printing and Binding by West Publishing Company.

 TEXT IS PRINTED ON 10% POST CONSUMER RECYCLED PAPER  PRINTED WITH SOY INK™

British Library Cataloguing-in-Publication Data. A catalogue record for this book is available from the British Library.

COPYRIGHT © 1986, 1989, 1992

COPYRIGHT © 1995

By WEST PUBLISHING COMPANY
By WEST PUBLISHING COMPANY
610 Opperman Drive
P.O. Box 64526
St. Paul, MN 55164–0526

Library of Congress Cataloging-in-Publication Data

Madura, Jeff.
   International financial management / Jeff Madura.—4th ed.
      p. cm.
   Includes index.
   ISBN 0–314–04161–3
   1. International finance.   2. Foreign exchange.   3. Asset
-liability management.   4. Banks and banking, International.
5. International business enterprises—Finance.   I. Title.
HG3881.M2765 1995
658.15′99—dc20   94–17237
                                                                        CIP

PRODUCTION CREDITS

Artwork David J. Farr, ImageSmythe, Inc. and Publication Services
Composition Carlisle Communications, Ltd.
Copyediting Beth Bulger
Cover Design Three Fish Design
Cover Photo Hong Kong, Central © Westlight
Text Design John Edeen

ABOUT THE AUTHOR

Jeff Madura is presently the Sun Bank Professor of Finance at Florida Atlantic University. He has written several textbooks, including *Financial Markets and Institutions*. His research on international finance has been published in numerous journals, including *Journal of Financial and Quantitative Analysis, Journal of Money, Credit and Banking, Journal of Banking and Finance, Journal of International Money and Finance, Applied Financial Economics, Journal of Financial Research, Journal of Multinational Financial Management,* and *Global Finance Journal.* He has received awards for excellence in teaching and research, and has served as a consultant for international banks, securities firms, and other multinational corporations.

To My Parents

CONTENTS IN BRIEF

CONTENTS

CHAPTER 8

RELATIONSHIPS BETWEEN INFLATION, INTEREST RATES, AND EXCHANGE RATES 205

PART 4

SHORT-TERM ASSET AND LIABILITY MANAGEMENT   371

CHAPTER 13

FINANCING INTERNATIONAL TRADE   373

PREFACE

The globalization of business is well documented in financial reports of large and small corporations. This trend has been motivated by the reduction in cross-border barriers, as has recently occurred in Eastern Europe, in some Latin American countries, and in the Pacific Basin. As markets become more internationally integrated, foreign markets will have more influence on corporate performance. Therefore, an understanding of international financial management is becoming even more critical to a company's success.

INTENDED MARKET

This text presumes an understanding of basic corporate finance. It is suitable for both undergraduate and master's level courses in international financial management. Some master's courses may attempt to maximize student comprehension by assigning the more difficult questions and problems, as well as the case problems and projects in each chapter.

ORGANIZATION OF THE TEXT

This text is organized first to provide a background on the international environment and then to focus on the managerial aspects from a corporate perspective. Part 1 (Chapters 1 to 5) introduces the major markets that serve international business. Part 2 (Chapters 6 to 8) describes relationships between exchange rates and economic variables, and explains the forces that influence these relationships. Part 3 (Chapters 9 to 12) begins the managerial perspective, with a focus on the measurement and management of exchange rate risk. Part 4 (Chapters 13 to 15) concentrates on the corporate management of short-term assets and liabilities. Part 5 (Chapters 16 to 21) describes the management of long-term assets and liabilities. Part 6 (Chapters 22 and 23) describes international financial management from a banker's perspective.

Each chapter is self-contained, so that professors can use classroom time to focus on the more comprehensive concepts and rely on the text to cover the other concepts. Chapters can be rearranged without a loss in continuity. Regardless of the sequence of chapters desired, it is highly recommended that the Wall Street Journal Case be assigned in each chapter, along with selected Questions.

APPROACH OF THE TEXT _____

The approach of the text is to reinforce the key concepts in the following ways:

1. OPENING DIAGRAM: A diagram is provided at the beginning of each part to illustrate in general terms how the key concepts to be covered in that part are related. This offers some intuition about the organization of chapters in that part.
2. OBJECTIVES: The key concepts are identified within a bulleted list of the objectives at the beginning of the chapter.
3. EMPHASIS: The key concepts are thoroughly described in the chapter.
4. "IN PRACTICE" BOXES: The "In Practice" boxes within chapters offer additional insight on these concepts, as they explain how various techniques are used by practitioners.
5. "APPLIED RESEARCH" BOXES: The "Applied Research" boxes within chapters summarize recent research findings on the key concepts and theories presented.
6. SUMMARY: The key concepts are summarized at the end of the chapter in a bulleted list that corresponds to the list of objectives at the beginning of the chapter.
7. SELF-TEST: A "Self-Test" at the end of each chapter challenges students on the key concepts. The answers to these questions are provided in the back of the text.
8. END OF CHAPTER QUESTIONS AND PROBLEMS: Many of the Questions and Problems at the end of each chapter test the students knowledge of the key concepts.
9. WALL STREET JOURNAL (WSJ) CASE: The "WSJ Case" at the end of each chapter provides a Wall Street Journal article that illustrates how the chapter's key concepts apply to real world situations. Questions at the end of the WSJ Case test the students understanding of how the key concepts are used in practice.
10. CASE PROBLEM: The Case Problem at the end of each chapter integrates the key concepts within each chapter. Some of these problems involve the use of a computer spreadsheet, such as Lotus 1-2-3.
11. PROJECTS: At the end of each chapter, projects are recommended for students who wish to more thoroughly understand one or more of the key concepts. A data bank provided in the back of the text can be used for some of the projects.
12. INTEGRATIVE PROBLEM: The Integrative Problem at the end of each part integrates the key concepts across chapters within that part.

CHANGES IN THIS EDITION _____

- All chapters have been updated to incorporate recent trends and events.
- The chapter titled "Government Influence on Exchange Rates" (Chapter 6) includes a section on the recent Exchange Rate Mechanism (ERM) crisis in Europe.
- Where appropriate, the effects of the North American Free Trade Agreement (NAFTA) and other policies promoting free trade are discussed.
- The chapter titled "Financing International Trade" (Chapter 13) has incorporated a discussion of the latest trade financing techniques.
- The chapter titled "Multinational Capital Budgeting (Chapter 17) has been substantially revised to demonstrate how international conditions can influence the capital budgeting process.
- The chapter titled "Multinational Cost of Capital and Capital Structure" (Chapter 18) has been substantially revised, to demonstrate how international conditions affect the cost of capital and capital structure. The link between this chapter and multinational capital budgeting is emphasized.
- The chapter titled "Country Risk Analysis" (Chapter 19) has been revised to emphasize the relationships between country risk, the cost of capital, and multinational capital budgeting.
- A "Wall Street Journal Case" has been added at the end of each chapter, which provides a reprinted article from *The Wall Street Journal* that is related to the chapter. The article is followed by questions that test the student's ability to apply concepts in the chapter.
- An "Integrative Problem" has been added at the end of each part of the text. This problem is designed to integrate the key concepts throughout the various chapters within that part.

SUPPLEMENTS FOR THE PROFESSOR _____

The following supplements are available for the professor:

1. An Instructor's Manual, which contains the chapter theme, topics to stimulate class discussion, and answers to end of chapter Questions, *WSJ* Case Problems, and Integrative Problems.
2. A computer diskette (contained within the Instructor's Manual) of the data bank that is provided in the back of the text.
3. A Test Bank.
4. A computerized Test Bank called "WesTest," which is a microcomputer test generation program for IBM PCs and compatibles, and the MacIntosh family of computers.
5. Transparency masters that reflect many of the exhibits illustrated in the text.
6. Acetate transparencies that reflect some of the key exhibits in the text (available to qualified adoptors).
7. A video cassette on one of two films (available to qualified adoptors):
- "Anatomy of a Corporate Takeover"
- "How Wall Street Works"

ACKNOWLEDGMENTS _____

Several people have contributed to the textbook. First, the motivation to write the textbook was primarily due to encouragement by professors Robert L. Conn (Miami University of Ohio), E. Joe Nosari and William Schrode (Florida State University), Anthony E. Scaperlanda (Northern Illinois University), and Richard A. Zuber (University of North Carolina at Charlotte).

Many of the revisions and expanded sections contained in this edition are due to comments and suggestions of students who used previous editions. In addition, several professors reviewed various drafts of the text and had a major influence on the contents and organization of the text. They are acknowledged in alphabetical order:

Raj Aggarwal
John Carroll University

Alan Alford
Northeastern University

H. David Arnold
Auburn University

Robert Aubey
University of Wisconsin

James C. Baker
Kent State University

Gurudutt Baliga
University of Delaware

Bharat B. Bhalla
Fairfield University

Rita Biswas
State University of New York
at Albany

Sarah Bryant
George Washington University

Francisco Carrada-Bravo
American Graduate School
of International Management

Andreas C. Christofi
Penn State University–Harrisburg

Alan Cook
Baylor University

W. P. Culbertson
Louisiana State University

Andrea L. DeMarkey
Villanova University

Robert Driscill
Ohio State University

Paul Fenton
Bishop's University

Stuart Fletcher
Appalachian State University

Robert D. Foster
American Graduate School
of International Management

Deborah W. Gregory
University of Georgia

Julian E. Gaspar
Texas A & M University

Nicholas Gressis
Wright State University

Indra Guertler
Babson College

Ann M. Hackert
Idaho State University

John M. Harris, Jr.
Clemson University

Ghassem Homaifar
Middle Tennessee State University

Nathaniel Jackendoff
Temple University

Kurt R. Jesswein
Laredo State University

Manuel L. Jose
University of Akron

Rauv Kalra
Moorhead State University

Ho-Sang Kang
University of Texas at Dallas

Coleman S. Kendall
University of Illinois–Chicago

Dara Khambata
American University

Suresh Krishman
Pennsylvania State University

Boyden E. Lee
New Mexico State University

Carl Luft
DePaul University

K. Christopher Ma
Texas Tech University

Wendell McCulloch, Jr.
California State University—
Long Beach

Carl McGowan
University of Michigan at Flint

Edward Omberg
San Diego State University

Ali M. Parhizgari
Florida International University

Anne Perry
American University

Frances A. Quinn
Merrimack College

S. Ghon Rhee
University of Rhode Island

Ashok Robin
Rochester Institute of Technology

Jacobus T. Severiens
Kent State University

Peter Sharp
California State University—
Sacramento

Dilip K. Shome
Virginia Tech University

Joseph Singer
University of Missouri—
Kansas City

Naim Sipra
University of Colorado at Denver

Jacky So
Southern Illinois University
at Edwardsville

Luc Soenen
California Polytechnic State University—
San Luis Obisbo

Ahmad Sorhabian
California State Polytechnic
University—Pomona

Amir Tavakkol
Kansas State University

Stephen G. Timme
Georgia State University

Mahmoud S. Wahab
University of Hartford

Ralph C. Walter III
Northeastern Illinois University

Elizabeth Webbink
Rutgers University

Glenda Wong
De Paul University

Marilyn Wiley
Florida Atlantic University

Emilio Zarruk
Florida Atlantic University

This edition also benefited from the input of Lynn Addiscott (Price Water-house), Victor Kalafa (W. R. Grace & Co.), Mike Dosal (Barnett Bank of Central Florida, Orlando), Jean-Claude Cossett (Laval University), Anna Martin (Florida Atlantic University), and Alan Tucker (Temple University), and Donna Wolfe (Medacom).

The people at West Publishing Company were once again very helpful. Editors Esther Craig and John Szilagyi were helpful in all stages of the book writing process. My previous editor, Dick Fenton, had a major influence on the changes made on updated editions. A special thanks is due to the production editors, Laura Nelson and Brenda Owens, for their efforts to assure a quality final product.

Finally, I wish to thank my parents, Arthur and Irene Madura, and my wife, Mary, for their moral support. Without their influence, this textbook would not exist.

PART 1

THE INTERNATIONAL FINANCIAL ENVIRONMENT

Part I (Chapters 1 through 5) provides an overview of the multinational corporation (MNC) and environment in which it operates. Chapter 1 explains the goals of the MNC, along with the motives and risks of international business. Chapter 2 describes the international flow of funds between countries. Chapter 3 describes the international financial markets and how these markets facilitate ongoing operations. Chapter 4 explains how exchange rates are determined, while Chapter 5 provides a background on the currency futures and options markets. Managers of MNCs must understand the international environment described in these chapters in order to make proper decisions.

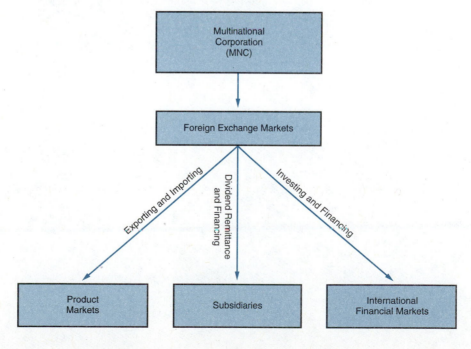

CHAPTER 1

MULTINATIONAL FINANCIAL MANAGEMENT: AN OVERVIEW

Firms continually enact strategies to improve their cash flows, and therefore enhance shareholder wealth. Some strategies involve expansion within a local area. These strategies can normally be implemented without much difficulty because information about the market is already known, and a business does not need to be altered much. Other strategies involve the penetration of foreign markets. Since foreign markets can be distinctly different from local markets, they create opportunities for improving the firm's cash flows. Many barriers to entry into foreign markets have been reduced or removed recently, thereby encouraging firms to pursue international business (producing and/or selling goods in foreign countries). Consequently, many firms have evolved into multinational corporations (MNCs), which are defined as firms that engage in some form of international business.

Initially, firms may merely attempt to export products to a particular country or import supplies from a foreign manufacturer. Over time, however, many of them recognize additional foreign opportunities and eventually establish subsidiaries in foreign countries. Some businesses, such as Dow Chemical, Exxon, American Brands, and Colgate-Palmolive, commonly generate more than half their sales in foreign countries. Westinghouse Electric Corporation operates in 16 foreign countries, and its annual international revenues normally exceed $2 billion. Honeywell has 42 subsidiaries and several other joint-venture projects scattered around the world. Eastman Kodak has subsidiaries in 32 foreign countries. Rockwell International Corp. operates in 26 foreign countries. All of these companies have enjoyed substantial growth as a result of their efforts to capitalize on international business opportunities. As another example, consider CPC International Inc., which operates in 47 different countries and has recently acquired some foreign businesses to strengthen its international position, including Santa Rosa of Italy and Nutrial of France. And perhaps the prime example is the Coca-Cola Company, distributing its products in over 160 countries and using 40 different currencies. Approximately 80 percent of its total annual operating income is typically generated outside the United States.

An understanding of international financial management is crucial to not only the large MNCs with numerous foreign subsidiaries, but also to the small firms that conduct international business. Many small U.S. firms generate more than 20 percent of their sales in foreign markets, including AMSCO International (Pennsylvania), Ferro (Ohio), Interlake (Illinois), Medtronic (Minnesota), Sybron (Wisconsin) and Synoptics (California). International business is not restricted to large firms and does not require that firms be located on the coast or near the border of a foreign country. The small U.S. firms that conduct international business tend to focus on the niches that have made them successful in the U.S. They tend to penetrate specialty markets where they will not have to compete with large firms that could capitalize on economies of scale. While some of the small firms have established subsidiaries, many of them use exporting to penetrate foreign markets. Seventy-five percent of U.S. firms that export have less than 100 employees.

International business is even important to companies that have no intention of engaging in international business, since these companies must recognize how their foreign competitors will be affected by movements in exchange rates, foreign interest rates, labor costs, and inflation. Such economic characteristics can affect the foreign competitors' cost of production and pricing policy.

Companies must also recognize how domestic competitors that obtain foreign supplies or foreign financing will be affected by economic conditions in foreign countries. If these domestic competitors are able to reduce their costs by capitalizing on opportunities in international markets, they may be able to reduce their prices without reducing their profit margins. This could allow them to increase market share at the expense of the purely domestic companies.

The idea of globalization is not new to MNCs based in other countries. European firms have historically conducted much international business, which is facilitated by their proximity to numerous foreign markets. Japanese firms have used international business as a means of growth. Japanese-based MNCs such as Canon, Hitachi, Matsushita, Mitsubishi, Nippon Steel, Olympus, and Ricoh have maintained a global presence for many years. While their global expansion was slowed by the global recession during the 1991–1993 period, many Japanese-based MNCs still pursued joint business relationships with firms in foreign markets to enhance their technology. MNCs based in other countries (including the U.S.) also used this strategy to remain globally competitive.

Newly appointed chief executive officers (CEOs) of today's MNCs recognize the importance of international business. Many of them, such as the CEOs of Rockwell International Corp., Ford Motor Company, Motorola, and Whirlpool, have been heavily involved in foreign projects and therefore have a more global view than their predecessors. New CEOs will likely be more willing to transfer operations around the globe.

This chapter provides a background on the goals of an MNC, and potential returns and risk from engaging in international business. The specific objectives of this chapter are to

- identify the main goal of the MNC and conflicts with that goal,
- describe the key theories that justify international business, and
- explain the common methods used to conduct international business.

GOAL OF THE MNC

The commonly accepted goal of an MNC is to maximize shareholder wealth. Developing a goal is necessary since all decisions should contribute to its accomplishment. Thus, if the objective were to maximize earnings in the near future, the firm's policies would be different than if the objective were to maximize shareholder wealth.

Any proposed corporate policy should consider not only potential earnings, but also risks. If the benefits to be derived from a corporate policy outweigh the costs and risks to the extent that the policy will help maximize shareholder wealth, this policy should be implemented. The following quote from an annual report of CPC International substantiates how international business can maximize shareholder wealth:

As our international business has grown and strengthened, we have benefited from the fact that the economies and currencies of most foreign countries have also strengthened over the long term, adding to the value of our shareholders' investment.

An MNC should make decisions using the same objective as the purely domestic firm. Yet, there is a much wider range of opportunities for the MNC, causing its decisions to be more complex.

Conflicts against the MNC Goal

It has often been argued that managers of a firm may make decisions that conflict with the firm's goal to maximize shareholder wealth. For example, a decision to establish a subsidiary in one location versus another may be based on the location's personal appeal to the manager rather than on its potential benefits to shareholders. Decisions to expand may be determined by the desires of managers to make their respective divisions grow in order to receive more responsibility and compensation. If a firm were composed of only one owner who was also the sole manager, a conflict of goals would not occur. However, for corporations with shareholders who differ from their managers, a conflict of goals can exist. This conflict is often referred to as the **agency problem.**

The agency costs of assuring that managers maximize shareholder wealth are normally larger for MNCs than for purely domestic firms, for the following reasons. First, MNCs that have subsidiaries scattered around the world may experience larger agency problems because it is more difficult to monitor managers of distant subsidiaries in foreign countries. Second, foreign subsidiary managers raised in different cultures may not follow uniform goals. Third, the sheer size of the larger MNCs can also create large agency problems.

Financial managers of an MNC with several subsidiaries may be tempted to make decisions that maximize the values of their respective subsidiaries. This objective will not necessarily coincide with maximizing the value of the overall MNC. While this discrepancy will be discussed in detail later in the text, a simple example can illustrate why a conflict may exist. Consider a subsidiary manager that obtained financing from the parent firm (headquarters) to develop and sell a new product. The manager estimated the costs and benefits of the project from the subsidiary's perspective and determined that the project was feasible. However, the manager neglected to realize that any earnings from this project remitted to the parent would be taxed heavily by the host government. The estimated after-tax benefits received by the parent were more than offset by the cost of financing the project. While the subsidiary's individual value was enhanced, the MNC's overall value was reduced. If financial managers are to maximize the wealth of their MNC's shareholders, they must implement policies that maximize the value of the overall MNC rather than the value of their respective subsidiaries. For many MNCs, major decisions by subsidiary managers must be approved by the parent. However, it is difficult for the parent to monitor all decisions made by subsidiary managers.

The magnitude of agency costs can vary with the management style of the MNC. A centralized management style, as illustrated at the top of Exhibit 1.1, can reduce agency costs because it allows managers of the parent to control foreign subsidiaries, and therefore reduces the power of subsidiary managers. However, the parent's managers may make poor decisions for the subsidiary because they are not as informed as subsidiary managers about financial characteristics of the subsidiary. Conversely, a decentralized management style, as illustrated at the bottom of Exhibit 1.1, may result in higher agency costs if subsidiary managers make decisions that do not focus on maximizing the value of the entire MNC. Yet, this style gives more control to those managers who are closer to the subsidiary's operations and environment.

Given the obvious tradeoff between centralized and decentralized management styles, some MNCs attempt to achieve the advantages of both styles. That is, they allow subsidiary managers to make the key decisions about their

EXHIBIT 1.1 Management Styles of MNCs

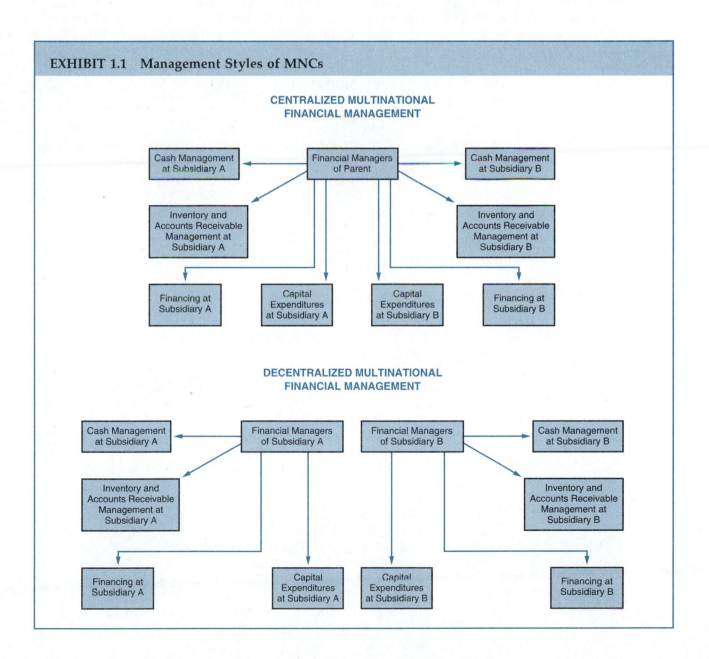

MNC PERCEPTIONS OF AGENCY COSTS: A SURVEY

A recent study by Boseman surveyed Australian-based MNCs to gain insight into their planning and ownership strategies. The companies surveyed commonly mentioned that the objectives of foreign operations conflicted with corporate objectives. The study concluded that this conflict becomes pronounced as foreign operations grow. The initial establishment of foreign operations is usually narrowly focused and in line with the MNC's overall goals. However, as the foreign operations expand and become diversified, the initial intentions for the foreign operations are forgotten. Managers of these operations become more concerned with the local conditions and attempt to maximize the value of their single entities as if they were independent of the MNC parent. Thus, there is less regard for how the entity can contribute to the overall value of the MNC. An MNC can attempt to prevent this conflict from occurring by rewarding foreign managers according to their contribution to the MNC as a whole.

respective operations, but the decisions are monitored by the parent's management to assure that they are in the best interests of the entire MNC.

Non-U.S. managers tend to focus less on short-term performance than do U.S. managers. This difference may cause non-U.S. managers to make decisions for foreign subsidiaries of the U.S.-based MNCs that are inconsistent with maximizing shareholder wealth. Yet, it could also be argued that a longer-term perspective may be beneficial, since a short-term focus could cause managers to make decisions that adversely affect the MNC's long-term performance.

Constraints Interfering with the MNC Objective

When financial managers of MNCs attempt to maximize their firm's value, they are confronted with various constraints that can be classified as environmental, regulatory, or ethical in nature.

Environmental Constraints.   Each country enforces its own environmental constraints. Some countries may enforce more of these restrictions on a subsidiary whose parent is based in a different country. Building codes, disposal of production waste materials, and pollution controls are examples of the restrictions that force subsidiaries to incur additional costs. Many European countries have recently imposed tougher anti-pollution laws as a result of severe pollution problems.

Regulatory Constraints.   Each country also enforces its own regulatory constraints pertaining to taxes, currency convertibility rules, earnings remittance restrictions, and other regulations that can affect cash flows of a subsidiary established there. Because these regulations can influence cash flows, they must be recognized by financial managers when assessing policies. Also, any change in these regulations may require revision of existing financial policies, so financial managers should not only recognize the regulatory restrictions that exist in a given country but also monitor them for any potential changes over time.

Ethical Constraints.   There is no consensus standard of business conduct that applies to all countries. A business practice that is perceived to be unethical in one country may be totally ethical in another. For example, the U.S.-based MNCs are well aware of common business practices in some less developed countries that would be declared illegal in the United States. Bribes to governments in order to receive special tax breaks or other favors are one example. The MNCs face a dilemma. If they do not participate in such practices, they may be at a competitive disadvantage. Yet, if they do participate, they receive a poor reputation in countries that do not approve such practices. Some U.S.-based MNCs have made the costly choice to restrain from business practices that are legal in certain foreign countries but not legal in the United States. That is, they follow a worldwide code of ethics. This may enhance their worldwide credibility, which can increase global demand for the products they produce.

THEORIES OF INTERNATIONAL BUSINESS

The commonly used theories for why firms become motivated to expand their business internationally are (1) the theory of comparative advantage, (2) the imperfect markets theory, and (3) the product cycle theory. The three theories overlap to a degree and can complement each other in developing a rationale for the evolution of international business.

Theory of Comparative Advantage

Multinational business has generally increased over time. Part of this growth is due to the increasing realization that specialization by countries can increase production efficiency. Some countries, such as Japan and the United States, have a technology advantage, while countries such as Jamaica, Mexico, and South Korea have an advantage in the cost of basic labor. Since these advantages cannot be easily transported, countries tend to use their advantages to specialize in the production of goods that can be produced with relative efficiency. This explains why countries such as Japan and the U.S. are large producers of computer components, while countries such as Jamaica and Mexico are large producers of agricultural and handmade goods.

Specialization in some products may result in no production of other products, so that trade between countries is essential. This is the argument made by the classical **theory of comparative advantage.** Due to comparative advantages, it is understandable why firms are able to penetrate foreign markets. Many of the Virgin Islands rely completely on international trade for most products, while they specialize in tourism. While the production of some goods is possible on these islands, there is more efficiency in the specialization of tourism. That is, the islands are better off using some revenues earned from tourism to import products than attempting to produce all the products that they need.

Imperfect Markets Theory

Countries differ with respect to resources available for the production of goods. Yet, even with such comparative advantages, the volume of international business would be limited if all resources could be easily transferred among countries. If markets were perfect, factors of production (except land) would be mobile and freely transferable. The unrestricted mobility of factors creates equality in costs and returns and removes the comparative cost advantage, the rationale for international trade and investment. However, the real world suffers from **imperfect market** conditions where factors of production are somewhat immobile. There are costs and often restrictions related to the transfer of labor and other resources used for production. There may also be restrictions on funds and other resources transferred among countries. Because markets for the various resources used in production are "imperfect," firms often capitalize on a foreign country's resources. Imperfect markets provide an incentive for firms to seek out foreign opportunities.

Product Cycle Theory

One of the more popular explanations for why firms evolve into MNCs is introduced in the **product cycle theory.** According to this theory, firms become established in the home market as a result of some perceived advantage they would have over existing competitors, such as a need by the market for at least one more supplier of the product. Because information about markets and competition is more readily available at home, a firm is likely to first establish itself in its home country. Foreign demand for the firm's product will initially be accommodated by exporting. As time passes, the firm may feel the only way to retain its advantage over competition in foreign countries is to produce the product in foreign markets, thereby reducing its transportation costs. Over time, the competition in the foreign markets may increase as other producers become more familiar with the firm's product. Thus, the firm may develop strategies to prolong the foreign demand for its product. A common approach is to attempt differentiating the product so that other competitors cannot offer exactly the same product. These phases of the cycle are illustrated in Exhibit 1.2. As an example, 3M Company uses one new product to penetrate foreign markets. After entering the market, it expands its product line. It now has over $6 billion per year in international sales, about 50 percent of its total sales.

There is more to the product cycle theory than is summarized here. This discussion merely suggests that as a firm matures, it may recognize additional opportunities outside its home country. Whether the firm's foreign business diminishes or expands over time will depend on how successful it is at maintaining some advantage over its competition. The advantage could represent an edge in its production or financing approach that reduces costs. Alternatively, the advantage could reflect an edge in its marketing approach that generates and maintains a strong demand for its product.

Increasing Globalization

Economies have become increasingly globalized as firms engage in international trade and investment. A primary force behind the globalization is the reduction in tariffs and other barriers imposed by country governments. For example, PepsiCo Inc. (owner of Kentucky Fried Chicken, Pizza Hut, and Taco Bell) has recently entered various markets in the Caribbean and Asia that were previously restricted, in pursuit of its goal to be in any country where people desire chicken,

EXHIBIT 1.2   International Product Life Cycle

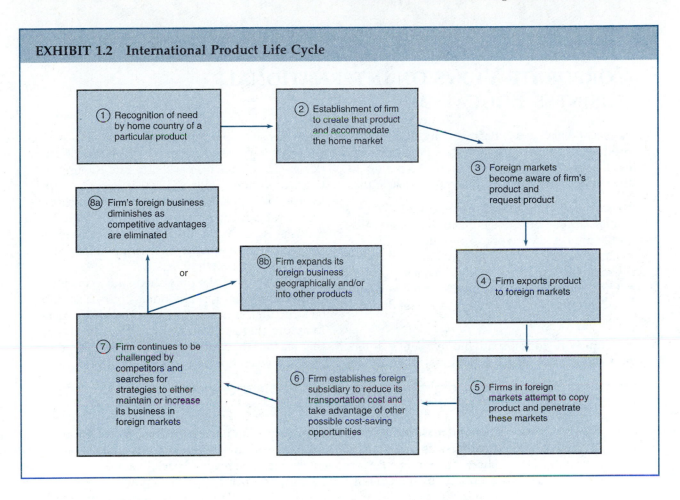

pizza, or tacos. Many U.S.-based MNCs, including Bausch & Lomb, Colgate-Palmolive, and General Electric, have been penetrating less developed countries such as Argentina, Chile, Mexico, India, China, and Hungary. New opportunities in these countries have resulted from the removal of government barriers.

A second driving force behind the globalization of business is the increasing standardization of products and services across countries. This allows firms to sell their products across countries, without costly product revisions. The previous disparity in product specifications represented an implicit trade barrier because of the extra cost associated with making the product acceptable in particular countries. Standardization greatly reduces the inconvenience of transporting goods and has already resulted in a significant increase in international business.

Globalization has also been stimulated by the movement toward free enterprise, whereby several national governments have sold some of their operations to corporations and other investors. This so-called **privatization** has already taken place in some Latin American countries such as Brazil and Mexico, in Eastern European countries, such as Poland and Hungary, and in such Caribbean territories as the Virgin Islands. Privatization allows for greater international business as foreign firms can acquire operations sold by national governments.

CORPORATE VIEWS ON INTERNATIONAL BUSINESS EDUCATION

A recent survey by Beamish and Calof was conducted to determine corporate perceptions of international business education. According to the survey responses, most companies state that

- International awareness is important.
- International business education is most valuable after related work experience.
- Their needs for executive skills include a background in international business.
- The combination of an international business background with a foreign language is marketable.

Executives rated international marketing, international finance, and international trade as the three most important international business studies for career progress within their businesses. They were also asked to rate the importance of various skills that were necessary for international positions within their businesses. The most important skills, based on their responses, were communications skills, leadership skills, interpersonal skills, adaptability, and ethical and moral standards.

The authors of the published study conclude that the content of international courses should be structured in consultation with practitioners to assure that the course content is useful. For this reason, they encourage the interchange of ideas between business schools and MNCs.

The reasons for promoting privatization have varied across countries. Privatization was used in Chile to prevent a few investors from controlling all the shares, and in France to prevent the possible reversal back to a more nationalized economy. In the United Kingdom, privatization was promoted to spread stock ownership across investors, which allows more people to have a direct stake in the success of British industry.

The primary reason why the market value of a firm may increase in response to privatization is the anticipated improvement in managerial efficiency. The goal of maximizing shareholder wealth is more focused than in management of a state-owned business, since the state must consider the economic and social ramifications of any business decision. Also, managers of a privately owned enterprise are more motivated to assure profitability because their careers may depend on it. For these reasons, privatized firms will search for local and global opportunities that could enhance their value. The trend toward privatization will undoubtedly create a more competitive global marketplace.

INTERNATIONAL BUSINESS METHODS

There are several methods by which firms conduct international business. The most common methods are these:

- international trade
- licensing
- franchising
- joint ventures

AN EXPERT'S VIEW OF INTERNATIONAL BUSINESS EDUCATION

John H. Dunning, a well-known expert on business and previous president of the Academy of International Business, offered some general comments and suggestions about international business. Some of his main points are summarized below:

- Since exchange rate movements have become more volatile, effective risk management strategies are needed.
- The role of governments in influencing costs and benefits of international business has increased. This implies that some attention should be given to government intervention and the assessment of each country's political risk.
- There has been a surge in the demand for international education, including college courses, conferences, and executive training courses. The supply of qualified instructors has not

kept up with demand. Business schools are beginning to respond to the demand by offering more courses. In the United States and Canada, there are relatively few universities that offer major programs in international business. In many European countries, such as France, Sweden, Switzerland, and the United Kingdom, international business programs are more commonly offered.

- Many business courses attempt to include an international dimension simply by tacking international applications on at the end of the course. This provides less international education than if international applications were infused throughout the course. Courses in some smaller countries such as Hong Kong, Singapore, Sweden, and Switzerland are more internationalized, as these countries recognize their reliance on international business.

- acquisitions of existing operations
- establishing new foreign subsidiaries.

Each method is discussed in turn, with some emphasis on its risk and return characteristics.

International Trade

International trade is a relatively conservative approach that can be used by firms to penetrate markets (by exporting) or to obtain supplies at a low cost (by importing). There is minimal risk to this approach, since the firm does not place any of its capital at risk. If the firm experiences a decline in its exporting or importing, it can normally reduce or discontinue this part of its business at a low cost.

Many large U.S.-based MNCs, including Boeing, DuPont, General Electric, and IBM, generate more than $4 billion in annual sales from exporting. Yet, more than 20 percent of the value of all U.S. exports is provided by small businesses.

Licensing

Licensing obligates a firm to provide its technology (copyrights, patents, trademarks, or trade names) in exchange for fees or some other specified benefits. For example, a soft drink producer may lend its formula and trademark to a foreign firm, so that the foreign firm can produce and sell the soft drink in another country. The soft drink producer that provides the technology would receive fees or a portion of the foreign revenues. Licensing allows firms to use their technology in foreign markets without a major investment in foreign countries, and without the transportation costs that result from exporting. A major disadvantage of licensing is that it is difficult for the firm providing the technology to assure quality control in the foreign production process.

Franchising

Franchising obligates a firm to provide a specialized sales or service strategy, support assistance, and possibly an initial investment in the franchise in exchange for periodic fees. For example, McDonalds, Pizza Hut, Subway Sandwiches, Micro Age Computers, and Dairy Queen have franchises that are owned and managed by local residents in many foreign countries. Like licensing, franchising allows firms to penetrate foreign markets without a major investment in foreign countries. The recent relaxation of barriers in foreign countries throughout Eastern Europe and South America has resulted in numerous franchising arrangements.

Joint Ventures

A **joint venture** is a venture that is jointly owned and operated by two or more firms. Many firms penetrate foreign markets by engaging in a joint venture with firms that reside in those markets. Most joint ventures allow two firms to apply their respective comparative advantages in a given project. For example, General Mills Inc. joined in a venture with Nestle SA, so that the cereals produced by General Mills could be sold through the overseas sales distribution network established by Nestle.

Xerox Corp. and Fuji Co. (of Japan) engaged in a joint venture which allowed Xerox Corp. to penetrate the Japanese market and allowed Fuji to enter the photocopying business. Sara Lee Corp. and Southwestern Bell have engaged in joint ventures with Mexican firms, as such ventures have allowed entry into Mexico's markets. There are numerous joint ventures between automobile manufacturers, as each manufacturer can offer its technological advantages. General Motors has ongoing joint ventures with automobile manufacturers in several different countries, including Hungary and the Soviet states.

Acquisitions of Existing Operations

Firms frequently acquire existing operations in foreign countries as a means of penetrating foreign markets. This method allows a firm to have full control over its foreign business, and to quickly obtain a large portion of foreign market share. However, it is normally riskier than the other methods previously mentioned because of the large investment required. In addition, if the foreign operations perform poorly, it may be difficult to sell the operations at a reasonable price.

Some firms engage in partial international acquisitions in order to obtain a stake in foreign operations. This requires a smaller investment than full international acquisitions, and therefore exposes the firm to less risk. However, the firm will not have complete control over foreign operations that are partially acquired.

Establishing New Foreign Subsidiaries

Firms can also penetrate foreign markets by establishing new operations in foreign countries to produce and sell their products. Like a foreign acquisition, this method requires a large investment. The establishment of new subsidiaries may be preferred to foreign acquisitions because the operations can be tailored exactly to the firm's needs. In addition, the investment amount may be less than that required to purchase existing operations. However, the firm will not reap any rewards from the investment until the subsidiary is built, and a customer base is established.

Summary of Methods

The methods of increasing international business extend from the relatively simple approach of international trade to the more complex approach of acquiring foreign firms or establishing new subsidiaries. Any method of increasing international business that requires a direct investment in foreign operations is normally referred to as **direct foreign investment** (DFI). International trade and licensing are not normally considered to be DFI because they do not involve direct investment in foreign operations. Franchising and joint ventures tend to require some investment in foreign operations, but to a limited degree. Foreign acquisitions and the establishment of new foreign subsidiaries require substantial investment in foreign operations and represent the largest portion of DFI.

INCREASED GLOBALIZATION

Increased globalization is relevant not only to MNCs, but to purely domestic firms as well. These firms may be subject to more foreign competition, especially if they are located in countries where international barriers are being removed.

Growth in International Trade

The volume of international trade (exports plus imports) relative to gross national product (GNP) is reported for some major countries in Exhibit 1.3. Note that the international trade volume as a percentage of GNP is generally much larger for Canada and European countries than it is for the United States or Japan. Yet, the importance of trade has increased over time for most countries. While Japan is very dependent on its exports, it has maintained economic growth even when importing countries experience a slowdown. Japan diversifies its exports across numerous countries so that it is not substantially influenced by a single country's economic conditions.

Growth in Direct Foreign Investment

The direct foreign investment (DFI) positions by U.S. firms and by non-U.S. firms in the U.S. are illustrated in Exhibit 1.4. These positions represent foreign acquisitions and the establishment of foreign subsidiaries. They reflect investment in real assets of foreign countries. The DFI positions in the U.S. and outside the U.S. have risen substantially over time, which confirms increasing globalization.

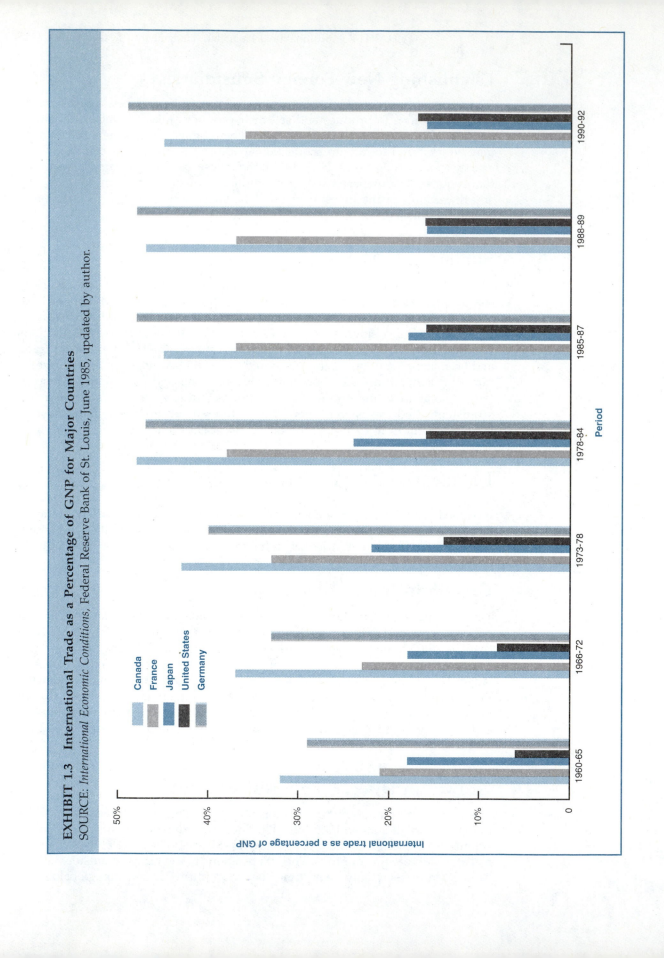

EXHIBIT 1.3　International Trade as a Percentage of GNP for Major Countries
SOURCE: *International Economic Conditions*, Federal Reserve Bank of St. Louis, June 1985, updated by author.

**EXHIBIT 1.4
Comparative Direct
Foreign Investment
Positions**

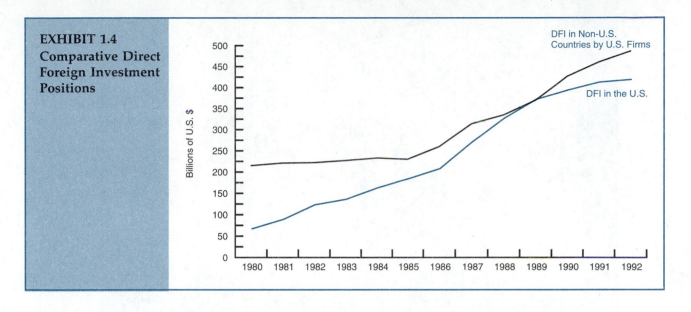

Both DFI positions leveled off during recessionary periods (such as in the early 1980s and in the early 1990s), but have increased during periods of strong economic growth.

The distribution of DFI by U.S. firms is illustrated in Exhibit 1.5. The United Kingdom and Canada are the biggest targets. Latin American countries received a larger portion of DFI in aggregate than Asian countries. This may be attributed to some barriers in Asia. The DFI by U.S. firms in Latin American countries may increase substantially as these countries open their markets to U.S. firms.

Relationship between Globalization and Profitability

A study by Daniels and Bracker found that U.S. companies with a higher degree of international business experienced superior profit performance. Since the results could have been somewhat distorted by industry differences, they reassessed the relationship for specific industries. They found that for the majority of industries studied, U.S. companies within a given industry that had a higher degree of international business experienced superior profit performance. While the results cannot be generalized for all firms, it appears that increasing international business may enhance a firm's profitability.

INTERNATIONAL OPPORTUNITIES AND RISK

Because of possible cost advantages from producing in foreign countries or possible revenue opportunities from demand by foreign markets, the growth potential becomes much greater for firms that consider international business. Exhibit 1.6 illustrates how a firm's growth can be affected by foreign investment and financing opportunities. The hypothetical investment opportunities for both a purely domestic firm and an MNC with similar operating characteristics are shown here. Each horizontal step represents a specific project. Each proposed project is anticipated to generate a marginal return to the firm.

EXHIBIT 1.5   Distribution of DFI by U.S. Firms   (in billions of $)

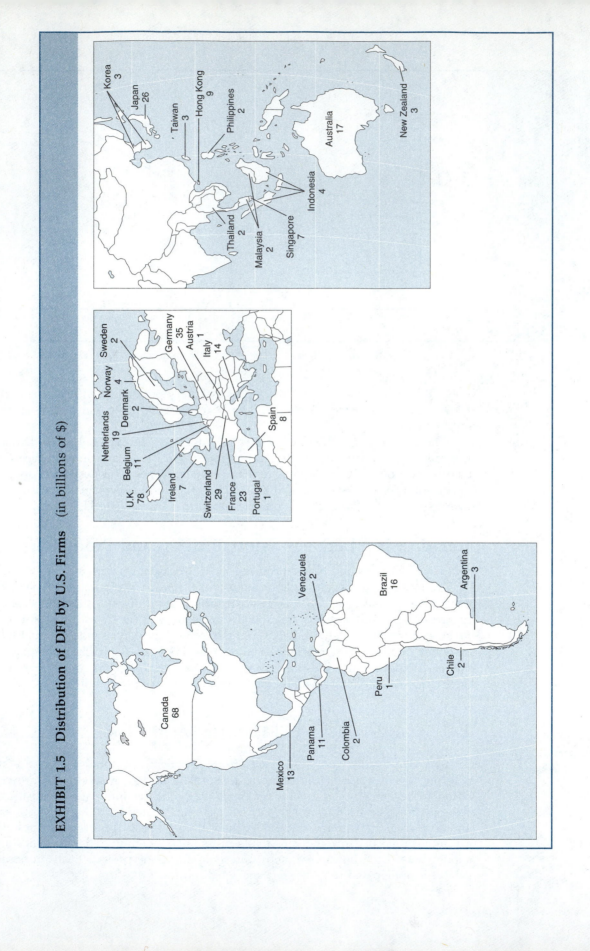

**EXHIBIT 1.6
Cost-Benefit
Evaluation for
Purely Domestic
Firms versus MNCs**

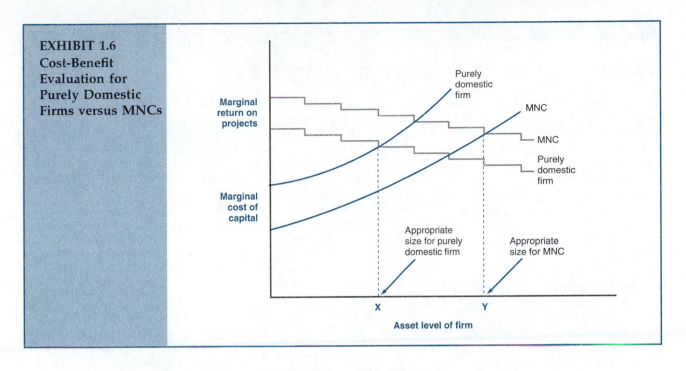

Moving from left to right in Exhibit 1.6, the projects are prioritized according to marginal return. Assume that these projects are independent of each other and that their expected returns as shown have been adjusted to account for risk. With these assumptions, a firm would select the project with the highest marginal return as most feasible and would undertake this project. Then, it would undertake the proposed project with the next highest marginal return, and so on. The marginal return on projects for the MNC is above that of the purely domestic firm, because of the expanded opportunity set of possible projects from which to select.

Exhibit 1.6 also displays cost-of-capital curves for the MNC and purely domestic firm. The cost of capital is shown to increase with asset size for either type of firm. This is based on the premise that creditors or shareholders require a higher rate of return as the firm grows. Growth in asset size requires increased debt, which forces the firm to increase its periodic interest payments to creditors. Consequently, the firm has a greater probability of being unable to meet its debt obligations. To the extent that creditors and shareholders require a higher return for a more highly indebted firm, the cost of capital to the firm rises with its volume of assets. The MNC is shown to have an advantage in obtaining capital funding at a lower cost than can the purely domestic firm. This is due to the larger opportunity set of funding sources around the world from which it has to choose.

Once the marginal cost of financing projects exceeds the marginal return on projects, the firm should not pursue such projects. As shown in Exhibit 1.6, a purely domestic firm will continue to accept projects up to point X. After that point, the marginal cost of additional projects exceeds the expected benefits.

When foreign resources, funds, and potential projects are considered, the firm's volume of feasible projects would be greater. The MNC's projects become

APPLIED RESEARCH

DEVELOPING A GLOBAL COMPETITIVE ADVANTAGE

An extensive study by Porter offers some interesting insight on the ability of firms to develop a global competitive advantage over other firms in the industry. Some of Porter's key points are listed below.

- Firms develop competitive advantages through innovation. The advantage is maintained when competitors are slow to respond.
- Most competitive advantages can be imitated. For example, South Korean firms have successfully created substitutes for color televisions and VCRs produced by Japanese firms. Also, Brazilian firms have created substitutes for casual leather footwear produced by Italian firms.
- A competitive advantage can be sustained only by continually upgrading it over time. For example, Japanese automobile producers initially penetrated the U.S. and other markets by producing inexpensive cars, using relatively low labor costs at that time to develop a competitive advantage. Since then, they have developed large modern plants to benefit from economies of scale. They have recently focused on customer satisfaction to retain their competitive advantage.
- Innovation may be more achievable when there is an investment in research and development. Since the rewards from research and development are not immediate, some firms that are short-run oriented will not make the investment and therefore will be less innovative. U.S. companies tend to be somewhat short-run oriented as their shareholders are looking for immediate performance. Conversely, German and Swiss firms tend to be more long-run oriented as their shareholders usually hold on to shares for a long period of time. Commercial banks in these countries invest heavily in stock, whereas U.S. commercial banks cannot invest in stock.
- Firms should be very selective when engaging in joint ventures for innovation. Alliances tend to be costly because they require the coordination of two separate operations and sets of goals.

The concepts above are applied to countries rather than individual firms. Porter suggests that because competition motivates innovation, the use of government intervention (such as trade barriers or direct subsidies) to protect an industry will discourage innovation. Thus, those countries that are more protected by their governments will be at a competitive disadvantage.

unacceptable after point Y. This optimal level of assets exceeds that of the purely domestic firm. The difference here is due to cost advantages and opportunities in foreign countries. This comparison illustrates why firms may desire to become internationalized.

There are several limitations to the concept illustrated in Exhibit 1.6. First, there may be some cases where there are no feasible foreign opportunities for a firm. In addition, an argument could be made that foreign projects are riskier than domestic projects and therefore result in a higher cost of capital. Finally, some critics contend that the marginal cost of capital will not rise as more projects are added if the firm diversifies its projects appropriately. Nevertheless, the exhibit offers insight as to why firms expand internationally. Moreover, it illustrates why the optimal size of a given firm will typically be greater if that firm considers foreign opportunities.

In addition to capitalizing on cost advantages and opportunities, firms that enter foreign markets can also reduce their exposure to their local economy. That is, diversifying their business internationally reduces the sensitivity of their performance to the home country conditions. For example, while a U.S. recession may lower the U.S. demand for a firm's product, the non-U.S. demand may be unaffected.

Opportunities in Europe

Over time, economic and political conditions can change, creating new opportunities in international business. A classic example is Europe in the late 1980s and early 1990s. In the late 1980s, industrialized countries in Europe agreed to make regulations more uniform and to remove many taxes on goods traded between these countries. This agreement, supported by the Single European Act of 1987, was followed by a series of negotiations among countries to begin phasing in policies that achieved uniformity by 1992. The act allows firms in a given European country greater access to supplies from firms in other European countries.

Many firms, including European subsidiaries of U.S.-based MNCs, have capitalized on the agreement by attempting to penetrate markets in border countries. Before the Single European Act, some subsidiaries conducted business only in their host country because opportunities in border countries were discouraged by taxes and other barriers. As these barriers were reduced in the late 1980s, firms began to enter new markets. By producing more of the same product and distributing it across European countries, firms may be more able to achieve economies of scale. CPC International announced that it would be able to increase efficiency by streamlining manufacturing operations as a result of the reduction in barriers. Reynolds Metals Company completed the unification of its European operations under the management of its European headquarters in Switzerland to prepare for a more unified Europe.

In 1989 another historic event occurred in Europe when the Berlin Wall separating East Germany from West Germany was removed. This was symbolic of new relations between East Germany and West Germany, and was followed by efforts to reunify the two countries. In addition, it created momentum to encourage free enterprise in all East European countries. As with the Single European Act, this event opened up new opportunities for MNCs. A key motive for pursuing opportunities in Eastern Europe was the lack of products available there. Continual shortages of goods encouraged MNCs to penetrate this market. Coca-Cola Company, Reynolds Metals Company, CPC International, General Motors, and numerous other MNCs aggressively pursued expansion in Eastern Europe as a result of the momentum toward free enterprise.

While the Single European Act of 1987 and the momentum toward free enterprise in Eastern Europe offered new opportunities to MNCs, they also posed new risks. As the Single European Act removed cross-border barriers, it exposed firms to additional competition. As in other historical examples of deregulation, the more efficient firms benefit at the expense of less efficient firms.

Opportunities in Mexico

As a result of the North American Free Trade Agreement (NAFTA) of 1993, trade barriers between the U.S. and Mexico were eliminated. Some U.S. firms attempted to capitalize on this by exporting goods to Mexico that had been previously restricted by barriers. Other firms established subsidiaries in Mexico to produce their goods at a lower cost than is possible in the U.S., and then sell the goods in the U.S. The removal of trade barriers essentially allowed U.S. firms to penetrate product and labor markets that previously had not been accessible.

The removal of trade barriers between the U.S. and Mexico allows Mexican firms to export some products to the U.S. that were previously restricted. Thus, U.S. firms that produce these goods are now subject to competition from Mexican exporters. Given the low cost of labor in Mexico, some U.S. firms will lose some of their market share. The effects should normally be most pronounced in the labor-intensive industries.

Opportunities Elsewhere

Within a month after the NAFTA accord, the momentum for free trade continued with a GATT (General Agreement on Tariffs and Trade) accord. This accord was the conclusion of trade negotiations from the so-called Uruguay round that had begun seven years earlier. It called for the reduction or elimination of trade restrictions on specified imported goods over a ten-year period across 117 countries. The accord was expected to generate more international business for firms that had previously been unable to penetrate foreign markets because of trade restrictions.

International Risk

While international business can reduce an MNC's exposure to its home country's economic conditions, it usually increases an MNC's exposure to (1) exchange rate movements, (2) foreign economic conditions, and (3) political risk. Each of these forms of exposure is briefly described below, and is discussed in more detail in various sections of the text. These forms of exposure should be considered by the MNCs that plan to pursue international business.

Exposure to Exchange Rate Movements. Most international business results in the exchange of one currency for another to make payment. Since exchange rates fluctuate over time, the cash outflows required to make payments change accordingly. Consequently, the number of units of a firm's home currency needed to purchase foreign supplies can change even if the suppliers have not adjusted their prices.

Exchange rate fluctuations can also affect the foreign demand for a firm's product. When the home currency strengthens, products denominated in that currency become more expensive to foreign customers, which may cause a decline in the demand, and therefore a decline in cash inflows.

For MNCs with subsidiaries in foreign countries, exchange rate fluctuations affect the value of cash flows remitted by subsidiaries to the parent. When the parent's home currency is strong, the remitted funds will convert to a smaller amount of the home currency.

Exposure to Foreign Economies. When MNCs enter foreign markets to sell products, the demand for these products is dependent on the economic conditions in those markets. Thus, the cash flows of the MNC are subject to foreign economic conditions. For example, U.S. firms such as DuPont and Nike experienced lower-than-expected cash flows because of weak European economies in the 1992–93 period.

Exposure to Political Risk. When MNCs establish subsidiaries in foreign countries, they become exposed to **political risk,** which represents political actions taken by the host government or the public that affect the MNC's cash flows (political risk is often viewed as a subset of **country risk,** which is explained later). For example, the host government may impose higher taxes on U.S.-based subsidiaries in retaliation for actions of the U.S. government. Alternatively, the host government may decide to buy out a subsidiary at whatever price it decides is fair.

PREVIEW OF TEXT

Each of the following chapters provides specific information on strategies used by managers of MNCs. Exhibit 1.7 shows how Chapters 2 through 21 can be used by managers to satisfy the MNC's return and risk objectives, and therefore maximize its stock price. The international financial markets described in Chapters 2 through 5 facilitate international business transactions. Chapters 6 through 8 allow managers to understand how factors affect exchange rates, so that they can manage the MNC's exchange rate risk (as explained in Chapters 9 through 12).

The short-term financial decisions of an MNC can be classified as short-term financing (Chapters 13 and 14) versus short-term investment (Chapter 15), while

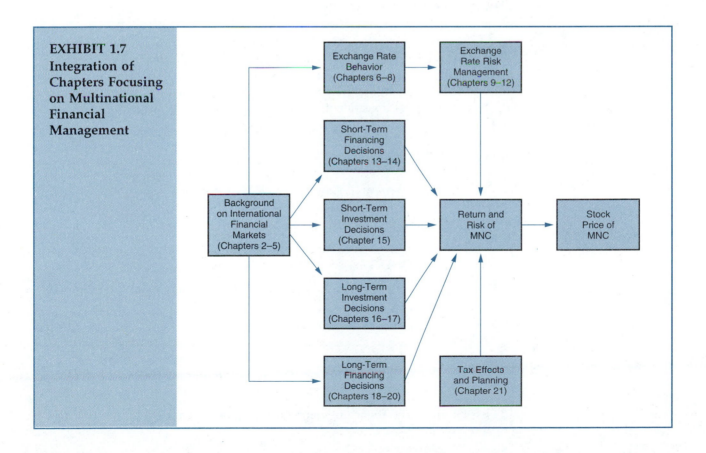

**EXHIBIT 1.7
Integration of Chapters Focusing on Multinational Financial Management**

the long-term financial decisions of an MNC can be classified as long-term investment (Chapters 16 and 17) versus long-term financing (Chapter 18 through 20).

Chapters 2 through 8 have a macro perspective, as they discuss international markets and economic conditions in general terms. Conversely, Chapters 9 through 21 have a micro perspective, as they emphasize the managerial decisions faced by individual MNCs. The macro chapters provide the background necessary to make micro (managerial) decisions.

SUMMARY

■ The main goal of the MNC is to maximize shareholder wealth. When managers are tempted to serve their own interests instead of those of shareholders, an agency problem exists. Managers also face environmental, regulatory, and ethical constraints that can conflict with the goal of maximizing shareholder wealth.

■ International business is justified by three key theories. The theory of comparative advantage suggests that each country should use its comparative advantage to specialize in its production, and rely on other countries to meet other needs. The imperfect markets theory suggests that because of imperfect markets, factors of production are immobile, which encourages countries to specialize based on the resources they have. The product cycle theory suggests that after firms are established in their home countries, they commonly expand their product specialization in foreign countries.

■ The most common methods in conducting international trade are international trade, licensing, franchising, joint ventures, acquisitions of foreign firms, and formation of foreign subsidiaries. Methods such as licensing and franchising involve little or low capital investment, but distribute some of the profits to other parties. Acquisition of foreign firms and formation of foreign subsidiaries involve a substantial capital investment, but offer the potential for large returns.

SELF-TEST FOR CHAPTER 1

(Answers are provided in Appendix A in the back of the text.)

1. Describe typical reasons why MNCs expand internationally.

2. Describe the changes in Europe, Canada, and Mexico that have created new opportunities for U.S.-based MNCs.

3. Describe the more obvious risks faced by MNCs that expand internationally.

QUESTIONS

1. Explain the agency problem of MNCs. Why might agency costs be larger for the MNC as opposed to a purely domestic firm?

2. Explain how the theory of comparative advantage relates to the need for international business.

3. Explain how the existence of imperfect markets has led to the establishment of subsidiaries in foreign markets.

4. If perfect markets existed, would wages, prices, and interest rates among countries be more similar or less similar than under conditions of imperfect markets? Why?

5. Explain how the product cycle theory relates to the growth of the MNC.

6. How does access to international opportunities affect the size of corporations? Describe a scenario wherein the size of the corporation is not affected by access to international opportunities.

7. What factors cause some firms to become more internationalized than others?

8. What are some potential disadvantages of international business that are often not relevant to domestic business? Briefly state how an MNC can be adversely affected by these disadvantages.

9. Briefly describe the change in the importance of world trade over time. If the trend continues, what does this suggest about the importance of international financial management?

10. As an overall review of this chapter, identify possible reasons for growth in international business. Then, list the various disadvantages that may discourage international business.

11. Describe constraints that interfere with the MNC's objective.

12. Describe the trends in the volume of U.S. direct investment abroad over time.

13. The managers of Loyola Corporation recently had a meeting to discuss new opportunities in Europe as a result of the recent integration between European countries. They decided not to penetrate new markets because of their present focus on expanding market share in the U.S. Financial managers of Loyola Corporation developed forecasts for earnings based on the 12 percent market share (defined here as its percentage of total European sales) that Loyola presently has in Europe. Is 12 percent an appropriate estimate for next year's European market share? If not, would it likely overestimate or underestimate the actual European market share next year?

14. Would the agency problem be more pronounced for Berkeley Corporation, which has its parent company make most major decisions for its foreign subsidiaries, or Oakland Corporation, which has a decentralized approach?

15. Explain why more standardized product specifications across countries can increase global competition.

16. How can German subsidiaries of U.S.-based MNCs capitalize on the removal of the Berlin Wall that separated East and West Germany?

17. Describe privatization and explain why it may allow for a greater degree of international business.

18. Describe the Single European Act and explain how it may affect international business by U.S. firms.

19. Review the table of contents and identify whether each of the chapters from Chapter 2 through Chapter 21 have a macro or micro perspective.

20. Explain why MNCs such as Coca Cola and PepsiCo Inc. still have numerous opportunities for international expansion.

21. An MNC desires to penetrate a foreign market with either a licensing agreement with a foreign firm or the acquisition of a foreign firm. Explain the differences in potential return and risk between a licensing agreement with a foreign firm, versus the acquisition of a foreign firm.

'King of Beers' Wants to Rule More of Japan

By YUMIKO ONO
Staff Reporter of THE WALL STREET JOURNAL

TOKYO—Stuck with a lowly market share in Japan for more than a decade, the "King of Beers" is taking dramatic steps to live up to its name.

Last month, Anheuser-Busch Cos. launched a joint venture with Kirin Brewery Co., which has about half the Japanese beer market. Under the agreement, Budweiser Japan Co., as the venture is called, will market and distribute Bud through Kirin's channels, as well as establish its own, and use Kirin's brewing facilities. Kirin says that for its 10% investment, it will learn about the world-wide beer market from the American brewer.

The venture is a bold move for the St. Louis-based brewer, whose foothold in the Japanese market for 12 years has been limited to a licensing agreement with Suntory Ltd., the weakest of Japan's four major brewers. Through Suntory, Budweiser has become Japan's favorite foreign beer—but that doesn't mean much. Last year's sales were a meager 1.2% of Japan's beer market, or about 10.1 million cases, while Bud's U.S. market share was 21.6%, or about 330 million cases.

For decades, beer has been Japan's most popular alcoholic beverage, accounting for more than 70% of the country's annual alcoholic consumption. The average Japanese consumer drinks 54 liters a year, compared with the 91 liters his American counterpart drinks.

"We want to make Budweiser into a mainstream beer" in Japan, says Jeffrey Ewins, marketing director of Budweiser Japan. It has set an ambitious goal of quadrupling its share to 5% in 10 years.

While it's unusual for a U.S. company in Japan to dismiss a partner for a rival, Anheuser's move is one example of an increasing trend among foreign companies with experience in Japan to try to expand their operational control.

But there are risks to such arrangements. Two years ago, when Borden Inc. dissolved a 20-year licensing agreement with Meiji Milk Products Co. to sell ice cream on its own, its sales plummeted. Borden found it was more difficult than expected to cultivate new sales channels. It has bounced back—but still sells below earlier levels.

Anheuser believes it can avoid that fate. The venture, in which the brewer has a 90% stake, will give it a wider sales network and more control in marketing its beer. The venture can hold its own promotional campaigns. Anheuser's licensing agreement left it completely dependent on Suntory's weak distribution channels and advertising—and the Japanese brewer thought Bud didn't need much promoting.

The joint venture quickly started an aggressive marketing campaign, beginning with its signature Clydesdale horses pulling a cartful of Buds through downtown Tokyo. Salesmen are handing out the characteristic bowtie-shaped neon signs to restaurants in major cities. And the company started airing its U.S. commercials in Japan.

"The world's No. 1 beer," says the deep-voiced Japanese narrator, as a man dives into a swimming pool. "You want to drink more and more."

But that line is getting harder to sell because people are drinking less. In the first eight months of this year, beer sales were down 2.2% to 1.19 billion gallons—the first drop in eight years. Budweiser Japan officials expect to sell a flat 10 million cases next year.

Promoting the End of a Trend

The company also is trying to reinvent Bud's image. For years, Suntory marketed Budweiser as a fashionable, expensive beer that handsome American actors guzzled in movies, and suggested that young couples sip the drink in chic bars. At one point, Budweiser's screwcap bottle became a tool to test how hip college students were. Trend-conscious students laughed at colleagues who tried in vain to open a bottle with an opener.

But now that Budweiser's cachet is fading, the venture says it's trying to appeal to a new consumer: heavy-drinking, middle-aged men. To reach them, it has launched full-page newspaper ads proclaiming that "the age when beers became trends and fashion is over."

QUESTIONS

1. Explain how the joint venture can enable Anheuser Busch to achieve its objective of maximizing shareholder wealth.

2. Explain how the joint venture can limit the risk of the international business.

3. Many international joint ventures are intended to circumvent barriers that normally prevent foreign competition. What barrier in Japan is Anheuser Busch circumventing as a result of the joint venture? What barrier in the U.S. is Kirin circumventing as a result of the joint venture?

4. Explain how Anheuser Busch could lose some of its market share in countries outside of Japan as a result of this particular joint venture.

RANGER SUPPLY COMPANY
Motivation for International Business

Ranger Supply Company is a large manufacturer and distributor of office supplies. It is based in New York, but sends supplies to firms throughout the U.S. It markets its supplies through periodic mass mailings of catalogues to those firms. Its clients can make orders over the phone, and Ranger ships the supplies upon demand. Ranger has had very high production efficiency in the past. This is partially attributed to low employee turnover and high morale, as employees are guaranteed job security until retirement.

Ranger already holds a large proportion of the market share in distributing office supplies in the U.S. Its main competition in the U.S. is from one U.S. firm and one Canadian firm. A British firm has a small share of the U.S. market but is at a disadvantage because of its distance. The British firm's marketing and transportation costs in the U.S. market are relatively high.

While Ranger's office supplies are somewhat similar to those of its competitors, it has been able to capture most of the U.S. market because of its high efficiency, which has resulted in low prices charged to the retail stores. It expects a decline in the aggregate demand for office supplies in the U.S. in future years. However, it anticipates strong demand for office supplies in Canada and in Eastern Europe over the next several years. Executives of Ranger have begun to consider exporting as a method of offsetting the possible decline in domestic demand for its products.

a) Ranger Supply Company plans to attempt penetrating either the Canadian market or the East European market through exporting. What factors deserve to be considered in deciding which market is more feasible?

b) One financial manager has been responsible for developing a contingency plan in case whichever market was chosen imposed export barriers over time. This manager proposed that Ranger should establish a subsidiary in the country of concern under such conditions. Is this a reasonable strategy? Are there any obvious reasons why this strategy could fail?

PROJECTS

Throughout the semester, you can apply the concepts in the text to the real world by reviewing an annual report of an MNC. Write to the "Investor Relations Department" of an MNC that you are interested in for an annual report so that you can review how that MNC conducts multinational financial management. In general, annual reports do not provide details of managerial decisions, but are still helpful for illustrating concepts in this text.

Many of these MNCs have toll-free phone numbers available, so that you can call their "Investor Relations" or "Shareholder's Services" departments to request annual reports. Call directory assistance to see if the MNC you are interested in has a toll-free number.

2. Look in a recent annual report of an MNC that interests you. Summarize any comments made in the annual report about

- the MNC's level of international sales
- the MNC's plans to expand overseas in the future
- the impact of the MNC's foreign business on its recent performance.

Does it appear that the MNC has benefited from its international operations? Explain.

REFERENCES

Aggarwal, Raj. "Investment Performance of U.S.-Based Multinational Companies: Comments and a Perspective of International Diversification of Real Assets." *Journal of International Business Studies* (Spring-Summer 1980), pp. 98–104.

Anderson, Otto. "On the Internationalization Process of Firms: A Critical Analysis." *Journal of International Business Studies,* (Second Quarter 1993), pp. 209–231.

Auster, Ellen. "International Corporate Linkages: Dynamic Forms in Changing Environments." *Columbia Journal of World Business* (Summer 1987), pp. 3–6.

Beamish, Paul W. and Jonathan L. Calof. "International Business Education: A Corporate View." *Journal of International Business Studies* (Fall 1989), pp. 553–564.

Bennett, Thomas, and Craig S. Hakkio. "Europe 1992: Implications for U.S. Firms." *Economic Review, Federal Reserve Bank of Kansas City* (April 1989), pp. 3–17.

Boseman, Glenn. "The Australian Multinational-Parent and Subsidiary Relationships." *Management International Review* 26, no. 2 (1986), pp. 43–51.

Daniels, J. D., and J. Bracker, "Profit Performance: Do Foreign Operations Make a Difference?" *Management International Review,* no. 1 (1989), pp. 46–56.

Dunning, John H. "The Study of International Business: A Plea for a More Interdisciplinary Approach." *Journal of International Business Studies* (Fall 1989), pp. 411–436.

Haar, Jerry. "A Comparative Analysis of the Profitability Performance of the Largest U.S., European, and Japanese Multinational Enterprises." *Management International Review,* no. 3 (1989), pp. 5–18.

Kim, W. Chan, and Renee A. Mauborgne. "Effectively Conceiving and Executing Multinationals' Worldwide Strategies." *Journal of International Business Studies,* (Third Quarter 1993), pp. 419–448.

Laczniak, Gene R., and Jacob Naor. "Global Ethics: Wrestling with the Corporate Conscience." *Business* (July–September 1985), pp. 3–9.

Madura, Jeff, and Lawrence C. Rose. "Are Product Specialization and International Diversification Compatible?" *Management International Review,* no. 3 (1987), pp. 37–44.

Porter, Michael E. "The Competitive Advantage of Nations." *Harvard Business Review* (March–April 1990), pp. 73–93.

Rybczynski, T. M. "The European Community and the World Economy." *Business Economics* (October 1989), pp. 24–29.

Tung, Rosalie L., and Edwin L. Miller. "Managing in the Twenty-first Century: The Need for Global Orientation." *Management International Review,* no. 1 (1990): pp. 5–18.

Vernon, Raymond. "International Investment and International Trade in the Product Life Cycle." *Quarterly Journal of Economics* (May 1966), pp. 190–207.

CHAPTER 2

INTERNATIONAL FLOW OF FUNDS

International business is facilitated by markets that allow for the flow of funds between countries. The transactions arising from international business cause money flows from one country to another. The balance of payments represents a measure of international money flows, and is discussed in this chapter. The specific objectives of this chapter are to

- explain the key components of the balance of payments, and
- explain how international transactions are influenced by economic and other factors.

BALANCE OF PAYMENTS _____

The **balance of payments** is a measurement of all transactions between domestic and foreign residents over a specified period of time. The use of the words "all transactions" can be somewhat misleading, since some transactions may be estimated. The recording of transactions is done by **double-entry bookkeeping.** That is, each transaction is recorded as both a credit and a debit. Thus, total credits and debits will be identical for a country's balance of payments in aggregate; however, for any subset of the balance-of-payments statement, there may be a deficit or surplus position.

A balance-of payments statement can be broken down into various components. Those that receive the most attention are the current account and the capital account.

Current Account

The **current account** is the broadest measure of a country's international trade in goods and services. Its primary component is the **balance of trade,** which is simply the difference between merchandise exports and imports. A deficit in the balance of trade represents a greater value of imported goods than exported goods. Conversely, a surplus reflects a greater value of exported goods than imported goods.

The annual current account balance of the United States since 1979 is shown in Exhibit 2.1. The United States has had a negative current account balance since the early 1980s. The U.S. current account deficit grew to almost $150 billion in 1987, but has declined since then.

The distribution of exports by U.S. firms versus imports by U.S. firms in 1992 is shown in Exhibit 2.2. For each country, the U.S. exports are shown (rounded to the nearest billion). For example, U.S. exports to Canada were about $90 billion. For most countries, the amount imported by the U.S. is somewhat similar to the amount exported. However, there are some major imbalances. For example, the exports to Japan ($48 billion) were substantially less than the imports from Japan ($100 billion). U.S. imports from China exceeded U.S. exports to China by about $20 billion. U.S. imports from Taiwan exceeded exports to Taiwan by $10 billion. These three imbalances resulted in a U.S. trade deficit of $82 billion, which is close to the total U.S. trade deficit in 1992.

The **balance on goods and services** is measured as the balance of trade plus the net amount of payments of interest and dividends to foreign investors and from foreign investment, as well as receipts and payments resulting from international tourism and other transactions. The current account represents the balance on goods and services plus **unilateral transfers,** which reflect government and private gifts and grants.

As an example of how international transactions affect the current account balance, consider U.S. tourists who spend money in London. These expenditures reflect an outflow of funds from the United States. They will reduce the U.S. current account balance and increase Great Britain's current account balance. Conversely, if British tourists come to Walt Disney World in the United States, their spending represents an inflow of funds into the United States. Thus, the

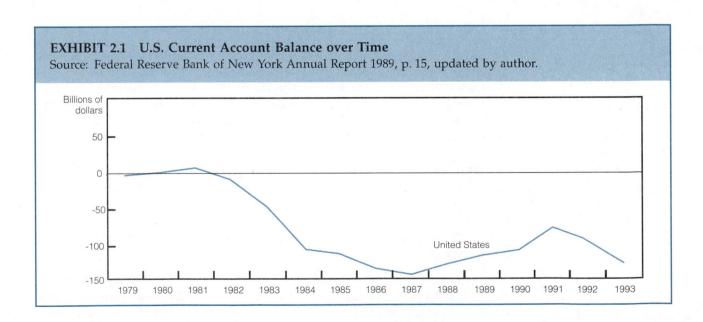

EXHIBIT 2.1   U.S. Current Account Balance over Time
Source: Federal Reserve Bank of New York Annual Report 1989, p. 15, updated by author.

EXHIBIT 2.2 Distribution of Export Markets for U.S. Firms (in billions of $)
Source: *Survey of Current Business*, 1993. Numbers are rounded to the nearest billion.

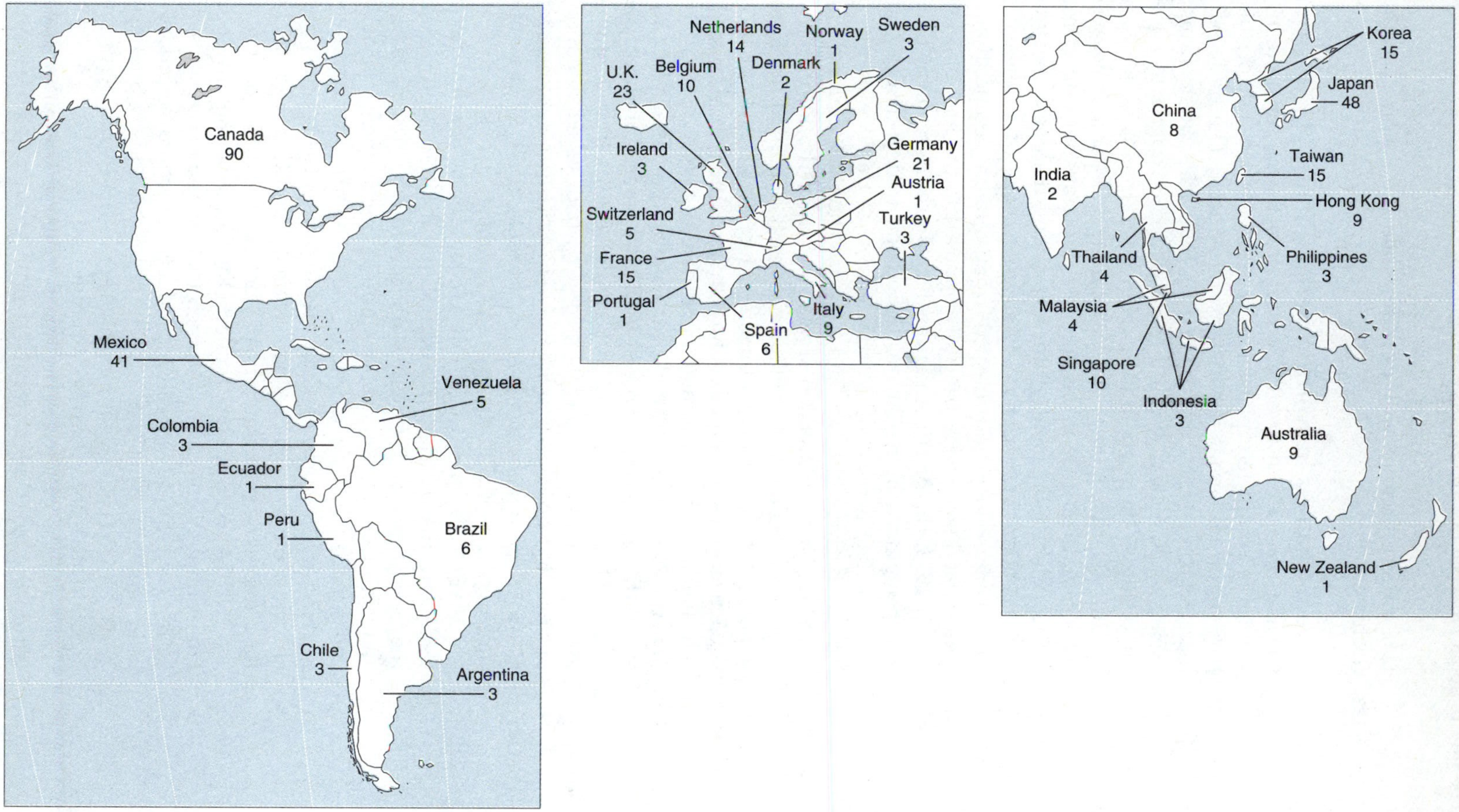

U.S. current account will increase while the current account in Great Britain decreases.

Recent Changes in North American Trade.   In January 1988, the U.S. and Canada agreed to a free trade pact, which was initiated in January 1989 and would be completely phased in by 1998. As a result of this agreement, trade barriers on numerous products were reduced. The trade pact was expected to increase competition within various industries. Some firms that had focused exclusively on domestic business were encouraged to consider exporting or importing as the barriers were removed.

In 1990, the U.S. was also negotiating a free trade pact with Mexico. Canada requested that it be included in the negotiations to complete a three-way agreement. The momentum for completing the pact was slowed because of the slow economies experienced by all three countries in the early 1990s. Industries that were somewhat protected from foreign competition, such as farming, textiles, and steel, were generally opposed to the idea of a free trade pact.

In 1993, the North American Free Trade Agreement (NAFTA) was passed, which removed numerous restrictions on trade between Canada, Mexico, and the U.S. The agreement is an extension of the 1989 treaty that reduced trade barriers between the U.S. and Canada. The three countries involved in NAFTA have combined production similar to that of the European Community, and a larger population (365 million versus 330 million in Europe). NAFTA also removes some restrictions on direct foreign investment in Mexico. Before the agreement, most of the direct foreign investment in Mexico was restricted to the so-called *maquiladoras* located near the U.S. border.

A recent survey by the Roper Organization of 455 U.S. manufacturing firms found that 81 percent favored NAFTA, 12 percent opposed, and 7 percent had no opinion. Numerous U.S. firms, including Bridgestone/Firestone, Caterpillar Tractor Co., DuPont Co., and Hoover Co., had stated intentions to expand their business in Mexico as a result of NAFTA. Thirty-eight percent of the firms were considering capital investment in Mexico, while 27 percent of the firms were considering capital investment in Canada.

NAFTA has encouraged other countries in South America to consider free trade agreements. Chile has expressed a desire to sign such an agreement with the U.S; Mexico and Venezuela are considering free trade pacts with each other and with Central American countries. The momentum for free trade has been enhanced by the movement in these countries toward free markets and less government interference. Countries in the southern cone of South America have already removed trade barriers against each other. Ultimately, there is potential for a free trade pact throughout North and South America.

NAFTA could adversely affect other countries not involved in the agreement. For example, Jamaica is concerned that its apparel business with the U.S. could be replaced by Mexico. Many products that could be produced by Mexico have been produced by islands in the Caribbean and by Southeast Asian countries. Thus, Mexico could gain market share in the exporting of these products to the U.S., at the expense of other countries.

There are some concerns that NAFTA will result in protectionism for firms within the bloc (like a "fortress North America"). These concerns are similar to those raised regarding other free trade blocs, such as in Europe. However, Mexican firms are positioned to gain market share even without such protectionism, as long as they can produce at a lower cost than firms based in other countries.

Opponents of NAFTA argue that the agreement will reduce the number of U.S. jobs as a result of lower labor costs there. However, proponents of NAFTA argue that there will be a redistribution of U.S. jobs: as the low-skilled jobs are transferred to Mexico, some high-skilled jobs will be created as a result of increased trade to Mexico. They also suggest that a portion of the income earned in Mexico resulting from NAFTA will be spent on U.S. goods.

There is some concern that the U.S. will need a massive retraining program to allow for the redistribution of U.S. jobs. Any government-sponsored programs would further increase the U.S. budget deficit.

Opponents of NAFTA argue that environmental standards will not be enforced in Mexico, which would give Mexico an extra advantage beyond its labor cost advantage. However, a counterargument is that the free trade pact could enhance Mexico's economy and help finance the environmental expenses there.

Related concerns about NAFTA include differences in safety and health laws for workers, and in child labor laws. These differences may give Mexico an extra cost advantage. Again, a counterargument is that Mexico may upgrade such laws if its economy is improved.

The effects of NAFTA will not be fully realized for many years. As with most guidelines that loosen trade barriers, those firms that were prevented by the barriers from pursuing international business may benefit. Conversely, those firms that were protected by the barriers may lose. The effects on many firms depend on how those firms respond to reduced trade barriers. Some firms that will face more competition must either become more efficient or consider diversifying into other industries in which they can compete more effectively.

Recent Changes in European Trade.   Since the Single European Act was implemented to remove explicit and implicit barriers to trade, exports and imports between European countries have increased. The integration among European countries could have a major impact on the balance of trade between European countries and non-European countries. Some analysts suggest that while European countries reduce barriers on trade within Europe, they will band together to raise barriers on imports coming from non-European countries. This approach has been referred to as "Fortress Europe", whereby European businesses are protected from exporters outside of Europe. In general, the "Fortress Europe" approach may be considered undesirable because it can result in less international trade. However, to the extent that it is simply used as a threat to discourage excessive trade barriers by non-European countries rather than enforced continuously, it may actually encourage free trade.

Another recent event that will affect trade is the momentum for free enterprise in the former East Germany and other countries in Eastern Europe. Consumers in these countries will have more freedom to purchase imported goods, which should enhance net exports of other European countries in the near future. However, as time passes and private enterprise evolves in Eastern Europe, firms residing there may be able to develop some comparative advantages.

Once the West European countries use East European markets to purchase goods as well as sell goods, the change in net exports will be less predictable.

Trade Agreements Around the World. International trade has grown in response to trade agreements among countries. Some of the more well-known free trade areas are shown in Exhibit 2.3. Many trade agreements specify reductions in trade barriers, while others specify free trade between the countries in the group.

In December 1993, a **General Agreement on Tariffs and Trade (GATT)** accord between 117 countries called for lower tariffs around the world. The accord resulted from the so-called Uruguay round of trade negotiations that had begun seven years earlier. The accord was expected to be implemented in 1995, at which time the GATT will be succeeded by a new agency called the World Trade Organization. The provisions of the accord reduced some tariffs by 30 percent on average and removed other tariffs over a five- to ten-year period. Existing tariffs were not reduced in some protected industries. In general, more progress was made on reducing tariffs in manufacturing industries than in service industries. Many of the large MNCs that have subsidiaries in numerous countries were affected less by the accord because they already had been producing their goods in the foreign markets they serve, and therefore had circumvented the tariffs. The accord was a major boost to exporting firms that had been previously subject to tariffs. Yet, because some of the tariffs will not be removed until after the year 2000, the complete effects of the accord will take time.

The GATT accord occurred just shortly after the NAFTA accord and continued the momentum for free trade. Even after the GATT accord, many countries were negotiating for the additional reduction in barriers imposed on their trade.

Capital Account

The **capital account** reflects changes in country ownership of long-term and short-term assets. Long-term foreign investment measures all capital investments made between countries, including both direct foreign investment and purchases of securities with maturities exceeding one year. Short-term foreign investment measures flows of funds invested in securities with maturities of less than one year. Because of the short maturity, investors of such securities will often maintain their funds in a given country for only a short time, causing short-term investment flows to be quite volatile over time.

To illustrate the importance of international capital flows, consider that Japanese investors typically purchase between 15 and 30 percent of the 30-year bonds issued by the U.S. Treasury. In addition, Japanese investors are responsible for as much as 25 percent of the volume of stocks traded on the New York Stock Exchange. Some analysts suggest that actions by Japanese investors triggered the two biggest stock market declines in the 1980s. The October 19, 1987 crash began after Japanese investors sold a very large amount in U.S. Treasury bond holdings, precipitating an abrupt increase in interest rates. The October 13, 1989 stock market decline began after two Japanese banks decided not to financially support a proposed $6.75 billion purchase of UAL Corporation by UAL's managers. This event appeared to make investors believe that other possible takeovers would not be completed because of insufficient backing by investors.

EXHIBIT 2.3 Trade Agreements Around the World

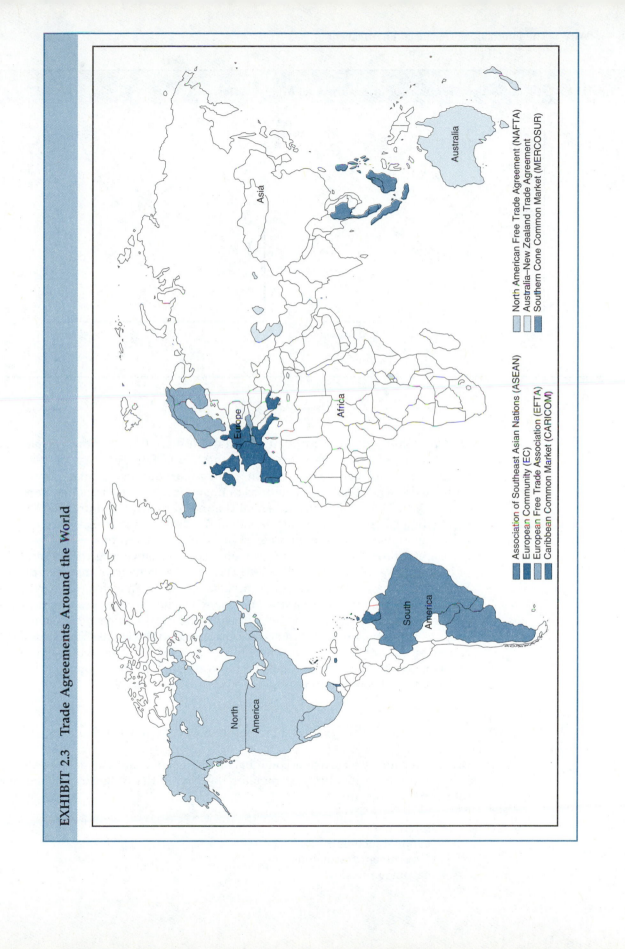

Association of Southeast Asian Nations (ASEAN)
European Community (EC)
European Free Trade Association (EFTA)
Caribbean Common Market (CARICOM)

North American Free Trade Agreement (NAFTA)
Australia–New Zealand Trade Agreement
Southern Cone Common Market (MERCOSUR)

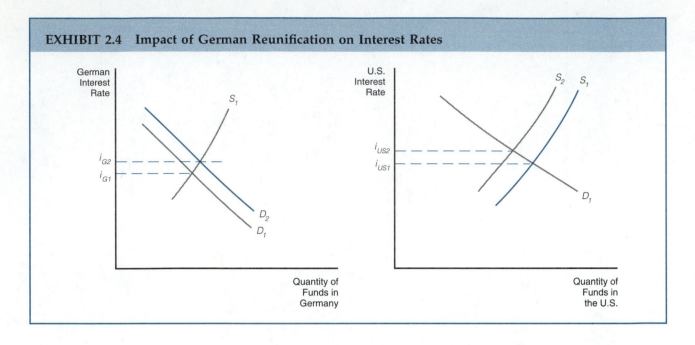

EXHIBIT 2.4   Impact of German Reunification on Interest Rates

Recent Changes in European Capital Flows.   Capital flows respond to changing regulations over time. When the Single European Act of 1987 was implemented to achieve integration throughout Europe, capital flows were redirected toward European countries to finance the new projects that would be undertaken. The result was less capital channeled to other countries, so that the supply of available funds became less than the demand for funds. Consequently, there was upward pressure on interest rates in those countries.

Capital flows between countries were also affected during the reunification of East and West Germany in late 1989. The encouragement of free enterprise in East Germany caused a substantial increase in the demand for funds there. By February 1990, interest rates in West Germany reached a seven-year high. Capital flows were redirected toward East Germany and West Germany to finance new projects. Consequently, less funds were channeled to the United States and other countries, causing interest rates there to rise (see Exhibit 2.4). Thus, interest rate movements across countries can be highly correlated, as the amounts of flows to and from most countries are influenced by the same factors.

FACTORS AFFECTING THE CURRENT ACCOUNT

Because a country's current account balance can significantly affect its economy, it is important to identify and monitor the factors that influence it. The most influential factors are

- Inflation
- National income
- Government restrictions
- Exchange rates.

Impact of Inflation

If a country's inflation rate increases relative to the countries with which it trades, its current account would be expected to decrease, other things being equal. Consumers and corporations within the country will most likely purchase more goods overseas (due to high local inflation), while the country's exports to other countries will decline.

Impact of National Income

If a country's income level (national income) increases by a higher percentage than those of other countries, its current account is expected to decrease, other things being equal. As the real income level (adjusted for inflation) rises, so does consumption of goods. A percentage of that increase in consumption will most likely reflect an increased demand for foreign goods. To illustrate the potential impact of national income on the current account balance, consider the frequent requests by the U.S. that other countries stimulate their respective economies, so that the foreign demand for U.S. goods increases. Yet, when countries are not willing to enact stimulative policies, the U.S. government must search for other solutions to its large balance of trade deficit.

The removal of the Iron Curtain boosted Europe's economy in late 1989 and in 1990, which led to a higher demand for U.S. goods. In fact, the United States experienced a surplus balance of trade with Western Europe over the first four months of 1990, a major improvement from the $1.3 billion deficit in 1989. However, slow economic growth in Japan and Europe during the early 1990s adversely affected the demand for U.S. exports. Meanwhile, relatively strong economic growth in Latin American countries and in China resulted in a higher demand for U.S. products by these countries. These examples substantiate the sensitivity of export volume to the economic strength of countries that purchase the exports.

Impact of Government Restrictions

If a country's government imposes a tax on imported goods (often referred to as a **tariff**), the prices of foreign goods to consumers are effectively increased. Tariff rates imposed by the U.S. government are on average lower than those imposed by other governments. However, some industries are more highly protected by tariffs than others. American apparel products and farm products have historically received more protection against foreign competition as a result of high tariffs on related imports. An increase in the use of tariffs is expected to increase the U.S. current account balance, unless other governments retaliate.

There are significant differences in tariffs among countries. For example, the United States recently charged a tariff of 13.5 cents per case of foreign beer, while Canada charged 24 cents per case, most European countries charged $2.93 per case, and China charged $14.64 per case.

In addition to tariffs, a government can reduce its country's imports by enforcing a **quota,** or a maximum limit that can be imported. Quotas have been commonly applied to a variety of goods imported by the U.S. and other countries.

Trade restrictions may save jobs, but only at a cost. A recent study by the Institute for International Economics estimated the cost per job saved to be

$705,000 for the U.S. automobile industry and $1 million for the specialty steel industry. Furthermore, trade restrictions tend to only benefit some industries at the expense of others, as other countries retaliate by imposing their own trade restrictions. In this case, imports by both countries may be reduced so that the current account level might not be much different from where it was before the first round of trade restrictions.

As an example of trade restrictions, the U.S. government enforced quotas on U.S.-imported specialty steel in July 1983 at the request of the U.S. steel industry to help the industry compete against foreign producers. The quotas were imposed on steel imported from European countries. This action is not considered legal based on the General Agreement on Tariffs and Trade (GATT) provisions established in 1947. The GATT rules allow for trade restrictions only in retaliation against illegal trade actions of other countries, such as a government's subsidizing of exports. The U.S. government-enforced trade restrictions were deemed illegal because they were simply intended to give the U.S. steel industry a competitive edge in its home market. Consequently, the U.S. government was forced to accept restrictions of equal value on U.S. exports. A group of European countries announced shortly thereafter that they would retaliate by imposing tariffs and quotas on U.S. chemicals, plastics, and sporting goods exported to their countries. The U.S. government felt that such retaliatory actions were excessive and considered counter-retaliation on other goods imported by the U.S. from these European countries. In this example, the U.S. steel industry benefited from the U.S. government-enforced trade restrictions, but the chemicals, plastics, and sporting goods industries were adversely affected by the retaliatory actions of the European countries.

During the 1990s, U.S. steel companies continued their claim that steel exported to the U.S. was being subsidized by foreign governments, allowing foreign steel firms an unfair advantage. In 1993, the U.S. International Trade Commission, which is charged with the task of reviewing such claims, ruled that many of the claims were unfounded.

In some industries, government restrictions on foreign trade remain. For example, the large U.S. automobile manufacturers have pressured the U.S. government to request that the Japanese government limit auto exports from Japan to the United States. The Japanese government has complied with this request, and has limited auto exports since 1985.

The government also has other ways in which it can influence the current account, beyond imposing restrictions. For example, in 1991 the French government provided huge subsidies to two of its massive electronics firms. Some European countries criticized this action since it was inconsistent with the recent removals of restrictions and subsidies that had inhibited free trade.

The general long-run movement toward free trade is continually interrupted by controversies between countries over the alleged **dumping** of products (selling at unfairly low prices). Dumping is often perceived to be the result of government subsidies to the exporters. In most cases, tariffs are imposed by the U.S. in an attempt to offset any subsidies that may give the exporters an unfair price advantage. Foreign governments commonly retaliate by imposing their own trade barriers on imports from the U.S. These interruptions to the free trade trend will likely continue because of the difficulty in determining whether products are being dumped, which leads to trade disagreements between countries.

ARE JAPANESE TRADE BARRIERS EXCESSIVE?

Sometimes *implicit* government trade barriers can have a significant impact on international trade. Japan is noted for its implicit barriers, such as extremely stringent product standards on imported products. Some economists argue that these barriers are to blame for the lingering U.S. trade deficit with Japan. Others, however, attribute the deficit to Japan's superior quality and production efficiency.

Japan's economy has substantially benefited since World War II from its participation in international trade. It has had large balance of trade surpluses since the early 1980s. Some countries openly criticized Japan for using excessive protectionist policies to maximize exports and limit imports, and Japan reacted to such criticism by reducing its trade barriers to a degree.

A related study by Bergstrand used regression analysis to determine the factors that affect the level of U.S. exports to and imports from Japan. (See Appendix B for a description of regression analysis.) The analysis found that most of the variation in exports and imports is related to economic variables (such as country prices and incomes) and exchange rates, but not to government trade barriers. This suggests that the imposition of trade barriers has not had a significant impact on the trade balance.

However, a 1993 study by the Council of Economic Advisers found that Japanese trade barriers are excessive, and cost American exporters $18 billion per year. The study also concluded that U.S. trade barriers are negligible, and do not have much effect on Japanese exporters. The concerns about Japanese barriers caused the U.S. government to pursue negotiations with Japan in 1994 in an attempt to resolve this issue. The U.S. government believed that a reduction in Japanese barriers could help to reduce the annual U.S. trade deficit with Japan of about $50 billion per year.

Impact of Exchange Rates

Each country's currency is valued in terms of other currencies through the use of exchange rates, so that currencies can be exchanged to facilitate international transactions. The values of most currencies can fluctuate over time because of market and government forces (as discussed in detail in Chapter 4). If a country's currency begins to rise in value against other currencies, its current account balance should decrease, other things being equal. Goods exported by the country will become more expensive to the importing countries if its currency strengthens. As a consequence, the demand for such goods will decrease. For example, a tennis racket selling in the United States for $100 would require a payment of DM200 by a German importer if the dollar were worth 2 marks (DM1 = $.50). Yet, if the dollar were worth 3 marks (DM1 = $.33), it would take DM300 to buy that racket, which could discourage German demand for it. A strong local currency is expected to reduce the current account balance if the traded goods are **price-elastic** (sensitive to price changes).

Just as a strong dollar is expected to cause a lower (or more negative) U.S. balance of trade, a weak dollar is expected to cause a higher balance of trade. The dollar's weakness lowers the price paid for U.S. goods by foreign customers, and can cause an increase in the demand for U.S. products. A weak dollar also tends to increase the dollar price paid for foreign goods, and reduces the U.S. demand for foreign goods.

In June 1992, a Japanese automobile worth 3 million yen was priced at $23,622 in the U.S., based on the exchange rate of 127 yen per dollar (¥1 = $.0078) at that time. In June 1993, the same automobile without any price increase would have been priced at $28,037, based on the prevailing exchange rate of 107 yen per dollar (¥1 = $.0093) at that time. In the first 6 months of 1993, Japanese exports declined to their lowest level in 14 years. This decline was partially attributed to the yen's strength.

In some periods, such as in the late 1970s and early 1980s, there is an inverse relationship between the dollar's value and the U.S. balance of trade. However, in other periods the relationship does not hold, for reasons explained shortly.

Interaction of Factors

Since the factors that affect the balance of trade interact, their simultaneous influence on the balance of trade is complex. For example, as a high U.S. inflation rate reduces the current account, it places downward pressure on the value of the dollar (as discussed in detail in Chapter 4). Since a weaker dollar can improve the current account, it may partially offset the impact of inflation on the current account.

CORRECTING A BALANCE OF TRADE DEFICIT

By reconsidering some of the factors that affect the balance of trade, it is possible to develop some common methods for correcting a deficit. Any policy that will increase foreign demand for the country's goods and services will improve the balance of trade position. Foreign demand may increase if export prices become more attractive. This can occur when the country's inflation is low or when its currency's value is reduced, thereby making the prices cheaper from a foreign perspective.

A floating exchange rate could possibly correct any international trade imbalances in the following way. A deficit in a country's balance of trade suggests that the country is spending a greater amount of funds on foreign products than it is receiving from exports to foreign countries. Because it is selling its currency (to buy foreign goods) in greater volume than the foreign demand for its currency, the value of its currency should decrease. This decrease in value should encourage more foreign demand for its goods in the future. While this theory seems rational, it does not always work in the manner stated. It is possible that, instead, a country's currency will remain stable or appreciate even when it has a balance of trade deficit. Other forces on the currency's value can offset the forces created by the balance of trade deficit. For example, consider a situation where foreign investors are purchasing the currency to invest in the country's securities. This demand for the currency places upward pressure on its value, thereby offsetting the downward pressure caused by the trade imbalance. Consequently, a country cannot always rely on currency movements to correct a trade deficit.

Why a Weak Home Currency Is Not a Perfect Solution

Even if a country's home currency weakens, its balance of trade will not necessarily improve. One reason is the possibility of a revised pricing policy by foreign competition in response to exchange rate movements. To illustrate,

MEASURING THE IMPACT OF EXCHANGE RATE MOVEMENTS ON INTERNATIONAL TRADE

The responsiveness to exports, imports, or the balance of trade to exchange rates can be measured using regression analysis. For example, a recent study by Chmura analyzed how exchange rates affected U.S. textile imports. The following regression equation was applied:

$$(\% \triangle \text{ imports})_t = b_0 + b_1 ER_{t-1} + b_2 GNP_{t-1} + \mu_t$$

where b_0, b_1, and b_2 represent regression coefficients, ER represents the percentage change in the real exchange rate of the dollar, GNP represents the percentage change in real GNP, t represents the quarter, and u represents an error term.

The real exchange rate of the dollar is a trade-weighted exchange rate adjusted for inflation. The real GNP also adjusts for inflation. Notice that the relationship expressed in the equation is designed to capture the lagged impact of the independent variables on imports. The regression model was applied to quarterly data from 1977 to 1986.

The results of the regression model follow:

$$(\% \triangle \text{ imports})_t = -29.41 + 1.33\ ER_{t-1} + 2.91\ GNP_{t-1}$$

The regression coefficient of 1.33 implies that a 1 percent change in the real exchange rate of the dollar was followed by a 1.33 percent change in U.S. textile imports one quarter later. Furthermore, $b_2 = 2.91$, so that a 1 percent change in GNP was followed by a 2.91 percent change in textile imports one quarter later. Both relationships are statistically significant. The results indicate the likely increase in textile imports that results from a given increase in the inflation-adjusted dollar value and GNP growth.

This analysis could be applied to each industry separately or to all industries consolidated. Furthermore, forecasts of imports in future periods could be developed by applying the regression coefficients to forecasted values of the trade-weighted exchange rate and GNP.

consider a German tire manufacturer that charged DM120 per tire to U.S. tire stores, when the German mark was valued at $.50. The dollar cost to the tire store is $60 (DM120 × $.50) per tire. If the mark's value appreciates to $.60, the dollar cost to the tire store is now $72 (DM120 × $.60) per tire. The German tire manufacturer could reduce its price to DM100, which would result in the original dollar price of $60 per tire (DM100 × $.60). By compensating for the exchange rate effects, the German firm can possibly retain the U.S. demand for its tires.

When the dollar weakened in 1986 and 1987, and U.S. prices became more attractive to non-U.S. customers, many non-U.S. companies lowered their prices to remain competitive with the U.S. firms. Thus, the U.S. demand for foreign goods was not affected much, because foreign producers lowered prices to compensate U.S. importers for the weaker dollar.

A second reason why the dollar's general weakness does not always affect the current account is that currencies of some other countries may have also weakened, allowing their local firms the same competitive advantages of U.S. firms. For example, while the dollar weakened against many European currencies in 1986 and 1987, the dollar's exchange rate with the currencies of Hong Kong, Singapore, South Korea, and Taiwan remained somewhat stable. As some U.S. firms terminated their demand for goods produced in European countries, they increased their demand for goods produced in Asian countries. Consequently, the dollar's weakness against European countries caused a change in international trade behavior, but did not eliminate the U.S. current account deficit.

A third reason why a weak dollar will not always reduce the U.S. trade deficit is that international trade transactions are prearranged and cannot be immediately adjusted. Thus, non-U.S. importing companies may be attracted to U.S. firms as a result of the weaker dollar, but do not immediately sever their relationships with suppliers from other countries. Over time, they may begin to take advantage of the weaker dollar by purchasing U.S. imports if they believe that the weakness will continue. The lag time between the dollar's weakness and the non-U.S. firm's increased demand for U.S. products has sometimes been estimated to be 18 months or even longer.

There is also a lagged relationship between the value of the dollar and the amount of U.S. imports, for the same reason. U.S. importers will not immediately switch to purchase U.S.-made goods when the dollar weakens. They may have established long-term relations with non-U.S. suppliers, or they may believe that there are no qualified substitutes for these goods in the United States. Given a stable amount of imports purchased and a weaker dollar, the dollar value of imports rises. Therefore, the U.S. balance of trade may actually deteriorate in the short run as a result of dollar depreciation. It only improves once U.S. and non-U.S. importers respond to the change in purchasing power that is caused by the weaker dollar. This represents the so-called **J curve effect,** as illustrated in Exhibit 2.5. The further decline in the trade balance before a reversal creates a trend that can look like the letter J.

A fourth reason why exchange rates will not always improve the U.S. balance of trade is that there are unique relationships between those importers and exporters that are under the same ownership. Many firms purchase products that are produced by their subsidiaries, in what is referred to as **intracompany trade.** This type of trade makes up more than 50 percent of all international trade. The trade between the two parties will normally continue in spite of

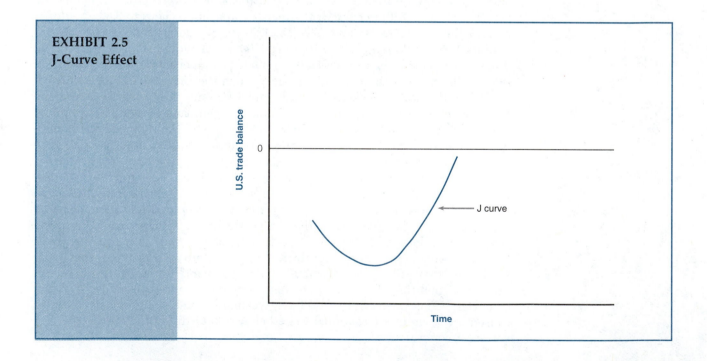

**EXHIBIT 2.5
J-Curve Effect**

exchange rate movements, because a decline in intracompany trade adversely affects the producer in the intracompany agreement. Thus, the impact of exchange rate movements on intracompany trade patterns is limited.

FACTORS AFFECTING THE CAPITAL ACCOUNT

As with trade flows, national governments have authority over capital (money) flows that enter the country. A country's government could, for example, impose a special tax on income accrued by local investors who invested in foreign markets. A tax such as this would likely discourage people from sending their funds to foreign markets and could therefore increase the country's capital account. Other countries affected by this tax, however, could retaliate by imposing a similar tax on their local people. The ultimate impact would be a reduction in foreign investing by investors across various countries.

Capital flows are also influenced by capital controls enforced by countries. Over the years, there has been a gradual liberalization of controls on international capital flows. Some countries, such as Canada, Germany, and the United States, have historically enforced relatively few capital controls. Other countries, such as Finland, Spain, and Sweden, have commonly imposed very restrictive controls on outflows of domestic currency. This imposition is typically designed to deal with a structural weakness in the country's balance of payments position.

The anticipated exchange rate movements by investors in securities can also affect the capital account. If a country's home currency is expected to strengthen, foreign investors may be willing to invest in the country's securities to benefit from the currency movement. Conversely, a country's capital account balance is expected to decrease if its home currency is expected to weaken, other things being equal.

When attempting to assess why a country's capital account changed or how it will change in the future, all factors must be considered simultaneously. A particular country may experience a reduction in its capital account even when its interest rates are attractive, if its home currency is expected to depreciate.

AGENCIES THAT PROMOTE INTERNATIONAL FLOWS

A variety of agencies have been established to facilitate international trade and financial transactions. These agencies often represent a collection of nations. A description of some of the more important agencies follows.

International Monetary Fund

The United Nations Monetary and Financial Conference held in Bretton Woods, New Hampshire, in July 1944 was called to develop a structured international monetary system. As a result of this conference, the **International Monetary Fund (IMF)** was formed. The major objectives of the IMF set by the charter are to (1) promote cooperation among countries on international monetary issues, (2) promote stability in exchange rates, (3) provide temporary funds to member countries attempting to correct imbalances of international payments, (4) promote free mobility of capital funds across countries, and (5) promote free trade. It is clear from these objectives that the IMF goals encourage increased internationalization of business.

Before 1973, when exchange rates were maintained within tight boundaries, the IMF concentrated on removing currency exchange restrictions and assuring currency convertibility, with the goal of encouraging international trade. The inception of floating exchange rates in 1973 and the onset of the 1974-75 recession caused concern by the IMF that countries would attempt reducing their respective currency values to stimulate exports and reduce imports. Thus, the IMF offered financing arrangements to countries experiencing large balance of trade deficits.

During the international debt crisis that erupted in August 1982, the IMF provided financing to many of the countries experiencing debt-repayment difficulties. It worked with each of these countries individually to develop and implement policies that would improve their balance of trade positions.

One of the key duties of the IMF is its **compensatory financing facility (CFF),** which attempts to reduce the impact of export instability on country economies. While it is available to all IMF members, it is mainly used by developing countries. A country experiencing financial problems due to reduced export earnings must demonstrate that the reduction is temporary and beyond its control. In addition, it must be willing to work with the IMF in resolving the problem.

Each member country of the IMF is assigned a quota based on a variety of factors reflecting that country's economic status. Members are required by the IMF to pay this assigned quota. The amount of funds that each member can borrow from the IMF is dependent on its particular assigned quota.

The financing by the IMF is measured in **special drawing rights (SDRs).** The SDR is not a currency but simply a unit of account. It is an international reserve asset created by the IMF and allocated to member countries to supplement currency reserves. The SDR's value fluctuates in accordance with the value of five major currencies: (1) U.S. dollar, (2) German mark, (3) French franc, (4) Japanese yen, and (5) British pound. This five-currency composite, designed on January 1, 1981, replaced a more complex 16-currency formula before that time. Each of the five currencies represented by the revised formula was assigned weights (in accordance with their international importance) to determine the SDR value. The U.S. dollar received a 42 percent weight, while the German mark received a 19 percent weight, and remaining currencies each received a 13 percent weight.

World Bank

The **International Bank for Reconstruction and Development (IBRD),** also referred to as the **World Bank,** was established in 1944. Its primary objective is to make loans to countries in order to enhance economic development. For example, the World Bank recently planned to lend Mexico about $4 billion over a ten-year period for environmental projects that would facilitate industrial development near the U.S. border. Its main source of funds is sale of bonds and other debt instruments to private investors and governments. The philosophy behind the World Bank's objective is profit-oriented. Therefore, loans are not subsidized, but are extended at market rates to governments (and their agencies) that are likely to make repayment.

One of the World Bank's key facilities is the **Structural Adjustment Loan (SAL)** facility established in 1980. The SALs are intended to enhance a country's long-term economic growth. For example, SALs have been provided to Turkey and to some of the less developed countries (LDCs) that are attempting to improve their balance of trade.

Because the World Bank provides only a small portion of the financing needed by developing countries, it attempts to spread its funds by entering into **cofinancing agreements.** Cofinancing is performed in the following ways:

- *Official aid agencies.* Development agencies may join the World Bank in financing development projects in low-income countries.
- *Export credit agencies.* The World Bank cofinances some capital-intensive projects that are also financed through export credit agencies.
- *Commercial banks.* The World Bank has joined with commercial banks to provide financing for private sector development. In recent years, more than 350 banks from all over the world have participated in cofinancing, including Bank of America, Bankers Trust, Chemical Bank and Citibank.

The World Bank has recently established the **Multilateral Investment Guarantee Agency (MIGA),** which offers various forms of political risk insurance. This is an additional means (along with its SALs) by which the World Bank can encourage the development of international trade and investment.

The World Bank is one of the largest borrowers in the world; its borrowings have amounted to the equivalent of $70 billion. Its loans are well-diversified among numerous currencies and countries. It has received the highest credit rating (AAA) possible.

International Financial Corporation

In 1956 the **International Financial Corporation (IFC)** was established to promote private enterprise within countries. Like the IMF, it is composed of a collection of nations as members. While it aims to enhance economic development, it uses the private rather than government sector to achieve its objectives. It not only provides loans to corporations, but also purchases stock, thereby becoming part owner in some cases, rather than just a creditor. The IFC typically provides 10 percent to 15 percent of the necessary funds in the private enterprise projects in which it invests, and the remainder of the project must be financed through other sources. Thus, the IFC acts as a catalyst as opposed to a sole supporter for private enterprise development projects. It traditionally has obtained financing from the World Bank but can borrow within the international financial markets.

International Development Association

The **International Development Association (IDA)** was created in 1960 with country development objectives somewhat similar to those of the World Bank. Yet, its loan policy is more appropriate for less prosperous nations. The IDA extends loans at low interest rates to poor nations that cannot qualify for or afford loans from the World Bank.

Bank for International Settlements

The **Bank for International Settlements (BIS)** attempts to facilitate cooperation among countries with regard to international transactions. It also provides assistance to countries experiencing a financial crisis. The BIS is sometimes referred to as the "central banks' central bank" or the "lender of last resort." It played an important role in supporting some of the less developed countries during the international debt crisis in the early and mid-1980s. It commonly provides financing for central banks in Latin American and East European countries.

Regional Development Agencies

There are several other agencies with more regional (as opposed to global) objectives relating to economic development. These include, for example, the Inter-American Development Bank (focusing on the needs of Latin America), the Asian Development Bank (established to enhance social and economic development in Asia), and the African Development Fund (focusing on development in African countries).

In 1990 the European Bank for Reconstruction and Development was created to help the East European countries adjust from communism to capitalism. Twelve West European countries hold 51 percent interest, while Eastern European countries hold 13.5 percent interest. The United States is the biggest shareholder, holding 10 percent interest. There are 40 member countries in aggregate.

SUMMARY

■ The key components of the balance of payments are the current account and the capital account. The current account represents a broad measure of the country's international trade balance. The capital account is a measure of the country's long-term and short-term capital investments, including direct foreign investment and investment in securities.

■ A country's current account is affected by inflation, national income, government restrictions, and exchange rates. High inflation, a high national income, low or no restrictions on imports, and a strong local currency tend to result in a strong demand for imports and a current account deficit. While some countries attempt to correct current account deficits by reducing the value of their currencies, this strategy is not always successful.

SELF-TEST FOR CHAPTER 2

(Answers are provided in Appendix A in the back of the text.)

1. Briefly explain how changes in various economic factors affect the U.S. current account balance.

2. Explain why U.S. tariffs will possibly change the composition of U.S. exports but will not necessarily reduce a U.S. balance of trade deficit.

3. Explain how capital flows were affected in 1992, when Germany's interest rates increased.

QUESTIONS

1. What is the current account generally composed of?

2. What is the capital account generally composed of?

3. Discuss the trend in the U.S. current account position since 1980. How can you explain the trend?

4. How would a relatively high home inflation rate affect the home country's current account, other things being equal?

5. How would a weakening home currency affect the home country's current account, other things being equal?

6. How can government restrictions affect international payments among countries?

7. Is a negative current account harmful to a country? Discuss.

8. More than 500 U.S. firms have developed offices or factories in China. Many other U.S. firms have become exporters to China in recent years. However, the U.S. government has periodically threatened to restrict business between the U.S. and China until China improves its human rights record. The U.S. Chamber of Commerce has estimated that heavy restrictions of U.S.-China business could cause layoffs of 150,000 U.S. workers. Should the U.S. use trade restrictions as a means of encouraging improvements in human rights in some countries? If so, how will this affect U.S. firms that are considering business in less developed countries?

9. It is sometimes suggested that a floating exchange rate will adjust to reduce or eliminate any current account deficit. Explain why this adjustment would occur. Why does the exchange rate not always adjust to a current account deficit?

10. What are some of the major objectives of the IMF?

11. From 1985 to 1987 the dollar substantially depreciated but the U.S. demand for particular foreign imports was not significantly affected. Explain why.

12. If a U.S. importer is charged higher prices for its imported supplies, what will influence its decision to switch to a U.S. supplier?

13. From 1986 to 1988 the dollar depreciated against most major currencies but not against the currencies of South Korea and Singapore. Explain why the balance of trade between the United States and these countries would shift in reaction to the dollar's depreciation against major currencies. Would the U.S. balance of trade deficit have been larger or smaller if the dollar depreciated against all currencies during this period? Explain.

14. Explain how a country can assess the historical impact of exchange rate movements on its imports. How can we use this information to forecast the expected impact of exchange rate movements on future imports?

15. In 1989 South Korea's export growth stalled. Some South Korean firms suggested that South Korea's primary export problem is the weakness in the Japanese yen. How would you interpret this statement?

16. In 1990, the U.S. balance of trade deficit was about $100 billion, which was the smallest deficit in several years. The smaller trade deficit was attributed to a strong demand for U.S. exports. What do you think is the underlying reason for the strong demand for U.S. exports?

17. In recent years there has been considerable momentum to reduce or remove trade barriers in an effort to achieve "free trade". Yet, one disgruntled executive of an exporting firm stated, "Free trade is not conceivable; we are always at the mercy of the exchange rate. Any country can use this mechanism to impose implicit trade barriers". What does this statement mean?

18. The Single European Act was expected to promote more cross-border trade within Europe. Yet, there was some concern that firms exporting to Europe would lose business. Why?

19. Explain why events in Japan can influence financial markets in the United States.

20. Explain how the German reunification could affect U.S. interest rates.

CASE: INTERNATIONAL FINANCIAL FLOWS

Americans Snap Up Securities Overseas at Record Pace

BY MICHAEL R. SESIT
Staff Reporter of THE WALL STREET JOURNAL

LONDON–Pulled by booming overseas stock markets and pushed by low U.S. interest rates, Americans are gobbling up foreign securities at a record pace.

This "huge wall of money from American investors" – in the words of Adaline Ko, a director at Fleming Investment Management Ltd. here – will continue pouring into overseas markets, money managers and analysts predict. . . .

In the second quarter of this year, U.S. investors purchased a record net $13.2 billion of foreign stocks, according to the Securities Industry Association, or SIA. It marked the 20th consecutive quarter that Americans have added shares to their portfolios in companies such as British drug giant Glaxo Holdings PLC, Mexican telephone concern Telefonos de Mexico SA and NV Royal Dutch Petroleum Co. During that period, U.S. investors have bought $109 billion of foreign stocks, lifting total overseas equity holdings to $210 billion. . . . .

He added that while U.S. investors expected foreign markets to rise early this year, many hesitated investing abroad because they felt a rising dollar would diminish those

gains. But the dollar hasn't risen as expected. "Now they are chasing after that growth," said Mr. Grubb.

Noting that U.S. pension funds currently hold roughly 6% to 7% of their total assets in international stocks and bonds, Bob Michaelson, chief global investment officer for Citibank Global Asset Management here, said that "most are targeting 10%, and some of the most sophisticated are up to 20%."

Americans' non-U.S. stock portfolios have nearly doubled during the past two and a half years, pointed out David Strongin, director of international finance at the SIA in New York. "Americans are diversifying their equity portfolios at a much faster pace than many experts had anticipated," he said.

Accelerating the move into foreign securities is the combination of slow U.S. growth, low U.S. interest rates and the expectation that falling interest rates in Europe will fire up stock and bond markets there. In addition, Mr. Strongin of the SIA said the actual and planned selloff of government-owned industries in many countries, relaxation of restrictions on foreign investment and rapid economic growth in the Third World is "serving as a powerful attraction for U.S. capital."

"There are numerous investment products in the U.S.; but in the low-interest rate environment, a lot of them have turned into wallflowers," he said. Meanwhile, "Americans are learning that it isn't such an insular

world out there, and that there are opportunities outside our markets."

During the first half of this year, U.S. investors purchased a net $21.7 billion of foreign stocks, nearly double the amount they bought in the first six months of 1992 and 67% of the total they bought in all of last year. A little more than half of the $21.7 billion went into European stock markets, with British shares accounting for $5.2 billion. Americans' next-favorite major foreign market was Canada, followed by Japan, Hong Kong, Italy, Spain and Germany. American investors also purchased a net $2.3 billion of Latin American shares in the first half, including $980 million in Mexico.

The $1.8 billion of Hong Kong stocks they added to their portfolios is astounding, given that the Hong Kong stock market is one-fourteenth the size of Japan's, in which Americans invested a net $2.3 billion. Because so many Hong Kong companies do business in China and have manufacturing facilities there, the colony's stock market is considered a play on the mainland's fast-growing economy.

So far, the bet has paid off. Hong Kong shares are up 57% this year in dollar terms, according to the Dow Jones World Stock Index. A rising yen, which increases the value of Japanese assets when translated into dollars, has propelled the Japanese stock market 47% higher. Meanwhile, Germany is up 30%, Italy 29%, Spain 24%, Britain 12%

Continued

CASE: INTERNATIONAL FINANCIAL FLOWS

Continued

and Canada 11%. By contrast, the U.S. component of the Dow Jones world index has climbed 7.7%.

"With the lower yields on cash deposits in the states, the [U.S.] stock and bond markets haven't performed well; and U.S. investors were looking around for alternative investments," said Richard Davidson, a European strategist at Morgan Stanley International here. "The reason that Europe got so much attention is because continental Europe remained in recession, interest rates were at extremely high levels early this year, and the bet that everyone was following was that European interest rates had to come down dramatically," he said.

American's growing comfort with international stocks and bonds could be upset, money managers warn, by an eventual rise in U.S. interest rates. That would increase the attraction of U.S. bonds, strengthen the dollar and therefore reduce the value of foreign securities. Higher U.S. rates also could send rumbles through emerging stock markets that are closely tied to the U.S. economy and currency.

Money managers also worry that some overseas stock markets may be overvalued. Noting that stocks in Europe are selling at an average of 22 times prospective 1993 earnings, compared with a 10-year historical average of about 14.5, Mr. Davidson of Morgan Stanley said: "There will be earnings growth next year, but it still won't be enough to make current valuations defendable."

But even those who see relative bargains in Europe don't discount a temporary U.S. investor retreat. "Right now, companies in Europe are at lower levels of valuation than comparable U.S. companies with similar growth prospects," said Richard Mace, a portfolio manager at Fidelity Investments in Boston. But he added that "a sharp rally in equity prices or a substantial decline in bond yields would make foreign markets look relatively less attractive."

Mr. Mace said he "wouldn't be surprised to see a 10% correction anytime." But he quickly added: "Those corrections are often buying opportunities."

Questions

1. It was mentioned that expectations of a strong dollar can affect the tendency of U.S. investors to invest abroad. Explain this effect.

2. It was mentioned that low U.S. interest rates can affect the tendency of U.S. investors to invest abroad. Explain this effect.

3. In general terms, what is the attraction of the foreign investments to U.S. investors?

MAPLELEAF PAPER COMPANY
Assessing the Effects of Changing Trade Barriers

Mapleleaf Paper Company is a Canadian firm that produces a particular type of paper that is not produced in the U.S. It focuses most of its sales in the U.S. In the past year for example, 180,000 of its 200,000 rolls of paper were sold to the U.S., with the remaining 20,000 rolls sold in Canada. It has a niche in the U.S., but because there are some substitutes, the U.S. demand for the product is sensitive to any changes in price. In fact, it had estimated that the U.S. demand rises (declines) three percent for every one percent decline (increase) in the price paid by U.S. consumers, other things held constant.

A 12 percent tariff had historically been imposed on the exports to the U.S. Then on January 2, a free trade agreement between the U.S. and Canada was implemented, eliminating the tariff. Mapleleaf was ecstatic about the news, as it had been lobbying for the free trade agreement for several years.

The Canadian dollar was worth $.76. Mapleleaf hired a consulting firm to forecast the value of the Canadian dollar in the future. The firm expected the Canadian dollar to be worth about $.86 by the end of the year and then stabilize after that. The expectations of a stronger Canadian dollar were driven by an anticipation that numerous Canadian firms would capitalize on the free trade agreement more than U.S. firms, which would cause the increase in the U.S. demand for Canadian goods to be much higher than the increase in the Canadian demand for U.S. goods. (However, no other Canadian firms were expected to penetrate the U.S. paper market.) Mapleleaf expected no major changes in the aggregate demand for paper in the U.S. paper industry. It was also confident that its only competition would continue to be two U.S. manufacturers that produce imperfect substitutes of the paper. Its sales in Canada were expected to grow by about 20 percent by the end of the year because of an increase in the overall Canadian demand for paper and then remain level after that. Mapleleaf invoiced its exports in Canadian dollars and planned to maintain its present pricing schedule, since its costs of production were relatively stable. Its U.S. competitors would also continue their pricing schedule. Mapleleaf was confident that the free trade agreement would be permanent. It immediately began to assess its long-run prospects in the U.S.

a) Based on the information provided, develop a forecast of Mapleleaf's annual production (in rolls) needed to accommodate demand in the future. Since orders for this year have already occurred, focus on the years following this year.

b) Explain the underlying reasons for the change in the demand and the implications of this exercise.

c) Would the general effects on Mapleleaf be similar to the effects on a U.S. paper producer that exports paper to Canada? Explain.

PROJECT

Once a month, the U.S. balance of trade figures are announced. Look in *The Wall Street Journal* or other business periodicals to assess this announcement and determine how the U.S. trade deficit has changed. What explanation is given for the change in the trade deficit? Is the change in the trade deficit attributed to a change in the U.S. dollar's value? Explain.

REFERENCES

Baldwin, Robert E. "Determinants of Trade and Foreign Investment: Further Evidence." *Review of Economics and Statistics* (Fall 1979), pp. 40–48.

Bergstrand, Jeffrey H. "United States-Japanese Trade: Predictions Using Selected Economic Models." *New England Economic Review*, Federal Reserve Bank of Boston (May–June 1986), pp. 24–37.

Chmura, Christine. "The Effect of Exchange Rate Variation on U.S. Textile and Apparel Imports." *Economic Review*, Federal Reserve Bank of Richmond (May–June 1987), pp. 17–22.

Coughlin, Cletus C. and Geoffrey E. Wood. "An Introduction to Non-Tariff Barriers to Trade." *Review*, Federal Reserve Bank of St. Louis (January–February 1989), pp. 32–46.

Fieleke, Norman S. "The Terms of Which Nations Trade." *New England Economic Review* (November–December 1989), pp. 3–12.

_____ . "International Payments Imbalances in the 1980s: An Overview." *New England Economic Review*, Federal Reserve Bank of Boston, (March–April 1989), pp. 4–14.

_____ . "Europe in 1992." *New England Economic Review*, Federal Reserve Bank of Boston, (May–June 1989), pp. 14–26.

Forrestal, Robert P. "The Rising Tide of Protectionism." *Economic Review*, Federal Bank of Atlanta (March–April 1987), pp. 4–10.

Hung, Wansing, Yoonbai Kim, and Kenichi Ohno. "Pricing Exports: A Cross-Country Study." *Journal of International Money and Finance* (February 1993), pp. 3–28.

Kroner, Kenneth F., and William D. Lastrapes. "The Impact of Exchange Rate Volatility on International Trade: Reduced Form Estimates Using the GARCH-in-mean Model." *Journal of International Money and Finance* (June 1993), pp. 298–318.

Obstfeld, Maurice. "Balance-of-Payments Crises and Devaluation." *Journal of Money, Credit, and Banking* (May 1984), pp. 208–217.

Rugman, Alan M., and Alain Verbeke. "Multinational Corporate Strategy and the Canada-U.S. Free Trade Assignment. *Management International Review* no. 3 (1990): pp. 253–266.

CHAPTER 3

INTERNATIONAL FINANCIAL MARKETS

Due to growth in international business over the last 30 years, various international financial markets have been developed. The specific objectives of this chapter are to describe the background and corporate use of the following international financial markets:

- foreign exchange market
- Eurocurrency market
- Eurocredit market
- Eurobond market, and
- international stock markets.

FOREIGN EXCHANGE MARKET

The **foreign exchange market** allows currencies to be exchanged in order to facilitate international trade or financial transactions. The system for establishing exchange rates has changed over time. From 1876 to 1913, exchange rates were dictated by the **gold standard.** Each currency was convertible into gold at a specified rate. Thus, the exchange rate between two currencies was determined by their relative convertibility rates per ounce of gold. Each country used gold to back its currency.

In 1914, World War I began, and the gold standard was suspended. Some countries reverted to the gold standard in the 1920s, but abandoned it as a result of a banking panic in the U.S. and Europe following the Great Depression. In the 1930s, some countries attempted to peg their currency to the dollar or the British pound, but there were frequent revisions. As a result of the instability in the foreign exchange market and the severe restrictions on international transactions during this period, the volume of international trade declined.

In 1944, an arrangement between countries (known as the **Bretton Woods Agreement**) called for fixed exchange rates between currencies. This arrangement lasted until 1971, as governments would intervene to prevent exchange rates from moving more than 1 percent above or below their initially established levels.

By 1971 the U.S. dollar appeared to be overvalued, since the foreign demand for U.S. dollars was substantially less than the supply of dollars for sale (to be exchanged for other currencies). Representatives from the major nations met to discuss how to deal with this dilemma. As a result of this conference, which became known as the **Smithsonian Agreement,** the U.S. dollar was devalued relative to the major currencies. The degree to which the dollar was devalued varied with each foreign currency. Not only was the dollar's value reset, but exchange rates were allowed to fluctuate by 2¼ percent in either direction from the newly set rates. This was the first step in letting market forces (supply and demand) determine the appropriate price of a currency. Although boundaries still existed for exchange rates, they were widened, allowing for the currency values to more freely move toward their appropriate levels.

Even after the Smithsonian Agreement, governments were still having difficulty maintaining exchange rates within the stated boundaries. By March 1973 the more widely traded currencies were allowed to fluctuate in accordance with market forces, and the official boundaries were eliminated.

Bank Participation

The term "foreign exchange market" should not be thought of as a specific building or location where traders exchange currencies. Requests by companies to exchange one currency for another with commercial banks are normally made by telephone. The most common type of foreign exchange transaction is for immediate exchange at the so-called **spot rate.** The market in which these transactions occur is known as the **spot market.** The average daily foreign exchange trading by banks around the world now exceeds $1 trillion. The average daily foreign exchange trading in the U.S. alone now exceeds $200 billion. While there are hundreds of banks in the world that can handle foreign exchange transactions, only 20 or so large banks accommodate 50 percent of the total volume of transactions. The U.S. dollar is not part of every transaction. Foreign currencies can be traded for each other. For example, a French firm may need British pounds to pay for imports from Great Britain. Much of the foreign exchange trading is conducted by banks in London, New York, and Tokyo. Thus, these cities are perceived to represent the three largest foreign exchange trading centers.

Small corporations may request quotes of foreign currencies over the phone from local banks and conduct the trade through mail. If they are not nationally known, they are somewhat restricted from contacting banks outside the local area (since such banks are not aware these firms exist).

A commercial bank's volume of trading in each foreign currency will coincide with the currency's use in international trade and finance. Exhibit 3.1 illustrates the distribution of foreign exchange turnover by banking institutions in the United States. The pie chart illustrates the importance of the Japanese yen and German mark, together comprising more than 58 percent of the total foreign exchange turnover. The British pound, Swiss franc, Canadian dollar, and French franc are also frequently traded. The six currencies listed here make up more than 90 percent of the foreign exchange turnover.

At any given point in time, the exchange rate between two currencies should be similar across the various banks that provide foreign exchange services. If

**EXHIBIT 3.1
Foreign Exchange
Turnover Reported
by U.S. Banks**
SOURCE: *FRBNY,*
Summary of Results of
U.S. Foreign Exchange
Market Turnover
Survey.

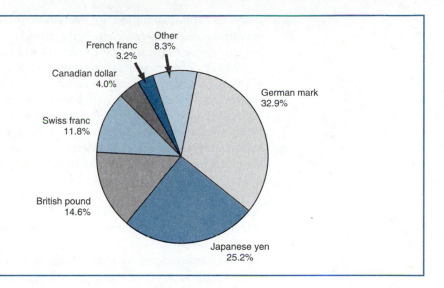

there were a large discrepancy, customers or other banks would purchase large amounts of a currency from whatever bank quoted a relatively low price and immediately sell it to whatever bank quoted a relatively high price. Such actions should cause adjustments in the exchange rate quotations that would eliminate any discrepancy.

If a bank begins to experience a shortage in a particular foreign currency, it can purchase that currency from other banks. This trading between banks occurs in what is often referred to as the **interbank market.** Within this market, banks can obtain quotes, or they can contact brokers who sometimes act as middlemen, matching one bank desiring to sell a given currency with another bank desiring to buy that currency. About 10 foreign exchange brokerage firms handle much of the interbank transaction volume.

While foreign exchange trading is conducted only during normal business hours in a given location, these hours vary among locations due to different time zones. Thus, at any given time on a weekday there is a bank open and ready to accommodate foreign exchange requests.

When the foreign exchange market opens in the U.S. each morning, the opening exchange rate quotations will be based on the prevailing exchange rate by banks in London and other locations where the foreign exchange markets have been open. For example, the quoted price of the British pound could be $1.80 at the previous close of the U.S. foreign exchange market, but by the time the market opens the following day, the opening price may be $1.76. In this example, news occurring in the morning before the U.S. market opened could have caused changes in the supply and demand conditions for British pounds in the London foreign exchange market, which reduced the quoted price for the pound.

With the newest electronic devices, foreign currency trades are negotiated on computer terminals, and a push of a button confirms the trade. Traders now use electronic trading boards that allow them to instantly register transactions and check their banks' positions in various currencies. Also, several U.S. banks have developed night trading desks. The largest banks established these night trading desks to capitalize on foreign exchange movements at night and to accommodate corporate requests for currency trades. Even some medium-sized banks have begun to use night trading to accommodate corporate clients.

Many foreign transactions do not require an exchange of currencies, but allow for a given currency to cross country borders. For example, the U.S. dollar is commonly accepted by merchants in many countries as a medium of exchange, especially in those countries where the home currency is either weak or subject to foreign exchange restrictions, such as Argentina, Bolivia, Brazil, China, Cuba, Indonesia, Russia, and Vietnam. Many merchants accept U.S. dollars because they can use them to purchase goods from other countries. The U.S. dollar is the official currency of Liberia and Panama.

Attributes of Banks That Provide Foreign Exchange. The following characteristics of banks are important to customers in need of foreign exchange:

1. *Competitiveness of quote.* A savings of 1¢ per unit on the order of 1 million units of currency is worth $10,000.
2. *Special relationship with the bank.* The bank may offer cash management services or be willing to make a special effort to obtain even hard-to-find foreign currencies for the corporation.
3. *Speed of execution.* Banks may vary in the efficiency with which they handle a trade that has been ordered. A corporation needing the currency will prefer a bank that conducts the transaction promptly and properly handles any paperwork.
4. *Advice about current market conditions.* Some banks may provide assessments of foreign economies and relevant activities in the international financial environment that relate to corporate customers.
5. *Forecasting advice.* Some banks may provide forecasts of the future state of foreign economies, the future value of exchange rates, etc.

This list suggests that a corporation needing a foreign currency should not automatically choose a bank that will sell that currency at the lowest price. Most corporations that often need foreign currencies develop a close relationship with at least one major bank in case they ever need favors from a bank.

Bid/Ask Spread of Banks

Commercial banks provide foreign exchange transactions for a fee. At any given point in time a bank's **bid** (buy) quote for a foreign currency will be less than its **ask** (sell) quote. The **bid/ask spread** is intended to cover the costs involved in accommodating requests to exchange currencies.

To understand how a bid/ask spread could affect you, assume you have $1,000 and plan to travel from the United States to Great Britain. Assume further that the bank's bid rate for the British pound is $1.52 and its ask rate is $1.60. Before leaving on your trip, you go to this bank to exchange dollars for pounds. Your $1,000 will be converted to 625 pounds (£), as follows:

$$\frac{\text{Amount in U.S. dollars to be converted}}{\text{Price charged by bank per pound}} = \frac{\$1,000}{\$1.60} = £625$$

Now suppose that because of an emergency you cannot take the trip, and you reconvert the £625 back to U.S. dollars, just after purchasing the pounds. If the exchange rate has not changed, you will receive

£625 × (Bank's bid rate of $1.52 per pound) = $950.

Due to the bid/ask spread, you have $50 (5 percent) less than what you started with. Obviously, the dollar amount of the loss would be larger if you originally converted more than $1,000 into pounds.

The nominal bid/ask spread will look much smaller for currencies worth less than the British pound. For example, the Japanese yen is worth less than a penny. If the bank's bid price for yen is $.007, its ask price may be $.0074. In this case, the nominal bid/ask spread is $.0074 − $.007, or just four-hundredths of a penny. Yet, the bid/ask spread in percentage terms is actually slightly higher for the yen in this example than for the pound in the previous example. To prove this, consider a traveler who sells $1,000 for yen at the bank's ask price of $.0074. The traveler receives about ¥ 135,135 (computed as $1,000/$.0074). If the traveler decides to cancel the trip and converts the yen back to dollars, then, assuming no changes in the exchange rate, the bank will sell these yen back at the bank's bid price of $.007 for a total of about $946 (computed by ¥ 135,135 × $.007), $54 (or 5.4 percent) less than what the traveler started with. This spread exceeds that of the British pound (5 percent in the previous example). A common way to compute the bid/ask spread in percentage terms follows:

$$\text{Bid/ask spread} = \frac{\text{Ask rate} - \text{Bid rate}}{\text{Ask rate}}$$

Using this formula, the bid/ask spreads are computed in Exhibit 3.2 for both the British pound and the Japanese yen.

Notice that these numbers coincide with those derived earlier. Such spreads are common for so-called "retail" transactions serving consumers. For larger so-called "wholesale" transactions between banks or for large corporations the spread will be much smaller. The spread is normally greater for those currencies that are less frequently traded.

EXHIBIT 3.2
Computation of the Bid/Ask Spread

Currency	Bid Rate	Ask Rate	$\dfrac{\text{Ask Rate} - \text{Bid Rate}}{\text{Ask Rate}} = $ Bid/Ask Percentage spread	
British pound	$1.52	$1.60	$\dfrac{\$1.60 - \$1.52}{\$1.60} =$	.05 *or* 5%
Japanese yen	$ .0070	$ .0074	$\dfrac{\$.0074 - \$.007}{\$.0074} =$	.054 *or* 5.4%

The bid/ask spread as defined here represents the discount in the bid rate as a percentage of the ask rate. An alternative bid/ask spread uses the bid rate as the denominator instead of the ask rate, and measures the percentage markup of the ask rate above the bid rate. The spread would be slightly higher when using this formula because the bid rate used in the denominator is always less than the ask rate.

In the following discussion and in examples throughout much of the text, the bid/ask spread will be ignored. That is, only one price will be shown for a given currency. This allows one to concentrate on understanding other relevant concepts. These examples depart slightly from reality, because the bid and ask prices are in a sense assumed to be equal. While the ask price will always exceed the bid price by a small amount in reality, the implications from examples should nevertheless hold, even though the bid/ask spreads are not accounted for. In particular examples where the bid/ask spread can contribute significantly to the concept, it will be accounted for.

Exchange Rate Risk at Banks

Because currency values fluctuate over time, a bank holding foreign currencies may gain or lose as a consequence. There are various ways a bank can reduce exposure to this risk. However, some banks do not attempt to hedge their open positions in foreign currencies if they expect the currencies to rise in value over time. Large commercial banks commonly generate foreign exchange earnings of $50 million or more during a given quarter.

Forward Contracts

Up to this point the discussion in this chapter has focused on foreign exchange trading in the spot market. There are also **forward contracts** available which allow for the purchasing or selling of currencies in future periods. Within the forward contract, a **forward rate** is specified. This represents the exchange rate at which currencies will be exchanged at a future point in time. When multinational corporations (MNCs) anticipate future need or future receipt of a foreign currency, they can set up forward contracts to lock in the rate at which they can purchase or sell a particular foreign currency. Virtually all MNCs use forward contracts. Some MNCs, such as CPC International and TRW, have forward contracts outstanding worth more than $100 million to hedge various positions.

How MNCs Use Forward Contracts. Consider a firm that will need 1,000,000 German marks in 90 days to purchase German imports. Assume that it can buy German marks from immediate delivery at the spot rate of $.50 per mark. At this spot rate, the firm would need $500,000 (computed as DM1,000,000 × $.50 per mark). However, it may not have the funds right now to exchange for marks. It could wait 90 days and then exchange dollars for marks at the spot rate existing at that time. Yet, the firm does not know what the spot rate will be at that time. If it rises to $.60 by then, the firm will need $600,000 (computed as DM1,000,000 × $.60 per mark). This represents an additional outlay of $100,000 due simply to the firm's waiting 90 days to make payment. Clearly, if the firm knew that the mark value was going to rise to $.60, it would have purchased the marks 90 days earlier just to avoid the additional expense. Even if it did not have the money at the time, it would have been better off borrowing U.S. dollars and using these dollars to buy the marks.

A preferable situation would be for a firm to be able to "lock in" the rate it will pay for marks 90 days from now without having to exchange dollars for marks immediately. This is exactly what the forward contract can do. The forward contract is an agreement between the firm and the bank to exchange currencies at a specified rate (the forward rate) in a specified number of days. The most common forward periods are for 30, 60, 90, 180, and 360 days, although other periods are available. The forward rate of a given currency will typically vary with the length (number of days) of the forward period.

Corporations also use the forward market to lock in the rate at which they can sell foreign currencies. This strategy is used to hedge against the possibility of those currencies depreciating over time.

Just as is the case with spot rates, there is a bid/ask spread on forward rates. For example, a given bank may have set up a contract with one firm where it will sell the firm marks 90 days from now at $.510 per mark. This represents the ask rate. At the same time, it may have agreed to purchase (bid) marks 90 days from now from some other firm at $.505 per mark.

Forward contracts are even available at some banks on currencies of developing countries, such as Chile, Mexico, South Korea, Taiwan, and Thailand. Since these markets have relatively small amounts of orders for forward contracts, banks are less able to match up willing buyers and sellers. This lack of liquidity causes banks to widen the bid/ask spread when quoting forward contracts. The contracts in these countries are generally available only for short-term horizons.

Premium or Discount on the Forward Rate.   If the forward rate exceeds the existing spot rate, it contains a premium. If it is less than the existing spot rate, it contains a discount. This premium or discount is normally computed on an annual basis as shown in Exhibit 3.3. For example, assume the forward exchange rates shown in Column 2 of Exhibit 3.3 were quoted for the British pound. Based on those forward rates, the forward discount has been computed for each maturity. The forward discounts can first be computed in decimal form, which is easily converted into percentage form.

EXHIBIT 3.3 Computation of Forward Rate Premiums or Discounts	Type of Exchange Rate for British Pounds	Value	Maturity	Forward Premium or Discount for the British Pound
	Spot rate	$1.8632		
	30-day forward rate	$1.8621	30 days	$\frac{\$1.8621 - \$1.8632}{\$1.8632} \times \frac{360}{30} = -.71\%$
	90-day forward rate	$1.8586	90 days	$\frac{\$1.8586 - \$1.8632}{\$1.8632} \times \frac{360}{90} = -.99\%$
	180-day forward rate	$1.8526	180 days	$\frac{\$1.8526 - \$1.8632}{\$1.8632} \times \frac{360}{180} = -1.14\%$

Forward rates typically differ from the spot rate for any given currency. If the forward rate were the same as the spot rate, and interest rates of the two countries differed, it would be possible for some investors (under certain assumptions) to use **arbitrage** so as to earn higher returns than would be possible domestically without incurring additional risk. Consequently, the forward rate will usually contain a premium (or discount) that reflects the difference between the home interest rate and the foreign interest rate.

Tailor-Made for MNCs. The forward contract between a firm and its bank can be tailored to accommodate the needs of the firm. Forward contract periods for two years or even longer are available for widely traded currencies. Some banks offer even five-year forward contracts to some large corporations.

Because forward contracts accommodate large corporations, the forward transaction will often be valued at $1 million or more. Forward contracts are not normally used by consumers or small firms. In some cases, a bank may request an initial deposit by the corporation to assure that it will fulfill its obligation. In other cases, the bank may fully trust the corporation and will not require an initial deposit.

Interpreting Foreign Exchange Quotations

Exchange rate quotations for most currencies are provided in *The Wall Street Journal* and in business sections of many newspapers on a daily basis. An example is disclosed in Exhibit 3.4. The quotations normally reflect the ask prices for large transactions. Since exchange rates change throughout the day, the exchange rates quoted in a newspaper reflect only one specific point in time during the day. Quotations that represent the value of a foreign currency in dollars (number of dollars per currency) are referred to as **direct quotations.** Conversely, quotations that represent the number of units of a foreign currency per dollar are referred to as **indirect quotations.** For example, if the French franc is worth $.20, the direct quotation of the franc would be $.20, while the indirect quotation of the franc would be 5.000 (5 francs per dollar). The indirect quotation is the reciprocal of the corresponding direct quotation.

The discussion of exchange rate movements can be confusing because some comments refer to direct quotations while other comments refer to indirect quotations. For consistency, direct quotations are used throughout this text unless an example can be clarified with the use of indirect quotations. The direct quotations are easier to link with comments about any foreign currency. For example, the increased value of the German mark is more obvious when using direct quotations to show a movement from $.50 to $.55.

Notice from Exhibit 3.4 that the forward rates for common maturities are disclosed just below the spot rate for six widely traded currencies. Forward rates for other maturities would have to be obtained directly from a bank. The forward premiums and discounts for those currencies whose forward rates are quoted can be calculated in a manner similar to that illustrated in Exhibit 3.3.

SDR and ECU. The term **SDR** near the bottom of Exhibit 3.4 represents **special drawing rights,** which are international reserve assets that were initially allocated by the International Monetary Fund to specific countries, and are

EXHIBIT 3.4
Foreign Exchange Rate Quotations
Source: *The Wall Street Journal* (June 14, 1994): p. C15. Reprinted by permission of *The Wall Street Journal* © 1994 Dow Jones & Company, Inc. All rights reserved worldwide.

CURRENCY TRADING

EXCHANGE RATES

Monday, June 13, 1994

The New York foreign exchange selling rates below apply to trading among banks in amounts of $1 million and more, as quoted at 3 p.m. Eastern time by Bankers Trust Co., Dow Jones Telerate Inc. and other sources. Retail transactions provide fewer units of foreign currency per dollar.

Country	U.S. $ equiv. Mon.	U.S. $ equiv. Fri.	Currency per U.S. $ Mon.	Currency per U.S. $ Fri.
Argentina (Peso)	1.01	1.01	.99	.99
Australia (Dollar)	.7350	.7348	1.3605	1.3609
Austria (Schilling)	.08639	.08534	11.58	11.72
Bahrain (Dinar)	2.6522	2.6522	.3771	.3771
Belgium (Franc)	.02953	.02916	33.86	34.30
Brazil (Cruzeiro real)	.0004636	.0004719	2157.17	2119.00
Britain (Pound)	1.5205	1.5090	.6577	.6627
30-Day Forward	1.5197	1.5081	.6580	.6631
90-Day Forward	1.5184	1.5067	.6586	.6637
180-Day Forward	1.5169	1.5052	.6592	.6644
Canada (Dollar)	.7236	.7276	1.3820	1.3743
30-Day Forward	.7228	.7267	1.3836	1.3761
90-Day Forward	.7208	.7248	1.3874	1.3796
180-Day Forward	.7174	.7221	1.3939	1.3848
Czech. Rep. (Koruna)				
Commercial rate	.0342818	.0341309	29.1700	29.2990
Chile (Peso)	.002423	.002426	412.64	412.25
China (Renminbi)	.114943	.114943	8.7000	8.7000
Colombia (Peso)	.001201	.001190	832.90	840.51
Denmark (Krone)	.1553	.1538	6.4380	6.5032
Ecuador (Sucre)				
Floating rate	.000465	.000464	2149.01	2154.01
Finland (Markka)	.18209	.18082	5.4919	5.5303
France (Franc)	.17817	.17643	5.6125	5.6680
30-Day Forward	.17798	.17624	5.6187	5.6742
90-Day Forward	.17774	.17596	5.6263	5.6830
180-Day Forward	.17758	.17575	5.6314	5.6900
Germany (Mark)	.6077	.6002	1.6455	1.6660
30-Day Forward	.6074	.5998	1.6464	1.6672
90-Day Forward	.6071	.5993	1.6473	1.6687
180-Day Forward	.6073	.5993	1.6467	1.6687
Greece (Drachma)	.004032	.003993	248.00	250.45
Hong Kong (Dollar)	.12925	.12924	7.7370	7.7375
Hungary (Forint)	.0096126	.0095639	104.0300	104.5600
India (Rupee)	.03212	.03212	31.13	31.13
Indonesia (Rupiah)	.0004613	.0004617	2168.02	2166.00
Ireland (Punt)	1.4844	1.4679	.6737	.6812
Israel (Shekel)	.3277	.3288	3.0520	3.0410
Italy (Lira)	.0006272	.0006214	1594.49	1609.37
Japan (Yen)	.009713	.009653	102.95	103.60
30-Day Forward	.009731	.009671	102.76	103.40
90-Day Forward	.009775	.009713	102.30	102.95
180-Day Forward	.009844	.009783	101.58	102.22
Jordan (Dinar)	1.4599	1.4577	.6850	.6860
Kuwait (Dinar)	3.3568	3.3568	.2979	.2979
Lebanon (Pound)	.000594	.000594	1682.50	1683.50
Malaysia (Ringgit)	.3858	.3852	2.5923	2.5960
Malta (Lira)	2.6178	2.6008	.3820	.3845
Mexico (Peso)				
Floating rate	.2962524	.2981959	3.3755	3.3535
Netherland (Guilder)	.5423	.5354	1.8440	1.8678
New Zealand (Dollar)	.5887	.5893	1.6987	1.6969
Norway (Krone)	.1402	.1385	7.1346	7.2196
Pakistan (Rupee)	.0327	.0327	30.61	30.60
Peru (New Sol)	.4694	.4716	2.13	2.12
Philippines (Peso)	.03765	.03724	26.56	26.85
Poland (Zloty)	.00004380	.00004382	22833.01	22820.00
Portugal (Escudo)	.005823	.005760	171.74	173.60
Saudi Arabia (Riyal)	.26667	.26667	3.7500	3.7500
Singapore (Dollar)	.6530	.6521	1.5315	1.5335
Slovak Rep. (Koruna)	.0307314	.0307314	32.5400	32.5400
South Africa (Rand)				
Commercial rate	.2764	.2761	3.6178	3.6215
Financial rate	.2092	.2089	4.7800	4.7880
South Korea (Won)	.0012402	.0012405	806.30	806.10
Spain (Peseta)	.007398	.007338	135.18	136.28
Sweden (Krona)	.1276	.1262	7.8383	7.9252
Switzerland (Franc)	.7209	.7118	1.3871	1.4048
30-Day Forward	.7209	.7118	1.3871	1.4048
90-Day Forward	.7213	.7121	1.3863	1.4042
180-Day Forward	.7226	.7132	1.3839	1.4021
Taiwan (Dollar)	.036958	.036934	27.06	27.08
Thailand (Baht)	.03971	.03961	25.18	25.25
Turkey (Lira)	.0000312	.0000311	32091.87	32205.77
United Arab (Dirham)	.2723	.2723	3.6725	3.6725
Uruguay (New Peso)				
Financial	.202429	.200401	4.94	4.99
Venezuela (Bolivar)				
Floating rate	.00607	.00602	164.80	166.00
SDR	1.41776	1.41238	.70534	.70802
ECU	1.17220	1.15920	....	....

Special Drawing Rights (SDR) are based on exchange rates for the U.S., German, British, French and Japanese currencies. Source: International Monetary Fund.

European Currency Unit (ECU) is based on a basket of community currencies.

exchanged between governments to cover debt obligations. The SDR's value is based on a weighted index of five currencies: U.S. dollar, British pound, French franc, German mark, and Japanese yen. It has been used as a unit of account to denominate the value of international bonds, international airline fares, and other international transactions. Its use as a unit of account has caused various firms to monitor its value over time relative to their home currencies.

The term ECU at the bottom of Exhibit 3.4 represents the European Currency Unit, which was originally established as a unit of account to settle debt obligations between various European governments. Some European governments have their currency tied to the ECU. The ECU's value is a weighted average of several European currencies.

The ECU is now used to denominate some deposits and loans in the Eurocurrency market. Securities denominated in ECUs have been issued in Germany, Switzerland, France, Belgium, Netherlands, Luxembourg, and the United Kingdom. ECU loans have been provided to both MNCs and governments.

Cross Exchange Rates

Most exchange rate quotation tables express currencies relative to the dollar. Yet, there are some instances where one is concerned about the exchange rate between two non-dollar currencies. For example, if a British firm needs marks to buy German goods, it is concerned about the German mark value relative to the British pound. The type of rate desired here is known as a **cross exchange rate,** since it reflects the amount of one foreign currency per unit of another foreign currency. Cross exchange rates can be easily determined with the use of foreign exchange quotations. The general formula follows.

$$\text{Value of 1 unit of Currency A in units of Currency B} = \frac{\text{Value of Currency A in \$}}{\text{Value of Currency B in \$}}$$

For example, if the pound is worth $1.80, and the German mark is worth $.60, the value of the British pound (£) in German marks (DM) is calculated as follows:

$$\text{Value of £ in DM} = \frac{\text{Value of £ in \$}}{\text{Value of DM in \$}}$$

$$= \frac{\$1.80}{\$.60}$$

$$= 3.00.$$

Thus, a British pound is worth DM3.00. An alternative way of expressing the pound-mark exchange rate is as the number of pounds equal to one mark. This figure can be computed by taking the reciprocal: 1/3.00 equals about .333, which suggests that a mark is worth about £.333 according to the information provided.

Currency Futures and Options Markets

Some MNCs involved in international trade use the currency futures and options markets to hedge their positions. A **currency futures** contract specifies a standard volume of a particular currency to be exchanged on a specific settlement date. An MNC that desires to hedge payables would buy futures contracts to lock in the price paid for a foreign currency at a future point in time. Conversely, an MNC that desires to hedge receivables would sell futures contracts to lock in the price received in exchange for a foreign currency at a future point in time. Futures contracts are somewhat similar to forward contracts, except that they are sold on an exchange while forward contracts are offered by commercial banks. Additional details on futures contracts, including other differences from forward contracts, are provided in Chapter 5.

Currency options contracts can be classified as calls or puts. A **currency call option** provides the right to buy a specific currency at a specific price (called the **strike price** or **exercise price**) within a specific period of time. It is used to hedge future payables. A **currency put option** provides the right to sell a specific currency at a specific price within a specific period of time. It is used to hedge future receivables.

CROSS EXCHANGE RATE QUOTATIONS

Cross exchange rate quotations are summarized for major currencies each day in *The Wall Street Journal,* as shown here. Each country is listed in the left column, with various currencies listed in the columns. For example, the top row represents quotations of exchange rates from Canada's perspective. Each number in the top row represents the number of Canadian dollars per currency listed at the top of the column. The second row represents quotations of exchange rates from France's perspective. Each number in that row represents the number of French francs per currency listed at the top of the column.

Key Currency Cross Rates — Late New York Trading June 14, 1994

	Dollar	Pound	SFranc	Guilder	Peso	Yen	Lira	D-Mark	FFranc	CdnDlr
Canada	1.3853	2.1039	.99877	.75186	.41089	.01349	.00087	.84172	.24674	....
France	5.6143	8.526	4.0478	3.0471	1.66522	.05466	.00351	3.4113	....	4.0528
Germany	1.6458	2.4995	1.1866	.89324	.48815	.01602	.00103	....	.29314	1.1880
Italy	1601.0	2431.4	1154.29	868.93	474.86	15.588	....	972.78	285.16	1155.7
Japan	102.71	155.99	74.052	55.745	30.464	....	.06415	62.407	18.294	74.14
Mexico	3.3715	5.1203	2.4308	1.8299	....	.03283	.00211	2.0485	.6005	2.4338
Netherlands ..	1.8425	2.7982	1.3284	....	.54649	.01794	.00115	1.1195	.32818	1.3300
Switzerland ...	1.3870	2.1064	....	.75278	.41139	.01350	.00087	.84275	.24705	1.0012
U.K.	.65846	....	.47474	.35737	.19530	.00641	.00041	.40008	.11728	.47532
U.S.	....	1.5187	.72098	.54274	.29660	.00974	.00062	.60761	.17812	.72187

Source: Dow Jones Telerate Inc.

SOURCE: *The Wall Street Journal* (June 15, 1994): p. C17. Reprinted by permission of *The Wall Street Journal* © 1994 Dow Jones & Company, Inc. All rights reserved worldwide.

Currency call and put options can be purchased on an exchange. They offer more flexibility than the forward or futures contracts because they do not require any obligation. That is, the firm can elect not to exercise the option.

Currency options have become a popular means of hedging. Coca-Cola Company has replaced about 30 to 40 percent of its forward contracting with currency options. FMC, a U.S. manufacturer of chemicals and machinery, now emphasizes currency options in place of forward contracts to hedge its foreign sales. A recent study by the Whitney Group found that 85 percent of U.S.-based MNCs use currency options. Additional details about currency options, including other differences from futures and forward contracts, are provided in Chapter 5.

EUROCURRENCY MARKET

Within each given country, financial markets exist in order to most efficiently transfer funds from surplus units (savers) to deficit units (borrowers). These markets are overseen by various regulators that attempt to enhance their safety and efficiency. The primary reason for the existence of financial institutions that make up these financial markets is to provide information and expertise. The surplus units do not typically know who needs to borrow funds at any particular point in time. Furthermore, they often cannot adequately evaluate the credit risk of any potential borrowers, nor establish the documentation necessary when providing loans. Financial institutions specialize in collecting funds from surplus units and then repackaging and transferring the funds to deficit units.

Development of the Eurocurrency Market

Like domestic firms, MNCs sometimes obtain funding through short-term loans from local financial institutions, or through issuing short-term securities such as commercial paper. However, they can also obtain funds from the financial institutions in foreign markets. The role of international financial intermediation emerged in the 1960s and 1970s as MNCs expanded their operations. During this period, the Eurodollar market, or what is now referred to as the **Eurocurrency market,** grew to accommodate the increasing international business. The Euro-dollar market was created as corporations in the U.S. deposited U.S. dollars in European banks. These European banks were willing to accept dollar deposits, since they could then lend dollars to corporate customers based in Europe. Because the U.S. dollar is widely used even by foreign countries as a medium for international trade, there is a consistent need for dollars in Europe. U.S. dollar deposits placed in banks located in Europe and other continents became known as **Eurodollars.** The growth of the Eurodollar market was partially due to U.S. regulations in 1968, which limited foreign lending by U.S. banks. Foreign subsidiaries of U.S.-based MNCs could obtain U.S. dollars from banks in Europe. In addition, ceilings were placed on the interest rates of dollar deposits in the U.S. This motivated the transfer of dollars to the Eurodollar market where such regulations were nonexistent. Furthermore, reserve requirements were nonexistent for Eurodollar deposits. Thus, banks could reduce the spread between what they paid on such deposits and charged on loans, and still make a reasonable profit. This added to the popularity of the Eurodollar market, since banks could offer attractive deposit rates to corporations and governments with excess cash and attractive loan rates to corporations and governments with deficient funds.

Composition of the Eurocurrency Market

The Eurocurrency market is composed of several large banks (referred to as **Eurobanks**) that accept deposits and provide loans in various currencies. Countries within the Organization of Petroleum Exporting Countries (OPEC) also use the Eurocurrency market to deposit a portion of their petroleum revenues. The deposits usually have been denominated in U.S. dollars, since OPEC generally requires payment for oil in dollars. Those dollar deposits by OPEC countries are sometimes referred to as **petrodollars.** The Eurocurrency market has historically recycled the oil revenues from the oil-exporting countries to other countries. That is, oil revenues deposited in the Eurobanks are sometimes lent to those oil-importing countries that are short of cash. As these countries purchase more oil, funds are again transferred to oil-exporting countries, which in turn results in new deposits. This recycling process has been an important source of funds for some countries.

Eurocurrency market transactions normally represent large deposits and loans, often the equivalent of $1 million or more. Large financial transactions such as these can reduce operating expenses for a bank. This is another reason why Eurobanks can offer attractive rates on deposits and loans.

When a currency is deposited in or loaned from a Eurobank, it is often described with a "Euro" prefix attached to it. For example, a loan in Swiss francs by a Eurobank is referred to as a "Euro-Swiss franc" loan, while a deposit of Japanese yen in a Eurobank is called a "Euroyen" deposit. One should not become confused by the "Euro" prefix. The interest rate for each Eurocurrency is somewhat representative of that currency's rate in its home country. That is, the Eurodollar loan rate may be just slightly less than a similar dollar loan in the United States, and the Euro-Swiss franc loan rate may be just slightly less than the loan rate for Swiss francs in Switzerland. However, the rates charged for loans in different foreign currencies vary substantially among currencies, since funds denominated in each currency have their own supply and demand.

Asian Dollar Market

The Eurocurrency market can be broadly defined to include banks in Asia that accept deposits and make loans in foreign currencies (mostly dollars). Yet, this market is sometimes referred to separately as the **Asian dollar market.** Most activity takes place in Hong Kong and Singapore. The only significant difference between the Asian market and the Eurocurrency market is location. Like the Eurocurrency market, the Asian dollar market grew to accommodate needs of businesses that were using the U.S. dollar (and some other foreign currencies) as a medium of exchange for international trade. These businesses could not rely on banks in Europe because of the inconvenience of distance and different time zones. In addition, the government of Singapore eliminated its 40 percent withholding tax on interest paid to nonresidents in 1968. In 1973 it reduced its tax on bank profits on Asian dollar offshore loans from 40 percent to 10 percent. Other taxes were also reduced or eliminated, thereby encouraging growth in the Asian dollar market. In the mid-1970s, oil-exporting countries added to the growth by establishing large dollar deposits in this market.

The major sources of Asian dollar deposits are MNCs with excess cash and government agencies. Major borrowers in this market are manufacturers.

The primary function of banks in the Asian dollar market is to channel funds from depositors to borrowers. Another function is interbank lending and borrowing. Banks participating in this market frequently lend to or borrow from each other. This activity typically results from their primary role as a financial intermediary. Banks that have more qualified loan applicants than they can accommodate use the interbank market to obtain additional funds. Banks in the Asian market commonly borrow from or lend to banks in the Eurocurrency market. Dollar loan demand has historically been relatively high at the Hong Kong banks, partially because of their contacts with businesses in South Korea, Taiwan, and the Philippines. Hong Kong banks have often borrowed from Singapore banks through the interbank market in order to obtain sufficient funds.

The potential benefits to a country that allows an offshore banking market to be established include increased employment and higher tax revenues. However, the banks that operate in these markets tend to pull customers away from the local banking markets.

EUROCREDIT MARKET

Multinational corporations and domestic firms sometimes obtain medium-term funds through term loans from local financial institutions, or through the issuance of notes (medium-term debt obligations) in their local markets. However, MNCs also have access to medium-term funds through Eurobanks located in foreign markets. Loans of one year or longer extended by Eurobanks are commonly called **Eurocredits** or **Eurocredit loans.** Such loans in the **Eurocredit market** have become popular since corporations and government agencies often desire to borrow for a term exceeding one year, and a common maturity for Eurocredit loans is five years.

Because Eurobanks accept short-term deposits and sometimes provide longer term loans, their asset and liability maturities do not match. This can adversely affect a bank's performance during periods of rising interest rates, since it may have locked in a rate on its Eurocredit loans while its rate paid on short-term deposits is rising over time. To avoid this risk, Eurobanks now commonly use floating rate Eurocredit loans. The loan rate floats in accordance with the movement of some market interest rate, such as the **London Interbank Offer Rate (LIBOR),** which is the rate commonly charged for loans between Eurobanks. For example, a Eurocredit loan may have a loan rate that adjusts every six months and is set at "LIBOR plus 3 percent." The premium paid above LIBOR will depend on the credit risk of the borrower.

In some cases, a corporation or government agency needs to borrow more funds than any single Eurobank is willing to lend. For this reason, **syndicated Eurocredit loans** have become popular. The banks participating in the syndicate combine funds to create a large loan for the borrower. Since each bank channels only a portion of the total loan to the borrower, no single bank is totally exposed to the risk that the borrower may fail to repay the loan. The risk is spread among the banks within the syndicate.

EUROBOND MARKET

MNCs, like domestic firms, can obtain long-term debt by issuing bonds in their local markets. MNCs can access long-term funds in foreign markets by issuing bonds in the international bond markets. International bonds are typically classified as either foreign bonds or Eurobonds. A **foreign bond** is issued by a borrower foreign to the country where the bond is placed. For example, a U.S. corporation may issue a bond denominated in German marks, which is sold to investors in Germany. In some cases, a firm may issue a variety of bonds in various countries. The currency denominating each type of bond is determined by the country where it is sold. Thus, a U.S. corporation may issue mark-denominated bonds that are placed in Germany, Swiss franc-denominated bonds that are placed in Switzerland, and so on. These foreign bonds are sometimes specifically referred to as **parallel bonds.**

Eurobonds are sold in countries other than the country represented by the currency denominating them. They have been very popular during the last decade as a means of attracting long-term funds.

Eurobonds are underwritten by a multinational syndicate of investment banks and simultaneously placed in many countries, providing a wide spectrum of fund sources to tap. The underwriting process takes place within a stepwise sequence. The multinational managing syndicate sells the bonds to a large underwriting crew. In many cases, a special distribution to regional underwriters is allocated before the bonds finally reach the bond purchasers. One problem with the distribution method is that the second- and third-stage underwriters do not always follow up on their promise to sell the bonds. The managing syndicate is therefore forced to redistribute the unsold bonds or to sell them directly, which creates "digestion" problems in the market and adds to the distribution cost. To avoid such problems, bonds are often distributed in higher volume to the underwriters that have fulfilled their commitments in the past at the expense of those that have not. This has helped the Eurobond market maintain its desirability as a bond placement center.

Eurobonds have several distinguishing features. They usually are issued in bearer form, and coupon payments are made yearly. Some Eurobonds carry a convertibility clause allowing them to be converted into a specified number of common stock shares. Eurobonds typically have few, if any, protective covenants, which is an advantage to the issuer. Also, call provisions are contained within even the short-maturity Eurobonds. Some Eurobonds, called **floating rate notes** (FRNs), have a variable rate provision that adjusts the coupon rate over time according to prevailing market rates.

Various currencies are commonly used to denominate Eurobonds. The U.S. dollar is used the most, denominating 70 to 75 percent of the Eurobonds, and it was even more dominant in earlier years.

Eurobonds have a secondary market. The market makers are in many cases the same underwriters who sell the primary issues. A technological advancement called **Euro-clear** helps to inform all traders about outstanding issues for sale, thus allowing a more active secondary market. The middlemen, or intermediaries, within the secondary market are based in ten different countries, with those in the United Kingdom dominating the action. They can act not only as brokers, but also as dealers that hold inventories of Eurobonds. Many of these intermediaries, such as Bank of America International, Salomon Brothers, and Citicorp International, are subsidiaries of U.S. parent corporations.

Development of the Eurobond Market

The emergence of the Eurobond market is partially the result of the **Interest Equalization Tax** (IET) imposed by the U.S. government in 1963 in order to discourage U.S. investors from investing in foreign securities. Thus, non-U.S. borrowers that historically had sold securities to U.S. investors began to look elsewhere for funds.

During the last decade, corporations from all over the world have begun to attract long-term funds from foreign sources by issuing bonds internationally. This form of borrowing can sometimes escape regulations that would be imposed on domestically placed bonds, and can also take advantage of lower interest rates often available in foreign countries. However, for an internationally traded bond, the commonly used currency of the issuer often differs from that of the purchaser. Therefore, one of the parties may be exposed to exchange rate risk.

Before 1984, investors that directly purchased U.S.-placed bonds were subject to a 30-percent withholding tax. The issuers of these bonds retained 30 percent of the interest payments to satisfy the withholding tax laws. A variety of tax treaties between the United States and other countries existed, causing this withholding tax to affect investors in some countries more than those in others. Because of the withholding tax, many U.S. bonds were issued in the Eurobond market through financing subsidiaries in the Netherlands Antilles. A tax treaty allowed interest payments from Antilles subsidiaries of U.S.-based corporations to non-U.S. investors to be exempt from the withholding tax. U.S. firms that used this method of financing were able to sell their bonds at a relatively high price because of the tax exemption. Thus, they obtained funds at a relatively low cost. Some U.S. firms did not use this financing method, since it entailed the cost of their establishing financing subsidiaries in the Netherlands Antilles, and because they knew this method of circumventing the withholding tax might be prohibited by the U.S. government at some point in the future. Indeed, in July 1984, the U.S. government abolished the withholding tax and allowed U.S. corporations to issue bearer bonds directly to non-U.S. investors. The result was a large increase in the volume of bonds sold by U.S. corporations to non-U.S. investors. In addition, mutual funds containing U.S. securities are accessible to foreign investors. Furthermore, primary dealers of U.S. Treasury notes and bonds have opened offices in London, Tokyo, and other foreign cities to accommodate the foreign demand for these securities.

Eurobond market activity has become more popular each year. U.S. corporate use of this market has generally increased over time, due to the popularity of convertible issues and FRNs. A sizable portion of offerings within the market are energy-related or derived from government agency needs for funds. While ratings are available for most Eurobond issues, there has been a tendency of the purchasers to ignore ratings in favor of a well-known name. This provides an advantage for well-known U.S. firms that have not been assigned the highest rating. About one-fourth of the debt issues in the Eurobond market are for less than $100 million, while more than one-third of the issues are for more than $300 million.

INTERNATIONAL STOCK MARKETS

MNCs and domestic firms commonly obtain long-term funding by issuing stock locally. Yet, MNCs can also attract funds from foreign investors by issuing stock in international markets. New issues of stock are increasingly being floated in international markets for a variety of reasons. Non-U.S. corporations that need large amounts of funds will sometimes issue the stock in the United States (these are called **Yankee stock offerings**) due to the liquidity of the new-issues market there. That is, a foreign corporation may be more likely to sell an entire issue of stock in the U.S. market, whereas in other, smaller markets, the entire issue may not necessarily sell.

The U.S. investment banks commonly serve as underwriters of the stock targeted for the U.S. market, and receive underwriting fees ranging from about 3 to 6 percent of the value of stock issued. Since many financial institutions in the U.S. purchase non-U.S. stocks as investments, non-U.S. firms may be able to place an entire stock offering within the U.S.

Firms that issue stock in the U.S. typically are required to satisfy more stringent disclosure rules on their financial condition. However, they are exempt from some of these disclosure rules when they qualify for a Securities and

Exchange Commission guideline (called Rule 144a) through a direct placement of stock to institutional investors.

Many of the recent stock offerings in the U.S. by non-U.S. firms have resulted from privatization programs in Latin America and Europe, whereby businesses that were previously government-owned are being sold to U.S. shareholders. Given the large size of some of these businesses, the local stock markets are not large enough to digest stock offerings. Consequently, U.S. investors are financing many privatized businesses based in foreign countries.

When a non-U.S. firm issues stock in its own country, its shareholder base is quite limited, as a few large institutional investors may own most of the shares. By issuing stock in the U.S., such a firm diversifies its shareholder base, which can reduce share price volatility caused when large investors sell shares.

Non-U.S. firms also obtain equity financing by using **American depository receipts** (ADRs), which are certificates representing bundles of stock. The use of ADRs circumvents some disclosure requirements imposed on stock offerings in the U.S., yet enables non-U.S. firms to tap the U.S. market for funds.

Although the U.S. market offers an advantage for new stock issues due to size, the registration requirements can sometimes cause delays in selling the new issues. For this reason, some U.S. firms have issued new stock in foreign markets in recent years. Other U.S. firms are issuing stock in foreign markets simply to enhance their global image. The existence of various markets for new issues provides a choice for corporations in need of equity. This competition between various new-issues markets should increase the efficiency of new issues.

International stock issues tend to sell better in foreign markets when the issuing MNC has a global image. Yet, some less well-known MNCs also issue stock in foreign markets to establish a global image. In addition, the issuance of stock across several markets may avoid the downward price pressure that could occur if the entire issue were sold in a single market.

The locations of the MNC's operations can influence the decision about where to place stock, as the MNC may desire a country where it is likely to generate enough future cash flows to cover dividend payments. The stocks of some U.S.-based MNCs are widely traded on numerous stock exchanges around the world. For example, the stock of Coca-Cola Company is traded on stock exchanges in the United States, Frankfurt, and Switzerland. The stock of TRW Inc. is traded on stock exchanges in the United States, London, and Frankfurt. CPC International, Allied-Signal, and many other U.S.-based MNCs have their stock listed on more than five different stock exchanges overseas. By listing their stock on foreign stock exchanges, MNCs can easily have their stock traded by foreign investors who have access to those stock exchanges.

A summary of the major stock markets is provided in Exhibit 3.5. Numerous other exchanges are also available. The exhibit shows how the percentage of individual versus institutional ownership of shares varies across stock markets.

Large MNCs have begun to simultaneously float new stock issues in various countries. Investment banks underwrite stocks through one or more syndicates across countries. The global distribution of stock can reach a much larger market, so greater quantities of stock can be issued at a given price.

As a result of recent events, the stock markets have progressed toward a global around-the-clock trading system. The event known as the "Big Bang" allowed for the opening of a computerized network (called SEAQ) in London in October 1986 that is somewhat similar to the NASDAQ system in the United

EXHIBIT 3.5 Characteristics of Stock Exchanges
SOURCE: *Institutional Investor* (March 1989): pp. 197–204.

Stock Exchange	Number of Companies Listed	Market Capitalization (in millions of dollars)	Average Daily Volume (in millions of shares)	Trading Hours	Percent of Shares Owned by Individuals	Percent of Shares Owned by Institutions or Funds	Restrictions on Foreign Ownership
Australia	1,506	$164,930	102.8	10:15–12:15 2:00–3:15	10%	90%	Only on strategic industries such as uranium.
Belgium	340	50,535	N/A	10:00–3:30	N/A	N/A	Some financial institutions are subject to a maximum limit.
Canada (Montreal)	1,188	368,917	5.36	9:30–4:00	52	48	
Canada (Toronto)	N/A	N/A	N/A	9:30–4:00	N/A	N/A	*See* Montreal exchange
Canada (Vancouver)	2,334	4,515	14	6:30–1:30	80	20	None
France	888	244,998	N/A	10:00–5:00	30	20	Investors in non-EC countries are subject to a maximum limit.
Hong Kong	308	71,697	N/A	10:00–12:30 2:30–3:30	N/A	N/A	None
Italy	211	135,428	N/A	10:00–1:45	N/A	N/A	None
Japan (Osaka)	N/A	N/A	118.9	9:00–11:00 1:00–3:00	N/A	N/A	None
Japan (Tokyo)	N/A	N/A	1,040	9:00–11:00 1:00–3:00	23.6	72	None
South Korea	N/A	57,007	9.7	9:40–11:40 1:20–3:20	68	29.3	Nonresidents can invest in stocks only through mutual funds.
Mexico	309	N/A	32.9	10:30–1:30	58.33	41.67	N/A

EXHIBIT 3.5 *continued*

Netherlands	572	91,720	N/A	10:00–4:30	N/A	N/A	None
New Zealand	387	15,208	6.5	9:30–11:00 2:15–3:30	N/A	N/A	Foreigners must have approval for ownership of 24% or more.
Norway	137	13,090	N/A	10:00–3:00	22.5	15	Limits are imposed on foreign ownership of stocks.
Singapore	326	N/A	N/A	10:00–12:30 2:30–4:00	25	75	Restrictions apply for stocks in some industries.
Switzerland (Basel)	483	N/A	N/A	9:10–1:30	N/A	N/A	Registered shares are restricted to residents.
Switzerland (Geneva)	494	100,032	N/A	9:00–1:15	N/A	N/A	*See* Basel exchange.
Switzerland (Zurich)	2,914	125,403	N/A	9:30–1:15	10	N/A	*See* Basel exchange.
Taiwan	N/A	92,008	354	9:00–12:00	40.7	50.1	Foreign investors are required to apply for a remittance permit.
United Kingdom	2,656	N/A	N/A	9:00–5:00	20	80	None
United States (N.Y.)	1,681	2,400,000	161	9:30–4:00	N/A	N/A	None
Germany	741	186,601	7,354	11:30–1:30	N/A	N/A	None

APPLIED RESEARCH

SHAREHOLDER REACTIONS TO OVERSEAS LISTINGS

A recent study by Howe and Kelm assessed how shareholders react to overseas stock listings by U.S.-based MNCs. Five possible reasons for a favorable reaction were cited:

1. Improved relationship between the MNC and foreign government
2. Increased demand for stock as a result of attracting investors in foreign markets
3. Increased access to foreign financial markets as a result of placing stock in these markets
4. Increased ability to use stock for foreign takeovers
5. Increased investor perception as a result of being accepted on foreign stock exchanges.

Potential disadvantages of overseas listings were also cited:

1. Listing costs of overseas listings
2. Costs of providing information to foreign financial market participants
3. Costs of complying with foreign disclosure requirements.

The authors attempted to determine how shareholders reacted to MNCs with new listings. They estimated abnormal returns in a period from 90 trading days before the actual listing to 40 trading days after the listing. They found that the abnormal returns were consistently negative, and in some cases statistically significant.

Some MNCs had a second overseas listing, and others had even a third listing. The authors separately assessed the abnormal returns for a second overseas listing and a third overseas listing. In general, the abnormal returns were significantly negative for both.

Overall, the results suggest that shareholders react unfavorably toward overseas listings. Therefore, the costs involved in overseas listing outweigh the potential benefits. The results in this study are based on a sample; shareholders of any particular MNC may possibly react favorably if the potential benefits to that MNC are more likely to be realized. In addition, if the costs of overseas listing are reduced in the future (if disclosure requirements are standardized globally), shareholder reaction to overseas listings may change.

States. In addition, the London stock exchange now allows large investment firms in the United States and Japan to trade there. Stocks traded on London, Japanese, and U.S. exchanges allow for trading almost around the clock.

USE OF INTERNATIONAL FINANCIAL MARKETS

Exhibit 3.6 illustrates the foreign cash flow movements of a typical MNC. These cash flows can be classified into five corporate functions, all of which generally require use of the foreign exchange markets. The spot market, forward market, currency futures market, and currency options market are all classified as foreign exchange markets.

The first function is foreign trade with business clients. Exports generate foreign cash inflows, while imports require cash outflows. A second function is direct foreign investment, or the acquisition of foreign real assets. This function requires cash outflows but generates future inflows through remitted dividends back to the MNC parent or the sale of these foreign assets. A third function is short-term investment in foreign securities. The Eurocurrency market is commonly used for this purpose. A fourth function is short-term financing in the Eurocurrency market. A fifth function is longer-term financing in the Eurocredit, Eurobond, or international stock markets.

EXHIBIT 3.6   Foreign Cash Flow Chart of an MNC

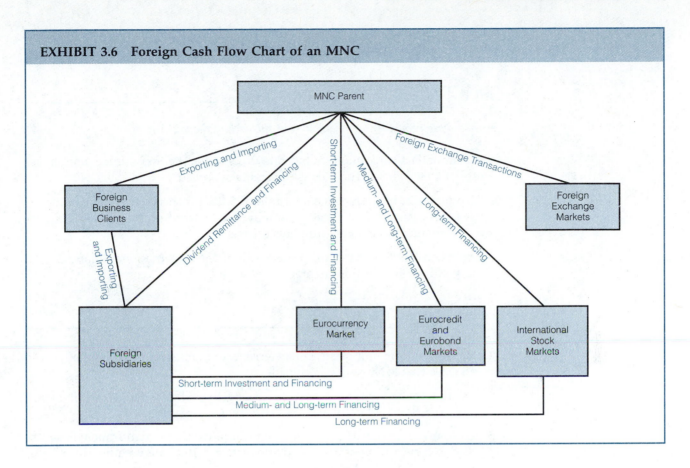

SUMMARY

■ The foreign exchange market allows currencies to be exchanged in order to facilitate international trade or financial transactions. Commercial banks serve as financial intermediaries in this market. They stand ready to exchange currencies on the spot, or at a future point in time with the use of forward contracts.

■ The Eurocurrency market is composed of several large banks that accept deposits and provide short-term loans in various currencies. This market is primarily used by governments and large corporations.

■ The Eurocredit market is composed of the same commercial banks that serve the Eurocurrency market. These banks convert some of the deposits received into Eurocredit loans (for medium-term periods) to governments and large corporations.

■ The Eurobond market facilitates the international transfers of long-term credit, which enables governments and large corporations to borrow funds from various countries. Eurobonds are underwritten by a multinational syndicate of investment banks, and are placed in various countries.

■ Just as the Eurocurrency, Eurocredit, and Eurobond markets enable firms to borrow funds in foreign countries, international stock markets enable firms to obtain equity financing in foreign countries. Thus, these markets have helped MNCs finance their international expansion.

SELF-TEST FOR CHAPTER 3

(Answers are provided in Appendix A in the back of the text.)

1. A commercial bank quotes a bid rate of $.784 for the Swiss franc, and an ask rate of $.80. What is the bid/ask percentage spread?

2. A commercial bank quotes a spot rate of $.190 for the French franc and a 90-day forward rate of $.188. Determine the forward premium (or discount) of the French franc on an annualized basis.

3. Briefly explain how MNCs can make use of each international financial market described in this chapter.

QUESTIONS

1. List some of the important characteristics of bank foreign exchange services that MNCs should consider.

2. Assume that a bank's bid price for Canadian dollars is $.7938, while its ask price is $.81. What is the bid/ask percentage spread?

3. Compute the forward discount or premium for the French franc whose 90-day forward rate is $.102 and spot rate is $.10. State whether your answer is a discount or premium.

4. Of what use is a forward contract to an MNC?

5. How can a forward contract backfire?

6. If a dollar is worth 1.7 German marks, what is the dollar value of a mark?

7. Assume a French franc is worth $.17 and a Japanese yen is worth $.008. What is the cross rate of the French franc with respect to yen? That is, how many yen equal a franc?

8. Explain how the Eurocurrency, Eurocredit, and Eurobond markets differ from one another.

9. Briefly describe the historical developments that led to floating exchange rates as of 1973.

10. What is the function of the Eurocurrency market?

11. Briefly describe the reasons for growth in the Eurocurrency market during the last twenty years.

12. Why do interest rates vary among countries?

13. With regard to Eurocredit loans, who are the common borrowers?

14. What is LIBOR, and how is it used in the Eurocredit market?

15. Why would a bank desire to participate in syndicated Eurocredit loans?

16. Discuss some reasons for the popularity of the Eurobond market.

17. Compute the forward discount or premium for the British pound whose 180-day forward rate is $1.75 and spot rate is $1.78. State whether your answer is a discount or premium.

18. The Wolfpack Corporation is a U.S. exporter that invoices its exports to the United Kingdom in British pounds. If it expects that the pound will appreciate against the dollar in the future, should it hedge its exports with a forward contract? Explain.

19. Explain why firms may consider issuing stock in foreign markets.

20. Bullet Inc., a U.S. firm, is planning to issue new stock in the United States during this month. The only decision it has left is the specific day in which the stock should be issued. Why do you think this firm monitors results of the Tokyo stock market every morning?

Currency Traders Welcome Upheaval
Europe's Turmoil Means Jobs, Chance for Big Profits

BY GLENN WHITNEY
Staff Reporter of THE WALL STREET
JOURNAL

LONDON – Amid the gnashing of teeth over the virtual demise of Europe's tightly controlled monetary system, one group is trying hard to hide its glee: foreign-exchange traders.

A common currency, Europe's goal by the year 2000, would have been bad for them. With fewer currencies to trade, they figured, fewer people would be needed to trade them. Instead, there will be even more fluctuation for currencies, and potentially more risk for anyone doing business internationally.

"Let's just say we're certainly not worried about where to find work anymore," says Per Kaalby, foreign-exchange manager at Bayerische Vereinsbank AG in Munich. "Everyone needs to look at Europe country-by-country now, and that requires more resources, more people and more potential for profit."

Mr. Kaalby estimates foreign-exchange turnover at his bank has increased 200% to 300% in the past week. Although growth won't continue at that pace, he predicts it will stay well above average. As a result, Bayerische Vereinsbank plans new hedging services for clients, which typically involve buying and selling currency contracts to manage risks.

Others are preparing to expand as well. Chase Manhattan Bank in London, the U.S. bank's global headquarters for currency trading, has steadily boosted staffing since turmoil began in the Exchange Rate Mechanism last year. (The ERM is a joint float of nine European currencies that fluctuate within proscribed ranges against one another.) Albert Maasland, the group's head of sales and marketing, says Chase, a unit of Chase Manhattan Corp., has hired about 12 traders and salesmen in the past six months, a 20% increase in currency-related personnel, and plans to add more.

Worries About Exposure

"We're executing three or four times the amount of business compared to about a year ago," Mr. Maasland says. "A lot of our clients who used to take comfort in the tight ERM bands, now find they have to worry about covering their exposure and that gives us plenty to do."

Other institutions such as Merrill Lynch & Co.'s Merrill Lynch Ltd. unit, Barclays Bank PLC and Union Bank of Switzerland also are considering beefing up their foreign-exchange trading desks and increasing their coverage of some smaller European economies like Spain, Belgium and the Scandinavian countries.

Chris Deuters, head of global foreign exchange at Lehman Brothers in London, says his firm, a unit of American Express Co., is used to analyzing Germany and the Benelux nations (Belgium, the Netherlands and Luxembourg) virtually as a single entity.

"Suddenly that's not meaningful anymore," he notes. "We have to look at each country individually, and that could mean a greater need for staff."

To be sure, the new opportunities for commercial banks, brokerage firms and derivatives exchanges are likely to dishearten European politicians. The French in particular vowed repeatedly "to break the back" of speculators.

Need for more Trading

The potential wrath of European authorities is no small concern of those in the market. David Clark, the treasurer at HSBC Holdings PLC and president of the International Foreign Exchange Association, worries that setbacks to the ERM might drive politicians to reinstate capital controls or impose taxes on currency transactions. None of the major international financial centers now has such controls or taxes.

Still, nearly everyone agrees there will be an increased need to trade European currencies, and London – as the world's largest center for foreign-exchange trading – will probably benefit most. A majority of the world's major banks, including those from the U.S., base their global currency trading operations in London.

According to a recent survey by the Bank of England and the Bank for International Settlements, of the $1.1 trillion in daily foreign-exchange trading, institutions in the U.K. trade the equivalent of $300 billion a day in currencies of all countries,

Continued

CASE: IMPACT OF THE ERM CRISIS ON FOREIGN EXCHANGE SERVICES

Continued

while the figure is $192 billion for the U.S. and $126 billion in Japan.

Mr. Clark of HSBC, whose holdings include Hongkong & Shanghai Banking Corp. and Midland Bank, predicts the amount of trading in European currencies probably will double over the next two to three years, led in part by sharply increased use of derivatives such as "FX options," which allow an investor to buy or sell a currency at a fixed price at a later date.

In addition, several factors are combining to make the international foreign-exchange market and parallel markets that have sprung up around it a brave new world for even experienced traders.

For the first time, they will be keeping track of 10 to 12 major currencies instead of three or four. The currencies will all be effectively free-floating in a 30% range vs. a narrow range of just 4.5% before the crisis last weekend. And there are no longer the stiff foreign-exchange and capital controls that helped limit currency fluctuations before much of Europe established the ERM in 1979. With the new wide bands, currencies such as the Spanish peseta for the first time will be tested by the full weight of the freewheeling global market.

A Changed Investment World

What's more, the investment world has changed radically since the ERM has been in operation. U.S. investors have poured ever-increasing sums into European markets. In 1993 they purchased a net $18.03 billion in European stocks, compared with $1.91 billion in 1985, according to the U.S. Securities Industry Association. Experts predict that trend will accelerate as Europe gradually recovers from recession, creating new investment opportunities. With more money at stake, the need for U.S. investors to protect against greater currency risk will grow.

European companies themselves also have ranged outside their home countries, establishing alliances and partnerships and building factories where the chance of widely fluctuating costs and revenues has increased sharply following the ERM's virtual collapse.

At ABB Asea Brown Boverl Ltd., a Swiss-Swedish electrical engineering group, the unravelling of the ERM already has meant more-active currency management. ABB has 12 treasury centers worldwide, each handling its own exposure. "One thing is clear – a year ago we could almost have done without dealing with currency risk within Europe. Now we definitely have to ride out much more volatility," says Dieter Kempkes, executive vice president in charge of trading.

While the foreign-exchange market in European currencies will almost certainly be more active day-to-day, the occasional frenzied periods of currency attacks might be a thing of the past. That is because given the new very wide bands, most ERM currencies are unlikely to fall to their floors, the point at which central banks must buy the currency.

Those obligatory purchases were what funded huge one-time gains by speculators in the ERM. The new, more liberalized ERM is likely to benefit those financial houses with steady flows of business, rather than speculators keen on making big bets.

In the past short-sellers sold a currency over a brief but intense period, forcing the central banks to buy. The market pressure eventually became unbearable, forcing authorities to devalue that currency rather than spend billions of dollars to protect it. After the devaluation the short-sellers could "cover" their positions by buying at the new lower rate.

"The new bands eliminate the predatory element that existed in the ERM. When you remove the tight bands, you remove the motivation for speculating over whether the bands will hold," says Malcolm Barr, international economist at Chemical Banking Corp.'s Chemical Bank unit in London.

Source: The Wall Street Journal (August 5, 1993): P. A4. Reprinted by permission of *The Wall Street Journal* © 1993 Dow Jones & Company, Inc. All rights reserved worldwide.

Questions

1. Explain why the widening of the ERM bands causes a greater need for foreign exchange traders.

2. If Europe ever adopts a single currency, how would the demand for foreign exchange traders be affected?

3. Explain the comment from Lehman Brothers that some countries were previously viewed as a single entity when ERM bands were tight, but now each country must be assessed individually.

4. Describe the recent increase in international financial flows throughout Europe, and how these flows affect the need for foreign exchange traders.

GRETZ TOOL COMPANY
Using International Financial Markets

Gretz Tool Company is a large U.S.-based multinational corporation with subsidiaries in eight different countries. The parent of Gretz provided an initial cash infusion to establish each subsidiary. However, each subsidiary has had to finance its own growth since then. The parent and subsidiaries of Gretz typically use Citicorp (the largest bank in the U.S., with branches in numerous countries) when possible to facilitate any flow of funds necessary.

a) Explain the various ways in which Citicorp could facilitate Gretz's flow of funds, and identify the type of financial market where that flow of funds occurs. For each type of financing transaction, specify whether Citicorp would serve as the creditor or just an intermediary.

b) The vice-president of Finance for Gretz recently stated how ironic it was that he could not use Citicorp for some financial transactions in the U.S., but that Citicorp could facilitate virtually all financial transactions overseas. What do you think this means?

c) Recently, the French subsidiary called on Citicorp for a medium-term loan and was offered the following alternatives:

Loan Denominated in:	Annualized Rate
French francs	13%
U.S. dollars	11
German marks	10
Japanese yen	8

What characteristics do you think would help the French subsidiary determine which currency to borrow?

PROJECT

Look at a recent copy of *The Wall Street Journal,* and fill in the quotes for spot and forward rates in the following table. Also compute the forward rate premiums in this table.

	Currency					
	British pound	Canadian dollar	French franc	Japanese yen	Swiss franc	German mark
Spot rate						
30-day forward rate						
30-day forward premium or discount						
90-day forward rate						
90-day forward premium or discount						
180-day forward rate						
180-day forward premium or discount						

REFERENCES

Bernauer, Kenneth. "The Asian Dollar Market." *Economic Review,* Federal Reserve Bank of San Francisco (Winter 1983), pp. 47–63.

Chang, Carolyn W., and Jack S. K. Chang. "Forward and Futures Prices: Evidence from the Foreign Exchange Markets." *Journal of Finance* (September 1990), pp. 1333–1336.

Chrystal, K. Alec. "A Guide to Foreign Exchange Markets." *Review* (March 1984), pp. 5–18.

Cornell Bradford, and Marc R. Reinganum. "Forward and Futures Prices: Evidence from the Foreign Exchange Markets." *Journal of Finance* (December 1981), pp. 1035–1045.

Grilli, Vittorio, and Nouriel Roubini. "Liquidity, Capital Controls, and Exchange Rates." *Journal of International Money and Finance* (April 1993), pp. 139–153.

Howe, John S. and Kathryn Kelm. "The Stock Price Impacts of Overseas Listings." *Financial Management* (Autumn 1987), pp. 51–56.

Howe, John S., and Jeff Madura. "The Impact of International Listings on Risk: Implications for Capital Market Integration." *Journal of Banking and Finance.* (December 1990), pp. 1133–1142.

Howe, John S., Jeff Madura, and Alan L. Tucker. "International Listings and Risk." *Journal of International Money and Finance* (February 1993), pp. 99–110.

Logue, Dennis E., and George S. Oldfield. "What's So Special About Foreign Exchange Markets?" *Journal of Portfolio Management* (Spring 1977), pp. 19–24.

CHAPTER 4

EXCHANGE RATE DETERMINATION

Firms that conduct international business must continuously monitor exchange rates because their cash flows are highly dependent on them. This chapter provides a foundation for understanding how exchange rates are determined.

The specific objectives of this chapter are to

- explain how exchange rate movements are measured,
- explain how the equilibrium exchange rate is determined, and
- examine factors that affect the equilibrium exchange rate.

MEASURING EXCHANGE RATE MOVEMENTS _____

An exchange rate measures the value of one currency in units of another currency. As economic conditions change, exchange rates can change substantially. To illustrate, Exhibit 4.1 shows the value of the British pound over time. The percentage changes from year to year are displayed in the third column. A decline in a currency's value is often referred to as **depreciation.** When the British pound depreciates against the U.S. dollar, this means that the U.S. dollar is strengthening relative to the pound. This increase in a currency value is often referred to as **appreciation.**

Exhibit 4.1 shows that the pound value has experienced cycles. In the 1975–1977 period, the pound was generally depreciating against the dollar. In the 1978–1980 period, it appreciated against the dollar. In the 1981–1985 period, it again depreciated against the dollar. The pound appreciated against the dollar in the 1985–1988 period, but has been erratic since then.

When the spot rates of two specific points in time are compared, the spot rate as of the more recent date is denoted as S and the spot rate as of the earlier date is denoted as S_{t-1}. The percentage change in the value of a foreign currency is computed as

EXHIBIT 4.1   Fluctuation of the British Pound Value Over Time

First trading day of July in year:	Approximate spot rate of British pound	Approximate percentage change from year before	Approximate number of pounds one could have purchased with $10,000
1975	$2.180	—	4,587
1976	1.788	−17.9%	5,592
1977	1.720	−3.8	5,814
1978	1.853	7.7	5,397
1979	2.176	17.5	4,595
1980	2.360	8.4	4,237
1981	1.924	−18.5	5,198
1982	1.734	−9.9	5,767
1983	1.527	−11.9	6,549
1984	1.357	−11.1	7,369
1985	1.306	−3.7	7,656
1986	1.530	+17.2	6,536
1987	1.610	+5.2	6,211
1988	1.709	+6.1	5,851
1989	1.550	−9.3	6,452
1990	1.742	+12.4	5,740
1991	1.635	−6.1	6,116
1992	1.898	+16.1	5,269
1993	1.4920	−21.4	6,702

$$\text{Percent } \Delta \text{ in foreign currency value} = \frac{S - S_{t-1}}{S_{t-1}} \times 100$$

A positive percentage change represents appreciation of the foreign currency, while a negative percentage change represents depreciation. For example, from July 1, 1992, to July 1, 1993, the percentage change in the spot rate was

$$\frac{\$1.492 - \$1.898}{\$1.898} \times 100 = -21.4\%$$

The negative sign implies depreciation of the pound. Such large percentage changes in a currency as those annual percentage changes disclosed in Exhibit 4.1 would not normally exist on a daily or weekly basis. Yet, rates of change of as much as 5 percent have occurred over a 24-hour period for some currencies.

On some days, most foreign currencies appreciate against the dollar, although by different degrees. On other days most currencies depreciate against the dollar, but by different degrees. There are also some days on which some currencies appreciate while others depreciate against the dollar; the media reports on this scenario by stating that "the dollar was *mixed* in trading."

EXCHANGE RATE EQUILIBRIUM

While it is easy to measure the percentage change in the value of a currency, it is more difficult to explain why the value changed, or to forecast how it may change in the future. To achieve either of these objectives, the concept of an **equilibrium exchange rate** must be understood, as well as the factors that affect the equilibrium rate.

Before considering why an exchange rate changes, realize that an exchange rate at a given point in time represents a *price* of a currency. Like any other products sold in markets, the price of a currency is determined by the demand for that currency relative to supply. Thus, for each possible price of a British pound, there would be a corresponding demand for pounds and a corresponding supply of pounds for sale. At any point in time, a currency should exhibit the price at which the demand for that currency is equal to supply—and this represents the equilibrium exchange rate. Of course, conditions can change over time, causing the supply or demand for a given currency to adjust, which would force movement in the currency's price. This topic is more thoroughly discussed in this section.

Demand for a Currency

The British pound is used here to explain exchange rate equilibrium. Exhibit 4.2 shows a hypothetical number of pounds that would be demanded under various possibilities for the exchange rate. At any one point in time there is only one exchange rate. The exhibit shows the quantity of pounds that would be demanded for various exchange rates. The reason for the downward-sloping demand schedule is that U.S. corporations would be encouraged to purchase more British goods when the pound was worth less, since it would take fewer dollars to obtain the desired amount of pounds.

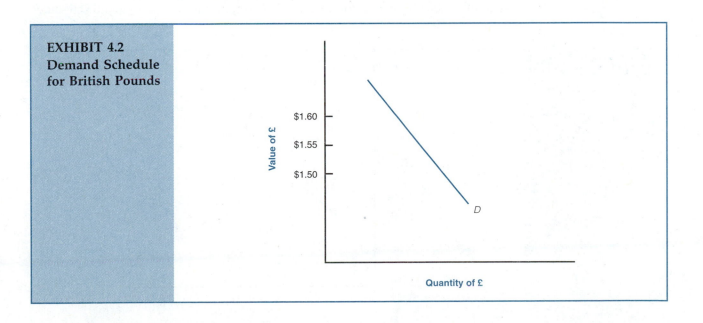

EXHIBIT 4.2
Demand Schedule for British Pounds

Supply of a Currency for Sale

Up to this point, only the U.S. demand for pounds has been considered, but the British demand for U.S. dollars must also be considered. This can be referred to as a British *supply of pounds for sale,* since pounds are supplied in the foreign exchange market in exchange for U.S. dollars.

A supply schedule of pounds for sale in the foreign exchange market can be developed in a manner similar to method for the demand schedule for pounds. Exhibit 4.3 shows the quantity of pounds for sale (supplied to the foreign exchange market in exchange for dollars) corresponding to each possible exchange rate. Notice from the supply schedule in Exhibit 4.3 that there is a positive relationship between the British pound value and the quantity of British pounds for sale (supplied), which can be explained as follows. When the pound is valued high, British consumers and firms are more likely to purchase U.S. goods. Thus, they supply a greater number of pounds to the market, to be exchanged for dollars. Conversely, when the pound is valued low, the supply of pounds for sale is less, reflecting less British desire to obtain U.S. goods.

The demand and supply schedules for British pounds are combined in Exhibit 4.4. At an exchange rate of $1.50, the quantity of pounds demanded would exceed the supply of pounds for sale. Consequently, the banks that provide foreign exchange services would experience a shortage of pounds at that exchange rate. At an exchange rate of $1.60, the quantity of pounds demanded would be less than the supply of pounds for sale. Therefore, banks providing foreign exchange services would experience a surplus of pounds at that exchange rate. According to Exhibit 4.4, the equilibrium exchange rate is presently $1.55, since this rate equates the quantity of pounds demanded to the supply of pounds for sale.

FACTORS THAT INFLUENCE EXCHANGE RATES _____

The equilibrium exchange rate will change over time as supply and demand schedules change. The factors that cause currency supply and demand schedules

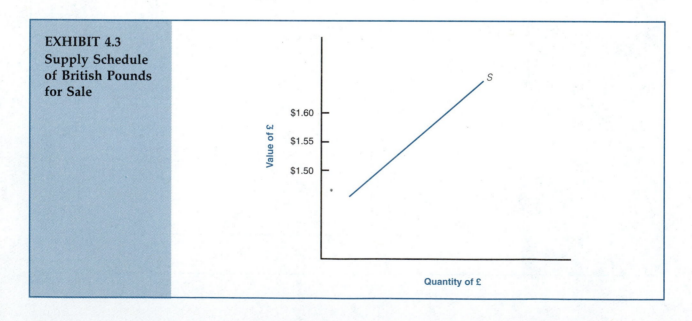

EXHIBIT 4.3
Supply Schedule of British Pounds for Sale

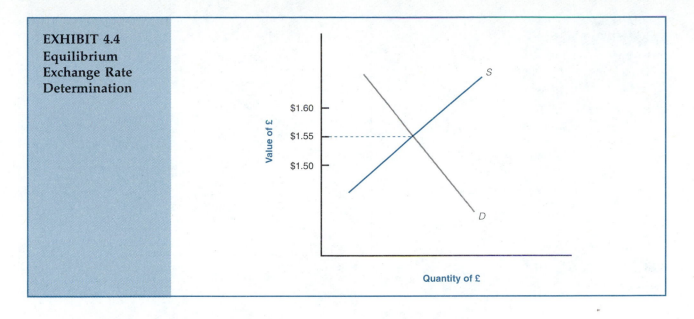

EXHIBIT 4.4
Equilibrium Exchange Rate Determination

to change are discussed here by relating each factor's influence to the demand and supply schedules graphically displayed in Exhibit 4.4.

Relative Inflation Rates

Changes in relative inflation rates can affect international trade activity, which influences the demand and supply of currencies, and therefore influences exchange rates. What would happen to the demand and supply schedules displayed in Exhibit 4.4 if U.S. inflation suddenly increased substantially while British inflation remained the same? (Assume that both British and U.S. firms sell goods that can serve as substitutes for each other.) The sudden jump in U.S. inflation should cause an increase in the U.S. demand for British goods, and therefore also cause an increase in the U.S. demand for British pounds. In addition, the jump in U.S. inflation should reduce the British desire for U.S. goods and therefore reduce the supply of pounds for sale. These market reactions are illustrated in Exhibit 4.5. At the previous equilibrium exchange rate of $1.55, there would be a shortage of pounds in the foreign exchange market. The increased U.S. demand for pounds and the reduced supply of pounds for sale places upward pressure on the value of the pound. According to Exhibit 4.5, the new equilibrium value is $1.57.

In reality, the actual demand and supply schedules, and therefore the true equilibrium exchange rate, will reflect several factors simultaneously. The point of the preceding example is to logically work through the mechanics of the way higher inflation in a country can affect an exchange rate. Each factor is assessed one at a time to determine its separate influence on exchange rates, holding all other factors constant. Then, all factors can be tied together to fully explain why an exchange rate moves the way it does.

As another example, assume there is a sudden and substantial increase in British inflation while U.S. inflation is low. Based on this information, answer the following questions: (1) How is the demand schedule for pounds affected? (2) How is the supply schedule of pounds for sale affected? (3) Will the new

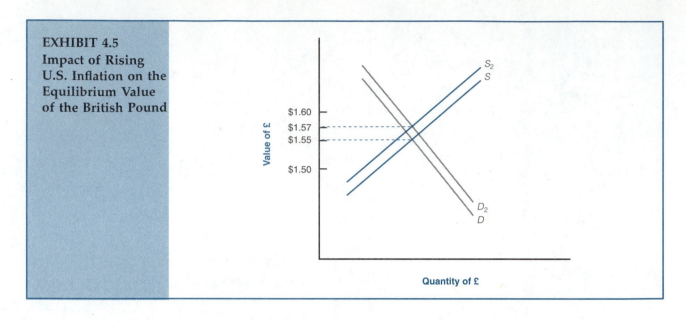

EXHIBIT 4.5
Impact of Rising U.S. Inflation on the Equilibrium Value of the British Pound

equilibrium value of the pound increase, decrease, or remain unchanged? The answers based on the information given are (1) the demand schedule for pounds should shift inward, (2) the supply schedule of pounds for sale should shift outward, and (3) the new equilibrium value of the pound will decrease. Of course, the actual amount by which the pound value will decrease depends on the magnitude of the shifts. There is not enough information to determine the exact magnitude of shifts.

Relative Interest Rates

Changes in relative interest rates affect investment in foreign securities, which influences the demand and supply of currencies, and therefore influences exchange rates. Assume that U.S. interest rates rise while British interest rates remain constant. In this case, U.S. corporations will likely reduce their demand for pounds, since the U.S. rates are now more attractive relative to British rates, and there is less desire for British bank deposits. Since U.S. rates will now look more attractive to British corporations with excess cash, the supply of pounds for sale by British corporations should increase as they establish more bank deposits in the United States. Due to an inward shift in demand for pounds and an outward shift in supply of pounds for sale, the equilibrium exchange rate should decrease. This is graphically represented in Exhibit 4.6. If U.S. interest rates decreased relative to British interest rates, we would expect the opposite shifts of those just stated.

To illustrate how changes in interest rate differentials can affect exchange rates, consider the lifting of the Iron Curtain that separated East and West Germany in November 1989. The reunification of East and West Germany resulted in a strong demand for loanable funds to develop the East German economy, which led to an abrupt increase in German interest rates. Consequently, the gap between U.S. and German interest rates was eliminated, and U.S. investors invested more of their funds into German securities (and other German assets). The flow of funds to Germany caused an increase in the U.S. demand for

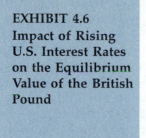

**EXHIBIT 4.6
Impact of Rising
U.S. Interest Rates
on the Equilibrium
Value of the British
Pound**

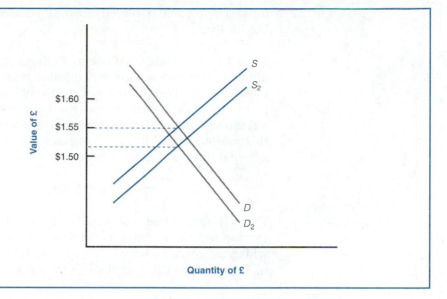

German marks, placing upward pressure on the mark's value. The mark continued to strengthen, reaching an all-time high in 1991. The strength of the mark was attributed not only to higher German interest rates, but also to a major decline in U.S. interest rates. By 1991, German interest rates had surpassed U.S. interest rates. Many investors attempted to capitalize on the relatively high German interest rates by shifting their funds to Germany. This action placed additional upward pressure on the mark's value.

To further illustrate the influence of relative interest rates on exchange rates, consider the following excerpts from the "Treasury and Federal Reserve Foreign Exchange Operations," contained in issues of the *Federal Reserve Bank of New York Quarterly Review:* "The dollar came under strong downward pressure during the May–July [1992] period, declining over 10 percent against the German mark and most other European currencies, nearly 5 percent against the Japanese yen. . . . The dollar's decline was a product of . . . . declines in both short- and long-term dollar interest rates which contrasted with an upward tendency in European interest rates."

"Interest rate considerations were the dominant factor in exchange rate movements during the period [August–October 1992]. Interest rate differentials provided a strong incentive for capital flows into the higher-yielding securities denominated in German marks and other currencies thought to be closely linked to the mark."

"From the beginning of May to the end of June [1993] the dollar rose against the mark by nearly 8 percent. During this period, market participants expected that the German Bundesbank would continue to ease short-term interest rates . . . ."

In some cases, an exchange rate between two countries' currencies can be affected by changes in a third country's interest rate. For example, in early 1987 the Canadian interest rate increased and became more attractive to some Japanese investors than the U.S. rate. This caused Japanese investors to purchase fewer dollar-denominated securities. That is, the supply of yen to be exchanged for dollars was smaller than it would have been without the increase in Canadian interest rates, which placed upward pressure on the value of yen against the U.S. dollar.

Real Interest Rates. While a relatively high interest rate may attract foreign inflows (to invest in securities offering high yields), the relatively high interest rate may reflect expectations of relatively high inflation. Since high inflation can place downward pressure on the local currency, this may discourage some foreign investors from investing in securities denominated in that currency. For this reason, it is helpful to consider the **real interest rate,** which adjusts the nominal interest rate for inflation:

$$\text{Real interest rate} = \text{Nominal interest rate} - \text{Inflation rate.}$$

The real interest rate is commonly compared among countries to assess exchange rate movements, because it combines nominal interest rates and inflation, both of which influence exchange rates. Other things held constant, there should be a high correlation between the real interest rate differential and the dollar's value.

Relative Income Levels

A third factor affecting exchange rates is relative income levels. Assume that the U.S. income level substantially rises while the British income level remains unchanged. Consider the impact of this scenario on the (1) demand schedule for pounds, (2) supply schedule of pounds for sale, and (3) equilibrium exchange rate. First, the demand schedule for pounds will shift outward, reflecting an increase in U.S. income and therefore increased demand for British goods. Second, the supply schedule of pounds for sale is not expected to change. Therefore, the equilibrium exchange rate of the pound is expected to rise, as shown in Exhibit 4.7. When the indirect effect of changing income levels on exchange rates through effects on interest rates is considered, the impact may differ from the theory presented above, as will be explained shortly.

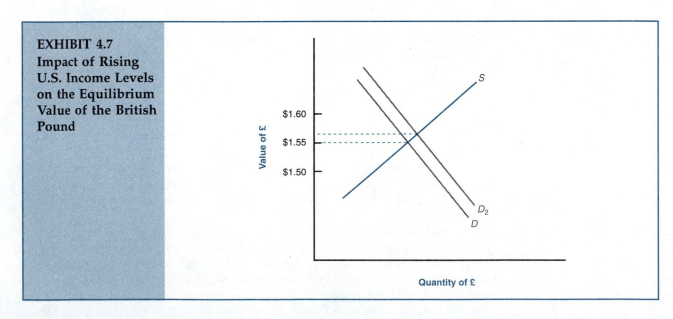

EXHIBIT 4.7
Impact of Rising U.S. Income Levels on the Equilibrium Value of the British Pound

Government Controls

A fourth factor affecting exchange rates is government controls. The governments of foreign countries can influence the equilibrium exchange rate in many ways, including (1) the imposition of foreign exchange barriers, (2) the imposition of foreign trade barriers, (3) intervening (buying and selling currencies) in the foreign exchange markets, and (4) affecting macro variables such as inflation, interest rates, and income levels. Chapter 6 covers these methods in detail. At this point, one example will be given to illustrate potential governmental influence. Recall the example in which U.S. interest rates rose relative to British interest rates. The expected reaction was an increase in British supply of pounds for sale to obtain more U.S. dollars (in order to capitalize on high U.S. money market yields). Yet, if the British government placed a heavy tax on interest income earned by its people from foreign investments, this could discourage the exchange of pounds for dollars.

Expectations

A fifth factor affecting exchange rates is market expectations of future exchange rates. Like other financial markets, foreign exchange markets react to any news that may have a future effect. For example, news of a potential surge in U.S. inflation may cause currency traders to sell dollars, anticipating a future decline in the dollar's value. This response places immediate downward pressure on the dollar.

Many institutional investors (such as commercial banks and insurance companies) take currency positions based on anticipated interest rate movements in various countries. For example, they may temporarily invest funds in Germany if they expect German interest rates to increase, because such a rise may

---

IN PRACTICE

BLACK MARKETS FOR CURRENCIES

In some countries (such as China, some East European countries, and some Latin American countries), the exchange rate is maintained by the government at an official rate. The rate may be allowed to change within established boundaries, depending on supply and demand conditions. However, when the actual supply and demand conditions cause an equilibrium exchange rate that is outside of these boundaries, a black market is commonly created. Consider the case of China, in which the official exchange rate for the yuan was about 17.5 (5.7 yuan per dollar) in 1993. At this exchange rate, the Chinese demand for dollars exceeds the supply of dollars available. Firms that need dollars to pay for foreign imports are often unable to obtain dollars at currency exchange centers in China, because dollars are not always available. Thus, there is a black market rate of about 10 yuan per dollar. This market is not legal, but is large and growing. It is used not only by small street vendors, but also by large import-export firms throughout China. Even government-owned bank branches have used the black market to obtain dollars. The black market tends to become very popular in any country where the local currency cannot be officially exchanged for dollars or some other widely used currency.

cause further capital flows into Germany, which could place upward pressure on the mark's value. By taking a position based on expectations, they can fully benefit from the change in the mark's value, because they will have purchased marks before the change occurred. While there is an obvious risk here that their expectations may be wrong, the point here is that expectations can influence exchange rates because they commonly motivate institutional investors to take foreign currency positions.

The transactions within the foreign exchange markets facilitate either trade or financial flows. The trade-related foreign exchange transactions are generally less responsive to news. However, financial flow transactions are very responsive to news, since the decisions to hold securities denominated in a particular currency is often dependent on anticipated changes in currency values. To the extent that news affects anticipated currency movements, it affects the demand for currencies and the supply of currencies for sale. Because of such speculative transactions, foreign exchange rates can be very volatile.

Day-to-day speculation on future exchange rate movements is commonly driven by signals of future interest rate movements, but can also be driven by other factors. Some examples of how the dollar's value responded to speculation and the cause of speculation are described below.

Date	Status of Dollar	Explanation
October 24, 1991	Weakened	Economic indicators for U.S. were poor (causing an expected decline in future U.S. interest rates)
October 29, 1991	Weakened	U.S. consumer confidence indicators declined (causing an expected decline in future U.S. interest rates)
January 16, 1992	Weakened	Correction following a week-long rally (speculators believed there was an overreaction)
January 30, 1992	Strengthened	Federal Reserve Chairman Alan Greenspan suggests that the Fed is unlikely to cut U.S. interest rates
July 15, 1992	Weakened	Expectations of a tight German monetary policy (could cause higher German interest rates)
April 19, 1993	Weakened	Foreign exchange market participants interpreted President Clinton's comments as a desire to weaken the dollar's value against the Japanese yen (to reduce the trade deficit with Japan)
June 15, 1993	Strengthened	Comments from the Bundesbank signalled a possible decline in German interest rates

Since signals of the future economic conditions that affect exchange rates can change quickly, the speculative positions in currencies may adjust quickly, causing unclear patterns in exchange rates. For example, consider the following summaries of the dollar's movements during March 1–4, 1993 by *The Wall Street Journal*.

March 1, 1993	The dollar strengthened because of the possibility of lower German interest rates.
March 2, 1993	The dollar weakened because of doubts about when German interest rates would decline.
March 3, 1993	The dollar did not change much, as there was continued speculation about if and when the German interest rates would decline.
March 4, 1993	The dollar weakened, partially because German interest rates did not decline.

These examples illustrate how the dollar's value is affected by speculative positions taken in response to anticipation of economic conditions. Speculators cannot wait for the economic conditions to occur, because by then, the exchange rates already will have adjusted.

Interaction of Factors

Trade-related factors and financial factors sometimes interact. For example, an increase in income levels sometimes causes expectations of higher interest rates. So even though a stronger income level can result in more imports, it may also indirectly attract more financial inflows (assuming interest rates increase). When considering the interaction, an increase in income levels is frequently expected to strengthen the local currency, because the favorable financial flows may overwhelm the unfavorable trade flows. Exhibit 4.8 separates payment flows between countries into trade-related and finance-related flows, and summarizes the factors that affect these flows.

Over a particular period, some factors may place upward pressure on the value of a foreign currency while other factors place downward pressure on the currency's value. For example, assume the simultaneous existence of (1) a sudden increase in U.S. inflation and (2) a sudden increase in U.S. interest rates. If the British economy were relatively unchanged, the increase in U.S. inflation

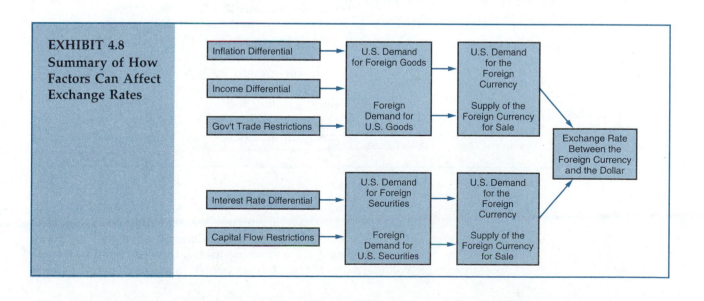

EXHIBIT 4.8 Summary of How Factors Can Affect Exchange Rates

USING ECONOMIC REPORTS TO ASSESS EXCHANGE RATES

Foreign exchange traders at banks and institutional money managers who frequently make international investments monitor reports of specific economic conditions because of the effects these conditions can have on exchange rates. If foreign exchange traders and institutional money managers revise their international currency positions as a report becomes public, they influence the demand and supply conditions for specific currencies, and exchange rates are therefore affected on that day. The most relevant reports for this purpose are summarized below:

a) Monthly balance of trade statistics. In the middle of every month, the U.S. balance of trade with all other countries for two months earlier is reported. This report is sometimes used as a possible signal about what the balance of trade will be in the future, which can influence the exchange rate movements.

b) Monthly employment levels. Each month, the U.S. employment level is provided. This figure is an indicator for economic growth because it can be used to determine the increase (or decrease) in the work force. Some analysts interpret any change in the employment level to signal a change in economic growth.

c) Other economic indicators. In recent years, foreign exchange participants have responded strongly to any economic news that signals a possible change in U.S. interest rates. This can be confirmed by reviewing the "Foreign Exchange" section of the *Wall Street Journal*. Signals of lower interest rates

tend to cause increased U.S. investment in foreign currencies, while signals of higher U.S. interest rates cause reduced U.S. investment in foreign currencies. Participants closely monitor U.S. economic indicators that may affect future interest rates, and therefore indirectly affect exchange rates. The most popular economic indicators that are frequently measured by the U.S. government and disclosed in business periodicals are

- Personal Income
- Personal Spending
- Industrial Production
- Capacity Utilization
- Purchasing Manager's Index
- Gross Domestic Product
- Factory Orders
- Initial Jobless Claims.

When the announcement of the economic index is more favorable than what has been anticipated, the prospects for higher-than-expected economic growth lead to prospects for higher-than-expected U.S. interest rates, which could result in more foreign capital flows in the U.S., and a stronger dollar. This places an immediate upward pressure on the value of the dollar.

When the announcement of the economic index is less favorable than what has been anticipated, the prospects for lower-than-expected economic growth lead to prospects for lower-than-expected U.S. interest rates, which could result in more foreign capital flows out of the U.S., and a weaker dollar. This places immediate downward pressure on the value of the dollar.

would place upward pressure on the pound's value while the increase in U.S. interest rates would place downward pressure on the pound's value. The sensitivity of an exchange rate to these factors is dependent on the volume of international transactions between the two countries. If the two countries engage in a large volume of international trade but very small international capital flows, the relative inflation rates would likely be more influential. However, if the two countries engage in a large volume of capital flows, interest rate fluctuations may be most influential.

Example.   Assume that Morgan Company, a U.S.-based multinational corporation (MNC), desires to forecast the direction of the German mark and Japanese yen, since it commonly purchases supplies from Germany and Japan. The following one-year projections have been developed for economic conditions by financial analysts of Morgan:

Factor	U.S.	Germany	Japan
Change in interest rates	−1%	−2%	−4%
Change in inflation	+2%	−3%	−6%

Assume that the United States and Germany conduct a large volume of international trade but engage in minimal capital flow transactions. Also assume that the United States and Japan conduct very little international trade but frequently engage in capital flow transactions. What should Morgan expect regarding the future value of the German mark and Japanese yen?

The German mark should be influenced most by trade-related factors because of Germany's assumed heavy trade with the United States. The expected inflationary changes should place upward pressure on the value of the mark. Interest rates are not expected to have much of a direct impact on the mark because of the assumed infrequent capital flow transactions between the United States and Germany.

The Japanese yen should be most influenced by interest rates because of Japan's assumed heavy capital flow transactions with the United States. The expected interest rate changes should place downward pressure on the yen. The inflationary changes are not expected to have much of a direct impact on the yen because of the assumed infrequent trade between the two countries.

An understanding of exchange rate equilibrium does not guarantee accurate forecasts of future exchange rates, since that will depend in part on how the factors that affect exchange rates will change in the future. Even if analysts fully realize how factors influence exchange rates, this does not mean they can predict how those factors will change. The art of forecasting exchange rates is discussed in Chapter 9.

How Factors Have Influenced Exchange Rates

The dollar's value changes by different magnitudes relative to each foreign currency of concern. In many cases, analysts measure the dollar's general strength or weakness with an index. That is, several currencies are consolidated into a single composite. The weight assigned to each currency is determined by its relative importance in international trade and/or finance. For simplicity, most indexes are based on only the industrialized countries. However, an index representing currencies of the industrialized countries would not be useful for assessing how the dollar's changing value has affected trade with less developed countries (LDCs).

MODELING EXCHANGE RATE MOVEMENTS

A recent study by Frankel offers some interesting insight into exchange rate movements. Frankel states that the high degree of volatility in exchange rate movements should not be surprising because the macroeconomic variables such as inflation and interest rates that influence exchange rate movements are also volatile. Numerous regression models have been used to determine the impact of macroeconomic variables on exchange rate movements. The models have often been disappointing in that the coefficients have the wrong sign or are not significant, and the R-squared value is low. Thus, the empirical results do not strongly support the theories of exchange rate determination. One possible explanation is that the macroeconomic variables do influence exchange rate movements according to theory, but the timing of the impact varies across currencies and over time. Therefore, it is difficult for a regression model to consistently detect the impact of macroeconomic variables on exchange rate movements. In addition, factors other than the macroeconomic variables may be influencing exchange rate movements. Some of these factors, such as implicit trade barriers, are difficult to incorporate in a model, but without them, the model is misspecified, and the true relationship between macroeconomic variables and exchange rate movements is not captured.

In the late 1970s, the dollar weakened against most currencies, primarily because of a relatively high U.S. inflation rate. In 1980, U.S. interest rates hit an all-time high that was at least partially due to the high U.S. inflation and growth in the late 1970s. The high interest rates caused a slowdown in the economy. While inflation was lowered, so was total spending. The combination of high U.S. interest rates, a somewhat depressed U.S. economy, and low inflation caused the dollar to strengthen against most currencies. It continued to strengthen throughout the early 1980s and often set all-time high records in 1984 and early 1985.

The dollar's value declined consistently from 1985 to 1988, mainly because of the large balance of trade deficit during that period. In 1989, the dollar strengthened as relatively high U.S. interest rates had attracted capital inflows from foreign countries. In addition, the U.S. balance of trade deficit had declined.

In 1990, the dollar weakened during the Persian Gulf War. The weakness was partially attributed to expectations of higher oil prices and therefore higher U.S. inflation. It strengthened as the war ended, but resumed its decline in late 1991 and 1992 as U.S. interest rates declined. Its decline against the German mark was more pronounced, as relatively high German mark interest rates had attracted capital flows from the U.S. However, in 1993, it strengthened against some European currencies as European interest rates declined.

SPECULATING ON ANTICIPATED RATES

Many commercial banks and other types of firms attempt to capitalize on their speculation of anticipated exchange rate movements. To illustrate how a bank may attempt to capitalize on the expected change in a currency's value, assume the following:

- Chicago Bank expects the exchange rate of the German mark (DM) to appreciate from its present level of $.50 to $.52 in 30 days.
- Chicago Bank is able to borrow $20 million on a short-term basis from other banks.
- Present short-term interest rates (annualized) in the interbank market are as follows:

Currency	Lending Rate	Borrowing Rate
Dollars	6.72%	7.2 %
German marks (DM)	6.48%	6.96%

Because brokers sometimes serve as intermediaries between banks, the lending rate differs from the borrowing rate. Given the information, Chicago Bank could

1. Borrow $20 million.
2. Convert the $20 million to DM40 million (computed as $20,000,000/ $.50).
3. Lend the marks at 6.48 percent annualized, which represents a .54 percent return over the 30-day period [computed as 6.48% × (30/360)]. After 30 days, the bank would receive DM40,216,000 [computed as DM40,000,000(1 + .0054)].
4. Use the proceeds of the mark loan repayment (on Day 30) to repay the dollars borrowed. The annual interest on the dollars borrowed is 7.2 percent, or .6 percent over the 30-day period [computed as 7.2% × (30/360)]. The total dollar amount necessary to repay the loan is therefore $20,120,000 [computed as $20,000,000 × (1 + .006)].

Assuming that the exchange rate on Day 30 is $.52 per mark as anticipated, the number of marks necessary to repay the dollar loan is DM38,692,308 (computed as $20,120,000/$.52 per mark). Given that the bank accumulated DM40,216,000 from its mark loan, it would earn a speculative profit of DM1,523,692, which is the equivalent of $792,320 (given a spot rate of $.52 per mark on Day 30). This speculative profit would be earned by the bank without using any funds from deposit accounts, since the funds would have been borrowed through the interbank market.

If Chicago Bank expected that the mark would depreciate, it could attempt to make a speculative profit by taking positions opposite to those described in the previous example. To illustrate, assume that the bank expects an exchange rate of $.48 for the mark on Day 30. It could borrow marks, convert them to dollars, and lend the dollars out. On Day 30, it could close out these positions. Using the rates quoted in the previous example, and assuming the bank can borrow DM40 million, the following steps could be taken:

1. Borrow DM40 million.
2. Convert the DM40 million to $20 million (computed as DM40,000,000 × $.50).

3. Lend the dollars at 6.72 percent, which represents a .56 percent return over the 30-day period. After 30 days, the bank would receive $20,112,000 [computed as $20,000,000 × (1 + .0056)].

4. Use the proceeds of the dollar loan repayment (on Day 30) to repay the marks borrowed. The annual interest on the marks borrowed is 6.96 percent, or .58% over the 30-day period [computed as 6.96 × (30/360)]. The total marks necessary to repay the loan is therefore DM40,232,000 [computed as DM40,000,000 × (1 + .0056)].

Assuming that the exchange rate on Day 30 is $.48 per mark as anticipated, the number of dollars necessary to repay the mark loan is $19,311,360 (computed as DM40,232,000 × $.48 per mark). Given that the bank accumulated $20,112,000 from its dollar loan, it would earn a speculative profit of $800,640 (computed as $20,112,000 − $19,311,360).

Most money center banks continue to take some speculative positions in foreign currencies. In fact, some banks' currency trading profits have averaged over $100 million per quarter in the early 1990s.

The appendix to this chapter illustrates how banks may attempt to speculate in the foreign exchange market. The potential return from foreign currency speculation is high for banks that have large borrowing capacity. Yet, foreign exchange rates are very volatile, and a poor forecast could result in a large loss. One of the best known bank failures, Franklin National Bank in 1974, was primarily attributed to massive speculative losses from foreign currency positions.

SUMMARY

■ Exchange rate movements are commonly measured by the percentage change in their values over a specified period, such as a month or a year. MNCs closely monitor exchange rate movements over the period in which they have cash flows denominated in the foreign currencies of concern.

■ The equilibrium exchange rate between two currencies at any point in time is based on the demand and supply conditions. Changes in the demand for a currency or the supply of a currency for sale will affect the equilibrium exchange rate.

■ The key economic factors that can influence exchange rate movements through their effects on demand and supply conditions are relative inflation rates, interest rates, and income levels, as well as government controls. As these factors cause a change in international trade or financial flows, they affect the demand for a currency or the supply of currency for sale, and therefore affect the equilibrium exchange rate.

■ The two factors that are most closely monitored by foreign exchange market participants are relative inflation and interest rates. If a foreign country experiences high inflation (relative to the U.S.), its exports to the U.S. should decrease (U.S. demand for its currency decreases), its imports should increase (supply of its currency to be exchanged for dollars increases), and there is downward pressure on its currency's equilibrium value.

■ If a foreign country experiences an increase in interest rates (relative to U.S. interest rates), the inflow of U.S. funds to purchase its securities should increase

(U.S. demand for its currency increases), the outflow of its funds to purchase U.S. securities should decrease (supply of its currency to be exchanged for U.S. dollars decreases), and there is upward pressure on its currency's equilibrium value.

■ All relevant factors must be considered simultaneously to assess the likely movement in a currency's value.

SELF-TEST FOR CHAPTER 4

(Answers are provided in Appendix A in the back of the text.)

1. Briefly describe how various economic factors can affect the equilibrium exchange rate of the Japanese yen's value with respect to that of the dollar.

2. A recent shift in the interest rate differential between the U.S. and Country A had a large effect on the value of Currency A. However, the same shift in the interest rate differential between the U.S. and Country B had no effect on the value of Currency B. Explain why the effects may vary.

3. Smart Banking Corp. can borrow $5 million at 6% annualized. It can use the proceeds to invest in Canadian dollars at 9% annualized over a six-day period. The Canadian dollar is worth $.95 and is expected to be worth $.94 in six days. Based on this information, should Smart Banking Corp. borrow U.S. dollars and invest in Canadian dollars? What would be the gain or loss in U.S. dollars?

QUESTIONS

1. Assume the spot rate of the British pound is $1.73. The expected spot rate one year from now is assumed to be $1.66. What percentage depreciation does this reflect?

2. Assume the U.S. inflation rate becomes high relative to German inflation. Other things being equal, how should this affect the (a) U.S. demand for German marks, (b) supply of marks for sale, and (c) equilibrium value of the mark?

3. Assume the U.S. interest rates fall relative to British interest rates. Other things being equal, how should this affect the (a) U.S. demand for British pounds, (b) supply of pounds for sale, and (c) equilibrium value of the pound?

4. Assume the U.S. income level rises at a much higher degree than does the German income level. Other things being equal, how should this affect the (a) U.S. demand for German marks, (b) supply of marks for sale, and (c) equilibrium value of the mark?

5. Assume the Japanese government relaxes its controls on imports by Japanese companies. Other things being equal, how should this affect the (a) U.S. demand for Japanese yen, (b) supply of yen for sale, and (c) equilibrium value of the yen?

6. What is the expected relationship between the relative real interest rates of two countries and the exchange rate of their currencies?

7. Discuss the historical trend of the dollar's value from the middle 1970s to the early 1990s.

8. Explain why a public forecast by a respected economist about future interest rates could affect the value of the dollar today. Why do some forecasts by well-respected economists have no impact on today's value of the dollar?

9. Assume that substantial capital flows occur between the United States, Country A, and Country B, in all directions. If interest rates in Country A declined, how could this affect the value of Currency A against the dollar? How might this decline in Country A's interest rates possibly affect the value of Currency B against the dollar?

10. Tarheel Company plans to determine how changes in U.S. and German real interest rates will affect the value of the U.S. dollar. (See Appendix B.)

    a) Describe a regression model that could be used to achieve this objective. Also explain the expected sign of the regression coefficient.

    b) If Tarheel Company thought that the existence of a quota in particular historical periods may have affected exchange rates, how might this be accounted for in the regression model?

11. From 1985 through 1987 the dollar weakened against most major currencies. Why do you think the dollar weakened over this period?

12. Blue Demon Bank expects that the French franc (FF) will depreciate against the dollar from its spot rate of $.15 to $.14 in 10 days. The following interbank lending and borrowing rates exist:

	Lending rate	Borrowing rate
U.S. dollar	8.0%	8.3%
French franc	8.5%	8.7%

Assume that Blue Demon Bank has a borrowing capacity of either $10 million or FF70 million in the interbank market, depending on which currency it wants to borrow.

a) How could Blue Demon Bank attempt to capitalize on its expectations without using deposited funds? Estimate the profits that could be generated from this strategy.

b) Assume all the preceding information, with this exception: assume that Blue Demon Bank expects the French franc to appreciate from its present spot rate of $.15 to $.17 in 30 days. How could it attempt to capitalize on its expectations without using deposited funds? Estimate the profits that could be generated from this strategy.

13. Assume that the United States heavily invests in government and corporate securities of Country K. In addition, residents of Country K heavily invest in the United States. Approximately $10 billion worth of investment transactions occur between these two countries each year. The total dollar value of trade transactions per year is about $8 million. This information is expected to also hold in the future.

    Because your firm exports goods to Country K, your job as international cash manager requires you to forecast the value of Country K's currency (the "krank") with respect to the dollar. Explain how each of the following conditions will affect the value of the krank, holding other things equal. Then aggregate all of these impacts to develop an overall forecast of the krank's movement against the dollar.

    a) The U.S. inflation has suddenly increased substantially, while Country K's inflation remains low.

    b) The U.S. interest rates have increased substantially, while Country K's interest rates remain low. Investors of both countries are attracted to high interest rates.

    c) The U.S. income level has increased substantially, while Country K's income level has remained unchanged.

    d) The United States is expected to place a small tariff on goods imported from Country K.

    e) Combine all expected impacts to develop an overall forecast.

14. Every month, the U.S. trade deficit figures are announced. The foreign exchange traders often react to this announcement and even attempt to forecast the figures before they are announced.

    a) Why do you think the trade deficit announcement sometimes has such an impact on foreign exchange trading?

    b) In some periods, foreign exchange traders do not respond to a trade deficit announcement, even when the announced deficit is very large. Offer an explanation for such a lack of response.

15. As the barriers are removed to allow free trade and capital flows across European countries, there is much interest in creating a single European currency that would be used by all countries by 1997. The German government stated that a single European currency would only be appropriate if those European countries with relatively high inflation are able to reduce their inflation rates. Why do you think this would be a necessary condition for the implementation of a single European currency?

16. The currencies of some Latin American countries depreciate against the U.S. dollar on a daily basis. What do you think is the major factor that places such severe downward pressure on the value of these currencies? What obvious change in Latin American economic policy is needed to prevent further depreciation of Latin American currencies?

17. As the "Iron Curtain" separating East and West Germany was removed in the fall of 1989, would you have anticipated appreciation or depreciation of the German mark against the dollar? Why?

18. Analysts commonly attribute the appreciation of a currency to expectations that economic conditions will strengthen. Yet, this chapter suggests that when other factors are held constant, increased national income could increase imports, and cause the local currency to weaken. In reality, other factors are not constant. What other factor is likely to be affected by increased economic growth, which could place upward pressure on the value of the local currency?

19. In the early 1990s, Russia was attempting to import more goods, but had little to offer other countries in terms of potential exports. In addition, Russia's inflation rate was high. Explain the type of pressure that these factors placed on the Russian currency.

CASE: FOREIGN EXCHANGE TRADING DURING THE ERM CRISIS

European Exchange-Rate Chaos Is Bedlam For Currency Traders at Chase Manhattan

By RANDALL SMITH
Staff Reporter of THE WALL STREET JOURNAL

NEW YORK—"It's been bedlam—people are trying to get prices and can't find them," says Paul Farrell, one of the senior currency traders at Chase Manhattan Bank, on one of the foreign exchange market's wildest days ever.

Britain has just raised its interest rates twice to defend the pound, but it isn't working. The pound is slipping. The entire European exchange-rate system is in doubt. Rumors are flying, and the dollar is rallying.

Thirty-five floors above Chase Manhattan Plaza yesterday morning, a small army of 50 traders and salespeople is trying to ride the billion-dollar waves sweeping across the currency markets. Hunched over banks of phones and green electronic quote screens, they bark out customer orders or price quotes as currency trading machines emit a series of ever-louder, high-pitched beeps, seeking prices from Chase.

"We knew this week would be wild, but not like this," says Geoff Koester, a European currency trader seated near Mr. Farrell. "It's all been unraveling." Now, Chase's traders want to avoid risks and mistakes at all costs. "The whole idea is just be square," Mr. Koestner explains. "Do the deal. Make the money and get out."

The traders are arrayed in neat rows of six across at black formica desks. As one trader gets a substantial customer order, he stands up and shouts out for exchange-rate quotes from other Chase traders who specialize in the currencies involved. Then the other traders try to fill the customer's order as quickly as possible—before the market moves or the order is canceled. Usually, one or two traders will be standing at any given time, swapping prices and orders. This day, seven or eight are standing at once; some-

times, nearly the entire roomful of traders are on their feet.

Chase, which ranked No. 5 among big U.S. banks with $215 million in 1991 foreign-exchange trading profits, is doing twice its normal trading volume—and making more than twice a normal day's profits, says James Borden, Chase's head of foreign exchange.

With the currency market so chaotic, the spread between bids and offering prices is far wider than usual. For Chase, that can be good news, as it makes much of its currency-trading profits from such bid-asked spreads, instead of betting heavily on the market's direction.

At 11:15 a.m., a grave Mr. Farrell stands up and tells other traders: "The central banks are gone here"—meaning the world's central banks appear to have temporarily abandoned their efforts to support the wobbling British pound.

A few moments later, Joseph Greene, a sandy-haired, bespectacled "sterling-mark" trader, stands and announces that a customer wants to sell £100 million and buy German marks. "There are no prices!" shouts Arnold Neimanis, who trades marks and is on the phone constantly to other brokers who are making price quotes.

Instead of making a bid—and taking the risk of holding the pounds with the market so disorderly—the Chase traders persuade the customer to allow them to execute the order bit by bit. Over the next few minutes, Chase executes half the trade, £5 million at a time; but the customer decides to stop at £50 million.

To veteran currency traders such as Mr. Farrell, the signs of turmoil are everywhere. Normally, he says, currency bid-asked spreads move in orderly progressions, for example, 10-20, then 15-25, then 20-30. The numbers denote the last two digits of a currency's price, such as 1.5220 marks per dollar.

Dealers give price quotes without necessarily knowing whether the customer wants to buy or sell, and so must be prepared to buy or sell at the quoted price. At 10-20, the dealer would be offering to buy dollars at 1.5210 or sell at 1.5220.

Today, the progression is more like 10-30, then 50-80.

Around 11:45, Rick Walsh, a trader who sits opposite Mr. Neimanis, warns him urgently: "Don't be exposed. They're buying dollars on the floor"—meaning the dollar may be moving up sharply against the mark. A few moments later, Mr. Neimanis calls out: "Just buy it, just buy it." Seated next to him, Russell Lascala marvels, "This dollar is going to the moon!"

Source: *The Wall Street Journal* (September 17, 1992): p. C1. Reprinted by permission of *The Wall Street Journal.* © 1992 Dow Jones & Company, Inc. All rights reserved worldwide.

Questions

1. Explain why the spread between the bid and the offering (ask) prices may widen during a period when exchange rate movements are volatile.

2. What is meant by the comment that traders at Chase Manhattan are swapping prices and orders?

3. Why did Chase Manhattan attempt to execute a large order (a customer wanting to sell £100 million) in pieces rather than all at once? Do you think Chase was the ultimate purchaser of the British pounds?

<table>
<tr><td>CASE
PROBLEM</td></tr>
</table>

BRUIN AIRCRAFT INC.
Factors Affecting Exchange Rates

Bruin Aircraft Inc. is a designer and manufacturer of airplane parts. Its production plant is based in California. About one-third of its sales are exports to the United Kingdom. While Bruin invoices its exports in dollars, the demand for its exports is highly sensitive to the value of the British pound. In order to maintain its parts inventory at a proper level, it must forecast the total demand for its parts, which is somewhat dependent on the forecasted value of the pound. The treasurer of Bruin was assigned the task of forecasting the value of the pound (against the dollar) for each of the next five years. He was planning to request from the firm's chief economist forecasts on all the relevant factors that could affect the pound's future exchange rate. He decided to organize his worksheet by separating demand-related factors from supply-related factors, as illustrated by the headings below:

Factors that can affect the value of the pound	Check (✔) here if the factor influences the U.S. demand for pounds	Check (✔) here if the factor influences the supply of pounds for sale

a) Help the treasurer by identifying the factors in the first column and then checking the second or third (or both) columns. Include any possible government-related factors and be specific (tie your description to the specific case background provided here).

PROJECT

Use *The Wall Street Journal* or some other business periodical to obtain the recent spot rate and the spot rate one year ago for major currencies. Compute the percentage change in the currency and offer reasons why the change may have occurred. Use the following table:

	Currency			
	British pound	Canadian dollar	Japanese yen	German mark
Recent spot rate				
Spot rate last year				
Percentage change				
Reason for change				

REFERENCES

Backus, David K., Allan W. Gregory, and Chris I. Telmer. "Accounting for Forward Rates in Markets for Foreign Currency." *Journal of Finance* (December 1993), pp. 1887–1908.

Bollerslev, Tim and Ian Domowitz. "Trading Patterns and Prices in the Interbank Foreign Exchange Market." *Journal of Finance* (September 1993), pp. 1421–1443.

Boyle, Glenn. "International Interest Rates, Exchange Rates, and Stochastic Structure of Supply." *Journal of Finance* (June 1990), pp. 655–672.

Chrystal, K. Alec. "A Guide to Foreign Exchange Markets." *Review* (March 1984), pp. 5–18.

Cornell, Bradford, and Marc R. Reinganum. "Forward and Futures Prices: Evidence from the Foreign Exchange Markets." *Journal of Finance* (December 1981), pp. 1035–1045.

Frankel, Jeffrey. "Flexible Exchange Rates: Experience versus Theory." *Journal of Portfolio Management* (Winter 1989), pp. 45–54.

Hakkio, Craig S. "Interest Rates and Exchange Rates—What is the Relationship?" *Economic Review,* Federal Reserve Bank of Kansas City (November 1986), pp. 33–43.

Lim, G. C. "Testing for the Fundamental Determinants of the Long Run Real Exchange Rate." *Journal of Banking and Finance* (June 1992), pp. 625–642.

Logue, Dennis E., and George S. Oldfield. "What's So Special About Foreign Exchange Markets?" *Journal of Portfolio Management* (Spring 1977), pp. 19–24.

Marrinan, Jane. "Exchange Rate Determination: Sorting Out Theory and Evidence." *New England Economic Review* (November-December 1989), pp. 39–51.

Officer, Lawrence, H. "The Purchasing Power Parity Theory of Exchange Rates: A Review Article." *IMF Staff Papers* (March 1976), pp. 1–60.

Woo, Wing Thye. "Some Evidence of Speculative Bubbles in the Foreign Exchange Market." *Journal of Money, Credit, and Banking* (November 1987), pp. 499–514.

FOREIGN EXCHANGE TRADING IN THE REAL WORLD

The following article by David Edwards appeared in the periodical MBA, June–July 1978. It was titled, "The Trading Room: It's Not A Gentlemen's Game." This article illustrates what foreign exchange trading is like in the real world.

Switzerland. The business week began at dinner Sunday night in the Dolder Grand Hotel, overlooking Lake Zurich. Hanas, the Treasurer from the local branch of an American bank, had been asked to dine by the chief traders from the Big Three Swiss banks. The meal, while elegant and copious, drew scant comment from the four of them. Through course after course they gossiped about finance, and politics as it affects finance, guarding their words. Little of importance was revealed until coffee when one of the three chief traders turned to Hanas and informed him that they had each decided to sell a billion dollars during the coming week. The signal had been given. Hanas left his cigar unfinished.

As Hanas rides the trolley along the Bahnhofstrasse on Monday morning, he is indistinguishable from the hordes of watchmakers who ride with him. He knows that if the Big Three are selling dollars, the currency will certainly continue to decline. He was at dinner because he works for an influential bank with branches all over the world and because he is one of the fastest traders in Europe. He will be instrumental in pushing the dollar down. He arrives at work at 7:15 and proceeds to sell $6 million against Swiss francs two time zones backward to Bahrain while the rest of the speculative community finishes breakfast.

England. At 7:30 in Kingston Hill, Jimmy Pritchard boards the London train. He looks much like his neighbors from the stock broker belt. For a minute he even feels like one of them. They wear bowler hats and pin-stripe suits and open the pages of the *Financial Times* as if on cue.

You can tell a currency trader from one of the big American banks by what he reads in the *Financial Times*. Jimmy Pritchard doesn't really read at all. He turns to check Friday's closing price for the dollar in New York (and sees that it was on shaky ground in Singapore), the Federal funds rate, the money supply—one column after another of statistics.

One news item catches his eye. The Federal Reserve in New York has raised the discount rate, pushing up all interest rates in America to make dollar investments more attractive to holders of foreign currencies. "Those bloody fools," he thinks, "do they really think it matters?"

Few of the men on the train know what the numbers mean. Currency traders comprise a tiny fraction of the thousands who work in the City. While brokers and managers spend their days persuading and cajoling, calculating, and projecting, pouring over contracts and shuffling papers, the traders play the fastest game in the world.

Money is a commodity. Traders like Hanas and Jim and their counterparts in other banks manipulate currencies in denominations of millions in transactions that take as little as ten seconds. They are street fighters, accustomed to thinking on their feet, making as many as 50 decisions a day about more money than 100 executives earn in their lifetimes. They have risen through the ranks of international banking to their niches in this esoteric specialty, acquiring hard nerves and a few refined tastes along the way.

When Jimmy arrives in his office adjacent to the trading room, the light for Zurich on his console is already flashing. He picks up the phone.

"Broschnagel took me in last night," Hanas tells him. "The other two have agreed to follow his lead this morning. I called New York this morning and woke Freeman up. It was one o'clock there. Free has agreed. We all follow their lead. I will sell $70 million this morning. Free thought 50 was more appropriate for you."

Jimmy says, "Hanas, I don't know. . . ."

"Look, Jimmy, I'm doing you a favor. When the Big Three move, the market moves. We follow. I'll call Frankfurt. Free wants Fritz to go 50 short also."

"All right, Hanas. Talk to you soon."

"My boys will let you know when we go."

Jimmy looks through the one-way glass at his 25 traders, already as nervous as race horses awaiting the start of the day. They sit at their consoles like NASA engineers monitoring a space shot. They each have perhaps forty direct lines to Europe with automatic dialing machines. Press a button to get a quotation on dollar-mark. Press another to price Norwegian krona against South African Rand.

The light on his intercom flashes.

"Hey, Jim, you've got another American trainee today." Bloody hell. "But this one's a lady. Been telling me how tough it was growing up in Texas and getting her M.B.A. over in France."

Jimmy enters the trading room. Except for the vault, this is the most restricted space in the bank. All around him people are writing, talking, scanning their video screens. Telexes pound out their messages silently under plexiglass cases. Newswires from the United States, Asia, and Europe bring events of the outside world into this soundproof, electronic, command bunker. Television screens give each of the bank's branches' latest price for currency in the currency of the host country. No one deals in those prices, unless trading is slow.

The trainee sits at Jimmy's desk holding a small Fendi purse under her left arm, left hand clutching a stenographer's notebook and a pen. Her right hand is poised to shake with her tutor for the week. . . .

"Hello, miss. I'm Jimmy Pritchard."

She rises, "E. L. Waters."

"What's your real name?" He watches her eyes widen with surprise briefly as she hears him speak. It has happened many times. These American trainees all think that English bankers should speak like Cambridge graduates. Instead they hear the rough strains of East London. It will be a long time before anyone from Oxford or Cambridge replaces this Cockney.

"Emmy Lou," she answers.

"Well, Emmy Lou, how long are you going to be with us?"

"My boss in credit analysis wants me to spend a week here."

Three men have gathered at Jimmy's desk. "Emmy Lou Waters, I'd like you to meet Henry Davids, our chief spot trader, the man who handles our speculative position, buying and selling with other banks. Mark Ricks runs the Eurocurrency deposit and loan operation, lending and borrowing in the inter-bank market and funding our speculative positions. And Duncan Willis who works with our commercial clients when they need to buy or sell one currency against another." They all shake hands with the newcomer.

Jimmy begins to spit out orders to his lieutenants. "We're going to hit the dollar again today. Henry, you take the lead."

"Right."

"But don't run it all into marks. Spread the book out. Free has given us an additional 50 million limit. Dump 20 million against the mark, 10 against Swiss francs, and 20 against sterling for starters. With the way the dollar is going down today, even the pound will have color in her cheeks by tonight."

Mark says, "There will always be an England."

"Save your energy, because you've got to borrow everything Henry's going to sell today. Borrow through Friday and don't pay more than seven and an eighth."

"My Eurodollar book's 2 billion short right now," Mark says. "Don't forget, last month we lent another billion to other banks for six months at eight. I'm covering the deposits on a day to day basis by having New York take the money in the New York Fed funds market at 7¼ percent. With the way the Fed is raising interest rates, we might lose our shirts on that billion. And everyone's near their limits. We may not be able to cover our positions through the other banks."

"I won't forget." Jimmy glances at the young American who is writing furiously in her notebook. He smiles. By the time she leaves this room she will have learned a whole new language.

He addresses the commercial chief. "Duncan, don't open your mouth before ten. Let Henry kick the hell out of the dollar. Then get your boys to go through the list of multi-nationals. Tell them the dollar might be a little soft. They'll watch the prices start to fall and by noon they'll run into your arms."

Mark says to Emmy Lou, "We do all the work and he has all the fun with our customers."

Jimmy says, "Duncan, we're counting on you to buy back this position for us from your commercials."

The three lieutenants return to their posts.

The trainee says, "I'd like you to define a few terms if you don't mind."

Jimmy wonders where she learned to talk, but before she can raise her notebook to read, one of the telex girls shouts, "I've got a Scandinavian bank on the line. They want to know the opening cable."

Jimmy calls, "How many times do I have to tell you, not until nine." His voice has the indulgent tone of a father, rather than annoyance. He's been at his job too long to lose his temper over anything so small.

Activity in the room is beginning to heat up. Everywhere, telephone consoles are blinking. People are shouting to one another and scribbling on slips of paper. Jimmy excuses himself for a minute and confers with Henry. Emmy Lou begins to write again, picking jargon out of the air at random.

"Marks spot next 2⅞-3⅙ . . . tom. next 2¹⁵/₁₆ . . . spot a week 3-3¼ sorry for wide . . . week fixed dollar 6¹⁵/₁₆-7¹/₁₆." Only about half the people in the room are speaking English. The rest are using French and German.

Jimmy returns, "I suggest that you don't try to get all the details at once. Just get a feel for the whole. Otherwise your notes will read like cursing in a comic strip."

"May I ask you a few basic questions?"

"Certainly."

She turns back in her notebook to a page where she had carefully written questions the night before.

"Where is the foreign exchange market?"

He smiles at her, again paternally. He has been asked a thousand times.

"The foreign exchange market is not like a stock exchange. The thousands of telephone lines and telexes in this room are connected to others in rooms very much like this in a few banks around the world. We do business with one another. You've probably read about nasty currency speculators in the newspapers. That's us."

"I heard you say before that Mark has to borrow the dollars you are going to sell. How can you sell borrowed money?"

"It's really very simple. Mark borrows say $50 million in the Eurodollar market for four nights. We sell them today against other currencies and then place the pounds, marks, and francs on deposit. On Friday we buy $50 million at a lower price than we sold them for and use the fifty to pay off the interbank deposit. We get to keep the leftover pounds, francs, and marks."

"You mean you make money pushing the dollar down?"

"Exactly. And don't say 'you' when you mean 'we'. You work for this bank too, Emmy Lou."

At 8:59, Henry's men are punching the buttons on their consoles to get quotations from brokers all over Europe. At the stroke of nine, the telexes begin to click furiously, but under their plexiglass casings, the clicking is reduced to a hum. The start of trading is an explosion, and the blast is felt in the sudden surge of energy everywhere in the room. People begin to shout back and forth. Lights on the consoles flash all around.

A Dane on loan to Henry from the Copenhagen branch shouts, "Opening dollar-mark here, 75-85."

Henry yells, "Give'em five million at 75."

Immediately another trader says, "Dollar-mark now 65-75."

Henry asks, "How many dollars is he paying for at 65?"

"He pays for five."

"$5 million his. Be sure and get the name this time."

Jimmy sits with his pupil. His console is blazing with lights and he leisurely listens in on conversations in different parts of the room. Life at his console is serene compared to the beehive in front of him. He watches with amusement as her uncomprehending eyes stare at the scene below.

"What happened?" she asks.

He explains patiently, "This is a two way market, Emmy Lou. That's why we give two prices—bid and offered. We began selling dollars for marks, receiving 2.1575 marks for each dollar. Henry sold $5 million at that rate in the first transaction of the day. At that moment he could have bought dollars at 2.1585. We always use the last two digits in the price. The prices change very rapidly as you can see, for the next $5 million brought only 2.1565 marks when we sold them."

"Why did Henry say 'be sure and get the name this time'?"

"He was speaking to one of the junior traders. Sometimes they ring off without knowing whom they're dealing with."

"You mean he can sell five million dollars to someone and not know who it is?"

"It's an honest mistake. Embarrassing though to call up a few banks and ask if you've just sold them $5,000,000."

On the flow the frenzy continues and the dollar declines.

A woman shouts from a telex, "Merck, Finck in Munich wants your dollar-mark price."

Henry replies, "It's down further. Tell him 50-65. Sorry for wide."

"He gives you $5 million at 50."

Henry curses under his breath. The low price was intended to discourage anyone from selling dollars to him." Get every German bank on the line you can."

The Dane says, "Got Deutsche-Duss here."

The junior trader says, "Commerce Hamburg."

"What's it with Dusseldorf?"

"45-55."

"Same in Hamburg."

"Give'em $10 million apiece."

The Dane yells, "Ten dollars at 45. Done." Into the mouthpiece of the phone he says, "Dusseldorf, where do you want your dollars? Morgan in New York? Done. Pay the marks to our Frankfurt office."

Jimmy explains to Emmy Lou that this is a quiet market that is moving quickly because they have hit it hard. Only $50 million will move the price. He reminds her that his colleagues in Zurich and Frankfurt are selling dollars. He points to the television monitor that he has been watching out of the corner of his eye.

"Look how much the Dollar-Swiss price has fallen. Hanas, our man there, and the Big Three Swiss are pounding the dollar."

She asks, "I heard you tell the others that you wanted them to sell $50 million. It sounds like you must have passed that already. Why don't you just go home now?"

"We have to buy and sell. In order to maintain that $50 million short position, we might have to turn over $700 million today."

"Why do you have to buy dollars if you don't want them?"

"If you get called you have to quote. That's the unwritten rule of this market. There are certain things we can do to discourage others from trying to sell to us like bidding at lower prices, but this is a rapidly moving market and when others see how prices are dropping, they try to dump dollars on us just as we dump on them."

"What happens if you don't buy?"

"Then we don't sell either. No one calls us. No one answers our calls. All this activity comes to a grinding halt."

"The electronic silent treatment."

"Right."

At ten o'clock, Duncan Willis begins his calling. He starts with the assistant treasurer of the largest British chemical company.

"Clive, this is Duncan Willis at the bank. We've seen the dollar soften this morning. I wanted to keep you up to date because your account officers have told us about the size of your dollar exposure. Personally, I think you ought to get out of it, but not right away. We think it might recover a bit."

Across the room, Henry and his traders have just sold another $30 million.

Duncan says, "I'll call you back as soon as we establish the trend for the dollar."

By eleven o'clock, Duncan and his men will have conveyed the same message to every multinational corporation in London.

From the opposite end of the trading room, a short thin man approaches Jimmy's desk. His name is Reggie Carton. Jimmy winces. Carton's two qualifications for his job at the bank are that he speaks proper schoolboy English and that he has had the tenacity to survive fifteen years of trying to become a foreign exchange trader. Now he heads the bank's domestic sterling desk, which funds sterling loans in England and in the former colonies known as sterling protectorates. Like other American banks in London, this one has a tiny sterling deposit base, and no capital at all in England, so in order to make loans in pounds, it is necessary to borrow them from British banks in denominations of one million pounds and up, much as Mark Ricks acquires Eurocurrencies in the interbank market.

Carton looks indignant. "I've got Mr. 80-80 from Athens on the phone," he says. "He wants to borrow another 5 million pounds of domestic sterling for three months in the name of our Bahrain branch. He claims it's to finance sterling trade bills they are holding in Jordan."

"Jimmy, I'm sick and tired of this. You know he doesn't have any commercial business in Jordan. He's turning a loophole in the exchange control laws into a way of life. We're not supposed to let pounds out of England. They are just borrowing sterling from us so they can place it in the Euromarket at higher rates with one of our other branches."

"For Crissakes," Jimmy answers, "Stop being such a moralist. Give it to him. It's no skin off your nose. If he borrows sterling from us at ten percent and places it with Paris at thirteen, it's his business.

"If he gets caught, his knickers are in a twist, not yours. Anyway, when was the last time the Old Lady audited our Jordanian office to find out if we really had the trade bills we claimed?"

Emmy Lou asks, "Who is Mr. 80-80 and who is the old lady?"

Jimmy says, "80-80 is Collins, the treasurer of our Middle East operations. Last year the bank made $80,000,000 in North Africa and the Middle East. The money market operation accounted for 80 percent of that. Every time Collins goes to New York, he can't keep his mouth shut about how much money he's made. The old lady, that's the Bank of England."

Carton becomes more upset. "Jimmy, this is an English branch of an American bank, accountable to British exchange control laws.

"*Oui, monsieur,* now get out of here and don't rip Collins off on the price."

Suddenly, the din among the traders turns into a roar. Henry yells, "Jimmy, we're in trouble and it's getting worse."

Jimmy leaves his seat and hurries to Henry's side.

"It's stopped falling," the spot trader tells him. "It's up 75 points. I don't understand it. I was getting dollars in all morning, and I had trouble getting rid of them faster than they came in. Eight minutes ago, the Scandinavians started buying at 50. It started moving up. Now it's 25 on the next big number. I have Societe Generale in Paris and Commerce Hamburg on the line, both wanting prices for large."

Jimmy looks at the television screen.

"The first thing you'd better do is get a price. Check the London brokers. I'll take care of it. Hand me the phone."

Henry says, "They're paying 25."

Jimmy takes the receiver. "Let me have Soc-Gen first." "Large" for Commerce Hamburg could mean $50 million and up which would move the market, either way, faster than he wanted it to move. By comparison, the Paris bank is small and safe. Commerce Hamburg is a gunslinger. *"Bon-jour, Vingt-cinque—trente-cinque."* He listens for a moment, then releases the button on the phone so that the party on the other end cannot hear what he says. "The son of a bitch wants $10 million at 35. I'll let him have only five. Stall Commerce Hamburg. Tell him anything, but don't give him a price. They're panicking in Paris. *Non, monsieur, cinque million. Trente-cinque.*"

One of the traders says, "Now they're paying fifty here in London."

Jimmy sprints the twenty-five yards back to his console. As he runs, he calls out his orders.

"Get me Hanas in Zurich and Fritz in Frankfurt on the same line." When he reaches his desk, the light for Zurich and Frankfurt are already flashing, but before he picks up the phone he says, "Get me our branches in Paris, Amsterdam, Brussels, and Milan in that order."

He picks up the phone. The others are already speaking to one another. Jimmy breaks in, "Cut it short. We're in trouble."

They both say, "I know."

Jimmy says, "Are either of your central banks intervening in the market?"

Fritz answers, "No, it's that maniac in Hamburg. He's taking his profit by turning that $300 million short position he took last week. One of these days I'm going. . . ."

"Cut it out, Fritz."

"It's my market he's playing with."

Hanas asks, "Well, what are we going to do about it?"

Jimmy speaks calmly and with the weight of authority in his tone. "This is what we'll do. We've got to march in step on this before the son of a bitch pushes the dollar up to where it was last week. Do what I say. I'll take the heat from New York if it comes to that. Take him out. Both of you sell him an additional $100 million. I'll drop $100 million here in London. We're all going to go to our daylight limits including the other branches, to set the line. I've got them on the phone now. Stuff him with whatever he needs. He won't know what hit him."

Hanas says, "Jimmy, if it doesn't work, they'll fry you. If it does, the Chairman will have his 15 percent."

"Tell your three friends in Zurich they owe us."

Within 90 seconds, Jimmy has given instructions to the other branches. They all recognize the logic of his tactics instantly.

The traders turn to their posts to unload the $100 million. The atmosphere remains charged. Jimmy sits back in his chair and keeps his eyes on the television screen.

A light blinks on his console. It's his Italian boss, the London treasurer, who sits in another part of the branch.

"Jimmy, how are things going?"

"Fine, Franco. We had a bit of a bother. Nothing we can't handle. Can I help you with something?" He hangs up. He knows his tactics will work. If you gorge the only big buyer, give him more than he needs, he will end up selling too. Hamburg knew better than to do this now.

Twenty minutes later, the dollar resumes its decline.

At 11:30, Duncan taps Jimmy on the shoulder.

"I know you've got problems," says Duncan , "but so do I."

"Anything I can do?"

"I hope so. The treasurer of Pepoco Oil is on line 29, and he's so mad the wire's ready to melt."

"What does he want?"

"To sell dollars and buy Belgian francs because he's got to make a payment in Luxemburg."

"How much?"

"Five million. . . ."

"So what's the problem?"

"He wants last Tuesday's price."

Jimmy folds his arms. A bemused look appears on his face.

Duncan says, "The difference is fifty thousand dollars."

"And if he doesn't get it?"

"He's implying that he'll take all the Sheik's general deposits away and place them with another bank."

Jimmy turns away. "I should have known." Pepoco had good reason to think they could call their shots in this situation. The oil company always took the payments for the Sheik's oil and kept it on deposit until the oil arrived at its destination. Then they turned the principle and the interest it had earned in the intervening four months over to the Sheik. Of course, if they kept 50 million pounds at one bank at rates below market interest, they would expect the bank to do them some favors, and this was a case in point. Jimmy reaches for the phone. He is angry and he grips the receiver so tight that his knuckles turn white, but his voice remains calm.

"I want you to know," he says, "that we are doing this for you at considerable cost to us. We want very much to maintain our relationship. If you absolutely must do this, I am willing to comply. That's what a relationship is all about. Goodbye."

"By the way, Duncan, how are you doing with your commercials?"

"Fine. This morning we shook $30 million loose from the trees at an average price of 35 points under the market. This afternoon we should get another 60. The multinationals are still running."

At 11:50, Jimmy punches the least-used button on his console, the one for his secretary's office. He asks her to make reservations for two at Simpson's on the Strand. She is more than happy to do this, since the only work she has done since last Wednesday is to pass one expense voucher. Jimmy produces little paper. His work disappears into the circuits of the electronic world he inhabits.

Simpson's has been serving . . . London's financial district in baronial elegance for centuries. The doorman in his red uniform greets Jimmy with a cheerful but respectful, "Good morning, sir." . . .

They sit in the largest of several dining rooms, which has about fifty tables. The waiters wear tuxedos. Their pink faces contrast with Jimmy's trading room pallor. The wine steward takes Jimmy's order of a pint of bitter stoically, but he disapproves of the woman's decision not to drink at all.

Emmy Lou asks Jimmy, "How do you feel?"

"Right now I'm three quarters-seven eighths, but after this beer arrives I'll be seven eighths-fifteen sixteenths."

"I assume that means you'll feel better."

"That's right."

"I'm exhausted," she says. "I felt like I was watching you run a war."

"You get used to it." The beer arrives, and Jimmy drinks quietly.

"Don't you feel nervous at all?"

"Today is Monday. The week ends on Friday."

"How much money are you going to make by Friday?" she asks.

"Look at it this way. Our commercial department can make a $100 million loan after six months of negotiations and the bank is lucky to clear one percent a year, or $1 million. If that loan were to an LDC, say Zaire, and it defaults, or its loan is "restructured" as we say now, then the bank must lend $100 million to get back its one percent margin. But this morning I sold $50 million and if the dollar declines two percent by Friday the way I expect it to, by the time I close my position I will make well over $1 million. That's in one week. Add to that the money we earn in the normal course of trading like the $100,000,000 I sold this morning to take Commerce Hamburg out which I will buy back at lower prices this afternoon. On top of that our commercial foreign exchange department is buying and selling below and above the market levels. The money market, then, is the most profitable sector of international banking."

"What happens when the dollar can't go any lower?"

"If we're lucky, the United States will start selling the gold reserves from Fort Knox to support it. We'll buy a piece of it. Then we'll start borrowing marks to sell against dollars and turn all our short positions. Then the dollar will rise, but not as fast as it fell."

"How long have you worked for the bank?" she asks.

"Twenty years."

"How long have you been a currency trader?"

"About fifteen."

A man of forty-five with jet black hair and an expensive suit appears at their table. Jimmy rises. The new man is four inches taller than him. His face is lined and sagging.

"Franco Orico, I'd like you to meet Emmy Lou Waters who has been sent to us by Credit Analysis." The Italian shakes her hand. "Emmy Lou, Franco is my boss."

"Very pleased to meet you," Franco says. "And how do you like working for our slow friends in Credit Analysis? Are they still taking six months to approve loans?"

She blushes. "I'm not sure. I'm just a trainee."

"Of course," says Franco. "And tell me, how do you like watching an expert at work?"

"I'm not sure that I understand it all, but I'm impressed."

Franco turns to Jimmy. His lined face becomes taut with concern. "I heard more about this 'bit of a bother' you had during the morning."

"It's over."

"Maybe you are enjoying too much freedom," Franco smiles at Emmy Lou. "Good afternoon, Miss Waters. Jimmy will answer all your questions." He leaves.

Jimmy sits down again. He is angry and afraid that it shows. Five days a week he turns over seven hundred million dollars plus another billion in Eurocurrencies, shaving a bit here, scraping there, massaging the market—last year his Group accounted for $45 million profit—all for the bank. Then one day something happens, something he cannot foresee, and he handles it like a master, but does anyone tip his hat? Does anyone even say thanks? No. Instead, he is humiliated in front of a trainee.

Jimmy says, "You know, Franco used to work for Bardolo. You've probably never heard of Bardolo but he's the one who helped Sindon kill one of your New York City banks a few years ago, in 1974, the last time the dollar took a real beating."

"The last time?" . . . "This has happened before?" . . .

Jimmy takes a long drink from his beer. . . . He knows what she is thinking, that he is responsible for debasing her precious dollar.

"Why are you selling the dollar? I want to know. I work for this bank too."

"Because everyone else is selling it except for that bloody fool in Hamburg."

"But why? Is it because of America's balance of trade deficit?"

"No, that's just part of the rationalization we give the press when it falls." She is clearly startled. He continues, "Last spring we began watching the dollar. We know the United States was building up a large deficit. But the commercials, particularly the oil companies, weren't selling dollars, and we couldn't understand it. We didn't know at the time that the Saudi petrodollars were being recycled into the United States Treasury. We started to sell in anticipation of commercial selling. We got out of the dollar before they did, which caused the commercials to run after us. We bought their dollars cheaper than we had sold ours, which allowed us to double up and sell them again. For the past six months, the dollar's decline has been making headlines. People are wringing their hands. It's the best streak we've had since 1974."

"But wasn't there a $30 billion deficit last year?"

Jimmy drinks, then says, "Maybe Americans are buying more oil than they should be. However, your own Commerce Department announced last month that foreign holdings of U.S. government securities increased over $20 billion last year, most of it from O.P.E.C. In other words, the Saudis put back everything they took. Add to that West Germany's recent agreement with the United States to support the dollar to the tune of $20 billion, and suddenly there is no trade deficit. And still the dollar has been going down. Now we say that fear of U.S. inflation is the reason for the dollar's continued weakness."

"That's ridiculous. You're creating the inflation in the U.S. Every time the dollar goes down it costs more to import goods and that inflation doesn't wait for the production cycle. It's immediate. I read the paper! The new chairman of our Federal Reserve Board said the dollar's decline since December has added ¾ of 1 percent to our cost of living!"

"Now wait a minute. That's the way it is. We both work for the bank. You want those first-class plane tickets and subsidized apartments on Park Avenue in New York and Park Lane in London. Stop making judgments about where they come from. I know plenty of people like you who went to business school because life hadn't kept its promises. . . . You wanted something better. Now, Miss Waters, you've got it. So leave your moral baggage outside the door of my trading room."

He leans back in his seat and finishes the last of his bitter. . . . [Emmy Lou] seems not angry, but chastened. She will serve the bank well, once she is convinced that's where all her loyalties belong.

"There's a saying in England," Jimmy tells her, "A cockney is someone born within the sound of the great bell of Bow Church. That's home for me."

"Where is it?"

"About a mile from here." The food arrives. Jimmy pulls his linen napkin into his lap. "But when I set foot in the bank, for the first, I was as far from the Bells of Bow as you are from Texas."

After lunch Jimmy broke up an argument between Henry and a junior trader. Henry had sold $10 million to a bank in Geneva over the phone. The trader wrote up the deal as a purchase. Luckily someone found the mistake before the entries were passed by the booking section.

Later, the Bahrain branch placed $40 million with London for six months at 8 percent and then took a deposit of $40 million back from the London branch for a week at 7 percent.

Jimmy called Athens, headquarters for the Middle East, and complained about Bahrain's irresponsibility. Bahrain would be making a profit of 1 percent on $40 million. London would lose 1 percent. The man in Athens said he would be more careful in the future, something he promised Jimmy an average of once a week, year in and year out.

The afternoon ended on a positive note. New York panicked. At three o'clock in London, it is nine a.m. in New York. Everyone had heard on the Today Show and Good Morning America of the pounding the greenback had taken in Europe. When the New York banks opened for business, they all sold, pushing the dollar lower. Henry's traders bought back all the dollars they had sold in the morning. Jimmy had made $1,235,000 and the week had just begun. On Tuesday the foreign exchange profit would disappear into "interest earned through a series of swaps," lowering the cost of funding his loan portfolio.

On the train going home, Jimmy looked at the men around him. Many of them were dozing. He wondered what they had been doing all day that could possibly have induced this exhaustion. Some were reading of scandal in the afternoon tabloid while others read paperback books. At the front of the car, a spirited game of bridge was being played. The sound of the bidding penetrated the rhythmic pounding of the train as it rolled forward. Cards and all other forms of gambling had always bored Jimmy, but horse racing especially bored him. It takes a horse two minutes to make a circuit of the track.

The rest were talking to one another. Jimmy thought about the years he had spent in the trading room, and he realized that he had never had a conversation on the train going home. What would he say to people? "Had a hard day at the office. Commerce Hamburg almost cost me a million at 11 this morning, but I fixed them at 11:01. Then at 11:02. . . ."

Had anyone taken the trouble to compare, they would have seen that while Jimmy dressed like the rest, they differed in some particulars. Jimmy's shoes were more worn than those of his neighbors. His shirt was from Marks and Spencer, not from Turnbull and Asser. The fact was that Jimmy had never developed expensive tastes. But how many of them could run the trading room? You think differently when you spend five days a week running as if your life depended on it. In general, it was not a gentleman's game.

CHAPTER 5

CURRENCY FUTURES AND OPTIONS

This chapter is devoted entirely to the currency futures market and currency options market, often used by speculators interested in trading currencies simply to achieve profits, but also used by firms to cover their foreign currency positions. Since firms commonly use currency futures and options, it is important to understand the background of these markets and how they can help achieve corporate goals. The specific objectives of this chapter are to

- explain how currency futures contracts are used to speculate or hedge based on anticipated exchange rate movements, and
- explain how currency options contracts are used to speculate or hedge based on anticipated exchange rate movements.

CURRENCY FUTURES MARKET

In 1919 the Chicago Mercantile Exchange (CME) was established as a commodity futures exchange to meet the needs of farmers and users of agricultural goods. In 1972 the CME allowed for futures in some short-term securities, gold, and foreign currencies.

Currency Futures Contracts versus Forward Contracts

Currency futures are contracts specifying a standard volume of a particular currency to be exchanged on a specific settlement date. They are similar to forward contracts in that they allow the purchaser to lock in the price to be paid for a given currency at a future point in time. Yet, their characteristics differ from those of forward contracts. They are traded face to face, unlike forward contracts, which are negotiated over the telephone. Face-to-face transactions require a

117

trading floor, which is provided by the Chicago Mercantile Exchange. Deals are executed by brokers. Contracts have to be standardized, or floor trading would be slowed down considerably as brokers would have to assess contract specifications. Recall that forward contracts, unlike futures contracts, are tailor-made.

The trading volume of currency futures has consistently increased over time; and as growth in international transactions continues, the market should grow as well. Futures contracts are available for several widely traded currencies at the Chicago Mercantile Exchange (see Exhibit 5.1), and the contract for each currency specifies a standardized number of units. Typical settlement dates are the third Wednesdays in March, June, September, and December.

Since corporations have specialized needs, they normally prefer the forward contracts. Consider a U.S. corporation, which as of January 2 realizes it will need 450,000 marks on February 11 (40 days later). If it attempts to lock in the future purchase price of marks with a futures contract, the closest contract settlement date is the third Wednesday of March. Also, the amount needed in marks (450,000) is more than the standardized amount (125,000) specified in the contracts. The best the firm could do is to buy three mark futures contracts (worth 375,000 marks) or four contracts (worth 500,000 marks). Conversely, the forward market can be tailored to meet the individual needs of the firm. That is, the firm can call a bank and request a forward contract specifying 450,000 marks in 40 days.

Some individual speculators and small firms are not able to set up forward contracts with banks since they have no other working relationship with banks. Also, the normal transaction amount for forward contracts is much larger than individual speculators or small firms may typically desire. Exhibit 5.2 summarizes the comparison of the forward and futures markets.

Pricing Currency Futures

The price of currency futures will normally be similar to the forward rate for a given currency and settlement date. To understand why, assume that the currency futures price on the pound is $1.50 and that forward contracts for a similar period are available for $1.48. Firms may attempt to purchase forward contracts and simultaneously sell currency futures contracts. If they could exactly match the settlement dates of the two contracts, they could generate guaranteed profits of $.02 per unit. These actions would place downward pressure on the

EXHIBIT 5.1
Currency Futures Contracts Traded on the Chicago Mercantile Exchange

Currency	Units per Contract
Australian dollar	100,000
British pound	62,500
Canadian dollar	100,000
German mark	125,000
Japanese yen	12,500,000
Swiss franc	125,000

**EXHIBIT 5.2
Comparison of the
Forward and
Futures Markets**
SOURCE: Reprinted
with the permission of
the Chicago Mercantile
Exchange.

	Forward	Futures
Size of contract	Tailored to individual needs.	Standardized.
Delivery date	Tailored to individual needs.	Standardized.
Participants	Banks, brokers, and multinational companies. Public speculation not encouraged.	Banks, brokers and multinational companies. Qualified public speculation encouraged.
Security deposit	None as such, but compensating bank balances or lines of credit required.	Small security deposit required.
Clearing operation	Handling contingent on individual banks and brokers. No separate clearinghouse function.	Handled by exchange clearinghouse. Daily settlements to the market price.
Marketplace	Over the telephone worldwide.	Central exchange floor with worldwide communications.
Regulation	Self-regulating.	Commodity Futures Trading Commission; National Futures Association.
Liquidation	Most settled by actual delivery. Some by offset, at a cost.	Most by offset: very few by delivery.
Transaction costs	Set by "spread" between bank's buy and sell prices.	Negotiated brokerage fees.

currency futures price. The futures contract and forward contracts of a given currency and settlement date should have the same price, or else guaranteed profits are possible (assuming no transaction costs).

The currency futures price differs from the spot rate, for the same reasons that a forward rate differs from the spot rate. If a currency's spot and futures prices were the same and the currency's interest rate were higher than the U.S. rate, U.S. speculators could lock in a higher return than they would receive on U.S. investments. They could purchase the foreign currency at the spot rate, invest the funds at the attractive interest rate, and simultaneously sell currency futures to lock in the exchange rate, at which they could reconvert the currency back to dollars. If the spot and futures rates were the same, there would be neither gain nor loss on the currency conversion. Thus, the higher foreign interest rate would provide a higher yield on this type of investment. The actions of investors to capitalize on this opportunity would place upward pressure on the spot rate and downward pressure on the currency futures price, causing the futures price to fall below the spot rate.

Interpreting Currency Futures Contracts Information

Assume that as of January 15, the German mark futures price for March is $.5900. By purchasing this futures contract on January 15, one is obligated to purchase marks for $.5900 per mark on the third Wednesday of March. Alternatively, anyone who sold this futures contract as of January 15 would be obligated to deliver (sell) marks for $.5900 per mark on the third Wednesday of March. Given that the mark futures contract represents DM125,000, the amount in dollars to be paid (received) when purchasing (delivering) the marks on the third Wednesday in March is $73,750 (computed as $.5900 per unit $\times$ 125,000 units).

Closing Out a Futures Position

If a firm holding a currency futures contract decides before settlement date that it no longer wants to maintain such a position, it can close out its position by selling an identical futures contract. The gain or loss to the firm from its previous futures position is dependent on the price of purchasing futures versus selling futures.

The price of a futures contract changes over time in accordance with movements in the spot rate. For example, if the spot rate of a currency increased substantially over a one-month period, the futures price would likely increase by about the same amount. In this case, the purchase and subsequent sale of a futures contract would be profitable. Conversely, a decline in the spot rate over time would correspond with a decline in the currency futures price, meaning that the purchase and subsequent sale of a futures contract would result in a loss. While the purchasers of the futures contract could decide not to close out their position under such conditions, the losses from that position could increase over time.

Sellers of futures contracts could close out their position by purchasing a currency futures contract with a similar settlement date. Most currency futures contracts are closed out before the settlement date.

Credit Risk of Currency Futures Contracts

Each currency futures contract represents an agreement between a client and the exchange clearinghouse, even though the exchange has not taken a position. To illustrate, assume you call a broker to request the purchase of a German mark futures contract with a March settlement date. Meanwhile, another person unrelated to you calls a broker to request the sale of a similar futures contract. Neither party needs to worry about the credit risk of the counterparty. The exchange clearinghouse assures that you will receive whatever is owed to you as a result of your currency futures position.

To minimize its risk in such a guarantee, the CME imposes **margin requirements** to cover fluctuations in the value of a contract, meaning that the participant must place a deposit on the contract. The initial margin requirement is typically between $1,000 and $2,000 per currency futures contract. However, if the value of the futures contract declines over time, the buyer may be asked to add to the initial margin. Margin requirements are not always required for forward contracts due to the more personal nature of the agreement; the bank knows the firm it is dealing with and may trust it to fulfill its obligation.

Corporate Use of Currency Futures

Corporations that have open positions in foreign currencies can consider the purchase or sale of futures contracts to offset such positions. The ownership of futures contracts locks in the price at which a firm can purchase a currency. For example, assume a U.S. firm orders German goods and upon delivery will need to send DM500,000 to the German exporter. Thus, the U.S. firm could purchase German mark futures contracts today, which would lock in the price to be paid for marks at a future settlement date. By holding futures contracts, the firm does not have to worry about changes in the spot rate of the mark over time.

Alternatively, a firm may consider selling a futures contract when it plans to receive a currency it will not need (perhaps from exporting products invoiced in the foreign currency preferred by the importer). By selling a futures contract, the firm is locking in the price at which it will be able to sell this currency as of settlement date. Such an action can be appropriate if the firm expects this currency to depreciate against its home currency. The manner in which a firm can use futures contracts to cover, or **hedge,** its currency positions is described more thoroughly in Chapter 11.

Speculation with Currency Futures

Currency futures contracts are sometimes purchased by speculators who are simply attempting to capitalize on their expectation of a currency's future movement. If, for example, they expect the British pound will appreciate in the future, they might purchase a futures contract that will lock in the price at which they can buy pounds at a specified settlement date. On the settlement date, they can purchase their pounds at the rate specified by the futures contract, and then sell these pounds at the spot rate. If the spot rate has appreciated by this time in accordance with their expectations, they will profit from this strategy.

Currency futures are often sold by speculators who expect that the spot rate of a currency will be less than the rate for which they would be obligated to sell it. For example, assume a mark futures contract specifies a price of $.54 per unit. Also assume speculators expect the spot rate of the mark will be $.50 on the settlement date. They could profit from selling a futures contract as follows. If their expectations are correct, they will be able to purchase 125,000 marks for $62,500 in the spot market as of settlement date. Then, by selling their marks at $.54 per mark as specified by the futures contract, they will receive $67,500, and their gain will be $5,000 ($67,500 − $62,500). Of course, expectations are often incorrect. It is because of different expectations that some speculators prefer to purchase a futures contract while other speculators prefer to sell the same contract at a given point in time.

Transaction Costs of Currency Futures

Brokers that fulfill orders to buy or sell futures contracts charge a transaction or brokerage fee in the form of a bid/ask spread. That is, they buy a futures contract for one price (their "bid" price) and simultaneously sell the contract to someone else for a slightly higher price (their "ask" price). The difference between a bid

SPECULATING WITH CURRENCY FUTURES

Results of the following strategy in the currency futures markets were analyzed in a study by Thomas, and in a second study by Madura and Cash. In each period, futures on currencies whose prices exhibited *discounts* (where the futures price was less than the spot rate) were purchased. Futures on currencies whose prices exhibited *premiums* (where the futures price exceeded the spot rate per unit) were sold. If the futures price of a currency futures contract was, on average, an unbiased estimator of the spot rate that would exist at the settlement date, this strategy would earn zero profits on average. However, the study revealed large profits on average from this strategy, suggesting that those currencies with futures discounts did not depreciate on average to the degree implied by the futures discount. In addition, those currencies with futures premiums

did not appreciate on average to the degree implied by the futures premium.

A second strategy that uses historical exchange rate movements to bet on currency futures was also assessed. A review of historical exchange rate movements suggests that exchange rates tend to move in cycles. This tendency may allow speculators to use recent movements to speculate with currency futures contracts. To determine whether such a system might work, the following simple strategy was applied. At the beginning of each quarter, the movement in a foreign currency was assessed. If the currency appreciated against the dollar in the previous period, this outcome was used as a forecast for the prevailing quarter. Thus, currency futures contracts on this currency were purchased to benefit from this expectation. Conversely, if the cur-

rency depreciated against the dollar in the previous period, futures contracts on this currency were sold with the expectation that the currency would continue to depreciate. The results of this strategy were assessed for five different currencies over a period from 1982 through 1987. For the Swiss franc and the Japanese yen, the strategy was profitable about 70 percent of the time. The other currencies did not have as favorable results but still led to profits on average. It should be emphasized that the strategy is risky, as some substantial losses were incurred in various quarters. However, the average gain during profitable quarters exceeded the average loss during loss quarters for all five currencies. Based on the generally favorable results from this simplified strategy, there may be potential for more consistent profits using a more sophisticated strategy.

and an ask price on a futures contract may be as little as $7.50. Yet, even this amount is larger in percentage terms than the transaction fees for forward contracts.

CURRENCY OPTIONS MARKET

In late 1982 exchanges in Amsterdam, Montreal, and Philadelphia allowed for trading in standardized foreign currency options. Since that time, options have been offered on the Chicago Mercantile Exchange and the Chicago Board Options Exchange. A **currency option** is an alternative type of contract that can be purchased or sold by speculators and firms. Currency options are presently available for seven currencies on the Philadelphia exchange: (1) British pound, (2) Canadian dollar, (3) German mark, (4) Japanese yen, (5) Swiss franc, (6) French franc, and (7) Australian dollar.

The options exchanges in the U.S. are regulated by the Securities and Exchange Commission. Options can be purchased or sold through brokers for a commission. The commission per transaction is commonly $30 to $60 for a single option currency option, but can be much lower per contract when the transaction involves multiple contracts. Brokers require that a margin be maintained during

IN PRACTICE

CURRENCY FUTURES QUOTATIONS

Currency futures quotations are summarized each day in *The Wall Street Journal*, as shown here. Each currency is listed in bold, with the specified number of units per contract to the right. Each row under a given currency represents a particular settlement month as specified in the left margin. For any particular currency and settlement month, the opening, high, low, and settle (closing) futures prices are disclosed. Changes in the futures price from the previous trading day are also disclosed. Notice that there is also a futures contract available for a U.S. dollar index, which is measured in relation to a composite of currencies. The popularity of any currency futures contract is indicated by the "open interest" in the right-hand column, which represents the number of existing contracts that have not been offset.

SOURCE: *The Wall Street Journal* (June 15, 1994): p. C16. Reprinted by permission of *The Wall Street Journal*, © 1994 Dow Jones & Company, Inc. All rights reserved worldwide.

CURRENCY

	Open	High	Low	Settle	Change	Lifetime High	Low	Open Interest
JAPAN YEN (CME)—12.5 million yen; $ per yen (.00)								
Sept	.9791	.9830	.9760	.9794	+ .0016	1.0017	.8942	54,789
Dec	.9850	.9897	.9850	.9862	+ .0015	1.0070	.9525	1,923
Mr95	.9938	.9950	.9932	.9934	+ .0014	1.0125	.9680	356
Est vol 23,679; vol Mon 31,363; open int 80,211, −3,944.								
DEUTSCHEMARK (CME)—125,000 marks; $ per mark								
Sept	.6071	.6089	.6064	.6074	+ .0007	.6130	.5600	61,586
Dec	.6078	.6091	.6071	.6076	+ .0006	.6105	.5590	1,190
Mr95	....	....	....	.6084	+ .0009	.6110	.5798	658
Est vol 33,300; vol Mon 76,906; open int 137,745, +871.								
CANADIAN DOLLAR (CME)—100,000 dlrs.; $ per Can $								
Sept	.7204	.7214	.7173	.7192	− .0015	.7740	.7068	27,778
Dec	.7169	.7169	.7140	.7158	− .0016	.7670	.7038	2,207
Mr95	.7127	.7127	.7120	.7127	− .0017	.7605	.7020	598
June	.7090	.7090	.7085	.7096	− .0018	.7600	.6990	152
Est vol 9,255; vol Mon 12,588; open int 42,717, −884.								
BRITISH POUND (CME)—62,500 pds.; $ per pound								
Sept	1.5192	1.5220	1.5144	1.5174	− .0008	1.5220	1.4440	34,084
Dec	....	....	....	1.5156	− .0008	1.5180	1.4400	266
Est vol 9,611; vol Mon 22,927; open int 50,221, +6,527.								
SWISS FRANC (CME)—125,000 francs; $ per franc								
Sept	.7211	.7244	.7205	.7218	+ .0009	.7244	.6590	38,462
Dec	.7244	.7257	.7217	.7227	+ .0006	.7257	.6885	640
Est vol 17,435; vol Mon 38,511; open int 53,899, +7,050.								
AUSTRALIAN DOLLAR (CME)—100,000 dlrs.; $ per A.$								
Sept	.7345	.7349	.7277	.7299	− .0049	.7412	.6645	7,898
Est vol 1,602; vol Mon 2,067; open int 11,944, −259.								
U.S. DOLLAR INDEX (FINEX)—1,000 times USDX								
June	92.14	92.22	92.05	92.14	− .02	99.04	91.74	575
Sept	92.41	92.54	92.28	92.41	− .05	98.55	92.08	7,382
Dec	....	....	92.68	92.68	− .05	99.00	92.96	2,039
Est vol 1,400; vol Mon 6,076; open int 9,999, +2,949.								
The index: High 92.28; Low 92.02; Close 92.17								

the life of the contract. The margin is increased for clients whose option positions have deteriorated. This protects against possible losses if the clients do not fulfill their obligations.

In addition to the exchanges on which currency options are available, some commercial banks and brokerage firms have begun to offer them. They are tailored to the specific needs of the firm. Since these options are not standardized, all the terms must be specified in the contracts. The number of units, desired strike price, and expiration date can be tailored to the specific need of the client. The minimum size of currency options, offered by financial institutions is normally about $5 million. Since these transactions are conducted with a specific financial institution rather than an exchange, there are no credit guarantees. Thus, the agreement made is only as safe as the parties involved. For this reason, financial institutions may require some collateral from any individuals or firms desiring to purchase or sell currency options. Currency options are classified as either **calls** or **puts.** Each is discussed here.

CURRENCY CALL OPTIONS

The **currency call option** grants the right to buy a specific currency at a specific price within a specific period of time. The price at which the owner is allowed to buy that currency is known as the **exercise price** or **strike price,** and there are monthly expiration dates for each option.

Call options are desirable when one wishes to lock in the price to be paid for a currency in the future. If the spot rate of the currency rises above the strike price, owners of call options can "exercise" their options by purchasing the currency at the strike price, which will be cheaper than the prevailing spot rate. This strategy is somewhat similar to that used by purchasers of futures contracts, but the futures contracts require an obligation, which the currency option does not. The owner can choose to let the option expire on the expiration date without ever exercising it. Owners of expired call options will have lost the premium they initially paid, but that is the most they can lose.

Currency options quotations are summarized each day in *The Wall Street Journal,* as shown in Exhibit 5.3. Each currency is listed in bold letters. While currency options have typically expired near the middle of the specified month, some of them expire at the end of the specific month and are designated as EOM. Each row under a listed currency represents a particular strike (or exercise) price, as designated in the first column. The expiration month is in the second column. The next two columns represent the volume of contracts traded and premium for call options with that strike price, while the final two columns represent the volume of contracts traded and premium for put options (discussed later) with that strike price. Some options are listed as "European Style," which means that those options can be exercised only upon expiration.

EXHIBIT 5.3
Currency Options Quotations

SOURCE: *The Wall Street Journal* (June 17, 1994) p. C13. *The Wall Street Journal,* © 1994 Dow Jones & Company, Inc. All rights reserved worldwide.

OPTIONS
PHILADELPHIA EXCHANGE

		Calls Vol. Last		Puts Vol. Last	
FFranc			179.75		
250,000 French Franc EOM-European style.					
18¼	Jul	5145	0.96	...	...
18½	Jul	5145	0.40	...	...
CDollr			71.95		
50,000 Canadian Dollar EOM-European style					
71½	Jun	8	0.33	...	...
73	Jun	24	0.03	...	...
73½	Jun	8	0.03	...	...
British Pound			151.98		
31,250 British Pound EOM-cents per unit.					
152½	Jun	...	...	15	0.84
31,250 British Pounds-European Style.					
152½	Jul	32	1.07	...	...
31,250 British Pounds-cents per unit.					
150	Jul	...	...	32	0.44
150	Aug	...	...	10	1.06
152½	Jul	16	0.90	...	...
157½	Aug	180	0.36	...	...
160	Sep	50	0.30	...	...
British Pound-GMark			248.28		
31,250 British Pound-German Mark cross.					
246	Jul	...	...	4	0.66
Canadian Dollar			71.95		
50,000 Canadian Dollars EOM-cents per unit.					
71½	Jun	...	...	9	0.19
50,000 Canadian Dollars-European Style.					
71	Jul	...	...	10	0.17
50,000 Canadian Dollars-cents per unit.					
72	Sep	...	...	2	1.05
72½	Jul	60	0.13	...	...
72½	Sep	...	...	5	1.45
73	Jul	50	0.08	...	...
73	Sep	...	...	28	1.75
73½	Sep	...	...	2	2.26
75½	Sep	...	...	2	3.95
76½	Sep	...	...	28	4.88
French Franc			179.75		
250,000 French Francs EOM-10ths of a unit per unit.					
17¾	Jun	...	...	30	0.26
250,000 French Francs-10ths of a cent per unit.					
17¾	Sep	...	...	8	2.48
18	Sep	...	...	10	3.84
250,000 French Francs-European Style.					
17½	Jul	...	...	200	0.42

		Calls Vol. Last		Puts Vol. Last	
GMark-JYen			63.20		
62,500 German Mark-Japanese Yen cross.					
62½	Sep	...	...	4	1.09
German Mark			61.31		
62,500 German Marks EOM-cents per unit.					
59½	Jun	...	...	100	0.02
60½	Jun	...	...	380	0.13
61	Jun	100	0.58	15	0.27
61½	Jun	130	0.27	10	0.42
62,500 German Marks-European Style.					
58½	Jul	...	...	250	0.04
59	Sep	...	...	340	0.40
59½	Jul	...	...	750	0.12
61½	Jul	48	0.61	...	...
61½	Aug	50	0.82	...	...
62	Jul	50	0.36	...	...
62	Sep	340	0.86	...	...
62½	Jul	750	0.23	...	...
63	Jul	750	0.12	...	...
63½	Jul	250	0.10	...	...
64	Sep	340	0.32	...	...
62,500 German Marks-cents per unit.					
58½	Aug	...	...	25	0.15
59	Aug	...	...	10	0.20
59	Sep	...	...	7	0.41
59½	Jul	...	...	11	0.12
60	Jul	...	...	20	0.20
60	Aug	...	...	50	0.43
60	Aug	...	...	302	0.69
60½	Jul	...	...	365	0.34
60½	Aug	...	...	13	0.59
60½	Sep	...	...	252	0.88
61	Jul	20	0.81	10	0.53
61	Sep	...	...	177	1.11
61½	Jul	30	0.60	20	0.55
62	Jul	638	0.37	...	...
62	Aug	...	...	1	1.38
62	Sep	1	0.88	11	1.62
62½	Jul	40	0.24	...	...
63	Sep	314	0.54	...	...
Japanese Yen			96.82		
6,250,000 Japanese Yen EOM-100ths of a cent per unit.					
98	Jun	10	0.23	...	...

		Calls Vol. Last		Puts Vol. Last	
6,250,000 Japanese Yen EOM.					
96½	Jun	15	0.76	...	...
97½	Jul	9	1.06	...	...
6,250,000 Japanese Yen-100ths of a cent per unit.					
93	Sep	...	...	11	0.55
94	Aug	...	...	7	0.43
94	Sep	...	...	2	0.77
95	Jul	...	...	5	0.40
95	Sep	...	...	10	1.10
96	Aug	5	2.17	...	...
96½	Jul	6	1.30	4	0.77
97	Sep	...	...	5	1.93
100	Sep	48	1.07	...	...
103	Jul	30	0.09	...	...
6,250,000 Japanese Yen-European Style.					
96½	Jul	25	1.51	...	...
98	Aug	5	1.41	...	...
98½	Jul	20	0.68	...	...
101	Sep	10	0.84	...	...
Swiss Franc			72.97		
62,500 Swiss Franc EOM-cents per unit.					
72	Jun	...	...	15	0.11
73	Jun	...	...	4	0.50
62,500 Swiss Francs EOM.					
71½	Jun	...	...	8	0.05
62,500 Swiss Francs-European Style.					
71½	Jul	100	1.70	100	0.27
72	Jul	24	1.39	...	...
73	Sep	24	1.46	...	...
62,500 Swiss Francs-cents per unit.					
68	Sep	...	...	10	0.15
72	Jul	...	...	8	0.47
72	Aug	5	1.67	...	...
72	Sep	...	...	50	1.00
72½	Jul	30	1.10	6	0.59
73	Jul	10	0.80	...	...
73	Aug	...	...	4	1.15
73	Sep	17	1.43	133	1.54
73½	Jul	...	...	25	1.05
74	Jul	...	...	5	1.38
74	Aug	5	0.70	...	...
74	Sep	...	...	11	2.03
74½	Jul	3	0.28	...	...
Call Vol 55,493				Open Int ... 366,412	
Put Vol 5,081				Open Int ... 354,270	

A currency call option is classified as *in the money* when the present exchange rate exceeds the strike price, *at the money* when the present exchange rate equals the strike price, and *out of the money* when the present exchange rate is less than the strike price. For a given currency and expiration date, an in-the-money call option will require a higher premium than options that are at the money or out of the money.

Factors Affecting Call Option Premiums

Premiums of call options vary due to three main factors:

1. *Level of existing spot price relative to strike price.* The higher the spot rate relative to the strike price, the higher will be the option price. This is due to the higher probability of buying the currency at a substantially lower rate than what you could sell it for. This relationship can be verified by comparing premiums of options for a specified currency and expiration date that have different strike prices.

2. *Length of time before the expiration date.* It is generally expected that the spot rate has a greater chance of rising high above the strike price if it has a longer period of time to do so. A settlement date in June allows two additional months beyond April for the spot rate to move above the strike price. This explains why June option prices exceed April and May option prices given a specific strike price. This relationship can be verified by comparing premiums of options for a specified currency and strike price that have different expiration dates.

3. *Potential variability of currency.* The greater the variability of the currency, the higher the probability that the spot rate will be above the strike price. Thus, more volatile currencies will have higher call option prices. For example, the Canadian dollar is a more stable currency than most other currencies. If all other factors are similar, Canadian call options should be less expensive than call options on other foreign currencies.

Hedging with Currency Call Options

Corporations with open positions in foreign currencies can sometimes use currency call options to cover these positions. If, for example, a U.S. firm orders Swiss goods, it may need to send Swiss francs to the Swiss exporter upon delivery. A Swiss franc call option locks in the rate at which a U.S. firm can exchange dollars for Swiss francs. This exchange of currencies at the specified strike price on the call option contract can be executed at any time before the expiration date. In essence, the call option contract has specified the maximum price the U.S. firm must pay to obtain these Swiss francs. Yet, if the Swiss franc's value remains below the strike price, the U.S. firm can purchase Swiss francs at the prevailing spot rate when it needs to pay for its imports and can simply let its call option expire.

Sometimes a firm anticipates a possible need for a foreign currency but is not yet certain of that need. Consider a firm that bids on a project required by the German government. If the bid is accepted, the firm will need approximately DM625,000 to purchase German materials and services. However, the firm will not know whether the bid is accepted until three months from now. In this case, it could purchase call options with a three-month expiration date. Ten call option contracts would cover the entire amount of potential exposure. If the bid is accepted, the firm can use the options to purchase the marks needed. If the mark has depreciated over time, the firm will likely let the options expire.

Assume that the exercise price on marks is $.50 and the call option premium is $.02 per unit. The firm will pay $1,250 per option (since there are 62,500 units per mark option) or $12,500 for the 10 option contracts. With the options, the maximum amount necessary to purchase the DM625,000 is $312,500 (computed as $.50 per mark × DM625,000). The amount of dollars needed could be less if the mark's spot rate were below the exercise price at the time the marks were purchased.

Even if the project's bid is rejected, the currency call option will be exercised if the mark's spot rate exceeds the exercise price before the option expires. Any gain from exercising may partially or even fully offset the premium paid for the options.

As another example, a U.S. firm involved in a foreign acquisition bid may purchase call options on the currency that would be needed to purchase the foreign company's shares. The call options hedge the U.S. firm against the potential appreciation of the currency that may be needed if the acquisition occurs. If the acquisition does not occur and the spot rate remains below the strike price, the firm can let the call options expire. If the acquisition does not occur and the spot rate exceeds the strike price, the firm can exercise the option and sell the foreign currency in the spot market. This may offset part or all of the premium paid for the option.

These examples suggest that options may be more appropriate than futures or forward contracts for some situations. Chrysler Corporation uses options for about 50 percent of its hedging transactions and forward contracts for the remaining 50 percent. Intel Corporation uses options to hedge its order backlog in semiconductors. If an order is cancelled, it has the flexibility to let the options contract expire. With a forward contract, it would be obligated to fulfill its obligation even though the order was cancelled. When Air Products and Chemicals was hired to perform some projects, it needed capital equipment from Germany. The purchase of equipment was contingent on whether the firm was hired for the projects. The company used options to hedge this possible future purchase.

Speculating with Currency Call Options

Because this text focuses on multinational financial management, the corporate use of currency options is more important than the speculative use. The use of options for hedging is discussed in detail in Chapter 11. Speculative trading is discussed here in order to provide more of a background on the currency options market.

Individuals may speculate in the currency options market based on their expectation of the future movements in a particular currency. For example, speculators who expect that the Japanese yen will appreciate can purchase Japanese yen call options. Once the spot rate of Japanese yen appreciates, they can exercise their option by purchasing yen at the strike price, then sell the yen at the prevailing spot rate.

Just as is the case with currency futures, for every buyer of a currency call option, there must be a seller. A seller (sometimes called a **writer**) of a call option is obligated to sell a specified currency at a specified price (the strike price) up to a specified expiration date. Speculators may sometimes want to sell a currency call option on a currency that is expected to depreciate in the future. The only way a currency call option will be exercised is if the spot rate is higher than the strike price. Thus, a seller of the currency call option will receive the premium when the option is purchased and can keep the entire amount if the option is not exercised. When it appears that an option will be exercised, there will still be sellers of options. However, such options will sell for high premiums due to the high risk that the option will be exercised at some point.

Numerical Examples.   Suppose that Jim is a speculator who buys a British pound call option with a strike price of $1.40 and a December settlement date. The current spot price as of that date is about $1.39. Jim pays a premium of $.012 per unit for the call option. Assume there are no brokerage fees. Just before the settlement date, the spot rate of the British pound reaches $1.41. At this time, Jim exercises the call option and then immediately sells the pounds at the spot rate to a bank. To determine Jim's profit or loss, first compute his revenues from selling the currency, then subtract from this amount the purchase price of pounds when exercising the option, and also subtract the purchase price of the option. The computations follow. Assume one option contract specifies 31,250 units.

	Per Unit	Per Contract
Selling price of £	$1.41	$44,063 ($1.41 × 31,250 units)
− Purchase price of £	− $1.40	− $43,750 ($1.40 × 31,250 units)
− Premium paid for option	− $ .012	− $375 ($.012 × 31,250 units)
= Net profit	− $ .002	− $62 (− $.002 × 31,250 units)

Assume that Linda was the seller of the call option purchased by Jim. Also assume that Linda would only purchase British pounds if and when the option was exercised, at which time she must provide the pounds at the exercise price of $1.40. Using the information in this example, Linda's net profit from selling the call option is derived below:

	Per Unit	Per Contract
Selling price of £	$1.40	$43,750 ($1.40 × 31,250 units)
− Purchase price of £	− $1.41	− $44,063 ($1.41 × 31,250 units)
+ Premium received	+ $ .012	+ $375 ($.012 × 31,250 units)
= Net profit	$ .002	$62 ($.002 × 31,250 units)

As a second example, assume the following information:

- Call option premium on Swiss francs (SF) = $.01 per unit
- Strike price = $.44
- 1 option contract represents SF62,500

A speculator who had purchased this call option decided to exercise the option shortly before the expiration date, when the spot rate reached $.49. The

---

EXHIBIT 5.4   Results from Speculating in Currency Call Options Over Two-Month Periods

First Trading Day of Year (When British Pound Call Options Were Purchased)	Spot Rate at Time of Purchase	Exercise Price of Call Option with March Expiration Date	Premium Paid for Option
1987	$1.47	$1.500	$.0175
1988	1.87	1.850	.0530
1989	1.82	1.825	.0254
1990	1.61	1.600	.0256
1991	1.94	1.950	.0276
1992	1.87	1.875	.0248
1993	1.50	1.500	.0318

francs were immediately sold in the spot market by the speculator. Given this information, the net profit to the speculator was

	Per Unit	Per Contract
Selling price of SF	$.49	$30,625 ($.49 × 62,500 units)
− Purchase price of SF	− $.44	− $27,500 ($.44 × 62,500 units)
− Premium paid for option	− $.01	− $625 ($.01 × 62,500 units)
= Net profit	$.04	$2,500 ($.04 × 62,500 units)

If the seller of the call option did not obtain francs until the option was about to be exercised, the net profit to the seller of the call option was

	Per Unit	Per Contract
Selling price of SF	$.44	$27,500 ($.44 × 62,500 units)
− Purchase price of SF	− $.49	− $30,625 ($.49 × 62,500 units)
− Premium received	+ $.01	+ $625 ($.01 × 62,500 units)
= Net profit	− $.04	− $2,500 (−$.04 × 62,500 units)

When brokerage fees are ignored, the currency call purchaser's gain will be the seller's loss. The currency call purchaser's expenses represent the seller's revenues, and the purchaser's revenues represent the seller's expenses. Yet, because it is possible for purchasers and sellers of options to close out their positions, the relationship described here will not hold unless both parties begin and close out their positions at the same time.

An owner of a currency option may simply sell the option to someone else before the expiration date rather than exercising it. The owner can still earn

EXHIBIT 5.4 *Continued*

Spot Rate on March 1 (When Option Was Exercised, if at all)	Net Profit Per Unit	Net Profit per Contract (Assuming 31,250 Pounds Per Contract)	Net Profit as a Percentage of the Initial Investment
$1.54	$ .0225	$ 703	128%
1.77	−.0530	−1,656	−100
1.74	−.0254	−794	−100
1.68	.0544	1,700	212
1.92	−.0276	−862	−100
1.76	−.0248	−775	−100
1.43	−.0318	−994	−100

profits, since the option premium changes over time, reflecting the probability that the option can be exercised and the potential profit from exercising it.

Actual Results From Speculation.   Exhibit 5.4 provides the actual gain or loss from purchasing specific British pound call options in recent periods. The call option was purchased on the first trading day of each year and was exercised on March 1 of that year (if at all). The results for currency call options were very favorable in 1987 and 1990, when the British pound appreciated. Conversely, the results were less favorable in the early 1990s, because the British pound had weakened over this period.

The gains or losses do not appear large on a per unit basis, but are sometimes very large when measured as a percentage of the initial investment. For example, in 1990 the gain on call option contracts on British pounds was 212 percent, while the losses were −100 percent (a loss of the entire investment) in the following three years.

At any point in time, there are options on a particular currency with varied exercise prices. The actual profits from speculating will depend on the particular option purchased. Yet, most currency call options tend to perform very well when the underlying currency appreciates substantially before the expiration date.

Break-Even Point From Speculation.   The purchaser of a call option will break even if the revenue from selling the currency equals the payments for (1) the currency (at the strike price) and (2) the option premium. In other words, regardless of the number of units in a contract, a purchaser will break even if the spot rate at which the currency is sold is equal to the strike price plus the option premium. In the previous example, the strike price is $1.40 and the option premium is $.012. Thus, in order for the purchaser to break even, the spot rate existing at the time the call is exercised must be $1.412 ($1.40 + $.012). Of course, speculators would not have purchased the call option if they thought the spot rate would only reach this break-even point without going higher before the expiration date. The computation of the break-even point is useful for a speculator deciding whether to purchase a currency call option.

CURRENCY PUT OPTIONS

The owner of a **currency put option** is granted the right to sell a currency at a specified price (the strike price) within a specified period of time. As with currency call options, the owner of a put option is not obligated to exercise the option. Therefore, the maximum potential loss to the owner of the put option is the price (or premium) paid for the option contract.

A currency put option is classified as *in the money* when the present exchange rate is less than the strike price, *at the money* when the present exchange rate equals the strike price, and *out of the money* when the present exchange rate exceeds the strike price. For a given currency and expiration date, an in-the-money put option will require a higher premium than options that are at the money or out of the money.

Factors Affecting Currency Put Option Premiums

The three main factors influencing call option premiums also influence put option premiums. First, the spot rate of a currency relative to the strike price is important. The lower the spot rate is relative to the strike price, the more valuable will be the put option, since there is a higher probability that the put option will be exercised. Recall that just the opposite relationship held for the call option. A second factor influencing the put option premium is the length of time until the expiration date. As with currency call options, the longer the time is to expiration, the greater will be the put option premium. A longer period creates a higher probability for the currency to move within a range where it would be feasible to exercise the option (whether it's a put or a call). These relationships can be verified by assessing quotations of put option premiums for a specified currency. A third factor that influences the put option premium is the variability of a currency. As with currency call options, the greater the variability is, the greater will be the put option premium, again reflecting a higher probability that the option may be exercised.

Hedging with Currency Put Options

Corporations with open positions in foreign currencies can use currency put options in some cases to cover these positions. For example, assume a U.S. firm has exported products to Canada and invoiced the products in Canadian dollars (at the request of the Canadian importers). This firm may be concerned that the Canadian dollars it is receiving will depreciate over time. To insulate itself against possible depreciation, it could purchase Canadian dollar put options, which would entitle the firm to sell Canadian dollars at the specified strike price. In essence, the firm would lock in the minimum rate at which it could exchange Canadian dollars for U.S. dollars over a specified period of time. Yet, if the Canadian dollar appreciated over this time period, the firm could let the put options expire and sell the Canadian dollars received at the prevailing spot rate.

Speculating with Currency Put Options

Individuals may speculate with currency put options based on their expectations of the future movements in a particular currency. For example, speculators who expect that the British pound will depreciate could purchase British pound put options, which would entitle them to sell British pounds at a specified strike price. If the pound's spot rate did depreciate as expected, they could then purchase pounds at the spot rate and exercise their put options by selling these pounds at the strike price.

Speculators could also attempt to profit from selling currency put options. The seller of such options is obligated to purchase the specified currency at the strike price from the owner who exercises the put option. Speculators who believe the currency will appreciate (or at least will not depreciate) may consider selling a currency put option. If the currency appreciated over the entire period, the option would not be exercised. This is an ideal situation for put option sellers, since they keep the premiums received when selling the options and bear no cost.

Numerical Example. To illustrate how to determine the net profit from speculating with put options, assume the following information:

- Put option premium on British pound (£) = $.04 per unit
- Strike price = $1.40
- 1 option contract represents £31,250

A speculator who had purchased this put option decided to exercise the option shortly before the expiration date, when the spot rate of the pound was $1.30. The pounds were purchased in the spot market at that time by the speculator. Given this information, the net profit to the purchaser of the put option was

	Per Unit	Per Contract
Selling price of £	$1.40	$43,750 ($1.40 × 31,250 units)
− Purchase price of £	− $1.30	− $40,625 ($1.30 × 31,250 units)
− Premium paid for option	− $ .04	− $1,250 ($.04 × 31,250 units)
= Net profit	$ .06	$1,875 ($.06 × 31,250 units).

Assuming that the seller of the put option sold the pounds received immediately after the option was exercised, the net profit to the seller of the put option was

	Per Unit	Per Contract
Selling price of £	$1.30	$40,625 ($1.30 × 31,250 units)
− Purchase price of £	− $1.40	− $43,750 ($1.40 × 31,250 units)
+ Premium received	+ $ .04	+ $1,250 ($.04 × 31,250 units)
= Net profit	− $ .06	− $1,875 (− $.06 × 31,250 units).

The seller of the put options could simply refrain from selling the pounds (after being forced to buy them at $1.40 per pound) until the spot rate of the pound rose. However, there is no guarantee that the pound will reverse its direction and begin to appreciate. The seller's net loss could potentially be greater if the pound's spot rate continued to fall, unless the pounds were sold immediately.

EXHIBIT 5.5   Results from Speculating in Currency Put Options Over Two-Month Periods

First Trading Day of Year (When British Pound Put Options were Purchased)	Spot Rate at Time of Purchase	Exercise Price of Put Option with March Expiration Date	Premium Paid for Option
1987	$1.47	$1.430	$.0070
1988	1.87	1.850	.0340
1989	1.82	1.825	.0400
1990	1.61	1.600	.0364
1991	1.94	1.950	.0578
1992	1.87	1.875	.0416
1993	1.50	1.500	.0442

Whatever an owner of a put option gains, the seller loses, and vice versa. This relationship would hold if brokerage costs did not exist, and if the buyer and seller of options entered and closed their positions at the same time. Brokerage fees for currency options exist, however, and are very similar in magnitude to those of currency futures contracts.

Actual Results From Speculation.   Exhibit 5.5 provides the actual gain or loss from purchasing specific British pound put options in recent two-month periods (from January to March). The put option was purchased on the first trading day of each year and was exercised on March 1 of that year (if at all). The results for currency put options were favorable in periods such as 1992 and 1993, when the British pound was typically weakening against the dollar. Conversely, the entire investment was lost in 1987 and 1990 when the pound appreciated. A comparison of results for put options (in Exhibit 5.5) to those for call options (in Exhibit 5.4) confirms that put options perform poorly when call options perform well, and vice versa.

Speculating With Combined Put and Call Options.   For volatile currencies, one possible speculative strategy is to purchase a **straddle,** which represents both a put option and a call option. This may seem unusual, since owning a put option is appropriate for expectations that the currency will depreciate while owning a call option is appropriate for expectations that the currency will appreciate. However, it is possible that the currency will depreciate (at which time the put is exercised) and then reverse direction and appreciate (allowing for profits when exercising the call). Also, one might anticipate that the currency will be substantially affected by current economic events, but be uncertain of the exact way in which it will be affected. By purchasing a put option and a call option, the speculator will gain if the currency moves substantially in either direction. Although two options are purchased and only one is exercised, the gains could more than offset the costs.

EXHIBIT 5.5 *Continued*

Spot Rate on March 1 (When Option Was Exercised, if at all)	Net Profit Per Unit	Net Profit per Contract (Assuming 31,250 pounds Per Contract)	Net Profit as a Percentage of the Initial Investment
$1.54	− $ .0070	−$ 219	−100%
1.77	.0460	1,437	135
1.74	.0450	1,406	112
1.68	−.0364	−1,137	−100
1.92	−.0278	869	−48
1.76	.0734	2,294	176
1.43	.0258	806	58

CONTINGENCY GRAPHS FOR OPTIONS

Assume that a British pound call option is available, with a strike price of $1.50 and a call premium of $.02. The speculative profits to be earned are dependent on the future spot rate of the pound. Assume that the speculator plans to exercise the option on the settlement date (if appropriate at that time) and will immediately sell the pounds received in the spot market. Under these conditions, a **contingency graph** can be created to measure the profit or loss per unit (see the upper left graph in Exhibit 5.6). Notice that if the future spot rate is $1.50 or less, the net gain per unit is −$.02 (ignoring transaction costs). This represents the loss of the premium per unit paid for the option, as the option would not be exercised. At $1.51, $.01 per unit would be earned by exercising the option, but considering the $.02 premium paid, the net gain would be −$.01. At $1.52, $.02 per unit would be earned by exercising the option, which would offset the $.02 premium per unit. This is the break-even point. At any rate above this point, the premium paid would be more than offset by the gain from exercising the option, resulting in a positive net gain.

A contingency graph could also be developed for the seller of this call option. The lower left graph shown in Exhibit 5.6 assumes that this seller would purchase the pounds in the spot market just as the option was exercised (ignoring transaction costs). At future spot rates of less than $1.50, the net gain to the seller would be the premium of $.02 per unit, as the option would not have been exercised. If the future spot rate were $1.51, the seller would have lost $.01 per unit on the option transaction (paying $1.51 for pounds in the spot market and selling pounds for $1.50 to fulfill the exercise request). Yet, this loss would be more than offset by the premium of $.02 per unit, resulting in a net gain of $.01 per unit. The break-even point is at $1.52, and the net gain to the seller of a call option becomes negative at all rates higher than that point. Notice that the contingency graphs for the buyer and seller of this call option are mirror images of one another in our example.

EXHIBIT 5.6   Contingency Graphs for Currency Options

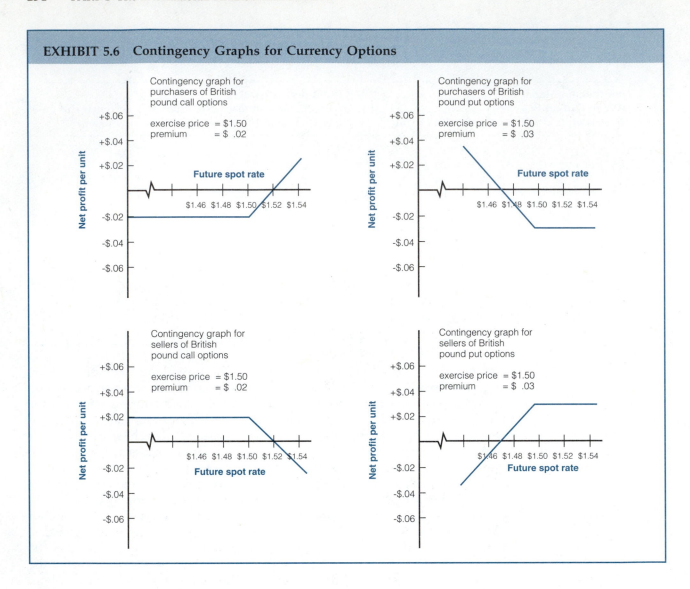

A contingency graph for a buyer of a put option can also be developed. The upper right graph in Exhibit 5.6 shows the net gains to a buyer of a British pound put option with an exercise price of $1.50 and a premium of $.03 per unit. If the future spot rate were above $1.50, the option would not be exercised. At a future spot rate of $1.48, the put option would be exercised. However, considering the premium of $.03 per unit, there would be a net loss of $.01 per unit. The break-even point in this example is $1.47, since this is the future spot rate that would generate $.03 per unit from exercising the option to offset the $.03 premium. At any future spot rates of less than $1.47, the buyer of the put option would earn a positive net gain.

A contingency graph for the seller of this put option is shown in the lower right graph in Exhibit 5.6. It is the mirror image of the contingency graph for the buyer of a put option.

IN PRACTICE

EXECUTING CURRENCY OPTION TRADES

The way currency option trades are made is perhaps best illustrated by following a typical trade through the Philadelphia Stock Exchange; the other exchanges follow essentially similar procedures. Suppose a customer wants to buy a British pound option with a $1.45 exercise price and June expiration date at the best price available on the market. The trading process begins when the customer calls a broker who is a member of the exchange and places the order. The broker books and clocks the order, then relays it electronically to the broker's booth on the exchange trading floor. The broker's floor trader then walks over to the other pound contract traders standing near the screens on which trades are reported, and shouts out his bid of, say, 1¢. Option price bids are quoted at cents per unit of the underlying currency, and a bid of 1¢ on a 12,500 British pound contract is equal to a premium of $125.

The floor trader's bid would be answered by offers to sell from other traders, at (say) 1.25¢, and 1.15¢. The offers may be coming from three kinds of traders: specialists, market makers, or floor brokers acting as agents for other customers. **Specialists** are firms designated by the exchange to maintain orderly trading and manage the limit orders for each currency. Some customers give their brokers orders to buy or sell only when prices reach a certain limit (say, "buy at 130.00" or "sell at 150.00"), and the specialist coordinates these orders. A **Market maker** is a member firm that buys and sells for its own account, and must make a bid or offer on a customer's order if called upon to do so by the specialist. In return for standing ready to trade even when it is not always in their interest to do so, market makers enjoy reduced margin requirements, and are able to execute trades for their own accounts faster than traders who must use a broker.

The floor trader takes the lowest offer—in this case 1.15¢, implying a premium of $143.75—and "matches tickets" with the selling trader, confirming the trade in pencil on printed paper slips. The buying trader hands the slips to the specialist, who staples them and gives them to an exchange employee who puts the information into the exchange's computerized reporting system. As soon as the trade is in the exchange's reporting system it is flashed onto the trading floor screens and private wire service screens. By SEC rules, the trade must be reported on the system within 90 seconds of when it occurs. The broker's floor trader then wires confirmation of the trade back to the broker, who advises his customer that the trade has been completed. If the option seller is another customer rather than a market maker, the seller's order will have followed a similar path through the customer's broker to the exchange floor, with one difference: the seller's broker will have required a margin deposit from its customer to protect the broker, the exchange's clearing corporation, and the option buyer from default.

SOURCE: Brian Gendreau. "New Markets in Foreign Currency Options," Federal Reserve Bank of Philadelphia, *Business Review* (July–August 1984).

There are various reasons why an option buyer's net gain will not always represent an option seller's net loss. The buyer may be using call options to hedge a foreign currency, rather than to speculate. In this case, the buyer does not evaluate the options position taken by measuring a net gain or loss; the option is used simply for protection. In addition, sellers of call options on a currency in which they presently maintain a position would not need to purchase the currency at the time an option is exercised. They could simply liquidate their position in order to provide the currency to the person exercising the option.

EUROPEAN CURRENCY OPTIONS

The discussion of currency options up to this point has been solely related to American-style options. European-style currency options are also available for speculating and hedging in the foreign exchange market. They are similar to American-style options except that they must be exercised on the expiration date if they are to be exercised at all. Consequently, they do not offer as much flexibility; however, this is not relevant to some situations. For example, firms that purchase options to hedge future foreign currency cash flows will probably not desire to exercise their options before the expiration date anyway. If European-style options are available for the same expiration date as American-style options and can be purchased for a slightly lower premium, some corporations may prefer them for hedging.

EFFICIENCY OF FUTURES AND OPTIONS

Speculators may believe that speculation in the currency futures and/or currency options markets can consistently generate abnormally large profits. This would not be possible if such foreign exchange markets were "efficient." In an efficient foreign exchange market, any available contracts would be priced to reflect all relevant information; thus, speculators would not be able to exploit existing information to earn abnormally large profits. Any valuable information would already have caused an adjustment in "sell" or "buy" requests, thereby forcing the contract price to reflect that information.

To assess the efficiency of the currency futures market, Thomas developed a trading strategy based on interest rate differentials. This strategy generated a return of about 10.3 percent above the three-month Treasury bill rate on average, suggesting that currency futures are not priced efficiently (if the excess return is assumed to more than compensate for the risk involved).

The efficiency of the currency options market has also been tested. Research by Bodurtha and Courtadon and by Tucker found that when accounting for transaction costs, the currency options market is efficient. This suggests that option prices generally reflect all available information.

A speculative strategy requires the speculator to incur risk, since the actual results from investing funds in a speculative instrument are uncertain. While a high return (profit as a percent of the amount invested) can sometimes be achieved by speculating in foreign exchange markets, there is considerable risk involved. "Abnormal" profits from a speculative strategy would reflect above-average returns *after* accounting for the risk involved. Individuals who speculate in futures and options markets must believe that they know something the market doesn't. Yet, corporations may use these markets even if they believe in market efficiency. Their positions in currency futures and currency options are usually intended to reduce exposure to fluctuating exchange rates rather than to earn a speculative profit.

SUMMARY

■ A currency futures contract specifies a standard volume of a particular currency to be exchanged on a particular date. Such a contract can be purchased by speculators who expect that currency to appreciate. If the currency appreciates, the value of the futures contract rises, allowing the speculators to benefit when they close out their positions.

A currency futures contract can be sold by speculators who expect that currency to depreciate. If the currency depreciates, the value of the futures contract declines, allowing the speculators to benefit when they close out their positions.

Futures contracts on a particular currency can be purchased by corporations that have payables in that currency, and wish to hedge against the possible appreciation of that currency. Conversely, these contracts can be sold by corporations that have receivables in that currency, and wish to hedge against the possible depreciation of that currency.

■ Currency options are classified as call options or put options. Call options allow the right to purchase a specified currency at a specified exchange rate by a specified expiration date. Put options allow the right to sell a specified currency at a specified exchange rate by a specified expiration date.

Call options on a specific currency can be purchased by speculators who expect that currency to appreciate. Put options on a specific currency can be purchased by speculators who expect that currency to depreciate.

Currency call options are commonly purchased by corporations that have payables in a currency that is expected to appreciate. Currency put options are commonly purchased by corporations that have receivables in a currency that is expected to depreciate.

SELF-TEST FOR CHAPTER 5

(Answers are provided in Appendix A in the back of the text.)

1. A call option on Swiss francs is available with a strike price of $.60 and is purchased by a speculator for the premium of $.06 per unit. Assume there are 62,500 units in this option contract. If the Swiss franc's spot rate is $.65 at the time the option is exercised, what is the net profit per unit to the speculator? What is the net profit for 1 contract? What would the spot rate need to be at the time the option is exercised for the speculator to break even? What is the net profit per unit to the seller of this option?

2. A put option on French francs is available with a strike price of $.19, and is purchased by a speculator for the premium of $.02. If the French franc's spot rate is $.14 on the expiration date, should the speculator exercise the option on this date or let the option expire? What is the net profit per unit to the speculator? What is the net profit per unit to the seller of this put option?

3. Longer-term currency options are becoming more popular for hedging exchange rate risk. Why do you think some firms decide to hedge by using other techniques instead of purchasing long-term currency options?

QUESTIONS

1. Compare and contrast the forward and futures contracts.

2. How can currency futures be used by corporations?

3. How can currency futures be used by speculators?

4. What is a currency call option?

5. What is a currency put option?

6. When should a firm consider purchasing a call option for hedging?

7. When should a firm consider purchasing a put option for hedging?

8. When should a speculator purchase a call option on German marks?

9. When should a speculator purchase a put option on German marks?

10. List the factors that affect currency call option premiums, and briefly explain the relationship that exists for each.

11. List the factors that affect currency put option premiums, and briefly explain the relationship that exists for each.

12. Assume a speculator purchased a call option on Swiss francs for $.02 per unit. The strike price was $.45, and the spot rate at the time the franc was exercised was $.46. Assume there are 62,500 units in a Swiss franc option. What was the net profit on this option to the speculator?

13. Assume a U.S. speculator purchased a put option on British pounds for $.04 per unit. The strike price was $1.80, and the spot rate at the time the pound was exercised was $1.59. Assume there are 31,250 units in a British pound option. What was the net profit on the option?

14. Assume a U.S. speculator sold a call option on German marks for $.01 per unit. The strike price was $.36, and the spot rate at the time the option was exercised was $.42. Assume the speculator did not obtain marks until the option was exercised. Also assume there are 62,500 units in a German mark option. What was the net profit to the seller of the call option?

15. Assume a U.S. speculator sold a put option on Canadian dollars for $.03 per unit. The strike price was $.75, and the spot rate at the time the Canadian dollar was exercised was $.72. Assume the speculator immediately sold off the Canadian dollars received when the option was exercised. Also assume there are 50,000 units in a Canadian dollar option. What was the net profit to the seller of the put option?

16. What are the advantages and disadvantages to a corporation that uses currency options rather than a forward contract to hedge against exchange rate fluctuations?

17. Assume that the transactions listed in Column 1 of the following table are anticipated by U.S. firms that have no other foreign transactions. Place an "X" in the table wherever you see a possible way to hedge each of the transactions.

	Forward Contract		Futures Contract		Options Contract	
	Forward Purchase	Forward Sale	Buy Futures	Sell Futures	Purchase a Call	Purchase a Put
a. Georgetown Company plans to purchase German goods denominated in marks.						
b. Harvard Inc. will sell goods to Japan, denominated in yen.						
c. Yale Corporation has a subsidiary in France that will be remitting funds to the U.S. parent.						
d. Brown Inc. needs to pay off existing loans soon that were denominated in French francs.						
e. Princeton Company may purchase a company in Japan in the near future (but the deal may not go through).						

18. Assume that the British pound's spot rate has moved in cycles over time. How might you try to use futures contracts on pounds to capitalize on this tendency? How could you determine whether such a strategy would have been profitable in previous periods?

19. Assume that on November 1 the spot rate of the British pound was $1.58 and the price on a December futures contract was $1.59. Assume that the pound depreciated over November, so that by November 30 it was worth $1.51.

    a) What do you think happened to the futures price over the month of November? Why?

    b) If you had known that this would occur, would you have purchased or sold a December futures contract in pounds on November 1? Explain.

20. Assume that a March futures contract on marks was available in January for $.54 per unit. Also assume that forward contracts were available for the same settlement date at a price of $.55 per mark. How could speculators capitalize on this situation, assuming zero transaction costs? How would such speculative activity affect the difference between the forward contract price and the futures price?

21. LSU Corporation purchased German mark call options for speculative purposes. If these options are exercised, LSU will immediately sell the marks in the spot market. Each option was purchased for a premium of $.03 per unit, with an exercise price of $.55. LSU plans to wait until the expiration date before considering whether to exercise the options. Of course, it will exercise the options at that time only if it is feasible to do so. In the following table, fill in the net profit (or loss) per unit to LSU

Corporation based on the listed possible spot rates of the mark that may exist on the expiration date.

Possible spot rate of the mark on the expiration date	Net profit (or loss) per unit to LSU Corporation if that spot rate occurs
$.56	
.58	
.60	
.62	
.65	
.67	

22. Auburn Company has purchased Swiss franc put options for speculative purposes. Each option was purchased for a premium of $.02 per unit, with an exercise price of $.66 per unit. Auburn Company will purchase the francs just before it exercises the options (if it is feasible to exercise the options). It plans to wait until the expiration date before considering whether to exercise the options. In the following table, fill in the net profit (or loss) per unit to Auburn Company based on the listed possible spot rates of the franc that may exist on the expiration date.

Possible spot rate of the franc on the expiration date	Net profit (or loss) per unit to Auburn Company if that spot rate occurs
$.56	
.59	
.64	
.67	
.69	
.71	

23. Bama Corporation has sold British pound call options for speculative purposes. The option premium was $.06 per unit and the exercise price was $1.58. Bama will purchase the pounds on the day the options are exercised (if the options are exercised) in order to fulfill its obligation. In the following table, fill in the net profit (or loss) to Bama Corporation if the listed spot rate exists at the time the purchaser of the call options considers exercising them.

Possible spot rate at the time the purchaser of call options considers exercising them	Net profit (or loss) per unit to Bama Corporation if that spot rate occurs
$1.53	
1.55	
1.57	
1.60	
1.62	
1.64	
1.68	

24. Bulldog Inc. has sold French franc put options at a premium of $.01 per unit, and with an exercise price of $.16 per unit. It has forecasted the French franc's lowest level over the period of concern as shown in the following table. If that level occurs and the put options are exercised at that time, determine the net profit (or loss) per unit to Bulldog Inc.

Possible value of French franc	Net profit (or loss) to Bulldog Inc. if that value occurs
$.12	
.13	
.14	
.15	
.16	

25. A U.S. professional football team plans to play an exhibition game in the United Kingdom next year. Assume all expenses will be paid by the British government, and a check of 1 million pounds will be provided to the team. The team anticipates that the pound will depreciate substantially by the scheduled date of the game. In addition, the National Football League must approve the deal, and approval (or disapproval) will not occur for three months. How could the team hedge its position? What is there to lose by waiting three months to see if the exhibition game is approved before hedging?

CASE: PANIC IN CURRENCY FUTURES TRADING

Chicago Merc Roiled by Dollar-Propping

By Jeffrey Taylor
Staff Reporter of THE WALL STREET JOURNAL

CHICAGO—The concerted effort by the Federal Reserve and other central banks to prop up the sagging U.S. dollar has wreaked havoc in the currency pits of the Chicago Mercantile Exchange.

On Monday, for instance, small fortunes were made and lost on the Merc floor in just the first hour after the Fed and central banks in Europe began buying U.S. dollars. It marked the first dollar-support move by the U.S. government since February 1991.

Since Monday, big institutional investors such as banks and commodity funds have been flooding the Merc pits with orders for currency futures and options contracts. Harried traders in multicolored jackets stand on the descending tiers of the pits, some trading for big investors and others trying to scalp profits as contract prices gyrate.

"The market has been wild," says David Silverman, a trader who makes his living buying and selling contracts in the Merc's mark futures pit. "Since the intervention, it's been reacting sharply to any little piece of news it can find."

Until Monday, the dollar's value against European currencies had been sinking steadily for months. The dollar's weakness had, in turn, created a sustained bull market in prices of the Merc's futures and options contracts for the mark. British pound and Swiss franc—contracts that track these cur-

rencies' heretofore rising value against the dollar.

The Longs Got Trapped

It was because of this bull market in the Merc currency pits that Monday's unexpected central-bank intervention had such a catastrophic effect on futures prices, traders say. As the dollar took off, "Everybody was trying to sell," says Jim Otiff, a floor broker in the British pound futures pit. "There were people who got trapped in long positions—a lot of bloodshed. It looked like sheer panic and it was a bit frightening."

Nowhere was the action hotter than in the mark futures pit. Although news-service display boards above the Merc floor had yet to flash the first headlines about the central banks' move, Mr. Silverman and other floor traders became aware of it almost immediately because of a rush of selling in their pit.

Shortly after 9 a.m. Monday, Mr. Silverman says, a floor broker who is known to handle trades for large commodity funds offered to sell 700 mark futures contracts—a huge order that represented about $50 million of marks—at the going market price. Under normal circumstances, brokers bring such big orders to the pit gradually—parceling them out bit by bit so as not to disrupt the market and send prices reeling.

"You know something is up when a customer is trying to sell 700 contracts at once without putting a price limit on," Mr. Silverman says. "This customer was basically saying: 'Sell $50 million worth of German marks and I don't care what price you do it at.'"

Mark Futures Tumble

More big sell orders quickly followed. Within seconds, the prices of mark futures contracts—which had been rising more or less steadily for months—were tumbling in what looked like a death spiral. Happily for Mr. Silverman, he was already holding a short position—a bet that the mark would decline against the dollar. This turned into a highly profitable trade, netting Mr. Silverman a profit that he declines to disclose.

Not all of Mr. Silverman's trades that morning were so lucrative. At one point, thinking that the plunging mark had hit bottom, he bought 20 futures contracts from a floor broker. "The next thing I knew, I was selling the contracts 36 points lower," he says. Each "point" represents a loss or profit of $12.50 a contract; at this rate, Mr. Silverman's trade produced a loss of $8,750 in less than five minutes.

The central banks' intervention had a similar explosive effect in the pit where futures contracts on British pounds are traded. As the pound's value against the dollar plunged, so did futures prices. In the pit, institutional clients began flooding Mr. Otiff, the floor broker, with orders.

By Monday afternoon, Mr. Otiff had lost his voice from screaming bids and offers at the top of his lungs. For the next two days, he was reduced to using sign language to announce his trades; during an interview yesterday, he spoke in a raspy whisper.

Many futures speculators who do their trading by phone were caught by surprise and had big losses; some others, however, had anticipated the central banks' move.

Continued

CASE: PANIC IN CURRENCY FUTURES TRADING

Continued

Kevin Lawrie, vice president, foreign exchange, at Bank of Boston, spent most of Monday protecting the bank's positions in global currency markets. Mr. Lawrie also trades currency futures contracts for his personal account, ordering the transactions through a broker who fills them on the Merc floor. "Going into last weekend," he says, "I was long four different currencies" in a wager that the dollar would remain weak.

But, "by Monday, the dollar was close to its historic low against the mark" Mr. Lawrie says. "There had been talk the previous week about intervention, so I decided to cut my long positions. I beat the intervention by about 10 minutes and when it happened, I had a good laugh about it."

Since the intervention, trading volume at the Merc has surged. On Monday, for instance, the exchange traded 62,253 mark futures contracts and 34,780 mark options contracts, up sharply from the average daily volume of 44,500 and 20,500 contracts, respectively. On the same day, the trading volume in pound futures and options was 18,599 and 4,640 contracts, respectively, up from average daily volume of 12,700 and 2,500 contracts.

And the lasting effect of Monday's central-bank intervention has been traders'

lingering fear that more such moves may be on the way. On Tuesday and again yesterday, the market was extremely sensitive to any news that seemed to signal what the Fed's intentions about the dollar might be.

For example, Fed Chairman Alan Greenspan, testifying before the Senate Banking Committee Tuesday afternoon, rolled the Merc's currency futures pits. Shortly before the 3 p.m. EDT close of trading, Mr. Greenspan expressed his view that the dollar's weakness didn't benefit the U.S. economy—contradicting the beliefs of some economists who feel that a weak dollar can help narrow the trade deficit by encouraging U.S. exports. Moments after Mr. Greenspan's remark, Mr. Otiff says, "we had a whole new wave of selling" in the pound futures pit.

Source: *The Wall Street Journal* (July 23, 1992): p. C1. Reprinted by permission of *The Wall Street Journal,* © 1992 Dow Jones & Company, Inc. All rights reserved worldwide.

Questions

1. Explain the logic of how central bank intervention caused sheer panic for currency futures traders with long positions.

2. Explain the concern caused when a floor broker was willing to sell 700 mark futures contracts (representing a value of about $50 million of marks) at the going market rate. What might this action signal to other brokers?

3. Explain why speculators with short (sell) positions could benefit as a result of the central bank intervention.

4. Some traders with long (buy) positions may have responded immediately to the central bank intervention by selling futures contracts. Why would some speculators with long positions leave their positions unchanged or even increase their positions by purchasing more futures contracts in response to the central bank intervention?

CASE
PROBLEM

CAPITAL CRYSTAL INC.
Using Currency Futures and Options

Capital Crystal Inc. is a major importer of crystal from Germany. The crystal is sold to prestigious retail stores throughout the U.S. The imports are denominated in German marks (DM). Every quarter, Capital needs DM500 million. It is presently attempting to determine whether it should use currency futures or currency options to hedge imports three months from now, if it will hedge at all. The spot rate of the mark if $.60. A three-month futures contract on the mark is available for $.59 per unit. A call option on the mark is available with a three-month expiration date and an exercise price of $.60. The premium to be paid on the call option is $.01 per unit.

Capital is very confident that the value of the mark will rise to at least $.62 in three months. It has been very accurate in its previous forecasts of the mark's value. The management style of Capital is very risk-averse. Managers receive a bonus at the end of the year if they satisfy minimal performance standards. The bonus is fixed, regardless of how high above the minimum level one's performance is. If performance is below the minimum, there is no bonus, and future advancement within the company is unlikely.

a) As a financial manager of Capital, you have been assigned the task of choosing among three possible strategies: (1) hedge the DM position by purchasing futures, (2) hedge the DM position by purchasing call options, or (3) do not hedge. Offer your recommendation and justify it.

b) Assume the previous information that was provided, except for this difference: Capital has revised its forecast of the mark to be worth $.57 three months from now. Given this revision, recommend whether Capital should (1) hedge the DM position by purchasing futures, (2) hedge the DM position by purchasing call options, or (3) not hedge. Justify your recommendation. Is your recommendation consistent with maximizing shareholder wealth?

PROJECTS

1. Using recent quotes from *The Wall Street Journal*, select a currency call option with an expiration date that occurs before the end of your school term. On that date, assume you will either (1) exercise your call option and sell the currency in the spot market or (2) let the option expire. Just before the end of your school term, determine your net profit or loss from this strategy as a percentage of your initial investment (the premium you originally paid).

2. Repeat the preceding project using a currency put instead of a currency call option.

3. Look in a recent issue of *The Wall Street Journal* to find Japanese yen call options. For any single expiration date, assess the relationship between exercise prices and premiums. Explain that relationship.

4. Repeat the preceding project using puts rather than calls.

5. Look in a recent issue of *The Wall Street Journal* and compare the Japanese yen call options that are available with a specific exercise price. Assess the relationship between the remaining time to the expiration date and the premium. Explain the relationship.

6. Repeat the preceding project using puts instead of calls.

REFERENCES

Adams, Paul and Steve Wyatt. "Biases in Option Prices: Evidence from the Foreign Currency Option Market." *Journal of Banking and Finance* (December 1987), pp. 549–562.

Biger, Nahum and John Hull. "The Valuation of Currency Options." *Financial Management* (Spring 1983), pp. 24–28.

Bodurtha, James and Georges Courtadon. "Tests of an American Option Pricing Model on the Foreign Currency Options Market." *Journal of Financial Quantitative Analysis* (June 1987), pp. 153–168.

Bodurtha, James N., Jr., and Georges R. Courtadon. "Efficiency Tests of the Foreign Currency Options Market." *Journal of Finance* (March 1986), pp. 151–161.

Carlozzi, Nicholas. "Exchange Rate Volatility: Is Intervention the Answer?" *Business Review,* Federal Reserve Bank of Philadelphia, (November–December 1983), pp. 3–10.

Chrystal, K. Alec. "A Guide to Foreign Exchange Markets." *Review,* Federal Reserve Bank of St. Louis, (March 1984), pp. 5–18.

Doukas, John and Abdul Rahman. "Unit Root Tests: Evidence from the Foreign Exchange Futures Market." *Journal of Financial and Quantitative Analysis* (March 1987), pp. 101–108.

Gendreau, Brian. "New Markets in Foreign Currency Options." *Business Review*, Federal Reserve Bank of Philadelphia, (July–August 1984), pp. 3–12.

Grammatikos, Theoharry. "Intervalling Effects and the Hedging Performance of Foreign Currency Futures." *Financial Review* (February 1986), pp. 21–36.

Hill, Joanne and Thomas Schneeweis. "The Hedging Effectiveness of Foreign Currency Futures." *Journal of Financial Research* (Spring 1982), pp. 95–104.

Hilliard Jimmy, Jeff Madura, and Alan L. Tucker. "Currency Option Pricing with Stochastic Domestic and Foreign Interest Rates." *Journal of Financial and Quantitative Analysis* (June 1991), pp. 139–151.

Johnson, Larry J. "Foreign-Currency Options, Ex Ante Exchange-Rate Volatility, and Market Efficiency: An Empirical Test." *Financial Review* (November 1986), pp. 433–450.

Kroner, Kenneth F. and Jahangir Sultan, "Time-Varying Distributions and Dynamic Hedging with Foreign Currency Futures," *Journal of Financial and Quantitative Analysis,* (December 1993), pp. 535–551.

Madura, Jeff and George Cash. "Investing in Currency Futures Contracts." *Journal of Business and Economic Perspectives* (Fall 1989), pp. 123–126.

Madura, Jeff and E. Theodore Veit. "Use of Currency Options in International Cash Management." *Journal of Cash Management,* (January–February 1986), pp. 42–48.

Maldonado, Rita and Anthony Saunders. "Foreign Exchange Futures and the Law of One Price." *Financial Management* (Spring 1983), pp. 19–23.

Shastri, Kuldeep and Kishore Tandon. "Valuation of American Option on Foreign Currency." *Journal of Banking and Finance* (June 1987), pp. 245–269.

Shastri, Kuldeep, and Kishore Tandon. "Valuation of Foreign Currency Options: Some Empirical Tests." *Journal of Financial and Quantitative Analysis* (June 1986), pp. 145–160.

Thomas, Lee R. III. "A Winning Strategy for Currency-Futures Speculation." *Journal of Portfolio Management* (Fall 1985), pp. 65–69.

Tucker, Alan L. "Empirical Tests of the Efficiency of the Currency Option Market." *Journal of Financial Research* (Winter 1985), pp. 275–285.

USING CURRENCY OPTION PRICING MODELS

Pricing models have been developed to price currency options. Based on information about an option (such as the exercise price and time to maturity) and about the currency (such as its spot rate, standard deviation, and interest rate), pricing models can derive the premium on a currency option. The currency option pricing model of Biger and Hull (1983) is

$$c = e^{-r^*T} S \cdot N(d_1) - e^{-rT}X \cdot N(d_1 - \sigma\sqrt{T})$$

where

$d_1 = \{[\ln(S/X) + (r - r^* + (\sigma^2/2))T]/\sigma\sqrt{T}\}$

c = the price the currency call option

S = the underlying spot exchange rate

X = the exercise price

r = the U.S. riskless rate of interest

r^* = the foreign riskless rate of interest

σ = the instantaneous standard deviation of the return on a holding of foreign currency

T = the time to option maturity expressed as a fraction of a year

$N(\cdot)$ = the standard normal cumulative distribution function.

This equation is based on the stock option pricing model (OPM) when allowing for continuous dividends. Since the interest gained on holding a foreign security (r^*) is equivalent to a continuously paid dividend on a stock share, this version of the OPM holds completely. The key transformation in adapting the stock OPM to value currency options is the substitution of exchange rates for stock prices. Thus, the percentage change of exchange rates is assumed to follow a diffusion process with constant mean and variance.

Bodurtha and Courtadon (1987) have tested the predictive ability of the currency option of the pricing model. They compute pricing errors from the model using 3,326 call options for the period of February 28, 1983 to September 21, 1983. The model's average percentage pricing error for all sample call options was −6.90 percent, which is smaller than the corresponding error reported for the dividend-adjusted Black-Scholes stock OPM. Hence, the currency option pricing model has been more accurate than the counterpart stock OPM.

The model developed by Biger and Hull is sometimes referred to as the European model because it does not account for early exercise. Yet, Bodurtha and Courtadon (1987) found that the application of an American currency options pricing model does not improve predictive accuracy. Their average percentage pricing error was −7.07 percent for all sample call options when using the American model.

Shastri and Tandon (1986) employ simulation analysis to demonstrate that the application of an American valuation formula does not systematically alter currency call options valuation. An early exercise, similar to that associated with discontinuous dividend payments on common stocks, should not be an important pricing factor.

Given all other parameters, the currency option pricing model can be used to impute the standard deviation σ. This implied parameter represents the option's market assessment of currency volatility over the life of the option.

THE INTERNATIONAL FINANCIAL ENVIRONMENT

Mesa Co. specializes in the production of small fancy picture frames, which are exported from the U.S. to the United Kingdom. Mesa invoices the exports in pounds and converts the pounds to dollars when they are received. The British demand for these frames is positively related to economic conditions in the United Kingdom. Assume that British inflation and interest rates are similar to the rates in the U.S. Mesa believes the U.S. balance of trade deficit from trade between the U.S. and the United Kingdom is expected to adjust to changing prices between the two countries, while capital flows will adjust to interest rate differentials. Mesa believes that the value of the pound is very sensitive to changing international flows, and is moderately sensitive to changing international trade flows. The following information was considered by Mesa:

- the U.K. inflation is expected to decline, while the U.S. inflation is expected to rise
- British interest rates are expected to decline, while U.S. interest rates are expected to increase.

1. Explain how the international trade flows should initially adjust in response to the changes in inflation (holding exchange rates constant). Explain how the international capital flows should adjust in response to the changes in interest rates (holding exchange rates constant).

2. Using the information provided, will Mesa expect the pound to appreciate or depreciate in the future? Explain.

3. Mesa believes international capital flows shift in response to changing interest rate differentials. Is there any reason why the changing interest rate differentials in this example will not necessarily cause international capital flows to change significantly? Explain.

4. Based on your answer to Question 2, how would Mesa's cash flows be affected by the expected exchange rate movements? Explain.

5. Based on your answer to Question 4, should Mesa consider hedging its exchange rate risk? If so, explain how it could hedge using forward contracts, futures contracts, and currency options.

EXCHANGE RATE BEHAVIOR

Part 2 (Chapters 6 through 8) focuses on critical relationships pertaining to exchange rates. Chapter 6 explains how governments can influence exchange rate movements and how such movements can affect economic conditions. Chapter 7 explores the relationships among foreign currencies. It also explains how the forward exchange rate is influenced by the differential between interest rates of any two countries. Chapter 8 discusses prominent theories regarding the impact of inflation on exchange rates, and the impact of interest rate movements on exchange rates.

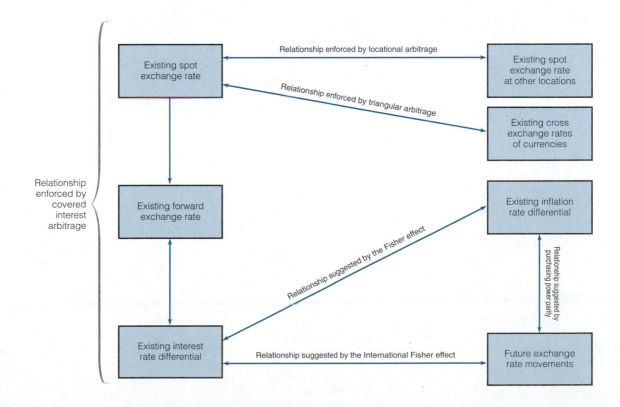

CHAPTER 6

GOVERNMENT INFLUENCE ON EXCHANGE RATES

Government policies affect exchange rates, which can influence a country's economy and financial markets. Because the performance of a multinational corporation (MNC) is affected by both the economy and exchange rates, it is important to understand how the government affects exchange rates. The specific objectives of this chapter are to

- describe the exchange rate systems used by various governments,
- explain how the governments can use direct intervention to influence exchange rates,
- explain how the governments can use indirect intervention to influence exchange rates, and
- explain how government intervention in the foreign exchange market can affect economic conditions.

EXCHANGE RATE SYSTEMS _____

Exchange rate systems can be classified according to the degree by which exchange rates are controlled by the government. Exchange rate systems normally fall into one of the following categories:

- Fixed
- Freely floating
- Managed float
- Pegged.

Each of these exchange rate systems is discussed in turn.

Fixed Exchange Rate System

In a **fixed exchange rate system,** exchange rates are either held constant or allowed to fluctuate only within very narrow boundaries. If an exchange rate begins to move too much, governments can intervene to maintain it within the boundaries. The methods used by governments to control exchange rates are mentioned later in this chapter.

From 1944 to 1971, exchange rates were typically fixed according to a system planned at the Bretton Woods conference (in Bretton Woods, New Hampshire, 1944), by representatives from various countries. Because this arrangement, known as the **Bretton Woods Agreement,** lasted from 1944 to 1971, that period is sometimes referred to as the Bretton Woods era. Each currency was valued in terms of gold; for example, the U.S. dollar was valued as 1/35 ounce of gold. Since all currencies were valued in terms of gold, their values with respect to each other were fixed. Governments intervened in the foreign exchange markets to ensure that exchange rates drifted no more than 1 percent above or below the initially set rates.

During the Bretton Woods era, the United States often experienced balance of trade deficits, which may imply that the dollar's value was too strong, since the use of dollars for foreign purchases exceeded the demand by foreign countries for dollar-denominated goods. By 1971 it appeared that some currency values would need to be adjusted in order to restore a more balanced flow of payments between countries. As of December 1971, a conference among representatives of various countries concluded with the **Smithsonian Agreement,** which called for a devaluation of the U.S. dollar by about 8 percent against other currencies. In addition, boundaries for the currency values were expanded to ±2.25 percent of the rates initially set by the agreement. However, international payments imbalances continued, and as of February 1973, the dollar was again devalued. By March 1973 most governments of the major countries were no longer attempting to maintain their home currency values within the boundaries established by the Smithsonian Agreement.

Under a fixed exchange rate environment, the managerial duties of an MNC are less difficult. However, there is still the risk that the government will alter the value of a specific currency. Currency devaluation can boost a country's exports, and therefore productivity (and jobs), since it encourages foreign consumers and firms to purchase goods denominated in that devalued currency. Revaluation (increasing the value) of a currency can increase competition that local firms receive from foreign firms, since foreign currencies can be purchased cheaply. Revaluation is a useful strategy by governments to restrain inflation, since it may prevent local firms from substantially raising the prices of their products. Of course, not all currencies can be revalued or devalued simultaneously. If the U.S. dollar, for example, is devalued against other currencies, this implies the other currencies have been revalued against the U.S. dollar.

Freely Floating Exchange Rate System

In a **freely floating exchange rate system,** exchange rate values would be determined by market forces without intervention by various governments. Under such a system, MNCs would need to devote substantial resources to measuring and managing exposure to exchange rate fluctuations.

Advantages of a Freely Floating Exchange Rate System.

From a macro viewpoint, where the stability of the entire world is concerned, a freely floating system could be preferable to a fixed exchange rate system. To illustrate, assume there are only two countries in the world: the United States and Great Britain. These countries trade frequently with each other. Now assume a fixed exchange rate system. If the United States experiences a much higher inflation rate than Great Britain, we might expect U.S. consumers to buy more goods in Great Britain and British consumers to reduce their imports of U.S. goods (due to the high U.S. prices). This reaction would force U.S. production down and unemployment up. It could also cause higher inflation in Great Britain due to the excessive demand for British goods relative to the supply of British goods produced. Thus, the high inflation in the United States could cause high inflation in Great Britain. In the mid- and late 1960s, the U.S. experienced relatively high inflation, and was accused of "exporting" this inflation to some European countries.

The results would not necessarily be the same in a freely floating exchange rate environment. As a consequence of high U.S. inflation, the increased U.S. demand for British goods would place upward pressure on the value of the British pound. As a second consequence of high U.S. inflation, the reduced British demand for U.S. goods would imply a reduced supply of pounds for sale (exchanged into dollars), which would also place upward pressure on the British pound value. The pound would appreciate due to these market forces (it would not be allowed to appreciate under the fixed rate system). This appreciation would make British goods more expensive to the U.S. consumers—as expensive as U.S. goods, even though British producers did not raise their prices. The higher prices would simply be due to the pound's appreciation, requiring a greater number of U.S. dollars to buy the same number of pounds as before. In Great Britain, the actual price of the goods as measured in British pounds might possibly be unchanged. Even though U.S. prices increased, British consumers would continue to purchase U.S. goods because their pounds could be exchanged for more U.S. dollars (due to the British pound's appreciation against the U.S. dollar).

This discussion indicates that U.S. inflation would have a greater impact on inflation in other countries within a fixed exchange rate system than it would in a floating exchange rate system. Problems experienced in one country would not necessarily be as contagious to other countries in a freely floating exchange rate environment. In our example, Great Britain is somewhat insulated from the U.S. inflation due to movement in the exchange rate.

Consider a second common economic problem: unemployment. Under a fixed rate system, high U.S. unemployment will cause a reduction in U.S. income and a decline in U.S. purchases of British goods. Consequently, productivity in Great Britain might decrease and its unemployment rise. Under a floating rate system, the decline in U.S. purchases of British goods would reflect a reduced U.S. demand for British pounds. Such a shift in demand could cause the pound to depreciate against the dollar (under the fixed rate system, the pound would not be allowed to depreciate). The depreciation of the pound would make British goods look cheap to U.S. consumers, offsetting the possible reduction in demand for these goods that could result from a lower level of U.S. income. As was true with inflation, a sudden change in unemployment appears to be less influential on a foreign country under a floating rate system than under a fixed rate system.

An additional advantage of freely floating rates is that a central bank is not required to constantly maintain exchange rates within specified boundaries. Therefore, it is not forced to implement an intervention policy that may have an unfavorable effect on the economy just to control exchange rates. Furthermore, governments can implement policies without concern as to whether the policies will maintain the exchange rates within specified boundaries. Finally, if exchange rates were not allowed to float, investors would invest funds in whatever country had the highest interest rate. This would likely cause governments in countries with low interest rates to restrict investors' funds from leaving the country. Thus, there would be more capital flow restrictions, and financial market efficiency would be reduced.

Disadvantages of a Freely Floating System. In the previous examples, Great Britain is somewhat insulated from the problems experienced in the United States due to the freely floating exchange rate system. While this is an advantage in protecting one country (Great Britain), it can be a disadvantage to the country that initially experienced the economic problems. For instance, if the United States experiences high inflation, the dollar may weaken, thereby insulating Great Britain from the inflation, as discussed earlier. However, from the U.S. perspective, a weaker U.S. dollar causes import prices to be higher. This can increase the price of U.S. materials and supplies, which will in turn increase U.S. prices of finished goods. In addition, higher foreign prices (from the U.S. perspective) can force U.S. consumers to purchase domestic products. As U.S. producers recognize that their foreign competition has been reduced due to the weak dollar, they can more easily raise their prices without losing their customers to foreign competition.

As a second example, consider a situation in which the U.S. unemployment rate is increasing. This tends to force the value of the dollar up as the demand for imports decreases. A stronger dollar will then reignite the desire for foreign goods, since they can be purchased cheaply. Yet, such a reaction can actually be detrimental to the United States during periods of high unemployment.

The preceding examples illustrate that a country's problems can sometimes be compounded by freely floating exchange rates. On the other hand, our earlier examples show that in a fixed exchange rate environment a country's problems are more contagious to other countries. The designation of one system as more desirable may depend on a country's political environment, economic conditions, goals, and policies.

Managed Float Exchange Rate System

The exchange rate system that exists today for some currencies lies somewhere between fixed and freely floating. It resembles the freely floating system in that exchange rates are allowed to fluctuate on a daily basis and official boundaries do not exist. Yet, it is similar to the fixed system in that governments can and sometimes do intervene to prevent their currencies from moving too much in a certain direction. This type of system is known as a **managed float,** or "dirty" float (as opposed to a "clean" float where rates float freely without government intervention). The various forms of intervention used by governments to manage exchange rate movements are discussed later in this chapter.

Criticism of a Managed Float System.   Some critics suggest that a managed float system allows a government to manipulate exchange rates in a manner that could benefit its own country at the expense of others. For example, a government may attempt to weaken its currency to stimulate a stagnant economy. The increased aggregate demand for products that results from such a policy may reflect a decreased aggregate demand for products in other countries, as the weakened currency attracts foreign demand. While this criticism is valid, it could apply as well to the fixed exchange rate system, where governments have the power to devalue their currencies.

Pegged Exchange Rate System

Some countries use a **pegged exchange rate** arrangement, in which their home currency's value is pegged to a foreign currency, or to some unit of account. While the home currency's value is fixed in terms of the foreign currency (or unit of account) to which it is pegged, it moves in line with that currency against other currencies. One of the best-known **pegged exchange rate** arrangements was established by the European Economic Community (EEC) in April 1972, when EEC members determined that their currencies were to be maintained within established limits of each other. This arrangement became known as the **snake.** Market pressure caused some currencies to move outside their established limits. Consequently, some members withdrew from the snake arrangement; it was difficult to maintain, and some currencies were realigned.

Due to continued problems with the snake arrangement, the European Monetary System (EMS) was pushed into operation as of March 1979. The EMS concept is similar to the snake arrangement, but the specific characteristics differ. Under the EMS arrangement, exchange rates of member countries are held together within specified limits and are also tied to the European Currency Unit (ECU). The ECU is not a currency but simply a unit of account. It is a weighted average of exchange rates of the member countries, each weight determined by a member's relative gross national product and activity in intra-European trade. The currencies of these member countries were allowed to fluctuate by no more than 2.25 percent (6 percent for some currencies) from the initially established par values. In 1993, these boundaries were widened substantially, allowing more fluctuation in exchange rates between European currencies.

The method of linking European currency values with the ECU has become known as the exchange rate mechanism (ERM). The participating governments intervene in the foreign exchange markets to maintain the exchange rates within boundaries established by the ERM. Other European currencies are pegged to the ECU and are therefore tied to the ERM currencies within narrow ranges. However, these governments have not committed to maintaining their currencies within the specified ranges.

Each currency tied to the ECU is assigned a so-called **central exchange rate** with respect to the ECU. From these assigned rates, the central exchange rate between any two currencies can be determined. For example, assume that the central rates of the French franc and German mark with respect to the ECU are 6.90 and 2.06, respectively. Given this information, we can determine that the central rate between the German mark (DM) and French franc (FF) is

$$\begin{aligned}
\text{Central rate of FF} \atop \text{in units per DM} &= \frac{\text{Central rate of FF in units per ECU}}{\text{Central rate of DM in units per ECU}} \\
&= \frac{6.90}{2.06} \\
&= 3.35
\end{aligned}$$

Alternatively, the central rate of the mark in units per franc could be determined by inverting the ratio shown here, to obtain .298.

If the exchange rate between the French franc and the German mark approaches either the lower or the upper limit, central banks will intervene to maintain the exchange rate within these limits. If the central banks cannot maintain the exchange rate within the limits, they may realign the central rates of each currency with respect to the ECU.

Impact of Exchange Rates on Countries with Pegged Currencies. To illustrate how a currency that is pegged to the U.S. dollar can be affected by other exchange rate movements, consider a world of three countries: (1) the United States, (2) a country called FLOAT whose currency fluctuates against the dollar, and (3) a country called PEG whose currency is pegged to the dollar. Assume that FLOAT's currency is presently valued at $.50 while PEG's currency is valued at $1.20. This implies that the cross exchange rate between FLOAT and PEG's currencies is 2.4 units of FLOAT's currency for each unit of PEG's currency (computed as $1.2/$.50 = 2.4). Assume that each country trades with the other two countries, and that some of the products traded are also produced in the other countries. Now assume that over the next six months, FLOAT's currency depreciates against the dollar and is worth only $.40 by the end of this six-month period. The most obvious result is an increase in the U.S. demand for FLOAT's products, because FLOAT's products can be purchased with fewer dollars. In addition, there is a decrease in FLOAT's demand for U.S. products, because these products cost more to FLOAT's firms and consumers. Yet, PEG's trade positions are also affected as follows.

When FLOAT's currency depreciates against the dollar, it also depreciates against PEG's currency, since PEG's currency is pegged to the dollar. In this example, the cross rate has changed to three units of FLOAT's currency for each unit of PEG's currency (computed as $1.2/$.40 = 3). This causes FLOAT's consumers and firms to reduce their demand for PEG's products, and PEG's consumers and firms to increase their demand for FLOAT's products.

Even though the value of PEG's currency with respect to the U.S. dollar is unchanged, the trade between the U.S. and PEG will be affected. Because U.S. consumers and firms can purchase FLOAT's products with fewer dollars, they will substitute FLOAT's exports for PEG's exports. In addition, PEG's consumers and firms will substitute FLOAT's exports for U.S. exports, because the price they pay for FLOAT's exports has been reduced.

Overall, the depreciation of FLOAT's currency against the dollar (and therefore against PEG's currency) causes an increase in FLOAT's exports to the other two countries and a decrease in FLOAT's demand for imports from those countries. In addition, the volume of trade between the United States and PEG decreases. FLOAT's economy is stimulated by these actions.

If our example is revised to assume appreciation of FLOAT's currency against the U.S. dollar, the opposite effects will likely occur. The United States and PEG will increase their demand for each other's products and reduce their demand for FLOAT's products. FLOAT will increase demand for U.S. and PEG's products. In general, the economies of the U.S. and PEG will be stimulated by this event.

The validity of this theory can be reinforced with a realistic example. Because the Korean won is essentially pegged to the dollar, while the Japanese yen floats against the dollar, significant adjustments in international trade occurred during the dollar's decline in 1986. Japanese products became more expensive to U.S. importers (except when the Japanese firms reduced the price to fully compensate for the weak dollar). Consequently, some U.S. importers switched to South Korean manufacturers of autos, steel, and videocassette recorders.

South Korea could be adversely affected during a strong-dollar period. Some U.S. importers may switch back to Japan when the dollar is stronger, since their relative purchasing power for Japanese imports will increase.

Classification of Exchange Rate Arrangements

Exhibit 6.1 categorizes exchange rate arrangements used by various countries. Several small countries peg their currencies to the U.S. dollar, while others peg their currencies to the French franc or a currency composite. The European countries that peg their currencies to the ECU are listed under the heading "Cooperative arrangements."

The Mexican peso has a controlled exchange rate that applies to international trade and a floating market rate that applies to tourism. The floating market rate is influenced by central bank intervention. In November 1987 the Mexican central bank removed its support of the Mexican peso, and the peso's value declined by about 25 percent against the dollar in a single day. The exchange rate became so volatile that some banks refused to accept pesos in exchange for dollars. In recent years, Mexico has reduced its inflation rate, and has been able to stabilize the value of the peso.

Governments of other Latin American countries have recently been successful in reducing the volatility of their currencies. As funds have flowed into Latin American countries to be invested in government bonds and in privatized companies, there is some demand for Latin American currencies, which has offset the typical outflow of funds from these countries. Argentina intervenes frequently to stabilize its currency's value. Chile intervenes to maintain its currency within 10 percent of its initially established exchange rate with respect to major currencies. The currencies of Brazil and Venezuela typically depreciate every day, but at a rate controlled by the government.

Some East European countries that recently opened their markets have tied their currencies to a single widely traded currency. The arrangement was sometimes temporary, as these countries were searching for the proper exchange rate that would stabilize or enhance their economic conditions. For example, the government of Slovakia devalued its currency (the koruna) in an attempt to increase the foreign demand for its goods and reduce unemployment.

Proposal For A Single European Currency.   One of the issues involved in the efforts to integrate European business is the possibility of a common currency for all European countries. In 1991, the Maastricht treaty called for the goal of a

EXHIBIT 6.1   Exchange Rate Arrangements[1]

			Currency pegged to		
US Dollar	French Franc	Russian ruble	Other currency	SDR	Other composite[2]
Angola	Benin	Armenia	Bhutan (Indian Rupee)	Libya	Algeria
Antigua & Barbuda	Burkina Faso	Azerbaijan	Estonia (deutsche mark)	Myanmar	Austria
Argentina	Cameroon	Belarus	Kirbati (Australian dollar)	Rwanda	Bangladesh
Bahamas, The	C. African Rep.	Georgia	Lesotho (South African Rand)	Seychelles	Botswana
Barbados	Chad	Kazakhstan	Namibia (South African Rand)		Burundi
			Swaziland (South African Rand)		
Belize	Comoros	Moldova			Cape Verde
Djibouti	Congo	Turkmenistan			Cyprus
Dominica	Côte d'Ivoire				Fiji
Grenada	Equatorial Guinea				Hungary
Iraq	Gabon				Iceland
Liberia	Mali				Jordan
Marshall Islands	Niger				Kenya
Oman	Senegal				Kuwait
Panama	Togo				Malawi
St. Kitts & Nevis					Malta
St. Lucia					Mauritania
St. Vincent and					Mauritius
the Grenadines					Morocco
Suriname					Nepal
Syrian Arab Rep.					Papua New Guinea
Yemen, Republic of					
					Solomon Islands
					Tanzania
					Thailand
					Tonga
					Vanuatu
					Western Samoa
					Zimbabwe

[1]For members with dual or multiple exchange markets, the arrangement shown is that in the major market.
[2]Comprises currencies which are pegged to various "baskets" of currencies of the members' own choice, as distinct from the SDR basket.
[3]Exchange rates of all currencies have shown limited flexibility in terms of the U.S. dollar.
[4]Refers to the cooperative arrangement maintained under the European Monetary System.

single European currency by the year 1999. One major advantage of a single European currency is the complete elimination of exchange rate risk between European currencies, which could encourage more trade and capital flows across European borders. There is some degree of exchange rate risk within the exchange rate mechanism because exchange rates can move within boundaries, and the central exchange rates between European currencies may be realigned by the European governments. If there were a single currency, realignment would not be a possibility. In addition, foreign exchange transactions costs associated with transactions between European countries would be eliminated. The goal of a single European currency is consistent with the goal of the Single European Act to remove trade barriers between European borders, since exchange rate risk is

EXHIBIT 6.1 *Continued*

Flexibility Limited in terms of a Single Currency or Group of Currencies			More Flexible		
Single currency[3]	Cooperative arrangements[4]	Adjusted according to a set of indicators[5]	Other managed floating		Independently floating
Bahrain	Belgium	Chile	Cambodia	Afghanistan,	Lebanon
Qatar	Denmark	Columbia	China, P.R.	Islamic State of Albania	Lithuania
Saudi Arabia	France	Madagascar	Croatia	Australia	Mongolia
United Arab Emirates	Germany		Ecuador	Bolivia	Mozambique
	Ireland		Egypt	Brazil	New Zealand
	Luxembourg		Greece	Bulgaria	
	Netherlands		Guinea	Canada	Nigeria
	Portugal		Guinea-Bissau	Costa Rica	Norway
	Spain		Indonesia	Dominican Rep.	Paraguay
			Israel	El Salvador	Peru
			Korea	Ethiopia	Philippines
			Lao P.D. Rep.	Finland	
			Malaysia	Gambia, The	Romania
			Maldives	Ghana	Russia
			Mexico	Guatemala	Sierra Leone
			Nicaragua		South Africa
			Pakistan	Guyana	Sudan
			Poland	Haiti	
			Sao Tome	Honduras	Sweden
			& Principe	India	Switzerland
			Singapore	Iran, I.R. of	Trinidad and Tobago
			Slovenia	Italy	Uganda
			Somalia	Jamaica	Ukraine
			Sri Lanka	Japan	
			Tunisia	Kyrgyz Rep.	United Kingdom
			Turkey	Latvia	United States
			Uruguay		Zaïre
			Venezuela		Zambia
			Viet Nam		

[5]Includes exchange arrangements under which the exchange rate is adjusted at relatively frequent intervals, on the basis of indicators determined by the respective member countries.
SOURCE: International Monetary Fund, 1994.

an implicit trade barrier. A single European currency would cause a single money supply throughout Europe, rather than a separate money supply for each currency. Thus, European monetary policy would be consolidated, as any effects on the supply of money would affect all European countries using that one currency as their form of money.

A major concern of a single European currency is based on the concept of a single European monetary policy. Each country's government may prefer to implement its own monetary policy. It would have to adapt to a system in which it had only partial input to the European monetary policy that would be implemented in all European countries, including its own. The system would be analogous to that used in the U.S., where there is a single currency across states. Just as the monetary policy in the U.S. cannot be separated across different states, European monetary policy with a single European currency could not be separated across European countries. While country governments may disagree on the ideal monetary policy to enhance their local economies, they would all have to agree on a single European monetary policy. Any given policy used in a particular period may enhance some countries and adversely affect others.

There are some other concerns that could prevent the implementation of a single currency. For example, at what exchange rate would all currencies be cashed in to be exchanged for the single currency to be used? It would be difficult to reach agreement on this question for each European country's home currency. Also, some economists believe that changing exchange rates serve as a stabilizer for international trade. Thus, the lack of an exchange rate mechanism could possibly cause greater trade imbalances between countries.

EXCHANGE RATE MECHANISM (ERM) CRISIS

The exchange rate mechanism experienced severe problems in the fall of 1992, as economic conditions and goals varied among European countries. The German government focused on controlling inflation and implemented a tight monetary policy, which increased German interest rates. Money flowed out of other European countries into Germany to capitalize on the relatively high German interest rates. Since exchange rates between European currencies were tied (within boundaries), European investors could capitalize on the high German interest rates without much concern about exchange rate risk. The flow of funds out of other European countries reduced the supply of funds in these countries. Consequently, interest rates increased in these countries as well, at a time when their respective governments were attempting to lower interest rates in order to stimulate their economies. The end result was less aggregate spending in countries because of the increase in interest rates. Such a result was especially undesirable during 1992, because some European countries were in the midst of a recession.

This example illustrates the degree to which European economies are integrated as a result of the ERM. When exchange rates are tied, a high interest rate in one country has a strong influence on interest rates in the other countries. Funds will flow to the country with a more attractive interest rate, which reduces the supply of funds in the other countries and places upward pressure on their interest rates. The flow of funds should continue until the interest rate differential has been eliminated or reduced. This process will not necessarily apply to countries outside the ERM, because the exchange rate risk may discourage the flow of funds to the countries with relatively high interest rates. However, since the ERM requires central banks to maintain the exchange rates between currencies within specified boundaries, investors moving funds among the participating European countries are less concerned about exchange rate risk.

In the fall of 1992, the central banks of European countries attempted to maintain exchange rates through direct intervention in the foreign exchange markets. They also attempted to increase interest rates, which would discourage investors from investing in marks to capitalize on high German interest rates. However, this form of intervention was conflicting with the goals of stimulating

European economies. In an attempt to stabilize the ERM, the central banks of some European countries were prevented from using more stimulative monetary policies.

Tensions rose in Europe during this period as countries were forced to maintain higher interest rates in response to Germany's desire to do so. This type of tension is common when several countries attempt to stabilize their exchange rates within narrow boundaries. The monetary policy of one country affects the local interest rate, which influences capital flows, and therefore interest rates, of the other countries. Consequently, the monetary policy of one country can be transmitted to the others. If all countries desired the same monetary policy (whether it be a stimulative policy to enhance economic growth or a restrictive policy to prevent inflation), the effects of one country's monetary policy on other countries would not be as damaging. However, European countries tend to have different goals.

In the fall of 1992, Germany had experienced a large budget deficit in financing the reunification of East and West Germany. The German government was more concerned about inflation and less concerned about unemployment because its economy was relatively strong. However, other European governments were more concerned about stimulating their economies to reduce their high unemployment levels.

In October 1992, the British and Italian governments suspended their participation in the ERM, because their own goals for a stronger economy could not be satisfied if their interest rates were to be so highly influenced by the German interest rates. This suspension of participation in the ERM meant that their currencies were no longer tied to the German mark and other European currencies. Therefore, even if interest rates were higher in some European countries, funds in Great Britain and in Italy would not necessarily flow to those countries because of exchange rate risk. In this way, the British and Italian interest rates would be more dependent on local conditions than on the conditions of other European countries.

The effects of the ERM on France during the fall of 1992 are illustrated in Exhibit 6.2. The left graph reflects Germany's tight monetary policy, which shifted the "supply of funds" curve from S_{G1} to S_{G2}, and therefore increased German interest rates from i_{G1} to i_{G2}. The middle graph reflects a flow of funds out of France (to capitalize on higher German interest rates), which caused a shift in the supply of funds from S_{F1} to S_{F2}, and an increase in French interest rates from i_{F1} to i_{F2}. The right graph reflects the inverse relationship between a country's interest rates and its business investment. Firms spend less when they must finance their expenditures at higher interest rates. Thus, the higher interest rates in France caused a reduction in business investment from B_{F1} to B_{F2}. Given that the unemployment rate in France was about 10 percent at the time, the effects on business investment were quite severe.

The adverse economic effects were not isolated in France. Ireland's unemployment rate was 17 percent at the time, and high interest rates were preventing any possible stimulus in Ireland's economy. Since Great Britain suspended its ties with the ERM, the British pound depreciated substantially against European currencies, including the Irish punt (mainly because of the relatively high interest rates in these countries). About one-third of Ireland's exports are to Great Britain. The Irish punt appreciated by about 15 percent against the British pound, causing a reduced British demand for Irish goods. Ireland responded to the crisis

EXHIBIT 6.2   Impact of Increased German Interest Rates on French Interest Rates

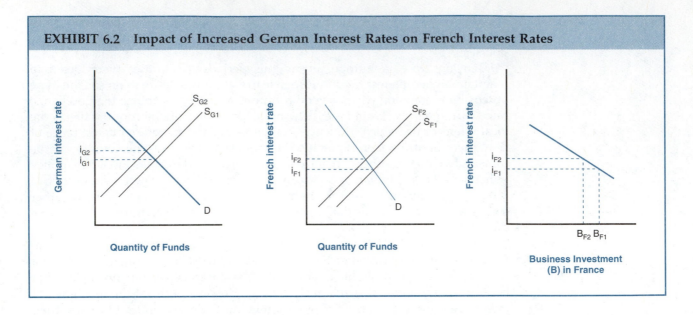

by devaluing its currency against other European currencies, in an attempt to enhance exports and stimulate its economy.

Meanwhile, while Denmark attempted to maintain its currency position in the ERM, Finland, Norway, and Sweden allowed their currencies to decline against ERM currencies in an attempt to stimulate their economies. Since 20 percent of Denmark's trade is with these three countries, its exports were severely affected by the change in exchange rates.

GOVERNMENT INTERVENTION

Each country has a government agency that may intervene in the foreign exchange markets to control its currency's value. In the United States, for example, the central bank is the Federal Reserve System (the Fed). Central banks have more duties than intervention in the foreign exchange market. They attempt to control the growth of money supply in their respective countries in a way that will favorably affect economic conditions.

Reasons for Government Intervention

The degree to which the home currency is controlled, or "managed," varies among central banks. Three common reasons for central banks to manage exchange rates are

- Smoothing exchange rate movements
- Establishing implicit exchange rate boundaries
- Reacting to temporary disturbances.

If a central bank is concerned that its economy will be affected by abrupt movements in its home currency's value, it may attempt to smooth the currency movements over time. Its actions may keep business cycles less volatile. It may also increase international trade by reducing exchange rate uncertainty. Furthermore, smoothing currency movements may reduce fears in the financial markets and speculative activity that could cause a major decline in a currency's value.

Some central banks attempt to maintain their home currency rates within some unofficial, or implicit, boundaries. Analysts are commonly quoted as forecasting that a currency will not fall below or rise above a particular benchmark value because the central bank would intervene to prevent that.

The Federal Reserve periodically intervened between 1983 and 1985 in an attempt to reverse the U.S. dollar's upward momentum and from 1986 through the beginning of 1988 to reverse the dollar's downward momentum. This implies that the Fed may have established implicit boundaries for the dollar. Yet, even if boundaries did exist, they would likely be modified over time. A very weak or strong dollar would be more tolerable in some periods than in others.

In some cases, a central bank may intervene to insulate a currency's value from a temporary disturbance. For example, the news that oil prices will rise could cause expectations of a future decline in the Japanese yen value, since Japan exchanges yen for dollars to purchase oil from oil-exporting countries. Foreign exchange market speculators may exchange yen for dollars in anticipation of this decline. The Japanese government may therefore intervene to offset the immediate downward pressure on the yen caused by such market transactions.

Several studies have found that government intervention does not have a permanent impact on exchange rate movements. In many cases, intervention is overwhelmed by market forces. Central banks operate, however, on the theory that currency movements would be even more volatile in the absence of intervention.

Direct Intervention

The Fed's direct method of intervention to force dollar depreciation is to exchange dollars that it holds as reserves for other foreign currencies in the foreign exchange market. This so-called "flooding the market with dollars" places downward pressure on the dollar. If the Fed desires to strengthen the dollar, it can exchange foreign currencies for dollars in the foreign exchange market, thereby placing upward pressure on the dollar.

The effects of direct intervention on the value of the British pound is illustrated in Exhibit 6.3. To strengthen the pound's value (or to weaken the dollar), the Fed exchanges dollars for pounds, which reflects an outward shift in the demand for pounds in the foreign exchange market (as shown in the left graph). Conversely, to weaken the pound's value (or to strengthen the dollar), the Fed exchanges pounds for dollars, which reflects an outward shift in the supply of pounds for sale in the foreign exchange market (as shown in the right graph).

Direct intervention is usually most effective when there is a coordinated effort among central banks. If all central banks simultaneously attempt to strengthen or weaken the dollar in the manner just described, they can exert greater pressure on the dollar's value.

Examples of Direct Intervention. In September 1985 the central banks of the United States, Germany, Great Britain, France, and Japan implemented a

EXHIBIT 6.3   Effects of Direct Central Bank Intervention in the Foreign Exchange Market

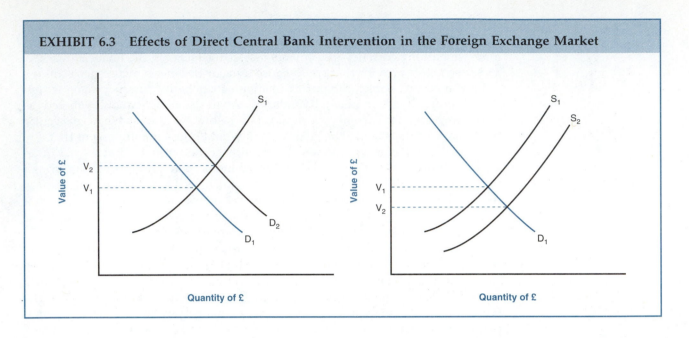

coordinated program to weaken the dollar. These actions were the result of an agreement among country representatives in the Plaza Hotel in New York in September 1985, an agreement now referred to as the **Plaza Accord.** The foreign exchange markets were flooded with billions of dollars as these central banks exchanged dollars for foreign currencies. This action added momentum to the dollar's fall. However, while direct intervention was frequently used in 1986 and 1987 to strengthen the dollar, it still continued to weaken.

The dollar began to strengthen in 1988. As it continued to strengthen in the summer of 1989, there was some concern by the industrialized countries that a stronger dollar could adversely affect the world economy. Five central banks intervened on September 14, 1989, precipitating an abrupt 2 percent decline in the dollar's value relative to the British pound and the German mark. However, additional central bank intervention in the following month was overwhelmed by market transactions. With the growth in foreign exchange activity, central bank intervention is less effective. The volume of foreign exchange transactions on a single day exceeds the combined values of reserves at all central banks.

In 1992, the dollar was weak, causing the Federal Reserve to intervene by purchasing dollars with European currencies. In 1993, the concern was focused on the Japanese yen, which appreciated against the dollar by 13 percent over the first five months of 1993 and reached a post–World War II high. The Federal Reserve intervened seven times on May 27, 1993 to prevent further momentum. Specifically, the Fed repeatedly purchased dollars with yen in the foreign exchange market on this day. The efforts may have temporarily slowed the yen's momentum, but did not weaken the yen.

Conditions That Precipitate Direct Intervention.   To illustrate the conditions that lead to central bank intervention, consider the following excerpts from "Treasury and Federal Reserve Foreign Exchange Operations," a feature contained in issues of the *Federal Reserve Bank of New York Quarterly Review:* "...The dollar's tendency in February [1992] to appreciate less against the yen than against the mark in part reflected expectations of official intervention to support the yen. At the time, Japanese officials were making increasingly strong and frequent statements indicating that they would not tolerate an excessive yen decline.... The Desk [Federal Reserve] entered the Tokyo market on February 17, in cooperation with the Japanese authorities, to sell a total of $100 million against yen. This operation was followed on February 20 with the sale, again in Tokyo, of an additional $50 million against yen.

... Participants began to adopt large short-dollar positions [by borrowing dollars and investing in marks] on the premise that the dollar faced little risk of appreciation but good prospects of a future decline. This perception of the dollar as a one-way bet ... caused the currency's decline to accelerate. Concerned with developments in the market, the U.S. monetary authorities intervened on July 20 [1992] in concert with a number of foreign central banks, purchasing $170 million [with marks]. The concerted operation calmed the market, and the dollar traded quietly through the remainder of the period.

... When the data, released on Friday, August 7 [1992], appeared to confirm economic weakness, ... the U.S. authorities intervened to stabilize the dollar. When pressures reemerged the following Tuesday, the U.S. authorities again intervened in an operation joined by other central banks. Over the two days, the U.S. authorities bought a total of $600 million [with marks], ... but the operations did not interrupt the tendency of the dollar to decline.... The U.S. authorities intervened on August 21 and 24, in cooperation with other monetary authorities, buying a total of $500 million. But when these operations did not appear to discourage the bidding for marks, the U.S. authorities refrained from further intervention."

Nonsterilized Versus Sterilized Intervention.   When the Fed intervenes in the foreign exchange market without adjusting for the change in money supply, it is engaging in **nonsterilized intervention.** For example, if the Fed exchanges dollars for foreign currencies in the foreign exchange markets in an attempt to strengthen foreign currencies (weaken the dollar), the dollar money supply increases.

If the Fed desires to intervene in the foreign exchange market while retaining the dollar money supply, it uses **sterilized intervention,** achieved by simultaneous transactions in the foreign exchange markets and Treasury securities markets. For example, if the Fed desires to strengthen foreign currencies (weaken the dollar) without affecting the dollar money supply, it (1) exchanges dollars for foreign currencies, and (2) sells some of its holdings of Treasury securities for dollars. The net effect is an increase in investors' holdings of Treasury securities and a decrease in bank foreign currency balances.

The difference between nonsterilized and sterilized intervention is illustrated in Exhibit 6.4: in one scenario, the Federal Reserve attempts to strengthen the German mark (top of exhibit), and in a second scenario, the Federal Reserve attempts to weaken the German mark (bottom of exhibit). For each scenario, this exhibit shows how the sterilized intervention (graph on the right) involves an exchange of Treasury securities for dollars that offsets the dollar flows resulting from the exchange of currencies. That is, the sterilized intervention achieves the same exchange of currencies in the foreign exchange market as nonsterilized intervention, but involves an additional transaction to prevent adjustments in the dollar money supply.

**EXHIBIT 6.4
Forms of Central
Bank Intervention
in the Foreign
Exchange Market**

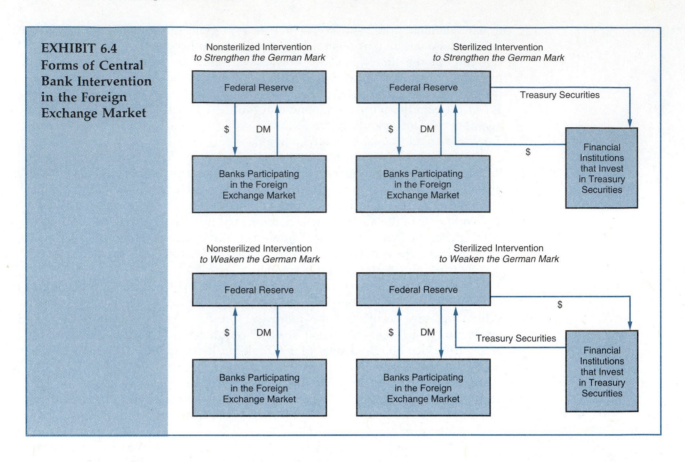

Speculating on Direct Intervention.   Some traders in the foreign exchange market attempt to determine when Federal Reserve intervention is occurring, and the extent of the intervention, in order to capitalize on the anticipated results of the intervention effort. Normally, the Federal Reserve attempts to intervene without being noticed. However, dealers at the major banks that trade with the Fed often pass the information to other market participants. Also, when the Fed deals directly with numerous commercial banks, markets are well aware that the Fed is intervening. To hide its strategy, the Fed may pretend to be interested in selling dollars when it is actually buying dollars, or vice versa. It calls commercial banks and obtains both bid and ask quotes on currencies, so that the banks are not sure whether the Fed is considering purchases or sales of these currencies.

Intervention strategies vary among central banks. Some arrange for one large order when they intervene; others arrange several smaller orders, of the equivalent of $5 million to $10 million. Even if traders determine the extent of central bank intervention, they still cannot know with certainty the impact of that intervention on exchange rates.

Indirect Intervention

The Fed can affect the dollar's value indirectly by influencing the factors that determine it. For example, the Fed could attempt to lower interest rates by increasing the U.S. money supply (assuming that inflationary expectations are not affected). Lower U.S. interest rates tend to discourage foreign investors from investing in U.S. securities, thereby placing downward pressure on the value of the dollar. Or to boost the dollar's value, the Fed could attempt to increase interest rates by reducing the U.S. money supply. It has commonly used this strategy along with direct intervention in the foreign exchange market.

As an example of how the foreign exchange market reacts to the indirect influence of the federal government, the dollar declined substantially on June 2, 1987, when it was announced that Paul Volcker would resign as chairman of the Fed. Volcker was known for his anti-inflationary efforts. Market participants anticipated higher U.S. inflation—and thus possible weakening of the dollar—because of his resignation. These expectations led to large sales of dollars in the foreign exchange market and an immediate decline in the dollar's value.

Recent research by Batten and Thornton found that some changes in the Fed's discount rate caused a significant reaction in the foreign exchange markets. This suggests that foreign exchange market participants should monitor Fed actions to anticipate how those actions will affect the economic variables (such as market interest rates) that influence exchange rates. Just as market participants monitor direct intervention, they also should monitor indirect intervention.

To illustrate the potential influence of indirect intervention on exchange rates, consider the following excerpts from exchange rate reports by the Federal Reserve Bank of New York.

"The Bundesbank [central bank of Germany] moved to increase interest rates on December 19 [1991]. . . . By contrast, the Federal Reserve reduced its discount rate by more than had been expected. . . . As the foreign exchange market responded to these divergent moves in interest rates, the dollar continued to decline against the German mark. . . ."

"The German Bundesbank reduced its official discount rate . . . by 100 basis points [1%] in a series of steps undertaken during the February–April [1993] period. . . . Following official rate reductions, the mark depreciated slightly against many European currencies."

Another good example of indirect intervention to influence exchange rate movements is the effort in Brazil to break the cycle between high inflation and the consistent depreciation in the Brazilian currency (the cruzado). Brazil's inflation rate has exceeded 70 percent in some months. First, the Brazilian government dismantled some large state-owned corporations in order to encourage competition in industries such as mining and steel. Second, it planned to reduce restrictions on imports. Third, it planned to reduce inflation by negotiating with businesses to limit wages and prices. Government officials also wanted to reduce money supply growth in Brazil. With such high inflation in Brazil, direct intervention in foreign exchange markets is not likely to have a lasting impact. Indirect intervention does not provide an immediate cure, but may be more effective in the long run.

EXCHANGE RATE TARGET ZONES

In recent years, many economists have criticized the present exchange rate system because of the wide swings in exchange rates of major currencies. Some have suggested that **target zones** be used for these currencies. A **central rate**

EXCHANGE RATE INTERVENTION AND CONFLICTS OF INTEREST

In 1991, the Federal Reserve System was faced with an interesting dilemma. The dollar had weakened considerably against most other major currencies. The dollar's weakness was primarily attributed to low U.S. interest rates relative to foreign interest rates. In order to stimulate the sagging U.S. economy, the Federal Reserve had pushed interest rates lower with a loose monetary policy (including a decrease in its discount rate). Meanwhile, Bundesbank (the German central bank) had raised interest rates in Germany to halt any momentum in inflation caused by a strong economy. The changes in interest rates have caused some global investors to shift their investments from the U.S. to Germany. In February 1991, when the dollar reached an all-time low against the mark, central banks used marks and other currencies to purchase U.S. dollars in the foreign exchange market. This attempt at direct intervention was overwhelmed by market forces resulting from interest rate differentials, which were partially attributed to the central banks. Thus the dollar continued to decline despite the direct intervention. The lesson from this example is that direct intervention in the foreign exchange market cannot usually offset exchange rate movements that are caused by economic conditions. The central banks would have been more successful in boosting the dollar's value if they had raised U.S. interest rates and lowered foreign interest rates. Yet this would have conflicted with their initial objectives of stimulating the U.S. economy and slowing German inflation.

would be established, with specific boundaries surrounding that rate (in a structure similar to the EMS). For example, the mark-dollar exchange rate might have a central rate of $.50 with boundaries of plus and minus 6 percent of that rate, resulting in an upper band of $.53 and a lower band of $.47. Such a target zone is similar to the bands used in the fixed exchange rate system, but a target zone system would likely allow wider boundaries. Proponents of the target zone system suggest that it would stabilize international trade patterns by reducing exchange rate volatility.

There are some complications involved in implementing a target zone system. First, what central rate should be established for each country? Second, how wide should the target zone be? The ideal target zone allows exchange rates to adjust to economic factors without causing wide swings in international trade and fear in financial markets.

Some governments may not agree on the appropriate central rates. For example, the U.S. government would probably prefer that the Japanese yen be assigned a central rate more highly valued than the market rate in order to reduce the U.S. balance of trade deficit with Japan. However, Japan's government may prefer a lower value for the yen. In addition, some governments may prefer a much wider target zone than others.

If target zones were implemented, governments would be responsible for intervening to maintain their currencies within the zones. If the zones were sufficiently wide, government intervention would rarely be necessary; however, such wide zones would basically resemble the exchange rate system as it exists today. Governments tend to intervene when a currency's value moves outside some implicitly acceptable zone.

Unless governments could maintain a currency's value within the target zone, this system could not provide stability in international markets. A country experiencing a large balance of trade deficit might intentionally allow its currency to float below the lower boundary in order to stimulate foreign demand for its exports. Wide swings in international trade patterns could result. Furthermore, financial market prices would be more volatile because financial market participants would expect some currencies to move outside of their zones. The result would be a system no different from what exists today.

In February 1987 representatives of the United States, Japan, West Germany, France, Canada, Italy, and the United Kingdom (also known as the **Group of Seven** or **G-7 countries**) signed the **Louvre Accord** to establish acceptable ranges (not disclosed to the public) for the dollar's value relative to other currencies. The Federal Reserve intervened heavily in the foreign exchange market for two months after the Louvre Accord, but has generally intervened only in small doses since then. Thus, central bank intervention policy since the Louvre Accord has been similar to the policy that existed before the Louvre Accord.

INTERVENTION AS A POLICY TOOL

The federal government of any country can implement its own fiscal and monetary policies to control its economy. In addition, it may attempt to influence the value of its home currency in order to improve its economy, weakening its currency under some conditions and strengthening it under others. In essence, the exchange rate becomes a tool, like tax laws and money supply, with which the government can work to achieve its desired economic objectives.

APPLIED RESEARCH

WILL THE LOUVRE ACCORD RESULT IN MORE STABLE EXCHANGE RATES?

If the Louvre Accord signed in February 1987 is effective in stabilizing exchange rates, there should be a decline in the volatilities of exchange rates. Recent research by Tucker and Madura tested for this as follows. First, the variance of each exchange rate's movements was estimated for some major currencies in a period just before the accord and just after the accord.

There was no significant difference in these variances.

As a second test, the market's anticipated volatility of each currency was measured before the accord and after the accord. The implied standard deviation obtained from the currency option pricing model was used as a proxy for the market's anticipated volatility. While there were significant shifts in vola-

tility, the shifts were negative for some currencies and positive for others. Overall, there was no discernible pattern. The results suggest that in general, actual and anticipated exchange rate volatility has not been reduced since the Louvre Accord. It appears that the market believes that coordinated central bank intervention will not stabilize foreign exchange markets.

Influence of a Weak Home Currency on the Economy

A weak home currency can stimulate foreign demand for products. A weak dollar, for example, can substantially boost U.S. exports and U.S. jobs. In addition, it may also reduce U.S. imports.

While a weak currency can reduce unemployment at home, it can lead to higher inflation. For example, in the late 1970s the U.S. dollar was weak, causing U.S. imports from foreign countries to be highly priced. The dollar was also weak in the early 1990s; this situation priced firms such as Bayer, Volkswagen, and Volvo out of the U.S. market. Under these conditions, U.S. companies were therefore able to raise their local prices, since it was difficult for foreign producers to compete. In addition, U.S. firms that are heavy exporters, such as Goodyear Tire & Rubber Co., Litton Industries, Merck, and Maytag Corp., also benefit from a weaker dollar.

Influence of a Strong Home Currency on the Economy

A strong home currency can encourage consumers and corporations of that home country to buy goods from other countries. This situation intensifies foreign competition and forces domestic producers to refrain from increasing prices. Therefore, we expect the country's overall inflation rate to be lower if its currency is strengthened, other things being equal.

While a strong currency is a possible cure for high inflation, it may cause higher unemployment due to the attractive foreign prices that result from a strong home currency. The ideal value of the currency depends on the perspective of the country and the officials who are involved with these decisions. The strength or weakness of a currency is just one of many factors that influence a country's economic conditions.

We can combine the above discussion of how exchange rates affect inflation with the discussion in Chapter 4 on how inflation can affect exchange rates, for a more complete picture of the dynamics of the exchange rate–inflation relationship. A weak dollar places upward pressure on U.S. inflation, which in turn places further downward pressure on the value of the dollar. A strong dollar places downward pressure on inflation and on U.S. economic growth, which in turn places further upward pressure on the dollar's value.

The interaction between exchange rates, government policies, and economic factors is illustrated in Exhibit 6.5. As already mentioned, factors other than the home currency's strength affect unemployment and/or inflation. Likewise, factors other than the unemployment or inflation level influence a currency's strength. The cycles that have been described here will often be interrupted by these other factors and therefore will not continue indefinitely.

SUMMARY

■ Exchange rate systems can be classified as fixed rate, freely floating, managed float, and pegged. In a fixed exchange rate system, exchange rates are either held constant or allowed to fluctuate only within very narrow boundaries. In a freely floating exchange rate system, exchange rate values are determined by market forces without intervention. In a managed float system, exchange rates are not

EXHIBIT 6.5   Impact of Government Actions on Exchange Rates

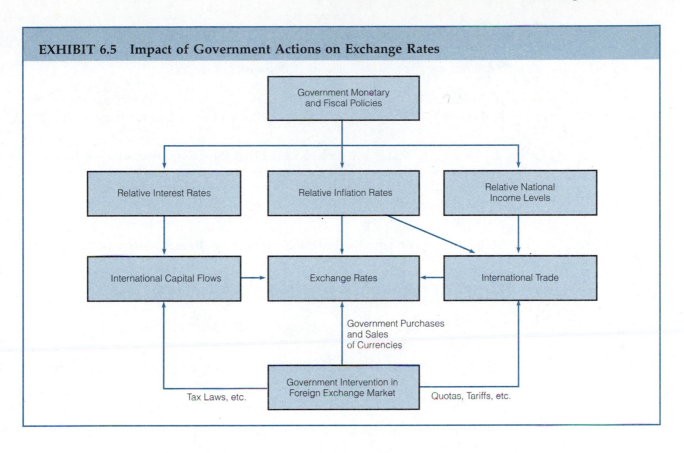

restricted by boundaries, but are subject to government intervention. In a pegged exchange rate system, a currency's value is pegged to a foreign currency or a unit of account, and moves in line with that currency (or unit of account) against other currencies.

■   Governments can use direct intervention by purchasing or selling currencies in the foreign exchange market, thereby affecting demand and supply conditions, and in turn affecting the equilibrium values of the currencies. When a government purchases a currency in the foreign exchange market, it places upward pressure on its equilibrium value. When a government sells a currency in the foreign exchange market, it places downward pressure on its equilibrium value.

■   Governments can use indirect intervention by influencing the economic factors that affect equilibrium exchange rates.

■   When government intervention is used to weaken the U.S. dollar, it stimulates the U.S. economy by reducing the U.S. demand for imports and increasing the foreign demand for U.S. exports. Thus, the weak dollar tends to reduce U.S. unemployment but can increase U.S. inflation.

When government intervention is used to strengthen the U.S. dollar, it can increase the U.S. demand for imports, which intensifies foreign competition. It can reduce U.S. inflation, but may cause a higher level of U.S. unemployment.

SELF-TEST FOR CHAPTER 6

(Answers are provided in Appendix A in the back of the text.)

1. Explain why it would be virtually impossible to set an exchange rate between the Japanese yen and the dollar and to maintain a fixed exchange rate.

2. Assume the Federal Reserve believes that the dollar should be weakened against the German mark. Explain how it could use direct and indirect intervention to weaken the dollar's value with respect to the mark. Assume that future inflation in the U.S. is expected to be low, regardless of the Fed's actions.

3. Briefly explain why the Federal Reserve may attempt to weaken the dollar.

QUESTIONS

1. Compare and contrast the fixed, freely floating, and managed float exchange rate systems.

2. What are some advantages and disadvantages of a freely floating exchange rate system versus a fixed exchange rate system?

3. Describe the background of the European Monetary System.

4. How can a central bank use direct intervention to change the value of a currency?

5. How can a central bank use indirect intervention to change the value of a currency?

6. The media frequently report that "the dollar's value strengthened against many currencies in response to the Federal Reserve's plan to increase interest rates." Explain why the dollar's value may change even before the Federal Reserve affects interest rates.

7. Assume there is concern that the United States may experience a recession. Provide recommendations to the Federal Reserve regarding how it should attempt to directly influence the dollar to prevent a recession. How might U.S. exporters react to this policy (favorably or unfavorably)? What about U.S. importing firms?

8. What is the impact of a weak home currency on the home economy, other things being equal?

9. What is the impact of a strong home currency on the home economy, other things being equal?

10. Explain the potential feedback effects of a currency's changing value on inflation.

11. Explain why a central bank may desire to smooth exchange rate movements.

12. Why do foreign market participants attempt to monitor the Fed's direct intervention efforts? How does the Fed attempt to hide its intervention actions?

13. In the fall of 1992, France was experiencing a relatively high unemployment rate. During this period, Great Britain and Italy suspended their participation in the exchange rate mechanism (ERM), but France continued to participate. Some analysts stated that France "paid a high price" for its continued participation in the ERM during this period. Interpret this statement.

14. In the fall of 1992, the interest rates of several European countries moved in tandem with the rise in German interest rates. Yet, U.S. interest rates were not moving in tandem with German interest rates. Explain why German interest rate movements tend to have a stronger effect on interest rates of other European countries than on U.S. interest rates.

15. In January 1992, the Fed used direct intervention by selling dollars in exchange for Japanese yen. Some analysts suggested that this action was politically motivated. Given the timing of this intervention, explain why this intervention may be perceived to be politically motivated.

16. Assume that the currency of South Korea is tied to the dollar. How would the following trade patterns be affected by the dollar's depreciation against the Japanese yen: (a) South Korean exports to Japan and (b) South Korean exports to the United States. Explain.

17. Assuming that U.S. bond prices are normally inversely related to U.S. inflation, offer your opinion on why expectations of a weak dollar can reduce bond prices, other things being equal.

18. When it was announced on June 2, 1987, that Paul Volcker would resign as chairman of the Federal Reserve, the dollar weakened substantially. Why?

19. Explain the meaning of target zones and how they would be implemented. What are their limitations?

20. Explain the difference between sterilized and nonsterilized intervention.

CASE: CENTRAL BANK INTERVENTION IN EUROPE

For Now, Central Bankers Regain Reins

By MICHAEL R. SESIT
Staff Reporter of THE WALL STREET JOURNAL.

LONDON — For the first time in weeks, European central banks seemed to be regaining the upper hand over currency traders.

The big question: Can they keep it? That depends, economists say, on how quickly they lower interest rates to nourish economic growth.

Yesterday, Europe's weaker currencies regained previously lost ground on the mark as Germany's central bank cut a key interest rate a bit. Several European bond markets continued to rally, and the German stock market surged 1.6%, carrying several others with it.

Switzerland's rose 1.3% and Sweden's 1.2%. Dutch stocks were up 0.8%, and the small Austrian stock market catapulted 3.2%. French shares fell 0.9% on what traders described as profit-taking after the market had risen 7% in three days.

Meanwhile, the dollar was mostly steady, although it fell to another record low against the yen. Some traders thought it might dip further before rising later this year.

What happens next depends on the speed with which European countries take advantage of the European Exchange Rate Mechanism's wider trading ranges, which were instituted after speculative selling pressure almost destroyed the ERM last week. The new structure allows most currencies in the nine-currency joint float to fluctuate by 15% up or down against a so-called central rate. Previously, most currencies were restricted to bands of only plus or minus 2.25%.

Apart from saving the ERM—at least in name—the motive behind the wider bands was to allow such countries as France and Denmark the leeway to try to recharge their recession-ridden economies with lower interest rates without having to suffer the humiliation of formally devaluing their currencies.

"Right now, people are trying to figure out what the next move of the authorities is," said Thomas Mayer, a senior economist at Goldman, Sachs International in Frankfurt. "The most natural consequence would be for the countries to orient monetary policy more toward their domestic needs."

France and Denmark, he said, need to heal their ailing economies. Mr. Mayer and others assert that with inflation in Denmark at 1%, and in France at just under 2%, both countries have a lot of leeway to lower interest rates without reigniting inflation fears.

Traders say that if these two countries don't begin to lower rates—as did Portugal on Monday and Spain yesterday—they will force them to do so by dumping their currencies as they did last week. "The markets will probably give them a couple of weeks to think things over," Mr. Mayer said.

But Alison Cottrell, an international economist at Midland Global Markets in London, disagreed: "You will have to see something out of France within a week."

She said that right now the currencies of France, Denmark and possibly Belgium aren't supported by the fact that their interest rates are higher than Germany's, "but because they are looked at as recovery plays."

"People are buying France not because they want francs but because they want the stocks and the bonds," she said, "That removes the temporary downside risk on the franc. So, you lose 1% on the currency and gain 10% on the stock market."

However, Ms. Cottrell warned that if France hesitated in lowering interest rates, "people will decide to take their money somewhere else."

Indeed, Golman Sachs's Mr. Mayer said: "The faster they do it, the shorter will be the period during which their currencies depreciate." When France and Denmark finally begin to lower interest rates, their currencies probably will fall against the mark. But because of Germany's economic malaise and relatively high 4.3% inflation rate, analysts contend that once France and Denmark show signs of economic recovery, their currencies will recapture some lost ground.

Stephen Dulake, a bond strategist at PaineWebber International (UK) Ltd. in London, predicted that interest rates in France and Denmark would begin to fall within four weeks.

Maybe so. But Nicholas Stevenson, a European equity strategist at S.G. Warburg & Co. in London, warned: "The Banque de France, freed of the constraint of the ERM's tight bands, may not cut its rates with the electric speed that money managers in London and New York expect." He also predicted that the Bundesbank would surprise investors by cutting rates faster than many expect.

Ironically, he said: "We'll probably end up where we would have ended up with [the former] ERM: a very steady decline in rates in the two major continental economies over the course of the year with their currencies remaining in fairly close alignment."

As a result, he said, in the very short term, "investors in the French stock market will be very disappointed by the lack of haste with which France cuts rates, and possibly pleasantly surprised by the willingness of the Bundesbank to cut German interest rates." . . .

Questions

1. Explain why Europe's weaker currencies increased in value following a cut in German interest rates by Bundesbank (the German central bank).

2. How does the widening of Europe's Exchange Rate Mechanism (ERM) affect the degree of central bank intervention?

3. At the time, France and Denmark had low inflation and weak economies. Explain how the central banks would be likely to adjust interest rates in these countries, and how their currencies (French franc and Danish krone) would respond to the central bank intervention.

CASE
PROBLEM

HULL IMPORTING COMPANY
Effects of Pegging the Pound to the ECU

CASE
PROBLEM

Hull Importing Company is a U.S.-based firm that imports small gift items and sells them to retail gift shops across the U.S. About half of the value of Hull's purchases comes from the United Kingdom, while the remaining purchases are from Germany. The imported goods are denominated in the currency of the country where they are produced. Hull normally does not hedge its purchases.

The German mark (along with other European currencies) was tied to the European Currency Unit through the European Monetary System. The mark's value with respect to the ECU was essentially pegged and could move only within boundaries. Conversely, the United Kingdom had not participated in this arrangement, so that the pound's value with respect to the ECU varied substantially.

In previous years, the mark and pound fluctuated substantially against the dollar (although not by the same degree). Hull's expenses are directly tied to these currency values because all of its products are imported. It has been successful because the imported gift items are somewhat unique and are attractive to U.S. consumers. However, Hull has been unable to pass on higher costs (due to a weaker dollar) to its consumers, because consumers would then switch to different gift items sold at other stores.

a) Hull wants to assess how the United Kingdom's policy of removing the pound's link with the ECU would affect the variability of its profits over time. Assume that the value of the ECU and the pound will exhibit about the same degree of volatility in their movements against the dollar. Offer any insight on how Hull's variability of profits may change.

b) Hull used to closely monitor government intervention by Bundesbank (the German central bank) on the value of the mark. Assume that during the 1990s, Bundesbank intervenes to strengthen the mark's value with respect to the dollar by 5 percent. Would this have a favorable or unfavorable effect on Hull's business? Would this have a larger or smaller effect on Hull's business since 1992, when the pound's value was no longer tied to the ECU? Explain.

PROJECT

Review *The Wall Street Journal* for the last few weeks (ignoring the weekends). Summarize any central bank intervention in the table below.

Date	Identify the central banks that intervened	Was the intervention intended to strengthen or weaken the dollar?	Describe movements of dollar on that day

REFERENCES

Batten, Dallas S., and Mack Ott. "What Can Central Banks Do About the Value of the Dollar?" *Review,* Federal Reserve Bank of St. Louis (May 1984), pp. 16-26.

Batten, Dallas S., and Daniel L. Thornton. "Discount Rate Changes and the Foreign Exchange Market." *Journal of International Money and Finance* (December 1984), pp. 279-92.

Carlozzi, Nicholas. "Exchange Rate Volatility: Is Intervention the Answer?" *Business Review,* Federal Reserve Bank of Philadelphia (November-December 1983), pp. 3-10.

Friedman, Milton, and Robert V. Roosa. "Free versus Fixed Exchange Rates: A Debate." *Journal of Portfolio Management* (Spring 1977), pp. 68-73.

Humpage, Owen F., and Nicholas V. Karamouzis. "Target Zones for Exchange Rates?" *Economic Commentary,* Federal Reserve Bank of Cleveland, August 1, 1986.

Kahn, George A. "International Policy Coordination in an Interdependent World." *Economic Commentary,* Federal Reserve Bank of Cleveland, August 1, 1986.

Klein, Michael W., and Eric S. Rosengren. "Foreign Exchange Intervention as a Signal of Monetary Policy," *New England Economic Review* (May/June 1991), pp. 39-50.

Pollard, Patricia. "Central Bank Independence and Economic Performance," *Review* (July/August 1993), pp. 22-36.

Rogoff, Kenneth. "On the Effects of Sterilized Intervention: An Analysis of Weekly Data." *Journal of Monetary Economics* (September 1984), pp. 133-150.

Tucker, Alan L., and Jeff Madura. "Impact of the Louvre on Actual and Anticipated Exchange Rate Volatility." *Journal of International Financial Markets, Institutions and Money* (No. 3, 1991), pp. 67-80.

Weber, Warren E. "Do Sterilized Interventions Affect Exchange Rates?" *Quarterly Review,* Federal Bank of Minneapolis (Summer 1986), pp. 14-23.

Whitt, Joseph A., Jr., Paul D. Koch, and Jeffrey A. Rosensweig. "The Dollar and Prices: An Empirical Analysis." *Economic Review,* Federal Reserve Bank of Atlanta (October 1986), pp. 4-18.

CHAPTER 7

INTERNATIONAL ARBITRAGE AND INTEREST RATE PARITY

If there are discrepancies within the foreign exchange market, in which quoted prices of currencies vary from what the market prices should be, certain market forces will realign the rates. The mechanics of this realignment take place as a result of international arbitrage. The specific objectives of this chapter are to

- explain the conditions that will result in various forms of international arbitrage, along with realignments that will occur in response to various forms of international arbitrage, and
- explain the concept of interest rate parity, and how it prevents arbitrage opportunities.

INTERNATIONAL ARBITRAGE

Arbitrage can be loosely defined as capitalizing on a discrepancy in quoted prices. In many cases, there is no investment of funds tied up for any length of time and no risk involved in the strategy. To illustrate, suppose two coin shops buy and sell coins. If Shop A is willing to sell a particular coin for $120, while Shop B is willing to buy that same coin for $130, a person can execute arbitrage by purchasing the coin at Shop A for $120 and selling it to Shop B for $130. The prices at coin shops can vary since demand conditions may vary among shop locations. If two coin shops are not aware of each other's prices, the opportunity for arbitrage may occur.

The act of arbitrage will cause prices to realign. In our example, arbitrage would cause Shop A to raise its price (due to high demand for the coin). At the same time, Shop B would reduce its bid price after receiving a surplus of coins as arbitrage occurs. The type of arbitrage discussed in this chapter is primarily international in scope; it is applied to foreign exchange and international money markets and takes three common forms:

- Locational arbitrage
- Triangular arbitrage
- Covered interest arbitrage.

Each form will be discussed in turn.

Locational Arbitrage

Commercial banks providing foreign exchange services will normally quote about the same rates on currencies, so shopping around may not necessarily lead to a more favorable rate. If the demand and supply conditions for a particular currency vary among banks, that currency may be priced at different rates among banks, and market forces will force realignment in the following manner.

Consider two banks that buy and sell currencies. Assume that there is no bid/ask spread, and that the single rate quoted at Bank A for a British pound is $1.60, while the single rate quoted at Bank B is $1.61. If you had funds available, you could use them to buy pounds at Bank A for $1.60 per pound and then sell pounds at Bank B for $1.61 per pound. Under the condition that there is no bid/ask spread and there are no other costs to conducting this arbitrage strategy, your gain would be $.01 per pound. The gain is risk-free in that you knew as you purchased pounds how much you could sell them for. Also, in this example you did not have to tie your funds up for any length of time. The term **locational arbitrage** implies capitalizing on the differential exchange rates between locations.

Since banks have a bid/ask spread on currencies, the next example accounts for this spread. The information on British pounds at both banks is revised to include the bid/ask spread in Exhibit 7.1. The information in this exhibit shows that you can no longer profit from locational arbitrage. If you buy pounds from Bank A at $1.61 (the bank's ask price) and then sell the pounds at Bank B at its bid price of $1.61, you just break even. The point of this example is to demonstrate that even when the bid prices between two banks or the ask prices between two banks are different, this does not guarantee that locational arbitrage will be possible. For you to achieve profits from locational arbitrage, the bid price of one bank must be higher than the ask price of another bank.

Realignment Due to Locational Arbitrage. An example in which locational arbitrage is possible can be helpful in demonstrating how market forces

EXHIBIT 7.1 Currency Quotes for Locational Arbitrage Example	Bank A			Bank B		
		Bid	Ask		Bid	Ask
	British pound quote	$1.60	$1.61	British pound quote	$1.61	$1.62

will cause a realignment in the exchange rates of the banks. Examine the quotations for the German mark at two banks as shown in Exhibit 7.2. Information contained in Exhibit 7.2 shows that you can obtain marks from Bank C at the ask price of $.500 and then sell marks to Bank D at the bid price of $.505. This represents one "round-trip" transaction in locational arbitrage. If you started with $10,000 and conducted one round-trip transaction, how many U.S. dollars would you end up with? The $10,000 is initially exchanged for DM20,000 ($10,000/$.50 per mark) at Bank C. Then the DM20,000 are sold for $.505 each, for a total of $10,100. Thus, your gain from locational arbitrage is $100. This does not sound like much relative to your investment of $10,000. However, consider that you have not had to tie up your funds. Your round-trip transaction could take place over a telecommunications network within a matter of minutes. Also, if you could use a larger sum of money for the transaction, your gains would be larger. Finally, you could continue to repeat your round-trip transactions until Bank C's ask price was no longer less than Bank D's bid price.

Quoted prices will react to the locational arbitrage strategy used by investors. Due to the high demand for marks at Bank C (resulting from arbitrage activity), a shortage of marks may soon develop there. As a result of this shortage, Bank C will raise its ask price for marks. The excess supply of marks at Bank D (resulting from sales of marks in exchange for U.S. dollars) will force Bank D to lower its bid price. As the currency prices are adjusted, gains from locational arbitrage will be reduced. Once the ask price of Bank C is not any lower than the bid price of Bank D, locational arbitrage will no longer occur. The time from which locational arbitrage occurs to the time at which prices adjust may be just a matter of minutes.

This discussion is not intended to make you believe you could pay for your education through part-time locational arbitrage. There are foreign exchange dealers who have computer terminals, comparing quotes from several banks, that will immediately signal to the dealer any opportunity to employ locational arbitrage. Thus, they will most likely beat you to the profits. The concept of locational arbitrage is relevant in that it explains why prices among banks at different locations will not normally differ by a significant amount. This applies not only to banks on the same street or within the same city, but to all banks across the world.

Triangular Arbitrage

Foreign exchange quotations are typically expressed in U.S. dollars, regardless of the country in which the quote is provided. Yet, there are many instances where the U.S. dollar is not part of the foreign exchange transaction. **Cross exchange rates** are used to determine the relationship between two nondollar currencies.

EXHIBIT 7.2 Currency Quotes for Second Locational Arbitrage Example	Bank C		Bank D	
	Bid	Ask	Bid	Ask
German mark quote	$.495	$.500	$.505	$.510

Given two nondollar currencies called X and Y, the value of X with respect to Y is determined as follows:

$$\text{Value of Currency X in units of Currency Y} = \frac{\text{Value of X in \$}}{\text{Value of Y in \$}}.$$

For example, if the British pound (£) is worth $1.50, while the German mark (or deutsche mark, DM) is worth $.50, the value of the British pound with respect to the mark is calculated

$$\text{Value of £ in units of DM} = \$1.50/\$.50 = 3.$$

The value of the DM in units of £ can also be determined from the cross exchange rate formula:

$$\text{Value of DM in units of £} = \$.50/\$1.50 = .33.$$

Notice that the value of a mark in units of pounds is simply the reciprocal of the value of a pound in units of marks. Assume that a quoted cross exchange rate differs from the appropriate cross exchange rate (as determined by the preceding formula). Under these conditions, **triangular arbitrage** can be used, whereby currency transactions are conducted in the spot market to capitalize on a discrepancy in the cross exchange rate between two currencies.

If the cross exchange rate is not set properly, arbitrage may be used to capitalize on the discrepancy. For example, assume that a bank has quoted the British pound (£) at $2.00, the French franc (FF) at $.20 and the cross exchange rate at £1 = FF11. Your first task is to use the pound value in U.S. dollars and franc value in U.S. dollars to develop the cross exchange rate that should exist between the pound and the franc. The cross rate formula discussed earlier reveals that the pound should be worth 10 francs. When quoting a cross exchange rate of £1 = FF11, the bank is exchanging too many francs for a pound, and is asking for too many francs in exchange for a pound. Based on this information, you could engage in triangular arbitrage by purchasing pounds with dollars, converting the pounds to francs, and then exchanging the francs for dollars. If you have $10,000, how many dollars will you end up with if you implement this triangular arbitrage strategy? To answer the question, consider the following steps.

- First, determine the number of pounds received for your dollars: $10,000 = £5,000, based on the bank's quote of $2.00 per pound.
- Second, determine how many francs you will receive in exchange for pounds: £5,000 = FF55,000, based on the bank's quote of 11 francs per pound.
- Finally, determine how many U.S. dollars you will receive in exchange for the francs: FF55,000 = $11,000, based on the bank's quote of $.20 per franc (5 francs to the dollar). The triangular-arbitrage strategy generates $11,000, which is $1,000 more than you started with.

Like locational arbitrage, triangular arbitrage does not tie up funds. Also, the strategy is risk-free, since there is no uncertainty about the prices at which you will buy and sell the currencies. To make the scenario more realistic, however, consider the information in Exhibit 7.3, which discloses bid and ask rates quoted by a bank. Using Exhibit 7.3, you can determine whether triangular arbitrage is possible by starting with some fictitious amount (say $10,000) of U.S. dollars, and estimating the number of dollars you would generate after implementing the strategy. The only difference between what is shown in Exhibit 7.3 and the above example is that bid/ask spreads are now considered.

In the above example, the triangular arbitrage strategy suggested exchanging dollars for pounds, pounds for francs, and then francs for dollars. Relate this strategy to the information disclosed in Exhibit 7.3. If you start out with $10,000, that will be converted into £5,000 (based on the bank's ask price of $2.00 per pound). Then the £5,000 are converted into FF54,000 (based on the bank's bid price for pounds of 10.8 francs per pound, £5,000 × 10.8 = FF54,000). Next, the FF54,000 are converted to $10,800 (based on the bank's bid price of $.200). The profit is $10,800 − $10,000 = $800. Any possible profit opportunities from triangular arbitrage should be only temporary since realignment in exchange rates occur, as explained below.

Realignment Due to Triangular Arbitrage.   The realignment that results from the triangular arbitrage activity is summarized in the second column of Exhibit 7.4. The realignment will likely occur quickly to prevent continued benefits from triangular arbitrage. The discrepancies assumed here are unlikely to occur within a single bank. A more likely case of triangular arbitrage would be three transactions at three separate banks.

Given three currencies, the exchange rate between each pair is displayed in Exhibit 7.5. If any two of these three exchange rates are known, the exchange rate of the third pair can be determined. When the actual cross exchange rate differs from the appropriate cross exchange rate, the exchange rates of the currencies are not in equilibrium. Triangular arbitrage would force the exchange rates back into equilibrium.

As with locational arbitrage, triangular arbitrage is not normally a strategy that most of us can take advantage of. This is especially true in light of the computer technology available to foreign exchange dealers, which can easily detect misalignment in cross exchange rates. The point of this discussion is that because of triangular arbitrage, cross exchange rates are usually aligned correctly. If they are not, triangular arbitrage will take place until the rates are aligned correctly.

EXHIBIT 7.3 Currency Quotes for a Triangular Arbitrage Example		Quoted Bid Price	Quoted Ask Price
	Value of a British pound in U.S. dollars	$1.99	$2.00
	Value of a French franc in U.S. dollars	$.200	$.201
	Value of a British pound in French francs (FF)	FF10.8	FF11.0

EXHIBIT 7.4
Impact of Triangular Arbitrage Example

Activity	Impact
1. Participants use dollars to purchase pounds.	Bank increases its ask price of pounds with respect to the dollar.
2. Participants use pounds to purchase French francs.	Bank reduces its bid price of the British pound with respect to the franc; that is, it reduces the number of francs to be exchanged per pound received.
3. Participants use French francs to purchase U.S. dollars.	Bank reduces its bid price of francs with respect to the dollar.

EXHIBIT 7.5
Relationship between Three Currencies

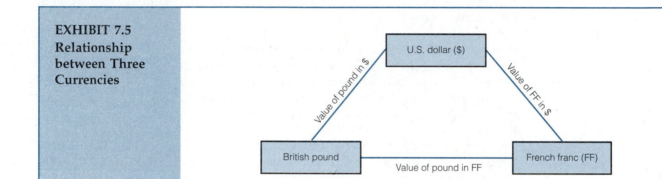

Covered Interest Arbitrage

Up to this point two types of arbitrage have been considered. Locational arbitrage forces any particular exchange rate to be similar among banks. Triangular arbitrage forces a quoted cross exchange rate to be appropriately priced. Another arbitrage concept, called **covered interest arbitrage,** tends to force a relationship between the interest rates of two countries and their forward exchange rate premium or discount. Covered interest arbitrage involves investing in a foreign country and covering against exchange rate risk. Some of the literature in international finance specifies that the funds to be invested be borrowed locally. In this case, the investors would not be tying up any of their own funds. Other research, however, does not make this specification. That is, the investors would use their own funds. In this case, the term arbitrage is loosely defined, since there is a positive dollar amount invested over a period of time. The following discussion is based on this latter meaning of covered interest arbitrage; yet, arbitrage under either interpretation should have a similar impact on currency values and interest rates.

To illustrate how covered interest arbitrage works, assume that you desire to capitalize on relatively high rates of interest in Great Britain, and you have funds available for 90 days. The interest rate is fixed; only the future exchange rate at which you will exchange pounds back to U.S. dollars is uncertain. A forward sale of pounds can be used to guarantee the rate at which you could exchange pounds for dollars at a future point in time. This actual strategy is as follows:

1. On Day 1, convert your U.S. dollars to pounds and set up a 90-day deposit account in a British bank.
2. On Day 1, engage in a forward contract to sell pounds 90 days forward.
3. In 90 days when the deposit matures, convert the pounds to U.S. dollars at the rate that was agreed upon in the forward contract.

The next example uses numbers to illustrate how this would work:

- You have $1,000,000 to invest.
- The current spot rate of the pound is $2.00.
- The 90-day forward rate of the pound is $2.00.
- The 90-day interest rate in the United States is 2 percent.
- The 90-day interest rate in Great Britain is 4 percent.

Based on this information, you could first convert the $1,000,000 to £500,000 and deposit the £500,000 in a British bank, then simultaneously set up a forward contract with a bank to sell the pounds at $2.00 per pound. By the time the deposit matures, you will have £520,000. The spot rate of the pound at the time the deposit matures is no longer important, since you have already locked in the rate at which you can sell the pounds through the forward contract. Based on the assumed 90-day forward rate of £1 = $2.00, you can convert the £520,000 into $1,040,000. This reflects a 4-percent return over the three-month period, which is 2 percent above the return on a U.S. deposit. In addition, the return on this foreign deposit has been locked in, since you know when you make the deposit exactly how much you will get back for the pounds you accumulate.

Recall that locational and triangular arbitrage do not tie up funds; thus, any profits are achieved instantaneously. In the case of covered interest arbitrage, the funds are tied up for a period of time (90 days, in our example). This would not be a valuable strategy if it earned 2 percent or less, since you could earn 2 percent on a domestic deposit. The term "arbitrage" here suggests that you can guarantee a return on your funds that exceeds the returns you could achieve domestically.

Realignment Due to Covered Interest Arbitrage.

As with the other forms of arbitrage, market forces resulting from covered interest arbitrage will cause a market realignment. Once the realignment takes place, excess profits from arbitrage are no longer possible.

In the above discussion, four variables (pound spot rate, British interest rate, U.S. interest rate, and pound forward rate) could be affected by covered interest arbitrage. It is difficult to forecast the exact magnitude of each change. Yet, it should be clear that each change reduces the excess return initially achieved from covered interest arbitrage.

The impact of covered interest arbitrage on exchange rates and interest rates is summarized in Exhibit 7.6. If we assume no adjustment in interest rates, covered interest arbitrage would be feasible until the forward rate of the pound was sufficiently below the spot rate to offset the interest rate advantage. Given

EXHIBIT 7.6
Impact of Covered Interest Arbitrage Example

Activity	Impact
1. Use dollars to purchase pounds in the spot market.	Upward pressure on the spot rate of the pound.
2. Engage in a forward contract to sell pounds forward.	Downward pressure on the forward rate of the pound.
3. Invest funds from the U.S. in Great Britain.	Possible upward pressure on U.S. interest rates and downward pressure on British interest rates.

that the British interest rate is 2 percent above the U.S. interest rate, U.S. investors could benefit from covered interest arbitrage until the forward rate was about 2 percent less than the spot rate.

If interest rates change in response to the flow of funds into Great Britain, the interest rate differential would be reduced. Consequently, it would take a smaller differential between the spot and forward rate of the pound to offset the interest rate differential.

Assume that the exchange rates and interest rates have changed as shown in Exhibit 7.7. With these new rates, covered interest arbitrage no longer provides a return to U.S. investors that is higher than the prevailing U.S. interest rate. This can be shown by computing the return earned from covered interest arbitrage, as follows (assume an initial investment of $1,000,000):

1. Convert $1,000,000 to pounds:

$$\$1,000,000/\$2.01 = £497,512.$$

2. Calculate accumulated pounds over 90 days at 3.5 percent:

$$£497,512 \times 1.035 = £514,925.$$

EXHIBIT 7.7
Adjustments in Exchange Rates and Interest Rates Due to Covered Interest Arbitrage

	Original Value	Value After Being Affected by Covered Interest Arbitrage
British pound spot rate in U.S. dollars	$2.00	$2.01
British pound 90-day forward rate in U.S. dollars	2.00	1.99
U.S. interest rate for 90 days	2%	2.47%
British interest rate for 90 days	4%	3.50%

3. Reconvert pounds to dollars (at the forward rate of $1.99) after 90 days:

$$£514,925 \times \$1.99 = \$1,024,701.$$

4. Determine yield earned from covered interest arbitrage:

$$(\$1,024,701 - \$1,000,000)/\$1,000,000 = .0247, \text{ or } 2.47\%.$$

This example shows that those individuals who initially conduct covered interest arbitrage cause exchange rates and interest rates to move in such a way that future attempts at covered interest arbitrage provide a return that is no better than what is possible domestically. At some point in the future, there may again be opportunities for excess profits through covered interest arbitrage. But as they are realized, the transactions from arbitrage will again affect exchange rates and interest rates such that further attempts at arbitrage are not feasible. Due to the market forces from covered interest arbitrage, a relationship between the forward rate premium and interest rate differentials should exist. This relationship is discussed in the following section.

INTEREST RATE PARITY (IRP)

Once market forces cause the interest rates and exchange rates to be such that covered interest arbitrage is no longer feasible, we are in an equilibrium state referred to as **interest rate parity (IRP).** In equilibrium, the forward rate differs from the spot rate by a sufficient amount to offset the interest rate differential between two currencies. In the above example, the U.S. investor receives a higher interest rate from the foreign investment, but there is an offsetting effect due to the investor's paying more per unit of foreign currency (at the spot rate) than what is received per unit when the currency is sold forward (at the forward rate). Recall that when the forward rate is less than the spot rate, this implies the forward rate exhibits a discount.

Derivation of Interest Rate Parity

The relationship between a forward premium (or discount) of a foreign currency and the interest rates representing these currencies according to IRP can be determined as follows. Consider a U.S. investor who attempts covered interest arbitrage. The return to a U.S. investor from using covered interest arbitrage can be determined given

- The amount of the home currency (U.S. dollars in our example) that is initially invested (A_h)
- The spot rate (S) in dollars when the foreign currency is purchased
- The interest rate on the foreign deposit (i_f)
- The forward rate (F) in dollars at which the foreign currency will be converted back to U.S. dollars

The amount of the home currency received at the end of the deposit period due to such a strategy (called A_n) is

$$A_n = (A_h/S)(1 + i_f)F$$

Since F is simply S times one plus the forward premium (called p), we can rewrite this equation as

$$A_n = (A_h/S)(1 + i_f)[S(1 + p)]$$
$$= A_h(1 + i_f)(1 + p).$$

The rate of return from this investment (called r) is as follows:

$$r = \frac{A_n - A_h}{A_h}$$
$$= \frac{[A_h(1 + i_f)(1 + p)] - A_h}{A_h}$$
$$= (1 + i_f)(1 + p) - 1.$$

If interest rate parity exists, then the rate of return achieved from covered interest arbitrage (r) should be equal to the rate available in the home country. Set the rate that can be achieved from using covered interest arbitrage to the rate that can be achieved from an investment in the home country (the return on a home investment is simply the home interest rate called i_h):

$$r = i_h.$$

By substituting into the formula the way in which r_j is determined, we obtain

$$(1 + i_j)(1 + p) - 1 = i_h.$$

By rearranging terms, we can find out what the forward premium of the foreign currency should be under conditions of interest rate parity:

$$(1 + i_f)(1 + p) - 1 = i_h$$
$$(1 + i_f)(1 + p) = (1 + i_h)$$
$$(1 + p) = \frac{(1 + i_h)}{(1 + i_f)}$$
$$p = \frac{(1 + i_h)}{(1 + i_f)} - 1$$

Numerical Example of Interest Rate Parity

As an example, assume that the French franc exhibits a six-month interest rate of 6 percent, while the U.S. dollar exhibits a six-month interest rate of 5 percent. From a U.S. investor's perspective, the U.S. dollar is the home currency. According to IRP, the forward rate premium of the franc with respect to the U.S. dollar should be

$$p = \frac{(1 + .05)}{(1 + .06)} - 1$$
$$= -.0094, \text{ or } -.94\% \text{ (not annualized)}.$$

Thus, the franc should exhibit a forward discount of about .94 percent. This implies that U.S. investors would receive .94 percent less when selling francs six months from now (based on a forward sale) than the price they pay for francs today at the spot rate. Such a discount would offset the interest rate advantage of the franc. If the French franc's spot rate is $.10, a forward discount of .94 percent means that the six-month forward rate is as follows:

$$F = S(1 + p)$$
$$= \$.10(1 - .0094)$$
$$= \$.09906.$$

The following numerical example confirms that if interest rate parity exists, covered interest arbitrage will not be feasible. Use the above information on the spot rate and six-month forward rate of the franc, as well as the French interest rate, to determine a U.S. investor's return from using covered interest arbitrage. Assume the investor begins with $1,000,000 to invest.

Step 1. On the first day, the U.S. investor converts $1,000,000 into francs (FF) at $.10 per franc:

$$\$1,000,000/\$.10 \text{ per franc} = \text{FF}10,000,000.$$

Step 2. On the first day, the U.S. investor also sells francs six months forward. The number of francs to be sold forward is the anticipated accumulation of francs over the six-month period, which is estimated as

$$\text{FF}10,000,000 \times (1 + 6\%) = \text{FF}10,600,000.$$

Step 3. After six months, the U.S. investor withdraws the initial deposit of francs along with the accumulated interest, amounting to a total of 10,600,000 francs. The investor converts the francs into dollars in accordance with the forward contract agreed upon six months earlier. The forward rate was $.09906, so the number of U.S. dollars received from the conversion is

$$\text{FF}10,600,000 \times (\$.09906 \text{ per franc}) = \$1,050,036.$$

Results. The act of covered interest arbitrage achieves a return of about 5 percent here. Rounding the forward discount at .94 percent causes the slight deviation from the 5 percent return.

The results suggest that in this instance, using covered interest arbitrage generates a return that is about what the U.S. investors would have received anyway if they had simply invested their funds domestically. This confirms that covered interest arbitrage is not worthwhile if interest rate parity exists.

The relationship between the forward premium (or discount) and the interest rate differential according to interest rate parity is simplified in an approximated form as follows:

$$p = \frac{F - S}{S} \simeq i_h - i_f$$

where

> p = forward premium (or discount)
> F = forward rate in dollars
> S = spot rate in dollars
> i_h = home interest rate
> i_f = foreign interest rate

This approximated form provides a reasonable estimate when the interest rate differential is small. The variables in this equation are not annualized. In our above example, the U.S. (home) interest rate is less than the foreign interest rate, so the forward rate contains a discount (the forward rate is less than the spot rate). The larger the degree by which the foreign interest rate exceeds the home interest rate, the larger will be the forward discount of the foreign currency specified by the IRP formula.

If the foreign interest rate is less than the home interest rate, the interest rate parity relationship suggests that the forward rate should exhibit a premium. There may be reason for investors to attempt covered interest arbitrage even if the home interest rate is higher than the foreign interest rate. Consider a situation in which the foreign interest rate is just slightly less than the home rate. In this case, interest rate parity would exist if the forward rate were just slightly larger than the spot rate (exhibiting a slight premium). Then, the amount U.S. investors gained from the forward rate premium would be offset by the slightly lower interest rate. However, if the forward rate exhibited a large premium, the U.S. investors could achieve a higher return through covered interest arbitrage than by investing domestically.

Graphic Analysis of Interest Rate Parity

The interest rate differential can be compared to the forward premium (or discount) with the aid of a graph like that in Exhibit 7.8. All the possible points that represent interest rate parity can be plotted by using the approximation expressed earlier and plugging in numbers. For example, if the foreign interest rate (i_f) exceeds the home interest rate (i_h) by 1 percent ($i_h - i_f = -1\%$), then the forward rate should exhibit a discount of 1 percent. This is represented by point A on the graph. If the foreign interest rate exceeds the home rate by 2 percent, then the forward rate should exhibit a discount of 2 percent, as represented by point B on the graph, and so on. For cases in which the foreign interest rate is less than the home interest rate, the forward rate should exhibit a premium approximately equal to that differential. For example, if the home interest rate exceeds the foreign rate by 1 percent ($i_h - i_f = 1\%$), then the forward premium should be 1 percent, as represented by point C. If the home interest rate exceeds the foreign rate by 2 percent ($i_h - i_f = 2\%$), then the forward premium should be 2 percent, as represented by point D, and so on. Any points lying on the diagonal line cutting the intersection of axes represent interest rate parity. For this reason, that diagonal line is referred to as the **interest rate parity (IRP) line.**

**EXHIBIT 7.8
Illustration of
Interest Rate Parity**

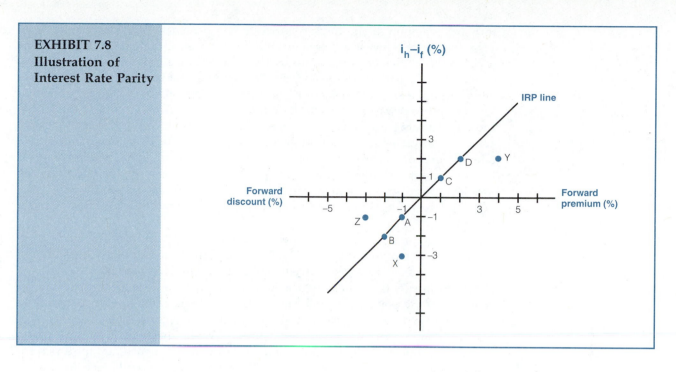

An individual or corporation could at any time examine all currencies to compare forward rate premiums (or discounts) to interest rate differentials. From a U.S. perspective, interest rates in Switzerland and Japan are sometimes lower than the home interest rates. Consequently, the forward rate of these currencies (Swiss franc and Japanese yen) will sometimes exhibit a premium. Thus, we would expect these currencies to be represented by points such as C or D or even points above D along the diagonal line in Exhibit 7.8. Conversely, countries such as Great Britain and France often have higher interest rates than the United States, and their forward rates often exhibit a discount. Thus, we would expect these currencies to be represented by points such as A or B.

Exhibit 7.8 can be used whether or not you annualize the rates, as long as you are consistent. That is, if you annualize the interest rates to determine the interest rate differential, you should also annualize the forward premium or discount.

What if a three-month deposit represented by a foreign currency offers an annualized interest rate of 10 percent, versus an annualized interest rate of 7 percent in the home country? Such a scenario is represented on the graph by $i_h - i_f = -3\%$. Also assume that the foreign currency exhibits an annualized forward discount of 1 percent. The combined interest rate differential and forward discount information can be represented by point X on the graph. Since point X is not on the IRP line, we should expect that covered interest arbitrage is beneficial for some investors. The investor attains 3 percent more for the foreign deposit, and this advantage is only partially offset by the 1 percent forward discount.

Assume that the annualized interest rate for the foreign currency is 5 percent, as compared to 7 percent for the home country. The interest rate differential expressed on the graph is $i_h - i_f = 2\%$. However, assume that the forward premium of the foreign currency is 4 percent (point Y in Exhibit 7.8). Thus, what the investor loses on the lower interest rate from the foreign investment is more than made up by the high forward premium.

Shift to the left side of the IRP line. Take point Z, for example. This represents a foreign interest rate that exceeds the home interest rate by 1 percent, while the forward rate exhibits a 3 percent discount. This point, like all points to the left on the interest rate parity line, represents a situation in which U.S. investors would achieve a lower return on a foreign investment than they would on a domestic one. The reason for this lower return is normally that either (1) the advantage of the foreign interest rate relative to the U.S. interest rate is more than offset by the forward rate discount (which reflects point Z), or (2) the degree by which the home interest rate exceeds the foreign rate more than offsets the forward rate premium.

However, for points such as these, covered interest arbitrage is feasible from the perspective of foreign investors. Consider British investors in Great Britain, where the interest rate is 1 percent higher than the U.S. interest rate, and the forward rate (with respect to the dollar) contains a 3-percent discount (as represented by point Z). British investors would sell their foreign currency in exchange for dollars, invest in dollar-denominated securities, and engage in a forward contract to purchase pounds forward. While they earn 1 percent less on a U.S. investment, they are able to purchase their home currency for 3 percent less than what they initially sold it for. This type of activity will place downward pressure on the spot rate of the pound and upward pressure on the pound's forward rate, until covered interest arbitrage is no longer feasible.

How to Test Whether Interest Rate Parity Exists

An investor or firm can plot all realistic points for various currencies on a graph such as that in Exhibit 7.8 to determine whether gains from covered interest arbitrage can be achieved. The location of the points provides an indication of whether covered interest arbitrage is worthwhile. For points to the right of the IRP line, investors in the home country should consider using covered interest arbitrage, since a return higher than the home interest rate (i_h) is achievable. Of course, as investors and firms take advantage of such opportunities, there will be a tendency for the point to move toward the IRP line. Covered interest arbitrage should continue until the IRP relationship holds.

The points to the left of the IRP line are not suitable for covered interest arbitrage by home-country investors, but are suitable for foreign investors. In our example, foreign investors would conduct covered interest arbitrage by purchasing and depositing the home currency (dollars), while simultaneously purchasing their currency forward for the date at which the U.S. deposit matures.

Interpretation of Interest Rate Parity

Interest rate parity is sometimes mistakenly summarized as follows: "If IRP exists, then foreign investors will earn the same returns as U.S. investors." To prove that this statement is incorrect, consider two countries: the U.S., with a 10 percent interest rate, and Great Britain, with a 14 percent interest rate. U.S. investors could achieve 10 percent domestically or attempt to use covered interest arbitrage. If they attempt covered interest arbitrage while IRP exists, then the result will be a 10 percent return, the same as that possible for them in the United States. If British investors attempt covered interest arbitrage while IRP exists, then the result will be a 14 percent return, the same as that possible for them in Great Britain. Thus, U.S. investors and British investors do *not* achieve the same nominal return here, even though IRP exists. An appropriate summary explanation of interest rate parity is that if interest rate parity exists, investors cannot use covered interest arbitrage to achieve higher returns than those achievable in their respective home countries.

Does Interest Rate Parity Hold?

To correctly determine whether IRP holds, it is necessary to compare the forward rate (or discount) and interest rate quotations that occur at the same time. If the forward rate and interest rate quotations do not reflect the same time of day, then results could be somewhat distorted. Due to limitations in access to data, it is difficult to get quotations that reflect the same point in time. Consequently, the testing of IRP is subject to some error. Yet, that should not discourage attempts to determine whether IRP exists. Empirical examination of IRP has been conducted by Aliber, Branson, Frenkel and Levich, Stokes and Neuburger, and others. The actual relationship between the forward rate premium and interest rate differentials generally supports IRP. While there are deviations, they are often not large enough to make covered interest arbitrage worthwhile, as we will now discuss in more detail.

Considerations When Assessing Interest Rate Parity

If IRP does not hold, there is still the possibility that covered interest arbitrage is not worthwhile. This is due to potential costs that arise from foreign investments but not from domestic investments. Such costs could include transaction costs, currency restrictions, and differential tax laws.

If an investor wishes to account for transaction costs, the actual point reflecting the interest rate differential and forward rate premium must be farther from the IRP line to make covered interest arbitrage worthwhile. Exhibit 7.9 identifies the areas that reflect potential for covered interest arbitrage *after* accounting for transaction costs. Notice the band surrounding the IRP line. For points not on the IRP line but within this band, covered interest arbitrage is not worthwhile (because the excess return is offset by costs). For points to the right (or below) the band, investors residing in the home country could gain through covered interest arbitrage. For points to the left (or above) the band, foreign investors could gain through covered interest arbitrage.

Even if covered interest arbitrage appears feasible after accounting for transaction costs, the act of investing funds overseas is subject to political risk. While the forward contract locks in the rate at which the foreign funds should be reconverted, there is no guarantee that funds will be allowed to be reconverted. A crisis in the foreign country could cause its government to restrict any exchange of the local currency for other currencies. In this case, the investor would be unable to use these funds until the foreign government eliminated the restriction. Investors may also perceive a slight default risk on foreign investments such as foreign Treasury bills, since they might not be assured that the

CROSS-CURRENCY COVERED INTEREST ARBITRAGE

A variation of covered interest arbitrage has been used to capitalize on differences in European interest rates. Assume that the German mark has a 4-percent discount. Since most European countries are linked within a narrow band, it is possible for U.S. investors to employ a variation of covered interest arbitrage to benefit from the high interest rates in Italy, while reducing exposure to exchange rate risk.

Assume the following information:

	Spot Rate	Forward Rate	Interest Rate
German mark (DM)	$.6120	$.5895	9%
Italian lira	$.00068	$.00062	15%
U.S. dollar	—	—	5%

Since the forward rate of the German mark contains a discount that offsets the Germany-U.S. interest rate differential (interest rate parity exists here), U.S. investors would not benefit from using covered interest arbitrage on German interest rates. Since the forward rate of the Italian lire contains a discount that offsets the Italy-U.S. interest rate differential, U.S. investors would not benefit from using covered interest arbitrage on Italian interest rates.

However, recognizing that the exchange rate between the German mark and Italian lira (which is presently 900 lire per mark) is maintained within narrow bands, U.S. investors could attempt a variation of covered interest arbitrage. Specifically, U.S. investors could

(1) Purchase lire with dollars, and invest the lire
(2) Sell German marks one year forward (even though there is no investment in marks, the forward discount on marks is not as large as it is on lire)
(3) Receive the principal and interest in lire at the end of one year
(4) Convert the lire principal and interest to marks
(5) Exchange the marks for dollars at the forward rate negotiated one year ago.

Using the data provided here, the steps are shown assuming an initial investment of $1 million and also assuming that the spot rate between the mark and the lira remains at 900 lire per mark.

(1) Convert $1 million into 1470.59 million lire (based on a spot rate of $.00068 for lire)
(2) Sell marks one year forward (assume that the amount of marks to be sold forward is negotiated to be between 1.7 million and 1.9 million marks)
(3) Receive 1,691.18 million lire in principal and interest from the investment at the end of one year (composed of principal plus 15% interest)
(4) Convert the 1,691.18 million lire to DM1.879 million (based on an exchange rate of 900 lire per mark)
(5) Exchange the DM1.879 million into $1.1077 million based on the forward exchange rate negotiated one year ago (computed as DM1.879 million marks × $.5895 per mark).

This strategy results in a gain of 10.77 percent for U.S. investors, which is clearly superior to the U.S. interest rate of 5 percent. However, this gain is not guaranteed, because the spot rate between the mark and lire at the end of one year is not guaranteed. In this example, the spot rate is assumed to remain unchanged. While the exchange rate is normally kept within bands by central banks, there is some risk that the mark-lira exchange rate could change and cause adverse results. For example, assume that the mark is revalued by 10 percent (from 900 lire per mark to 990 lire per mark). This would cause step (4) in the example to result in the conversion of 1,691.18 million lire to about DM1.7083 million. Thus, step (5) would show an exchange of 1.7083 million marks into $1.007 million (computed as DM1.7083 million × $.5895 per mark). This strategy would now result in a gain of only .7 percent for U.S. investors. This result is less favorable because the foreign currency the U.S. investors have invested in (lire) has weakened against the foreign currency that they sold forward (the mark). Thus, there is a risk here that does not exist in the conventional form of covered interest arbitrage. The risk is less severe if the central banks are more likely to maintain the exchange rate between the two foreign currencies of concern within narrow bands.

**EXHIBIT 7.9
Potential for
Covered Interest
Arbitrage When
Considering
Transaction Costs**

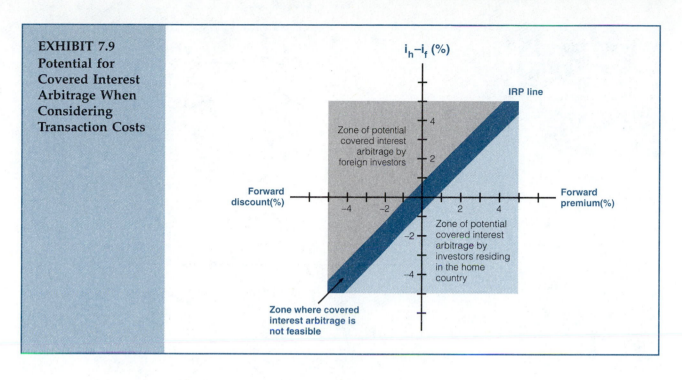

foreign government will guarantee full repayment of interest and principal upon default.

Firms and investors recognize the impact that taxes may have on income. Because tax laws vary among countries, investors and firms that set up deposits in other countries must be aware of the existing tax laws. It is possible that covered interest arbitrage could be feasible when considering before-tax returns but not necessarily when considering after-tax returns. Such a scenario would be due to differential tax rates.

If IRP does not hold, the possibility of covered interest arbitrage deserves consideration. However, the existence of all these factors could eliminate the possibility of abnormal returns from covered interest arbitrage. Covered interest arbitrage should be attempted only if abnormal returns remain after considering transaction costs, potential currency restrictions, and taxes.

RELATION BETWEEN SPOT AND FORWARD RATES

Because of interest rate parity, a foreign currency's forward rate will normally move in tandem with the spot rate. This correlation of movement depends on interest rate movements, as shown in Exhibit 7.10. Currency A's spot rate (S_A) and forward rate (F_A) are shown, along with a comparison of the U.S. interest rate ($i_{U.S.}$) and Country A's interest rate (i_A). From time t_0 to t_1, i_A exceeds $i_{U.S.}$, and F_A is therefore less than S_A by approximately that interest rate differential. The size of the interest rate differential declines over this period, causing the discount on F_A to decline along with it. At time t_1, the interest rates of the two countries are equal, so that F_A is equal to S_A. From time t_1 to t_2, i_A is below $i_{U.S.}$, causing F_A to be above S_A. At the beginning of this period, the premium on F_A

EXHIBIT 7.10 Relationship between Interest Rate Differentials and Forward Rate Premiums Over Time

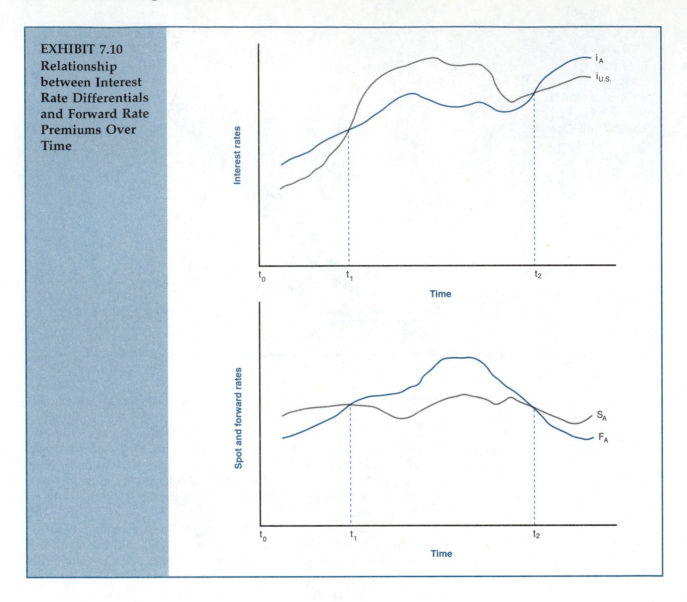

rises because the differential between $i_{U.S.}$ and i_A becomes larger. As time t_2 approaches, the interest rate differential narrows until $i_A = i_{U.S.}$ at time t_2, causing F_A to equal S_A. After time t_2, i_A exceeds $i_{U.S.}$, forcing F_A to fall below S_A.

SUMMARY

■ Locational arbitrage may occur if foreign exchange quotations differ among banks. The act of locational arbitrage should force the foreign exchange quotations of banks to become realigned, and locational arbitrage will no longer be possible.

■ Triangular arbitrage is related to cross exchange rates. A cross exchange rate between two currencies is determined by the values of these two currencies with respect to a third currency. If the actual cross exchange rate of these two currencies differs from the rate that should exist, triangular arbitrage is possible. The act of triangular arbitrage should force cross exchange rates to become realigned, at which time triangular arbitrage will no longer be possible.

■ Covered interest arbitrage is based on the relationship between the forward rate premium and the interest rate differential. The size of the premium or discount exhibited by the forward rate of a currency should be about the same as the differential between the interest rates of the two countries of concern. In general terms, the forward rate of the foreign currency will contain a discount (premium) if its interest rate is higher (lower) than the U.S. interest rate. If the forward premium deviates substantially from the interest rate differential, covered interest arbitrage is possible. This type of arbitrage represents a foreign short-term investment in a foreign currency covered by a forward sale of that foreign currency in the future. In this manner, the investor is not exposed to fluctuation in the foreign currency's value.

■ Interest rate parity (IRP) is a theory which states that the size of the forward premium (or discount) should be equal to the interest rate differential between the two countries of concern. When IRP exists, covered interest arbitrage is not feasible, because any interest rate advantage in the foreign country will be offset by the discount on the forward rate. Thus, the act of covered interest arbitrage would generate a return that is no higher than what would be generated by a domestic investment.

SELF-TEST FOR CHAPTER 7 _____

(Answers are provided in Appendix A in the back of the text)

1. Assume that the following spot exchange rates exist today:

$$DM = \$.60$$
$$FF = \$.15$$
$$DM = FF4.$$

Assume no transaction costs. Based on these exchange rates, can triangular arbitrage be used to earn a profit? Explain.

2. Assume the following information:

Spot rate of £ = $1.60
180-day forward rate of £ = $1.56
180-day British interest rate = 4%
180-day U.S. interest rate = 3%.

Based on this information, is covered interest arbitrage by U.S. investors feasible? Explain.

3. Using the information in the previous question, does interest rate parity exist? Explain.

4. Explain in general terms how various forms of arbitrage can remove any discrepancies in the pricing of currencies.

5. Assume that the British pound's one-year forward rate exhibits a discount. Assume that interest rate parity continually exists. Explain how the discount on the British pound's one-year forward discount would change if British one-year interest rates rose by 3 percentage points while U.S. one-year interest rates rose by 2 percentage points.

QUESTIONS

1. Explain the concept of locational arbitrage and the scenario necessary for it to be plausible.

2. Assume the following information:

	Bank X	Bank Y
Bid price of Swiss francs	$.401	$.398
Ask price of Swiss francs	$.404	$.400

Given this information, is locational arbitrage possible? If so, explain the steps that would reflect locational arbitrage, and compute the profit from this arbitrage if you had $1,000,000 to use.

3. Based on the information in the previous question, what market forces would occur to eliminate any further possibilities of locational arbitrage?

4. Explain the concept of triangular arbitrage and the scenario necessary for it to be plausible.

5. Assume the following information for a particular bank:

	Quoted Price
Value of Canadian dollar in U.S. dollars	$.90
Value of German mark in U.S. dollars	$.30
Value of Canadian dollar in German marks	DM3.02

Given this information, is triangular arbitrage possible? If so, explain the steps that would reflect triangular arbitrage, and compute the profit from this strategy if you had $1,000,000 to use.

6. Based on the information in the previous question, what market forces would occur to eliminate any further possibilities of triangular arbitrage?

7. Explain the concept of covered interest arbitrage and the scenario necessary for it to be plausible.

8. Assume the following information:

Spot rate of Canadian dollar	= $.80
90-day forward rate of Canadian dollar	= $.79
90-day Canadian interest rate	= 4%
90-day U.S. interest rate	= 2.5%

Given this information, what would be the yield (percentage return) to a U.S. investor who used covered interest arbitrage? (Assume the investor invests $1,000,000.)

9. Based on the information in the previous question, what market forces would occur to eliminate any further possibilities of covered interest arbitrage?

10. Assume the following information:

Spot rate of French franc	= $.100
180-day forward rate of French franc	= $.098
180-day French interest rate	= 6%
180-day U.S. interest rate	= 5%

Given this information, is covered interest arbitrage worthwhile for French investors? Explain your answer.

11. Explain the concept of interest rate parity. Provide a rationale for its possible existence.

12. Describe a method for testing whether interest rate parity exists.

13. Why are transaction costs, currency restrictions, and differential tax laws important when evaluating whether covered interest arbitrage can be beneficial?

14. Assume that the existing U.S. one-year interest rate is 10 percent and the Canadian one-year interest rate is 11 percent. Also assume that interest rate parity exists. Should the forward rate of the Canadian dollar exhibit a discount or a premium? If U.S. investors attempted covered interest arbitrage, what would be their return? If Canadian investors attempted covered interest arbitrage, what would be their return?

15. Why would investors consider covered interest arbitrage in a foreign country where the interest rate is lower than their home interest rate?

16. Consider investors that invest in either U.S. or British one-year Treasury bills. Assume zero transaction costs and no taxes.

a) If interest rate parity exists, then the return for U.S. investors who use covered interest arbitrage would be the same as the return for U.S. investors who invest in U.S. Treasury bills. Is this statement true or false? If false, correct the statement.

b) If interest rate parity exists, then the return for British investors who use covered interest arbitrage would be the same as the return for British investors who invest in British Treasury bills. Is this statement true or false? If false, correct the statement.

17. Assume that the Swiss forward rate presently exhibits a premium of 6 percent, and that interest rate parity exists. How will this premium change if U.S. interest rates decrease, in order for interest rate parity to be maintained? Why might we expect the premium to change?

18. In the early 1980s the forward rate premiums of several currencies were higher than they are now. What does this imply about interest rate differentials between the United States and foreign countries today compared to those in the early 1980s?

19. If the relationship that is specified by interest rate parity does not exist at any period, but does exist on average, then covered interest arbitrage should not be considered by U.S. firms. Do you agree or disagree with this statement? Explain.

20. The one-year Swiss interest rate is 6 percent. The one-year U.S. interest rate is 10 percent. The spot rate of the Swiss franc is $.50. The forward rate of the Swiss franc is $.54. Is covered interest arbitrage feasible for U.S. investors? Is it feasible for Swiss investors? Explain why each of these opportunities for covered interest arbitrage is or is not feasible.

21. Assume that the one-year U.S. interest rate is 11 percent, while the one-year interest rate in a specific less developed country (LDC) is 40 percent. Assume that a U.S. bank is willing to purchase the currency of that country from you one year from now at a discount of 13 percent. Would covered interest arbitrage be worth considering? Is there any reason why you should not attempt covered interest arbitrage in this situation? (Ignore tax effects.)

22. Why do you think currencies of countries with high inflation rates tend to have forward discounts?

23. In 1989 and 1990 the German economy expanded significantly in response to European integration and the reunification of West and East Germany. How might these conditions affect the forward discount of the German mark?

24. Assume that the 30-day forward premium of the Canadian dollar was −1 percent, while the 90-day forward premium of the Canadian dollar was 2 percent. Explain the likely interest rate conditions that would cause these conditions. Does this ensure that covered interest arbitrage is worthwhile?

Kohl, Playing Down Money Crisis, Says Germany Still Supports Maastricht Pact

By Terence Roth
Staff Reporter of The Wall Street Journal

FRANKFURT - German Chancellor Helmut Kohl said Europe's latest currency crisis could delay implementation of the Maastricht treaty for a couple of years, but he reaffirmed Germany's commitment to the plan for European economic and political union.

The decision last week to expand the range in which European currencies could fluctuate against each other wasn't a decision against Maastricht, Mr. Kohl said, commenting publicly for the first time on the recent crisis in the European Monetary System. In an interview yesterday on Germany's Sat.1 cable-TV channel, he argued that the problems facing plans for European monetary union don't rise primarily from the EMS crisis but the extent to which economic and fiscal policies still need to converge.

Separately, German officials responded coolly to reports that British Prime Minister John Major was hoping to resurrect his earlier proposal for the introduction of the European currency unit as a parallel currency to Europe's national currencies. Bonn led opposition to the plan in the runup to the Maastricht treaty, "and we still don't believe this is a good idea," said a German official.

In his television interview, Mr. Kohl sought to dispel speculation that the currency crisis has caused a rift in Franco-German relations, fueling doubts about Europe's unity process under the Maastricht treaty. Franco-German relations remained intact, he said, asserting that "We didn't isolate the French."

Wider Range in Trading

On Aug. 2, to defuse the EMS crisis, European Community finance ministers agreed to let most currencies fluctuate as much as 15% up or down against each other, compared with a previous general range of 2.25%. Under the Exchange Rate Mechanism, or ERM, nations commit themselves to support their currencies within a specified trading range, and must intervene in the markets as needed. The wider ranges were agreed upon to prevent more nations from pulling out of the ERM, as certain currencies came under fire by speculators. While the trading-band change kept the EMS alive, at least in name, some say it amounted to a de facto suspension of the trading scheme.

In the interview, Mr. Kohl said that, prior to the Aug. 2 decision to widen trading bands, he personally opposed a French proposal to temporarily float the mark from ERM to ease tensions in the currency grid. He said he told the French that he doubted whether it was a plan that other governments could accept. Mr. Kohl's prediction was at least borne out by Dutch officials, who had insisted that if the mark left the ERM, the guilder would follow, which was more than the French had bargained for.

Mr. Kohl said he agreed with French Prime Minister Edouard Balladur's proposal that European Community government leaders discuss the timetable for a single European currency at a special EC summit in October, Maastricht guidelines currently foresee the adoption of a single currency and common central bank in Europe in 1997 at the earliest.

The German chancellor defended the Bundesbank's tight anti-inflation policies, which many analysts believe touched off the currency crisis. He conceded that Europe's recession has strained the monetary system. But he warned against easing Maastricht's strict guidelines for national economies, a checklist of limits on deficits, inflation and national debt.

German Ratification Is Expected

"If that results in the delay of the currently foreseen timetable by one to two years, then in what way does that change the process?" Mr. Kohl said, "What is decisive is that something will happen in this decade which nobody would have believed possible in 90 years of this century: That after two world wars it is possible to really build this Europe, a Europe of individual countries, into which Germans and the French can bring in their identities, but under a European roof."

Germany is the only EC country not to have ratified the Maastricht treaty. But Mr. Kohl said he hopes that Germany's Federal Constitutional Court will rule against complaints claiming unlawful dilution of German sovereignty. He said he hoped to be able to bring a German ratification to the October EC summit, where he said Germany will stick to its insistence on Frankfurt as the location for a future European central bank.

"I'm actually very optimistic," he said. Mr. Kohl added that putting the European central bank in Germany was "obvious," and that the other countries understood this, if some only reluctantly.

"The D-mark is, after all, the reference currency of Europe. It is nothing we should be ashamed of," Mr. Kohl said. "It is the result of sensible, hard work of the Germans and smart policies, not the least from the Bundesbank."

Source: *The Wall Street Journal* (August 10, 1993): p. A11. Reprinted by permission of *The Wall Street Journal*. © 1993 Dow Jones & Company, Inc. All rights reserved worldwide.

Questions

1. The bands of Europe's exchange rate mechanism (ERM) can restrict currency movements. Attempt to create a scenario in which a European firm could engage in arbitrage by investing in other European currencies to achieve high interest earnings, even without covering the position in the forward market. Such a strategy can be feasible when exchange rates are restricted.

2. Refer back to your answer to the previous question. Could U.S. firms benefit from arbitrage in the same manner as European firms? Explain.

3. Before the ERM bands widened, the spot and forward exchange rates between any two European currencies were almost identical. When the ERM bands were widened, there was a wider gap between the spot and forward exchange rates. Explain why this would occur, using interest rate parity in your explanation.

CASE PROBLEM

ZUBER INC.
Using Covered Interest Arbitrage

Zuber Inc. is a U.S.-based MNC that has been aggressively pursuing business in Eastern Europe since the Iron Curtain was lifted in 1989. One of the Eastern Bloc countries has allowed for its currency's value to be market-determined. The spot rate of the currency is $.40. The country also has begun to allow investments by foreign investors, as a method of attracting funds to help build its economy. Its interest rate on one-year securities issued by the federal government is 14 percent, which is substantially higher than the 9-percent rate presently offered on one-year U.S. Treasury securities.

A local bank began to create a forward market for the local currency. This bank was recently privatized and has been trying to make a name for itself in international business. The bank has quoted a one-year forward rate of $.39.

As an employee in Zuber's international money market division, you have been asked to assess the possibility of investing short-term funds in this country. You are in charge of investing $10 million over the next year. Your objective is to earn the highest return possible, while maintaining safety (since the funds will be needed by the firm next year).

Since the exchange rate has just become market-determined, there is a high probability that the currency's value will be very volatile for several years as it seeks out its true equilibrium value. The expected value of the currency in one year is $.40, but there is a high degree of uncertainty about this. The actual value in one year may be as much as 40 percent above or below this expected value.

a) Would you be willing to invest the funds in this country without covering your position? Explain.

b) Suggest how you could attempt covered interest arbitrage. What is the expected return from using covered interest arbitrage?

c) What risks are involved in using covered interest arbitrage here?

d) If you had to choose between investing your funds in U.S. Treasury bills at 9 percent or using covered interest arbitrage, what would be your choice? Defend your answer.

PROJECTS

1. Look up the spot rate and 180-day forward rate of the British pound in a recent issue of *The Wall Street Journal.* Also, look up (in the "Money Rates" section) U.S. and British 180-day interest rates. Assume these rates are applicable for investors and reflected investments with equal risk. Determine whether a U.S. investor would benefit from utilizing covered interest arbitrage.

2. Using a recent issue of *The Wall Street Journal*, fill in the first three blanks that follow this question. Using those three exchange rates, determine the cross exchange rates and fill in the next three blanks. (Assume that cross exchange rates are properly aligned so that triangular arbitrage is not profitable.)

Spot rate of British pound in $ = $ _____

Spot rate of Swiss franc in $ = $ _____

Spot rate of the Japanese yen in $ = $ _____

Spot rate of the British pound in SF   = SF _____

Spot rate of the British pound in yen = ¥ _____

Spot rate of the Swiss franc in yen   = ¥ _____

3. Determine whether covered interest arbitrage would have been profitable from a U.S. perspective, using the Data Bank in the back of this text on a country of your choice. Assess several historical points in time.

REFERENCES

Adler, Michael, and Bernard Dumas. "International Portfolio Choice and Corporation Finance: A Synthesis." *Journal of Finance* (June 1983), pp. 925-984.

Aliber, Robert Z. "The Interest Rate Parity Theorem: A Reinterpretation." *Journal of Political Economy* (December 1973), pp. 1451-1459.

Branson, William H. "The Minimum Covered Interest Differential Needed for International Arbitrage Activity." *Journal of Political Economy* (December 1979), pp. 1029-1034.

Cornell, Bradford. "Spot Rates, Forward Rates, and Market Dynamics." *Journal of Political Economy* (December 1976), pp. 1161-1176.

Dooley, Michael P., and Peter Isard. "Capital Controls, Political Risks, and Deviations from Interest-Rate Parity." *Journal of Political Economy* (April 1980), pp. 370-384.

Dutton, Marilyn Miller, "Real Interest Rate Parity New Measures and Tests," *Journal of International Money and Finance,* (February 1993), pp 62-77.

Frenkel, Jacob A., and Richard M. Levich. "Transaction Costs and Interest Arbitrage: Tranquil Versus Turbulent Periods." *Journal of Political Economy* (December 1977), pp. 1209-1226.

_____ . "Covered-Interest Arbitrage and Unexploited Profits Reply." *Journal of Political Economy* (April 1979), pp. 418-422.

Geweke, J., and E. Feige. "Some Joint Tests of the Efficiency of Markets for Forward Foreign Exchange." *Review of Economics and Statistics* (October 1979), pp. 334-341.

Popper, Helen, "Long-term Covered Interest Parity: Evidence from Currency Swaps," *Journal of International Money and Finance,* (August 1993), pp 439-448.

Rhee, S. Ghon and Rosita P. Chang, "Intra-Day Arbitrage Opportunities in Foreign Exchange and Eurocurrency Markets," *Journal of Finance,* March 1992, pp 363-379.

Solnik, Bruno. "International Parity Conditions and Exchange Risk: A Review." *Journal of Banking and Finance* (August 1978), pp. 281-293.

Stokes, Houston H., and Hugh Neuburger. "Interest Arbitrage, Forward Speculation and the Determination of the Forward Exchange Rate." *Columbia Journal of World Business* (Winter 1979), pp. 86-98.

RELATIONSHIPS BETWEEN INFLATION, INTEREST RATES, AND EXCHANGE RATES

Inflation rates and interest rates can have a strong impact on exchange rates, as explained in Chapter 4. Given their potential importance, they deserve to be studied more closely. The specific objectives of this chapter are to

- explain the purchasing power parity (PPP) theory, and its implications for exchange rate changes,
- explain the international Fisher effect (IFE) theory, and its implications for exchange rate changes, and
- compare the PPP theory, IFE theory, and theory of interest rate parity (IRP), which was introduced in the previous chapter.

PURCHASING POWER PARITY (PPP)

In Chapter 4, the expected impact of relative inflation rates on exchange rates was discussed. Recall from this discussion that when one country's inflation rate rises relative to that of another, the demand for its currency declines as its exports decline (due to its higher prices). In addition, consumers and firms in the country with higher inflation tend to increase their importing. Both of these forces place downward pressure on the currency of the high-inflation country. Inflation rates often vary among countries, causing international trade patterns and exchange rates to adjust accordingly.

One of the most popular and controversial theories in international finance is the **purchasing power parity (PPP) theory,** which focuses on the inflation–exchange rate relationship. There are various forms of PPP theory. The **absolute form,** also called the "law of one price," suggests that prices of similar products of two different countries should be equal when measured in a common currency. If a discrepancy in prices as measured by a common currency exists, the demand should shift so that these prices should converge. For example, if the same product is produced by the United States and the United Kingdom, and the price in the United Kingdom is lower when measured in a common currency, the demand for that product should increase in the United Kingdom while it declines in the United States. Consequently, the actual price charged in each country may be affected and/or the exchange rate may adjust. Both forces would cause the prices of the products to be similar when measured in a common currency. Realistically, the existence of transportation costs, tariffs, and quotas may prevent the absolute form of PPP. If transportation costs were high in this example, the demand for the products might not shift in the manner suggested. Thus, the discrepancy in prices would continue.

The **relative form** of PPP is an alternative version that accounts for the possibility of market imperfections such as transportation costs, tariffs, and quotas. This version acknowledges that because of these market imperfections, prices of similar products of different countries will not necessarily be the same when measured in a common currency. However, it states that the rate of change in the prices of products should be somewhat similar when measured in a common currency, as long as the transportation costs and trade barriers are unchanged. To illustrate the relative form of PPP, assume that two countries initially have zero inflation. Also assume that the current exchange rate between the two countries' currencies is in equilibrium. As time passes, both countries may experience inflation; for PPP to hold, the exchange rate should adjust to offset the differential in the inflation rates of the two countries. If this occurs, the prices of goods in either country should appear similar to consumers. That is, consumers should note little difference in their purchasing power in the two countries.

Derivation of Purchasing Power Parity

Assume that the price indexes of the home country (h) and a foreign country (f) are equal. Now assume that over time, the home country experiences an inflation rate of I_h, while the foreign country experiences an inflation rate of I_f. Due to inflation, the price index of goods in the consumer's home country (P_h) becomes

$$P_h(1 + I_h).$$

The price index of the foreign country (P_f) will also change due to inflation in that country:

$$P_f(1 + I_f).$$

If $I_h > I_f$, and the exchange rate between the currencies of the two countries does not change, then your purchasing power is greater on foreign goods than on home goods. In this case, PPP does not exist. If $I_h < I_f$, and the exchange rate between the currencies of the two countries does not change, then your purchasing power is greater on home goods than on foreign goods. In this case also, PPP does not exist.

The theory of PPP suggests that the exchange rate will not remain constant, but will adjust to maintain the parity in purchasing power. If inflation occurs and the exchange rate of the foreign currency changes, the foreign price index from the home consumer's perspective becomes

$$P_f(1 + I_f)(1 + e_f),$$

where e_f represents the percentage change in the value of the foreign currency. According to PPP theory, the percentage change in the foreign currency (e_f) should change to maintain parity in the new price indexes of the two countries. We can solve for e_f under conditions of PPP by setting the formula for the new price index of the foreign country equal to the formula for the new price index of the home country, as follows:

$$P_f(1 + I_f)(1 + e_f) = P_h(1 + I_h).$$

Solving for e_f, we obtain

$$(1 + e_f) = \frac{P_h(1 + I_h)}{P_f(1 + I_f)}$$

$$e_f = \frac{P_h(1 + I_h)}{P_f(1 + I_f)} - 1.$$

Since P_h equals P_f (because price indexes were initially assumed equal in both countries), they cancel, leaving

$$e_f = \frac{(1 + I_h)}{(1 + I_f)} - 1$$

This formula reflects the relationship between relative inflation rates and the exchange rate according to PPP. Notice that if $I_h > I_f$, e_f should be positive. This implies that the foreign currency will appreciate when the home country's inflation exceeds the foreign country's inflation. Conversely, if $I_h < I_f$, then e_f should be negative. This implies that the foreign currency will depreciate when the foreign country's inflation exceeds the home country's inflation.

Numerical Examples of Purchasing Power Parity

As a numerical example, assume that the exchange rate is in equilibrium initially. Then the home currency experiences a 5 percent inflation rate, while the foreign country experiences a 3 percent inflation rate. According to PPP, the foreign currency will adjust as shown:

$$e_f = \frac{1 + I_h}{1 + I_f} - 1$$

$$= \frac{1 + .05}{1 + .03} - 1$$

$$= .0194, \text{ or } 1.94\%.$$

The implications are that the foreign currency should appreciate by 1.94 percent in response to the higher inflation of the home country relative to the foreign country. If this exchange rate change does occur, the price index of the foreign country will be as high as that in the home country from the perspective of consumers in the home country. Even though the inflation is lower in the foreign country, appreciation of the foreign currency pushes the foreign country's price index up from the perspective of consumers in the home country. When considering the exchange rate effect, price indexes of both countries rise by 5 percent from the home country perspective. Thus, the purchasing power on foreign goods is equal to that on the home goods.

In a second example, again assume that the exchange rate is in equilibrium initially. Then the home country experiences a 4 percent inflation rate, while the foreign country experiences a 7 percent inflation rate. According to PPP, the foreign currency will adjust as shown:

$$e_f = \frac{(1 + I_h)}{(1 + I_f)} - 1$$
$$= \frac{1 + .04}{1 + .07} - 1$$
$$= -.028, \text{ or } -2.8\%.$$

The implications are that the foreign currency should depreciate by 2.8 percent in response to the higher inflation of the foreign country relative to the home country. If this exchange rate does occur, the price index of the home country will be as high as that in the foreign country. Even though the inflation is lower in the home country, the depreciation of the foreign currency places downward pressure on the foreign country's price index from the perspective of the consumers in the home country. When considering the exchange rate impact, price indexes of both countries rise by 4 percent. Thus, PPP would still exist, due to the adjustment in the exchange rate.

A more simplified but less precise relationship based on PPP is

$$e_f \simeq I_h - I_f.$$

That is, the exchange rate percentage change should be approximately equal to the differential in inflation rates between two countries. This simplified formula is appropriate only when the inflation differential is small. To illustrate the use of this simplified formula, consider two countries, the United States and Great Britain, which trade extensively with each other. Assume an equilibrium state in which the exchange rate of the British pound is initially worth $2.00. Now assume that the United States experiences a 9 percent inflation rate, while Great Britain experiences a 5 percent inflation rate. Under these conditions, PPP theory would suggest that the British pound should appreciate by approximately 4 percent, the differential in inflation rates.

Rationale behind Purchasing Power Parity Theory

If two countries produce products that are substitutes for each other, the demand for products should adjust as inflation rates differ. In our above example, prices increase in the United States by 9 percent, versus 5 percent in Great Britain. This should initially cause U.S. consumers to increase imports from Great Britain and British consumers to lower their demand for the U.S. goods (since prices of British goods have increased by a lower rate). Such forces place upward pressure on the British pound value. The shifting in consumption from the United States to Great Britain will continue until the British pound value has appreciated to the extent that (1) the prices paid for British goods by U.S. consumers are no lower than the prices for the comparable products made in the United States, and (2) the prices paid for U.S. goods by British consumers are no higher than the prices for the comparable products made in Great Britain. The level of appreciation in the pound needed to achieve this new equilibrium situation is approximately 4 percent, as will be verified here.

Given British inflation of 5 percent and the pound's appreciation of 4 percent, U.S. consumers would be paying about 9 percent more for the British goods than they paid in the initial equilibrium state. This is equal to the 9 percent increase in prices of U.S. goods from the U.S. inflation. Consider a situation in which the pound appreciated by only 1 percent. In this case, the increased price of British goods to U.S. consumers would be approximately 6 percent (5 percent inflation and 1 percent appreciation in the British pound), which is less than the 9 percent increase in the price of U.S. goods to U.S. consumers. Thus, we would expect U.S. consumers to continue to shift their consumption to British goods. Purchasing power parity suggests that the increasing U.S. consumption of British goods by U.S. consumers would persist until the pound appreciated by about 4 percent. Any level of appreciation lower than this would represent more attractive British prices relative to U.S. prices from the U.S. consumer's viewpoint.

From the British consumer's point of view, the price of U.S. goods would have initially increased by 4 percent more than British goods. Thus, British consumers would continue to reduce imports from the United States until the pound appreciated enough to make U.S. goods no more expensive than British goods. Once the pound appreciated by 4 percent, this would partially offset the increase in U.S. prices of 9 percent from the British consumer's perspective. To be more precise, the net effect is that the prices of U.S. goods would increase by approximately 5 percent to British consumers (9 percent inflation minus the 4 percent savings to British consumers due to the pound's 4 percent appreciation).

Using Purchasing Power Parity to Forecast

The new value of the spot exchange rate of a given currency (called S_{t+1}) would be a function of the initial spot rate that existed in equilibrium (called S) and the inflation differential, as shown here:

$$S_{t+1} = S \left[1 + \frac{(1 + I_h)}{(1 + I_f)} - 1 \right]$$
$$= \frac{S(1 + I_h)}{(1 + I_f)}.$$

The approximate version (which provides reasonable estimates when the inflation differential is small) is

$$S_{t+1} = S[1 + (I_h - I_f)].$$

Recall that in our previous example, the pound was assigned an initial value of $2.00. Then the 4 percent inflation differential occurred, which, according to PPP theory, would cause the approximate adjustment:

$$S_{t+1} = S[1 + (.09 - .05)]$$
$$= \$2.00(1.04)$$
$$= \$2.08.$$

To test your understanding, consider a second example. Assume that France and the United States trade extensively with each other and that both countries produce somewhat similar products. Assume that initially the equilibrium value of the French franc (FF) is $.20. Then, assume that the U.S. experiences 1 percent inflation, while France experiences 6 percent inflation. According to PPP theory, the spot rate of the franc will adjust as follows:

$$S_{t+1} = S[1 + (.01 - .06)]$$
$$= \$.20[1 + (-.05)]$$
$$= \$.19.$$

Graphic Analysis of Purchasing Power Parity

Using PPP theory, we should be able to assess the potential impact of inflation on exchange rates. Exhibit 8.1 is a graphic representation of PPP theory. The points on the exhibit suggest that given the inflation differential between the home and

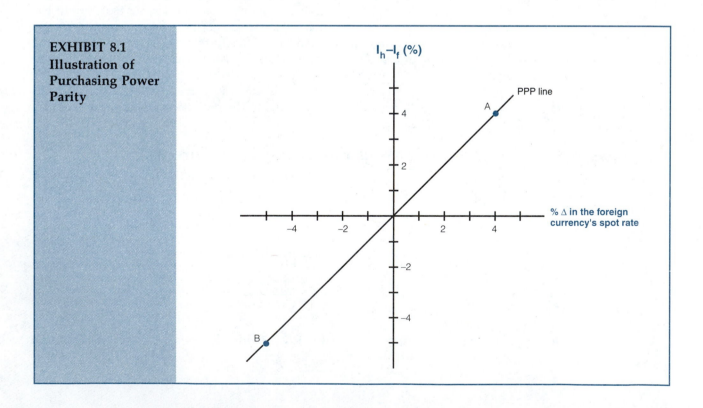

**EXHIBIT 8.1
Illustration of
Purchasing Power
Parity**

the foreign country of X percent, the foreign currency should adjust by X percent due to that inflation differential. The diagonal line connecting all these points together is known as the **PPP line.** Point A represents our example in which the U.S. (to be considered as the home country here) and British inflation rates were assumed to be 9 percent and 5 percent, respectively, so that $I_h - I_f = 4\%$. Recall that this led to the anticipated appreciation in the British pound of 4 percent, as illustrated by point A. Point B reflects the example in which the U.S. and French inflation rates were assumed to be 1 percent and 6 percent respectively, so that $I_h - I_f = -5\%$. Recall that this led to anticipated depreciation of the French franc by 5 percent, as illustrated by point B. If the exchange rate does respond to inflation differentials according to PPP theory, the actual points should lie on or close to the PPP line.

Exhibit 8.2 identifies areas of purchasing power disparity. Assume an initial equilibrium situation, then a change in the inflation rates of the two countries. If the exchange rate does not move as PPP theory would suggest, there is a disparity in the purchasing power of the two countries.

Point C in Exhibit 8.2 represents home inflation (I_h) in excess of foreign inflation (I_f) by 4 percent. Yet, the foreign currency appreciated by only 1 percent in response to this inflation differential. Consequently, purchasing power disparity exists. The home consumer's purchasing power on foreign goods has become more favorable relative to the purchasing power on the home country's goods. The PPP theory would suggest that such a disparity in purchasing power should exist only in the short run. Over time, as the home country consumers take advantage of the disparity by purchasing more foreign goods, upward pressure on the foreign currency's value will cause point C to move toward the PPP line.

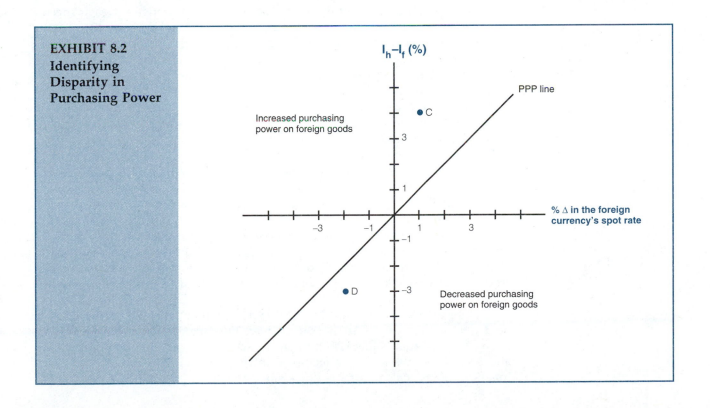

**EXHIBIT 8.2
Identifying
Disparity in
Purchasing Power**

All points to the left of (or above) the PPP line represent more favorable purchasing power on foreign goods than on home goods.

Point D in Exhibit 8.2 represents home inflation below foreign inflation by 3 percent. Yet, the foreign currency has depreciated by only 2 percent. Again, purchasing power disparity exists. The purchasing power on foreign goods has become less favorable relative to the purchasing power on the home country's goods. The PPP theory would suggest that the foreign currency in this example should have depreciated by 3 percent to fully offset the 3 percent inflation differential. Since the foreign currency did not weaken to this extent, the home country consumers may discontinue their purchasing of goods in the foreign country, causing the foreign currency to weaken to the extent anticipated by PPP theory. If so, point D would move toward the PPP line. All points to the right of (or below) the PPP line represent more favorable purchasing power on home country goods than on foreign goods.

Testing the Purchasing Power Parity Theory

The PPP theory not only provides an explanation of how relative inflation rates between two countries can influence an exchange rate, but it also provides information that could be used to forecast exchange rates. Substantial research has been conducted to examine whether PPP exists. The results of these tests will be discussed shortly. But first, how would you go about testing whether PPP exists? One simple method would be to choose two countries (say, the United States and a foreign country) and compare their differential in inflation rates to the percentage change in the foreign currency's value during several time periods. We could plot on a graph similar to Exhibit 8.2 each point representing the inflation differential and exchange rate percentage change for each specific time period, and then determine whether these points closely resemble the PPP line as drawn in Exhibit 8.2. If the points deviate significantly from the PPP line, then the percentage change in the foreign currency is not being influenced by the inflation differential in the manner PPP theory suggests.

As an alternative test of PPP, several foreign countries could be compared with the home country over a given time period. Each foreign country would exhibit an inflation differential relative to the home country, which could be compared to the exchange rate change during the period of concern. Thus, a point could be plotted on a graph such as Exhibit 8.2 for each foreign country analyzed. If the points deviated significantly from the PPP line, then the exchange rates would not be responding to the inflation differentials in accordance with PPP theory. PPP theory can be tested for any countries on which inflation information is available.

Much research has been conducted to test whether PPP exists. Recent studies by Mishkin, Adler and Dumas and by Abuaf and Jorion found evidence of significant deviations from PPP, persisting for lengthy periods. Another related study by Adler and Lehman provided evidence against PPP even over the long term.

However, recent research by Hakkio found that when an exchange rate deviated far from the value that would have been expected according to PPP, it moved toward that value. While the relationship between inflation differentials and exchange rates is not perfect even in the long run, it supports the use of inflation differentials to forecast long-run movements in exchange rates.

To further examine whether PPP is valid, Exhibit 8.3 illustrates the relationship between relative inflation rates and exchange rate movements over time. The inflation differential shown in each of the four graphs (each graph represents one foreign currency) is measured as the U.S. inflation rate minus the foreign inflation rate. The annual differential in inflation between the United States and each foreign country is represented on the vertical axis of Exhibit 8.3. In addition, the annual exchange rate percentage change of each foreign currency (relative to the U.S. dollar) is represented on the horizontal axis. If PPP existed during the period examined, the points plotted on the graph should be near an imaginary 45-degree line, which would split the axes (like the PPP line shown in Exhibit 8.2). The annual inflation differentials and exchange rate percentage changes from 1981 to 1993 are plotted.

While the results for each graph are different, some general comments apply to all graphs. The percentage changes in exchange rates are typically much more

EXHIBIT 8.3   Comparison of Annual Inflation Differentials and Exchange Rate Movements for Four Major Countries

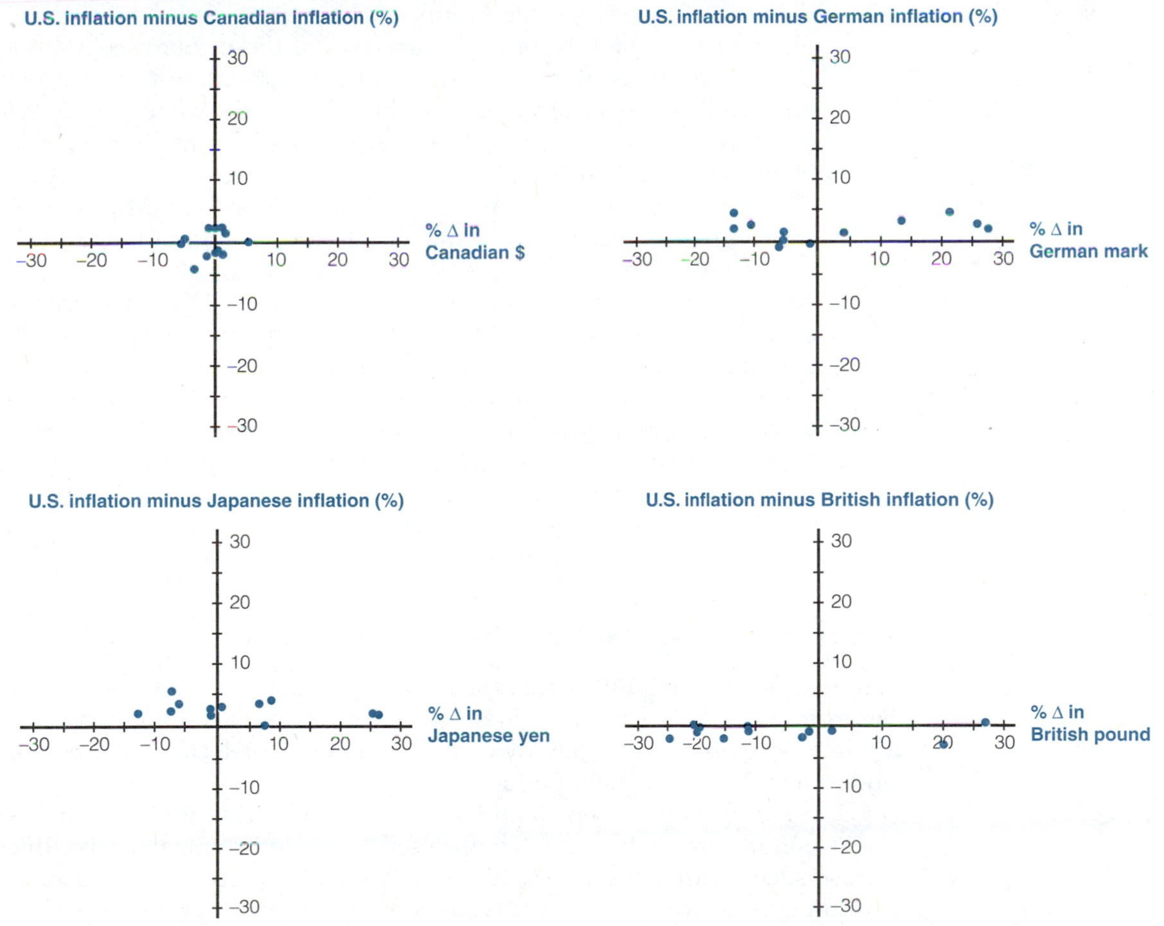

U.S. inflation minus Canadian inflation (%)

U.S. inflation minus German inflation (%)

U.S. inflation minus Japanese inflation (%)

U.S. inflation minus British inflation (%)

volatile than the inflation differentials. Thus, the exchange rates are changing to a greater degree than would be anticipated by PPP theory. In some years, even the direction of a currency could not have been anticipated by PPP theory. The results in Exhibit 8.3 suggest that the relationship between inflation differentials and exchange rate movements often becomes distorted.

Why Purchasing Power Parity Does Not Occur

Two of the most commonly proposed reasons that PPP does not consistently occur follow:

1. *Other influential factors.* Exchange rates are affected by other factors in addition to the inflation differential. Recall that differentials in interest rate and income levels as well as government controls are important. To illustrate, assume the French inflation rate is 5 percent above the U.S. inflation rate. From this information, PPP theory would suggest the French franc should depreciate by 5 percent against the U.S. dollar. Yet, if the government of France imposed trade barriers on U.S. exports, French consumers and firms could not adjust their spending in reaction to the inflation differential. Therefore, the exchange rate will not adjust.

   In the early 1990s, some European countries experienced higher inflation than the U.S. Yet, the currencies of these countries did not depreciate against the dollar because their high interest rates attracted large capital flows from U.S. investors. During the same period, Hong Kong, Singapore, and South Korea experienced relatively high inflation. However, the currencies of these countries did not depreciate against the dollar because of the large capital flows from U.S. firms and investors to capitalize on the higher interest rates and to invest in privatized businesses.

2. *No substitutes for traded goods.* The idea behind PPP theory is that as soon as the prices become relatively higher in one country, the other country will discontinue importing and shift to domestic purchases instead of importing. This shift influences the exchange rate. However, what if substitute goods are not available domestically? For example, if French inflation increases by 5 percent more than the U.S. inflation rate, U.S. consumers may not necessarily find suitable substitute goods at home. Thus, they may continue to buy the highly priced French goods and the French franc may *not* depreciate as it was originally expected to.

Limitation in Tests of Purchasing Power Parity

A limitation in testing PPP is that the results will vary with the base period used. For example, if 1978 is used as a base period, most subsequent periods will show a relatively overvalued dollar; by contrast if 1984 is used, the dollar may appear undervalued in subsequent periods.

The base period chosen should reflect an equilibrium position, since subsequent periods are evaluated in comparison to it. Unfortunately, it is difficult to choose such a base period. In fact, one of the main reasons for abolishing fixed exchange rates was the difficulty in identifying an appropriate equilibrium exchange rate.

STATISTICAL TEST OF PPP

A somewhat simplified statistical test of purchasing power parity could be developed by applying regression analysis to historical exchange rates and inflation differentials. To illustrate, let's focus on one particular exchange rate. The quarterly percentage changes in the foreign currency value (e_f) can be regressed against the inflation differential that existed at the beginning of the quarter, as shown here:

$$e_f = a_0 + a_1 \left[\frac{(1 + I_{U.S.})}{(1 + I_f)} - 1 \right] + \mu,$$

where a_0 is a constant, a_1 is the slope coefficient, and μ is an error term. Regression analysis would be applied to quarterly data to determine the regression coefficients. The hypothesized values of a_0 and a_1 are 0 and 1.0, respectively. These coefficients imply that for a given inflation differential, there is an equal offsetting percentage change in the exchange rate, on average. The appropriate t-test for each regression coefficient requires a comparison to the hypothesized value, and division by the standard error (s.e.) of the coefficient, as follows:

Test for $a_0 = 0$:   Test for $a_1 = 1$

$$t = \frac{a_0 - 0}{\text{s.e. of } a_0} \qquad t = \frac{a_1 - 1}{\text{s.e. of } a_1}.$$

The t-table would then be used to find the critical t-value. If either t-test finds that the coefficients differ significantly from what is expected, the relationship between the inflation differential and the exchange rate differs from that stated by PPP theory. It should be mentioned that the appropriate lag time between the inflation differential and exchange rate is subject to controversy. See the related references at the end of this chapter for a more comprehensive explanation of tests on PPP theory.

INTERNATIONAL FISHER EFFECT (IFE)

Along with PPP theory, another major theory in international finance is the **international Fisher effect (IFE)** theory. It uses interest rate rather than inflation rate differentials to explain why exchange rates change over time, but it is closely related to the PPP theory because interest rates are often highly correlated with inflation rates. According to the so-called **Fisher effect,** nominal risk-free interest rates contain a real rate of return and anticipated inflation. If investors of all countries require the same real return, interest rate differentials between countries may be the result of differentials in expected inflation.

Recall that PPP theory suggests that exchange rate movements are caused by inflation rate differentials. If real rates of interest are the same across countries, any difference in nominal interest rates could be attributed to the difference in expected inflation. The IFE theory suggests that foreign currencies with relatively high interest rates will depreciate because the high nominal interest rates reflect expected inflation. The nominal interest rate would also incorporate the *default risk* of an investment. The following examples focus on investments that are risk-free, so that default risk will not have to be accounted for.

Assume that investors in the United States expect a 6 percent rate of inflation over one year, and require a real return of 2 percent over one year; the nominal interest rate on one-year Treasury securities would be 8 percent. If investors in all countries required the same real rate of return for one year, then the differential in nominal interest rates among any two countries would represent their respective inflation differentials. For example, assume that the nominal interest

APPLIED RESEARCH

PURCHASING POWER PARITY IN THE LONG RUN

Purchasing power parity (PPP) can be tested by assessing a "real" exchange rate between two currencies over time. The real exchange rate is the actual exchange rate adjusted for inflationary effects in the two countries of concern. In this way, the exchange rate serves as a measure of purchasing power. If a currency weakens by 10 percent, but its home inflation is 10 percent more than inflation in the foreign country, the real exchange rate has not changed. The degree of weakness in the currency is offset by the lower inflationary effects on foreign goods.

If the real exchange rate reverts to some mean level over time, this would suggest that it is constant in the long run, and any deviations from the mean are temporary. Conversely, if the real exchange rate follows a random walk, this implies that it moves randomly without any predictable pattern. That is, it does not tend to revert to some mean level, and therefore cannot be viewed as constant in the long run. Under these conditions, the notion of purchasing power parity is rejected because the movements in the real exchange rate appear to be more than temporary deviations from some equilibrium value.

A recent study by Abuaf and Jorion tested PPP by assessing the long-run pattern of the real exchange rate. They state that the typical findings rejecting PPP in previous studies are questionable because of limitations in the methods used to test PPP. The authors find that the notion of a constant real exchange rate in the long run cannot be rejected, offering some support for PPP in the long run. They suggest that deviations from PPP are substantial in the short run, but are reduced by about half in three years. Thus, even though exchange rates deviate from the levels predicted by PPP in the short run, their deviations are reduced over the long run.

While this study shows some support for PPP in the long run, the findings are not totally conclusive. Furthermore, the authors found some evidence that PPP does not hold in the short run, which is consistent with other studies, and suggests that short-term movements in exchange rates cannot be ignored by firms.

rate is 8 percent in the United States and 5 percent in Japan. If investors in both countries require a real return of 2 percent, then the differential in expected inflation is 3 percent (6 percent in the United States versus 3 percent in Japan). According to PPP theory, the Japanese yen would be expected to appreciate by the expected inflation differential of 3 percent. If the exchange rate changes as expected, Japanese investors that attempt to capitalize on the higher U.S. interest rate would earn a return similar to what they could have earned in their own country. While the U.S. interest rate is 3 percent higher, the Japanese investors would have repurchased their yen for 3 percent more than the price at which they sold yen.

To reinforce the concept, assume that the nominal interest rate in France is 13 percent. Given that investors in France also require a real return of 2 percent, the expected inflation rate in France must be 11 percent. According to PPP theory, the French franc is expected to depreciate by approximately 5 percent against the dollar (since the French inflation rate is 5 percent higher). Therefore, U.S. investors would not benefit from investing in France, because the 5 percent interest rate differential would be offset by investing in a currency that would be worth 5 percent less by the end of the period. U.S. investors would earn 8 percent on the French investment, which is the same they could earn in the United States.

Given this information, the expected inflation differential between France and Japan is 8 percent. According to PPP theory, this inflation differential suggests that the French franc should depreciate by 8 percent against the yen. Therefore, even though Japanese investors would earn an additional 8 percent interest on a French investment, the franc would be valued at 8 percent less by the end of the period. Under these conditions, the Japanese investors would earn a return of 5 percent, which is the same as what they would earn on an investment in Japan. These possible investment opportunities, along with some others, are summarized in Exhibit 8.4. Note that wherever investors of a given country invest their funds, the expected nominal return is the same.

Derivation of the International Fisher Effect

The precise relationship between the interest rate differential of two countries and the expected exchange rate change according to IFE can be derived as follows. First, the actual return to investors who invest in money market securities (such as short-term bank deposits) in their home country is simply the interest rate offered on those securities. However, the actual return to investors who invest in a foreign money market security depends on not only the foreign interest rate (i_f), but also the percent change in the value of the foreign currency (e_f) denominating the security. The formula for the actual or so-called "effective" (exchange rate adjusted) return on a foreign bank deposit (or any money market security) is

$$r = (1 + i_f)(1 + e_f) - 1.$$

According to the IFE, the effective return on a home investment should on average be equal to the effective return on a foreign investment. That is,

$$r = i_h.$$

Where r is the effective return on the foreign deposit and i_h is the interest rate on the home deposit. We can determine the degree by which the foreign currency must change in order to make investments in both countries generate similar returns. Take the previous formula for what determines r, and set it equal to i_h as follows:

$$r = i_h$$
$$(1 + i_f)(1 + e_f) - 1 = i_h.$$

Now solve for e_f:

$$(1 + i_f)(1 + e_f) = (1 + i_h)$$
$$(1 + e_f) = \frac{(1 + i_h)}{(1 + i_f)}$$
$$e_f = \frac{(1 + i_h)}{(1 + i_f)} - 1.$$

As verified here, the IFE theory contends that when $i_h > i_f$, e_f will be positive. That is, the foreign currency will appreciate when the foreign interest rate is

EXHIBIT 8.4 Illustration of the International Fisher Effect (IFE) from Various Investor Perspectives

Investors residing in	Attempt to invest in	Expected inflation differential (home inflation minus foreign inflation)	Expected percentage change in currency needed by investors	Nominal interest rate to be earned	Return to investors after considering exchange rate adjustment	Inflation anticipated in home country	Real return earned by investors
Japan	Japan	—	—	5%	5%	3%	2%
	U.S.	3% − 6% = −3%	−3%	8	5	3	2
	France	3% − 11% = −8%	−8	13	5	3	2
U.S.	Japan	6% − 3% = 3%	3	5	8	6	2
	U.S.	—	—	8	8	6	2
	France	6% − 11% = −5	5	13	8	6	2
France	Japan	11% − 3% = 8%	8	5	13	11	2
	U.S.	11% − 6% = 5%	5	8	13	11	2
	France	—	—	13	13	11	2

lower than the home interest rate. This appreciation will improve the foreign return to investors from the home country, making returns on foreign securities similar to returns on home securities. Conversely, when $i_f > i_h$, e_f will be negative. That is, the foreign currency will depreciate when the foreign interest rate exceeds the home interest rate. This depreciation will reduce the return on foreign securities from the perspective of investors in the home country, making returns on foreign securities no higher than returns on home securities.

As a numerical example, assume that the interest rate on a one-year insured home bank deposit is 11 percent and the interest rate on a one-year insured foreign bank deposit is 12 percent. For the actual returns of these two investments to be similar from the perspective of investors in the home country, the foreign currency would have to change over the investment horizon by the following percentage:

$$e_f = \frac{(1 + i_h)}{(1 + i_f)} - 1$$

$$= \frac{(1 + .11)}{(1 + .12)} - 1$$

$$= -.0089, \text{ or } -.89\%.$$

The implications are that the foreign currency denominating the foreign deposit would need to depreciate by .89 percent in order to make the actual return on the foreign deposit equal to 11 percent from the perspective of investors in the home country. This would then make the return on the foreign investment equal to the return on a domestic investment. A more simplified but less precise rule of the IFE is

$$e_f \simeq ih - i_f.$$

That is, the exchange rate percentage change over the investment horizon will equal the interest rate differential between two countries. This approximation provides reasonable estimates only when the interest rate differential is small. For example, if the British rate on six-month deposits were 2 percent above the U.S. interest rate, the British pound would depreciate by approximately 2 percent over six months, according to IFE. If this occurred, U.S. investors would earn about the same return on British deposits as they would on U.S. deposits. Thus, there would be no advantage to the foreign investments, even though they exhibited a higher interest rate than domestic investments.

Graphic Analysis of the International Fisher Effect

Exhibit 8.5 displays the set of points that conform to the argument behind IFE theory. For example, point E reflects a situation in which the foreign interest exceeded the home interest rate by three percentage points. Yet, the foreign currency has depreciated by 3 percent, to offset its interest rate advantage. Thus, an investor setting up a deposit in the foreign country would achieve a return similar to what is possible domestically. Point F represents a home interest rate 2 percent above the foreign interest rate. If investors from the home country establish a foreign deposit, they are at a disadvantage regarding the foreign

**EXHIBIT 8.5
Illustration of IFE
Line**
(when exchange rate
changes perfectly
offset interest rate
differentials)

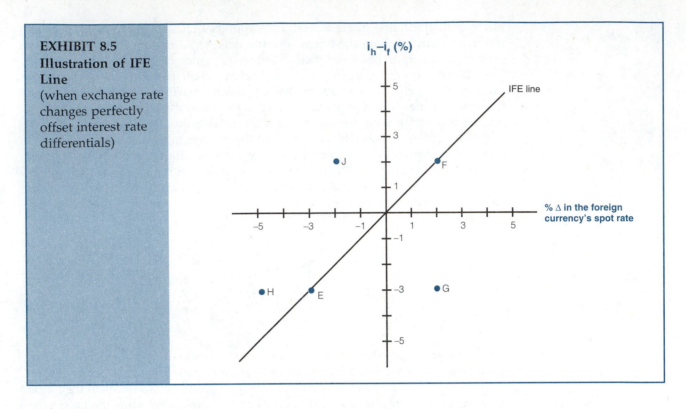

interest rate. However, IFE theory suggests that the currency should appreciate by 2 percent to offset the interest rate disadvantage.

Point F in Exhibit 8.5 can also illustrate the IFE from a foreign investor's perspective. The home interest would appear attractive to the foreign investor. However, IFE theory suggests the foreign currency will appreciate by 2 percent, which, from the foreign investor's perspective, implies the home country's currency denominating the investment instruments would depreciate to offset the interest rate advantage.

All the points along the so-called **IFE line** in Exhibit 8.5 reflect exchange rate adjustment to offset the differential in interest rates. This means an investor will end up achieving the same yield (adjusted for exchange rate fluctuations) whether investing at home or in a foreign country.

To be precise, IFE theory does not suggest this relationship will exist over each time period. The point of IFE theory is that if a corporation periodically makes foreign investments to take advantage of higher foreign interest rates, it will achieve a yield that is sometimes above and sometimes below the domestic yield. Periodic investment by a U.S. corporation that attempts to capitalize on the higher interest rates would on the average, therefore, achieve a similar yield if it simply made domestic deposits periodically.

Points below the IFE line generally reflect the higher returns from investing in foreign deposits. For example, point G in Exhibit 8.5 suggests that the foreign interest rate exceeds the home interest rate by 3 percent. In addition, the foreign currency has appreciated by 2 percent. The combination of the higher foreign interest rate plus the appreciation of the foreign currency will cause the foreign yield to be higher than what is possible domestically. If actual data were

APPLIED RESEARCH

STATISTICAL TEST OF IFE

A somewhat simplified statistical test of the international Fisher effect can be developed by applying regression analysis to historical exchange rates and the nominal interest rate differential. The percentage changes in the foreign currency value (e_f) can be regressed against the nominal interest rate differential that existed at the beginning of the quarter:

$$e_f = a_0 + a_1 \left[\frac{1 + i_{U.S.}}{1 + i_f} - 1 \right] + \mu$$

where a_0 is a constant, a_1 is the slope coefficient, and μ is an error term. Regression analysis would determine the regression coefficients. The hypothesized values of a_0 and a_1 are 0 and 1.0, respectively. These coefficients imply that a given differential in nominal interest rates is offset on average by an equal percentage change in the exchange rate.

The appropriate t-test for each regression coefficient requires a comparison to the hypothesized value and then division by the standard error (s.e.) of the coefficients, as follows:

Test for $a_0 = 0$

$$t = \frac{a_0 - 0}{\text{s.e. of } a_0}$$

Test for $a_1 = 1$

$$t = \frac{a_1 - 1}{\text{s.e. of } a_1}$$

The t-table is then used to find the critical t-value. If either t-test finds that the coefficients differ significantly from what was hypothesized, the IFE is refuted.

compiled and plotted, and the vast majority of points were below the IFE line, this would suggest that investors of the home country could consistently increase their investment returns by establishing foreign bank deposits. Such results would refute the IFE theory.

Points above the IFE line generally reflect returns from foreign deposits that are lower than the returns possible domestically. For example, point H reflects a foreign interest rate that is 3 percent above the home interest rate. Yet, point H suggests that the exchange rate of the foreign currency has depreciated by 5 percent, to more than offset its interest rate advantage.

As another example, point J represents a situation in which an investor of the home country is hampered in two ways by investing in a foreign deposit. First, the foreign interest rate is lower than the home interest rate. Second, the foreign currency has depreciated during the time the foreign deposit has been held. If actual data were compiled and plotted, and the vast majority of points were above the IFE line, this would suggest that investors of the home country would receive consistently lower returns from foreign investments as opposed to investments in the home country. Such results would refute the IFE theory.

If the actual points (one for each period) of interest rates and exchange rate changes were plotted over time on a graph such as Exhibit 8.5, we could determine whether the points are systematically below the IFE line (suggesting higher returns from foreign investing), above the line (suggesting lower returns from foreign investing), or evenly scattered on both sides (suggesting a balance of higher returns from foreign investing in some periods, and lower foreign returns in other periods).

Exhibit 8.6 is an example of a set of points that tend to support the IFE theory. The implications are that returns from short-term foreign investments are on the average about equal to the returns that are possible domestically. Notice that each individual point reflects a change in the exchange rate that does not

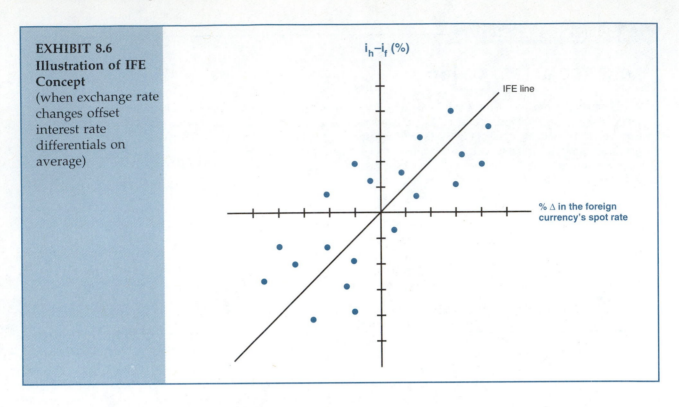

**EXHIBIT 8.6
Illustration of IFE
Concept**
(when exchange rate
changes offset
interest rate
differentials on
average)

exactly offset the interest rate differential. In some cases, the exchange rate change does not fully offset the interest rate differential. In other cases, the exchange rate change has more than offset the interest rate differential. Overall, the results balance out such that the interest rate differentials are *on the average* offset by changes in the exchange rates. Thus, foreign investments have generated yields that are on the average equal to those of domestic investments.

If foreign yields are expected to be about equal to domestic yields, a U.S. firm would most probably prefer the domestic investments, because the yield on domestic short-term securities (such as bank deposits) is known in advance. However, the yield to be attained from foreign short-term securities is uncertain, due to the uncertainty of the spot exchange rate that will exist when the security matures. Investors generally prefer an investment whose return is known over an investment whose return is uncertain, assuming that all other features of the investments are similar.

Tests of the International Fisher Effect

Whether the IFE holds in reality depends on the particular time period examined. From 1974 to 1977, the U.S. interest rates were generally lower than foreign interest rates. As IFE theory would predict, these foreign currencies weakened during this period. In 1978–1979, the U.S. interest rates were generally higher than foreign interest rates, and the foreign currency values strengthened during this period (again supporting IFE theory to an extent). However, during the 1980–1984 period, the foreign currencies consistently weakened far beyond what would have been anticipated according to IFE theory. Furthermore, during the

1985–1987 period, foreign currencies strengthened to a much greater degree than suggested by the interest differential. While the IFE theory may hold during some time frames, there is evidence that it does not consistently hold.

If the IFE holds, then a strategy of borrowing in one country and investing the funds in another country should not provide a positive return on average. The reason is that exchange rates should adjust to offset interest rate differentials on the average. Research by Madura and Nosari simulated a speculative strategy whereby the currency with the lowest quoted interest rate was borrowed by a U.S. speculator and converted and invested in the currency exhibiting the highest interest rate. At the end of the investment period, the funds were withdrawn and loan repayment was made. This strategy was continued periodically over time. If the IFE held for these periods, the *spread* (difference between return on the investment and cost of borrowing) should have been zero on average (in the absence of transaction costs). The trend of spreads during the various periods is illustrated in Exhibit 8.7, showing that the spread was usually positive.

The process described here was repeated from the perspective of speculative investors in seven other major countries. Regardless of the perspective, the spread was found to be significantly above zero, on average. These results refute the IFE theory.

A related study by Thomas tested the IFE theory by examining the results of (1) purchasing currency futures contracts of currencies with high interest rates that contained discounts (relative to the spot rates) and (2) selling futures on currencies with low interest rates that contained premiums. If the high-interest-rate currencies depreciated and the low-interest-rate currencies appreciated to the extent suggested by the IFE theory, the strategy described here would not generate significant profits. However, 123 (57 percent) of the 216 transactions created by this strategy were profitable. In addition, the average gain was much higher than the average loss. The rate of return averaged 77 percent on an annual basis. This study indicates that the IFE does not hold—which is not to say that all MNCs should immediately place all excess cash in high-interest-rate currencies. There is significant risk in such a strategy, as verified by the existence of losses generated in some periods of the study.

EXHIBIT 8.7

Assessing Speculative Spreads to Determine Whether the IFE Holds

SOURCE: Akron Business and Economic Review (Winter 1984), p. 51.

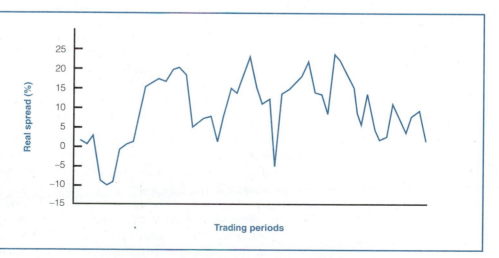

Why the International Fisher Effect Does Not Occur

Earlier in this chapter, we have mentioned that purchasing power parity has not held over certain periods. Since the international Fisher effect is based on purchasing power parity, it does not consistently hold either. Because there are factors other than inflation that affect exchange rates, the exchange rates do not adjust in accordance with the inflation differential. Assume a nominal interest rate in a foreign country that is 3 percent above the U.S. rate because expected inflation in that country is 3 percent above expected U.S. inflation. Even if these nominal rates properly reflect inflationary expectations, the exchange rate of the foreign currency will react to other factors in addition to the inflation differential. If these other factors place upward pressure on the foreign currency's value, they will offset the downward pressure placed by the inflation differential. Consequently, foreign investments will achieve higher returns for the U.S. investors than domestic investments will.

COMPARISON OF IRP, PPP, AND IFE THEORIES

At this point, it may be helpful to compare three related theories of international finance: (1) interest rate parity (IRP), discussed in Chapter 7, (2) purchasing power parity (PPP), and (3) the international Fisher effect (IFE). Exhibit 8.8 summarizes the main theme of each theory. Note that all three theories relate to the determination of exchange rates. Yet, they differ in their implications. The theory of IRP focuses on why the forward rate differs from the spot rate and on the degree of difference that should exist. This relates to a specific point in time. Conversely, PPP theory and IFE theory focus on how a currency's spot rate will change over time. While PPP theory suggests that the spot rate will change in accordance with inflation differentials, IFE theory suggests that it will change in accordance with interest rate differentials. PPP is nevertheless related to IFE because inflation differentials influence the nominal interest rate differentials between two countries.

SUMMARY

■ Purchasing power parity (PPP) theory specifies a precise relationship between relative inflation rates of two countries and their exchange rate. In inexact terms, PPP theory suggests that the equilibrium exchange rate will adjust by the same magnitude as the differential in inflation rates between two countries. While PPP continues to be a valuable concept, there is evidence of sizable deviations from the theory in the real world.

■ The international Fisher effect (IFE) specifies a precise relationship between relative interest rates of two countries and their exchange rates. It suggests that an investor who periodically invests in foreign interest-bearing securities will on average achieve a return similar to what is possible domestically. This implies that the exchange rate of the country with high interest rates will depreciate to offset the interest rate advantage achieved by foreign investments. However, there is evidence that during some periods the IFE does not hold. Thus, investment in foreign short-term securities may achieve a higher return than

EXHIBIT 8.8   Comparison of IRP, PPP, and IFE Theories

Theory	Key Variables of Theory		Summary of Theory
Interest rate parity (IRP)	Forward rate premium (or discount)	Interest rate differential	The forward rate of one currency with respect to another will contain a premium (or discount) that is determined by the differential in interest rates between the two countries. As a result, covered interest arbitrage will provide a return that is no higher than a domestic return.
Purchasing power parity (PPP)	Percentage change in spot exchange rate	Inflation rate differential	The spot rate of one currency with respect to another will change in reaction to the differential in inflation rates between the two countries. Consequently, the purchasing power for consumers when purchasing goods in their own country will be similar to their purchasing power when importing goods from the foreign country.
International Fisher effect (IFE)	Percentage change in spot exchange rate	Interest rate differential	The spot rate of one currency with respect to another will change in accordance with the differential in interest rates between the two countries. Consequently, the return on uncovered foreign money market securities will on average be no higher than the return on domestic money market securities from the perspective of investors in the home country.

what is possible domestically. If a firm attempts achieving this higher return, however, it does incur the risk that the currency denominating the foreign security might depreciate against the investor's home currency during the investment period. In this case, the foreign security could generate a lower return than a domestic security, even if it exhibits a higher interest rate.

■ The PPP theory focuses on the relationship between the inflation rate differential and future exchange rate movements. The IFE focuses on the interest rate differential and future exchange rate movements. The theory of interest rate parity (IRP) focuses on the relationship between the interest rate differential and the forward rate premium (or discount) at a given point in time.

If IRP exists, it is not possible to benefit from covered interest arbitrage. Investors can still attempt to benefit from high foreign interest rates if they remain uncovered (do not sell the currency forward). But IFE suggests that this strategy will not generate higher returns than what are possible domestically, because the exchange rate is expected to decline on average by the amount of the interest rate differential.

SELF-TEST FOR CHAPTER 8 _____

(Answers are provided in Appendix A in the back of the text.)

1. A U.S. importer of Japanese computer supplies pays for the supplies in yen. The importer is not concerned about the possible increase in Japanese prices (charged in yen) because of the likely offsetting effect caused by purchasing power parity (PPP). Explain what this means.

2. Use what you know about tests of PPP to answer this question. Using the information in the first question, explain why the U.S. importer of Japanese supplies would be concerned about its future payments.

3. Before the 1990s, currencies of the Eastern Bloc countries were not convertible into dollars. Assume that these currencies are set against the dollar, but that large inflation occurs in these countries over time. Use purchasing power parity to explain how the values of these currencies will be affected.

4. Assume that the Canadian dollar's spot rate is $.85 and that the Canadian and U.S. inflation rates are similar. Then assume that the Canadian experiences 4 percent inflation, while the U.S. experiences 3 percent inflation. According to purchasing power parity, what will be the new value of the Canadian dollar after it adjusts to the inflationary changes? (You may use the approximate formula to answer this question).

5. Assume that the Australian dollar's spot rate is $.90 and that the Australian and U.S. one-year interest rates were initially 6 percent. Then assume that the Australian one-year interest rate increases by 5 percentage points, while the U.S. one-year interest rate remains unchanged. Using this information and the international Fisher effect (IFE) theory, forecast the spot rate for one year ahead.

6. In the previous question, the Australian interest rates increased from 6 percent to 11 percent. According to the international Fisher effect (IFE), what is the underlying factor that would cause such a change? Give an explanation based on IFE of the forces that would cause a change in the Australian dollar. If U.S. investors believed in the IFE, would they attempt to capitalize on the higher Australian interest rates? Explain.

QUESTIONS _____

1. Explain the theory of purchasing power parity (PPP). Based on this theory, what is the general forecast of the values of currencies in highly inflated countries?

2. Explain the rationale behind purchasing power parity theory.

3. Explain how you could determine whether purchasing power parity exists.

4. Inflation differentials between the U.S. and industrialized countries have typically been a few percentage points in any given year. Yet, there have

been many years in which annual exchange rates between the corresponding currencies have changed by 10 percent or more. What does this information suggest about purchasing power parity (PPP)?

5. Explain why purchasing power parity does not hold.

6. Describe a limitation in testing whether purchasing power parity holds.

7. Explain the international Fisher effect (IFE). What are the implications of IFE to firms with excess cash that consistently invest in foreign Treasury bills?

8. What is the rationale for the existence of the international Fisher effect?

9. Assume U.S. interest rates are generally above foreign interest rates. What does this suggest about the future strength or weakness of the dollar based on the international Fisher effect? Explain.

10. Compare and contrast interest rate parity (discussed in the previous chapter), purchasing power parity (PPP), and the international Fisher effect (IFE).

11. One assumption made in developing the international Fisher effect is that all investors in all countries require the same real return. What does this mean?

12. How could you use regression analysis to determine whether the relationship specified by purchasing power parity (PPP) exists on average? Specify the model, and describe how you would assess the regression results to determine if there is a *significant* difference from the relationship suggested by PPP.

13. Describe a statistical test for the international Fisher effect.

14. If investors in the United States and Canada required the same real return, and the nominal rate of interest were 2 percent higher in Canada, what would this imply about expectations of U.S. inflation and Canadian inflation? What do these inflationary expectations suggest about future exchange rates?

15. Some countries with high inflation rates tend to have high interest rates. Why?

16. Currencies of some Latin American countries, such as Brazil and Argentina, consistently weaken against most other currencies. What concept in this chapter would explain this occurrence?

17. Japan has typically had lower inflation than the United States. How would one expect this to affect the Japanese yen's value? Why has this expected relationship not always occurred?

18. Assume that the nominal interest rate in Mexico is 48 percent and the interest rate in the United States is 8 percent for one-year securities that are free from default risk. What would the international Fisher effect suggest about the differential in expected inflation in these two countries? Using this information and the purchasing power parity theory, describe the expected nominal return to U.S. investors who invest in Mexico.

19. Shouldn't the international Fisher effect discourage investors from attempting to capitalize on higher foreign interest rates? Why do some investors continue to invest overseas, even when they have no other transactions overseas?

20. Assume that the inflation rate in France is expected to increase substantially. How would this affect French nominal interest rates and the French exchange rate? If the international Fisher effect holds, how would the nominal return to U.S. investors who invest in France be affected by the higher inflation in France? Explain.

21. How is it possible for purchasing power parity to hold, if the international Fisher effect does not?

22. Explain why the international Fisher effect may not hold.

23. Assume that the spot exchange rate of the British pound is $1.73. How would this spot rate adjust according to purchasing power parity if Great Britain experiences an inflation rate of 7 percent while the United States experiences an inflation rate of 2 percent?

24. Assume the spot exchange rate of the Swiss franc is $.70. The one-year interest rate is 11 percent in the United States and 7 percent in Switzerland. What would be the spot rate in one year according to the international Fisher effect? (You may use the approximate formula to answer this question.)

25. As of today, assume the following information is available:

	U.S.	France
Real rate of interest required by investors	2%	2%
Nominal interest rate	11%	15%
Spot rate rate	—	$.20
One-year forward rate	—	$.19

a) Use the forward rate to forecast the percentage change in the French franc over the next year.

b) Use the differential in expected inflation to forecast the percentage change in the French franc over the next year.

c) Use the spot rate to forecast the percentage change in the French franc over the next year.

26. During February 1990, interest rates of the German mark rose to their highest level in seven years. The increase was mostly attributed to the strong demand for funds in West Germany as a result of the reunification effort with East Germany. Explain how the forward premium of the German mark would likely be affected by this event. How would the forecast of the percentage change in the mark be affected by the increased German interest rates, according to the international Fisher effect?

27. Would PPP be more likely to hold between the United States and Hungary if trade barriers were completely removed and if Hungary's currency were allowed to float without any government intervention? Explain.

28. Would IFE be more likely to hold between the United States and Hungary if trade barriers were completely removed and if Hungary's currency were allowed to float without any government intervention? Explain.

CASE: INFLATION AND EXCHANGE RATES IN RUSSIA

Ruble Plunges Over 15% to Low Against Dollar

By a WALL STREET JOURNAL *Staff Reporter*

MOSCOW—As Russia strains under political chaos and worsening inflation, the ruble fell to its lowest level ever against the dollar.

The Russian currency dropped more than 15% of its value yesterday, trading at 1,299 to the dollar at the Moscow Interbank Currency Exchange, which sets Russia's benchmark exchange rate. That compares with 1,102 rubles to the dollar Wednesday and 1,036 Tuesday, just before President Boris Yeltsin ordered the nation's legislature to disband. The currency's previous low had been 1,116 to the dollar on June 15.

Adding fuel to the ruble's weakness is inflation, which has begun to edge up again. In August, alone, inflation spurted to between 25% and 30%, compared with July's monthly level of about 19%. According to Grigory Yavlinsky, an independent economist, inflation is rising about 1% a day this month.

To help fight the problem, Russia's Central Bank yesterday raised its discount rate to 180% from 170%. When reflecting interest-rate compounding, the annual discount rate works out to more than twice the previous level. Still, it is well below the annual inflation rate, currently about 800%.

Source: *The Wall Street Journal* (September 24, 1993): p. A82. Reprinted by permission of The Wall Street Journal. © 1993 Dow Jones & Company, Inc. All rights reserved worldwide.

QUESTIONS

1. Explain why the Russian inflation of about 800 percent was placing severe pressure on the value of the Russian ruble.

2. Does the effect of Russian inflation on the decline of the ruble's value support the theory of purchasing power parity (PPP)? How might the relationship be distorted by political conditions in Russia?

3. Does it appear that the prices of Russian goods will be equal to the prices of U.S. goods from the perspective of Russian consumers (after considering exchange rates)? Explain.

4. Given the 800 percent inflation and the decline in the ruble, will the effects offset each other for U.S. importers? That is, how will U.S. importers of Russian goods be affected by the conditions?

**CASE
PROBLEM**

FLAME FIXTURES INC.
Business Application of Purchasing Power Parity

Flame Fixtures Inc. is a small U.S. business in Arizona that produces and sells lamp fixtures. Its costs and its revenues have been very stable over time. Its profits have been adequate, but Flame has been searching for means of increasing profits in the future. It has recently been negotiating with a Mexican firm called Coron' Company, from which it would purchase some of the necessary parts. Every three months Coron' Company would send a specified number of parts with the bill invoiced in Mexican pesos. By having the parts produced by Coron', the company is expected to save about 20 percent on production costs. Coron' is only willing to work out a deal if it is assured that it will receive a minimum specified amount of orders every three months over the next ten years, for a minimum specified amount. Flame will be required to use its assets to serve as collateral in case it does not fulfill its obligation.

The price of the parts will change over time in response to the costs of production. Flame recognizes that the cost to Coron' will increase substantially over time, as a result of the very high inflation rate in Mexico. Therefore, the price charged in pesos will likely rise substantially every three months. However, Flame feels that because of the concept of purchasing power parity (PPP), its dollar payments to Coron' will be very stable. According to PPP, if Mexican inflation is much higher than U.S. inflation, the peso will weaken against the dollar by that difference. Since Flame does not have much liquidity, it could experience a severe cash shortage if its expenses were much higher than anticipated.

The demand for Flame's product has been very stable, and is expected to continue that way. Since the U.S. inflation rate is expected to be very low, Flame will likely continue pricing its lamps at today's prices (in dollars). It believes that by saving 20 percent on production costs, it will substantially increase its profits. It is about ready to sign a contract with Coron' Company.

a) Describe a scenario that could cause Flame to save even more than 20 percent on production costs.

b) Describe a scenario that could cause Flame to actually incur higher production costs than if it simply had the parts produced in the U.S.

c) Do you think that Flame will experience stable dollar outflow payments to Coron' over time? Explain. (Assume that the number of parts ordered is constant over time).

d) Do you think that Flame's risk changes at all as a result of its new relationship with Coron' Company? Explain.

PROJECT _____

Use data from the Data Bank in the back of this text to determine whether a U.S. investor could have earned a higher return (on average) on consecutive investments in the United Kingdom than in the U.S. Assess several historical periods. What do your results imply about the international Fisher effect?

REFERENCES _____

Abuaf, Niso, and Philippe Jorion. "Purchasing Power in the Long Run." *Journal of Finance* (March 1990), pp. 157–174.

Adler, Michael, and Bernard Dumas. "International Portfolio Choice and Corporate Finance: A Synthesis." *Journal of Finance* (June 1983), pp. 925–984.

Adler, Michael, and Bruce Lehmann. "Deviations from Purchasing Power Parity in the Long Run." *Journal of Finance* (December 1983), pp. 1471–1487.

Brittain, Bruce. "Tests of Theories of Exchange Rate Determination." *Journal of Finance* (May 1977), pp. 519–529.

Cornell, Bradford. "Inflation, Relative Price Changes, and Exchange Risk." *Financial Management* (Autumn 1980), pp. 30–34.

____. "Relative Price Changes and Deviations from Purchasing Power Parity." *Journal of Banking and Finance* (September 1979), pp. 263–279.

Cumby, Robert E., and Maurice Obstfeld. "A Note on Exchange-Rate Expectations and Nominal Interest Differentials: A Test of the Fisher Hypothesis." *Journal of Finance* (June 1981), pp. 697–703.

Dornbusch, Rudiger. "Flexible Exchange Rates and Interdependence." *International Monetary Fund Staff Papers* (March 1983), pp. 3–38.

Dueker, Michael J., "Hypothesis Testing with Near-Unit Roots: The Case of Long-run Purchasing Power Parity," *Review,* Federal Reserve Bank of St. Louis, July/August 1993, pp 37–48.

Frenkel, Jacob A. "Purchasing Power Parity: Doctrinal Perspective and Evidence from the 1920s." *Journal of International Economics* (May 1978), pp. 169–192.

____. "Flexible Exchange Rates, Prices, and the Role of News: Lessons from the 1970s." *Journal of Political Economy* (August 1981), pp. 665–705.

Fung, Hung-Gay and Wai-Chung, Lo, "Deviations from Purchasing Power Parity," *Financial Review,* November 1992, pp 553–570.

Geweke, J., and E. Feige. "Some Joint Tests of the Efficiency of Markets for Forward Foreign Exchange." *Review of Economics and Statistics* (October 1979), pp. 334–341.

Hakkio, Craig S., "Interest Rates and Exchange Rates—What Is the Relationship?" *Economic Review,* Federal Reserve Bank of Kansas City (November 1986), pp. 33–43.

_____ . "Is Purchasing Power Parity a Useful Guide to the Dollar?" *Economic Review,* Federal Reserve Bank of Kansas City (Third Quarter 1992), pp. 37–51.

Huang, Roger. "Risk and Parity in Purchasing Power." *Journal of Money, Credit, and Banking* (August 1990), pp. 338–356.

Kahn, George A., "Inflation and Disinflation: A Comparison across Countries." *Economic Review,* Federal Reserve Bank of Kansas City, (February 1985), pp. 23–42.

Kim, Yoonbai. "Purchasing Power in the Long Run: A Cointegration Approach." *Journal of Money, Credit, and Banking* (November 1990), pp. 491–503.

Koveos, Peter, and Bruce Seifert, "Purchasing Power Parity and Black Markets." *Financial Management* (Autumn 1985), pp. 40–46.

Krugman, Paul R. "Purchasing Power Parity and Exchange Rates." *Journal of International Economics* (August 1978), pp. 397–407.

Madura, Jeff, and E. Joe Nosari. "Speculative Trading in the Eurocurrency Market." Akron Business and Economic Review (Winter 1984), pp. 48–52.

Manzur, Meher. "An International Comparison of Prices and Exchange Rates: A New Test of Purchasing Power Parity." *Journal of International Money and Finance* (March 1990), pp. 75–91.

Mishkin, Frederic S., "Are Real Interest Rates Equal across Countries? An Empirical Investigation of International Parity Conditions." *Journal of Finance* (December 1984), pp. 1345–1357.

Thomas, Lee R., "A Winning Strategy for Currency-futures Speculation." *Journal of Portfolio Management* (Fall 1985), pp. 65–69.

Thornton, Daniel L. "Tests of Covered Interest Rate Parity." *Review,* Federal Reserve Bank of St. Louis. (July–August 1989), pp. 55–66.

Tootell, Geoffrey M.B., "Purchasing Power Parity Wtihin the U.S.," *New England Economic Review,* July/August 1992, pp. 15–24.

Whitt, Joseph A., Jr. "Purchasing-Power Parity and Exchange Rates in the Long Run." *Economic Review,* Federal Reserve Bank of Atlanta (July–August 1989), pp. 18–32.

Whitt, Joseph A. Jr., Paul D. Koch, and Jeffrey A. Rosensweig, "The Dollar and Prices: An Empirical Analysis," *Economic Review,* Federal Reserve Bank of Atlanta (October 1986), pp. 4–18.

Wolff, Christian, "Forward Foreign Exchange Rates, Expected Spot Rates, and Premia: A Signal-Extraction Approach," *Journal of Finance (June 1987)*, pp. 395–406.

EXCHANGE RATE BEHAVIOR

1. As an employee of the foreign exchange department for a large company, you have been given the following information.

Beginning of Year
Spot rate of £ = $1.596
Spot rate of SF = $.70
Cross Exchange rate: £1 = SF2.28
One-year Forward rate of SF = $.71
One-year Forward rate of £ = $1.58004
One-year U.S. interest rate = 8.00%
One-year British interest rate = 9.09%
One-year Swiss interest rate = 7.00%

Determine whether triangular arbitrage is feasible, and if so, how it would be conducted to make a profit.

2. Using the information in Question 1, determine whether covered interest arbitrage is feasible, and if so, how it would be conducted to make a profit.

3. Based on the information in Question 1 for the beginning of the year, use the international Fisher effect (IFE) theory to forecast the annual percentage change in the British pound's value over the year.

4. Assume that at the beginning of the year, the pound's value is in equilibrium. Assume that over the year, the British inflation rate is 6 percent, while the U.S. inflation rate is 4 percent. Assume that any change in the pound's value due to the inflation differential has occurred by the end of the year. Using this information and the information provided in Question 1, determine how the pound's value changed over the year.

5. Assume that the pound's depreciation over the year has been attributed directly to central bank intervention. Explain the type of direct intervention that would place downward pressure on the value of the pound.

EXCHANGE RATE RISK MANAGEMENT

Part 3 (Chapters 9 through 12) explains the various functions involved in managing exposure to exchange rate risk. Chapter 9 describes various methods used to forecast exchange rates and explains how to assess forecasting performance. Chapter 10 demonstrates how to measure exposure to exchange rate movements. Given a firm's exposure and forecasts of future exchange rates, Chapters 11 and 12 explain how to hedge that exposure.

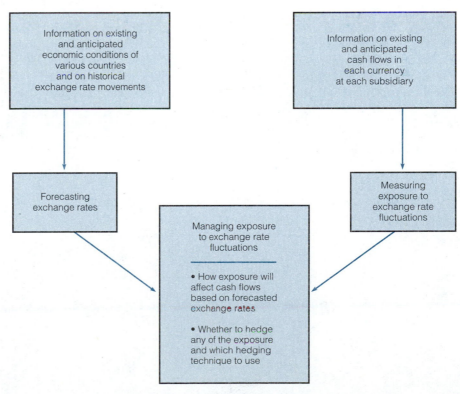

CHAPTER 9

FORECASTING EXCHANGE RATES

The decisions of a multinational corporation (MNC) are influenced by exchange rate projections. The specific objectives of this chapter are to

- explain how firms can benefit from forecasting exchange rates,
- describe the common techniques used for forecasting, and
- explain how forecasting performance can be evaluated.

WHY FIRMS FORECAST EXCHANGE RATES

Virtually every operation of an MNC can be influenced by changes in exchange rates. Several corporate functions for which exchange rate forecasts are necessary follow:

1. *Hedging decision.* MNCs are constantly confronted with the decision of whether to hedge future payables and receivables in foreign currencies. Whether a firm hedges may be determined by its forecasts of foreign currency values. As a simple example, consider a firm in the United States that plans to pay for steel imported from France in 90 days. If the forecasted value of the French franc in 90 days is sufficiently below the 90-day forward rate, the MNC may decide not to hedge.

2. *Short-term financing decision.* When large corporations borrow, they have access to several different currencies. The currency they borrow will ideally (1) exhibit a low interest rate and (2) weaken in value over the financing period. If, for example, a U.S. firm borrowed Swiss francs, and the Swiss franc depreciated against the U.S. dollar over the financing period, the firm could pay back the loan with fewer dollars (when converting those dollars in exchange for the amount owed in francs). This financing decision should therefore be influenced by exchange rate forecasts of any currencies available for financing.

3. *Short-term investment decision.* Corporations sometimes have a substantial amount of excess cash available for a short term. Large deposits can be

established in several currencies. The ideal currency for deposits would (1) exhibit a high interest rate and (2) strengthen in value over the investment period. Consider, for example, a U.S. corporation that has excess cash deposited into a British bank account, and assume the British pound has appreciated against the dollar by the end of the deposit period. As the British pounds are withdrawn and exchanged for U.S. dollars, more dollars will be received, due to the pound's appreciation against the dollar. Exchange rate forecasts of the currencies denominating available deposit accounts should therefore be considered when determining where to invest the short-term cash.

4. *Capital budgeting decision.* When an MNC attempts to determine whether to establish a subsidiary in a given country, a capital budgeting analysis is conducted. Forecasts of the future cash flows used within the capital budgeting process will be dependent on future currency values. This dependency can be due to (1) future inflows or outflows denominated in foreign currencies that will require conversion to the home currency, and/or (2) the influence of future exchange rates on demand for the corporation's products. There are several additional ways by which exchange rates can affect the estimated cash flows, but the main point here is that accurate forecasts of currency values will improve the estimates of the cash flows, and therefore enhance the MNC's decision-making abilities.

5. *Long-term financing decision.* Corporations that issue bonds to secure long-term funds may consider denominating the bonds in foreign currencies. As with short-term financing, corporations would prefer the currency borrowed (denominating the debt) to depreciate over time against the currency they are receiving from sales. To estimate the cost of issuing bonds denominated in a foreign currency, forecasts of exchange rates are required.

6. *Earnings assessment.* When earnings of an MNC are reported, subsidiary earnings are consolidated and translated into the currency representing the parent firm's home country. For example, consider an MNC with its home office in the United States and subsidiaries in Switzerland and Great Britain. The Swiss subsidiary's earnings in Swiss francs must be measured by translation to U.S. dollars. The British subsidiary's earnings in pounds must also be measured by translation to U.S. dollars. "Translation" does not suggest that the earnings are physically converted to U.S. dollars. It is simply a recording process to periodically report consolidated earnings in a single currency. Using the scenario just described, appreciation of the Swiss franc will boost the Swiss subsidiary's earnings when reported in (translated to) U.S. dollars. Forecasts of exchange rates thus play an important role in the overall forecast of an MNC's consolidated earnings.

The need for accurate exchange rate projections should now be clear. The following section describes forecasting methods available.

FORECASTING TECHNIQUES

The numerous methods available for forecasting exchange rates can be categorized into four general groups: (1) technical, (2) fundamental, (3) market-based, and (4) mixed.

Technical Forecasting

Technical forecasting involves use of historical exchange rate data to predict future values. For example, the fact that a given currency has increased in value over four consecutive days may provide an indication of how the currency will move tomorrow. In some cases, a more complex statistical analysis is applied in technical forecasting. For example, a computer program can be developed to detect particular historical trends.

There are also several **time series models** that examine moving averages and thus allow a forecaster to develop some rule, such as, "The currency tends to decline in value after a rise in moving average over three consecutive periods." Normally, consultants who use such a method will not disclose their particular rule for forecasting. If they did, their potential clients might apply the rules themselves rather than pay for the consultant's advice.

Technical forecasting of exchange rates is similar to technical forecasting of stock prices. If the pattern of currency values over time appears random, then technical forecasting is not appropriate. Unless historical trends in exchange rate movements can be identified, examination of past movements will not be useful for indicating future movements.

Technical factors have sometimes been cited as the main reason for changing speculative positions that cause an adjustment in the dollar's value. For example, *Wall Street Journal* summaries of dollar movements on particular days are shown below:

Date	Status of Dollar	Explanation
Oct. 14, 1992	Weakened	Technical factors overwhelmed economic news
Nov. 18, 1992	Weakened	Technical factors triggered sales of dollars
Dec. 16, 1992	Weakened	Technical factors triggered sales of dollars
Apr. 14, 1993	Strengthened	Technical factors indicated that dollars had been recently oversold, triggering purchase of dollars

These examples suggest that technical forecasting appears to be widely used by speculators who frequently attempt to capitalize on day-to-day exchange rate movements.

Technical forecasting models have helped some speculators in the foreign exchange market at various times. However, a model that has worked well in one particular period will not necessarily work well in another. With the abundance of technical models existing today, some are bound to generate speculative profits in any given period.

Many foreign exchange participants argue that even if a particular technical forecasting model is shown to lead consistently to speculative profits, it will no longer be useful once other participants begin to use it. The trading based on its recommendation would push the currency value to a new position immediately. Speculators using technical exchange rate forecasting often incur large transaction costs due to frequent trading. In addition, it can be time-consuming to monitor currency movements in the search for any systematic pattern. Furthermore, speculators need sufficient capital to absorb losses that may occur.

From the corporate point of view, use of technical forecasting may be limited in that it typically focuses on the near future, which is not that helpful for developing corporate policies. Also, it rarely provides point estimates or a range of possible future values, as pointed out by Goodman. Because technical analysis will not typically estimate future exchange rates in precise terms, it is not, by itself, an adequate forecasting tool for corporate treasurers of MNCs.

Fundamental Forecasting

Fundamental forecasting is based on fundamental relationships between economic variables and exchange rates. Given current values of these variables along with their historical impact on a currency's value, corporations can develop exchange rate projections. For example, high inflation in a given country can lead to depreciation in the currency representing that country. Of course, all other factors that may influence exchange rates should also be considered.

A forecast may arise simply from a subjective assessment of the degree to which general movements in economic variables in one country are expected to affect exchange rates. From a statistical perspective, a forecast would be based on quantitatively measured impacts of factors on exchange rates. While some of the full-blown fundamental models are beyond the scope of this text, a simplified discussion follows.

Example of Fundamental Forecasting. The focus here is on only two of the many factors that affect currency values. Before identifying them, consider that the corporate objective is to forecast the percentage change (rate of appreciation or depreciation) in the British pound with respect to the U.S. dollar during the next quarter. For simplicity, assume the firm's forecast for the British pound is dependent on only two factors that affect the pound's value:

1. Inflation in the United States relative to inflation in Great Britain
2. Income growth in the United States relative to income growth in Great Britain (measured as a percentage change).

The first step is to determine how these variables have affected the percentage change in the pound value based on historical data. This is commonly achieved with regression analysis. First, quarterly data can be compiled for the inflation and income growth levels of both Great Britain and the United States. The dependent variable is the quarterly percentage change in the British pound value (called *BP*). The independent (influential) variables may be set up as follows:

1. Previous quarterly percentage change in the inflation differential (U.S. inflation rate minus British inflation rate), referred to as *INF*
2. Previous quarterly percentage change in the income growth differential (U.S. income growth minus British income growth), referred to as *INC*.

The regression equation can be defined as

$$BP = b_0 + b_1INF + b_2INC + \mu,$$

where b_0 is a constant, b_1 measures the sensitivity of *BP* to changes in *INF*, b_2 measures the sensitivity of *BP* to changes in *INC*, and μ represents an error term. A set of historical data would be needed to obtain previous values of *BP*, *INF*, and

INC. Using this data set, regression analysis will generate the values of the regression coefficients (b_0, b_1, and b_2). That is, regression analysis determines the direction and degree to which *BP* is affected by each independent variable. The coefficient b_1 will exhibit a positive sign if, when *INF* changes, *BP* changes in the same direction (other things held constant). A negative sign indicates that *BP* and *INF* move in opposite directions. In the equation given, b_1 is expected to exhibit a positive sign, because when inflation in the United States relative to Great Britain increases, this exerts upward pressure on the pound's value.

The regression coefficient b_2 (which measures the impact of *INC* on *BP*) is expected to be positive, since when U.S. income growth exceeds British income growth, there is upward pressure on the pound's value. These relationships have already been thoroughly discussed in Chapter 4.

Once regression analysis is employed to generate values of the coefficients, these coefficients can be used to forecast. To illustrate, assume the following values: $b_0 = .002$, $b_1 = .8$, and $b_2 = 1.0$. The coefficients can be interpreted as follows. For a one-unit percentage change in the inflation differential, the pound is expected to change by .8 percent in the same direction, other things held constant. For a one-unit percentage change in the income differential, the British pound is expected to change by 1.0 percent in the same direction, other things held constant. To develop forecasts, assume that the most recent quarterly percentage change in *INF* (the inflation differential) is 4 percent, and that in *INC* (the income growth differential) it is 2 percent. Using this information along with our estimated regression coefficients, the forecast for *BP* is

$$\text{BP} = b_0 + b_1\,\text{INF} + b_2\,\text{INC}$$

$$= .002 + .8(4\%) + 1(2\%)$$

$$= .2\% + 3.2\% + 2\%$$

$$= 5.4\%.$$

Thus, given the current figures for inflation rates and income growth, the pound should appreciate by 5.4 percent during the next quarter.

This example is simplified to illustrate how fundamental analysis can be implemented for forecasting. A full-blown model may include many more than two factors. Yet, the application would still be somewhat similar. A large time series database (perhaps 50 or more periods) would be necessary to warrant any confidence in the relationships detected by such a model.

Use of Sensitivity Analysis for Fundamental Forecasting.

When a regression model is used for forecasting, and the values of the influential factors have a lagged impact on exchange rates, the actual value of those factors can be used as input for the forecast. For example, if the inflation differential has a lagged impact on exchange rates, the inflation differential in the previous period may be used to forecast the percentage change in the exchange rate over the future period. However, some factors may have an instantaneous influence on exchange rates. Since these factors are not known, forecasts must be used. Firms recognize that poor forecasts of these factors can cause poor forecasts of the exchange rate movements, so they may attempt to account for the uncertainty by using **sensitivity analysis,** in which more than one possible outcome is considered for the factors exhibiting uncertainty.

To illustrate how sensitivity analysis can be applied to the forecasting of exchange rate movements, assume that Phoenix Corporation develops a regression model to forecast the percentage change in the German mark's value. We will simplify our example by assuming that the real interest rate differential and the inflation differential are the only factors that affect exchange rate movements, as shown in this regression model:

$$e_t = a_0 + a_1 \, \mathrm{INT}_t + a_2 \, \mathrm{INF}_{t-1} + \mu$$

where

$$e_t = \text{percentage change in the exchange rate over period } t$$
$$\mathrm{INT}_t = \text{real interest rate differential over period } t$$
$$\mathrm{INF}_{t-1} = \text{inflation differential in the previous period}$$
$$a_0, a_1, a_2 = \text{regression coefficients}$$
$$\mu = \text{error term.}$$

Historical data are used to determine values for e_f, along with values for INT_t and INF_{t-1} for several periods (preferably, 30 or more periods are used to build the database). The length of each historical period (quarter, month, etc.) should match the length of the period for which the forecast is needed. The historical data needed per period for the German mark model are (1) percentage change in mark value, (2) U.S. real interest rate minus German real interest rate, and (3) U.S. inflation rate in the previous period minus German inflation rate in the previous period. Assume that regression analysis has provided the following estimates for the regression coefficients:

Regression Coefficient	Estimate
a_0	.001
a_1	−.7
a_2	.6

The negative sign of a_1 suggests a negative relationship between INT_t and the mark's movements, while the positive sign of a_2 suggests a positive relationship between INF_{t-1} and the mark's movements.

To forecast the mark's percentage change over the upcoming period, INT_t and INF_{t-1} must be estimated. Assume that INF_{t-1} was 1 percent. However, INT_t is not known at the beginning of the period and must therefore be forecasted. Assume that Phoenix Corporation has developed the following probability distribution for INT_t:

Probability	Possible Outcome
20%	−3%
50%	−4%
30%	−5%
100%	

A separate forecast of e_t can be developed from each possible outcome of INT_t, as follows:

Forecast of INT	Forecast of e_t	Probability
–3%	.1% + (–.7)(–3%) + .6(1%) = 2.8%	20%
–4%	.1% + (–.7)(–4%) + .6(1%) = 3.5%	50%
–5%	.1% + (–.7)(–5%) + .6(1%) = 4.2%	30%

If other currencies were to be forecasted, the probability distributions of their movements over the upcoming period could also be developed in a similar manner. For example, the percentage change in the Japanese yen could be forecasted by regressing historical percentage changes in the yen's value against (1) the differential between U.S. real interest rates and Japanese real interest rates, and (2) the differential between U.S. inflation in the previous period and Japanese inflation in the previous period. The regression coefficients estimated by regression analysis for the yen model will differ from those for the mark model. The estimated coefficients could then be used along with estimates for the interest rate differential and inflation rate differential to develop a forecast of the percentage change in the yen. Sensitivity analysis could be used to reforecast the yen's percentage change based on alternative estimates of the interest rate differential.

Use of PPP For Fundamental Forecasting. Recall that the theory of purchasing power parity (PPP) specifies the fundamental relationship between the inflation differential and the exchange rate. In simple terms, PPP states that the currency of the relatively inflated country will depreciate by an amount that reflects that country's inflation differential. If this theory were accurate in reality, there would not be a need to even consider alternative forecasting techniques. However, using the inflation differential of two countries to forecast their exchange rate is not always accurate. Problems arise because (1) the timing of the impact of inflation fluctuations on changing trade patterns, and therefore on exchange rates, is not known with certainty, (2) data used to measure relative prices of two countries may be somewhat inaccurate, (3) barriers to trade can disrupt the trade patterns that should emerge in accordance with PPP theory, and (4) other factors, such as the interest rate differential between countries, can also affect exchange rates. For these reasons, the inflation differential by itself is not sufficient to most accurately forecast exchange rate movements. Yet, it should be included in any fundamental forecasting model.

Limitations of Fundamental Forecasting. While fundamental forecasting accounts for the expected fundamental relationships between factors and currency values, the following limitations exist:

- Uncertain timing of impact
- Forecasts needed for factors with instantaneous impact
- Omission of other relevant factors from model
- Change in sensitivity of currency movements to each factor over time.

First, the precise timing of the impact of some factors on a currency's value is not known. It is possible that the impact of inflation on exchange rates will not completely occur until two, three, or four quarters later. The regression model would need to be adjusted accordingly.

A second limitation (as mentioned earlier) is related to those factors that exhibit an immediate impact on exchange rates. Their inclusion in a fundamental forecasting model would be useful only if forecasts could be obtained for them. Forecasts of these factors should be developed for a period that corresponds to the period in which a forecast for exchange rates is necessary. In this case, the accuracy of the exchange rate forecasts will be somewhat dependent on the forecasting accuracy of these factors. Even if firms knew exactly how movements in these factors affected exchange rates, their exchange rate projections could be inaccurate if they could not predict the values of the factors.

A third limitation is that there may be factors that deserve consideration in the fundamental forecasting process that cannot be easily quantified. For example, what if large German exporting firms experienced an unanticipated labor strike, causing shortages? This would reduce the availability of German goods for U.S. consumers, and therefore reduce U.S. demand for German marks. Such an event, which would place downward pressure on the German mark value, is not normally incorporated into the forecasting model.

A fourth limitation of the fundamental model is that coefficients derived from the regression analysis will not necessarily remain constant over time. In the previous example, the coefficient for INF was .6, suggesting that for a one-unit change in INF, the mark would appreciate by .6 percent. Yet, if the German or U.S. governments imposed new trade barriers, or eliminated existing barriers, the impact of the inflation differential on trade (and therefore on the mark's exchange rate) could be affected.

These limitations of fundamental forecasting are discussed to emphasize that even the most sophisticated forecasting techniques (fundamental or otherwise) are not going to provide consistently accurate forecasts. MNCs that use forecasting techniques must allow for some margin of error, and recognize the possibility of error when implementing corporate policies.

Market-Based Forecasting

The process of developing forecasts from market indicators, known as **market-based forecasting,** is usually based on either (1) the spot rate or (2) the forward rate.

Use of the Spot Rate.   To clarify why the spot rate can serve as a market-based forecast, assume the British pound is expected to appreciate against the dollar in the very near future. This will encourage speculators to buy the pound with U.S. dollars today in anticipation of its appreciation, and these purchases could force the pound's value up immediately. Conversely, if the pound is expected to depreciate against the dollar, speculators will sell off pounds now, hoping to purchase them back at a lower price after they decline in value. Such action could force the pound to depreciate immediately. Thus, the current value of the pound should reflect the expectation of the pound's value in the very near future. Corporations can use the spot rate to forecast, since it represents the market's expectation of the spot rate in the near future.

Use of the Forward Rate.   To understand why the forward rate can serve as a forecast of the future spot rate, consider the following example. Assume the

30-day forward rate of the British pound is $1.40, and the general expectation of speculators is that the future spot rate of the pound will be $1.45 in 30 days. If speculators expect the future spot rate to be $1.45, and the prevailing forward rate is $1.40, they might buy pounds 30 days forward at $1.40 and then sell them when received (in 30 days) at the spot rate existing then. If their forecast is correct, they will earn $.05 ($1.45 − $1.40) per pound. If a large number of speculators implement this strategy, the substantial forward purchases of pounds will cause the forward rate to increase until this speculative demand stops. Perhaps this speculative demand will terminate when the forward rate reaches $1.45, since at this rate, no profits will be expected by implementing the strategy described. This example shows that the forward rate should move toward the market's general expectation of the future spot rate. In this sense, the forward rate serves as a market-based forecast, since it reflects the market's expectation of the spot rate at the end of the forward horizon (30 days from now in the example above).

While the focus of this chapter is on corporate forecasting rather than speculation, it is speculation that helps to push the forward rate to the level that reflects the general expectation of the future spot rate. If corporations are convinced the forward rate is a reliable indicator of the future spot rate, they can simply monitor this publicly quoted rate to develop exchange rate projections.

Long-Term Forecasting With Forward Rates. While forward rates are sometimes available for two to five years, such rates are rarely quoted. However, the quoted interest rates on risk-free instruments of various countries can be used to determine what the forward rates would be under conditions of interest rate parity. For example, assume that the U.S. five-year interest rate is 10 percent, annualized, while the British five-year interest rate is 13 percent. The five-year compounded return on investments in each of these countries is computed as follows:

Country	Five-year compounded return
U.S.	$(1.10)^5 - 1 = 61\%$
U.K.	$(1.13)^5 - 1 = 84\%$

Thus, the appropriate five-year forward rate premium (or discount) of the British pound would be

$$p = \frac{(1 + i_{U.S.})}{(1 + i_{U.K.})} - 1$$

$$= \frac{1.61}{1.84} - 1$$

$$= -.125, \text{ or } -12.5\%.$$

The results of our computation suggest that the five-year forward rate of the pound should contain a 12.5 percent discount. That is, the spot rate of the pound is expected to depreciate by 12.5 percent over the five-year period for which the forward rate is used to forecast.

Skepticism About the Forward Rate Forecast.   One reason firms might not accept the forward rate as a predictor is because of a second market force. Recall that according to interest rate parity, the forward premium (or discount) is determined by the interest rate differential. If, for example, the 30-day interest rate of the British pound is above the 30-day U.S. interest rate, we expect the forward rate on the pound to exhibit a discount. The size of the discount will be such that U.S. investors cannot achieve abnormal returns by using covered interest arbitrage (converting dollars to pounds, investing pounds in a British 30-day account, and simultaneously selling pounds 30 days forward in exchange for dollars). Based on this information, consider that the forward rates of some currencies such as the British pound and French franc, are usually below their current spot rates. That is, they almost always exhibit a forward discount (since their interest rates are typically above the U.S. rates). The discount within the forward rate suggests that the pound and French franc should depreciate, even when all other factors suggest that these currencies will appreciate.

Mixed Forecasting

Because no single forecasting technique has been found to be consistently superior to the others, some MNCs may prefer to use a combination of forecasting techniques. This method is referred to as **mixed forecasting.** Various forecasts for a particular currency value could be developed using several forecasting techniques. Each of the techniques used could be assigned weights in such a way that the weights totalled 100 percent, with the techniques thought to be more reliable being assigned higher weights. The actual forecast of the currency by the MNC would be a weighted average of the various forecasts developed.

FORECASTING SERVICES

The corporate need to forecast currency values has prompted the emergence of several consulting firms, including Business International, Conti Currency, Predex, and Wharton Econometric Forecasting Associates. In addition, some large investment banks, such as Goldman Sachs, and commercial banks, such as Citibank, Chemical Bank, and Chase Manhattan Bank, offer forecasting services. Many consulting services use at least two different types of analysis to generate separate forecasts, and then determine the weighted average of the forecasts.

Some forecasting services, such as Capital Techniques, FX Concepts, and Preview Economics, focus on technical forecasting, while other services, such as Corporate Treasury Consultants Ltd. and WEFA, focus on fundamental forecasting. Many services, such as Chemical Bank, and Forexia Ltd. use both technical and fundamental forecasting. In some cases, the technical forecasting techniques are emphasized by the forecasting firms for short-term forecasts, while fundamental techniques are emphasized for long-run forecasts.

Forecasts are even provided for currencies that are not widely traded. Firms provide forecasts on any currency for time horizons of interest to their clients, ranging from one day to ten years from now. In addition, some firms will offer advice on international cash management, assessment of exposure to exchange rate risk, and hedging. Many of the firms provide their clients with forecasts and recommendations monthly, or even weekly, for an annual fee.

Recently, most forecasting services have been inaccurate regarding currency values. Given the recent volatility in foreign exchange markets, it is quite difficult to forecast currency values. One way for a corporation to determine whether a forecasting service is valuable is to compare the accuracy of its forecasts to that of alternative publicly available and free forecasts. The forward rate serves as a benchmark for comparison here, since it is quoted in many newspapers and magazines. A study by Richard Levich compared the forecasts of several currency forecasting services regarding nine different currencies to the forward rate. Only 5 percent of the forecasts (when considering all forecasting firms and all currencies forecasted) for one month ahead were more accurate than the forward rate, while only 14 percent of forecasts for three months ahead were more accurate. These results are frustrating to the corporations that have paid $25,000 per year or more for expert opinions. Perhaps some corporate clients of these consulting firms believe the fee is worth it even when the forecasting performance is poor, if other services (such as cash management) are included in the package. It is also possible that a corporate treasurer, in recognition of the potential for error in forecasting exchange rates, may prefer to pay a consulting firm for its forecasts. Then the treasurer is not (in a sense) directly responsible for corporate problems that result from inaccurate currency forecasts. Not all MNCs hire consulting firms to do their forecasting. For example, Kodak, Inc., once used a service, but became dissatisfied with it and has now developed its own forecasting system.

EVALUATION OF FORECAST PERFORMANCE

An MNC that forecasts exchange rates must monitor its performance over time to determine whether the forecasting procedure is satisfactory. For this purpose, a measurement of the forecast error is required. There are various ways to compute forecast errors. Only one possible measurement will be discussed here and is defined as follows:

$$\text{Absolute forecast error as a percentage of the realized value} = \frac{|\text{Forecasted value} - \text{Realized value}|}{\text{Realized value}}$$

The error is computed using an absolute value, since this avoids a possible offsetting effect when determining the mean forecast error. For example, consider a simplified example, in which the forecast error is .05 in the first period and −.05 in the second period (if the absolute value is not taken). The mean error here over the two periods is zero. Yet, that is misleading, since the forecast was not perfectly accurate in either period. The absolute value avoids such a distortion.

When measuring forecast performance of different currencies, it is often useful to adjust for their relative sizes, so forecasting ability can be compared among currencies. As an example, consider the following forecasted and realized values by a U.S. firm during one period:

IN PRACTICE

USING TRADE DEFICIT ANNOUNCEMENTS TO FORECAST EXCHANGE RATES

Some foreign exchange market participants speculate according to the dollar's expected movements over the next few days or weeks, since their speculative positions may last only that long. They are less concerned about long-term relationships between economic factors and exchange rates than they are about how the market may react on any given day to news. In the late 1980s and early 1990s, monthly trade deficit announcements were closely monitored by speculators. The announcements carried an implicit forecast of future exchange rates that was used by speculators to take positions, as described below.

In October 1987 the August trade deficit of $15.68 billion was announced. Foreign exchange market participants were expecting more favorable news and reacted to the announcement by switching from dollars to other currencies. Their actions caused an immediate decline in the dollar's value. Within seconds of the trade report, the dollar declined against the German mark by .5 percent. Even though the trade deficit had already occurred, the an-

nounced deficit amount created forecasts about future trade, and therefore modified forecasts of the dollar's value.

In January 1988 the announced November trade deficit was lower than anticipated, causing forecasts of a stronger dollar. The reaction by foreign exchange market participants caused the dollar to strengthen immediately. In February 1988 the announced December trade deficit was lower than anticipated, and a similar market reaction occurred.

In the early months of 1991, trade deficit announcements revealed a smaller trade deficit for the U.S. than anticipated. The dollar strengthened immediately in response to the signals provided by these announcements. In some months during 1993 and 1994, the dollar weakened in response to announcements of large trade deficits. Each month, a new monthly trade deficit is announced, and new implicit forecasts of the dollar's value are created. Each implicit forecast lasts only until the next trade deficit announcement, or until other news related to exchange rates is provided.

	Forecasted Value	Realized Value
British pound	$1.35	$1.50
French franc	$ .12	$ .10

In this case, the difference between the forecasted value and the realized value is $.15 for the pound, compared to $.02 for the franc. This does not necessarily imply that the forecast of the franc is more accurate. When considering the size of what is forecasted (dividing the difference by the realized value), one can see that the British pound has been predicted with more accuracy on a percentage basis. With the data given, the forecasting error (as defined earlier) of the British pound is

$$\frac{|\ \$1.35 - \$1.50\ |}{\$1.50} = \frac{\$.15}{\$1.50} = .10, \text{ or } 10\%.$$

In comparison, the forecast error of the French franc is

$$\frac{|\ .12 - .10\ |}{.10} = \frac{.02}{.10} = .20, \textit{ or } 20\%.$$

Thus, the French franc has been predicted with less accuracy.

Forecast Accuracy Over Time

Has there been any improvement in forecasting in recent years? The answer depends on the method used to develop forecasts. With regard to the forward rate as a predictor, the magnitude of the absolute errors is shown for the British pound over time in Exhibit 9.1. The size of the errors changes over time. However, there does not appear to be a consistent movement toward larger or smaller errors.

The year 1981 stands out as a period in which forecasts were worse than ever. Recall that U.S. interest rates were extremely high at the time, which attracted foreign (including British) demand for U.S. dollars to buy U.S. securities. Consequently, the British pound depreciated to such a degree that the 90-day forecasts based on the forward rate were off by as much as $.32 per pound.

The forecasting analysis discussed here has concentrated on the British pound. Data for other major currencies are available in the data bank near the end of the text, so that one can evaluate forecasting performance for these currencies using the method that has been described.

Forecast Accuracy among Currencies

The ability to forecast currency values may vary with the currency of concern. For example, Exhibit 9.2 discloses the mean forecast errors of six major currencies over the 1983–1992 period. These errors are derived when the 90-day forward rate is being used to forecast. The Canadian dollar stands out as the currency most accurately predicted. Its mean error is roughly one-third of the mean errors of the other currencies. This is important information, since a financial manager of a U.S. firm can feel more confident about the number of dollars to be received (or needed) on Canadian transactions. Conversely, it appears much more difficult to forecast the future value of the Swiss franc. The higher degree of accuracy when forecasting the Canadian dollar versus the other currencies is attributed to less volatility in the Canadian dollar's exchange rate over time.

Search for Forecast Bias

The difference between the forecasted and realized exchange rates for a given point in time represents a nominal forecast error. A time series of nominal forecast errors is illustrated in Exhibit 9.3. Negative errors over time represent underestimating, while positive errors represent overestimating. If the errors are consistently positive or negative over time, then a bias in the forecasting procedure does exist. In this example, it appears that a bias did exist in distinct periods. During the strong-pound periods, the forecasts underestimated, while in weak-pound periods, the forecasts overestimated.

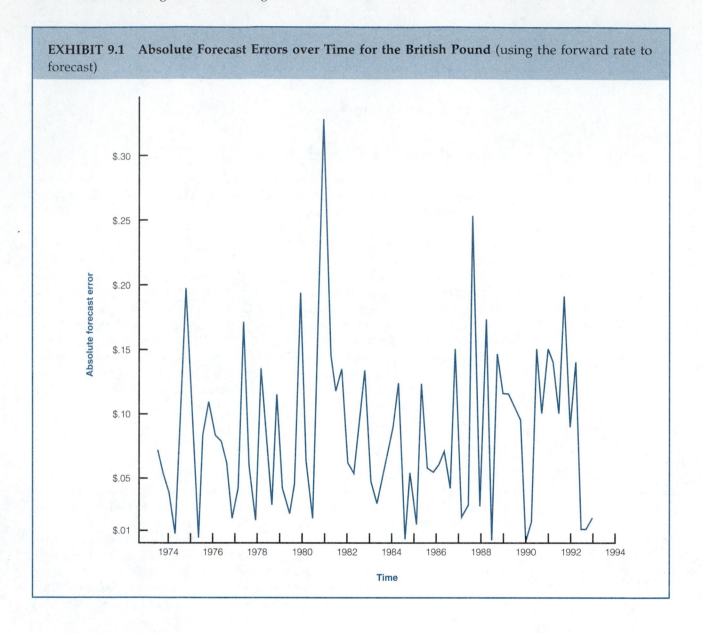

EXHIBIT 9.1   Absolute Forecast Errors over Time for the British Pound (using the forward rate to forecast)

**EXHIBIT 9.2
Comparison of
Forecast Errors
among Six
Currencies**

Currency	Mean Absolute Forecast Error as a Percentage of the Realized Value
British pound	8.9%
Canadian dollar	3.5
French franc	9.6
German mark	10.9
Japanese yen	9.0
Swiss franc	11.7

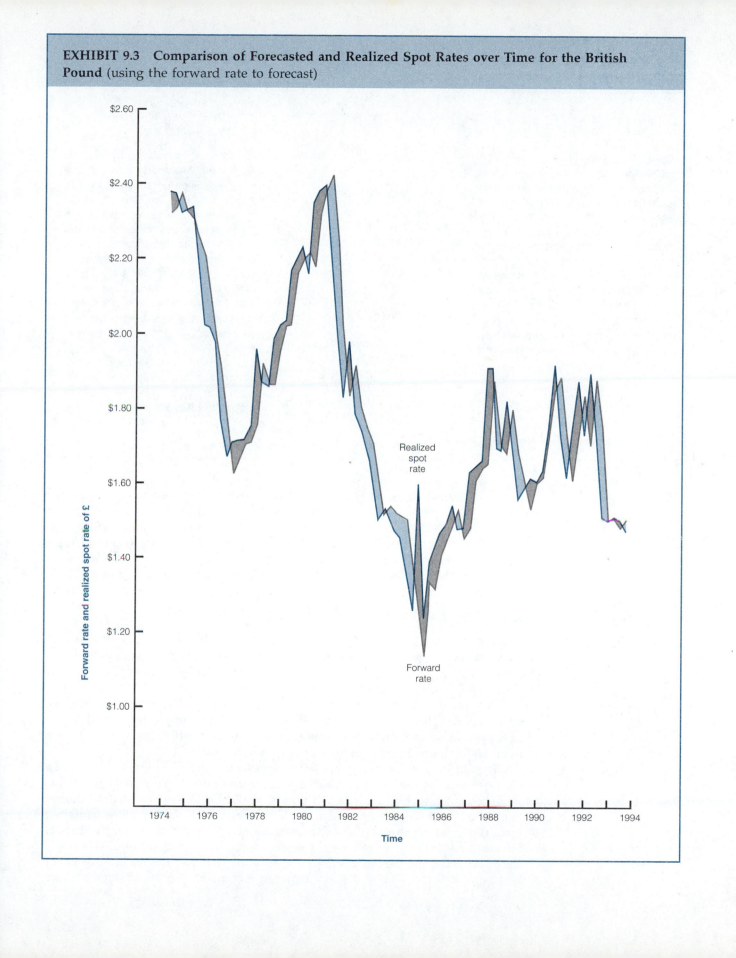

EXHIBIT 9.3 Comparison of Forecasted and Realized Spot Rates over Time for the British Pound (using the forward rate to forecast)

APPLIED RESEARCH

STATISTICAL TEST OF FORECAST BIAS

If the forward rate is an unbiased predictor of the future spot rate, this implies that alternative forecasts cannot consistently outperform the forward rate as a predictor. If the forward rate is unbiased, it fully reflects all available information about the future spot rate. Any forecast errors would be the result of events that could not have been anticipated from existing information at the time of the forecast. A conventional method of testing for a forecast bias is to apply the following regression model to historical data:

$$S = a_0 + a_1 F_{t-1} + \mu_t$$

where

S = spot rate at time

F_{t-1} = forward rate at time $t-1$

μ_t = error term

a_0 = intercept

a_1 = regression coefficient.

If the forward rate is unbiased, the intercept should equal zero and the regression coefficient a_1 should equal 1.0. The t-test for a_1 is

$$t = \frac{a_1 - 1}{\text{standard error of } a_1}.$$

If $a_0 = 0$ and a_1 is significantly less than 1.0, this implies that the forward rate is systematically overestimating the spot rate. For example, if $a_0 = 0$ and $a_1 = .90$, the future spot rate is estimated to be 90 percent of the forecast generated by the forward rate. Conversely, if $a_0 = 0$ and a_1 is significantly greater than 1.0, this implies that the forward rate is systematically underestimating the spot rate. For example, if $a = 0$ and $a_1 = 1.1$, the future spot rate is estimated to be 1.1 times the forecast generated by the forward rate. When a bias is detected and anticipated to persist in the future, future forecasts may incorporate the bias detected. Using the example in which $a_1 = 1.1$, future forecasts of the spot rate may incorporate this information by multiplying the forward rate times 1.1 to create a forecast of the future spot rate.

By detecting a bias, an MNC may be able to revise its forecast to adjust for the bias so it can improve its forecasting accuracy. For example, if the errors are consistently positive, an MNC could adjust today's forward rate downward to reflect the bias detected. Over time, a forecasting bias can change (from underestimating to overestimating, or vice versa). Any adjustment to the forward rate used as a forecast would need to reflect the anticipated bias for the period of concern.

Graphic Evaluation of Forecast Performance

Performance from forecasting can be examined with the use of a graph that compares forecasted values with the realized values for various time periods. As a hypothetical example, consider the corporate exchange rate projections for Currency Q with respect to the U.S. dollar which appear in Exhibit 9.4.

The predicted and realized exchange rate values in Exhibit 9.4 can be compared graphically, as shown in Exhibit 9.5. For example, in period 1, the predicted value of Currency Q was $.20 and the realized value was $.16. This point is illustrated in Exhibit 9.5 and designated with a "1."

The 45-degree line in Exhibit 9.5 represents perfect forecasts. To clarify, consider a case in which the realized value turned out to be exactly what was predicted over several periods. All points would be located on that 45-degree line in Exhibit 9.5. For this reason, the line is referred to as the **perfect forecast line.** While in our example the forecasts are not perfectly accurate, the perfect forecast line still can be useful for assessing forecasting performance. The closer the points reflecting the eight periods are vertically to the 45-degree line, the better is the forecast. The vertical distance between each point and the 45-degree line is

EXHIBIT 9.4
Hypothetical Evaluation of Forecast Performance

Period	Predicted Value of Currency Q for End of Period	Realized Value of Currency Q as of End of Period
1	$.20	$.16
2	.18	.14
3	.24	.16
4	.26	.22
5	.30	.28
6	.22	.26
7	.16	.14
8	.14	.10

EXHIBIT 9.5
Comparison of Forecasted and Realized Spot Rates

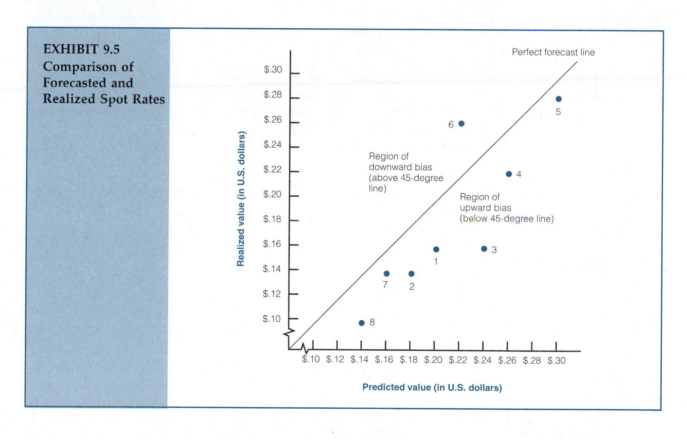

the forecast error. For example, the 45-degree line is $.04 above the point representing period 1. This implies that the forecast for period 1 was $.04 above the realized value. All points below the 45-degree line reflect overestimation by the forecasts. In Exhibit 9.5 seven of the eight points are in this range. Thus, it appears that the forecasts tend to be *upward biased* (typically above the realized value).

All points above the 45-degree line reflect underestimation by the forecasts. In Exhibit 9.5, only one of the eight points is in this range. None of the eight points is on the 45-degree line. This means that Currency Q was not predicted with perfect accuracy in any of the eight periods.

If points appear to be scattered evenly on both sides of the 45-degree line, then the forecasts are said to be *unbiased,* since they are not consistently above or below the realized values. Such results do not offer much insight on how to improve forecasts.

Whether evaluating the size of forecast errors or attempting to search for a bias, more reliable results are obtained when examining a large number of periods. Only eight periods have been evaluated here, in order to provide a simplified example.

The forecast evaluation procedure described here is applied to the British pound and shown in Exhibit 9.6. Separating the entire period into subperiods (as shown in Exhibit 9.7) reveals a forecast bias in various time periods.

Comparison of Forecasting Techniques

When an MNC evaluates its forecasting performance, it must realize that errors will commonly occur. To at least minimize the errors, it may desire to compare forecasting errors of various available methods. This can be done by plotting the points relating to both methods on a graph similar to Exhibit 9.5. The points pertaining to each method could be distinguished by a particular mark or color. The performance of the two methods could be evaluated by comparing distances of points from the 45-degree line. In some cases, neither forecasting method may stand out as superior when compared graphically. If so, a more precise comparison could be conducted by computing the forecast errors for all periods for each method, and then comparing these errors.

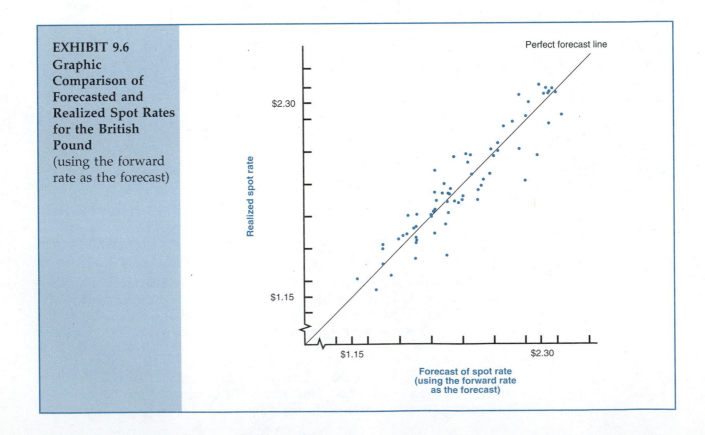

EXHIBIT 9.6
Graphic Comparison of Forecasted and Realized Spot Rates for the British Pound (using the forward rate as the forecast)

EXHIBIT 9.7 Graphic Comparison of Forecasted and Realized Spot Rates in Different Subperiods for the British Pound (using the forward rate as the forecast)

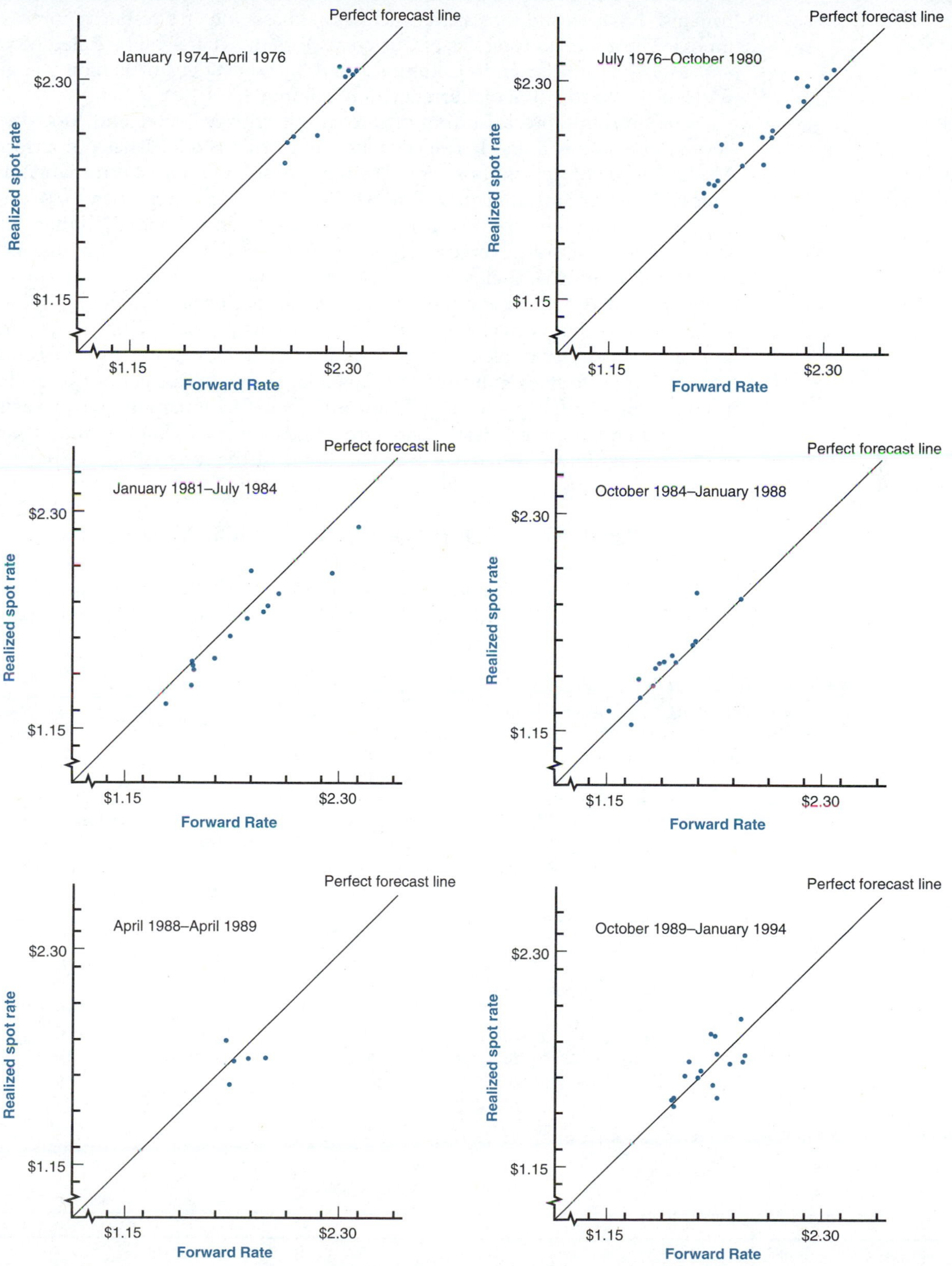

As an example, the data from Exhibit 9.4 will be used as one set of forecasts assumed to be developed by a U.S. firm for Currency Q's value. Assume that the firm also has a second forecast for each period based on an alternative forecasting model. The assumed forecasts of Currency Q, using what shall be called Model 1 and Model 2, are shown in Columns 2 and 3, respectively, of Exhibit 9.8, along with the realized value of Currency Q in column 4.

The absolute forecast errors of forecasting with Model 1 and Model 2 are shown in columns 5 and 6, respectively. Notice that Model 1 has outperformed Model 2 in six of the eight periods. The mean absolute forecast error when using Model 1 is $.04, meaning that forecasts with Model 1 are off by $.04 on the average. While Model 1 is not perfectly accurate, it does a better job than Model 2, whose mean absolute forecast error is $.07. Overall, predictions with Model 1 are on the average $.03 closer to the realized value.

For an MNC to do a complete comparison of performance among forecasting techniques, it should evaluate as many periods as possible. Only eight periods are used in our example, since that is enough to illustrate how to compare forecasting performance. If the MNC has a large number of periods to evaluate, it could statistically test for significant differences in forecasting errors using a *t*-test or a nonparametric test. Results from such a test would determine whether there is a significant difference in the accuracy of the forecasting techniques.

FORECASTING UNDER MARKET EFFICIENCY

If the foreign exchange rate market is **weak-form efficient,** then historical and current exchange rate information is not useful for forecasting exchange rate

EXHIBIT 9.8   Comparison of Forecast Techniques

(1)	(2)	(3)	(4)	(5)	(6)	(7) = (5) − (6)
Period	Predicted value of Currency Q by Model 1	Predicted value of Currency Q by Model 2	Realized value of Currency Q	Absolute forecast error using Model 1	Absolute forecast error using Model 2	Difference in absolute forecast errors (Model 1 − Model 2)
1	$.20	$.24	$.16	$.04	$.08	−$ .04
2	.18	.20	.14	.04	.06	−.02
3	.24	.20	.16	.08	.04	.04
4	.26	.20	.22	.04	.02	.02
5	.30	.18	.28	.02	.10	−.08
6	.22	.32	.26	.04	.06	−.02
7	.16	.20	.14	.02	.06	−.04
8	.14	.24	.10	.04	.14	−.10
				Sum = .32	Sum = .56	Sum = −.24
				Mean = .04	Mean = .07	Mean = −.03

movements, since today's exchange rates reflect all of this information. That is, technical analysis would not be capable of improving forecasts. If the foreign exchange market is **semistrong-form efficient,** then *all* relevant public information is already reflected in today's exchange rates. If today's exchange rates fully reflected any historical trends in exchange rate movements, but not other public information on expected interest rate movements, the foreign exchange market would be weak-form efficient, but not semistrong-form efficient. Much research has tested the efficient market hypothesis for foreign exchange markets. Research by Cornell and Dietrich and others suggests that foreign exchange markets appear to be weak-form efficient and semistrong-form efficient.

If foreign exchange markets are **strong-form efficient,** then all relevant public *and* private information is already reflected in today's exchange rates. This form of efficiency cannot be tested, since private information is not available.

Even though foreign exchange markets are generally found to be at least semistrong-form efficient, forecasts of exchange rates by MNCs may still be worthwhile. Their goal is not necessarily to earn speculative profits, but to use reasonable exchange rate forecasts to implement policies. When MNCs assess proposed policies, they usually prefer to develop their own forecasts of exchange rates over time rather than simply use market-based rates as a forecast of future rates. MNCs are often interested in more than a point estimate of an exchange rate one year, three years, or five years from now. They prefer to determine a variety of scenarios and assess how exchange rates may change for each scenario. Even if today's forward exchange rate properly reflects all available information, it does not indicate to the MNC the possible deviation of the realized future exchange rate from what is expected. MNCs need to determine the range of various possible exchange rate movements in order to assess the degree to which their operating performance could be affected.

SUMMARY

■ Multinational corporations need exchange rate forecasts to make decisions on hedging payables and receivables, short-term financing and investment, capital budgeting, and long-term financing.

■ The most common forecasting techniques can be classified as (1) technical, (2) fundamental, (3) market-based, and (4) mixed. Unfortunately, these techniques have generally performed rather poorly in recent years. Yet, due to the high variability in exchange rates, it should not be surprising that forecasts will not always be accurate. Also, floating rates have been in existence only since the early 1970s; this has not allowed much time to improve forecasting ability by experience.

■ Forecast methods can be evaluated by comparing the actual values of currencies to the values predicted according to the forecast method. This comparison should be conducted over several periods in order to draw meaningful implications. Two criteria used to evaluate performance of a forecast method are bias and accuracy. When comparing the forecast accuracy between two currencies, the absolute forecast error should be divided by the realized value of the currency to control for differences in the relative values of currencies.

SELF-TEST FOR CHAPTER 9

(Answers are provided in Appendix A in the back of the text)

1. Assume that the annual U.S. return is expected to be 7 percent for each of the next four years, while the annual interest rate in Mexico is expected to be 20 percent. Determine the appropriate four-year forward rate premium or discount on the Mexican peso, which could be used to forecast the percentage change in the peso over the next 4 years.

2. Consider the following information:

Currency	90-Day Forward Rate	Spot Rate That Occurred 90 Days Later
Canadian dollar	$.80	$.82
Japanese yen	$.012	$.011

   If the forward rate was used as the forecast of the future spot rate, determine whether the Canadian dollar or the Japanese yen was forecasted with more accuracy, based on the absolute forecast error as a percentage of the realized value.

3. Assume that the forward rate and spot rate of the Italian lira are normally similar at a given point in time. Assume that the Italian lira has depreciated consistently and substantially over the last three years. Would the forward rate have been biased over this period? If so, would it typically have overestimated or underestimated the future spot rate of the lira (in dollars)? Explain.

4. An analyst has stated that the German mark seems to increase in value over the two weeks following announcements by Bundesbank (the German central bank) that it would raise interest rates. If this statement is true, what are the inferences regarding weak or semistrong form efficiency?

5. Assume that the Mexican interest rates are much higher than U.S. interest rates. Also assume that interest rate parity (discussed in Chapter 7) exists. If you use the forward rate of the Mexican peso to forecast the Mexican peso's future spot rate, would you expect the peso to appreciate or depreciate? Explain.

6. Warden Co. is considering a project in Venezuela, which will be very profitable if the local currency (bolivar) appreciates against the dollar. If the bolivar depreciates, the project will result in losses. Warden Co. forecasts that the bolivar will appreciate. The bolivar's value has historically been very volatile. As a manager of Warden Co., would you be comfortable with this project? Explain.

QUESTIONS

1. Explain corporate motives for forecasting exchange rates.

2. Explain the technical technique for forecasting exchange rates.

3. Explain the fundamental technique for forecasting exchange rates.

4. Explain the market-based technique for forecasting exchange rates.

5. Explain the mixed technique for forecasting exchange rates.

6. What are some limitations of using technical forecasting to predict exchange rates?

7. What are some limitations of using a fundamental technique to forecast exchange rates?

8. What is the rationale for using market-based forecasts?

9. Explain how to assess performance in forecasting exchange rates.

10. Explain how to detect a bias in forecasting exchange rates.

11. You are hired as a consultant to assess a firm's ability to forecast. The firm has developed a point forecast for two different currencies. It wants to determine which currency was forecast with greater accuracy. The information is provided.

Period	Yen Forecast	Actual Yen Value	Pound Forecast	Actual Pound Value
1	$.0050	$.0051	$1.50	$1.51
2	.0048	.0052	1.53	1.50
3	.0053	.0052	1.55	1.58
4	.0055	.0056	1.49	1.52

12. You are hired as a consultant to determine whether there is a bias from forecasting the percentage change in the Dutch guilder (DG). A set of 200 data points was used to develop the following regression equation.

$$\text{Actual } \% \Delta \text{ in DG over period } t = a_0 + a_1 (\text{Forecasted } \% \Delta \text{ in DG over period } t)$$

The regression results are as follows:

Coefficient	Standard error
$a_0 = .006$	.011
$a_1 = .800$	.05

Based on these results, is there a bias in the forecast? Verify your conclusion. If there is a bias, explain whether it is an overestimate or an underestimate.

13. Syracuse Corporation believes that future real interest rate movements will affect exchange rates, and has applied regression analysis to historical data in order to assess the relationship. It will use the regression coefficient derived from this analysis along with forecasted real interest rate

movements in order to predict exchange rates in the future. Explain at least three limitations of this method.

14. Lexington Company is a U.S.-based MNC with subsidiaries in most major countries. Each subsidiary is responsible for forecasting the future exchange rate of its local currency, relative to the U.S. dollar. Comment on this policy. How might Lexington Company assure consistent forecasts among the different subsidiaries?

15. Assume that the following regression model was applied to historical quarterly data:

$$e_t = a_0 + a_1 INT_t + a_2 INF_{t-1} + \mu_t$$

where

e_t = percentage change in exchange rate of the franc in period t

INT_t = average real interest rate differential (U.S. interest rate minus French interest rate) over period t

INF_{t-1} = inflation differential (U.S. inflation rate minus French inflation rate) in the previous period

a_0, a_1, a_2 = regression coefficients

μ_t = error term.

Assume that the regression coefficients were estimated as follows:

$$a_0 = 0.0$$
$$a_1 = .9$$
$$a_2 = .8.$$

Also assume that the inflation differential in the most recent period was 3 percent. The real interest rate differential in the upcoming period is forecasted as follows:

Interest Rate Differential	Probability
0%	30%
1	60
2	10

If Stillwater Inc. uses this information to forecast the French franc's exchange rate, what will be the probability distribution of the franc's percentage change over the upcoming period?

16. Assume that the four-year annualized interest rate in the United States is 9 percent and the four-year interest rate in Switzerland is 6 percent. Assume interest rate parity holds for a four-year horizon. Assume that the spot rate of the Swiss franc is $.60. If the forward rate is used to forecast exchange rates, what will be the forecast for the Swiss franc's spot rate in four years?

What percentage appreciation or depreciation does this forecast imply over the four-year period?

17. Assume that foreign exchange markets were found to be weak-form efficient. Does this suggest anything about utilizing technical analysis to speculate in the foreign exchange markets?

18. If MNCs believed that foreign exchange markets are strong-form efficient, why would they develop their own forecasts of future exchange rates? Why wouldn't they simply use today's quoted rates as indicators about future rates? After all, today's quoted rates should reflect all relevant information.

19. Most foreign currencies appreciated substantially against the dollar during the 1985–1987 period. Would market-based forecasts have overestimated or underestimated the realized values over this period? Explain.

20. The director of currency forecasting at Champaign-Urbana Corporation made the statement, "The most critical task of forecasting exchange rates is not to derive a point estimate of a future exchange rate, but to assess how wrong our estimate might be." What does this statement mean?

21. Assume that in the 1990s, some countries in East Europe allow the exchange rates of their currencies to fluctuate against the dollar. Would the fundamental technique based on historical relationships be useful for forecasting future exchange rates of these currencies? Explain.

22. Royce Company is a U.S. firm with future receivables one year from now in Canadian dollars and British pounds. Its pound receivables are known with certainty, while its estimated Canadian dollar receivables are subject to a 2 percent error in either direction. The dollar values of both types of receivables are similar. There is no chance of default by the customers involved. The treasurer of Royce stated that the estimate of dollar cash flows to be generated from the British pound receivables is subject to greater uncertainty than that of the Canadian dollar receivables. Explain the rationale for such a statement.

23. In the early months of 1991, most major currencies declined substantially against the dollar. Do you think the 30-day forward rates of major currencies were unbiased predictors of their respective future spot rates over these months? Explain.

24. Assume that you obtain a quote for a one-year forward rate on the Mexican peso. Over the next year, the peso depreciates by 12 percent. Do you think the forward rate overestimated the spot rate one year ahead in this example? Explain.

25. The treasurer of Glencoe Inc. detected a forecast bias when using the 30-day forward rate to forecast future spot rates over various periods. He believed he could use such information to determine whether imports ordered every week should be hedged (payment is made 30 days after each order.) The president of Glencoe stated that in the long run, the forward rate is unbiased and suggested that the treasurer should not waste time trying to "beat the forward rate," but should just hedge all orders. Who is correct?

CASE: USING ECONOMIC INFORMATION TO FORECAST EXCHANGE RATES

Currency Traders, Analysts Expect the Dollar To Post Its Oft-Predicted Rebound This Year

By Michael R. Sesit
Staff Reporter of *The Wall Street Journal*

Play it again, Sam.

For the past two years, currency analysts and traders predicted that a recovering U.S. economy and rising U.S. interest rates, coupled with slowing European economies and lower rates in Europe would spell a stronger dollar. They were wrong.

Guess what? They're singing the same tune again for 1993.

"Interest rate differentials will narrow in favor of the dollar. The U.S. economy will grow faster than most of its trading partners. U.S. equity markets look relatively attractive," says Lawrence A. Veit, an international economist at Brown Brothers Harriman & Co. "Some of the political and social uncertainties that exist abroad will not exist in the U.S., and we start from a position of the dollar being undervalued."

Many of these factors are already behind the dollar's rebound late last year from record lows in September.

In six months, Mr. Veit sees the dollar trading at 1.69 marks and 126 yen and the British pound at $1.42. By year end, Mr. Veit projects the U.S. currency to be at 1.80 marks and 118 yen. The pound, he says, will have plummeted to $1.31. As recently as early September, it traded above $2.

At the end of 1992, the dollar stood at 1.6209 marks and 124.84 yen, compared with 1.5170 marks and 124.85 yen at the start of 1992. On Dec. 31, 1991, the pound sold for $1.8690; a year later it stood at $1.5100.

In between, a lot happened. After climbing 11% to 1.6860 marks in late March on prospects of a weaker German economy and lower German interest rates plus a stronger U.S. economic recovery, the dollar began to tumble when those expectations failed to materialize.

By Sept. 2, the dollar was trading at a post-World War II low of 1.3862 marks; it also fell to record lows against the Swiss franc and a five-year low against the British pound. In late September, the dollar hit a record low of 118.6 yen, after having climbed to a 1992 high of 135 yen in April.

Going into 1992, "everybody was very bullish about the dollar, about [U.S.] economic recovery, and Germany was expected to cut their rates in February," explains George Magnus, chief international fixed-income economist at S. G. Warburg & Co. in London. But the Bundesbank actually raised interest rates initially to battle inflationary pressures associated with the spiralling costs of bailing out the former East Germany. What's more, U.S. rates fell, instead of stabilizing. "It was a major disappointment," says Mr. Magnus.

Germany's reluctance to lower interest rates and Europe's failed attempt at political, monetary and economic union claimed other victims as well. In a European currency crisis that began in September, Britain and Italy were forced to pull the pound and lira out of Europe's system of semifixed exchange rates and Spain and Portugal had to devalue their currencies within the system. In addition, Finland, Sweden and Norway were forced to abandon their currencies' unofficial links to the system.

Expecting the French franc and Danish krone to come under sustained attack early this year, Paul Chertkow, head of global currency research at UBS Phillips & Drew in London, says that Europe's Exchange Rate Mechanism "is going to be in grave jeopardy; a devaluation of the French franc would signal the death knell of the ERM itself." While Mr. Chertkow expects Germany and France to vigorously defend the franc, Geoffrey Dennis, an international economist and strategist at James Capel Inc., notes: "It's no longer seen as a heinous crime to devalue."

He and others are a lot more positive about the dollar's outlook in 1993. "We aren't going to be surprised again by a renewed downturn in U.S. interest rates; it does look as if the American economy is going to shift gears," says Mr. Magnus of S. G. Warburg. Moreover, he says that the downturn in German interest rates has already begun and that "German rates are going to fall substantially" in 1993.

Predicting that the U.S. currency will rise to 1.65–1.70 marks by spring, Mr. Magnus sees it rising to 1.85–2.0 marks by the end of 1993.

Key to the strong dollar scenario is the narrowing gap between U.S. and German short-term interest rates. James Capel forecasts that differential will shrink from about 5.70 percentage points in late 1992 to 2.25 points by the end of 1993.

The dollar is also poised to rise from a technical standpoint, says Capel's Mr. Dennis. "In early 1992, people jumped on the [dollar] rally for fear of missing it" and got stung, he says. But now, seeking to avoid past mistakes, "they are taking profits on the way up."

To a large degree, the bullish dollar theme is as much a tale of European woe as American cheer. Europe, analysts argue, is wrought with political and social uncertainties. Eastern Europe could explode the way Yugoslavia has. The European Community is foundering and the leaders of Britain, France, Germany and Italy are all politically weak.

"There is going to be a sense of political stability in the U.S. over the next four years," says Mr. Dennis. "With all the tension, turmoil and economic gloom in Europe, that's going to be a tremendous plus for the dollar."

Mr. Magnus of S. G. Warburg says: "Investors are going to be very hesitant about holding European currencies because of economic and political paralysis."

Continued

CASE: USING ECONOMIC INFORMATION TO FORECAST EXCHANGE RATES

Continued

Importantly, "the foreign-exchange market will conclude that the German problems aren't cyclical but structural," says UBS's Mr. Chertkow, noting that the country will need to borrow roughly 200 billion marks in 1993, or about 6% of its gross domestic product. He adds that "Germany's domestic financial problems, as a result of reunification, will continue to be exacerbated by the need to assist Germany's east European neighbors in order to minimize the social unrest in those countries from spreading across its borders."

By contrast, U.S. growth will pick up, inflation will remain under control, and the U.S. current account deficit will be small. "That shouldn't restrain the dollar's recovery," contends Mr. Chertkow.

What's more, Mr. Veit of Brown Brothers Harriman says: "The painful industrial restructuring America is going through at the moment will make the country even more competitive."

Many analysts predict Japan's economic slump will initially weaken the yen a bit before the currency strengthens later in the year on the back of the country's huge and expanding current account surplus. Also, following another round of cuts in official interest rates, the Bank of Japan is expected to keep rates stable to higher.

Of course, there are risks to the strong dollar scenario. The U.S. recovery could peter out, or the new Clinton administration could go on a spending program that balloons the U.S. budget deficit.

Source: *The Wall Street Journal* (January 4, 1993), p. R13. Reprinted by permission of *The Wall Street Journal,* © 1993 Dow Jones & Company, Inc. All rights reserved worldwide.

Questions

1. During the ERM crisis, Germany's interest rates increased, while U.S. interest rates declined. How did this affect the market's "bullish" opinion about the dollar?

2. What is meant by the statement that "the dollar is also poised to rise from a technical standpoint"?

3. What fundamental factors are given attention by the analysts that offered forecasts of the dollar's value? Explain each factor.

WHALER PUBLISHING COMPANY
Forecasting Exchange Rates

Whaler Publishing Co. specializes in producing textbooks in the United States and marketing these books in foreign universities where the English language is used. Its sales are invoiced in the currency of the country where the textbooks are sold. The expected revenues from textbooks sold to university book stores are as follows:

University Book Stores In:	Local Currency	Today's Spot Exchange Rate	Expected Revenues from Book Stores This Year
Australia	Australian Dollars (A$)	$ .7671	A$38,000,000
Canada	Canadian Dollars (C$)	.8625	C$35,000,000
New Zealand	New Zealand Dollars (N$)	.5985	N$33,000,000
United Kingdom	Pounds (£)	1.9382	£34,000,000

Whaler is comfortable with the estimated foreign currency revenues in each country. However, it is very uncertain about the U.S. dollar revenues to be received from each country. At this time (which is the beginning of year 16), Whaler is using today's spot rate as its best guess of the exchange rate at which the revenues from each country will be converted into U.S. dollars at the end of this year (which implies a zero percentage change in the value of each currency). Yet, it recognizes the potential error associated with this type of forecast. Therefore it desires to incorporate the risk surrounding each currency forecast by creating confidence intervals for each currency. First, it must derive the annual percentage change in the exchange rate over each of the last fifteen years for each currency to derive a standard deviation in the percentage change of each foreign currency. By assuming that the percentage changes in exchange rates are normally distributed, it plans to develop two ranges of forecasts for the annual percentage change in each currency: (1) one standard deviation in each direction from its best guess to develop a 68 percent confidence interval, and (2) two standard deviations in each direction from its best guess to develop a 95 percent confidence interval. These confidence intervals can then be applied to today's spot rates to develop confidence intervals for the future spot rate one year from today.

The exchange rates at the beginning of each of the last 16 years for each currency (with respect to the U.S. dollar) are as follows:

WHALER PUBLISHING COMPANY
Continued

Beginning of Year	Australian $	Canadian $	New Zealand $	British Pound
1	$1.2571	$.9839	$1.0437	$2.0235
2	1.0864	.9908	.9500	1.7024
3	1.1414	.9137	1.0197	1.9060
4	1.1505	.8432	1.0666	2.0345
5	1.1055	.8561	.9862	2.2240
6	1.1807	.8370	.9623	2.3850
7	1.1279	.8432	.8244	1.9080
8	.9806	.8137	.7325	1.6145
9	.9020	.8038	.6546	1.4506
10	.8278	.7570	.4776	1.1565
11	.6809	.7153	.4985	1.4445
12	.6648	.7241	.5235	1.4745
13	.7225	.8130	.6575	1.8715
14	.8555	.8382	.6283	1.8095
15	.7831	.8518	.5876	1.5772
16	.7671	.8625	.5985	1.9382

The confidence intervals for each currency can be applied to the expected book revenues to derive confidence intervals in U.S. dollars to be received from each country. Complete this assignment for Whaler Publishing Company, and also rank the currencies in terms of uncertainty (degree of volatility). Since the exchange rate data provided are real, the analysis will indicate (1) how volatile currencies can be, (2) how much more volatile some currencies are than others, and (3) how estimated revenues can be subject to a high degree of uncertainty as a result of uncertain exchange rates. [If you use a spreadsheet to do this case, you may want to retain it, since the case in the following chapter is an extension of this case.]

PROJECT

1. Assess the forecasting accuracy of the forward rate using a currency of your choice and the data bank in the back of this text. Use a procedure similar to that used within this chapter on the British pound. Is the forward rate of your currency more accurate than the forward rate of the pound (based on results shown in this chapter)? Did your forward rate exhibit an upward or downward bias in any periods? Explain.

REFERENCES

Bekaert, Geert, and Robert J. Hodrick. "On Biases in the Measurement of Foreign Exchange Premiums." *Journal of International Money and Finance* (April 1993), pp. 115–138.

Bilson, John F. "The Speculative Efficiency Hypothesis." *Journal of Business* (July 1982), pp. 435–451.

Cavaglia, Stefano, William F. C. Verschoor, and Christian C. P. Wolff. "Further Evidence on Exchange Rate Expectations." *Journal of International Money and Finance* (February 1993), pp. 78–98.

Chiang, Thomas C. "On the Predictors of the Future Spot Rates—A Multi-Currency Analysis." *The Financial Review* (February 1986), pp. 69–83.

Cornell, Bradford. "Spot Rates, Forward Rates and Exchange Market Efficiency." *Journal of Financial Economics* (August 1977), pp. 55–66.

Cornell, Bradford, and J. Kimball Dietrich. "The Efficiency of the Market for Foreign Exchange Under Floating Exchange Rates." *Review of Economics and Statistics* (February 1978), pp. 111–120.

Finnerty, J. E., J. Owers, and F. J. Creran. "Foreign Exchange Forecasting and Leading Economic Indicators: The U.S.–Canadian Experience." *Management International Review* (1987), no. 2, pp. 59–70.

Frankel, Jeffrey. "Tests of Rational Expectations in the Forward Exchange Market." *Southern Economic Journal* (April 1980), pp. 1083–1001.

Giddy, Ian H., and Gunter Dufey. "The Random Behavior of Flexible Exchange Rates: Implications for Forecasting." *Journal of International Business Studies* (Spring 1975), pp. 1–32.

Goodman, Stephen H. "Foreign Exchange Rate Forecasting Techniques: Implications for Business and Policy." *Journal of Finance* (May 1979), pp. 415–427.

———. "No Better Than the Toss of a Coin." *Euromoney* (December 1978), pp. 75–85.

Hansen, Lars Peter, and Robert J. Hodrick. "Forward Exchange Rates as Optimal Predictors of Future Spot Rates: An Econometric Analysis." *Journal of Political Economy* (October 1980), pp. 829–853.

Levich, Richard M. "How the Rise of the Dollar Took Forecasters by Surprise." *Euromoney* (August 1982), pp. 98–111.

———. "Are Forward Exchange Rates Unbiased Predictors of Future Spot Rates?" *Columbia Journal of World Business* (Winter 1979), pp. 49–61.

———. "Currency Forecasters Lose Their Way." *Euromoney* (August 1983), pp. 140–148.

Levich, Richard M., and Lee R. Thomas III. "The Significance of Technical Trading-Rule Profits in the Foreign Exchange Market: A Bootstrap Approach." *Journal of International Money and Finance* (October 1993), pp. 451–474.

Longworth, David. "Testing the Efficiency of the Canadian U.S. Exchange Market Under the Assumption of a No Risk Premium." *Journal of Finance* (March 1981), pp. 43–49.

Madura, Jeff. "Detecting Bias in Forward Exchange Rates." *Journal of Business Forecasting* (Fall 1983), pp. 19–20.

Ott, Mack and Paul T. W. M. Veugelers. "Forward Exchange Rates in Efficient Markets: The Effects of News and Changes in Monetary Policy Regimes." *Review,* Federal Reserve Bank of St. Louis (June–July 1986), pp. 5–15.

Rosenberg, Michael R. "Is Technical Analysis Right for Currency Forecasting?" *Euromoney* (July 1981), pp. 125–130.

Sweeney, Richard J. "Beating the Foreign Exchange Market," *Journal of Finance* (March 1986), pp. 163–182.

Wolff, Christian, "Exchange Rates, Innovations, and Forecasting." *Journal of International Money and Finance* (March 1988), pp. 49–62.

CHAPTER 10

MEASURING EXPOSURE TO EXCHANGE RATE FLUCTUATIONS

Exchange rate risk can be broadly defined as the risk that a company's performance will be affected by exchange rate movements. Multinational corporations (MNCs) closely monitor their operations to determine how they are exposed to various forms of exchange rate risk. The specific objectives of this chapter are to

- discuss the relevance of an MNC's exposure to exchange rate risk,
- explain how transaction exposure can be measured,
- explain how economic exposure can be measured, and
- explain how translation exposure can be measured.

IS EXCHANGE RATE RISK RELEVANT?

Some critics may suggest that a firm's exposure to exchange rate risk is not relevant and that firms therefore need not measure or manage their exposure. One argument for exchange rate irrelevance is that, according to purchasing power parity (PPP) theory, exchange rate movements should be matched by price movements. For example, consider the case of Office Import Company, a U.S. importer of office supplies that distributes these supplies throughout the country. Assume that Office Import Company presently competes against several U.S. companies that produce their own office supplies. If the dollar depreciates, Office Import Company will need more dollars to cover its import payments. Yet, according to PPP, a decline in the dollar would be associated with relatively high inflation in the United States. Thus, while the local competitors would not be affected by the dollar's decline, their cost of producing supplies would increase as a result of inflation. And although Office Import Company would be adversely affected by the dollar's decline, it would avoid the higher production costs in the

United States. It may therefore be argued that this offsetting effect makes exchange rate risk irrelevant. However, PPP does not necessarily hold. It is quite possible that the exchange rate will not change in accordance with the inflation differential between the two countries. Since a perfect offsetting effect is unlikely, the firm's competitive capabilities may indeed be influenced by exchange rate movements. Even if PPP did hold over a very long period of time, this would not comfort firms that are focusing on the next two to five years.

A second argument for exchange rate irrelevance is that investors in MNCs could hedge this risk on their own. For example, if investors in Office Import Company are aware that performance may be affected by exchange rate fluctuations, they may choose to take positions (in futures contracts or options contracts) to offset any adverse impact of dollar depreciation on Office Import Company. The reasoning is that exchange rate risk is not relevant to corporations because shareholders can deal with this risk individually.

Why Exchange Rate Risk is Relevant

The argument above assumes that investors have complete information on corporate exposure to exchange rate fluctuations as well as the capabilities to correctly insulate their individual exposure. To the extent that investors prefer that corporations perform the hedging for them, exchange rate exposure is relevant to corporations.

Volatile foreign earnings can also cause more volatile growth and downsizing cycles within a firm, which is more costly than slow stable growth. Hedging can reduce the firm's volatility of cash flows because the firm's payments and receipts are not forced to fluctuate in accordance with currency movements. This can reduce the possibility of bankruptcy, which allows the firm easier access to credit from creditors or suppliers, and may allow the firm to borrow at lower interest rates (because the perceived risk is lower). Hedging may also allow the firm to more accurately forecast future payments and receipts, which can enhance its cash budgeting decisions.

Numerous MNCs, including Colgate, Eastman Kodak, and Merck, have attempted to stabilize their earnings with hedging strategies. Merck found a high correlation between its historical foreign earnings and research and development spending. When the dollar was weak, foreign sales were higher, and funds were available for research and development. However, when the dollar was strong, Merck's foreign earnings declined, and it had less funds available for research and development. To stabilize its research and development program, it decided to stabilize its foreign earnings by implementing a five-year hedging plan.

As mentioned in the previous chapter, exchange rates cannot be forecasted with perfect accuracy, but the firm can at least measure its exposure to exchange rate fluctuations. If the firm is highly exposed to exchange rate fluctuations, it can consider techniques to reduce its exposure. Such techniques are identified in the following chapter. Before choosing among them, the firm should first measure its degree of exposure.

Exposure to exchange rate fluctuations comes in three forms:

- Transaction exposure
- Economic exposure
- Translation exposure.

Each type of exposure will be discussed in turn.

TRANSACTION EXPOSURE

The value of a firm's cash inflows received in various currencies will be affected by respective exchange rates of these currencies when converted into the currency desired. Similarly, the value of a firm's cash outflows in various currencies will be dependent on the respective exchange rates of these currencies. The degree to which the value of future cash transactions can be affected by exchange rate fluctuations is referred to as **transaction exposure.**

Because of the high variability in exchange rates, transaction risk is critical to an MNC. Two steps are involved in measuring transaction exposure: (1) determine the projected net amount of inflows or outflows in each foreign currency, and (2) determine the overall risk of exposure to those currencies. Each of these steps is discussed in turn.

Transaction Exposure to "Net" Cash Flows

Measurement of transaction exposure requires projections of the consolidated net amount in currency inflows or outflows for all subsidiaries, categorized by currency. Subsidiary X may have net inflows of £500,000, while Subsidiary Y may have net outflows of £600,000. The consolidated net inflows here would be −£100,000. If the pound depreciates before the individual cash flows take place, this will have an unfavorable impact on Subsidiary X, since the pounds will be worth less when converted to the desired currency. However, the pound's depreciation will have a favorable impact on Subsidiary Y, since it will not need as much of its currency to make payments denominated in pounds. The net effect of the pound's depreciation on the MNC is minor, since there is an offsetting effect. The net effect could be substantial, though, if most subsidiaries had future inflows of British pounds. Estimating the consolidated net cash inflows is a useful first step when assessing an MNC's exposure, since it helps to determine the MNC's overall position in each currency.

Example. Consider a U.S.-based MNC called Miami Company that estimates its consolidated cash flows for one period ahead, as shown in Exhibit 10.1. All estimated inflows and outflows for a currency are combined to determine the "net" position in that currency. Any offsetting positions in a currency are of no concern, since they do not contribute to transaction exposure of the entire MNC. The largest open (non-offset) currency position in Exhibit 10.1 is in French francs, from the U.S.-based MNC's perspective. Its net cash flow position shows a net inflow of 40 million units.

Assume that Miami Company uses the information in Exhibit 10.1 to develop a range of possible exchange rates that may exist at the end of the period. Applying the range of possible exchange rates to the number of units of each currency to be received or needed one period ahead, the MNC could determine a possible range in its local currency (the U.S. dollar in our example) of inflows or outflows related to each foreign currency. Exhibit 10.2 illustrates how this can be done. The first row of the exhibit shows an expected net outflow of 4 million Canadian dollars, as was given earlier. Based on the range in the

EXHIBIT 10.1   Consolidated Net Cash Flow Assessment of Miami Company

Currency	Total Inflow	Total Outflow	Net Inflow or Outflow	Current Exchange Rate	Net Inflow or Outflow as Measured in U.S. Dollars
Canadian dollar	C$2,000,000	C$6,000,000	C$4,000,000 (outflow)	$.80	$3,200,000 (outflow)
German mark	DM10,000,000	DM12,000,000	DM2,000,000 (outflow)	$.50	$1,000,000 (outflow)
French franc	FF100,000,000	FF60,000,000	FF40,000,000 (inflow)	$.10	$4,000,000 (inflow)
Swiss franc	SF1,000,000	SF6,000,000	SF5,000,000 (outflow)	$.60	$3,000,000 (outflow)

EXHIBIT 10.2   Estimating the Range of Net Inflows or Outflows for Miami Company

Currency	Net Inflow or Outflow	Range of Possible Exchange Rates at End of Period	Range of Possible Net Inflows or Outflows in U.S. Dollars (Based on Range of Possible Exchange Rates)
Canadian dollar (C$)	C$4,000,000 (outflow)	$.79 to $.81	$3,160,000 to $3,240,000 (outflow)
German mark (DM)	DM2,000,000 (outflow)	$.48 to $.52	$960,000 to $1,040,000 (outflow)
French franc (FF)	FF40,000,000 (inflow)	$.09 to $.11	$3,600,000 to $4,400,000 (inflow)
Swiss franc (SF)	SF5,000,000 (outflow)	$.56 to $.64	$2,800,000 to $3,200,000 (outflow)

possible exchange rate of the Canadian dollar of from $.79 to $.81, the range of possible net inflows or outflows is from $3,160,000 at the low end (computed as C$4,000,000 × $.79 per unit) to $3,240,000 at the high end (computed as C$4,000,000 × $.81 per unit). This range of possible net inflows or outflows expressed in the MNC parent's local currency is displayed in the last column of Exhibit 10.2. Notice from that column that the range of possible U.S. dollar outflows needed to obtain Swiss francs is actually larger than the range of possible U.S. dollar outflows needed to obtain Canadian dollars. This occurs because the range of possible exchange rates for the Swiss franc is wider than the range for the Canadian dollar. The main point of this comparison is that a firm's transaction exposure in any foreign currency is not based merely on the size of its open position in that currency. It is also based on the range of possible exchange rates that may occur for each foreign currency.

In this example, the net inflows or outflows in each foreign currency are provided, but the exchange rates at the end of the period are assumed uncertain. In reality, the net inflows or outflows in each foreign currency would also be uncertain. Thus, the MNC might develop a range of possible net inflows and outflows of each currency instead of a point estimate. If so, the second column of Exhibit 10.2 would show a range. At this point, the measurement of exposure in each currency becomes more complex. Some methods, though, such as sensitivity analysis or simulation, could be used to generate a range of estimates for exposure in each currency, based on the given ranges of the possible net inflows or outflows in each currency, as well as the possible exchange rates.

In the example, the net cash flow situation is assessed for only one period. This period could reflect a month, a quarter, or a year. MNCs may desire to assess their transaction exposure during several periods. To do this, the same methods that were described could be applied to each period. The farther into the future the MNC attempts to measure transaction exposure, the less accurate will be the measurement. This is due to greater uncertainty about inflows or outflows in each foreign currency, as well as future exchange rates, over periods farther into the future. The net exposure identified in Exhibits 10.1 and 10.2 will be assessed after the following discussion of currency variability and correlations.

Transaction Exposure Based on Currency Variability

In the above example, the ranges of projected exchange rates for the end of the period are given without any explanation as to how they were derived. Each MNC may have its own method for developing exchange rate projections. Some methods have been described in the previous chapter. While it is sometimes impossible to predict future currency values with much accuracy, an MNC can evaluate historical data in order to at least assess the potential degree of movement for each currency.

The standard deviation statistic serves as one possible way to measure the degree of movement for each particular currency. To demonstrate the use of such information, consider a U.S.-based MNC trying to assess currency movements. It could evaluate the historical variability in each foreign currency based on the standard deviation statistics. The second column of Exhibit 10.3 displays the

EXHIBIT 10.3 Standard Deviations of Exchange Rate Movements	Currency	Time Period		
		1972–1992	1972–1982	1983–1992
	British pound	.0564	.0493	.0630
	Canadian dollar	.0212	.0214	.0210
	French franc	.0606	.0589	.0622
	German mark	.0657	.0645	.0678
	Japanese yen	.0609	.0592	.0631
	Swiss franc	.0745	.0763	.0734

standard deviation of six foreign currencies (based on quarterly data) during the 1972–1992 period. From this exhibit, it is clear that some currencies fluctuate much more than others. For example, the standard deviation of the French franc's exchange rate movements is about 6 percent, which is almost three times that of the Canadian dollar. Other currencies also exhibit more than triple the variability of the Canadian dollar. Based on this information, a U.S.-based MNC may feel that an open asset or liability position in Canadian dollars is not as worrisome as an open position in other currencies. That is, the potential for these other currencies to deviate far from their projected future values is greater than the same potential for the Canadian dollar (from the U.S. firm's perspective). Yet, there is more to consider than the currency's standard deviation when assessing transaction exposure, as will be discussed shortly.

Currency Variability over Time

The variability of a currency will not necessarily remain consistent from one time period to another. Columns 3 and 4 in Exhibit 10.3 illustrate how standard deviations can change over time. Most currencies were more volatile against the dollar in the 1983–1992 period than in the 1972–1982 period.

Since currency variability levels change over time, the MNC's assessment of a currency's future variability will not be perfect when a previous time period is used as the indicator. However, the MNC can benefit from information such as that in Exhibit 10.3 if it is used wisely. While the MNC may not be able to predict a currency's future variability with perfect accuracy, it can identify currencies whose values are *most likely* to be stable or highly variable in the future. For example, the Canadian dollar consistently exhibits lower variability than any of the other currencies in the future. Thus, the U.S.-based MNC is less concerned with open positions in the Canadian dollar relative to most other foreign currencies, even though it is not sure what the Canadian dollar's variability will be in the future.

Transaction Exposure Based on Currency Correlations

While the above analysis can help an MNC measure its transaction exposure, currency correlations must also be assessed. Consider two U.S.-based MNCs (called American MNC and National MNC) that have consolidated the anticipated net inflows or outflows for all currencies of all subsidiaries. Assume American MNC is exposed to a large volume of Canadian dollar inflows while National MNC is exposed to a large volume of German mark inflows and French franc outflows. Which MNC is more exposed to transaction risk? It may seem that National MNC is more exposed, since its exposure is to two currencies that fluctuate to a high degree against the U.S. dollar. American MNC may appear to be less exposed, since the Canadian dollar is quite stable. This reasoning ignores the important concept of currency correlations, which will now be discussed.

Assume for the moment that the German mark and the French franc values relative to the U.S. dollar are highly positively correlated. This means that when the mark appreciates against the U.S. dollar, so will the French franc, and by about the same degree. Also, if one of these currencies is depreciating against the U.S. dollar, the other currency is following a similar pattern. Relate this information to National MNC, which has future inflows in marks and future outflows in French francs. If these currencies simultaneously depreciate against the U.S. dollar, the mark inflows will be worth less when converted to U.S. dollars, and it will take fewer U.S. dollars to pay for the outflows denominated in French francs. Two highly correlated currencies act almost as if they are the same currency. The transaction exposure to inflows of one currency and outflows of the other currency are then offset. Normally, currencies do not move exactly in tandem over time. Yet, even if the currencies move in the same direction to a degree, a partial offsetting effect will take place when one currency represents an inflow while the other currency represents an outflow.

When the MNC has two or more inflow currencies, it can still benefit from assessing correlations. Consider these inflows as a portfolio. The lower the correlations are in this case, the lower will be the overall variability of the portfolio of cash inflows. From a U.S. MNC's perspective, variability provides a measure of the potential degree to which the portfolio's dollar value may fluctuate. This reflects the uncertainty about what the portfolio will be worth. MNCs would normally prefer to have a cash inflow portfolio that exhibits low variability, since there is less chance that the value of such a portfolio will substantially deviate from what is expected. A portfolio of currencies with low (or negative) correlations can reduce portfolio variability, because all the currencies would not all be moving in the same direction at about the same magnitude (as they would be if they were highly correlated). Thus, there is an offsetting effect, making the overall movement of the portfolio over time more stable. A similar methodology could be used by the MNC to assess the various consolidated net outflow currencies (or the portfolio of cash outflows).

Measurement of Currency Correlations.   The correlations among currency movements can be measured by their *correlation coefficients*, which indicate the degree to which two currencies move in relation to each other. Thus, MNCs could use such information when deciding their degree of transaction exposure. The extreme case is perfect positive correlation, which is represented by a correlation coefficient equal to 1.00. Correlations can also be negative, reflecting an inverse relationship between individual movements, the extreme case being −1.00. The correlation coefficients (based on quarterly data) for currency pairs in three different periods are illustrated in Exhibit 10.4. First consider the top number in each cell, which represents the 1972–1992 period. It is clear that some currency pairs exhibit a much higher correlation than others. For example, the German mark/French franc correlation is .87 and the German mark/Swiss franc correlation is .88. At the other extreme, the Canadian dollar has a very low correlation with other currencies. Currency correlations are generally positive; this implies that currencies tend to move in the same direction against the U.S. dollar (though by different degrees). The positive correlation may not always occur on a day-to-day basis, but it appears to hold over longer periods of time for most currencies. This is especially true of European currency movements against the dollar.

Scenarios.   To illustrate how MNCs would assess exposure based on currency movements, consider the historical exchange rate fluctuations as shown in Exhibit 10.5 for Currencies X, Y, and Z. Assume you are treasurer of a U.S.-based MNC when examining the following two scenarios.

Scenario 1. Assume that you expect as of one year from now to need $10 million for the purchase of Currency X and another $20 million to purchase Currency Y. You also expect to receive about $30 million when converting inflows

EXHIBIT 10.4
Correlations among Exchange Rate Movements
*The top number in each cell represents the entire 1972–1992 period, while the middle number in each cell represents an early subperiod (1972–1982), and the lower number in each cell represents the more recent subperiod (1983–1992).

	British pound	Canadian dollar	French franc	German mark	Japanese yen	Swiss franc
British pound	1.00					
	1.00					
	1.00					
Canadian dollar	.22	1.00				
	.01	1.00				
	.39	1.00				
French franc	.63	.05	1.00			
	.55	.06	1.00			
	.69	.02	1.00			
German mark	.67	.13	.87	1.00		
	.60	.09	.85	1.00		
	.73	.17	.89	1.00		
Japanese yen	.58	.16	.60	.67	1.00	
	.45	.01	.55	.54	1.00	
	.69	.32	.65	.78	1.00	
Swiss franc	.64	.16	.78	.88	.73	1.00
	.55	.08	.77	.83	.65	1.00
	.73	.26	.81	.94	.83	1.00

EXHIBIT 10.5
Illustration of Currency Movements for Scenarios

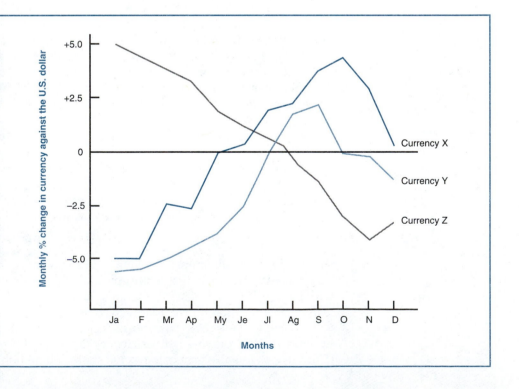

of Currency Z one year from now. There is much transaction exposure in this scenario, as explained below.

Exhibit 10.5 suggests that Currencies X and Y are highly correlated with each other, but negatively correlated with Currency Z. If Currencies X and Y appreciate against the U.S. dollar, more dollars will be needed to purchase them. And if they appreciate against the dollar, Currency Z will likely depreciate against the dollar, based on its historical co-movements with Currencies X and Y. Since Currency Z is to be received by the MNC in the future, this cash inflow will convert to fewer U.S. dollars if it does depreciate. Thus, the MNC could possibly end up receiving fewer dollars and paying out more dollars than it currently expects to.

Scenario 2. Assume that you expect as of one year from now to need $10 million for the purchase of Currency X, and another $20 million to purchase Currency Y (as in Scenario 1). Also, assume that you expect to need another $30 million to purchase Currency Z one year from now. Finally, assume that you have no projected inflows in foreign currencies. There is not much transaction risk in this scenario, when you consider all currencies simultaneously. Based on the correlations that appear to exist as shown in Exhibit 10.5, the changes in values of Currencies X and Y will be somewhat offset by opposite movements in Currency Z. For example, if Currencies X and Y appreciate by 20 percent, the MNC will need $36 million instead of $30 million to buy these currencies. Yet, Currency Z will likely depreciate under this situation. A perfect offset would occur if Currency Z depreciated by 20 percent, so that it would take only $24 million to purchase the necessary amount of Currency Z. Then, the additional $6 million needed to purchase Currencies X and Y would be offset by the $6 million saved due to depreciation of Currency Z. A perfect offset is not likely to occur, but the point here is to be able to detect positions that could somewhat offset each other.

In summary, the first step when assessing transaction exposure is to determine the size of the position in each currency. The second step is to determine how that individual currency position could affect the firm. This is accomplished by assessing the standard deviations and correlations of the currencies. Even if a particular currency is perceived as risky, its impact on the firm's overall variability will not be severe if the firm has taken just a minor position in that currency. For this reason, both of these steps must be considered simultaneously when developing an overall assessment of the firm's transaction risk.

Currency Correlations over Time

Notice from Exhibit 10.4 that correlations are not constant over time. Therefore, the MNC cannot use previous correlations to predict future correlations with perfect accuracy. There are some pairs of currencies whose co-movements are somewhat stable over time, however, so the correlations disclosed in Exhibit 10.4 can provide valuable information for MNCs. For example, the European currencies are consistently highly correlated with each other. At the other extreme, the Canadian dollar consistently appears to move almost independently of the other currencies, based on its continued low correlations with them.

The actual movements of some major currencies against the U.S. dollar are shown in Exhibit 10.6. In this exhibit, it is clear that the Swiss and German currencies are highly correlated. In fact, all European currencies shown here tend to move in tandem. The characteristics of currencies illustrated by Exhibit 10.6 support the information provided earlier on currency correlations.

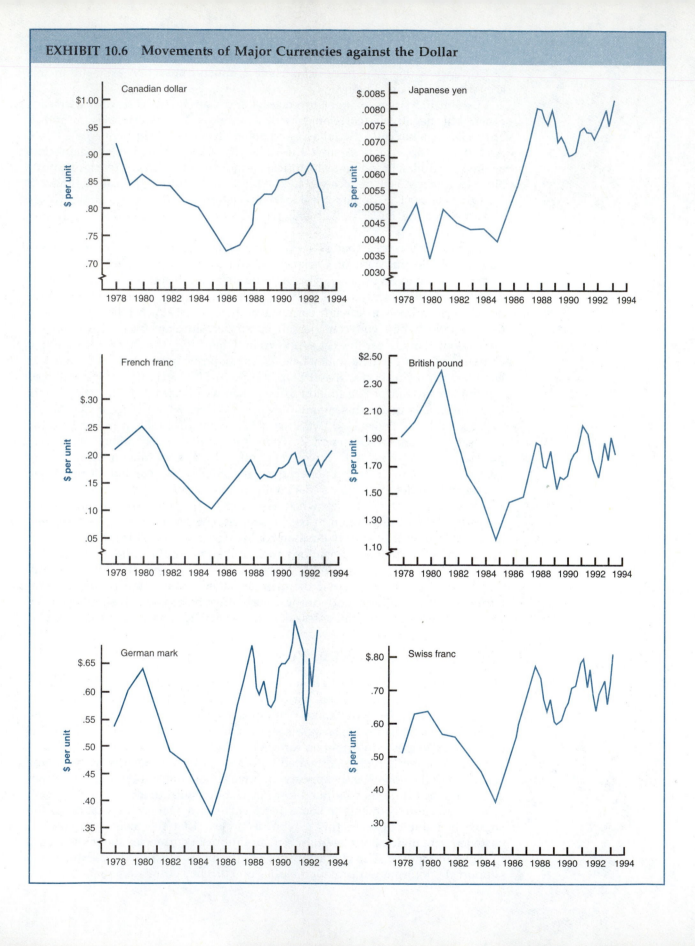

EXHIBIT 10.6   Movements of Major Currencies against the Dollar

Assessing Transaction Exposure: An Example

The concept of currency correlations can be applied to the earlier example of Miami Company's transaction exposure, as displayed in Exhibit 10.1. If European currencies such as the German mark, French franc, and Swiss franc are highly correlated, then the exposures to the cash inflows and outflows in these currencies will offset each other to a degree. Miami Company anticipates cash inflows in French francs equivalent to $4 million, and cash outflows in German marks and Swiss francs with a combined equivalent of $4 million. Thus, if a weak-dollar cycle occurs, it will be adversely affected by its exposure to German marks and Swiss francs, but favorably affected by its French franc exposure. During a strong-dollar cycle, it will be adversely affected by the French franc exposure, but favorably affected by the German mark and Swiss franc exposure. Under these conditions, the only exposure of concern to the firm would be the Canadian dollar. Since the firm has an outflow position in Canadian dollars, it could be adversely affected if the Canadian dollar appreciates against the U.S. dollar. Yet, because the Canadian dollar is somewhat stable with respect to the U.S. dollar over time, the risk of substantial appreciation of the Canadian dollar is low. In general, the overall transaction exposure of the firm to possible changes in exchange rates is low, because of the offsetting effects of the European currencies and the stability of the Canadian dollar.

Additional Example. To test your ability to assess transaction exposure, consider the exposure of Boston Company to exchange rate fluctuations. Boston's transaction exposure is summarized in Exhibit 10.7. Notice that the only difference between Boston Company and Miami Company is that Boston's French franc exposure represents a cash outflow rather than an inflow, and its Canadian dollar exposure represents a cash inflow rather than an outflow. Assume as before that the European currencies are now highly correlated. Boston Company will be adversely affected by a weak-dollar cycle, since it will need more dollars to make payment on each currency position. There is no offsetting effect as there is for Miami Company, since the Canadian dollar is the only inflow currency, and it does not move in tandem with the European currencies. It should be recognized that Boston Company is more likely to benefit from a strong-dollar cycle, since it will need less dollars to make payment on each currency position (and its inflows in Canadian dollars will not likely be affected much by the dollar's strength). Whether Boston Company decides to hedge its exposure will depend on its forecasts of exchange rates.

EXHIBIT 10.7 Transaction Exposure of Boston Company	Currency	Net Inflow or Outflow
	Canadian dollar	C$4 million (inflow)
	German mark	DM2 million (outflow)
	French franc	FF40 million (outflow)
	Swiss franc	SF5 million (outflow)

ECONOMIC EXPOSURE

The degree to which a firm's present value of future cash flows can be influenced by exchange rate fluctuations is referred to as **economic exposure** to exchange rates. Transaction exposure is a subset of economic exposure. However, the influence of exchange rate fluctuations on a firm's cash flows is not always due to transaction of currencies. This will become clear shortly. Some of the more common variables representing an MNC's cash flows subject to economic exposure are listed in the first column of Exhibit 10.8. They are categorized as affecting inflows or outflows. The second column of Exhibit 10.8 suggests how each of these variables may be affected by appreciation of the firm's local currency, while the third column suggests how each variable is affected by depreciation of the firm's local currency. A discussion of the impact of local currency appreciation on each variable follows.

EXHIBIT 10.8
Economic Exposure to Exchange Rate Fluctuations

Variables That Influence the Firm's Local Currency Inflows	Impact of Local Currency Appreciation on Variables	Impact of Local Currency Depreciation on Variables
Local sales (relative to foreign competition in local markets)	Decrease	Increase
Firm's exports denominated in local currency	Decrease	Increase
Firm's exports denominated in foreign currency	Decrease	Increase
Interest received from foreign investments	Decrease	Increase
Variables That Influence the Firm's Local Currency Outflows		
Firm's imported supplies denominated in local currency	No Change	No Change
Firm's imported supplies denominated in foreign currency	Decrease	Increase
Interest owed on foreign funds borrowed	Decrease	Increase

Economic Exposure to Local Currency Appreciation

The following discussion of economic exposure to local currency appreciation is related to Column 2 in Exhibit 10.8. With regard to the firm's cash inflows, its local sales (within the firm's country) are expected to decrease as a result of appreciation in the local currency. This is due to the increased foreign competition, as local customers could obtain foreign substitute products cheaply with their strengthened currency. The extent of reduced local sales would depend on the degree of foreign competition within the local market.

Cash inflows from exports denominated in the local currency would likely be reduced as a result of appreciation in the local currency. The reason is that foreign importers would need more of their own currency to pay for these products. Exports denominated in the foreign currency would also likely cause reduced cash inflows, but for a different reason. Demand for the firm's product by foreign importers would not change, since they could use their own currency and would not need to obtain the firm's local currency. However, when the firm received the foreign currency inflows, it would convert them to its local currency. If the local currency had appreciated, these inflows would convert to a reduced amount. Finally, any interest or dividends received from foreign investments would convert to a reduced amount in local currency inflows if the local currency had strengthened.

With regard to the firm's cash outflows, the cost of imported supplies denominated in the local currency would not be directly affected by any changes in exchange rates. However, the cost of imported supplies denominated in the foreign currency would be reduced if the local currency appreciated. In addition, any interest to be paid on financing in foreign currencies would be reduced (in terms of the local currency) if the local currency appreciated. This would be due to exchange of the strengthened local currency for the foreign currency in order to make interest payments.

Overall, appreciation in the firm's local currency causes a reduction in both cash inflows and outflows. Thus, it is difficult to generalize whether net cash flows will increase or decrease due to the local currency's appreciation. The impact of local currency appreciation on a firm's net cash flows depends on whether the inflow variables are affected more or less than the outflow variables. If, for example, the firm is in the exporting business but obtains its supplies and borrowed funds locally, its inflow variables will be reduced by a greater degree than its outflow variables. In this case, net cash flows will be reduced. Conversely, cash inflows of a firm concentrating its sales locally with little foreign competition will not be severely reduced by appreciation of the local currency. If such a firm obtains supplies and borrowed funds overseas, its outflows will be reduced. Overall, this firm's net cash flows will be enhanced by the appreciation of its local currency.

A prominent example of an MNC's economic exposure is Caterpillar Inc., which has relied heavily on exports for a large portion of its sales. The strengthening of the dollar increases the price paid by importers for Caterpillar's products. Caterpillar is especially vulnerable to the value of the dollar because its key competitor is Komatsu of Japan, whose exports are denominated in Japanese yen. When the value of the yen was relatively weak, many firms switched from Caterpillar to Komatsu. Caterpillar's performance improved substantially in periods when the yen and other foreign currencies strengthened against the dollar.

Economic Exposure to Local Currency Depreciation

If the firm's local currency depreciates (see Column 3 of Exhibit 10.8), the variables will be affected in a manner opposite to the way they are influenced by appreciation. Local sales should increase due to reduced foreign competition (since prices denominated in strong foreign currencies would seem high to the local customers). The firm's exports denominated in the local currency would appear cheap to importers, thereby increasing foreign demand for them. Even exports denominated in the foreign currency could increase cash flows, since a given amount in foreign currency inflows to the firm would convert to a larger amount of the local currency. In addition, interest or dividends from foreign investments would now convert to more of the local currency.

With regard to cash outflows, imported supplies denominated in the local currency would not be directly affected by any change in exchange rates. However, the cost of imported supplies denominated in the foreign currency would rise, since it would take more of the weakened local currency to obtain the foreign currency needed. Any interest payments paid on financing in foreign currencies would increase.

In general, depreciation of the firm's local currency causes an increase in both cash inflows and outflows. Because a partial offsetting effect is likely, it is difficult to generalize as to whether net cash flows will increase or decrease due to the local currency's depreciation. The end result depends on whether inflow variables are affected more than outflow variables. A firm that concentrates on exporting and obtains supplies and borrowed funds locally would likely benefit from a depreciated local currency. This was the case for Caterpillar during the 1985–1988 period, when the dollar weakened substantially against most major currencies. Conversely, a firm that concentrates on local sales, has very little foreign competition, and obtains foreign supplies (denominated in foreign currencies) would likely be hurt by a depreciated local currency.

Indirect Economic Exposure

The impact of a change in the local currency on inflow and outflow variables can sometimes be indirect, and therefore different from what is expected. For example, consider a U.S. firm that imports wood from Canada, and assume the imports are denominated in U.S. dollars. If the U.S. dollar depreciates, the U.S. firm is not directly affected, since its payment is in U.S. dollars and it will not need to obtain Canadian dollars. However, the Canadian exporter, upon receipt of the payment in U.S. dollars, may convert them to Canadian dollars. If the U.S. dollar has depreciated, the Canadian exporter will receive less in Canadian dollars. To offset this reduction in its inflows, it may charge the U.S. firm higher prices in the future. Such a policy would increase the U.S. firm's cash outflows needed to pay for imports denominated in U.S. dollars. The impact here would be indirect.

Economic Exposure of Domestic Firms

While our focus is on the financial management of MNCs, even purely domestic firms are affected by economic exposure. For example, consider a local steel producer that purchases all of its supplies locally and sells all of its steel locally.

Because the firm's transactions are solely in the local currency, it is not subject to transaction exposure. However, if there is foreign competition within the local markets this firm sells to, then it is subject to economic exposure. If the exchange rate of the foreign competitor's invoice currency depreciates against the local currency, then customers interested in steel products may shift their purchases toward the foreign steel producer. Consequently, demand for the local firm's steel will likely decrease, and so will net cash inflows. This example illustrates how a firm can be subject to economic exposure without being subject to transaction exposure.

Economic Exposure of MNCs

The degree of economic exposure to exchange rate fluctuations will likely be much greater for a firm involved in international business than for a purely domestic firm. As an example of an MNC's economic exposure, General Corporation arranged to sell software to Mexican customers in the early 1980s. However, the Mexican peso was devalued by 40 percent against the dollar, substantially increasing the Mexican customer's purchase price. Consequently, sales by General Corporation to Mexico declined. As another example, DuPont Company suffered a similar setback due to the weakness of foreign currencies against the dollar during 1983. The treasurer of DuPont estimated the 1983 losses to be as high as $100 million as a result of exchange rate effects in that year. The losses were due to weak foreign currency cash flows being converted to U.S. dollars, and a decline in the demand for DuPont's exports.

DuPont Company and many other U.S.-based MNCs benefited from the weaker dollar in the 1985–1988 period, and also during the 1990–1991 period. The volume of their exports increased substantially in response to a weaker dollar. DuPont's performance is very sensitive to exchange rates, because its export business is valued at over $3 billion.

During the first five months of 1993, the Japanese yen appreciated against the dollar by 13 percent, and reached a post–World War II high. This allowed many U.S. firms to increase their U.S. market share at the expense of Japanese exporters, who were priced out of the U.S. market.

The impact of the U.S. dollar's movements varies across U.S.-based MNCs because of their differences in operating characteristics. Even those U.S.-based MNCs that can be classified as heavy exporters may be affected differently, depending on how their competitors react to exchange rate movements. A U.S. exporter whose foreign competitors are willing to reduce their profit margin during a weak-dollar period may not necessarily benefit from the exchange rate movements.

The effects of exchange rate movements on MNCs can also vary with the currency of concern, since exchange rates can change by varying degrees. For example, while the Japanese yen appreciated against the dollar in the first half of 1993, some European currencies depreciated. Thus, U.S.-based MNCs with exports concentrated in Europe were adversely affected by their exposure, while those with exports concentrated in Japan were favorably affected.

The numerous examples provided above illustrate that (1) exchange rate movements can affect an MNC's performance, (2) the impact is sometimes favorable, and (3) the impact is dependent on the MNC's degree of exposure to the specific currency of concern.

IMPACT OF A WEAK DOLLAR ON EUROPEAN BUSINESS

To understand the potential impact of the dollar's value on corporate performance, consider the effects of the weak dollar on European firms. Volvo, Volkswagen, Jaguar, Airbus, Air France, Daimler Benz, and other European firms experienced a significant decline in U.S. demand because they were priced out of the U.S. market when the dollar weakened. Jaguar (a British-owned firm at the time) experienced losses of about $100 million in 1990, as its exports declined in response to the weak dollar. Since Jaguar had normally received about 40 percent of its revenues from exports to the U.S., its performance was very sensitive to the weakening of the dollar. During the beginning of 1991 when the British pound was worth almost $2, Jaguar's exports to the United States had declined by about 66 percent. Airbus was also adversely affected by the weak dollar. It receives dollars for its work contracts, while its expenses are in French francs. The dollar revenues when converted to francs were diminished by the exchange rate.

Some European governments have attempted to cushion the exchange rate effects on firms. For example, the French government provided Air France with capital. The German government provided subsidies to Daimler Benz.

The weak dollar concerns not only European exporters, but also European firms that may compete with U.S. exporters in the European markets. Some of these firms prefer that trade barriers be imposed on U.S. firms. Consequently, the momentum for free trade has been slowed.

The desire for free trade is somewhat dependent on the exchange rate. When the dollar was stronger in the early 1980s, some U.S. firms desired that trade barriers be enforced to prevent excessive foreign competition. As the dollar weakened considerably during the early 1990s, the European firms used the same argument. Some firms that either are involved in international trade or compete with foreign exporters would identify the exchange rate as the most critical factor affecting their performance.

Measuring Economic Exposure

While economic exposure can force either a favorable or an unfavorable impact on a company, it is critical for the company to assess the potential degree of exposure that exists, and then determine whether it should attempt to insulate itself against this exposure. Assessing the economic exposure of an MNC with subsidiaries scattered across countries is difficult, due to the interaction of cash flows denominated in various currencies into, out of, and within the MNC. The overall impact of a given currency's fluctuation on all of the subsidiaries is extremely complex.

Sensitivity of Earnings to Exchange Rates.
One method of measuring an MNC's economic exposure is to classify the cash flows into different income statement items and subjectively predict each income statement item based on a forecast of exchange rates. Then an alternative exchange rate scenario can be considered and the forecasts for the income statement items revised. By reviewing how the earnings forecast in the income statement changes in response to alternative exchange rate scenarios, the firm can assess the influence of currency movements on earnings and cash flows. If the firm's costs and revenues are

affected to a similar degree, it will be somewhat insulated from exchange rate movements.

To illustrate this procedure, consider Madison Inc., which is a U.S.-based company that conducts a portion of its business in Canada. Its U.S. sales are denominated in U.S. dollars, while its Canadian sales are denominated in Canadian dollars. Its pro forma income statement for next year is shown in Exhibit 10.9. The income statement items are segmented into those for the U.S. (Column 2) and for Canada (Column 3). Assume that Madison Inc. desires to assess how its income statement items would be affected by three possible exchange rate scenarios for the Canadian dollar over the period of concern: (1) $.75, (2) $.80, and (3) $.85. These scenarios are separately analyzed in the second, third, and fourth columns of Exhibit 10.10.

If the U.S. sales are unaffected by the possible exchange rates, the impact of exchange rates on all income statement items can be assessed from the information contained in Exhibit 10.9. However, to make the example more realistic, assume that Madison's sales in the United States are higher when the Canadian dollar (C$) is stronger, since Canadian competitors will be priced out of the U.S. market. To be specific, assume the following forecasts for U.S. sales corresponding to each possible exchange rate scenario:

Possible Exchange Rate of C$	Forecasted U.S. Sales (in Millions)
$.75	$300
.80	304
.85	307

The impact of an exchange rate on local sales for any firm would depend on the foreign competition of concern. Historical data could be used to assess how local sales had been affected by exchange rates in the past. For our example, the

EXHIBIT 10.9 Revenue and Cost Estimates: Madison Inc. (in millions of U.S. dollars and Canadian dollars)

	U.S. Business	Canadian Business
Sales	$304	C$ 4
Cost of goods sold	$ 50	C$200
Gross profit	$254	−C$196
Operating expenses		
Fixed	$ 30	—
Variable	$ 30.72	—
Total	$ 60.72	—
Earnings before interest and taxes	$193.28	−C$196
Interest expense	$ 3	C$ 10
Earnings before taxes (EBT)	$190.28	−C$206

EXHIBIT 10.10
Impact of Possible Exchange Rate Movements on Earnings (in millions)

	Exchange Rate Scenario					
		C$=$.75		C$=$.80		C$=$.85
Sales						
(1) U.S.		$300		$304		$307
(2) Canadian	C$4=	$ 3	C$4 =	$ 3.2	C$4 =	$ 3.4
(3) Total		$303		$307.2		$310.4
Cost of goods sold						
(4) U.S.		$ 50		$ 50		$ 50
(5) Canadian	C$200 =	$150	C$200 =	$160	C$200 =	$170
(6) Total		$200		$210		$220
(7) Gross profit		$103		$ 97.2		90.4
Operating expenses						
(8) U.S.: Fixed		$ 30		$ 30		$ 30
(9) U.S.: Variable (10% of total sales)		$ 30.3		$ 30.72		$ 31.04
(10) Total		$ 60.3		$ 60.72		$ 61.04
(11) EBIT		$ 42.7		$ 36.48		$ 29.36
Interest expense						
(12) U.S.		$ 3		$ 3		$ 3
(13) Canadian	C$10 =	$ 7.5	C$10 =	$ 8	C$10 =	$ 8.5
(14) Total		$ 10.5		$ 11		$ 11.5
(15) EBT		$ 32.2		$ 25.48		$ 17.86

impact of the exchange rate on local sales is given, so there is no need to assess historical data.

Given this information, Madison Inc. can determine how its pro forma statement would be affected by each exchange rate scenario, as shown in Exhibit 10.10. The assumed impact of exchange rates on U.S. sales is shown in Row 1. Row 2 shows the amount in U.S. dollars to be received as a result of Canadian sales (after converting the forecasted C$4 million of Canadian sales into U.S. dollars). Row 3 represents the estimated U.S. dollars to be received from total sales, which is determined by combining Rows 1 and 2. Row 4 shows the cost of goods sold in the U.S. Row 5 converts the estimated C$200 million cost of goods sold into U.S. dollars for each exchange rate scenario. Row 6 measures the estimated U.S. dollars needed to cover the total cost of goods sold, which is determined by combining Rows 4 and 5. Row 7 estimates the gross profit in U.S. dollars, as determined by subtracting Row 6 from Row 3. Rows 8 through 10 show estimated operating expenses, and Row 11 subtracts total operating expenses from gross profit to determine earnings before interest and taxes (EBIT). Row 12 estimates the interest expenses paid in the United States, while Row 13 estimates the U.S. dollars needed to make interest payments in Canada. Row 14 combines Rows 12 and 13 to estimate total U.S. dollars needed to make all interest payments. Row 15 shows earnings before taxes (EBT), estimated by subtracting Row 14 from Row 11.

The effect of exchange rates on Madison's revenues and costs can now be reviewed. Exhibit 10.10 illustrates how both U.S. sales and the dollar value of Canadian sales would increase as a result of a stronger Canadian dollar. Because Madison's Canadian cost of goods sold exposure (C\$200 million) is much greater than its Canadian sales exposure (C\$4 million), there is a negative overall impact of a strong Canadian dollar on gross profit. The total amount in U.S. dollars needed to make interest payments is also higher when the Canadian dollar is stronger. In general, Madison Inc. would be adversely affected by a stronger Canadian dollar. It would be favorably affected by a weaker Canadian dollar, since the reduced value of total revenues would be more than offset by the reduced cost of goods sold and interest expenses.

A general conclusion from our example is that firms with more (less) in foreign costs than in foreign revenues will be unfavorably (favorably) affected by a stronger foreign currency. Yet, the precise anticipated impact can be determined only by utilizing the procedure described here, or some alternative procedure. Our example is based on a one-period time horizon. If firms have developed forecasts of sales, expenses, and exchange rates for several periods ahead, they can assess their economic exposure over time. Their economic exposure will be affected by any change in operating characteristics over time.

Sensitivity of Cash Flows to Exchange Rates.   Another possible method of assessing the firm's economic exposure to currency movements is to apply regression analysis to historical cash flow and exchange rate data as follows:

$$PCF_t = a_0 + a_1 e_t + \mu_t,$$

where

PCF_t = percentage change in inflation-adjusted cash flows measured in the firm's home currency over period t

e_t = percentage change in the exchange rate of the currency over period t

μ_t = random error term

a_0 = intercept

a_1 = slope coefficient.

The regression coefficient a_1, estimated by regression analysis, would indicate the sensitivity of PCF_t to e_t. If the firm anticipated no major adjustments in its operating structure, it would expect the sensitivity detected from regression analysis to be somewhat similar in the future.

This regression model may be revised to handle more complex situations. For example, if additional currencies were to be assessed, they could be included in the model as additional independent variables. Each currency's impact would be measured by the estimate of its respective regression coefficient. If an MNC were influenced by numerous currencies, it could measure the sensitivity of PCF_t to an index (or composite) of currencies.

Some MNCs may prefer to use their stock price as a proxy for the firm's value, and then assess how their stock price changes in response to currency movements. Regression analysis could also be applied to this situation, by replacing PCF_t with the percentage change in stock price in the models specified here.

Some researchers, including Adler and Dumas, suggest the use of regression analysis for this purpose. By assigning stock returns as the dependent variable, regression analysis can indicate how firm value is sensitive to exchange rate fluctuations. The specifics of the regression model are provided in Appendix 10A.

Some companies may assess the impact of exchange rates on particular corporate characteristics, such as earnings, exports, or sales. For example, Toyota Motor Corporation has measured the sensitivity of exports to the yen exchange rate (relative to the U.S. dollar). Consequently, the firm can forecast the expected impact of a forecasted yen value on future exports.

TRANSLATION EXPOSURE

The exposure of the MNC's consolidated financial statements to exchange rate fluctuations is known as **translation exposure.** For example, if the assets or liabilities of the MNC's subsidiaries are translated at something other than historical exchange rates, the balance sheet will be affected by fluctuations in currency values over time. In addition, subsidiary earnings translated into the reporting currency on the consolidated income statement are subject to changing exchange rates. The importance of translation exposure is questioned in the following section. Then the determinants of translation exposure are identified. Finally, a description of the current accounting rules' impact on translation exposure is provided, and some examples of translation exposure are offered.

Does Translation Exposure Matter?

Translation of financial statements for consolidated reporting purposes does not affect an MNC's cash flows. For this reason, some analysts suggest that translation exposure is not relevant. Other analysts argue that because consolidated financial statements are representative of an MNC's performance, translation exposure is relevant. In the middle 1970s, a survey found that most firms identified translation exposure to be more important than transaction exposure. In 1977, a repeat of the survey found transaction exposure to be perceived as more important. This attitude appears to hold today. Each company has its own opinion as to whether it should attempt to hedge translation exposure. As an example, Kodak, Inc., does not spend much time hedging translation exposure, but is more concerned with transaction exposure.

MNCs not concerned with translation exposure could argue that the subsidiary earnings do not actually have to be converted into the parent's currency. Therefore, if the subsidiary's local currency is currently weak, the earnings could be retained rather than converted and sent to the parent. The earnings could be reinvested in the subsidiary's country if feasible opportunities exist. Because the subsidiary's earnings do not necessarily have to be exchanged for the parent's currency, the translation of a weakened subsidiary currency might distort the true performance of the subsidiary. If financial analysts recognize this distortion,

APPLIED RESEARCH

ESTIMATED IMPACT OF EXCHANGE RATES ON PROFITS

A recent article by Hung attempts to determine how profits of U.S. manufacturing firms have been affected by changes in exchange rates. Hung shows that exchange rates can affect domestic profits of U.S. firms by influencing the degree of competition from imports, as well as the demand for the U.S. firm's exports. In addition, profits from foreign operations of U.S. firms are influenced by translation effects.

Hung's analysis found the following results:

- A 1 percent increase in the dollar's value (relative to an index of foreign currencies) resulted in a .19 percent decline in U.S. export prices, as U.S. firms sometimes lower prices to partially compensate for an expensive dollar. The profits of U.S. firms are reduced not only by the price adjustment, but also by the reduction in foreign demand as the dollar strengthens.

- A model was developed to explain the variation in U.S. manufacturing profits over time. The model expressed these profits as a function of (1) foreign economic conditions (which can affect the foreign demand for U.S. exports and U.S. products produced overseas), (2) U.S. economic conditions, (3) price variables (which affect the competitiveness of U.S. firms), and (4) the real inflation-adjusted value of the U.S. dollar. Regression analysis was used to test the model. Based on the analysis, a 10 percent increase in the value of the dollar lowers manufacturing profits by about 6 percent. This result supports the typical view that a strong dollar adversely affects the performance of U.S. firms.

With 1980 used as a base year, the dollar's real value over the 1981–1990 period was 13.2 percent higher than its value in the base year. Hung estimates that as a result of the relatively strong average real value of the dollar over this decade, profits of U.S. manufacturing firms were reduced by about $190 billion.

they will not automatically assign a poor evaluation to MNCs whose consolidated earnings are reduced due to weakened subsidiary currencies.

Because all firms are not convinced that translation exposure is irrelevant, it is important to understand what influences a firm's degree of exposure to translation gains and losses. This topic is discussed in the following section.

Determinants of Translation Exposure

Translation exposure is dependent on

- The degree of foreign involvement by foreign subsidiaries
- The locations of foreign subsidiaries
- The accounting methods used.

Degree of Foreign Involvement. The greater the percentage of an MNC's business conducted by its foreign subsidiaries, the larger will be the percentage of a given financial statement item that is susceptible to translation exposure. For example, the foreign involvement of some MNCs may be mostly in the form of exporting. These MNCs don't have much of their business conducted by foreign subsidiaries. Thus, the consolidated financial statement will not be substantially affected by exchange rate fluctuations (although such firms may exhibit a high degree of transaction and economic exposure).

Locations of Foreign Subsidiaries. The locations of the subsidiaries can also influence the degree of translation exposure, since the financial statement items of each subsidiary are typically measured by that country's home currency. For example, consider the reporting situation of a U.S. MNC with a German subsidiary. The German subsidiary's assets, liabilities, earnings, etc., are measured in German marks. The MNC must develop consolidated quarterly financial statements that require translation of the German subsidiary figures into U.S. dollar terms. If the subsidiaries are located in countries such as Canada, where the currency is somewhat stable against the U.S. dollar, then translation risk will be lower.

Accounting Methods.   Finally, the MNC's degree of accounting exposure can be greatly affected by the accounting procedures it uses to translate when consolidating financial statement data. Under the Financial Accounting Standards Board No. 52 (FASB-52), adopted in December 1981, the consolidated accounting rules for U.S.-based MNCs changed dramatically. Listed are some of the more important points of FASB-52:

1. The functional currency of an entity is the currency of the economic environment in which the entity operates.
2. The current exchange rate as of the reporting date is used to translate the assets and liabilities of a foreign entity from its functional currency into the reporting currency.
3. The weighted average exchange rate is used to translate revenue, expenses, and gains and losses of a foreign entity from its functional currency into the reporting currency.
4. Translated income gains or losses due to changes in foreign currency values are not recognized in current net income but are reported as a second component of stockholder's equity; an exception to this rule is a foreign entity located in a country with high inflation.
5. Realized income gains or losses due to foreign currency transactions are recorded in current net income, although there are some exceptions.

Under FASB-52, consolidated earnings are sensitive to the functional currency's weighted average exchange rate. Consider a British subsidiary of a U.S.-based MNC that earned £10,000,000 in Year 1 and £10,000,000 in Year 2. When these earnings are consolidated along with other subsidiary earnings, they are translated at the weighted average exchange rate in that year. Assume the weighted average exchange rate is $1.90 in Year 1 and $1.50 in Year 2. The translated earnings for each reporting period in U.S. dollars are determined as follows:

Reporting Period	Assumed Local Earnings of British Subsidiary	Weighted Average Exchange Rate of Pound over the Reporting Period	Translated U.S. Dollar Earnings of British Subsidiary
Year 1	£10,000,000	$1.90	$19,000,000
Year 2	£10,000,000	$1.50	$15,000,000

Notice that even though local earnings in pounds were the same in each year, consolidated MNC dollar earnings translated from the British subsidiary were reduced by $4 million in Year 2. The discrepancy here is due to the change in the weighted average of the British pound exchange rate. It is possible that financial analysts may give the MNC a poor evaluation due to its British subsidiary's reduced earnings (when measured in dollars) in Year 2. Yet, the drop in earnings is not the fault of the British subsidiary, but rather of a weakened British pound that makes its Year 2 earnings look small (when measured in U.S. dollars). The pound's exchange rate has varied by the amount shown in the example during the 1990s, which partially explains the variability in earnings of MNCs over time.

Consider a U.S.-based MNC with subsidiaries concentrated in Europe. The functional currencies for reporting purposes will likely be highly correlated. Consequently, during a strong-dollar cycle, all functional currencies are likely to weaken against the dollar by about the same degree, and the impact on reported earnings could be substantial. If an MNC's functional currencies are not highly correlated, reported consolidated earnings are likely to be less sensitive to exchange rate movements, since some of the functional currency values may move in opposite directions or by smaller degrees than others.

Examples of Translation Exposure

Consolidated earnings of Black & Decker, Coca Cola, and other MNCs are very sensitive to exchange rates because more than a third of their assets and sales are overseas. Their earnings in foreign countries are reduced when foreign currencies depreciate against the dollar.

The earnings of numerous U.S.-based MNCs were favorably affected by the weakened dollar over the 1985–1988 period. The boost in earnings was primarily attributed to the foreign subsidiary earnings that were translated into dollars at a higher exchange rate.

In 1989 some currencies depreciated against the dollar, reducing the reported sales and profits of many U.S.-based MNCs. For example, CPC International stated that its reported non-U.S. sales were $50 million less as a result of weaker foreign currencies in 1989. During the early 1990s, many currencies experienced volatile cycles, causing wide swings in the translation effects on the consolidated earnings of U.S.-based MNCs. The effect of translation exposure on consolidated earnings can be documented by reviewing the annual reports of MNCs.

SUMMARY

■ MNCs with less risk can obtain funds at lower financing costs. Since they may experience more volatile cash flows because of exchange rate movements, exchange rate risk can affect their financing costs. Thus, MNCs may benefit from hedging exchange rate risk.

■ Transaction exposure represents the exposure of an MNC's future cash transactions to exchange rate movements. MNCs can measure their transaction exposure by determining their future payables and receivables positions in various currencies, along with the variability levels and correlations of these currencies. From this information, they can assess how their revenues and costs may change in response to various exchange rate scenarios.

■ Economic exposure represents any exposure of an MNC's cash flows (direct or indirect) to exchange rate movements. MNCs can attempt to measure their economic exposure by determining the extent to which their cash flows will be affected by their exposure to each foreign currency.

■ Translation exposure represents the exposure of an MNC's consolidated financial statements to exchange rate movements. To measure translation exposure, MNCs can forecast their earnings in each foreign currency, and then determine the potential exchange rate movements of each currency relative to their home currency.

SELF-TEST FOR CHAPTER 10

(Answers are provided in Appendix A in the back of the text)

1. Given that shareholders can diversify away an individual firm's exchange rate risk by investing in a variety of firms, why are firms concerned about exchange rate risk?

2. A U.S. firm considers importing its supplies from either Canada (denominated in C$) or France (denominated in FF) on a monthly basis. The quality is the same for both sources. Once the firm completes the agreement with a supplier, it will be obligated to continue using that supplier for at least three years. Based on existing exchange rates, the dollar amount to be paid (including transportation costs) would be the same. The firm has no other exposure to exchange rate movements. Given that the firm prefers to have less exchange rate risk, which alternative is preferable? Explain.

3. Assume your U.S. firm presently exports to Germany on a monthly basis. The goods are priced in marks. Once material is received from a source, it is quickly used to produce the product in the U.S., and then exported. Presently, there is no other exposure to exchange rate risk. You have a choice of purchasing the material from Canada (denominated in C$), from France (denominated in FF) or from within the U.S. (denominated in U.S.$). The quality and your expected cost is similar across the three sources. Which source would be preferable, given that you prefer minimal exchange rate risk?

4. Using the information in the previous question, consider the proposal to price the exports to Germany in dollars, and to use the U.S. source for material. Would this proposal eliminate the exchange rate risk?

5. Assume that the dollar is expected to strengthen over the next several years against European currencies. Explain how this will affect the consolidated earnings of U.S.-based MNCs with subsidiaries in Europe.

QUESTIONS

1. Why would an MNC consider examining only its "net" cash flows in each currency when assessing its transaction exposure?

2. Your employer, a large MNC, has asked you to assess its transaction exposure. Its projected cash flows are as follows for the next year:

Currency	Total Inflow	Total Outflow	Current Exchange Rate in U.S. Dollars
French francs (FF)	FF4,000,000	FF2,000,000	$ .15
British pounds (£)	£2,000,000	£1,000,000	$1.50
German marks (DM)	DM3,000,000	DM4,000,000	$ .30

Provide your assessment as to your firm's degree of economic exposure (as to whether the exposure is high or low). Substantiate your answer. Use any background data available to you in order to answer your question.

3. What factors affect a firm's degree of transaction exposure in a particular currency? For each factor, explain the desirable characteristics that would reduce transaction exposure.

4. Are currency correlations perfectly stable over time? What does your answer imply about using past data on correlations as an indicator for the future?

5. If a firm has net receivables in several currencies that are highly correlated with each other, what does this imply about the firm's overall degree of transaction exposure?

6. Compare and contrast transaction exposure and economic exposure.

7. How should appreciation of a firm's home currency generally affect its cash inflows? Why?

8. How should depreciation of a firm's home currency generally affect its cash outflows? Why?

9. Assume that Firm Z is in the exporting business and that it obtains its supplies and borrows funds locally. How would depreciation of this firm's local currency likely affect its net cash flows? Why?

10. Why are even the cash flows of a purely domestic firm exposed to exchange rate fluctuations?

11. Assume an MNC hires you as a consultant to assess its degree of economic exposure to exchange rate fluctuations. How would you handle this task? Be specific.

12. a) In using regression analysis to assess a firm's degree of economic exposure to exchange rate movements, what is the use of breaking the database into subperiods? (See Appendix 10A.)
    b) Assume the regression coefficients based on assessing economic exposure were much higher in this second subperiod than in the first subperiod. What does this tell you about the firm's degree of economic exposure over time? Why might such results occur? (See Appendix 10A.)

13. a) Present an argument for why translation exposure is relevant to an MNC.
    b) Present an argument for why translation exposure is not relevant to an MNC.

14. What factors affect the firm's degree of translation exposure? Explain how each factor influences translation exposure.

15. How have MNCs changed over time (based on surveys) with respect to their attitude about the importance of transaction exposure versus translation exposure?

16. How does FASB-52 differ from FASB-8? (See Appendix 10C.)

17. Consider a period in which the U.S. dollar weakens against most foreign currencies. How will this affect the reported earnings of a U.S.-based MNC with subsidiaries all over the world?

18. Consider a period in which the U.S. dollar strengthens against most foreign currencies. How will this affect the reported earnings of a U.S.-based MNC with subsidiaries all over the world?

19. Walt Disney World built an amusement park in France that opened in 1992. How do you think this project will affect Disney's overall economic exposure to exchange rate movements? Explain.

20. Using the cost and revenue information below for DeKalb Inc., determine how the costs, revenues, and earnings items would be affected by three possible exchange rate scenarios: (1) DM = $.50, (2) DM = $.55, (3) DM = $.60. (Assume U.S. sales will be unaffected by the exchange rate). Assume that DM earnings will be remitted to the U.S. at the end of the period.

Revenue and Cost Estimates: DeKalb Company
(in millions of U.S. dollars and German marks)

	U.S. Business	German Business
Sales	$ 800	DM 800
Cost of goods sold	$ 500	DM 100
Gross profit	$ 300	DM 700
Operating expenses	$ 300	
Earnings before interest and taxes	0	DM 700
Interest expenses	$ 100	0
Earnings before taxes	–$ 100	DM 700

21. Aggie Company produces chemicals. It is a major exporter to Germany, where its main competition is from other U.S. exporters. All of these companies invoice the products in U.S. dollars. Is Aggie's transaction exposure likely to be significantly affected if the mark strengthens or weakens? Explain. If the mark weakened for several years, can you think of any change that might occur within the global chemicals market?

22. Longhorn Company produces hospital equipment. Most of its revenues are in the United States. About half of its expenses require outflows in German marks (to pay for German materials). Most of Longhorn's competition is from U.S. firms that have no international business at all. How will Longhorn Company be affected if the mark strengthens?

23. Lubbock Inc. produces furniture and has no international business. Its major competitors import most of their furniture from Switzerland, then sell it out of retail stores in the United States. How will Lubbock Inc. be affected if the Swiss franc strengthens over time?

24. Sooner Company is a U.S. wholesale company that imports expensive high-quality luggage and sells it to retail stores around the United States. Its main competitors also import high-quality luggage and sell it to retail stores. None of these competitors hedge their exposure to exchange rate movements. The treasurer of Sooner Company told the board of directors that the firm's performance would be more volatile over time if it hedged its exchange rate exposure. How could a firm's cash flows be more stable as a result of such high exposure to exchange rate fluctuations?

25. Boulder Inc. exports chairs to Germany (invoiced in U.S. dollars) and competes against local German companies. If purchasing power parity exists, why would Boulder not benefit from a stronger mark?

26. Toyota Motor Corporation measures the sensitivity of exports to the yen exchange rate (relative to the U.S. dollar). Explain how regression analysis could be used for such a task. Identify the expected sign of the regression coefficient if Toyota primarily exported to the United States. If Toyota established plants in the United States, how might the regression coefficient on the exchange rate variable change?

27. How can a U.S. company use regression analysis to assess its economic exposure to fluctuations in the British pound?

28. Cornhusker Company is an exporter of products to France. It wants to know how its stock price is affected by changes in the franc's exchange rate. It believes that the impact may occur with a lag of one to three quarters. How could regression analysis be used to assess the impact?

29. Vegas Corporation is a U.S. firm that exports most of its products to Germany. It historically invoiced its products in German marks to accommodate the importers. However, it was adversely affected when the mark weakened against the dollar. Since Vegas did not hedge, its mark receivables were converted into a relatively small amount of dollars. After a few more years of continual concern about possible exchange rate movements, Vegas called its customers and requested that they pay for future orders with dollars instead of marks. At this time, the mark was valued at $.51. The customers decided to oblige, since the number of marks to be converted to dollars when importing the goods from Vegas was still slightly smaller than the number of marks that would be needed to buy the product from a German manufacturer. Based on this situation, has transaction exposure changed for Vegas Corporation? Has economic exposure changed? Explain.

30. Saab, the Swedish automobile manufacturer, purchases many of its components from Germany. It exports many of its automobiles to the United States. Recently, the Swedish kronor depreciated against the German mark and appreciated against the U.S. dollar. Holding other factors constant, how would Saab's performance be affected by these currency movements?

31. A German company called Bonz Company has heavy exposure in French francs as a result of importing French supplies denominated in French francs. Stark Company, also German, has heavy exposure in Canadian dollars as a result of importing Canadian supplies denominated in Canadian dollars. Both firms receive German mark cash flows on all their products sold. Neither firm hedges payments on the imports. Assume that the values of imported supplies ordered by the firms are about the same. Also assume that other characteristics of the firms are similar. Which firm will likely experience more volatile profit streams over time? Why?

32. The French franc appreciated against most other European currencies in the 1992–1993 period. How would you expect this to affect EuroDisney's business?

CASE: DOW CHEMICAL'S EXCHANGE RATE EXPOSURE

Dow Chemical to Use Only the Mark For All Its Business Dealings in Europe

By Scott McMurray
And Robert L. Simison
Staff Reporters of THE WALL STREET JOURNAL

Dow Chemical Co., reacting to the chaos in European currency markets, said it will use German marks as the common currency for all its European business transactions.

Dow's move comes as Europe's bankers and politicians are deeply divided over the outlook for a single currency. It also echoes the widespread frustration among European businessmen who favor a single currency. However, no businessman contacted plans, as yet, to follow Dow's lead and embrace the mark.

The move shifts currency risks from Dow to customers who used to do business in other currencies, said Fernand Kaufmann, Dow's sales and commercial vice president for Europe. The move late last week also effectively raises prices in European markets where local currencies have been devalued. For that reason, it may not stick in light of the depressed world-wide market for chemicals and plastics, competing chemical companies said.

Dow's action anticipates the day when a single European currency will "benefit both manufacturers and customers in terms of simplification and fairness," Mr. Kaufmann said. Dow's new policy, for instance, would nullify any advantage that a Dow customer in one country might have over competitors in another country based on currency swings, he said.

Rivals took a more down-to-earth view of Dow's intentions. "We commend them for the attempt to raise prices in Europe," said John Fitzpatrick, assistant treasurer of Union Carbide Corp., Danbury, Conn.

Dow, which is based in Midland, Mich., said customers who buy polystyrene, polyethylene and urethane chemical products will continue to be billed in local currencies. But invoices will reflect prices set in marks. Dow said the move was aimed at insulating its European earnings from sharp currency swings.

"Our major cost elements, energy and hydrocarbons in particular, are dollar-denominated, and our total operating costs are on an increasing trend," Mr. Kaufmann said in a statement. He said Dow was initiating the mark-based pricing structure "to avoid an erosion of our margins."

Mr. Kaufmann said Dow Europe, excluding consumer specialty products, posted a narrow operating loss in the second quarter—its first in a decade—and has been trying to push prices up. "The currency turmoil complicated this plan," he said.

Dow reported a 20% decline in second-quarter net income to $186 million, or 68 cents a share, from $233 million, or 86 cents a share, a year earlier. Last year, Europe accounted for 31%, or $5.88 billion, of Dow's $18.81 billion in sales.

Du Pont Unlikely to Follow

Leading Dow competitors said they weren't inclined to line up behind the mark. Du Pont Co., Wilmington, Del., "doesn't have any plans at present" to change from doing business in local currencies, said a Du Pont Europe spokesman. Germany's BASF AG and Belgium's Solvay & Cie. said their currency hedging strategies provided adequate protection against unstable currency markets.

In Italy, ECP EniChem Polimeri, the polyethylene subsidiary of Italy's ENI state energy group, said it will make selective price increases on various products. EniChem said it bases its prices on local currencies and doesn't plan to follow Dow in a

mark-based price structure. On the other hand, a spokesman for Montedison S.A. in Italy said the company's Himont polypropylene subsidiary has based its prices on marks for years to avoid risks from currency fluctuations.

Nor were companies from other industries adopting a Euromark strategy. International Business Machines Corp., Armonk, N.Y., is organized in Europe on a country-by-country basis, and transacts business and pays taxes in those currencies. "It would be an additional currency risk for us to bill in marks," said Joerg Winkelmann, an IBM Europe spokesman.

Honeywell's Method

Honeywell Inc., Minneapolis, said the industrial controls company conducts business among its European units in European Currency Units, or ECUs, and with its U.S. parent in dollars. In negotiating contracts with customers, Honeywell said, its local subsidiaries often obtain currency-index provisions to protect against sharp swings.

In the steel industry, Luxembourg's giant Arbed S.A. said it is concerned about the currency turmoil. But, said Albert Rinnen, a finance executive, "we can't impose on our clients to be paid in Deutsche marks. Belgian francs or pesetas. It's not that easy to sell steel in this kind of climate."

A spokesman for the Netherlands' NV Phillips Electronics says the company is more worried about high interest rates than fluctuating currencies. If the instability were to persist, however, the Dutch electronics giant says it might need to make some "strategic changes" in its pricing policy. But it declined to elaborate.

Unilever, the Anglo-Dutch consumer products giant, says it has been little affected by the currency upheavals. "We produce consumer goods in 87 countries. Our individual local companies mainly produce for

Continued

CASE: DOW CHEMICAL'S EXCHANGE RATE EXPOSURE

Continued

their own market,'' a spokesman said. If anything, he added, the weakness of the dollar helps because it tends to reduce raw materials costs.

Some companies are downright sanguine about the vicissitudes of the past two weeks. "We are extremely relaxed" about the current situation, says a spokesman for Paris-based L'Oreal S.A., the giant cosmetics company. "We aren't at all worried. We've dealt with this kind of problem for 85 years. We've seen even more brutal fluctuations in the past."

Source: *The Wall Street Journal* (28 September 1992), p. A5C. Reprinted by permission of *The Wall Street Journal*, © 1992 Dow Jones & Company, Inc. All rights reserved worldwide.

Questions

1. Why might Dow Chemical benefit from pricing all of its European products in German marks?

2. Dow Chemical's strategy (of pricing all of its European products in German marks) was announced shortly after the exchange rate mechanism (ERM) was adjusted to allow much wider bands around the exchange rates between European currencies. Explain why the ERM adjustment may have caused Dow Chemical to implement the strategy.

3. Why might Dow Chemical's cash flows be adversely affected by its strategy of pricing European products in marks?

WHALER PUBLISHING COMPANY
Measuring Exposure to Exchange Rate Risk

Recall the situation of Whaler Publishing Company from the previous chapter. Whaler needed to develop confidence intervals of four exchange rates in order to derive confidence intervals for U.S. dollar cash flows to be received from four different countries. Each confidence interval was isolated on a particular country.

Assume that Whaler would like to estimate the range of its aggregate dollar cash flows to be generated from other countries. A computer spreadsheet should be developed to facilitate this exercise. Whaler plans to simulate the conversion of the expected currency cash flows to dollars, using each of the previous years as a possible scenario (recall that exchange rate data are provided in the original case in Chapter 9). Specifically, Whaler will determine the annual percentage change in the spot rate of each currency for a given year. Then it will apply that percentage to the respective existing spot rates to determine a possible spot rate in one year for each currency. Recall that today's spot rates are assumed to be as follows:

Australian dollar	= $ .7671
Canadian dollar	= $ .8625
New Zealand dollar	= $ .5985
British pound	= $1.9382

Once the spot rate is forecasted for one year ahead for each currency, the U.S. dollar revenues received from each country can be forecasted. For example, from Year 1 to Year 2, the Australian dollar declined by about 13.6%. If this percentage change occurs this year, the spot rate of the Australian dollar will decline from today's rate of $.7671 to about $.6629. In this case, the A$38,000,000 to be received would convert to $25,190,200. The same tasks must be done for the other three currencies as well, in order to estimate the aggregate dollar cash flows under this scenario.

This process can be repeated, using each of the previous years as a possible future scenario. There will be 15 possible scenarios, or 15 forecasts of the aggregate U.S. dollar cash flows. Each of these scenarios is expected to have an equal probability of occurring. By assuming that these cash flows are normally distributed, Whaler uses the standard deviation of the possible aggregate cash flows for all 15 scenarios to develop 68% and 95% confidence intervals surrounding the "expected value" of the aggregate level of U.S. dollar cash flows to be received in one year.

CASE
PROBLEM

WHALER PUBLISHING COMPANY (CONTINUED)

a) Perform these tasks for Whaler in order to determine these confidence intervals on the aggregate level of U.S. dollar cash flows to be received. The methodology described above is used by Whaler, rather than the simple combining of results of individual countries (from the previous chapter), since exchange rate movements may be correlated.

b) Review the annual percentage changes in the four exchange rates. Do they appear to be positively correlated? Estimate the correlation coefficient between exchange rate movements, with either a calculator or a spreadsheet package. Based on this analysis, you can fill out the correlation coefficient matrix below:

	A$	C$	N$	£
A$	1.00			
C$		1.00		
N$			1.00	
£				1.00

Would aggregate dollar cash flows to be received by Whaler be more risky than they would if the exchange rate movements were completely independent? Explain.

c) One executive of Whaler suggested that a more efficient way of deriving the confidence intervals would be simply to use the exchange rates instead of the percentage changes as the scenarios, and derive U.S. dollar cash flow estimates directly from them. Do you think this method would be as accurate as the method now used by Whaler? Explain.

PROJECTS

1. Select an MNC and assess the sensitivity of its stock returns to historical exchange rate movements using the procedure described in Appendix 10A. Several software packages, including LOTUS, have regression packages that can perform regression analysis.

2. Review the annual report of an MNC, and summarize how the MNC was affected by recent changes in the U.S. dollar's value. Explain why the MNC was favorably or unfavorably affected by the dollar's recent movement. Summarize the MNC's translation exposure and the effect of the dollar's recent movements on consolidated earnings.

3. Using the data bank in the back of the text, estimate the standard deviation of

a) percentage changes in the British pound over the last 20 quarters.

b) percentage changes in the German mark over the last 20 quarters.

c) percentage changes in the Japanese yen over the last 20 quarters.

d) percentage changes in an equally weighted portfolio of these three currencies; the percentage change in the portfolio is equal to $(1/3 \times \%\Delta$ in pound$) + (1/3 \times \%\Delta$ in mark$) + (1/3 \times \%\Delta$ in yen$)$.

Compare the standard deviation of the portfolio to those of the individual currencies. Explain why the portfolio's standard deviation is lower. See Appendix 10B for related information.

REFERENCES

Adler, Michael, and Bernard Dumas. "Exposure to Currency Risk: Definition and Measurement." *Financial Management* 13, no. 2 (Summer 1984), pp. 41-50.

Beaver, William, and Mark Wolfson. "Foreign Currency Translation Gains and Losses: What Effect Do They Have and What Do They Mean." *Financial Analysts Journal* (March-April 1984), pp. 28-36.

Bodnar, Gordon M., and William M. Gentry. "Exchange Rate Exposure and Industry Characteristics: Evidence from Canada, Japan, and the USA." *Journal of International Money and Finance* (February 1993), pp. 29-45.

Choi, Jongmoo Jay. "A Model of Firm Valuation with Exchange Exposure." *Journal of International Business Studies* (Summer 1986), pp. 153-160.

Flood, Eugene, Jr., and Donald R. Lessard. "On the Measurement of Operating Exposure to Exchange Rates: A Conceptual Approach." *Financial Management* (Spring 1986), pp. 25-36.

Glen, Jack, and Philippe Jorion. "Currency Hedging for International Portfolios." *Journal of Finance* (December 1993), pp. 1865-1886.

Hung, Juan. "Assessing the Exchange Rate's Impact on U.S. Manufacturing Profits." *FRBNY Quarterly Review* (1992-93), pp. 44-63.

Jacque, Laurent L. "Management of Foreign Exchange Risk: A Review Article." *Journal of International Business Studies* (Spring-Summer 1981), pp. 81-99.

Jorion, Philippe. "The Exchange Rate Exposure of U.S. Multinationals." *Journal of Business* (July 1990), pp. 331-336.

_____ . "The Pricing of Exchange Rate Risk in the Stock Market." *Journal of Financial and Quantitative Analysis* (September 1991), pp. 363-376.

Kwok, Chuck C. Y. "Examining Event Study Methodologies in Foreign Exchange Markets." *Journal of International Business Studies* (Second Quarter 1990), pp. 189-224.

Lessard, Donald R., and John B. Lighthouse. "Volatile Exchange Rates Can Put Operations at Risk." *Harvard Business Review* (July-August 1986), pp. 107-114.

Luehrman, Timothy A. "The Exchange Rate Exposure of a Global Competitor." *Journal of International Business Studies* (Second Quarter 1990), pp. 225-242.

Madura, Jeff. "Empirical Measurement of Systematic Exchange Rate Risk." *Journal of Portfolio Management* (Summer 1983), pp. 43-46.

_____ . "Assessment of Exchange Rate Risk from Various Country Perspectives." *International Review of Economics and Business* (July 1990), pp. 655-666.

Madura, Jeff, and E. Joe Nosari. "Utilizing Currency Portfolios to Mitigate Exchange Rate Risk." *Columbia Journal of World Business* (Spring 1984), pp. 96-99.

Nance, Deana R., Clifford W. Smith Jr., and Charles W. Smithson. "On the Determinants of Corporate Hedging." Journal of Finance (March 1993), pp. 267-284.

Soenen, Luc. "The Optimal Currency Cocktail—A Tool for Strategic Foreign Exchange Management." *Management International Review* 25, no. 2 (1985), pp. 12-22.

ALTERNATIVE MEASURES OF ECONOMIC EXPOSURE

A method of measuring an MNC's economic exposure to exchange rates is illustrated, followed by a method of measuring an MNC's economic exposure to country conditions.

ECONOMIC EXPOSURE TO EXCHANGE RATES

To provide an actual example of an MNC's economic exposure to exchange rate fluctuations, quarterly data on the stock of a company (name withheld) and on several currencies were compiled for an eight-year period. Regression analysis was then conducted to determine how the percentage change in a company's stock price was affected by fluctuations in each exchange rate. The stock price represents firm value and should reflect shareholders' assessment of future cash flow.

Regression analysis was conducted separately for each currency as follows:

$$r_t = a_0 + a_1 USI_t + a_2 e_t + \mu_t$$

where r_t reflects the percentage change in the stock price of the company, USI_t is the percentage change in an index of U.S. stocks, e_t is the percentage change in a particular currency's value, a_0, a_1, and a_2 are regression coefficients, and μ_t is an error term. The index of U.S. stocks is included in the analysis, since it is thought to exert a major influence on any particular U.S. stock. Thus, the regression analysis is set up to determine whether e has any impact on r_t above and beyond the influence of USI. The regression model will generate values for a_0, a_1 and a_2. The regression coefficient a_2 will suggest how movements in the currency of concern affects the company's value. Regression analysis can then be repeated to analyze the impact of each currency on the company's value.

The individual impacts of four different currencies on the company's stock value are provided in Exhibit 10A.1. The data set was split into two equal subperiods. Results are shown for each subperiod. The data were segmented so we could assess whether the impact of an individual currency on the company changed over time. Four separate regressions were run for each subperiod to assess the sensitivity of a U.S.-based MNC's stock returns to each of the four currencies. Notice from Exhibit 10A.1 that a_2 is typically negative. This implies that as the value of the currency appreciates against the U.S. dollar, the company stock value falls, and vice versa. The larger the size of the regression coefficient, the greater is the sensitivity of the firm's value to movements in the foreign currency.

From Exhibit 10A.1, it appears that movements in the Canadian dollar and German mark exerted the most influence on the company value in the earlier subperiod. In the more recent subperiod, the Swiss franc movements were most influential, although the size of the regression coefficient did not differ substantially among the four currencies. While the regression coefficients were generally negative for these currencies, they may be positive when applied to some other companies.

The MNC could repeat the regression analysis for a more recent time period so as to determine whether its firm value is becoming more sensitive to exchange rate fluctuations. It would do this by comparing the regression coefficients based on the recent subperiod with those derived in the earlier subperiod for each currency. If the coefficients increased in size, then the MNC's degree of economic exposure to exchange rate fluctuations would have increased, and vice versa.

The impact of each currency was weaker in the more recent subperiod shown in the exhibit. For example, the Canadian dollar's a_2 coefficient was $-.81$ in the earlier subperiod, which implies that a 1 percent change in the Canadian dollar would cause a .81 percent change (in the opposite direction) in the company's value. However, in the more recent subperiod, the coefficient a_2 was $-.06$, suggesting that a 1 percent change in the Canadian dollar would cause a .06 percent change (in the opposite direction) in the company's value. This reflects a weaker impact than in the earlier subperiod. Because there are so many variables that may influence the movements in a company's stock, it is difficult to perfectly disentangle the individual impacts of each variable. Yet the regression analysis applied to separate subperiods at least indicates whether the company has become more or less exposed to an individual currency's movements.

A company may become more exposed or sensitive to an individual currency's movements over time for several reasons, including

- Reduction in hedging
- Greater involvement in the country represented by that currency
- Increased use of that currency to purchase goods.

The opposite pattern for these factors could reduce exposure to an individual currency. The regression analysis discussed earlier could help determine whether a particular corporate policy has increased or reduced the MNC's economic exposure.

Recent research by Bodnar and Gentry assessed exchange rate effects on firms of particular U.S. industries. They created a portfolio of firms for each industry and used regression analysis to measure the influence of exchange rate movements on portfolio stock returns. They found that portfolios of export-oriented industries were favorably affected by a weak home currency, while import-oriented industries were adversely affected by a weak home currency. They also replicated their analysis for Canadian and Japanese industries, and found that Canadian and Japanese industries were more exposed to exchange rate movements than U.S. industries. The authors suggest that these results can be explained by the higher degree of international business conducted by Canadian and Japanese firms.

ECONOMIC EXPOSURE TO COUNTRY CONDITIONS

Regression analysis can be used to assess the sensitivity of a company's performance to economic conditions. First, a measure of the economy's condition is needed for each country. Two possible measures are gross national product and national income, but these variables do not indicate the anticipated future condition of the economy. The stock price index for each country, on the other hand, reflects not only the current conditions but also expectations about the future.

To assess the exposure of an MNC to country economies, regression analysis can set the MNC's firm value as a function of the stock indexes for all countries of concern. In general, we would expect the regression coefficients to be positive, since the MNC's value should increase if the stock index of a particular country increases (since a higher stock index reflects favorable economic conditions). For some countries, the regression coefficient may be close to zero, implying the MNC is hardly exposed to the economic conditions of foreign countries. Information such as this can identify those countries whose economies have more influence on the MNC's value. Using stock indexes, the regression equation can be written as

$$r_t = c_0 + c_1 HI_t + c_2 FI_t + \mu_t,$$

where r_t is the return of the company's stock, HI_t is the return on the country's home stock index, FI_t is the return on the foreign stock index, and μ_t is an error term. The coefficient c_0 is a constant, while c_1 and c_2 are regression coefficients measuring the sensitivity of r_t to HI and FI respectively. Regression analysis in the form described here was conducted for a specific U.S.-based MNC, and the results of the analysis are displayed in Exhibit 10A.2.

The regression analysis was run separately for four different foreign countries to determine the separate impact of each country. In addition, the time period was split into two subperiods to determine whether the influence of any country had changed over time. From Exhibit 10A.2, the German economy appears to have had the greatest influence on the MNC of concern. This statement holds for either subperiod. In the more recent subperiod, for example, a 1 percent change in the German index coincided with a 1.4 percent change (in the same direction) in the company's stock price. The French economy appears to have had a relatively minor influence on this MNC's value.

With regard to the sensitivity of the company to foreign economies over time, the MNC appeared to be generally more sensitive in the more recent time period than in the earlier time period. The only exception was its sensitivity to the French economy, which remained stable over time. Increased sensitivity to foreign economies over time could be due to a greater amount of business in these countries.

EXHIBIT 10A.1 Sensitivity of a Company's Stock Value to Currency Movements Based on Regression Analysis	Currency	Regression Coefficient a_2: Earlier Subperiod	Regression Coefficient a_2: More Recent Subperiod
	Canadian dollar	−.81	−.06
	French franc	.05	.05
	German mark	−.73	−.01
	Swiss franc	−.26	−.27

EXHIBIT 10A.2 Sensitivity of a Company's Stock Value To Country Economies Based on Regression Analysis	Stock Index of:	Regression Coefficient in Earlier Subperiod	Regression Coefficient in More Recent Subperiod
	Canada	.5	.7
	France	.1	.1
	Germany	.9	1.4
	Switzerland	.3	.8

ESTIMATING THE VARIABILITY OF A CURRENCY PORTFOLIO

To illustrate how the variability of foreign currency cash flows is affected by correlations, consider a simplified example in which an MNC has only two foreign currencies. Fifty percent of the MNC's funds are expected to come from Currency A, and the remaining funds from Currency B. Assume that over an annual period, the standard deviation of exchange rate movements is 4 percent for Currency A and 4 percent for Currency B. Also assume that these two currencies are perfectly positively correlated, so that their correlation coefficient is 1.00. The standard deviation of this two-currency portfolio (σ_p) can be determined from the following equation:

$$\sigma_P = \sqrt{W_A^2\sigma_A^2 + W_B^2\sigma_B^2 + 2W_AW_B\sigma_A\sigma_B CORR_{AB}},$$

where

W_A = percentage of funds to be received from receivables in Currency A

W_B = percentage of funds to be received from receivables in Currency B

σ_A = standard deviation of exchange rate movements for Currency A

σ_B = standard deviation of exchange rate movements for Currency B

$CORR_{AB}$ = correlation coefficient of exchange rate movements between Currencies A and B.

Using the information provided, the variability of the combined (portfolio) cash flows of Currencies A and B can be estimated as

$$\sigma_P = \sqrt{.5^2(.04)^2 + .5^2(.04)^2 + 2(.5)(.5)(.04)(.04)(1.0)}$$
$$= \sqrt{.0004 + .0004 + .0008}$$
$$= \sqrt{.0016}$$
$$= .04, \text{ or } 4\%.$$

Notice that the standard deviation in the portfolio is as high as the standard deviation of either individual currency. The diversification between these two currencies does not reduce variability, because the currency movements are perfectly positively correlated. Diversification between currencies with a low correlation could substantially reduce the variability of the portfolio of inflow currencies. For example, if the two currencies had a correlation coefficient of .2, the portfolio variability (assuming 50 percent weight to each currency) would be

$$\sigma_P = \sqrt{.5^2(.04)^2 + .5^2(.04)^2 + 2.(.5)(.5)(.04)(.04)(0.2)}$$
$$= \sqrt{.0004 + .0004 + .00016}$$
$$= \sqrt{.00096}$$
$$= \text{about } .031, \text{ or } 3.1\%.$$

A negative correlation coefficient between Currencies A and B would reduce the portfolio variability to even a greater degree. For example, consider an extreme example in which Currencies A and B are perfectly negatively correlated, as represented by a correlation coefficient of −1.00. The portfolio variability (assuming 50 percent weight to each currency) would be

$$\sigma_P = \sqrt{.5^2(.04)^2 + .5^2(.04)^2 + 2(.5)(.5)(.04)(.04)(-1.0)}$$
$$= \sqrt{.0004 + .0004 + (-.0008)}$$
$$= \sqrt{0}$$
$$= 0.$$

The portfolio's exchange rate movements against the dollar would be stable because of the offsetting effects between Currencies A and B, if they are perfectly negatively correlated. Such a situation would normally be favorably perceived by an MNC, since the home currency value of the portfolio of foreign currencies could be virtually insulated from movements in these currencies.

It is unlikely that the MNC will be able to structure its foreign cash flows so that it is totally insulated against exchange rate movements. However, the examples given here demonstrate that a set of foreign currency cash inflows is less volatile if the correlations are low. The cash flows would also be less volatile if the standard deviations of the individual currencies were lower. This can be verified by assuming a standard deviation of less than 4 percent for each currency in the preceding examples and recomputing the portfolio's standard deviation.

FASB-52 versus FASB-8

The provisions of FASB No. 52 differ from FASB No. 8 (used before December 1981) in various ways. First, FASB-8 was based on the **monetary/nonmonetary approach** in translating financial statements for consolidation purposes. That is, current exchange rates (as of the reporting date) were used to measure monetary assets and liabilities, while historic exchange rates were used to measure nonmonetary items. Inventory and fixed assets are examples of nonmonetary items. The values of nonmonetary items were translated at the exchange rate in effect at the date of purchase. Because some items were measured at historical rates while other items were measured at current rates, the consolidated accounting statements could become distorted. Since FASB-52 requires all assets and liabilities to be measured at current exchange rates, such a distortion should no longer occur. Thus, translation exposure should be reduced, due to the elimination of this distortion.

A second difference between FASB-8 and FASB-52 is the way translation gains and losses are recorded. Under FASB-8, they were included in the reported net income. Under FASB-52, they are included not in the income statement, but instead in shareholders' equity in a **cumulative translation adjustment (CTA) account.** This is expected to reduce the variability of consolidated net income, since only realized changes in net income will be recorded in the income statement.

To illustrate the difference between FASB-8 and FASB-52 as related to translation exposure, consider the following situation for a company called SUB, which has been in operation for one year. SUB is a subsidiary of a U.S.-based MNC. The financial statements for this company are disclosed in Exhibit 10C.1. The financial statements are translated according to FASB-8 and FASB-52.

Notice that the assets of SUB are translated to a greater amount under FASB-8 than under FASB-52. This is due to the translation of inventory and fixed assets at the historical rate under FASB-8, versus the current rate under FASB-52. If the functional currency (the local currency used by SUB) appreciated over time, the total assets would be valued higher under FASB-52, since all assets would be translated at the higher current rate.

The liabilities are translated to the same amount for FASB-8 as for FASB-52. This similarity occurs because both reporting rules use the current rate to translate liabilities.

Stockholders' equity is translated to a larger amount under FASB-8 than under FASB-52. Even though common stock is translated at the historical rate under both reporting rules, retained earnings is a plug figure dependent on the difference between assets and the sum of liabilities plus common stock. Since assets are larger for FASB-8, the amount in retained earnings is forced to be larger.

The gross income translated to U.S. dollars is lower under FASB-8 than under FASB-52, due to FASB-8 use of the historical rate to translate cost of sales. A functional currency that is strong when the costs of sales are incurred but weakens by the time the financial statements are disclosed will show a relatively low gross income (since revenues are translated at the low current rate). If the functional currency appreciated against the dollar from the time costs were incurred to the time of financial statement disclosure, the gross income would be relatively high. Under FASB-52, sales and cost of sales are translated using a weighted average of exchange rates over the reporting period. Thus, even if most costs are incurred when the functional currency is strong against the dollar, and most sales are generated later, when the functional currency is weak, the net income will not be distorted (since cost of sales will not be translated at the historical exchange rate).

When operating expenses are deducted from gross income to determine net income, they are translated at the weighted average exchange rate under both FASB-8 and FASB-52. However, because of the difference in computing translated gross income, the reported net income in U.S. dollars by SUB will vary between the two accounting rules.

Since this is SUB's first year in operation and no cash dividends were paid, the retained earnings account is equal to net income under FASB-8. The difference between this net income figure of $7.8 million and the operating profit of $4.3 million is the translation gain of $3.5 million. Under FASB-52, the translation gain or loss is not incorporated within the income statement. Instead, it is included as a component of retained earnings. Exhibit 10C.1 shows that the retained earnings account under FASB-52 was divided into *accumulated earnings* (as determined by the income statement) and the *cumulative translation account* (which measures the translation gain or loss). Since retained earnings are forced to be $2 million, and accumulated earnings are translated at $5.1 million, the cumulative translation account is the residual of −$3.1 million.

The translation of costs into the reporting currency according to the historical exchange rate can be misleading. If the subsidiary used its local currency when incurring the costs, the fact that its currency was strong against the dollar at that time did not affect the actual cost to the subsidiary. In addition, the inclusion of translation gains and losses in the income statement can be misleading, since these gains and losses were not actually realized. These distortions to translated net income due to FASB-8 rules have been alleviated by FASB-52 with its use of the weighted average exchange rate during the reporting period for both revenues and expenses, and its omission of translation gains and losses from the income statement. Although MNCs will always be faced with translation gains and losses due to the sometimes wide fluctuations in exchange rates, FASB-52 appears to help present a more accurate picture of the true financial position and results of operations by foreign subsidiaries.

Although FASB-52 should reduce an MNC's exposure to translation risk, it cannot totally eliminate it. Recall that the stockholders' equity account is increased due to a translation gain or reduced due to a translation loss. Thus, financial ratios such as return on equity (net income/equity) and leverage (debt/equity) are influenced by translation gains and losses.

EXHIBIT 10C.1   Translation of a Subsidiary's Financial Statements under FASB-8 and FASB-52 Rules (figures are in thousands)

Assets	Value in Functional Currency	FASB-8 Translation Rates	Translation to U.S. Dollars Under FASB-8	FASB-52 Translation Rates	Translation to U.S. Dollars Under FASB-52
Cash	4,000	Current; $1.50	6,000	Current; $1.50	$ 6,000
Inventory	6,000	Historical; $1.80	10,800	Current; $1.50	9,000
Fixed assets	10,000	Historical; $1.90	19,000	Current; $1.50	15,000
Total Assets	20,000		35,800		$30,000
Liabilities and equity					
Accounts payable	2,000	Current; $1.50	3,000	Current; $1.50	3,000
Long-term debt	10,000	Current; $1.50	15,000	Current; $1.50	15,000
Common stock	5,000	Historical; $2.00	10,000	Historical; $2.00	10,000
Retained earnings	3,000	Forced	7,800	Forced	2,000*
Total liab. and equity	20,000		35,800		$30,000
Income Statement					
Sales	12,000	Weighted avg.; $1.70	20,400	Weighted avg.; $1.70	20,400
−Cost of sales	8,000	Historical; $1.80	14,400	Weighted avg.; $1.70	13,600
Gross profit	4,000		6,000		6,800
−Operating expenses	1,000	Weighted avg.; $1.70	1,700	Weighted avg.; $1.70	1,700
Operating profit	3,000		4,300		5,100
Gain on translation			3,500		
Net income	3,000		7,800		5,100

*The forced translation amount of $2,000,000 represents −$3,100,000 for the cumulative translation amount, and $5,100,000 in accumulated earnings.

11

MANAGING TRANSACTION EXPOSURE

Recall from the previous chapter that there are three forms by which a multinational corporation (MNC) is exposed to exchange rate fluctuations: (1) transaction exposure, (2) economic exposure, and (3) translation exposure. This chapter focuses on the management of transaction exposure, while the following chapter focuses on the management of economic and translation exposure. The specific objectives of this chapter are to

- identify the commonly used techniques for hedging transaction exposure,
- explain how each technique can be used to hedge future payables and receivables,
- compare the advantages and disadvantages among hedging techniques, and
- suggest other methods of reducing exchange rate risk when hedging techniques are not available.

TRANSACTION EXPOSURE

Transaction exposure exists when the future cash transactions of a firm are affected by exchange rate fluctuations. For example, a U.S. firm that purchases German goods may need marks to buy the goods. While it may know exactly how many marks it will need, it doesn't know how many dollars will be needed to be exchanged for those marks. This uncertainty occurs because the exchange rate between marks and dollars fluctuates over time. Also consider a U.S.-based MNC that will be receiving a foreign currency. Its future receivables are exposed, since it is uncertain of the dollars it will obtain when exchanging the foreign currency received.

If transaction exposure does exist, the firm faces three major tasks. First, it must identify the degree of transaction exposure. Second, it must decide whether to hedge this exposure. Finally, if it decides to hedge part or all of the exposure, it must choose among the various hedging techniques available. Each of these tasks is discussed in turn.

Identifying Net Transaction Exposure

Before the MNC makes any decisions related to hedging, it should identify the individual **net transaction exposure** on a currency-by-currency basis. The term "net" here refers to the consolidation of all expected inflows and outflows for a particular time and currency. The management at each subsidiary plays a vital role in the process of reporting its expected inflows and outflows. Then a centralized group consolidates subsidiary reports in order to identify, for the MNC as a whole, the expected net positions in each foreign currency during several upcoming periods. The MNC can identify its exposure by reviewing this consolidation of subsidiary positions. For example, one subsidiary may have net receivables in German marks three months from now, while a different subsidiary may have net payables in marks. If the mark appreciates, this will be favorable to the first subsidiary and unfavorable to the second subsidiary. However, the impact on the MNC as a whole is at least partially offset. Each subsidiary may desire to hedge its net currency position in order to avoid the possible adverse impacts on its performance due to fluctuation in the currency's value. However, the overall performance of the MNC could already be insulated by the offsetting positions between subsidiaries. Therefore, hedging the position of each individual subsidiary may not be necessary.

To determine the net exposure in each currency over all subsidiaries, the MNC should first identify each subsidiary's position in all currencies. Exhibit 11.1 shows an example for an MNC that has four subsidiaries and deals in four currencies. Review the position in Currency 1 from Exhibit 11.1. Two subsidiaries have net inflows in Currency 1, while the other two subsidiaries have net outflows in Currency 1. On a consolidated basis, the MNC has an expected net

EXHIBIT 11.1   Example of Net Exposure of Currencies for Each Subsidiary as of a Particular Point in Time

Subsidiary	Net Position in Each Particular Currency Measured in the Parent Currency (in 1,000s of units):			
	Currency 1	Currency 2	Currency 3	Currency 4
London	+100	−60	−80	− 30
Munich	− 50	−30	+50	− 20
Paris	− 60	−50	+70	+100
Toronto	+ 30	+70	−10	− 50
Consolidated net exposure for each currency	+ 20	−70	+30	+ 0

inflow of 20,000 units in Currency 1. Each currency's consolidated net inflows have been computed by accounting for all subsidiary positions. Since the currency positions for each subsidiary will change over time, the net exposure per currency will change as well.

It may be difficult for management of an individual subsidiary to be comfortable with remaining exposed to currency fluctuations. But the goal in multinational financial management is to maximize the value of the overall multinational corporation, not any particular subsidiary. The role of subsidiary management is still important, even if currency exposure is managed by the parent. It involves reporting current and projected financial data, as well as assessing the economic environment and potential trends. Because subsidiary management is local to the subsidiary, it may perform these duties better than the centralized management group at the headquarters.

The view that consolidated net positions in cash flows are more important than each individual subsidiary's net positions is disputed by some. Critics claim that when a subsidiary requests a loan locally, the creditors will evaluate the individual subsidiary rather than the MNC as a whole. In this case, a large unhedged foreign currency position in a particular subsidiary could be perceived as a risk by creditors. In the event that this open (unhedged) position increases the risk of the subsidiary, the creditors may either deny the loan request or charge a higher loan rate. In this case, the creditors are more interested in the subsidiary's financial data than in the overall exposure and performance of the MNC.

If the subsidiary hedges a position to reduce its individual risk, this action may actually increase the overall exposure of the MNC. There may be an offsetting effect here when the MNC is viewed as a whole. If one subsidiary desires to hedge its position (in order to reduce its individual exposure and earn a better evaluation by local creditors), then there is no longer an offsetting effect for the MNC as a whole. The other subsidiary would now need to hedge its position for the MNC to avoid exposure. Hedging by both subsidiaries could eliminate the exchange rate exposure, but transaction costs are incurred. Appropriate communication among subsidiaries along with a centralized currency exposure management division can sometimes avoid such costs. For a centralized approach to be successful, an adequate reporting system by each subsidiary is necessary.

Examples.   As an example of centralization used to measure net transaction exposure, consider Eastman Kodak Company's centralized currency management approach. Kodak bills subsidiaries in their local currencies. The rationale for a change in strategies was to shift the foreign exchange exposure from subsidiaries to the parent company. Because the parent was reorganized to concentrate its resources and expert personnel, it centralized the currency exposure management. The parent now receives foreign currencies from its subsidiaries overseas and converts them to U.S. dollars. It can maintain the currencies as foreign deposits if it believes such currencies will strengthen against the U.S. dollar in the near future.

Another example is Borg-Warner Corporation, which has set up a central clearinghouse system that also reflects a centralized management approach. Thus, its assessment and management of currency exposure is conducted on the entire portfolio of all subsidiaries, rather than on each subsidiary individually.

A final example of centralized management is Fiat, the Italian auto manufacturer. Fiat has implemented such a system to monitor 421 subsidiaries dispersed among 55 countries. A key to its success is a comprehensive reporting system that keeps track of its aggregate cash flows in each currency. The net inflow or outflow position for each currency can then be assessed as to whether and how the position should be balanced out.

These examples support the centralized approach to hedging, in which net transaction exposure in each currency must be identified. Then, the firm can assess the degree of net exposure in each currency by using the techniques described in the previous chapter. For example, it can determine whether any of the net inflow currencies are highly correlated with the net outflow currencies. If so, it may consider not hedging for these currencies, since an offsetting effect should occur. There will likely be some net currency positions that are not offsetting, and the MNC must decide whether to hedge these positions. A discussion of this issue follows.

Is Hedging Worthwhile?

Before MNCs take the time to consider various techniques for hedging, they may question whether hedging is worthwhile. Consider the firm that is deciding whether to hedge its periodic future payables denominated in a foreign currency. The forward contract is a common hedging device against this foreign currency position. If the spot rate in the future exceeds today's forward rate, then the MNC will save money by hedging its net payables (as opposed to no hedge). If the spot rate in the future is less than today's forward rate, then the MNC will lose money by hedging its net payables. A forward rate that serves as an unbiased forecast of the future spot rate will underestimate and overestimate the future spot rate with equal frequency. In this case, periodic hedging with the forward rate will be more costly in some periods and less costly in other periods. On the average, it will not reduce the MNC's costs. Thus, it could be argued that hedging is not worthwhile.

Many MNCs, such as Black and Decker, Eastman Kodak Co., Merck & Co., and Zenith Electronics Corp., choose to hedge only in those situations in which they expect the currency to move in a direction that will make hedging feasible. That is, they may hedge future payables if they foresee appreciation in the currency denominating the payables. In addition, they may hedge future receivables if they foresee depreciation in the currency denominating the receivables. For example, Zenith hedges its imports of Japanese components only when it expects the yen to appreciate.

Some MNCs, such as Seagram Company, tend to hedge most or all of their net positions in foreign currency. These MNCs do not necessarily expect that hedging will always be beneficial. In fact, such MNCs may even believe that hedging will on the average result in the same cash inflows or outflows as not hedging. Yet, they may prefer knowing what their future cash inflows or outflows in terms of their home currency will be in each period, since this could enhance corporate planning. A hedge allows the firm to know the future cash flows (in terms of the home currency) that will result from any foreign transactions that have already been negotiated.

In general, decisions on whether to hedge, how much to hedge, and how to hedge will vary with the MNC management's degree of risk aversion, and its forecasts of exchange rates. MNCs that are more conservative tend to hedge more of their exposure.

Most MNCs do not perceive their foreign exchange management as a profit center. The main responsibility is to (1) measure the potential exposure to exchange rate movements, which is necessary to assess the risk, (2) determine whether the exposure should be hedged, and (3) determine how the exposure should be hedged, if at all. Thus, it is normally inappropriate for the foreign exchange management group to set a profit goal, as it may even use some hedges that will likely result in slightly worse outcomes than no hedges at all, just to avoid the possibility of a major adverse movement in exchange rates.

Adjusting the Invoice Policy to Manage Exposure

In some circumstances, the U.S. firm may be able to modify its pricing policy to hedge against transaction exposure. That is, the firm may be able to invoice (price) its exports in the same currency that will be needed to pay for imports. For example, assume the firm has continual payables in Swiss francs, perhaps because a Swiss exporter sends goods to the U.S. firm under the condition that the goods be invoiced in Swiss francs. Consequently, the U.S. firm is now exposed to fluctuations in the value of the Swiss franc. Assume the U.S. firm exports products (invoiced in U.S. dollars) to other corporations in Switzerland. It could modify its invoicing policy from U.S. dollars to Swiss francs in order to match its future payables in Swiss francs. In this way, the Swiss franc receivables from these exports can be used to pay off the U.S. firm's future payables in Swiss francs.

It would be difficult, if not impossible, to (1) invoice the precise amount for exports in Swiss francs in order to exactly match the Swiss franc payables and (2) perfectly match the timing of inflows and outflows. Because the matching of assets and liabilities in foreign currencies does have its limitations, it will not completely hedge all of the firm's exposed positions in foreign currencies. Therefore, other hedging techniques deserve consideration.

Techniques to Eliminate Transaction Exposure

If the MNC decides to hedge part or all of its transaction exposure, it may select from the following hedging techniques:

- Futures hedge
- Forward hedge
- Money market hedge
- Currency option hedge.

Each of these hedging techniques is discussed in turn, with examples provided. After all techniques have been discussed, a comprehensive example illustrates how all the techniques can be compared to determine the appropriate technique to hedge a particular position.

Futures Hedge

Currency futures can be used by firms that desire to hedge transaction exposure. A futures contract hedge is very similar to that of a forward contract (to be discussed shortly), except that forward contracts are common for large transactions, whereas futures contracts may be more appropriate for firms that prefer to hedge in smaller amounts.

A firm that buys a currency futures contract is entitled to receive a specified amount in a specified currency for a stated price on a specified date. To hedge payment on future payables in a foreign currency, the firm may desire to purchase a currency futures contract representing the currency it will need in the near future. By holding this contract, it locks in the amount of its home currency needed to make payment on the payables.

While currency futures can reduce the firm's transaction exposure, they sometimes backfire on the firm. If the firm is hedging payables, the locked-in futures price for the currency could end up being higher than the future spot rate of the currency (if the currency depreciates over time). If the firm expected the currency's value to depreciate by the time it would need to make payment, it would not purchase a currency futures contract.

A firm that sells a currency futures contract is entitled to sell a specified amount in a specified currency for a stated price on a specified date. To hedge the home currency value of future receivables in a foreign currency, the firm may desire to sell a currency futures contract representing the currency it will be receiving. This way the firm knows how much of its home currency it will receive after converting the foreign currency receivables into its home currency. By locking in the exchange rate at which it will be able to exchange the foreign currency for its home currency, it insulates the value of its future receivables from the fluctuations in the foreign currency's spot rate over time.

As with the purchase of currency futures, a sale of currency futures can backfire. In our example in which the firm is hedging future receivables, the locked-in currency futures price at which the firm will sell the foreign currency may end up being lower than the spot rate of the currency (if the foreign currency appreciates over time). Nonetheless, due to the uncertainty of future currency values, the firm may be more comfortable hedging than remaining exposed to exchange rate fluctuations.

Forward Hedge

Forward contracts are commonly used by large corporations that desire to hedge. To use the forward contract hedge, the MNC purchases that currency denominating the payables forward. For example, if a U.S.-based MNC must pay a Swiss supplier 1,000,000 francs in 30 days, it can request from a bank a forward contract to accommodate this future payment. The bank agrees to provide the Swiss francs to the MNC in 30 days in exchange for U.S. dollars. The forward contract specifies the exchange rate at which the currencies will be exchanged. This exchange rate reflects the so-called 30-day forward rate. The MNC hedges its position by locking in the rate it will pay for Swiss francs in 30 days. Thus, it now knows the number of dollars it will need to exchange for francs.

If the U.S.-based MNC expects receivables in Swiss francs in 30 days, it would like to lock in the rate at which it can sell these francs for dollars. In this case, a request for a forward sale of Swiss francs is appropriate. Many MNCs commonly implement the forward hedging technique. For example, Du Pont Company often has the equivalent of $300 million to $500 million in forward contracts at any one time, to cover open currency positions.

Forward Hedge versus No Hedge on Payables.   The decision as to whether to hedge a position with a forward contract or to keep it unhedged can be made by comparing the known result of hedging to the possible results of remaining unhedged. To illustrate, assume that a U.S. firm will need £100,000 in 90 days to pay for British imports. Assume that today's 90-day forward rate of the British pound is $1.40. To assess the future value of the British pound, the firm may develop a probability distribution, as shown in Exhibit 11.2. This is graphically illustrated in Exhibit 11.3, which breaks down the probability distribution. Both exhibits can be used to determine the probability that a forward hedge will be more costly than no hedge. This is achieved by estimating the **real cost of hedging** payables (RCH_p). The real cost of hedging measures the additional expenses beyond those incurred without hedging. The term "real" here does not mean "inflation-adjusted." The real cost of hedging payables is measured as

$$RCH_p = NCH_p - NC_p,$$

where

$$NCH_p = \text{nominal cost of hedging payables}$$

$$NC_p = \text{nominal cost of payables without hedging.}$$

When the real cost of hedging is negative, this implies that hedging is more favorable than not hedging. The RCH_p is estimated for each scenario in Column 5 of Exhibit 11.2. While NCH_p is certain, NC_p is uncertain, causing RCH_p to be uncertain.

While the firm doesn't know RCH_p in advance, it can at least use the information in Exhibits 11.2 and 11.3 to decide whether a hedge is feasible. First, it could estimate the expected value of the RCH_p. This expected value is determined by

$$\text{Expected value of } RCH_p = \sum P_i RCH_{p,i},$$

EXHIBIT 11.2   Feasibility Analysis for Hedging

Possible Spot Rate of £ in 90 Days	Probability	Nominal Cost of Hedging £100,000	Amount in $ Needed to Buy £100,000 If Firm Remains Unhedged	Real Cost of Hedging £100,000
$1.30	5%	$140,000	$1.30 × 100,000 = $130,000	$10,000
$1.32	10	$140,000	$1.32 × 100,000 = $132,000	$ 8,000
$1.34	15	$140,000	$1.34 × 100,000 = $134,000	$ 6,000
$1.36	20	$140,000	$1.36 × 100,000 = $136,000	$ 4,000
$1.38	20	$140,000	$1.38 × 100,000 = $138,000	$ 2,000
$1.40	15	$140,000	$1.40 × 100,000 = $140,000	$ 0
$1.42	10	$140,000	$1.42 × 100,000 = $142,000	−$ 2,000
$1.45	5	$140,000	$1.45 × 100,000 = $145,000	−$ 5,000

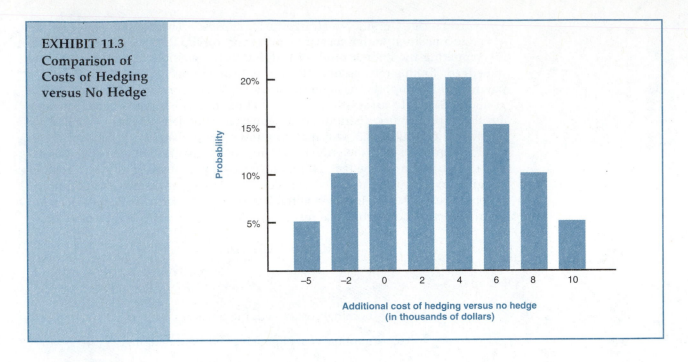

EXHIBIT 11.3
Comparison of Costs of Hedging versus No Hedge

Probability

20%

15%

10%

5%

−5   −2   0   2   4   6   8   10

Additional cost of hedging versus no hedge (in thousands of dollars)

where P_i represents the probability that the ith outcome will occur. In our example, the expected value of the RCH_p can be computed as

$$E(RCH_p) = \Sigma P_i RCH_{p,i}$$
$$= 5\%(10,000) + 10\%(8,000) + 15\%(6,000)$$
$$+ 20\%(4,000) + 20\%(2,000) + 15\%(0)$$
$$+ 10\%(-2,000) + 5\%(-5,000)$$
$$= \$500 + \$800 + \$900$$
$$+ \$800 + \$400 + 0$$
$$- \$200 - \$250$$
$$= \$2,950.$$

While this expected value is useful in assessing RCH_p, it does not clearly indicate the overall probability that hedging will be more costly. Such additional information could be determined by reviewing Exhibit 11.2 or 11.3. The data indicate there is a 15 percent chance that the RCH_p will be negative (that the nominal cost of hedging will be lower than remaining unhedged). Some firms may be more comfortable hedging, since this way they will know the exact amount of U.S. dollars needed for future purchases. Other firms may be willing to remain unhedged if the projected unhedged cost will most likely be less than the nominal cost of hedging. In our example, the probability of incurring a lower cost when remaining unhedged is 85 percent. The hedge versus no-hedge decision will be based on the firm's degree of risk aversion. Firms with a greater desire to avoid risk would be expected to hedge their open positions in foreign currencies more often than firms that are less concerned with risk.

If the forward rate is an accurate predictor of the future spot rate, the RCH_p will be zero. Because the forward rate often underestimates or overestimates the future spot rate, RCH_p differs from zero. If, however, the forward rate is an unbiased predictor of the future spot rate, RCH_p will be zero on average, as the differences between the forward rate and future spot rate will offset each other over time. If a firm believes that the forward rate is an unbiased predictor of the future spot rate, it will consider hedging its payables, since the forecasted RCH_p is zero, and the transaction exposure can be eliminated.

Forward Hedge versus No Hedge on Receivables.   For firms with exposure in receivables, the real cost of hedging receivables (RCH_r) can be estimated as

$$RCH_r = NR_r - NRH_r,$$

where

NR_r = nominal home currency revenues received without hedging

NRH_r = nominal home currency revenues received from hedging.

This equation is structured so that the real cost of hedging receivables is positive when hedging results in lower revenues than not hedging. This allows for consistency between RCH_p and RCH_r, since a negative (positive) value of either implies that hedging has had a more (less) favorable result than not hedging.

As with payable positions, firms can determine whether to hedge receivable positions by first developing a probability distribution for the future spot rate, and then using it to develop a probability distribution of RCH_r. If the RCH_r was likely to be negative, hedging would be preferred. If the RCH_r was likely to be positive, the firm would need to evaluate whether the potential benefits from remaining unhedged were worth the risk. If the forward rate was believed to be an unbiased predictor of the future spot rate, firms would consider hedging their receivables positions at an expected real cost of zero (ignoring transaction costs).

The RCH has been defined here in terms of the MNC's home currency (U.S. dollars, in our example). It can also be expressed as a percentage of the nominal hedged amount. This may be a useful measurement when comparing the RCH for various currencies. For example, if a U.S. firm were hedging various currencies in different amounts, a comparison of the dollar amount of RCH among currencies would be distorted by the dollar amount of payables or receivables hedged. For this reason, RCHs for each currency should be measured as a percentage of their respective hedged amounts if they are to be compared.

The RCH cannot be determined until the payables or receivables period is over. Firms should be pleased when they hedge if the RCH turns out to be very low, and especially pleased if it is negative. Conservative firms, however, may feel hedging is worthwhile even if the RCH turns out to be high.

The real cost of hedging British pounds over time (from a U.S. firm's perspective) is displayed in Exhibit 11.4. The top graph shows the real cost of hedging payables, while the lower graph shows the real cost of hedging receivables. Ninety-day periods were used to measure the real costs of hedging. The costs were measured on a per-unit basis. The real cost of hedging pound payables (shown in the top graph of Exhibit 11.4) was high in the early 1980s,

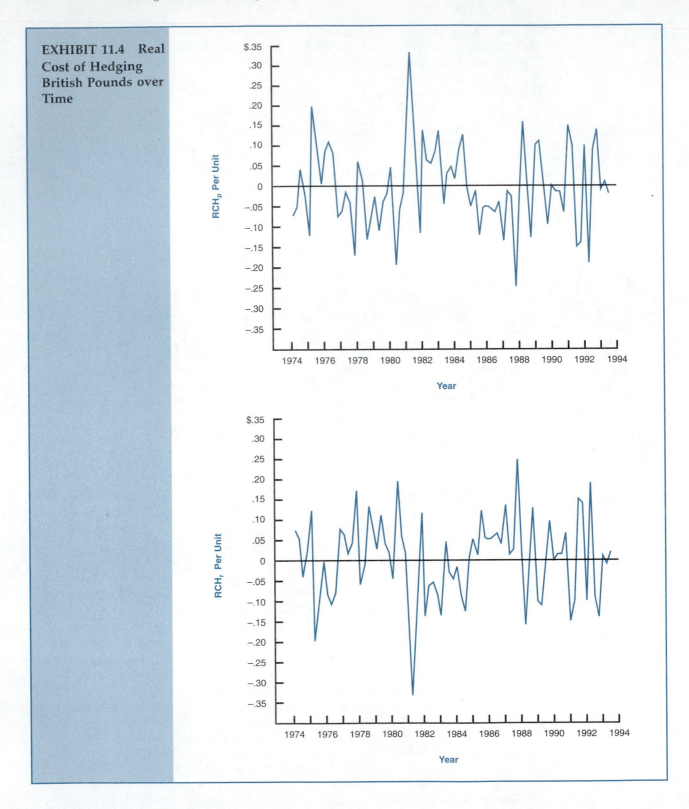

EXHIBIT 11.4 Real Cost of Hedging British Pounds over Time

since the pound was weakening over this period. Thus, the existing spot rate at the time payables were due was typically below the forward rate available at the beginning of each corresponding 90-day period. The real cost of hedging pound payables was commonly negative in the late 1970s, late 1980s, and early 1990s, since the pound was strengthening over these periods.

The real cost of hedging receivables is shown in the bottom graph of Exhibit 11.4. Since transaction costs were ignored when measuring the real costs of hedging in Exhibit 11.4, the real cost of hedging receivables is the exact opposite of the real cost of hedging payables.

Money Market Hedge

A **money market hedge** involves taking a money market position to cover a future payables or receivables position. The money market hedge on payables will be discussed separately from the hedge on receivables.

Money Market Hedge on Payables.

First, a simplified money market hedge, in which the firm has excess cash, will be illustrated. Then, a second example will show how a firm can use a money market hedge to hedge payables, even if it does not have excess cash.

If a firm has excess cash, it can create a short-term deposit in the foreign currency that it will need in the future. For example, if a U.S. firm needs SF1,000,000 in 30 days and it can earn 6 percent annualized (.5 percent for 30 days) on a Swiss security over this period, the amount needed to purchase a Swiss one-month security is

$$\text{Deposit amount to hedge SF payables} = \frac{\text{SF } 1,000,000}{1 + .005}$$

$$= \text{SF } 995,025.$$

Assuming that the franc's spot rate is $.65, $646,766 is needed to purchase the Swiss securities (computed as SF995,025 × $.65). In 30 days, the security will mature and provide SF1,000,000 to the U.S. firm, which can then be used to cover its payables. Regardless of how the Swiss exchange rate changes over this period, the U.S. firm's Swiss investment will be able to cover the payables position.

In many cases, firms would prefer to hedge payables without using their cash balances. A money market hedge can still be used in this situation, but it requires two money market positions: (1) borrowed funds in the home currency, and (2) a short-term investment in the foreign currency. To illustrate, reconsider the above example, in which SF1,000,000 is needed in 30 days. Recall that $646,766 is needed to obtain the investment of SF995,025, which in turn will accumulate to the SF1,000,000 needed in 30 days. If the U.S. firm has no excess cash, it can borrow $646,766 from a U.S. bank, and exchange those dollars for francs in order to purchase the Swiss security.

Because the Swiss investment will cover the future payables position, the U.S. firm needs to be concerned only about the dollars owed back on the loan in 30 days. The firm's money market hedge used to hedge payables can be summarized as follows:

HOW INTEREST RATE MOVEMENTS CAN AFFECT THE COST OF HEDGING

Interest rate movements and the forces behind interest rate parity can have an indirect impact on the costs of hedging imports or exports. The unification of East and West Germany in late 1989 placed upward pressure on German interest rates, ultimately causing these rates to rise above U.S interest rates. Consequently, the forces behind interest rate parity caused the forward rate on the German mark to be less than the spot rate. (If it was not, covered interest arbitrage would be possible). This was a marked change from the 1980s, when the mark's forward rate consistently exhibited a premium. The shift from a forward premium to a discount was beneficial to U.S. firms that consistently hedge their mark payables, while it adversely affected U.S. firms that consistently hedge their mark receivables. However, one must also consider that the same force that caused a forward discount on the mark (rising German interest rates relative to U.S. interest rates) also placed upward pressure on the spot rate of the mark in the early 1990s. Thus, even though U.S. importers could now buy marks forward at a discount, the discount from a very high spot rate still made the hedged payables seem expensive. Conversely, U.S. firms sold marks forward at a discount to hedge mark receivables. But, the dollar value of receivables was still substantial because of the mark's strength in the early 1990s.

STEP 1. Borrow $646,766 from a U.S. bank; assume a .7 percent interest rate over the 30-day loan period.

STEP 2. Convert the $646,766 to SF995,025, given the exchange rate of $.65 per franc.

STEP 3. Use the francs to purchase a Swiss security that offers .5 percent over one month.

STEP 4. Repay the U.S. loan in 30 days, plus interest; the amount owed is $651,293 (computed as $646,766 × 1.007).

Consider a U.S. firm that plans to implement either a forward contract hedge or a money market hedge to cover its future payables. Which of these two hedging techniques would be most appropriate for the MNC? The answer can be determined by comparing the payment dictated by the forward contract to the loan repayment made on borrowed funds when using the money market hedge. The forward hedge and the money market hedge are directly comparable, as long as the firm's cash balances are not used in the money market hedge. Thus, a firm can determine which hedge is preferable before implementing a hedge. Of course, it cannot determine whether either hedge will outperform an unhedged strategy until the period of concern has elapsed.

Money Market Hedge on Receivables. Consider a U.S. firm that expects to receive DM400,000 in 90 days. A simplified money market hedge could be implemented if the firm needed to borrow U.S. funds for 90 days anyway. Instead of borrowing dollars, it could borrow marks and convert them into dollars for use. Assuming an annualized interest rate of 8 percent, or 2 percent over the 90-day period, the amount of marks to be borrowed to hedge the future receivables would be

$$\text{Borrowed amount to hedge DM receivables} = \frac{\text{DM } 400{,}000}{1 + .02}$$

$$= \text{DM } 392{,}157.$$

If the firm borrows DM392,157 and converts those marks to dollars, then the receivables can be used to pay off the mark loan in 90 days. Meanwhile, the proceeds of the loan can be used for whatever purpose the firm desires.

In some cases, the firm may not need to borrow funds for a 90-day period. In these situations, a money market hedge can still be used to hedge receivables if the firm takes two positions in the money markets: (1) borrow the foreign currency representing future receivables, and (2) invest in the home currency. To illustrate, reconsider the previous example of DM400,000 in receivables. Even if the U.S. firm does not have a use for the DM392,157 borrowed, it can invest them in a 90-day U.S. security. Assuming that a mark is worth $.55, the marks borrowed can be converted to $215,686. Assuming an annualized U.S. interest rate of 7.2 percent (1.8 percent over 90 days) on 90-day securities, the U.S. investment will be worth $219,568 (computed as $215,686 × 1.018) in 90 days. Since the receivables can cover the existing loan, the firm will have $219,568 as a result of enacting the money market hedge.

The results of the money market hedge in this example can be compared to the results of a forward hedge in order to determine which type of hedge is preferable. Since the results of either hedge are known beforehand, the firm can implement the one that is more feasible. As with hedging payables, the firm will not know whether the chosen hedge on receivables will outperform an unhedged strategy until the period of concern has elapsed.

Implications of IRP for the Money Market Hedge. If interest rate parity (IRP) exists, and transaction costs do not exist, the money market hedge will yield the same results as the forward hedge. This is so because the forward premium on the forward rate reflects the interest rate differential between the two currencies. The hedging of future payables with a forward purchase will be similar to borrowing at the home interest rate and investing at the foreign interest rate. The hedging of future receivables with a forward sale will be similar to borrowing at the foreign interest rate and investing at the home interest rate. Even if the forward premium generally reflects the interest rate differential between countries, the existence of transaction costs may cause the results from a forward hedge to differ from those from the money market hedge.

Currency Option Hedge

Firms recognize that hedging techniques such as the forward hedge and money market hedge can backfire when a payables currency depreciates or a receivables currency appreciates over the hedged period. In these situations, an unhedged strategy would likely outperform the forward hedge or money market hedge. The ideal type of hedge would insulate the firm against adverse exchange rate movements but allow the firm to benefit from favorable exchange rate movements. Currency options exhibit these attributes. However, a firm must assess whether the advantages of a currency option hedge are worth the price (premium) paid for it. Details on currency options are provided in Chapter 5. The following discussion illustrates how they can be used in hedging.

Hedging Payables with Currency Call Options. A currency call option provides the right to buy a specified amount of a particular currency at a specified price (the exercise price) within a given period of time. Yet, unlike a futures or forward contract, the currency call option *does not obligate* its owner to buy the currency at that price. To illustrate, consider a firm that has payables in British pounds. If the spot rate of the pound remains lower than the exercise price throughout the life of the option, the firm that needs pounds could let the option expire and simply purchase them at the existing spot rate. On the other hand, if the spot rate of the pound appreciates over time, the call option allows the firm to purchase pounds at the exercise price. That is, the firm owning a call option has locked in a maximum price (the exercise price) to pay for the currency. It also has the flexibility, though, to let the option expire and obtain the currency at the existing spot rate when the currency is to be sent for payment.

Consider Clemson Corporation, which has payables of £100,000 90 days from now. Assume there is a call option available with an exercise price of $1.60. Clemson doesn't have to exercise its call option if it can obtain pounds at a lower spot rate. Assume that the option premium is $.04 per unit. For options that cover the 100,000 units, the total premium is $4,000 (100,000 × $.04).

Assume that Clemson expects the spot rate of the pound to be either $1.58, $1.62, or $1.66 when the payables are due. The effect of each of these scenarios on Clemson's cost of payables is shown in Exhibit 11.5. The first two columns simply identify the scenario to be analyzed. The third column shows the premium per unit paid on the option, which is the same regardless of the spot rate that occurs when payables are due. The fourth column shows the amount that Clemson would pay per pound for the payables under each scenario, assuming that it owned call options. If Scenario 1 occurs, Clemson will let the options expire and purchase pounds in the spot market for $1.58 each. If Scenarios 2 or 3 occur, Clemson will exercise the options and therefore purchase pounds for $1.60 per unit. The fifth column is the sum of the third and fourth columns, as it determines the amount paid per unit when including the premium paid on the call option. The sixth column converts the fifth column into a total dollar cost, based on the £100,000 hedged.

Hedging Receivables with Currency Put Options. Like the currency call option, the currency put option can also be a valuable hedging device. The currency put option provides the right to sell a specified amount in a particular currency at a specified price (the exercise price) within a given period of time. It could be used by firms to hedge future receivables in foreign currencies, since it guarantees a certain price (the exercise price) at which the future receivables can be sold. The currency put option *does not obligate* its owner to sell the currency at a specified price. If the existing spot rate of the foreign currency is above the exercise price when the firm receives the foreign currency, the firm can sell the

EXHIBIT 11.5 Use of Currency Call Options for Hedging British Pound Payables   (exercise price = $1.60; premium = $.04)

(1)	(2)	(3)	(4)	(5) = (4) + (3)	(6)
Scenario	Spot Rate When Payables Are Due	Premium per Unit Paid on Call Options	Amount Paid per Unit When Owning Call Options	Total Amount Paid per Unit (including the Premium) When Owning Call Options	$ Amount Paid for £100,000 When Owning Call Options
1	$1.58	$.04	$1.58	$1.62	$162,000
2	1.62	.04	1.60	1.64	164,000
3	1.66	.04	1.60	1.64	164,000

currency received at the spot rate and let the put option expire. The application of put options for hedging will now be discussed.

Assume that Knoxville Inc. expects to receive DM600,000 in about 90 days. If Knoxville is concerned about the possibility of the mark's depreciation against the dollar, it could purchase put options to cover its receivables. Assume that the mark put options considered here have an exercise price of $.50 and a premium of $.03 per unit. Also assume that Knoxville anticipates the spot rate in 90 days to be either $.44, $.46, or $.51. The amount to be received as a result of owning currency put options is shown in Exhibit 11.6. Columns 2 through 5 are on a per unit basis. Column 6 is determined by multiplying the per unit amount received in Column 5 by 600,000 units.

EXHIBIT 11.6 Use of Currency Put Options for Hedging German Mark Receivables   (exercise price = $.50; premium = $.03)

(1)	(2)	(3)	(4)	(5) = (4) − (3)	(6)
Scenario	Spot Rate When Payment on Receivables Is Received	Premium per Unit on Put Options	Amount Received per Unit When Owning Put Options	Net Amount Received per Unit (after Accounting for Premium Paid)	Dollar Amount Received from Hedging DM600,000 Receivables with Put Options
1	$.44	$.03	$.50	$.47	$282,000
2	.46	.03	.50	.47	282,000
3	.51	.03	.51	.48	288,000

EXHIBIT 11.7   Review of Techniques for Hedging Transaction Exposure

Hedging Technique	To Hedge Payables	To Hedge Receivables
1. Futures hedge	Purchase a currency futures contract (or contracts) representing the currency and amount related to the payables.	Sell a currency futures contract (or contracts) representing the currency and amount related to the receivables.
2. Forward hedge	Purchase a forward contract representing the currency and amount related to the payables.	Sell a forward contract representing the currency and amount related to the receivables.
3. Money market hedge	Borrow local currency and convert to currency denominating payables. Invest these funds until they are needed to cover the payables.	Borrow the currency denominating the receivables, convert it to the local currency, and invest it. Then pay off the loan with cash inflows from the receivables.
4. Currency option hedge	Purchase a currency call option (or options) representing the currency and amount related to the payables.	Purchase a currency put option (or options) representing the currency and amount related to the receivables.

Comparison of Hedging Techniques

Each of the hedging techniques is briefly summarized in Exhibit 11.7. When using a futures hedge, forward hedge, or money market hedge, the firm can estimate the funds (denominated in its home currency) that it will need for future payables, or the funds it will receive after converting foreign currency receivables. Thus, it can compare the costs or revenues and determine which of these hedging techniques is appropriate. However, the cash flow associated with the currency option hedge cannot be determined with certainty, because the costs of purchasing payables and the revenues generated from receivables are not known ahead of time.

To reinforce an understanding of the hedging techniques, a comprehensive example is provided here. Assume that Fresno Corporation will need £200,000 in 180 days. It considers using (1) a forward hedge, (2) a money market hedge, (3) an option hedge, or (4) no hedge. Its analysts develop the following information, which can be used to assess the alternative solutions:

- Spot rate of pound as of today = $1.50.
- 180-day forward rate of pound as of today = $1.47.
- Interest rates are as follows:

	U.K.	U.S.
180-day deposit rate	4.5%	4.5%
180-day borrowing rate	5.0%	5.0%

- A call option on pounds that expires in 180 days has an exercise price of $1.48 and a premium of $.03.
- A put option on pounds that expires in 180 days has an exercise price of $1.49 and a premium of $.02.
- Fresno Corporation forecasted the future spot rate in 180 days as follows:

Possible Outcome	Probability
$1.43	20%
$1.46	70%
$1.52	10%

Each alternative solution to the existing problem is assessed in Exhibit 11.8. Now these solutions will be compared to determine the best one.

Each of the alternative solutions has been analyzed to estimate the nominal dollar cost of paying for the payables denominated in pounds. The cost is known with certainty for the forward rate hedge and money market hedge. However, the cost when either using the call option or remaining unhedged is dependent on the spot rate 180 days from now. The costs of the four alternatives are also compared with the use of probability distributions, as shown in Exhibit 11.9. A review of this exhibit shows that the forward hedge is superior to the money market hedge, since the dollar cost is definitely less. A comparison of the forward hedge to the call option hedge shows that there is an 80 percent change that the call option hedge will be more expensive. Thus, the forward hedge appears to be the optimal hedge.

The probability distribution of outcomes for the no-hedge strategy appears to be more favorable than that for the forward hedge. Fresno Corporation is likely to perform best if it remains unhedged, but it should choose the forward hedge if it prefers to hedge. If Fresno does not hedge, it should periodically reassess the hedging decision. For example, after 60 days it should repeat the analysis shown here, based on the applicable spot rate, forward rate, interest rates, call option information, and forecasts of the spot rate 120 days into the future (when the payables are due).

A similar analysis of transaction exposure could be conducted if a firm desired to hedge receivables. For example, assume that Gator Corporation anticipates no payables in pounds, but will receive £300,000 in 180 days. The same information on the spot, forward, and options prices is used to compare hedging techniques and an unhedged strategy in Exhibit 11.10.

The dollar amounts to be received from each of the four alternatives are compared in Exhibit 11.11. It appears that the money market hedge is the optimal hedge for this example. The money market hedge would be outperformed by the no-hedge strategy if the spot rate of the pound in 180 days were $1.52. There is only a 10 percent probability of that outcome, though. Therefore, the firm will likely decide to hedge its receivables position.

While this example includes the assessment of one particular currency option, several alternative currency options are normally available with different exercise prices. When hedging payables, a firm could reduce the premium paid by choosing a call option with a higher exercise price. Of course, the trade-off is that the maximum amount to be paid for the payables would be higher. Similarly, a firm hedging receivables could reduce the premium paid by choosing

EXHIBIT 11.8   Comparison of Hedging Alternatives for Fresno Corporation

Forward Hedge
Purchase pounds 180 days forward

$$\text{Dollars needed in 180 days} = \text{Payables in £} \times \text{Forward rate of £}$$
$$= £\,200,000 \times \$1.47$$
$$= \$294,000$$

Money Market Hedge
Borrow \$, Convert to £, Invest £, Repay \$ loan in 180 days

$$\begin{matrix}\text{Amount in £} \\ \text{to be invested}\end{matrix} = \frac{£200,000}{(1 + .045)}$$
$$= £191,388$$

$$\left\{\begin{matrix}\text{Amount in \$} \\ \text{needed to convert} \\ \text{into £ for deposit}\end{matrix}\right\} = £191,388 \times \$1.50$$
$$= \$287,081$$

$$\left\{\begin{matrix}\text{Interest and principal} \\ \text{owed on \$ loan after} \\ \text{180 days}\end{matrix}\right\} = \$287,081 \times (1 + .05)$$
$$= \$301,435$$

Call Option
Purchase call option (the following computations assume that the option is to be exercised on the day pounds are needed, or not at all. Exercise price = \$1.48; premium = \$.03.)

Possible Spot Rate in 180 days	Premium per Unit Paid for Option	Exercise Option?	Total Price (Including Option Premium) Paid per Unit	Total Price Paid for £200,000	Probability
\$1.43	\$.03	No	\$1.46	\$292,000	20%
\$1.46	\$.03	No	\$1.49	\$298,000	70%
\$1.52	\$.03	Yes	\$1.51	\$302,000	10%

Remain Unhedged
Purchase £200,000 in the spot market 180 days from now

Future Spot Rate Expected in 180 Days	Dollars Needed to Purchase £200,000	Probability
\$1.43	\$286,000	20%
\$1.46	\$292,000	70
\$1.52	\$304,000	10

EXHIBIT 11.9
Nominal Dollar Cost of Pound-Denominated Payables

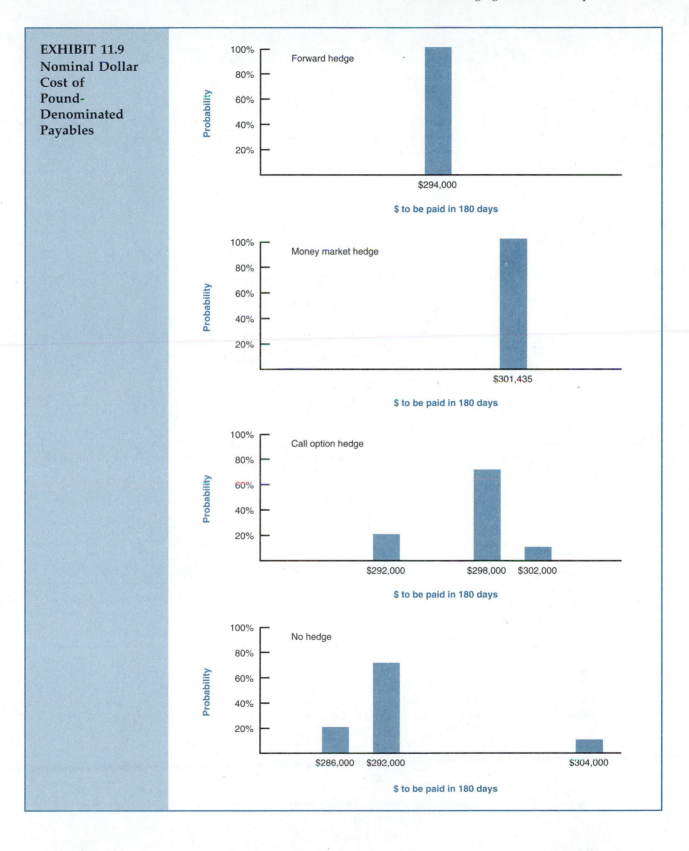

EXHIBIT 11.10   Comparison of Hedging Alternatives for Gator Corporation

Forward Hedge
Sell pounds 180 days forward

$$\text{Dollars to be received in 180 days} = \text{Receivables in £} \times \text{Forward rate of £}$$
$$= £300,000 \times \$1.47$$
$$= \$441,000$$

Money Market Hedge
Borrow £, convert to $, invest $, use receivables to pay off loan in 180 days

$$\text{Amount in £ Borrowed} = \frac{£300,000}{(1 + .05)}$$
$$= £285,714$$
$$\substack{\$ \text{ received} \\ \text{from converting £}} = £285,714 \times \$1.50 \text{ per £}$$
$$= \$428,571$$
$$\$ \text{ accumulated after 180 days} = \$428,571 \times (1 + .045)$$
$$= \$447,857$$

Put Option Hedge
Purchase put option (assume the options are to be exercised on the day pounds are to be received, or not at all. Exercise price = \$1.49; premium = \$.02.)

Possible Spot Rate in 180 days	Premium per Unit Paid for Option	Exercise Option?	Total Dollars Received per Unit (After Accounting for the Premium)	Total Dollars Received from Converting £300,000	Probability
$1.43	$.02	Yes	$1.47	$441,000	20%
1.46	.02	Yes	1.47	441,000	70
1.52	.02	No	1.50	450,000	10

Remain Unhedged

Possible Spot Rate in 180 Days	Total Dollars Received from Converting £300,000	Probability
$1.43	$429,000	20%
1.46	438,000	70
1.52	456,000	10

**EXHIBIT 11.11
Dollars Received
from Pound-
Denominated
Receivables**

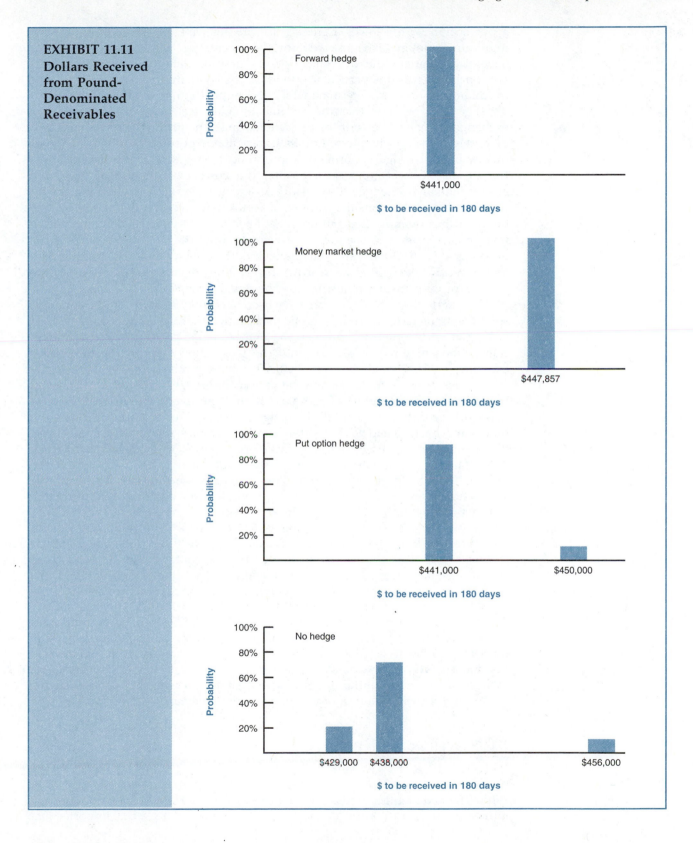

a put option with a lower exercise price. In this case, the tradeoff is that the minimum amount to be received for the receivables would be lower. Firms generally compare the available options first to determine which is most appropriate. Then this particular option can be compared to the other hedging techniques in order to determine which technique (if any) should be used.

It should be clear that the optimal hedging technique is dependent on exchange rate projections. If the projections cause the firm to believe that it will definitely be adversely affected by its transaction exposure, a forward hedge or money market hedge is normally appropriate. Conversely, if the firm believes that it may benefit from its exposure, the currency option hedge is more appropriate (if any hedge is used at all). As a realistic example of choosing among hedging techniques, consider the case of Merck, with worldwide sales of over $6 billion. It has recently used put options to hedge its receivables denominated in foreign currencies, because it did not want to forgo the potential benefits if the dollar weakened. Under this type of scenario, the option would not be exercised, as the receivables would be worth more at the prevailing spot rate. Yet, the options provide insurance just in case the dollar strengthens.

The examples provided so far have been simplified to focus on the comparison of hedging techniques. It is implicitly assumed that the amount to be hedged is known with certainty. However, the precise dollar amount in many foreign transactions may not be known until the transaction date. In the receivables example, it is assumed that the £300,000 will be received in 180 days. If the receivables amount could actually be as low as £200,000, should the firm still hedge the expected inflow of £300,000? If the firm overhedges, it will have to make up the difference to fulfill the hedging strategy. For example, if it uses the money market hedge to hedge £300,000, and receivables amount to only £200,000, it will have to purchase £100,000 in the spot market to achieve the £300,000 needed to pay off the loan. If the pound appreciates over the 180-day period, the firm will need a large amount in dollars to obtain the £100,000. This example shows how **overhedging** (hedging a larger amount in a currency than the actual transaction amount) can adversely affect a firm.

A solution to avoid overhedging is to hedge only the minimum known amount in the future transaction. In our example, if the future receivables may be as low as £200,000, the firm could hedge this amount. However, under these conditions the firm may not have completely hedged its position. If the actual transaction amount turns out to be £300,000 as expected, the firm will be only partially hedged and will need to sell the extra £100,000 in the spot market.

This dilemma is very common for firms, since the precise amount in a foreign currency to be received at the end of a period can be uncertain, especially for firms heavily involved in exporting. Based on this example, it should be clear that most MNCs cannot completely hedge all of their transactions. Nevertheless, by hedging a portion of those transactions that affect them, they can reduce the sensitivity of their cash flows to exchange rate movements.

LIMITATION OF REPEATED SHORT-TERM HEDGING

While the hedging techniques described in this chapter can be useful, they have limited effectiveness for the long term. To illustrate, consider a U.S. importer that

---

APPLIED RESEARCH

HEDGING PERFORMANCE OF CURRENCY OPTIONS VERSUS FORWARDS

A recent study by Madura simulated a process of hedging a position in each of five major currencies, to study the effectiveness of hedging with currency options as opposed to forward contracts in each quarter. The study was conducted first from the perspective of a U.S. importing firm, and then from that of a U.S. exporting firm. From the importer's perspective, the results were mixed. In some quarters, the importer would have been better off with currency call options, while in other quarters the forward purchase would have been preferable. Of course, the superiority of one technique over another would not have been determined until after the periods were over. On average, there was no significant difference in the amount paid for imports between

hedging with currency call options and doing so with forward purchases. This result held for each of the five currencies. From the U.S. exporter's perspective, there was on average no significant difference between using currency put options and using forward sales to hedge receivables for four of the currencies. For the Japanese yen, the dollar value of the receivables was significantly higher when using put options than it was when using forward sales.

A comparison was also conducted between currency options and an unhedged strategy. From an importer's perspective, there was no significant difference on average in the amount paid between using currency call options and using an unhedged strategy. One exception

was the German mark, in which the unhedged strategy was superior.

From an exporter's perspective, there was no significant difference on average in the amount received between hedging with currency put options and using an unhedged strategy. One exception was the British pound, in which the unhedged strategy was superior.

Overall, currency options generally performed about as well as forward contracts or the unhedged strategy, and they may alleviate any concerns managers have about exchange rate movements. Furthermore, they offer the opportunity to benefit if exchange rates move in a favorable direction. The results of this study suggest that currency options should be given serious consideration.

specializes in importing particular Japanese stereos in one large shipment per year and then selling them to retail stores throughout the year. Assume that today's exchange rate of the Japanese yen is $.005, and that the stereos are worth ¥60,000, or $300. Further assume that the forward rate of the yen generally exhibits a premium of 2 percent. Exhibit 11.12 shows the dollar/yen exchange rate to be paid by the importer over time. As the spot rate changes, the forward rate will often change by a similar amount. Thus, if the spot rate increases by 10 percent over the year, the forward rate may increase by about the same amount, and the importer will pay 10 percent more for next year's shipment of stereos (assuming no change in the yen price quoted by the Japanese exporter). The use of a one-year forward contract during a strong-yen cycle is preferable to no hedge in this case, but will still result in subsequent increases in prices paid by the importer each year. This illustrates that the use of short-term hedging techniques does not completely insulate a firm from exchange rate exposure, even if they are repeatedly used over time.

If the hedging techniques could be applied to longer-term periods, they could more effectively insulate the firm from exchange rate risk over the long run. To illustrate, the stereo importer could, as of Time 0, create a hedge for shipments to arrive at the end of each of the next several years. The forward rate for each hedge would be based on the spot rate as of today, as shown in Exhibit 11.13. During a strong-yen cycle, such a strategy would save a substantial

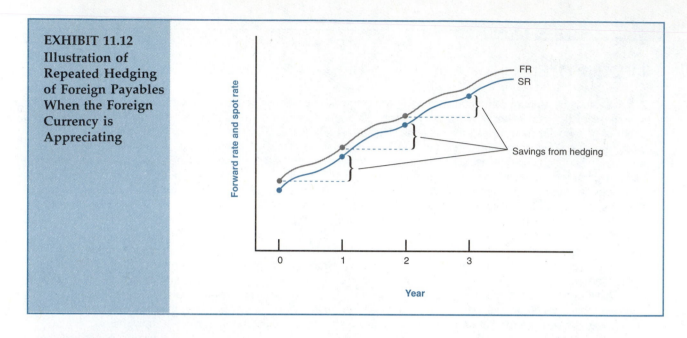

EXHIBIT 11.12
Illustration of Repeated Hedging of Foreign Payables When the Foreign Currency is Appreciating

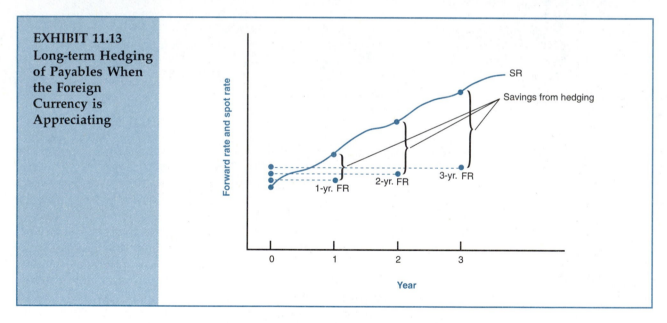

EXHIBIT 11.13
Long-term Hedging of Payables When the Foreign Currency is Appreciating

amount of money. However, the limitation of this strategy is that the amount in yen to be hedged farther into the future is more uncertain, since the shipment size will be dependent on economic conditions or other factors at that time. If a recession occurs, the importer may reduce the number of stereos ordered, but the amount in yen to be received by the importer is dictated by the forward contract that was created. If the stereo manufacturer goes bankrupt, or simply experiences stockouts, the importer is still obligated to purchase the yen, even if a shipment is not forthcoming.

HEDGING LONG-TERM
TRANSACTION EXPOSURE

Some MNCs are certain of having cash flows denominated in foreign currencies for several years, and attempt to use long-term hedging. For example, Walt Disney Company has hedged its Japanese yen cash flows that would be remitted to the United States (from the Japanese theme park) 20 years ahead. Eastman Kodak Co. and General Electric Co. incorporate foreign exchange management into their long-term corporate planning. Thus, techniques for hedging long-term exchange rate exposure are needed.

For firms that can accurately estimate foreign currency payables or receivables that will occur several years from now, there are three commonly used techniques to hedge such long-term transaction exposure:

- Long-term forward contract
- Currency swap
- Parallel loan.

Each technique is discussed in turn.

Long-Term Forward Contract

Until recently, **long-term forward contracts,** or long forwards, were seldom used. Today the long forward is quite popular. Most large international banks will routinely quote forward rates for terms of up to five years for British pounds, Canadian dollars, German marks, and Swiss francs. Long forwards are especially attractive to firms that have set up fixed-price exporting or importing contracts over a long period of time and want to protect their cash flow from exchange rate fluctuations.

Like a short-term forward contract, the long forward can be tailored to accommodate the specific needs of the firm. Maturities of up to 10 years or more can sometimes be set up for the major currencies. Because a bank is trusting that a firm will fulfill its long-term obligation specified in the forward contract, it will consider only very creditworthy customers.

Currency Swap

A **currency swap** is a second technique for hedging long-term transaction exposure to exchange rate fluctuations. It can take many forms. One type of currency swap accommodates two firms that have different long-term needs. Consider a U.S. firm, hired to build an oil pipeline in Great Britain, that expects to receive payment in British pounds in five years when the job is completed. At the same time, a British firm is hired by a U.S. bank for a long-term consulting project. Assume that payment to this British firm will be in U.S. dollars and that much of the payment will occur in five years. The U.S. firm will be receiving British pounds in five years and the British firm will be receiving U.S. dollars in five years. These two firms could arrange a currency swap that allows for an exchange of pounds for dollars in five years at some negotiated exchange rate. In this way, the U.S. firm could lock in the number of U.S. dollars the British pound payment will convert to in five years. Likewise, the British firm could lock in the number of British pounds the U.S. dollar payment will convert to in five years.

To create a currency swap, firms need to find other firms that can accommodate their needs. There are brokers employed by large banks and investment firms that act as middlemen for swaps. They are notified by those corporations that want to eliminate transaction exposure to specific currencies at certain future dates. Using this information, they can match up firms when one firm needs the currency the other firm wants to dispose of (and vice versa). The brokers receive a fee for their service.

Currency swaps have been commonly used. Now that long-term forward contracts are available, however, the popularity of currency swaps may diminish, due to the more extensive documentation required on swap arrangements.

Over time, the currency swap obligation may become undesirable to one of the parties involved. Using our example, if the British pound appreciates substantially over time, the U.S. company that agreed to swap pounds for dollars will be worse off than if it had been able to obtain its dollars in the spot market. Of course, it did not know this when it engaged in a swap agreement. The swap agreement may require periodic payments from one party to the other to account for exchange rate movements, so as to reduce the possibility that one party will not fulfill its obligation by the time the swap is supposed to occur.

Parallel Loan

A **parallel loan** (or "back-to-back loan") involves an exchange of currencies between two parties, with a promise to re-exchange currencies at a specified exchange rate and future date. It represents two swaps of currencies, one swap at the inception of the loan contract and another swap at the specified future date. A parallel loan is interpreted by accountants as a loan and is therefore recorded on financial statements.

ALTERNATIVE HEDGING TECHNIQUES _____

Sometimes a firm is not able to completely eliminate its transaction exposure. For example, a firm cannot always accurately forecast the sales (representing inflow payments) on products and/or the purchases (representing outflow payments) on supplies denominated in foreign currencies. Thus, it does not know the precise amount to hedge in each foreign currency. In addition, projected costs of the hedging techniques may seem too high to be worthwhile. Finally, there is also the possibility that the currencies a firm is exposed to cannot be hedged, perhaps due to the nonexistence of a forward market or currency options market for such currencies. Even the money market hedge may not be possible if there are barriers to foreign investing or borrowing in the home country of a particular currency. Also, the swap arrangement may be difficult to set up if the currency is not widely traded, since there would not be an active market for swaps in that currency.

When a perfect hedge is not available (or is too expensive) to eliminate transaction exposure, the firm should consider methods to at least reduce exposure. Such methods include

- Leading and lagging
- Cross-hedging
- Currency diversification.

Each method is discussed in turn.

Leading and Lagging

The act of leading and lagging represents an adjustment in the timing of payment request or disbursement to reflect expectations about future currency movements. For example, consider a multinational corporation based in the United States that has subsidiaries dispersed around the world. The focus here will be on a subsidiary in Great Britain that purchases some of its supplies from a subsidiary in Germany. Assume these supplies are denominated in German marks. If the British subsidiary expects the pound will soon depreciate against the mark, it may attempt to accelerate the timing of its payment before the pound depreciates. This strategy is referred to as **leading.**

As a second possibility, consider a scenario in which the British subsidiary expects the pound will soon appreciate against the mark. In this case, the British subsidiary may attempt to stall its payment until after the pound appreciates. In this way it could use fewer pounds to obtain the marks needed for payment. This strategy is referred to as **lagging.** General Electric and other well-known MNCs commonly use leading and lagging strategies in countries that allow them.

Some country governments limit the length of time involved on leading and lagging strategies, so that the flow of funds into or out of a country is not disrupted. Consequently, a multinational corporation must be aware of government restrictions of any countries in which it conducts business before using these strategies.

Cross-hedging

Cross-hedging is a common method of reducing transaction exposure when the currency cannot be hedged. Assume a U.S. firm has payables in Currency X 90 days from now. Because it is worried that Currency X may appreciate against the U.S. dollar, it may desire to hedge this position. If forward contracts and the other hedging techniques are not possible for this currency, the firm may consider cross-hedging, in which case it needs to first identify a currency that can be hedged and is highly correlated with Currency X. It could then set up a 90-day forward contract on this currency. If two currencies are highly correlated relative to the U.S. dollar (that is, they move in a similar direction against the U.S. dollar), then the exchange rate between these two currencies should be somewhat stable over time. When purchasing the one currency 90 days forward, the U.S. firm can then exchange that currency for Currency X. The effectiveness of this strategy depends on the degree to which these two currencies are positively correlated. The stronger the positive correlation, the more effective will be the cross-hedging strategy.

To illustrate a second use of cross-hedging, consider a U.S. firm that has net inflows denominated in German marks and net outflows denominated in Swiss francs. Because these two currencies often move in tandem against the U.S. dollar, a cross-hedge exists. If by chance the mark depreciates, the U.S. firm will obtain fewer dollars when exchanging those marks received. Of course, the Swiss franc will probably also have depreciated (though not necessarily by the same degree) against the dollar. Thus, fewer dollars will be needed to obtain francs when sending outflow payments. Regardless of whether these currencies depreciate or appreciate against the U.S. dollar, the U.S. firm in this example will be

APPLIED RESEARCH

REDUCING EXCHANGE RATE RISK THROUGH DIVERSIFICATION

A recent study by Soenen provides insight on the potential reduction in exchange rate risk (as measured by variance) attributed to diversification. First, the average variance of monthly percentage changes in exchange rates was estimated for each currency (with respect to the U.S. dollar). Then the average variance of randomly selected two-currency, equally weighted currency portfolios was estimated. The procedure was replicated for other portfolios containing more currencies. The objective was to determine the degree to which risk could be reduced on average by adding additional currencies to the portfolio. In general, one would expect that a more diversified portfolio of currencies should exhibit less risk. However, to the extent that the movements of most currencies against the dollar are positively correlated, the benefits from diversification may be limited after some point. The results are disclosed in the next column. The results suggest that diversification can effectively reduce risk. However, once the portfolio contains four to six currencies, adding more currencies has a negligible effect on variance. The implications are that while firms can reduce the risk by diversifying among currencies, diversification beyond some small number of currencies will not necessarily reduce risk any further. Results would vary with the particular currencies chosen, though.

Number of Currencies in Portfolio	Average Variance	Average Percentage Risk Reduction Relative to a Single Foreign Currency
1	10.360%	–
2	8.536	17.6%
4	7.099	31.5
6	6.993	32.5
8	6.700	35.3
10	6.680	35.5
12	6.600	36.3

somewhat insulated from the exchange rate fluctuations if the two currencies are highly positively correlated.

Currency Diversification

A third method for reducing transaction exposure is currency diversification. Consider a multinational firm based in the U.S. that is heavily involved in exporting and importing and has more inflows than outflows in each foreign currency. In this case, the MNC will be hurt by a strong dollar, since the foreign currencies received will not be worth as many dollars. If all the inflows are denominated in one or a few foreign currencies, substantial depreciation of one of these currencies would severely affect the *dollar value* of the firm's inflows. However, substantial depreciation in one foreign currency would not be as damaging if that currency were only one of several to which the firm was exposed. This is so because the single currency would represent only a small portion of total inflows and would therefore not severely affect the dollar value of the total inflows. Some MNCs, such as Coca Cola, PepsiCo, and Phillip Morris, claim that their exposure to exchange rate movements is significantly reduced because they diversify their business among numerous countries.

The dollar value of future inflows in foreign currencies will be more stable if the foreign currencies received are *not* highly positively correlated. The reason is that lower positive correlations or negative correlations can reduce the variability of the dollar value of all foreign currency inflows. If the foreign currencies were highly correlated with each other, diversifying among them would not be a very effective way to reduce risk. If one of the currencies substantially depreciated, the others would do so as well, given that all these currencies move in tandem.

SUMMARY

- MNCs use the following techniques to hedge transaction exposure: (1) futures hedge, (2) forward hedge, (3) money market hedge, and (4) currency options hedge.

- To hedge payables, a futures or forward contract on the foreign currency can be purchased. Alternatively, a money market hedge strategy can be used, in which the MNC borrows its home currency and converts the proceeds into the foreign currency that will be needed in the future. Finally, call options on the foreign currency can be purchased.
  To hedge receivables, a futures or forward contract on the foreign currency can be sold. Alternatively, a money market hedge strategy can be used, in which the MNC borrows the foreign currency to be received and converts the funds into its home currency; the loan is to be repaid by the receivables. Finally, put options on the foreign currency can be purchased.

- Futures contracts and forward contracts normally yield similar results. Forward contracts are more flexible because they are not standardized. The money market hedge yields results similar to those of the forward hedge if interest rate parity exists. The currency options hedge has an advantage over the other hedging techniques in that it does not have to be exercised if the MNC would be better off unhedged. Yet, a premium must be paid to purchase the currency options, as there is a cost for the flexibility they provide.

- When hedging techniques are not available, there are still some methods of reducing transaction exposure, such as leading and lagging, cross-hedging, and currency diversification.

SELF-TEST FOR CHAPTER 11

(Answers are provided in Appendix A in the back of the text)

1. Montclair Co., a U.S. firm, plans to use a money market hedge to hedge its payment of A$3,000,000 for Australian goods in one year. The U.S. interest rate is 7%, while the Australian interest rate is 12%. The spot rate of the Australian dollar is $.85, while the one-year forward rate is $.81. Determine the amount of U.S. dollars needed in one year if a money market hedge is used.

2. Using the information in the above question, would Montclair Co. be better off hedging the payables with a money market hedge or with a forward hedge?

3. Using the information about Montclair in the first question, explain the possible advantage of a currency option hedge over a money market hedge for Montclair Co. What is a possible disadvantage of the currency option hedge?

4. Sanibel Co. purchases British goods (denominated in £) every month. It negotiates a one-month forward contract at the beginning of every month to hedge its payables. Assume the British pound appreciates consistently over the next five years. Will Sanibel be affected? Explain.

5. Using the information in the Question 4, suggest how Sanibel Co. could more effectively insulate itself from the possible long-term appreciation of the British pound.

6. Hopkins Co. will receive SF2,000,000 in three months. It believes the 3-month forward rate will be an accurate forecast of the future spot rate. The 3-month forward rate of the Swiss franc is $.68. A put option is available with an exercise price of $.69 and a premium of $.03. Would Hopkins prefer a put option hedge to no hedge? Explain.

QUESTIONS

1. Quincy Corporation estimates the following cash flows in 90 days at its subsidiaries as follows:

Subsidiary	Net Position in Each Currency Measured in the Parent's Currency		
	Currency 1	Currency 2	Currency 3
A	+200	−300	−100
B	+100	− 40	− 10
C	−180	+200	− 40

Determine the consolidated net exposure of the MNC to each currency.

2. Assume that Stevens Point Company has net receivables of 100,000 Swiss francs in 90 days. The spot rate of the franc is $.50, and the Swiss interest rate is 2 percent over 90 days. Suggest how the U.S. firm could implement a money market hedge. Be precise.

3. Assume that Vermont Company has net payables of 200,000 French francs in 180 days. The French interest rate is 7 percent over 180 days, and the spot rate of the French franc is $.10. Suggest how the U.S. firm could implement a money market hedge. Be precise.

4. Assume that Citadel Company purchases some goods in Germany that are denominated in marks. It also sells goods denominated in U.S. dollars to some German firms. At the end of each month, it has a large net payables position in German marks. How can this U.S. firm use an invoicing strategy to reduce this transaction exposure? List any limitations on the effectiveness of this strategy.

5. Explain how a U.S. corporation could hedge net receivables in British pounds with futures contracts.

6. Explain how a U.S. corporation could hedge net payables in Japanese yen with futures contracts.

7. Explain how a U.S. corporation could hedge net receivables in French francs with a forward contract.

8. Explain how a U.S. corporation could hedge payables in Canadian dollars with a forward contract.

9. Assume that Loras Corporation needs 100,000 Swiss francs 180 days from now. It is trying to determine whether or not to hedge this position. It has developed the following probability distribution for the Swiss franc:

Possible Value of Swiss Franc in 180 days	Probability
$.40	5%
.45	10
.48	30
.50	30
.53	20
.55	5

The 180-day forward rate of the Swiss franc is $.52. The spot rate of the Swiss franc is $.49. Develop a table showing a feasibility analysis for hedging. That is, determine the possible differences between the costs of hedging and those of not hedging. What is the probability that hedging will be more costly to the firm than not hedging?

10. Using the information in Question 9, determine the expected value of the additional cost of hedging.

11. If hedging is expected to be more costly than not hedging, why would a firm even consider hedging?

12. Assume that Suffolk Company negotiated a forward contract to purchase 200,000 British pounds in 90 days. The 90-day forward rate was $1.40 per British pound. The pounds to be purchased were to be used to purchase British supplies. On the day the pounds were delivered in accordance with the forward contract, the spot rate of the British pound was $1.44. What was the real cost of hedging the payables for this U.S. firm?

13. Repeat Question 12, except assume that the spot rate of the British pound was $1.34 on the day the pounds were delivered in accordance with the forward contract. What was the real cost of hedging the payables in this example?

14. Assume that Bentley Company negotiated a forward contract to sell 100,000 Canadian dollars in one year. The one-year forward rate on the Canadian dollar was $.80. This strategy was designed to hedge receivables in Canadian dollars. On the day the Canadian dollars were to be sold off in accordance with the forward contract, the spot rate of the Canadian dollar was $.83. What was the real cost of hedging receivables for this U.S. firm?

15. Repeat Question 14, except assume that the spot rate of the Canadian dollar was $.75 on the day the Canadian dollars were to be sold off in accordance with the forward contract. What was the real cost of hedging receivables in this example?

16. Assume the following information:

90-day U.S. interest rate	4%
90-day German interest rate	3%
90-day forward rate of German mark	$.400
Spot rate of German mark	$.404

Assume that Santa Barbara Company in the United States will need 300,000 marks in 90 days. It wishes to hedge this payables position. Would it be better off using a forward hedge or a money market hedge? Substantiate your answer with estimated costs for each type of hedge.

17. Assume the following information:

180-day U.S. interest rate	8%
180-day British interest rate	9%
180-day forward rate of British pound	$1.50
Spot rate of British pound	$1.48

Assume that Riverside Corporation from the United States will receive 400,000 pounds in 180 days. Would it be better off using a forward hedge or a money market hedge? Substantiate your answer with estimated revenues for each type of hedge.

18. Why would a firm consider hedging net payables or net receivables with currency options rather than forward contracts? What are the disadvantages of hedging with currency options as opposed to forward contracts?

19. Relate the use of currency options to hedging net payables and receivables. That is, when should currency puts be purchased, and when should currency calls be purchased?

20. Can an MNC determine whether currency options will be more or less expensive than a forward hedge when considering both hedging techniques to cover net payables? Why or why not?

21. How can a firm hedge long-term currency positions? Elaborate on each method.

22. Under what conditions would an MNC's subsidiary consider use of a "leading" strategy to reduce transaction exposure?

23. Under what conditions would an MNC's subsidiary consider use of a "lagging" strategy to reduce transaction exposure?

24. Explain how cross-hedging can be used by a firm to reduce transaction exposure.

25. Explain how currency diversification can be used by a firm to reduce transaction exposure.

26. a) Assume that Carbondale Company expects to receive SF500,000 in one year. The existing spot rate of the Swiss franc is $.60. The one-year forward rate of the Swiss franc is $.62. Carbondale created a probability distribution for the future spot rate in one year as follows:

Future Spot Rate	Probability
$.61	20%
.63	50
.67	30

Assume that one-year put options on francs are available, with an exercise price of $.63 and a premium of $.04 per unit. One-year call options on francs are available with an exercise price of $.60 and a premium of $.03 per unit. Assume the following money market rates:

	U.S.	Switzerland
Deposit rate	8%	5%
Borrowing rate	9	6

Given this information, determine whether a forward hedge, money market hedge, or currency options hedge would be most appropriate. Then compare the most appropriate hedge to an unhedged strategy, and decide whether Carbondale should hedge its receivables position.

b) Assume that Baton Rouge Inc. expects to need SF1 million in one year. Using any relevant information in Part A of this question, determine whether a forward hedge, money market hedge, or a currency options hedge would be most appropriate. Then compare the most appropriate hedge to an unhedged strategy, and decide whether Baton Rouge should hedge its payables position.

27. SMU Corporation has future receivables on DM4,000,000 in one year. It must decide whether to use options or a money market hedge to hedge this position. Use any of the following information to make the decision. Verify your answer by determining the estimate (or probability distribution) of dollar revenues to be received in one year for each type of hedge.

Spot rate of DM	$.54
One-year call option	exercise point = $.50; premium = $.07
One-year put option	exercise price = $.52; premium = $.03

	U.S.	Germany
One-year deposit rate	9%	6%
One-year borrowing rate	11	8

	Rate	Probability
Forecasted spot rate of DM	$.50	20%
	.51	50
	.53	30

28. As treasurer of Tucson Corporation, you must decide how to hedge (if at all) future receivables of 250,000 marks 90 days from now. Put options are available for a premium of $.03 per unit and an exercise price of $.49 per mark. The forecasted spot rate of the mark in 90 days follows:

Future Spot Rate	Probability
$.44	30%
.40	50
.38	20

Given that you hedge your position with options, create a probability distribution for dollars to be received in 90 days.

29. As treasurer of Tempe Corporation, you are confronted with the following problem. Assume the one-year forward rate of the British pound is $1.59. You plan to receive 1 million pounds in one year. There is a one-year put option available. It has an exercise price of $1.61. The spot rate as of today is $1.62, and the option premium is $.04 per unit. Your forecast of the percentage change in the spot rate was determined from the following regression model:

$$e_t = a_0 + a_1 \, DINF_{t-1} + a_2 \, DINT_t + \mu,$$

where

$$e_t = \text{percentage change in British pound value over period } t$$

$$DINF_{t-1} = \text{differential in inflation between the United States and the United Kingdom in period } t-1$$

$$DINT_t = \text{average differential between United States interest rate and British interest rate over period } t$$

$$a_0, a_1, \text{ and } a_2 = \text{regression coefficients}$$

$$\mu = \text{error term.}$$

The regression model was applied to historical annual data, and the regression coefficients were estimated as follows:

$$a_0 = 0$$

$$a_1 = 1.1$$

$$a_2 = .6.$$

Assume last year's inflation rates were 3 percent for the United States and 8 percent for the United Kingdom. Also assume that the interest rate differential ($DINT_t$) is forecasted as follows for this year:

Forecast of $DINT_t$	Probability
1%	40%
2	50
3	10

Using any of the available information, decide whether the treasurer should choose the forward hedge or a put option hedge. Show your work.

30. Would a U.S. firm's real cost of hedging Swiss franc payables every 90 days have been positive, negative, or about zero on average over a period in which the dollar weakened consistently? What does this imply about the forward rate as an unbiased predictor of the future spot rate? Explain.

31. If interest rate parity exists, would a forward hedge be more favorable, equally favorable, or less favorable than a money market hedge on French franc payables? Explain.

32. Would a U.S. firm's real cost of hedging Japanese yen receivables have been positive, negative, or about zero on average over a period in which the dollar weakened consistently? Explain.

33. If you are a U.S. importer of German goods, and you believe that today's forward rate of the mark is a very accurate estimate of the future spot rate, do you think German mark call options would be a more appropriate hedge than the forward hedge? Explain.

34. You are an exporter of goods to the United Kingdom, and you believe that today's forward rate of the British pound substantially underestimates the future spot rate. Company policy requires you to hedge your British pound receivables in some way. Would a forward hedge or a put option hedge be more appropriate? Explain.

35. Explain how a French firm can use the forward market to hedge periodic purchases of U.S. goods denominated in U.S. dollars.

36. Explain how a German firm can use the forward market to hedge periodic sales of goods sold to the U.S. that are invoiced in dollars.

37. Explain how a French firm can use the forward market to hedge periodic purchases of Japanese goods denominated in yen.

38. Cornell Company purchases computer chips denominated in yen on a monthly basis from a Japanese supplier, in a transaction. To hedge its exchange rate risk, this U.S. firm negotiates a three-month forward contract three months before the next order will arrive. In other words, Cornell is always covered for the next three monthly shipments. Because Cornell consistently hedges in this manner, it is not concerned with exchange rate movements. Is Cornell insulated from exchange rate movements? Explain.

39. Malibu Inc. is a U.S. company that imports British goods. It plans to use call options to hedge payables of £100,000 in 90 days. Three call options are available which have an expiration date 90 days from now. Fill in the number of dollars needed to pay for the payables (including the option premium paid) for each option available under each possible scenario.

Scenario	Spot Rate of Pound 90 Days from Now	Exercise Price = $1.74; Premium = $.06	Exercise Price = $1.76; Premium = $.05	Exercise Price = $1.79; Premium = $.03
1	$1.65			
2	1.70			
3	1.75			
4	1.80			
5	1.85			

If each of the five scenarios had an equal probability of occurrence, which option would you choose? Explain.

U.S. Firms Abroad Ride Shifting Waves of Currency

Antidotes to Monetary Turmoil Include Hedging, Shortening Payment Terms

By Leslie Scism
Staff Reporter of The Wall Street Journal

Most companies love nothing more than locking in customers for a good long time. But when **LuxCel Group** Inc. set up shop to sell paging devices in the Crimean city of Yalta last month, it adamantly refused to sign long-term service contracts for them.

With local currencies in the former Soviet Union spiraling downward, there was nothing that LuxCel wanted less than a customer boasting a three-year contract. Instead, the 30-employee company, based in Paramus, N.J., limits ruble-denominated service pacts to three months.

As small and midsize companies such as LuxCel increasingly operate abroad, they are busy honing techniques to protect themselves against falling foreign currencies. The task is rapidly gaining urgency.

In recent days, monetary turmoil in Europe has exposed American companies operating there to greater foreign-exchange risk than they ordinarily face. While violent currency swings may be unlikely, American business can count on continued volatility because European countries have agreed to allow far more fluctuation in their exchange rates now.

Losses From Plunging Currency

Meanwhile, currencies plunge in value in the former Soviet Union, Brazil and elsewhere. It all means that fortunes can be lost by holding the wrong currency at the wrong time.

"We're just as worried as the big companies," says Mitchell Reback, director of finance for **Neutrogena** Corp., a 700-employee Los Angeles concern that derives 25% of its revenue from overseas.

The most common danger: A local currency may lose value between a sale's close in a local currency and payment of the bill. When payment day arrives, the American business owner could end up with currency worth much less in dollars than anticipated.

For companies that can get away with it, the preferred way is to bill in dollars and let customers bear the brunt of shifting exchange rates. "If you have a strong marketing position, you can play the hardball game of saying, 'I want to be paid in my own currency,' " says Robert Bush, controller of **Wedco Technology** Inc.

Sizable Revenue From Europe

Wedco, which custom-grinds plastics and other materials for companies in the U.S. and Europe, is the dominant player in its small niche. The Bloomsbury, N.J., concern earned about a third of its $30.3 million in revenue in Western Europe last year.

European customers sometimes balk at paying dollars, Mr. Bush says. "But we say, 'I'm sorry, this is the way we do it.' Obviously, we could lose some sales, but it [billing in dollars] takes a tremendous worry off our shoulders."

Wedco's market dominance also allows it to eliminate currency-fluctuation risk connected to inventory. Some manufacturers purchase raw materials in one country to sell, in processed form, in another. If currency fluctuations suddenly make materials more expensive, the manufacturer must pass on the higher cost to customers—or swallow it. To avoid this trap, many companies try to buy raw materials in the country where they sell finished goods, or shift purchases to countries with weakening currencies.

Wedco's own solution: Force the customer to supply its own raw materials. Again, some balk. Faced with a recession in Europe causing slackening demand, Wedco acquiesces in cases involving "longstanding customers," the controller says.

Circon Corp., a Santa Barbara, Calif., maker of medical endoscopes and video systems, collects dollars for about 50% of its European sales. If the company can't get payment in greenbacks, it tries to minimize risk by negotiating a "very short term of payment, 10 or 15 days," says Richard Auhll, chairman.

American businesses buying from European vendors also seek shelter. **Suprema Specialties** Inc., Paterson, N.J., buys cheese from Italian cooperatives. Commonly ordering six months in advance, it negotiates a price in dollars to be due upon shipment. Because the cooperatives have an oversupply of cheese, "they'll take any kind of payment possible," says Paul Lauriero, executive vice president.

Many companies achieve the same effect—locking in dollar-denominated prices—by buying "forward contracts" from banks. These contracts obligate the parties to exchange one currency for another at a future date and at a pre-determined rate. Some companies also purchase "option contracts," which give concerns the right, but not the obligation, to exchange one currency for another at a future date at a set rate. Even for small companies, this protection generally costs well under 1% of the amount involved.

Some companies, such as Neutrogena, say big banks are often reluctant to spend the time necessary to counsel small or midsize

Continued

CASE: HOW U.S. FIRMS ARE MANAGING EXCHANGE RATE RISK

Continued

players on appropriate hedging strategies. But **Checkpoint Systems** Inc., a maker of surveillance systems, scanning equipment and antitheft tags, says it finds banks eager to help. The Thorofare, N.J., concern is now talking to banks about hedging payables and receivables abroad, says Steven Selfridge, chief financial officer.

Solution in Financial Hedging

Telematics International Inc., a Fort Lauderdale, Fla., computer-networking systems company that gets about half its $67.3 million in sales overseas, turned to financial hedging seven months ago. That was after the company recorded $632,000 in losses for 1992 because it didn't hedge its currency exposure. "We were exposed" to the plum-

meting British pound, says John Dooley, an assistant treasurer.

Source: *The Wall Street Journal* (August 6, 1993): p. B2. Reprinted by permission of *The Wall Street Journal,* ©1993 Dow Jones & Company, Inc. All rights reserved worldwide.

Questions

1. Does Wedco's strategy of pricing its materials for European customers in dollars avoid economic exposure? Explain.

2. Explain why Circon Corp. negotiates a very short term of payment when selling products overseas.

3. Explain why the earnings of Telematics International Inc. were affected by changes in the value of the pound. Why would Telematics leave its exposure unhedged?

CASE PROBLEM

BLACKHAWK COMPANY
Forecasting Exchange Rates and the Hedging Decision

This case is intended to illustrate how forecasting exchange rates and hedging decisions are related. Blackhawk Company plans to purchase DM800,000 one quarter from now to pay for imports. As Treasurer of Blackhawk, you are responsible for determining whether and how to hedge this payables position. Several tasks will need to be completed for you to make these decisions. The entire analysis can be performed using LOTUS.

Your first goal is to assess three different models for forecasting the value of DM at the end of the quarter (also called the future spot rate, or FSR):

- Using the forward rate (FR) at the beginning of the quarter
- Using the spot rate (SR) at the beginning of the quarter
- Estimating the historical influence of the inflation differential during each quarter on the percentage change in the DM (which leads to a forecast of the FSR of the DM).

The historical data to be used for this analysis are provided in the following table.

Quarter	Spot Rate of DM at Beginning of Quarter	90-Day Forward Rate of DM at Beginning of Quarter	Spot Rate of DM at End of Quarter	Last Quarter's Inflation Differential	Percentage Change in DM Over Quarter
1	$.3177	$.3250	$.3233	−.05%	1.76%
2	.3233	.3272	.3267	−.46	1.05
3	.3267	.3285	.3746	.66	14.66
4	.3746	.3778	.4063	.94	8.46
5	.4063	.4093	.4315	.58	6.20
6	.4315	.4344	.4548	.23	5.40
7	.4548	.4572	.4949	.02	8.82
8	.4949	.4966	.5153	1.26	4.12
9	.5153	.5169	.5540	.86	7.51
10	.5540	.5574	.5465	.54	−1.35
11	.5465	.5510	.5440	1.00	−.46
12	.5440	.5488	.6309	1.09	15.97
13	.6309	.6365	.6027	.78	−4.47
14	.6027	.6081	.5409	.23	−10.25
15	.5491	.5538	.5320	.71	−3.11
16	.5320	.5365	.5617	1.18	5.58
17	.5617	.5667	.5283	.70	−5.95
18	.5283	.5334	.5122	−.31	−3.05
19	.5122	.5149	.5352	.62	4.49
20	.5352	.5372	.5890	.87	10.05
21(Now)	.5890	.5878	(to be forecasted)	.28	(to be forecasted)

CASE PROBLEM

BLACKHAWK COMPANY (CONTINUED)

a) Use regression analysis to determine whether the forward rate is an unbiased estimator of the spot rate at the end of the quarter.

b) Use the simplified approach of assessing the signs of forecast errors over time. Do you detect any bias when using the FR to forecast? Explain.

c) Determine the average absolute forecast error when using the forward rate to forecast.

d) Determine whether the spot rate of the DM at the beginning of the quarter is an unbiased estimator of the spot rate at the end of the quarter using regression analysis.

e) Use the simplified approach of assessing the signs of forecast errors over time. Do you detect any bias when using the SR to forecast? Explain.

f) Determine the average absolute forecast error when using the spot rate to forecast. Is the spot rate or the forward rate a more accurate forecast of the future spot rate (FSR)? Explain.

g) Use the following regression model to determine the relationship between the inflation differential (called DIFF, and defined as the U.S. inflation minus German inflation) and the percentage change in the DM (called PDM):

$$PDM = b_0 + b_1 \, DIFF$$

Once you have determined the coefficients b_0 and b_1, use them to forecast PDM based on a forecast of 2% for DIFF in the upcoming quarter. Then apply your forecast for PDM to the prevailing spot rate (which is $.589) to derive the expected FSR of the DM.

h) Blackhawk plans to develop a probability distribution for the FSR. First, it will assign a 40 percent probability to the forecast of FSR derived from regression analysis in the previous question. Second, it will assign a 40 percent probability to the forecast of FSR based on either the forward rate or the spot rate (whichever was more accurate according to your earlier analysis). Third, it will assign a 20 percent probability to the forecast of FSR based on either the forward rate or spot rate (whichever was less accurate according to your earlier analysis).
Fill in the table that follows:

Probability	FSR
40%	
40	
20	

| CASE PROBLEM | # BLACKHAWK COMPANY (CONTINUED) |

i) Assuming that Blackhawk does not hedge, fill in the following table.

Probability	Forecasted Dollar Amount Needed to Pay for Imports in 90 Days
40%	
40	
20	

j) Based on the probability distribution for the FSR, use the table that follows to determine the probability distribution for the real cost of hedging if a forward contract is used for hedging (recall that the prevailing 90-day forward rate is $.5878).

Probability	Forecasted Dollar Amount Needed if Hedged With a Forward Contract	Forecasted Amount Needed if Unhedged	Forecasted Real Cost of Hedging Payables
40%			
40			
20			

k) If Blackhawk hedges its position, it will use either a 90-day forward rate, a money market hedge, or a call option. The following data is available at the time of its decision.

- Spot rate   = $.589
- 90-Day forward rate   = $.5878
- 90-Day U.S. borrowing rate   =   2.5%
- 90-Day U.S. investing rate   =   2.3%
- 90-Day German borrowing rate   =   2.4%
- 90-Day German investing rate   =   2.1%
- Call option on DM has a premium of $.01 per unit
- Call option on DM has an exercise price of $.60

CASE PROBLEM

BLACKHAWK COMPANY (CONTINUED)

Determine the probability distribution of dollars needed for a call option if used (include the premium paid) by filling out the table below:

Probability	FSR	Dollars Needed to Pay for Payables
40%		
40		
20		

l) Compare the forward hedge to the money market hedge. Which is superior? Why?

m) Compare either the forward hedge or the money market hedge (whichever is better) to the call option hedge. If you hedge, which technique should you use? Why?

n) Compare the hedge you believe is the best to an unhedged strategy. Should you hedge or remain unhedged? Explain.

PROJECTS

1. Assume that your company needed 100,000 units of a foreign currency every quarter to purchase foreign supplies. Use the data bank in the back of the text to determine the real cost of hedging with that currency. (Choose a currency.) Identify periods in which the real cost of hedging was typically positive. Was the dollar strengthening or weakening in those periods? Explain. (This exercise could easily be set up on a spreadsheet first to reduce your computational time).

2. Repeat this project, except assume that you will receive 100,000 units of a foreign currency every quarter.

REFERENCES

Bodnar, Gordon M., and William M. Gentry. "Exchange Rate Exposure and Industry Characteristics: Evidence from Canada, Japan, and the USA." *Journal of International Money and Finance* (February 1993), pp. 29–45.

Boothe, Robert, and Jeff Madura. "Reducing Exposure to Exchange Rate Risk: A Case Study." *Long-Range Planning* (June 1985), pp. 98–101.

Calderon-Rossell, Jorge R. "Covering Foreign Exchange Risks of Single Transactions: A Framework for Analysis." *Financial Management* (Autumn 1979), pp. 78–85.

Chrystal, K. Alec. "A Guide to Foreign Exchange Markets," *Review,* Federal Reserve Bank of St. Louis (March 1984), pp. 5–18.

Dufey, Gunter, and S. L. Srinivasulu. "The Case for Corporate Management of Foreign Exchange Risk." *Financial Management* (Winter 1983), pp. 54–62.

Glen, Jack, and Philippe Jorion. "Currency Hedging for International Portfolios." *Journal of Finance* (December 1993), pp. 1865–1886.

Hammer, Jerry A., "Hedging Performance and Hedging Objectives: Tests of New Performance Measures in the Foreign Currency Market." *Journal of Financial Research* (Winter 1990), pp. 307–324.

Hekman, Christine R. "Measuring Foreign Exchange Exposure: A Practical Theory and Its Application." *Financial Analysts Journal* (September–October 1983), pp. 59–65.

Hung, Juan. "Assessing the Exchange Rate's Impact on U.S. Manufacturing Profits." *FRBNY Quarterly Review* (1992–93), pp. 44–63.

Jacque, Laurent L. "Management of Foreign Exchange Risk: A Review Article." *Journal of International Business Studies* (Spring–Summer 1981), pp. 81–99.

Jorion, Philippe. "The Pricing of Exchange Rate Risk in the Stock Market." *Journal of Financial and Quantitative Analysis* (September 1991), pp. 363–376.

Kaufold, Howard, and Michael Smirlock. "Managing Corporate Exchange and Interest Rate Exposure." *Financial Management* (Autumn 1986), pp. 64–72.

Kwok, Chuck. "Hedging Foreign Exchange Exposures: Independent vs. Integrative Approaches." *Journal of International Business Studies* (Summer 1987), pp. 33–52.

Lessard, Donald R., and John B. Lightstone. "Volatile Exchange Rates Can Put Operations at Risk." *Harvard Business Review* (July–August 1986), pp. 107–114.

Logue, Dennis E., and George S. Oldfield. "Managing Foreign Assets When Foreign Exchange Markets Are Efficient." *Financial Management* (Summer 1977), pp. 16–22.

Madura, Jeff. "Assessment of Exchange Rate Risk from Various Country Perspectives." *International Review of Economics and Business* (July 1990), pp. 655–666.

_____ . "Hedging With American Currency Options: A Five-Year Appraisal." *Journal of Business and Economic Perspectives* (Spring 1990), pp. 35–38.

_____ . "The Real Costs of Hedging in the Forward Exchange Market: An Empirical Investigation." *Management International Review,* no. 2 (1984), pp. 24–27.

Madura, Jeff, and Richard Fosberg. "Intertemporal Exchange Rate Risk: Implications for Corporate Exposure." *International Review of Economics and Business* (October–November 1988), pp. 1053–1060.

Madura, Jeff, and E. Joe Nosari. "Utilizing Currency Portfolios to Mitigate Exchange Rate Risk." *Columbia Journal of World Business* (Spring 1984), pp. 96–99.

Madura, Jeff, and L. A. Soenen. "Asymmetric Risk Aversion and the Real Costs of Hedging in the Foreign Exchange Market." *European Journal of Accounting and Finance* (July–August 1985), pp. 304–309.

Madura, Jeff, and E. Theodore Veit. "Use of Currency Options for International Cash Management." *Journal of Cash Management* (January–February 1986), pp. 42–48.

Makin, John H. "Portfolio Theory and the Problem of Foreign Exchange Risk." *The Journal of Finance* 33 (May 1978), pp. 517–534.

Nance, Deana R., Clifford W. Smith Jr., and Charles W. Smithson. "On the Determinants of Corporate Hedging." *Journal of Finance* (March 1993), 267–284.

Rodriguez, Rita M. "Corporate Exchange Risk Management: Theme and Aberrations." *Journal of Finance* (May 1981), pp. 427–439.

_____ . "Management of Foreign Exchange Risk in U.S. Multinationals." *Sloan Management Review* (Spring 1978), pp. 31–49.

Soenen, Luc A. "Risk Diversification Characteristics of Currency Cocktails." *Journal of Economics and Business* (May 1989), pp. 177–189.

Soenen, L. A., and E. F. Van Winkel, "The Real Costs of Hedging in the Forward Exchange Market." *Management International Review,* no. 1 (1982), pp. 53–59.

Srinivasulu, S. L. "Currency Denomination of Debt: Lessons from Rolls-Royce and Laker Airways." *Business Horizons* (September–October 1983), pp. 19–23.

Stanley, Marjorie T., and Stanley B. Block. "Portfolio Diversification of Foreign Exchange Risk: An Empirical Study." *Management International Review,* no. 1 (1980), pp. 83–92.

Swanson, Peggy, and Stephen Caples. "Hedging Foreign Exchange Risk Using Forward Foreign Exchange Markets: An Extension." *Journal of International Business Studies* (Spring 1987), pp. 75–82.

Westerfield, Janice M. "How U.S. Multinationals Manage Currency Risk." *Business Review* (March–April 1980), pp. 19–27.

CHAPTER 12

MANAGING ECONOMIC EXPOSURE AND TRANSLATION EXPOSURE

The means by which multinational corporations (MNCs) can manage the exposure of their international transactions to exchange rate movements (referred to as transaction exposure) are described in the previous chapter. However, cash flows of MNCs may still be sensitive to exchange rate movements (economic exposure), even if anticipated international transactions are hedged. Furthermore, the consolidated financial statements of MNCs may still be exposed to exchange rate movements (translation exposure). The specific objectives of this chapter are to

- explain how an MNC's economic exposure can be hedged, and
- explain how an MNC's translation exposure can be hedged.

In general, it is more difficult to effectively hedge economic or translation exposure than to hedge transaction exposure, for reasons explained in this chapter.

MANAGING ECONOMIC EXPOSURE

From a U.S. firm's perspective, transaction exposure represents only the exchange rate risk when converting net foreign cash inflows to U.S. dollars, or when purchasing foreign currencies to send payments. Economic exposure represents any impact of exchange rate fluctuations on a firm's future cash flows. Corporate cash flows can be affected by exchange rate movements in ways not directly associated with foreign transactions. Thus, firms cannot just focus on hedging their foreign currency payables or receivables, but must also attempt to determine how all their cash flows will be affected by possible exchange rate movements.

Assessing Economic Exposure

To illustrate how economic exposure can be managed, reconsider the case of Madison Inc. discussed in Chapter 10. Madison's economic exposure to exchange rate movements can be assessed by determining the sensitivity of expenses and revenues to various possible exchange rate scenarios. The original revenue and expense information from Exhibit 10.10 of Chapter 10 is restated in Exhibit 12.1. The U.S. revenues are assumed to be sensitive to different exchange rate scenarios because of the foreign competition. Canadian sales are anticipated to be C$4 million, regardless of the exchange rate scenario. Yet, the dollar amount received from these sales will depend on the scenario. The cost of goods sold attributable to U.S. orders is assumed to be $50 million, and insensitive to exchange rate movements. The cost of goods sold attributable to Canadian orders is assumed to be C$200 million. The U.S. dollar amount of this cost varies with the exchange rate scenario. The gross profit shown in Exhibit 12.1 is determined by subtracting the total dollar value of cost of goods sold from the total dollar value of sales.

EXHIBIT 12.1   Original Impact of Exchange Rate Movements on Earnings: Madison Inc.
              (in millions)

		C$ = $.75		C$ = $.80		C$ = $.85
Sales						
(1) U.S.		$300		$304		$307
(2) Canadian	C$4 =	$ 3	C$4 =	$ 3.2	C$4 =	$ 3.4
(3) Total		$303		$307.2		$310.4
Cost of goods sold						
(4) U.S.		$ 50		$ 50		$ 50
(5) Canadian	C$200 =	$150	C$200 =	$160	C$200 =	$170
(6) Total		$200		$210		$220
(7) Gross profit		$103		$ 97.2		90.4
Operating expenses						
(8) U.S.: Fixed		$ 30		$ 30		$ 30
(9) U.S.: Variable (10% of total sales)		$ 30.3		$ 30.72		$ 31.04
(10) Total		$ 60.3		$ 60.72		$ 61.04
(11) Earnings before interest and taxes		$ 42.7		$ 36.48		$ 29.36
Interest expense						
(12) U.S.		$ 3		$ 3		$ 3
(13) Canadian	C$10 =	$ 7.5	C$10 =	$ 8	C$10 =	$ 8.5
(14) Total		$ 10.5		$ 11		$ 11.5
(15) Earnings before taxes		$ 32.2		$ 25.48		$ 17.86

Operating expenses are separated into fixed and variable. The fixed expenses are $30 million per year, while the projected variable expenses are dictated by projected sales. The earnings before interest and taxes are determined by the total U.S. dollar amount of gross profit minus the total U.S. dollar amount of operating expenses. The interest owed to U.S. banks is insensitive to the exchange rate scenario. However, the projected amount of dollars needed to pay interest on existing Canadian loans varies with the exchange rate scenario. Earnings before taxes are estimated by subtracting total interest expenses from earnings before interest and taxes.

Exhibit 12.1 enables Madison to assess how its income statement items would be affected by different exchange rate movements. A stronger Canadian dollar results in an increase in Madison's U.S. sales and in the dollar revenues earned from Canadian sales. However, it also increases Madison's cost of materials purchased from Canada and its amount in dollars needed to pay interest on loans from Canadian banks. The higher expenses more than offset the higher revenues in the strong Canadian dollar scenario. Thus, the amount of Madison's earnings before taxes is inversely related to the strength of the Canadian dollar.

If the Canadian dollar strengthens consistently over the long run, Madison's cost of goods sold and interest expenses will likely rise at a higher rate than U.S. dollar revenues. Consequently, it may wish to enact some policies to create a more balanced impact of Canadian dollar movements on its revenues and expenses. At the present time, its high exposure to exchange rate movements is due to its expenses being more susceptible than its revenues to the changing value of the Canadian dollar. A policy to either increase Canadian sales or reduce orders of Canadian materials would provide more balance.

How Restructuring Can Reduce Economic Exposure

Madison could create more balance by increasing Canadian sales. It believes that it can achieve Canadian sales of C$20 million if it spends $2 million more on advertising (which is part of its fixed operating expenses). The increased sales will also require an additional expenditure of $10 million on materials from U.S. suppliers. In addition, it plans to reduce its reliance on Canadian suppliers and increase its reliance on U.S. suppliers. This strategy is expected to reduce the cost of goods sold attributable to Canadian suppliers by C$100 million and increase the cost of goods sold attributable to U.S. suppliers by $80 million (not including the $10 million increase resulting from increased sales to the Canadian market). Furthermore, it plans to borrow additional funds in the United States and retire some existing loans from Canadian banks. The result will be an additional interest expense of $4 million to U.S. banks and a reduction of C$5 million owed to Canadian banks. The anticipated impact of these strategies on the projected income statement is shown in Exhibit 12.2. For each of the three exchange rate scenarios, the initial projections are in the left column, while the revised projections (as a result of the proposed strategy) are in the right column.

Each of the revised estimates of the income statement items will be explained. First, the projected total sales increase, in response to intentions of penetrating the Canadian market. Second, the U.S. cost of goods sold is now $90 million higher than before, resulting from a $10 million increase to accommodate increased Canadian sales, and an $80 million increase due to the shift from Canadian suppliers to U.S. suppliers. The Canadian cost of goods sold decreases from C$200 million to C$100 million as a result of this shift. The revised fixed

EXHIBIT 12.2 Impact of Possible Exchange Rate Movements on Earnings under Two Alternative Operational Structures   (in millions)

	Exchange Rate Scenario C$ = $.75		Exchange Rate Scenario C$ = $.80		Exchange Rate Scenario C$ = $.85	
	Original Operational Structure	Proposed Operational Structure	Original Operational Structure	Proposed Operational Structure	Original Operational Structure	Proposed Operational Structure
Sales						
U.S.	$300	$300	$304	$304	$307	$307
Canadian	C$4 = $ 3	C$20 = $ 15	C$4 = $ 3.2	C$20 = $ 16	C$4 = $ 3.4	C$20 = $ 17
Total	$303	$315	$307.2	$320	$310.4	$324
Cost of goods sold						
U.S.	$ 50	$140	$ 50	$140	$ 50	$140
Canadian	C$200 = $150	C$100 = $ 75	C$200 = $160	C$100 = $ 80	C$200 = $170	C$100 = $ 85
Total	$200	$215	$210	$220	$220	$225
Gross profit	103	100	$ 97.2	100	$ 90.4	$ 99
Operating expenses						
U.S.: Fixed	$ 30	$ 32	$ 30	$ 32	$ 30	$ 32
U.S.: Variable (10% of total sales)	$ 30.3	$ 31.5	$ 30.72	$ 32	$ 31.04	$ 32.4
Total	$ 60.3	$ 63.5	$ 60.72	$ 64	$ 61.04	$ 64.4
Earnings before interest and taxes	$ 42.7	$ 36.5	$ 36.48	$ 36	$ 29.36	34.6
Interest expense						
U.S.	$ 3	$ 7	$ 3	$ 7	$ 3	$ 7
Canadian	C$10 = $ 7.5	C$5 = $ 3.75	C$10 = $ 8	C$5 = $ 4	C$10 = $ 8.5	C$5 = $ 4.25
Total	$ 10.5	$ 10.75	$ 11	$ 11	$ 11.5	$ 11.25
Earnings before taxes	$ 32.2	$ 25.75	$ 25.48	$ 25	$ 17.86	$ 23.35

operating expenses of $32 million include the increase in advertising expenses necessary to penetrate the Canadian market. The variable operating expenses are revised because of revised estimates for total sales. The interest expenses are revised because of the increased loans from the U.S. banks and reduced loans from Canadian banks.

If Madison increases its Canadian dollar inflows and reduces its Canadian dollar outflows as proposed, its revenues and expenses will be affected by Canadian dollar movements in a somewhat similar manner. Thus, its performance will be less susceptible to movements in the Canadian dollar. Exhibit 12.3 illustrates the sensitivity of Madison's earnings before taxes to the three exchange rate scenarios (derived from Exhibit 12.2). The reduced sensitivity of Madison's proposed restructured operations to exchange rate movements is obvious.

The way a firm restructures its operations to reduce economic exposure to exchange rate risk depends on the form of exposure. For Madison Inc., future expenses are more sensitive than future revenues to the possible values of a foreign currency. Therefore, economic exposure could be reduced by increasing the sensitivity of revenues and reducing the sensitivity of expenses to exchange rate movements. Firms that have a greater quantity of exchange rate-sensitive revenues than of expenses, however, would reduce economic exposure by decreasing the quantity of exchange rate-sensitive revenues, or by increasing the quantity of exchange rate-sensitive expenses.

It should be mentioned that some revenues or expenses may be more exchange rate-sensitive than others. Therefore, simply matching quantity of exchange rate-sensitive revenues to the quantity of exchange rate-sensitive expenses may not completely insulate a firm from exchange rate risk. The firm can best evaluate a proposed restructuring of operations by forecasting various income-statement items for various possible exchange rate scenarios (as shown in Exhibit 12.2) and then assessing the sensitivity of earnings to these different scenarios.

Expediting the Analysis With Computer Spreadsheets.   Determining the sensitivity of earnings before taxes to alternative exchange rate scenarios could

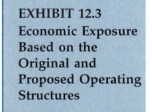

**EXHIBIT 12.3
Economic Exposure Based on the Original and Proposed Operating Structures**

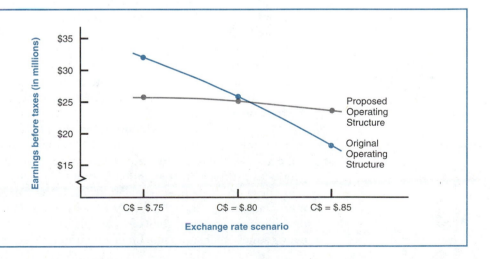

also be expedited by computer. A spreadsheet similar to Exhibit 12.2 could be created. Forecasts could be input by the analyst for items such as sales, cost of goods sold, and fixed operating expenses. The remaining items could be defined by formula, so that they could be estimated by computer after forecasts of the other items were input. For example, the exchange rate forecast influences projections of (1) dollars received from Canadian sales, (2) cost of goods sold attributable to purchases of Canadian materials, and (3) amount in dollars needed to cover the Canadian interest payments. The firm could revise the input in accordance with proposed restructured operations, in order to determine how economic exposure would be affected. A computerized spreadsheet would allow the analyst to assess several possible operational structures.

Recall that Madison Inc. assessed one alternative operational structure in which it increased foreign Canadian sales by C$16 million, reduced its purchases of Canadian materials by C$100 million, and reduced its interest owed to Canadian banks by C$5 million. If it had computerized the spreadsheet, it could easily have assessed the impact of alternative strategies, such as increasing Canadian sales by other amounts, and/or reducing the Canadian expenses by other amounts. This would have offered Madison more information about its economic exposure under various operational structures, and would therefore have enabled it to devise the operational structure that would reduce economic exposure to the degree desired.

Issues Involved in the Restructuring Decision

When deciding how to restructure operations to reduce economic exposure, one must address the following questions:

- Should the firm attempt to increase or reduce sales in new or existing foreign markets?
- Should the firm increase or reduce its dependency on foreign suppliers?
- Should the firm establish or eliminate production facilities in foreign markets?
- Should the firm increase or reduce its level of debt denominated in foreign currencies?

Each of these four questions reflects a different part of the firm's income statement. This first relates to foreign cash inflows and the remaining ones to foreign cash outflows. Some of the more common solutions to balancing a foreign currency's inflows and outflows are summarized in Exhibit 12.4. Any restructuring of operations that can reduce the periodic difference between a foreign currency's inflows and outflows can reduce the firm's economic exposure to that currency's movements.

MNCs that have production and marketing facilities in various countries may be able to shift their allocation of operations in order to reduce any adverse impact of economic exposure. For example, consider a U.S.-based MNC that produces products in the United States, France, Germany, and Great Britain, and sells these products to several countries. If the German mark strengthens against many currencies, the MNC may boost production in Great Britain, expecting a decline in demand for the German subsidiary's products. The MNC parent may even request that some machinery be transported from Germany to Great Britain

IN PRACTICE

HEDGING "SOFT" CURRENCIES

Firms that recently capitalized on the free enterprise in Eastern Europe have a peculiar type of exposure to exchange rate risk. The "soft" currencies of the Eastern Europe countries are not convertible into so-called "hard" currencies that are traded around the world. Firms are using a variety of strategies to deal with this problem. For example, Digital Equipment Corp. opened a sales office in Hungary. Since most of its customers there are from Western Europe, it requires payment in hard currencies.

In April 1990, PepsiCo reached an agreement with the Soviet Union to double its production of Pepsi and to build Pizza Huts in Moscow. The deal is valued at about $3 billion. Rather than accept the Soviet currency (rubles), which was not convertible into dollars or any other widely traded currency, PepsiCo received ten ships (mostly oil tankers) and vodka made in the Soviet Union.

The ruble's value was perceived to be weak, so that even if it was convertible, it was expected to be devalued with respect to other currencies over time. Thus, the cash flows to PepsiCo would be reduced by devaluation, especially if conversion of all rubles were not allowed until after the devaluation. While PepsiCo has avoided exchange rate risk, its future cash flows from this deal are still uncertain. How much can the ships and vodka be sold for in the United States? However, even though the ultimate cash flows to PepsiCo from this deal are not known, there is less uncertainty than there would be if the company had accepted rubles.

The Hungarian subsidiary of Digital Equipment Corp. requires payment for its computers in a "hard" currency, which can be converted to dollars. Some McDonald's restaurants in the Soviet Union accept several hard currencies as payment. Gillette Company negotiated to exchange rubles for dollars on a Soviet joint venture. This was a major achievement, since the Soviet Union normally has not allowed such an exchange. The exchange rate for this deal has been set at six rubles per dollar.

EXHIBIT 12.4 How to Restructure Operations to Balance the Impact of Currency Movements on Cash Inflows and Outflows	Type of Operation	Recommended Action When a Foreign Currency Has a Greater Impact on Cash Inflows	Recommended Action When a Foreign Currency Has a Greater Impact on Cash Outflows
	Sales in foreign currency units	Reduce foreign sales	Increase foreign sales
	Reliance on foreign supplies	Increase foreign supply orders	Reduce foreign supply orders
	Proportion of debt structure representing foreign debt	Restructure debt to increase debt payments in foreign currency	Restructure debt to reduce debt payments in foreign currency

and allocate more marketing funds to the British subsidiary at the expense of the German subsidiary. This type of strategy may force the firm to forgo economies of scale that could be achieved if production were concentrated at one particular subsidiary while other subsidiaries focused on warehousing and distribution.

How Honda Restructured to Reduce Exposure

To illustrate how the shifting of production can reduce economic exposure, consider the actual case of Honda, the Japanese automobile producer. By developing plants in the U.S. to produce automobiles for sale there, Honda not only circumvents possible trade restrictions, but also can reduce its economic exposure to exchange rate risk. When the automobiles were exported to the U.S., the U.S. demand for Hondas would decline in response to appreciation of the yen, because the dollar cost of the purchase increased. Thus, Honda's cash flows were adversely affected as the strong yen caused less demand for its exports. By producing automobiles in the U.S. and invoicing them in dollars, Honda is trying to ensure that the U.S. demand for these automobiles should not be so sensitive to the value of the Japanese yen. However, Honda is not completely insulated from exchange rate risk, for two reasons. First, the Honda plants in the U.S. purchase various components from Japan (invoiced in yen), causing the dollar costs of these components to rise when the yen appreciates. Second, earnings remitted from Honda's plants in the U.S. to its parent in Japan will convert to a smaller number of yen when the yen appreciates. Nevertheless, the transfer of production to the location where the product is sold has reduced the economic exposure.

MANAGING TRANSLATION EXPOSURE

Translation exposure results when an MNC translates each subsidiary's financial data to its home currency for consolidated financial statements. Because cash flow is not affected, some people would argue that it is not necessary to hedge or even reduce accounting exposure. Still, some firms are concerned with translation exposure because of its potential impact on reported consolidated earnings. Based on a recent survey of firms by *Institutional Investor* magazine, more than one-third of firms believe that the hedging of translation exposure is a major concern.

Some MNCs attempt to avoid translation exposure by matching foreign liabilities with foreign assets. For example, Phillip Morris uses foreign financing to match its level of foreign assets.

Use of Forward Contracts to Hedge Translation Exposure

MNCs can use forward contracts to hedge translation exposure, as described in the following example. Consider a U.S.-based MNC that has just one subsidiary located in Great Britain. Assume the British subsidiary as of the beginning of its fiscal year forecasts earnings at £20,000,000. Assume this subsidiary plans to reinvest the entire amount in earnings in Great Britain and does not plan to remit any earnings back to the parent in the United States. While there is no foreseeable

IN PRACTICE

ECONOMIC EXPOSURE OF LAKER AIRWAYS

To illustrate the importance of hedging economic exposure, consider the case of Laker Airways, a British Airline. Srinivasulu reports that Laker generated about half of its revenues in dollars and half in British pounds. However, a large proportion of its expenses (such as fuel, oil, and debt payments) were denominated in dollars. As the dollar strengthened in 1981, Laker needed larger amounts in pounds to cover the dollar-denominated expenses.

In January 1981, Laker borrowed $131 million from a group of U.S. and European banks.

The debt was denominated in U.S. dollars and therefore required debt repayments in U.S. dollars. By borrowing U.S. dollars in 1981, Laker further increased its degree of economic exposure. As the dollar continued to strengthen, the firm's revenues could not adequately cover its dollar-denominated expenses. Consequently, Laker Airways went bankrupt. It might have survived if it had reduced its economic exposure, either by reducing its dollar-denominated expenses or by increasing its dollar-denominated revenues.

transaction exposure from the future earnings (since the pounds will remain in Great Britain), translation exposure does exist for the MNC.

The British earnings would be translated at the weighted average value of the pound over the course of the year. If the British pound is currently worth $1.50, and if its value was constant during the year, the forecasted translation of British earnings into U.S. dollars would be $30 million (computed as £20,000,000 × $1.50 per pound).

The MNC may be concerned that the translated value of British earnings will be reduced if the pound's average value decreases during the year. To hedge this translation exposure, it could implement a forward hedge on the expected earnings by selling £20,000,000 one year forward. Assume the forward rate at that time is $1.50, the same as the spot rate. At the end of the year, the MNC could buy £20,000,000 at the spot rate and fulfill its forward contract obligation to sell £20,000,000. If the pound depreciates during the fiscal year, then the MNC will be able to purchase pounds at the end of the fiscal year at a cheaper rate than it could sell them for ($1.50 per pound) to fulfill the forward contract. Thus, it will have generated income that could offset the translation loss.

The precise level of income generated by the forward contract will depend on the spot rate of the pound at the end of the fiscal year. Under conditions in which the pound depreciates, the translation loss will be somewhat offset by the gain generated from the forward contract position.

Limitations of Hedging Translation Exposure

There are four limitations in hedging translation exposure:

- Inaccurate earnings forecasts
- Inadequate forward contracts for some currencies
- Accounting distortions
- Increased transaction exposure.

Inaccurate Earnings Forecasts.   A subsidiary's forecasted earnings for the end of the year are not guaranteed. In our example, British earnings were projected to be 20 million pounds. If the actual earnings turned out to be much higher, the translation loss in the previous example would likely exceed the gain generated from the forward contract strategy.

Inadequate Forward Contracts for Some Currencies.   A second limitation is that forward contracts are not available for all currencies. Thus, an MNC with subsidiaries in some smaller countries may not be able to obtain forward contracts for the currencies of concern.

Accounting Distortions.   A third limitation is that the forward-rate gain or loss reflects the difference between the forward rate and future spot rate, whereas the translation gain or loss reflects the average exchange rate over the period of concern. In addition, the translation losses are not tax deductible, whereas gains on forward contracts used to hedge translation exposure are taxed.

Increased Transaction Exposure.   The fourth and most critical limitation with a hedging strategy (forward or money market hedge) on translation exposure is that the MNC may be increasing its transaction exposure. For example, consider a situation in which the subsidiary's currency appreciates during the fiscal year, resulting in a translation gain. If the MNC enacts a hedge strategy at the start of the fiscal year, this strategy will generate a transaction loss that will somewhat offset the translation gain. Some MNCs may not be comfortable with this offsetting effect. The translation gain is simply a paper gain; that is, the reported dollar value of earnings is higher due to the subsidiary currency's appreciation. Yet, the parent does not receive any more income due to this appreciation if the subsidiary reinvests the earnings. The MNC parent's net cash flow is not affected. Conversely, the loss resulting from a hedge strategy is a *real* loss. That is, the net cash flow to the parent will be reduced due to this loss. In this example, the MNC reduces its translation exposure at the expense of increasing its transaction exposure.

Alternative Solution to Hedging Translation Exposure

Perhaps the best way for MNCs to deal with translation exposure is to clarify how their consolidated earnings have been affected by exchange rate movements. In this way, shareholders and potential investors will be more aware of the translation effect. An unusually low level of consolidated earnings may not discourage shareholders and potential investors if it is attributed to translation of subsidiary earnings at low exchange rates.

Some MNCs do not consider hedging translation exposure because they do not perceive this exposure to be relevant. For example, Phillips Petroleum has stated in its annual report that translation exposure is not hedged because translation effects do not influence cash flows. Many other MNCs follow similar policies.

SUMMARY

■ Economic exposure can be managed by balancing the sensitivity of revenues and expenses to exchange rate fluctuations. To accomplish this, however, the firm must first recognize how its revenues and expenses are affected by exchange rate fluctuations. For some firms, revenues are more susceptible. These firms are most concerned that their home currency will appreciate against foreign currencies, since the unfavorable effects on revenues will more than offset the favorable effect on expenses. Conversely, firms whose expenses are more exchange rate-sensitive than their revenues are most concerned that their home currency will depreciate against foreign currencies. When firms reduce their economic exposure, they reduce not only these unfavorable effects, but also the favorable effects if the home currency value moves in the opposite direction.

■ Translation exposure can be reduced by creating a short position in the foreign currency used to measure a subsidiary's income. If the foreign currency depreciates against the home currency, the adverse impact on the consolidated income statement can be offset by the gain on a short position in that currency. If the foreign currency appreciates over the time period of concern, there will be a loss on the short position that is offset by a favorable effect on the reported consolidated earnings. However, many MNCs would not be satisfied with a "paper gain" that offsets a "cash loss."

SELF-TEST FOR CHAPTER 12

(Answers are provided in Appendix A in the back of the text)

1. Salem Exporting Co. purchases chemicals from U.S. sources, and uses them to make pharmaceutical products that are exported to Canadian hospitals. Salem prices its products in C$, and is concerned about the possibility of the long-term depreciation of C$ against the dollar. It periodically hedges its exposure with short-term forward contracts, but this does not insulate against the possible trend of continuing C$ depreciation. How could Salem offset some of its exposure resulting from its export business?

2. Using the information in Question 1, give a possible disadvantage of offsetting exchange rate exposure from the export business.

3. Coastal Corp. is a U.S. firm with a subsidiary in the United Kingdom. It expects that the pound will depreciate this year. Explain Coastal's translation exposure. How could Coastal hedge its translation exposure?

4. Arlington Co. has substantial translation exposure in European currencies. The treasurer of Arlington Co. suggests that the translation effects are not relevant because the earnings generated by the European subsidiaries are not being remitted to the U.S. parent, but are simply reinvested in Europe. Yet, the vice-president of finance of Arlington Co. is concerned about translation exposure because the stock price is highly dependent on the consolidated earnings, which are dependent on the exchange rates at which the earnings are translated. Who is correct?

5. Lincolnshire Co. exports 80 percent of its total production of goods in New Mexico to Latin American countries. Kalafa Co. sells all the goods it produces in the U.S., but has a subsidiary in Spain that usually generates about 20 percent of its total earnings. Compare the translation exposure of these two U.S. firms.

QUESTIONS

1. St. Paul Company does business in the United States and Germany. It is attempting to assess its economic exposure and has compiled the following information.

   a) Its U.S. sales are somewhat affected by the German mark's value, because it faces competition from German exporters. It forecasts the U.S. sales based on the following three exchange rate scenarios.

Exchange Rate of Mark	Revenue from U.S. Business (in millions)
DM = $.48	$100
DM = .50	105
DM = .54	110

   b) Its German mark revenues on sales to Germany invoiced in marks are expected to be DM600 million.

   c) Its anticipated cost of goods sold is estimated at $200 million from the purchase of U.S. materials and DM100 million from the purchase of German materials.

   d) Fixed operating expenses are estimated at $30 million.

   e) Variable operating expenses are estimated at 20 percent of total sales (after including German sales, translated to a dollar amount).

   f) Interest expense is estimated at $20 million on existing U.S. loans, and the company has no existing German loans.
   Create a forecasted income statement for St. Paul Company under each of the three exchange rate scenarios. Explain how St. Paul's projected earnings before taxes are affected by possible exchange rate movements. Explain how it can restructure its operations to reduce the sensitivity of its earnings to exchange rate movements, without reducing its volume of business in Germany.

2. Baltimore Inc. is a U.S.-based MNC that obtains 10 percent of its supplies from European manufacturers. Sixty percent of its revenues are due to exports to Europe, where its product is exported and invoiced in European currencies. Explain how Baltimore Inc. could attempt to reduce its economic exposure to exchange rate fluctuations.

3. UVA Company is a U.S.-based MNC that obtains 40 percent of its foreign supplies from Switzerland. It also borrows Swiss francs from Swiss banks

and converts the francs to dollars to support U.S. operations. It presently receives about 10 percent of its revenues from Swiss customers. Its sales to Swiss customers are denominated in francs. Explain how UVA Company can reduce its economic exposure to exchange rate fluctuations.

4. Albany Corporation is a U.S.-based MNC that has a large government contract with Germany. The contract will continue for several years and generate more than half of Albany's total sales volume. The German government pays Albany in German marks. About 10 percent of Albany's operating expenses are in German marks; all other expenses are in U.S. dollars. Explain how Albany Company can reduce its economic exposure to exchange rate fluctuations.

5. When an MNC restructures its operations to reduce its economic exposure, it may sometimes forgo economies of scale. Explain.

6. Explain how a U.S.-based MNC's consolidated earnings are affected if the dollar weakens against most foreign currencies.

7. Explain how a firm can hedge its translation exposure.

8. Explain some limitations of hedging translation exposure.

9. Would a more established MNC or a less established MNC be more capable of effectively hedging its given level of translation exposure? Why?

10. If U.S.-based MNCs are concerned with how shareholders react to changes in consolidated earnings, but prefer not to hedge their translation exposure, how can they attempt to reduce shareholder reaction to a decline in consolidated earnings that results from a strengthened dollar?

11. Carlton Company and Palmer Inc. are U.S.-based MNCs with subsidiaries in Germany that distribute medical supplies (produced in the United States) to customers throughout Europe. Both subsidiaries purchase the products at cost and sell the products at 90 percent markup. The other operating costs of the subsidiaries are very low. Carlton Company has a research and development center in the United States which focuses on improving its medical technology. Palmer Inc. has a similar center that is based in France. The parent of each firm subsidizes its respective research and development center on an annual basis. Which firm is subject to a higher degree of economic exposure? Explain.

12. Nelson Company is a U.S. firm with annual export sales of about DM800 million. Its main competitor is Mez Company, also based in the United States, with a subsidiary in Germany that generates about DM800 million in annual sales. Any earnings generated by the subsidiary are reinvested to support its operations. Based on the information provided, which firm is subject to a higher degree of translation exposure? Explain.

U.S. Companies Move to Limit Currency Risk

A WALL STREET JOURNAL *News Roundup*

The European currency crisis is changing the way some U.S. companies do business on the Continent.

The continuing turmoil in Europe's Exchange Rate Mechanism, combined with the decision early Monday by European Community nations to let their currencies fluctuate more widely, is raising the financial risks and creating increased uncertainty for U.S. companies that have European operations. Some companies say they expect to be insulated from the tumult by currency hedging and other strategies already in place, but others are taking additional steps to protect themselves.

"This overall is not good news for Gillette or any companies doing business in Europe," Gian Camuzzi, Gillette Co.'s senior assistant treasurer, said of the currency crisis.

It may be better news in the long run. John Barter, chief financial officer of AlliedSignal Inc., a Morristown, N.J., technology company with automotive, aerospace and engineered-material businesses, said he expected Europe's currency plan to "restimulate the European economy" by allowing many countries to lower their interest rates rather than having to keep rates high to support weaker currencies.

Moving Manufacturing

But for now, many businesses are focusing on protecting themselves. Those with the flexibility to move production to softer-currency countries have a distinct advantage. FMC Corp. is already shifting some business to European countries whose currencies are weakening. During the weekend, the Chicago-based manufacturer decided to fill a customer's order for food-packaging machinery from one of its plants in Italy, rather than from a plant in the U.S. says FMC treasurer Cheryl Francis. With the lira having dropped in value over the past few months and under pressure again in recent days, making machines costs FMC less in Italy than in the U.S.

Moving production within Europe can also pay off. Rob Bazelaar, managing director of Peerless Manufacturing Co.'s Peerless Europe operations, said the company two years ago adopted a subcontracting system for its European manufacturing, and work can be shifted around the Continent as needed. "I have the advantage of not being stuck in one country," Mr. Bazelaar said. "I can have things manufactured anywhere I want to." Peerless, a Dallas-based company that designs and manufactures filters and separators, has a good deal of subcontracting in France and Germany, and Mr. Bazelaar expects the work assigned to French subcontractors to increase.

Gillette has manufacturing facilities in several European countries. But even so, said the company's Mr. Camuzzi, its razor-blade business in France will be hurt because it sells German-made blades there. The appreciation of the Deutsche mark against the franc leaves the Boston-based company with the choice of raising prices or cutting profit margins on the blades it sells in France.

Adjusting Prices

Mr. Camuzzi said he expects Gillette to increase prices in France. The Boston-based company "definitely" will adjust its prices around Europe, Mr. Camuzzi said, not only to maintain profits, but also to deter private enterprises from buying up the company's products in one country to sell in others. "Otherwise, we'll have a flow of products coming out of France and going into Germany," he said.

Gillette also plans to do more currency hedging, Mr. Camuzzi said. In hedging, companies protect themselves against currency fluctuations in accounts payable and receivable by establishing positions in the currencies in question. "If you have a receivable in marks and a payable in francs, we will eliminate the position rather than carry it on the books," Mr. Camuzzi said.

Walt Disney Co. hedges "substantially more than half" of its foreign income against currency fluctuations, said Richard D. Nanula, senior vice president and chief financial officer, and doesn't expect to change that strategy. The company sees a possible happy ending to the currency crisis: "If the franc were to weaken," as the latest currency agreement allows, "it will make France and Euro Disney a cheaper visit from surrounding countries," Mr. Nanula said. Moreover, "if the French don't have to worry about protecting their currency, they can lower interest rates, and lowering interest rates potentially will put people back to work in France. That may translate into more visits to our theme park."

Source: The Wall Street Journal (August 3, 1993): p. A10. Reprinted by permission of *The Wall Street Journal,* © 1993 Dow Jones & Company, Inc. All rights reserved worldwide.

Questions

1. Explain why the establishment of several production sites across European countries by FMC Corp. can reduce exposure to exchange rate fluctuations.

2. Peerless Manufacturing Co. has subcontractors in France and in Germany. Explain how Peerless can manage its exposure to exchange rates better by having subcontractors in two different countries.

3. When Gillette has receivables in marks and payables in francs, it is concerned about its exchange rate risk. Why is this type of risk more pronounced since the widening of the Exchange Rate Mechanism (ERM) bands?

4. Explain how the widening of the ERM bands can increase the volatility of cash flows of EuroDisney (based in France).

CASE PROBLEM

MADISON, INC.
Assessing Economic Exposure

The situation for Madison, Inc. was described in this chapter to illustrate how alternative operational structures could affect economic exposure to exchange rate movements. Ken Moore, the vice-president of finance at Madison, Inc., was seriously considering a shift to the proposed operational structure described in the text. He was determined to stabilize the earnings before taxes and believed that the proposed approach would achieve this objective. The firm expected that the Canadian dollar would consistently depreciate over the next several years. Over time, it has been very accurate in its forecasts. Moore paid little attention to the forecasts, stating that regardless of how the Canadian dollar changed, future earnings would be more stable under the proposed operational structure. He also was constantly reminded of how the strengthened Canadian dollar from 1986 to 1991 had adversely affected the firm's earnings. In fact, he was somewhat concerned that he might even lose his job if the adverse effects from economic exposure continued throughout the 1990s.

a) Would a revised operational structure at this time be in the best interests of the shareholders? Would it be in the best interests of the vice-president?

b) How could a revised operational structure possibly be feasible from the vice-president's perspective but not from the shareholders' perspective? Explain how the firm might be able to ensure that the vice-president make decisions related to economic exposure that were in the best interests of the shareholders.

PROJECT

1. Many annual reports of MNCs indicate where their operations are located. Use this information to suggest how the MNC could restructure its operations (without reducing its foreign business) to reduce exposure. Refer back to the chapter for an example. Your analysis may need to be more generalized than the example used in the chapter because you will not have specific details.

REFERENCES

Bodnar, Gordon M., and William M. Gentry. "Exchange Rate Exposure and Industry Characteristics: Evidence from Canada, Japan, and the USA." *Journal of International Money and Finance* (February 1993), pp. 29–45.

Boothe, Robert, and Jeff Madura. "Reducing Exposure to Exchange Rate Risk: A Case Study." *Long-Range Planning* (June 1985), pp. 98–101.

Calderon-Rossell, Jorge R. "Covering Foreign Exchange Risks of Single Transactions: A Framework for Analysis." *Financial Management* (Autumn 1979), pp. 78–85.

Glen, Jack, and Philippe Jorion. "Currency Hedging for International Portfolios." *Journal of Finance* (December 1993), pp. 1865–1886.

Hung, Juan. "Assessing the Exchange Rate's Impact on U.S. Manufacturing Profits." *FRBNY Quarterly Review* (1992–93), pp. 44–63.

Jacque, Laurent L. "Management of Foreign Exchange Risk: A Review Article." *Journal of International Business Studies* (Spring–Summer 1981), pp. 81–99.

Jorion, Philippe. "The Pricing of Exchange Rate Risk in the Stock Market." *Journal of Financial and Quantitative Analysis* (September 1991), pp. 363–376.

Kaufold, Howard, and Michael Smirlock. "Managing Corporate Exchange and Interest Rate Exposure." *Financial Management* (Autumn 1986), pp. 64–72.

Logue, Dennis E., and George S. Oldfield. "Managing Foreign Assets When Foreign Exchange Markets Are Efficient." *Financial Management* (Summer 1977), pp. 16–22.

Madura, Jeff. "Assessment of Exchange Rate Risk from Various Country Perspectives." *International Review of Economics and Business* (July 1990), pp. 655–666.

Madura, Jeff, and E. Joe Nosari. "Utilizing Currency Portfolios to Mitigate Exchange Rate Risk." *Columbia Journal of World Business* (Spring 1984), pp. 96–99.

Madura, Jeff, and Alan L. Tucker. "Intertemporal Shifts in Actual and Anticipated Exchange Rate Volatility." *Journal of Global Business* (Summer 1990), pp. 5–10.

Nance, Deana R., Clifford W. Smith Jr., and Charles W. Smithson. "On the Determinants of Corporate Hedging." *Journal of Finance* (March 1993), pp. 267–284.

Srinivasulu, S. L. "Currency Denomination of Debt: Lessons from Rolls-Royce and Laker Airways." *Business Horizons* (September–October 1983), pp. 19–23.

Westerfield, Janice M. "How U.S. Multinationals Manage Currency Risk." *Business Review* (March–April 1980), pp. 19–27.

Yang, James G. S. "Managing Multinational Exchange Risks." *Management Accounting* (February 1986), pp. 45–52.

EXCHANGE RATE RISK MANAGEMENT

Vogl Co. is a U.S. firm conducting a financial plan for the next year. It has no foreign subsidiaries, but more than half of its sales are from exports. Its foreign cash inflows to be received from exporting and cash outflows to be paid for imported supplies over the next year are disclosed below:

Currency	Total Inflow	Total Outflow
Canadian dollar (C$)	C$32,000,000	C$2,000,000
German mark (DM)	DM5,000,000	DM1,000,000
French franc (FF)	FF11,000,000	FF10,000,000
Swiss franc (SF)	SF4,000,000	SF8,000,000

The spot rates and one-year forward rates as of today are

Currency	Spot Rate	One-year Forward Rate
C$	$.90	$.93
DM	.60	.59
FF	.18	.15
SF	.65	.64

1. Based on the information provided, determine the net exposure of each foreign currency in dollars.

2. Are any of the exposure positions offsetting to some degree?

3. When using today's spot rate as a forecast of the Canadian dollar in 90 days, would you hedge the Canadian dollar position?

4. Assume that the Canadian dollar net inflows may range from C$20,000,000 to C$40,000,000 over the next year. Explain the risk of hedging C$30,000,000 in net inflows. How can Vogl Co. avoid such a risk? Is there any tradeoff resulting from your strategy to avoid that risk?

5. Vogl Co. recognizes that its year-to-year hedging strategy only hedges the risk over a given year, but does not insulate it from long-term trends in the C$ value. It has considered establishing a subsidiary in Canada. The goods

would be sent from the U.S. to the Canandian Subsidiary and distributed by the subsidiary. The proceeds received would be reinvested in Canada by the Canadian subsidiary. Would Vogl Co. eliminate its Canadian dollar exposure by using the strategy? Explain.

SHORT-TERM ASSET AND LIABILITY MANAGEMENT

Part 4 (Chapters 13 through 15) focuses on the MNC's management of short-term assets and liabilities. Chapter 13 describes methods by which MNCs can finance their international trade. Chapter 14 identifies sources of short-term funds and explains the criteria used by MNCs to make their short-term financing decisions. Chapter 15 describes how MNCs optimize their cash flow and explains the criteria used to make their short-term investment decisions.

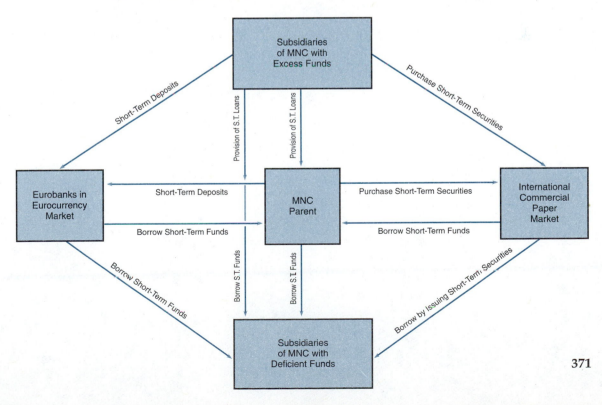

CHAPTER 13

FINANCING INTERNATIONAL TRADE

The international trade activities of multinational corporations (MNCs) have grown in importance over time. This trend is attributed primarily to the various ways in which the commercial banks can finance and facilitate international trade. While banks also finance domestic trade, their role in financing international trade is more critical due to the additional complications involved. First, the exporter might question the importer's ability to make payment. Second, even if the importer is creditworthy, the government might impose exchange controls that prevent payment to the exporter. Third, the importer might not trust that the exporter will ship the goods ordered. Fourth, even if the exporter does ship the goods, trade barriers or time lags in international transportation might delay arrival time.

The specific objectives of this chapter are to

- describe methods of payment for international trade,
- explain common trade finance methods, and
- describe the major agencies that facilitate international trade with export insurance and/or loan programs.

PAYMENT METHODS FOR INTERNATIONAL TRADE

In any international trade transaction, credit is provided by either the supplier (exporter), the buyer (importer), one or more financial institutions, or any combination of these. The supplier may have sufficient cash flow to fund the entire trade cycle, beginning with the production of the product until payment is eventually made by the buyer. This form of credit is known as **supplier credit.** In some cases, the exporter may require bank financing to augment its cash flow. On the other hand, the supplier may not desire to provide financing, in which case the buyer will have to finance the transaction itself, either internally or externally, through its bank. Banks on both sides of the transaction can thus play an integral part in trade financing.

In general, five basic methods of payment are used to settle international transactions, each with a different degree of risk to the exporter and importer (Exhibit 13.1):

- Prepayment
- Letters of credit
- Drafts (sight/time)
- Consignment
- Open account.

Prepayment

Under the **prepayment** method, the exporter will not ship the goods until the buyer has remitted payment to the exporter. Payment is usually made in the

---

EXHIBIT 13.1   Comparison of Payment Methods

Method	Usual Time of Payment	Goods Available to Buyers	Risk to Exporter	Risk to Importer
Prepayment	Before shipment	After payment	None	Relies completely on exporter to ship goods as ordered
Letter of credit	When shipment is made	After payment	Very little or none, depending on credit terms	Assured shipment made, but relies on exporter to ship goods described in documents
Sight draft; documents against payment	On presentation of draft to buyer	After payment	If draft unpaid, must dispose of goods	Same as above unless importer can inspect goods before payment
Time draft; documents against acceptance	On maturity of drafts	Before payment	Relies on buyer to pay drafts	Same as above
Consignment	At time of sale by buyer	Before payment	Allows importer to sell inventory before paying exporter	None; improves cash flow of buyer
Open account	As agreed	Before payment	Relies completely on buyer to pay account as agreed	None

form of an international wire transfer to the exporter's bank account or a bank draft. This method affords the supplier the greatest degree of protection, and it is normally requested of first-time buyers whose creditworthiness is unknown or whose countries are in financial difficulty. Most buyers, however, are not willing to bear all the risk by prepaying an order.

Letters of Credit (L/C)

A **letter of credit (L/C)** is an instrument issued by a bank on behalf of the importer (buyer) promising to pay the exporter (beneficiary) upon presentation of shipping documents in compliance with the terms stipulated therein. In effect, the bank is substituting its credit for that of the buyer. This method is a compromise between seller and buyer because it affords certain advantages to both parties. The exporter is assured of receiving payment from the issuing bank as long as it presents documents in accordance with the L/C. It is important to point out that the issuing bank is obligated to honor drawings under the L/C regardless of the buyer's ability or willingness to pay. On the other hand, the importer does not have to pay for the goods until shipment has been made and documents are presented in good order. However, the importer still must rely upon the exporter to ship the goods as described in the documents, since the L/C does not guarantee that the goods purchased will be those invoiced and shipped. Letters of credit will be described in greater detail later in this chapter.

Drafts

A **draft** (or **bill of exchange**) is an unconditional promise drawn by one party, usually the exporter, instructing the buyer to pay the face amount of the draft upon presentation. The draft represents the exporter's formal demand for payment from the buyer. A draft affords the exporter less protection than an L/C, since the banks are not obligated to honor payments on the buyer's behalf.

Most trade transactions handled on a draft basis are processed through banking channels. In banking terminology, they are known as **documentary collections.** In a documentary collection transaction, banks on both ends act as intermediaries in the processing of shipping documents and the collection of payment. If shipment is made under a sight draft, the exporter is paid once shipment has been made and the draft is presented to the buyer for payment. The buyer's bank will not release the shipping documents to the buyer until the buyer has paid the draft. This is known as **documents against payment.** It is a practice that provides the exporter with some protection, since the banks will release the shipping documents only according to the exporter's instructions. The buyer needs the shipping documents to pick up merchandise. The buyer does not have to pay for the merchandise until the draft has been presented.

If a shipment is made under a time draft, the exporter provides instructions to the buyer's bank to release shipping documents against acceptance (signing) of the draft. This method of payment is sometimes referred to as **documents against acceptance.** By accepting the draft, the buyer is promising to pay the exporter at the specified future date. This accepted draft is also known as a **trade acceptance,** which is different from a banker's acceptance. In this type of transaction, the buyer is able to obtain the merchandise prior to paying for it. It is the buyer's responsibility to honor that draft at maturity. In this case, the exporter is providing the financing and is dependent upon the buyer's financial integrity to pay the draft at maturity. Shipping on a time draft basis provides some added comfort, in that banks at both ends are used as collection agents. In addition, a draft serves as a binding financial obligation in case the exporter wishes to pursue litigation on uncollected receivables. The added risk is that if the buyer fails to pay the draft at maturity, the bank is not obligated to honor payment. The exporter is assuming all the risk and must analyze the buyer accordingly.

Consignment

Under a **consignment** arrangement, the exporter ships the goods to the importer while still retaining actual title to the merchandise. The importer has access to the inventory, but does not have to pay for the goods until they have been sold to a third party. The exporter is trusting the importer to remit payment for the goods sold at that time. If the importer fails to pay, the exporter has limited recourse, since there is no draft involved and the goods have already been sold. As a result of the high risk, the consignment method is seldom used except by affiliated and subsidiary companies trading with the parent company.

Open Account

The opposite of prepayment is the **open account** transaction in which the exporter ships the merchandise and expects the buyer to remit payment according to the agreed-upon terms. The exporter is relying fully upon the financial creditworthiness, integrity, and reputation of the buyer. As might be expected, this method is used when seller and buyer have a great deal of experience with each other and mutual trust. Despite the risks involved, open account transactions are expanding, particularly among the industrialized nations.

TRADE FINANCE METHODS

As mentioned in the section above, banks on both sides of the transaction play a critical role in financing international trade. Some of the more popular methods of financing international trade include

- Accounts receivable financing
- Factoring
- Letters of credit (L/C)
- Banker's acceptances
- Short-term bank loans
- Forfaiting
- Countertrade.

Each of these methods is described in turn.

Accounts Receivable Financing

In some cases, the exporter of goods may be willing to ship goods to the importer without an assurance of payment from a bank. This could take the form of an open account shipment or a time draft. Prior to shipment, the exporter should have conducted its own credit check on the importer to determine creditworthiness. If the exporter is willing to wait for payment, it is extending credit to the buyer.

If the exporter needs funds immediately, it may require financing from a bank. In what is referred to as **accounts receivable financing,** the bank will provide a loan to the exporter secured by an assignment of the account receivable. The bank's loan is made to the exporter based on its creditworthiness. In the event the buyer fails to pay the exporter for whatever reason, the exporter is still responsible to repay the bank.

Accounts receivable financing involves additional risks, such as government restrictions and exchange controls, that may prevent the buyer from paying the exporter. As a result, the loan rate is often higher than domestic accounts receivable financing. The length of a financing term is usually one to six months.

Factoring

When an exporter ships goods before receiving payment, the accounts receivable balance increases. Unless the exporter has received a loan from a bank, it is initially financing the transaction, and it must monitor the collections of receivables. Since there is a danger that the buyer will never pay at all, the exporting firm may consider selling the accounts receivable to a third party, known as a **factor.** In this type of financing, the exporter sells the accounts receivable without recourse. The factor then assumes all administrative responsibilities involved in collecting from the buyer and the associated credit exposure. As one would expect, the factor performs its own credit approval process on the foreign buyer before purchasing the receivable. For providing this service, the factor usually purchases the receivable at a discount and also receives a flat processing fee.

Factoring provides several benefits to the exporter. First, by selling the accounts receivable, the exporter does not have to worry about the administrative duties involved in maintaining and monitoring an accounts receivable accounting ledger. Second, the factor assumes the credit exposure to the buyer, so the exporter does not have to maintain personnel to assess the creditworthiness of foreign buyers. Finally, the sale of the receivable to the factor provides immediate payment and improves the exporter's cash flow.

Since it is the importer who must be creditworthy from a factor's point of view, **cross-border factoring** is often used. This involves a network of factors in various countries who assess credit risk. The exporter's factor contacts a correspondent factor in the buyer's country to assess the importer's creditworthiness and handle the collections of the receivable. Factoring services are usually provided by the factoring subsidiaries of commercial banks, commercial finance companies, and other specialized finance houses.

Letters of Credit (L/C)

Introduced earlier, the letter of credit (L/C) is one of the oldest forms of trade finance still in existence. Because of the protection and benefits it accords to both exporter and importer, it is a critical component of many international trade transactions. The L/C is an undertaking by a bank to make payments on behalf of a specified party to a beneficiary under specified conditions. The beneficiary (exporter) is paid upon presentation of the required documents in compliance with the terms of the L/C. The L/C process normally involves two banks, the exporter's bank and the importer's bank. The issuing bank is substituting its credit for that of the importer. It has essentially guaranteed payment to the exporter, provided the exporter complies with the terms and conditions of the L/C.

It is important to mention that the L/C does not ensure that the buyer will receive what was ordered. Banks deal in documents only, not merchandise. The bank's decision to pay is based upon an examination of documents, not receipt of or inspection of the merchandise. Therefore the buyer must trust the seller to ship the goods in accordance with the L/C and the buyer's purchase order.

Sometimes the exporter is uncomfortable with the issuing bank's promise to pay, since the bank is located in a foreign country. Even if the issuing bank is well known worldwide, the exporter may be concerned that the foreign government might impose exchange controls or other restrictions that would prevent payment by the issuing bank. For this reason, the exporter may request that a local bank confirm the L/C and thus assure that all the responsibilities of the issuing bank will be met. The confirming bank is obligated to honor drawings made by the beneficiary in compliance with the L/C regardless of the issuing bank's ability to make that payment. Consequently, the confirming bank is trusting that the foreign bank issuing the L/C is sound. The exporter, however, need worry only about the credibility of the confirming bank.

Trade-related letters of credit are known as **commercial letters of credit** or **import/export letters of credit.** There are basically two types: revocable and irrevocable. A **revocable letter of credit** can be cancelled or revoked at any time without prior notification to the beneficiary, and it is seldom used. An **irrevocable letter of credit** (see Exhibit 13.2) cannot be cancelled or amended without the beneficiary's consent. The bank issuing the letter of credit is known as the **"issuing" bank.** The correspondent bank in the beneficiary's country to which the issuing bank sends the L/C is commonly referred to as the **"advising" bank.** The bank that agrees to examine documents under the L/C and pay the beneficiary is called the **"negotiating" bank.** An irrevocable L/C obligates the issuing bank to honor all drawings presented in conformity with the terms of the L/C. Letters of credit are normally issued in accordance with the provisions contained in "Uniform Customs and Practice for Documentary Credits," published by the International Chamber of Commerce.

The bank issuing the L/C makes payments once the required documentation has been presented in accordance with the payment terms. The importer must pay the issuing bank the amount of the L/C plus accrued fees associated with obtaining the L/C. The importer will usually have an account established at the issuing bank to be drawn upon for payment, so that the issuing bank does not tie up its own funds. However, if the importer does not have sufficient funds in his account, the issuing bank is still obligated to honor all valid drawings against the L/C. This is why the bank's decision to issue an L/C on behalf of an importer involves an analysis of the importer's creditworthiness and is analogous to the decision to make a loan. The documentary credit procedure is described in the flowchart in Exhibit 13.3.

In what is commonly referred to as a *refinancing of a sight L/C*, the bank arranges to fund a loan to pay out the L/C instead of charging the importer's

EXHIBIT 13.2
Example of an
Irrevocable Letter
of Credit

Name of issuing bank

Address of issuing bank

Name of exporter

Address of exporter

We establish our irrevocable letter of credit:
for the account of (*importer name*),
in the amount of (*value of exports*),
expiring (*date*),
available by your draft at (*time period*) days sight, and accompanied by:
   (any invoices, packing lists, bills of lading, etc., that need to be presented
   with the letter of credit)
Insurance provided by (*exporter or importer*)
covering shipment of (*merchandise description*)
From: (*port of shipment*)
To: (*port of arrival*)

(Authorized Signature)

EXHIBIT 13.3   Documentary Credit Procedure

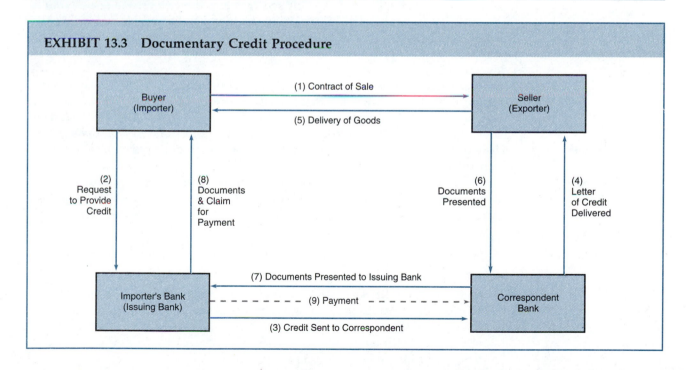

account immediately. The importer is responsible for repaying the bank both principal and interest at maturity. This is just another method of providing extended payment terms to a buyer when the exporter insists upon payment at sight.

The bank issuing the L/C makes payment to the beneficiary (exporter) upon presentation of documents that meet the conditions stipulated in the L/C. Letters of credit are payable either at sight (upon presentation of documents) or at a specified future date. The typical documentation required under an L/C includes a draft (sight or time), a commercial invoice, and a bill of lading. Depending upon the agreement, product, or country, other documents (such as a certificate of origin, inspection certificate, packing list, or insurance certificate) might be required. The three most common L/C documents are as follows.

Draft.   Also known as a **bill of exchange,** a draft (introduced earlier) is an unconditional promise drawn by one party, usually the exporter, requesting the importer to pay the face amount of the draft at sight or at a specified future date. If the draft is drawn at sight, it is payable upon presentation of documents. If it is payable at a specified future date (a time draft), and it is accepted by the importer, it is known as a trade acceptance. A **banker's acceptance** is a time draft drawn on and accepted by a bank. When presented under a letter of credit, the draft represents the exporter's formal demand for payment. The time period, or **tenor,** of most time drafts is usually anywhere from 30 to 180 days.

Bill of Lading.   The key document in an international shipment under an L/C is the **bill of lading (B/L).** It serves as a receipt for shipment and a summary of freight charges; most important, it conveys title to the merchandise. If the merchandise is to be shipped by boat, the carrier will issue what is known as an **ocean bill of lading.** When the merchandise is shipped by air, the carrier will issue an **airway bill.** The carrier presents the L/C to the exporter (shipper), who in turn presents it to the bank along with the other required documents.

A significant feature of a B/L is its negotiability. A straight B/L is consigned directly to the importer. Since it does not represent title to the merchandise, the importer does not need it to pick up the merchandise. However, when a B/L is made out to order, it is said to be in negotiable form. The exporter normally endorses the B/L to the bank once payment is received from the bank.

The bank would not endorse the B/L over to the importer until payment had been made. The importer needs the original B/L to pick up the merchandise. With a **negotiable B/L,** title passes to the holder of the endorsed B/L. Because a negotiable B/L grants title to the holder, banks can take the merchandise as collateral. Some of the usual provisions contained within a B/L include

- A description of the merchandise
- Identification marks on the merchandise
- Evidence of loading (receiving) ports
- Names of the exporter (shipper)
- Name of the importer
- Status of freight charges (prepaid or collect)
- Date of shipment.

Commercial Invoice.   The exporter's (seller's) description of the merchandise being sold to the buyer is the **commercial invoice,** which normally contains the following information:

- Name and address of seller
- Name and address of buyer
- Date
- Terms of payment
- Price, including freight, handling, and insurance if applicable
- Quantity, weight, packaging, etc.
- Shipping information.

Under an L/C shipment, the description of the merchandise outlined in the invoice must correspond exactly to that contained in the L/C.

Variations of the L/C.   There are several variations of the L/C that are useful in financing trade. A **standby letter of credit** can be used to guarantee invoice payments to a supplier. It promises to pay the beneficiary if the buyer fails to pay as agreed. It is a performance-related instrument used extensively in the United States in lieu of bid bonds, performance bonds, and other contractual obligations. Internationally, standby L/Cs are used often with government-related contracts and serve as bid bonds, performance bonds, or advance payment guarantees. In an international or domestic trade transaction the seller would agree to ship to the buyer on standard open account terms as long as the buyer provided a standby L/C for a specified amount and term. As long as the buyer pays the seller as agreed, the standby L/C is never funded. However, if the buyer fails to pay, the exporter may present documents under the L/C and request payment from the bank. The buyer's bank is essentially guaranteeing that the buyer will make payment to the seller.

A **transferable letter of credit** is a variation of the standard commercial L/C that allows the first beneficiary to transfer all or a part of the original L/C to a third party. The new beneficiary has the same rights and protection as the original beneficiary. This type of L/C is used extensively by brokers, or middlemen, who are not the actual suppliers. For example, the broker asks the foreign buyer to issue an L/C for $100,000 in his favor. The L/C must contain a clause stating the L/C is transferable. The broker has located a supplier who will provide the product for $80,000. However, the end supplier has requested payment in advance from the broker. With a transferable L/C, the broker can transfer $80,000 of the original L/C to the end supplier under the same terms and conditions, except for the amount, the latest shipment date, the invoice, and the period of validity. When the end supplier ships the product, it presents its documents to the bank. When the bank pays the L/C, $80,000 is paid to the end supplier and $20,000 goes to the broker. In effect, the broker has utilized the credit of the buyer to finance the entire transaction.

An **assignment of proceeds** under an L/C is another method of financing a transaction involving a middleman. The original beneficiary of the L/C may pledge (or assign), to the end supplier, the proceeds under an L/C. The end supplier has the assurance from the bank that if and when documents are presented in compliance with the terms of the L/C, the bank will pay the end supplier according to the assignment instructions. This assignment is valid only if the beneficiary (middleman) presents documents that comply with the L/C. The end supplier must recognize that the issuing bank is under no obligation to pay the end supplier if the original beneficiary never ships the goods, or fails to comply with the terms of the L/C.

Banker's Acceptances

Introduced earlier, a **banker's acceptance** (shown in Exhibit 13.4) is a bill of exchange, or time draft, drawn on and accepted by a bank. It is the accepting bank's obligation to pay the holder of the draft at maturity.

The first step in the creation of a banker's acceptance is for the importer to order goods from the exporter. The importer then requests its local bank to issue an L/C on its behalf. The L/C will allow the exporter to draw a time draft on the bank in payment for the exported goods. The exporter presents the time draft, along with shipping documents, to its local bank, and the exporter's bank sends the time draft along with the shipping documents to the importer's bank. The importer's bank accepts the draft, thereby creating the banker's acceptance. If the exporter does not want to wait until the specified date to receive payment, it can request that the banker's acceptance be sold in the money market. In this case, the funds received from the sale of a banker's acceptance are less than they would be if the exporter waited to receive payment. Such a discount reflects the time value of money.

A money market investor may be willing to buy the banker's acceptance at a discount and hold it until payment is due. This investor will then receive full payment, because the banker's acceptance represents a future claim on funds of the bank represented by the acceptance. The bank will make full payment at the date specified, since it expects to receive this amount plus an additional fee from the importer.

If the exporter holds the acceptance until maturity, it provides the financing for the importer, as it does with accounts receivable financing. In this case, the key difference between use of a banker's acceptance and accounts receivable financing is that a banker's acceptance guarantees payment to the exporter by a bank. However, if the exporter sells the banker's acceptance in the secondary market, it is no longer providing the financing for the importer. The holder of the banker's acceptance is financing instead.

A banker's acceptance can be beneficial to the exporter, importer, and issuing bank. The exporter does not need to worry about the credit risk of the importer and can therefore penetrate new foreign markets without concern about the credit risk of potential customers. In addition, there is little exposure to political

EXHIBIT 13.4
Banker's Acceptance

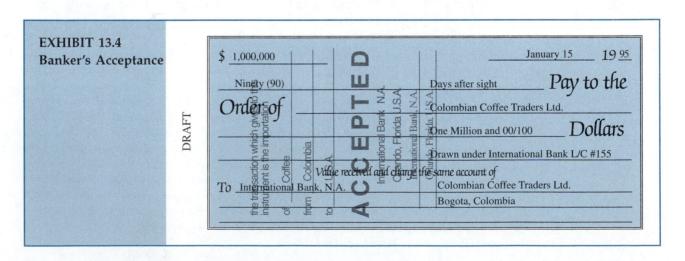

risk or to exchange controls imposed by a government. Banks are normally allowed to meet their payment commitments even under the existence of controls. Yet, an importer may have greater difficulty in making payment to the exporter if controls are imposed. Without a banker's acceptance, an exporter might not receive payment, even if the importer is willing to pay, due to exchange controls. Finally, the exporter can sell the banker's acceptance at a discount before payment is due and thus obtain funds up front from the issuing bank.

The importer benefits from a banker's acceptance in that it has greater access to foreign markets when purchasing supplies and other products. Without banker's acceptances, exporters may be unwilling to accept the credit risk of importers. Due to the documents presented along with the acceptance, the importer is assured that goods have been shipped. Even though the importer has not paid in advance, this assurance is valuable, since the importer may need to know if and when supplies and other products will arrive. Finally, because the banker's acceptance allows the importer to pay at a later date, the importer's payment is financed until the maturity date of the banker's acceptance. Without an acceptance, the importer would likely be forced to pay in advance, thereby tying up funds.

The bank accepting the drafts benefits in that it earns a commission for creating an acceptance. The commission that the bank charges the customer reflects the perceived creditworthiness of the customer. The interest rate charged the customer, which is commonly referred to as the **all-in rate,** consists of the discount rate plus the acceptance commission. In general, the all-in rate for acceptance financing is lower than prime-based borrowings, as shown in the following comparison:

	Loan	Acceptance
Amount:	$1,000,000	$1,000,000
Term:	180 Days	180 Days
Rate:	Prime + 1.5%	BA Rate + 1.5%
	10.0% + 1.5% = 11.5%	7.60% + 1.5% = 9.10%
Interest Cost:	$57,500	$45,500

In this example, the interest savings for a six-month period is $12,000. Since the banker's acceptance is a marketable instrument with an active secondary market, the rates on acceptances usually fall between those of short-term Treasury bills and those of commercial paper. Investors are usually willing to purchase acceptances as an investment because of their yield, safety, and liquidity. When a bank creates, accepts, and sells the acceptance, it is actually using the investor's money to finance the bank's customer. As a result, the bank has created an asset at one price, sold it at another, and retained a commission (spread) as its fee.

Banker's acceptance financing can also be arranged through the refinancing of a sight letter of credit. In this case, the exporter (beneficiary) of the letter of credit may insist upon payment at sight. So that the importer can obtain terms, the bank arranges to finance the payment of the sight letter of credit under a separate acceptance-financing agreement. The importer (borrower) simply draws drafts upon the bank, which in turn accepts and discounts the drafts. Proceeds are used to pay the exporter. At maturity, the importer is responsible for repayment to the bank.

Acceptance financing can also be arranged without the use of a letter of credit under a separate acceptance agreement. Similar to a regular loan agreement, it stipulates the terms and conditions under which the bank is prepared to finance the borrower using acceptances instead of promissory notes. As long as the acceptances meet one of the underlying transaction requirements, the bank and borrower can utilize banker's acceptances as an alternative financing mechanism. The life cycle of a banker's acceptance is illustrated in Exhibit 13.5.

EXHIBIT 13.5   Life Cycle of a Typical Banker's Acceptance

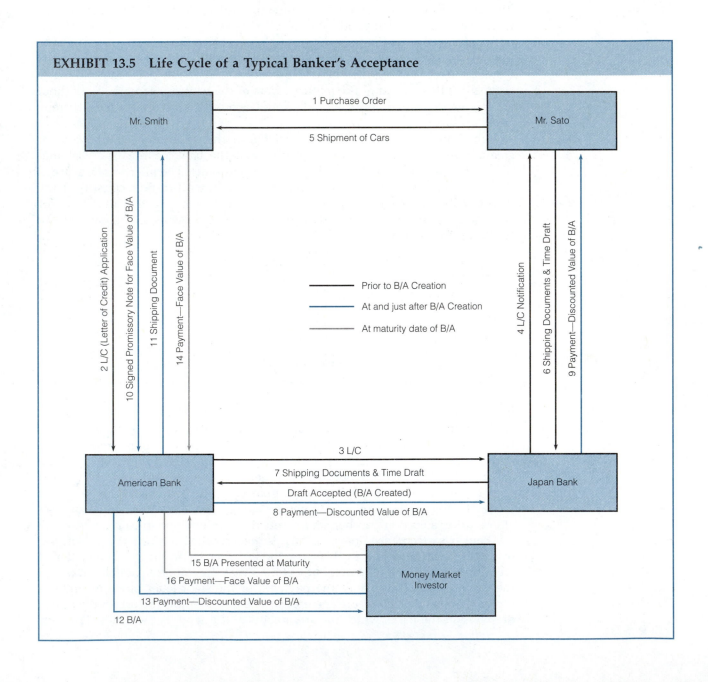

Short-Term Bank Loans

As just explained, a banker's acceptance can allow an exporter to receive funds immediately, yet allow an importer to delay its payment until a future date. The bank may even provide short-term loans beyond the banker's acceptance period. In the case of an importer, the purchase from overseas usually represents the acquisition of inventory. The loan finances the working capital cycle that begins with the purchase of inventory and continues with the sale of the goods, creation of an account receivable, and conversion to cash. With an exporter, the short-term loan might finance the manufacture of the merchandise destined for export (pre-export financing) or the time period from when the sale is made until payment is received from the buyer. For example, the firm may have imported foreign beer, which it plans to distribute to grocery and liquor stores. The bank can not only provide a letter of credit for trade finance, but also finance the importer's cost from the time of distribution and collection of payment.

Forfaiting

Because capital goods are often quite expensive, an importer may not be able to make payment on the goods within a short time period. Thus, longer-term financing may be required here. The exporter could be able to provide financing for the importer but may not desire to do so, since the financing may extend over several years. In this case, a type of trade finance known as **forfaiting** could be used. Forfaiting refers to the purchase of financial obligations, such as bills of exchange or promissory notes, without recourse to the original holder, usually the exporter. In a forfait transaction, the importer would issue a promissory note in favor of the exporter to pay for the imported capital goods. The term generally ranges from three to seven years. The exporter would then sell the notes, without recourse, to the forfaiting bank. In some respects, this is similar to factoring, in that the forfaiter (or factor) assumes responsibility for the collection of payment from the buyer and the underlying credit risk and country risk. Since the forfaiting bank assumes the risk of nonpayment, it should asses the creditworthiness of the importer as if it were extending a medium-term loan. Forfait transactions are normally collateralized by a bank guarantee or letter of credit issued by the importer's bank for the term of the transaction. Since financial information is usually difficult to obtain on the importer, the forfaiting bank places a great deal of reliance on the bank guarantee as the collateral in the event the buyer fails to pay as agreed. It is this guarantee backing up the transaction that has fostered the growth of the forfait market, particularly in Europe, as a practical means of trade finance.

Forfaiting transactions usually are in excess of $500,000 and can be denominated in most currencies. For some larger transactions, more than one bank may be involved. In this case, a syndicate is formed wherein each participant assumes a proportionate share of the underlying risk and profit. A forfaiting firm may decide to sell the promissory notes of the importer to other financial institutions willing to purchase them. However, the forfaiting firm is still responsible for payment on the notes in the event the importer is unable to pay.

Countertrade

The term **countertrade** denotes all types of foreign trade transactions in which the sale of goods to one country is linked to the purchase or exchange of goods from that same country. Some types of countertrade, such as barter, have been in existence for thousands of years. However, only recently has countertrade gained popularity and importance. The growth in various types of countertrade has been fueled by large balance of payments disequilibriums, foreign currency shortages, and LDC debt problem, and stagnant worldwide demand. As a result, many multinationals have been confronted with countertrade opportunities, particularly in Asia, Latin America, and Eastern Europe. The most common types of countertrade include barter, compensation, and counterpurchase.

Barter represents the exchange of goods between two parties without the use of any currency as a medium of exchange. Most barter arrangements are one-time transactions governed by one contract. An example would be the exchange of 100 tons of wheat from Canada for 20 tons of shrimp from Ecuador.

In a **compensation** or clearing-account arrangement, the delivery of goods to one party is compensated for by the seller's buying back a certain amount of product from that same party. The transaction is governed by one contract, and the value of the goods is expressed in monetary terms. The buy-back arrangement could be for a fraction of the original sale (**partial compensation**) or more than 100 percent of the original sale (**full compensation**). An example of compensation would be the sale of phosphate from Morocco to France in exchange for purchasing a certain percentage of fertilizer. In some countries, this is also referred to as an industrial cooperation arrangement. Such arrangements often involve the construction of large projects, such as power plants, in exchange for the purchase of the project's output over an extended period of time. For example, a hydroelectric plant was sold by Brazil to Argentina in exchange for Brazil's purchase of a percentage of the plant's output over a long-term contract.

The term **counterpurchase** denotes the exchange of goods between two parties under two distinct contracts expressed in monetary terms. Delivery and payment of both goods are technically separate transactions. An example would be the sale of televisions by Lucky-Goldstar (based in Korea) to Yugoslavia in exchange for Lucky-Goldstar's marketing of Yugo cars in Korea.

The countertrade market is still developing. The primary participants are governments and multinationals, with assistance provided by specialists in the field, such as attorneys, financial institutions, and trading companies. The transactions are usually very complex and large. Many variations of countertrade exist, and the terminology used by the various market participants is still forming. Nonetheless, despite the economic inefficiencies of countertrade, it has grown in significance and is used by the experienced traders and governments.

AGENCIES THAT MOTIVATE INTERNATIONAL TRADE

Due to the inherent risks of international trade, insurance against various forms of risk is desirable. Some agencies provide insurance, or combine it with various loan-support programs or guarantees.

The prominent agencies providing this service in the United States are

- Export-Import Bank of the U.S. (Eximbank)
- Private Export Funding Corporation (PEFCO)
- Overseas Private Investment Corporation (OPIC).

Each of these agencies is described in turn.

Export-Import Bank of the United States

Eximbank was established in 1934 with the original intention to facilitate Soviet-American trade. Its mission today is to finance and facilitate the export of American goods and services and maintain the competitiveness of American companies in overseas markets. It operates as an independent agency of the U.S. government and, as such, carries the full faith and credit of the United States. In over 50 years, Eximbank has supported over $190 billion in U.S. exports. In fact, since 1988 Eximbank has financed, guaranteed, or insured over $14 billion in U.S. exports.

The programs of Eximbank are designed to meet two broad objectives: (1) by assuming the underlying credit and country risk, encourage private lenders to finance export trade, and (2) provide direct loans to foreign buyers when private lenders are unwilling to do so. To satisfy these objectives, the Eximbank conducts various programs that are classified into three broad groups: (1) guarantees, (2) loans, and (3) insurance.

Guarantee Programs.

The two most widely used guarantee programs are the **Working Capital Guarantee Program** and the **Medium-Term Guarantee Program.** The Working Capital Guarantee Program encourages commercial banks to extend short-term export financing to eligible exporters by providing a comprehensive guarantee which covers 100 percent of the loan's principal and interest. Eximbank's guarantee protects the lender against the risk of default by the exporter. It does not protect the exporter against the risk of nonpayment by the foreign buyer. The loans are fully collateralized by export receivables and export inventory and require the payment of guarantee fees to Eximbank. The export receivables are usually supported with export credit insurance or a letter of credit.

The **Medium-Term Guarantee** Program encourages commercial lenders to finance the sale of U.S. capital equipment and services to approved foreign buyers. The Eximbank guarantees 100 percent of the loan's principal and interest. The financed amount cannot exceed 85 percent of the contract price. This program is designed to finance products sold on a medium-term basis, with repayment terms of generally between one and five years. The guarantee fees paid to Eximbank are determined by the repayment terms and buyer's risk.

Loan Programs.

Two of the most popular loan programs are the **Direct Loan Program** and the **Intermediary Loan Program.** Under the **Direct Loan Program,** Eximbank offers fixed-rate loans directly to the foreign buyer to purchase U.S. capital equipment and services on a medium-term or long-term basis. The total financed amount cannot exceed 85 percent of the contract price, while the U.S. content must exceed 50 percent of the contract's value. Repayment terms depend upon the amount, but are typically one to five years for medium-term transactions and seven to ten years for long-term transactions. Eximbank's lending rates are generally below market rates.

The **Intermediary Loan Program** enables commercial banks to extend fixed-rate, medium-term loans to eligible foreign buyers. The Eximbank provides fixed-rate funding to the commercial bank, which in turn extends a fixed-rate loan at the Eximbank lending rates to the foreign borrower. As with the other programs, the loan amount cannot exceed 85 percent of the contract price. An important covenant of this program is that the Eximbank is only providing fixed-rate funding to the lender. The lender is obligated to repay Eximbank even if the foreign borrower defaults. If the lender wishes to protect itself from the risk of nonpayment by the foreign borrower, it must utilize one of the other guarantee or insurance programs.

Insurance Programs.   Eximbank offers several insurance policies to banks. The most widely used is the **Bank Letter of Credit Policy.** This policy enables banks to confirm letters of credit issued by foreign banks supporting a purchase of U.S. exports. Without this insurance, some banks would not be willing to assume the underlying commercial and political risk associated with confirming a letter of credit. The banks are insured up to 100 percent for sovereign (government) banks and 95 percent for all other banks. The premium is based on the type of buyer, repayment term, and country. The **Financial Institution Buyer Credit Policy** is issued in the name of the bank. The policy provides insurance coverage for loans by banks to foreign buyers on a short-term basis.

Export Credit Insurance

The Foreign Credit Insurance Association (FCIA) was formed in 1961 as a group of private insurance companies that, in cooperation with Eximbank, would insure foreign receivables against the risk of nonpayment due to commercial defaults or political risk defaults. However, as a result of heavy losses sustained in the 1980s, many of the private insurers pulled out of the group. In 1992, Eximbank began to issue, service, and underwrite its export credit insurance policies directly.

A variety of short-term and medium-term insurance policies are available to exporters, banks, and other eligible applicants. Basically, all the policies provide insurance protection against the risk of nonpayment by foreign buyers. If the foreign buyer fails to pay the exporter because of commercial reasons such as cash flow problems or insolvency, Eximbank will reimburse the exporter between 90 and 100 percent of the insured amount, depending upon the type of policy and buyer. If the loss is due to political factors, such as foreign exchange controls or war, Eximbank will reimburse the exporter for 100 percent of the insured amount. The insurance policies can be used by exporters as a marketing tool by enabling them to offer more competitive terms while protecting them against the risk of nonpayment. The exporter can also use the insurance policy as a financing tool by assigning the proceeds of the policy to a bank as collateral. Certain restrictions may apply to particular countries, depending upon Eximbank's experience, as well as existing economic and political conditions.

The **New-Export Policy** provides enhanced coverage to new exporters. Small firms with very few export credit sales are eligible for this policy. The policy will insure short-term credit sales (under 180 days) to approved foreign buyers. In addition to providing 95 percent coverage against commercial risk defaults and 100 percent against political risk, the policy offers lower premiums and no annual commercial risk loss deductible. The exporter can assign the policy to a bank as collateral. The **Umbrella Policy** operates in a slightly different manner. The policy itself is issued to an "administrator," such as a bank, trading company, insurance broker, or government agency. The policyholder administers the policy for multiple exporters and relieves the exporters of the administrative responsibilities associated with the policy. The short-term insurance protection is similar to the New-Export policy and does not have a commercial risk deductible. The proceeds of the policy may be assigned to a bank for financing purposes.

The **Multi-Buyer Policy** is used primarily by the experienced exporter. It provides insurance coverage on short-term export sales to many different buyers. Premiums are based on an exporter's sales profile, credit history, losses, terms of repayment, country and other factors. Based upon the exporter's experience and the buyer's creditworthiness, Eximbank may grant the exporter authority to preapprove specific buyers up to a certain limit.

The **Single-Buyer Policy** allows an exporter to selectively insure certain short-term transactions to preapproved buyers. Premiums are based on repayment term and transaction risk. There is also a Medium-Term Policy to cover sales to a single buyer for terms of between one and five years.

Private Export Funding Corporation (PEFCO)

PEFCO, a private corporation, is owned by a consortium of commercial banks and industrial companies. In cooperation with Eximbank, PEFCO provides medium- and long-term fixed-rate financing to foreign buyers. Eximbank guarantees all export loans made by PEFCO. Most PEFCO loans are to finance large projects, such as aircraft and power generation equipment, and as a result have very long terms (5 to 25 years). Since commercial banks usually do not extend such long terms, PEFCO fills a void in the market. PEFCO raises its funds in the capital markets through the issuance of long-term bonds. These bonds are readily marketable, since they are in effect secured by Eximbank-guaranteed loans.

Overseas Private Investment Corporation (OPIC)

OPIC, formed in 1971, is a self-sustaining federal agency responsible for insuring direct U.S. investments in foreign countries against the risks of currency inconvertibility, expropriation, and other political risks. Through the direct loan or guaranty program, OPIC will provide medium- to long-term financing to U.S. investors undertaking an overseas venture. In addition to the general insurance and finance programs, OPIC offers specific types of coverage for exporters bidding on or performing foreign contracts. American contractors can insure themselves against contractual disputes and even the wrongful calling of standby letters of credit.

Other Considerations

Beyond the insurance and financing, there are U.S. tax provisions that encourage international trade. Beginning in 1985, the Foreign Sales Corporation (FSC) replaced the Domestic International Sales Corporation (DISC) as the primary tax vehicle to promote U.S. exports. DISC provided a U.S. exporter with a tax deferral on a percentage of its income generated through export sales. The new FSC rules allow for the exporter to receive up to a 15 percent tax exemption on income earned through the FSC. However, the FSC must be incorporated offshore and meet certain procedural and administrative requirements.

SUMMARY

■ The common methods of payment for international trade are (1) prepayment (before goods are sent), (2) letters of credit, (3) drafts, (4) consignment, and (5) open account.

■ The most popular methods of financing international trade are (1) accounts receivable financing, (2) factoring, (3) letters of credit, (4) banker's acceptances, (5) short-term bank loans, (6) forfaiting, and (7) countertrade.

■ The major agencies that facilitate international trade with export insurance and/or loan programs are (1) Export-Import Bank, (2) Private Export Funding Corporation, and (3) Overseas Private Investment Corporation.

SELF-TEST FOR CHAPTER 13

(Answers are provided in Appendix A in the back of the text)

1. Explain why so many international transactions require international trade credit facilitated by commercial banks.

2. Explain the difference in the risk to the exporter between accounts receivable financing and factoring.

3. Explain how the Export-Import Bank can encourage U.S. firms to export to less developed countries where there is political risk.

QUESTIONS

1. How can a banker's acceptance be beneficial to (1) an exporter? (2) an importer? (3) a bank?

2. Why would an exporter provide financing for an importer? Is there much risk in this activity? Explain.

3. What is the role of a factor within international trade transactions? How can a factor aid an exporter?

4. What is the role today of the Export-Import Bank of the United States?

5. What are bills of lading, and how do they facilitate international trade transactions?

6. What is forfaiting? Specify the type of traded goods for which forfaiting is applied.

7. Briefly describe the role of PEFCO.

8. In this chapter, numerous forms of government insurance and guarantee programs are described. What motivates a government to establish so many programs?

9. Describe how the desirability for foreign trade would be affected if banks did not provide trade-related services.

10. What is countertrade?

11. Briefly describe the Working Capital Guarantee Program administered by the Export-Import Bank.

12. Describe the Direct Loan Program that is administered by the Export-Import Bank.

13. Describe the New-Export Policy.

14. Describe the role of the Overseas Private Investment Corporation (OPIC).

CASE: LETTERS OF CREDIT IN RUSSIA

Entrepreneurs Risk Stumbling as They Rush Into Russia

One Seafood Firm May Be Stuck With 7 Million Pounds of Frozen Fish

BY EUGENE CARLSON
Staff Reporter of THE WALL STREET JOURNAL

Russia's road to capitalism is full of potholes that can jar an unsuspecting Western business owner.

Seafood exporter Michael Graham discovered this last month when the fax machine in his Mobile, Ala., office delivered a disturbing message. It said that the foreign trade bank of the Russian republic, admitting to a "technical error," had canceled a $20.8 million irrevocable letter of credit it had issued five months earlier to Mr. Graham's firm, Ocean Traders of North America.

The surprise action puts into jeopardy an export order for 16,000 tons of fish that Mr. Graham had negotiated in December with a Russian customer. Since then, Mr. Graham had been stockpiling frozen fish on the Gulf Coast, and paying fishermen, wholesalers, and cold storage firms, to meet a mid-June shipping deadline.

Mr. Graham had assumed that the letter of credit, a device routinely used by importers and exporters to finance trade deals, was virtual insurance that he would be paid for his fish shipment. Letters of credit, recognized world-wide as a kind of foreign trade currency, are designed to guarantee that an exporter will be paid for a shipment by making a bank, rather than the ultimate customer, the payer. In theory, an irrevocable letter of credit can't be canceled without consent of all parties.

"We sincerely apologize for the trouble caused," the Russian bank, known as Rosvneshtorgbank, said in a two-page wire to New York's Chase Manhattan Bank, which is advising Mr. Graham.

The Gulf Coast seafood entrepreneur is livid. "I'm sitting here with seven million pounds of fish," says Mr. Graham, "and these guys are saying 'Oops. Sorry. We made a technical error, and we're not going to honor our obligation.' This could very easily put me out of business."

Other American entrepreneurs trying to do business in the former Soviet Union are encountering bureaucratic grief. Mr. Graham's problem is only a blip in the capitalist revolution now rolling through Russia, and other former Soviet republics and satellites. But revolutions don't follow a rule book, and the 27-year-old Mr. Graham is learning the hard way that entrepreneurs who do business in a society in economic flux can get burned.

The glitches, such as the one confronting Mr. Graham, come at a time when Russia's leaders are desperately seeking economic credibility through steps such as joining the International Monetary Fund, making the national currency convertible on foreign exchange markets and privatizing state-owned companies. But a huge gulf remains between the reform policies espoused by President Boris Yeltsin and the nuts-and-bolts decisions that bureaucrats make every day, experts say.

William McHenry, a Russia specialist at Georgetown University's business school, blames much of the problem on the unfamiliarity of Russia's new breed of capitalist theorists with capitalist realities. "The people who took over are younger, and more democratically oriented, but they don't have that much business experience," he says.

Ironically, Russia's free-market bureaucrats are stumbling over routine economic procedures that ran like clockwork under the

Communist bureaucrats. Mitch McCauley, an officer dealing in loans to Russia at the U.S. Export-Import Bank in Washington, says the old regime had a "stellar" reputation for paying its foreign debts. "That was one thing they had going for them. They never defaulted," he says.

There is sympathy for Mr. Graham's plight in Washington. "I don't believe [Rosvneshtorgbank has] the basis for backing out of the letter of credit," says Mr. McCauley. He says Ex-Im bank, a federal government agency, has specifically asked the Russian bank to pay off on Mr. Graham's export order.

"Mike knows what he's doing. He's pushing all the right buttons," says Mr. McCauley.

Mr. Graham started Ocean Traders a year ago. Prior to striking out on his own, he headed an international subsidiary of his family's seafood-trading company, Deep Sea Foods Inc. of Mobile.

The Russian fish order called for a total of 16,000 tons of frozen Atlantic mackerel, Gulf mullet, chub mackerel and pollock to be shipped by June 17. The buyer was Protec, a state-owned company that supplies equipment and food to Russia's armed forces.

Over the past five months, Mr. Graham has accumulated about a fifth of the total fish order. Payments to fish dealers and cold storage operators have cost about $700,000 so far, he says. Fees to banks and lawyers will push the total higher.

In a letter of explanation to the Ex-Im Bank, Rosvneshtorgbank Chairman Valery Telegin says the deal with Mr. Graham was all a mistake. He says his bank isn't authorized to do commercial transactions such as

Continued

CASE: LETTERS OF CREDIT IN RUSSIA

Continued

the fish contract between Protec and Ocean Traders. Moreover, he says, Protec lacks the hard currency to cover its obligations under the letter of credit.

The Russian foreign trade bank also reportedly is pressuring Chase Manhattan. Mr. Graham says that Robert Keller, an officer in the bank's North American trade division, this week read him a letter from Rosvneshtorgbank, in which the Russian bank threatened to cut off any future correspondent banking relations with Chase unless it persuades Mr. Graham to drop his letter of credit claim.

Mr. Keller "beseeched me to return the letter of credit," Mr. Graham says.

A Chase spokesman confirmed that the Russian bank told Chase it was canceling Mr. Graham;s letter of credit. But he said he "can't confirm" that Rosvneshtorgbank threatened Chase's correspondent banking relations. The Russian bank couldn't be reached for comment.

Meanwhile, Ex-Im Bank has said it would be happy to include Mr. Graham's fish deal under the new export-insurance program it opened last month with Russia. That would guarantee that Mr. Graham gets paid. There's just one hitch. The agreement setting up the export insurance program says all exports to Russia covered by Ex-Im Bank insurance must be approved by Rosvneshtorgbank.

With about one month remaining until the letter of credit expires, Mr. Graham says he is willing to sell his Russian customer the fish he has bought so far, so he can stop his losses.

He also has started shopping for other customers overseas. Unfortunately for Mr. Graham, the fish he has accumulated is considered an inferior food fish and enjoys little demand in North America. Ocean Traders has contacted potential customers in Egypt, Senegal and Algeria, but no one has bitten.

Mr. Graham says he is sympathetic to Russia's democratic goals, but isn't about to knuckle under. Indeed, he says he is thinking about a lawsuit. But taking on even an underfinanced sovereign nation is a tall order. "I don't know how many assets they have in the United States—whether it would be beating a dead horse," he sighs. "It's just me against the Russians."

Source: *The Wall Street Journal* (May 15, 1992): p. B2. Reprinted by permission of *The Wall Street Journal* © 1992 Dow Jones & Company, Inc. All rights reserved worldwide.

Questions

1. Explain how the irrevocable letter of credit would normally facilitate the business transaction between the Russian importer and Ocean Traders of North America (the U.S. exporter).

2. Explain how the cancellation of the letter of credit could create a trade crisis between the U.S. and Russia firms.

3. Why do you think situations like this (the cancellation of the letter of credit) are rare in industrialized countries?

4. Can you think of any alternative strategy that the U.S. exporter could have used to protect itself more when dealing with a Russian importer?

RYCO CHEMICAL COMPANY
Using Countertrade

Ryco Chemical Company produces a wide variety of chemical products that are sold to manufacturing firms. Some of the chemicals used in its production are imported from Concellos Chemical Company in Brazil. Concellos uses some chemicals in its production that are produced by Ryco (although Concellos has historically purchased these chemicals from another U.S. chemical company rather than from Ryco). The Brazilian cruzeiro has been depreciating continuously against the dollar, so that Concellos' cost of obtaining chemicals is always rising. Concellos would probably pay two times as much for these chemicals this year because of the weak cruzeiro. It would likely attempt to pass on most of its higher costs to its customers in the form of higher prices. However, it may not always be able to pass on higher costs from a weak cruzeiro, because its competitors make all their chemicals locally and their costs are directly tied to Brazil's inflation. Its competitors sell all their goods locally. This year, Concellos planned to charge Ryco a price in cruzeiros that was substantially above last year's price.

Representatives from Ryco were flying to Brazil to discuss its trade problems with Concellos. Specifically, Ryco wants to avoid its exposure to the high inflation rate in Brazil. This adverse effect is somewhat offset by the consistent decline in the value of the cruzeiro, allowing Ryco to obtain more cruzeiros with a given amount of dollars every year. However, the offset is not perfect and Ryco wants to create a better hedge against Brazilian inflation.

a) Describe a countertrade strategy that could reduce Ryco's exposure to Brazilian inflation.

b) Would Concellos be willing to consider this strategy? Is there any favorable effect on Concellos that may motivate Concellos to accept the strategy?

c) Assume that countertrade is agreed upon by both parties. Why would the cost of obtaining imports still rise over time for Concellos? Would Concellos earn lower profits as a result?

CHAPTER 14

SHORT-TERM FINANCING

All firms make short-term financing decisions periodically. Beyond the trade financing discussed in the previous chapter, multinational corporations (MNCs) obtain short-term financing to support other operations as well. Because MNCs have access to additional sources of funds, their short-term financing decisions are more complex than those of other companies. The specific objectives of this chapter are to

- explain why MNCs consider foreign financing,
- explain how MNCs determine whether to use foreign financing, and
- illustrate the possible benefits of financing with a portfolio of currencies.

SOURCES OF SHORT-TERM FINANCING _____

MNC parents and their subsidiaries typically use various methods of obtaining short-term funds to satisfy their liquidity needs. One method increasingly used in recent years is the issuing of **Euronotes,** or unsecured debt securities. The interest rates on these notes are based on LIBOR (the interest rate Eurobanks charge on interbank loans). They typically have maturities of one, three, or six months. Some MNCs continually roll them over as a form of intermediate-term financing. Commercial banks underwrite the notes for MNCs, and some commercial banks purchase them for their own investment portfolios.

In addition to Euronotes, MNCs also issue **Euro-commercial paper** to obtain short-term financing. Dealers issue this paper for MNCs without the backing of an underwriting syndicate, so a selling price is not guaranteed to the issuers. Maturities can be tailored to the investor's preferences. Dealers make a secondary market by offering to repurchase Euro-commercial paper before maturity.

Another popular source of short-term funds by MNCs is direct loans from Eurobanks, typically utilized to maintain a relationship with Eurobanks. If other sources of short-term funds become unavailable, MNCs will rely more heavily on direct loans from Eurobanks. Most MNCs maintain credit arrangements with various banks around the world. For example, Westinghouse has credit arrangements with more than 100 foreign and domestic banks.

INTERNAL FINANCING BY MNCs

Before an MNC's parent or subsidiary in need of funds searches for outside funding, it should determine whether there are any available internal funds. That is, it should check other subsidiaries' cash flow positions. If, for example, earnings have been high at particular subsidiaries and a portion of funds generated is simply invested locally in money market securities, the parent may request these funds from the subsidiaries. This is especially feasible during periods when the cost of obtaining funds in the parent's home country is relatively high.

Parents of MNCs can also attempt to be financed by subsidiaries through increasing their markups on supplies they send to the subsidiaries. In this case, the funds given to the parent by the subsidiary will never be returned. This method of supporting the parent can sometimes be more feasible than the previously discussed methods, if it avoids restrictions or taxes enforced by national governments (discussed more thoroughly in Chapter 15). Yet, this method itself may be restricted or limited by host governments where subsidiaries are located.

WHY MNCs CONSIDER FOREIGN FINANCING

Regardless of whether an MNC parent or subsidiary decides to obtain financing from subsidiaries or from some other source, it also must decide which currency to borrow. Even if it needs its home currency, it may prefer to borrow a foreign currency. Reasons for this preference follow.

Foreign Financing to Offset Foreign Receivables

A large firm may finance in a foreign currency to offset a net receivables position in that foreign currency. For example, consider a U.S. firm that has net receivables denominated in German marks. If it needs short-term funds, it can borrow marks and convert them to U.S. dollars for the purpose for which it needs funds. Then, the net receivables in marks will be used to pay off the loan. In this example, financing in a foreign currency reduces the firm's exposure to fluctuating exchange rates. This strategy is especially appealing if the interest rate of the foreign currency is low.

Foreign Financing to Reduce Costs

Even when an MNC parent or subsidiary is not attempting to cover foreign net receivables, it may still consider borrowing foreign currencies if the interest rates on such currencies are attractive. Financing in foreign currencies is common as a result of the development of the Eurocurrency market. The cost of financing can vary with the currency borrowed in the Eurocurrency market. A Eurocurrency loan may offer a slightly lower rate than a loan in the same currency through the home country. Therefore, a U.S.-based MNC, for example, may be able to obtain a lower rate when borrowing U.S. dollars in the Eurocurrency market than it could from a local bank. Yet, the U.S. MNC may also consider financing in a foreign currency through the Eurocurrency market, even if it needs U.S. dollars. Assume the Eurodollar financing rate is 12 percent, while the Euro-Swiss franc financing rate is 8 percent. The U.S. MNC can borrow Swiss francs and immediately convert those francs to dollars for use. Once the loan repayment is due, the U.S. firm will need to obtain Swiss francs in order to pay off the loan. If the Swiss franc value in terms of U.S. dollars has not changed from the time the loan was given until the loan is repaid, the U.S. firm will pay 8 percent on that loan.

Exhibit 14.1 illustrates how interest rates differ among currencies. The Swiss interest rate is typically lowest, while British and Canadian interest rates are often much higher. In some periods, there is a 7 percent differential between the highest and lowest interest rates.

DETERMINING THE EFFECTIVE FINANCING RATE

In reality, the value of the currency borrowed will most likely change with respect to the borrower's local currency over time. The actual cost of financing by the debtor firm will depend on (1) the interest rate charged by the bank that provided the loan, and (2) the movement in the borrowed currency's value over the life of the loan. Thus, the actual or "effective" financing rate may differ from the quoted interest rate. This point is illustrated in the following example.

A U.S. firm is given a one-year loan of SF1,000,000 at the quoted interest rate of 8 percent. When the U.S. firm receives the loan, it converts the Swiss francs to U.S. dollars to pay a supplier for materials. The exchange rate at that time is $.50 per SF, so the SF1,000,000 is converted to $500,000 (computed as SF1,000,000 × $.50 per SF = $500,000). One year later, the U.S. firm pays back the loan of SF1,000,000 plus interest of SF80,000 (interest computed as 8% × SF1,000,000). Thus, the total amount in Swiss francs needed by the U.S. firm is SF1,000,000 + SF80,000 = SF1,080,000 francs. Assume the Swiss franc appreciates from $.50 to $.60 by the time the loan is to be repaid. The firm will need to convert $648,000 (computed as SF1,080,000 × $.60 per SF) to the necessary number of francs for loan repayment.

To compute the effective financing rate, first determine the amount in dollars beyond the amount borrowed that was paid back. Then divide by the number of dollars borrowed (after converting the francs to dollars). Given that the firm borrowed the equivalent of $500,000 and paid back $648,000 for the loan, the effective financing rate in this case is $148,000/$500,000 = 29.6%. If the exchange rate remained constant throughout the life of the loan, the total loan repayment would have been $540,000, representing an effective rate of $40,000/$500,000 = 8%. Since the Swiss franc appreciated substantially in our example, the effective financing rate was very high. If the U.S. firm had anticipated the Swiss franc's substantial appreciation, it would not have borrowed the francs.

The effective financing rate (called r_f) is derived as follows:

$$r_f = (1 + i_f)\left[1 + \left(\frac{S_{t+1} - S}{S}\right)\right] - 1,$$

EXHIBIT 14.1   Short-Term Interest Rates for Various Countries
SOURCE: *International Economic Conditions*, Federal Reserve Bank of St. Louis, updated by author.

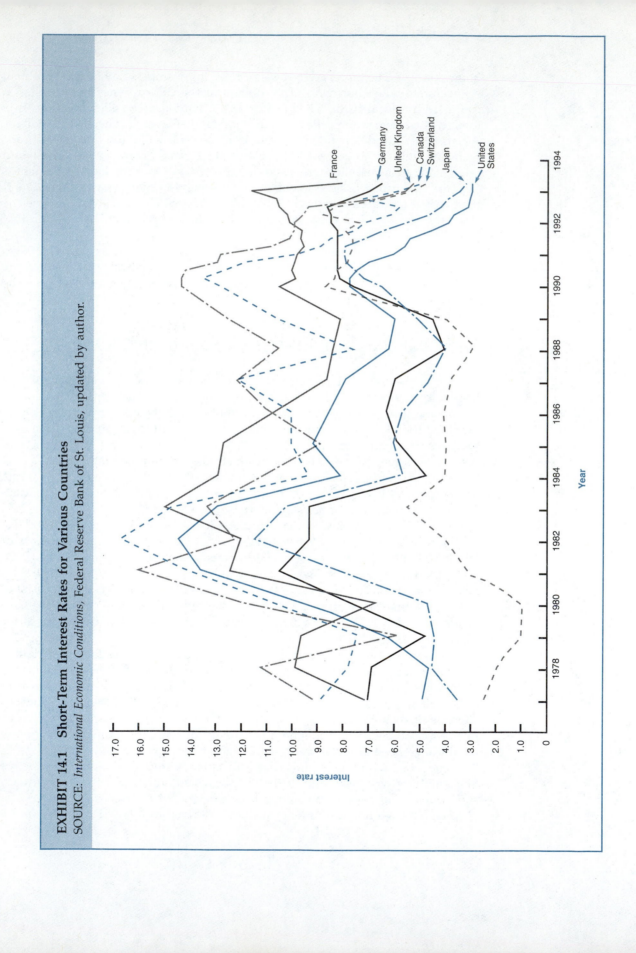

where i_f represents the financing rate of the foreign currency, and S and S_{t+1} represent the spot rate of the foreign currency at the beginning and end of the financing period, respectively. Since the terms in parentheses reflect the percentage change in the foreign currency's spot rate (denoted as e_f), the preceding equation can be rewritten as

$$r_f = (1 + i_f)(1 + e_f) - 1.$$

In the example, e_f reflects the percentage change in the Swiss franc (against the U.S. dollar) from the day francs were borrowed until the day they were paid back by the U.S. firm. The Swiss franc appreciated from $.50 to $.60, or by 20 percent over the life of the loan. With this information and the quoted interest rate of 8 percent, the effective financing rate on Swiss francs by the U.S. firm can be computed as

$$r_f = (1 + i_f)(1 + e_f) - 1$$
$$= (1 + .08)(1 + .20) - 1$$
$$= .296 \text{ or } 29.6\%,$$

which is the same rate determined from the alternative computational approach.

To test your understanding of financing in a foreign currency, consider a second example for the U.S. firm. Based on a quoted interest rate of 8 percent for the Swiss franc, and depreciation in the franc from $.50 (on the day funds were borrowed) to $.45 (on the day of loan repayment), what is the effective financing rate of a one-year loan from the viewpoint of a U.S. firm? The answer can be determined by first computing the percentage change in the Swiss franc's value: ($.45 − $.50)/$.50 = −10%. Next, the quoted interest rate (i_f) of 8% and the percentage change in the Swiss franc (e_f) of −10% can be inserted into the formula for the effective financing rate (r_f):

$$r_f = (1 + .08)[1 + (-.10)] - 1$$
$$= [(1.08)(.9)] - 1$$
$$= -.028 \text{ or } -2.8\%.$$

A *negative* effective financing rate implies the U.S. firm actually paid fewer dollars in total loan repayment than the number of dollars borrowed. Such a result can occur if the Swiss franc depreciates substantially over the life of the loan. This does not imply that a loan will be basically "free" anytime the currency borrowed depreciates over the life of the loan. Yet, depreciation of any amount will cause the effective financing rate to be less than the quoted interest rate, as can be substantiated by reviewing the formula for the effective financing rate.

The examples provided so far suggest that a firm should not consider only the quoted interest rates of foreign currencies when choosing which currency to borrow. The expected rate of appreciation or depreciation should also be considered.

CRITERIA CONSIDERED FOR FOREIGN FINANCING _____

There are various criteria an MNC must consider in its international financing decision, including

- Interest rate parity
- The forward rate as a forecast
- Exchange rate forecasts.

These criteria can influence the MNC's decision regarding which currency or currencies to borrow. Each is discussed in turn.

Interest Rate Parity

Recall that covered interest arbitrage was described in Chapter 7 as a foreign short-term investment with a simultaneous forward sale of the foreign currency denominating the foreign investment. From a financing perspective, covered interest arbitrage can be conducted as follows. First, borrow a foreign currency and convert that currency to the home currency for use. Also, simultaneously purchase the foreign currency forward to lock in the exchange rate of the currency needed to pay off the loan. If the foreign currency's interest rate is low, this may appear to be a feasible strategy. However, such a currency will normally exhibit a forward premium that reflects the differential between its interest rate and the home interest rate.

This can be shown by recognizing that the financing firm will be affected no longer by the percentage change in exchange rates, but instead by the percentage difference between the spot rate at which the foreign currency was converted to the local currency and the forward rate at which the foreign currency was repurchased. The difference reflects the forward premium (unannualized). The unannualized forward premium (p) can substitute for e_f in the equation introduced earlier, to determine the effective financing rate when covering in the forward market under conditions of interest rate parity:

$$r_f = (1 + i_f)(1 + p) - 1.$$

If interest rate parity exists, we have seen in Chapter 7 that

$$p = \frac{(1 + i_h)}{(1 + i_f)} - 1,$$

where i_h represents the home currency. When this equation is used to reflect financing rates, we can substitute the formula for p to determine the effective financing rate of a foreign currency under conditions of interest rate parity:

$$r_f = (1 + i_f)(1 + p) - 1$$

$$= (1 + i_f)\left[1 + \frac{(1 + i_h)}{(1 + i_f)} - 1\right] - 1$$

$$= i_h.$$

Thus, if interest rate parity exists, the attempt of covered interest arbitrage to finance with a low interest rate currency will result in an effective financing rate similar to the domestic rate.

Exhibit 14-2 summarizes the implications of a variety of scenarios relating to interest rate parity. Even if interest rate parity exists, financing with a foreign currency may still be feasible, but it would have to be conducted on an uncovered basis (without use of a forward hedge). That is, foreign financing may result in a lower financing cost than domestic financing, but it cannot be guaranteed (unless the firm has receivables in that same currency).

The Forward Rate as a Forecast

Assume the forward rate (F) of the foreign currency borrowed is used by firms as a predictor of the spot rate that will exist at the end of the financing period. The expected effective financing rate from borrowing a foreign currency would be forecasted by substituting F for S_{t+1} in the following equation:

EXHIBIT 14.2 Implications of Interest Rate Parity for Financing	Scenario	Implications
	1. Interest rate parity holds.	Foreign financing and a simultaneous hedge of that position in the forward market will result in financing costs similar to those in domestic financing.
	2. Interest rate parity holds, and the forward rate is an accurate forecast of the future spot rate.	Uncovered foreign financing will result in financing costs similar to those in domestic financing.
	3. Interest rate parity holds, and the forward rate is expected to overestimate the future spot rate.	Uncovered foreign financing is expected to result in lower financing costs than those in domestic financing.
	4. Interest rate parity holds, and the forward rate is expected to underestimate the future spot rate.	Uncovered foreign financing is expected to result in higher financing costs than those in domestic financing.
	5. Interest rate parity does not hold; the forward premium (discount) exceeds (is less than) the interest rate differential.	Foreign financing with a simultaneous hedge of that position in the forward market results in higher financing costs than those in domestic financing.
	6. Interest rate parity does not hold; the forward premium (discount) is less than (exceeds) the interest rate differential.	Foreign financing with a simultaneous hedge of that position in the forward market results in lower financing costs than those in domestic financing.

$$r_f = (1 + i_f)\left[1 + \frac{S_{t+1} - S}{S}\right] - 1$$

$$r_f = (1 + i_f)\left[1 + \frac{F - S}{S}\right] - 1.$$

As already shown, the right side of this equation is equal to the home currency financing rate if interest rate parity exists. If the forward rate is an accurate estimator of the future spot rate S_{t+1}, the foreign financing rate will be similar to the home financing rate.

When interest rate parity exists here, the forward rate can be used as a break-even point to assess the financing decision. When a firm is financing with the foreign currency (and not covering the foreign currency position), the effective financing rate will be less than the domestic rate if the future spot rate of the foreign currency (spot rate at the time of loan repayment) is less than the forward rate (at the time the loan is granted). Conversely, the effective financing rate in a foreign loan will be greater than the domestic rate if the future spot rate of the foreign currency turns out to be greater than the forward rate.

If the forward rate is an unbiased predictor of the future spot rate, then the effective financing rate of a foreign currency will on average be equal to the domestic financing rate. In this case, firms that consistently borrow foreign currencies will not achieve lower financing costs. While the effective financing rate in some periods may turn out to be lower than the domestic rate, it will be higher in other periods, causing an offsetting effect. Firms that believe the forward rate is an unbiased predictor of the future spot rate will prefer borrowing their home currency, where the financing rate is known with certainty and is not expected to be any higher on average than foreign financing.

Exchange Rate Forecasts

While the forecasting capabilities of firms are somewhat limited, some firms may make decisions based on cycles in currency movements. Firms may use the recent movements as a forecast of future movements to determine whether they should borrow a foreign currency. This strategy would have been successful on average if utilized in the past. It will be successful in the future if currency movements continue to move in one direction for long periods of time.

Once the firm develops a forecast for the exchange rate's percentage change over the financing period (e_f), it can use this forecast along with the foreign interest rate to forecast the effective financing rate of a foreign currency. The forecasted rate can then be compared to the domestic financing rate. For example, assume a U.S. firm needs funds for one year, and is aware that the one-year interest rate in U.S. dollars is 12 percent and the interest rate from borrowing Swiss francs is 8 percent. Assume the U.S. firm forecasts that the Swiss franc will appreciate from its current rate of $.45 to $.459, or by 2 percent over the next year. The expected value for e_f (written as $E(e_f)$) will therefore be 2 percent. Thus, the expected effective financing rate [$E(r_f)$] will be

$$E(r_f) = (1 + i_f)[1 + E(e_f)] - 1$$

$$= (1 + .08)(1 + .02) - 1$$

$$= .1016, \text{ or } 10.16\%.$$

In this example, financing in Swiss francs is expected to be less expensiv than financing in U.S. dollars. However, the value for e_f is forecasted and therefore is not known with certainty. Thus, there is no guarantee that foreign financing will truly be less costly.

Deriving a Value for e_f that Equates Domestic and Foreign Rates.

The U.S. firm may attempt at least to determine what value of e_f would make the effective rate from foreign financing the same as domestic financing. To determine this value, begin with the effective financing rate formula and solve e_f as shown:

$$r_f = (1 + i_f)(1 + e_f) - 1$$

$$(1 + r_f) = (1 + i_f)(1 + e_f)$$

$$\frac{(1 + r_f)}{(1 + i_f)} = (1 + e_f)$$

$$\frac{(1 + r_f)}{(1 + i_f)} - 1 = e_f.$$

Since the U.S. financing rate is 12 percent in our example above, that rate is plugged in for r_f. We can also plug in 8 percent for i_f, so that the break-even value of e_f is

$$e_f = \frac{(1 + r_f)}{(1 + i_f)} - 1$$

$$= \frac{(1 + .12)}{(1 + .08)} - 1$$

$$= .037037, \text{ or } 3.7037\%.$$

This suggests the Swiss franc must appreciate by about 3.7 percent over the loan period to make the Swiss franc loan as costly as a loan in U.S. dollars. Any smaller degree of appreciation would make the Swiss franc loan less costly. The U.S. firm can use this information when determining whether to borrow U.S. dollars or Swiss francs. If it expects the Swiss franc to appreciate by more than 3.7 percent over the loan life, it should prefer borrowing in U.S. dollars. If it expects the Swiss franc to appreciate by less than 3.7 percent, or to depreciate, its decision is more complex. If the potential savings from financing with the foreign currency outweighs the risk involved, then the firm should choose that route. The final decision here will be influenced by the firm's degree of risk aversion.

Use of Probability Distributions.

To gain more insight in the financing decision, the firm may wish to develop a probability distribution for the percentage change in value for a particular foreign currency over the financing horizon. As discussed in Chapter 9, even expert forecasts are not always accurate. Thus, it is sometimes useful to develop a probability distribution when forecasting, instead of relying on a single point estimate. Using the probability distribution of possible percentage changes in the currency's value, along with the currency's interest rate, the firm can determine the probability distribution of the possible effective financing rates for the currency. Then, it can compare this distribution to the known financing rate of the home currency in order to make its financing decision. An example follows.

Assume a U.S. firm is deciding whether to borrow Swiss francs for one year. It finds that the quoted interest rate for the Swiss franc is 8 percent, and the quoted rate for the U.S. dollar is 15 percent. The firm then develops a probability distribution for the Swiss franc's possible percentage change in value over the life of the loan. The probability distribution is displayed in Exhibit 14.3. The first row in Exhibit 14.3 shows there is a 5 percent probability of a 6 percent depreciation in the Swiss franc over the loan life. If the Swiss franc does depreciate by 6 percent, the effective financing rate would be 1.52 percent. This implies there is a 5 percent probability that the U.S. firm will incur a 1.52 percent effective financing rate on its loan. The second row shows there is a 10 percent probability of a 4 percent depreciation in the Swiss franc over the loan life. If the Swiss franc does depreciate by 4 percent, the effective financing rate would be 3.68 percent. This implies there is a 10 percent probability that the U.S. firm will incur a 3.68 percent effective financing rate on its loan. For each possible percentage change in the Swiss franc's value, there is a corresponding effective financing rate. We can associate each possible effective financing rate (Column 3) with a probability of that occurring (Column 2). From these two columns we can attain an expected value for the effective financing rate of the Swiss franc. An expected value of the effective financing rate is determined by multiplying each possible effective financing rate by its associated probability. Based on the information in Exhibit 14.3, the expected value of the effective financing rate, referred to as $E(r_f)$, is computed:

$$
\begin{aligned}
E(r_f) &= 5\%(1.52\%) + 10\%(3.68\%) + 15\%(6.92\%) + 20\%(9.08\%) \\
&\quad + 20\%(12.32\%) + 15\%(14.48\%) \\
&\quad + 10\%(16.64\%) + 5\%(18.80\%) \\
&= .076\% + .368\% + 1.038\% + 1.816\% \\
&\quad + 2.464\% + 2.172\% + 1.664\% + .94\% \\
&= 10.538\%.
\end{aligned}
$$

EXHIBIT 14.3 Analysis of Financing with a Foreign Currency	Possible Rate of Change in the Swiss Franc Over the Life of the Loan (e_f)	Probability of Occurrence	Effective Financing Rate If This Rate of Change in the Swiss Franc Does Occur (r_f)
	−6%	5%	(1.08)[1 + (−6%)] − 1 = 1.52%
	−4	10	(1.08)[1 + (−4%)] − 1 = 3.68
	−1	15	(1.08)[1 + (−1%)] − 1 = 6.92
	+1	20	(1.08)[1 + (1%)] − 1 = 9.08
	+4	20	(1.08)[1 + (4%)] − 1 = 12.32
	+6	15	(1.08)[1 + (6%)] − 1 = 14.48
	+8	10	(1.08)[1 + (8%)] − 1 = 16.64
	+10	5	(1.08)[1 + (10%)] − 1 = 18.80
		100%	

It has been determined that the expected value of the effective financing rate for borrowing Swiss francs is 10.538 percent. Given this information, should the U.S firm borrow Swiss francs or U.S. dollars? The answer may depend on what the interest rate is for a U.S. dollar loan. Recall that it is assumed to be 15 percent. If you are the treasurer of the U.S. firm, are you going to borrow U.S. dollars (and pay 15 percent interest) or borrow Swiss francs (with an expected value of 10.538 percent for the effective financing rate)? You may choose to borrow U.S. dollars, since you desire to know with certainty the rate you will pay for your loan. However, you may be willing to borrow Swiss francs if you feel the potential reduction in financing costs from a Swiss franc loan outweighs the risk involved. What is the risk in this case? Using Exhibit 14.3, you can see that the risk reflects the 5 percent chance (probability) that the effective financing rate on Swiss francs will be 18.8 percent, and the 10 percent chance that the effective financing rate on Swiss francs will be 16.64 percent. Either of these possibilities represents a greater expense to the U.S. firm than would be incurred if it borrowed U.S. dollars. For this reason, some of the more conservative firms may choose to avoid the uncertainty by simply borrowing U.S. dollars. Other firms may be willing to borrow francs and tolerate the risk.

To further assess the decision regarding which currency to borrow, the information in Columns 2 and 3 of Exhibit 14.3 is used to develop a probability distribution in Exhibit 14.4. This exhibit illustrates the probability of each possible effective financing rate that may occur if the U.S. firm borrows Swiss francs. Notice that the U.S. interest rate (15 percent) is included in Exhibit 14.4 for comparison purposes. There is no distribution of possible outcomes for the U.S. rate, since the rate of 15 percent is known with certainty (no exchange rate risk exists). There is a 15 percent probability that the U.S. rate will be lower than the effective rate on Swiss francs and an 85 percent chance that the U.S. rate will be greater than the effective rate on Swiss francs. This information can assist the firm in its financing decision.

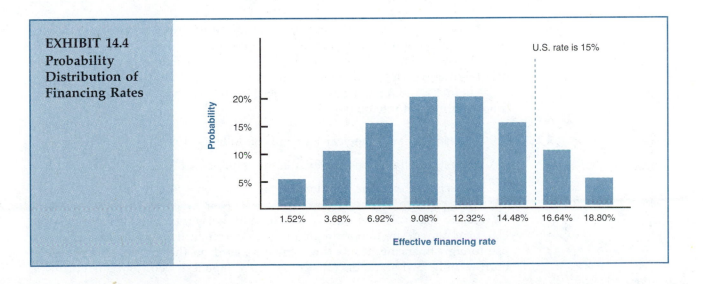

EXHIBIT 14.4 Probability Distribution of Financing Rates

ACTUAL RESULTS FROM FOREIGN FINANCING _____

The fact that some firms utilize foreign financing suggests that they believe reduced financing costs can be achieved. To assess this issue, the effective financing rates of the Swiss franc and the U.S. dollar are compared in Exhibit 14.5 from the perspective of a U.S. firm. The data are segmented into annual periods. The fourth column measures the effective financing rate for the Swiss franc (based on information provided in Columns 2 and 3), while the fifth column shows the U.S. rate. The sixth column represents the difference. A positive difference suggests a lower U.S. financing rate, while a negative difference suggests lower costs when financing with Swiss francs.

The borrowing of Swiss francs was most advantageous from 1980 through 1984. During these years, the franc depreciated substantially, so that the effective financing rate on francs was usually negative from a U.S. firm's perspective. The difference between Swiss franc and dollar financing rates during these years ranged from 14 percent to 34.5 percent. As an extreme example, the Swiss franc's effective financing rate was −24.9 percent in 1984, versus 9.6 percent for dollars, causing a difference of 34.5 percent. A U.S. firm that borrowed francs rather than dollars to obtain a $1,000,000 loan would therefore have reduced financing costs by $345,000 (34.5% × $1,000,000).

The results of borrowing francs have not always been so favorable. In the mid-1980s, the franc appreciated, causing its effective financing rate (from a U.S. perspective) to be high. Therefore, U.S. firms that borrowed francs during this time incurred much higher financing costs than they would have if they had borrowed dollars.

Exhibit 14.5 demonstrates the potential savings in financing costs that can be achieved if the foreign currency depreciates against the firm's home currency. It also demonstrates how the foreign financing could backfire if the firm's expectations are incorrect and the foreign currency appreciates over the financing period.

FINANCING WITH A PORTFOLIO OF CURRENCIES _____

While foreign financing can result in significantly lower financing costs, the variance in foreign financing costs over time is higher. MNCs may be able to achieve lower financing costs without excessive risk by financing with a portfolio of foreign currencies, as demonstrated here.

Assume a U.S. firm needs to borrow $100,000 for one year and obtains the following interest rate quotes:

Interest rate for a one-year loan in U.S. dollars = 15%

Interest rate for a one-year loan in Swiss francs = 8%

Interest rate for a one-year loan in Japanese yen = 9%.

Due to relatively low quotes for a loan in Swiss francs or Japanese yen, the U.S. firm may desire to borrow in a foreign currency. If the U.S. firm decides to use foreign financing, it has three choices based on the information given: (1) borrow only Swiss francs, (2) borrow only Japanese yen, and (3) borrow a

EXHIBIT 14.5   Comparison of Financing with SF versus $

Financing Date	One-Year Foreign (Swiss) Interest Rate	Percentage Change in Exchange Rate of SF Over One-Year Period	Effective Financing Rate of SF	One-Year U.S. Interest Rate	Difference
1/75	4.0%	–3.1%	.8%	5.8%	–5.0%
1/76	2.0	7.0	9.1	5.0	4.1
1/77	3.5	22.5	26.8	5.3	21.5
1/78	2.0	23.4	25.8	7.2	18.6
1/79	3.0	2.6	5.7	10.0	–4.3
1/80	4.0	–10.3	–6.7	11.6	–18.3
1/81	2.3	–2.1	.1	14.1	–14.0
1/82	2.9	–9.9	–7.3	10.7	–18.0
1/83	1.3	–8.5	–7.3	8.6	–15.9
1/84	1.8	–26.2	–24.9	9.6	–34.5
1/85	3.3	24.5	28.6	7.5	21.1
1/86	3.8	27.9	32.8	6.0	26.8
1/87	3.2	24.8	28.8	5.8	23.0
1/88	3.2	–15.0	–12.3	6.0	–18.3
1/89	4.0	–2.7	1.2	7.7	–6.5
1/90	7.4	18.0	26.7	7.7	19.0
1/91	7.7	–4.4	3.0	6.0	–3.0
1/92	7.4	–6.9	0.0	3.1	–3.1
1/93	5.1	–0.8	4.3	3.0	1.3

mixture or portfolio of francs and yen. Assume the U.S. firm has established possible percentage changes in the spot rate from the time the loan would begin until loan repayment for both the Swiss franc and Japanese yen, as shown in Column 2 of Exhibit 14.6. For each possible percentage change that might occur, a probability of that occurrence is disclosed in the third column. Based on the assumed interest rate of 8 percent for the Swiss franc, the effective financing rate is computed for each possible percentage change in the Swiss franc's spot rate over the loan life. There is a 30 percent chance the Swiss franc will appreciate by 1 percent over the loan life. If the Swiss franc appreciates by 1 percent, the effective financing rate will be 9.08 percent. Thus, there is a 30 percent chance that the effective financing rate will be 9.08 percent. Furthermore, there is a 50 percent chance that the effective financing rate will be 11.24 percent and a 20 percent chance that it will be 17.72 percent. Given that the U.S. loan rate is 15 percent, there is only a 20 percent chance that the financing in Swiss francs will result in a higher financing cost than that of domestic financing.

The lower section of Exhibit 14.6 provides information on Japanese yen. For example, the yen has a 35 percent chance of depreciating by 1 percent over the loan life, and so on. Based on the assumed 9 percent interest rate and the exchange rate fluctuation forecasts, there is a 35 percent chance that the effective financing rate will be 7.91 percent, a 40 percent chance that it will be 12.27

EXHIBIT 14.6   Development of Possible Effective Financing Rates

Currency	Possible Percentage Change in the Spot Rate Over the Loan Life	Probability of That Percentage Change in the Spot Rate Occurring	Computation of Effective Financing Rate Based on That Percentage Change in the Spot Rate
Swiss franc	1%	30%	$(1.08)[1 + (.01)] - 1 = .0908$, or 9.08%
Swiss franc	3	50	$(1.08)[1 + (.03)] - 1 = .1124$, or 11.24%
Swiss franc	9	20	$(1.08)[1 + (.09)] - 1 = .1772$, or 17.72%
		100%	
Japanese yen	−1%	35%	$(1.09)[1 + (-.01)] - 1 = .0791$, or 7.91%
Japanese yen	3	40	$(1.09)[1 + (.03)] - 1 = .1227$, or 12.27%
Japanese yen	7	25	$(1.09)[1 + (.07)] - 1 = .1663$, or 16.63%
		100%	

percent, and a 25 percent chance that it will be 16.63 percent. Given the 15 percent rate on U.S. dollar financing, there is a 25 percent chance that financing in Japanese yen will be more costly than domestic financing. Before examining the third possible foreign financing strategy (the portfolio approach), determine the expected value of the effective financing rate for each foreign currency by itself. This is accomplished by totaling the products of each possible effective financing rate and its associated probability as follows:

Currency	Computation of Expected Value of Effective Financing Rate
Swiss francs	(30%) (9.08%) + 50% (11.24%) + 20% (17.72%) = 11.888%
Japanese yen	(35%) (7.91%) + 40% (12.27%) + 25% (16.63%) = 11.834%

The expected financing costs of the two currencies are almost the same. The individual degree of risk (that the costs of financing will turn out to be higher than domestic financing) is about the same for each currency. If the U.S firm does choose to finance with only one of these foreign currencies, it is difficult to pinpoint (based on our analysis) which currency is more appropriate. Now, consider the third and final foreign financing strategy: the portfolio approach.

Using the information in Exhibit 14.6, there are three possibilities for the Swiss franc's effective financing rate. The same holds true for the Japanese yen. If a U.S. firm borrows half of its needed funds in each of the foreign currencies, then there will be nine possibilities for this portfolio's effective financing rate, as shown in Exhibit 14.7. The first two columns list all possible joint effective financing rates. The third column computes the joint probability of that occurrence. The fourth column shows the computation of the portfolio's effective financing rate based on the possible rates disclosed for the individual currencies shown in the first two columns.

EXHIBIT 14.7   Analysis of Financing with Two Foreign Currencies

(1)		(2)	(3)	(4)
Possible Joint Effective Financing Rates			**Computation of Joint Probability**	**Computation of Effective Financing Rate of Portfolio (50% of Total Funds Borrowed in Each Currency)**
Swiss Franc	Japanese Yen			
9.08%	7.91%		(30%) (35%) = 10.5%	.5 (9.08%) + .5 (7.91%) = 8.495%
9.08	12.27		(30%) (40%) = 12.0	.5 (9.08%) + .5 (12.27%) = 10.675
9.08	16.63		(30%) (25%) = 7.5	.5 (9.08%) + .5 (16.63%) = 12.885
11.24	7.91		(50%) (35%) = 17.5	.5 (11.24%) + .5 (7.91%) = 9.575
11.24	12.27		(50%) (40%) = 20.0	.5 (11.24%) + .5 (12.27%) = 11.755
11.24	16.63		(50%) (25%) = 12.5	.5 (11.24%) + .5 (16.63%) = 13.935
17.72	7.91		(20%) (35%) = 7.0	.5 (17.72%) + .5 (7.91%) = 12.815
17.72	12.27		(20%) (40%) = 8.0	.5 (17.72%) + .5 (12.27%) = 14.995
17.72	16.63		(20%) (25%) = 5.0	.5 (17.72%) + .5 (16.63%) = 17.175
			100.0%	

An examination of the top row will help to clarify the table. This row suggests that one possible outcome of borrowing both Swiss francs and Japanese yen is that they will exhibit effective financing rates of 9.08 percent and 7.91 percent, respectively. The probability of the Swiss franc rate's occurring is 30 percent, while the probability of the Japanese yen rate's occurring is 35 percent. Recall that these percentages were given in Exhibit 14.6. The joint probability that both of these rates will occur simultaneously is (30%)(35%) = 10.5%. Assuming that half (50%) of the funds needed are to be borrowed from each currency, the portfolio's effective financing rate will be .5(9.08%) + .5(7.91%) = 8.495% (if those individual effective financing rates occur for each currency).

A similar procedure was used to develop the remaining eight rows in Exhibit 14.7. From this table, there is a 10.5 percent chance that the portfolio's effective financing rate will be 8.495 percent, a 12 percent chance that it will be 10.675 percent, and so on.

Exhibit 14.8 displays the probability distribution for the portfolio's effective financing rate that was derived in Exhibit 14.7. This exhibit shows that financing with a portfolio (50 percent financing in Swiss francs with the remaining 50 percent financed in Japanese yen) has only a 5 percent chance of being more costly than domestic financing. These results are more favorable than those of either individual foreign currency, as is explained next.

Portfolio Diversification Effects. When both foreign currencies are borrowed, the only way the portfolio will exhibit a higher effective financing rate than the domestic rate is for *both* currencies to experience their maximum possible level of appreciation (which is 9 percent for the Swiss franc and 7 percent for the Japanese yen). If only one does, the severity of its appreciation

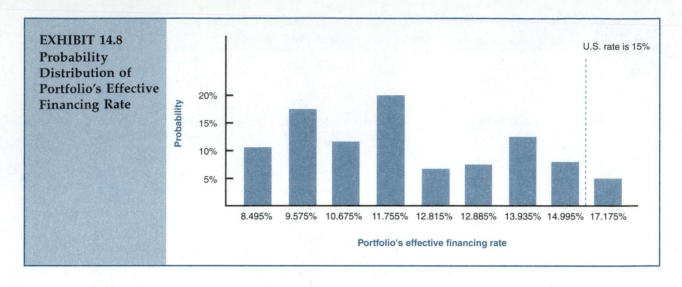

EXHIBIT 14.8
Probability Distribution of Portfolio's Effective Financing Rate

will be somewhat offset by the other currency's not appreciating to such a large extent. The probability of maximum appreciation is 20 percent for the Swiss franc and 25 percent for the Japanese yen. The joint probability of both of these events occurring simultaneously is (20%)(25%) = 5%. This is an advantage of financing in a portfolio of foreign currencies. In this example, the U.S. firm has a 95 percent chance of attaining lower costs with the foreign portfolio than with domestic financing.

The expected value of the effective financing rate for the portfolio can be determined by multiplying the percentage financed in each currency by the expected value of that currency's individual effective financing rate. Recall that the expected value was 11.888 percent for the Swiss franc and 11.834 percent for the Japanese yen. Thus, for a portfolio representing 50 percent of funds borrowed in each currency, the expected value of the effective financing rate is .5(11.888%) + .5(11.834%) = 11.861%. Based on an overall comparison, the expected value of the portfolio's effective financing rate is very similar to that from financing solely in either foreign currency. However, the risk (of incurring a higher effective financing rate than the domestic rate) when financing with the portfolio is substantially less.

In the example, the computation of joint probabilities requires the assumption that the movements in the two currencies are independent. If movements of the two currencies were actually highly positively correlated, then financing in a portfolio of currencies would not be as beneficial as demonstrated, since there is a strong likelihood of both currencies experiencing a high level of appreciation simultaneously. If the two currencies are not highly correlated, they are less likely to simultaneously appreciate to such a degree. Thus, the chances that the portfolio's effective financing rate will exceed the U.S. rate are reduced when the currencies included in the portfolio are not highly positively correlated.

The present example includes two currencies in the portfolio. Financing with a more diversified portfolio of additional currencies that exhibit low interest rates may even increase the probability that foreign financing will be less costly than domestic financing, since several currencies are not likely to move in tandem and therefore simultaneously appreciate to offset the advantage of their low interest rates. Again, the degree to which these currencies are correlated with each other is important here. If all currencies are highly positively correlated with each other, financing with such a portfolio would not be very different from financing with a single foreign currency.

Repeated Financing with a Currency Portfolio

A firm that repeatedly finances in a currency portfolio would normally prefer to compose a financing package that exhibits a somewhat predictable effective financing rate on a periodic basis. The more volatile a portfolio's effective financing rate over time, the more uncertainty (risk) there is about the effective financing rate that will exist in any period. The degree of volatility depends on the standard deviations and paired correlations of effective financing rates of the individual currencies within the portfolio.

We can use the portfolio variance as a measurement for degree of volatility. The variance of a two-currency portfolio's effective financing rate [$VAR(r_p)$] over time is computed as

$$VAR\,(r_p) = w^2_A\sigma^2_A + w^2_B\sigma^2_B + 2w_Aw_B\sigma_A\sigma_B CORR_{AB},$$

where w_A and w_B represent the percentage of total funds financed from Currencies A and B respectively, σ^2_A and σ^2_B represent the individual variances of each currency's effective financing rate over time, and $CORR_{AB}$ reflects the correlation coefficient of the two currencies' effective financing rates. Since the percentage exchange rate change plays an important role in influencing the effective financing rate, it should not be surprising that $CORR_{AB}$ is strongly affected by the correlation between the exchange rate fluctuations of the two currencies. A low correlation between currency fluctuations may force $CORR_{AB}$ to be low.

To illustrate how the variance in a portfolio's effective financing rate is related to characteristics of the component currencies, assume the following information based on historical information of several three-month periods:

Mean effective financing rate of Canadian dollar for three months = 3%

Mean effective financing rate of Swiss franc for three months = 2%

Standard deviation of Canadian dollar's effective financing rate = .04

Standard deviation of Swiss franc's effective financing rate = .09

Correlation coefficient of effective financing rates of these two currencies = .10.

Given this information, the mean effective rate on a portfolio (r_p) of funds financed 50 percent by Canadian dollars and 50 percent by Swiss francs is determined by totaling the weighted individual effective financing rates:

$$r_p = w_Ar_A + w_Br_B$$
$$= .5(.03) + .5(.02)$$
$$= .015 + .01$$
$$= .025 \; or \; 2.5\%.$$

The variance of this portfolio's effective financing rate over time is

$$VARr_p = .5^2(.04)^2 + .5^2(.09)^2 + 2(.5)(.5)(.04)(.09)(.10)$$

$$= .25(.0016) + .25(.0081) + .00018$$

$$= .0004 + .002025 + .00018$$

$$= .002605.$$

This example suggests how an MNC can use historical data to determine the mean effective financing rate and variance of a two-currency portfolio. Thus, it can compare various financing packages to see which package would have been most appropriate. The MNC may be more interested in estimating the mean return and variability for repeated financing in a particular portfolio in the future. There is no guarantee that past data will be indicative of the future. Yet, if the individual variability and paired correlations are somewhat stable over time, the historical variability of the portfolio's effective financing rate should provide a reasonable forecast.

This analysis is not restricted to just two currencies. The mean effective financing rate for a currency portfolio of any size will be determined by totaling the respective individual effective financing rates weighted by the percentage of funds financed with each currency. Solving the variance of a portfolio's effective financing rate becomes more complex as more currencies are added to the portfolio, but computer software packages are commonly applied to more easily determine the solution.

SUMMARY

■ MNCs may use foreign financing to offset anticipated cash inflows in foreign currencies, so that exposure to exchange rate risk is minimized. Alternatively, some MNCs may use foreign financing in an attempt to reduce their financing costs. Foreign financing costs may be lower if the foreign interest rate is relatively low, or if the foreign currency borrowed depreciates over the financing period.

■ MNCs can determine the effective financing rate that they expect for any foreign currency over the period in which financing will be needed. The expected effective financing rate is dependent on the quoted interest rate of the foreign currency and the forecasted percentage change in the currency's value over the financing period.

■ When MNCs borrow a portfolio of currencies that have a low interest rate, they can increase the probability of achieving relatively low financing costs, if the currencies' values are not highly correlated.

SELF-TEST FOR CHAPTER 14

(Answers provided in Appendix A in the back of the text)

1. Assume that the interest rate in Italy is 9 percent. A U.S. firm plans to borrow Italian lire, convert them to dollars and repay the loan in one year.

What will be the effective financing rate if the lira depreciates by 6 percent? If the lira appreciates by 3 percent?

2. Using the information in Question 1, and assuming a 50 percent chance of either scenario occurring, determine the expected value of the effective financing rate.

3. Assume the Swiss one-year interest rate is 5%, while the U.S. one-year interest rate is 8%. What percentage change in the Swiss franc would cause a U.S. firm borrowing francs to incur the same effective financing rate as it would if it borrowed dollars?

4. The spot rate of the German mark is $.62. The one-year forward rate of the German mark is $.60. The German one-year interest rate is 9%. Assume the forward rate is used to forecast the future spot rate. Determine the expected effective financing rate for a U.S. firm that borrows marks to finance its U.S. business.

5. A U.S. company plans to repeatedly borrow two European currencies with low interest rates to finance its U.S. operations. Will the variance of the two-currency portfolio's effective financing rate be much lower than the variance of either individual currency's effective financing rate? Explain.

QUESTIONS _____

1. Explain why an MNC parent would consider financing from its subsidiaries.

2. Discuss the use of specifying a break-even point when financing in a foreign currency.

3. Discuss the development of a probability distribution of effective financing rates when financing in a foreign currency. How is this distribution developed?

4. Once the probability distribution of effective financing rates from financing in a foreign currency is developed, how can it be used in deciding whether to finance in the foreign currency or the home currency?

5. How can a firm finance in a foreign currency and not necessarily be exposed to exchange rate risk?

6. Explain how a firm's degree of risk aversion enters into its decision on whether to finance in a foreign currency or a local currency. What motivates the firm to even consider financing in a foreign currency?

7. Assume a U.S.-based MNC needs $3 million for a one-year period. Within one year, it will generate enough U.S. dollars to pay off the loan. It is considering three options: (1) borrowing U.S. dollars at an interest rate of 6 percent, (2) borrowing Swiss francs at an interest rate of 3 percent, or (3) borrowing German marks at an interest rate of 4 percent. The MNC has forecasted that the Swiss franc will appreciate by 1 percent over the next year, and that the German mark will appreciate by 3 percent. What is the expected "effective" financing rate for each of the three options? Which

option appears to be most feasible? Why might the MNC not necessarily choose the option reflecting the lowest effective financing rate?

8. How is it possible for a firm to incur a negative effective financing rate?

9. If interest rate parity does not hold, what strategy should a U.S. firm consider when it needs short-term financing? Assume a U.S. firm needs dollars. It borrows German marks at a lower interest rate than that for dollars. If interest rate parity exists and if the forward rate of the mark is a reliable predictor of the future spot rate, what does this suggest about the feasibility of such a strategy? If the MNC expects the current spot rate to be a more reliable predictor of the future spot rate, what does this suggest about the feasibility of such a strategy?

10. A firm needs local currency. Assume the local one-year loan rate is 15 percent, while a foreign one-year loan rate is 7 percent. By how much must the foreign currency appreciate to cause the foreign loan to be more costly than a local loan?

11. A U.S.-based MNC decides to borrow Japanese yen for one year. The interest rate on the borrowed yen is 8 percent. The MNC has developed the following probability distribution for the yen's degree of fluctuation against the dollar:

Possible Degree of Fluctuation of Yen against the Dollar	Percentage Probability
−4%	20%
−1	30
0	10
3	40

Given this information, what is the expected value of the effective financing rate of the Japanese yen from the U.S. corporation's perspective?

12. Assume that interest rate parity exists. If a firm believed that the forward rate was an unbiased predictor of the future spot rate, would it expect to achieve lower financing costs by consistently borrowing a foreign currency with a low interest rate?

13. Assume a U.S firm considers obtaining 40 percent of its one-year financing in Canadian dollars and 60 percent in Swiss francs. The forecasts of appreciation in the Canadian dollar and Swiss franc for the next year are as follows:

Currency	Possible Percentage Change in the Spot Rate Over the Loan Life	Probability of That Percentage Change in the Spot Rate Occurring
Canadian dollar	4%	70%
Canadian dollar	7	30
Swiss franc	6	50
Swiss franc	9	50

The interest rate on the Canadian dollar is 9 percent, and the interest rate on the Swiss franc is 7 percent. Develop the possible effective financing rates of the overall portfolio and the probability of each possibility based on the use of joint probabilities.

14. Why might a corporation attempt to borrow a portfolio of foreign currencies even when it needs to make payments in its local currency?

15. Does borrowing a portfolio of currencies offer any possible advantages over the borrowing of a single foreign currency?

16. If a firm borrows a portfolio of currencies, what characteristics of the currencies will affect the potential variability of the portfolio's effective financing rate? What characteristics would be desirable from a borrowing firm's perspective?

17. Boca Inc. needs $4 million for one year. It presently has no business in Germany but plans to borrow marks from a German bank, because the German interest rate is three percentage points lower than the U.S. rate. Assume that interest rate parity exists; also assume that Boca believes that the one-year forward rate of the mark exceeds the future spot rate one year from now. Will the expected effective financing rate be higher, lower, or the same as financing with dollars? Explain.

18. Jacksonville Corporation is a U.S.-based firm that needs $600,000. It has no business in Switzerland but is considering one-year financing with Swiss francs, because the annual interest rate would be 5 percent versus 9 percent in the United States. The spot rate of the Swiss franc is presently $.62, while the forward rate is $.6436.

    a) Can Jacksonville benefit from borrowing Swiss francs and simultaneously purchasing francs one year forward to avoid exchange rate risk? Explain.

    b) Assume that Jacksonville does not cover its exposure and uses the forward rate to forecast the future spot rate. Determine the expected effective financing rate. Should Jacksonville finance with Swiss francs? Explain.

    c) Assume that Jacksonville does not cover its exposure and expects that the Swiss franc will appreciate by either 5 percent, 3 percent, or 2 percent, with an equal probability of each occurrence. Use this information to determine the probability distribution of the effective financing rate. Should Jacksonville finance with Swiss francs? Explain.

19. Assume that the U.S. interest rate is 7 percent and the Swiss interest rate is 4 percent. Assume that the Swiss franc's forward rate has a premium of 4 percent. Is the following statement true? "Interest rate parity does not hold; therefore U.S. firms could lock in a lower financing cost by borrowing Swiss francs and purchasing francs forward for one year." Explain your answer.

20. Orlando Inc. is a U.S.-based MNC with a subsidiary in Mexico. Its Mexican subsidiary needs a one-year loan of 10 million pesos for operating expenses. Since the Mexican interest rate is 70 percent, it is considering

borrowing dollars, which it would convert to pesos to cover the operating expenses. By how much would the dollar have to appreciate against the peso to cause such a strategy to backfire? (The one-year U.S. interest rate is 9%.)

21. Assume the following information. Raleigh Corporation needs to borrow funds for one year to finance an expenditure in the United States. The following interest rates are available:

	Borrowing Rate
U.S.	10%
Swiss	6%
Japan	5%

The percentage change in the spot rates of the Swiss franc and Japanese yen over the next year are as follows:

Swiss Franc		Japanese Yen	
Probability	Percentage Change in Spot Rate	Probability	Percentage Change in Spot Rate
10%	5%	20%	6%
90%	2%	80%	1%

If Raleigh Corporation borrows a portfolio, 50 percent of funds from francs and 50 percent of funds from yen, determine the probability distribution of the effective financing rate of the portfolio. What is the probability that Raleigh will incur a higher effective financing rate from borrowing this portfolio than from borrowing dollars?

EC Fiscal Woes Seen As Threat To Unity Treaty

Governors of Central Banks Urge Steps To Bolster The Credibility of EMS

BY TERENCE ROTH
Staff Reporter of THE WALL STREET JOURNAL

BASEL, Switzerland—European Community central bank governors warned their governments that the Maastricht treaty for greater European unity was at risk unless budget deficits were curbed and agreement on policies improved.

In an annual report issued this week, the committee of governors also urged steps to restore credibility to the European Monetary System, claiming that imbalances in monetary and fiscal policies persist.

Steps to reduce budget deficits and public-sector debt must be taken now, the bankers said, "if the credibility of member countries' policies and treaty obligations are to be maintained and overburdening of monetary policies is to be avoided."

Despite government calls for accelerated interest-rate cuts, EC central banks declared that fighting inflation would continue to be the top priority this year, suggesting the rates may not fall as quickly as governments would like. To finance markets, it appears that governments and central banks are talking past each other.

(The report was released prior to yesterday's interest-rate cuts by Germany's Bundesbank.)

"We aren't speaking different languages, but the emphasis can be different," said committee Chairman Wim Duisenberg, head of the Dutch central bank.

Only two of the 12 EC countries, France and Luxembourg, meet the public debt and budget deficit conditions required for entering a monetary union. The bankers' report cites an EC Commission forecast that the average budget deficit of EC countries in 1993 would rise a half-percentage point to 5.75% of EC gross domestic product, nearly double the 3% limit set by the Maastricht Treaty. The biggest offenders continue to be Italy, Greece and Belgium on deficits and public debt, which Maastricht limits to 60% of GDP.

Warnings of fault lines come at a time of relative calm in the EMS Exchange Rate Mechanism. The French franc survived France's March elections, but currency analysts say Europe's spreading recession, Britain's delayed ratification of Maastricht, the second Danish Maastricht referendum and Spain's June 6 elections all could spark another ERM crisis.

"Political events tend to enhance uncertainty," said Mr. Duisenberg. "If the Danish vote is no, then there is no Maastricht treaty anymore; it's as simple as that." Ten nations have ratified the treaty. . . .

The central banks said the 1992 crisis, which resulted in devaluation of Spanish, Portuguese and Irish currencies and a sharp drop in the Italian lira and British sterling, showed that the EMS must remain flexible and that exchange-rate realignments "may be needed if major economic imbalances arise." But they also emphasized that a realignment won't fix deeper problems raised by divergent fiscal, monetary and wage policies.

In a warning to market speculators, the governors said that central banks would cooperate closely to defend currency levels backed by strong economic cloud—an obvious reference to the French franc, which, with the same argument, the banks and governments supported against speculators last year. Mr. Duisenberg said there was no limit on the extent of central bank intervention.

Mr. Duisenberg said five years without economic convergance and without changes in currency parities was a major cause of September's ERM crisis—when the Bundesbank alone spent more than 90 billion marks to defend partner currencies. The next error, he said, was stretching a major currency realignment over six months because of political resistance from governments of affected currencies.

"It should have been done over one long weekend in Brussels," Mr. Duisenberg said. "We will never do that again," adding that EC central bank governors have since increased the frequency of private meetings to discuss ERM currency parities.

Britain and Italy, whose currencies were suspended from their fixed ERM parities in September, were warned to watch for "a pickup in inflationary dangers." The same warning went to Spain, Portugal and Ireland, giving exporters a competitive edge while also increasing inflation dangers. There are no plans to restore the lira or sterling to ERM soon, Mr. Duisenberg said.

Referring to the annual report, he said Europe needs a new dose of fiscal restraint, wage moderation and improved convergence in economic performance to restore credibility to the ERM and allow completion of the process toward monetary union.

"Unless we reach those targets, a real EMU has no chance," he said. With Europe in recession, meeting Maastricht criteria could become more difficult, Mr. Duisenberg said. But he added that the central bankers committee fears that the problems aren't solely cyclical. "Our fear is that there is a structural deterioration of government finances in some EC countries."

Continued

CASE: INTERNATIONAL FINANCING SINCE THE ERM CRISIS

Continued

Questions

1. Since interest rates across European currencies have become more diverse and the Exchange Rate Mechanism (ERM) bands have widened, explain how short-term financing decisions for European firms might change.

2. Consider an Italian firm that wishes to support its Italian operations with short-term funds. Given Italy's relatively high interest rates, the firm decides to borrow other European currencies (at lower interest rates) to support its Italian operations. The firm is somewhat concerned that the European currencies will appreciate substantially against the lira, which could more than offset the lower interest rate. Is this adverse scenario more likely now than it was before the ERM bands were widened? Explain.

3. Consider a U.S. firm that frequently uses short-term financing in pounds to support its British operations. The interest expenses will depend on British interest rate levels over time. Do you think the firm's interest expenses over time will be more or less volatile now that Great Britain has removed itself from the ERM (meaning that it no longer ties its interest rates to those of other countries)?

FLYER COMPANY
Composing the Optimal Currency Portfolio for Financing

As treasurer for Flyer Company, you must develop a strategy for short-term financing. The firm, based in the United States, presently has no transaction exposure to currency movements. Assume the following data as of today:

Currency	Spot Exchange Rate	Annualized Interest Rate
Australian dollar	$ .75	13.0%
British Pound	1.70	12.5
Canadian Dollar	.86	11.0
French franc	.17	11.5
German mark	.60	7.0
Italian lira	.0008	12.0
Japanese yen	.006	8.0
Swedish krona	.16	9.0
Swiss franc	.71	6.0
U.S. dollar	1.00	9.0

Your forecasting department has provided you with the following forecasts of the spot rates one year from now:

	Strong $ Scenario	Somewhat Stable $ Scenario	Weak $ Scenario
Australian dollar	$ .66	$ .76	$ .85
British pound	1.58	1.73	1.83
Canadian dollar	.85	.85	.91
French franc	.14	.173	.18
German mark	.53	.59	.63
Italian lira	.00073	.00079	.00086
Japanese yen	.0055	.0062	.0072
Swedish krona	.15	.155	.17
Swiss franc	.62	.69	.78
U.S. dollar	1.00	1.00	1.00

The probability of the strong dollar scenario is 30 percent, the probability of the somewhat stable dollar scenario is 40 percent, and the probability of the weak dollar scenario is 30 percent. Based on the information provided, prescribe the composition of the portfolio that would achieve the minimum expected effective financing rate based on each of the following risk preferences:

CASE PROBLEM

FLYER COMPANY (CONTINUED)

1. Risk-neutral	Focus on minimizing the expected value of your effective financing rate, without any constraints.
2. Balanced	Borrow no more than 25 percent in any foreign currency.
3. Conservative	Borrow at least 60 percent U.S. dollars and no more than 10 percent of the funds from any individual foreign currency.
4. Ultraconservative	Do not create any exposure to exchange rate risk.

Fill out the following table:

	Portfolio's Effective Financing Rate Based on a:			
Risk Preference	**Strong $ Scenario**	**Stable $ Scenario**	**Weak $ Scenario**	**Expected Value of Effective Financing Rate**
Risk-neutral portfolio				
Balanced portfolio				
Conservative portfolio				
Ultraconservative portfolio				

Which portfolio would you prescribe for your firm? Why?

PROJECT

1. Use the interest rate and exchange rate data from the data bank in the back of the text to determine a U.S. firm's effective financing rate when borrowing German marks on a quarterly basis. Identify the periods in which this strategy would have resulted in very low effective financing rates. Was the dollar strengthening or weakening in those periods? (A computer spreadsheet could easily be created to reduce your computational time.)

REFERENCES

Biger, Nahum. "Exchange Risk Implications of International Portfolio Diversification." *Journal of International Business Studies* (Fall 1979) pp. 64–74.

Eaker, M. R., and J. Lenowitz. "Multinational Borrowing Decisions and the Empirical Exchange Rate Evidence." *Management International Review*, no. 1 (1986), pp. 24–32.

Finney, Malcolm, and Nigel Meade. "A Practical Approach to Corporate Borrowing and Exchange Rate Risk." *Euromoney* (October 1978), pp. 191–197.

Folks, William R. "Optimal Foreign Borrowing Strategies with Operations in Forward Exchange Markets." *Journal of Financial and Quantitative Analysis* (June 1978), pp. 245–254.

Levy, Haim. "Optimal Portfolio of Foreign Currencies with Borrowing and Lending." *Journal of Money, Credit, and Banking* (August 1981), pp. 325–341.

Lin, Antsong, and Peggy E. Swanson. "Measuring Global Money Market Interrelationships: An Investigation of Five Major World Currencies." *Journal of Banking and Finance* (June 1993), pp. 609–628.

Madura, Jeff. "Borrowing Abroad: How to Choose the Best Mix of Foreign Currencies." *Journal of Business Forecasting* (Winter 1982–83), pp. 9–11.

_____ . "Model for Financing in International Money Markets." *International Review of Economics and Business* (October-November 1986), pp. 1049–1056.

_____ . "Development and Evaluation of International Financing Models." *Management International Review* 25, no. 4 (1985), pp. 17–27.

Madura, Jeff, and E. Joe Nosari. "Optimal Portfolio of Foreign Currencies with Borrowing and Lending." *Journal of Money, Credit, and Banking* (November 1982), p. 531.

CHAPTER 15

INTERNATIONAL CASH MANAGEMENT

The term **cash management** can be broadly defined to mean optimization of cash flows and investment of excess cash. From an international perspective, cash management is very complex because of different laws among countries that pertain to cross-border cash transfers. In addition, exchange rate fluctuations can affect the value of cross-border cash transfers. The specific objectives of the chapter are to

- explain the difference in analyzing cash flows between a subsidiary perspective and a parent perspective,
- explain the various techniques used to optimize cash flows,
- explain common complications in optimizing cash flows, and
- explain the potential benefits and risks from foreign investing.

CASH FLOW ANALYSIS: SUBSIDIARY PERSPECTIVE

The management of working capital (such as inventory, accounts receivable, and cash) has a direct influence on the amount and timing of cash flow. Working capital management and the management of cash flow are integrated. We discuss them here first before focusing on cash management. Exhibit 15.1 is used to complement the discussion.

Begin with outflow payments by the subsidiary to purchase raw materials or supplies. The subsidiary will normally have a more difficult time forecasting future outflow payments if its purchases are international rather than domestic, because of exchange rate fluctuations. In addition, the possibility exists of substantially higher payments due to appreciation of the invoice currency. Consequently, the firm may wish to maintain a large inventory of supplies and raw materials so that it can cut down on purchases if the invoice currency appreciates, and instead draw from its inventory. Still another possibility is that

423

EXHIBIT 15.1   Cash Flow from a Subsidiary's Perspective

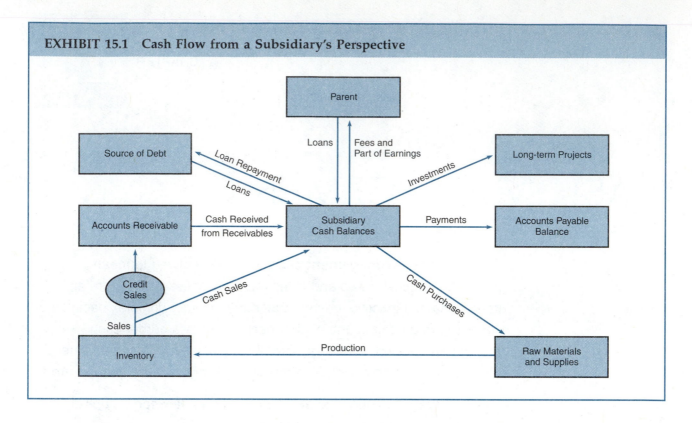

imported goods from another country could be restricted by the importer's government (through quotas, etc.). In this event, a larger inventory would give a firm more time to search for alternative sources of supplies or raw materials. A subsidiary with domestic supply sources would not experience such a problem, and therefore would not need as large an inventory.

Outflow payments for supplies will be influenced by future sales. If the sales volume is substantially influenced by exchange rate fluctuations, its future level becomes more uncertain, which makes outflow payments for supplies more uncertain. Such uncertainty may force the subsidiary to maintain larger cash balances in order to cover any unexpected increase in supply requirements.

Subsidiaries use their raw materials and/or supplies in their production process. If their finished goods are exported overseas, the sales volume may be more volatile than if the goods were sold only domestically. This could be so due to the fluctuating exchange rate of the invoice currency. Demand for these finished goods by importers will most likely decrease if the invoice currency appreciates. The sales volume of exports is also susceptible to business cycles of the importing countries. If the goods were sold domestically, the exchange rate fluctuations would not have a direct impact on sales, although they would still have an indirect impact, since they would influence prices paid by local customers for imports from foreign competitors.

Sales can often be increased when credit standards are relaxed. However, it is important to focus on cash inflows due to sales rather than on sales themselves. Looser credit standards may cause a slowdown in cash inflows from sales, which could offset the benefits of increased sales. Accounts receivable management is an important part of the subsidiary's working capital management because of its potential impact on cash inflows.

The subsidiary may be expected to periodically send dividend payments and other fees to the parent. These fees could represent royalties or charges for overhead costs incurred by the parent that benefit the subsidiary. An example is research and development costs incurred by the parent, which would improve the quality of goods produced by the subsidiary. Whatever the reason, payments by the subsidiary to the parent are often necessary. When dividend payments and fees are often known in advance and denominated in the subsidiary's currency, forecasting cash flows is easier for the subsidiary. The level of dividends paid by subsidiaries to the parent is dependent on liquidity needs, potential uses of funds at various subsidiary locations, expected movements in the currencies of subsidiaries, and host-country government regulations.

After accounting for all outflow and inflow payments, the subsidiary will find itself with either excess or deficient cash. Thus, it will periodically need to either invest its excess cash or borrow to cover its cash deficiencies. If it anticipates a cash deficiency, short-term financing is necessary, as described in the previous chapter. If it anticipates excess cash, it must determine how the excess cash should be used. Investing in foreign currencies can sometimes be attractive, but exchange rate risk makes the effective yield uncertain. This issue is discussed later in this chapter.

Liquidity management is a crucial component of a subsidiary's working capital management. Subsidiaries commonly have access to numerous lines of credit and overdraft facilities in various currencies. Therefore, they may maintain adequate liquidity without substantial cash balances. While liquidity is important for the overall multinational corporation (MNC), it cannot be properly measured by liquidity ratios. Potential access to funds is more relevant than cash on hand.

CENTRALIZED CASH FLOW MANAGEMENT

Each subsidiary should manage its working capital by simultaneously considering all of the points discussed thus far. Often, though, each subsidiary is more concerned with its own operations than with the overall operations of the MNC. Thus, a **centralized cash management** group may need to monitor, and possibly manage, the parent-subsidiary and inter-subsidiary cash flows. This role is critical, since it can often benefit individual subsidiaries in need of funds or overly exposed to exchange rate risk. Kraft's treasury department, for example, is centralized to manage liquidity, funding, and foreign exchange requirements of its global operations. And Monsanto's centralized system for pooling different currency balances from various subsidiaries in Asia creates an estimated annual savings of $250,000 per year.

Exhibit 15.2 may be helpful throughout our discussion of cash flow management. It is a simplified cash flow diagram for an MNC with two subsidiaries in different countries. While each MNC may handle its payments in a different manner, Exhibit 15.2 is based on simplified assumptions that will help illustrate some key concepts of multinational cash management. The exhibit reflects the assumption that the two subsidiaries periodically send fees and dividends to the parent and often send excess cash to the parent (where the centralized cash

EXHIBIT 15.2   Cash Flow of the Overall MNC

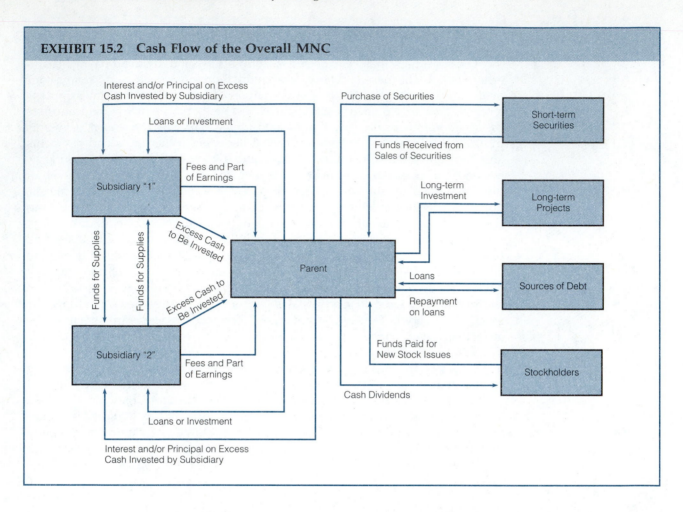

management process is assumed to take place). These cash flows represent the incoming cash to the parent from the subsidiaries. The parent's cash outflows to the subsidiaries include loans and the return of cash previously invested by the subsidiaries. The subsidiaries also have cash flows between themselves, due to purchasing of supplies from each other.

While each subsidiary is managing its working capital, there is a need to monitor and manage the cash flows between the parent and the subsidiaries, as well as between the individual subsidiaries. This task of international cash management should be delegated to a centralized cash management group. International cash management can be segmented into two functions: (1) optimizing cash flow movements, and (2) investing excess cash. These two functions are discussed in turn.

TECHNIQUES TO OPTIMIZE CASH FLOWS

Cash inflows can be optimized by

- accelerating cash inflows
- minimizing currency conversion costs

- minimizing the tax on cash flow
- managing blocked funds
- managing inter-subsidiary cash transfers.

Each of these tasks is discussed in turn.

Accelerating Cash Inflows

The first goal in international cash management is to accelerate cash inflows, since the more quickly the inflows are received, the more quickly they can be invested or used for other purposes. Several managerial practices are advocated for this endeavor, some of which may be implemented by the individual subsidiaries. First, a corporation may establish **lockboxes** around the world, which are post office box numbers to which customers are instructed to send payment. When set up in appropriate locations, a lockbox can help reduce mailing time (**mail float**). The processing of incoming checks at a lockbox is normally taken care of by a bank on a daily basis. A second method for accelerating cash inflows is the **preauthorized payment,** which allows a corporation to charge a customer's bank account up to some limit. Both the preauthorized payment and lockboxes are even used in a domestic setting. Because international transactions may have a relatively long mailing time, these methods to accelerate cash inflows can be quite valuable for an MNC.

Minimizing Currency Conversion Costs

Another technique for optimizing cash flow movements, **netting,** can be implemented with the joint effort of subsidiaries or by the centralized cash management group. This technique optimizes cash flow by reducing the administrative and transaction costs that result from currency conversion. Consider an MNC with two subsidiaries located in different countries. Any time one subsidiary purchases goods from a second subsidiary, it may need a foreign currency to make payment. The second subsidiary may do the same when purchasing goods from the first subsidiary. Both subsidiaries could avoid (or at least reduce) the transaction costs of currency conversion if they netted out the payments—that is, if they accounted for all of their transactions over a given period to determine one net payment.

Over time, the use of netting has become increasingly popular. Its key benefits are as follows. First, it reduces the number of cross-border transactions between subsidiaries, thereby reducing the overall administrative cost of such cash transfers. Second, it reduces the need for foreign exchange conversion, since transactions occur less frequently, thereby reducing the transaction costs associated with foreign exchange conversion. Third, the process of netting forces tight control over information on transactions between subsidiaries. Thus, there is a more coordinated effort among all subsidiaries to accurately report and settle their various accounts. Finally, cash flow forecasting is easier, since only net cash transfers are made at the end of each period, rather than individual cash transfers throughout the period. Improved cash flow forecasting can enhance financing and investment decisions.

A **bilateral netting system** involves transactions between two units: between the parent and a subsidiary, or between two subsidiaries. A **multilateral netting system** usually involves a more complex interchange among the parent and several subsidiaries. For most large MNCs, a multilateral netting system would be necessary to effectively reduce administrative and currency conversion costs. Such a system is normally centralized, so that all necessary information is consolidated. From the consolidated cash flow information, net cash flow positions for each pair of units (subsidiaries, or whatever) is determined, and the actual reconciliation at the end of each period can be dictated. The centralized group may even maintain inventories of various currencies so currency conversion for the end-of-period net payments can be completed without significant transaction costs.

Exhibit 15.3 is an example of an inter-subsidiary payments matrix that totals each subsidiary's individual payments against each other subsidiary. For example, the first row implies the Canadian subsidiary owes the French subsidiary the equivalent of $40,000, the Canadian subsidiary owes the British subsidiary the equivalent of $80,000, and so on. During this same period, these subsidiaries have also received goods from the Canadian subsidiary, for which payment is due. In the second column (under Canada), the table suggests the French subsidiary owes the Canadian subsidiary the equivalent of $60,000, the British subsidiary owes the Canadian subsidiary the equivalent of $90,000, and so on.

Since subsidiaries owe each other, currency conversion costs can be reduced by requiring that only the net payment be extended. Using the intersubsidiary table, the schedule of net payments is determined as shown in Exhibit 15.4. Since the Canadian subsidiary owes the French subsidiary the equivalent of $40,000, but is owed the equivalent of $60,000 by the French subsidiary, the net payment required is from the French subsidiary to the Canadian subsidiary, amounting to the equivalent of $20,000. Exhibits 15.3 and 15.4 convert all figures to U.S. dollar equivalents to allow for consolidating payments in both directions so the net payment can be determined.

There can be some limitations to multilateral netting due to foreign exchange controls. Although the major industrialized countries typically do not impose such controls on netting, some other countries do. For a third class of countries, netting is prohibited. Thus, an MNC with subsidiaries around the world may be able to implement the multilateral netting system only over some of its subsidiaries. Obviously, this will limit the degree to which the netting system can reduce administration and transaction costs.

Minimizing Tax on Cash Flow

To further optimize cash flows, the MNC must consider the tax consequences of altering its cash flow. If, for example, the host country government of a particular subsidiary places a high withholding tax on subsidiary earnings remitted to the parent, the parent of the MNC may instruct the subsidiary to temporarily refrain from remitting earnings and to reinvest them in that host country instead. As an alternative approach, the MNC may instruct the subsidiary to set up a research and development division that will benefit subsidiaries elsewhere. The main purpose behind this strategy is to search for a way to efficiently use the funds abroad if the funds cannot be sent to the parent without excessive taxation.

Another possible strategy to deal with such high taxation is to adjust the **transfer pricing** policy. To illustrate, suppose that Oakland Corporation has established two subsidiaries to capitalize on low production costs. One of these subsidiaries (called Hitax Sub) is located in a country whose government charges

EXHIBIT 15.3   Inter-Subsidiary Payments Matrix

Payments Owed by Subsidiary Located in:	U.S. Dollar Value (in Thousands) of Payments Owed to Subsidiary Located in:						
	Canada	France	Great Britain	Japan	Switzerland	U.S.	Germany
Canada	—	40	80	90	20	40	60
France	60	—	40	30	60	50	30
Great Britain	90	20	—	20	10	0	40
Japan	100	30	50	—	20	30	10
Switzerland	10	50	30	10	—	50	70
U.S.	10	60	20	20	20	—	40
Germany	40	30	0	60	40	70	—

EXHIBIT 15.4   Netting Schedule

Net Payments to be Made by Subsidiary Located in:	Net U.S. Dollar Value (in Thousands) of Payments Owed to Subsidiary Located in:						
	Canada	France	Great Britain	Japan	Switzerland	U.S.	Germany
Canada	—	0	0	0	10	30	20
France	20	—	20	0	10	0	0
Great Britain	10	0	—	0	0	0	40
Japan	10	0	30	—	10	10	0
Switzerland	0	0	20	0	—	30	30
U.S.	0	10	20	0	0	—	0
Germany	0	0	0	50	0	30	—

a 50 percent tax rate on before-tax earnings. Hitax Sub produces partially finished products and sends them to the other subsidiary (called Lotax Sub), where the final assembly takes place. The host government of Lotax Sub charges a 20 percent tax on before-tax earnings. To simplify the example, assume that no dividends are to be remitted to the parent in the near future. Given this information, pro forma income statements would be as shown in the top part of Exhibit 15.5 for Hitax Sub (Column 2), Lotax Sub (Column 3), and the consolidated subsidiaries (Column 4). The income statement items are reported in U.S. dollars to more easily illustrate how a revised transfer pricing policy can affect earnings.

The sales level shown for Hitax Sub matches the cost of goods sold for Lotax Sub, implying that all Hitax Sub sales are to Lotax Sub. The additional expenses incurred by Lotax Sub to complete the product are classified as operating expenses.

IN PRACTICE

CHARACTERISTICS OF MULTINATIONAL NETTING SYSTEMS

Numerous MNCs, such as Monsanto and Baxter Laboratories, use netting procedures to substantially reduce transaction costs. A recent survey of MNCs by Srinivasan and Kim revealed the following:

- About 82 percent of the respondents net their intra-company payments.
- The most popular type of netting is multilateral netting.
- About 86 percent of the firms that net payments between subsidiaries do so on a monthly basis. Some firms use a bimonthly basis.
- Most respondents that use netting systems develop the netting schedule by forecasting actual cash flows to and from subsidiaries.

Only a small percentage of respondents use a mathematical model to determine the net payments, but most respondents use internally created computer programs to facilitate their analysis.

- Some of the MNCs have built-in safety mechanisms to change data right up to the settlement day. Some of the MNCs that do not have safety mechanisms stated that the forecasted information is normally reliable, so safety mechanisms are not necessary.

Overall, the results suggest that netting is a commonly used tool to reduce currency conversion costs and that the specific netting procedure varies among MNCs.

Notice from Exhibit 15.5 that both subsidiaries have the same earnings before taxes. Yet, because of the differences in tax rates, Hitax Sub will earn an after-tax income of $7.5 million less than Lotax Sub. If Oakland Corporation could revise its transfer pricing, its consolidated earnings after taxes would be increased. To illustrate, suppose that the price of products sent from Hitax Sub to Lotax Sub is reduced, causing the sales of Hitax Sub to decline from $100 million to $80 million. This would also reduce the cost of goods sold of Lotax Sub by $20 million. The revised pro forma income statement resulting from the change in the transfer pricing policy is shown in the bottom part of Exhibit 15.5. The difference in forecasted earnings before taxes between the two subsidiaries is now $40 million, although the consolidated amount has not changed. Because earnings have been shifted from Hitax Sub to Lotax Sub, the consolidated tax payments are reduced to $11.5 million from the original estimate of $17.5 million. Thus, the corporate taxes imposed on earnings are now forecasted to be $6 million less than originally expected.

It should be mentioned that there are some limitations to such an adjustment in the transfer pricing policy, since host governments may enforce laws that restrict such practices when the intent is to avoid taxes. Transactions between subsidiaries of a firm are supposed to be priced using the principle of "arm's-length" transactions. That is, the price should be set as if the buyer is unrelated to the seller, and should not be adjusted simply to shift tax burdens. However, since there is some flexibility on transfer pricing policies, MNCs from all countries attempt to establish transfer pricing policies that are within legal limits,

EXHIBIT 15.5
Impact of Transfer Pricing Adjustment on Pro Forma Earnings and Taxes: Oakland Corporation
(*in thousands*)

	Original Estimates		
	Hitax Sub	*Lotax Sub*	*Consolidated*
Sales	$100,000	$150,000	$250,000
Less: cost of good sold	50,000	100,000	150,000
Gross profit	50,000	50,000	100,000
Less: operating expenses	20,000	20,000	40,000
Earnings before interest and taxes	30,000	30,000	60,000
Interest expense	5,000	5,000	10,000
Earnings before taxes	25,000	25,000	50,000
Taxes (50% for Hitax and 20% for Lotax)	12,500	5,000	17,500
Earnings after taxes	12,500	20,000	32,500

	Revised Estimates Based on Adjusting Transfer Pricing Policy		
	Hitax Sub	*Lotax Sub*	*Consolidated*
Sales	$80,000	$150,000	$230,000
Less: cost of good sold	50,000	80,000	130,000
Gross profit	30,000	70,000	100,000
Less: operating expenses	20,000	20,000	40,000
Earnings before interest and taxes	10,000	50,000	60,000
Interest expense	5,000	5,000	10,000
Earnings before taxes	5,000	45,000	50,000
Taxes (50% for Hitax and 20% for Lotax)	2,500	9,000	11,500
Earnings after taxes	2,500	36,000	38,500

but also reduce tax burdens. Even if the transfer price reflects the "fair" price that would normally be charged in the market, one subsidiary can still charge another for technology transfers, research and development expenses, or other forms of overhead expenses incurred.

Financing strategies may also be used to deal with high taxation. For example, the parent of Oakland Corporation may provide only minimal financial support to Hitax Sub, thereby forcing it to borrow and incur annual interest expenses. Debt becomes a more attractive source of funds when the tax rates are high. In fact, the parent may attempt to have Hitax Sub borrow more funds than needed and channel funds to subsidiaries in other countries. Hitax Sub would receive the largest tax benefit from borrowing because of the high tax rate. This strategy represents one more way in which the high-tax subsidiary subsidizes other subsidiaries. Such a strategy reduces that subsidiary's profits but increases

WHAT FACTORS AFFECT AN MNC's TRANSFER PRICING DECISION?

A recent study by Tang attempted to determine which factors were most important in an MNC's transfer pricing decision. A survey of 80 companies yielded the following information:

- The overall profit to the company was the most important factor affecting the transfer pricing decision. Most respondents were in agreement as to the importance of this factor.
- Other factors that had a strong influence in the transfer pricing decision were (1) the competitive position of subsidiaries in foreign countries, (2) the performance evaluation of subsidiaries, (3) restrictions imposed by host governments on remitted earnings, (4) the need for cash by foreign subsidiaries, (5) the interests of local partners in foreign subsidiaries, and (6) rules and requirements of financial reporting for foreign subsidiaries.
- Some other, less influential factors were (1) rates of inflation in foreign countries, (2) the volume of interdivisional transfer, (3) the risk of expropriation in foreign countries, and (4) domestic government requirements on direct foreign investments.

For more information, see the article from which this brief summary is drawn.

cash flow for the MNC overall. Some host country governments may attempt to prevent MNCs from implementing such a strategy.

Another method of reducing taxes is through the establishment of a **reinvoicing center.** The main objective is to shift profits to subsidiaries where tax rates are low. Title to goods passes through the reinvoicing center, but the goods do not. The invoice is normally denominated in the currency of the exporting subsidiary. The reinvoicing centers serve as a centralized payments facility, and subsidiaries are charged a fee for using the facility. This arrangement essentially shifts profits from other subsidiaries to the reinvoicing center and therefore reduces overall taxes incurred by the MNC.

Managing Blocked Funds

Cash flows can also be affected by a host government's blockage of funds, which might occur if the government requires all funds to remain within the country in order to create jobs and reduce unemployment. To deal with funds blockage, the MNC may implement the same strategies used in the case of high host country government taxation. To make efficient use of these funds, the subsidiary may be instructed by the MNC to set up a research and development division, which incurs costs and possibly generates revenues for other subsidiaries.

Another strategy is to use transfer pricing in a manner that will increase the expenses incurred by the subsidiary. A host country government is likely to be more lenient on funds sent to cover expenses than on earnings remitted to the parent.

When subsidiaries are restricted from transferring funds to the parent, the parent may instruct the subsidiary to obtain financing from a local bank rather

IN PRACTICE

OPTIMIZING SUBSIDIARY-PARENT CASH FLOWS

A recent survey by Grosse of chief financial officers of the U.S.-based MNCs that have subsidiaries in Latin America produced some interesting results:

- About 67 percent of the firms utilize intersubsidiary financing.
- Only 7 percent of the firms provide financing to the parent by a subsidiary.
- About 67 percent of the firms use leading and lagging strategies.
- About 80 percent of the firms prefer loans to equity funding for financing subsidiary development. The author presumes the reason to be that subsidiaries are not prohibited from using funds to cover debt repayment, whereas they are sometimes prohibited from remitting funds back to the parent.
- About 53 percent of the firms transfer parts to subsidiaries for partial or complete assembly. Of these firms, 57 percent use an arm's-length transfer pricing policy. Other firms that have partial assembly performed by subsidiaries use a "cost-plus" or similar method for determining transfer pricing.

These results are not necessarily representative of all U.S.-based MNCs, since the survey focused on MNCs with Latin American subsidiaries. Nevertheless, the results suggest that some of the techniques mentioned in this chapter for optimizing cash flow are commonly utilized.

than from the parent. By borrowing through a local intermediary, the subsidiary is assured that its earnings can be distributed to pay off previous financing. If the earnings were to be sent to the parent, the host government could enforce a blockage of funds.

As an example of managing blocked funds, subsidiaries of a U.S. MNC based in the Philippines were prevented from exchanging their Philippine pesos into U.S. dollars to send these dollars home. To deal with such restrictions, one general manager reportedly loaded pesos into his luggage and took them to Hong Kong, where he converted them into U.S. dollars. A better way of dealing with such restrictions is to find a use for the currency within the host country. For example, in the case of the Philippine government restriction, one company held its corporate meeting in Manila so it could use the pesos to pay the expenses of the meeting (hotel, food, etc.) in pesos. This approach is somewhat similar to sending the funds to the parent, since it is likely that the parent would have paid the expenses of the corporate meeting had it been held in the parent's country.

Inter-Subsidiary Cash Transfers

Proper management of cash flows can also be beneficial to a subsidiary in need of funds. Assume that Short Sub needs funds, while Long Sub has excess funds. If Long Sub purchases supplies from Short Sub, it could provide financing by paying for its supplies earlier than necessary. This technique is often called **leading.** Alternatively, if Long Sub sells supplies to Short Sub, it could provide financing by allowing Short Sub to lag its payments. This technique is called **lagging.** The leading or lagging strategy can make efficient use of cash and therefore reduce debt. Some host governments prohibit the practice by requiring that a payment between subsidiaries occurs at the time at which goods are transferred. An MNC would need to be aware of any existing laws that restricted use of this strategy.

COMPLICATIONS IN OPTIMIZING CASH FLOW

Most complications encountered in optimizing cash flow can be classified into four categories:

- Company-related characteristics
- Government restrictions
- Characteristics of banking systems
- Distortion of subsidiary performance.

Each complication is discussed in turn.

Company-Related Characteristics

In some cases, optimizing cash flow can become complicated, due to characteristics of the MNC. For example, if one of the subsidiaries delays payments to other subsidiaries for supplies received, the other subsidiaries may be forced to borrow until the payments arrive. A centralized approach that monitors all inter-subsidiary payments should be able to minimize such problems.

Government Restrictions

The existence of government restrictions can disrupt a cash flow optimization policy. For example, some governments prohibit the use of a netting system, as noted earlier. In addition, some countries periodically prevent cash from leaving the country, thereby preventing net payments from being made. These problems can arise even for MNCs that do not experience any company-related problems.

Characteristics of Banking Systems

The abilities of banks to facilitate cash transfers for MNCs will vary among countries. Banks in the United States are advanced in this field, but banks in some other countries do not offer services needed by MNCs. For example, MNCs prefer some form of zero-balance account, where excess funds can be used to make payments but earn interest until they are used. In addition, some MNCs benefit from the use of lockboxes. Such services are not available in some countries. In addition, there may be insufficient updating on the MNC's bank account information, or fees for banking services may not be broken down in a detailed manner. Without full use of banking resources and information, international cash management is limited in its effectiveness. In addition, an MNC with subsidiaries in, say, eight different countries will typically be dealing with eight different banking systems. Much progress has been made in foreign banking systems in recent years. As time passes, and a more uniform global banking system emerges, such problems may be alleviated.

Distortion of Subsidiary Performance

The various techniques that can be used by an MNC to optimize cash flow will often distort the profits of each individual subsidiary. For example, a change in the transfer pricing policy or inter-subsidiary cash transfer could be beneficial to the MNC overall. Yet, from the perspective of individual subsidiaries, earnings of one subsidiary may increase at the expense of another subsidiary. While the executives of a subsidiary may recognize the overall benefits to the MNC, they may worry that their jobs will be at stake due to the distorted earnings reports. That is, one subsidiary's reported earnings will look worse than they really are. The low earnings may be totally due to transfer pricing policies or leading and lagging strategies designed to deal with high taxes, currency blockage, etc. The parent, in its evaluation of performance of individual subsidiaries, must take into account such policies. If these policies are ignored, executives will be more concerned with maximizing earnings of their individual subsidiaries without concern for the overall MNC. This constitutes a goal conflict between the subsidiary executives and the owners (shareholders) of the MNC. The shareholder's goal is to maximize the value of the firm. If the executives make decisions that maximize their subsidiary earnings rather than shareholder wealth, then their philosophy will restrict the MNC from fully satisfying its owners. To ensure that there is no goal conflict, each subsidiary's performance should be based not on individual earnings, but instead on its contribution to the overall value of the MNC. Thus, executives will be rewarded based on how their decisions affect the overall value of the MNC.

If a subsidiary exists as a part of the MNC that is not wholly owned by the parent, the goal conflict will be more pronounced. The minority owners of the subsidiary will prefer that this particular subsidiary do what is best for itself rather than for the overall MNC. Such a conflict can sometimes make management of an MNC's cash flow quite complicated.

The centralized cash management division of an MNC cannot always accurately forecast events that affect parent-subsidiary or inter-subsidiary cash flows. It should, however, be ready to react to any event by considering (1) any potential adverse impact on cash flows, and (2) how to avoid such an adverse impact. If the cash flow situation between the parent and subsidiaries results in a cash squeeze on the parent, it should have sources of funds (credit lines) available. On the other hand, if it has excess cash after considering all outflow payments, it must consider where to invest funds. This decision is thoroughly examined here.

INVESTING EXCESS CASH

Along with optimizing cash flow, the other key function of international cash management is investing excess cash. International money markets have grown to accommodate corporate investment of excess cash, one of the key markets being the Eurocurrency market. The dollar volume of deposits has more than doubled since 1980. Eurodollar deposits commonly offer MNCs a slightly higher yield than bank deposits in the United States. Many MNCs utilize the Eurocurrency market as a temporary use of funds. For example, Westinghouse maintains over $400 million in Eurodollar deposits. Many MNCs also establish deposits in non-dollar currencies in the Eurocurrency market. While Eurodollar deposits still dominate the market, the relative importance of non-dollar currencies has increased over time.

In addition to their use of the Eurocurrency market, MNCs can also purchase foreign Treasury bills and commercial paper. Improved telecommunications systems have increased access to these securities in foreign markets and allow for a greater degree of integration among money markets in various countries.

There are several aspects of short-term investing that deserve consideration by the MNC. First, should the excess cash of all subsidiaries remain separated or be pooled together? Second, how can the MNC determine the effective yield expected from each possible alternative? Third, what does interest rate parity suggest about short-term investing? Fourth, how can the quoted forward rate be used to evaluate the short-term investment decision? Fifth, how can forecasted exchange rates influence the short-term investment decision? Finally, is it worthwhile to diversify investments among currencies? Each of these questions is discussed in turn.

Centralized Cash Management

An MNC's short-term investing policy can either maintain separate investments for all subsidiaries or employ a centralized approach. Recall that the function of optimizing cash flow could be improved by a centralized approach, since all subsidiary cash positions could be monitored simultaneously. With regard to the investing function, centralization allows for more efficient usage of funds, and possibly higher returns. The term *centralized* implies that excess cash from each subsidiary is pooled together until it is needed by a particular subsidiary. To understand the advantages of such a system, consider that the rates paid on short-term investments such as bank deposits are often higher for larger denominations. Thus, if two subsidiaries have excess cash of $50,000 each for one month, the rates on their individual bank deposits may be lower than the rate they could obtain if they pooled the funds into a single $100,000 bank deposit. In this manner, the centralized (pooling) approach generates a higher rate of return on excess cash.

The centralized approach can also improve the efficiency of working capital management by reducing the MNC's overall financing costs. To illustrate, suppose that Subsidiary A has excess cash during the next month of $50,000, while Subsidiary B needs to borrow $50,000 for one month. If cash management is not centralized, Subsidiary A may use the $50,000 to purchase a one-month bank certificate earning, say, 10 percent (on an annualized basis). At the same time, Subsidiary B may borrow from a bank for one month at a rate of, say, 12 percent. The bank must charge a higher rate on loans than it offers on deposits. With a centralized approach, Subsidiary B could borrow Subsidiary A's excess funds, thereby reducing its financing costs. This approach is limited, since the excess cash of one subsidiary may be denominated in a currency different from that needed by the other subsidiary. While the cash transfer is still possible, the chance of exchange rate fluctuations could discourage it.

The pooling of invested funds and matching of subsidiaries with excess funds may result in excessive transaction costs. For example, consider an MNC whose subsidiaries are transacting in several different currencies. A fully centralized approach would require all excess funds to be pooled and converted to a single currency for investment purposes. In this case, the advantage of pooling may be offset by the transaction costs incurred when converting to a single currency. Centralized cash management could still be valuable, though. The short-term cash available in each currency could be pooled together so there would be a separate pool for each currency. The excess cash of subsidiaries in a particular currency could still be used to satisfy other subsidiary deficiencies in that currency. In this way, funds could be transferred from one subsidiary to another without incurring transaction costs that banks charge for exchanging currencies. This strategy would be especially feasible if all subsidiary deposits were deposited in branches of a single bank, so that funds could easily be transferred among subsidiaries.

Our discussion of using excess cash has emphasized two suggestions: (1) pool together short-term cash denominated in a particular currency whenever possible in order to get the highest return on short-term bank deposits with a given maturity, and (2) attempt to accommodate short-term financing needs of subsidiaries with excess funds available at other subsidiaries whenever possible.

When a firm has any cash remaining, it may consider whether to cover any payables positions in foreign currencies. If the firm has future cash outflows in foreign currencies that are expected to appreciate, it may desire to cover such positions by creating short-term deposits in those currencies. The maturity of a deposit would ideally coincide with the date at which the funds are needed.

Any remaining funds can be invested in domestic or foreign short-term securities. In some periods, foreign short-term securities will have higher interest rates than domestic interest rates. The differential can be substantial, as is illustrated in Exhibit 15.6. However, firms must account for the possible exchange rate movements when assessing the potential yield on foreign investments, as explained below.

Determining the Effective Yield

Consider a U.S. firm that invests in a deposit denominated in the currency reflecting the highest interest rate, and then converts the funds back to dollars when the deposit matures. This strategy will not necessarily be feasible, since the currency denominating the deposit may depreciate over the life of the deposit. If it does, the advantage of a higher interest rate may be more than offset by the degree of depreciation in the currency representing the deposit. It is the deposit's **effective yield,** not its interest rate, that is most important to the cash manager. The effective yield of a bank deposit considers both the interest rate and the rate of appreciation (or depreciation) of the currency denominating the deposit, and can therefore be very different from the quoted interest rate on a deposit denominated in a foreign currency. An example follows to illustrate this point.

Assume a large U.S. corporation with $1,000,000 in excess cash creates a one-year deposit in French francs (FF) at 6 percent. The exchange rate of the French franc at the time of the deposit is $.20. The U.S. dollars are first converted to FF5,000,000 (since $1,000,00/$.20 per franc = FF5,000,000), then deposited in a Eurobank. One year later, the Eurobank will pay the U.S. corporation a total of FF5,300,000 (the initially deposited FF5,000,000 plus interest of 6% × FF5,000,000 = FF300,000). Assume the U.S. corporation has no use for francs. Also assume the exchange rate of the French franc is $.19 as the deposit is withdrawn. The FF5,300,000 francs converts to $1,007,000 (computed as FF5,300,000 × $.19 per franc). The yield on the investment is:

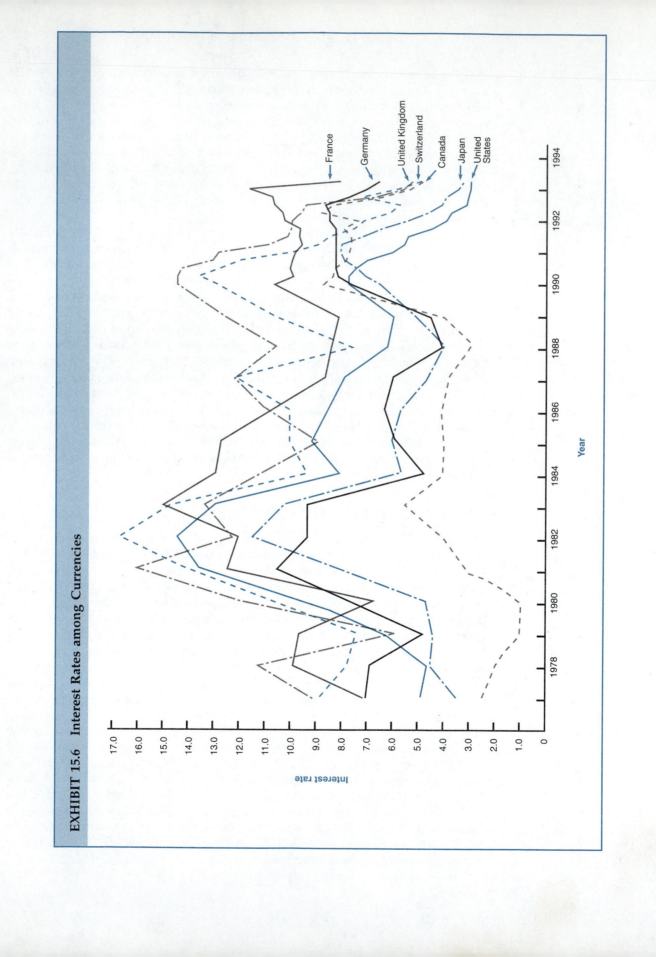

EXHIBIT 15.6 Interest Rates among Currencies

$$\frac{\$1,007,000 - \$1,000,000}{\$1,000,000} = .007, \text{ or } .7\%.$$

This example demonstrates how the yield on a foreign deposit can be influenced by a change in the exchange rate. If the U.S. corporation had decided to set up a Eurodollar deposit instead, it would have earned more than .7 percent. In addition, it would not have been exposed to exchange rate fluctuations if it planned to use the proceeds to cover expenses in the United States. However, the results of a foreign deposit would not always be unfavorable, as in our example. If the franc appreciated from $.20 to $.21 over the life of the deposit, then the FF5,300,000 received from the Eurobank as the deposit matures would be worth $1,113,000. In this case, the effective yield on the one-year deposit to the U.S. corporation would be

$$\frac{\$1,113,000 - \$1,000,000}{\$1,000,000} = .113, \text{ or } 11.3\%.$$

This effective yield for the U.S. corporation is due to both the interest rate on the deposit and the appreciation of the franc against the U.S. dollar.

The examples provided here illustrate how appreciation of a currency denominating the foreign deposit over the deposit period will force the effective yield to be above the quoted interest rate. Conversely, depreciation will create the opposite effect.

The above computation of the effective yield on foreign deposits is conducted in a logical manner. A quicker method is shown below:

$$r = (1 + i_f)(1 + e_f) - 1,$$

where r is the effective yield on the foreign deposit, i_f is the quoted interest rate, and e_f is the percentage change (from the day of deposit to the day of withdrawal) in the value of the currency representing the foreign deposit. The term i_f is used in Chapter 14 to represent the interest rate when borrowing a foreign currency. In this chapter, the interest rate of concern is the deposit rate on the foreign currency. In our example, e_f represents the percentage change in the French franc (against the U.S. dollar) from the date francs are purchased (and deposited) until the day they are withdrawn (and converted back to U.S. dollars). In our first example, the French franc depreciated from $.20 to $.19, or by 5 percent, over the life of the deposit. Using this information as well as the quoted deposit rate of 6 percent, we find that the effective yield to the U.S. firm on this deposit denominated in French francs is

$$r = (1 + i_f)(1 + e_f) - 1$$
$$= (1 + .06)[1 + (-.05)] - 1$$
$$= .007, \text{ or } .7\%.$$

which is the same rate computed using the first approach.

To test your ability to use the formula for the effective yield, apply it to our revised example, in which the French franc appreciated from $.20 to $.21, or by 5 percent. Based on the quoted interest rate of 6 percent, and the appreciation of 5 percent, the effective yield is

$$r = (1 + i_f)(1 + e_f) - 1$$
$$= (1 + .06)(1 + .05) - 1$$
$$= .113, \text{ or } 11.3\%,$$

which is the same rate computed earlier for this revised example.

The effective yield could be negative, if the currency denominating the deposit depreciated to an extent that more than offset the interest accrued from the deposit. For example, if a U.S. corporation sets up a foreign deposit that has a quoted interest rate of 5 percent, and the currency depreciates against the dollar by 7 percent, the effective yield is

$$r = (1 + .05)[1 + (-.07)] - 1$$
$$= -.0235, \text{ or } -2.35\%.$$

The result here suggests that the firm will end up with 2.35 percent less in funds than it initially deposited.

Up to this point, only bank deposits have been considered. There may also be other short-term foreign securities available. Any available securities denominated in a particular currency should have somewhat similar yields. As with bank deposits, the effective yield on all other securities denominated in a foreign currency is influenced by the fluctuation of that foreign currency's exchange rate. Our discussion will continue with a focus on bank deposits for short-term foreign investment. Yet, the implications of our discussion can be applied to other short-term securities as well.

Implications of Interest Rate Parity

Recall that covered interest arbitrage is described in Chapter 7 as a foreign short-term investment with a simultaneous forward sale of the foreign currency denominating the foreign investment. One might think that a foreign currency with a high interest rate would be an ideal candidate for covered interest arbitrage. However, such a currency will normally exhibit a forward discount that reflects the differential between its interest rate and the investor's home interest rate. This relationship is based on the theory of interest rate parity, as discussed in Chapter 7. Investors cannot lock in a higher return when attempting covered interest arbitrage, if interest rate parity exists.

Even if interest rate parity does exist, short-term foreign investing may still be feasible, but would have to be conducted on an uncovered basis (without use of the forward market). That is, short-term foreign investing may result in a higher effective yield than domestic investing, but it cannot be guaranteed.

Use of the Forward Rate as a Forecast

If interest rate parity exists, the forward rate can still be a useful indicator to the U.S. firm's investment decision. Consider the following information:

One-year U.S. interest rate = 12%

One-year French interest rate = 15%

Spot rate of French franc = $.20

One-year forward rate of French franc = $.1948

Amount of excess funds available at U.S. firm = $400,000.

The U.S. firm may first consider using covered interest arbitrage by investing in French francs and covering the position. This would result in the purchasing of 2,000,000 francs (computed as $400,000/$.20 per franc). At the end of one year, the U.S. firm will receive 2,300,000 francs (computed as 2,000,00 francs × 1.15). It can lock in the number of U.S. dollars received when converting those francs back to dollars by selling francs one year forward. At the forward rate of $.1948, this amounts to $448,040 (2,300,000 francs × $.1948 per franc). The effective yield here is

$$\frac{\$448,040 - \$400,000}{\$400,000} = .12, \text{ or } 12\%.$$

This is no more lucrative for the U.S. firm than simply investing in the United States.

Now consider a second possibility, in which the U.S. firm does not cover in the forward market. Assume the actual spot rate at the time the deposit matures turns out to be $.1948. This is the same exchange rate that the U.S. firm could have negotiated in the forward market when the deposit was created. We know from the previous example that at this exchange rate, the investment will yield about 12 percent, the same as the yield on a U.S. investment.

If the franc's actual spot rate after one year turns out to be more than $.1948, the total U.S. dollars received from the investment will be more than $448,040, and the effective yield will be more than 12 percent (and therefore more rewarding than a U.S. investment). If the actual spot rate after one year turns out to be less than $.1948, the total U.S. dollars received will be less than $448,040, and the effective yield will be less than 12 percent (and therefore less rewarding than the U.S. investment). This example demonstrates that if interest rate parity exists, we can use the forward rate as a break-even point to assess the short-term investment decision. When investing in the foreign currency (and not covering the foreign currency position), the effective yield will be more than the domestic yield if the spot rate of the foreign currency after one year is more than the forward rate at the time the investment is undertaken. Conversely, the yield of a foreign investment will be lower than the domestic yield if the spot rate of the foreign currency after one year turns out to be less than the forward rate at the time the investment is undertaken.

Relationship with the International Fisher Effect. When interest rate parity exists, MNCs that use the forward rate as a predictor of the future spot rate expect the yield on foreign deposits to equal that on U.S. deposits. While the forward rate is not necessarily an accurate predictor, it can still be a reasonable forecasting tool if it provides unbiased forecasts of the future spot rate. Being unbiased suggests that it underestimates or overestimates the future spot rate with equal frequency. Thus, the effective yield on foreign deposits is equal to the domestic yield, on average. MNCs that consistently invest in foreign short-term securities will earn a yield similar on average to what they could earn on domestic securities.

Our discussion here is closely related to the international Fisher effect (IFE), discussed in Chapter 8. Recall that the international Fisher effect suggests that the exchange rate of a foreign currency is expected to change by an amount reflecting the differential between its interest rate and the U.S. interest rate. The rationale behind this theory is that a high nominal interest rate reflects an expectation of high inflation, which could weaken the currency (according to purchasing power parity). If interest rate parity exists, the forward premium or discount reflects that interest rate differential and represents the expected percentage change in the currency's value when the forward rate is used as a predictor of the future spot rate. The IFE suggests that firms cannot consistently earn short-term yields on foreign securities which are higher than those on domestic securities, since the exchange rate is expected to adjust to the interest rate differential on average. If interest rate parity holds and the forward rate is an unbiased predictor of the future spot rate, we can expect the IFE to hold.

The IFE may appear to hold for some currencies and not for others. To determine whether IFE holds, the effective yield from investing in a foreign currency can be compared to that of domestic investing. If the effective yields of the two alternative investments in short-term securities are similar over time on average, then the results would support the IFE. This comparison is conducted in Exhibit 15.7 for a firm that has invested its excess cash in Britain money market securities rather than in U.S. money market securities because of the relatively high British interest rates. The top graph shows that when the British pound appreciated, as in the 1977–1980 period and the 1985–1988 period, the effective yield from the British investment was much higher than the British interest rate. As an extreme example, in 1987 the one-year yield on the British investment exceeded 40 percent.

However, the risk of the British investment is possible depreciation of the pound, which occurred some periods (such as in the 1981–1984 period). In these periods, the effective yield on the British investment was negative. As an extreme example, in 1981 the pound depreciated against the dollar by 20 percent, and the effective yield on the British investment was −8.98 percent. This implies that the firm would have received less funds from its money market investment than what it initially invested. Overall, the top graph shows how the effective yield of a foreign investment is dependent on the currency's movement over the investment period.

The lower graph compares the effective yield on the British investment (derived in the top graph) to the U.S. interest rate. This graph illustrates how a foreign investment can generate much higher returns when the foreign currency strengthens, but much lower returns when the foreign currency weakens.

The key implications of interest rate parity and the forward rate as a predictor of future spot rates for foreign investing are summarized in Exhibit 15.8. This exhibit explains the conditions necessary in order for investment in foreign short-term securities to be feasible.

Use of Exchange Rate Forecasts

While MNCs do not know how a currency's value will change over the investment horizon, they can use the formula for the effective yield provided earlier in this chapter and plug in their forecast for the percentage change in the foreign currency's exchange rate (e_f). Since the interest rate of the foreign currency

EXHIBIT 15.7   Investing Cash in British Pounds Versus Dollars

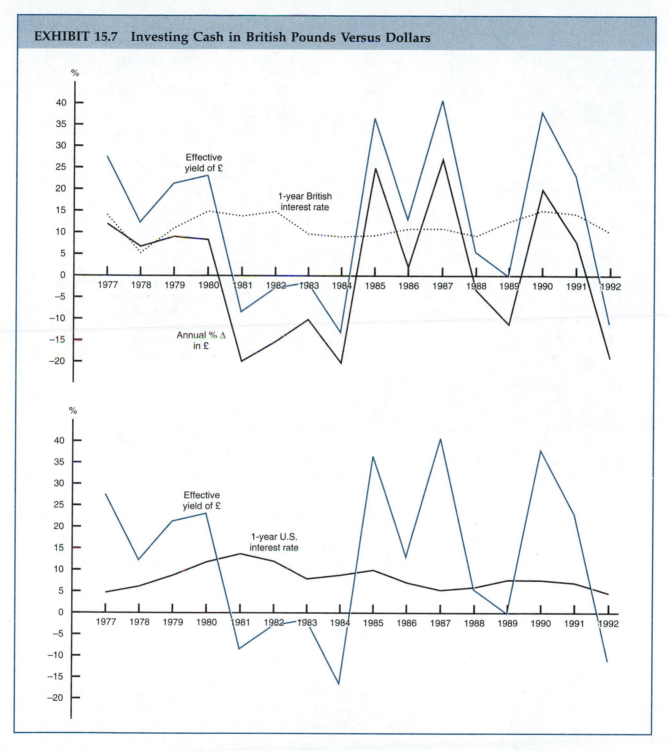

deposit (i_f) is known, the effective yield can be forecasted given a forecast of e_f. This projected effective yield on a foreign deposit can then be compared with the yield when investing in the firm's local currency. For example, assume a U.S. firm has funds available for one year. It is aware that the one-year interest rate on a U.S.

**EXHIBIT 15.8
Considerations
When Investing
Excess Cash**

Scenario	Implications for Investing in Foreign Money Markets
1. Interest rate parity exists.	Covered interest arbitrage is not worthwhile.
2. Interest rate parity exists, and the forward rate is an accurate forecast of the future spot rate.	An uncovered investment in a foreign security is not worthwhile.
3. Interest rate parity exists, and the forward rate is an unbiased forecast of the future spot rate.	An uncovered investment in a foreign security will on average earn an effective yield similar to an investment in a domestic security.
4. Interest rate parity exists, and the forward rate is expected to overestimate the future spot rate.	An uncovered investment in a foreign security is expected to earn a lower effective yield than an investment in a domestic security.
5. Interest rate parity exists, and the forward rate is expected to underestimate the future spot rate.	An uncovered investment in a foreign security is expected to earn a higher effective yield than an investment in a domestic security.
6. Interest rate parity does not exist; the forward premium (discount) exceeds (is less than) the interest rate differential.	Covered interest arbitrage is feasible for investors residing in the home country.
7. Interest rate parity does not exist; the forward premium (discount) is less than (exceeds) the interest rate differential.	Covered interest arbitrage is feasible for foreign investors but not for investors residing in the home country.

dollar deposit is 11 percent and the interest rate on a French franc deposit is 14 percent. Assume that the U.S. firm forecasts the French franc will depreciate from its current rate of $.1600 to $.1584, or a 1 percent decrease. The expected value for e_f [$E(e_f)$] will therefore be −1 percent. Thus, the expected effective yield [$E(r)$] on a French franc-denominated deposit is

$$E(r) = (1 + i_f)[1 + E(e_f)] − 1$$
$$= (1 + 14\%)[1 + (−1\%)] − 1$$
$$= 12.86\%.$$

In this example, investing in a French franc deposit is expected to be more rewarding than investing in a U.S. dollar deposit. Keep in mind that the value for e_f is forecasted, and therefore is not known with certainty. Thus, there is no guarantee that foreign investing will truly be more lucrative.

Deriving the Value of e_f That Equates Foreign and Domestic Yields. In recognition that e_f is uncertain, the U.S. firm may attempt to at least determine what value of e_f would make the effective yield from foreign investing the same as that from investing in a U.S. dollar deposit. To determine this value, begin with the effective yield formula and solve for e_f as follows:

$$r = (1 + i_f)(1 + e_f) - 1$$

$$(1 + r) = (1 + i_f)(1 + e_f)$$

$$\frac{(1 + r_f)}{(1 + i_f)} = (1 + e_f)$$

$$\frac{(1 + r_f)}{(1 + i_f)} - 1 = e_f.$$

Since the U.S. deposit rate was 11 percent in our previous example, that is the rate to be plugged in for r. We can also plug in 14 percent for i_f, so the break-even value of e_f would be

$$e_f = \frac{(1 + r)}{(1 + i_f)}$$

$$= \frac{(1 + 11\%)}{(1 + 14\%)} - 1$$

$$= -2.63\%.$$

This suggests that the French franc must depreciate by about 2.63 percent to make the French franc deposit generate the same effective yield as a deposit in U.S. dollars. Any smaller degree of depreciation would make the French-franc deposit more rewarding. The U.S. firm can use this information when determining whether to invest in a U.S. dollar or French franc deposit. If it expects the French franc to depreciate by more than 2.63 percent over the deposit period, it will prefer investing in U.S. dollars. If it expects the French franc to depreciate by less than 2.63 percent, or to appreciate, its decision is more complex. If the potential reward from investing in the foreign currency outweighs the risk involved, then the firm should choose that route. The final decision here will be influenced by the firm's degree of risk aversion.

Use of Probability Distributions.   Since even expert forecasts are not always accurate, it is sometimes useful to develop a probability distribution, instead of relying on a single prediction. An example of how a probability distribution is applied follows.

Assume a U.S. firm is deciding whether to invest in French francs for one year. It finds that the quoted interest rate for the French franc is 14 percent, and the quoted interest rate for a U.S. dollar deposit is 11 percent. The firm then develops a probability distribution for the French franc's possible percentage change in value over the life of the deposit. The probability distribution is displayed in Exhibit 15.9. From the first row in the exhibit, we see that there is a 5 percent probability of a 10 percent depreciation in the French franc over the deposit life. If the French franc does depreciate by 10 percent, the effective yield will be 2.60 percent. This implies there is a 5 percent probability of the U.S. firm's earning a 2.60 percent effective yield on its funds. From the second row in the exhibit, we see there is a 10 percent probability of an 8 percent depreciation in the

EXHIBIT 15.9
Analysis of Investing in a Foreign Currency

Possible Rate of Change in the French Franc Over the Life of the Investment (e_f)	Probability of Occurrence	Effective Yield if This Rate of Change in the French Franc Does Occur
−10%	5%	$(1.14)[1 + (−.10)] − 1 = .0260$, or 2.60%
−8	10	$(1.14)[1 + (−.08)] − 1 = .0488$, or 4.88
−4	15	$(1.14)[1 + (−.04)] − 1 = .0944$, or 9.44
−2	20	$(1.14)[1 + (−.02)] − 1 = .1172$, or 11.72
+1	20	$(1.14)[1 + (.01)] − 1 = .1514$, or 15.14
+2	15	$(1.14)[1 + (.02)] − 1 = .1628$, or 16.28
+3	10	$(1.14)[1 + (.03)] − 1 = .1742$, or 17.42
+4	5	$(1.14)[1 + (.04)] − 1 = .1856$, or 18.56
	100%	

French franc over the deposit period. If the French franc does depreciate by 8 percent, the effective yield will be 4.88 percent, which means there is a 10 percent probability of the U.S. firm's generating a 4.88 percent effective yield on this deposit. For each possible percentage change in the French franc's value, there is a corresponding effective yield. Each possible effective yield (Column 3) is associated with a probability of that yield's occurring (Column 2). An *expected value* of the effective yield of the French franc is derived by multiplying each possible effective yield by its corresponding probability. Based on the information in Exhibit 15.9, the expected value of the effective yield, referred to as $E(r)$, is computed this way:

$$E(r) = 5\%(2.60\%) + 10\%(4.88\%) + 15\%(9.44\%) + 20\%(11.72\%)$$
$$+ 20\%(15.14\%) + 15\%(16.28\%) + 10\%(17.42\%)$$
$$+ 5\%(18.56\%)$$

$$= .13\% + .488\% + 1.416\%$$
$$+ 2.344\% + 3.028\%$$
$$+ 2.442\% + 1.742\% + .928\%$$

$$= 12.518\%.$$

Thus, the expected value of the effective yield when investing in French francs is approximately 12.5 percent.

To further assess the question of which currency to invest in, the information in Columns 2 and 3 from Exhibit 15.9 is used to develop a probability distribution in Exhibit 15.10, which illustrates the probability of each possible effective yield that may occur if the U.S. firm invests in French francs. Notice that the U.S. interest rate (11 percent) is known with certainty and is included in Exhibit 15.10 for comparison purposes. A comparison of the French franc's probability distribution against the U.S. interest rate suggests that there is a 30 percent probability that the U.S. rate will be more than the effective yield from investing in French francs, and a 70 percent chance that it will be less.

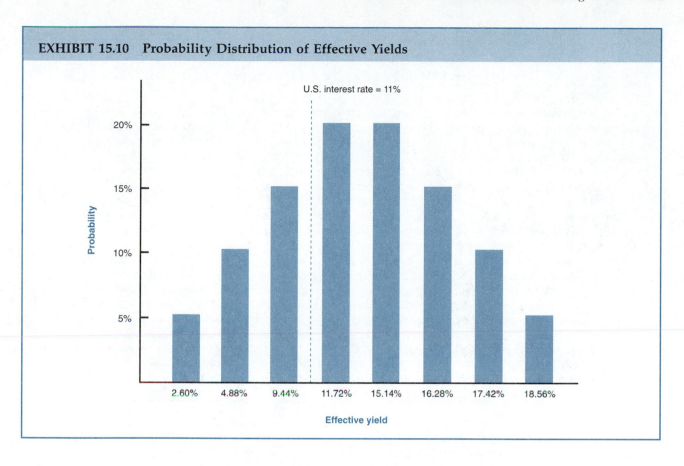

EXHIBIT 15.10   Probability Distribution of Effective Yields

If you are the treasurer of the U.S. firm, are you going to invest in U.S. dollars (and earn 11 percent with certainty) or invest in French francs (with an expected value of 12.5 percent for the effective yield)? You may choose to invest in a U.S. dollar deposit, since you prefer knowing with certainty the yield you will earn from your investment. Or you may feel the potential reward from investing in francs outweighs the risk involved. The risk is the 5 percent chance (probability) that the effective yield on the French franc deposit will be 2.60 percent, or the 10 percent chance the effective yield on the French franc deposit will be 4.88 percent, or the 15 percent chance the effective yield on French francs will be 9.44 percent. Each of these possibilities represents a lower return to the U.S. firm than what it would have earned if it had invested in a U.S. dollar deposit. This explains why some of the more conservative firms choose to avoid the uncertainty and invest in U.S. dollars.

Diversifying Cash Across Currencies

Because an MNC is not sure how exchange rates will change over time, it may prefer to diversify cash among securities with different currency denominations. This way it avoids the possibility of incurring substantial losses due to a particular currency's depreciation. Limiting the percentage of excess cash invested in each currency will reduce the MNC's exposure to exchange rate risk. The degree to which a portfolio of investments denominated in various currencies will reduce risk depends on the currency correlations. Ideally, the currencies

APPLIED RESEARCH

COMPOSING EFFICIENT MONEY MARKET PORTFOLIOS

For over two decades, researchers have demonstrated potential gains from international diversification of financial assets. Most of the research has focused on stocks, but a few studies have focused on the investment in money market securities, and these studies are relevant to MNCs, which sometimes have large amounts of short-term cash available to invest. Levy applied a so-called mean-variance model to historical interest rate and exchange rate data. This model was used to identify "efficient" portfolios, defined as having the minimum variance for a given mean return. Levy found that the efficient portfolios dominated the individual currencies. That is, there was an efficient portfolio that could match the return of each individual currency and had less risk than that currency. These results imply that there are possible benefits from an internationally diversified money market portfolio.

Levy applied the model to various country perspectives and demonstrated that the composition of the efficient portfolios varies with the perspective. This is because a currency may have appreciated to different degrees against other currencies, and may have led to higher yields for investors in specific countries.

A related study by Cotner and Seitz found that the composition of efficient portfolios changes over time; this is attributed to changes in the returns from investing in various currencies and changes in the co-movements between these returns (which affect the variance, or risk, of the portfolio). Consequently, MNCs may not know the composition of efficient portfolios until the investment period is over. Nevertheless, the study suggests that internationally diversified money market portfolios deserve consideration. Even if an MNC cannot create an efficient portfolio, it may still be able to achieve a more desirable return-risk combination when diversifying its investment among currencies.

represented within the portfolio will exhibit low or negative correlations with each other. The potential benefits from investing in a portfolio of currencies is more thoroughly discussed in Appendix 15.

Using Dynamic Hedging to Hedge Investments

Some commercial banks, such as Chase Manhattan Corporation, have begun to offer **dynamic hedging** for firms that invest in short-term securities denominated in foreign currencies. Unlike some other hedging techniques, dynamic hedging does not guarantee the home currency cash flows to be received at a future point in time. It reflects periodic hedging by the bank, wherein hedges are applied when the currencies held are expected to depreciate and removed when they are expected to appreciate. In essence, the objective is to protect against downside risk while benefiting from the favorable movement of exchange rates.

Consider a manager assigned to perform dynamic hedging for a U.S. firm that has invested in British pounds. If the pound begins to decline and is expected to depreciate further, the manager will sell pounds forward for a future date at which the pound's value is expected to turn upward. If the manager is very confident that the pound will depreciate in the short run, most or all of the position will be hedged. Now assume that the pound begins to appreciate before the forward contract date. Since the contract will preclude the potential benefits from appreciation of the pound, the manager may buy pounds forward to offset the existing forward sale contracts. In this way, the manager has removed the existing hedge. Of course, if the forward rate at the time of the forward purchase exceeds the forward rate that existed at the time of the forward sale, a cost is incurred to remove the hedge.

The manager may decide to remove only part of the hedge, offsetting only some of the existing forward sales with forward purchases. With this approach, the position is still partially protected if the pound depreciates further. Overall, the performance from using portfolio insurance is dependent on the manager's ability to forecast the direction of exchange rate movements.

SUMMARY

■ Each subsidiary of an MNC can assess its cash flows by estimating expected cash inflows and outflows to forecast its balance in each currency. This will indicate whether it will have excess cash to invest or a cash deficiency. The MNC's parent may prefer to use a centralized perspective, in which the cash flow positions of all subsidiaries are consolidated. In this way, funds could be transferred among subsidiaries to accommodate cash deficiencies at particular subsidiaries.

■ The common techniques to optimize cash flows are (1) accelerating cash inflows, (2) minimizing currency conversion costs, (3) minimizing tax on cash flow, (4) managing blocked funds, and (5) implementing inter-subsidiary cash transfers.

■ The efforts by MNCs to optimize cash flows are complicated by (1) company-related characteristics, (2) government restrictions, (3) characteristics of banking systems, and (4) distortion of subsidiary performance.

■ MNCs can possibly achieve higher returns when investing excess cash in foreign currencies that either have relatively high interest rates or may appreciate over the investment period. However, if the foreign currency depreciates over the investment period, this may offset any interest rate advantage of that currency.

SELF-TEST FOR CHAPTER 15

(Answers are provided in Appendix A in the back of the text)

1. Explain why a parent may prefer to charge some subsidiaries higher prices for the supplies it provides them than it charges other subsidiaries.

2. Country X typically has a high interest rate, and its currency is expected to strengthen against the dollar over time. Country Y typically has a low interest rate, and its currency is expected to weaken against the dollar over time. Both countries have imposed a "blocked funds" restriction over the next four years on the two subsidiaries owned by a U.S. firm. Which subsidiary will be more adversely affected by the blocked funds, assuming that there are limited opportunities for corporate expansion in both countries?

3. Assume that the Australian one-year interest rate is 14%. Also assume the Australian dollar is expected to appreciate by 8% over the next year against

the U.S. dollar. What is the expected effective yield on a one-year deposit in Australia by a U.S. firm?

4. Assume that the one-year forward rate is used as the forecast of the future spot rate. The French franc's spot rate is $.20, while its one-year forward rate is $.19. The French one-year interest rate is 11%. What is the expected effective yield on a one-year deposit in France by a U.S. firm?

5. Assume the Venezuela one-year interest rate is 90%, while the U.S. one-year interest rate is 6%. Determine the break-even value for the percentage change in Venezuela's currency (the bolivar) that would cause the effective yield to be the same for a one-year deposit in Venezuela as for a one-year deposit in the U.S.

6. Assume interest rate parity exists. Would U.S. firms possibly consider placing deposits in countries with high interest rates? Explain.

QUESTIONS

1. Discuss the general functions involved in international cash management.

2. What is netting, and how can it improve an MNC's performance?

3. How can an MNC implement leading and lagging techniques to help subsidiaries in need of funds?

4. Explain how the MNC's optimization of cash flow can distort the profits of each subsidiary.

5. How can a centralized cash management system be beneficial to the MNC?

6. Why would a firm consider investing short-term funds overseas?

7. Assume a U.S.-based MNC has $2,000,000 in cash available for 90 days. It is considering the use of covered interest arbitrage, since the British 90-day interest rate is higher than the U.S. interest rate. What will determine whether this strategy is feasible?

8. Assume a U.S.-based MNC has $1,000,000 in cash available for 30 days. It can earn 1 percent on a 30-day investment in the U.S. Alternatively, if it converts the dollars to French francs, it can earn $1\frac{1}{2}$ percent on a French deposit. The spot rate of the French franc is $.12. The spot rate 30 days from now is expected to be $.10. Should this firm invest its cash in the U.S. or in France? Substantiate your answer.

9. Assume a U.S.-based MNC has $3,000,000 in cash available for 180 days. It can earn 7 percent on a U.S. Treasury bill or 9 percent on a British Treasury bill. The British investment does require conversion of dollars to British pounds. Assume that interest rate parity holds and that the MNC believes the 180-day forward rate is a reliable predictor of the spot rate to be realized 180 days from now. Would the British investment provide an effective yield that is below, above, or equal to the yield on the U.S. investment? Explain your answer.

10. Repeat Question 9, but this time assume that the firm expects the 180-day forward rate of the pound to substantially overestimate the spot rate to be realized in 180 days.

11. Repeat Question 9, but this time assume that the firm expects the 180-day forward rate of the pound to substantially underestimate the spot rate to be realized in 180 days.

12. Assume the one-year U.S. interest rate is 10 percent, and the one-year Canadian interest rate is 13 percent. If a U.S. firm invests its funds in Canada, what percentage will the Canadian dollar have to depreciate to make its effective yield the same as the U.S. interest rate, from the U.S. firm's perspective?

13. A U.S.-based MNC plans to invest its excess cash in France for one year. The one-year French interest rate is 19 percent. The probability of the French franc's percentage change in value during the next year is as follows:

Possible Rate of Change in the French Franc Over the Life of the Investment	Probability of Occurrence
−3%	20%
4	50
10	30

What is the expected value of the effective yield based on this information? Given that the U.S. interest rate for one year is 17 percent, what is the probability that a one-year investment in francs will generate a lower effective yield than could be generated if the U.S. firm simply invested domestically?

14. If a U.S. firm believes that the international Fisher effect holds, what are the implications regarding a strategy of continually attempting to generate high returns by investing in currencies with high interest rates?

15. A U.S. firm considers placing 30 percent of its excess funds in a one-year French franc deposit and the remaining 70 percent of its funds in a one-year Canadian dollar deposit. The French one-year interest rate is 15 percent, while the Canadian one-year interest rate is 13 percent. The possible percentage changes in the two currencies for the next year are forecasted as follows:

Currency	Possible Percentage Change in the Spot Rate over the Investment Horizon	Probability of that Percentage Change in the Spot Rate Occurring
French franc	−2%	20%
French franc	1	60
French franc	3	20
Canadian dollar	1	50
Canadian dollar	4	40
Canadian dollar	6	10

Given this information, determine the possible effective yields of the portfolio and the probability associated with each possible portfolio yield.

Given a one-year U.S. interest rate of 16 percent, what is the probability that the portfolio's effective yield will be lower than the yield achieved from investing in the United States? (See Appendix 15).

16. Why would a firm consider investing in a portfolio of foreign currencies instead of just a single foreign currency?

17. Tallahassee Company has $2 million in excess cash that it has invested in Mexico at an annual interest rate of 60 percent. The U.S. interest rate is 9 percent. By how much would the Mexican peso have to depreciate to cause such a strategy to backfire?

18. San Antonio Corporation has several subsidiaries in less developed countries that trade goods and supplies with each other. Explain how transfer pricing could be used by San Antonio Corporation to reduce its overall tax payments.

19. Dallas Company has determined that the French interest rate is 16 percent, while the U.S. interest rate is 11 percent for one-year Treasury bills. The one-year forward rate of the French franc has a discount of 7 percent. Does interest rate parity exist? Can Dallas Company achieve a higher effective yield by using covered interest arbitrage than by investing in U.S. Treasury bills? Explain.

20. Corpus Company has a subsidiary in Country X that produces computer components and sells them to another subsidiary in Country Y, where the production process is completed. The tax rate in Country X is 50 percent, while the tax rate in Country Y is 20 percent. The pro forma income statements of the Corpus subsidiaries are shown in Exhibit A. Assume that Corpus headquarters adjusts its transfer pricing policy so that sales by Subsidiary X are reduced from $400,000 to $320,000 (this also affects the cost of goods sold at Subsidiary Y by the same amount). Determine the change in total tax payments of the consolidated subsidiaries as a result of this revised transfer pricing policy.

EXHIBIT A
Corpus Company
Pro Forma Income
Statements

	Subsidiary X	Subsidiary Y	Consolidated Subsidiaries
Sales	$400,000	$700,000	$1,100,000
Less: cost of goods sold	220,000	400,000	620,000
Gross profit	180,000	300,000	480,000
Less: operating expenses	80,000	100,000	180,000
Earnings before interest and taxes	100,000	200,000	300,000
Interest expense	10,000	30,000	40,000
Earnings before taxes	90,000	170,000	260,000
Taxes (50% for Sub X and 20% for Sub Y)	45,000	34,000	79,000
Earnings after taxes	45,000	136,000	181,000

CASE: INTERNATIONAL CASH MANAGEMENT SINCE THE ERM CRISIS

Use the *Wall Street Journal* article in the case from Chapter 14 as the article for this case. The article focuses on changes in the European Exchange Rate Mechanism (ERM), which have implications for international cash management.

QUESTIONS

1. As interest rates across European currencies become more diverse, and the Exchange Rate Mechanism (ERM) bands widen, explain how international cash management for U.S. firms might change.

2. Will diversifying cash among European currencies cause more or less stability in a U.S. firm's cash portfolio now, as opposed to previous years, when the ERM band was tighter? That is, how have the benefits from diversification changed?

3. Some MNCs have cash inflows in one European currency and cash outflows in others over any given month. A centralized division overseeing this situation may argue that if the dollar equivalent amounts of the cash inflows and outflows in European currencies are about equal, the firm's exposure is negligible. Explain how this view may have been affected since ERM bands have been widened.

CASE PROBLEM

ISLANDER CORPORATION
Composing the Optimal Currency Portfolio for Investing

As treasurer for the Islander Corporation, you must develop a strategy for investing the excess cash that will be available for the next year. The firm, based in the United States, presently has no transaction exposure to foreign currency movements. Assume the following data as of today:

Currency	Spot Exchange Rate	Annualized Interest Rate
Australian dollar	.75	13.00
British pound	1.70	12.5
Canadian dollar	.86	11.0
French franc	.17	11.5
German mark	.60	7.0
Italian lira	.0008	12.0
Japanese yen	.006	8.0
Swedish krona	.16	9.0
Swiss franc	.71	6.0
U.S. dollar	1.00	9.0

Your forecasting department has provided you with the following forecasts of the spot rates one year from now:

	Strong $ Scenario	Somewhat Stable $ Scenario	Weak $ Scenario
Australian dollar	$ .66	$ .76	$ .85
British pound	1.58	1.73	1.83
Canadian dollar	.85	.85	.91
French franc	.14	.173	.18
German mark	.53	.59	.63
Italian lira	.00073	.00079	.00086
Japanese yen	.0055	.0062	.0072
Swedish krona	.15	.155	.17
Swiss franc	.62	.69	.78
U.S. dollar	1.00	1.00	1.00

The probability of the strong dollar scenario is 30 percent, the probability of the somewhat stable dollar scenario is 40 percent, and the probability of the weak dollar scenario is 30 percent. Based on the information provided, prescribe the composition of the investment portfolio that would maximize the expected value of the effective yield for each of four possible risk preferences:

CASE PROBLEM

ISLANDER CORPORATION (CONTINUED)

1. Risk-neutral   Focus on maximizing the expected value of your effective yield, without any constraints.

2. Balanced   Invest no more than 25 percent in any foreign currency.

3. Conservative   Invest at least 50 percent of the funds in the U.S. dollar and no more than 10 percent of the funds in any individual foreign currency.

4. Ultraconservative Do not create any exposure to exchange rate risk.

Fill out the following table:

| | Forecasted Effective Yield for: | | | |
Risk Preference	Strong $ Scenario	Somewhat Stable $ Scenario	Weak $ Scenario	Expected Value of Effective Yield
Risk-neutral portfolio				
Balanced portfolio				
Conservative portfolio				
Ultraconservative portfolio				

Which portfolio would you prescribe for your firm? Why? (You may find it helpful to draw bar charts that show the probability distribution of effective yields for each of the portfolios, placing one bar chart above another).

PROJECT

Use the interest rate and exchange rate data in the back of the text to determine a U.S. firm's effective (exchange rate-adjusted) yield when investing in French francs on a quarterly basis. Identify the periods in which this strategy would have resulted in very low effective yields. Was the dollar strengthening or weakening in those periods? (A computerized spreadsheet could easily be created to reduce your computational time.)

REFERENCES

Abdallah, Wagdy M. "How to Motivate and Evaluate Managers with International Transfer Pricing Systems." *Management International Review,* no. 1 (1989), pp. 65–71.

Cotner, John, and Neil Seitz. "A Simplified Approach to Short-Term International Diversification." *Financial Review* (May 1987), pp. 249–266.

Grosse, R. "Financial Transfers in the MNE: The Latin America Case." *Management International Review* 26 (1986), pp. 33–44.

Levy, Haim. "Optimal Portfolio of Foreign Currencies with Borrowing and Lending." *Journal of Money, Credit, and Banking* 13 (August 1981), pp. 326–341.

Lewis, Karen K. "The Behavior of Eurocurrency Returns Across Different Holding Periods and Monetary Regimes." *Journal of Finance* (September 1990), pp. 1211–1236.

Lin, Antsong, and Peggy E. Swanson. "Measuring Global Money Market Interrelationships: An Investigation of Five Major World Currencies." *Journal of Banking and Finance* (June 1993), pp. 609–628.

Madura, Jeff, and E. Joe Nosari. "Global Money Management: One Approach." *Financial Executive* (June 1984), pp. 42–47.

_____ . "Optimal Portfolio of Foreign Currencies with Borrowing and Lending." *Journal of Money, Credit, and Banking* (November 1982), p. 531.

_____ . "Speculation in International Money Markets." *Atlantic Economic Journal* (July 1983), pp. 87–90.

_____ . "Speculative Trading in the Eurocurrency Market." *Akron Business and Economic Review* (Winter 1984), pp. 48–52.

Soenen, L. A. "International Cash Management: A Study of the Practices of U.K.-Based Companies." *Journal of Business Research* (August 1986), pp. 345–354.

Srinivasan, Venkat, and Yong H. Kim. "Payments Netting in International Cash Management: A Network Optimization Approach," *Journal of International Business Studies* (Summer 1986), pp. 1–20.

Swanson, Peggy E. "The International Transmission of Interest Rates." *Journal of Banking and Finance* (December 1988), pp. 563–573.

Swanson, Peggy E., and William S. Y. How. "Portfolio Diversification by Currency Denomination: An Approach to International Cash Management with Implications for Foreign Exchange Markets." *Quarterly Review of Economics and Business* (Spring 1986), pp. 95–103.

Tang, Roger Y. W. "Environmental Variables of Multinational Transfer Pricing: A U.K. Perspective." *Journal of Business, Finance, and Accounting* (Summer 1982), pp. 179–189.

INVESTING IN A PORTFOLIO OF CURRENCIES

Large financial corporations may consider investing in portfolios of currencies, as illustrated in the following example. Assume a U.S. firm needs to invest $100,000 for one year and obtains these interest rate quotes:

Interest rate for a one-year deposit in U.S. dollars = 11%

Interest rate for a one-year deposit in French francs = 14%

Interest rate for a one-year deposit in British pounds = 13%

Due to relatively high quotes for a deposit in French francs or British pounds, it is understandable that the U.S. firm may desire to invest in a foreign currency. If the U.S. firm decides to use foreign investing, it has three choices based on the information given here:

- Invest in only French francs
- Invest in only British pounds
- Invest in a mixture (or portfolio) of francs and pounds.

Assume the U.S. firm has established possible percentage changes in the spot rate from the time the deposit would begin until maturity for both the French franc and British pound, as shown in Column 2 of Exhibit 15A.1. We shall first discuss the French franc. For each possible percentage change that might occur, a probability of that occurrence is disclosed in the third column. Based on the assumed interest rate of 14 percent for the French franc, the effective yield is computed for each possible percentage change in the French franc's spot rate over the loan life. In Exhibit 15A.1, there is a 20 percent chance the French franc will depreciate by 4 percent during the deposit period. If it does, the effective yield will be 9.44 percent. Thus, there is a 20 percent chance the effective yield will be 9.44 percent. Furthermore, there is a 50 percent chance the effective yield will be 12.86 percent and a 30 percent chance it will be 16.28 percent. Given that the U.S. deposit rate is 11 percent, there is a 20 percent chance that investing in French francs will result in a lower effective yield than investing in a U.S. dollar deposit.

The lower section of Exhibit 15A.1 provides information on the British pound. The pound has a 30 percent chance of depreciating by 3 percent during the deposit period, and so on. Based on the 13 percent interest rate for a British pound deposit, there is a 30 percent chance the effective yield will be 9.61 percent, a 30 percent chance it will be 13 percent, and a 40 percent chance it will

EXHIBIT 15A.1   Development of Possible Effective Yields

Currency	Possible Percentage Change in the Spot Rate over the Deposit Life	Probability of that Percentage Change in the Spot Rate Occurring	Computation of Effective Yield Based on that Percentage Change in the Spot Rate
French franc	−4%	20%	$(1.14)[1 + (−4\%)] − 1 = 9.44\%$
French franc	−1%	50%	$(1.14)[1 + (−1\%)] − 1 = 12.86\%$
French franc	+2%	30%	$(1.14)[1 + (2\%)] − 1 = 16.28\%$
		100%	
British pound	−3%	30%	$(1.13)[1 + (−3\%)] − 1 = 9.61\%$
British pound	0%	30%	$(1.13)[1 + (0\%)] − 1 = 13.00\%$
British pound	2%	40%	$(1.13)[1 + (2\%)] − 1 = 15.26\%$
		100%	

be 15.26 percent. Keeping in mind the 11 percent rate on a U.S. dollar deposit, there is a 30 percent chance that investing in British pounds will be less rewarding than investing in a U.S. dollar deposit.

Before examining the third possible foreign investing strategy (the portfolio approach) available here, determine the expected value of the effective yield for each foreign currency, summing the products of each possible effective yield and its associated probability as follows:

Currency	Computation of Expected Value of Effective Yield:
French franc	$(20\%)(9.44\%) + 50\%(12.86\%) + 30\%(16.28\%) = 13.202\%$
British pound	$(30\%)(9.61\%) + 30\%(13.00\%) + 40\%(15.26\%) = 12.887\%$

The expected value of the French franc's yield is slightly higher. In addition, the individual degree of risk (the chance the return on investment will be lower than the return on a U.S. deposit) is higher for the pound. If the U.S. firm does choose to invest in only one of these foreign currencies, it may choose the French franc, since its return and risk characteristics are more favorable. Yet, before making its decision, the firm should consider the possibility of investing in a currency portfolio, as discussed here.

The information in Exhibit 15A.1 shows three possibilities for the French franc's effective yield. The same holds true for the British pound. If a U.S. firm invests half of its available funds in each of the foreign currencies, then there will be nine possibilities for this portfolio's effective yield. These possibilities are shown in Exhibit 15A.2. The first two columns list all possible joint effective yields. The third column computes the joint probability of each possible occurrence. The fourth column shows the computation of the portfolio's effective yield based on the possible rates disclosed for the individual currencies shown in

EXHIBIT 15A.2 Analysis of Investing in Two Foreign Currencies

Possible Joint Effective Yield		Computation of Joint Probability	Computation of Effective Yield of Portfolio (50% of Total Funds Invested in Each Currency)
French Franc	*British Pound*		
9.44%	9.61%	(20%)(30%) = 6%	.5 (9.44%) + .5 (9.61%) = 9.525%
9.44	13.00	(20%)(30%) = 6	.5 (9.44%) + .5(13.00%) = 11.22
9.44	15.26	(20%)(40%) = 8	.5 (9.44%) + .5(15.26%) = 12.35
12.86	9.61	(50%)(30%) = 15	.5 (12.86%) + .5 (9.61%) = 11.235
12.86	13.00	(50%)(30%) = 15	.5 (12.86%) + .5(13.00%) = 12.93
12.86	15.26	(50%)(40%) = 20	.5 (12.86%) + .5(15.26%) = 14.06
16.28	9.61	(30%)(30%) = 9	.5 (16.28%) + .5 (9.61%) = 12.945
16.28	13.00	(30%)(30%) = 9	.5 (16.28%) + .5(13.00%) = 14.64
16.28	15.26	(30%)(40%) = 12	.5 (16.28%) + .5(15.26%) = 15.77
		100%	

the first two columns. The top row of the table suggests that one possible outcome of investing in both French francs and British pounds is an effective yield of 9.44 percent and 9.61 percent, respectively. The probability that this French franc's effective yield will occur is 20 percent, while the probability that the British pound's effective yield will occur is 30 percent. The joint probability that both of these effective yields will occur simultaneously is (20%)(30%) = 6%. Assuming that half (50%) of the funds available are invested in each currency, the portfolio's effective yields will be .5(9.44%) + .5(9.61%) = 9.525% (if those individual effective yields do occur).

A similar procedure was used to develop the remaining eight rows in Exhibit 15A.2. There is a 6 percent chance the portfolio's effective yield will be 11.22 percent, an 8 percent chance that it will be 12.35 percent, and so on.

Exhibit 15A.2 shows that investing in the portfolio will likely be more rewarding than investing in a U.S. dollar deposit. While there is a 6 percent chance the portfolio's effective yield will be 9.525 percent, all other possible portfolio yields (see column 4) are more than the U.S. deposit rate of 11 percent.

Recall that investing solely in French francs has a 20 percent chance of being less rewarding than investing in the U.S. deposit, while investing solely in British pounds has a 30 percent chance of being less rewarding. The analysis in Exhibit 15A.2 suggests that investing in a portfolio (50 percent invested in French francs, with the remaining 50 percent invested in British pounds) has only a 6 percent chance of being less rewarding than domestic investing. These results will be explained.

When an investment is made in both currencies, the only time the portfolio will exhibit a lower yield than the U.S. deposit is when *both* currencies experience their maximum possible levels of depreciation (which is 4 percent depreciation for the French franc and 3 percent depreciation for the British pound). If only one of these events occurs, its severity will be somewhat offset by the other currency's not depreciating to such a large extent.

In our example, the computation of joint probabilities requires the assumption that the movements in the two currencies are independent. If movements of the two currencies were actually highly correlated, then investing in a portfolio of currencies would not be as beneficial as demonstrated here, because there would be a strong likelihood that both currencies would experience a high level of depreciation simultaneously. If the two currencies are not highly correlated, they will not be expected to simultaneously depreciate to such a degree.

The present example includes two currencies in the portfolio. Investing in a more diversified portfolio of additional currencies that exhibit high interest rates can even increase the probability that foreign investing will be more rewarding than the U.S. deposit. This is due to the low probability that all currencies will move in tandem and therefore simultaneously depreciate to offset their high interest rate advantages. Again, the degree to which these currencies are correlated with each other is important here. If all currencies were highly positively correlated with each other, investing in such a portfolio would not be very different from investing in a single foreign currency.

REPEATED INVESTING IN A CURRENCY PORTFOLIO

A firm that repeatedly invests in foreign currencies may normally prefer to compose a portfolio package that will exhibit a somewhat predictable effective yield on a periodic basis. The more volatile a portfolio's effective yield over time, the more uncertainty (risk) there is about the yield that portfolio will exhibit in any period. The portfolio's variability depends on the standard deviations and paired correlations of effective yields of the individual currencies within the portfolio.

We can use the portfolio variance as a measurement for degree of volatility. The variance of a two-currency portfolio's effective yield (σ_p^2) over time is computed as

$$\sigma_p^2 = w_A^2\sigma_A^2 + w_B^2\sigma_B^2 + 2w_Aw_B\sigma_A\sigma_BCORR_{AB}$$

where w_A and w_B represent the percentage of total funds invested in Currencies A and B respectively, σ_A^2 and σ_B^2 represent the individual variances of each currency's effective yield overtime, and $CORR_{AB}$ reflects the correlation coefficient of the two currencies' effective yields. Since the percentage exchange rate change plays an important role in influencing the effective yield, it should not be surprising that $CORR_{AB}$ is strongly affected by the correlation between the exchange rate fluctuations of the two currencies. A low correlation between currency fluctuations can force $CORR_{AB}$ to be low.

To illustrate how the variance in a portfolio's effective yield is related to characteristics of the component currencies, consider the following example. The following information is based on several three-month periods:

Mean effective yield of British pound over 3 months = 4%

Mean effective yield of French franc over 3 months = 5%

Standard deviation of British pound's effective yield = .06

Standard deviation of French franc's effective yield = .10

Correlation coefficient of effective yields of these two currencies = .20.

Given the information above, the mean effective yield on a portfolio (r_p) of funds invested as 50 percent into British pounds and 50 percent into French franc is determined by summing the weighted individual effective yields:

$$r_p = .5(.04) + .5(.05)$$

$$= .02 + .025$$

$$= .045, \text{ or } 4.5\%.$$

The variance of this portfolio's effective financing rate over time is

$$\sigma_p^2 = .5^2(.06)^2 + .5^2(.10)^2 + 2(.5)(.5)(.06)(.10)(.20)$$

$$= .25(.0036) + .25(.01) + .5(.0012)$$

$$= .0009 + .0025 + .0006$$

$$= .004.$$

There is no guarantee that past data will be indicative of the future. Yet, if the individual variability and paired correlations are somewhat stable over time, the historical variability of the portfolio's effective yield should be a reasonable forecast of the future portfolio variability.

SHORT-TERM ASSET AND LIABILITY MANAGEMENT

Kent Co. is a large U.S. firm with no international business. It has two branches within the U.S., an eastern branch and a western branch. Each branch presently makes investing or financing decisions independently, as if it were a separate entity. The eastern branch has excess cash of $15 million to invest for the next year. It can invest its funds in Treasury bills denominated in dollars, or in any of the three foreign currencies in which it does business. The only restriction enforced by the parent is that a maximum of $5 million can be invested or financed in any foreign currency, in order to limit the exposure to any single foreign currency.

The western branch needs to borrow $15 million over one year to support its U.S. operations. It can borrow funds in any currency in which it does business (although any foreign funds borrowed would need to be converted to dollars to finance the U.S. operations). The only restriction enforced by the parent is that a maximum equivalent of $5 million can be borrowed in any single currency. A large bank serving the Eurocurrency market has offered Kent Co. the following terms:

Currency	Annual Interest Rate on Deposits	Annual Interest Rate Charged on Loans
U.S. Dollars	6%	9%
Australian dollars	11%	14%
Canadian dollars	7%	10%
German marks	9%	12%
Japanese yen	8%	11%

The parent of Kent Co. has created one-year forecasts of each currency (shown below) which can be used by the branches in making their investing or financing decisions:

Currency	Spot Exchange Rate	Forecasted Annual Percentage Change in Exchange Rates
Australian dollar	$.70	−4%
Canadian dollar	$.80	−2%
German mark	$.60	+3%
Japanese yen	$.008	0%

1. Determine the investment portfolio composition for Kent's eastern branch that would maximize the expected effective yield, while satisfying the restriction imposed by the parent.

2. What is the expected effective yield of the investment portfolio?

3. Based on the expected effective yield for the portfolio and the initial investment amount of $15 million, determine the annual interest to be earned on the portfolio.

4. Determine the financing portfolio composition for Kent's western branch that would minimize the expected effective financing rate, while satisfying the restriction imposed by the parent.

5. What is the expected effective financing rate of the total amount borrowed?

6. Based on the expected effective financing rate for the portfolio, and the total amount of $15 million borrowed, determine the expected loan repayment amount beyond the principal borrowed.

7. When the expected interest received by the eastern branch and paid by the western branch of Kent Co. are consolidated, what is the net amount of interest received?

8. If the eastern branch and the western branch worked together, the eastern branch could loan its $15 million to the western branch. Yet, one could argue that the branches could not take advantage of interest rate differentials or expected exchange rate effects among currencies. Given the data provided in this example, would you recommend that the two branches make their short-term investment or financing decisions independently, or that the eastern branch lend its excess cash to the western branch? Explain.

LONG-TERM ASSET AND LIABILITY MANAGEMENT

Part 5 (Chapters 16 through 21) focuses on the multinational corporation's (MNC's) management of long-term assets and liabilities. Chapter 16 explains how MNCs can benefit from international business. Chapter 17 describes the information MNCs must have in considering multinational projects and demonstrates how the capital budgeting analysis is conducted. Chapter 18 explains the capital structure decision for MNCs, which affects the cost of financing new projects. Chapter 19 explains how MNCs assess country risk, while Chapter 20 describes the MNC's long-term financing decision, and Chapter 21 focuses on multinational planning.

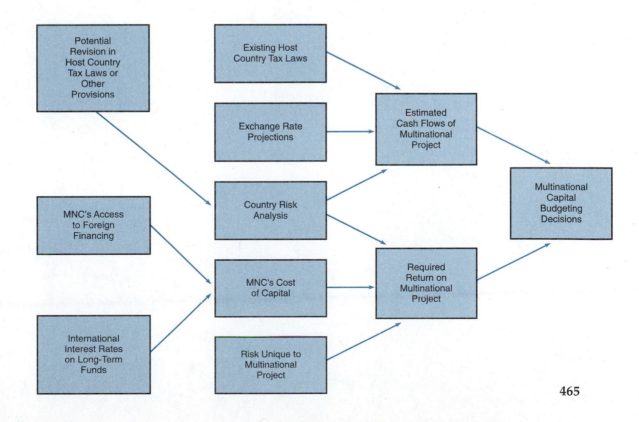

CHAPTER 16

DIRECT FOREIGN INVESTMENT

The global expansion of multinational corporations (MNCs) has become more widespread following the actions of many governments to remove various barriers. MNCs commonly capitalize on foreign business opportunities by engaging in **direct foreign investment** (DFI), which represents investment in real assets (such as land, buildings, or even existing plants) in foreign countries.

MNCs conduct DFI through joint ventures with foreign firms, acquisitions of foreign firms, and formations of new foreign subsidiaries. Any of these types of DFI can generate high returns when managed properly. However, DFI requires a substantial investment, and can therefore place much capital at risk. Moreover, when the investment does not perform as well as expected, the MNC may be unable to easily sell the foreign project it created. Given these return and risk characteristics of DFI, MNCs tend to analyze carefully the potential benefits and costs before implementing any type of DFI. The specific objectives of this chapter are to

- describe common motives for initiating direct foreign investment, and
- illustrate the benefits of international diversification.

BENEFITS OF DIRECT FOREIGN INVESTMENT

Direct foreign investment is commonly considered by MNCs because it can improve profitability and enhance shareholder wealth. There are several ways in which DFI can boost revenues or reduce costs. DFI can

1. Attract new sources of demand
2. Enter markets in which superior profits are possible
3. Fully benefit from economies of scale
4. Use foreign factors of production
5. Use foreign raw materials
6. Use foreign technology
7. Exploit monopolistic advantages
8. React to exchange rate movements
9. React to trade restrictions
10. Diversify internationally

1. *Attract new sources of demand.* A corporation often reaches a stage at which growth is limited in its home country. This may be due to intense competition for the product it sells. Even if there is little competition, its market share in its home country may already be near its potential peak. Thus, a possible solution is to consider foreign markets where there is potential demand. For example, Blockbuster Entertainment Corp. has recently established video stores in Australia, Chile, Japan, and several European countries where the video rental concept is relatively new. With over two thousand stores in the U.S., Blockbuster's growth potential in the U.S. was limited.

   Many of the developing countries, such as Argentina, Chile, Mexico, Hungary, and China, have been perceived as the most attractive sources of new demand. Many MNCs have penetrated these countries since barriers have been removed. Because the consumers in these countries have historically been restricted from purchasing goods produced by firms outside their countries, the markets for some goods are not well established and offer much potential for penetration by MNCs. As an example, Diebold Corp. has penetrated the Chinese market for bank safety deposit boxes. In 1993, the demand within China alone for these boxes was greater than Diebold's typical annual production.

2. *Enter markets in which superior profits are possible.* If other corporations within the industry have proven that excessive earnings can be realized in other markets, an MNC may also decide to sell in those markets. It may plan to undercut the prevailing, excessively high prices. A common problem with this strategy is that previously established sellers in a new market may prevent a new competitor from taking away their business by lowering their prices just as the new competitor attempts to break into this market.

3. *Fully benefit from economies of scale.* The corporation that attempts to sell its primary product in new markets may increase its earnings and shareholder wealth due to **economies of scale** (lower average cost per unit resulting from increased production). Such a motive is more likely for firms that utilize much machinery.

   As the Single European Act removed trade barriers, it allowed MNCs to achieve greater economies of scale. For example, some U.S.-based MNCs have consolidated their European plants, as the removal of tariffs between European countries allows economies of scale at one European plant without excessive exporting cost. The act also enhances economies of scale by making regulations on television ads, automobile standards, and other products and services uniform across European countries. As a result, Colgate-Palmolive Company, Prime Computer, and other MNCs are manufacturing more homogeneous products that can be sold in all European countries, rather than differentiating them to meet country-specific standards.

4. *Use foreign factors of production.* Labor and land costs can vary dramatically among countries. MNCs often attempt to set up production in locations where land and labor are cheap. Due to market imperfections (as discussed in Chapter 1) such as imperfect information, relocation transaction costs, barriers to industry entry, etc., specific labor costs do not necessarily become equal among markets. Thus, it is worthwhile for MNCs to survey markets to determine whether they can benefit from cheaper costs by producing in those markets.

   The minimum daily wage rate is less than $4.10 in Mexico, versus over $30 in the United States. Baxter Travenol has established manufacturing plants in Mexico and Malaysia to capitalize on lower costs of production (primarily wage rates). Honeywell has some of its joint ventures in countries where production costs are low, such as Korea and India. It also has established subsidiaries in countries where production costs are low, such as Mexico, Malaysia, Hong Kong, and Taiwan.

   Japanese companies are increasingly using Mexico and other low-wage countries for production. For example, Sony Corporation recently established a plant in Tijuana. Matsushita Electrical Industrial Company has a large plant in Tijuana.

   Numerous U.S.-based MNCs have subsidiaries in Mexico for similar reasons, including Black & Decker Corp., Eastman Kodak Co., Ford Motor Co., General Electric Co., RCA Corp., Smith Corona, and Zenith Radio Corp. The growth in such subsidiaries has contributed significantly to Mexico's economy.

   Many German-based MNCs, including Daimler-Benz (producer of Mercedes), BMW, and Volkswagen, have recently established plants outside of Germany to reduce their labor costs. In 1992, when the average German manufacturing wage was about $24 per hour (including benefits), BMW decided to establish a plant in South Carolina. Firms in Germany or any other high-wage countries are more likely to establish foreign subsidiaries when their operations are labor-intensive.

5. *Use foreign raw materials.* Due to transportation costs, a corporation attempts to avoid importing raw materials from a given country, especially when it plans to then sell the finished product back to consumers in that foreign country. Under such circumstances, a more feasible solution may be to develop the product in the country where the raw materials are located.

6. *Use foreign technology.* Corporations are increasingly establishing overseas plants or acquiring existing overseas plants to learn about the technology of foreign countries. This technology is then used to improve their production processes at all subsidiary plants around the world.

7. *Exploit monopolistic advantages.* Industrial organization theory states that firms may become internationalized if they possess resources or skills not available to competing firms. If a particular firm possesses advanced technology and has exploited this advantage successfully in local markets, it may attempt to exploit it internationally as well. Technology is not restricted to developing a new product. It can even represent a more efficient production, marketing, or financing process. To the extent to which the firm has an advantage over competitors, it should be able to benefit from becoming internationalized.

8. *React to exchange rate movements.* When a foreign currency is perceived by a firm to be undervalued, the firm may consider direct foreign investment in that country, as the initial outlay should be relatively low. For example, assume that a U.S. firm could build a manufacturing plant in the United Kingdom for £40 million. The dollar cost of this project would have been $77.2 million at the beginning of 1991, when the British pound was valued at $1.93. However, just six months later, the dollar cost of this project would have been $65.2 million (or $12 million less), since the pound's value had declined to $1.63 by that time. Since the decision regarding whether to engage in direct foreign investment is partially dependent on the cost, exchange rate movements may influence this decision.

   Japanese companies substantially increased their DFI in the United States, Taiwan, South Korea, and Southeast Asia in the mid-1980s and in 1993, because the yen's strength at those times allowed for relatively low initial outlays to establish subsidiaries. A related reason for such DFI is to offset the changing demand for a company's exports due to exchange rate fluctuations. For example, when Japanese automobile manufacturers build plants in the U.S., they can reduce exposure to exchange rate fluctuations by incurring dollar costs that offset dollar revenues. While MNCs do not simply engage in large projects as an indirect means of speculating on currencies, the feasibility of proposed projects may be dependent on existing and expected exchange rate movements. In this way, the tendency to use direct foreign investment is influenced by exchange rates.

9. *React to trade restrictions.* In some cases, an MNC uses direct foreign investment as a defensive rather than an aggressive strategy. For example, Japanese automobile manufacturers established plants in the United States in anticipation that their exports to the United States would be subject to more stringent trade restrictions. Japanese companies recognized the potential trade barriers that could either limit or prohibit their exports. Since 1980 there have been numerous trade restrictions enforced on automobile imports by the United States.

10. *Diversity internationally.* Since country economies do not move perfectly in tandem over time, net cash flow from sales of products across countries should be more stable than comparable sales if the products were sold in a single country. By diversifying sales (and possibly even production) internationally, a firm can make its net cash flows less volatile. Thus, the possibility of a liquidity deficiency is less likely. In addition, the firm may enjoy a lower cost of capital, as shareholders and creditors perceive the MNC's risk to be lower as a result of more stable cash flows. Potential benefits to MNCs that diversify internationally are more thoroughly examined later in the chapter.

IN PRACTICE

INVESTMENT OPPORTUNITIES IN EUROPE

A survey of CEOs from the United States, Canada, Europe, and the Pacific Basin was conducted to get their views on opportunities in Europe as cross-border barriers are eliminated and regulations are standardized across countries. The responses are summarized below:

Possible Result	Percentage Expecting Result
Easier cross-border transit	94%
Easier labor movement	84
Uniform technical standards	78
More European exports	76
Greater role of U.S. firms in Europe	75
More foreign ownership of European firms	75
Greater role of Japanese firms in Europe	72
Lower consumer prices in Europe	57
Standardized corporate taxes in Europe	56

European Country	Percentage Planning to Expand Business into Country
Spain	64%
Germany	62
France	60
United Kingdom	59
Italy	55
Netherlands	42
Portugal	41
Belgium	38
Ireland	27
Greece	21
Denmark	19
Luxembourg	19

	Percentage Expecting a Fortress Europe	Percentage Not Expecting a Fortress Europe
European CEOs	39%	61%
American CEOs	75	25
Japanese CEOs	79	21
Pacific Rim CEOs	87	13

The CEOs were also asked where in Europe they planned to expand their business. Overall, the survey suggests that CEOs expect major changes in Europe, and are planning to capitalize on the new opportunities.

The CEOs were also asked whether a protectionist Europe ("Fortress Europe") would emerge.

The results suggest a clear difference in opinion between European CEOs and other CEOs. The expectation of a "Fortress Europe" by many non-European CEOs may partially explain their desire to establish a greater presence within Europe.

Summary of Benefits of Direct Foreign Investment

The optimal method for a firm to penetrate a foreign market is partially dependent on the characteristics of the market. For example, direct foreign investment by U.S. firms is common in Europe, but not so common in Asia, where the people are accustomed to purchasing products from Asians. Thus, licensing arrangements or joint ventures may be more appropriate when firms are expanding into Asia. Exhibit 16.1 summarizes the possible benefits of DFI, and explains the means by which MNCs could use DFI to achieve those benefits.

EXHIBIT 16.1   Summary of Benefits Resulting from Direct Foreign Investment

Possible Benefit	Means of Using DFI to Achieve This Benefit
1. Attract new sources of demand.	Establish a subsidiary or acquire a competitor in a new market.
2. Enter markets in which superior profits are possible.	Acquire a competitor that has controlled its local market.
3. Fully benefit from economies of scale.	Establish a subsidiary in a new market that can sell products produced elsewhere; this allows for increased production and possibly greater production efficiency.
4. Use foreign factors of production.	Establish a subsidiary in a market that has relatively low costs of labor or land; sell the finished product to countries where the cost of production is higher.
5. Use foreign raw materials.	Establish a subsidiary in a market in which raw materials are cheap and accessible; sell the finished product to countries in which the raw materials are more expensive.
6. Use foreign technology.	Participate in a joint venture in order to learn about a production process or other operations.
7. Exploit monopolistic advantages.	Establish a subsidiary in a market in which competitors are unable to produce the identical product; sell products in that country.
8. React to exchange rate movements.	Establish a subsidiary in a new market in which the local currency is weak but expected to strengthen over time.
9. React to trade restrictions.	Establish a subsidiary in a market in which tougher trade restrictions will adversely affect the firm's export volume.
10. Diversify internationally.	Establish subsidiaries in markets whose business cycles differ from those where existing subsidiaries are based.

Most MNCs pursue DFI based on their expectations of capitalizing on one or more of the potential benefits summarized in Exhibit 16.1.

While most attempts to increase international business are motivated by one or more of the benefits listed here, there are some corresponding disadvantages as well. For example, the potential cost savings associated with establishing a subsidiary in a less developed country are obvious. However, the expense of establishing the subsidiary, the uncertainty of inflation and exchange rate movements, and the political risk should not be ignored. Decisions to invest in a foreign country must weigh the potential benefits against such costs or additional risks.

BENEFITS OF INTERNATIONAL DIVERSIFICATION

A numerical example is presented next to illustrate how an international project can reduce the firm's risk to a greater degree than a local project can. Then the potential diversification benefits from multiple projects are discussed.

Numerical Example of Diversification Benefits

Consider a U.S. firm that plans to invest in a new project that will be located either in the United States or in Great Britain. Once the project is completed, it will constitute 30 percent of the firm's total funds invested in itself. Assume the firm's current investment in its business (the remaining 70 percent) is exclusively in the United States. Characteristics of the proposed project are forecasted for a five-year period for both a U.S. and a British location, as shown in Exhibit 16.2.

Assume the firm plans to assess the feasibility of each proposed project based on expected return and on risk, using a five-year time horizon. Also assume the firm's expected annual after-tax return on investment on its prevailing business is 20 percent, and its variability of returns (as measured by standard deviation) is expected to be .10. The firm can assess its expected overall performance based on developing the project in the United States. Then it can repeat the analysis based on developing the business in Great Britain. It is essentially comparing two portfolios. The first portfolio is 70 percent of its total funds invested in its prevailing U.S. business, plus the remaining 30 percent of funds invested in a new project located in the United States. The second portfolio again represents 70 percent of the firm's total funds invested in its prevailing business, but the remaining 30 percent of funds in a new project located in Great Britain. Therefore, 70 percent of each portfolio's investment is identical. The difference is reflected in the remaining 30 percent of funds invested.

If the new project is located in the United States, the overall firm's expected after-tax return (r_p) is

$$r_p = (70\%) \quad (20\%) \quad + \quad (30\%) \quad (25\%) \quad = \quad 21.5\%$$

% of funds invested in prevailing business	Expected return on prevailing business	% of funds invested in new U.S. project	Expected return on new U.S. project	Firm's overall expected return

		Characteristics of Proposed Project if Located in the United States	Characteristics of Proposed Project if Located in Great Britain
EXHIBIT 16.2 Evaluation of Proposed Projects in Alternative Locations	Mean expected annual return on investment (after taxes)	25%	25%
	Standard deviation of expected annual after-tax returns on investment	.09	.11
	Correlation of expected annual after-tax returns on investment with after-tax returns of prevailing U.S. business	.80	.02

This computation is based on weighting the returns according to the percentage of total funds invested in each investment.

If the firm calculates its overall expected return when locating the new project in Great Britain instead of the United States, the results would remain unchanged. This is because the new project's expected return is the same regardless of the country of location. Therefore, in terms of return, neither new project has an advantage.

With regard to risk, the new project is expected to exhibit slightly less variability in returns during the five-year period if located in the United States (see Exhibit 16.2). Since firms typically prefer more stable returns on their investments, this is an advantage. However, estimating the risk of the individual project without consideration of the overall firm would be a mistake. The expected correlation of the new project's returns with those of the prevailing business must also be considered. Recall that portfolio variance is determined by the individual variability of each component as well as their pairwise correlations. The variance of a portfolio (σ_p^2) composed of only two investments (A and B) is computed as

$$\sigma_p^2 = w_A^2\, \sigma_A^2 + w_B^2\, \sigma_B^2 + 2w_A w_B\, \sigma_A\, \sigma_B\, (\text{CORR}_{AB}),$$

where w_A and w_B represent the percentage of total funds allocated to Investments A and B, respectively; σ_A and σ_B are the standard deviations of returns on Investments A and B, respectively, and CORR_{AB} is the correlation coefficient of returns between Investments A and B. This equation for portfolio variance can be applied to the problem at hand. The portfolio reflects the overall firm. First, compute the overall firm's variance in returns assuming it locates the new project in the U.S. (based on the information provided in Exhibit 16.2). This variance (σ_p^2) is

$$\sigma_p^2 = (.70)^2 (.10)^2 + (.30)^2 (.09)^2 + 2 (.70)(.30)(.10)(.09)(.80)$$

$$= (.49)(.01) + (.09)(.0081) + .003024$$

$$= .0049 + .000729 + .003024$$

$$= .008653.$$

If the firm decides to locate the new project in Great Britain instead of the United States, its overall variability in returns will be different, because that project differs from the new U.S. project in terms of individual variability in returns and correlation with the prevailing business. The overall variability of the firm's returns based on locating the new project in Great Britain is estimated by variance in the portfolio returns (σ_p^2):

$$\sigma_p^2 = (.70)^2 (.10)^2 + (.30)^2 (.11)^2 + 2(.70) (.30) (.10) (.11) (.02)$$

$$= (.49) (.01) + (.09) (.0121) + .0000924$$

$$= .0049 + .001089 + .0000924$$

$$= .0060814$$

Thus, the firm will generate more stable returns if the new project is located in Great Britain. The firm's overall variability in returns is almost 29.7 percent less if the new project is located in Great Britain rather than in the United States.

The reason for the reduced variability when locating in the foreign country is based on the correlation of the new project's expected returns with the expected returns of the prevailing business. If the new project is located in the firm's home country (the United States), its returns are expected to be more highly correlated with those of the prevailing business than they would be if the project were located in Great Britain. When economic conditions of two countries (such as the United States and Great Britain) are not highly correlated, then a firm may reduce its risk by diversifying its business in both countries rather than concentrating in just one.

Diversification Benefits of Multiple Projects

By extending the previous example to multiple projects, one can gain further insight on the benefits from international diversification. Consider a set of 60 possible U.S. projects, each of which has expected returns to a firm over the next five years. Assume that the variance of each project's expected returns has been estimated, and that the average variance of these 40 projects also has been determined. Now consider all possible sets of two projects combined (and equally weighted). If the returns on these projects are not all perfectly positively correlated, the average variance of a typical two-project portfolio will be less than the average variance of individual projects. Similarly, the variance of all possible three-project portfolios (equally weighted) should be even lower. As more projects are added, the portfolio variance should decrease on average. Initially, the average reduction in variance of returns (a measure of risk) associated with the addition of one more project is substantial. However, after some point, the average reduction in variance becomes negligible, meaning that the remaining risk cannot be diversified away by adding more U.S. projects. This is illustrated as the U.S. curve in Exhibit 16.3.

Now consider another set of 40 projects, of which some are in the United States and the rest are in various foreign countries. If the procedure just described is applied to this set, the outcome will be similar to the global curve in Exhibit 16.3. Notice that the degree of risk reduction resulting from adding an additional project is greater for the global set than for the U.S. set. For any given number of projects, the global portfolio has less risk. The advantage to the global set is attributed to the lower correlations between returns of projects implemented in different economies.

Risk-Return Analysis of International Projects

Like any investor, an MNC with projects positioned around the world is concerned with the risk and return characteristics of the projects. The portfolio of all projects reflects the MNC in aggregate. From a conceptual perspective, the MNC's global strategy of developing projects can be examined using Exhibit 16.4. Each point on the graph reflects a specific project that either has been implemented or is being considered. The return axis may be measured by potential return on assets or return on equity. The risk may be measured by potential fluctuation in the returns generated by each project.

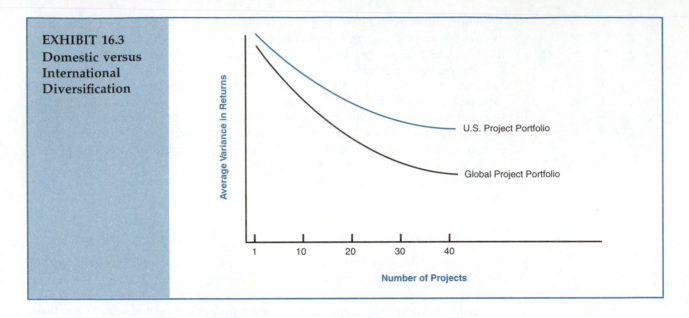

**EXHIBIT 16.3
Domestic versus
International
Diversification**

Average Variance in Returns

U.S. Project Portfolio

Global Project Portfolio

1   10   20   30   40

Number of Projects

Exhibit 16.4 shows that Project A has the highest expected return of all the projects. While the MNC could devote most of its resources toward this project to attempt to achieve such a high return, its risk is possibly too high by itself. In addition, such a project may not be able to absorb all available capital anyway, if its potential market for customers is limited. Thus, the MNC develops a portfolio of projects. By combining Project A with several other projects, the MNC may decrease its expected return. On the other hand, risk could also be reduced substantially. If the MNC appropriately combines projects, its project portfolio may be able to achieve a risk-return trade-off exhibited by any of the points on the curve in Exhibit 16.4. This curve represents a frontier of efficient project

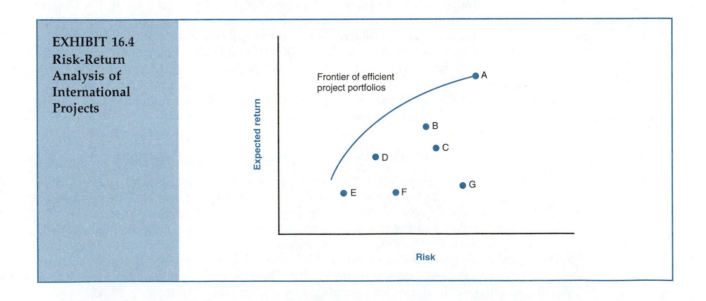

**EXHIBIT 16.4
Risk-Return
Analysis of
International
Projects**

Expected return

Frontier of efficient
project portfolios

● A

● B

● C

● D

● E   ● F   ● G

Risk

EFFECT OF INTERNATIONAL INVOLVEMENT ON CORPORATE RISK

Can a firm truly reduce risk by increasing its degree of international business? Certain studies shed considerable light on this question.

One particular study by Agmon and Lessard examined this issue by assessing the relationship between *betas* (a measure of risk) and the degree of international business among MNCs. First, MNCs were placed into portfolios categorized by their percentages of sales outside the United States. Then the betas of each portfolio were computed. The relationship between the foreign sales percentage and beta is shown in the exhibit. The beta was generally lower for portfolios of MNCs that had a high proportion of foreign sales. For example, the portfolio of MNCs with 1 percent to 7 percent of sales outside the United States exhibited a beta value of 1.04. At the other extreme, the portfolio of U.S. MNCs with 42 percent to 62 percent of their sales outside the United States exhibited a beta value of .88.

The general reduction in risk (less sensitivity to the U.S. market) of MNCs with a greater percentage of foreign sales substantiates the theory that increased internationalization can reduce risk. Yet, it should be emphasized that even the well-diversified U.S. MNCs are somewhat vulnerable to economic events in the United States.

Research by Madura and Rose assessed the impact of international diversification *and* the impact of diversity (sales across economies) on an MNC's risk. They found that for MNCs with less than 21 percent of foreign sales, there was an inverse relationship between degree of international business and beta. This supports Agmon and Lessard's findings. For MNCs with a relatively large percent of foreign sales (over 34 percent), they found no relationship.

They also found that higher diversity is associated with higher risk. This result is somewhat surprising,

since spreading a business across countries was expected to offer greater diversification benefits than concentrating in a single foreign country could. The results may suggest that some MNCs are unable to conduct business effectively in numerous countries, perhaps because of large costs associated with adapting to cultural differences and country-specific regulations.

A second test of the relationship between percentage of foreign sales and risk was conducted by Rugman, who used the standard deviation of stock returns rather than the beta as a measure of risk for the firm. His analysis of MNCs found a negative relationship between percentage of foreign sales and standard deviation of stock returns. The negative relationship suggests that MNCs with a greater degree of foreign business are less risky (their stock price is less volatile); this conclusion coincides with the findings just summarized here.

Relationship Between Degree of Foreign Involvement and Risk for MNCs

Portfolio Number	Proportion of Sales Outside the U.S. (%)	Computed Value of Beta as a Measure of Risk
1	1–7	1.04
2	7–10	1.06
3	10–13	.98
4	13–17	.82
5	17–21	.98
6	21–25	.98
7	25–28	.82
8	28–35	.99
9	35–42	.86
10	42–62	.88

SOURCE: These results were drawn from "Investor Recognition of Corporate International Diversification," *Journal of Finance* (September 1977), p. 98, reprinted with permission of the *Journal of Finance*.

portfolios that exhibit desirable risk-return characteristics, in that no single project could outperform any of these portfolios. The term "efficient" refers to a minimum risk for a given expected return. Project portfolios outperform the individual projects because of the diversification attributes discussed earlier. The lower, or more negative, the correlation in project returns over time, the lower will be the project portfolio risk. As new projects are proposed, the frontier of efficient project portfolios may shift. An MNC is better off if the efficient frontier is further to the left, since this reflects less risk.

Along the frontier of efficient project portfolios, no portfolio can be singled out as "optimal" for all MNCs. This is because MNCs vary in their willingness to accept risk. If the MNC is very conservative and has the choice of any portfolios represented by the frontier in Exhibit 16.4, it will probably prefer one that exhibits low risk (near the bottom of the frontier). Conversely, a more aggressive strategy would be to implement a portfolio of projects that exhibit risk-return characteristics such as those near the top of the frontier.

The actual location of the frontier of efficient project portfolios depends on the business in which the firm is involved. Consider an MNC that sells steel solely to European nations and is considering other related projects. Its frontier of efficient project portfolios would exhibit considerable risk (because it sells just one product to countries whose economies move in tandem). Yet, another MNC that sells a wide range of products to countries all over the world could reduce its project portfolio risk to a greater degree. Therefore, its frontier of efficient project portfolios would be closer to the vertical axis. This comparison is illustrated in Exhibit 16.5. Of course, this comparison assumes the multi-product MNC is knowledgeable about all of its products and the markets to which it sells.

Our discussion suggests that MNCs can achieve more desirable risk-return characteristics from their project portfolios if they sufficiently diversify among products *and* geographical markets. This also relates to the advantage an MNC has over a purely domestic firm with only a local market. The MNC may be able to develop a more efficient portfolio of projects than its domestic counterpart.

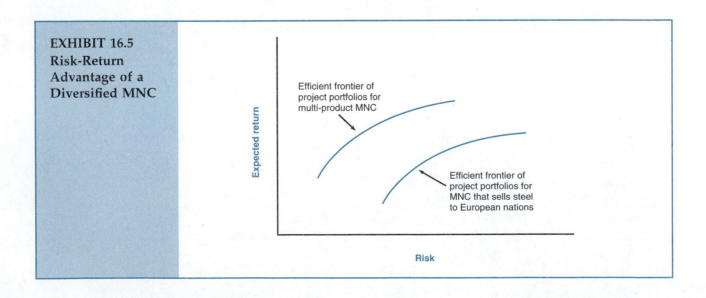

**EXHIBIT 16.5
Risk-Return
Advantage of a
Diversified MNC**

DECISIONS SUBSEQUENT TO DFI

Once DFI takes place, periodic decisions are necessary to determine whether further expansion should take place in a given location. In addition, as the project generates earnings, the MNC must decide whether to have the funds remitted to the parent or used by the subsidiary. If the subsidiary has a use for the funds that would be of more value than the parent's use, the subsidiary should retain the funds. Of course, a certain percentage of the funds will be needed to maintain operations, but the remaining funds could be sent to the parent, sent to another subsidiary, or reinvested for expansion purposes.

Facts relevant to the decision regarding whether the subsidiary should reinvest the earnings should be analyzed on a case-by-case basis. That is, there is no simple guideline to follow. The appropriate decision depends on the economic conditions in the subsidiary's country and the parent's country, as well as restrictions imposed by the host country government. Exhibit 16.6 provides a breakdown of earnings from U.S. DFI in various regions during 1992. The total earnings for each region are divided into "distributed" (sent to parent or elsewhere) and "reinvested" earnings. Notice how the reinvestment ratio (computed as reinvested earnings divided by total earnings) varies among regions. The ratio is highest in the less developed countries, reflecting more opportunities for expansion in these countries.

HOST GOVERNMENT VIEW OF DFI

DFI may be perceived as a cause of or the remedy for national problems. For example, DFI may provide needed employment or technology. However, locally owned companies may lose business due to the new competition. These effects could lead to proposals for increased protectionism.

The ability of a host government to attract DFI is dependent on the country's markets and resources, as well as government regulations and incentives. Countries such as Singapore and Hong Kong have attracted substantial DFI

EXHIBIT 16.6
Earnings From Direct Foreign Investment Abroad by U.S.-Based MNCs in 1992
(*in millions of dollars*)
SOURCE: *Survey of Current Business*, U.S. Department of Commerce.

Location	Earnings Total	Distributed	Reinvested	Reinvestment Ratio
All areas	50,914	33,294	17,620	.35
Canada	2,463	1,958	504	.20
Europe	21,017	16,479	4,538	.22
Latin America (and other Western Hemisphere nations)	13,656	6,075	7,582	.56
Asia and Pacific	11,337	6,465	4,873	.43

because they enforce few restrictions. Conversely, Japan has attracted a very limited amount of DFI because of major barriers to entry.

Some governments offer incentives by reducing production restrictions. For example, Mexico recently reduced its restrictions on automobiles produced there. It had required that Mexican parts make up 65 percent of an automobile produced for the domestic market and 30 percent of one produced for export. This policy was changed to encourage automobile manufacturers from other countries to establish plants in Mexico. Mexico also recently announced that it would allow foreign companies to own 100 percent of their subsidiaries established in Mexico.

Each government must weigh the advantages and disadvantages of DFI in its country. Some types of DFI will be more attractive to some governments than others. The ideal DFI solves problems such as unemployment and lack of technology without taking business away from local firms. An example would be a production plant that uses local labor and produces goods that are not direct substitutes of other locally produced goods. In this case, the plant will not cause a reduction in sales by local firms. A second ideal situation would be a plant that uses local labor and then exports the products (assuming no other local firm exports such products to the same areas).

In most cases, there may be both advantages and disadvantages to a country's allowing a given type of DFI into the country. If the advantages appear to outweigh the disadvantages, the government may attempt to provide additional incentives in order to encourage the DFI to take place. Such incentives could include tax breaks on the income earned there, rent-free land and buildings, low-interest loans, subsidized energy, and reduced environmental (pollution, etc.) restrictions. The degree to which a government would offer such incentives depends on the extent to which the MNC's DFI would benefit that country.

As an example of government incentive, consider the recent decision by Allied Research Associates Inc. to build a production facility and office in Belgium. The Belgian government subsidized a large portion of the expenses, offering tax concessions and favorable interest rates on loans to Allied.

SUMMARY _____

■ MNCs may be motivated to initiate direct foreign investment because they can attract new sources of demand, or enter markets where superior profits are possible. These two motives are normally based on opportunities to generate more revenue in foreign markets. There are numerous other motives for using direct foreign investment that are typically related to cost efficiency, such as using foreign factors of production, raw materials, or technology.

There are other motives for direct foreign investment that MNCs consider to protect their foreign market share, such as reacting to exchange rate movements or trade restrictions.

■ International diversification is a common motive for direct foreign investment. It allows an MNC to reduce its exposure to domestic economic conditions. In this way, the MNC may be able to stabilize its cash flows and reduce its risk. Such a goal is desirable because it may reduce the firm's cost of financing.

International projects can possibly allow MNCs to achieve lower risk than what is possible from only domestic projects, without reducing their expected returns. International diversification tends to be more capable of risk reduction when the direct foreign investment is targeted for countries whose economies are somewhat unrelated to an MNC's home country economy.

SELF-TEST FOR CHAPTER 16

(Answers are provided in Appendix A in the back of the text)

1. Offer some reasons for U.S. firms' preference of direct foreign investment in Canada over DFI in Mexico.

2. Offer some reasons for U.S. firms' preference of direct foreign investment in Mexico over DFI in Canada.

3. One U.S. executive stated that Switzerland was not considered as a location for direct foreign investment because of the Swiss franc's value. Interpret this statement.

4. Why do you think joint ventures are a common strategy used by U.S. firms to enter China?

5. Why would the U.S. offer large incentives to a foreign automobile manufacturer for establishment of a production subsidiary in the U.S.? Isn't this strategy indirectly subsidizing the foreign competitors of U.S. firms?

QUESTIONS

1. Describe some potential benefits to the MNC as a result of direct foreign investment (DFI). Elaborate on each type of benefit.

2. Packer Inc., a U.S. producer of computer diskettes, plans to establish a subsidiary in Germany in order to penetrate the German market. Executives of Packer believe that the mark's value is relatively strong and will weaken against the dollar over time. If their expectations about the mark value are correct, how will this affect the feasibility of the project? Explain.

3. Bear Company and Viking Inc. are automobile manufacturers that desire to benefit from economies of scale. Bear Company has decided to establish distributorship subsidiaries in various countries, while Viking Inc. has decided to establish manufacturing subsidiaries in various countries. Which firm is more likely to benefit from economies of scale?

4. Raider Chemical Company and Ram Inc. had similar intentions to reduce the volatility of their cash flows. Raider implemented a long-range plan to establish 40 percent of its business in Canada. Ram Inc. implemented a long-range plan to establish 30 percent of its business in Europe and Asia, scattered among 12 different countries. Which company would more effectively reduce cash flow volatility once the plans are achieved?

5. If the United States placed long-term restrictions on imports, would the amount of direct foreign investment by non-U.S. MNCs in the United States increase, decrease, or be unchanged? Explain.

6. In 1972 Tandy Corporation established a manufacturing facility in South Korea to produce computer components. One of the attractions was the relatively low cost of labor. In 1989 Tandy closed the facility, as the cost advantage dissipated. Why do you think the relative cost advantage has dissipated in South Korea and other Asian countries such as Hong Kong, Singapore, and Taiwan? (Ignore possible exchange rate effects.)

7. Offer your opinion on why economies of some less developed countries with strict restrictions on international trade and direct foreign investment are somewhat independent from economies of other countries. Why would MNCs desire to enter such countries? If these countries relaxed their restrictions, would their economies continue to be independent of other economies? Explain.

8. Dolphin Inc., a U.S.-based MNC with a German subsidiary, expects that the German mark will appreciate for several years. How might Dolphin Inc. adjust its policy on remitted earnings from the German subsidiary?

9. Bronco Corporation has decided to establish a subsidiary in Taiwan that would produce stereos and sell them in Taiwan. It expects that its cost of producing these stereos will be one-third the cost of producing them in the United States. Assuming that its production cost estimates are accurate, is Bronco's strategy sensible? Explain.

10. What do the studies mentioned in the chapter reveal about the relationship between degree of international business and risk of MNCs? What do these results imply about the feasibility of increasing international business?

11. Starter Corp. of New Haven, Connecticut produces sportswear that is licensed by professional sports teams. It recently decided to expand in Europe. What are the potential benefits for this firm to use direct foreign investment?

12. What potential benefits do you think were most important in the decision of Walt Disney Company to build a theme park in France?

13. Once an MNC establishes a subsidiary, DFI remains an ongoing decision. What does this statement mean?

14. Why would foreign governments provide MNCs with incentives to undertake DFI there?

15. This chapter concentrates on possible benefits to a firm that increases its international business. What are some risks of international business that may not exist for local business?

CASE: U.S. DIRECT FOREIGN INVESTMENT IN CHINA

Enticed by Visions of Enormous Numbers, More Western Marketers Move Into China

By Valerie Reitman
Staff Reporter of The Wall Street Journal

BEIJING - "Give China a chance," exhorts one of hundreds of fractured-English billboards supplanting the Communist propaganda of yore, "Shall return the world a miracle."

Procter & Gamble Co. has already taken China up on its invitation in a big way: Department stores in Beijing, Shanghai and Canton (also called Guangzhou) feature fancy front-entrance counters flaunting P&G's Head & Shoulders, Pantene and Rejoice (known as Pert Plus in the U.S.) shampoos, as well as an array of other P&G products.

Playing catch-up to P&G, which started a joint venture in southern China five years ago with state-owned Guangzhou Soap Factory, big consumer-products markers around the world are now rushing to start, or in some cases expand, operations in the homeland of nearly one of every four of the world's consumers.

For example, Unilever Group, the Anglo-Dutch behemoth, just announced plans to sink $60 million into factories to churn out ice cream and Omo detergent in Shanghai, where it already produces Lux brand soap and shampoo. Kao Corp., the Japanese giant that invented superconcentrated detergents, says it expects to begin manufacturing in China soon. Johnson & Johnson, already making Band-Aids in Shanghai, plans another factory there to produce baby shampoo. And Colgate-Palmolive Co. is constructing a new toothpaste factory in southern China.

Curing 'Winkles'

The foreign companies are lured by 1.2 billion would-be buyers of shampoo, toothpaste, and detergent, not to mention the goods known in China as the "three bigs." Those longed-for objects — once a watch, bicycle and a sewing machine — evolved in the 1980s into the color television set, washing machine and tape recorder, only to give way today to the VCR, air conditioner and stereo.

The makers of household products are counting on their quality and Western cachet to edge out local products such as E&E Nourishing Lotion with Caterpillar Fungus, which claims to cure "winkles." And they are keenly aware that they are involved with the fastest-growing economy on the globe. "China is showing explosive growth," says Craig Tate, Colgate's Asian division chief. "You only have to spend time in the stores to get an idea of the size of the opportunity."

Indeed, with saturated markets and ferocious competition elsewhere, China represents probably the last major marketing frontier on the planet. "There will never be a start-up as big as China," says Peter Hempstead, P&G's China chief.

P&G has sales in China of about $130 million a year (at the official exchange rate), up about 50% from the previous year, according to Zhang Yong De, an official with the Guangzhou Free Trade Zone, which has a 5% interest in P&G's joint venture. (P&G confirms the sales figure is "in the ballpark.") According to Mr. Hampstead, the company has begun eking out a small profit on its hair-care line but not yet on its other lines.

With all the potential, there are steep hurdles to making a buck here - and many new entrants aren't counting on making money for years. Among the obstacles: an overheating economy choked by soaring inflation; difficulty converting Chinese yuan into foreign currency for importing supplies and repatriating profits; an abysmal infrastructure that can turn a rail shipment traveling from Canton to Beijing into a month-long odyssey; and the logistical nightmare of supplying thousands of tiny mom-and-pop stores that can afford to stock only a few bottles at a time.

Even more troubling: the possibility that fledgling economic freedoms in China could be derailed.

Moreover, Western products are still a luxury for most Chinese, particularly in the rural areas where peasants barely subsist. The 14 cents needed to buy P&G's popular single-use shampoo pouches can be a huge extravagance, even for many residents of the most prosperous East Coast cities.

Nonexistent Market Research

Among marketers' most formidable challenges is accurately forecasting the size of China's potential and gearing production to meet it. Given nonexistent market research and the dramatic recent growth in incomes, just how much soap can be sold in China? No one has any idea.

P&G may have been over-optimistic. It bought fewer containers than promised from one of its packaging suppliers, M.C. Bottling Co. Mr. Hempstead acknowledges that P&G "may have been way off on some sizes" but has met projections overall in most areas.

While some estimate China has 100 million customers affluent enough to buy Western goods, Mr. Hempstead sees double or triple that in dozens of cities beyond Beijing and Shanghai. Moreover, the Chinese urban consumer tends to have a proportionally large disposable income, since rents tend to be very low. "The Chinese consumer is increasingly demanding, affluent and resembling her sisters in Hong Kong and Taiwan," says Mr. Hempstead.

Consider stylishly dressed hotel clerk Wang Lang, shopping recently in the Guangzhou Department Store in Canton. Though she makes just $50 a month in her job, she considers the $6 bottle of Rejoice a bargain since it combines both shampoo and conditioner and can last a month. "If I were to go to the beauty shop, it would cost $1.75 every time," she says.

But P&G's ever-escalating prices deter others. In the face of four price increases on Pantene in the past year, Zhang Yong De, the Guangzhou Free Trade Zone official, and his wife, who together earn $350 a month, switched to a Chinese alternative. Besides, he says, P&G's products are "made for Westerners" and may be too greasy for fine Chinese hair. "Chinese eat rice," he says. "Westerners eat wheat. The [shampoo's] ingredients just do not fit the Chinese people." (P&G's Mr. Hempstead agrees "it's probably true that there are differences" in that Chinese hair is finer than others, but he says the differences aren't substantial.)

Continued

CASE: U.S. DIRECT FOREIGN INVESTMENT IN CHINA

Continued

Mr. Zhang's wife and college-age daughter, however, swear by P&G's Whisper sanitary napkins. P&G defined a chronic need for them after seeing normally well-dressed employees wearing old dark clothes and shunning their bicycles two or three days a month because of leakage in local products. Some Chinese women now shell out up to 10 times more than local alternatives for Whisper.

P&G makes its products at its sprawling plant located in an industrial park with about 160 others companies in Canton. Outside the park, standing in striking contrast to old economic ideals, a billboard of China's most powerful leader, Deng Xiaoping, hails the park as "China's future hope."

To reduce its need for foreign exchange, which costs about 1.5 times the official exchange rate, P&G tries to buy supplies locally, although it still needs to import about half its requirements. P&G began making surfactants in Canton for its sham-poos last year to avoid high import tariffs, for example.

And it continues to blaze ahead, buying an adjacent plot for an undisclosed expansion of its four factory buildings in Canton. It will likely add manufacturing in northern China, as well, since its Canton plant has no rail access - a must for shipping detergent. A likely candidate for another joint venture is the soap factory in Tianjin, near Shanghai, which P&G recently contracted to produce Safeguard soap.

Says Mr. Hempstead, "It's obvious to anyone who sees the size of the potential, with the logistics of China, that we will have a need for multiple sites."

Source: *The Wall Street Journal* (July 12, 1993), pp. B1, B10. Reprinted by permission of *The Wall Street Journal.* © 1993 Dow Jones & Company, Inc. All rights reserved worldwide.

QUESTIONS

1. Explain in general terms the motivation for the recent direct foreign investment by Proctor & Gamble, Unilever, and Colgate-Palmolive Co. in China.

2. Describe some of the obstacles faced by U.S. firms, such as Proctor & Gamble and Colgate-Palmolive Co., that have engaged in direct foreign investment in China.

3. Johnson & Johnson plans a factory in Shanghai to produce baby shampoo. Why do you think Johnson & Johnson will produce the shampoo there rather than simply exporting the shampoo from the U.S.?

CASE PROBLEM

BLUES CORPORATION
Capitalizing on the Opening of East European Borders

Blues Corporation has an established reputation having done business in the United States for over fifty years. Executives of Blues Corporation were elated over the reunification between East and West Germany in November 1989. During 1990 and 1991 they developed a strategy for capitalizing on German reunification, which set the stage for various East European countries to open their borders. Most of Blues' business is in the United States. It has a subsidiary in the western section of Germany, which produces goods and exports them to other European countries. Blues Corporation produces numerous consumer goods that could possibly be produced or marketed in East European countries. The following issues were raised at a recent executive meeting. Offer your comments about each issue.

a) Blues Corporation is considering shifting its European production facility from the former West Germany to the former East Germany. There are two key factors motivating this shift. First, the labor cost is lower in eastern Germany. Second, there is an existing facility in the former East Germany (presently government-owned) that is for sale. Blues would like to transform the facility and use its technology to increase the production efficiency. It estimates that it would need only one-fourth of the workers in that facility. What other factors deserve to be considered before the decision is made?

b) Blues Corporation expects that it could penetrate the East European markets. It would need to invest considerable funds in promoting its consumer goods in East Europe, since its goods are not well-known in that area. Yet, it believes that this strategy could pay off in the long run because it could underprice the competition. At the present time, the main competition consists of government-owned businesses that are perceived to be inefficiently run. The lack of competitive pricing in this market is the primary reason for Blues Corporation to consider marketing its product in Eastern Europe. What other factors deserve to be considered before a decision is made?

c) Blues Corporation is presently experiencing a cash squeeze because of a reduced demand for its goods in the United States (although management expects the demand in the United States to increase soon). It is presently near its debt capacity and prefers not to issue stock at this time. Blues Corporation will purchase a facility in Eastern Europe or enact a heavy promotion program in Eastern Europe only if it can raise funds by divesting a significant amount of its U.S. assets. The market values of its assets are temporarily depressed, but some of the executives think an immediate move is necessary to fully capitalize on the East European market. Would you recommend that Blues Corporation divest some of its U.S. assets? Explain.

CASE PROBLEM

PENGUIN COMPANY
Assessing Global Competition

Penguin Company produces automobile parts that are used by all automobile companies around the world. It's headquarters is in the United States, where it generates about 75 percent of its sales. Its foreign sales are conducted through exporting, as it does not have subsidiaries overseas. Its main competition comes from several companies in Hong Kong and a few companies in Taiwan, which produce similar products. These companies dominate most of the non-U.S. markets.

The Hong Kong companies have existed for a long period of time and have traditionally held about 50 percent of market share. In the last few years, their market share has risen. They have strong banking relationships with several major banks and have often successfully engaged in joint venture programs with many different foreign firms. Their manufacturing of the auto parts is performed exclusively in Hong Kong and exported to all major markets.

There are three Taiwan companies which also produce auto parts. These companies are relatively new, although they are growing at a rapid pace.

The specific auto parts produced by these companies could be duplicated by other companies only at great expense. A substantial amount in research and development resources was invested to achieve the technology to mass-produce these parts according to automobile manufacturers' specifications. Consequently, there are presently significant barriers to entry in this subset of the auto parts industry.

In recent years, the gain in global market share by the Hong Kong companies has come at the expense of Penguin Company. This year Penguin Company has appealed to the U.S. government that the Hong Kong companies must be selling their product below cost. It is suspected that the Hong Kong government is subsidizing their cost in order to maintain a high level of employment. The Hong Kong companies maintain that it is their work efficiency, not government subsidies, that have allowed them to increase their global market share. Penguin Company is especially concerned because the Hong Kong companies have just begun a major marketing effort to capture a larger portion of the U.S. market. For this reason, Penguin Company continues to pressure the U.S. government to correct this "unfair entrance into the U.S. markets." The Taiwan companies also appear to be more cost-effective than Penguin Company, but they have not penetrated the U.S. market. Their volume of business is not yet large enough to justify a large marketing drive in the United States. The Taiwan companies also do not have the resources to compete against the Hong Kong companies for the U.S. market.

PENGUIN COMPANY (CONTINUED)

a) Evaluate the situation from the perspective of the U.S. government. That is, define the options the U.S. government has, and evaluate the viability of each option.

b) Evaluate the situation from the perspective of the Hong Kong companies. Should they be willing to spend large sums of money on marketing costs in their effort to gain a large share of the U.S. market? Defend your conclusion. What factors must be considered in their analysis?

c) If the Hong Kong companies decide to continue their marketing drive in the United States, they may consider establishing production plants in the United States, rather than exporting the products. What factors should be considered when making the decision? That is, what factors would affect the estimated cash inflows and outflows of such a decision? How does the expectation of a weaker U.S. dollar in the future affect the idea of establishing a subsidiary?

d) Evaluate the situation from the perspective of Penguin Company. Besides its appeal to the U.S. government, what other options might it consider in order to survive?

e) Evaluate the situation from the perspective of a global mutual fund portfolio manager whose portfolio is made up mostly of Hong Kong, Taiwan, and U.S. stocks (presently about one-third investment in each group). Is there any reason to consider adjusting the allocation of funds among the three countries discussed here? Explain any relevant events that could affect the stock values of the portfolio, and state how you would revise the allocation amount to each country (if at all).

Part of a portfolio manager's job is to continually evaluate the future prospects of existing companies, and to buy or sell stocks based on anticipation. Are there any particular types of companies that could benefit or lose as a result of any actions that may be taken by the U.S. government, Penguin Company, or its competitors? Identify these types of companies, and explain how they may benefit or lose. Suggest which companies should be most closely monitored as a result of the situation.

PROJECT

Review recent annual reports of an MNC of your choice and summarize why it has increased its international operations over time. Various factors that motivate international business are identified in this chapter. Determine which factors were probably most influential in motivating the MNC's expansion into other countries.

REFERENCES

Aggarwal, R. "Investment Performance of U.S.-Based Multinational Companies: Comments and a Perspective on International Diversification on Real Assets." *Journal of International Business Studies* (Spring–Summer 1980), pp. 98–104.

_____ . "Multinationality and Stock Market Valuation: An Empirical Study of U.S. Markets and Companies." *Management International Review* (1979), pp. 5–21.

Agmon, Tamir, and Donald Lessard. "Investor Recognition of Corporate International Diversification." *Journal of Finance* (September 1977), pp. 1049–1058.

Black, Joseph H., Jeff Madura, and Lawrence C. Rose. "Corporate Risk Response to Competing Diversification Strategies: An International Perspective." *Journal of International Finance* (Fall 1989), pp. 57–72.

Errunza, Vihang R., and L. Senbet. "The Effects of International Operations on the Market Value of the Firm: Theory and Evidence." *Journal of Finance* (May 1981), pp. 401–417.

Essayyad, Musa, and H. K. Wu. "The Performance of U.S. International Mutual Funds." *Quarterly Journal of Business and Economics* (Autumn 1988), pp. 32–46.

Eun, Cheol S., and Bruce G. Resnick. "Estimating the Correlation Structure of International Share Prices." *Journal of Finance* (December 1984), pp. 1311–1324.

Fatemi, Ali M. "Shareholder Benefits from Corporate International Diversification." *Journal of Finance* (December 1984), pp. 1325–1344.

Fosberg, Richard H., and Jeff Madura. "Risk Reduction Benefits from International Diversification: A Reassessment." *Journal of Multinational Financial Management*, no. 1 (1991), pp. 35–42.

Ghertman, Michel. "Foreign Subsidiary and Parents' Roles During Strategic Investment and Divestment Decisions." *Journal of International Business Studies* (Spring 1988), pp. 47–67.

Hisey, Karen B., and Richard E. Caves. "Diversification Strategy and Choice of Country: Diversifying Acquisitions Abroad by U.S. Multinationals, 1978–1980." *Journal of International Business Studies* (Summer 1985), pp. 51–64.

Jacquillat, Bertrand, and Bruno Solnik. "Multinationals Are Poor Tools for Diversification." *Journal of Portfolio Management* (Winter 1978), pp. 8–12.

Kahley, William J. "U.S. and Foreign Direct Investment Patterns." *Economic Review.* Federal Reserve Bank of Atlanta (November–December 1989), pp. 42–57.

Kim, Wi Saeng, and Esmeralda O. Lyn. "FDI Theories and the Performance of Foreign Multinationals Operating in the U.S." *Journal of International Business Studies* (First Quarter 1990), pp. 41–54.

Madura, Jeff. "Influence of Foreign Markets on Multinational Stocks: Implications for Investors." *Review of International Economics and Business*, October–November 1989, pp. 1009–1018.

_____ . "International Portfolio Construction." *Journal of Business Research* (Spring 1985), pp. 87–95.

Madura, Jeff, and Wallace Reiff. "A Hedge Strategy for International Portfolios." *Journal of Portfolio Management* (Fall 1985), pp. 70–74.

Madura, Jeff, and Lawrence C. Rose. "Are Product Specialization and International Diversification Compatible?" *Management International Review* no. 3 (1987), pp. 37–44.

_____ . "Impact of International Sales Degree and Diversity on Corporate Risk." *International Trade Journal* (Spring 1989), pp. 261–276.

Mann, Catherine L., "Determinants of Japanese Direct Investment in U.S. Manufacturing Industries," *Journal of International Money and Finance,* (October 1993), pp 523–542.

Officer, Dennis T., and J. Ronald Hoffmeister. "ADRs: A Substitute for the Real Thing?" *Journal of Portfolio Management* (Winter 1987), pp. 61–65.

Rolfe, Robert J., David A. Ricks, Martha M. Pointer, and Mark McCarthy, "Determinants of FDI Incentive Preferences of MNEs," *Journal of International Business Studies,* (Second Quarter, 1993), PP 335–355.

Roll, Richard. "The International Crash of October 1987." *Financial Analysts Journal* (October 1988), pp. 19–35.

Rugman, Alan R. "Foreign Operations and the Stability of U.S. Corporate Earnings: Risk Reduction by International Diversification." *Journal of Finance* (March 1975), pp. 233–234.

_____ . "International Diversification by Financial and Direct Investment." *Journal of Economics and Business* (Fall 1977), pp. 31–37.

Solnik, Bruno H. "Why Not Diversify Internationally Rather Than Domestically?" *Financial Analysts Journal* (July/August 1974), pp. 48–54.

Stulz, Rene M. "On the Determinants of Net Foreign Investment." *Journal of Finance* (May 1983), pp. 459–468.

Tucker, Alan L. "International Investing: Are ADRs an Alternative?" *AAII Journal* (November 1987), pp. 10–12.

INTERNATIONAL STOCK DIVERSIFICATION

A substantial amount of research has demonstrated that investors in stocks can benefit by diversifying internationally. The stocks of most firms are highly influenced by the country in which those firms reside (although some firms are more vulnerable to economic conditions than others).

Since stock markets partially reflect the current and/or forecasted state of their countries economies, they do not move in tandem. Thus, particular stocks of the various markets are not expected to be highly correlated. This contrasts with a purely domestic portfolio, in which most stocks are often moving in the same direction and by a somewhat similar magnitude.

To assess how country stock markets move relative to one another, correlation coefficients of monthly stock market returns have been computed for the 1972–1992 period. Each country's stock index represents a sample of stocks. The correlation coefficients of stock index returns for nine major countries are displayed in Exhibit 16A.1. Some pairs of indexes, such as the United States/ Canada, and Germany/Netherlands, exhibit relatively high correlations. For the most part, though, stock index correlations range between .30 and .50. Consequently, investors should be able to reduce variability in portfolio returns by diversifying among stocks from several countries.

EXHIBIT 16A.1   Correlations of Stock Market Movements in Major Countries

	Canada	France	Germany	Japan	Netherlands	Sweden	Switzerland	U.K.
France	.54							
Germany	.31	.53						
Japan	.42	.40	.31					
Netherlands	.45	.54	.66	.47				
Sweden	.44	.40	.48	.39	.56			
Switzerland	.54	.50	.66	.32	.69	.49		
U.K.	.51	.44	.45	.45	.54	.31	.60	
U.S.	.57	.33	.42	.42	.43	.40	.56	.55

POTENTIAL RISK REDUCTION FOR THE FUTURE _____

If correlations are generally increasing over time, stock index values are moving more in tandem. Therefore, the variability of portfolios composed of these individual indexes would increase. This issue is assessed below.

Data on country stock index returns have been divided into two subperiods. The correlations between stock indexes for both subperiods have been computed and are displayed in Exhibit 16A.2. The correlations of the earlier subperiod are shown at the top of each cell and those of the more recent subperiod at the bottom of each cell. Overall, thirty-one of the thirty-six correlations increased over time, suggesting that stock market correlations are increasing over time. Thus, the potential benefits from international stock markets may have been reduced over time. However, this may be offset by the new opportunities that have resulted from the opening of additional foreign stock markets.

MARKET MOVEMENTS DURING THE 1987 CRASH _____

Further evidence on the relationships between stock markets is obtained by assessing market movements during the stock market crash in October 1987. Exhibit 16A.3 shows the stock market movements for four major countries during the crash. While the magnitude of the decline was not exactly the same,

---

EXHIBIT 16A.2   Comparison of Stock Market Correlations During Two Subperiods
*1 = January 1972-December 1981
**2 = January 1982-December 1992

	Sub-period	Canada	France	Germany	Japan	Nether-lands	Sweden	Switzer-land	U.K.
France	1*	.54							
	2**	.53							
Germany	1	.14	.29						
	2	.43	.71						
Japan	1	.37	.24	.49					
	2	.46	.55	.22					
Netherlands	1	.42	.44	.54	.69				
	2	.51	.63	.72	.34				
Sweden	1	.13	.14	.26	.27	.29			
	2	.64	.58	.55	.45	.71			
Switzerland	1	.54	.32	.38	.50	.51	.14		
	2	.57	.64	.78	.22	.78	.64		
U.K.	1	.47	.37	.50	.41	.56	.18	.67	
	2	.66	.61	.51	.60	.59	.53	.61	
U.S.	1	.33	.07	.31	.43	.43	.01	.45	.47
	2	.87	.62	.49	.44	.56	.67	.65	.77

INTERNATIONAL STOCK MARKET QUOTATIONS

International stock market prices are quoted for major stock markets each day in *The Wall Street Journal*, as shown here. Each country is identified in the left column. For any given country, the stock index value is quoted, along with the percentage change in the index value (from the previous day) in the country's local currency (see the second and third columns). In addition, the closing value of the index for the day and the percentage change are also measured in U.S. dollars to reflect a U.S. investor's perspective. The twelve-month high and low and twelve-month percentage change are also measured from the U.S. perspective.

DOW JONES WORLD STOCK INDEX

Wednesday, July 13, 1994

REGION/ COUNTRY	DJ EQUITY MARKET INDEX, LOCAL CURRENCY	PCT. CHG.	CLOSING INDEX	CHG.	PCT. CHG.	12-MO HIGH	12-MO LOW	12-MO CHG.	PCT. CHG.	FROM 12/31	PCT. CHG.
Americas			107.13	+ 0.24	+ 0.23	115.99	105.21	− 0.81	− 0.75	− 5.05	− 4.50
Canada	111.27	+ 0.11	93.10	+ 0.36	+ 0.39	107.30	88.37	− 0.27	− 0.29	− 7.25	− 7.23
Mexico	160.79	− 0.96	145.04	− 1.47	− 1.00	203.25	116.19	+ 26.19	+ 22.04	− 37.84	− 20.69
U.S.	424.86	+ 0.25	424.86	+ 1.05	+ 0.25	456.27	416.31	− 1.33	− 0.31	− 17.33	− 3.92
Europe			115.92	+ 0.34	+ 0.29	122.60	98.44	+ 16.94	+ 17.11	− 0.17	− 0.14
Austria	108.86	− 0.14	107.40	− 0.96	− 0.89	111.50	85.39	+ 22.01	+ 25.78	+ 2.58	+ 2.46
Belgium	118.54	− 0.05	117.37	− 1.34	− 1.13	123.06	98.83	+ 15.26	+ 14.95	+ 5.83	+ 5.22
Denmark	106.93	+ 0.21	104.78	− 0.85	− 0.81	106.98	80.33	+ 23.46	+ 28.85	+ 9.05	+ 9.46
Finland	216.45	+ 1.15	176.33	+ 0.84	+ 0.48	176.64	107.62	+ 64.39	+ 57.52	+ 37.66	+ 27.16
France	117.86	+ 1.52	115.83	+ 1.17	+ 1.02	124.46	100.32	+ 14.08	+ 13.84	− 1.95	− 1.66
Germany	123.24	+ 0.28	121.07	− 0.66	− 0.54	125.38	96.04	+ 23.58	+ 24.19	+ 2.14	+ 1.80
Ireland	138.68	− 0.12	116.13	− 0.41	− 0.35	125.99	94.54	+ 20.85	+ 21.88	+ 4.17	+ 3.73
Italy	156.27	+ 1.81	126.75	+ 1.69	+ 1.35	143.55	81.75	+ 29.21	+ 29.95	+ 27.65	+ 27.90
Netherlands	132.24	+ 0.78	129.05	+ 0.16	+ 0.12	131.59	105.81	+ 22.51	+ 21.13	+ 3.31	+ 2.63
Norway	128.28	+ 1.62	113.70	+ 1.10	+ 0.98	118.78	88.83	+ 23.15	+ 25.56	+ 10.42	+ 10.09
Spain	126.19	+ 1.03	96.66	+ 0.23	+ 0.24	106.94	78.01	+ 14.37	+ 17.46	+ 1.78	+ 1.87
Sweden	152.23	+ 1.05	111.31	+ 0.09	+ 0.08	122.77	89.67	+ 21.02	+ 23.29	+ 7.25	+ 6.96
Switzerland	147.78	− 1.26	154.25	− 3.06	− 1.95	172.92	121.91	+ 28.64	+ 22.80	− 4.02	− 2.54
United Kingdom	126.81	+ 1.20	106.18	+ 1.00	+ 0.95	118.15	95.06	+ 10.30	+ 10.74	− 6.12	− 5.45
Asia/Pacific			126.24	− 0.09	− 0.07	127.24	98.67	+ 14.09	+ 12.56	+ 19.48	+ 18.25
Australia	115.03	+ 0.27	111.65	+ 0.53	+ 0.48	128.45	93.84	+ 17.18	+ 18.18	− 1.63	− 1.44
Hong Kong	199.51	+ 2.71	200.67	+ 5.31	+ 2.72	279.65	153.12	+ 42.91	+ 27.20	− 69.69	− 25.78
Indonesia	193.27	+ 1.07	177.87	+ 2.27	+ 1.29	248.28	148.55	+ 25.09	+ 16.42	− 56.06	− 23.96
Japan	97.58	+ 0.45	123.98	− 0.47	− 0.38	125.40	91.51	+ 12.89	+ 11.61	+ 28.28	+ 29.54
Malaysia	204.52	+ 0.66	215.04	+ 1.30	+ 0.61	284.09	154.04	+ 59.48	+ 38.24	− 54.95	− 20.35
New Zealand	133.47	+ 0.75	149.36	+ 1.08	+ 0.73	172.58	114.65	+ 32.54	+ 27.86	− 2.16	− 1.43
Singapore	149.19	+ 1.09	159.78	+ 1.40	+ 0.88	184.75	114.99	+ 43.91	+ 37.90	− 19.43	− 10.84
Thailand	210.07	+ 1.81	198.73	+ 3.29	+ 1.68	256.46	121.80	+ 73.91	+ 59.21	− 45.17	− 18.52
Asia/Pacific (ex. Japan)			158.90	+ 2.29	+ 1.46	199.98	124.49	+ 33.57	+ 26.79	− 34.69	− 17.92
World (ex. U.S.)			120.89	+ 0.08	+ 0.07	121.54	102.52	+ 14.12	+ 13.23	+ 10.36	+ 9.38
DJ WORLD STOCK INDEX			115.77	+ 0.15	+ 0.13	119.04	105.71	+ 8.55	+ 7.98	+ 4.70	+ 4.23

Indexes based on 6/30/82=100 for U.S., 12/31/91=100 for World.   ©1994 Dow Jones & Co. Inc., All Rights Reserved

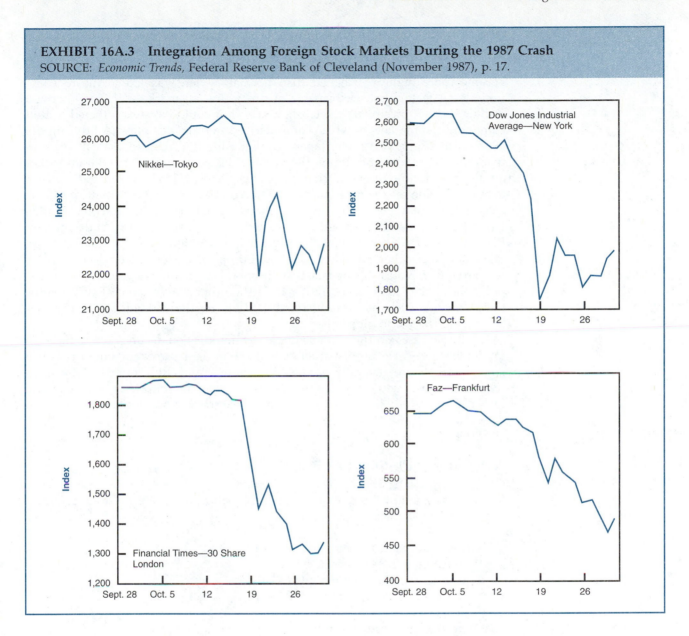

EXHIBIT 16A.3   Integration Among Foreign Stock Markets During the 1987 Crash
SOURCE: *Economic Trends,* Federal Reserve Bank of Cleveland (November 1987), p. 17.

all four markets were adversely affected. When institutional investors anticipated a general decline in stocks, they sold some stocks from all markets, rather than just the U.S. market.

Many stock markets experienced larger declines in prices than the United States did. For example, during the month of October 1987, the U.S. market index declined by about 21 percent, while the German market index declined by about 23 percent and the United Kingdom index by 26 percent. The stock market indices of Australia and Hong Kong decreased by more than 50 percent over this same month.

Some critics have suggested that the institutional forces in the United States (such as computer-assisted trading, specialists, and concurrent trading in stock index futures), along with a strong U.S. influence on the world, caused a worldwide crash. Yet, a study by Roll shows no evidence that the United States was the sole culprit. Roll shows that during October 1987 country stock indices became more highly correlated than normal, which was likely due to some underlying factor that was capable of disrupting all markets. If computerized trading did not precipitate the crash, however, it could have exacerbated it. Roll compared the markets in which computerized trading was prevalent during the 1987 crash (Canada, France, Japan, United Kingdom, United States) to other markets. In local currency terms, the five markets with computerized trading had an average decline of about 21 percent over October 1987, versus a 28 percent average decline for the other markets. This comparison suggests that computerized trading may even have reduced market volatility. Asian markets such as Hong Kong, Malaysia, and Singapore experienced substantial market declines on Black Monday (October 19, 1987) several hours before the U.S. market even opened. In fact, other markets throughout Europe also experienced declines prior to the United States. It appears that the non-U.S. markets could have caused paranoia in the U.S. market, rather than the other way around. Thus, institutional factors such as computerized trading in the United States did not precipitate the worldwide crash.

Roll also assessed the possible impact of liquidity on declines across markets in October 1987. He used market capitalization as a proxy for liquidity, since larger markets are generally perceived as more liquid. Roll found no statistical relationship between market capitalization and the magnitude of decline across markets. Therefore, liquidity did not influence market performance during the crash.

METHODS USED TO INVEST INTERNATIONALLY

If investors attempt international stock diversification, there are four common approaches available:

- Direct purchases of foreign stocks
- Investment in MNC stocks
- American depository receipts (ADRs)
- International mutual funds (IMFs)

Each approach is discussed in turn.

Direct Purchases of Foreign Stocks

Foreign stocks could be purchased on foreign stock exchanges. This requires the services of brokerage firms that can contact floor brokers who work on the foreign stock exchange of concern. However, this approach is inefficient because of market imperfections such as insufficient information, transaction costs, and tax differentials among countries.

An alternative method of investing directly in foreign stocks is to purchase stocks of foreign companies that are sold on the local stock exchange. In the United States, for example, Royal Dutch Shell (of the Netherlands), Sony (of Japan), and many other foreign stocks are sold on U.S. stock exchanges. Because the number of foreign stocks listed on any local stock exchange is typically quite limited, this method by itself may not be adequate to achieve full benefits of international diversification.

Investment in MNC Stocks

The operations of an MNC represent international diversification. Like an investor with a well-managed stock portfolio, an MNC can reduce risk (variability in net cash flows) by diversifying sales not only among industries, but also among countries. In this sense, the MNC as a single firm can achieve stability similar to that of an internationally diversified stock portfolio.

If MNC stocks behave as an international portfolio, then they should be sensitive to the stock markets of the various countries in which they operate. A study by Jacquillat and Solnik assessed the sensitivity of MNC returns to various stock market movements during the 1966–1974 period, using the following regression model:

$$R_{MNC} = a_o + a_1 R_L + b_1 R_{I,1} + b_2 R_{I,2} + \ldots + b_n R_{I,n} + u,$$

where R_{MNC} is the average return on a portfolio of MNCs from the same country, a_o is the intercept, R_L is the return on the local stock market, $R_{I,1}$ through $R_{I,n}$ are returns on foreign stock indices I_1 through I_n and u is an error term. The regression coefficient a_1 measures the sensitivity of MNC returns to their local stock market, while coefficients b_1 through b_n measure the sensitivity of MNC returns to the various foreign stock markets. The time series regression analysis found that MNCs based in a particular country were typically affected only by the local stock market, and were not affected by other stock market movements. This same result occurred for the MNC portfolio of each country.

A recent study by Madura reassessed the sensitivity of MNC returns to various stock markets over the 1974–1987 period. A reassessment was necessary, since many MNCs have significantly increased their international operations since the period used by Jacquillat and Solnik to evaluate MNCs. The increased international involvement of MNCs could have caused them to behave more as an internationally diversified stock portfolio. Based on a procedure similar to that of Jacquillat and Solnik, this study again showed that MNC stock returns respond only to the local stock market returns, and not to the movements of any other markets. Thus, MNCs are not an effective means to achieve international diversification.

American Depository Receipts

Another approach is to purchase **American depository receipts (ADRs),** which are certificates representing ownership of foreign stocks. There are more than 1,000 ADRs available in the United States, primarily traded on the over-the-counter (OTC) stock market. Because most of these ADRs are not actively traded, their prices are typically not reported on a consistent basis. This may change over time, however, as they are becoming increasingly popular.

Officer and Hoffmeister assessed the viability of ADRs as a means of international diversification. They found that while ADR returns were more volatile than U.S. stock returns, combined portfolios of ADRs and U.S. stocks exhibited significantly lower variability than portfolios solely composed of U.S. stocks. Thus, they concluded that ADRs could effectively enable U.S. investors to reduce risk. Related research by Tucker compared the benefits of ADRs to foreign stocks by comparing the marginal benefits of adding ADRs to a U.S. stock portfolio to those of adding foreign stocks. The degree of risk reduction with ADRs was quite similar to that with foreign stocks. These results imply that ADRs are an effective means of international diversification, and therefore that investment in ADRs may be an adequate substitute for direct investment in foreign stocks. However, the limited number of ADRs available and the relatively high transaction costs may encourage some investors to use an alternative approach.

International Mutual Funds

A final approach to consider is purchasing shares of **international mutual funds (IMFs),** which are portfolios of stocks from various countries. Several investment firms, such as Fidelity, Vanguard, and Merrill Lynch, have constructed IMFs for their customers. Like domestic mutual funds, IMFs are popular due to (1) the low minimum investment necessary to participate in the funds, (2) the presumed expertise of the portfolio managers, and (3) the high degree of diversification achieved by the portfolios' inclusion of several stocks. Yet, an IMF is often thought to be more capable of reducing risk than a purely domestic mutual fund, since it includes foreign securities. An IMF represents a prepackaged portfolio, so investors who use it do not need to construct their own portfolios. While some investors prefer to construct their own portfolios, the existence of numerous IMFs on the market today allows investors to select the one that most closely resembles the type of portfolio they would have constructed on their own. Moreover, there are some investors who feel more comfortable with a professional manager composing the international portfolio.

Research by Essasyyad and Wu assessed the performance of 18 international mutual funds over the 1977–1984 period. Fifteen of the 18 IMFs exhibited a higher mean monthly return than the Standard & Poor's (S&P) 500 index. In addition, 16 of the IMFs exhibited a lower coefficient of variation (defined as standard deviation of returns divided by mean return) than the S&P 500 index, suggesting a lower level of risk per unit of return.

To further assess risk, the authors measured the betas of the IMFs, using the S&P 500 index as a proxy for the market. Four of the 18 IMFs had a beta that was not statistically different from zero. For the 18 IMFs, the average percentage of variation in returns explained by market movements was only about 24 percent. This confirms that IMF return patterns differ substantially from U.S. market returns, a desirable attribute for portfolio diversification.

EXCHANGE RATE RISK OF FOREIGN STOCKS _____

As the foreign currency denominating a foreign stock appreciates, the return to the investor is enhanced. However, if the foreign currency depreciates, the return is reduced. The volatility of exchange rates causes returns on foreign stocks to be volatile as well.

Reducing Exchange Rate Risk of Foreign Stocks

The exchange rate risk resulting from foreign stock holdings can be reduced by diversification among stocks of different countries. For example, a U.S. investor can reduce exchange rate risk by spreading whatever funds are to be used for foreign investments across various non-U.S. countries. If correlations between foreign currency movements (against the U.S. dollar) are low or negative, exchange rate risk can be effectively reduced through diversification.

Many foreign currencies move in tandem against the dollar, especially the European currencies that are pegged to the European Currency Unit (ECU). Because these currencies are essentially fixed relative to one another (within boundaries), they are forced to move by a similar magnitude and direction against the dollar. Thus, if one of these currencies depreciates substantially against the dollar, the others will as well, and all foreign stocks denominated in these currencies will be adversely affected to a similar degree. Investors would achieve more effective diversification of currencies by spreading the foreign investment across continents.

Another method of reducing exchange rate risk is to take short positions in the foreign currencies denominating the foreign stocks. For example, a U.S. investor holding French stocks who expects the stocks to be worth FF1 million one year from now could sell forward contracts (or futures contracts) representing FF1 million. The stocks could be liquidated at that time and the francs could be exchanged for dollars at a locked-in price.

Limitations of Hedging. While hedging the exchange rate risk of an international stock portfolio can be effective, it has three limitations. First, the number of foreign currency units to be converted to dollars at the end of the investment horizon is unknown. If the units received from liquidating the foreign stocks are more (less) than the amount hedged, the investor has a net long (short) position in that foreign currency, and the return will be unfavorably affected by its depreciation (appreciation). Nevertheless, while investors may not perform a perfect hedge for this reason, they should normally be able to hedge most of their exchange rate risk.

A second limitation of hedging exchange rate risk is that the investors may decide to retain the foreign stocks beyond the initially planned investment horizon. Of course, they can create another short position after the initial short position is terminated. If they ever decide to liquidate the foreign stocks prior to the forward delivery date, the hedge will be less effective. They could use the proceeds to invest in foreign money market securities denominated in that foreign currency in order to postpone conversion to dollars until the forward delivery date. But this prevents them from using the funds for other opportunities until that delivery date.

A third limitation of hedging is that forward rates for some currencies may not exist, or may exhibit a large discount. This limitation generally does not apply to the widely traded currencies.

Effects of Hedging. Some research has been performed on hedging investments in foreign stocks. A study by Madura and Reiff estimated the returns of country stock indices with and without hedging (from a U.S. perspective), in order to determine the degree of risk reduction achievable from hedging. They developed an **efficient frontier** of unhedged portfolios and compared it to an efficient frontier of hedged portfolios. The hedged portfolios generally exhibited about half the variance for a given return level. These results are due to higher variances of unhedged stock index returns, and higher correlations between the unhedged stock index returns.

While the development of ex post efficient portfolios shows potential risk-return levels that could have been achieved, such optimal results are difficult to achieve in reality. A study by Eun and Resnick assessed the performance of hedged and unhedged portfolios on an ex ante basis. That is, only information prior to the decision dates was used to compose the portfolios. Their study found that the hedged portfolios resulted in much lower risk than the unhedged portfolios, even on an ex ante basis. The hedged portfolios consistently outperformed unhedged portfolios, suggesting that the benefits of international diversification are best realized by hedging against exchange rate risk.

CHAPTER 17

MULTINATIONAL CAPITAL BUDGETING

Multinational corporations (MNCs) evaluate international projects by using multinational capital budgeting, which compares the benefits and costs of these projects. Given that many MNCs spend more than $100 million per year on international projects, multinational capital budgeting is a critical function. Many international projects are irreversible, and cannot be easily sold to other corporations at a reasonable price. Proper use of multinational capital budgeting can separate the international projects worthy of implementation from those that are not.

The most popular form of capital budgeting is to determine the project's net present value by estimating the present value of the project's future cash flows, and subtracting the initial outlay required for the project. Multinational capital budgeting typically involves a similar process. However, special circumstances of international projects that affect the future cash flows or the discount rate used to discount cash flows make multinational capital budgeting more complex. The specific objectives of this chapter are to

- compare the capital budgeting analysis of an MNC's subsidiary versus its parent,
- demonstrate how multinational capital budgeting can be applied to determine whether an international project should be implemented, and
- explain how the risk of international projects can be assessed.

SUBSIDIARY VERSUS PARENT PERSPECTIVE _____

Should capital budgeting for a multinational project be conducted from the viewpoint of the subsidiary that will administer the project or the parent that will most likely finance much of the project? Some would say the subsidiary's perspective should be used, since it will be responsible for administering the project. In addition, since the subsidiary is a subset of the MNC, what is good for the subsidiary would appear to be good for the MNC. This reasoning, however, is not necessarily correct. One could argue that if the parent is financing the project, then it should be evaluating the results from its point of view. The feasibility of the capital budgeting analysis can vary with the perspective, because the net after-tax cash inflows to the subsidiary can differ substantially from those to the parent. Such a difference is due to several factors, some of which are discussed here.

Tax Differentials

Assume the parent considers expanding a subsidiary's marketing department. Also assume the host country government imposes a very low tax rate on earnings generated by the subsidiary. If the earnings due to the project will someday be remitted to the parent, the MNC needs to consider how the parent's government taxes these earnings. If the parent's government imposes a high tax rate on the remitted funds, the project may be feasible from the subsidiary's point of view, but not from the parent's point of view. Under such a scenario, the parent should not consider implementing such a project, even though it appears feasible from the subsidiary's perspective.

Restricted Remittances

Consider a potential project to be implemented in a country where the government restrictions require that a percentage of the subsidiary earnings remain in the country. Since the parent may never have access to such funds, the project is not attractive to the parent. Yet, the project may be attractive to the subsidiary. One possible solution to such a problem is to let the subsidiary obtain partial financing for the project within the host country. In this case, the portion of funds not allowed to be sent to the parent can be used to cover the financing costs over time.

Excessive Remittances

Consider a parent that charges its subsidiary very high administrative fees, since management is centralized at the headquarters. To the subsidiary, the fees represent an expense. To the parent, the fees represent revenue that may substantially exceed the actual cost of managing the subsidiary. In this case, the project's earnings may appear low from the subsidiary's perspective and high from the parent's perspective. The feasibility of the project again depends on perspective. In most cases, neglecting the parent's perspective will distort the true value of a foreign project.

Exchange Rate Movements

When earnings are remitted to the parent, they are normally converted from the subsidiary's local currency to the parent's currency. The amount received by the parent is therefore influenced by the existing exchange rate. If the subsidiary project is assessed from the subsidiary's perspective, the cash flows forecasted for the subsidiary do not have to be converted to the parent's currency.

Subsidiary Versus Parent Perspective: An Example

To illustrate how the capital budgeting analysis may vary among perspectives, consider the following simplified example. Buckeye Corporation, a U.S.-based MNC, has a subsidiary in Mexico that produces and sells farm equipment. Buckeye believes the subsidiary could also develop an equipment repair business. The following projections and relevant data have been compiled for the analysis:

- The anticipated initial investment (or initial outlay) is 9.6 billion pesos, which at the existing exchange rate of $.001 per peso, converts to $9.6 million.
- The business will generate an estimated 5 billion pesos per year for four years.
- The business will be sold in four years; the host government will acquire the business in four years with no compensation to Buckeye; however, the host government imposes no taxes on income earned by the business. It does impose a withholding tax of 20 percent on any funds remitted to the U.S. parent.
- The exchange rate of the Mexican peso is forecasted as follows:

End of Year	Value of Mexican peso
1	$.0008
2	$.0006
3	$.0004
4	$.0003

- The U.S. government will tax any dollar earnings received by the parent from its subsidiary at a 20 percent rate.
- The required rate of return on the project is 18 percent. The required rate of return is dependent on existing economic conditions, the firm's capital structure, and the project's risk, as discussed in the following chapter.

Based on this information, the capital budgeting analysis is conducted as shown in Exhibit 17.1. The top panel is an analysis from the subsidiary's perspective, and assumes the subsidiary has made the initial investment itself. The present value of the cash flows to be generated is provided, along with the cumulative net present value (NPV). The cumulative NPV is useful not only for estimating the project's NPV, but also for determining how long it takes to generate a positive NPV. For projects that may be terminated sooner than planned (due to an unanticipated host government takeover, etc.), there is a desire to achieve a positive NPV as soon as possible. The analysis in Exhibit 17.1 shows that the project has a positive NPV by the end of Year 3.

This same project is analyzed from the parent's perspective in the lower panel of Exhibit 17.1. Now assume that the parent provides the initial invest-

EXHIBIT 17.1   Capital Budgeting Analysis: Buckeye Corporation   *(in thousands)*

	Year 0	Year 1	Year 2	Year 3	Year 4
Subsidiary Perspective					
Initial investment	P9,600,000				
Periodic cash flows		P5,000,000	P5,000,000	P5,000,000	P5,000,000
PV of cash flows (at 18%)		P4,237,288	P3,590,922	P3,043,154	P2,578,944
Cumulative NPV		–P5,362,712	–P1,771,790	P1,271,364	P3,850,308
Parent Perspective					
Initial investment	$9,600				
Total cash flows from subsidiary		P5,000,000	P5,000,000	P5,000,000	P5,000,000
Withholding tax if cash flows were remitted to parent (20%)		P1,000,000	P1,000,000	P1,000,000	P1,000,000
Remitted funds after withholding tax		P4,000,000	P4,000,000	P4,000,000	P4,000,000
Exchange rate of Mexican peso		$.0008	$.0006	$.0004	$.0003
Funds to parent		$3,200	$2,400	$1,600	$1,200
Taxes by U.S. government (20%)		$640	$480	$320	$240
After-tax funds to parent		$2,560	$1,920	$1,280	$960
PV of cash flows (at 18%)		$2,169	$1,379	$779	$495
Cumulative NPV		–$7,431	–$6,052	–$5,273	–$4,778

ment. The differences in cash flows to the parent occur for three reasons. First, there is a 20 percent withholding tax on any funds remitted to the parent, which reduces the amount in pesos to be remitted. Second, the pesos will be converted into dollars before they are remitted to the parent. Because the peso is expected to depreciate, the amount in dollars to be received in each successive year is reduced. Finally, the U.S. government plans to impose a 20 percent tax on the remitted earnings received by the parent, which will reduce the parent cash flows (our analysis assumes that all funds remitted represent earnings). From the parent's perspective, the NPV is negative even at the end of the four-year period. Thus, the project should not be undertaken. This conclusion conflicts with the analysis conducted from the subsidiary's perspective.

In the example above, the required rate of return for the parent is assumed to be the same as the required rate of return for the subsidiary. In reality, the required rates of return may be different. Yet, the more relevant point is that the parent's perspective is appropriate in attempting to determine whether a project will enhance the firm's value. Given that the parent's shareholders are its owners, it should make decisions that satisfy its shareholders. Each project, whether foreign or domestic, should ultimately generate sufficient cash flows to the parent in order to enhance shareholder wealth. Any projects that can create a positive net present value for the parent should enhance shareholder wealth.

One exception to the rule of using a parent's perspective occurs when the foreign subsidiary is not wholly owned by the parent, and when the foreign project is partially financed with retained earnings of the parent and of the subsidiary. In this case, the foreign subsidiary has a group of shareholders that it must satisfy. Any arrangement made between the parent and the subsidiary

**EXHIBIT 17.2
Process of
Remitting
Subsidiary Earnings
to the Parent**

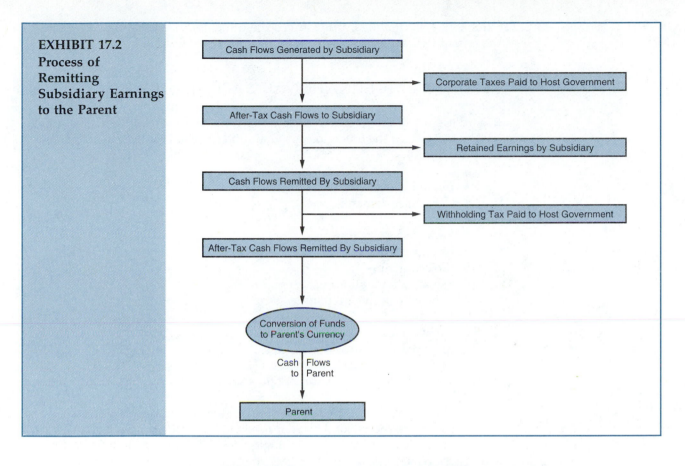

should be acceptable to the two entities only if the arrangement enhances the values of both entities. The decisions are not intended to transfer wealth from one entity to another, but are in the interest of both groups of shareholders.

While this exception has been recognized, most foreign subsidiaries of MNCs are wholly owned by the parents. Examples in this text implicitly assume that the subsidiary is wholly owned by the parent (unless noted otherwise), and therefore focus on the parent's perspective.

Exhibit 17.2 illustrates the process from the time earnings are generated by the subsidiary until remitted funds are received by the parent. The exhibit shows that the earnings are reduced initially by corporate taxes paid to the host government. Then, some of the earnings are retained by the subsidiary (either by choice of the subsidiary or according to host government rules), with the residual targeted as funds to be remitted. Those funds that are remitted may be subject to a withholding tax by the host government. The remaining funds are converted to the parent's currency (at the prevailing exchange rate) and remitted to the parent. Given the various factors shown here that can drain subsidiary earnings, the cash flows actually remitted by the subsidiary may represent only a small portion of the earnings generated by the subsidiary. As an extreme example, the subsidiary may retain and reinvest all earnings generated, which defers the remittance of earnings to the parent until some future point in time. The feasibility of the project from the parent's perspective is dependent not on the subsidiary cash flows, but on the cash flows that it ultimately receives. While

Exhibit 17.2 is simplified, it illustrates the difficulty in estimating cash flows to the parent that are initially generated by a foreign subsidiary.

INPUT FOR MULTINATIONAL CAPITAL BUDGETING _____

Regardless of the long-term project to be considered, an MNC will normally require forecasts of the following economic and financial characteristics related to the project:

1. Initial investment
2. Consumer demand
3. Price
4. Variable cost
5. Fixed cost
6. Project lifetime
7. Salvage (liquidation) value
8. Fund-transfer restrictions
9. Tax laws
10. Exchange rates
11. Required rate of return.

Each of these characteristics is briefly described in turn.

1. *Initial investment.* The parent's initial investment in a project may constitute the major source of funds to support a particular project. Funds initially invested in a project may include not only whatever is necessary to start the project, but also additional funds, such as working capital to support the project over time. Such funds are needed to finance inventory, wages, etc., until the revenues from the project are generated. Because cash inflows will not always be sufficient to cover upcoming cash outflows, working capital is needed throughout a project's lifetime.
2. *Consumer demand.* An accurately forecasted consumer demand for a product is quite valuable when projecting a cash flow schedule. However, future demand is often difficult to forecast. For example, if the project is a plant in Germany that produces automobiles, the MNC must forecast what percentage of the auto market in Germany it can pull from prevailing auto producers. Once a market share percentage is forecasted, projected demand can be computed with ease. Yet, the forecast of market share is subject to error. Demand forecasts can sometimes be aided by historical data on what market share other MNCs in the industry pulled when they entered this market. However, historical data are not always an accurate indicator of the future. In addition, many projects reflect a first attempt, so there are no predecessors to review as an indicator of the future.
3. *Price.* The price at which the product could be sold can be forecasted using competitive products in the markets as a comparison. However, a long-term capital budgeting analysis requires projections for not only the upcoming period, but the expected lifetime of the project as well.

The future prices will most likely be responsive to the future inflation rate in the host country (where the project is to take place). Yet, the future inflation rate is not known. Thus, future inflation rates must be forecasted in order to develop projections of the product price over time.

4. *Variable cost.* Like the price estimate, variable-cost forecasts can be developed from assessing prevailing comparative costs of the components (such as hourly labor costs, etc.) that make it up. Such costs should normally move in tandem with the future inflation rate of the host country. Even if the variable cost per unit can be accurately predicted, the projected total variable cost (variable cost per unit times quantity produced) may be far off if the demand is inaccurately forecasted.

5. *Fixed cost.* On a periodic basis, the fixed cost may be easier to predict than the variable cost, since it is not normally sensitive to changes in demand. It is, however, sensitive to any change in the host country's inflation rate from the point at which the forecast is made until the point at which the fixed costs are incurred.

6. *Project lifetime.* While it is difficult to assess the life of some projects, other projects are designated specific lifetimes, at the end of which they will be liquidated. This makes the capital budgeting analysis easier to apply. It should be recognized that the MNC does not always have complete control over the lifetime decision. In some cases, political events may force a liquidation of the project earlier than planned. The probability that such events will occur varies among countries.

7. *Salvage (liquidation) value.* The after-tax salvage value of most projects is difficult to forecast. It will depend on several factors, including the success of the project and the attitude of the host government toward the project. As an extreme possibility, the host government could take over the project without adequately compensating the MNC.

8. *Fund-transfer restrictions.* In some cases, a host government will prevent a subsidiary's earnings from being sent to the parent. This restriction may reflect an attempt to encourage additional local spending, or to avoid excessive sales of the local currency in exchange for some other currency. Since the fund-transfer restrictions prevent cash from coming back to the parent, projected net cash flows from the parent's perspective will be affected by the restrictions. If the parent is aware of these restrictions, it can incorporate them when projecting net cash flows. However, the host government may adjust its fund-transfer restrictions over time, in which case the MNC can only forecast the future fund-transfer restrictions and incorporate these forecasts into the analysis.

9. *Tax laws.* The tax laws of each individual country are complex. Under some circumstances, they allow tax deductions or credits for the MNC due to tax payments by subsidiaries to their respective host countries. Because after-tax cash flows are necessary for an adequate capital budgeting analysis, tax effects must be accounted for. MNCs can normally handle this task. However, tax laws are not permanent. Because they are changed often, it is difficult to know how they affect a project over time.

10. *Exchange rates.* Any international project will be affected by exchange rate fluctuations during the life of the project, but these movements are often very difficult to forecast. There are methods of hedging against them, though most hedging techniques are used to cover short-term positions. While it is possible to hedge over longer periods (with long-term forward contracts or currency swap arrangements), the MNC has no way of knowing the amount of funds that it should hedge. This is because it is only guessing at its future costs and revenues due to the project. Thus, the MNC may decide not to hedge the projected foreign currency net cash flows. Unfortunately, even if these cash flows are predicted with perfect accuracy, an MNC that does not hedge may improperly estimate the project cash flows to be received by the parent as a result of inaccurate exchange rate forecasts during the life of the project.

11. *Required rate of return.* Once the relevant cash flows of a proposed project are estimated, they can be discounted at the project's required rate of return, which may differ from the MNC's cost of capital because of that particular project's risk. The MNC's cost of capital is discussed in the following chapter.

Additional considerations will be discussed after a simplified multinational capital budgeting example is provided. In the real world, magic numbers aren't provided to MNCs for insertion into their computers. The challenge revolves around accurately forecasting the variables relevant to the project evaluation. If garbage (inaccurate forecasts) is input into the computer, the analysis output generated by the computer will also be garbage. Consequently, an MNC may take on a project by mistake. Since such a mistake may be worth millions of dollars, it is understandable that MNCs need to assess the degree of uncertainty for any input that is used in the project evaluation. This is discussed more thoroughly later in this chapter.

MULTINATIONAL CAPITAL BUDGETING EXAMPLE

Capital budgeting for the MNC is necessary for all long-term projects that deserve consideration. The projects may range from a small expansion of a subsidiary division to the creation of a new subsidiary. The example that follows reflects the possible development of a new subsidiary. It begins with assumptions that simplify the capital budgeting analysis. Then, additional considerations are discussed in order to emphasize the potential complexity of such an analysis.

The forthcoming example illustrates one of many possible methods available that would achieve the same result. Also, keep in mind that a real-world problem would involve more extenuating circumstances than those shown here.

Example: Background

Spartan Inc., a U.S.-based manufacturer of high-quality tennis rackets, has recently considered exporting rackets to Switzerland. However, it anticipates that the Swiss government will prohibit these exports in retaliation for recent trade restrictions placed by the U.S. government on some Swiss exports. Consequently,

Spartan is considering the development of a subsidiary in Switzerland that could manufacture and sell the tennis rackets locally. Various departments of Spartan Inc. were asked to supply relevant information for a capital budgeting analysis. In addition, some executives of Spartan Inc. met with government officials of Switzerland regarding the proposed subsidiary. All relevant information follows.

1. *Initial investment.* An estimated 20 million Swiss francs (SF), which includes funds to support working capital, would be needed for the project. Given the existing spot rate of $.50 per Swiss franc, the dollar amount of the parent's initial investment is $10 million.

2. *Project life.* The project is expected to end in four years. The host government of Switzerland has promised to make a payment to the parent in order to purchase the plant after four years.

3. *Price and demand.* The estimated price and demand schedules during each of the next four years are shown here:

Year	Price per Racket	Demand in Switzerland
1	SF350	60,000 units
2	SF350	60,000 units
3	SF360	100,000 units
4	SF380	100,000 units

4. *Costs.* The variable costs (for materials, labor, etc.) per unit were estimated and consolidated as shown here:

Year	Variable costs (VC) per Racket
1	SF200
2	SF200
3	SF250
4	SF260

The expense of leasing extra office space is SF1 million per year. Other annual overhead expenses are expected to be SF1 million per year.

5. *Exchange rates.* The spot exchange rate of the Swiss franc is $.50. The spot rate is used by Spartan Inc. as its best forecast of the exchange rate that will exist in the future periods. Thus, the forecasted exchange rate for all future periods is $.50.

6. *Host country taxes on income earned by subsidiary.* The Swiss government will allow Spartan Inc. to establish the subsidiary and will impose a 20 percent tax rate on income. In addition, it will impose a 10 percent withholding tax on any funds remitted by the subsidiary to the parent.

7. *U.S. government taxes on income earned by Spartan subsidiary.* The U.S. government will allow a tax credit on taxes paid in Switzerland, so that earnings remitted by the parent will not be taxed by the U.S. government.

8. *Cash flows from Spartan subsidiary to parent.* The Spartan subsidiary plans to send all net cash flow received back to the parent firm at the

end of each year. The Swiss government promises no restrictions on the cash flows to be sent back to the parent firm, but does impose a 10 percent withholding tax on any funds sent to the parent, as mentioned above.

9. *Depreciation.* The Swiss government will allow the subsidiary of Spartan Inc. to depreciate the cost of the plant and equipment at a maximum rate of SF2 million per year, which is the rate to be used by the subsidiary.

10. *Salvage value.* The Swiss government will send a payment of SF12 million to the parent to assume ownership of the subsidiary at the end of four years. Assume there is no capital gain or loss on the sale of the subsidiary.

11. *Required rate of return.* Spartan Inc. requires a 15 percent return on this project.

Example: Analysis

The capital budgeting analysis will be conducted from the parent's perspective, based on the assumption that the subsidiary is intended to generate cash flows that will ultimately be passed on to the parent. Thus, the net present value from the parent's perspective is based on a comparison of the present value of the cash flows received by the parent to the initial outlay by the parent. As illustrated earlier in this chapter, an international project's NPV is dependent on whether a parent or subsidiary perspective is used. Since the U.S. parent's perspective is used, the cash flows of concern are the dollars ultimately received by the parent as a result of the project. The initial outlay of concern is the investment by the parent. The required rate of return is based on the cost of capital used by the parent to make its investment, with an adjustment for the risk of the project. If the establishment of the subsidiary is beneficial to Spartan's parent, the present value of future cash flows (including the salvage value) ultimately received by the parent should exceed the parent's initial outlay.

The capital budgeting analysis to determine whether Spartan Inc. should establish the subsidiary is provided in Exhibit 17.3 (review this exhibit as you read on). The first step is to incorporate demand and price estimates in order to forecast total revenue (see Lines 1 through 3). Then, the expenses are summed to forecast total expenses (see Lines 4 through 9). Next, before-tax earnings are computed (in Line 10) by subtracting total expenses from total revenues. Host government taxes (Line 11) are then deducted from before-tax earnings to determine after-tax earnings for the subsidiary (Line 12).

The depreciation expense is added to the after-tax subsidiary earnings to compute the net cash flow to the subsidiary (Line 13). All of these funds are to be remitted by the subsidiary, so Line 14 is the same as Line 13. The subsidiary can afford to send all net cash flow to the parent, since its loan from the local bank is providing the working capital to support corporate operations. The funds remitted to the parent are subject to a 10 percent withholding tax (Line 15), so the actual amount of funds to be sent after these taxes is shown in Line 16. The salvage value of the project is shown in Line 17. The funds to be remitted must first be converted into dollars at the exchange rate (Line 18) existing at that time. The parent's cash flow from the subsidiary is shown in Line 19. The periodic funds received from the subsidiary are not subject to U.S. corporate taxes, since

20 pts
on
final

EXHIBIT 17.3   Capital Budgeting Analysis: Spartan Inc.

	Year 0	Year 1	Year 2	Year 3	Year 4
1. Demand		60,000	60,000	100,000	100,000
2. Price per unit		SF350	SF350	SF360	SF380
3. Total revenue = (1) × (2)		**SF21,000,000**	**SF21,000,000**	**SF36,000,000**	**SF38,000,000**
4. Variable cost per unit		SF200	SF200	SF250	SF260
5. Total variable cost = (1) × (4)		SF12,000,000	SF12,000,000	SF25,000,000	SF26,000,000
6. Annual lease expense		SF1,000,000	SF1,000,000	SF1,000,000	SF1,000,000
7. Other fixed annual expenses		SF1,000,000	SF1,000,000	SF1,000,000	SF1,000,000
8. Noncash expense (depreciation)		SF2,000,000	SF2,000,000	SF2,000,000	SF2,000,000
9. Total expenses = (5) + (6) + (7) + (8)		**SF16,000,000**	**SF16,000,000**	**SF29,000,000**	**SF30,000,000**
10. Before-tax earnings of subsidiary = (3) − (9)		SF5,000,000	SF5,000,000	SF7,000,000	SF8,000,000
11. Host government tax (20%)		SF1,000,000	SF1,000,000	SF1,400,000	SF1,600,000
12. After-tax earnings of subsidiary		SF4,000,000	SF4,000,000	SF5,600,000	SF6,400,000
13. Net cash flow to subsidiary = (12) + (8)		**SF6,000,000**	**SF6,000,000**	**SF7,600,000**	**SF8,400,000**
14. SF remitted by subsidiary (100% of CF)		SF6,000,000	SF6,000,000	SF7,600,000	SF8,400,000
15. Withholding tax on remitted funds (10%)		SF600,000	SF600,000	SF760,000	SF840,000
16. SF remitted after withholding taxes		**SF5,400,000**	**SF5,400,000**	**SF6,840,000**	**SF7,560,000**
17. Salvage value					SF12,000,000
18. Exchange rate of SF		$.50	$.50	$.50	$.50
19. Cash flows to parent		$2,700,000	$2,700,000	$3,420,000	$9,780,000
20. PV of parent cash flows (15% discount rate)		**$2,347,826**	**$2,041,588**	**$2,248,706**	**$5,591,747**
21. Initial investment by parent	$10,000,000				
22. Cumulative NPV		−$7,652,174	−$5,610,586	−$3,361,880	$2,229,867

---

it was assumed the taxes paid in Switzerland would represent a credit offsetting taxes owed to the U.S. government.

Although several capital budgeting techniques are available, a commonly used technique is to estimate the cash flows and salvage value to be received by the parent and compute the net present value (NPV) of the project, as shown here:

$$NPV = -IO + \sum_{t=1}^{n} \frac{CF_t}{(1 + k)^t} + \frac{SV_n}{(1 + k)^n}$$

where

IO = initial outlay (investment)

CF_t = cash flow in period t

SV_n = salvage value

k = required rate of return on the project

n = lifetime of the project (number of periods).

The *present value (PV)* of each period's net cash flow is computed using a 15 percent discount rate (Line 20). The discount rate should reflect the parent's cost of capital with an adjustment for the project's risk. Finally, the cumulative NPV (Line 22) is determined by consolidating the discounted cash flows for each period, and subtracting the initial outlay (in Line 21). For example, as of the end of Year 2, the cumulative NPV was –$5,610,586. This was determined by consolidating the $2,347,826 in Year 1, the $2,041,588 in Year 2, and subtracting the initial investment of $10,000,000. The critical value in Line 22 is in the last period, since this reflects the NPV of the project.

In our example, the cumulative NPV as of the end of the last period is $2,229,867. Because the NPV is positive, the MNC may accept this project, if the discount rate of 15 percent has fully accounted for the project's risk. However, if the analysis has not yet accounted for risk, the decision may be to reject the project. The manner by which the MNC can account for risk in capital budgeting is discussed shortly.

FACTORS TO CONSIDER IN MULTINATIONAL CAPITAL BUDGETING

The example of Spartan Inc. ignores a variety of factors that may affect the capital budgeting analysis, namely

1. Exchange rate fluctuations
2. Inflation
3. Financing arrangement
4. Blocked funds
5. Uncertain salvage value
6. Impact of project on prevailing cash flows
7. Host government incentives

Each of these factors is discussed in turn.

Exchange Rate Fluctuations

Recall that Spartan Inc. uses the Swiss franc's current spot rate ($.50) as a forecast for all future periods of concern. While the company realizes that the exchange rate will typically change over time, it does not know whether the franc will strengthen or weaken in the future. While the difficulty in accurately forecasting exchange rates is well known, a multinational capital budgeting analysis could at least incorporate other scenarios for exchange rate movements, such as a pessimistic scenario and an optimistic scenario. From the parent's point of view, appreciation of the franc would be favorable, since the franc inflows would someday be converted to more U.S. dollars. Conversely, depreciation would be unfavorable, since the weakened francs would convert to fewer U.S. dollars over time.

Weak-franc and strong-franc scenarios are illustrated in Exhibit 17.4. At the top of the table, the anticipated after-tax franc cash flows (including salvage value), are shown for the subsidiary, from Lines 16 and 17 in Exhibit 17.3. The amount in U.S. dollars that these francs convert to depends on the exchange rates existing in the various periods in which they are converted. The number of francs multiplied by the forecasted exchange rate will determine the estimated number of dollars received by the parent.

Notice from Exhibit 17.4 the differences in cash flow received by the parent in the strong-franc scenario from those received in the weak-franc scenario. A strong franc is clearly beneficial, as verified by the increased dollar value of cash flows received. The large differences in cash flow received by the parent in the different scenarios illustrate the impact of exchange rate expectations on the feasibility of an international project.

The NPV forecasts based on projections for exchange rates are illustrated in Exhibit 17.5. The estimated NPV is highest if the franc is expected to strengthen and lowest if it is expected to weaken. The estimated NPV is negative for the weak-franc scenario but positive for the stable-franc and strong-franc scenarios. This project's true feasibility would depend on the probability distribution of

---

EXHIBIT 17.4   Analysis Using Different Exchange Rate Scenarios: Spartan Inc.

	Year 0	Year 1	Year 2	Year 3	Year 4
SF remitted after withholding taxes (including salvage value)		SF5,400,000	SF5,400,000	SF6,840,000	SF19,560,000
Strong-Franc Scenario					
Exchange rate of SF		$.54	$.57	$.61	$.65
Cash flows to parent		$2,916,000	$3,078,000	$4,172,400	$12,714,000
PV of cash flows (15% discount rate)		$2,535,652	$2,327,410	$2,743,421	$7,269,271
Initial investment by parent	$10,000,000				
Cumulative NPV		−$7,464,348	−$5,136,938	−$2,393,517	$4,875,754
Weak-Franc Scenario					
Exchange rate of SF		$.47	$.45	$.40	$.37
Cash flows to parent		$2,538,000	$2,430,000	$2,736,000	$7,237,200
PV of cash flows (15% discount rate)		$2,206,957	$1,837,429	$1,798,964	$4,137,893
Initial investment by parent	$10,000,000				
Cumulative NPV		−$7,793,043	−$5,955,614	−$4,156,650	−$18,757

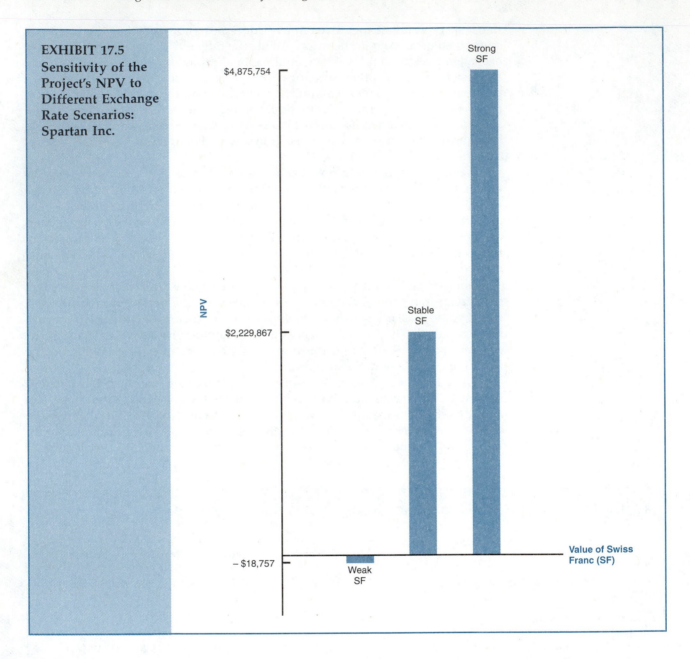

EXHIBIT 17.5
Sensitivity of the Project's NPV to Different Exchange Rate Scenarios: Spartan Inc.

these three scenarios for the franc during the project's lifetime. If there is a high probability that the weak-franc scenario will occur, this project should not be accepted.

Inflation

Our example implicitly considers inflation, since variable cost per unit and product prices generally have been rising over time. However, inflation can be quite volatile from year to year in some countries, and can therefore strongly influence a project's net cash flows. Inaccurate inflation forecasts could lead to inaccurate net cash flow forecasts. The inflation rate in many less developed countries may be 200 percent or more in any given year. It would be virtually impossible for any subsidiary in these countries to accurately forecast inflation each year.

While both costs and revenues should be affected in the same direction by inflation fluctuations, their magnitudes may be very different from each other. This is especially true when the project involves importing partially manufactured components and selling the finished product locally. The local economy's inflation will most likely have a stronger impact on revenues than on costs in such cases.

The joint impact of inflation and exchange rate fluctuations on a subsidiary's net cash flows may produce a partial offsetting effect, from the viewpoint of the parent. The exchange rates of highly inflated countries tend to weaken over time. Thus, even if subsidiary earnings are inflated, they will be deflated when converted into the parent's home currency (if the subsidiary's currency has weakened). Such an offsetting effect is not exact or consistent, though. Because inflation is only one of many factors that influence exchange rates, there is no guarantee a currency will depreciate when the local inflation rate is relatively high. Therefore, one cannot ignore the impact of inflation and exchange rates on net cash flows.

Even if relatively high inflation does cause a currency to weaken, the impact on net cash flows of a project will not necessarily be offsetting. Suppose an MNC's subsidiary in a highly inflated country generates highly inflated earnings and invests them in local securities for several years. If and when the inflation subsides and the local currency strengthens, the subsidiary could convert the accumulated earnings to the parent's home currency and send these funds to the parent. This example illustrates why MNCs cannot neglect the impact of inflation and/or exchange rates on cash flows.

Financing Arrangement

Many foreign projects are partially financed by foreign subsidiaries. To illustrate how this foreign financing can influence the feasibility of the project, consider the following revisions in the example of Spartan Inc. Assume that the subsidiary borrows SF10 million to purchase the offices that are leased in the initial example. Assume that interest payments on this loan (of SF1 million) are to be paid by the subsidiary annually, and the principal (SF10 million) will be paid at the end of Year 4, when the project is terminated. Since the Swiss government permits a maximum of SF2 million per year in depreciation for this project, the subsidiary's depreciation rate will remain unchanged. The offices are expected to have a market value of SF10 million at the end of Year 4, at which time they will be sold.

Domestic capital budgeting problems would not include debt payments in the measurement of cash flows, because all financing costs are captured by the discount rate. However, foreign projects are more complicated, especially when partial financing of the investment in the foreign project is provided by the foreign subsidiary. While consolidating the initial investment made by the parent and the subsidiary simplifies the capital budgeting process, it can cause significant estimation errors. The estimated foreign cash flows that are ultimately remitted to the parent and are subject to exchange rate risk will be overstated if the foreign interest expenses are not explicitly considered as cash outflows for the foreign subsidiary. Thus, a more accurate approach is to separate the investment made by the subsidiary from the investment made by the parent. The capital budgeting analysis can focus on the parent's perspective by comparing the present value of the cash flows received by the parent to the initial investment by the parent.

Given the revised assumptions, the following revisions must be made to the capital budgeting analysis:

1. Since the subsidiary is borrowing funds to purchase the offices, the lease payments of SF1 million per year will not be necessary. However, the subsidiary will pay interest payments of SF1 million per year as a result of the loan. Thus, the annual cash outflows for the subsidiary are still the same.
2. The subsidiary must pay the SF10 million in loan principal at the end of four years. However, since the subsidiary expects to receive SF10 million (in 4 years) from the sale of the offices it purchases with the funds provided by the loan, it can use the proceeds of the sale to pay the loan principal.

Since the subsidiary's maximum depreciation expense allowed by the Swiss government already has been taken even before the subsidiary owned the offices, it cannot increase its annual depreciation expenses. In this example, the cash flows ultimately received by the parent when the subsidiary obtains financing to purchase offices are similar to the cash flows determined in the original example (when the offices are to be leased). If the numbers were not offsetting, the capital budgeting analysis would be conducted in the revised example to determine whether the NPV from the parent's perspective is higher than that in the initial example.

Recall that in the original example, the offices are leased by the subsidiary, while in the revised example the offices are purchased with borrowed funds by the subsidiary. Consider one more alternative arrangement, in which the parent uses its own funds to purchase the offices. That is, its initial investment is $15 million, composed of the original $10 million investment as explained earlier, plus an additional $5 million to obtain an extra SF10 million to purchase the offices. This example is provided because it illustrates how the capital budgeting analysis changes when the parent takes a bigger stake in the investment. Given the revised assumption that the parent rather than the subsidiary will purchase the offices, the following revisions must be made to the capital budgeting analysis:

1. The subsidiary will not have any loan payments (since it will not need to borrow funds), as the offices are to be purchased by the parent. Since the offices are to be purchased, there will be no lease payments either.
2. The initial investment by the parent is $15 million instead of $10 million.
3. The salvage value to be received by the parent is SF22 million instead of SF12 million, because the offices are assumed to have a market value of SF10 million at the end of Year 4. The SF10 million to be received from selling the offices can be added to the SF12 million to be received from selling the rest of the subsidiary.

The capital budgeting analysis for Spartan Inc. under this revised financing strategy in which the parent finances the entire $15 million investment is shown in Exhibit 17.6. This analysis uses our original exchange rate projections of $.50 per Swiss franc for each period. The numbers that are directly affected by the revised financing arrangement are bracketed. Other numbers are also affected indirectly as a result. For example, the subsidiary's after-tax earnings increase as a result of avoiding interest or lease payments on its offices. The NPV of the project under this alternative financing arrangement is positive, but less than in the original arrangement. Given the higher initial outlay of the parent and the lower NPV, this arrangement in which the parent finances the $15 million investment is not as feasible as the arrangement in which the offices are either leased or purchased with funds borrowed by the subsidiary.

EXHIBIT 17.6   Analysis with an Alternative Financing Arrangement: Spartan Inc.

	Year 0	Year 1	Year 2	Year 3	Year 4
1. Demand		60,000	60,000	100,000	100,000
2. Price per unit		SF350	SF350	SF360	SF380
3. **Total revenue = (1) x (2)**		**SF21,000,000**	**SF21,000,000**	**SF36,000,000**	**SF38,000,000**
4. Variable cost per unit		SF200	SF200	SF250	SF260
5. Total variable cost = (1) x (4)		SF12,000,000	SF12,000,000	SF25,000,000	SF26,000,000
6. Annual lease expense		[SF 0]	[SF 0]	[SF 0]	[SF 0]
7. Other fixed annual expenses		SF1,000,000	SF1,000,000	SF1,000,000	SF1,000,000
8. Noncash expense (deprec.)		SF2,000,000	SF2,000,000	SF2,000,000	SF2,000,000
9. **Total expenses = (5) + (6) + (7) + (8)**		**SF15,000,000**	**SF15,000,000**	**SF28,000,000**	**SF29,000,000**
10. Before-tax earnings of subsidiary = (3) − (9)		SF6,000,000	SF6,000,000	SF8,000,000	SF9,000,000
11. Host government tax (20%)		SF1,200,000	SF1,200,000	SF1,600,000	SF1,800,000
12. After-tax earnings of subsidiary		SF4,800,000	SF4,800,000	SF6,400,000	SF7,200,000
13. **Net cash flow to subsidiary = (12) + (8)**		**SF6,800,000**	**SF6,800,000**	**SF8,400,000**	**SF9,200,000**
14. SF remitted by subsidiary (100% of CF)		SF6,800,000	SF6,800,000	SF8,400,000	SF9,200,000
15. Withholding tax on remitted funds (10%)		SF680,000	SF680,000	SF840,000	SF920,000
16. **SF remitted after withholding taxes**		**SF6,120,000**	**SF6,120,000**	**SF7,560,000**	**SF8,280,000**
17. Salvage value					[SF22,000,000]
18. Exchange rate of SF		$.50	$.50	$.50	$.50
19. Cash flows to parent		$3,060,000	$3,060,000	$3,780,000	$15,140,000
20. **PV of parent cash flows (15% discount rate)**		**$2,660,870**	**$2,313,780**	**$2,485,411**	**$8,656,344**
21. Initial investment by parent	[$15,000,000]				
22. Cumulative NPV		−$12,339,130	−$10,025,350	−$7,539,939	$1,116,405

One reason the subsidiary financing is more feasible than complete parent financing is that the financing rate on the loan is lower than the parent's required rate of return on funds provided to the subsidiary. Yet, if local loans had a relatively high interest rate, the use of local financing would not likely be as attractive.

In general, this revised example shows that the increased investment by the parent causes more exchange rate exposure to the parent, for the following reasons. First, since the parent provides the entire investment, there is no foreign financing required. Consequently, there are no interest payments paid by the subsidiary, and the cash flows to be remitted to the parent are larger. Second, the salvage value to be remitted to the parent is larger. Given the larger payments to the parent, the cash flows ultimately received by the parent are more susceptible to exchange rate movements.

The exposure is not as large when the offices are purchased by the subsidiary, because the subsidiary financing forces some of the financing expenses to be incurred by the subsidiary. The subsidiary financing essentially shifts some of the expenses to the same currency as that received by the subsidiary, and therefore reduces the amount that will ultimately be converted into dollars for remittance to the parent.

Some foreign projects are completely financed with retained earnings of existing foreign subsidiaries. These projects are difficult to assess from the parents' perspectives, because their direct effects are normally focused on the subsidiaries. One approach is to view a subsidiary's investment in a project as an opportunity cost, since the funds could be remitted to the parent rather than invested in the foreign project. Thus, the initial outlay from the parent's perspective is the amount in funds that it would have received from the subsidiary if the funds were remitted rather than invested in this project. The cash flows from the parent's perspective reflect those cash flows ultimately received by the parent as a result of the foreign project.

Even if the project generates earnings for the subsidiary that are reinvested by the subsidiary, the key cash flows from the parent's perspective are those that it ultimately receives from the project. In this way, any international factors that will affect the cash flows (such as withholding taxes and exchange rate movements) are incorporated into the capital budgeting process. As explained earlier in the chapter, some foreign projects may be favorable from the subsidiary perspective, but not the parent perspective. Under these conditions, a subsidiary that intends to use its retained earnings for a foreign project should be instructed by the parent to remit these earnings instead. If the foreign project has a negative net present value from the parent's perspective, this implies that the parent should have alternative uses for the funds that are more feasible.

Blocked Funds

In some cases, the host country may block funds the subsidiary attempts to send to the parent. For example, some countries may require that earnings generated by the subsidiary be reinvested locally for at least three years before they can be remitted. This can possibly affect the accept/reject decision on a project. Reconsider the example of Spartan Inc., assuming that all funds are blocked until the subsidiary is sold. This forces the subsidiary to reinvest those funds until that time. Blocked funds penalize a project if the return on such reinvestment is less than the required rate of return on the project.

Assume that these funds are used to purchase marketable securities that are expected to yield 5 percent annually, after taxes. A reevaluation of Spartan's cash flows (from Exhibit 17.3) to incorporate the blocked-funds restriction is shown in Exhibit 17.7. The withholding tax is not applied until the funds are remitted to the parent, which is in Year 4. The original exchange rate projections are used here. In addition, the risk of the project is greater, because the parent does not recover any funds until the project is terminated. Thus, all parent cash flows depend on the exchange rate four years from now.

If the foreign subsidiary has a loan outstanding, it may be able to better utilize blocked funds by repaying the local loan. For example, the SF6 million at the end of Year 1 could be used to reduce the outstanding loan balance rather than invested in marketable securities, assuming that the lending bank allows early repayment. The local loan could be paid off early, if this is permitted by the lending institution.

Uncertain Salvage Value

The salvage value of an MNC's project typically has a significant impact on the project's NPV. When the salvage value is uncertain, the MNC may desire to incorporate various possible outcomes for the salvage value and reestimate the NPV based on each possible outcome. It may even desire to estimate the break-even salvage value, (also called break-even terminal value), which is the salvage value necessary to achieve a zero NPV for the project. If the actual salvage value is expected to equal or exceed the break-even salvage value, the project is feasible. The break-even salvage value (called SV_n) can be determined by setting NPV equal to zero and rearranging the capital budgeting equation, as follows:

EXHIBIT 17.7   Capital Budgeting with Blocked Funds: Spartan Inc.

	Year 0	Year 1	Year 2	Year 3	Year 4
SF to be remitted by subsidiary		SF6,000,000	SF6,000,000	SF7,600,000	SF8,400,000
					SF7,980,000
SF accumulated by reinvesting					SF6,615,000
funds to be remitted					SF6,945,750
					SF29,940,750
Withholding tax (10%)					SF2,994,075
SF remitted after withholding tax					SF26,946,675
Salvage value					SF12,000,000
Exchange rate					$.50
Cash flows to parent					$19,473,338
PV of parent cash flows (15% discount rate)					$11,133,944
Initial investment by parent	$10,000,000				
Cumulative NPV		−$10,000,000	−$10,000,000	−$10,000,000	$1,133,944

$$NPV = -IO + \sum_{t=1}^{n} \frac{CF_t}{(1+k)^t} + \frac{SV_n}{(1+k)^n}$$

$$O = -IO + \sum_{t=1}^{n} \frac{CF_t}{(1+k)^t} + \frac{SV_n}{(1+k)^n}$$

$$\left[IO - \sum_{t=1}^{n} \frac{CF_t}{(1+k)^t} \right] = \frac{SV_n}{(1+k)^n}$$

$$\left[IO - \sum_{t=1}^{n} \frac{CF_t}{(1+k)^t} \right] (1+k)^n = SV_n.$$

To illustrate the use of break-even salvage value, reconsider the Spartan Inc. example and assume that Spartan is not guaranteed a price for the project. The break-even salvage value for that project can be determined by (1) estimating the present value of future cash flows (excluding the salvage value), (2) subtracting the discounted cash flows from the initial outlay, and (3) multiplying the difference times $(1 + k)^n$. Using the original cash flow information from Exhibit 17.3, the present value of cash flows can be determined:

IN PRACTICE

ATTITUDES ABOUT THE PAYBACK PERIOD FOR FOREIGN PROJECTS

A *Wall Street Journal* survey of chief executive officers (CEOs) suggests some differences in attitudes about foreign projects across geographical regions. CEOs were asked what their payback period (period in which the initial investment in a project is recovered) has been when investing abroad. The average of responses for each group of CEOs is disclosed below:

CEOs from:	Average Payback Period
U.S. and Canada	4.3 Years
Pacific Rim	5.0
Europe	5.1
Japan	6.6

To assess the attitude about future projects, CEOs were asked if they were willing to accept projects with a longer payback. The percent of respondents in each group that replied yes is disclosed next:

CEOs from:	Percentage of Respondents Willing to Extend Payback Period
U.S. and Canada	32%
Pacific Rim	42
Europe	49
Japan	63

The comparative responses across groups to the two questions suggest that U.S. CEOs are more short-run-oriented than other CEOs, while Japanese CEOs are long-run-oriented. The disparity in attitudes may be the result of disparity in shareholder attitudes. U.S shareholders tend to have a short-run perspective when investing in stocks, while Japanese investors are long-run-oriented.

$$\text{PV of parent cash flows} = \frac{\$2,700,000}{(1.15)^1} + \frac{\$2,700,000}{(1.15)^2} + \frac{\$3,420,000}{(1.15)^3} + \frac{\$3,780,000}{(1.15)^4}$$

$$= \$2,347,826 + \$2,041,588 + \$2,248,706 + \$2,161,227$$

$$= \$8,799,347.$$

Given the present value of cash flows and the estimated initial outlay, the break-even salvage value is determined this way:

$$SV_n = \left[IO - \sum \frac{CF_t}{(1+k)^t} \right] (1+k)^n$$

$$= [\$10,000,000 - \$8,799,347](1.15)^4$$

$$= \$2,099,950$$

Given the original information in Exhibit 17.3, Spartan Inc. would accept the project only if the salvage value were estimated to be at least \$2,099,950 (assuming that the project's required rate of return is 15 percent).

Assuming the forecasted exchange rate of \$.50 per Swiss franc (2 francs per dollar), the project must sell for more than SF4,199,900 (computed as \$2,099,950 divided by \$.50) to exhibit a positive NPV (assuming no taxes are paid on this amount). If Spartan did not have a guarantee from the Swiss government, it could assess the probability that the subsidiary would sell for more than the break-even salvage value and then incorporate this assessment in its decision to accept or reject the project.

Impact of Project on Prevailing Cash Flows

In our example, there is no presumed impact of the new project on prevailing cash flows. In reality, however, there may often be an impact. Reconsider the Spartan Inc. example, assuming this time that (1) there is no concern about the Swiss government's imposing trade restrictions on imported tennis rackets; (2) Spartan Inc. still considers establishing a subsidiary in Switzerland because its production costs in Switzerland are expected to be lower than they would be in the United States; and (3) without a subsidiary, Spartan's export business to Switzerland is expected to generate net cash flows of \$1 million over the next four years. With a subsidiary, these cash flows would be forgone. The effects of these assumptions are shown in Exhibit 17.8. The previously estimated cash flows to the parent from the subsidiary (drawn from Exhibit 17.3) are restated in Exhibit 17.8. These estimates do not account for forgone cash flows, since the export business was assumed to be prohibited in the future. However, if the export business were allowed to exist, the forgone cash flows attributable to this business would have to be considered, as shown in Exhibit 17.8. The adjusted cash flows to the parent account for the project's impact on prevailing cash flows.

The present value of adjusted cash flows and cumulative NPV are also shown in Exhibit 17.8. The project's NPV is now negative, as a result of the adverse effect on prevailing cash flows. Thus, the project would not be feasible if the exporting business to Switzerland could be continued.

EXHIBIT 17.8   Capital Budgeting When Prevailing Cash Flows Are Affected: Spartan Inc.

	Year 0	Year 1	Year 2	Year 3	Year 4
Cash flows to parent, ignoring impact on prevailing cash flows		$2,700,000	2,700,000	$3,420,000	$9,780,000
Impact of project on prevailing cash flows		−$1,000,000	−$1,000,000	−$1,000,000	−$1,000,000
Cash flows to parent, incorporating impact on prevailing cash flows		$1,700,000	$1,700,000	$2,420,000	$8,780,000
PV of cash flows to parent (15% discount rate)		$1,478,261	$1,285,444	$1,591,189	$5,019,994
Initial investment	$10,000,000				
Cumulative NPV		−$8,521,739	−$7,236,295	−$5,645,106	−$625,112

It should be mentioned that some foreign projects may have a favorable impact on prevailing cash flows. For example, if a manufacturer of computer components established a foreign subsidiary to manufacture computers, the subsidiary might order the components from the parent. In this case, the sales volume of the parent would increase.

Host Government Incentives

Some foreign projects proposed by MNCs would have a favorable impact on economic conditions in a host country, and would therefore be encouraged by the host government. Any incentives offered by the host government must be incorporated within the capital budgeting analysis. For example, a low-rate host government loan or a reduced tax rate offered to the subsidiary would enhance periodic cash flows. If the government subsidized the initial establishment of the subsidiary, the MNC's initial investment would be reduced.

ADJUSTING PROJECT ASSESSMENT FOR RISK

If an MNC is unsure of the estimated cash flows of a proposed project, it needs to incorporate an adjustment for this risk. Three common methods used for adjusting the evaluation for risk are

- Risk-adjusted discount rate
- Sensitivity analysis
- Simulation.

Each method is described in turn.

Risk-Adjusted Discount Rate

The greater the uncertainty about a project's forecasted cash flows, the larger should be the discount rate applied to cash flows, other things being equal. This risk-adjusted discount rate tends to reduce the worth of a project by a degree that reflects the risk the project exhibits. This approach is easy to use, but it is criticized for being somewhat arbitrary. In addition, an equal adjustment to the discount rate over all periods does not reflect differences in the degree of uncertainty from one period to another. If the projected cash flows among periods have different degrees of uncertainty, the risk adjustment of the cash flows should vary also.

Consider a country whose political situation is slowly destabilizing. The probability of blocked funds, expropriation, etc., will increase over time. Thus, cash flows sent to the parent are less certain in the distant future than they are in the near future. A different discount rate should therefore be applied to each period in accordance with its corresponding risk. Even so, it will be a subjective adjustment that may not accurately reflect the risk.

Despite its subjectivity, the risk-adjusted discount rate is a commonly used technique, perhaps because of the ease with which one can arbitrarily adjust it. In addition, there is no alternative technique that will perfectly adjust for risk, although there are some (discussed next) that in certain cases may better reflect a project's risk.

Sensitivity Analysis

Once the MNC has estimated the NPV of a proposed project, it may want to consider alternative estimates for its input variables. For example, demand for the Spartan subsidiary's tennis rackets (in our earlier example) is estimated to be 60,000 in the first two years and 100,000 in the next two years. If demand were 60,000 in all four years, how would that change the NPV results? Alternatively, what if demand were 100,000 in all four years? Use of such *what-if* scenarios is referred to as **sensitivity analysis.** The objective is to determine how sensitive the NPV is to alternative values of the input variables. The estimates of any input variables can be revised to create new estimates for NPV. If the NPV is consistently positive during these revisions, then the MNC should become more comfortable with the project. If in many cases it is negative, the accept/reject decision for the project becomes more difficult.

The two exchange rate scenarios developed earlier represent a form of sensitivity analysis. The advantage of sensitivity analysis over the use of simple point estimates is that it reassesses the project based on various circumstances that may occur. Many computer software packages are available to perform sensitivity analysis.

Simulation

Simulation can be used for a variety of tasks, including the generation of a probability distribution for NPV based on a range of possible values for one or more input variables. Simulation is typically performed with the aid of a computer package. To illustrate how it can be applied to multinational capital budgeting, reconsider Spartan Inc., and assume that it expects the exchange rate to depreciate by 3 to 7 percent per year (with an equal probability of all values between this range occurring). Unlike a single point estimate, simulation can

MULTINATIONAL CAPITAL BUDGETING IN THE REAL WORLD

Surveys have been conducted on MNCs to identify how they practice capital budgeting. A brief review of survey results will determine whether actual practice of multinational capital budgeting coincides with the theory described in this chapter. A 1983 survey by Kim, Farragher, and Crick suggests that traditional capital budgeting techniques (such as NPV analysis or internal rate of return) are popular even for international projects. However, it was surprising to find that the payback method is commonly used. Twelve percent of U.S.-based MNCs and 31 percent of the non-U.S. based MNCs use it. Perhaps the payback method is preferred for projects for which the probability of a host government takeover is relatively high. Under such circumstances, recovering the initial outlay as quickly as possible becomes a critical objective. The survey found that more than 90 percent of MNCs adjust foreign projects for their individual levels of risk, although the ways in which they adjust vary.

Another survey by Stanley and Block inquired about the MNCs' estimation of cost of capital within the capital budgeting process. With regard to assessing projects of subsidiaries, the study found that 49 percent of the MNCs use the parent's cost of capital, 32 percent use the subsidiary's cost of capital, and some MNCs use both types. These results suggest that MNCs in some cases are considering the cost of obtaining funds locally rather than considering the MNC parent's cost.

The main purpose of providing survey results here is to illustrate that there are no unanimous solutions to issues in multinational capital budgeting. The MNCs analyze project characteristics differently. This does not mean that some MNCs are using an incorrect approach. The difference in analysis is most likely due to different backgrounds (industries, locations, etc.) and types of projects. The differences make multinational capital budgeting very challenging, since the appropriate approaches to implement may depend on the specific situation and type of firm involved.

consider the entire distribution of possibilities for the franc's exchange rate at the end of each year. It considers all point estimates for the other variables and randomly picks one of the possible values of the franc's depreciation level for each of the four years. Based on this random selection process, the NPV is determined.

The procedure just described represents one iteration. Then the process is repeated: the franc's depreciation for each year is again randomly selected (within the range of possibilities assumed earlier). Again, the NPV of the project if these exchange rate fluctuations actually occurred is computed. The simulation program may be run for, say, 100 iterations. This means that 100 different possible scenarios are created for the possible exchange rates of the franc during the four-year project period. Each iteration reflects a different scenario. The NPV of the project based on each scenario is then computed. Thus, simulation generates a distribution of NPVs for the project. The major advantage of simulation is that the MNC can examine the range of possible NPVs that may occur. From the information, it can determine the probability that the NPV will be positive, or greater than a particular level. The greater the uncertainty of the exchange rate, the greater will be the uncertainty of the NPV. The risk of a project will be greater if it involves the transaction of more volatile currencies, other things being equal.

In reality, many or all of the input variables necessary for multinational capital budgeting may be uncertain in the future. Probability distributions could be developed for all variables with uncertain future values. The final result is a distribution of possible NPVs that might occur for the project. The simulation technique does not put all of its emphasis on any one particular NPV forecast, but instead provides a distribution of the possible outcomes that may occur.

The project's cost of capital can be used as a discount rate when simulation is performed. The probability that the project will be successful can be estimated by measuring the area within the probability distribution in which the NPV>0. This area represents the probability that the present value of future cash flows will exceed the initial outlay. MNCs can also use the probability distribution to estimate the probability that the project will backfire by measuring the area in which NPV<0.

Simulation is difficult to do manually because of the iterations necessary to develop a distribution of NPVs. Yet, computer programs can run 100 iterations and generate results within a matter of seconds. The user of a simulation program must provide the probability distributions for the input variables that will affect the project's NPV. Like any model, the accuracy of results generated by simulation will be determined by the accuracy of the input.

SUMMARY

■ Capital budgeting conducted from an MNC's subsidiary perspective may generate different results and a different conclusion from those obtained if it is conducted from an MNC's parent perspective. The subsidiary perspective does not consider possible exchange rate and tax effects on cash flows transferred by the subsidiary to the parent. When a parent is deciding whether to implement an international project, it should determine whether the project is feasible from its own perspective.

■ Multinational capital budgeting requires any input that will help estimate the initial outlay, periodic cash flows, salvage value, and required rate of return on the project. Once these factors are estimated, the international project's NPV can be estimated, just as if it were a domestic project. However, it is normally more difficult to estimate these factors for an international project. Exchange rates create an additional source of uncertainty, because they affect the cash flows ultimately received by the parent as a result of the project. Other international conditions that can influence the cash flows ultimately received by the parent include the financing arrangement (parent versus subsidiary financing of the project), blocked funds by the host government, and host government incentives.

■ The risk of international projects can be accounted for by adjusting the discount rate used to estimate the project's net present value. However, the adjustment to the discount rate is subjective. An alternative method is to estimate the net present value based on various possible scenarios for exchange rates or any other uncertain factors. This method is facilitated by the use of sensitivity analysis or simulation.

SELF-TEST FOR CHAPTER 17 _____

(Answers are provided in Appendix A in the back of the text)

1. Two managers of a U.S. firm assessed a project proposed in Jamaica. Each manager used exactly the same estimates of the earnings to be generated by the project in Jamaica, as these estimates were provided by other employees. The managers agree on the proportion of funds to be remitted each year, the life of the project, and the discount rate to be applied. Both managers also assessed the project from the U.S. parent's perspective. Yet, one manager determined that this project had a large net present value, while the other manager determined that the project had a negative net present value. Explain the possible reasons for such a difference.

2. Pinpoint the parts of a multinational capital budgeting analysis that are sensitive for a proposed sales distribution center in Ireland, when the forecast of a stable economy in Ireland is revised to predict a recession.

3. New Orleans Exporting Co. focuses on producing small computer components which are then sold to Mexico. It plans to expand by establishing a plant in Mexico, which will produce the components and sell them locally. This plant will cut down on the amount of goods that will be transported from New Orleans. The firm has determined that the cash flows to be earned in Mexico would yield a positive net present value, after accounting for tax and exchange rate effects, converting cash flows to dollars, and discounting them at the proper discount rate. What other major factor must be considered in the estimation of the project's NPV?

4. Explain how the present value of the salvage value of a Portugal subsidiary will be affected (from the U.S. parent's perspective) by (a) an increase in the risk of the foreign subsidiary, and (b) an expectation that Portugal's currency (escudo) will depreciate against the dollar over time.

5. Wilmette Co. and Niles Co. (both from the U.S.) are assessing the acquisition of the same firm in Belgium, and have obtained the future cash flow estimates (in Belgian francs) from the firm. Wilmette would use its retained earnings from U.S. operations to acquire the subsidiary. Niles Co. would finance the acquisition mostly with a term loan (in francs) from Belgian banks. Neither firm has any other European business. Which firm's dollar cash flows would be affected more by future changes in the value of the franc (assuming that the Belgian firm is acquired)?

6. Assume a U.S. firm has been considering the divestiture of a Swedish subsidiary that produces ski equipment and sells it locally. A Swedish firm has already offered to acquire this Swedish subsidiary. Assume that the U.S. parent has just revised its projections of the Swedish krona's value downward. Will the proposed divestiture now seem more feasible or less feasible than it did before? Explain. (See the appendix.)

7. Review the capital budgeting example of Spartan Inc. discussed in this chapter. Identify the specific variables assessed within the process of estimating a foreign project's net present value (NPV) (from a U.S. perspective) that would cause the most uncertainty about the NPV.

QUESTIONS

1. Why should capital budgeting for subsidiary projects be assessed from the parent's perspective?

2. What additional factors deserve consideration in multinational capital budgeting that are not normally relevant for a purely domestic project?

3. What is the limitation of using point estimates of exchange rates within the capital budgeting analysis?

4. Explain how simulation can be used in multinational capital budgeting.

5. Why is simulation applicable to multinational capital budgeting? What can it do that other risk adjustment techniques cannot?

6. List the various techniques for adjusting risk in multinational capital budgeting. Describe any advantages or disadvantages of each technique.

7. Project X has an NPV estimated by your employees to be $1.2 million. Your employees state in their report that they have not accounted for risk, but that with such a large NPV, the project should be accepted, since even a risk-adjusted NPV would likely be positive. You have the final decision as to whether to accept or reject the project. What is your decision?

8. Describe in general terms how future appreciation of the German mark will likely affect the value (from the parent's perspective) of a project established in Germany today by a U.S.-based MNC. Will the sensitivity of the project value be affected by the percentage of earnings remitted to the parent each year?

9. Repeat Question 8, assuming future depreciation of the German mark.

10. Explain how the financing decision can influence the sensitivity of NPV to exchange rate forecasts.

11. Wolverine Corporation presently has no existing business in Germany but is considering the establishment of a subsidiary there. The following information has been gathered to assess this project:

   - The initial investment required is DM50 million. Given the existing spot rate of $.50 per mark, the initial investment in dollars is $25 million. In addition to the DM50 million initial investment on plant and equipment, DM20 million is needed for working capital and will be borrowed by the subsidiary from a German bank. The German subsidiary of Wolverine will pay interest only on the loan each year, at an interest rate of 14 percent. The loan principal is to be paid in 10 years.
   - The project will be terminated at the end of Year 3, when the subsidiary will be sold.

- The price, demand, and variable cost of the product in Germany are as follows:

Year	Price	Demand	Variable cost
1	DM500	40,000 units	DM30
2	DM511	50,000 units	DM35
3	DM530	60,000 units	DM40

- The fixed costs, such as overhead expenses, are estimated to be DM6 million per year.
- The exchange rate of the mark is expected to be $.52 at the end of Year 1, $.54 at the end of Year 2, and $.56 at the end of Year 3.
- The German government will impose an income tax of 30 percent on income. In addition, it will impose a withholding tax of 10 percent on earnings remitted by the subsidiary. The U.S. government will allow a tax credit on remitted earnings and will not impose any additional taxes.
- All cash flows received by the subsidiary are to be sent to the parent at the end of each year. The subsidiary will use its working capital to support ongoing operations.
- The plant and equipment are depreciated over 10 years, using the straight-line depreciation method. Since the plant and equipment are initially valued at DM50 million, the annual depreciation expense is DM5 million.
- In three years, the subsidiary is to be sold. Wolverine plans to let the acquiring firm assume the existing German loan. The working capital will not be liquidated, but will be used by the acquiring firm. Wolverine expects to receive DM52 million after subtracting capital gains taxes when it sells the subsidiary. Assume that this amount is not subject to a withholding tax.
- Wolverine requires a 20 percent rate of return on this project.

a) Determine the net present value of this project. Should Wolverine accept this project?

b) Assume that Wolverine also considers an alternate financing arrangement, in which the parent invests an additional $10 million to cover the working capital requirements, so that the subsidiary avoids the German loan. If this arrangement is used, the selling price of the subsidiary (after subtracting any capital gains taxes) is expected to be DM18 million higher. Is this alternative financing arrangement more feasible for the parent than the originally proposed arrangement? Explain.

c) Would the NPV of this project from the parent's perspective be more sensitive to exchange rate movements if the subsidiary used German financing to cover the working capital or if the parent invested more of its own funds to cover the working capital? Explain.

d) Assume Wolverine uses the original proposed financing arrangement and that funds are blocked until the subsidiary is sold. The funds to be remitted are reinvested at a rate of 6 percent (after taxes) until the end of Year 3. How is the project's NPV affected?

e) What is the break-even salvage value of this project, if Wolverine Corporation uses the original proposed financing arrangement and funds are not blocked?

f) Assume that Wolverine decides to implement the project, using the original proposed financing arrangement. Also assume that after one year, a German firm offers Wolverine a price of $27 million after taxes for the subsidiary, and that Wolverine's original forecasts for Years 2 and 3 have not changed. Should Wolverine divest the subsidiary? Explain. (See the appendix.)

12. Huskie Industries, a U.S.-based MNC, considers purchasing a small German manufacturing company that sells products only within Germany. Huskie has no other existing business in Germany and no cash flows in German marks. Would the proposed acquisition likely be more feasible if the mark is expected to appreciate or to depreciate over the long run? Explain.

13. When Walt Disney World considered establishing a theme park in France, were the forecasted revenues and costs associated with the French park sufficient to assess the feasibility of this project? Were there any other "relevant cash flows" that deserved to be considered?

14. Athens Inc. established a subsidiary in the United Kingdom that was independent of its operations in the United States. The subsidiary's performance was well above what was expected. Consequently, when a British firm approached Athens Inc. about the possibility of acquiring it, Athens' chief financial officer replied that the subsidiary was performing so well that it was not for sale. Comment on this strategy.

15. Lehigh Company established a subsidiary in Switzerland that was performing below the cash flow projections developed before the subsidiary was established. Lehigh anticipated that future cash flows would also be lower than the original cash flow projections. Consequently, Lehigh decided to inform several potential acquiring firms of its plan to sell the subsidiary. Lehigh then received a few bids. Even the highest bid was very low, but Lehigh accepted the offer. It justified its decision by stating that any existing project whose cash flows are not sufficient to recover the initial investment should be divested. Comment on this statement. (See the appendix).

16. Flagstaff Corporation is a U.S.-based firm with a subsidiary in Mexico. It plans to reinvest its earnings in Mexican government securities for the next ten years since the interest rate earned on these securities is so high. Then, after ten years, it will remit all accumulated earnings to the United States. What is a drawback of using this approach? (Assume the securities have no default or interest rate risk.)

17. Colorado Springs Company (based in the United States) plans to divest either its German or its Canadian subsidiary. Assume that if exchange rates stayed constant, the dollar cash flows each of these subsidiaries provided to the parent over time would be somewhat similar. However, the firm expects the German mark to depreciate against the U.S. dollar, and the Canadian dollar to appreciate against the U.S. dollar. The firm can sell

either subsidiary for about the same price today. Which one should it sell? (See the appendix.)

18. San Gabriel Corporation recently considered divesting its Italian subsidiary, and determined that the divestiture was not feasible. The required rate of return on this subsidiary was 17 percent. In the last week its required return on that subsidiary increased to 21 percent. If the sales price of the subsidiary has not changed, explain why the divestiture may now be feasible.

19. Ventura Corporation is a U.S.-based MNC which plans to establish a subsidiary in France. It is very confident that the French franc will appreciate against the dollar over time. The subsidiary will retain only enough revenues to cover expenses and will remit the rest to the parent each year. Would Ventura benefit more from exchange rate effects if its parent provided equity financing for the subsidiary, or if the subsidiary were financed by local banks in France? Explain.

20. Santa Monica Company is a U.S.-based MNC that was considering establishing a consumer products division in Germany, which would be financed by German banks. It completed its capital budgeting analysis in August 1989. Then, in November 1989, there was evidence of possible reunification between East and West Germany. In response, it increased its expected cash flows by 20 percent and did not adjust the discount rate applied to the project. Why was the discount rate affected by reunification?

21. Assume a less developed country called LDC removes its barriers to encourage direct foreign investment (DFI) in order to reduce its unemployment rate, presently at 15 percent. Also assume that several MNCs are likely to consider DFI in LDC. The inflation rate in recent years has averaged 4 percent. The hourly wage in LDC for manufacturing is the equivalent of about $5 per hour. As Piedmont Company developed cash flow forecasts to perform a capital budgeting analysis for a project in LDC, it assumed a wage rate of $5 in Year 1, and applied a 4 percent increase to each of the next ten years. The components produced are to be exported to its headquarters in the United States, where they will be used in the production of computers. Do you think Piedmont will overestimate or underestimate the net present value of this project? Why? (Assume that LDC's currency is tied to the dollar and will remain that way.)

22. Using the capital budgeting framework discussed in this chapter, explain the sources of uncertainty surrounding a proposed project in Hungary by a U.S. firm. In what ways is the estimated NPV of this project more uncertain than that of a similar project in a more developed European country?

CASE: PEPSICO'S INVESTMENT IN POLAND

PepsiCo to Invest $500 Million in Poland In Battle With Coke Over Eastern Europe

By MICHAEL J. MCCARTHY
Staff Reporter of THE WALL STREET JOURNAL

PepsiCo Inc. said it plans to invest $500 million in Poland, signaling that the country will become a major battleground as the company fights Coca-Cola Co.'s drive into Eastern Europe.

Coca-Cola has significantly expanded its presence in Eastern Europe over much of the past two years, with Pepsi offering mostly tactical resistance, like price discounting and new packaging. As a result, Coke's investments have produced big market-share gains in the former Communist countries where it had badly trailed Pepsi for more than two decades.

The five-year investment by PepsiCo also shows that the company increasingly is aiming its international-investment artillery squarely at emerging markets. Since April, PepsiCo has announced five-year plans to invest $115 million in the Budapest area of Hungary, and $750 million in Mexico.

PepsiCo's Polish investment furthers its strategy of expanding its beverage and food businesses together. Of the $500 million, about 40% will be used to build soft-drink plants and boost Pepsi distribution. Another 40% will be used to develop the company's snack-food operation, and the remainder is targeted for the nascent fast-food business in the former Communist country.

Poland is considered a treasure trove by U.S. consumer-product marketers, many struggling with a low-growth domestic market. With roughly 38 million people, Poland is the largest consumer market in the region, excluding the former Soviet Union, and has a population intensely interested in Western consumer goods.

To capitalize on that, PepsiCo yesterday opened a "three-in-one" restaurant in Poland, its first outside of the U.S. PepsiCo planted its attention-getting conglomeration of Pizza Hut, Taco Bell and Kentucky Fried Chicken at Warsaw's busy Solidarity Avenue and Bank Square intersection.

"Pepsi's products are treats for those who haven't had," said Emanuel Goldman, a beverage analyst for PaineWebber Inc.

Each of PepsiCo's business lines has vast potential for growth in Poland. The Western fast-food industry amounts to a dozen joints, such as McDonald's and Pizza Hut. Currently, Polish consumers eat less than half a pound of snack chips a year, well below the two pounds annually munched in some neighboring European countries to the west. As for soft drinks, Poles each drink about two gallons a year, roughly one-tenth the amount consumed in some Western European countries.

PepsiCo and Coke have been in Poland since 1972. But until the collapse of Communism, the cola giants had to operate under such heavy government regulation that they were able to muster a combined market share of only about 10%. Local soft drinks dominated the industry.

In the past three years, however, Coke and Pepsi have had substantial growth in Poland, where they now account for an estimated 60% of the market. In terms of U.S. dollars, the market roughly equates to $80 million, with Coke's 35% share edging out Pepsi's 25%, according to industry estimates. For both companies, Poland represents enormous potential growth.

PepsiCo said its beverage investment, roughly $200 million over the next five years, will be used for equipment upgrades, production expansions, marketing, promotion, advertising and employee training. Since 1990, Coke has pumped some $207 million into plants, trucks and equipment, said E. Neville Isdell, the Coca-Cola executive in charge of the company's Northeast Europe/Middle East group. Mr. Isdell said Coke has just begun advertising in Poland this summer and plans to invest an additional $50 million in new plants there in the next 12 months.

Aside from checking Atlanta-based Coke, Pepsi decided to invest more heavily in Poland because it had developed market expertise from its 40%-ownership of E. Wedel SA, Poland's biggest chocolate company. PepsiCo acquired the stake for $25 million in 1991, and now says it plans to increase its ownership to nearly 70% by next year. PepsiCo, based in Purchase, N.Y., also said it plans to open a new salty snack plant in Grodzisk, as part of its expanded investment in snack foods.

Wedel is one of PepsiCo's business partners in Poland that will help shoulder the $500 million investment, which PepsiCo described as the largest in the consumer-products industry in Poland. Pepsi said retail sales of its products in Poland are expected to exceed $100 million this year and $600 million by the end of the decade.

Source: *The Wall Street Journal* (August 11, 1993), p. B6. Reprinted by permission of *The Wall Street Journal,* © 1993 Dow Jones & Company, Inc. All rights reserved worldwide.

QUESTIONS

1. Given that the investment by PepsiCo Inc. in Poland was entirely in dollars, describe the exposure to exchange rate risk resulting from the project. Explain how the size of the parent's initial investment and the exchange rate risk would have been affected if PepsiCo Inc. had financed much of the investment with loans from banks in Poland.

2. Describe the factors that were likely considered by PepsiCo Inc. when estimating the future cash flows of the project in Poland.

3. What factors were likely considered by PepsiCo Inc. in deriving its required rate of return on the project in Poland?

<table>
<tr><td>CASE
PROBLEM</td></tr>
</table>

NORTH STAR COMPANY
Capital Budgeting

This case is intended to illustrate that the value of an international project is sensitive to various types of input. It also is intended to show how a computer spreadsheet format can facilitate capital budgeting decisions that involve uncertainty.

This case can be performed using LOTUS 1-2-3. The following present value factors may be helpful input in Lotus for discounting cash flows:

Years from Now	Present Value Interest Factor at 18%
1	.8475
2	.7182
3	.6086
4	.5158
5	.4371
6	.3704

For consistency in discussion of this case, you should develop your computer spreadsheet in a format somewhat similar to that in the Capital Budgeting chapter, with each year representing a column across the top. The use of a computer spreadsheet will significantly reduce the time needed to complete this case.

North Star Company considered establishing a subsidiary to capitalize on the removal of Eastern European border restrictions. The subsidiary would manufacture clothing in Germany and target the Eastern European countries for most of its business. Its sales would be invoiced in German marks (DM). It has forecasted net cash flows to the subsidiary as follows:

Year	Net Cash Flows to Subsidiary
1	DM 8,000,000
2	10,000,000
3	14,000,000
4	16,000,000
5	16,000,000
6	16,000,000

These cash flows do not include financing costs (interest expenses) on any funds borrowed in Germany. North Star Company also expects to receive DM30 million after taxes as a result of selling the subsidiary at the end of Year 6. Assume there will not be any withholding taxes imposed on this amount.

The exchange rate of the mark is forecasted below based on three possible scenarios of economic conditions:

NORTH STAR COMPANY (CONTINUED)

CASE PROBLEM

End of Year	Scenario I: Somewhat Stable Mark	Scenario II: Weak Mark	Scenario III: Strong Mark
1	.50	.49	.52
2	.51	.46	.55
3	.48	.45	.59
4	.50	.43	.64
5	.52	.43	.67
6	.48	.41	.71

The probability of each scenario is shown below:

	Somewhat Stable Mark	Weak Mark	Strong Mark
Probability	60%	30%	10%

Fifty percent of the net cash flows to the subsidiary would be remitted to the parent, while the remaining fifty percent would be reinvested to support ongoing operations at the subsidiary. North Star Company anticipates a 10 percent withholding tax on funds remitted to the United States.

The initial investment (including investment in working capital) by North Star in the subsidiary would be DM40 million. Any investment in working capital (such as accounts receivable, inventory, etc.) is to be assumed by the buyer in Year 6. The expected salvage value has already accounted for this transfer of working capital to the buyer in Year 6. The initial investment could be financed completely by the parent ($20 million, converted at the present exchange rate of $.50 per mark to achieve DM40 million). North Star Company will only go forward with its intentions to build the subsidiary if it expects to achieve a return on its capital of 18 percent or more.

The parent is considering an alternative financing arrangement. With this arrangement, the parent would provide $10 million (DM20 million), which means that the subsidiary would need to borrow DM20 million. Under this scenario, the subsidiary would obtain a 20-year loan and pay interest on the loan each year. The interest payments are DM1.6 million per year. In addition, the forecasted proceeds to be received from selling the subsidiary (after taxes) at the end of 6 years would be DM20 million (the forecast of proceeds is revised downward here because the equity investment of the subsidiary is less; the buyer would be assuming more debt if part of the initial investment in the subsidiary were supported by local bank loans). Assume the parent's required rate of return would still be 18 percent.

**CASE
PROBLEM**

NORTH STAR COMPANY (CONTINUED)

a) Which of the two financing arrangements would you recommend for the parent? Assess the forecasted NPV for each exchange rate scenario to compare the two financing arrangements and substantiate your recommendation.

b) In the first question, an alternative financing arrangement of partial financing by the subsidiary was considered, with an assumption that the required rate of return by the parent would not be affected. Is there any reason why the parent's required rate of return may increase when using this financing arrangement? Explain. How would you revise the analysis in the previous question under this situation? (This question requires discussion, not analysis.)

c) Would you recommend that North Star Co. establish the subsidiary even if the withholding tax is 20 percent?

d) Assume that there is some concern about the economic conditions in Germany which could cause a reduction in the net cash flows to the subsidiary. Explain how LOTUS could be used to reevaluate the project based on alternative cash flow scenarios. That is, how can this form of country risk be incorporated into the capital budgeting decision? (This question requires discussion, not analysis.)

e) Assume that North Star Company does implement the project, investing $10 million of its own funds, with the remainder borrowed by the subsidiary. Two years later, a U.S.-based corporation notifies North Star that it would like to purchase the subsidiary. Assume that the exchange rate forecasts for the somewhat stable scenario are appropriate for Years 3 through 6. Also assume that the other information already provided on net cash flows, financing costs, the 10% withholding tax, the salvage value, and the parent's required rate of return is still appropriate. What would be the minimum dollar price (after taxes) that North Star should receive to divest the subsidiary? Substantiate your opinion.

PROJECT

Assume that your firm's British subsidiary has been able to remit earnings of £400,000 at the end of each year since 1980. Based on the exchange rate at about that time each year, determine the dollar cash flows.

Repeat this analysis for your firm's Canadian subsidiary, which was able to remit C$800,000 at the end of each year since 1980. Is the standard deviation of the dollar cash flows higher for the British subsidiary or the Canadian subsidiary? Why? What does this project tell you about the exchange rate risk of a Canadian project versus a British project (from a U.S. perspective)?

REFERENCES

Booth, Laurence D. "Capital Budgeting Frameworks for the Multinational Corporation." *Journal of International Business Studies* (Fall 1982), pp. 114–123.

Collins, J. Markham, and William S. Sekely. "The Relationship of Headquarters Country and Industry Classification to Financial Structure." *Financial Management* (Autumn 1983), pp. 45–51.

Doukas, John, and Nickolaos G. Travlos. "The Effect of Corporate Multinationalism on Shareholders' Wealth: Evidence from International Acquisitions." *Journal of Finance* (December 1988), pp. 1161–1175.

Kester, W. Carl. "Capital and Ownership Structure: A Comparison of United States and Japanese Manufacturing Corporations." *Financial Management* (Spring 1986), pp. 5–16.

Kim, Suk H., Edward J. Farragher, and Trevor Crick. "Foreign Capital Budgeting Practices Used by the U.S. and Non-U.S. Multinational Companies." *The Engineering Economist* (Spring 1984), pp. 207–215.

Oblak, David J., and Roy J. Helm, Jr. "Survey and Analysis of Capital Budgeting Methods Used by Multinationals." *Financial Management* (Winter 1981), pp. 34–41.

Stanley, Margorie T., "Capital Structure and Cost of Capital for the Multinational Firm." *Journal of International Business Studies* (Spring–Summer 1981), pp. 103–120.

Stanley, Marjorie T., and Stanley B. Block. "A Survey of Multinational Capital Budgeting." *Financial Review* (March 1984), pp. 36–54.

―――― . "An Empirical Study of Management and Financial Variables Influencing Capital Budgeting Decisions for Multinational Companies in the 1980s." *Management International Review* (November 1983), pp. 61–71.

Srinivasan, Venkat, and Yong H. Kim. "Integrating Corporate Strategy and Multinational Capital Budgeting: An Analytical Framework." *Recent Developments in International Banking and Finance* (1988), pp. 381–397.

CAPITAL BUDGETING FOR INTERNATIONAL ACQUISITIONS AND DIVESTITURES

MNC are constantly assessing whether they should adjust their volume of international business by engaging in international acquisitions or divestitures. Methods of assessing the feasibility of international acquisitions are described first, followed by methods to assess the feasibility of international divestitures.

INTERNATIONAL ACQUISITIONS

An international acquisition of a firm is similar to other international projects in that it requires an initial outlay and is expected to generate cash flows whose present value will exceed the initial outlay. Numerous U.S.-based MNCs, including Rockwell International, Ford Motor Co., Scott Paper Co., Borden Inc., and Dow Chemical Co. have recently engaged in international acquisitions. Many more international acquisitions are taking place in Europe now, in response to the more uniform standards throughout Western Europe and momentum for free enterprise in Eastern Europe.

MNCs may view international acquisitions as a better form of direct foreign investment than establishing a new subsidiary. However, there are distinct differences between these two forms of direct foreign investment. Through an international acquisition, the firm can immediately expand its international business, since the target is already in place. Conversely, establishing a new subsidiary requires time. Second, an international acquisition can benefit from the customer relationships that have already been established. These advantages of an international acquisition over the establishment of a foreign subsidiary must be weighed against the higher costs of the acquisition. When viewed as a project, the international acquisition normally generates quicker and larger cash flows than the establishment of a new subsidiary, but requires a larger initial outlay. International acquisitions also necessitate the integration of parent management style with that of the foreign target.

Capital budgeting analysis can be used to determine whether a firm should be acquired. The net present value of a company from the acquiring firm's perspective (NPV_a) is

$$\text{NPV}_a = -\text{IO}_a + \sum_{t=1}^{n} \frac{\text{CF}_{a,t}}{(1+k)^t} + \frac{\text{SV}_a}{(1+k)^n}$$

where

IO_a = initial outlay needed by the acquiring firm to acquire the company

$CF_{a,t}$ = cash flow to be generated by the company for the acquiring firm

k = required rate of return on the acquisition of the company

SV_a = salvage value of the company (expected selling price of the company at a point in the future)

n = time at which the company will be sold.

The capital budgeting analysis of a foreign acquisition must account for the exchange rate of concern. For example, consider a U.S.-based MNC that assesses the acquisition of a foreign company. The dollar initial outlay ($IO_{U.S.}$) needed by the U.S. firm is determined by the acquisition price in foreign currency units (IO_f) and the spot rate of the foreign currency (S):

$$IO_{U.S.} = IO_f(S)$$

The dollar amount of cash flows to the U.S. firm is determined by the foreign currency cash flows ($CF_{f,t}$) per period remitted to the United States and the spot rate at that time (S_t):

$$CF_{a,t} = (CF_{f,t})S_t$$

This ignores any withholding taxes or blocked-funds restrictions imposed by the host government, and any income taxes imposed by the U.S. government. The dollar amount of salvage value to the U.S. firm is determined by the salvage value in foreign-currency units (SV_f) and the spot rate at that time (period n) when it is converted to dollars (S_n):

$$SV_a = (SV_f)S_n.$$

The net present value of a foreign takeover prospect can be derived by substituting the equalities just described in the capital budgeting equation:

$$NPV_a = -IO_a + \sum_{t=1}^{n} \frac{CF_{a,t}}{(1 + k)^t} + \frac{SV_a}{(1 + k)^n}$$

$$= -(IO_f)S + \sum_{t=1}^{n} \frac{(CF_{f,t})S_t}{(1 + k)^t} + \frac{(SV_f)S_n}{(1 + k)^n}.$$

This equation is simplified by ignoring blocked funds and tax considerations.

Factors Considered in International Acquisitions

Several factors must be considered when assessing a possible international acquisition, including

- Exchange rate movements
- Required return of acquiring firms
- Ability to use financial leverage
- Accounting and tax laws
- Country barriers.

Each of these factors is discussed.

Exchange Rate Movements.   The above equation suggests how existing and anticipated exchange rates affect the NPV of a foreign target:

- The lower the existing spot rate (S) is, the lower the price to be paid by the acquiring firm for the company, other things being equal.
- The higher the future spot rates are over each period (S_t), the higher the cash flows received by the acquiring firm, other things being equal.
- The higher the spot rate is when the company is sold (S_n), the higher the salvage value from the acquiring firm's perspective, other things being equal.

This discussion suggests that the ideal time to purchase a foreign company is when the spot rate of that company's currency is perceived to be very low and is expected to rise over time. Of course, estimates for the foreign initial outlay, foreign cash flows, and foreign salvage value also affect the NPV to be generated by the target. These other factors are also relevant to potential acquiring firms that reside in the same country as the target. Such firms do not, however, need to account for the exchange rates in the manner described above. Consequently, potential acquiring firms from other countries may perceive a company to have a much higher or lower value than local potential acquiring firms perceive it to. If the company's currency is expected to appreciate (depreciate) against other currencies in the future, potential acquiring firms in other countries would likely value the company higher (lower) today than potential acquirers based in the company's country.

Required Return of Acquiring Firms.   Another factor that affects the potential value of an acquisition is the required rate of return for the acquiring firm. Since the cost of capital varies among countries (as explained in the following chapter), so does the required rate of return. Thus, firms in some countries may find acquisitions more attractive than firms in other countries.

Ability to Use Financial Leverage.   Firms commonly finance a portion of their international acquisitions with borrowed funds. Firms in some countries have more flexibility to borrow, because investors and creditors in those countries are more receptive to higher degrees of financial leverage (as discussed in the following chapter). Those firms that have greater flexibility to borrow may be more successful in completing international acquisitions. Firms in the United States tend to have less financial leverage than firms in other countries. If the U.S. firms attempted to fund an acquisition with a substantial amount of debt, they might be penalized. Their cost of the debt would increase as creditors commanded a high premium to compensate for the high risk. Consequently, the return required might be too high, so that some international acquisitions would not be worthwhile.

Accounting and Tax Laws.   Accounting and tax laws can create competitive advantages for acquiring firms in some countries. For example, in most industrialized countries, goodwill (the purchase price of the firm minus the tangible assets) resulting from an acquisition does not affect the acquiring firm's earnings. However, U.S. firms must amortize goodwill against earnings, without any tax deductions. The U.S.-based MNCs are adversely affected because future reported earnings are reduced without any tax benefits. Since share prices of firms are somewhat influenced by earnings, the perceived value of the acquiring firm is adversely affected by the tax provision. Even with this disparity in accounting and tax laws, U.S. firms may benefit from foreign acquisitions. However, foreign firms subject to more favorable accounting and tax provisions may be able to bid higher prices for target firms.

Country Barriers.   Explicit and implicit barriers imposed by country governments do not necessarily offer advantages to specific acquiring firms, but instead prevent or discourage the acquisitions of particular targets. For example, **hostile takeovers** (acquisitions not desired by the target firms) are outlawed or strongly discouraged by governments in most countries. They are tolerated in the United States more than in other countries. Thus, a foreign firm may be able to acquire a U.S. firm through a hostile takeover, but a U.S. firm will probably not be able to acquire non-U.S. firms in this manner.

Regulations Imposed on International Acquisitions

All countries have one or more agencies that monitor mergers and acquisitions. The acquisition activity in any given country is somewhat influenced by the regulations enforced by these agencies. For example, in France, the Treasury can reject any deal if the acquirer is based outside the European Economic Community. It may also reject a deal if the target is in some closely monitored industry, such as defense or health care. The Monopolies Commission of France also reviews acquisitions to prevent any combined firms from controlling more than 25 percent of an industry or from severely reducing competition.

Acquisitions in Japan are reviewed by the Fair Trade Commission, while acquisitions in Germany are examined by the Antitrust Authority, and acquisitions in the United Kingdom are reviewed by several regulatory agencies. Acquisitions in the United States are also reviewed by several agencies, including the Securities and Exchange Commission, which regulates the conduct of acquisitions, and the Justice Department and Federal Trade Commission, which analyze the potential impact on competition.

Explicit and implicit barriers to even friendly acquisitions can vary among countries. At one extreme, the U.S. government has allowed even hostile takeovers (unless they violate antitrust laws), while Japan has historically discouraged all acquisitions. While formidable barriers to Japanese markets still remain, some U.S. and European MNCs have acquired Japanese firms. In recent years, U.S.-based MNCs such as Corning Glass Works, Data General, Eastman Kodak, and Motorola have acquired Japanese firms. The Japanese government is more receptive to acquisitions than it has been in the past, as long as the Japanese target firm is agreeable.

An implicit barrier to international acquisitions in some countries is the "red tape" involved, such as procedure and documentation requirements. An acquiring firm is subject to a different set of requirements in each country. Therefore, it has been difficult for a firm to become proficient at the process unless it concentrates on international acquisitions within a single foreign country. The current efforts to make regulations uniform across Europe will simplify the paperwork involved in acquisitions of European firms.

Acquisitions of Privatized Businesses

In recent years, government-owned businesses of many developing countries in Eastern Europe and South America have been sold to individuals or corporations. Many MNCs have capitalized on this wave of so-called privatization by acquiring the businesses being sold by governments. These businesses may be attractive because of the potential for MNCs to increase their efficiency. However, the valuation of these businesses is difficult for the following reasons.

First, the future cash flows are very uncertain because the businesses previously have been operating in environments of little or no competition. Thus, previous sales volume figures may not be useful indicators of future sales.

Second, if earnings of the foreign subsidiary are converted to the MNC parent's home currency, the exchange rate estimates are very uncertain. The exchange rates of the currencies in these countries were not determined by market forces, since the currencies were rarely traded in the foreign exchange markets. Thus, the exchange rates may change substantially over time as international trade and investment becomes more common.

Third, the discount rate used to measure the present value of the business is subject to error, because the cost of financing projects in these countries is so uncertain. Interest rates in the countries engaged in privatization have not been determined by market forces, since capital flows in and out of these countries were restricted. As barriers to international capital flows are removed, there is much uncertainty as to how interest rates will adjust. Since the cost of financing businesses in these countries is very uncertain, the discount rate is uncertain as well.

Finally, the lack of established stock markets in these countries prevents an MNC from deriving a value for a business based on comparable publicly held firms.

Even with the difficulties of measuring the value of privatized businesses, MNCs such as Gerber Products, PepsiCo, and Westinghouse have acquired these businesses as a means of entering new markets.

Trends in International Acquisitions

Exhibits 17A.1 and 17A.2 compare the volume and value of cross-border acquisitions involving U.S. firms. During the late 1980s, more U.S. firms served as targets than as acquirers in international acquisitions. The difference is partially attributed to some of the factors already described. U.S. firms that attempt to acquire non-U.S. firms tend to have less flexibility to borrow and are subject to less favorable tax laws and more stringent country barriers. Potential opportunities in the United States may also explain why many U.S. firms have been acquired by non-U.S. firms. However, this trend has changed in the 1990s as the acquisition activity (international and domestic) has declined. Non-U.S. firms have cut back on acquisitions of U.S. targets to a greater degree. In addition,

EXHIBIT 17.A1   Trends in International Acquisitions
SOURCE: *Mergers & Acquisitions* (May–June 1990, May–June 1993).

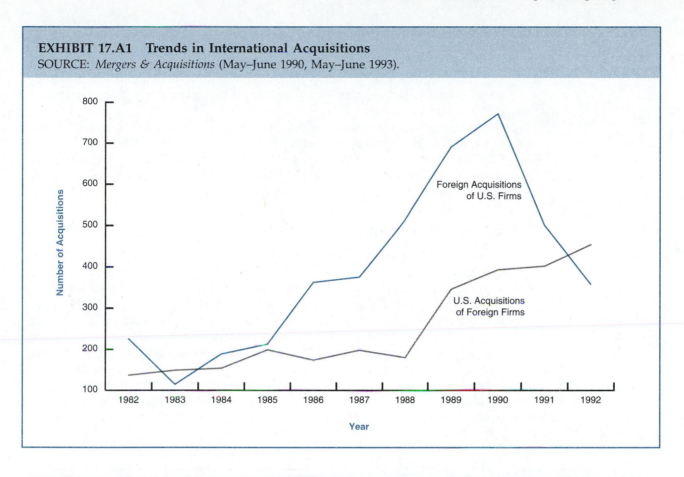

EXHIBIT 17.A2   Value of International Acquisitions
SOURCE: *Mergers & Acquisitions* (May–June 1990, May–June 1993).

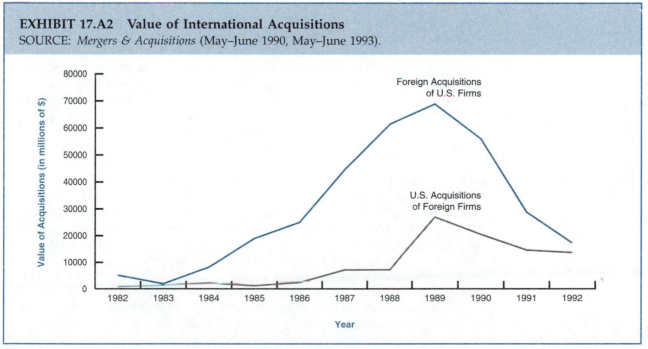

European firms have been attractive targets for U.S. firms attempting to establish a foothold in Europe following the more uniform regulations across European countries and the momentum for free enterprise in Eastern Europe. At present, U.S. firms acquire more targets in the United Kingdom than in any other country, while British and Canadian firms are the most common non-U.S. acquirers of U.S. targets.

Exhibit 17A.2 compares the values of U.S. acquisitions of foreign firms to those of foreign acquisitions of U.S. firms. The value of foreign acquisitions of U.S. firms was consistently higher throughout the 1980s. The difference was especially pronounced in the 1987–1989 period, when the dollar was significantly weaker than it had been in the mid-1980s.

Partial International Acquisitions

When an MNC wishes to expand in another country, but lacks an understanding of business in that country, it may consider partial international acquisitions. This type of investment normally allows the foreign target to continue operating, and may not necessarily cause the employee turnover that commonly occurs after a target's ownership changes. However, by acquiring a substantial fraction of the shares, the MNC may have some influence on the target's management, and be in a position to complete the acquisition in the future. Some MNCs buy stakes in foreign companies to have some control over their operations. For example, Coca Cola has purchased stakes in many foreign bottle companies that serve as the bottlers of its syrup. In this way, it can ensure that the bottle operations meet its standards.

DIVESTITURE ANALYSIS

Even after an MNC's accept/reject decisions are made, they should be reassessed at various times. Some foreign projects that have been rejected may become acceptable as a result of a reduction in the MNC's cost of capital, increased host government incentives, improved economic conditions in the host country, or more favorable projections of exchange rates. Foreign projects that have been implemented must be assessed to determine whether they should be continued or divested.

To illustrate how an MNC might reevaluate a project after it has been implemented, reconsider the example from this chapter in which Spartan Inc. proposed a Swiss subsidiary. Assume that the project is implemented, and after two years, the spot rate of the Swiss franc is $.46. In addition, forecasts have been revised for the remaining two years of the project, indicating that the Swiss franc should be worth $.44 in Year 3 and $.40 in the project's final year. Because these forecasts have an adverse effect on the project, Spartan Inc. considers divesting the subsidiary. For simplicity, assume that the original forecasts of the other variables remain unchanged, and that a potential acquirer has offered SF13,000,000 (after adjusting for any capital gains taxes) for the subsidiary if the acquirer can assume the existing local loan and retain the existing working capital. Spartan can conduct a divestiture analysis by comparing the after-tax proceeds from the possible sale of the project (in terms of U.S. dollars) to the present value of expected dollar inflows that the project will generate if it is not

EXHIBIT 17 A.3   Divestiture Analysis: Spartan Inc.

	End of Year 2 (Today)	End of Year 3 (One Year from Today)	End of Year 4 (Two Years from Today)
SF remitted after withholding taxes		SF6,840,000	SF19,560,000
Selling price	SF13,000,000		
Exchange rate	$.46	$.44	$.40
Cash flow received from divestiture	$5,980,000		
Cash flows forgone due to divestiture		$3,009,600	$7,824,000
PV of forgone cash flows (15% discount rate)		$2,617,044	$5,916,068

$$NPV_d = \$5,980,000 - (\$2,617,044 + \$5,916,068)$$
$$= \$5,980,000 - \$8,533,112$$
$$= -\$2,553,112$$

sold. This comparison will determine the net present value of the divestiture (NPV_d), as illustrated in Exhibit 17A.3. Since the present value of forgone cash flows exceeds the price at which the project could be sold, NPV_d is negative. Thus, the project should not be divested.

Some existing projects that seem profitable when analyzed separately can actually reduce the value of the MNC overall. For example, several U.S.-based corporations had subsidiaries in South Africa in the mid-1980s that appeared to be profitable. Yet, the presence of some of these corporations in South Africa caused reduced cash flows within the United States (due to the boycotting of products, etc.). Numerous U.S. corporations divested their South African subsidiaries in the late 1980s.

Many divestitures occur as a result of a revised assessment of industry or economic conditions. For example, numerous U.S. commercial banks divested foreign subsidiaries when they realized there was not enough business in the foreign markets to make the investment worthwhile. Warner-Lambert Company, Johnson & Johnson, and several other U.S.-based MNCs recently divested some of their Latin American subsidiaries when economic conditions deteriorated there.

CHAPTER 18

MULTINATIONAL COST OF CAPITAL AND CAPITAL STRUCTURE

The cost of capital has a major impact on a multinational corporation's (MNC's) value. To fund its operations, an MNC uses a capital structure (proportion of debt versus equity financing) that can minimize its cost of capital, and therefore maximize its value. The specific objectives of this chapter are to

- explain how corporate and country characteristics influence an MNC's cost of capital,
- explain why there are differences in the costs of capital among countries, and
- explain how corporate and country characteristics are considered by an MNC when it establishes its capital structure.

BACKGROUND ON COST OF CAPITAL

A firm's capital consists of equity (retained earnings and funds obtained by issuing stock) and debt (borrowed funds). The firm's cost of retained earnings reflects an opportunity cost: what the existing shareholders could have earned if they had received the earnings as dividends and invested the funds themselves. The firm's cost of new common equity (issuing new stock) reflects an opportunity cost: what the new shareholders could have earned if they had invested their funds elsewhere instead of in the stock. This cost exceeds that of retained earnings because it also includes the expenses associated with selling the new stock (flotation costs). The firm's cost of debt is easier to measure, because interest expenses are incurred by the firm as a result of borrowing funds. Firms attempt to use a specific capital structure, or mix of capital components, that will minimize their cost of capital. The lower a firm's cost of capital, the lower is its required rate of return on a given proposed project. Firms estimate their cost of capital before they conduct capital budgeting, because the net present value of any project is partially dependent on the cost of capital.

The firm's weighted average cost of capital (referred to as k_c) can be measured as

$$k_c = \left(\frac{D}{D + E}\right) k_d (1 - t) + \left(\frac{E}{D + E}\right) k_e$$

where D is the amount of the firm's debt, k_d is the before-tax cost of its debt, t is the corporate tax rate, E is the equity of the firm, and k_e is the cost of financing with equity. These ratios reflect the percentage of capital represented by debt and equity respectively.

There is an advantage to using debt rather than equity as capital, because the interest payments on debt are tax deductible. However, the greater the use of debt, the greater the interest expense is, and the higher the probability is that the firm will be unable to meet its expenses. Consequently, the rate of return required by potential new shareholders or creditors will increase to reflect the higher probability of bankruptcy.

The trade-off between debt's advantage (tax deductibility of interest payments) and its disadvantage (increased bankruptcy probability) is illustrated in Exhibit 18.1. The firm's cost of capital is shown to initially decrease as the ratio of debt to total capital increases. However, after some point (labeled X in Exhibit 18.1), the cost of capital rises as the ratio of debt to total capital increases. This implies that it is favorable to increase the use of debt financing until the point at which the bankruptcy probability becomes large enough to offset the tax advantage of using debt. To go beyond that point would increase the firm's overall cost of capital.

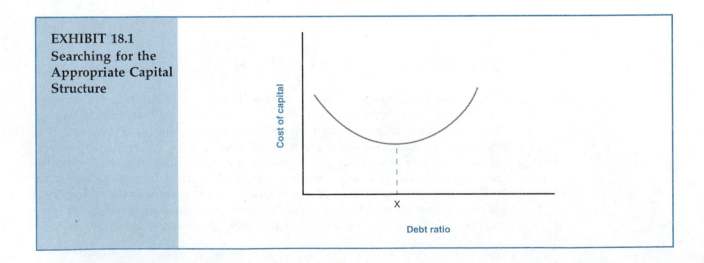

EXHIBIT 18.1
Searching for the Appropriate Capital Structure

Cost of Capital for MNCs _____

The cost of capital for MNCs may differ from that for domestic firms because of the following characteristics that differentiate MNCs from domestic firms.

1. *Size of firm.* MNCs that often borrow substantial amounts may be given preferential treatment by creditors, thereby reducing their cost of capital. Furthermore, their relatively large issues of stocks or bonds allow for reduced flotation costs (as a percentage of the amount of financing). Yet, this is due to their size and not to their internationalized business. That is, a domestic corporation may be given the same treatment if it is large enough. However, a firm's growth is more restricted if it is not willing to operate internationally. Because MNCs may more easily achieve growth, they may be more able than purely domestic firms to reach the necessary size to receive preferential treatment from creditors.

2. *Access to international capital markets.* MNCs are normally able to obtain funds through the international capital markets. Since the cost of funds can vary among markets, the MNC's access to the international capital markets may allow it to attract funds at a lower cost than that paid by domestic firms. In addition, subsidiaries may be able to obtain funds locally at a lower cost than that available to the parent, if the prevailing interest rates in the host country are relatively low. Such a form of financing can lower the cost of capital, and will not necessarily increase the MNC's exposure to exchange rate risk, since the revenues generated by the subsidiary will most likely be denominated in the same currency. In this case, the subsidiary is not relying on the parent for financing, although some centralized managerial support from the parent will most likely still exist.

3. *International diversification.* A firm's cost of capital is affected by the probability that it will go bankrupt. If a firm's cash inflows come from sources all over the world, there might be more stability in cash inflows. This reasoning is based on the premise that total sales will not be highly influenced by a single economy. To the extent that individual economies are independent of each other, net cash flows from a portfolio of subsidiaries should exhibit less variability, which may reduce the probability of bankruptcy and therefore reduce the cost of capital.

4. *Exposure to Exchange rate risk.* An MNC's cash flow could be more volatile than that of a domestic firm in the same industry, if it is highly exposed to exchange rate risk. If foreign earnings are remitted to the U.S. parent of an MNC, they will not be worth as much when the U.S. dollar is strong against major currencies. Thus, the capability of making interest payments on outstanding debt is reduced, and the probability of bankruptcy is higher. This could force creditors and shareholders to require a higher return, which increases the MNC's cost of capital.

   Overall, a firm more exposed to exchange rate fluctuations will normally have a wider (more dispersed) distribution of possible cash flows in future periods. Since the cost of capital should reflect that possibility, and since the possibility of bankruptcy would be higher if the cash flow expectations were more uncertain, exposure to exchange rate fluctuations could lead to a higher cost of capital.

5. *Exposure to Country risk.* An MNC that establishes foreign subsidiaries is subject to the possibility that the host country government may seize the MNC's subsidiary assets. The probability of such an occurrence is influenced by many factors, including the attitude of the host country government and the industry of concern. If assets are seized and fair compensation is not provided, the probability of the MNC's going bankrupt increases. The higher the percentage of an MNC's assets invested in foreign countries, and the higher the overall country risk of operating in these countries, the higher will be the MNC's probability of bankruptcy (and therefore cost of capital), other things being equal.

There are other forms of country risk not as critical as a host government takeover that could affect an MNC subsidiary's cash flows. These less critical types of risk (such as revised tax laws by host country governments, etc.), are not necessarily incorporated within the cash flow projections, since there is no reason to believe they will arise. Yet, because there is a possibility that these events will occur, the capital budgeting process should incorporate such risk. For example, Exxon has much experience in assessing the feasibility of potential projects in foreign countries. If it detects a radical change in government or tax policy, it adds a premium to the required return of related projects. The size of the premium is determined by financial planners and political analysts.

Five factors that may distinguish between the cost of capital for an MNC and that cost for a domestic firm in a particular industry have been assessed. In general, the first three factors listed (size, access to international capital markets, and international diversification) are favorable to an MNC's cost of capital, while exchange rate risk and country risk are unfavorable. It is impossible to generalize on whether MNCs have a cost of capital advantage over domestic firms. Each MNC should be assessed separately to determine whether the net effects of its international operations on the cost of capital are favorable.

Cost of Capital Comparison Using the CAPM

To assess how required rates of return of MNCs differ from those of purely domestic firms, the capital asset pricing model (CAPM) can be applied. It defines the required return (k_e) on a stock as

$$k_e = R_f + B(k_m - R_f),$$

where

$$R_f = \text{risk-free rate of return}$$

$$k_m = \text{market return}$$

$$B = \text{beta of stock.}$$

The CAPM suggests that the required return on a firm's stock is a positive function of (1) the risk-free rate of interest, (2) the market rate of return, and (3) the stock's beta. The beta represents the sensitivity of the stock's returns to market returns (a stock index is normally used as a proxy for the market). An MNC has no control over the risk-free rate of interest or over the market returns, but may be able to influence its beta. An MNC that increases its amount in foreign sales may be able to reduce its stock's beta and therefore reduce the return required by investors. In this way, it would reduce its cost of capital.

Advocates of the CAPM may suggest that a project's beta could be used to determine the required rate of return for that project. A project's beta represents the sensitivity of the project's cash flow to the market conditions. A project whose cash flow is insulated from market conditions will exhibit a low beta.

For a well-diversified MNC with cash flows generated by several projects, each project contains two types of risk: (1) unsystematic variability in cash flows unique to the firm, and (2) systematic risk. Capital asset pricing theory suggests that the unsystematic risk of projects can be ignored, since it will be diversified away. However, systematic risk is not diversified away, since all projects are similarly affected. The lower a project's beta, the lower is the project's systematic risk, and the lower would be the required rate of return for such a project. If projects of MNCs exhibit lower betas than projects of purely domestic firms, then the required rates of return on MNC projects should be lower. This translates into a lower overall cost of capital.

Capital asset pricing theory would most likely suggest that the MNC cost of capital is generally lower than that of domestic firms, due to the reasoning just presented. It should be emphasized, though, that unsystematic project risk is considered to be relevant by some MNCs. And if it is also considered within the assessment of a project's risk, the required rate of return will not necessarily be lower for MNC projects than projects of domestic firms. In fact, a large project in a less developed country with very volatile economic conditions and a high degree of country risk would be perceived as very risky by many MNCs, even if the expected cash flows of this project were uncorrelated with the U.S. market. This implies that MNCs may consider unsystematic risk as an important factor when determining a foreign project's required rate of return.

When assuming that markets are segmented, it is acceptable to use the U.S. market when measuring a U.S.-based MNC's project beta. If U.S. investors invest mostly in the U.S., their investments are systematically affected by the U.S. market. MNCs that adopt projects with low betas may be able to reduce their own betas (the sensitivity of their stock returns to market returns). Such firms are desirable to U.S. investors because they offer more diversification benefits as a result of having low betas.

Since markets are becoming more integrated over time, one could argue that a world market is more appropriate than a U.S. market for U.S.-based MNCs. That is, if investors purchased stocks across numerous countries, their stocks would be substantially affected by world market conditions, not just U.S. market conditions. Consequently, they would prefer to invest in firms that had low sensitivity to world market conditions to achieve more diversification benefits. MNCs that could adopt projects that were somewhat isolated from world market conditions might be able to reduce their overall sensitivity to these conditions, and could be viewed as desirable investments by investors.

While markets are becoming more integrated, U.S. investors still tend to focus on U.S. stocks, to capitalize on lower transaction and information costs. Thus, their investments are systematically affected by U.S. market conditions;

this causes them to be most concerned about the sensitivity of investments to the U.S. market.

In summary, we cannot say with certainty whether an MNC will have a lower cost of capital than a purely domestic firm in the same industry. However, we can use this discussion to understand how an MNC may attempt to take full advantage of the favorable aspects that reduce its cost of capital, while minimizing exposure to the unfavorable aspects that increase its cost of capital.

COSTS OF CAPITAL ACROSS COUNTRIES

An understanding of why the cost of capital can vary among countries is relevant for three reasons. First, it can explain why MNCs based in some countries may have a competitive advantage over others. Just as there are differences in technology or resources across countries, there are differences in the cost of capital, which can allow some MNCs to more easily increase their world market share. Second, MNCs may be able to adjust their international operations and sources of funds to capitalize on differences in the cost of capital among countries. Third, an understanding of differences in the costs of each capital component (debt and equity) can help explain why MNCs based in some countries tend to use a more debt-intensive capital structure than MNCs based elsewhere. Country differences in the cost of debt are described first, followed by country differences in the cost of equity.

Country Differences in the Cost of Debt

The cost of debt to a firm is primarily determined by the risk-free interest rate in the currency borrowed and the risk premium required by creditors. The cost of debt for firms is higher in some countries than in others because the corresponding risk-free rate is higher, or because the risk premium is higher. Explanations for country differences in the risk-free rate and in the risk premium follow.

Differences in the Risk-Free Rate. The risk-free rate is determined by the interaction of the supply and demand for funds. Any factors that influence the supply and/or demand will affect the risk-free rate. Some of the factors that have such an influence and vary among countries are tax laws, demographics, monetary policies, and economic conditions.

Tax laws in some countries offer more incentives to save than those in others, which can influence the supply of savings, and therefore, interest rates. A country's corporate tax laws related to depreciation and investment tax credits can also affect interest rates through their influence on the corporate demand for funds.

The demographics of a country influence the supply of savings available and the amount of loanable funds demanded. Since demographics differ among countries, so will supply and demand conditions, and therefore nominal interest rates. Countries with younger populations are likely to experience higher interest rates, since younger households tend to save less and borrow more.

The monetary policy implemented by each country's central bank influences the supply of loanable funds, and therefore interest rates. Countries that use a loose money policy (high money supply growth) may achieve lower nominal interest rates if they can maintain a low rate of inflation. Some theories suggest that a loose money policy will cause higher interest rates by raising inflationary expectations and the demand for loanable funds. The point here is that regardless of how a monetary policy affects interest rates, each central bank implements its own monetary policy, and this can cause differences in interest rates among countries.

Since economic conditions influence interest rates, they will also cause interest rates to vary across countries. The cost of debt in many less developed countries is much higher than that cost in industrialized countries, primarily because of economic conditions. The high expected rate of inflation causes creditors to require a high risk-free interest rate.

Differences in the Risk Premium.

The risk premium on debt must be large enough to compensate creditors for the risk that the borrower is unable to meet its payment obligations. This risk can vary among countries because of differences in economic conditions, relationships between corporations and creditors, government intervention, and degree of financial leverage.

If economic conditions in a particular country tend to be more stable, the risk of a recession is relatively low. Thus, the probability that a firm cannot meet its obligations is lower, allowing for a lower risk premium.

Relationships between corporations and creditors are closer in some countries than in others. In Japan, creditors stand ready to extend credit in the event of a corporation's financial distress, which reduces the risk of illiquidity. The cost of a Japanese firm's financial problems may be shared in various ways by the firm's management, business customers, and consumers. Since the financial problems are not borne entirely by creditors, there is more motivation for all parties involved to see that the problems are resolved. Thus, there is less likelihood (for a given level of debt) that Japanese firms will go bankrupt, which implies a lower risk premium on the debt of Japanese firms.

Governments in some countries are more willing to intervene and rescue failing firms. For example, in the United Kingdom many firms are partially owned by the government. It may be in the best interest of the government to rescue firms that it partially owns. Even if the government is not a partial owner, it may provide direct subsidies or extend loans to failing firms. In the United States, government rescues are not as well received, since taxpayers prefer not to bear the cost of corporate mismanagement. While there has been some government intervention in the United States to protect particular industries, the probability that a failing firm would be rescued by the government is lower there than in other countries. Therefore, the risk premium on a given level of debt would be higher for U.S. firms than for firms of other countries.

Firms in some countries have greater borrowing capacity because their creditors are willing to tolerate a higher degree of financial leverage. For example, firms in Japan and Germany have a higher degree of financial leverage than firms in the United States. If all other factors were equal, these high-leverage firms would have to pay a higher risk premium. However, all other factors are not equal. In fact, these firms are allowed to use a higher degree of financial leverage because of their unique relationships with the creditors and governments.

Comparative Costs of Debt Across Countries.

The before-tax cost of debt (as measured by corporate bond yields) for various countries is displayed in

EXHIBIT 18.2   Costs of Debt Across Countries

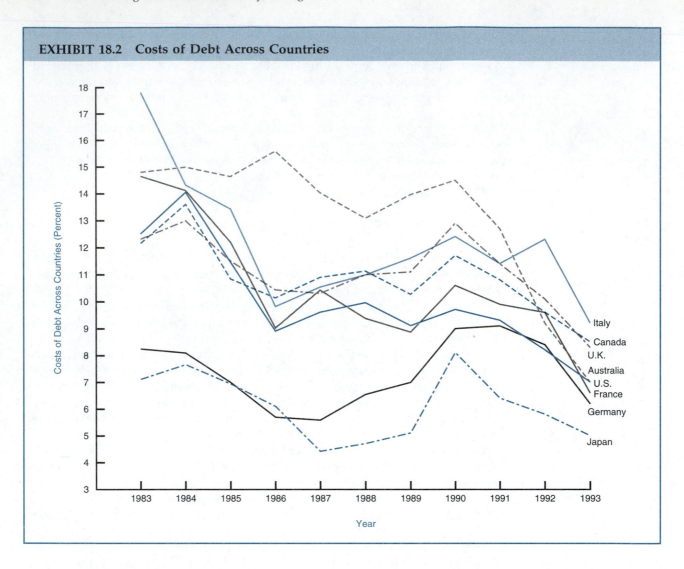

Exhibit 18.2. There is some positive correlation between country cost-of-debt levels over time. The nominal cost of debt for firms in each country peaked in 1980, declined sharply in the early 1980s, leveled off during the late 1980s, and declined in the early 1990s. The disparity in the cost of debt among the countries is due primarily to the disparity in their risk-free interest rates.

MNCs operating in countries with a high cost of capital will be forced to decline projects that might be feasible for MNCs operating in countries with a low cost of capital. In addition, MNCs in countries with a high cost of debt may be more likely to divest existing projects because of the high cost associated with funding them. As an example, Lloyds Bank of the United Kingdom decided to sell its U.S. commercial bank operations in 1989. Its reason was that the returns were not adequate, and it could do just as well by investing the funds in British money markets. If the nominal cost of capital for British firms had been lower, Lloyds Bank might have retained this project.

Country Differences in the Cost of Equity

A country's cost of equity represents an opportunity cost: what shareholders could earn on investments with similar risk if the equity funds were distributed to them. This return on equity can be measured as a risk-free interest rate that could have been earned by shareholders, plus a premium to reflect the risk of the firm. Since risk-free interest rates vary among countries, the costs of equity can vary distinctly among countries.

The cost of equity is also based on investment opportunities in the country of concern. In a country with many investment opportunities, potential returns may be relatively high, resulting in a high opportunity cost of funds, and therefore a high cost of capital. According to McCauley and Zimmer, a country's cost of equity can be estimated by first applying the price/earnings multiple to a given stream of earnings.

The price/earnings multiple is related to the cost of capital because it reflects the share price of the firm in proportion to the firm's performance (as measured by earnings). A high price/earnings multiple implies that the firm receives a high price when selling new stock for a given level of earnings, which means that the cost of equity financing is low. However, adjustments to the price/earnings multiples must be made for the effects of a country's inflation, earnings growth, and other factors.

Combining the Costs of Debt and Equity

The costs of debt and equity can be combined to derive an overall cost of capital. The relative proportions of debt and equity used by firms in each country must be applied to reasonably estimate this cost of capital. Given the differences in the costs of debt across countries, and the differences in the costs of equity across countries, it is understandable why the cost of capital may be lower for firms based in specific countries. Japan has commonly been cited as having a relatively low cost of capital. It normally has a relatively low risk-free interest rate, which not only affects the cost of debt but indirectly affects the cost of equity. In addition, the price/earnings multiples of Japanese firms are normally high, which allows Japanese firms to obtain equity funding at a relatively low cost. MNCs can attempt to access capital from countries where capital costs are low, but when the capital is used to support operations in other countries, the MNCs are normally exposed to exchange rate risk. Thus, the cost of capital may ultimately turn out to be higher than expected.

USING THE COST OF CAPITAL FOR ASSESSING FOREIGN PROJECTS

When an MNC's parent proposes an investment in a foreign project that has the same risk as the MNC itself, it can use its weighted average cost of capital as the required rate of return for the project. However, many foreign projects may exhibit different risk levels than those of the MNCs. There are various ways for an MNC to account for the risk differential in its capital budgeting process. First, it can account for the risk within its cash flow estimates. Various possible values for each input variable (such as demand, price, labor cost, etc.) can be incorporated to estimate net present values (NPVs) under alternative scenarios, and then derive a probability distribution of net present values (NPVs). When the weighted average cost of capital is used as the required rate of return, the probability distribution of NPVs can be assessed to determine the probability that the foreign project will generate a return that is at least equal to the firm's weighted average cost of capital. If the project exhibits much risk, an area of the probability distribution will reflect negative NPVs, which suggests that the project could backfire. This is a useful method to use in accounting for risk, because it explicitly incorporates the various possible scenarios in the NPV estimation, and therefore can measure the probability that a project may backfire. Computer software programs that perform sensitivity analysis and simulation can be used to facilitate the process.

An alternative method of accounting for a foreign project's risk is to adjust the firm's weighted average cost of capital for the risk differential. For example, if the foreign project were thought to exhibit more risk than the MNC exhibits, a premium could be added to the weighted average cost of capital to derive the required rate of return on the project. Then, the capital budgeting process would incorporate this required rate of return as the discount rate. If the foreign project exhibited lower risk, the MNC would use a required rate of return on the project that was less than its weighted average cost of capital.

This method is easy to use, but there is no perfect formula to adjust for the project's unique risk. Yet, some logic could be used to derive a reasonable risk adjustment. Recall that the weighted average cost of capital is simply the weighted average cost of equity plus the weighted average after-tax cost of debt. The MNC's parent could estimate its cost of equity and the after-tax cost of debt on the funds to be obtained to finance the foreign project. The after-tax cost of debt can be estimated with reasonable accuracy, since there is public information on the present costs of debt (bond yields) incurred by other firms whose risk level is similar to the foreign project. Recall that the cost of equity is an opportunity cost, what investors could earn on alternative equity investments with similar risk. The MNC could attempt to measure the expected return on a set of stocks that exhibited the same risk as its foreign project. This expected return could serve as the cost of equity. The required rate of return on the project would be the project's weighted cost of capital, based on the estimates explained here.

THE MNC's CAPITAL STRUCTURE DECISION

MNCs recognize the trade-off between using debt and using equity for financing their operations. The advantages of using debt as opposed to equity vary with corporate characteristics specific to the MNCs themselves and specific to the countries where the MNCs have established subsidiaries. Some of the more relevant corporate characteristics that can affect an MNC's capital structure are identified first, followed by country characteristics.

Influence of Corporate Characteristics

Characteristics unique to each MNC can influence its capital structure. Some of the more common firm-specific characteristics that affect the MNC's capital structure are identified here:

Stability of MNC's Cash Flows.   MNCs with more stable cash flows can handle more debt, because there is a constant stream of cash inflows to cover periodic interest payments. Conversely, MNCs with erratic cash flows may prefer less debt, because they are not assured of generating enough cash in each period to make larger interest payments on debt. MNCs that are diversified across several countries may have more stable cash flows, since the conditions in any single country should not have a major impact on their cash flows. Consequently, these MNCs may be able to handle a more debt-intensive capital structure.

MNC's Credit Risk.   MNCs that have lower credit risk (risk of default on loans provided by creditors) have more access to credit. Any factors that influence credit risk can affect an MNC's choice of using debt versus equity. For example, if an MNC's management is thought to be strong and competent, its credit risk may be low, which allows for easier access to debt. MNCs with assets that serve as acceptable collateral (such as buildings, trucks, and adaptable machinery) are more able to obtain loans, and may prefer to emphasize debt financing. Conversely, MNCs with assets that are not marketable have less acceptable collateral, and may need to use equity financing.

MNC's Access to Earnings.   MNCs that are more profitable may be able to finance most of their investment with retained earnings, and therefore use an equity-intensive capital structure. Conversely, MNCs that have small levels of retained earnings may rely on debt financing. Growth-oriented MNCs are less able to finance their expansion with retained earnings, and tend to rely on debt financing. Yet, MNCs with less growth need less new financing, and may rely on retained earnings (equity) rather than on debt.

Influence of Country Characteristics

In addition to characteristics unique to each MNC, the characteristics unique to each host country can influence the MNC's choice of debt versus equity financing, and therefore influence the MNC's capital structure. Specific country characteristics that can influence an MNC's choice of equity versus debt financing are described here.

Stock Restrictions in Host Countries.   Investors in some countries are restricted by their governments to invest in local stocks. Even when investors are allowed to invest in other countries, they may not have complete information about stocks of companies outside their home countries. This represents an implicit barrier to cross-border investing. Furthermore, potential adverse exchange rate effects and tax effects could discourage investors from investing outside their home countries. The impediments to worldwide investing can cause some investors to have fewer stock investment opportunities than others. Consequently, an MNC operating in countries where investors have less investment opportunities may be able to raise equity in those countries at a relatively low cost. This could entice the MNC to use more equity by issuing stock in these countries to finance its operations.

Interest Rates in Host Countries.   Because of government-imposed barriers on capital flows along with potential adverse exchange rate, tax, and country risk effects, loanable funds do not always flow to where they are needed most. Thus, the price of loanable funds (the interest rate) can vary across countries. MNCs may be able to obtain loanable funds (debt) at a relatively low cost in specific countries, while the cost of debt in other countries may be very high. Consequently, an MNC's preference for debt may depend on the costs of debt in the countries where it operates.

Strength of Host Country Currencies.

If an MNC is concerned about the potential weakness of currencies used in foreign countries, it may attempt to finance a large proportion of its foreign operations with those currencies rather than with parent funds. In this way, the amount in earnings to be remitted periodically by the subsidiaries would be smaller because of interest payments on local debt. This strategy reduces the MNC's exposure to exchange rate risk. Thus, this form of debt financing may be a desirable way to obtain capital when a subsidiary is highly exposed to exchange rate risk.

Country Risk in Host Countries.

If an MNC is exposed to a high degree of country risk, it may use much debt financing in the foreign countries. The local creditors which have lent funds to the MNC have a genuine interest in assuring that the MNC is treated fairly by the host government. In addition, if the MNC's operations in a foreign country are terminated by the host government, it will not lose as much if its operations are financed by local creditors. Under these circumstances, the local creditors will have to negotiate with the host government to obtain all or part of the funds they have lent after the host government liquidates the assets it confiscates from the MNC.

A less severe form of country risk is the possibility that the host government will temporarily block funds to be remitted by the subsidiary to the parent. Subsidiaries that are prevented from remitting earnings over a period may prefer to use local debt financing. This strategy would reduce the amount in funds to be blocked because interest would need to be paid on local debt. Thus, this form of debt financing is proper when country risk is a concern.

Tax Laws in Host Countries.

Foreign subsidiaries of an MNC may be subject to a withholding tax when they remit earnings. By using local debt financing rather than relying on parent financing, they may be able to reduce the amount that is to be remitted periodically, as they would make interest payments on the local debt. Thus, they may reduce the withholding taxes by using more local debt financing. Foreign subsidiaries may also consider the use of debt if high corporate tax rates are imposed by the host governments on foreign earnings, in order to benefit from the tax advantage of using debt where taxes are high (unless the higher amount of taxes paid would be fully offset by tax credits received by the parent).

Summary of Country Characteristics.

Overall, MNCs may prefer to use more debt when their foreign subsidiaries are subject to (1) low local interest rates, (2) potentially weak local currencies, (3) high degree of country risk, and (4) high taxes. Since the characteristics vary among host countries, some of an MNC's subsidiaries may benefit from a high degree of financial leverage, while others may not.

A study by Fatemi found that selected U.S.-based MNCs with at least 25 percent of their sales in foreign countries had significantly lower financial leverage than purely domestic firms. A related study by Lee and Kwok also found that MNCs had lower financial leverage, but that the results varied among industries. Even with these generalizations, it should be emphasized that the capital structure decision is dependent on numerous characteristics specific to the individual MNC, and to the countries where the MNC's subsidiaries are located.

To illustrate how the country of concern can influence the MNC's capital structure preference, consider a U.S.-based MNC that plans to establish a large subsidiary in a Latin American country. Historically, Latin American countries have had high inflation, high interest rates, and weak currencies. If the subsidiary is financed with local debt, it will incur a high interest rate. However, debt financing would help insulate the MNC's shareholders against country risk, as it minimizes the equity investment in the subsidiary. In addition, the use of local debt creates future cash outflows (interest payments) in the same currency as its cash inflows generated by the subsidiary. Thus, the use of debt not only minimizes the equity investment required, but also reduces the amount that will ultimately be remitted by the subsidiary to the parent in the future. This reduces the parent's exposure to exchange rate risk, which is especially relevant given the typical weakness of Latin American currencies. In this example, the advantages of local debt financing (it reduces exposure to country risk and exchange rate risk) must be weighed against the disadvantage (there is a high cost of debt). Other country-specific characteristics such as tax guidelines may also be considered here. The final decision can be made only after more specific details about the country characteristics are provided. Yet, this brief discussion clearly illustrates how each characteristic unique to the host country can affect the preference for debt versus equity financing.

CREATING THE TARGET CAPITAL STRUCTURE

An MNC may deviate from its target capital structure in each country where financing is obtained, yet still achieve its target capital structure on a consolidated basis. The following examples of particular foreign country conditions illustrate the motive behind deviating from a local target capital structure while still satisfying a global target capital structure.

First, consider that Country A does not allow MNCs with headquarters elsewhere to list their stock on its local stock exchange. Under these conditions, an MNC would likely decide to borrow funds through bond issuance or bank loans rather than by issuing stock in this country. By being forced to use debt financing here, the MNC might deviate from its target capital structure, which could raise its overall cost of capital. It might offset this concentration in debt by using complete equity financing in some other host country that allowed the firm's stock to be listed on the local exchange.

Consider a second example, in which Country B allows the MNC to issue stock there and list its stock on its local exchange. Also assume that the project to be implemented in that country will not generate net cash flows for five years. In this case, equity financing may be more appropriate. The MNC could issue stock, and by paying low or zero dividends, it could avoid any major cash outflows for the next five years. It might offset this concentration in equity by using mostly debt financing in some other host country.

As a third example, consider an MNC that desires financing in Country C, which is experiencing political turmoil. The use of local bank loans would be most appropriate, since local banks may be able to prevent the MNC's operations in that country from being affected by any political conditions. If the local banks are creditors, it is in their interest to assure that the MNC's operations are sufficiently profitable to repay its loans. These examples illustrate how the MNC's capital structure in each individual country may deviate from the global target capital structure established by the MNC.

The ideal sources of funds for all countries will not necessarily sum to match the global target capital structure. However, the parent's mix of debt and equity financing in its own country (where it has the flexibility to use either type) may be adjusted to achieve the global target capital structure.

The strategy of ignoring a "local" target capital structure in favor of a "global" target capital structure is rational as long as it is acceptable by foreign creditors and investors. However, if foreign creditors and investors monitor the local capital structure, they may require a higher rate of return on funds provided to the MNC. For example, the "local" target capital structures for the subsidiaries based in Country A (from the earlier example) and in Country C are entirely debt (unless some equity investment was provided by the parent). Creditors in these two countries may penalize the MNC for its highly leveraged local capital structure, even though its global capital structure is more balanced, because they believe that the subsidiaries in their respective countries may be unable to meet the high debt repayment levels. Their concern is valid only if the subsidiaries would not be rescued by the MNC's parent. If the parent plans to back the subsidiaries, it could guarantee debt repayment to the creditors in the foreign countries, which might reduce the risk perception and lower the cost of the debt. Many MNC parents stand ready to financially back their subsidiaries, since if they did not, their other subsidiaries would be unable to obtain financing.

Local Ownership of Foreign Subsidiaries

Some MNCs may allow a specific foreign subsidiary to issue stock to local investors or employees as a means of infusing equity into the subsidiary. Thus, the foreign subsidiary is referred to as "partially owned" rather than "wholly owned" by the MNC's parent. This strategy can affect the MNC's capital structure. It may be feasible when the MNC's parent can enhance the subsidiary's image and presence in the host country, or can motivate the subsidiary's managers by allowing them partial ownership.

One concern about a partially owned foreign subsidiary is a potential conflict of interest, especially when the managers are minority shareholders. These managers may make decisions that can benefit the subsidiary at the expense of the MNC overall. For example, they may use funds for projects that are feasible from their perspective but not from the parent's perspective.

Some countries will allow an MNC to establish a subsidiary there only if the subsidiary can sell shares. An MNC may be willing to tolerate a partially owned subsidiary to meet the host country requirements. In some cases, minority shareholders must maintain a minimum percentage of the capital. Thus, if the subsidiary attempts to expand, it may not be able to accept an equity investment from the parent if the investment causes the minority interest to fall below the minimum level.

One possible advantage of a partially owned subsidiary is that it may open up additional opportunities within the host country. The subsidiary's name may spread as a result of shares placed with minority shareholders in that country. In

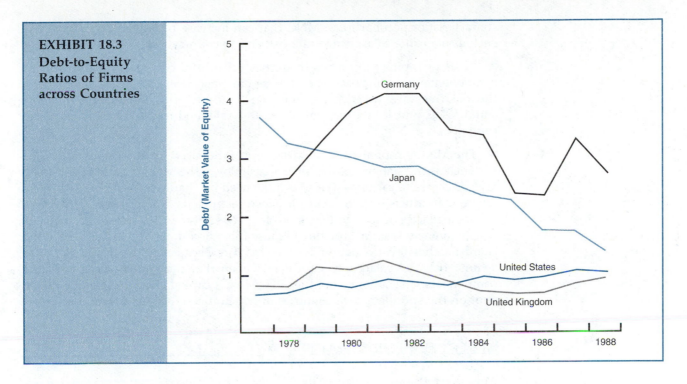

**EXHIBIT 18.3
Debt-to-Equity
Ratios of Firms
across Countries**

addition, a minority interest in a subsidiary by local investors may offer some protection against threats of any adverse actions by the host government. Minority shareholders benefit directly from a profitable subsidiary. Therefore, they could pressure their government to refrain from imposing excessive taxes, environmental constraints, or any other provisions that would reduce the profits of the subsidiary.

CAPITAL STRUCTURES ACROSS COUNTRIES

A comparison of debt-to-equity ratios among firms based in four countries is shown in Exhibit 18.3. The debt is measured by its book value, while the equity is measured by its market value. From this exhibit, it is clear that firms in Japan and Germany have used a much higher degree of financial leverage (on average) than have firms in the United States or the United Kingdom. However, the probability of bankruptcy may generally be lower for MNCs in other countries, since their respective governments may rescue them. Furthermore, banks in Japan and Germany commonly serve as creditors and large shareholders of firms, and have a vested interest in rescuing these firms.

SUMMARY

■ The cost of capital may be lower for an MNC than for a domestic firm because of characteristics peculiar to the MNC, including its size, access to international capital markets, and its degree of international diversification. Yet, there are some characteristics peculiar to an MNC that can increase the MNC's cost of capital, such as exposure to exchange rate risk and to country risk.

■ Costs of capital vary across countries because of country differences in the components that comprise the cost of capital. Specifically, there are differences in the risk-free rate, the risk premium on debt, and the cost of equity among countries. Countries with a higher risk-free rate tend to exhibit a higher cost of capital.

■ The MNC's capital structure decision is influenced by corporate characteristics such as the stability of the MNC's cash flows, the MNC's credit risk, and the MNC's access to earnings. It also is influenced by characteristics of the countries where it conducts business, such as stock restrictions, interest rates, strength of local currencies, country risk, and tax laws. Some characteristics favor an equity-intensive capital structure because they discourage the use of debt. Other characteristics favor a debt-intensive structure because of the desire to protect against risks by creating foreign debt. Given that the relative costs of capital components vary among countries, the MNC's capital structure may be dependent on the specific mix of countries in which it conducts its operations.

SELF-TEST FOR CHAPTER 18

(Answers are provided in Appendix A in the back of the text)

1. When Goshen Inc. focused only on domestic business in the U.S., it had a low debt level. As it expanded into other countries, it increased its degree of financial leverage (on a consolidated basis). What factors would have caused Goshen to increase its financial leverage (assuming that country risk was not a concern)?

2. Lynde Co. is a U.S.-based MNC with a large subsidiary in the Philippines, financed with equity from the parent. In response to news about possible turnover in the Philippines government, the subsidiary revised its capital structure by borrowing from local banks, and transferring the equity investment back to the U.S. parent. Explain the likely motive behind these actions.

3. Duever Co. (a U.S. firm) noticed that its financial leverage was substantially lower than most successful firms in Germany and Japan within the same industry. Is Duever's capital structure less than optimal?

4. Consider a U.S.-based MNC with a large subsidiary in Argentina, where interest rates are very high and the currency is expected to weaken. Assume the country risk is perceived by the MNC to be high. Explain the trade-off involved in financing the subsidiary with local debt versus doing so with an equity investment from the parent.

5. A U.S.-based MNC is considering a project to establish a plant for producing and selling consumer goods in an undeveloped country. Assume that the host country's economy is very dependent on oil prices, the local currency of the country is very volatile, and the country risk is very high. Also assume that the country's economic conditions are unrelated to U.S.

conditions. Should the required rate of return (and therefore the risk premium) on the project be higher or lower than that of other alternative projects in the U.S.?

QUESTIONS

1. Create an argument in support of an MNC's favoring a debt-intensive capital structure.

2. Create an argument in support of an MNC's favoring an equity-intensive capital structure.

3. Do U.S.-based MNCs in general have a higher or lower degree of financial leverage than U.S. domestic firms (based on recent research)?

4. Describe general differences between the capital structures of firms based in the United States and those of firms based in Japan. Offer an explanation for this difference.

5. Why might a firm use a "local" capital structure at a particular subsidiary that differs substantially from its "global" capital structure?

6. Explain how characteristics of MNCs can affect the cost of capital.

7. Explain why managers of a wholly owned subsidiary may be more likely to satisfy the shareholders of the MNC.

8. LaSalle Corporation is a U.S.-based MNC with subsidiaries in various less developed countries where stock markets are not well established. How can LaSalle still attempt to achieve its "global" target capital structure of 50 percent debt and 50 percent equity, even if it plans to use only debt financing for the subsidiaries in these countries?

9. Drexel Company is a U.S.-based company that is establishing a project in a politically unstable country. It is considering two possible sources of financing. Either the parent could provide most of the financing, or the subsidiary could be supported by local loans from banks in that country. Which financing alternative is most appropriate to protect the subsidiary?

10. Charleston Corporation has considered establishing a subsidiary in either Germany or the United Kingdom. The subsidiary would be mostly financed with loans from the local banks in the host country chosen. It determined that the revenue generated from British subsidiary would be slightly more favorable than the revenue generated by the German subsidiary, even after considering tax and exchange rate effects. The initial outlay is the same, and both countries appear to be politically stable. Charleston recently chose to establish the subsidiary in the United Kingdom because of the revenue advantage. Do you agree with its decision? Explain.

11. Fairfield Corporation, a U.S. firm, just established a subsidiary in a less developed country that consistently experiences an annual inflation rate of 80 percent or more. The country does not have an established stock market, but loans by local banks are available with a 90 percent interest

rate. Fairfield has decided to use a strategy in which the subsidiary is financed entirely with funds from the parent. It believes that in this way it can avoid the excessive interest rate in the host country. What is a key disadvantage of using this strategy that may cause Fairfield to be no better off than if it paid the 90 percent interest rate?

12. Veer Company is a U.S.-based MNC that has most of its operations in Japan. Noticing that the Japanese companies with which it competes use more financial leverage, it has decided to adjust its financial leverage to be in line with theirs. In this way, it should reap more tax advantages, with the heavy emphasis on debt. It believes that the market's perception of its risk will remain unchanged, since its financial leverage is still no higher than that of Japanese competitors. Comment on this.

13. Pullman Inc., a U.S. firm, has had much profitability, but prefers not to pay out higher dividends because its shareholders desire that the funds be reinvested. It plans for large growth in several less developed countries. Pullman Inc. would like to finance the growth with local debt in the host countries of concern to reduce exposure to country risk. Explain the dilemma faced by Pullman, and possible solutions.

14. Forest Co. produces goods in the U.S., Germany, and Australia, and sells the goods in the areas where they are produced. Foreign earnings are periodically remitted to the U.S. parent. As German interest rates have declined to a very low level, Forest Co. has decided to finance its German operations with borrowed funds in place of the parent's equity investment. Forest will transfer the U.S. parent's equity investment in the German subsidiary over to its Australian subsidiary. These funds will be used to pay off a floating rate loan, as Australian interest rates have been high and are rising. Explain the expected effects of these actions on the consolidated capital structure and cost of capital of Forest Co.

15. Using the information in Question 14, explain how the exposure of Forest Co. to exchange rate risk may have changed.

16. Explain why the cost of capital for a U.S.-based MNC with a large subsidiary in Brazil is larger than for a U.S.-based MNC in the same industry with a large subsidiary in Japan. Assume the subsidiary operations for each MNC are financed with local debt in the host country.

U.S., Mexican Firms Announce Wave Of Joint Ventures in the Wake of Nafta

By PAUL B. CARROLL
Staff Reporter of THE WALL STREET JOURNAL

MEXICO CITY — U.S. and Mexican companies are announcing a wave of joint ventures in Mexico, in their first steps toward taking advantage of the North American Free Trade Agreement.

Dozens of ventures have been announced in the month since Nafta was approved by the U.S. Congress—including such U.S. names as Trans Union Corp., Underwriters Laboratories Inc., Western Union Financial Services Inc. and GTE Corp.—and it appears that those are just the beginning.

"I've actually been surprised that there haven't been more announced," says Miguel Jauregui, a lawyer here who specializes in foreign investment. He says he thinks lots of other companies are prepared to unveil their plans but are waiting because they've gone into "holiday mode." "After the first of the year, we'll see a lot more announcements, and they'll probably go on for six months," he says.

The ventures are a welcome sign for the Mexican economy, which has been struggling all year and actually contracted in the third quarter.

The biggest problem has been that interest rates are several times as high as those in the U.S. The government has been reluctant to push those rates down too fast, because high rates here help attract the huge amounts of foreign capital that are needed to finance the economy's restructuring. But the joint ventures will provide a steady flow of foreign capital regardless of interest fees, giving the government a little more room to drive them down.

Nora Lustig, a senior fellow at the Brookings Institution, says the ventures should also reassure investors about the stability of the economy. Compared with the money Mexico has drawn in the past, mainly attracted to Treasury bills and the stock market, money invested in production and other joint ventures "is less volatile, more committed to staying in the country," she says.

Increasing Economic Efficiency
Ms. Lustig also says the ventures could "increase efficiency [in the Mexican economy] by bringing in foreign technology and competition." Down the road, she says, the ventures could even lead to an improvement in the notoriously weak Mexican safety standards, because the U.S. partners will be under more scrutiny on safety issues than Mexican companies traditionally have been.

The U.S. companies coming to Mexico say they are doing so through joint ventures, rather than on their own, largely because they don't know the market well yet and don't have the kind of name-recognition they have in the U.S.

Roger M. Laverty, chief executive officer of Smart & Final Inc., a Los Angeles-based warehouse-grocery chain, says the company decided that "the Mexican market offered great opportunities for our concept, but we also thought there were significant differences in the Mexican market that we weren't fully attuned to. Perhaps most important, we thought that the image of an American company coming down and 'showing' the local companies how to do things wouldn't play well."

As a result, Smart & Final yesterday launched a joint venture with Central Detallista SA, a regional grocery company in Mexico, and said the companies will jointly open several large stores in Mexico.

UL Forms Alliance
It would have been hard for Underwriters Laboratories, or UL, to go about its business of certifying the safety of electrical products on its own in Mexico. But the company, which lacks name recognition here, should be able to take advantage of an alliance it formed with a private Mexican certifier, the Asociacion Nacional de Normalizacion y Certificacion del Sector Electrico.

Similarly, almost nothing happens in telecommunications in Mexico except through the phone monopoly, Telefonos de Mexico SA. So GTE recently formed a company with Telmex that will let airplane passengers place phone calls to people on the ground in Mexico.

Trans Union recently announced an agreement with the Association of Mexican Banks to form a venture that will provide electronic credit ratings for Mexicans for the first time, something that would have been impossible for Trans Union to do by itself, given the fragmented state of credit records in Mexico.

Likewise, Western Union formed an alliance with Elektra, a Mexican chain of electronics stores. The venture gives Western Union an instant network of places where Mexicans can go to take advantage of a new service and wire money or collect wired funds.

Not every company, of course, decides that a joint venture is the way to go. Ford Motor Co., for instance, recently announced plans on its own to increase its operations in Mexico. But Ford, like other U.S. companies manufacturing in Mexico, doesn't need local expertise to make its products and is so well-established in Mexico that it doesn't need a partner's help to sell cars here, either.

SOURCE: *The Wall Street Journal* (December 21, 1993), p. A7. Reprinted by permission of *The Wall Street Journal,* © 1993 Dow Jones and Company, Inc. All rights reserved worldwide.

Continued

CASE: THE COST OF CAPITAL FOR SUBSIDIARIES IN MEXICO

Continued

QUESTIONS

1. Explain how the cost of capital for U.S. firms such as GTE Corp. and Underwriters Laboratories Inc. is affected by expansion into Mexico.

2. Explain the logic behind the Mexican government's reluctance to quickly reduce interest rates. Is there any disadvantage associated with a policy of allowing interest rates to remain high?

3. How might U.S.-based MNCs expand in Mexico without incurring the high Mexican interest expenses when financing the expansion? Are there any disadvantages associated with this strategy?

4. Are there any additional alternatives for the Mexican subsidiary to finance its business itself after it has been well established? How might this strategy affect the subsidiary's capital structure?

SABRE COMPUTER CORPORATION
Cost of Capital

Sabre Computer Corporation is a U.S.-based company that plans to participate in joint ventures in Mexico and in Germany. Each joint venture involves the development of a small subsidiary that helps produce computers. The main contribution of Sabre is the technology and a few key computer components used in the production process. The joint venture in Mexico specifies joint production of computers with a Mexican company owned by the government. The computers have already been ordered by educational institutions and government agencies throughout Mexico. Sabre has a contract to sell all the computers it produces in Mexico to these institutions and agencies at a price that is tied to inflation. Given the very high and volatile inflation levels in Mexico, Sabre wanted to assure that the contracted price would adjust to cover rising costs over time.

The venture will require a temporary transfer of several managers to Mexico, plus the manufacturing of key computer components in a leased Mexican plant. Most of these costs will be incurred in Mexico and will therefore require payment in pesos. Sabre will receive 30 percent of the revenue generated (in pesos) from computer sales. The Mexican partner will receive the remainder.

The joint venture in Germany specifies joint production of personal computers with a German computer manufacturer. The computers will then be marketed to consumers throughout the Eastern Bloc countries in Europe; these countries were generally off limits to computer manufacturers before 1990. Similar computers are produced by some competitors, but Sabre believes it can penetrate these markets because its products will be competitively priced. While the economies of the Eastern Bloc countries are expected to be somewhat stagnant, demand for personal computers is reasonably strong. The computers will be priced in marks, and Sabre will receive 30 percent of the revenue generated from sales.

CASE PROBLEM

SABRE COMPUTER CORPORATION (CONTINUED)

a) Assume Sabre plans to finance most of its investment in the Mexican subsidiary by borrowing Mexican pesos, and to finance most of its investment in the German subsidiary by borrowing German marks. The cost of financing is influenced by the risk-free rates in the respective countries and the risk premiums on funds borrowed. Explain how these factors will affect the relative costs of financing both ventures. Address this question from the perspective of the subsidiary, not from the perspective of Sabre's parent.

b) Will the joint venture experiencing the higher cost of financing (as determined in the previous question) necessarily experience lower returns to the subsidiary? Explain.

c) The German subsidiary has a high degree of financial leverage. Yet, the parent's capital structure is mostly equity. What will determine whether the creditors of the German subsidiary charge a high risk premium on borrowed funds because of the high degree of financial leverage?

d) One executive of Sabre suggested that since the cost of debt financing by highly leveraged German-owned companies is about 14 percent, its German subsidiary should be able to borrow at about the same interest rate. Do you agree? Explain. (Assume that the chances of the subsidiary's experiencing financial problems are the same as those for these other German-owned firms).

e) There is some concern that the economy in Germany could become inflated. Assess the relative magnitude of an increase in inflation on (1) the cost of funds, (2) the cost of production, and (3) revenue from selling the computers.

PROJECT

Review the annual report of an MNC of your choice. Offer your opinion as to whether this MNC's cost of capital is higher or lower than what it would be if all its operations were in the U.S.

REFERENCES

Adler, Michael. "The Cost of Capital and Valuation of a Two-Country Firm." *Journal of Finance* (March 1974), pp. 119–132.
_____. "International Portfolio Choice and Corporation Finance: A Synthesis." *Journal of Finance* (June 1983), pp. 925–984.

Collins, J. Markham, and William S. Sekely. "The Relationship of Headquarters Country and Industry Classification to Financial Structure." *Financial Management* (Autumn 1983), pp. 45–51.

Fatemi, Ali M. "The Effect of International Diversification on Corporate Financing Policy." *Journal of Business Research* (January 1988), pp. 17–30.

Howe, John, and Jeff Madura. "The Impact of International Listings on Risk: Implications for Capital Market Integration." *Journal of Banking and Finance* (December 1990), pp. 1133–1142.

Kester, W. Carl. "Capital and Ownership Structure: A Comparison of United States and Japanese Manufacturing Corporations." *Financial Management* (Spring 1986), pp. 5–16.

Lee, Kwang Chul, and Chuck C. Y. Kwok. "Multinational Corporations vs. Domestic Corporations: International Environmental Factors and Determinants of Capital Structure." *Journal of International Business Studies* (Summer 1988), pp. 195–217.

McCauley, Robert N., and Steven A. Zimmer. "Explaining International Differences in the Cost of Capital." *FRBNY Quarterly Review* (Summer 1989), pp. 7–28.

Meek, G. K., and S. J. Gray. "Globalization of Stock Markets and Foreign Listing Requirements: Voluntary Disclosures by Continental European Companies Listed on the London Stock Exchange." *Journal of International Business Studies* (Summer 1989): pp. 315–336.

Myers, Stewart C. "The Capital Structure Puzzle." *Journal of Finance* (July 1984), pp. 575–592.

Petry, Glenn H., and James Sprow. "International Trends and Events in Corporate Finance and Management: A Survey." *Financial Practice and Education* (Spring/Summer 1993), 21–28.

Prowse, Stephen D. "The Structure of Corporate Ownership in Japan." *Journal of Finance* (July 1992), pp. 1121–1140.

Saudagaran, Shahrokh. "An Empirical Study of Selected Factors Influencing the Decision To List on Foreign Stock Exchanges." *Journal of International Business Studies* (Spring 1988), pp. 101–127.

Sekely, William S., and J. Markham Collins. "Cultural Influences on International Capital Structure." *Journal of International Business Studies* (Spring 1988), pp. 87–100.

Senbet, Lemma W. "International Capital Market Equilibrium and the Multinational Firm Financing and Investment Policies." *Journal of Financial and Quantitative Analysis* (September 1979), pp. 425–450.

Stanley, Margorie T. "Capital Structure and Cost of Capital for the Multinational Firm." *Journal of International Business Studies* (Spring–Summer 1981), pp. 103–120.

THE CAPITAL STRUCTURE PUZZLE FOR MULTINATIONAL CORPORATIONS

The controversy surrounding an optimal capital structure has not been completely resolved and perhaps never will be. However, studies have provided insightful explanations that are consistent with corporate behavior. A well-known study by Myers proposes that firms seem to follow a pecking order, in which they prefer to use internal financing in order to avoid issue costs. If internal financing is not sufficient, firms use debt financing first, followed by equity financing. The administrative and underwriting costs associated with debt are less than those of equity. Furthermore, Myers suggests that when managers have more favorable information about a project to be financed, the use of debt will be preferable to the use of external equity.

In what he refers to as the capital structure puzzle, Myers offers a viable explanation for why firms within a single industry can have different capital structures. The objective of this appendix is to extend Myers' theory to a multinational framework. Specifically, the appendix explains how international conditions can cause a multinational corporation (MNC) to either accelerate the shift from one financing method to the next, or rearrange the pecking order. In this way, factors that can influence an MNC's capital structure are identified.

SIMPLIFIED PECKING ORDER MODEL _____

To assess the pecking order for an MNC, the following assumptions are used:

- There is a two-country world.
- The MNC's parent is in one country and its wholly owned subsidiary is in the other.
- The parent presently has the same capital structure as the subsidiary.
- The exchange rate between the currencies of the two countries is fixed.
- The expected cash flows to the headquarters are the same as those to the subsidiary.
- The corporate tax rates of the two countries are the same.
- There are no withholding taxes in the foreign country.
- The country risk in the foreign country is perceived to be the same as that in the home country.
- There are no restrictions on capital flows, causing interest rates to be the same in both countries.
- The MNC has the same degree of recognition in the foreign country as in the home country. It also has its stock traded on exchanges in both countries.

- The subsidiary and the parent are separate entities. The parent is not a guarantor for the subsidiary.
- Information is freely available worldwide.

These assumptions are relaxed later in order to reassess the pecking order for more complex situations.

Under the existing conditions, the headquarters behaves as a domestic firm. Using Myer's theory, the headquarters would prefer to use internal funds as a source of capital. If internal funds are not available, external debt financing would be second priority, followed by external equity financing. Since the subsidiary is a separate entity, its characteristics are similar to those of the headquarters. Therefore, it would share the same pecking order.

GLOBAL CONDITIONS THAT DISRUPT THE PECKING ORDER

The existence of market imperfections can force a rearrangement of financing priorities. In the following discussion, various global conditions that can affect the desirability of a financing choice are identified. These conditions are similar to those that have an effect on the MNC's capital structure (as discussed in this chapter). Throughout the following discussion, it is assumed that the subsidiary periodically remits any earnings beyond what it needs for internal financing to the parent.

Country Risk

If the country risk were higher in the foreign country, the subsidiary might consider a financing strategy that would strengthen its political position. External debt financing in the host country's credit markets would force local banks and other creditors to have a vested interest in the subsidiary's well-being. This type of financing creates an implicit insurance benefit. Alternatively, external stock financing by the subsidiary could allow local investors (including employees who purchase stock) to have a vested interest in the subsidiary, which creates an implicit insurance benefit. Even if internal funds were available, the parent might instruct the subsidiary to remit internal funds and use external funding to create the implicit insurance. This example suggests one way external funds can take precedent over internal funds at the subsidiary level. Yet, internal funds remitted to the parent might still be used by the parent before other alternative sources of funds. So it may be argued that the internal funds would still be first priority, but only the designated user of the funds (parent versus subsidiary) would change. However, if the parent had more internal funds than were needed, it might use some of the funds to pay extra dividends. In this case, the use of external financing by the subsidiary would not be fully offset by the parent's additional internal financing, and the pecking order would be partially rearranged.

Differential Interest Rates

When markets are segmented, the cost of capital will be dependent on the country in which the capital is raised. Differential costs of capital can influence the MNC's financing decisions. If interest rates were lower in the host country, the subsidiary might prefer external debt. Any internal funds might be transferred to the parent, especially if the parent did not have enough internal funds to support present needs. Assuming that the subsidiary generated revenues in the local currency, this strategy would not increase exposure to exchange rate risk. Revenues received by the subsidiary could be used to meet its debt obligations. In essence, the subsidiary's external debt financing would replace the parent's debt financing. However, the subsidiary's access to additional debt might be limited because of its high degree of financial leverage.

If markets were somewhat segmented, and the cost of capital in the subsidiary's country appeared too excessive, the parent might use its own funds to support projects implemented by the subsidiary. For example, if interest rates were higher in the host country, the parent might be more willing to provide its own internal funds so that the subsidiary did not need to use external financing. Consequently, the parent's internal funds would be reduced, so that it would more quickly resort to external financing.

Exchange Rate Expectations

The external financing of a subsidiary might also be rearranged to capitalize on exchange rate expectations. If the local currency were expected to weaken over time, remitted earnings could be accelerated if the subsidiary issued stock with a low dividend, rather than issuing debt. This would defer the repayment on funds used, thereby improving the subsidiary's cash flow in the near future and allowing the subsidiary to remit larger amounts to the parent.

If the subsidiary believed its local currency would appreciate against the parent's currency, it might retain more of its internal funds. Consequently, the parent could be forced to use more external financing.

If the parent anticipated that the subsidiary's local currency would appreciate against its own, it might provide an immediate cash infusion to finance growth in the subsidiary. As a result, there would be a transfer of internal funds from the parent to the subsidiary, which would possibly cause more external financing by the parent and less financing by the subsidiary. Over time, this strategy should allow the subsidiary to remit larger payments to the parent, which would increase the internal funds available to the parent.

If the parent anticipated that the subsidiary's local currency would depreciate against its own, it might require that the subsidiary obtain any necessary financing in the host country. In this way, the amount of funds to be remitted over time would be reduced, minimizing exposure to exchange rate movements. This strategy would reduce the internal funds available to the subsidiary, possibly resulting in more external financing by the subsidiary. If the parent thus used a smaller amount to finance the subsidiary's growth, it would have more internal funds available for its own investment and would need less external financing.

Blocked Funds

If the subsidiary were prevented from remitting funds, it would be forced to use more internal financing, and would need less external financing. Thus, the parent would have less internal funds to use for financing. This situation would not disrupt the rank order of financing, but might force the parent to use more external financing, as its internal funds would be depleted more quickly.

Withholding Taxes

If withholding taxes imposed by the host country on remitted earnings were high, the parent might attempt to transfer explicit or implicit costs to the subsidiary. Thus, the level of earnings generated by the subsidiary would be reduced, and the amount in internal funds available to the subsidiary would be reduced as well. This condition might influence the proportion of funds obtained from external sources. The subsidiary might be forced to use more external financing, while the parent would generate more earnings by transferring costs, and would have more internal funds available.

Differential Corporate Taxes

If host country corporate income taxes exceeded parent country income taxes, the parent might attempt to transfer costs to the subsidiary. Such a transfer pricing policy would ultimately allocate internal funds from the subsidiary to the parent, which would force the subsidiary to use more external financing and might reduce the amount of external financing required by the parent.

Higher host country taxes might also encourage the subsidiary to use heavy debt financing. Given a transfer of costs to the subsidiary, there would be a lack of internal funding anyway for the subsidiary, so that much debt financing might be needed.

Guarantees on Debt

If the parent backed the debt of the subsidiary, the subsidiary's borrowing capacity might be increased, while the borrowing capacity of the parent might be reduced. Therefore, the subsidiary might need less external equity financing.

Consolidating the Global Conditions

The discussion so far has focused on one global condition at a time. These effects of each condition when holding other conditions constant are summarized in Exhibit 18A.1. When the cost of the parent's operations can be fully absorbed by internal funds, the global conditions that cause higher external financing for the subsidiary will result in higher debt ratios for the MNC overall. These conditions are (1) a high level of country risk in the host country, (2) low host country interest rates, and (3) expected weakness of the host country currency, (4) high withholding taxes imposed by the host government, and (5) high corporate taxes imposed by the host government.

Conversely, the global conditions that cause lower external financing for the subsidiary will result in lower debt ratios for the MNC overall. These conditions are (1) high interest rates in the host country, (2) expected strength in the host country currency, and (3) blocked funds imposed by the host government.

IMPACT OF INCREASED EXTERNAL FINANCING

When global conditions increase the external financing of the subsidiary, the amount of internal financing needed by the subsidiary is reduced. As these extra internal funds are remitted to the parent, the parent will have a larger amount in

EXHIBIT 18A.1   Effect of Global Conditions on Financing

International Conditions	Amount of External Debt Financing by Subsidiary	Internal Funds Available to Parent	Amount of External Financing by Parent
Higher Country Risk In Host Country	Higher	Higher	Lower
Higher Interest Rates in Host Country	Lower	Lower	Higher
Lower Interest Rates in Host Country	Higher	Higher	Lower
Expected Weakness of Host Country Currency: Causing Accelerated Remittances	Higher	Higher	Lower
Expected Strength of Host Country Currency: Causing Deferred Remittances	Lower	Lower	Higher
Blocked Funds Imposed by Host Government	Lower	Lower	Higher
High Withholding Taxes Imposed by Host Government	Higher	Higher	Lower
Higher Corporate Taxes Imposed by Host Government	Higher	Higher	Lower
Parent Guarantees Subsidiary's Debt	Higher	Higher	Lower

internal funds for financing before it resorts to external financing. Assuming that the parent's operations absorb all internal funds and require some debt financing, there are offsetting effects on the capital structures of the subsidiary and the parent. The increased use of debt financing by the subsidiary is offset by the reduced debt financing of the parent. Yet, the cost of capital for the MNC overall could have changed for two reasons. First, the revised composition of debt could affect the interest charged on the debt. Second, it could affect the MNC's overall exposure to exchange rate risk, and therefore influence the risk premium on capital.

There are situations in which the increased use of debt financing of the subsidiary will not be offset by reduced debt financing of the parent. If the parent's operations can be fully financed with internal funds, the parent will not use external financing. In this case, international conditions that encourage increased use of debt financing by the subsidiary will result in a more debt-intensive capital structure for the MNC. Again, the cost of capital to the MNC could be affected by the increased external financing, for reasons already mentioned. Yet, an additional reason here is the use of a higher proportion of debt financing.

IMPACT OF REDUCED EXTERNAL FINANCING

When global conditions reduce the external financing of the subsidiary, the amount of internal financing needed by the subsidiary is increased. Consequently, it will remit fewer funds to the parent, reducing the amount in internal funds available to the parent. If the parent's operations absorb all internal funds and require some debt financing, there are offsetting effects on the capital structures of the subsidiary and parent. The reduction in debt financing of the subsidiary is offset by the increased use of debt financing of the parent. The cost of capital may change even if the MNC's capital structure does not, for reasons expressed earlier.

If the parent's operations can be fully financed with internal funds, the parent will not use external financing. Thus, the reduction in external financing of the subsidiary is not offset by increased external financing of the parent, and the MNC's overall capital structure becomes more equity-intensive.

Conditions That Encourage External Equity Financing

The present discussion has assumed that the MNC parent's operations either could be absorbed by internal funds or would require some external debt financing. Further steps down the pecking order were not necessary. For an MNC that could not satisfy all funding requirements with external debt financing, external equity financing would be next in line. Yet, there are some global conditions that may encourage the MNC to use external equity ahead of debt; which are discussed next.

Agency Costs. If the subsidiary in a host country cannot easily be monitored by investors from the parent's country, agency costs are higher. The subsidiary in a host country may be induced by the parent to issue stock rather than debt in the local market, so that the managers there are monitored to ensure maximization of the firm's stock price.

Listing Overseas. An MNC may be more capable of developing a global image if its stock is listed on a foreign stock exchange than if it uses debt financing. External equity financing may be prioritized ahead of debt financing under these circumstances.

If the subsidiary chooses external equity financing instead of debt financing, the MNC's overall capital structure will become more equity-intensive, unless it is offset by the parent's financing mix. The lack of debt financing by the subsidiary could increase the debt capacity of the parent, allowing the parent to borrow funds that the subsidiary has not. Essentially, the increase in external equity financing by the subsidiary could preclude the need for external equity financing by the parent.

CHAPTER 19

COUNTRY RISK ANALYSIS

Country risk represents the potentially adverse impact of a country's environment on the multinational corporation's (MNC's) cash flows. Thus, it is considered when the firm is assessing whether to conduct business within a particular country. Country risk can be partitioned into the country's political risk and its financial risk. The specific objectives of this chapter are to

- identify the common factors used by MNCs to measure a country's political risk,
- identify the common factors used by MNCs to measure a country's financial risk,
- explain the techniques used to measure country risk, and
- explain how the assessment of country risk is used by MNCs when making financial decisions.

WHY COUNTRY RISK ANALYSIS IS IMPORTANT _____

Country risk analysis is important to MNCs for the following reasons. First, it can be used by MNCs as a screening device to avoid countries with excessive risk. Research by Nigh found that events that heighten country risk tend to discourage U.S. direct foreign investment in that particular country. A second reason for assessing country risk is that it can be used to monitor countries where the MNC is presently engaged in international business. If the country risk level of a particular country begins to increase, the MNC may consider divesting its subsidiaries located there. A third reason for country risk analysis is to assess particular forms of risk for a proposed capital budgeting project considered for a foreign country.

U.S.-based MNCs could avoid country risk by simply avoiding international business. However, this strategy would eliminate several opportunities that could generate very high returns. If an MNC does not pursue specific international opportunities, its competitors will. The potential for very high returns is common in those countries that are less developed, and tend to have a higher degree of country risk. Thus, MNCs attempt to manage this return-risk tradeoff by closely assessing the country risk involved in possible foreign projects.

INCREASED AWARENESS OF COUNTRY RISK

In 1976 a division of Consolidated Foods, Inc., searched for an appropriate country for a new manufacturing plant. The company decided on a location described at the time as a "happy, sleepy country." The location was El Salvador. Within two years of this decision, political turmoil arose. In the process, a group of rebels held the division's president and about 120 employees hostage until the company agreed to provide wage increases. By 1979 the division was closed. This example illustrates how internal country problems can affect an MNC.

In the 1980s the crises in Iran, Afghanistan, and some Latin American countries made MNCs realize the importance of effective country risk analysis. While MNCs diversify their operations internationally to reduce their exposure to any individual country's problems, they should attempt to reduce risk further by anticipating where country crises are beginning to develop. If a crisis is anticipated well in advance, an MNC can avoid further direct foreign investment in that country, and/or withdraw its current operations from that country before the crisis intensifies.

In some cases, a country's problems may even affect firms that are not conducting business there. Consider the effect of the crisis in China in 1989 as an example. During the demonstrations at Tiananmen Square, supplies of styrene (used to produce consumer products) were not allowed in China. An excess global market supply resulted, causing the market price to decline. This had a significant influence on the earnings of companies that produce styrene, including Arco Chemical Company, a large U.S.-based MNC.

POLITICAL RISK FACTORS

An MNC must assess country risk not only in countries where it currently does business, but also in those in which it expects to market exports or establish subsidiaries. Several risk characteristics of a country may significantly affect performance, and the MNC should be concerned about the degree of impact likely for each.

As one might expect, there are many country characteristics related to the political environment that influence an MNC. The extreme form of political risk is the possibility that the host country will take over a subsidiary. In some cases of expropriation, some compensation (the amount decided by the host country government) is awarded. In other cases, the assets are confiscated and no compensation is provided. Such events can take place peacefully or by force. Some of the more common forms of political risk include

- Attitude of consumers in the host country
- Attitude of host government
- Blockage of fund transfers
- Currency inconvertibility

- War
- Bureaucracy.

Each of these characteristics will be examined.

Attitude of Consumers in the Host Country

A mild form of political risk (to an exporter) is a tendency of residents to purchase only homemade goods. Even if the exporter decided to set up a subsidiary in the foreign country, this philosophy could prevent its success. All countries tend to exert some pressure on consumers to purchase from locally owned manufacturers. (In the United States, consumers are encouraged to look for the "made in the U.S.A." label.) MNCs that consider entering a foreign market (or have already entered that market) must monitor the general loyalty of consumers toward homemade products. If consumers are very loyal to local products, a joint venture with a local company may be more feasible than an exporting strategy.

Attitude of Host Government

Various actions of a host government can affect the cash flow of an MNC. For example, a host government might impose pollution control standards (which affect costs) and additional corporate taxes (which affect after-tax earnings), as well as withholding taxes and fund transfer restrictions (which affect after-tax cash flows sent to the parent).

Some analysts use turnover in government members or philosophy as a proxy for a country's political risk. While this can significantly influence the MNC's future cash flows, it alone does not serve as a suitable representation of political risk. A subsidiary will not necessarily be affected by changing governments. Furthermore, a subsidiary can be affected by adjusted policies of the host government or by a changing attitude toward the subsidiary's home country (and therefore the subsidiary), even when the host government has no risk of being overthrown.

There are various ways in which the host government can make the MNC's operations coincide with its own goals. It may, for example, require the use of local employees for managerial positions at a subsidiary. In addition, it may require social facilities (such as an exercise room, non-smoking areas, etc.), or special environmental controls (air pollution control equipment, etc.). Furthermore, it is not uncommon for a host government to require special permits, impose extra taxes, or subsidize competitors. All of these examples represent political risk, in that they reflect a country's political characteristics and could influence an MNC's cash flows.

Blockage of Fund Transfers

Subsidiaries of MNCs often send funds back to the headquarters for loan repayments, purchases of supplies, administrative fees, remitted earnings, or several other possible purposes. In some cases, a host government may block fund transfers, which could force subsidiaries to undertake projects that are not optimal (just to make use of the funds). Alternatively, the MNC could invest the funds in local securities that would provide some return while they were blocked. But, this return might be inferior to other uses of the funds.

Currency Inconvertibility

Some governments do not allow their home currency to be exchanged into other currencies. Thus, the earnings generated by a subsidiary in these countries cannot be remitted to the parent through currency conversion. When the currency is inconvertible, an MNC parent may need to exchange it for goods to extract benefits from projects in that country.

War

Some countries tend to engage in constant battles with neighboring countries, or experience internal battles. This can affect the safety of employees hired by an MNC's subsidiary or by salespeople who attempt to establish export markets for the MNC. In addition, countries occasionally plagued with the threat of war typically have volatile business cycles, which make the MNC's cash flow generated from such countries more uncertain.

Bureaucracy

A final country risk factor is government bureaucracy, which can complicate the MNC's business. While this factor may seem irrelevant, it was a major deterrent for MNCs that had considered projects in Eastern Europe in the early 1990s. Many of the East European governments were not experienced at facilitating the entrance of MNCs into their markets.

FINANCIAL RISK FACTORS

Along with political factors, financial factors should also be considered when assessing country risk. One of the most obvious financial factors is the current and potential state of the country's economy. An MNC that exports to a country or develops a subsidiary in a country is highly concerned with that country's demand for its products. This demand is, of course, strongly influenced by the country's economy. A recession in the country could severely reduce demand for the MNC's exports or products sold by the MNC's local subsidiary. For example, in the early 1990s, the European business performance of Ford Motor Co., Nike, Walt Disney Co., and numerous other U.S.-based MNCs was severely affected by the European recession.

In some cases, financial distress in a country can encourage a government to implement policies that could limit the MNC's market penetration there. For example, Ford Motor Company was allowed by the Spanish government to set up production facilities in Spain only if it would abide by certain provisions. These included a limit of Ford's local sales volume to 10 percent of the previous year's local automobile sales. In addition, of the total volume of automobiles produced by Ford in Spain, two-thirds had to be exported. The motivation behind these provisions was creation of jobs for workers in Spain without seriously affecting local competitors. Allowing a subsidiary that primarily exports its product achieved this objective for Spain.

In this example, the MNC (Ford) was aware of the host government's restrictions before establishing a subsidiary. In some cases the rules change after the game has begun. That is, additional host government restrictions may be enforced after an MNC establishes a foreign subsidiary. For example, during the international debt crisis, many of the less developed countries were experiencing economic problems, so governments restricted local firms from importing goods from MNCs in an attempt to boost local sales.

Because the state of a country's economy is dependent on several financial factors, an MNC should consider all of these factors. Some of the more obvious ones include interest rates, exchange rates, and inflation. Higher interest rates tend to slow the growth of an economy and reduce demand for the MNC's products. Lower interest rates often stimulate the economy and increase demand for the MNC's products. Exchange rates can strongly influence the demand for the country's exports, which in turn affects the country's production and income level. Inflation can affect the purchasing power of consumers and therefore the consumer demand for an MNC's goods.

Interest rates, exchange rates, and inflation can also have an impact on each other, which makes the overall assessment of their impact on the economy more complex. Even if we know exactly how these factors influence a country's economy, we are unsure of their future values, so some uncertainty still remains. As an example, assume that for every percentage point decrease in interest rates in Country X, there will be a 2 percent increase in total production. However, it is not known with certainty how interest rates will change in the future. A firm may forecast a 3 percent decrease in interest rates, which would lead to a 6 percent increase in total production. Yet, if interest rates actually increase, production may actually decrease. Financial factors that indicate the government's purchasing power are also important in a case in which the government serves as a customer of the MNC. For example, a growing budget deficit may force the government to reduce its purchases of goods produced by the MNC and its subsidiaries.

As another example of government intervention, consider the wage-price freeze imposed by Brazil in 1990 and 1991 in order to reduce the inflationary spiral. This action slowed down the economy and affected sales of several subsidiaries of U.S.-based MNCs, including Armco, Inc., Black & Decker Corporation, and Quaker Oats Company.

The discussion up to this point emphasizes that country risk analysis goes far beyond an MNC's estimation of the probability that its subsidiary will be taken over by the local government. It includes an assessment of all factors (political and financial) related to the foreign country that influence the cash flow of the MNC. Also, after assessing country risk, the MNC must decide how to deal with it.

TYPES OF COUNTRY RISK ASSESSMENT

Although there is no consensus as to how country risk can best be assessed, some guidelines have been developed. The first step is to recognize the difference between (1) an overall risk assessment of a country without consideration of the MNC's business and (2) the risk assessment of a country as related to the MNC's type of business. The first type can be referred to as **macro-assessment** of country risk and the latter type as a **micro-assessment**. Each type is discussed in turn.

COUNTRY CHARACTERISTICS THAT AFFECT PROFITS

A recent survey by Petry and Sprow was conducted to determine what country characteristics could have the greatest potential impact on the profitability of large MNCs. Each characteristic was assigned a weight from 1 to 5, with 5 reflecting the most negative impact. An average weight across all MNCs was then computed, so that those characteristics with a larger average weight are perceived to have a larger negative impact on the MNC's profitability. The average weight for the seven most critical characteristics are disclosed here.

The authors also found that the weights assigned by MNCs in the consumer/retail sector were lower than those assigned by MNCs in the industrial sector. MNCs with a relatively large proportion of international business assigned higher weights, or greater importance, to restrictive practices and unstable currencies.

Country Characteristic	Average Weight
Restrictive Practices	3.44
Tariffs or Regulations	3.16
Unstable Currencies	3.07
Foreign Government Subsidies	3.07
Shaky Governments in Less Developed Countries	2.84
Third World Debt Problems	2.67
Varying Standards between Countries	2.58

Macro-Assessment of Country Risk

A macro-assessment involves consideration of all variables that affect country risk except for those unique to a particular firm or industry. This type of risk is convenient in that it remains the same for a given country, regardless of the firm or industry of concern; however, it excludes relevant information that could improve the accuracy of the assessment. While a macro-assessment of country risk is not ideal for any individual MNC, it serves as a foundation that can then be modified to reflect the particular business in which the MNC is involved.

Any macro-assessment model should consider both political and financial characteristics of the country being assessed. Political factors include the relationship of the host government with the MNC's home country government, the attitude of the people in the host country toward the MNC's government, the historical stability of the host government, the vulnerability of the host government to political takeovers within the government, and the probability of war between the host country and neighboring countries. Consideration of such political factors will indicate the probability of political events that may affect an MNC and the magnitude of the impact.

The financial factors of a macro-assessment model should include GNP growth, inflation trends, government budget levels (and the government deficit), interest rates, unemployment, the country's reliance on export income, the balance of trade, and foreign exchange controls. The list of financial factors could easily be extended several pages. The factors listed here represent just a subset of the financial factors considered when evaluating the financial strength of a country.

There is clearly some degree of subjectivity in identifying each of the relevant political and financial factors for a macro-assessment of country risk. There is also some subjectivity in determining the degree of importance of each factor in contributing to the overall macro-assessment for a particular country. For instance, one assessor may assign a much higher weight (degree of importance) to real GNP growth than another assessor. Finally, there is some subjectivity in predicting these financial factors. Because of the types of subjectivity mentioned here, it is not surprising that the risk assessors often differ in opinion after completing a macro-assessment of country risk.

Micro-Assessment of Country Risk

While a macro-assessment of country risk provides an indication of the country's overall status, it does not assess country risk from the perspective of the particular business of concern. Consider Country Z, which has been assigned a relatively low macro-assessment by most experts, due to its poor financial condition. Also consider two MNCs that are deciding whether to set up subsidiaries in Country Z. One MNC is considering the development of a subsidiary that would produce automobiles, while the other MNC plans to build a subsidiary that would produce military supplies. Country Z's government may be committed to purchasing a given amount of military supplies, regardless of how weak the economy is. Thus, the military supply subsidiary may be feasible, while the automobile subsidiary may not.

There is always the possibility that Country Z's government will search for a locally owned firm to produce military supplies, since it may desire more confidentiality about the supplies it is ordering. This possibility is an element of country risk, since it is a country characteristic (or attitude) that can affect the feasibility of a project. Yet, this specific characteristic is relevant only to the military supply subsidiary, and not to the automobile subsidiary. This example illustrates how an appropriate country risk assessment varies with the firm, industry, and project of concern, and therefore why the macro-assessment of country risk has its limitations. A micro-assessment is also necessary when evaluating the country risk as related to a particular project proposed by a particular firm.

In addition to political variables, financial variables are also necessary for micro-assessment of country risk. Micro factors would include the sensitivity of the firm's business to real GNP growth, inflation trends, interest rates, etc. Due to differences in business characteristics, some firms are more susceptible to the host country's economy than others.

In summary, the overall assessment of country risk consists of four parts:

1. Macro political risk
2. Macro financial risk
3. Micro political risk
4. Micro financial risk.

While these parts can be consolidated to generate a single country risk rating, it may be useful to keep them separate, so an MNC can realize the various ways by which its direct foreign investment or exporting operations are exposed to country risk.

Techniques to Assess Country Risk

Once a firm identifies all the macro and micro factors that deserve consideration in the country risk assessment, it may wish to implement a system for evaluating these factors and determining a country risk rating. There are various techniques available to achieve this objective. Some of the more popular techniques are

- Checklist approach
- Delphi technique
- Quantitative analysis
- Inspection visits
- Combination of techniques.

Each technique is briefly discussed in turn.

Checklist Approach

A checklist approach involves judgment on all the political and financial factors (both macro and micro) that contribute to a firm's assessment of country risk. Some factors (such as real GNP growth) can be measured from available data, while others (such as probability of entering into a war) must be subjectively measured. The factors should be converted if necessary to some numerical form in which they can be assessed for a particular country. Those factors thought to have a greater influence on country risk should be assigned greater weights. Both the measurement of some factors and the weighting scheme implemented are subjective.

Delphi Technique

The **Delphi technique** involves the collection of independent opinions on country risk without group discussion by the assessors who provide these opinions. The assessors here may be employees of the firm conducting the assessment or outside consultants. The MNC can average these country risk scores in some manner and even assess the degree of disagreement by measuring dispersion of opinions.

Quantitative Analysis

Once the financial and political variables have been measured for a period of time, models for quantitative analysis can attempt to identify the characteristics that influence the level of country risk. Discriminant analysis is a statistical tool commonly used for this purpose. To illustrate, assume there are some countries that historically can be classified as exhibiting tolerable risk, while other countries exhibit intolerable risk. Discriminant analysis can examine the financial and political factors of all of these countries and attempt to identify which factors help to distinguish (or discriminate) between a tolerable-risk country and an intolerable-risk country. For example, discriminant analysis may find that real growth in GNP is a crucial variable in explaining why a country is a good or bad risk. This information, along with the information determined for all other factors, can then be used in reassessing countries over time. If real GNP growth and other key variables begin to deteriorate for a particular country, this provides a signal that the country risk is increasing.

Regression analysis may also be used to assess risk, since it can measure the sensitivity of one variable to other variables. For example, a firm could regress a measure of its business activity (such as its percentage increase in sales) against country characteristics (such as real growth in GNP). Results from such an analysis will indicate the susceptibility of a particular business to a country's economy. This is valuable information to incorporate into the overall evaluation of country risk.

While statistical models can quantify the impact of variables on each other, they do have their limitations. For example, discriminant analysis applied to historical data may have found that strong real GNP growth can reduce a country's degree of country risk. But, if the firm cannot predict the real growth in GNP for a country, it may be difficult to predict how a country's risk will change over time. Because the country risk rating is to be used in assessing possible projects for the future, the ideal rating system would provide an early warning about countries that may cause problems for the firm in the future. Thus, the ideal quantitative techniques would identify characteristics that signalled problems well before they actually occurred (preferably before the firm's decision to take on a project in that country). At this point in time, such a quantitative model is not known to exist.

Inspection Visits

Inspection visits involve traveling to a country and meeting with government officials, firm executives, and/or consumers. Such meetings help clarify any uncertain opinions the firm has about a country. Indeed, some variables, such as inter-country relationships, may be difficult to assess without a trip to the host country.

Combination of Techniques

In some cases, it may be most appropriate to implement two or more of the techniques described above. This is common practice, since each technique has its own strengths and weaknesses. For example, the inspection visit may provide useful information, but does not by itself represent a complete country risk analysis. Individual evaluations of country risk could be generated by each technique for a particular country and, if significant differences showed up, further analysis could be conducted.

COMPARING RISK RATINGS AMONG COUNTRIES

An MNC may evaluate country risk for several countries, perhaps to determine where to establish a subsidiary. One approach to comparing political and financial ratings among countries, advocated by some foreign risk managers, is a

foreign investment risk matrix (FIRM), which displays the financial (or economic) risk by intervals ranging across the matrix from "acceptable" to "unacceptable." It also displays political risk by intervals ranging from "stable" to "unstable." An example of this matrix is shown in Exhibit 19.1. Each country can be positioned in its appropriate location on the matrix based on its political rating and financial rating.

Some countries, such as Country A in the exhibit, will be acceptable because they have a low degree of political and financial risk. Other countries, such as Country B, have low financial risk but high political risk. For Country C in the exhibit, the converse is true. Still others have a high degree of financial and political risk, such as Country D. A firm that uses this matrix must determine the acceptable and unacceptable zones. Based on the zones shown in Exhibit 19.1, Country A is acceptable for implementing projects, while Country B and Country D are unacceptable. Country C is in a so-called "unclear zone," suggesting further evaluation is necessary.

As already mentioned, the importance of political risk versus financial risk varies with the intent of the MNC. Those considering direct foreign investment to attract demand in that country must be highly concerned about financial risk. Those establishing a foreign manufacturing plant to capitalize on cheap production costs, planning to export the goods from there, should be more concerned with political risk.

While the FIRM approach can be useful for an MNC, it does not quantify an overall country risk rating for any individual country, since its financial and political ratings have not been weighted. An appropriate procedure for quantifying a country's overall risk is described next.

**EXHIBIT 19.1
Example of Foreign Investment Risk Matrix**
NOTE: This matrix was adapted from a matrix suggested by Bhalla; see *Euromoney,* June 1983, p. 70.

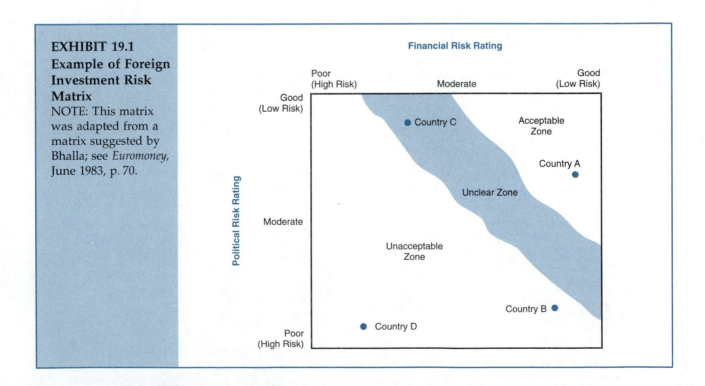

QUANTIFYING COUNTRY RISK: AN EXAMPLE

To develop an overall country risk rating, it is necessary to first construct separate ratings for political and financial risk. As discussed earlier in this chapter, both political risk and financial risk depend on a variety of factors. First, the political factors can be assigned values within some arbitrarily chosen range (such as values from 1 to 5, where 5 is the best value/lowest risk). Next, these political factors are assigned weights (representing degree of importance), which should add up to 100 percent. The assigned values of the factors times their respective weights can then be summed up to derive a political risk rating.

The process described for deriving the political risk rating can then be repeated to derive the financial risk rating. That is, values can be assigned (from 1 to 5, where 5 is the best value/lowest risk) to all financial factors. The assigned values of the factors times their respective weights can be summed up to derive a financial risk rating.

Once the political and financial ratings have been derived, a country's overall country risk rating as related to a specific project can be determined by assigning weights to the political and financial ratings according to their perceived importance. For example, if the political risk were thought to be much more influential on a particular project than the financial risk, it would receive a higher weight than the financial risk rating (both weights must total to 100 percent). The political and financial ratings multiplied by their respective

---

HOW EXECUTIVES ASSESS POLITICAL RISK

A recent survey by Mascarenhas and Atherton provided some interesting feedback on how executives perceive the techniques for political risk assessment used by their MNCs. In general, the executives believed that their companies' systems for assessing political risk were not being used to their fullest potential. Some of their main criticisms are summarized here:

1. *Delay in preparing report.* MNC managers sometimes must make quick decisions on foreign projects, but the political risk assessment may not be completed in time. In some cases, parts of the assessment are outdated by the time the entire assessment is complete.
2. *Assessments are reactive, not proactive.* Many political risk assessments are performed in response to a proposed project rather than in

anticipation that a project proposal may be forthcoming. This causes further delay in the political risk assessment.
3. *Data limitations.* Some of the data on political variables are difficult to quantify. In addition, the assessment of political risk requires information from foreign residents in the country of concern. It is often difficult to obtain relevant information from these residents.
4. *Distorted information.* From the transition of raw data on political variables to a finalized political risk assessment, the data can become distorted. This may occur because some variables are given more or less attention than deserved, or because managers may desire to contrive the data in such a way to support their preconceived opinion.

weights would determine the overall country risk rating for a country as related to a particular project.

As a simplified example, Exhibit 19.2 illustrates Cougar Company's country risk assessment of the hypothetical country Sunland. The company is assessing the establishment of a steel manufacturing plant there. From Exhibit 19.2, there are three political factors and five financial factors that contribute to the overall country risk rating in this example. In a realistic setting, many more factors might be included. Political risk factor A might reflect the degree of political tension within the country, political risk factor B the degree of political tension of the country with its neighboring countries, and so on. Financial risk factor A might reflect potential internal economic growth, and so on.

The number of relevant factors comprising both the political risk and the financial risk categories will vary with the country being assessed and the type of corporate operations planned for that country. The assignment of values to the factors, along with the degrees of importance (weights) assigned to the factors, will also vary with the country being assessed and type of corporate operations planned for that country.

To complete the example of deriving Sunland's overall country risk as related to Cougar Company's future plans, assume the company has assigned the values and weights to the factors as shown in Exhibit 19.3. In this example, the company generally assigns the financial factors higher ratings than the political factors. The financial condition of the country has therefore been assessed more favorably than the political condition. Political factor B is thought to be most important, based on a weighting of 60 percent, whereas political factors A and C receive the remaining 40 percent weighting. Financial factor E is

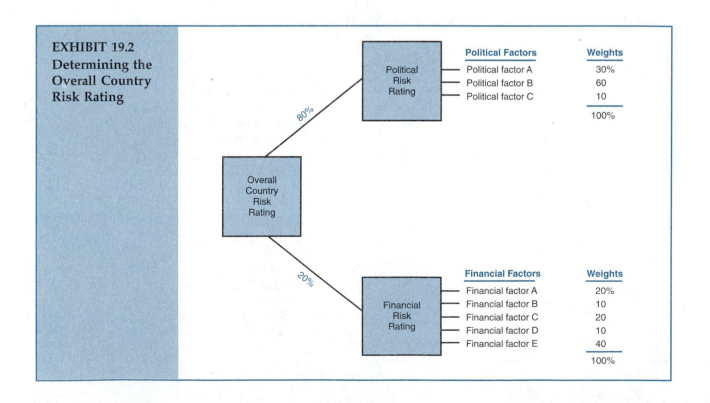

EXHIBIT 19.2
Determining the Overall Country Risk Rating

Political Factors	Weights
Political factor A	30%
Political factor B	60
Political factor C	10
	100%

Financial Factors	Weights
Financial factor A	20%
Financial factor B	10
Financial factor C	20
Financial factor D	10
Financial factor E	40
	100%

EXHIBIT 19.3   Derivation of the Overall Country Risk Rating Based on Assumed Information

(1)	(2)	(3)	(4) = (2) × (3)
Political Risk Factors	Rating Assigned by Company to Factor (Within a Range of 1–5)	Weight Assigned by Company to Factor According to Importance	Weighted Value of Factor
Political factor A	4	30%	1.2
Political factor B	2	60	1.2
Political factor C	3	10	.3
		100%	2.7 = Political risk rating
Financial Risk Factors			
Financial factor A	5	20%	1.0
Financial factor B	4	10	.4
Financial factor C	4	20	.8
Financial factor D	5	10	.5
Financial factor E	3	40	1.2
		100%	3.9 = Financial risk rating

(1)	(2)	(3)	(4) = (2) × (3)
Category	Rating As Determined Above	Weight Assigned by Company to Each Risk Category	Weighted Rating
Political risk	2.7	80%	2.16
Financial risk	3.9	20%	.78
		100%	2.94 = Overall country risk rating

thought to be very important, based on its 40 percent weighting, compared to 20 percent weights for factors A and C and 10 percent weights for factors B and D.

The political risk rating is determined by adding the products of assigned ratings (Column 2) and weights (Column 3) of the political risk factors. It equals 2.7, which may appear low based on the individual assigned values. Yet, political factor B carries a 60 percent weight and was assigned a low value, which explains the relatively low political risk rating.

The financial risk is computed to be 3.9, which again verifies that the financial condition of the country is better than its political condition. Once the political and financial ratings are determined, the overall country risk rating can be derived (as shown at the bottom of Exhibit 19.3), given the weights assigned to political and financial risk. Column 3 in the lower portion of Exhibit 19.3 suggests the company perceives political risk (receiving an 80 percent weight) to be much more important than financial risk (receiving a 20 percent weight) in this country as related to the proposed project. The overall country risk rating of 2.94 may appear low given the individual category ratings. This is due to the heavy weighting to political risk, which in this example is critical, from the firm's perspective. Should Cougar Company establish a steel manufacturing plant in a country that has an overall country risk rating of 2.94 (based on a scale of 1 to 5)? The answer depends on the risk tolerance of the firm, as discussed in the following section.

Before moving on, it should be emphasized that country risk assessors have their own individual procedures for quantifying country risk. The procedure described here is just one of many. Most procedures are similar, though, in that they somehow assign ratings and weights to all individual characteristics relevant to country risk assessment.

USE OF COUNTRY RISK ASSESSMENT _____

The first step for a firm after it has developed a country risk rating is to determine whether that rating suggests the risk is tolerable. If the country risk is too high, then the firm does not need to analyze the feasibility of the proposed project any further. Some firms may contend that no risk is too high when considering a project. Their reasoning is that if the potential return is high enough, the project is worth undertaking. However, there are cases in which the degree of country risk could be too high regardless of the project's expected return. Consider a proposed development of a subsidiary that appears very profitable in Country Z. If Country Z is often engaged in war, this places a threat on the life of any employees who would be transferred to that subsidiary. In this case, Country Z should be off limits, and the proposed project should not receive further consideration.

If the risk rating of a country is in the tolerable range, any project related to that country deserves further consideration. Capital budgeting analysis would be appropriate to determine whether the project is feasible.

Incorporating Country Risk in Capital Budgeting

Country risk can be incorporated in the capital budgeting analysis of a proposed project by adjustment of the discount rate, or by adjustment of the estimated cash flows. Each method is discussed below.

Adjustment of the Discount Rate. The discount rate of a proposed project is supposed to reflect the required rate of return on that project. Thus, the discount rate could be adjusted to account for the country risk. The lower the country risk rating, the higher is the perceived risk, and the higher is the discount rate applied to the project's cash flows. This approach is convenient in that one adjustment to the capital budgeting analysis can capture country risk. However, there is no precise formula for adjusting the discount rate to incorporate country risk. The adjustment is somewhat arbitrary, and may therefore cause feasible projects to be rejected or unfeasible projects to be accepted.

Adjustment of the Estimated Cash Flows. Perhaps the most appropriate method for incorporating forms of country risk in a capital budgeting analysis is to estimate how the cash flows would be affected by each form of risk. For example, if there is a 20 percent probability that the host government will temporarily block funds from the subsidiary to the parent, the MNC should estimate the project's net present value (NPV) under these circumstances, realizing that there is a 20 percent chance that this NPV will occur. (The estimation of a project's NPV when funds are blocked is demonstrated in Chapter 17.)

If there is a chance that the host government takeover will occur, the foreign project's NPV under these conditions should be estimated. Each possible form of risk has an estimated impact on the foreign project's cash flows, and therefore on the project's NPV. By analyzing each possible impact, the MNC can determine the probability distribution of NPVs for the project. Its accept/reject decision on the project will be based on its assessment of the probability that the project will generate a positive NPV, as well as the size of possible NPV outcomes. While this procedure may seem somewhat tedious, it directly incorporates forms of country risk into the cash flow estimates and explicitly illustrates the possible results from implementing the project. The more convenient method of adjusting the discount rate in accordance with the country risk rating does not indicate the probability distribution of possible outcomes.

To illustrate how country risk can be incorporated in capital budgeting, reconsider the example for Spartan Inc. that is discussed in Chapter 17. Assume for the moment that all the initial assumptions regarding Spartan's initial investment, project life, pricing policy, exchange rate projections, etc., apply here. However, two country risk characteristics will be incorporated here that are not included in the initial analysis. First, assume that there is a 30 percent chance that the withholding tax imposed by the Swiss government will be at a 20% rate rather than a 10% rate. Second, assume there is a 40 percent chance that the Swiss government will provide Spartan a payment (salvage value) of SF7 million rather than SF12 million. These two possibilities represent a form of country risk. Assume that these two possible situations are unrelated. To determine how the NPV is affected by each of these scenarios, a capital budgeting analysis similar to that shown in Exhibit 17.3 from Chapter 17 could be used. If this analysis were already on a spreadsheet, the NPV could be easily estimated by adjustment of line items no. 15 (withholding tax imposed on remitted funds) and no. 17 (salvage value). The capital budgeting analysis measures the effect of a 20% withholding tax rate in Exhibit 19.4. Since none of the items before line no. 14 are affected, these items are not shown here. If the 20% withholding tax rate is imposed, the NPV of the four-year project is $1,252,160.

Now consider the possibility of the lower salvage value, while using the initial assumption of a 10% withholding tax rate. The capital budgeting analysis accounts for the lower salvage value in Exhibit 19.5. The estimated NPV is $800,484, based on this scenario.

Finally, consider the possibility that the higher withholding tax and the lower salvage value occur. The capital budgeting analysis in Exhibit 19.6 accounts for both of these situations. The NPV is estimated to be −$177,223.

Once estimates for the NPV are derived for each scenario, the firm can attempt to determine whether the project is feasible. In our example, there are two country risk variables that are uncertain, and there are four possible NPV outcomes, as illustrated in Exhibit 19.7. Given the probability of each possible situation, and the assumption that the withholding tax outcome is independent from the salvage value outcome, joint probabilities can be determined for each

EXHIBIT 19.4   Analysis of Project Based on a 20% Withholding Tax: Spartan Inc.

	Year 0	Year 1	Year 2	Year 3	Year 4
14. SF remitted by subsidiary		SF6,000,000	SF6,000,000	SF7,600,000	SF8,400,000
15. Withholding tax imposed on remitted funds (20%)		SF1,200,000	SF1,200,000	SF1,520,000	SF1,680,000
16. SF remitted after withholding taxes		SF4,800,000	SF4,800,000	SF6,080,000	SF6,720,000
17. Salvage value					SF12,000,000
18. Exchange rate of SF		$.50	$.50	$.50	$.50
19. Cash flows to parent		$2,400,000	$2,400,000	$3,040,000	$9,360,000
20. PV of parent cash flows (15% discount rate)		$2,086,956	$1,814,745	$1,998,849	$5,351,610
21. Initial investment by parent	$10,000,000				
22. Cumulative NPV		−$7,913, 044	−$6,098,299	−$4,099,450	$1,252,160

EXHIBIT 19.5   Analysis of Project Based on a Reduced Salvage Value: Spartan Inc.

	Year 0	Year 1	Year 2	Year 3	Year 4
14. SF remitted by subsidiary		SF6,000,000	SF6,000,000	SF7,600,000	SF8,400,000
15. Withholding tax imposed on remitted funds (20%)		SF600,000	SF600,000	SF760,000	SF840,000
16. SF remitted after withholding taxes		SF5,400,000	SF5,400,000	SF6,840,000	SF7,560,000
17. Salvage value					SF7,000,000
18. Exchange rate of SF		$.50	$.50	$.50	$.50
19. Cash flows to parent		$2,700,000	$2,700,000	$3,420,000	$7,280,000
20. PV of parent cash flows (15% discount rate)		$2,347,826	$2,041,588	$2,248,706	$4,162,364
21. Initial investment by parent	$10,000,000				
22. Cumulative NPV		−$7,652,174	−$5,610,586	−$3,361,880	$800,484

pair of outcomes by multiplying the probabilities of the two outcomes of concern. Since the probability of a 20% withholding tax is 30 percent, the probability of a 10% withholding tax is 70 percent. Given that the probability of a lower salvage value is 40 percent, the probability of the initial estimate for the salvage value is 60 percent. Thus, scenario no. 1 (10% withholding tax and SF12 million salvage value) created in Chapter 17 has a joint probability (probability that both outcomes will occur) of (70%) × (60%) = 42%.

From Exhibit 19.7, scenario no. 4 is the only scenario in which there is a negative NPV. Since this scenario has a 12% chance of occurring, there is a 12% chance that the project proposed will adversely affect the value of the firm. Put

EXHIBIT 19.6   Analysis of Project Based on a 20% Withholding Tax and a Reduced Salvage Value: Spartan Inc.

	Year 0	Year 1	Year 2	Year 3	Year 4
14. SF remitted by subsidiary		SF6,000,000	SF6,000,000	SF7,600,000	SF8,400,000
15. Withholding tax imposed on remitted funds (20%)		SF1,200,000	SF1,200,000	SF1,520,000	SF1,680,000
16. SF remitted after withholding date		SF4,800,000	SF4,800,000	SF6,080,000	SF6,720,000
17. Salvage value					SF7,000,000
18. Exchange rate of SF		$.50	$.50	$.50	$.50
19. Cash flows to parent		$2,400,000	$2,400,000	$3,040,000	$6,860,000
20. PV of parent cash flows (15% discount rate)		$2,086,956	$1,814,745	$1,998,849	$3,922,227
21. Initial investment by parent	$10,000,000				
22. Cumulative NPV		−$7,913,044	−$6,098,044	−$4,099,450	−$177,223

EXHIBIT 19.7 Summary of Estimated NPVs Across the Possible Scenarios: Spartan Inc.

Scenario	Withholding Tax Imposed by Swiss Government	Salvage Value of Project	NPV	Probability
1	10%	SF12,000,000	$2,229,867	(70%)(60%) = 42%
2	20%	SF12,000,000	$1,252,160	(30%)(60%) = 18%
3	10%	SF7,000,000	$800,484	(70%)(40%) = 28%
4	20%	SF7,000,000	−$177,223	(30%)(40%) = 12%

$$E(NPV) = \$2,229,867 \ (42\%)$$

$$+ \ \$1,252,160 \ (18\%)$$

$$+ \ \$800,484 \ (28\%)$$

$$- \ \$177,223 \ (12\%)$$

$$= \$1,364,801$$

another way, there is an 88% chance that the project will enhance the firm's value. The expected value of the project's NPV could be measured as the sum of each scenario's estimated NPV multiplied by its respective probability across all four scenarios, as shown in the bottom of Exhibit 19.7. Most MNCs would accept the proposed project, given the likelihood that the project will have a positive NPV, and the limited loss that would occur even under the worst case scenario.

In this example, the initial assumptions for most input variables were used, as if these assumptions were known with certainty. However, it is possible to account for the uncertainty of country risk characteristics (as is done in our present example) while also allowing for uncertainty in the other variables as well. This process can be facilitated if the analysis is on a computer spreadsheet. For example, if the firm wished to allow for three possible exchange rate trends, it could adjust the exchange rate projections for each of the four scenarios assessed in the present example. Each scenario would reflect a specific withholding tax outcome, a specific salvage value outcome, and a specific exchange rate trend. There would be a total of 12 scenarios, with each scenario having an estimated NPV and a probability of occurrence. Based on the estimated NPV and the probability of each scenario, the firm could then measure the expected value of the NPV and the probability that the NPV would be positive.

Even after a project is accepted and implemented, country risk must continue to be monitored. With a labor-intensive MNC, the host country may feel it is benefiting from a subsidiary's existence (due to the subsidiary's employment of local people), and the chance of expropriation may be low. Yet, there are several other forms of country risk that need to be considered. Decisions regarding subsidiary expansion, fund transfers to the parent, and sources of financing can all be affected by any changes in country risk; and since country risk can change dramatically over time, periodic reassessment is required, especially for less stable countries.

Applications of Country Risk Analysis

There are some cases in which country risk assessment has enabled MNCs to avoid further involvement and even reduce current involvement in politically tense countries. For example, four months before the fall of the Shah of Iran, a country risk assessor for Gulf Oil detected severe political pressure building within Iran. Consequently, Gulf Oil began planning to deal with the subsequent loss of Iranian oil, which at the time amounted to 10 percent of its crude supplies.

APPLIED RESEARCH

Do MNCs in High-Risk Countries Achieve Higher Returns?

A recent study by Chase, Kuhle, and Walther assessed the relationship between the political risk of a country and the returns on direct foreign investment in that country. Since investors are assumed to be risk-averse, one would hypothesize higher expected returns for investment in riskier countries. The higher return would compensate the investor for the relatively high degree of uncertainty. If the same returns could be achieved in safer countries, one would assume the inves-

tors would confine their dealings to those countries. In essence, the expected returns in high-risk countries should contain a risk premium that compensates investors for the high risk.

To test this hypothesis, annual data on political risk ratings and returns on direct foreign investments were compiled for 46 countries. A strong positive risk-return relationship existed in the early 1980s, supporting the hypothesis that firms investing in high-risk countries earn

higher returns. However, the strong positive risk-return relationship did not exist in many other years. In fact, in some years there was a negative relationship between country risk and return.

In general, the results suggest that firms investing in high-risk countries are not always adequately compensated. That is, they might be able to achieve similar returns on direct foreign investment in less risky countries.

While dedicating resources to country risk assessment can be well worth the cost, the art of forecasting country crises is far from being perfected.

Whether MNCs hire outside consultants or use in-house staff to perform country risk analysis, they have often been unable to predict major trouble in various countries. For example, the Iranian crisis, Poland's financial crisis, and the economic deterioration of several Latin American countries were generally not detected well in advance. It is understandable that country risk systems are prone to errors. Consider the procedure discussed earlier in this chapter, in which individual country characteristics are assigned values which rate each characteristic. The values assigned are somewhat arbitrary. In addition, the assigning of weights to reflect the importance of each characteristic is also somewhat arbitrary. Thus, while an overall risk rating of a country can be useful, it cannot always detect upcoming crises.

The general inability of MNCs to predict country crises may also be due to too much reliance on statistics. Quantitative models, while valuable, cannot evaluate subjective data that cannot be quantified. In addition, historical trends of various country characteristics are not always useful for anticipating an upcoming crisis. Furthermore, warnings by country risk assessors are sometimes ignored by executives higher up in the company's organization.

Due to the exposure to error when assessing country risk, no system has been singled out as optimal. A survey of 193 corporations heavily involved in foreign business found that about half of the corporations have no formal means for making country risk assessments. This does not mean they neglect to assess country risk, but rather that there is no proven method to use. Some of the assessors' opinions of country risk are based simply on their conversations with other people whom they believe are reliable. While such an approach is quite simplistic, there is no clear-cut evidence that even the most sophisticated technique will more properly assess country risk.

Country Risk Analysis of Eastern Bloc Countries.
To illustrate the characteristics that are given much attention when assessing country risk, consider the assessment of Eastern Bloc countries in recent years. Hungary has generally received relatively high ratings because of its capable labor force, the recent ease in remitting profits from the country, and its government's efforts to promote direct foreign investment. Poland, Romania, and the countries that formerly made up Czechoslovakia and Yugoslavia have received low ratings because of internal political battles, large budget deficits, poor economic conditions, large government bureaucracies, and a lack of effort in welcoming direct foreign investment.

While these ratings may change over time, this assessment summary suggests the more relevant characteristics that influence the ratings of Eastern Bloc countries. Some other important characteristics assessed when measuring country risk in these countries are availability of hotels, office space, phone lines, and public transportation.

Country Risk Resulting From the Persian Gulf Crisis.
As a result of the Persian Gulf crisis, many MNCs attempted to reassess country risk. Terrorism became a major concern. Various methods were used by MNCs to protect against terrorism. Cross-country travel by executives was reduced, as MNCs used teleconference calls instead. Some MNCs with subsidiaries in Saudi Arabia

temporarily closed some of their operations, allowing employees from other countries to return home. Some projects that were being considered for countries that could be subject to terrorist attacks were postponed. Even projects that appeared to be feasible from a financial perspective were postponed because of the potential danger to employees.

In addition to the threat of terrorism, there were numerous other ways in which the Persian Gulf crisis influenced cash flows of MNCs. The effects varied with the characteristics of each MNC. The more obvious effects of the crisis were reduced travel and higher oil prices. The reduction in travel adversely affected airlines, hotels, restaurants, luggage manufacturers, photography-related firms (such as Eastman Kodak Co.), and cruise lines.

The Persian Gulf crisis is a clear example of how country risk can change over time. It would have been difficult to forecast that Iraq was going to invade Kuwait or to forecast the events following the invasion. MNCs recognize that some unpredictable events will unfold that will affect their exposure to country risk. Yet they can at least be prepared to revise their operations in order to reduce their exposure.

EXPOSURE TO HOST GOVERNMENT TAKEOVERS

While there are several possible benefits to direct foreign investment, country risk can offset such benefits. The most severe country risk is a host government takeover. This type of takeover may result in major losses, especially when the MNC does not have any power to negotiate with the host government.

Reducing Exposure to Host Government Takeovers

The most common strategies used to reduce exposure to a host-government takeover are

- Use a short-term horizon
- Rely on unique supplies or technology
- Hire local labor
- Borrow local funds
- Purchase insurance

Use a Short-Term Horizon.   This technique concentrates on recovering cash flow quickly, so that in the event of expropriation, losses are minimized. An MNC would also exert only a minimum effort to replace worn-out equipment and machinery at the subsidiary. It may even phase out its overseas investment by selling off its assets to local investors or the government in stages over time.

Rely on Unique Supplies or Technology.   If the subsidiary can bring in supplies from its headquarters (or a sister subsidiary) that cannot be duplicated locally, the host government will not be able to take over and operate the subsidiary without such supplies. Also, the supplies could be cut off by the MNC if the subsidiary were treated unfairly.

If the subsidiary can hide the technology in its production process, a government takeover will be less likely. The only way a takeover would work here would be if the MNC were willing to provide the necessary technology, and

PROTECTING AGAINST TERRORISM

One form of political risk is terrorism. In recent years, the threat of terrorism has increased, and MNCs have attempted to protect against it. Some of the terrorism by Middle East groups took place in Europe, where many U.S.-based MNCs have subsidiaries. Numerous U.S.-based MNCs with foreign subsidiaries have attempted to maintain a low profile in foreign countries so that terrorists will not use their subsidiaries to show their hatred for the United States. For example, NCH Corporation, a Texas-based chemical company with about 2,000 em- ployees in Europe, attempts to be perceived as a local business. Philbro-Saloman Inc. has developed contingency plans for evacuating its employees at European offices. U.S.-based MNCs such as Hercules Inc. and General Foods reacted to terrorism events by taking additional security measures to protect their property and employees. Heinz Company considered a proposal to transport European executives to the United States for business meetings rather than transporting U.S. executives to Europe.

the MNC would provide such information only under conditions of a friendly takeover, in which it received adequate compensation.

Hire Local Labor.   If local employees of the subsidiary were affected by the host government's takeover, they could pressure their government to avoid such action. However, the government could still let those employees retain their positions after taking over the subsidiary. Thus, this strategy has only limited effectiveness in avoiding or reducing a government takeover.

Borrow Local Funds.   If the subsidiary borrows funds locally, local banks will be concerned about its future performance. If for any reason a government takeover would reduce the probability that the banks would receive their loan repayments promptly, they might pressure the host government to avoid a takeover. However, the host government may guarantee repayment to the banks, so this strategy has only limited effectiveness. Nevertheless, it could still be preferable to a situation in which the MNC not only lost the subsidiary but also still owed home country creditors.

Purchase Insurance.   Insurance can be purchased to cover the risk of expropriation. For example, the U.S. government provides insurance through the Overseas Private Investment Corporation (OPIC). The insurance premiums paid by a firm depend on the degree of insurance coverage and the risk associated with the firm. Yet, any insurance policy will typically cover only a portion of the company's total exposure to country risk.

Many home countries of MNCs have investment guarantee programs that insure to some extent the risks of expropriation, wars, or currency blockage. Some guarantee programs have a one-year waiting period or longer before compensation is paid on losses due to expropriation. Also, some insurance policies do not cover all forms of expropriation. Furthermore, to be eligible for such insurance, the subsidiary might be required by the country to concentrate on exporting rather than on local sales. Even if a subsidiary qualifies for insurance, there is a cost. Any insurance will typically cover only a portion of the assets and may specify a maximum duration of coverage, such as 15 or 20 years. A subsidiary must weigh the benefits of this insurance against the cost of the policy's premiums and potential losses in excess of coverage. The insurance can be helpful, but it does not by itself prevent losses due to expropriation.

In 1993, Russia established an insurance fund to protect MNCs against various forms of country risk. This action was taken to encourage more direct foreign investment in Russia.

The World Bank recently established an affiliate called the Multilateral Investment Guarantee Agency (MIGA) to provide political insurance for MNCs with direct foreign investment in less developed countries. MIGA offers insurance against expropriation, breach of contract, currency inconvertibility, war, and civil disturbances.

SUMMARY

■ The factors used by MNCs to measure a country's political risk include attitude of consumers toward purchasing homemade goods, the host government's attitude toward the MNC, the blockage of fund transfers, currency inconvertibility, war, and bureaucracy. These factors can increase the costs of international business.

■ The factors used by MNCs to measure a country's financial risk are the country's interest rates, exchange rates, and inflation rates.

■ The techniques typically used by MNCs to measure the country risk are the checklist approach, the Delphi technique, quantitative analysis, and inspection visits. Since no one technique covers all aspects of country risk, a combination of these techniques is commonly used.

The measurement of country risk is essentially a weighted average of the political or financial factors that are perceived to comprise country risk. Each MNC has its own view as to the weights that should be assigned to each factor. Thus, the overall rating for a country may vary among MNCs.

■ Once country risk is measured, it can be incorporated into a capital budgeting analysis by adjustment of the discount rate. However, the adjustment is somewhat arbitrary and may cause improper decision making.

An alternative method of incorporating country risk analysis into capital budgeting is to explicitly account for each factor that affects country risk. For each possible form of risk, the MNC can recalculate the foreign project's net present value under the condition that the event (such as blocked funds, increased taxes, etc.) occurs.

SELF-TEST FOR CHAPTER 19

(Answers are provided in Appendix A in the back of the text.)

1. Key West Co. exports highly advanced phone system components to its subsidiary shops on islands in the Caribbean Sea. The components are purchased by consumers to improve their phone systems. These

components are not produced in other countries. Explain how political risk factors could adversely affect the profitability of Key West Co.

2. Using the information in Question 1, explain how financial risk factors could adversely affect the profitability of Key West Co.

3. Given the information in Question 1, do you expect that Key West Co. is more concerned about the adverse effects of political risk or those of financial risk?

4. In 1992, a bomb exploded in the World Trade Center. Explain what types of firms would be most concerned about an increase in country risk as a result of this event.

5. Rockford Co. plans to expand its successful business by establishing a subsidiary in Canada. However, it is concerned that after two years the Canadian government will either impose a special tax on any income sent back to the U.S. parent, or order the subsidiary to be sold at that time. The executives have estimated that either of these scenarios has a 15% chance of occurring. They have decided to add 4 percentage points onto the project's required rate of return to incorporate the country risk they were concerned about in the capital budgeting analysis. Is there a better way to more precisely incorporate the country risk of concern here?

QUESTIONS

1. List some forms of country risk other than a takeover of a subsidiary by the host government.

2. Identify common political factors for an MNC to consider when assessing country risk. Briefly elaborate on how each factor can affect the risk to the MNC.

3. Identify common financial factors for an MNC to consider when assessing country risk. Briefly elaborate on how each factor can affect the risk to the MNC.

4. Discuss the use of the foreign investment risk matrix (FIRM) to compare country risk among countries. Why do firms have different acceptable zones when using this matrix?

5. Describe the steps involved in assessing country risk once all relevant information has been gathered.

6. Describe the possible errors involved in assessing country risk. In other words, explain why country risk analysis is not always accurate.

7. Explain an MNC's strategy of diversifying projects internationally in order to maintain a low level of overall country risk.

8. Once a project is accepted, country risk analysis for the foreign country involved is no longer necessary, assuming that no other proposed projects are being evaluated for that country. Do you agree with this statement? Why or why not?

9. If the potential return is high enough, any degree of country risk can be tolerated. Do you agree with this statement? Why or why not?

10. An MNC has decided to call a well-known country risk consultant to conduct a country risk analysis on a small country in which the MNC plans to develop a large subsidiary. The MNC prefers to hire the consultant, since it plans to use its employees for other important corporate functions. The consultant uses a computer program that has assigned weights of importance linked to the various factors. The consultant will evaluate the factors for this small country and insert a rating for each factor into the computer. While the assigned weights to the factors are not adjusted by the computer, the factor ratings are adjusted for each particular country the consultant assesses. Do you think the MNC should use this consultant? Why or why not?

11. Explain the micro-assessment of country risk.

12. How could a country risk assessment be used to adjust a project's required rate of return? How could such an assessment be used to instead adjust a project's estimated cash flows?

13. Explain some methods of reducing exposure to existing country risk, while maintaining the same amount of business within a particular country.

14. Why do some subsidiaries maintain a low profile as to where their parents are located?

15. Do you think that a proper country risk analysis can replace a capital budgeting analysis of a project considered for a foreign country? Explain.

16. NYU Corporation considered establishing a subsidiary in Zenland; it performed a country risk analysis to help make the decision. It first retrieved a country risk analysis performed about one year earlier, when it had planned to begin a major exporting business to Zenland firms. Then it updated the analysis by incorporating all current information on the key variables that were used in that analysis, such as Zenland's willingness to accept exports, its existing quotas, and existing tariff laws. Is this country risk analysis adequate? Explain.

17. In the early 1990s, MNCs such as Alcoa DuPont, Heinz, and IBM donated products and technology to foreign countries where they have subsidiaries. How could these actions reduce some forms of country risk?

18. A U.S. firm plans a project in the United Kingdom, in which it would lease space for one year in a shopping mall to sell expensive clothes manufactured in the U.S. The project would end in one year, when all earnings would be remitted to the U.S. firm. Assume no additional corporate taxes would be incurred beyond those imposed by the British government. Since the firm would rent space, it would not have any long-term assets in the United Kingdom, and expects the salvage (terminal) value of the project to be about zero.

    Assume that the project's required rate of return is 18 percent. Also assume that the initial outlay required by the parent to fill the store with clothes is $200,000. The pre-tax earnings are expected to be £300,000 at the end of one year. The British pound is expected to be worth $1.60 at the end of one year, when the after-tax earnings will be converted to dollars and remitted to the U.S. The following forms of country risk must be considered:

- The British economy may weaken (probability = 30%), which would cause the expected pre-tax earnings to be £200,000.
- The British corporate tax rate on income earned by U.S. firms may increase from 40% to 50% (probability = 20%).

These two forms of country risk are independent. Calculate the expected value of the project's net present value (NPV) and determine the probability that the project will have a negative NPV.

19. Explain how capital budgeting analysis would need to be adjusted for Question 18 if there were three possible outcomes for the British pound, in addition to the possible outcomes for the British economic growth and the corporate tax rate.

CASE: COUNTRY RISK IN CHINA

China's New Currency Exchange Center, In Shanghai, Will Tighten Conversions

BY JOSEPH KAHN
Staff Reporter of THE WALL STREET JOURNAL

SHANGHAI—It is about to get a lot more difficult for foreign businesses in China to repatriate their profits.

In early April, the Beijing government plans to replace its array of "swap markets" across the country with a national inter-bank currency exchange center based in Shanghai. Chinese bankers and foreign analysts say the new foreign exchange system will enable financial markets to operate more efficiently and will lay the foundation for full convertibility of the Chinese yuan into dollars and other hard currencies.

Those are long-term goals, however. In the short run, the reform is likely to cause headaches for many foreign companies based in China—as well as for some Chinese companies engaged in foreign trade.

Scrutiny From People's Bank
The People's Bank of China, the country's central bank, for example, is expected to tighten restrictions on which companies can convert yuan and in what quantity they can do so. The bank also intends to scrutinize every transaction to determine if it adheres to the business charter negotiated by the company and the government, according to people familiar with the new exchange system.

"Beijing will directly manage the operation. The transactions will have to be more closely matched to policy," says Mao Yingliang, president of the Shanghai Branch of the People's Bank. Access to foreign currency "will become more standardized," he adds.

Creation of an inter-bank currency market is a key part of China's plan to overhaul its financial system. The first step was elimination of the country's dual-exchange rate on Jan. 1, but analysts say a range of other long-debated changes, including the establishment of a Western-style central banking system and the expansion of capital markets, are likely to be phased in more slowly than

originally envisioned. Indeed, the launch of the new foreign exchange system has been delayed for three months by indecision over its accessibility and by glitches in setting up a six-city computer link.

Meeting GATT Stipulation
The new exchange system will fulfill a requirement of the General Agreements on Tariffs and Trade, which governs most world trade, by setting up a framework for the yuan's eventual conversion. Its immediate impact will be to consolidate control of foreign exchange in the hands of central planners. The change comes during a campaign to reverse the country's soaring trade deficit and stem the flight of capital.

Under the new Western-style system, designated Chinese banks will handle all currency trading. The People's Bank will limit the volume of transactions and will intervene on the market whenever necessary to keep the exchange rate of the yuan within a narrow range against foreign currencies, Mr. Mao says.

Access to the market takes on particular importance in light of the recent wave of investment by foreign companies hoping to cash in on sales to the Chinese. Such companies want to be able to convert Chinese yuan so that they can repatriate their profits.

China theoretically requires all foreign-funded companies to "balance" foreign exchange, meaning they should not contribute to a net outflow of hard currency. But many companies have found the existing swap market system relatively flexible in practice, allowing them to trade Chinese currency for foreign exchange well before they meet targets for earning hard currency through exports.

'An Enforcement Mechanism'
"Many of the foreign companies are concerned about how [the new system] will impact their business," says Lai Chi-Sun, chief representative of Motorola Inc.'s Motorola China Inc. "We get the impression that the Chinese see this as an enforcement mechanism" for clamping down on the export of hard currency.

Motorola's Tianjin-based manufacturing operation depends heavily on imports of raw materials. It sells finished goods primarily to

the China market, making conversion of yuan-denominated profits a necessity. To date, Mr. Lai says, the company has had "liberal access" to swap markets.

He says government officials have failed to provide concrete details on how quickly his company will be required to balance its currency earnings, a process that he said will take at least several years. Manufacturing operations in China typically spend more hard currency than they earn in the initial stages of operations, because the operations often have to import machinery and raw materials.

Source: *The Wall Street Journal* (February 24, 1994), p. A13. Reprinted by permission of *The Wall Street Journal,* © 1994 Dow Jones & Company, Inc. All Rights Reserved Worldwide.

QUESTIONS

1. Explain why China's tightening of restrictions on currency convertibility can make some projects of U.S.-based MNCs unfeasible.

2. Explain how a U.S.-based MNC could have attempted to account for this type of country risk (tighter restrictions on currency convertibility), even if it was not sure that China would tighten restrictions.

3. It is sometimes argued that projects considered for China could be assessed using a higher discount rate to capture the possibility of new government policies, in order to account for this risk when estimating a project's NPV. Would this method properly distinguish between projects in China that will be worthwhile and those that will not?

KING INC.
Country Risk Analysis

CASE PROBLEM

King Inc., a U.S. firm, is considering the establishment of a small subsidiary in Bulgaria which would produce food products. All ingredients can be obtained or produced in Bulgaria. The final products to be produced by the subsidiary would be sold in Bulgaria and other Eastern Bloc countries. King Inc. is very interested in this project, since there is little competition in that area. Three high-level managers of King, Inc. have been assigned the task of assessing the country risk of Bulgaria. Specifically, the managers were asked to list all characteristics of Bulgaria that could adversely affect the performance of this project. The decision on whether to undertake this project will be made only once this country risk analysis is completed, and accounted for in the capital budgeting analysis. Since King Inc. has focused exclusively on domestic business in the past, it is not accustomed to country risk analysis.

a) What factors related to Bulgaria's government deserve to be considered?

b) What country-related factors can affect the demand for the food products to be produced by King Inc.?

c) What country-related factors can affect the cost of production?

PROJECT

Review the annual report of an MNC of your choice. Summarize the forms of country risk that the MNC is exposed to according to the report.

REFERENCES

Bhalla, Bharat, "How Corporations Should Weigh Up Country Risk." *Euromoney* (June 1983), pp. 66–72.

Boddewyn, Jean J. "Political Aspects of MNE Theory." *Journal of International Business Studies* (Fall 1988), pp. 341–363.

Brewer, Thomas L. "The Instability of Governments and the Instability of Controls on Funds Transfers by Multinational Enterprises: Implications for Political Risk Analysis." *Journal of International Business Studies* (Winter 1983), pp. 147–157.

Chase, C. D., J. L. Kuhle and C. H. Walther. "The Relevance of Political Risk in Direct Foreign Investment." *Management International Review*, no. 3 (1988), pp. 31–38.

Doz, Yves L., and C. K. Prahalad. "How MNCs Cope with Host Government Intervention." *Harvard Business Review* (March–April 1980), pp. 149–157.

Kobrin, Stephen J. "Political Risks: A Review and Reconsideration." *Journal of International Business Studies* (Spring–Summer 1979), pp. 67–80.

Leavy, Brian. "Assessing Country Risk for Foreign Investment Decisions." *Long-Range Planning* (June 1984), pp. 141–150.

Mascarenhas, B., and C. Atherton. "Problems in Political Risk Assessment." *Management International Review*, no. 3 (February 1983), pp. 22–32.

Petry, Glenn H. and James Sprow, "International Trends and Events in Corporate Finance and Management: A Survey," *Financial Practice and Education,* Spring/Summer 1993, pp. 21–28.

Nigh, Douglas. "The Effect of Political Events on U.S. Direct Foreign Investment: A Pooled Time-Series Cross-Sectional Analysis." *Journal of International Business Studies* (Spring 1985), pp. 1–17.

Saini, Krishan G., and Philip S. Bates. "A Survey of the Quantitative Approaches to Country Risk Analysis." *Journal of Banking and Finance* (June 1984), pp. 341–355.

Schmidt, David A. "Analyzing Political Risk." *Business Horizons* (July–August 1986), pp. 43–50.

Tallman, Stephen B. "Home Country Political Risk and Foreign Direct Investment in the U.S." *Journal of International Business Studies* (Summer 1988), pp. 219–234.

CHAPTER 20

LONG-TERM FINANCING

Multinational corporations (MNCs) typically use long-term sources of funds to finance long-term projects. They have access to domestic and foreign sources of funds. It is worthwhile for MNCs to consider all possible forms of financing before making their final decisions. The specific objectives of this chapter are to

- explain why MNCs consider long-term financing in foreign currencies
- explain how to assess the feasibility of long-term financing in foreign currencies, and
- explain how the assessment of long-term financing in foreign currencies is adjusted for bonds with floating interest rates.

LONG-TERM FINANCING DECISION

The long-term financing decision of the MNC involves some aspects similar to the decision about short-term financing. Recall that the "effective" cost of short-term financing considers both the quoted interest rate and the percentage change in the exchange rate of the currency borrowed over the loan life. Just as currencies exhibit different interest rates on short-term bank loans, bond yields can vary as well among currencies. Exhibit 20.1 illustrates the long-term bond yields for several different countries. The wide differentials in yields at any given point in time are evident. The yields shown in Exhibit 20.1 do not account for exchange rate fluctuations. That is, each yield shown reflects what an investor *within* the country of concern would have earned from bonds denominated in the local currency.

Because bonds denominated in foreign currencies sometimes have lower yields, U.S. corporations often consider issuing bonds in those countries denominated in these currencies. Since the actual financing cost to a U.S. corporation issuing a foreign currency-denominated bond is affected by that currency's value relative to the U.S. dollar during the financing period, there is no guarantee that the bond will be less costly than a U.S. dollar-denominated bond. The borrowing firm must make coupon payments in the currency denominating the bond. If this

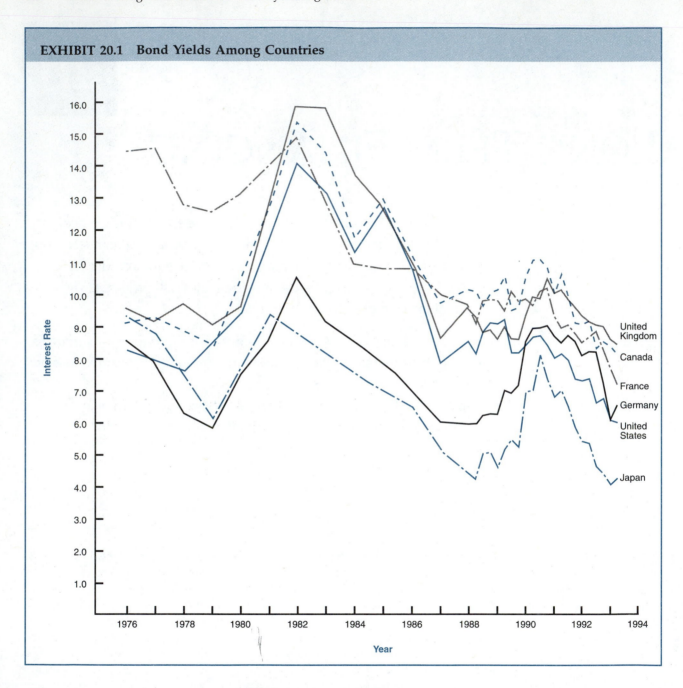

EXHIBIT 20.1 Bond Yields Among Countries

currency appreciates against the firm's home currency, the funds needed to make coupon payments will increase. For this reason, a firm will not always denominate debt in a currency that exhibits a low interest rate.

To make the long-term financing decision, the MNC must (1) determine the amount of funds needed, (2) forecast the price at which it can issue the bond, and (3) forecast periodic exchange rate values for the currency denominating the bond. This information can be used to determine the bond's financing costs, which can be compared with the financing costs the firm would incur using its home currency. Finally, the uncertainty of the actual financing costs to be

GLOBAL BOND MARKET QUOTATIONS

The prices and yields of government bonds in various countries are disclosed in *The Wall Street Journal,* as shown here. A bond index has been created for each country, which is monitored to measure returns in the local currency. The returns are measured as the percentage change from the previous day, from the previous month and from the beginning of the year. The index is also measured from a U.S. perspective to indicate the performance for U.S. investors. Notice how the year-to-date return for bonds

measured in local currency can vary substantially from the return for those same bonds measured from a U.S. perspective. The difference reflects the exchange rate effects on the returns to U.S. investors.

SOURCE: *The Wall Street Journal,* July 21, 1994, p. C22. Reprinted by permission of *The Wall Street Journal* © 1994, Dow Jones & Company, Inc. All rights reserved worldwide.

Total Rates of Return on International Bonds
In percent, based on Salomon Brothers' World Government Bond Index

| | — LOCAL CURRENCY TERMS — | | | | | — U.S. DOLLAR TERMS — | | | | |
	INDEX VALUE-a	1 DAY	1 MO	3 MOS	SINCE 12/31	INDEX VALUE-a	1 DAY	1 MO	3 MOS	SINCE 12/31
Japan	186.45	− 0.18	+ 1.32	+ 0.25	− 3.75	475.19	+ 0.09	+ 4.61	+ 4.86	+ 8.77
Britain	282.06	− 0.41	+ 3.56	− 0.02	− 8.16	377.24	− 1.10	+ 4.22	+ 4.23	− 3.84
Germany	196.49	− 0.38	+ 2.52	+ 1.12	− 1.44	395.56	− 0.97	+ 4.64	+ 9.38	+ 9.28
France	271.47	− 0.13	+ 3.37	− 0.44	− 4.45	488.54	− 0.57	+ 5.27	+ 7.99	+ 5.15
Canada	273.91	− 1.05	+ 1.98	− 1.94	− 7.99	261.17	− 1.08	+ 2.99	− 1.72	− 11.83
Netherlands	202.66	+ 0.02	+ 3.36	+ 1.22	− 2.96	410.63	− 0.68	+ 5.45	+ 9.60	+ 7.27
Non-U.S.	222.57	− 0.18	+ 2.10	− 0.20	− 3.86	404.32	− 0.42	+ 4.28	+ 5.51	+ 5.60
World*	238.98	− 0.28	+ 1.39	+ 0.16	− 3.60	319.72	− 0.43	+ 2.76	+ 3.71	+ 2.17

*Includes 14 international government bond markets   NA=Not Applicable   a-Dec. 31, 1984=100

incurred from foreign financing must be accounted for as well. To illustrate the borrower's analysis of financing with Eurobonds, an example is provided here.

Financing with a Stable Currency

Consider a U.S.-based MNC that needs to borrow $1,000,000 over a three-year period. This reflects a relatively small amount of funds and a short time period for bond financing, but will allow for a more simplified example. Assume the firm believes it can sell dollar-denominated bonds at par value if it provides a coupon rate of 14 percent. It also has the alternative of denominating the bonds in German marks to sell in the Eurobond market, in which case it would convert its borrowed marks to dollars to use as needed. Then, it would need to obtain marks annually to make the coupon payments. Assume the current exchange rate of the German mark is $.50. The firm needs DM2,000,000 (computed as $1,000,000/$.50 per mark) to obtain the $1 million it initially needs. The firm believes it can sell the mark-denominated bonds at par value if it provides a coupon rate of 10 percent.

The costs of both financing alternatives are illustrated in Exhibit 20.2. The outflow payment schedule of each financing method is provided here. The

EXHIBIT 20.2   Financing with Bonds Denominated in Dollars versus Marks

Financing Alternative	End of Year: 1	2	3	Annual Cost of Financing
1) Dollar-denominated bonds (coupon rate = 14%)	$140,000	$140,000	$1,140,000	14%
2) Mark-denominated bonds (coupon rate = 10%)	DM 200,000	DM 200,000	DM 2,200,000	—
Forecasted exchange rate of DM	$.50	$.50	$.50	—
Payment in dollars	$100,000	$100,000	$1,100,000	10%

outflow payments if the firm finances with dollar-denominated bonds are known. In addition, the number of marks needed at the end of each period is known if the firm finances with a mark-denominated bond. Yet, because the future exchange rate of the mark is uncertain, the number of dollars needed to obtain the marks each year is uncertain. If exchange rates do not change, the annual cost of financing with marks is 10 percent, which is less than the 14 percent annual cost of financing with dollars.

A comparison between the costs of financing with the two different currencies can be conducted by determining the annual cost of financing with each bond, from the U.S. firm's perspective. The comparison is shown in the last column of Exhibit 20.2. The annual cost of financing represents the discount rate at which the future outflow payments must be discounted so that their present value equals the amount borrowed. This is similar to the so-called yield to maturity, but is assessed here from the borrower's perspective rather than the investor's perspective. When the price at which the bonds are initially issued equals the par value and there is no exchange rate adjustment, the annual cost of financing is simply equal to the coupon rate. Thus, the annual cost of financing for the dollar-denominated bond would be 14 percent. If the mark's value were expected to change over time, the annual cost of financing could be easily determined with some calculators.

In our example, the mark-denominated debt appears to be less costly. However, it is unrealistic to assume that the mark will remain stable over time. Consequently, some MNCs may choose to issue dollar-denominated debt, even though it appears more costly. The potential savings from issuing bonds denominated in a foreign currency must be weighed against the potential risk of such a method. In this example, risk reflects the possibility that the mark will appreciate to a degree that causes mark-denominated bonds to be more costly than dollar-denominated bonds.

Financing with a Strong Currency

To illustrate the risk involved in financing with a bond denominated in marks, assume the mark has appreciated from $.50 to $.55 at the end of Year 1, to $.60 at

EXHIBIT 20.3 Financing with German Marks During a Strong-Mark Period

	End of Year:			Annual Cost of Financing
	1	2	3	
Payments in German marks	DM 200,000	DM 200,000	DM 2,200,000	—
Forecasted exchange rate of DM	$.55	$.60	$.65	—
Payments in dollars	$110,000	$120,000	$1,430,000	20.11%

the end of Year 2, and to $.65 by the end of Year 3. In this case, the payments made by the U.S. firm are displayed in Exhibit 20.3. From a comparison of the dollar outflows in this scenario with the outflows that would have occurred from a dollar-denominated bond, the risk to a firm from denominating a bond in a foreign currency is evident. The period of the last payment is particularly crucial for bond financing in foreign currencies. It includes not only the final coupon payment but the principal as well. Normally, exchange rates are more difficult to predict over longer time horizons. Thus, the time at which the principal is to be repaid is so far away that it may be virtually impossible to have a reliable estimate of the exchange rate at that time. For this reason, some firms may be uncomfortable issuing bonds denominated in foreign currencies.

Financing with a Weak Currency

Just as an appreciating currency increases the periodic outflow payments of the bond issuer, a depreciating currency will reduce outflow payments. To illustrate, consider the same information provided earlier on a three-year bond denominated in German marks. Also assume the mark depreciates from $.50 to $.48 at the end of Year 1, to $.46 at the end of Year 2, and to $.40 by the end of Year 3. In this case, the payments made by the U.S. firm are shown in Exhibit 20.4. When one compares the dollar outflows in this scenario with the outflows that would have occurred from a dollar-denominated bond (as shown in Exhibit 20.4), the potential savings from foreign financing are evident.

EXHIBIT 20.4 Financing with German Marks During a Weak-Mark Period

	End of Year:			Annual cost of financing
	1	2	3	
Payments in German marks	DM 200,000	DM 200,000	DM 2,200,000	—
Forecasted exchange rate of DM	$.48	$.46	$.40	—
Payments in dollars	$96,000	$92,000	$880,000	2.44%

Up to this point, three scenarios have been evaluated: (1) no change in the mark's exchange rate, (2) an appreciating mark, and (3) a depreciating mark. Exhibit 20.5 summarizes the results of the three scenarios, illustrating how exchange rates can influence the outflow payments from financing with bonds denominated in foreign currencies.

ACTUAL BOND FINANCING COSTS

Consider a U.S. firm that in January 1976 sold bonds denominated in British pounds with a par value of £10 million and a 10 percent coupon rate, thereby requiring coupon payments of £1 million at the end of each year. Assume this firm had no existing business in the United Kingdom, and therefore needed to exchange dollars for pounds to make the coupon payments each year. Exhibit 20.6 shows how the dollar payments would fluctuate each year according to the actual exchange rate at that time. In 1980, when the pound was worth $2.3950, the coupon payment was $2,395,000. Just four years later, the pound was worth $1.1592, causing the coupon payment to be $1,159,200. Thus, the firm's dollar coupon payment in 1984 was less that half of that paid in 1980, even though the number of pounds needed (£1 million) was the same each year. In general, the dollar coupon payments increased during the late 1980s (as the pound appreciated), and then declined during the early 1990s (as the pound depreciated). The strong influence of exchange rate movements on the cost of financing with bonds denominated in a foreign currency is very obvious in this exhibit. The actual effects would vary with the currency of denomination, since exchange rates do not move in perfect tandem against the dollar. Yet, the general trends in the financing costs are somewhat similar across currencies, because most exchange rate movements are positively correlated.

COMPARING BOND DENOMINATION ALTERNATIVES

A firm in need of long-term funds must decide which currency to use in denominating the bond. When considering a foreign currency for which it does not have future cash inflows, it must assess the potential strength or weakness of that currency. One approach to assessing the feasibility of each currency is to

EXHIBIT 20.5   Exchange Rate Effects on Outflow Payments for Mark-Denominated Bonds

Exchange Rate Scenario	Payment in Dollars At End of Year:			Annual cost of Financing
	1	2	3	
Scenario 1: No change in mark value	$100,000	$100,000	$1,100,000	10.00%
Scenario 2: Strong mark	$110,000	$120,000	$1,430,000	20.11%
Scenario 3: Weak mark	$ 96,000	$ 92,000	$ 880,000	2.44%

EXHIBIT 20.6
Actual Costs of Annual Financing With Pound-Denominated Bonds From a U.S. Perspective

End of Year	Exchange Rate	U.S. $ Needed to Cover Annual Coupon Payment of £1 million
1976	$1.7025	$1,702,500
1977	1.9200	1,920,000
1978	2.0435	2,043,500
1979	2.2145	2,214,500
1980	2.3950	2,395,000
1981	1.9280	1,928,000
1982	1.6200	1,620,000
1983	1.4525	1,452,500
1984	1.1592	1,159,200
1985	1.4445	1,444,500
1986	1.4745	1,474,500
1987	1.8570	1,857,000
1988	1.8095	1,809,500
1989	1.6055	1,605,500
1990	1.9255	1,925,500
1991	1.8707	1,870,700
1992	1.7827	1,782,700
1993	1.4925	1,492,500

forecast its exchange rate for each period for which an outflow payment would be provided to bondholders, and to determine the amount of the home currency needed to cover the payments according to those forecasted exchange rates. Because it is difficult to develop accurate point estimates of exchange rates, this approach can easily lead to poor decisions. Therefore, it is necessary to consider alternative techniques for projecting future exchange rates.

Use of Exchange Rate Probabilities

An alternative approach to projecting point estimates of future exchange rates is to develop a probability distribution for an exchange rate for each period for which payments are made to bondholders. In this case, the *expected value* of the exchange rate can be computed for each period by multiplying each possible exchange rate by its associated probability and totaling the products. Then, the exchange rate's expected value can be used to forecast the cash outflows necessary to pay bondholders over each period. The exchange rate's expected value may vary from one period to another. After developing probability distributions and computing the expected values, one can estimate the expected cost of financing and compare that with the cost of financing with a bond denominated in the home currency.

Using this approach, a single outflow estimate is derived for each payment period, and a single estimate is derived for the annual cost of financing over the life of the bond. Since this approach does not indicate the range of possible results that may occur, it is difficult to assess the probability that a bond denominated in a foreign currency will be more costly than a bond denominated in the home currency. It is possible to measure such risk through use of simulation, as explained next.

Use of Simulation

When a firm considers issuing bonds in a foreign currency, it can develop a probability distribution of the currency's exchange rate at the end of each year (or whenever coupons are to be paid). The U.S. firm can feed its probability distributions of exchange rates into a simulation computer program. Then, the program will randomly draw one of the possible values from the exchange rate distribution for the end of each year and determine the outflow payments necessary based on those exchange rates. Consequently, the cost of financing is determined. The procedure described up to this point represents one iteration. Next, the program will repeat the procedure by again randomly drawing one of the possible values from the exchange rate distribution at the end of each year. This will provide a new schedule of outflow payments reflecting those randomly selected exchange rates. The cost of financing for this second iteration is also determined. The simulation program continually repeats this procedure, perhaps 100 times or so (as many times as desired).

For every iteration, a possible scenario of future exchange rates is proposed, which is then used to determine the annual cost of financing if that scenario does occur. Thus, the simulation generates a probability distribution of annual financing costs that can then be compared with the known cost of financing if the

---

IN PRACTICE

CORPORATE USE OF THE EUROBOND MARKET

Many U.S.-based MNCs including Johnson & Johnson, Monsanto, RCA Corporation, Burroughs Corporation, General Electric, Procter & Gamble, Westinghouse, and IBM, utilize the Eurobond market as a source of funds. Some U.S.-based MNCs use the Eurobond market to issue bonds denominated in non-dollar currencies. While some of these bonds may be exposed to exchange rate risk, others are covered by incoming cash flows in the same currency. As an example, Sperry Corporation issued 10-year bonds in Switzerland. The coupon payments were to be made in Swiss francs. Because Swiss interest rates were lower than U.S. rates, Sperry was reducing its interest payments. While this strategy sometimes backfires on the issuer when the currency denominating the debt strengthens, Sperry had covered against

this possibility. Its Swiss subsidiaries used a portion of their dividends that they normally remitted to the parent to make interest payments on the bonds.

Some MNCs utilize a variety of currencies to denominate their currencies. For example, CPC International Inc. recently issued one set of bonds denominated in German marks and another set of bonds denominated in Swiss francs. Dow Chemical has bonds outstanding that are denominated in yen, marks, pounds, and even Kuwaiti dinar. Diversifying among currencies may be aimed at either reducing exchange rate risk (relative to the risk from denominating bonds in a single foreign currency) or matching the various incoming payments in various currencies.

bond is denominated in U.S. dollars (the home currency). Such a comparison will determine the probability that issuing bonds denominated in a foreign currency will be cheaper than dollar-denominated bonds.

FINANCING WITH FLOATING RATE EUROBONDS

Eurobonds are often issued with a floating, rather than fixed, coupon rate. This means the coupon rate will fluctuate over time in accordance with interest rates. For example, the coupon rate may somehow be tied to the **London Interbank Offer Rate (LIBOR),** which is a rate at which Eurobanks lend funds to each other. As LIBOR increases, so does the coupon rate of a floating rate bond. A floating coupon rate can be an advantage to the bond issuer during periods of decreasing interest rates, when otherwise the firm would be locked in at a higher coupon rate over the life of the bond. It can also be a disadvantage, during periods of rising interest rates.

When coupon rates are fixed, the only uncertain variable to be assessed for denominating a bond in a foreign currency is the exchange rate. If the coupon rate is floating, then projections are required not only for exchange rates but for interest rates as well. Recall that simulation can be used to examine the possible outcomes of bond financing based on various possible exchange rate scenarios. It can be used simultaneously to incorporate possible outcomes for the coupon rate over the life of the loan, and can develop a probability distribution of annual costs of financing.

EXCHANGE RATE RISK OF FOREIGN BONDS

When financing in bonds, one must assess not only the potential savings from denominating a bond in a foreign currency, but the risk resulting from exchange rate fluctuations as well. Not all foreign currencies exhibit the same risk. From a U.S. borrower's perspective, a bond denominated in Canadian dollars is less risky than a bond denominated in German marks (assuming it has no offsetting position in either of these currencies). This is because the Canadian dollar exhibits less fluctuation against the U.S. dollar over time, and therefore is less likely to deviate far from its projected future exchange rate. If all other characteristics of two bonds denominated in different currencies are similar, a U.S. borrower should prefer the bond denominated in the currency that is more stable.

Hedging Exchange Rate Risk

The exchange rate risk from financing with bonds in foreign currencies can be hedged with offsetting cash inflows in that currency, or with forward contracts, as explained below.

Offsetting Cash Inflows.   Some firms may have inflow payments in particular currencies, which could offset outflow payments related to bond financing. Thus, it may be possible to finance with bonds denominated in a foreign currency that exhibits a lower coupon rate without becoming exposed to exchange rate risk. Yet, it is unlikely that a firm would be able to perfectly match the timing and amount of the outflows in the foreign currency denominating the bond to the inflows in that currency. Therefore, some exposure to exchange rate fluctuations will exist. The exposure can be substantially reduced though, if the firm receives inflows in the particular currency denominating the bond. This can help to stabilize the firm's cash flow. Numerous MNCs, including Allied-Signal Inc. and Coca-Cola Company, issue bonds in some of the foreign currencies that they receive from operations.

Even when a firm does not expect to be receiving foreign currency inflows, it can sometimes issue bonds denominated in foreign currencies to stabilize net cash flows. For example, consider a U.S. firm that often exports products to Germany with the price denominated in U.S. dollars. If the dollar strengthens, exports become expensive to German purchasers, thereby discouraging their demand for the U.S. products. This would normally reduce cash inflows. However, if a mark-denominated bond had been previously issued, a stronger dollar would require fewer dollars to obtain the sufficient number of marks to make coupon payments, and this would reduce the cash outflows. Overall, the reduction in both cash inflows and outflows may have no significant impact on net cash flow. If the dollar weakened instead, the outflow payments to cover bond coupon payments would increase. The increased outflow payments would be at least partially offset, however, by increased cash flows due to an increased export business by the U.S. firm (resulting from the weak dollar).

Forward Contracts. When a bond denominated in a foreign currency has a lower coupon rate than the firm's home currency, the firm may consider issuing bonds denominated in that currency and simultaneously hedging its exchange rate risk through the forward market. Because the forward market can sometimes accommodate requests of five years or longer, such an approach may be possible. The firm could arrange to purchase the foreign currency forward for each time at which payments are required. However, the forward rate for each horizon will most likely be above the spot rate. Consequently, hedging these future outflow payments may not be less costly than the outflow payments needed if a dollar-denominated bond were issued. The relationship implied here is similar to interest rate parity discussed in earlier chapters, except that the point of view in this chapter is long-term rather than short-term.

LONG-TERM FINANCING IN MULTIPLE CURRENCIES

Up to this point, discussion has focused on choosing the most feasible currency for a bond. In some cases, the appropriate selection for a borrower may be not a single currency or bond, but a portfolio of currencies. Since the lifetime of bonds is too long to single out any particular currency as being safe, a portfolio of diversified currencies could reduce the risk incurred by the bond issuer. For example, a U.S. firm may denominate bonds in several foreign currencies rather than a single foreign currency, so that substantial appreciation of any one particular currency will not drastically increase the number of dollars necessary to cover the financing payments. To illustrate the potential advantage of bond diversification, consider the example of an MNC based in the U.S. that plans to issue bonds and has considered four alternatives:

1. Issue bonds denominated in U.S. dollars
2. Issue bonds denominated in Japanese yen
3. Issue bonds denominated in Swiss francs
4. Issue some bonds denominated in Japanese yen and some bonds denominated in Swiss francs.

Assume the MNC has no net exposure in either Japanese yen or Swiss francs. Also assume the coupon rate for a U.S. dollar-denominated bond is 14 percent, while for a yen- or franc-denominated bond the coupon rate is 8 percent. It is expected that any of these bonds could be sold at par value.

There is a substantial difference here between the coupon rates of the dollar-denominated bonds and those of bonds denominated in foreign currencies. If the Swiss franc appreciates against the U.S. dollar, the actual financing cost from issuing franc-denominated bonds may be higher than that of the dollar-denominated bonds. If the Japanese yen appreciates substantially against the U.S. dollar, the actual financing cost from issuing yen-denominated bonds may be higher than that of the dollar-denominated bonds. If the exchange rates of the Swiss franc and Japanese yen move in opposite directions against the U.S. dollar, then both types of bonds could not simultaneously be more costly than dollar-denominated bonds, so financing with both type of bonds would almost ensure that the overall financing cost to the U.S. firm would be less than the cost from issuing a dollar-denominated bond.

In reality, there is no guarantee the exchange rates of the Swiss franc and Japanese yen will move in opposite directions. However, if the currency movements are not highly correlated, it is unlikely that both currencies will simultaneously appreciate to an extent that will offset their lower coupon rate advantages. Therefore, financing in bonds denominated in more than one foreign currency can increase the probability that the overall cost of foreign financing will be less than that financing with the domestic currency (U.S. dollars, in our example). This example involves only two foreign currencies. In reality, a firm may consider several currencies that exhibit lower interest rates and issue a portion of its bonds in each of these currencies. Such a strategy can increase the other costs (advertising, printing, etc.) of issuing bonds, but those costs may be offset by a reduction in cash outflows to bondholders.

Currency Cocktail Bonds

There is a method by which a firm can finance in several currencies without issuing various types of bonds (thus avoiding higher transaction costs). It can develop a **currency cocktail bond,** denominated in not one, but a mixture (or "cocktail") of currencies. Within the Eurobond market, a cocktail bond may be preferred over the single-currency bond, since it can reduce exchange rate risk.

A currency cocktail simply reflects a multi-currency unit of account. Several currency cocktails have been developed to denominate international bonds, and some have already been used in this manner. Two of the more popular currency cocktails are the **European Currency Unit** (ECU) and the **Special Drawing Right** (SDR). The ECU is linked to the weighted currency values of European currencies, and its value changes only when the values of component currencies change. Because the ECU is determined by the values of European currencies, European Monetary System members are the major users.

The Special Drawing Right (SDR) composite was originally devised as an alternative foreign reserve asset, but is now used to denominate bonds and bank deposits and to price various services. The SDR is presently defined as a weighted composite of the U.S. dollar, German mark, Japanese yen, British pound, and French franc. The weight assigned to each currency is based on that currency's relative importance in international trade and finance.

USING SWAPS TO HEDGE FINANCING COSTS

When MNCs issue bonds that expose them to interest rate or exchange rate risk, they may use *swaps* to hedge the risk. **Interest rate swaps** can be used to hedge interest rate risk, while **currency swaps** can be used to hedge exchange rate risk.

Interest Rate Swaps

As the popularity of the Eurobond market has increased, so have interest rate swaps, which enable a firm to exchange fixed rate payments for variable rate payments. The interest rate swaps are used by bond issuers because they may reconfigure the future bond payments to a more preferable structure. For example, consider two firms that desire to issue bonds:

- Quality Company is a highly rated firm that prefers to borrow at a variable interest rate.
- Risky Company is a low-rated firm that prefers to borrow at a fixed interest rate.

Assume the rates these companies would pay for issuing either variable-rate or fixed-rate Eurobonds are as follows:

	Fixed-rate Bond	Variable-rate Bond
Quality Company	9%	LIBOR + ½%
Risky Company	10½%	LIBOR + 1%

LIBOR, the London interbank offer rate, changes over time. Based on the information given, Quality Company has a comparative advantage when issuing either fixed rate or variable rate bonds, but more of one with fixed rate bonds. Quality Company could issue fixed rate bonds while Risky Company issues variable rate bonds; then Quality could provide variable rate payments to Risky in exchange for fixed rate payments.

Assume that Quality Company negotiates with Risky Company to provide variable rate payments at LIBOR + ½ percent, in exchange for fixed rate payments of 9½ percent. The interest rate swap arrangement is shown in Exhibit 20.7. Quality Company benefits, since its fixed rate payments received on the swap exceed the payments owed to bondholders by ½ percent. Its variable rate payments to Risky Company are the same as what it would have paid if it issued variable rate bonds. Risky Company is receiving LIBOR + ½ percent on the swap, which is ½ percent less than what it must pay on its variable rate bonds. Yet, it is making fixed payments of 9½ percent, which is 1 percent less than what it would

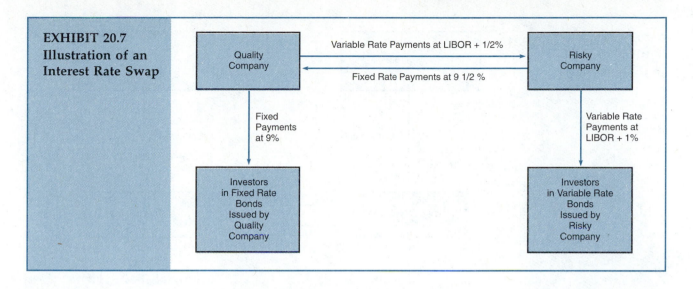

EXHIBIT 20.7 Illustration of an Interest Rate Swap

have paid if it issued fixed rate bonds. Overall, it saves ½ percent per year of financing costs.

Two limitations of the swap just described are worth mentioning. First, there is a cost of time and resources associated with searching for a suitable swap candidate and negotiating the swap terms. Second, there is a risk to each swap participant that the counter participant could default on payments. For this reason, financial intermediaries are usually involved in swap agreements. They match up participants and also assume the default risk involved. For their role, they charge a fee, which would reduce the estimated benefits in this example, but their involvement is critical to effectively match up swap participants and reduce concern about default risk.

Currency Swaps

Another swap used to complement bond issues, the **currency swap,** enables firms to exchange currencies at periodic intervals. Consider a U.S. firm, called Miller Company, that desires to issue a German mark-denominated bond, since it could make payments with mark inflows to be generated from existing operations. However, this firm is not well known to investors that would consider purchasing mark-denominated bonds. Also consider a firm, called Beck Company, that desires to issue dollar-denominated bonds because its inflow payments are mostly in dollars. However, it is not well known to the investors that would purchase these bonds. If Miller is known within the dollar-denominated market while Beck is known within the mark-denominated market, the following transactions would be appropriate. Miller could issue dollar-denominated bonds, while Beck issued mark-denominated bonds. Miller could provide mark payments to Beck in exchange for dollar payments. This swap of currencies would allow the companies to make payments to their respective bondholders without concern about exchange rate risk. This type of currency swap is illustrated in Exhibit 20.8

The large commercial banks that serve as financial intermediaries for currency swaps sometimes take positions. That is, they may agree to swap fixed

**EXHIBIT 20.8
Illustration of a
Currency Swap**

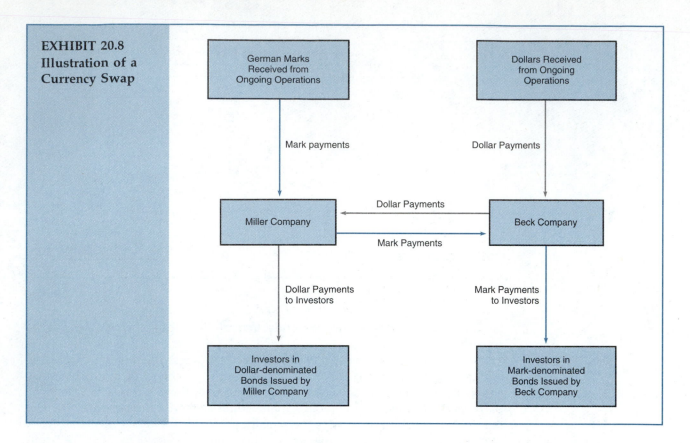

**EXHIBIT 20.9
Illustration of a
Parallel Loan**

1. Loans are
simultaneously
provided by parent of
each MNC to
subsidiary of the other
MNC.
2. At a specified time
in the future, the loans
are repaid in the same
currency that was
borrowed.

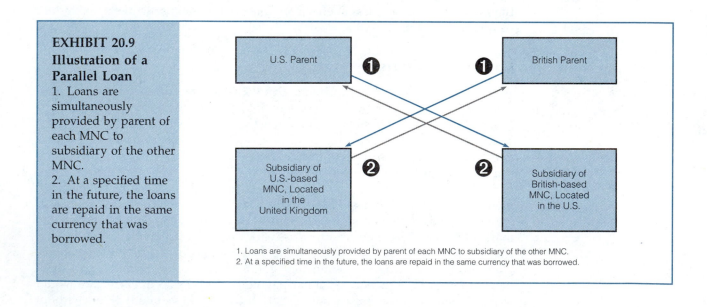

1. Loans are simultaneously provided by parent of each MNC to subsidiary of the other MNC.
2. At a specified time in the future, the loans are repaid in the same currency that was borrowed.

payments for variable payments or swap currencies with firms, rather than simply search for suitable swap candidates.

An alternative method by which firms could obtain financing in a foreign currency is the parallel (or back-to-back) loan, which represents simultaneous loans provided by two parties with an agreement to repay at a specified point in the future. For example, assume that the parent of a U.S.-based MNC desires to expand its British subsidiary, while the parent of a British-based MNC desires to expand its American subsidiary. The British parent provides pounds to the British subsidiary of the U.S.-based MNC, while the U.S. parent provides dollars to the American subsidiary of the British-based MNC (as shown in Exhibit 20.9). At the time specified by the loan contract, the loans are repaid. The British subsidiary of the U.S.-based MNC uses pound-denominated revenues to repay the British company that provided the loan. At the same time, the American subsidiary of the British-based MNC uses dollar-denominated revenues to repay the U.S. company that provided the loan.

SUMMARY

- Some MNCs may consider long-term financing in foreign currencies to offset future cash inflows in those currencies, and therefore reduce exposure to exchange rate risk. Other MNCs may consider long-term financing in foreign currencies to reduce financing costs. If a foreign interest rate is relatively low or the foreign currency borrowed depreciates over the financing period, long-term financing in that currency can result in low financing costs.

- An MNC can assess the feasibility of financing in foreign currencies by applying exchange rate forecasts to the periodic coupon payments and the principal payment. In this way, it determines the amount of its home currency that is necessary per period to cover the payments. The annual cost of financing can be estimated by determination of the discount rate that equates the periodic payments on the foreign financing to the initial amount borrowed (as measured in the domestic currency). The discount rate derived from this exercise represents the annual cost of financing in the foreign currency, which can be compared to the cost of domestic financing. The cost of long-term financing in a foreign currency is dependent on the currency's exchange rate over the financing period, and therefore is uncertain. Thus, the MNC will not automatically finance with a foreign currency that has a lower interest rate, since its exchange rate forecasts are subject to error. For this reason, the MNC may estimate the costs of foreign financing under various exchange rate scenarios over time.

- For Eurobonds that have floating interest rates, the coupon payment to be paid to investors is uncertain. This creates another uncertain variable (along with exchange rates) in estimating the amount in the firm's domestic currency which is required per period to make the payments. This uncertainty can be accounted for through estimation of the coupon payment amount necessary under various interest rate scenarios over time. Then, with the use of these estimates, the amount of the firm's domestic currency required to make the payments can be estimated, based on various exchange rate scenarios over time.

SELF-TEST FOR CHAPTER 20 _____

(Answers are provided in Appendix A in the back of the text.)

1. Explain why a firm may issue a bond denominated in a currency different from its home currency to finance local operations. Explain the risk involved.

2. A U.S.-based MNC is considering the issuance of a 20-year Swiss franc-denominated bond. The proceeds are to be converted to German marks to support the firm's German operations. The MNC has no Swiss operations, but prefers to issue the bond in francs rather than marks because the coupon rate is 2 percentage points lower. Explain the risk involved in this strategy. Do you think the risk here is greater or less than it would be if the bond proceeds were used to finance U.S. operations? Why?

3. Some large companies based in Latin American countries could borrow funds (through issuing bonds or borrowing from U.S. banks) at an interest rate that would be substantially less than the interest rates in their own countries. Assuming that they are perceived to be creditworthy in the U.S., why might they may still prefer to borrow in their local countries when financing local projects (even if they incur interest rates of 80 percent or more)?

4. A respected economist just announced a prediction that even though German inflation would not rise, German interest rates would rise consistently over the next five years. Paxson Co., a U.S. firm with no foreign operations, has recently issued a German mark-denominated bond to finance U.S. operations. It chose the mark denomination because the coupon rate was low. Its vice-president stated, "I'm not concerned about the prediction because we issued fixed rate bonds, and are therefore insulated from risk." Do you agree? Explain.

5. Long-term interest rates in some Latin American countries commonly exceed 100 percent annually. Offer your opinion on why these interest rates are so much higher than those of industrialized countries, and why some projects in these countries are feasible for local firms, even though the cost of funding the projects is so high.

QUESTIONS _____

1. What factors should be considered by a U.S. firm that plans to issue a floating rate Eurobond?

2. What is the advantage of using simulation to assess the bond financing position?

3. Explain the difference in the cost of financing with foreign currencies during the 1981-1984 (strong dollar) period, versus the 1990-1993 (weak dollar) period for a U.S. firm.

4. Explain how a U.S.-based MNC issuing bonds denominated in German marks may be able to offset a portion of this exchange rate risk.

5. Is the risk of issuing a floating rate Eurobond higher or lower than the risk of issuing a fixed rate Eurobond? Explain.

6. Columbia corporation is a U.S. company with no foreign currency cash flows. It plans to issue either (1) a bond denominated in German marks with a fixed interest rate, or (2) a bond denominated in U.S. dollars with a floating interest rate. It estimates its periodic dollar cash flows for each bond. Which bond do you think would have greater uncertainty surrounding these future dollar cash flows? Explain.

7. Why would a U.S. firm consider issuing bonds denominated in multiple currencies?

8. Why is the ECU bond popular?

9. Assume you are assessing the potential cost of financing with Eurobonds denominated in a foreign currency. What is the most critical point in time at which the exchange rate will have the greatest impact?

10. How would an investing firm differ from a borrowing firm in the features (i.e., interest rate and currency's future exchange rates) it would prefer a floating rate Eurobond to exhibit?

11. Assume that Seminole Inc. considers issuing a mark-denominated bond at its present coupon rate of 7 percent, even though it has no incoming mark cash flows to cover the bond payments. It is attracted to the low financing rate, since dollar bonds issued in the United States would have a coupon rate of 12 percent. Assume that either type of bond would have a four-year maturity and could be issued at par value. Seminole needs to borrow $10 million. Therefore, it will issue either dollar bonds with a par value of $10 million or mark bonds with a par value of DM20 million. The spot rate of the mark is $.50. Seminole has forecasted the mark's value at the end of each of the next four years, when coupon payments are to be paid:

End of Year	Exchange rate of DM
1	$.52
2	.56
3	.58
4	.53

Determine the expected annual cost of financing with marks. Should Seminole Corporation issue bonds denominated in dollars or in marks? Explain.

12. Assume that Hurricane Inc. is a U.S. company that exports products to Great Britain, invoiced in dollars. It also exports products to Germany, invoiced in dollars. It presently has no cash outflows in foreign currencies, and it plans to issue bonds in the near future. It could likely issue bonds at par value in (1) dollars, with a coupon rate of 12 percent, (2) marks, with a coupon rate of 9 percent, or (3) pounds, with a coupon rate of 15 percent. It expects that the mark and the pound will strengthen over time. How could Hurricane revise its invoicing policy and make its bond denomination decision to achieve low financing costs without excessive exposure to exchange rate fluctuations?

CASE: EURO DISNEY'S FINANCING DILEMMA

Restructuring of Euro Disney Hits Bond Snag

French Debtholders Pose Obstacle and Demand Rescue by Walt Disney

BY PETER GUMBEL
Staff Reporter of THE WALL STREET JOURNAL

PARIS—Talks aimed at salvaging the troubled **Euro Disney** SCA theme park have run into an unexpected obstacle even before they start: angry French bondholders, who are demanding representation at the negotiations and want **Walt Disney** Co. to come to their rescue.

Such demands would normally get short shrift in France, where small investors rarely have enough clout to defend their interests. But because of an odd discrepancy in the terms attached to an issue do Euro Disney bonds, bankers familiar with the situation say the holders in this case pose a particularly complex legal problem that could hamper the restructuring talks.

At the same time, credit-rating agencies and analysts have been examining the exposure of key banks involved in Euro Disney lending. While the risks generally seem well spread, they are concluding that some French banks, in particular recently privatized **Banque Nationale de Paris,** could face embarrassing losses.

The discrepancy concerns four billion French francs ($676.4 million) of convertible bonds issued in July 1991. The English-language text of the prospectus that was used for its launch in the London market stipulates that the terms can only be changed if there is unanimity of the holders. The French text, however, says that only a majority of holders is needed.

The difference reflects the lack of consistency in European issuing practices. But unless the bondholders can somehow be left out of the restructuring altogether, which seems unlikely, the dissimilar language could become a legal quagmire, some fear. "Dealing with the bondholders could be very problematic," admits an official at one big creditor bank involved in the negotiations. He adds that the restructuring itself promises to be anything but easy, not least because of the high stakes involved and the relatively short time in which the problems have to be resolved.

A Report for Creditors

Euro Disney's 60 creditor banks are scheduled to receive tomorrow a preliminary report from auditors KPMG Peat Marwick assessing both the resort's financial situation and its revamped business strategy. Formal negotiations with both Euro Disney and Walt Disney are expected to start a few days later, once the banks have agreed on their tactics.

Euro Disney's future viability depends on an agreement between the parties to reduce its 21 billion francs in debt, probably by at least 50%, through an expected mixture of debt write-downs and an injection of fresh capital.

At the moment, the park's revenue is more than eaten up by high interest charges, which amounted to about 1.7 billion francs in the last fiscal year, ended Sept. 30. Walt Disney, which owns 49% of Euro Disney SCA, the European operating company for the park, has said it is only prepared to continue funding the resort to the end of March.

The bondholders are represented by a French association headed by Colette Neuville, an activist who often campaigns for the rights of minority holders. A legal report for the bondholders issued yesterday pressed for them to be represented at the talks, and Georges Berlioz, the lawyer who drafted the report, threatened legal action if they were excluded. "If we are not invited, we will litigate our way in," Mr. Berlioz said in a telephone interview.

On one crucial point, Mr. Berlioz's report echoed demands made by the creditor banks themselves, namely that Walt Disney should carry much of the burden for an eventual restructuring.

Under Euro Disney's complex financial structure, involving a web of shareholdings and cross-holdings, Walt Disney largely limited its direct financial responsibility for the project. For example, most of the resort's debt isn't owed directly by Euro Disney to the creditor banks, but via a number of finance companies that own the park and its six hotels—and with which Euro Disney has no direct shareholder links.

While Walt Disney thus has only limited, legally enforceable ties to the resort, the bondholders and the banks insist that it nonetheless remains responsible. Creditor bankers, in the words of one senior official "want an asymmetrical sharing of the pain"—with Walt Disney bearing the brunt.

Walt Disney Keeps Mum

The U.S. company has avoided making public comments on the restructuring talks, and a spokesman wasn't available to comment on specific issues relating either to the bondholders or to a possible sharing of the restructuring burden.

Given the complexities of the talks, banking analysts and credit-rating agencies have been taking a close look at the risks to creditors, especially in the event that talks fail and Euro Disney closes-the still unlikely worst-case scenario.

French banks account for about 50% of Euro Disney's 14 billion francs in bank debt. By far the biggest creditor is France's state-owned **Caisse des Depots & Consigna- tions,** which has outstanding loans in excess of 4 billion francs. The organization, however, is the government's financing arm, and thus isn't usually scrutinized like other commercial banks.

Of the other lenders, rating agencies identify four main creditors: Banque Nationale de Paris, **Credit Agricole, Banque Indosuez** and the **Banques Populaire** group. Although the banks aren't divulging the extent of their loans, analysts say their exposure ranges between about 500 million francs and one billion francs each.

Behind this group, with a substantially smaller exposure, come several Japanese, British and German banks. And at least two U.S. banks—**Citicorp**'s Citibank unit and **J. P. Morgan** & Co.—also have outstanding loans. The banks all declined official comment.

"Obviously we are concerned," says Samuel S. Theodore, vice president of rating agency Moody's France SA, "but for most of the banks we don't feel that this exposure itself is going to be a rating event." Adds Scott Bugie, an analyst at Standard and

Continued

CASE: EURO DISNEY'S FINANCING DILEMMA

Continued

Poor's Corp. in Paris: "The risk is well spread. It's not going to bring any bank down."

Nonetheless, the risk of substantial losses for the main French banks involved is causing some concern. In particular, analysts say, a possible failure of Euro Disney would be severely embarrassing for Banque Nationale de Paris, which was privatized by the French government late last year.

Just this month, Moody's placed BNP under review for a possible downgrading, for reasons not connected to Euro Disney. Analysts believe the bank hasn't yet made any provisions for possible Euro Disney losses. BNP officials say privately that Chairman Michel Pebereau is concerned not to allow Euro Disney to drag down earnings so soon after privatization.

Source: *The Wall Street Journal* (February 1, 1994), p. A11. Reprinted by permission of *The Wall Street Journal* © 1994 Dow Jons & Company, Inc. All Rights Reserved Worldwide.

Questions

1. When bonds are issued across countries, and a separate prospectus is needed per country, the provisions may be inconsistent. Explain how the provisions of Euro Disney's convertible bonds were more complicated because of the discrepancies in the prospectuses.

2. Who is responsible to incur the losses associated with Euro Disney's financial problems? The creditors? Walt Disney (the parent)? Explain the controversy and offer your opinion.

3. The case of Euro Disney illustrates how disagreements can occur among creditors about provisions of the credit (bonds, loans) and also between the parent of a firm and the creditors. Why are these disagreements more likely for MNCs than for purely domestic firms? Is there a solution to avoid such disagreements?

DEVIL VCR CORPORATION
Long-Term Financing

Devil VCR Corporation is a U.S.-based company that produces videocassette recorders. It plans a major exporting program in Germany, with a focus on the East German consumers. Three years ago, Devil established a production facility in the United Kingdom, since it sells VCRs there. Devil plans to expand capacity there and will use that facility to produce the VCRs that are to be marketed in East Germany. The VCRs will be sold to distributors in East Germany, invoiced in German marks. The transportation expenses will be substantially less than they would if the VCRs were built in the United States. If the exporting program is very successful, Devil Corporation will probably build a facility in Germany, but plans to wait at least ten years.

Prior to this exporting program, Devil Corporation decided to develop a hedging strategy to hedge any cash flows to the U.S. parent. Its plan is to issue bonds to finance the entire investment in the exporting program. Virtually all expenses associated with this program are denominated in pounds. Yet, the revenue generated by the program is denominated in marks. Any revenue above and beyond expenses is to be remitted to the United States on an annual basis. Aside from the exporting program, the British subsidiary will generate just enough in cash flows to cover expenses, and therefore will not be remitting any earnings to the parent. Devil Corporation is considering three different ways to finance the program for ten years:

- Issue ten-year mark-denominated bonds at par value; coupon rate = 11%.
- Issue ten-year pound-denominated bonds at par value; coupon rate = 14%.
- Issue ten-year U.S. dollar-denominated bonds at par value; coupon rate = 11%.

The present exchange rates are £1 = $2, $1 = DM 2, and £1 = DM 4. The British subsidiary would need £20 million to expand the facility, and £2 million per year to produce the extra VCRs. The sale of VCR exports is expected to generate DM25 million per year. Devil can use the forward market if necessary. The forward rates for the next five years are as follows:

CASE PROBLEM	# DEVIL VCR CORPORATION (CONTINUED)

	£/$ Forward Rate		DM/$ Forward Rate		£/DM Forward Rate	
End of Year	Exchanging $ for £	Exchanging £ for $	Exchanging $ for DM	Exchanging DM for $	Exchanging DM for £	Exchanging £ for DM
1	$1.97	$1.95	$.500	$.495	DM 3.94	DM 3.92
2	1.94	1.91	.500	.495	3.82	3.79
3	1.90	1.86	.500	.490	3.80	3.76
4	1.87	1.83	.500	.490	3.74	3.69
5	1.83	1.78	.505	.485	3.66	3.60

a) Assume Devil VCR Corporation would prefer to minimize exchange rate risk if possible. Describe how Devil could issue bonds in a manner that would minimize exchange rate risk.

b) Estimate the earnings to be received by the U.S. parent (in dollars) as a result of the export project over the next five years. Assume Devil VCR Corporation desires to hedge any expected currency transactions when developing your estimates. Also assume no tax effects.

c) Explain why the exporting program will still likely create exchange rate risk (specifically, transaction exposure) for Devil VCR Corporation.

PROJECT

Review the annual report of an MNC of your choice. Did the MNC issue any bonds denominated in foreign currencies? Does the MNC generate cash flows in that currency that could be used to cover the coupon payments? (Give your opinion, if this is not clear from the annual report.) Summarize any statements made regarding the MNC's decision to finance with U.S. dollars versus foreign currencies.

REFERENCES

Adler Michael, and Bernard Dumas. "The Exposure of Long-Term Foreign Currency Bonds." *Journal of Financial and Quantitative Analysis* (November 1980), pp. 973–994.

"Coping with Globally Integrated Financial Markets." *Quarterly Review,* Federal Reserve Bank of New York (Winter 1987), pp. 1–5.

Fatemi, Ali. "The Effect of International Diversification on Corporate Financing Policy," *Journal of Business Research* (January 1988), pp. 17–30.

Finnerty, Joseph E., Thomas Schneeweis, and Shantoram P. Hegde. "Interest Rates in the Eurobond Markets." *Journal of Financial and Quantitative Analysis* (September 1980), pp. 743–755.

Kidwell, David S., M. Wayne Marr, and G. Rodney Thompson. "Eurodollar Bonds: Alternative Financing for U.S. Companies." *Financial Management* (Winter 1985), pp. 18–27.

Liu, Y. Angela, and L. Paul Hsueh. "Tax Effect on the Debt Denomination Decision of Multinational Projects." *Journal of International Business Studies* (First Quarter 1993), pp. 145–154.

Madura, Jeff, and Ann Marie Whyte. "International Linkage of Credit Risk Among Countries." *International Review of Economics and Business* (March 1991), pp. 255–265.

Madura, Jeff, and Richard Fosberg. "The Impact of Financing Sources on Multinational Projects." *Journal of Financial Research* (Spring 1990), pp. 61–69.

Mahajan, Arvind, and Donald R. Fraser. "Dollar Eurobond and U.S. Bond Pricing." *Journal of International Business Studies* (Summer 1986), pp. 22–36.

Park, Y. S. "Currency Swaps as a Long-term International Financing Technique," *Journal of International Business Studies* (Winter 1984), pp. 47–54.

Rhee, S. Ghon, Rosita P. Chang, and Peter E. Koveos. "The Currency-of-Denomination Decision for Debt Financing." *Journal of International Business Studies* (Fall 1985), pp. 143–150.

CHAPTER 21

GLOBAL STRATEGIC PLANNING

A common saying is that in this world, only two things are certain: death and taxes. While taxes will be imposed on earnings, the amount of taxes may depend on the multinational corporation's (MNC's) corporate tax planning. The specific objectives of this chapter are to

- describe international tax characteristics that affect an MNC's tax liability,
- explain how MNCs may use transfer pricing to reduce taxes,
- describe the types of financial policies enacted by MNCs that are subject to international tax laws,
- explain why some corporate policy decisions should be made on a centralized level rather than a subsidiary level, and
- explain the need for an MNC of an efficient accounting system.

INTERNATIONAL TAX CHARACTERISTICS

Tax laws can vary among countries in many ways, but any type of tax causes before-tax cash flows to vary from after-tax cash flows. Since the MNC is most concerned with after-tax cash flows, anticipated taxes must be accounted for.

Each country varies in the way it generates tax revenues. The United States relies on corporate and individual income taxes for federal revenues. Other countries may depend more on the *value-added tax* (VAT) or excise taxes. Since each country has its own philosophy on whom to tax and how much, it is not surprising that among countries corporations may be treated unequally in terms of taxes. Because systems and tax rates are unique to each country, corporations need to compare the various tax provisions of each country. The more important characteristics of a country to be considered within an MNC's international tax assessment are (1) corporate income taxes, (2) withholding taxes, (3) provision for carrybacks and carryforwards, (4) tax treaties, and (5) tax credits. A discussion of each characteristic follows.

Corporate Income Taxes

In general, countries impose taxes on corporate income generated within their borders, even if the parents of those corporations are based in other countries. Each country has its unique corporate income tax laws. The United States, for example, taxes the worldwide income of U.S. "persons"—a term that includes corporations. However, as a general rule, foreign income of a foreign subsidiary of a U.S. company is not taxed until it is transferred to the U.S. parent by payment of dividends or a liquidation distribution. This is the concept of deferral. There are statutory exceptions to deferral, such as when a controlled foreign subsidiary earns tax-haven income in excess of a certain percentage of gross earnings or when it invests in U.S. property. Such exceptions to deferral are not important to this discussion and are mentioned only to make the reader aware of their existence.

An MNC planning direct foreign investment in foreign countries must determine how the anticipated earnings from direct foreign investment will be affected. Tax rates vary among countries. As an extreme example, some countries in the Caribbean have attempted to entice direct foreign investment by MNCs through programs that exempt profits from federal income taxes. At the other extreme, some European countries impose corporate tax rates of about 50 percent (note that health care is usually subsidized by the government in these countries). Given differences in tax deductions, depreciation, business subsidies, and other factors, corporate tax differentials cannot be measured simply by comparing quoted tax rates across countries.

Corporate tax rates can also differ within a country, depending on whether the entity is a domestic corporation. Also, if it is considered to have a permanent establishment in a country, an unregistered foreign corporation may be subject to that country's tax laws on income earned within its borders. Generally, a permanent establishment includes an office or fixed place of business or a specified kind of agency (*independent* agents are normally excluded) through which active and continuous business is conducted. In some cases, the tax depends on the industry, or on the form of business used (corporation, branch, partnership, etc.).

Withholding Taxes

Various fund outflows from a subsidiary can be subject to withholding taxes by the host country. MNCs interested in direct foreign investment must account for this analysis. While a withholding tax does not affect a subsidiary's cash flows, it can affect after-tax cash flows to the parent (since the government of the host country may tax a portion of the transferred funds). As with corporate tax rates, the withholding tax rate can vary substantially among countries. Even within a country, the withholding tax can vary according to the purpose of the fund transfer. Dividends, interest, rents, and royalty fees are often paid by a subsidiary to the parent. Each of these fund transfers may be subject to a different withholding tax rate. Withholding taxes can be reduced by income tax treaties (discussed shortly).

Provision for Carrybacks and Carryforwards

Negative earnings from operations can often be carried back or forward to offset earnings in other years. The laws pertaining to these so-called **net operating loss carrybacks** and **carryforwards** can vary among countries. An MNC generally does not plan to generate negative earnings in foreign countries. Yet, if negative earnings occur, it is desirable to be able to use them to offset other years of positive earnings. Most foreign countries do not allow negative earnings to be carried back. Yet, virtually all countries allow some flexibility in carrying losses forward. For U.S. tax purposes, excess foreign tax credits generated in one year can be carried back for two years and then forward for up to five years to offset U.S. tax on foreign source income. In the case of a carryback, an amended U.S. return is filed and a refund of previously paid U.S. tax is requested.

Tax rates are shown in Exhibit 21.1 for several countries. This exhibit shows the extent to which these tax rates can vary among host countries.

EXHIBIT 21.1
Host Country Taxes Imposed on Income Earned by U.S. Firms

The source for many of these corporate tax rates is *Corporate Taxes*, published by the accounting firm Price Waterhouse, 1993. The tax rates may vary among companies, since tax incentives are available in many countries, which can significantly reduce the tax liability. Consult a tax guide such as the one identified above for more details on tax rates.

Country	Corporate Income Tax Rate[a]	Withholding Tax Rate on: Dividends	Interest	Royalties
Argentina	30%	0%	12%	18–24%
Australia	39	15	10	10
Austria	30	25	0	20
Bahamas	0	0	0	0
Barbados	40	15	12	15
Brazil	25	15	25	25
Bulgaria	40	5–15	10	5
Canada	32	10–15	15	10
China	30	10	10	10
France	33	5	0	0–5
Germany	46	5–25	0–25	0
Greece	35	0	0	0
Hong Kong	17	0	0	0
Hungary	40	15	0	0
Italy	36	5–15	12–15	5–10
Jamaica	33	10–15	12	10
Japan	37	10–15	10	10
Malaysia	34	0	0	15
Mexico	35	5–15	10–15	10
New Zealand	38	15	10	10
Norway	28	15	0	0
Russian Federation	32	0	0	0
Singapore	30	0	30	30
Spain	35	10	10	10
Sweden	30	15	0	0
Switzerland	22–35	5–15	5	0
Thailand	30	10	15	15
United Kingdom	33	0	0	0

Tax Treaties

The tax rates discussed so far may give the impression that by the time the parent receives any cash flow from its subsidiaries, there is not much left. Moreover, the parent's government could then tax the remaining earnings, which would reduce the after-tax earnings of the MNC even further. Actually, the severity of taxation is exaggerated here. Countries often establish income tax treaties, whereby one partner will reduce its taxes by granting a credit for taxes imposed on corporations operating within the other treaty partner's tax jurisdiction. Income tax treaties help avoid corporate exposure to double taxation. Some treaties apply to taxes paid on income earned by MNCs in foreign income. Other treaties apply to withholding taxes imposed by the host country on foreign earnings that are remitted to the parent.

Without such treaties, subsidiary earnings could be taxed by the host country and then again by the parent's country when received by the parent. To the extent that the parent uses some of these earnings to provide cash dividends for shareholders, triple taxation could result (since the dividend income is also taxed at the shareholder level). Because income tax treaties reduce taxes on earnings generated by MNCs, they help stimulate direct foreign investment. Many foreign projects are perceived as feasible only because of income tax treaties.

Tax Credits

Even without income tax treaties, an MNC may be allowed to credit income and withholding taxes paid in one country against taxes owed by the parent, if it meets certain requirements. Like income tax treaties, tax credits help to avoid double taxation and stimulate direct foreign investment. They also make international tax planning quite complicated. An MNC can benefit substantially from a knowledgeable tax planning department.

The tax credit policies can vary among countries (the U.S. policy is the most complicated), but they generally work like this. Consider a U.S.-based MNC subject to a U.S. tax rate of 34 percent. Assume that a foreign subsidiary of this corporation has generated earnings taxed at less than 34 percent by the host-country's government. The earnings remitted to the parent from the subsidiary will be subject to an additional amount of U.S. tax, to bring the total tax up to 34 percent. From the parent's point of view, the tax on its subsidiary's remitted earnings are 34 percent overall, so it does not matter whether the host country of the subsidiary or the United States receives most of the taxes. From the perspective of the governments of these two countries, however, the allocation of taxes is very important. If subsidiaries of U.S. corporations are established in foreign countries, and if these countries tax income at a rate close to 34 percent, they can generate large tax revenues from income earned by the subsidiaries. The tax revenues received by them are at the expense of the parent's country (the United States, in this case).

If the corporate income tax rate in a foreign country is greater than 34 percent, the United States generally does not impose any additional taxes on earnings remitted to a U.S. parent by foreign subsidiaries in that country. In fact, under present law, the U.S. allows the excess foreign tax to be credited against other taxes owed by the parent, due on the same type of income generated by subsidiaries in other lower-tax countries. In a sense, this suggests that some host countries could charge abnormally high corporate income tax rates to foreign subsidiaries and still attract direct foreign investment. If the MNC in our example has subsidiaries located in some countries with low corporate income taxes, the U.S. tax on earnings remitted to the U.S. parent will normally bring up the total tax to 34 percent. Yet, credits against excessive income taxes by high-tax countries on foreign subsidiaries could offset these taxes that would otherwise be paid to the U.S. government. Due to tax credits, therefore, an MNC might consider direct foreign investment in a country with excessive tax rates.

When transfer pricing shifts the tax liability to different subsidiaries, it affects the distribution of tax revenue received by countries. A study by the Internal Revenue Service in 1990 found that non-U.S. firms may have avoided about $50 million in taxes over five years. Over a recent ten-year period, more than 50 percent of all non-U.S. firms operating in the United States paid little or nothing in taxes. Ten non-U.S. automobile distributors generated $38 billion in revenue in the United States in 1987 and paid less than 1 percent in taxes to the United States. One non-U.S. electronics distributor paid more than $150 million in U.S. taxes over six years, while another similar firm paid no tax. The difference in tax was attributed to transfer pricing.

USE OF TRANSFER PRICING TO REDUCE TAXES

Once the tax laws of the various countries are fully understood, an MNC should design a network of cash flows that will optimize its value. In some cases, this may cause one subsidiary to gain at the expense of another subsidiary. For example, consider a U.S.-based MNC that has subsidiaries in a high-tax country called HT and in a low-tax country called LT. Assume both subsidiaries plan to retain all of their earnings for future projects. Under this scenario, the United States will not be taxing any of the foreign earnings (since none are remitted to the U.S. parent), and the taxes will be imposed only by the respective country governments of the subsidiaries. The MNC will benefit most if the subsidiary in LT generates the majority of the before-tax earnings. Assume the subsidiaries of these two foreign countries trade goods with each other. The MNC may devise a transfer pricing strategy whereby the subsidiary in LT charges abnormally high prices when exporting to the subsidiary in HT. Conversely, the subsidiary in HT could export goods to the subsidiary in LT at substantially reduced prices. The transfer pricing schedule suggested here should boost earnings of the LT subsidiary and reduce earnings of the subsidiary located in HT. However, after taxes, there is not an exact offsetting effect, since the tax rates differ in the two countries.

If more earnings can be transferred to the LT subsidiary, then the after-tax earnings from subsidiaries of both countries combined will be higher. This is due to the low tax rate imposed on any earnings in LT. The actual mechanics of international transfer pricing go far beyond the example provided here, and it should be emphasized that such transfer pricing strategies may not be allowed by some countries. The U.S. laws in this area are particularly strict, generally requiring inter-company transactions to be priced using the "arm's length" principle, which implies that the transactions should be priced in the same way as transactions between unrelated firms. The U.S. laws can even apply to inter-company transactions of foreign subsidiaries of a U.S.-based MNC. Also, the United States has a new "super royalty" rule that requires the income from the transfer of an intangible to be commensurate with the income generated by the intangible. Nevertheless, there are various ways MNCs can justify increasing prices at one subsidiary and reducing them at another.

There is substantial evidence that MNCs based in numerous countries use transfer pricing strategies to reduce their taxes. Moreover, several alternative methods circumvent transfer pricing restrictions. Various fees can be implemented for services, research and development, royalties, and administrative duties. While the fees may be imposed to shift earnings and minimize tax effects, the actual performance of each subsidiary is distorted. Yet, a centralized MNC approach could account for the transfer pricing strategy implemented when assessing the true performance of each subsidiary.

Some MNCs may reduce taxes in those high-tax countries where their subsidiaries have earned substantial profits by expanding there, with resulting additional costs that offset the profits. This strategy essentially defers the taxes until some future year in which profits are not offset by expenses from new expansion. Ideally, the MNCs continue such a strategy (assuming that business expansion is feasible) until the country's corporate tax rate is reduced.

INFLUENCE OF TAX LAWS ON MNC POLICIES _____

Some of the important functions of an MNC that can be affected by tax differentials among countries are

- Short-term financing
- Working capital management
- Capital structure policy
- Capital budgeting.

Short-Term Financing

Consider an MNC with one subsidiary that needs to borrow funds, and a second subsidiary in a different country that has excess funds. If the second subsidiary is located in a high-tax country, then the MNC's centralized management may request that it provide the loan at a very attractive rate to the subsidiary in need of funds. The lending subsidiary's performance may be reduced, since it could generate a better return on its funds if it used them elsewhere. The borrowing subsidiary's performance will be enhanced, due to the attractive terms of the loan. Without consideration of taxes, the reduced performance of the lending subsidiary would be equal to the increased performance of the borrowing subsidiary, and the MNC as a whole would not benefit. Yet, when taxes are considered, the MNC as a whole may indeed benefit from such a strategy, because any shifting of income from subsidiaries in high-tax countries to subsidiaries in low-tax countries can increase the after-tax inflows of the MNC as a whole. If it were not for the tax advantage, the borrowing subsidiary might have financed from some other source, such as a local bank. This example shows how financing decisions can be affected by tax characteristics of countries.

Working Capital Management

From a working capital management perspective, assume the subsidiary with excess cash wishes to invest that cash for three months. If it were not for the tax advantage, it would likely invest those funds elsewhere, rather than providing the low-rate loan to the other subsidiary. This shows how short-term investing (a role within working capital management) is affected by tax characteristics of countries.

Capital Structure Policy

Country tax characteristics can also be influential on the MNC's capital structure policy. Consider an MNC parent that plans to finance a large project for a foreign subsidiary and is considering the issuance of new stock to generate funds. If the subsidiary is based in a high-tax country, the MNC may prefer to have the subsidiary finance the project itself, by issuing bonds locally or within the Eurobond market. The interest expenses from bond payments will offset part of the income earned by the subsidiary, and reduce taxes. Thus, the decision on how to attract long-term funds can also depend on differences in tax laws among countries.

Capital Budgeting

From a capital budgeting perspective, consider an MNC that desires to establish a manufacturing plant in one of two possibly attractive locations. One location is in a high-tax country, and the second location is in a low-tax country. While there are obviously many factors to compare among locations, if the tax advantage of establishing the plant in the low-tax country is not offset by any disadvantages, the MNC will choose that site. Even though tax credits can reduce or eliminate the disadvantage exhibited by a high-tax host country, the credits will not necessarily be applied to all income. For example, if a subsidiary retains a large portion of its earnings rather than remitting them to the parent, the tax credits will not be as valuable.

For some capital budgeting situations, the current tax information of countries may not be sufficient to determine the tax effects, since tax incentives may be offered in particular circumstances, and tax rates can change over time. Consider an MNC that plans to establish a manufacturing plant in Country Y rather than Country X. Assume that while many economic characteristics favor Country X, the current tax rates within Country Y are lower. However, whereas tax rates in Country X have been historically stable and are expected to continue that way, they have been changing every few years in Country Y. In this case, the MNC must assess the future uncertainty of the tax rates. It cannot treat the current tax rate of Country Y as a constant when conducting a capital budgeting analysis. Instead, it must consider possible changes in the tax rates over time, and based on these possibilities, determine whether Country Y's projected tax advantages *over time* sufficiently outweigh the advantages of the Country X location. One approach to account for possible changes in the tax rates is to use sensitivity analysis, which measures the sensitivity of the net present value (NPV) of after-tax cash flows to various possible tax changes over time. For each tax scenario, a different NPV is projected. By accounting for each possible tax scenario, the MNC can develop a distribution of possible NPVs that may occur, and can then compare these for each country.

Accounting For Tax Uncertainty. An MNC may want to not only account for various possible tax scenarios for a project, but also consider possible scenarios for other important variables as well. The tax rate is only one of several variables relevant to the capital budgeting process whose future values are uncertain. A simulation model can be used to create ranges for each possible variable during each future period. For example, the corporate income tax rate in Country Y may be between 30 percent and 40 percent, the sales in units may be between 6 million and 8 million units, and so on. Different ranges can be set for each period when using a full-blown simulation model. Based on the host of possibilities, the simulation program can generate a distribution of possible NPVs that could occur for the project. The procedure can then be replicated for Country X, with ranges set for each variable so that the model can generate possible NPVs. Then the two distributions can be compared. The key point here is that any long-term corporate decisions affected by tax effects should account for any future changes in tax laws that may occur.

An MNC's tax planning department should be able to determine the tax effects of any corporate decision, provided it has complete information on all cash flows of the MNC, including cash flows among subsidiaries. There are two critical, broadly defined functions involved in tax planning for the MNC. The first is to be aware of all the current tax laws that exist for each country where the MNC does (or plans to do) business. This first function also includes any information that may indicate future changes in tax laws. The second function is to take the information generated from the first function and aid various corporate departments in their centralized decisions. Again, any decisions influenced by taxes must be perceived from the overall MNC's perspective, rather than from an individual subsidiary's perspective.

Both of the functions of tax planning for the MNC are obviously very important. The first function requires some perseverance and competence in order to obtain and understand information on current tax provisions among countries. It also requires some insight into how tax provisions may change over time. The second function requires analytical tools and the imagination necessary to fully account for the tax effects of possible corporate policies.

MULTINATIONAL CORPORATE POLICY

An efficient system of multinational corporate policy and planning requires that decisions be made to maximize the MNC as a whole. To achieve this goal, any decision making must avoid two common conflicts that arise. The first is a conflict of interests between a subsidiary's individual goals and the goals of the overall MNC. The second is a conflict of interests between the various corporate departments (financing, investing, etc.) of the MNC.

Agency Costs of International Business

MNCs with subsidiaries in foreign countries may experience major conflicts between manager and shareholder goals, which result in agency costs. Subsidiary managers are not necessarily concerned with the parent's perspective. They may view their subsidiaries as profit centers, and therefore make decisions that enhance local performance. For example, they may not be concerned with hedging the exchange rate risk when remitting earnings to the parent, or about withholding taxes imposed on remitted earnings, if they are concerned only with maximizing the earnings of their respective subsidiaries. By using such a narrow perspective, a subsidiary manager may invest in projects that enhance the subsidiary's earnings, but adversely affect the MNC overall.

Differences in customs between the parent and its subsidiaries may cause the subsidiaries to make decisions that are inconsistent with parent goals. In addition, differences in languages and accounting standards between the MNC's parent and its subsidiaries can make it difficult for the parent to monitor the operations of subsidiaries. These conditions can cause agency problems to be more severe for MNCs than for purely domestic firms.

Subsidiary Versus Centralized Management

An MNC makes some corporate decisions similar to those of a domestic firm, but often the decisions are more complex. Common decisions of MNCs involve

- Hedging exchange rate risk
- Financing
- Investing excess cash
- Transfer pricing
- Direct foreign investment (capital budgeting)
- Capital structure policy.

For many of these decisions, each subsidiary may develop its own assessment of the variables that will influence the outcome of the decision. Virtually all decisions are based on expectations. Thus, projections are needed so that managers can assess the feasibility of any possible decision.

To understand how subsidiary decisions could conflict with what is best for the MNC overall, consider the following examples. With regard to hedging, one subsidiary may hedge its cash inflows of foreign Currency X, while another does not hedge its cash outflows of Currency X. If neither subsidiary hedged, their exposure to fluctuations in Currency X could be offset in aggregate. However, since only one is hedging, the unhedged position of the other is exposed. To avoid exposure, this other subsidiary must also hedge.

Persistent hedging by subsidiaries results in high transaction costs, so hedging should be avoided if it is not necessary. A centralized system can detect individual exposures of each subsidiary, whereas a decision at the subsidiary level may often neglect the positions of other subsidiaries and therefore be inconsistent with maximizing the value of the overall MNC.

As another example, various subsidiaries may make decisions based on their individual exchange rate projections. Given that the exchange rate projections could be the determining factor of a corporate policy, the projections should be consistent among subsidiaries. A centralized system can develop the projections and then distribute them to the subsidiaries. Otherwise, each subsidiary will be using a different basis of reasoning for its policies. In addition, a situation in which each subsidiary is employing its own forecasting team is a waste of resources.

APPLIED RESEARCH

IMPACT OF MNC CHARACTERISTICS ON CENTRALIZATION

A recent study by Gates and Egel-hoff attempted to determine why MNCs have different degrees of centralization. They measured centralization as the average level in the organization that needs to approve decisions before they can be implemented. The average was determined from 22 important decisions common to MNCs, including 10 marketing decisions, 5 manufacturing decisions, and 7 financial decisions. Results of the study are summarized here, with a focus on financial centralization.

- Size of foreign operations was negatively related to the degree of financial centralization. This supports the theory that as an MNC grows, it must decentralize, so that it does not overload its managers.
- The size of the MNC was negatively correlated with the degree of financial centralization. The argument used above may explain this result.
- The extent of outside ownership in foreign subsidiaries was negatively correlated with the degree of financial centralization. The reason may be that foreign subsidiaries with more outside ownership are less legally dependent on the parent, encouraging decentralization.
- European-based MNCs had less financial centralization than U.S.-based MNCs. Perhaps this results from cultural differences.
- The age of the MNC was negatively correlated with the degree of financial concentration. The longer the foreign operations have existed, the more decentralized they become.

Many policy decisions of MNCs are based on economic and financial projections, and the centralized management should be largely responsible for these projections. The subsidiaries can assist by providing whatever information is useful for the development of the projections. Several variables need to be forecasted for each country where the MNC conducts business or plans to in the future, including currency exchange rates, inflation rates, interest rates, economic activity (national income, GNP, etc.), balance of trade, trade restrictions, currency restrictions, political problems, technology status, and special industry conditions. The MNC can apply projections of these macro variables to specific policy proposals in order to determine optimal policies for all financial management functions.

Centralization can make efficient use of resources by avoiding redundancy of operations. In addition, it prevents conflicts between subsidiaries with regard to projections. Centralized projections can be used by the subsidiaries to make some decisions on issues that require no other information about other subsidiaries. Other decisions (such as whether to hedge) that benefit from information on other subsidiaries can be made by the centralized management. An argument can be made that taking the decision-making power away from the subsidiaries reduces the control they have on their own performance. This argument has merit. Of course, if a centralized decision is in the best interests of the overall MNC, the subsidiary should abide by that decision even if it does not agree with it.

With a centralized approach, each subsidiary can either gain or lose due to a centralized decision. Therefore, performance evaluation of individual subsidiaries must account for the ways these decisions affect the subsidiaries. Any reduction in earnings due to centralized decisions should be accounted for. At the same time, earnings at other subsidiaries may be increased due to centralized decisions. The managers of these subsidiaries should not be more highly rewarded under such circumstances.

Role of Subsidiary due to Centralization

Because a centralized system places much of the responsibility on the centralized group, the managers of individual subsidiaries play a more passive role, simply following instructions handed down to them. This could reduce their motivation to increase efficiency at their respective subsidiaries, since each subsidiary's periodic performance is not as dependent on their decisions. That is, they no longer receive the credit for superior performance or the blame for poor performance. While this can be a serious problem, the advantages of a centralized system should outweigh any deficiencies. The potential lack of motivation at the subsidiary level due to centralized management can be alleviated if it is properly communicated to subsidiary personnel that the underlying goal is to maximize the value of the overall MNC, not the value of any particular subsidiary.

While the centralized management approach is strongly advocated here for decisions that affect various subsidiaries, it should be emphasized that the only way such an approach is feasible is if the reward system to personnel is based not on subsidiary performance, but instead on how well instructions are followed. Also, some decisions can be made at the subsidiary level, as long as they do not have a significant adverse impact on other individual subsidiaries, or on the overall MNC.

Conflict of Interests among Corporate Departments

The conflict of interests discussed thus far is among subsidiaries, or between a subsidiary and its headquarters. Another type of conflict can occur within the centralized management system. Consider the following decisions to be made by the MNC: (1) where to establish direct foreign investment, (2) type of business to engage in, and (3) optimal capital structure. Each of these decisions depends on the other two. Whether direct foreign investment is feasible in a particular location depends on the type of business in which it plans to expand. The capital budgeting analysis to determine whether the investment is feasible will be affected by the cost of capital. The cost of capital can be influenced by the capital structure of the MNC. The optimal capital structure depends on the type of business the MNC is involved in (that is, whether periodic inflow payments in such a business are stable or erratic). The interdependencies noted here illustrate that policy decisions should not be totally separated from each other. While an MNC may have various departments within the centralized system which make policy decisions, there should be interaction between departments.

Accounting and Control

A primary role in any corporate planning system is the monitoring of previous policy decisions. Ongoing evaluation of previous decisions will help distinguish policies that have worked from those that have not. In addition, reasons for the failure of some policies may be detected, and thus similar mistakes may be avoided in the future.

HOW MNCS USE STRATEGIC PLANNING

A recent study by Boseman surveyed managers of MNCs to determine managerial attitudes toward organization, planning, and control. Some of the key results of the survey as related to this chapter are summarized below:

- For 53 percent of the MNCs, area managers were responsible for operations (representing a decentralized system). For about 30 percent of the MNCs, the foreign operations reported to an International Division. For 17 percent of the MNCs, foreign operations reported to the parent.
- A related characteristic to responsibility is monitoring. For 35 percent of the MNCs, the foreign operations were monitored by the respective subsidiaries, while 47 percent were monitored by the parent. The remaining 18 percent used regional monitoring.
- Fifty-three percent of the MNCs organized their foreign operations to benefit from syner-

gistic coordination. That is, there were some integrated functions between the subsidiaries.

- Forty-one percent of the MNCs attempted to maximize their performance from opportunities on a country-by-country basis. Another 41 percent maximized performance on a global basis. The remaining 18 percent did so on a regional basis.
- Sixty-five percent of the MNCs used political forecasting for their strategic planning. Some political forecasting systems were on a country-by-country basis while others were on a global basis. Thirty-five percent used sociocultural forecasting for their strategic planning. Some MNCs even used both forecasting systems while others used neither.
- The most preferred form of foreign ownership was wholly owned subsidiaries, followed by majority ownership, and joint ventures with fifty-fifty ownership.

To minimize poor decision making, an efficient system of internal accounting control is necessary. The accounting system is largely the responsibility of each subsidiary, which must periodically report its status on all aspects of cash flow. For example, a subsidiary may report its actual cash flow in the previous week or month, as well as its anticipated cash flow in the upcoming week, month, or quarter. The cash flow figures should be separated into the various foreign currencies. The centralized system can consolidate this information from each subsidiary, to identify offsetting positions in particular currencies. Where offsetting positions do not exist, the decision on whether to hedge must be made. Short-term investment and financing decisions may also hinge on the cash flows anticipated by subsidiaries. Thus, it is critical that the subsidiaries provide accurate estimates. Comparison of actual data with their estimates over time will reveal any consistent over- or underestimating of cash flows, so that any such bias can be removed in future estimates. This principle, applied here to cash flow, can also be applied to all other financial characteristics reported by subsidiaries.

SUMMARY

- An MNC's tax liability is dependent on the tax characteristics of the countries where it operates. The more critical tax characteristics of any country are its corporate income taxes, withholding taxes, provision for carrybacks and carry-forwards, tax treaties, and tax credits.

■ MNCs may attempt to reduce taxes with their transfer pricing of transactions between subsidiaries. The transfer pricing policies are generally intended to transfer income to locations where the subsidiary is taxed at a lower rate. However, transfer pricing policies must be established within guidelines enforced by countries.

■ International tax laws can affect MNC decisions regarding short-term financing, working capital management, capital structure policy, and capital budgeting.

■ Centralized decision making can avoid redundancies and inconsistencies that may occur when tasks (such as exchange rate forecasts) are conducted at the subsidiary level. The subsidiaries still play an important role in providing whatever input may be necessary. Furthermore, the reward system for subsidiary managers must recognize that subsidiaries are not in complete control of their performance.

SELF-TEST FOR CHAPTER 21 _____

(Answers are provided in Appendix A in the back of the text.)

1. Explain how withholding tax laws could affect the feasibility of a project by a U.S. firm in a foreign country.

2. Explain how transfer pricing can affect the profitability of foreign subsidiaries.

3. Explain how a capital structure policy for a foreign subsidiary may be influenced by tax rules.

4. Explain how centralized management can reduce transactions costs associated with hedging, without increasing the MNC's exchange rate exposure.

5. Assume that each of an MNC's ten subsidiaries commonly exchanges six different currencies. Each subsidiary plans to create its own forecasts for each of the six currencies, since each subsidiary is confident in its own forecasting approach. Do you agree with this philosophy? Explain.

QUESTIONS _____

1. Discuss how the importance of tax planning at MNCs would change if tax rules were identical among all countries and did not change over time. (Your answer should imply why tax planning is critical to the MNC in reality.)

2. What corporate decisions can be affected when incorporating taxes into the decisions? Briefly elaborate on how each decision is affected by taxes.

3. In what general ways do countries differ with regard to their tax systems?

4. How can tax treaties between countries be beneficial to MNCs?

5. Explain how transfer pricing can be used to reduce the MNC's overall tax liability.

6. Briefly describe the role of tax planning by the MNC. What are its two key functions?

7. Describe the possible conflict of interests between a subsidiary and centralized management.

8. How could an MNC avoid a conflict of interests between a subsidiary and centralized management?

9. Explain why a conflict of interests can often arise between corporate departments at an MNC.

10. How could an MNC avoid conflicts of interests between its various corporate departments?

CASE: INTERNATIONAL REORGANIZATION OF AT&T

AT&T to Give Foreign Units More Autonomy

Each Is to Get Own CEO Under Plan to Increase Revenue From Overseas

BY JOHN J. KELLER
Staff Reporter of THE WALL STREET JOURNAL

NEW YORK—American Telephone & Telegraph Co., grappling with slow growth in the U.S., is setting up foreign units with their own chief executive officers to pursue the potentially huge new markets in Asia, Europe and Latin America.

The new CEOs, one of whom has already been appointed to head Asian operations, will have the power to set up individual country operations, set local pricing for AT&T products and services, and even hunt for mergers and joint ventures to help AT&T's global expansion.

AT&T Chairman and Chief Executive Officer Robert Allen has been frustrated with the company's slow progress in the foreign markets, which promise far higher growth. Despite his initial goal to derive half of AT&T's revenue from overseas operations by 2000, foreign sales account for only 24% of about $65 billion in total annual revenue today. Mr. Allen has been forced to back off somewhat, aiming to achieve the 50% mark 10 years from now.

Mr. Allen is said to believe that AT&T's current structure overseas is a drag on his goal. "We're launching something new. . . . As a result, AT&T will never be the same," Mr. Allen told senior officers a few weeks ago in a conference call, according to a transcript circulating around AT&T. "But [AT&T] will be faster, more effective and better able to seize the enormous opportunity that markets outside the U.S. represent for our company."

While AT&T's U.S. business grows at less than 5% a year, China, other nations in Asia, and countries in Latin America and Eastern Europe are modernizing archaic phone systems and promise big orders. China is expected to acquire $1.2 billion in new switching gear alone every year for the next three decades.

AT&T employs about 54,000 workers in foreign markets, of which about half are in AT&T's traditional lines of equipment and communication services and the rest in its NCR computer unit. But local management is spotty, and equipment and long-distance businesses report up through separate units based in Basking Ridge, N.J.

Virtually all major decisions are made in the U.S., requiring foreign proposals to snake their way up through myriad departments before getting approval. "That's much too far from our customers" to achieve on-site, rapid decision-making, said Victor Pelson, chief of AT&T Global Operations "The market is changing very rapidly."

AT&T is a relative newcomer in many overseas markets. The U.S. government forced the company to sell off its international business in the early 1920s. Those operations became ITT Corp. AT&T wasn't allowed back in until after its breakup in 1984, while rivals Alcatel-Alsthom of France, which ended up owning the ITT assets, and Sweden's LM Ericsson have been entrenched for decades.

As part of the new reorganization, AT&T has begun consolidating its overseas facilities, which include 39 plants in 24 countries, into three regional hubs. The new Asia/Pacific unit is based in Hong Kong; a European unit based in Brussels will also run Middle East and Africa businesses; a Latin America unit will be based in Coral Gables, Fla.

Hired to head AT&T's Asia unit is Walter Sousa, 50 years old, formerly the chief operating officer of Hong Kong-based Astec PLC and a 20-year veteran of Hewlett-Packard Co.'s Asian business. Other CEO appointments are expected early next year.

The new CEOs of these units will be full members of AT&T's powerful Global Operations team. Led by Mr. Pelson, the team includes the chief executives of AT&T's four groups: Communication Services, Network Systems, Multimedia and NCR Corp.

Recently, Mr. Allen assigned William Warwick, regarded as the AT&T executive who turned around AT&T's ailing consumer phone and chip businesses, to build an AT&T China unit.

Mr. Pelson said the China unit has been granted special autonomy under the revamped management structure. Mr. Warwick will be allowed to run his business independently of the new Asia CEO and expand the company into a full-fledged supplier of network equipment to the Chinese government and its chief research and development collaborator.

Source: *The Wall Street Journal* (December 13, 1993), pp. A3, A4. Reprinted by permssion of *The Wall Street Journal* © 1993 Dow Jones & Company, Inc. All Rights Reserved Worldwide.

QUESTIONS

1. Why could AT&T benefit from its international reorganization?

2. Why do you think AT&T consolidated its overseas facilities?

3. Why would AT&T grant special autonomy to the China unit, independent of the Asian region?

CASE PROBLEM

REDWING TECHNOLOGY COMPANY
Assessing Subsidiary Performance

Redwing Technology Company is a U.S.-based firm that makes a variety of high-technology components. Five years ago, it established subsidiaries in Canada, France, and Japan. The earnings generated by each subsidiary as translated (at the average annual exchange rate) into U.S. dollars per year are shown below:

	Translated Dollar Value of Annual Earnings in Each Subsidiary (in millions of $)		
Years Ago	Canada	France	Japan
5	$20	$21	$30
4	24	24	32
3	28	24	35
2	32	36	41
1	36	42	46

Each subsidiary had an equivalent amount in resources with which to conduct operations. The wage rates for the labor needed were similar across countries. The inflation rates, economic growth, and degree of competition were somewhat similar across countries. The average exchange rates of the respective currencies over the last five years are disclosed below:

Years Ago	Canadian Dollar	French Franc	Japanese Yen
5	$.84	$.10	$.0040
4	.83	.12	.0043
3	.81	.16	.0046
2	.81	.20	.0055
1	.79	.24	.0064

The earnings generated by each country were reinvested rather than remitted. There were no plans to remit any future earnings either.

REDWING TECHNOLOGY COMPANY (CONTINUED)

A committee of vice-presidents met to determine the performance of each subsidiary in the last five years. The assessment was to be used for (1) determining bonus compensation for the executive in charge of each subsidiary, and (2) determining where additional funds held by the parent should be invested. Since exchange rates of the related currencies were affected by so many different factors, the treasurer acknowledged that there was much uncertainty about their future direction. The treasurer did suggest, however, that last year's average exchange rate would probably serve as at least a reasonable guess of exchange rates in future years. He did not anticipate any of the currencies to experience consistent appreciation or depreciation.

a) Use whatever means you think appropriate to rank the performance of the executive in charge of each subsidiary. That is, which executive did the best job over the five-year period, in your opinion? Justify your opinion.

b) Use whatever means you think appropriate to determine which subsidiary deserves additional funds from the parent to push for additional growth. (Assume no constraint on potential growth in any country). Where would you recommend the parent's excess funds be invested, based on the information available? Justify your opinion.

c) Repeat Question (b), but assume that all earnings generated from the parent's investment would be remitted to the parent every year. Would your recommendation change? Explain.

d) A final task of the committee was to recommend whether any of the subsidiaries should be divested. One vice-president suggested that a review of the earnings translated into dollars shows that the performance of Canadian and French subsidiaries are very highly correlated. The VP concluded that having both of these subsidiaries did not achieve much in diversification benefits, and recommended that either the Canadian or French subsidiaries could be sold without forgoing any diversification benefits. Do you agree? Explain.

PROJECT _____

Review the annual report of an MNC of your choice. Based on the annual report, does it appear that the decision making is centralized or decentralized? Elaborate.

REFERENCES

Beaver, William, and Mark Wolfson. "Foreign Currency Translation Gains and Losses: What Effect Do They Have and What Do They Mean?" *Financial Analysts Journal* (March-April 1984), pp. 28–36.

Boseman, Glenn. "The Australian Multinational-Parent and Subsidiary Relationships." *Management International Review*, no. 2 (1986), pp. 43–51.

Burns, Jane O. "Transfer Pricing Decisions in U.S. Multinational Corporations." *Journal of International Business Studies* (Fall 1980), pp. 23–39.

Choi, Frederisk D.S., and I. J. Czechowicz. "Assessing Foreign Subsidiary Performance: A Multinational Comparison." *Management International Review* (April 1983), pp. 14–25.

Daniels, John D., and Jeffrey Bracker. "Profit Performance: Do Foreign Operations Make a Difference?" *Management International Review*, no. 1 (1989), pp. 46–56.

Gates, Stephen R., and William G. Egelhoff. "Centralization in Headquarters-Subsidiary Relationships." *Journal of International Business Studies* (Summer 1986), pp. 71–92.

Hamel, Gary, and C. K. Prahalad. "Do You Really Have a Global Strategy?" *Harvard Business Review* (July-August 1985), pp. 139–148.

Hoffman, Richard C. "The General Management of Foreign Subsidiaries in the U.S.A.: An Exploratory Study." *Management International Review*, no. 2 (1988), pp. 41–55.

Kreder, Martina, and Maria Zeller. "Control in German and U.S. Companies." Management International Review, no. 3 (1988), pp. 58–66.

Rugman, Alan M. and Alain Verbeke. "Foreign Subsidiaries and Multinational Strategic Management: An Extension and Correction of Porter's Single Diamond Framework." *Management International Review* (Second Quarter 1993), pp. 71–84.

LONG-TERM ASSETS AND LIABILITY MANAGEMENT

Gandor Co. is a U.S. firm that is considering a joint venture with a Chinese firm to produce and sell video cassettes. Gandor will invest $12 million in this project, which will help to finance the Chinese firm's production. For each of the first three years, 50 percent of the total profits will be distributed to the Chinese firm, while the remaining 50 percent will be converted to dollars to be sent to the U.S. The Chinese government intends to impose a 20 percent income tax on the profits earned by Gandor. The Chinese government has guaranteed that the after-tax profits (denominated in renminbi, the Chinese currency) can be converted to U.S. dollars at an exchange rate of RM1 = $.20 per unit and sent to Gandor Co. each year. At the present time, there is no withholding tax imposed on profits to be sent to the U.S. as a result of joint ventures in China. Assume that even after considering the taxes paid in China, there is an additional 10 percent tax imposed by the U.S. government on profits received by Gandor Co. After the first three years, all profits earned are allocated to the Chinese firm.

The expected total profits resulting from the joint venture per year are as follows:

Year	Total Profits from Joint Venture (in renminbi, RM)
1	RM60 million
2	RM80 million
3	RM100 million

Gandor's average cost of debt is 13.8 percent before taxes. Its average cost of equity is 18 percent. Assume the corporate income tax rate imposed on Gandor is normally 30 percent. Gandor uses a capital structure composed of 60 percent debt and 40 percent equity. Gandor automatically adds 4 percentage points to its cost of capital when deriving its required rate of return on international joint ventures. While this project has particular forms of country risk that are unique, Gandor plans to account for these forms of risk within its estimation of cash flows.

There are two forms of country risk that Gandor is concerned about. First, there is the risk that the Chinese government will increase the corporate income tax rate from 20 percent to 40 percent (20 percent probability). If this occurs, additional tax credits will be allowed, resulting in no U.S. taxes on the profits from this joint venture. Second, there is the risk that the Chinese government will impose a withholding tax of 10 percent on the profits that were to be sent to the U.S. (20 percent probability). In this case, additional tax credits will not be allowed, and Gandor will still be subject to a 10 percent U.S. tax on profits received from China. Assume the two types of country risk are mutually exclusive. That is, the Chinese government will only adjust one of its tax guidelines (the income tax or the withholding tax), if any.

1. Determine Gandor's cost of capital. Also determine Gandor's required rate of return for the joint venture in China.

2. Determine the probability distribution of Gandor's net present values for the joint venture. The capital budgeting analyses should be conducted for the three scenarios:
   Scenario 1. Based on original assumptions
   Scenario 2. Based on an increase in the corporate income tax by the Chinese government
   Scenario 3. Based on the imposition of a withholding tax by the Chinese government.

3. Would you recommend that Gandor participate in the joint venture? Explain.

4. What do you think would be the key underlying factor that would have the most influence on the profits earned in China as a result of the joint venture?

5. Is there any reason for Gandor to revise the composition of its capital (debt and equity) obtained from the U.S. when financing joint ventures like this?

6. When Gandor was assessing this proposed joint venture, some of the managers of Gandor Co. recommended that it borrow the Chinese currency rather than dollars to partially obtain the necessary capital for its initial investment. They suggested that such a strategy can reduce Gandor's exchange rate risk. Do you agree? Explain.

THE INTERNATIONAL BANKING ENVIRONMENT

Part 6 (Chapters 22 and 23) provides a background on international banking. Chapter 22 describes the development of international banking and explains the risks incurred by these banks. Chapter 23 concentrates on the risk of nonperforming foreign loans. It describes the events that led to the international debt crisis and explains how banks have attempted to deal with the crisis. It also illustrates how banks use country risk assessment as input to their international lending decisions.

CHAPTER **22**

INTERNATIONAL BANKING

Commercial banks play a vital role in facilitating international transactions. They help finance international trade and other operations. They hold inventories of various currencies so that corporations can obtain the necessary currency to purchase foreign goods or invest in foreign securities. In addition, they offer forward contracts to corporations that desire to lock in the rate at which a currency can be purchased or sold in advance. This chapter describes the international banking environment in which commercial banks operate. The specific objectives of this chapter are to

- describe motives of commercial banks for conducting international banking,
- provide a background on the Eurocurrency market,
- explain the risks incurred by banks involved in international operations, and
- describe key banking regulations among countries.

BACKGROUND

The primary function of international banking is to facilitate the international business of multinational corporations (MNCs). Many commercial banks have engaged in international banking by establishing (1) branch banks, (2) Edge Act corporations, and (3) international banking facilities. Each will be discussed in turn.

Branch Banks

A **branch** bank can provide virtually all of the services its parent provides, as long as it abides by host country regulations. Due to its relationship with its parent, it must also abide by regulations of its parent's home country. Branches of

645

large banks are popular, since they are household names internationally and can penetrate different geographical areas. They are convenient to MNCs' subsidiaries that may need local correspondence with banks. Due to branch banking, all subsidiaries of an MNC dispersed around the world can work with one or a few banks.

U.S. banks have commonly set up branches overseas in order to accept deposits and provide loans to foreign customers. Foreign branches of U.S. banks are not subject to the reserve requirements or interest ceilings that exist in the United States. Foreign branches of U.S. banks are concentrated in the United Kingdom, Brazil, Hong Kong, France, Japan, Singapore, and Germany. In addition to the branches, U.S. banks commonly establish **agencies,** which provide loans but do not accept deposits or provide trust services.

Edge Act Corporations

Due to the International Banking Act of 1978, **Edge Act corporations** (called "Edges") are allowed more flexibility in handling international transactions. Edges are used to establish international banking offices outside the home state. These operations focus on aiding corporations involved in international trade. Edges are supervised by the U.S. Federal Reserve System.

International Banking Facilities

International banking facilities (IBFs) represent a recent popular innovation in the international banking industry. An IBF is not a new physical facility, but instead a part of the existing bank. Created in the United States in late 1981, IBFs are allowed to accept deposits from or make loans to non-residents of the United States. Because IBFs are not subject to normal U.S. regulations, they are free from reserve requirements and interest rate ceilings. These advantages are similar to those of institutions located within the Eurocurrency market. The IBFs are subject to some restrictions, though. First funds borrowed by an IBF from its parent, like funds borrowed from an offshore branch, are subject to reserve requirements. Second, IBF transactions with customers must normally amount to $100,000 or more. This restricts the IBF business to large corporations or government agencies. Finally, IBFs are not allowed to insure certificates of deposit (CDs). This prevents possible competition by IBFs within U.S money markets.

The IBFs attract funds largely from foreign banks, foreign government agencies, and other IBFs. Their existence allows U.S. banks greater ability to provide international banking services. The fact that some banks have replaced their "offshore" banking with IBFs suggests that IBFs may be perceived as a substitute for offshore banking. IBFs sometimes have more tax benefits or lower transaction costs, or even less political risk, than offshore banking.

MOTIVATION FOR INTERNATIONAL BANKING

Large banks have served as primary suppliers of funds to foreign countries. They have found that higher returns can often be achieved, as foreign borrowers are willing to pay higher interest rates in order to obtain funds. In addition, lending to various foreign borrowers is an effective method for banks to diversify their loanable funds. Diversification of loanable funds can be achieved without lending funds overseas. However, if all the firms that borrow from a bank are from the same country, they may all be systematically influenced by the events that occur in that country (such as a recession, etc.). A portfolio of international loans is not expected to be as susceptible to a single economic event as a purely domestic loan portfolio.

Beyond the diversification argument, other motives exist for banks to expand globally. Foreign banking markets may have easy access to entry. Regulations may be more relaxed, as discussed in detail later in this chapter. Economies of scale (lower average cost per unit of output as volume increases) may result from international expansion of banking services. Finally, subsidiaries of MNCs located in foreign markets may request services from the bank which the headquarters uses in the home country. Thus, the establishment of foreign branch banking can further develop relationships already initiated with MNCs. The general growth of international trade and finance calls for banks that have a working knowledge of more than one country. Some banks have devoted resources to become established in various countries and become accustomed to differences in country cultures, politics, and economics. Yet, by providing global banking services, they have differentiated themselves from other regional or national banks. That is, they can provide services to customers that non-global banks are not accustomed to providing, which is one more reason why banks are motivated to expand internationally.

Effects of East European Reform

The lifting of the Iron Curtain in November 1989 attracted the attention of commercial banks around the world. The privatization of businesses has resulted in a substantial need for financing. Some of the more obvious ways in which banks can facilitate the trend towards privatization are (1) providing direct loans to businesses, (2) acting as underwriters on bonds or stock issued by firms, (3) providing letters of credit, and (4) providing consulting services on international trade, mergers, and other corporate activities.

Some U.S. banks have been conducting business in Eastern Bloc countries. For example, Chase Manhattan Bank and BankAmerica do business in Moscow, while Citibank does business in Hungary. First Chicago serves as an investment bank and financial advisor to Hungary, the Soviet states, and Yugoslavia. Several U.S. banks have formed alliances with financial institutions in Eastern Europe, to provide various services.

Effects of NAFTA

U.S. banks recently expanded into Mexico in response to the passage of the North American Free Trade Agreement (NAFTA). These U.S. banks can offer various corporate services to the MNCs expanding into Mexico, such as loans, foreign exchange services, and banker's acceptances. They also can facilitate the privatization of Mexican businesses that have been government-owned. These banks are also positioned to expand throughout Latin America if trade agreements are broadened to include Chile and other Latin American countries. The U.S. bank involvement in Latin America is now focused less on the provision of loans to governments, and more on the provision of various services to firms.

Migration of Non-U.S. Banks into the United States

As the non-U.S. firms expanded their business into the United States, so did the non-U.S. banks. The primary functions of non-U.S. banks within the United States are wholesale- rather than retail-oriented. That is, they emphasize deposits and loans in large denominations, rather than smaller retail transactions. They are located mainly in areas where multinational business is common, such as New York, Los Angeles, San Francisco, and Chicago. Their primary role is to serve the subsidiaries of MNCs whose parents reside in their home countries, although they also attempt to serve the headquarters of U.S.-based MNCs.

In recent years, Japanese banks have been most aggressive in penetrating the U.S. market. They now control more than 25 percent of the California market. One major reason for their growth is their very competitive corporate loans. They also have been known to provide letters of credit for lower fees than those charged by U.S. banks. Another reason for their growth is a relatively low cost of capital, which allows them to take on many ventures that would not be feasible for U.S. banks. Furthermore, the high savings rate of the Japanese allows for substantial growth in deposits in Japan, which may then be channeled to support operations in the United States.

THE EUROCURRENCY MARKET

The Eurocurrency market serves as an international banking center, at which lenders and borrowers from various countries are matched up. The financial intermediaries in this market, often referred to as **Eurobanks,** are located primarily in Europe, and many of the large U.S. banks have branches in Europe that serve as Eurobanks. The liabilities of Eurobanks are mainly time deposits in large amounts and of varied currency denominations. Their assets consist of short-term and medium-term loans to corporations and government agencies.

Development of the Eurocurrency Market

The growth of multinational business encouraged banks to establish branches where subsidiaries of MNCs were located. Banks that had already established relationships with MNCs' parents attempted to also develop relationships with their subsidiaries.

Because the U.S. dollar was the primary currency used to denominate internationally traded goods, there was a need for U.S. dollars around the world. This was especially true in Europe, where international trade was quite popular. Banks in Europe welcomed dollar-denominated deposits from corporations with excess cash, since they could lend them to corporations that needed dollars to make payments on imports. The widespread use of these so-called **Eurodollars** contributed to the growth of the Eurocurrency market.

In the early 1960s, funds were being transferred among countries not only to pay for imports, but also to purchase foreign securities. However, the Interest Equalization Tax (IET) imposed on U.S. investors as of 1963 discouraged foreign investments. In addition, the U.S.-based MNCs were asked by the U.S. government to obtain funding for foreign projects from foreign sources. Limitations were placed on U.S. banks regarding their volume of international lending. This government policy, along with the IET, was intended to ensure that U.S. funds would be available to finance development within the United States. Due to these policies, both non-U.S. corporations and U.S.-based MNCs in need of funds for projects outside the country were forced to look elsewhere for funds. The Eurocurrency market grew in response to the need for an international banking arena that could finance business outside the United States.

During the early 1970s, the worldwide demand for oil increased to meet the higher global production of goods and services. As the Organization of Petroleum Exporting Countries (OPEC) exported oil, the oil-importing countries needed to borrow more funds. In addition, the OPEC countries were receiving revenues they desired to invest. Both forces increased the growth of the Eurocurrency market. In fact, the Eurobanks within this market helped recycle the oil payments, as they accepted deposits from the cash-rich OPEC countries and converted these funds into loans for the oil-importing countries.

Reasons for Attractive Eurobank Rates

Beyond all the developments described up to this point, the popularity of the Eurocurrency market can also be attributed to the attractive deposit and loan rates offered by Eurobanks, due to four characteristics that distinguish them from other commercial banks. First, reserve requirements are not imposed on foreign currency deposits at Eurobanks, allowing them to reduce the spread between the average rate offered on deposits and the average rate charged on loans. Second, interest rate ceilings are not imposed on deposit rates as they were in the United States. Third, the transactions are typically of wholesale rather than retail nature; so each transaction represents a large amount of funds. This characteristic reduces costs to the Eurobanks, enabling them to offer attractive rates. Fourth, Eurobank deposits are not insured by government agencies, and therefore do not require insurance premiums to be paid by Eurobanks. This again allows the banks to offer attractive rates on their deposits and loans.

Due to these four characteristics, Eurobanks can afford to offer higher interest rates on their deposits, and charge lower rates on their loans. Furthermore, the absence of restrictions to entry into the Eurocurrency market assures that rates will remain competitive, since competition between Eurobanks should persist. If collective rate-setting among banks did occur, other banks would enter this market to maintain competition.

Risks to Depositors

While Eurocurrency deposits typically offer attractive interest rates, they pose some risks, too. First, there is a possibility that due to political turmoil, Eurocurrency deposits in these banks could be seized by foreign government authorities. Such an event is not likely for depositors who keep their funds in their home countries. Second, Eurocurrency deposits are typically not insured. Therefore, if a Eurobank defaults, reimbursement to the depositors is uncertain. Finally, a depositor's assessment of the financial soundness of Eurobanks is more difficult than an assessment of U.S. banks due to more stringent disclosure requirements in the United States. These risks or inconveniences discourage some corporations from maintaining Eurocurrency deposit balances.

Syndicated Eurocurrency Loans

While the Eurocurrency market concentrates on large-volume transactions, there are often times when no single Eurobank is willing to provide the amount needed by a particular corporation or government agency. In this case, a **syndicate** of Eurobanks may be composed. Each bank within the syndicate participates in the lending. A lead bank is responsible for negotiating terms with the borrower. Then the lead bank organizes a group of banks to underwrite the loans. The syndicate of banks is usually formed in about six weeks, or less if the borrower is well known, since the credit evaluation can then be conducted more quickly.

Borrowers who receive a syndicated loan incur various fees besides the interest on the loan. Front-end management fees are paid to represent the costs of organizing the syndicate and underwriting the loan. In addition, a commitment fee of about .25 percent or .50 percent is charged annually on the unused portion of the available credit extended by the syndicate.

Syndicated loans can be denominated in a variety of currencies. The interest rate depends on the currency denominating the loan, the maturity of the loan, and the creditworthiness of the borrower. Interest rates on syndicated loans are commonly adjustable according to movements in LIBOR (London Interbank Offer Rate), and the adjustment may occur every six months or every year.

Syndicated Eurocurrency loans not only reduce the default risk of a large loan to the degree of participation for each individual bank, but can also add an extra incentive for the borrower to repay the loan. If a government defaults on a loan to a syndicate, word will spread among banks quickly, and the government will likely have difficulty in obtaining future loans. Borrowers are therefore strongly encouraged to make prompt loan repayments on syndicated loans. From the perspective of the banks, syndicated Eurocurrency loans increase the probability of prompt repayment.

RISKS INCURRED BY A EUROBANK

The risks incurred by a Eurobank are somewhat similar to those of most commercial banks. First, its loans are subject to default risk. Second, it is exposed to exchange rate risk, since its assets may be denominated in a mix of currencies that does not perfectly match its liabilities. Finally, Eurobanks are exposed to interest rate risk, since the maturities of their liabilities will not always match the maturities of their assets. Each of these three types of risk will be discussed in turn.

Default Risk of Loans Provided by Eurobanks

The international loan portfolios of Eurobanks may be subject to a high degree of default risk, since Eurobanks may not be able to closely monitor the foreign companies to which they lend. In defense of the Eurobanks, their international loans are typically extended to the prominent corporations around the world, as well as to governments. This is generally perceived as a plus, since the largest corporations and governments have historically been reliable in paying back their loans. However, the recent international debt crisis has banks wondering whether any loan is safe. Eurobanks attempt to reduce the risk of their loan portfolios by employing effective credit evaluation on loan requests and by maintaining adequate diversification among industries and countries.

Exchange Rate Risk of Eurobanks

Eurobanks are also exposed to currency risk. That is, the currency composition of their assets may differ from that of their liabilities. While this risk may also exist for other commercial banks, it is more pronounced for Eurobanks, since they are always accepting foreign deposits and extending foreign loans.

Because a bank cannot always match its borrowed currencies with the currencies denominating loans, its performance will typically be exposed to exchange rate fluctuations. As a simplified example, consider that as of March 1, 1995, Bank A accepts $1 million in three-month U.S. dollar-denominated deposits and then uses the funds to provide a three-month mark-denominated loan amounting to DM2 million (by first converting the dollars to marks at an exchange rate of DM = $.50). In this case, the bank owes dollars to a depositor in the future, but has no expected future cash inflows in dollars. While it has matched maturities here, it has not matched currencies. This bank is "short" on dollars (since dollar-denominated liabilities exceed dollar-denominated assets) and "long" on marks (since mark-denominated assets exceed mark-denominated liabilities).

Assume that Bank A charges 12 percent annually (3 percent during the three-month loan period) on its mark-denominated loan and pays 8 percent annually (2 percent during the three-month loan period) on its dollar-denominated deposits. Since the exchange rate of the mark with respect to the dollar will not remain constant during the three-month period, the profit to the bank is exposed to any exchange rate adjustment that occurs. For example, if the mark's value declined to DM = $.48, the marks received upon loan repayment would convert to $988,800, which is not even sufficient to repay the depositor. If a bank is uncomfortable with its non-offsetting currency positions, it should search for another bank with which it can enact a currency swap. The swap arrangement could specify that as of June 1, 1995, Bank A would exchange marks for dollars with another bank according to a specified exchange rate. The swap locks in the rate at which Bank A can convert its marks (to be received) to dollars, thereby hedging against the possibility of the mark's depreciating over time.

Interest Rate Risk of Eurobanks

Eurobanks often face interest rate risk due to a maturity mismatch on their liabilities versus their assets. For example, if the source of funds reflects a shorter term to maturity than that of the loan it extends (with the use of these funds), the bank is subject to interest rate risk. Its spread between average interest earned on its assets and average interest paid out on its liabilities could be reduced during periods of rising interest rates. To insulate itself against this interest rate risk, the bank may arrange a swap with another bank that has mismatched maturities of the opposite type (average liability maturity exceeding average asset maturity).

As an example, consider Bank X, which as of January 2, 1996 received a one-month, $1 million deposit and will pay 9 percent annually (.75 percent for the month) on this deposit. Assume it has used the $1 million to make a three-month loan at 12 percent annually (3 percent for the three months). If by chance interest rates rise as of one month from now, the deposit rate paid by the bank will need to rise in order to attract more funds. Yet, the return on the $1 million loan given out is locked in for three months. Thus, the margin between interest received on loans and interest the bank pays on deposits will be narrowed. Consider a second bank, called Bank Y, which as of January 2, 1996 received a three-month, $1 million deposit and will pay 9 percent annually (2.25 percent for three months) on this deposit. Assume it has used the $1 million to make a one-month loan at 12 percent annually (1 percent over one month). If interest rates decline as of one month from now, the loan rate charged on a new loan by the bank at that time will need to be reduced in order to compete against rates of other banks. Yet, the rate on the $1 million deposit is locked in for three months. Thus, the margin between interest received on loans and interest the bank pays on deposits could be reduced.

Bank X is concerned about a reduced margin if interest rates rise, while Bank Y is concerned about a reduced margin if interest rates fall. The two banks can create a swap to insulate against the existing interest rate risk. In our example, Bank Y can, as of January 2, 1996, arrange to provide Bank X with a future loan of $1 million. This loan rate will be set at, say, 10.5 percent annually, and will be provided as of February 2. It will last for two months. At that time (April 2), Bank X will repay Bank Y for the loan with interest. This arrangement reflects a swap of funds from Bank Y to Bank X on February 2, in return for funds sent from Bank X to Bank Y on April 2.

Based on this example, the results for both banks are as follows. Bank X pays .75 percent over one month to a depositor, and 1.75 percent (10.5 percent annual rate) over two months for the loan from Bank Y. The cost of obtaining funds is therefore 2.50 percent over three months. The return to Bank X due to its three-month loan is 3 percent. If Bank X had not arranged for a swap, it could not have locked in its cost of obtaining funds, and would have faced the possibility of even a negative margin if interest rates increased over time.

Bank Y pays 2.25 percent over three months to a depositor. The return to Bank Y on its funds lent out is 1 percent over the first month, plus 1.75 percent over the next two months. The return amounts to 2.75 percent over three months. If Bank Y had not arranged for a swap, it could not have locked in its return on funds over the three-month period. Thus, it would have faced the possibility of even a negative margin if interest rates decreased over time.

If both banks had been able to match the maturities of their liabilities to those of their assets, they would not have needed a swap, since fluctuating interest rates would not have affected them. However, only a coincidence would cause the various maturities on liabilities to perfectly match those on assets for a bank. While the bank could actively pursue matched maturities, it might lose prospective customers if it restricted them to limited maturities on deposits or loans.

The use of floating-rate loans has effectively reduced interest rate risk, since the bank's interest received on assets should adjust as the interest paid on liabilities changes. Of course, the adjustment every six months or year still leaves the bank somewhat exposed, if its maturities on the liability side are shorter. Thus, the interest rate swap can further reduce exposure to maturity imbalances.

All Risks Combined

In reality, a Eurobank must attempt to manage its default risk, exchange rate risk, and interest rate risk simultaneously. Suppose a Eurobank receives most of its deposits in U.S. dollars with short-term maturities. On its asset side, assume that most loans have been long-term in nature, denominated in various European currencies, and focusing on a few selected industries. This Eurobank is exposed to a high degree of default risk, exchange rate risk, and interest rate risk. To reduce some of the risk, it may attempt to enter into currency swaps and interest rate swaps. Yet, it is unlikely to achieve perfect matching of maturities and currencies of its liabilities and its assets. Even if it did, default risk on the loans extended would remain. The discussion here does not imply that the risks incurred by Eurobanks are intolerable, but simply points out the challenge involved in managing all risks simultaneously.

BANKING REGULATIONS AMONG COUNTRIES

The United States has a complex regulatory system with the tightest restrictions in the world. In addition, the regulatory process is overseen by four agencies (Federal Reserve Board, Federal Deposit Insurance Corporation, Comptroller of the Currency, and state agencies). Banks in the United States are restricted to a maximum amount to be loaned to individual borrowers and are forced to write off nonperforming loans. In addition, they are not allowed to purchase stock for their asset portfolios.

Canadian banks are regulated by the Office of the Inspector General. They can purchase a limited amount of stock. They have no limits imposed on the loan amount to any individual borrower or country. Relative to most countries, Canadian banks enjoy fewer restrictions. The Bank of Canada serves as a lender of last resort to Canadian banks.

French banks are restricted to some extent from non-bank activities. However, they can own stock in non-bank companies. The Bank of France serves as a lender of last resort to French banks.

Japanese banks are supervised by the Ministry of Finance and the Bank of Japan. They are restricted from some but not all security underwriting activities. Limits are placed on loans to individual borrowers, although exceptions exist for public and guaranteed loans. Limits are not placed on loans to countries. The Bank of Japan assumes an active role in lending to Japanese banks in need of funds.

British banks are supervised by the Bank of England. They have much flexibility in entering into various forms of business, including investment banking services. The Bank of England serves as a lender of last resort to British banks.

German banks are overseen by the Federal Banking Supervisory Office and the Bundesbank (the German central bank). German banks are free to enter into various business activities, including investment banking services. Maximum limits are placed on individual loans. The Bundesbank serves as the lender of last resort to German banks.

Due to differences in regulations among countries, some banks are at a disadvantage when competing within the international banking environment.

Some differences in regulation are likely to persist, since each government maintains its own philosophy with regard to its role in regulating the banking industry.

Standardizing Regulations Across Countries

The trend toward globalization in the banking industry is attributed to the recent standardization of regulations around the world. Three of the more significant regulatory events allowing for a more competitive global playing field are (1) the International Banking Act, which placed U.S. and foreign banks operating in the United States under the same set of rules, (2) the Single European Act, which placed all European banks operating in Europe under the same set of rules, and (3) the uniform capital adequacy guidelines, which forced banks of 12 industrialized nations to abide by the same minimum capital constraints. A description of each of these events follows.

International Banking Act.   Passage of the **International Banking Act** (IBA) in 1978 restricted foreign-owned banks from accepting deposits across state lines. They were allowed to accept deposits in other states only by establishing Edge Act corporations (discussed earlier in this chapter). U.S.-owned banks were subject to similar restrictions at the time the IBA was passed.

The IBA also required that foreign-owned banks in the United States obtain deposit insurance and adhere to product and service restrictions enforced by the Bank Holding Company Act. In general, the IBA eliminated some comparative advantages of foreign-owned banks in the United States. Thus, the International Banking Act of 1978 had a favorable effect on the money center banks that had been competing with foreign banks on an unequal basis.

Single European Act.   One of the most significant events affecting the international banking is the **Single European Act,** which was phased in by 1992 throughout the European Economic Community (EEC) countries. Some of the more relevant provisions of the Single European Act for the banking industry are listed below:

- Capital can flow freely throughout Europe.
- Banks can offer a wide variety of lending, leasing, and securities activities in the EEC.
- The regulations regarding competition, mergers, and taxes will be similar throughout the EEC.
- A bank established in any one of the EEC countries will have the right to expand into any or all of the other EEC countries.

As a result of this act, the banks have expanded across European countries. Efficiency in the European banking markets will increase as banks can more easily cross countries without concern for country-specific regulations that have prevailed in the past.

Another key provision of the act is that banks entering Europe receive the same banking powers as other banks there. Similar provisions are allowed for non-U.S. banks that enter the United States.

Even some European savings institutions will be affected by more uniform regulations across European countries. Savings institutions throughout Europe are now evolving into full-service institutions, expanding into services such as insurance, brokerage, and mutual fund management.

Basel Accord. Before 1987, capital standards imposed on banks varied across countries, which allowed some banks to have a comparative global advantage over others. As an example, consider a bank in the United States that is subject to a 6 percent capital ratio, which is twice that of a foreign bank. The foreign bank could achieve the same return on equity as the U.S. bank by generating a return on assets that is only one-half that of the U.S. bank. In essence, the foreign bank's **equity multiplier** (assets divided by equity) would be double that of the U.S. bank, which would offset the low return on assets. Given these conditions, foreign banks could accept lower profit margins while still achieving the same return on equity. This would afford them a stronger competitive position. In addition, growth would be more easily achieved, as a relatively small amount of capital is needed to support an increase in assets.

Some analysts would counter that these advantages are somewhat offset by the higher risk perception of banks having low capital ratios. Yet, if the governments in those countries are more likely to back banks that experience financial problems, banks with low capital may not necessarily be too risky. Therefore, some non-U.S. banks would have globally competitive advantages over U.S. banks, without being subject to excessive risk. In December 1987, 12 major industrialized countries attempted to resolve the disparity by proposing uniform bank standards. In July 1988, central bank governors of the 12 countries agreed on standardized guidelines, in what was referred to as the **Basel Accord.** Capital was classified as either Tier 1 ("core") capital, or Tier 2 ("supplemental") capital (Tier 1 capital being at least 4 percent of risk-weighted assets). The use of risk weightings on assets implicitly created a higher required capital ratio for riskier assets. Off-balance sheet items were also accounted for, so that banks could not circumvent capital requirements by focusing on services (such as letters of credit and interest rate swaps) that are not explicitly shown on a balance sheet. Even with uniform capital requirements across countries, some analysts may still contend that U.S. banks are at a competitive disadvantage because they are subject to different accounting and tax provisions. Nevertheless, the uniform capital requirements represent significant progress toward a more level global field.

SUMMARY

■ Commercial banks conduct international banking in order to penetrate foreign markets and extend their business internationally. In addition, they can diversify their loan portfolios, which may reduce their credit risk. Commercial banks may also be encouraged to enter foreign markets that are subject to less regulation.

■ The Eurocurrency market facilitates the international flow of funds from corporations or governments with large amounts in excess funds to those with deficient funds. Eurobanks serve as financial intermediaries in this market. The

Eurocurrency market became popular in the 1970s, as OPEC countries had excess funds from oil revenues that were deposited into Eurobanks. The funds were typically lent to oil-importing countries.

■ Eurobanks that serve in the Eurocurrency market are exposed to default risk, exchange rate risk, and interest rate risk. Their exchange rate risk occurs because the currency composition of their assets differs from that of their liabilities.

■ Bank regulations have historically varied across countries. However, in recent years some of the regulations have become standardized. The International Banking Act created guidelines for foreign banks operating in the U.S. that were similar to the guidelines imposed on U.S. banks operating at home. The Single European Act placed all banks operating in Europe under the same set of rules. The uniform capital adequacy guidelines enforced similar risk-based capital requirements across banks residing in various industrialized countries. These standardized rules allow for more even competition among banks in the international banking environment.

SELF-TEST FOR CHAPTER 22

(Answers are provided in Appendix A in the back of the text.)

1. Consider a subsidiary of a U.S. bank that has used short-term dollar-denominated CDs as its main source of funds. Assume that it has exchanged the funds received for British pounds to provide six-year fixed-rate loans to British firms. Explain the possible exchange rate movements that would adversely affect this bank's performance.

2. Using the information in Question 1, explain the possible interest rate movements that would adversely affect the bank's performance.

3. A U.S. bank plans to establish a subsidiary in East Europe to provide loans to newly developed businesses. Since there is a shortage of funds in East Europe, the subsidiary plans to issue large CDs in the U.S., and then convert the proceeds to the currencies needed for loans to firms in East Europe. Do you believe the subsidiary's loan portfolio will be subject to a high degree of default risk? Explain. Will the subsidiary be subject to a high degree of exchange rate risk? Explain.

QUESTIONS

1. Discuss the motives that led to the growth of international banking.

2. What are IBFs, and how can they serve MNCs?

3. In what ways do banking regulations differ among countries?

4. Describe how a bank can become exposed to exchange rate risk.

5. Describe how a bank can reduce exposure to exchange rate risk.

6. Describe how a bank can become exposed to interest rate risk.

7. Describe how a bank can reduce exposure to interest rate risk.

8. Why did the Eurocurrency market become so popular?

9. What is syndicated lending? Why do banks sometimes prefer this form of lending?

10. Describe the possible differences in risk between a purely domestic bank and an international bank.

11. Why might a venture seem feasible for a Japanese bank, but not for a U.S. bank, even if the cash flows are similar? (Ignore exchange rate effects.)

12. Why might a bank be able to achieve greater economies of scale in Europe now than it could in the 1980s?

13. Why did differences in capital requirements give some banks a competitive advantage over others?

14. Even with uniform capital requirements, some banks may have competitive advantage over others because of differences in laws across countries. Explain.

15. Loras Bank planned to establish subsidiaries in various East European countries during the 1990s, even though it did not expect these subsidiaries to be profitable. Its logic was that this action was necessary to retain existing business. Interpret this statement.

European Banking Profits to Rely More On Trading and Contracting Out Tasks

By Nicholas Bray
Staff Reporter of THE WALL STREET JOURNAL.

LONDON - European banks are expected to increasingly rely on profits from securities and currency trading as well as cost savings from contracting out accounting and data-processing tasks, a new study says.

"Intensifying competition, weak balance sheets, profit pressures and new capital-adequacy requirements are forcing many banks to move away from ... traditional ... money transmission, lending and deposit-taking," the report, published by the Arthur Andersen accounting and consulting group, asserts.

Instead, much like big New York banks, European institutions are moving increasingly toward the trading of cash, securities and derivatives products as a source of profits, the study says. But uncertainty over whether they will be able to manage the complex risks inherent in these markets brings a new element of instability to a sector already pounded by recession and the effects of competition in traditional business areas.

Consolidation and New Entrants

Based on a survey of top executives at 400 leading banks and capital markets organizations across Europe, the report claims to be the most comprehensive study to date of practitioners' expectations for the banking sector. The survey was conducted during late 1992 and early 1993 by offices of the Andersen Worldwide Organization in 21 European countries. Subsequently, 50 industry experts participated in a workshop to analyze the survey's results and consider their implications.

One result of changing patterns, the report predicts, is likely to be continued consolidation through mergers and acquisitions. At the same time, however, new technologies are going to facilitate a process of fragmentation, as a host of nonbank players take advantage of easier access into the banks' traditional playground.

"We're definitely going to see consolidation, but also new entrants." said David Andrews, Andersen Consulting's head of financial services in Britain. "In the short term, we are entering a more dynamic market."

The entry of new niche players into financial markets will probably have little more than a marginal effect on the earnings of large established firms, but it "could ... cost existing smaller players dearly," the report says.

Changing Financial Patterns

Against this background, it asserts, the key to survival is likely to be banks' ability to position themselves in terms of size and structure, while at the same time segmenting their customer base to provide products tailored for specific groups.

Not surprisingly, the report contains the usual predictions about the need for slimming down work forces and reallocating employees to areas where they can produce more value in a changing environment. It dwells on changing financing patterns and the shift away from banks as intermediaries between borrowers and investors. It also predicts that banks will increasingly move to performance-related pay mechanisms as a way of motivating staff, and forecasts a sharp increase in the number of banking transactions done by telephone to 40% by the year 2000 from around 1% today.

Potentially its most illuminating findings, however, are those relating to outsourcing, or the transfer of routine tasks to outside subcontractors, and to the future role of currency and securities trading as a source of earnings.

Mirroring a trend in manufacturing industry, more and more banks said they expect to increase significantly the type and extent of operations subcontracted to outsiders. Along with the transfer of operations such as data-processing, accounting and computer systems maintenance, this process is also likely to promote the development of so-called white label products in such areas as mortgage servicing, where a central operator provides services for a range of banking clients.

One example already in operation in Britain is Barclays Bank's centralized mortgage-servicing unit in Leeds, which provides services under contract to a number of outside clients. Outsourcing is likely both to benefit banks that get rid of internal functions, by cutting costs and giving managers more time to concentrate on other tasks, and to assist the providers of such services, by enabling them to build up significant new profit centers.

In parallel, however, panelists forecast that their banks' profits will come increasingly from trading activities and proprietary trading, rather than from lending, their main traditional source of earnings.

Some banks surveyed already make as much as 35% of earnings out of trading. Over the longer term, many are aiming to raise such profits to the same level as those earned from lending, the report said.

QUESTIONS

1. Explain why the large international banks may consider focusing less on traditional lending and more on the trading of derivatives products. That is, what underlying factors could cause this strategy to be more profitable?

2. Explain how financial statement items might change for the large international banks that focus less on traditional lending and more on the trading of derivatives products.

3. What is a potential benefit to the international banks that plan to do more subcontracting (outsourcing)?

4. Given the potential changes in emphasis by international banks, offer your opinion on what the global banking environment will be like over the next decade.

5. How might some international banks attempt to benefit from the development of emerging markets around the world?

CASE PROBLEM

BANK OF CHICAGO
Exposure to Exchange Rate and Interest Rate Risk

The Bank of Chicago was a major participant in the Eurocurrency, Eurocredit, and Eurobond markets. Its branches in the Eurocurrency market accepted short-term deposits in nine different currencies. It used these funds to provide short-term or medium-term loans, or to purchase bonds in the Eurobond market. About one-third of its funds were allocated to each of these uses of funds. Its philosophy was to always use the same currency deposited to make its investments. In this way, it felt that it would avoid exposure to exchange rate risk. Whenever it needed funds in a particular currency, it would raise its deposit rates on that currency to attract more deposits.

The Bank of Chicago had very strong relations with the French government, but did not have any relations with German or Swiss governments. Therefore, it would often experience a very strong demand for French francs when the French government wanted to borrow funds, but experienced less demand for marks or Swiss francs. Consequently, it would sometimes experience a shortage of French francs, but have excess marks and Swiss francs. Whenever it had excess funds, it would loan them out on a daily basis in the interbank market. The annualized return was less than it would be if it could have provided long-term loans with these funds.

The Bank of Chicago was concerned about its exposure to interest rate risk, since some of its assets were less rate-sensitive than its liabilities. It decided to issue notes denominated in British pounds and use the proceeds to invest in British money market securities. As a result, the average rate sensitivity on all of its liability currencies in aggregate was more closely aligned with the average rate sensitivity on all of its asset currencies in aggregate.

a) What problems might arise as a result of the Bank of Chicago's philosophy of consistently using the same currency received to make a loan or investment?

b) If the Bank of Chicago did convert some of its excess deposits into French francs to accommodate the high demand for franc-denominated loans, would it be very susceptible to large losses resulting from exchange rate risk? Explain.

c) The recent issuance of British notes aligned the rate sensitivity on both sides of the balance sheet. Is the Bank of Chicago now insulated from interest rate risk? What scenarios could cause the bank to incur losses as a result of its interest rate sensitivities?

PROJECT _____

Once a year, special issues of *Business Week,* *Forbes,* and *Fortune* review the performance of numerous firms in the previous year. These issues normally come out in April. Find the section that is devoted to banking, and assess the performance of the ten largest banks that conduct a significant amount of international business. How did these banks perform relative to smaller banks? Attempt to explain why the international banks did better or worse than the smaller banks.

REFERENCES

Aggarwal, Raj, and Jon Durnford. "Market Assessment of International Banking Activity: A Study of U.S. Bank Holding Companies." *Quarterly Journal of Economics and Business* (Spring 1989), pp. 58-67.

Aharony, Joseph, Anthony Saunders, and Itzhak Swary. "The Effects of the International Banking Act on Domestic Bank Profitability." *Journal of Money, Credit and Banking* (November 1986), pp. 493-506.

Aliber, Robert Z. "International Banking: A Survey." *Journal of Money, Credit, and Banking* (November 1984), pp. 661-712.

Goodman, Laurie S. "The Pricing of Syndicated Eurocurrency Credits." Federal Reserve Bank of New York. *Quarterly Review* (Summer 1980), pp. 39-49.

Jain, Arvind, and Douglas Nigh. "Politics and the International Lending Decisions of Banks." *Journal of International Business Studies* (Summer 1989), pp. 349-359.

Lee, Suk Hun. "Relative Importance of Political Instability and Economic Variables on Perceived Instability and Economic Variables on Perceived Country Creditworthiness." *Journal of International Business Studies* (Fourth Quarter 1993), pp. 801–812.

Logue, Dennis E., and Pietra Rivoli. "Some Consequences of Banks' LDC Loans: A Note." *Journal of Financial Services Research* (May 1992), pp. 37–47.

Madura, Jeff, Alan L. Tucker, and Emilio Zarruk. "Reaction of Bank Share Prices to the Third-World Debt Reduction Plan." *Journal of Banking and Finance* (September 1992), pp. 853–868.

Maxwell, Charles E., and Lawrence J. Gitman. "Risk Transmission in International Banking: An Analysis of 48 Central Banks." *Journal of International Business Studies* (Summer 1989), pp. 268-279.

Schwartz, Eduardo S., and Salvador Zurita. "Sovereign Debt: Optimal Contract, Underinvestment, and Forgiveness." *Journal of Finance* (July 1992), pp. 981–1004.

Soenen, Luc A., and Raj Aggarwal. "Banking Relationships and Cash and Foreign Exchange Management: A Study of Companies in the United Kingdom, the Netherlands, and Belgium." *Management International Review*, no. 2 (1988), pp. 56-69.

Waheed, Amjad, and Ike Mathur. "The Effects of Announcements of Bank Lending Agreements on the Market Values of U.S. Banks." *Financial Management* (Spring 1993), pp. 119–127.

CHAPTER 23

THE INTERNATIONAL DEBT CRISIS AND BANK ASSESSMENT OF COUNTRY RISK

The previous chapter provides a background on the international banking environment. In the early 1980s, this environment was severely affected as several large borrowers experienced difficulty in repaying their international loans on time. This event, often referred to as the international debt crisis (IDC), is the focus of this chapter, as it continues to affect the banking industry. The specific objectives of this chapter are to

- describe the events that precipitated the crisis,
- explain how the large banks with heavy exposure to LDC loans have managed their loan portfolios since the crisis, and
- explain how banks assess country risk when considering international loans.

THE INTERNATIONAL DEBT CRISIS

During the early 1980s, many less developed countries (LDCs) began to incur large balance of trade deficits, largely because of the global recession that reduced demand by industrialized countries for LDC exports. The large balance of trade deficits caused deteriorated conditions in LDCs. Worsening conditions caused the debt level to rise. The loans to the Latin American countries were largely denominated in dollars. Consequently, loan repayment became more difficult when the dollar strengthened against the borrowers' currencies in the early 1980s.

661

Many of the loans to LDCs had floating interest rates (periodically adjusting to some market interest rate). For example, the percentage of floating-rate debt to total debt is provided in Exhibit 23.1 for five individual LDCs. Because the loans were generally of a floating-rate nature, the debt repayment amount was influenced by changes in the interest rates over time. When interest rates were rising, floating-rate loans became even more difficult to pay off.

The sudden emergence of loan rescheduling requests began in 1980. By 1983 more than 25 countries were victims of the IDC.

As a result of the IDC, many critics contend that international lending increases rather than decreases the risk on a bank's loan portfolio. Because the loan rescheduling during the IDC involved not just one but several LDCs, the idea of diversifying to reduce risk has lost some of its allure. During the IDC, it became clear that the economies of many LDCs are highly correlated with each other. Consequently, diversifying loans among them did not significantly reduce a foreign loan portfolio's risk from the banker's point of view.

THE DEBT CRISIS FROM A BANKER'S PERSPECTIVE

To understand the bankers' dilemma during the IDC, consider yourself a chief international loan officer for a bank with millions of dollars lent to each of several LDCs. Assume you receive phone calls from the governments of each of the debtor countries with the message, "We can't pay our outstanding loans, and probably will never be able to unless you help us with additional loans." You, as the chief international loan officer, must determine whether to provide more funds to these countries. If you do not, there is a chance you will never receive repayments on previous loans extended to these countries. However, if you do extend the loans, you still are not guaranteed that the countries will generate enough funds to repay them. It is possible that your bad debt will therefore be greater than if you cut off relations now with these debtor countries.

There is no perfect solution to such a problem. Yet, there are some aspects that deserve consideration. First, what are the attitudes of all of the other banks that are in a similar position? If you decide to provide more funds, but the other banks decide not to, these LDCs may have a difficult time rebuilding (since the support from only some of the banks would be insufficient). Conversely, if you do not extend additional loans while all other bankers do, then there is a better chance the countries will be able to rebuild and someday pay off their debts. In this case, your bank would not be given high priority in terms of loan repayment

EXHIBIT 23.1 **Percentage of Loans That Had Floating Rates in Five Different Countries** Source: *Federal Reserve Bank of San Francisco Weekly Letter* (September 23, 1983).	Country	Floating Rate Debt as a Percentage of Total Debt
	Argentina	66%
	Brazil	62
	Chile	74
	Mexico	78
	South Korea	55

or future loan requests by the countries, since you declined to provide further assistance when it was needed.

By meeting with other bankers, you could determine their attitudes toward solving the problem. Bankers did in fact meet frequently to discuss possible solutions during the IDC. Their negotiating ability was strengthened since they acted as a group. Another consideration for an international loan officer faced with this situation is your degree of involvement. A bank with only a very small portion of total loans extended to these countries may prefer to avoid getting further involved and be more willing to write off the outstanding loans as bad debt. Yet, a bank with a large percentage of its total loans provided to these troubled countries has more at stake. It may not be able to afford writing off the outstanding loans. Some of the banks had only a small percentage of loans extended to these LDCs, while other banks were more deeply involved. Such a variety of unique situations among banks caused some intense discussion as to the appropriate solution by bankers as a group.

GOVERNMENT INTERVENTION IN THE CRISIS

In 1983 there was much disagreement as Congress met to determine whether to provide additional funds to the **International Monetary Fund (IMF).** The IMF is an international agency that attempts to facilitate international trade and finance, and help countries experiencing balance of payment difficulties. It could channel funds to LDCs experiencing debt repayment problems. Most large U.S. banks favored additional IMF funding, since they believed it would reduce the LDCs' problems. In this case, they hoped that the countries would at some point repay their loans.

Other banks with little exposure to bad debt from foreign loans were generally not as favorable toward congressional appropriation of more funds to the IMF. In fact, some of their views reflected the feeling that those banks that extended the loans to these troubled countries should work out their problems without the aid of the government. That is, taxpayers should not be forced to provide the U.S. government with money for the IMF that would later be recycled into the hands of the large banks. Some bankers felt that if the U.S. government were willing to bail out the large banks (by appropriating funds to the IMF), then it should bail out smaller banks that might fail because many of their domestic loans were never repaid.

A possible response to that criticism is that small bank failures do not normally cause massive fear in the banking industry. Large bank failures, on the other hand (resulting from bad debt on loans extended to LDCs), could cause bank depositors to withdraw their funds from banks, thereby accelerating a possible collapse in the banking industry. Even though depositors are insured up to a stated maximum amount of funds, there would only be so much money to go around if several large banks did fail. The Federal Deposit Insurance Corporation (FDIC), which insures bank depositors, would not be able to cover all of them.

In November 1983 Congress passed the so-called **IMF Funding Bill,** which called for funds to be sent from the U.S. government to the IMF and then channelled to the LDCs. The IMF provided these funds based on promises by LDCs to improve various aspects of their financial condition, such as their balance of trade positions. The objective was for the troubled countries to spend more money at home in an effort to stimulate their respective economies. In Argentina's case, for example, the IMF requested an effort to cut the government's budget deficit and reduce its inflation rate. The IMF loans were a key to the LDCs' gaining access to additional commercial bank loans.

IMPACT OF THE DEBT CRISIS ON NON-BANK MNCS

The IMF package required LDCs to substantially improve their current account positions. As a result, government authorities imposed import restrictions and currency blockages in an effort to boost spending within these economies. Thus, not only were the large banks with outstanding loans to such countries adversely affected by the crisis, but all multinational corporations (MNCs) that either export to or maintain subsidiaries within these countries were affected as well. In 1983, some U.S. MNCs simply sold their subsidiaries. Others struggled to find local supplies for their operations that could serve as substitutes for the supplies they used to import.

The measures taken by the IMF and LDCs affected both the operations and the finances of many MNCs. For example, car sales by plants of the biggest three automobile manufacturers were off by 33 percent in Mexico during the first half of 1983, while truck sales declined 50 percent. Manufacturers in appliances and other industries shut down parts of their normal operations in Mexico. Minnesota Mining and Manufacturing (3M) Company discontinued sales of its video-cassettes and copying machines in Latin America. Du Pont's chemical exports to the Southern Hemisphere declined by 20 percent during 1983.

Litton Industries discovered that its $1 million on deposit at Mexican banks had been converted by the Mexican government into pesos (the Mexican currency). The peso's weakening over time reduced the dollar value of these deposits. Because the Mexican peso had been very weak throughout the crisis, MNC subsidiaries based in Mexico did not want to finance with other currencies. Their revenues were in pesos and they would have had to pay back their loans by converting the weak pesos to whatever currency was borrowed. The Mexican peso weakened against the U.S. dollar by 82 percent from mid-February 1982 to July 1983. Imagine the dollar cost of borrowing to a Mexican subsidiary during that period! To avoid incurring such enormous exchange and financing costs, many Latin American subsidiaries (where local currencies were very weak) began to use local currency financing. With this approach, the revenues received were in the same currency as that needed to pay off loans. However, the interest rates in some of these countries were outrageous. For example, the going interest rate on loans denominated in Brazilian cruzeiros was 205 percent as of July 1983, more than 20 times the prevailing interest rates in developed countries.

LOAN MANAGEMENT SINCE THE DEBT CRISIS

Banks heavily involved in lending to Latin American countries clearly had much at stake. Exhibit 23.2 identifies the amounts owed by some Latin American countries to U.S. banks. The banks were most exposed to the debt of Argentina, Brazil, Mexico, and Venezuela. During the late 1980s, the average exposure of U.S. money center banks to the combined debt of these countries was about 4

EXHIBIT 23.2		Total Debt	Debt Held by U.S. Banks
Debt of LDCs	Argentina	$ 49.6	$ 8.5
(billions of dollars)	Bolivia	4.2	0.14
Source: *Economic*	Brazil	104.5	23.9
Review, Federal Reserve	Chile	21.5	5.9
Bank of Kansas City	Colombia	13.6	2.6
(January 1987), p. 25.	Ecuador	7.7	2.1
	Mexico	97.3	24.8
	Peru	14.2	1.65
	Uruguay	4.7	0.89
	Venezuela	36.5	20.4

percent of their total assets. Exhibit 23.2 shows that creditors from other countries were also exposed to Latin American debt. U.S. banks were responsible for only 17 percent of Argentina's total debt, 23 percent of Brazil's debt, and 25 percent of Mexico's debt.

Sale of LDC Loans

During the international debt crisis, several banks reduced their LDC loan exposure to satisfy existing and potential shareholders. Some were willing to swap LDC loans to achieve a more diversified mix (which would reduce their exposure to any individual LDC). Foreign loans were sold at a sizable discount. Some Middle Eastern and European banks sold their entire Latin American loan portfolios. The banks attempting to sell their loans were essentially unwilling to restructure the loan terms and allow time for the LDCs to recuperate. They instead desired to sell the loans cheap and incur the losses immediately. The perceived probability of loan repayment can be assessed by reviewing the discounts on LDC loans sold in the secondary market. Exhibit 23.3 shows the market price for which loans to various countries were selling in the secondary loan market. There are large differences in the market value of debt across LDCs.

Increasing Loan Loss Reserves

In May 1987 Citicorp boosted its loan loss reserves by about $3 billion. This was a major event, because it indicated anticipation of large loan losses in the future. Other large banks in the United States followed Citicorp's strategy over the next two months. The stock market seemed to accept the news without any major negative reaction, even though the increased loan loss reserves would depress earnings. Market participants had apparently anticipated that the large banks would need to boost their loan loss reserves well in advance. The banks might have been able to avoid the increase in loan loss reserves temporarily, but eventually the likelihood of some LDC loan defaults would have required it. Perhaps the largest U.S. banks were more willing to boost loan loss reserves after observing the absence of any negative market reaction to Citicorp's announcement.

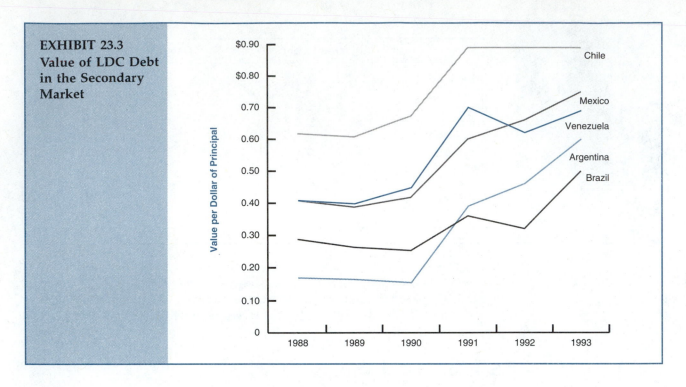

**EXHIBIT 23.3
Value of LDC Debt
in the Secondary
Market**

In September 1989 another round of increases in loan loss reserves began for some money center banks. The most publicized announcement was J.P. Morgan's increase by $2 billion, which boosted its loan loss reserve account to match its total LDC debt exposure. The total loan loss reserves at other money center banks represented only between 35 and 50 percent of medium- and long-term LDC debt.

Use of Debt-Equity Swaps

Many banks and non-bank MNCs have participated in **debt-equity swaps,** which can reduce the amount of LDC debt held by financial institutions in the following manner. A U.S.-based MNC can purchase (at a discount) some of an LDC's outstanding loans in the secondary market. It then trades the debt to the LDC government in exchange for some assets that are being liquidated by the government. Such assets could include airplanes, machinery, buildings, or even land. U.S.-based MNCs such as Allied-Signal Inc., Chrysler Corporation, and General Electric Company have engaged in debt-equity swaps. Allied-Signal has swapped debt for equity investments in Chile. Chrysler and General Electric have swapped debt for companies in Mexico. Many financial institutions that are holding LDC debt have also swapped some of the debt for equity investments. For example, Citicorp has traded debt for an equity investment in gold mining in Chile.

Given sufficient equity investment opportunities in LDCs, MNCs are encouraged to engage in debt-equity swaps. Consequently, the secondary market for LDC debt is more active. If debt-equity swaps were not possible, the only demand for existing LDC loans in the secondary market would be by financial institutions that are willing to assume greater exposure to LDC debt. The existence of debt-equity swaps allows other companies to purchase LDC debt obligations, even if they have no plans to hold these obligations. Because debt-equity swaps increase the demand for LDC loans in the secondary market, they reduce the size of the discount on these loans.

While debt-equity swaps enhance a bank's chances of selling LDC debt, they do not necessarily reduce the risk of banks that exchange LDC debt for LDC equity. Some equity investments in LDCs may be just as risky as the LDC loans that are traded in. Furthermore, banks that acquire equity interest in LDC assets may not have the expertise to manage those assets.

Implementation of the Brady Plan

Over the period from 1985 to 1988, a plan was endorsed as a means of mitigating the LDC debt crisis. The plan was based on voluntary actions by lenders to reduce their exposure. In December 1988 the World Bank proposed a gradual implementation of the plan, along with its commitment to provide loans to LDCs in place of bank loans and to impose economic reforms on the LDCs. During 1989 the plan gained momentum, as the International Monetary Fund (IMF) signaled its willingness to replace LDC debt maintained by banks. In what then became known as the **Brady Plan,** negotiations between banks and individual LDCs were encouraged in order to provide banks with the option of having their debt replaced by the World Bank and IMF by their trading it in at a discount.

In July 1989, banks reached an agreement with Mexico in which they were given the following options: (1) agree to a 35 percent cut in the principal or interest on loans, or (2) grant new loans equal to 25 percent of the Mexican loans. Essentially, the trade-off involved either recognizing losses on previous loans while reducing exposure, or increasing investment in LDCs without incurring immediate losses. The agreement could improve Mexico's position, because it reduced the amount Mexico owed on existing debt and also allowed for additional loans from banks. In this way, Mexico might be better able to improve its debt servicing, which would enhance investors' perceptions of Mexican debt maintained by banks. The agreement between banks and Mexico paved the way for agreements between banks and other LDCs.

BANK ASSESSMENT OF COUNTRY RISK

A bank's loan evaluation process includes a review of the environment surrounding the applicant. This represents an analysis of country risk. The IDC has convinced large international banks of the need to accurately assess country risk, which, from a banker's perspective, reflects the probability that a country will fail to meet its loan repayment schedule. A bank's assessment of country risk can affect lending decisions related not only to government requests for loans, but to foreign corporate loan requests as well. Country risk analysis from a bank's point of view will consider political and financial risk factors; it is similar to a country risk analysis from an MNC's direct foreign investment perspective. However, the manner in which political and financial factors affect a bank can differ substantially from the way they affect an MNC considering direct foreign investment. In addition, the importance attached to the various factors differs.

Effect of the Brady Plan on Bank Value

In 1989, the Brady Plan (also called the Debt Reduction Plan) was implemented. This plan contained provisions that would allow less developed countries (LDCs) to retire some of their outstanding debt at a discount. To the extent that the plan was expected to be beneficial, banks should have experienced higher stock prices. Research by Madura, Tucker, and Zarruk measured the effects of the Brady Plan on bank stock prices. Subsamples of banks exposed to LDC debt and of non-exposed banks were analyzed separately. The exposed banks experienced a strong favorable stock price response to news about the Brady Plan, while the non-exposed banks were unaffected. These results suggest that the favorable effects of the plan were isolated in those banks which had loans committed to LDCs.

The effects within the group of exposed banks appeared to vary across banks, as some of these banks were in a position to benefit more than others. Those banks that were most highly exposed appeared to benefit the most from the Brady Plan. In general, the Brady Plan was interpreted by the market as an indirect subsidy from the government to those large banks with exposure to LDC debt.

Country risk measurement by banks involves assessing whether funds will be available to the potential borrower in the future periods of a loan, so any condition that prevents prompt loan repayment can be categorized as a political or financial problem. Thus, a logical approach to country risk analysis involves assessing all relevant political and financial characteristics of a potential borrower.

Political Risk Factors

From a bank lending perspective, the most severe form of political risk would be the refusal to repay loans due to the borrowing country's political relationship with the bank or the bank's home country. However, there are other forms of political risk that are less severe but worth assessing. For example, a change in foreign government tax policy could have a significant impact on a foreign firm's ability to repay outstanding loans. In addition, a foreign government may decide to become the "owner" of a firm. The government's attitude toward fulfilling outstanding loan contracts can differ from that of the firm. A more indirect form of political risk is government blockage of currency convertibility, such that a particular currency cannot be obtained to repay loans denominated in that currency.

If the bank is lending funds to a foreign government, it must assess the government's commitment to repay loans. Because government philosophy changes over time, a bank must assess the possibility of a change in governmental ideology that may influence the commitment to repay outstanding loans.

While some assessments of political risk are kept confidential, others are publicly available. The *Institutional Investor* publishes a summary of country risk ratings by 75 to 100 banks. This summary is revised every six months. The political risk rating scale ranges from a high of 100 (reflecting the highest level of creditworthiness) to a low of zero.

The *Institutional Investor* ratings for several major countries as well as some less developed countries are displayed in Exhibit 23.4. For most industrialized countries, the ratings have been quite stable over time. Yet, they have been very erratic for some of the LDCs, such as Argentina, Brazil, and Mexico. The ideal risk rating system would be able to detect political and financial problems far

EXHIBIT 23.4 Country Risk Ratings among European and Latin American Countries (Ratings can range from zero to a high of 100) Source: *Institutional Invesetor*, 1993.

Country in Europe	Rating	Country in Latin America	Rating
Germany	90	Chile	52
Netherlands	89	Mexico	46
France	88	Columbia	40
United Kingdom	85	Venezuela	38
Belgium	80	Uruguay	34
Norway	78	Argentina	33
Denmark	77	Brazil	28
Spain	75	Paraguay	27
Italy	74	Ecuador	21
Ireland	70	Peru	15
Greece	49		
Czech Republic	46		
Turkey	45		
Hungary	45		
Poland	29		
Romania	24		
Bulgaria	20		
Albania	11		
Yugoslavia	8		

into the future. It should be emphasized that since the ratings here were conducted by bankers, they are assessed in the context of international lending.

Financial Risk Factors

Country risk assessors must thoroughly evaluate the financial condition of a foreign country, since it influences the probability of loan repayment by both the country's government and its corporations. The government of a financially strong country will normally generate sufficient tax revenues to promptly cover its debts. However, a financially weak country will most likely need to spend far more on its people than it receives in taxes from them, causing enormous budget deficits. To repay loans at a time like this requires new loans to be used in repaying the maturing loans. Governments may sometimes be reluctant to borrow more money for the purpose of covering maturing debt. The IDC is evidence that even governments are sometimes unable (or unwilling) to meet loan repayment obligations.

A strong economy in a given foreign country can substantially improve the performance (and therefore the ability to repay loans) of firms in that country. For this reason, a bank's country risk assessors evaluate the current and projected economic outlook of all countries in which loans are provided. In order to develop a projected economic outlook for a given country, several economic indicators are used, including gross national product (GNP), the unemployment rate, money supply, inflation, and interest rates. Indicators of strong economic growth within a country generally represent favorable news for firms requesting loans within that country. Yet a loan to a particular foreign firm is not safe just because its national economy is strong. Each firm reacts uniquely to economic trends. Consequently, it is critical that banks assess not only the current and

USING DISCRIMINANT ANALYSIS TO IDENTIFY CHARACTERISTICS THAT AFFECT COUNTRY RISK

The technique of discriminant analysis is useful for identifying factors that are distinctly different between two groups. It has historically been used to identify factors that distinguish (or discriminate) between successful and failing firms. It could even be used to identify characteristics that distinguish between good and bad sports teams, or between successful and unsuccessful employees of a firm.

Discriminant analysis is a popular technique for country risk assessment because it can attempt to identify factors that distinguish between those countries experiencing debt repayment problems and countries not experiencing problems. Once these factors are known, they can be closely monitored in the future.

The factors hypothesized to discriminate between two groups must first be identified, and they must be numerically measurable. Then historical data are used to measure the factors. Discriminant analysis generates a discriminant function that determines not only which factors distinguish between the two groups, but the type of influence each factor has.

Recent research by Morgan[1] used discriminant analysis to assess the influence of variables on the likelihood that a country would need to reschedule its loan repayments. Morgan found the following characteristics of countries whose loan payments were rescheduled:

- Their total debt to exports ratio was relatively high.
- Their proportion of floating-rate loans (relative to total loans) was relatively high.

- Their real growth rate in gross domestic product (GDP) was relatively low.

While discriminant analysis is useful for identifying characteristics that distinguish countries that rescheduled loans versus those that did not, its accuracy in predicting reschedulings will depend on whether those characteristics continue to have a similar impact on reschedulings. For example, from Morgan's results, one would expect that a country with a greater proportion of floating rate loans would have a higher probability of experiencing loan repayment problems. However, if interest rates decrease in the future, countries with a greater proportion of floating rate loans may be favorably affected.

---

projected economy, but also the type and degree of influence that country's economy has on each firm that has requested a loan. This implies that there is a two-step process for banks evaluating the economic influence on foreign loan applicants. The first step is to forecast the future economic strength of a country. The second is to forecast the applicant firm's future performance based on the forecast of the economy. This second step requires an understanding of how the firm's sales and profits are influenced by national business cycles.

COUNTRY RISK ASSESSMENT PROCEDURE

Assessment of a particular country's risk may involve anywhere from one person to twenty or more people at a particular bank. The assessment usually entails (1) preparation of country studies and reports, (2) use of scoring (or rating) systems in which various characteristics of each country are assessed in terms of contribution to risk, and (3) use of rating models that can aggregate the individual risk characteristics of a particular country in order to develop an overall rating. If any one of the techniques is conducted improperly, the overall risk assessment approach will be susceptible to significant errors. For example, inaccurate reporting of a country's current conditions will cause even the most accurate scoring system and rating model to generate incorrect country risk ratings. Each of the three steps to assess country risk is briefly discussed here.

With regard to the accumulation of information about potential borrowers, it is difficult to separate useful data from irrelevant data. For example, is a recent riot involving 500 people in a particular country relevant information to a country risk assessor? If the riot was a one-time event, the information is probably not critical. However, if this small riot could lead to greater tensions and therefore a massive revolt, then the information is valuable. To ascertain whether the event may lead to more critical events is difficult.

Once a bank has determined what information to incorporate, and how to rate each financial and political characteristic of a country, it must decide how to weigh the contribution of each characteristic. Because there is no perfect solution for any of these decisions, it is understandable that each bank has its own unique approach for assessing country risk. Even if two banks follow exactly the same procedure for assessing a particular country, their final decisions on whether to extend loans may differ. This is due to differences among banks regarding willingness to bear risk. An aggressive bank might lend to a borrower rated as a "moderate risk," while a more conservative bank might not.

Limitations and Solutions to Country Risk Analysis

There are two common mistakes that can result from country risk assessment: (1) a bank provides a loan it should not have, or (2) a bank does not provide a loan it should have. The consequence of the first error is a defaulted loan, while the consequence of the second error is possibly a lost customer. The first error is typically much more damaging to an international bank.

Given the limitations of any country risk assessment approach, banks must recognize that their decisions may turn out to be improper. To reduce the damage caused by providing loans that should not have been provided, banks could place a cap on total volume of loans extended to each particular country. This would limit the sensitivity of the overall loan portfolio to any single country's problems.

If a bank limits its loans to any single country but desires to provide a significant volume of foreign loans, it should diversify its loans among countries. Diversification helps protect the overall loan portfolio from substantially declining in value, since any one country's financial and political problems will affect only a small portion of the portfolio. However, there are some countries whose risk ratings tend to move together. Such countries typically share a common characteristic, such as having oil as their major export, or being located in the same geographical region. A portfolio of loans to such countries exhibits considerable risk, since their political and financial conditions tend to move in tandem. International lenders achieve more effective diversification by including countries whose political and financial condition trends are unrelated.

The diversification concept suggests that banks must consider more than a country's individual characteristics. Banks must also assess the contribution of that country risk to the risk of the overall loan portfolio. For example, consider a bank that has extended most of its international loans to countries that are heavy oil importers. The bank is currently assessing the creditworthiness of Country X, another oil importer, and Country Y, an oil exporter. Assume that both countries have requested loans. Also assume that based on the individual assessments,

EXAMPLE OF COUNTRY RISK ASSESSMENT

The following assessment method, described by Morgan, was used by a bank to measure country risk. This system was based on four major aspects of a country:

1. *Economic indicators*—to evaluate the country's financial condition
2. *Debt management*—to measure the country's ability to repay debt
3. *Political factors*—to assess political characteristics and political stability
4. *Structural factors*—to measure socioeconomic conditions, such as human resource base.

Short-term and medium-term models of these four aspects were developed in order to determine an overall short-term rating and an overall medium-term rating for a country. The segmentation into two time horizons was used because a country's economic outlook may vary with the time horizon used.

Each of the four models assigns a score between 0 and 100. Once the four models are complete, the overall rating is determined by weighing the importance of the models. An example of how the overall rating is determined is shown in Exhibit A. Notice that a grade is assigned for both the short- and medium-term horizons. The grades for this hypothetical example were higher in the short term than the medium term. The weight distribution differed between short- and medium-term horizons, since economic indicators were thought to be more important in the short-term horizon, while the political rating was more important for the medium-term horizon.

The overall numerical grade for each horizon can be converted into a rating. The conversion process converts grades into categories similar to those in Standard and Poor's rating system on securities. Based on the grades shown in Exhibit B, the country's short-term horizon received a rating of A, while the medium-term horizon received a grade of BBB.

EXHIBIT A
Example of Determining Country Risk Ratings

	Short-term Horizon			Medium-term Horizon		
	Weight	Grade	Weighted Grade	Weight	Grade	Weighted Grade
Debt management model	.3	80	24	.3	70	21
Economic indicator model	.3	90	27	.2	70	14
Political rating model	.2	60	12	.3	50	15
Structural rating model	.2	75	15	.2	60	12
			78			62

EXHIBIT B
Conversion of a Country's Grade into a Rating

Overall Grade Rating	Rating	
91–100	AAA	Excellent
81–90	AA	
71–80	A	
61–70	BBB	Average quality
51–60	BB	
41–50	B	
31–40	CCC	Low quality
21–30	CC	
11–20	C	
0–10	D	Excessive risk

Country X deserves a slightly higher individual credit rating. However, the economic conditions of Country X are susceptible to oil price changes in a manner similar to those of the other countries already within the bank's loan portfolio. Thus, if the market price of oil increases substantially, Country X will be adversely affected, along with the other countries in the bank's loan portfolio. Yet, Country Y would probably benefit from the rise in the market price of oil. From a loan portfolio perspective, a loan to Country Y may be perceived as safer, since it may reduce the risk of the overall loan portfolio. This example illustrates why banks must assess a country not only individually, but in terms of its contribution to the overall risk in the bank's loan portfolio.

SUMMARY

■   The international debt crisis was precipitated by a recession in the early 1980s that adversely affected many countries. Demand for exports of the LDCs declined. The dollar-denominated loans caused higher loan repayment amounts for LDCs in the early 1980s, when the dollar strengthened. Some of the loans had floating interest rates, which caused higher loan repayment amounts in the early 1980s, when U.S. interest rates rose.

■   Many large banks with heavy exposure to LDC loans sold some of these loans at a deep discount in the secondary loan market. They also increased their loan loss reserves, in anticipation that they would write off some of these loans. Some of the banks used debt-equity swaps, in which they swapped loans for an equity investment in the assets of LDCs.

■   When banks consider providing international loans, they assess country risk by assigning ratings to various political and financial characteristics of the country of concern. These characteristics reflect the country's perceived ability and willingness to make future debt payments. The country risk assessment procedure requires weighting the various factors that are presumed to affect country risk. Thus, the country risk rating is essentially a weighted average of ratings assigned to factors that comprise country risk. While most banks would consider the same factors, each bank assigns its own ratings to factors, and uses its own scheme for weighting the factors.

SELF-TEST FOR CHAPTER 23

(Answers are provided in Appendix A in the back of the text.)

1. Offer your own opinion on why banks were unable to recognize the potential financial problems of LDCs when they extended loans to these countries.

2. Should the banking system be more closely regulated to prevent another international debt crisis or any other banking crisis?

3. The bank's assessment of a country's financial condition is different from the assessment of a firm's financial condition, because a country does not have financial statements. What financial characteristics of a country are most critical, in your opinion, in determining whether the country is creditworthy?

QUESTIONS

1. Discuss the developments that led to the international debt crisis.

2. Discuss the IMF's role in attempting to resolve the international debt crisis.

3. What does the existence of the international debt crisis suggest about the previous country risk assessments conducted by banks?

4. Identify factors that would likely be used by banks to assess a government's creditworthiness.

5. Identify factors that would likely be used by banks to assess a foreign corporation's creditworthiness.

6. Why are country risk assessments by banks not always accurate?

7. With regard to the international debt crisis, would banks be better off acting as a group or individually in negotiating the rescheduling of loans? Discuss.

8. When a crisis (such as the international debt crisis) develops, should international banks receive any help from their governments to resolve the problem? To what extent should their governments become involved?

9. Why do banks sometimes rate countries differently? That is, what components of the country risk rating procedure can lead to different overall ratings among banks for a particular country?

10. Two common mistakes due to inaccurate country risk assessment by a bank are

   - Providing a loan it should not have
   - Not providing a loan it should have.

   Which of these mistakes is more critical? Elaborate.

11. There are a variety of statistical techniques (such as discriminant analysis) that are used to identify characteristics that can correctly discriminate between countries that have had debt repayment problems and countries that have not. Explain why such techniques may not correctly predict which countries will experience debt repayment problems in the future.

12. Explain debt-equity swaps and how they increase activity in the secondary loan market.

13. Why do you think the market did not react negatively to money center banks that boosted their loan loss reserves in 1987 and again in 1989? After all, didn't the boost in loan loss reserves signal problems involving LDC debt?

14. It has been suggested that the next international debt crisis could result from economic problems in Eastern European countries. Do you think that the Eastern European countries are as exposed to economic problems as the Latin American countries?

15. Briefly describe how the Brady Plan was intended to resolve international debt repayment problems.

'Bridge' Loans to Latin America Rise, But Some Wonder if the Toll Is Too High

By Craig Torres
Staff Reporter of The Wall Street Journal

NEW YORK With their scars barely faded from the Latin American lending of years past, big banks are back in the region making temporary "bridge" loans to Latin companies.

Bridge loans picked up a bad name in the U.S. corporate lending market awhile back. They are meant to last a few months, quickly replaced with long-term financing. When all works as planned, bridge loans can bring fat fees to lenders and speedy cash to borrowers. But Wall Street will never forget how the 1989 collapse in the junk-bond market turned giant "temporary" bridge loans into bridges to nowhere, generating big writeoffs.

Today, the bridge is back, often as a source of upfront cash for junk-rated Latin corporations that are planning bond issues. Bankers Trust New York Corp., Chase Manhattan Corp., Citicorp and J.P. Morgan & Co., as well as foreign banks such as Spain's Banco Santander, all are writing bridge loans to Latin American companies.

A Competitive Tool

In the race to win much-demanded Latin bond offerings today, banks use bridge loans as a competitive tool to differentiate themselves from their rivals at Wall Street investment banks.

Yet the Street doesn't seem envious. "From the standpoint of credit risk, it is not something we've seen as a good business to get into," says Emilio Lamar, managing director at Merrill Lynch & Co.'s international emerging markets unit. Stephen Dizard, managing director at Salomon Inc.'s Salomon Brothers, adds: "Put simply, we don't do bridge loans to win bond offerings. And I don't think we feel disadvantaged."

A Federal Reserve System official, who declined to be identified, comments, "Some of these bridge loans are incredible, given the track record over the long course of history in Latin America and the recent memory of the 1980s." The Fed official adds "The appetite for going out and lending extraordinary sums of money to shaky foreign debtors is back."

Bankers acknowledge the risks of bridge lending. Roland Wojewodzki, managing director at J.P. Morgan, says: "We are very cautious." He says J.P. Morgan prefers to write bridge loans only for acquisitions, and only after the bank discerns that the bridge can be repaid out of operating cash, if necessary.

"We have been extremely careful," says Joaquin Avila, managing director at Banco Santander's investment banking unit.

Moody's Investors Service Co. and Standard & Poor's Corp., as a matter of policy, won't rate a company higher than its home country. Chile is the only country in Latin America that has an investment grade rating from both agencies on its dollar-denominated debt. In effect, billions of dollars in Latin American corporate debt carry a below-investment grade, or "junk" rating. Some companies have investment-grade ratings on debt denominated in local currency, such as Mexican pesos, but only a select few have strong balance sheets and businesses, the agencies say.

Big Demand

High yielding Latin debt is much in demand today. Latin corporations have sold some $25 billion in dollar denominated debt to both mutual funds favored by small investors and institutions during the past year and a half. Several of these debt deals repaid bank bridge loans.

But bull markets in foreign bonds don't last forever. And political risk often is as dangerous as market risk in Latin America.

Chase Manhattan made a $150 million bridge loan to Venezuelan oil company Bariven in advance of a $400 million bond sale in March 1992. But as the bank prepared to sell the bonds, Venezuela plunged into civil turmoil following an attempted coup in February.

The bridge loan was repaid, but Chase ended up holding some of the Bariven 10-year bonds, which by late spring had fallen more than five points, or $50 for each $1,000 face amount.

Bankers Trust wrote a $230 million bridge loan for the working-capital needs of Bariven. A bond sale led by Bankers Trust in December 1991, two months before the coup attempt, repaid the bridge.

It was a timely exit for Bankers Trust. By March 1992, the bonds were down about two points, or $20 for each $1,000 face amount.

Latin American economies are still very young. There will be downturns, and defaults, predicts Ashwin Vasan, portfolio manager at Oppenheimer Management Corp. That's when banks will face serious conflict-of-interest issues if they try to sell bonds to bail out a bridge, he says. "When the company is in trouble, and the banks are leaving, watch out," he says.

"The conflict," says Brian O'Neill, senior vice president at Chase Manhattan Bank, "is if it is a bad credit, and you are paying yourself with the bonds' proceeds and getting your chestnuts out of the fire."

Bankers say bridge loans provide ready cash to Latin corporations making acquisitions or bidding for properties in privatizations. "Bridge lending is used as a competitive tool for a [bond] issuer to have funds immediately available," says Hugo Verdegaal, division executive for Citibank's international corporate finance department.

Latin borrowers know their debt is in demand. They know Latin underwriting rankings are important for banks. So they play the bankers against themselves. They demand proceeds before the bonds are even sold—simply because they know the banks will do it to compete for deals.

Citibank's Mr. Verdegaal says: "In a number of cases, the client for business purposes, or other reasons, would like to have the funds upfront. It is not customary to do that, but it is being done."

Bankers are watching each other. They're all are worried about the other guy. "What scares me most is that most banks just get into business to get market share,"

Continued

CASE: A NEW WAVE OF LOANS TO LESS DEVELOPED COUNTRIES

Continued

says Banco Santander's Mr. Avila. Few admit that this is exactly what they are doing, though. Argentine companies have so frequently arranged for upfront cash ahead of bond deals that it has become a joke among bankers. They say Argentine companies have a cash hotline to New York banks. The number? 1-800-B-R-I-D-G-E.

Bankers Trust sells its bridge loans soon after they are made. "They aren't kept on [Bankers Trust's] balance sheet," a Bankers Trust official explains. But they do end up on some other bank's or investor's balance sheet.

Mr. Wojewodzki, the J.P. Morgan managing director, recalls a haunting memory.

While driving in South America in 1981, he spotted a high, unfinished overpass. "I always think of that when we talk about bridge loans around here," he says. The road ended in the sky, a bridge to nowhere.

Source: *The Wall Street Journal* (August 25, 1993), pp. C1, C19. Reprinted by permission of *The Wall Street Journal,* © 1993 Dow Jones & Company, Inc. All Rights Reserved Worldwide.

QUESTIONS

1. Why do you think Chase Manhattan, J.P. Morgan, Citicorp, and other commercial banks offer bridge loans to less developed countries?

2. Do you believe these bridge loans offered by Bankers Trust New York Corp., Citicorp, and other banks to less developed countries (LDCs) are less risky than the loans provided to LDCs in the 1970s and 1980s? Explain.

3. Would banks use the same type of country risk analysis for bridge loans to less developed countries that they used for longer-term loans to LDCs?

BRIDGES TO LATIN AMERICA

Many of the celebrated Latin American bond deals are also financings designed to get banks out of risky bridge loans. Here's a list of some of the bridge loans extended by banks over the past two years, and a comment on the bonds that bailed them out.

Company/Location	Lead Lender	Amount (millions)	Comment
Cemex/Mexico	Citibank	$1,160	Giant bridge loan helped finance acquisitions by the cement company. Repaid through bond sales including $1 billion bond offering led by J P Morgan in June
Femsa/Mexico	J.P. Morgan	1,000	Bridge paid down with asset sales and $325 million bond offering led by Bear Steams, March 1992.
Bariven/Venezuela	Bankers Trust	230	Bridge loan for oil company's working capital. Repaid with $230 million bond issue. December 1991.
Bariven/Venezuela	Chase Manhattan	150	Bridge financed capital-equipment purchase. Repaid with $400 million bond offering. March 1992.
Astra/Argentina	Citibank Swiss Bank Banco Santander	100	Cash forwarded to Argentine energy company ahead of $100 million June 1992 bond offering
Tecpetrol/Argentina	Chase Manhattan	60	Bridge financed purchase of oil and gas properties from government. Repaid with $60 million bond sale in June.
Vitro/Mexico	Banco Santander	60	Bridge financed an acquisition. Repaid with $70 million bond issue in October 1992

CASE
PROBLEM

BANK OF BALTIMORE
Reducing Exposure to LDC Debt

CASE
PROBLEM

The Bank of Baltimore presently has $500 million book value in loans to Argentina. Given the recent economic problems experienced by Argentina, the Bank of Baltimore has not received any payments from that nation lately. It considers selling these loans immediately in the secondary market, and believes it would receive 28 cents on the dollar. Alternatively, it is considering a debt-equity swap, in which it would swap the debt in exchange for automobiles owned by the government. It has no direct use of these automobiles, but expects that it would be able to sell them for about 1 trillion Austral (the Argentine currency), although it would probably take about one year to complete each of the sales. The exchange rate is presently 4800 Austral to $1. However, the value of the Austral will probably depreciate by about 50 percent within one year.

a) Should the Bank of Baltimore sell the loans in the secondary market, or engage in a debt-equity swap? Defend your answer.

b) Another alternative is to swap the debt immediately for ownership of a privatized business in sheet metal production in Argentina. Based on a comprehensive valuation, the present value of this business is 720 billion Austral. Presently, there are no other firms bidding for this business. Should the bank choose this alternative?

PROJECT

Review the annual report of a large U.S. bank that historically has provided loans to less developed countries. Summarize any statements made regarding these loans. Is the bank offering new loans to these countries? Has it reduced its foreign loan exposure by selling loans? Has it increased its loan loss reserves in anticipation that loans may default?

REFERENCES

Boehmer, Ekkehart, and William L. Megginson. "Determinants of Secondary Market Prices for Developing Country Syndicated Loans." *Journal of Finance* (December 1990), pp. 1517–1540.

DeWitt, R. Peter, and Jeff Madura. "How Banks Assess Country Risk." *World of Banking* (January–February 1986), pp. 28–33.

Dornbusch, Rudiger. "International Debt and Economic Instability." *Economic Review*, Federal Reserve Bank of Kansas City (January 1987), pp. 15–32.

Doukas, John. "Syndicated Euro-Credit Sovereign Risk Assessments; Market Efficiency and Contagion Effects." *Journal of International Business Studies* (Summer 1989), pp. 255–267.

Lee, Suk Hun. "Relative Importance of Political Instability and Economic Variables on Perceived Instability and Economic Variables on Perceived Country Creditworthiness." *Journal of International Business Studies* (Fourth Quarter 1993), pp. 801–812.

Logue, Dennis E., and Pietra Rivoli. "Some Consequences of Banks' LDC Loans: A Note." *Journal of Financial Services Research* (May 1992), pp. 37–47.

Madura, Jeff, Alan L. Tucker, and Emilio Zarruk. "Reaction of Bank Share Prices to the Third-World Debt Reduction Plan." *Journal of Banking and Finance* (September 1992), pp. 853–868.

Morgan, John B. "A New Look at Debt Rescheduling Indicators and Models." *Journal of International Business Studies* (Summer 1986), pp. 37–54.

Morgan, John B. "Assessing Country Risk at Texas Commerce." *Banker's Magazine* (May–June 1985), pp. 23–29.

Sabi, Manijeh. "An Application of the Theory of Foreign Direct Investment to Multinational Banking in LDCs." *Journal of International Business Studies* (Fall 1988), pp. 433–447.

Schwartz, Eduardo S., and Salvador Zurita. "Sovereign Debt: Optimal Contract, Underinvestment, and Forgiveness." *Journal of Finance* (July 1992), pp. 981–1004.

Waheed, Amjad, and Ike Mathur. "The Effects of Announcements of Bank Lending Agreements on the Market Values of U.S. Banks." *Financial Management* (Spring 1993), pp. 119–127.

ANSWERS TO SELF-TEST QUESTIONS

ANSWERS TO SELF-TEST FOR CHAPTER 1 _____

1. MNCs can capitalize on comparative advantages (such as a technology or cost of labor) they have relative to firms in other countries, which allows them to penetrate those other countries' markets. Given a world of imperfect markets, comparative advantages across countries are not freely transferable. Therefore, MNCs may be able to capitalize on comparative advantages. Many MNCs initially penetrate markets by exporting, but ultimately establish a subsidiary in foreign markets, and attempt to differentiate their products as other firms enter those markets (product cycle theory).

2. In the late 1980s and early 1990s, West European countries removed numerous barriers, which allowed more potential for efficient expansion throughout Europe. Consequently, U.S. firms may be able to expand across European countries at a lower cost than before.

    During the same period, East European countries opened their markets to foreign firms and privatized many of the state-owned firms. This allowed U.S. firms to penetrate these countries to offer products that previously had been unavailable.

    In the early 1990s, the U.S., Canada, and Mexico agreed to cut trade barriers. Some U.S. firms may benefit by penetrating the Canadian and Mexican markets.

3. First, there is the risk of poor economic conditions in the foreign country. Second, there is country risk, which reflects the risk of changing government or public attitudes toward the MNC. Third, there is exchange rate risk, which can affect the performance of the MNC in the foreign country.

ANSWERS TO SELF-TEST FOR CHAPTER 2 _____

1. Each of three economic factors is described, holding other factors constant.

    a. *Inflation.* A relatively high U.S. inflation rate relative to other countries can make U.S. goods less attractive to U.S. and non-U.S. consumers, which results in less U.S. exports, more U.S. imports and a lower (or more negative) current account balance. A relatively low U.S. inflation rate would have the opposite effect.

    b. *National Income.* A relatively high increase in the U.S. national income (compared to other countries) tends to cause a large increase in demand for imports, and can cause a lower (or more negative) current account balance. A relatively low increase in the U.S. national income would have the opposite effect.

c. *Exchange Rates.* A weaker dollar tends to make U.S. products cheaper to non-U.S. firms, and makes non-U.S. products expensive to U.S. firms. Thus, U.S. exports are expected to increase, while U.S. imports are expected to decrease. However, some conditions can prevent these effects from occurring, as explained in the chapter. Normally, a stronger dollar causes U.S. exports to decrease and U.S. imports to increase, because it makes U.S. goods more expensive to non-U.S. firms and makes non-U.S. goods less expensive to U.S. firms.

d. *Government Restrictions.* When the U.S. government imposes new barriers on imports, the U.S. imports decline, causing the U.S. balance of trade to increase (or be less negative). When non-U.S. governments impose new barriers on imports from the U.S., the U.S. balance of trade may decrease (or be more negative). When governments remove trade barriers, the opposite effects are expected.

2. When the U.S. imposes tariffs on imported goods, foreign countries may retaliate by imposing tariffs on goods exported by the U.S. Thus, there is a decline in U.S. exports that may offset any decline in U.S. imports.

3. As Germany's interest rates increased, other European interest rates increased, and U.S. capital flow to these countries increased to capitalize on the relatively high interest rates.

ANSWERS TO SELF-TEST FOR CHAPTER 3

1. Bid/ask spread = (Ask rate − Bid rate)/Ask rate
   = ($.80 − $.784)/$.80
   = .02, or 2%

2. FR premium (or discount) = $\dfrac{\$.188 - \$.190}{\$.190} \times \dfrac{360}{90} \simeq .0421$, or −4.21%

3. MNCs use the spot foreign exchange market to exchange currencies for immediate delivery. They use the forward foreign exchange market and the currency futures market to lock in the exchange rate at which currencies will be exchange at a future point in time. They use the currency options market when they wish to lock in the maximum (minimum) amount to be paid (received) in a future currency transaction, but maintain flexibility in the event of favorable exchange rate movements.

   MNCs use the Eurocurrency market to engage in short-term investing or financing, or the Eurocredit market to engage in medium-term financing. They can obtain long-term financing by issuing bonds in the Eurobond market, or by issuing stock in the international markets.

ANSWERS TO SELF-TEST FOR CHAPTER 4

1. Economic factors affect the yen's value as follows:

   a. If U.S. inflation is higher than Japanese inflation, the U.S. demand for Japanese goods may increase (to avoid the higher U.S. prices), and the Japanese demand for U.S. goods may decrease (to avoid the higher U.S. prices). Consequently, there is upward pressure on the value of the yen.

b. If U.S. interest rates increase and exceed Japanese interest rates, the U.S. demand for Japanese interest-bearing securities may decline (since U.S. interest-bearing securities are more attractive), while the Japanese demand for U.S. interest-bearing securities may rise. Both forces place downward pressure on the yen's value.

c. If U.S. national income increases more than Japanese national income, the U.S. demand for Japanese goods may increase more than the Japanese demand for U.S. goods. Assuming that the change in national income levels does not affect exchange rates indirectly through effects on relative interest rates, the forces should place upward pressure on the yen's value.

d. If government controls reduce the U.S. demand for Japanese goods, they place downward pressure on the yen's value. If the controls reduce the Japanese demand for U.S. goods, they place upward pressure on the yen's value.

    The opposite scenarios of those described above would cause the expected pressure to be in the opposite direction.

2. U.S. capital flows with Country A may be larger than U.S. capital flows with Country B. Therefore, the change in the interest rate differential has a larger effect on the capital flows with Country A, causing the exchange rate to change. If the capital flows with Country B are nonexistent, interest rate changes do not change the capital flows, and therefore do not change the demand and supply conditions in the foreign exchange market.

3. Smart Banking Corp. should not pursue the strategy because a loss would result, as shown below.

a. Borrow $5 million

b. Convert $5 million to C$5,263,158 (based on the spot exchange rate of $.95 per C$).

c. Invest the C$ at 9% annualized, which represents a return of .15% over six days, so the C$ received after six days = C$5,271,053 (computed as C$5,263,158 × [1+.0015].

d. Convert the C$ received back to U.S. dollars after six days: C$5,271,053 = $4,954,789 (based on anticipated exchange rate of $.94 per C$ after six days).

e. The interest rate owed on the U.S. dollar loan is .10% over the six-day period. Thus, the amount owed as a result of the loan is $5,005,000 (computed as $5,000,000 × [1+.001].

f. The strategy is expected to cause a gain of ($4,954,789 − $5,005,000) = −$50,211.

ANSWERS TO SELF-TEST FOR CHAPTER 5 _____

1. The net profit to the speculator is −$.01 per unit.
    The net profit to the speculator for one contract is $625 (computed as −$.01 × 62,500 units).

The spot rate would need to be $.66 for the speculator to break even. The net profit to the seller of the call option is $.01 per unit.

2. The speculator should exercise the option.

   The net profit to the speculator is $.03 per unit.

   The net profit to the seller of the put option is −$.03 per unit.

3. The premium paid is higher for options with longer expiration dates (other things being equal). Firms may prefer not to pay such high premiums.

ANSWERS TO SELF-TEST FOR CHAPTER 6

1. Market forces cause the demand and supply of yen in the foreign exchange market to change, which causes a change in the equilibrium exchange rate. The central banks could intervene to affect the demand or supply conditions in the foreign exchange market, but they would not always be able to offset the changing market forces. For example, if there were a large increase in the U.S. demand for yen, and no increase in the supply of yen for sale, the central banks would have to increase the supply of yen in the foreign exchange market to offset the increased demand.

2. The Fed could use direct intervention by selling some of its dollar reserves in exchange for marks in the foreign exchange market. It could also use indirect intervention by attempting to reduce U.S. interest rates through monetary policy. Specifically, it could increase the U.S. money supply, which places downward pressure on U.S. interest rates (assuming that inflationary expectations do not change). The lower U.S. interest rates should discourage foreign investment in the U.S. and encourage increased investment by U.S. investors in foreign securities. Both forces tend to weaken the dollar's value.

3. A weaker dollar tends to increase the demand for U.S. goods, because the price paid for a specified amount in dollars by non-U.S. firms is reduced. In addition, the U.S. demand for foreign goods is reduced, because it takes more dollars to obtain a specified amount in foreign currency once the dollar weakens. Both forces tend to stimulate the U.S. economy, and therefore improve productivity and reduce unemployment in the U.S.

ANSWERS TO SELF-TEST FOR CHAPTER 7

1. No. The cross exchange rate between the mark and the franc is appropriate, based on the other exchange rates. There is no discrepancy to capitalize on.

2. No. Covered interest arbitrage involves the exchange of dollars for pounds. Assuming the investors begin with $1 million (the starting amount will not affect the final conclusion), the dollars would be converted to pounds as shown below:

$1 million/$1.60 per £ = £625,000.

The British investment would accumulate interest over the 180-day period, resulting in

$$£625,000 \times 1.04 = £650,000.$$

After 180 days, the pounds would be converted to dollars:

$$£650,000 \times \$1.56 \text{ per pound} = \$1,014,000.$$

This amount reflects a return of 1.4 percent above the amount U.S. investors initially started with. The investors could simply invest the funds in the U.S. at 3 percent. Thus, U.S. investors would earn less using the covered interest arbitrage strategy than investing in the U.S.

3. No. The forward rate discount on the pound does not perfectly offset the interest rate differential. In fact, the discount is 2.5 percent, which is larger than the interest rate differential. The U.S. investors do worse when attempting covered interest arbitrage than when investing their funds in the U.S. because the interest rate advantage on the British investment is more than offset by the forward discount.

    Further clarification may be helpful here. While the U.S. investors could not benefit from covered interest arbitrage, British investors could capitalize on covered interest arbitrage. While British investors would earn 1-percent interest less on the U.S. investment, they would be purchasing pounds forward at a discount of 2.5 percent at the end of the investment period. When interest rate parity does not exist, investors from only one of the two countries of concern could benefit from using covered interest arbitrage.

4. If there is a discrepancy in the pricing of a currency, one may capitalize on it by using the various forms of arbitrage described in the chapter. As arbitrage occurs, the exchange rates will be pushed toward their appropriate levels, because arbitrageurs will buy an underpriced currency in the foreign exchange market (increase in demand for currency places upward pressure on its value), and will sell an overpriced currency in the foreign exchange market (increase in the supply of currency for sale places downward pressure on its value).

5. The one-year forward discount on pounds would become more pronounced (by about one percentage point more than before), because the spread between the British interest rates and U.S. interest rates would increase.

ANSWERS TO SELF-TEST FOR CHAPTER 8 _____

1. If the Japanese prices rise because of Japanese inflation, the value of the yen should decline. Thus, even though the importer might need to pay more yen, it would benefit from a weaker yen value (it would pay fewer dollars for a given amount in yen). Thus, there could be an offsetting effect, if PPP holds.

2. Purchasing power parity does not necessarily hold. In our example, Japanese inflation could rise (causing the importer to pay more yen),

and yet the Japanese yen would not necessarily depreciate by an offsetting amount, or at all. Therefore, the dollar amount to be paid for Japanese supplies could increase over time.

3. High inflation will cause a balance of trade adjustment, whereby the U.S. will reduce its purchases of goods in these countries, while the demand for U.S. goods by these countries should increase (according to PPP). Consequently, there will be downward pressure on the values of these currencies.

4.
$$e_f = I_h - I_f$$
$$= 3\% - 4\%$$
$$= -.01 \text{ or } -1\%$$
$$S_{t+1} = S(1 + e_f)$$
$$= \$.85[1 + (-.01)]$$
$$= \$.8415$$

5.
$$e_f = \frac{(1 + i_h)}{(1 + i_f)} - 1$$
$$= \frac{(1 + .06)}{(1 + .11)} - 1$$
$$\approx -.045, \text{ or } -4.5\%$$
$$S_{t+1} = S(1 + e_f)$$
$$= \$.90\,[1 + (-.045)]$$
$$= \$.8595$$

6. According to the IFE, the increase in interest rates by 5 percentage points reflects an increase in expected inflation by 5 percentage points.

   If the inflation adjustment occurs, the balance of trade should be affected, as Australian demand for U.S. goods rises while the U.S. demand for Australian goods declines. Thus, the Australian dollar should weaken.

   If U.S. investors believed in the IFE, they would not attempt to capitalize on higher Australian interest rates because they would expect the Australian dollar to depreciate over time.

ANSWERS TO SELF-TEST FOR CHAPTER 9

1. U.S. four-year interest rate = $(1+.07)^4$ = 31.08% or .3108. Mexican four-year interest rate = $(1+.20)^4$ = 107.36% or 1.0736.

$$p = \frac{(1 + i_h)}{(1 + i_f)} - 1 = \frac{1.3108}{2.0736} - 1$$
$$= -.3679 \text{ or } -36.79\%.$$

2.
$$\text{Canadian dollar } \frac{|\$.80 - \$.82|}{\$.82} = 2.44\%$$

$$\text{Japanese yen } \frac{|\$.012 - \$.011|}{\$.011} = 9.09\%$$

The forecast error was larger for the Japanese yen.

3. The forward rate of the lira would have overestimated the future spot rate, because the spot rate would have declined by the end of each month.

4. Semistrong-form efficiency would be refuted, since the currency values do not adjust immediately to useful public information.

5. The peso would be expected to depreciate, because the forward rate of the peso would exhibit a discount (be less than the spot rate). Thus, the forecast derived from the forward rate is less than the spot rate, which implies anticipated depreciation of the peso.

6. As the chapter suggests, forecasts of currencies are subject to a high degree of error. Thus, if a project's success if very sensitive to the future value of the bolivar, there is much uncertainty. This project could easily backfire, because the future value of the bolivar is very uncertain.

ANSWERS TO SELF-TEST FOR CHAPTER 10 _____

1. Managers have more information about the firm's exposure to exchange rate risk than do shareholders, and may be able to hedge it more easily than shareholders could. Shareholders may prefer that the managers hedge for them. Also, cash flows may be stabilized as a result of hedging, which can reduce the firm's cost of financing.

2. The Canadian supplies would have less exposure to exchange rate risk because the Canadian dollar is less volatile than the French franc.

3. The French source would be preferable, because the FF and DM (mark) movements are highly correlated. Thus, if the DM depreciates (which reduces the dollar cash flows received by your firm), the FF will likely depreciate as well (which reduces your costs). This alternative offsets part of the exposure in DM, whereas using the U.S. source for material would not offset the exposure in DM.

4. No. If exports are priced in dollars, the dollar cash flows received from exporting will depend on German demand, which will be influenced by the mark's value. If the mark depreciated, German demand for the exports would likely decrease.

5. The earnings generated by the European subsidiaries will be translated to a smaller amount in dollar earnings if the dollar strengthens. Thus, the consolidated earnings of the U.S.-based MNCs will be reduced.

ANSWERS TO SELF-TEST FOR CHAPTER 11

1.

Amount of A$ to be invested today	=	A$3,000,000/(1+.12)
	=	A$2,678,571
Amount of U.S. $ to be borrowed to convert to A$	=	A$2,678,571 × $.85
	=	$2,276,786
Amount of U.S. $ needed in one year to pay off loan	=	$2,276,786 × (1+.07)
	=	$2,436,161

2. The forward hedge would be more appropriate. Given a forward rate of $.81, Montclair would need $2,430,000 in one year (computed as A$3,000,000 × $.81) when using a forward hedge.

3. Montclair could purchase currency call options in Australian dollars. The option could hedge against the possible appreciation of the Australian dollar. Yet, if the Australian dollar depreciates, Montclair could let the option expire and purchase the Australian dollars at the spot rate at the time it needs to send payment.

   A disadvantage of the currency call option is that a premium must be paid for it. Thus, if Montclair expects that the Australian dollar will appreciate over the year, the money market hedge would probably be a better choice, since the flexibility provided by the option would not be useful in this case.

4. Even though Sanibel Co. is insulated from the beginning of a month to the end of the month, the forward rate will become higher each month, because the forward rate moves with the spot rate. Thus, the firm will pay more dollars each month, even though it is hedged during the month. Sanibel will be adversely affected by the consistent appreciation of the pound.

5. Sanibel Co. could engage in a series of forward contracts today to cover the payments in each successive month. In this way, it locks in the future payments today, and does not have to agree to the higher forward rates that may exist in future months.

6. A put option on SF2,000,000 would cost $60,000. If the spot rate of the SF reached $.68 as expected, the put option would be exercised, which would yield $1,380,000 (computed as SF2,000,000 × $.69). Accounting for the premium costs of $60,000, the receivables amount would convert to $1,320,000. If Hopkins remains unhedged, it expects to receive $1,360,000 (computed as SF2,000,000 × $.68). Thus, the unhedged strategy is preferable.

ANSWERS TO SELF-TEST FOR CHAPTER 12

1. Salem could attempt to purchase its chemicals from Canadian sources. Then, if the C$ depreciates, the reduction in dollar inflows resulting from its exports to Canada will be partially offset by a reduction in dollar outflows needed to pay for the Canadian imports.

   An alternative possibility for Salem is to finance its business with Canadian dollars, but this would probably be a less efficient solution.

2. A possible disadvantage is that Salem would forego some of the benefits if the C$ appreciated over time.
3. The consolidated earnings of Coastal Corp. will be adversely affected if the pound depreciates, because the British earnings will be translated into dollar earnings for the consolidated income statement at a lower exchange rate. Coastal could attempt to hedge its translation exposure by selling pounds forward. If the pound depreciates, it will benefit from its forward position, which could help offset the translation effect.
4. This argument has no perfect solution. It appears that shareholders penalize the firm for poor earnings even when the reason for poor earnings is a weak pound that has adverse translation effects. It is possible that translation effects could be hedged to stabilize earnings, but Arlington may consider informing the shareholders that the major earnings changes have been due to translation effects and not to changes in consumer demand or other factors. Perhaps shareholders would not respond so strongly to earnings changes if they were well aware that the changes were primarily caused by translation effects.
5. Lincolnshire has no translation exposure, since it has no foreign subsidiaries. Kalafa has translation exposure resulting from its subsidiary in Spain.

ANSWERS TO SELF-TEST FOR CHAPTER 13

1. The exporter may not trust the importer or may be concerned that the government will impose exchange controls that prevent payment to the exporter. Meanwhile, the importer may not trust that the exporter will ship the goods ordered, and therefore may not pay until the goods are received. Commercial banks can help by providing guarantees to the exporter in case the importer does not pay.
2. In accounts receivable financing, the bank provides a loan to the exporter secured by the accounts receivable. If the importer fails to pay the exporter, the exporter is still responsible to repay the bank. Factoring involves the sales of accounts receivable by the exporter to a so-called "factor," so that the exporter is no longer responsible for the importer's payment.
3. The guarantee programs of the Export-Import Bank provide medium-term protection against the risk of nonpayment by the foreign buyer due to political risk.

ANSWERS TO SELF-TEST FOR CHAPTER 14

1.
$$r_f = (1 + i_f)(1 + e_f) - 1$$
$$\text{If } e_f = -6\%, r_f = (1 + .09)[1 + (-.06)] - 1$$
$$= .0246, \text{ or } 2.46\%$$
$$\text{If } e_f = 3\%, r_f = (1 + .09)(1 + .03) - 1$$
$$= .1227, \text{ or } 12.27\%$$

2.

$$E(r_f) = 50\%(2.46\%) + 50\%(12.27\%)$$

$$= 1.23\% + 6.135\%$$

$$= 7.365\%$$

3.

$$e_f = \frac{(1 + r_f)}{(1 + i)} - 1$$

$$= \frac{(1 + .08)}{(1 + .05)} - 1$$

$$= .0286, \text{ or } 2.86\%.$$

4.

$$E(e_f) = (\text{Forward rate} - \text{Spot rate})/\text{Spot rate}$$

$$= (\$.60 - \$.62)/\$.62$$

$$= -.0322, \text{ or } 3.22\%$$

$$E(r_f) = (1 + i_f)[1 + E(e_f)] - 1$$

$$= (1 + .09)[1 + (-.0322)] - 1$$

$$= .0548, \text{ or } 5.48\%$$

5. The two-currency portfolio will not exhibit much lower variance than either individual currency because European currencies tend to move together. Thus, the diversification effect is limited.

ANSWERS TO SELF-TEST FOR CHAPTER 15

1. Earnings of subsidiaries are taxed according to host government tax rates, which vary across countries. The parent would prefer to shift expenses over to those subsidiaries whose earnings will be heavily taxed. This form of transfer pricing can reduce taxes (but there are some restrictions that may prohibit this strategy).

2. The subsidiary in Country Y should be more adversely affected, because the blocked funds will not earn as much interest over time. In addition, the funds will likely be converted to dollars at an unfavorable exchange rate, because the currency is expected to weaken over time.

3.

$$E(e_f) = (1 + i_f)[1 + E(e_f)] - 1$$

$$= (1 + .14)(1 + .08) - 1$$

$$= .2312, \text{ or } 23.12\%.$$

4.

$$E(e_f) = (\text{Forward rate} - \text{Spot rate})/\text{Spot rate}$$

$$= (\$.19 - \$.20)/\$.20$$

$$= -.05, \text{ or } -5\%$$

$$E(e_f) = (1 + i_f)[1 + E(e_f)] - 1$$

$$= (1 + .11)[1 + (-.05)] - 1$$

$$= .0545, \text{ or } 5.45\%.$$

5.

$$e_f = \frac{(1 + r)}{(1 + i_f)} - 1$$

$$= \frac{(1 + .06)}{(1 + .90)} - 1$$

$$= -.4421 \text{ or } -44.21\%.$$

If the bolivar depreciates by less than 44.21% against the dollar over the one-year period, a one-year deposit in Venezuela will generate a higher effective yield than a one-year U.S. deposit.

6. Yes. Interest rate parity would discourage U.S. firms only from covering their investments in foreign deposits by using forward contracts. As long as the firms believe that the currency will not depreciate to offset the interest rate advantage, they may consider investing in countries with high interest rates.

ANSWERS TO SELF-TEST FOR CHAPTER 16

1. Possible reasons may include

- more demand for the product (depending on the product)
- better technology in Canada
- fewer restrictions (less political interference).

2. Possible reasons may include

- more demand for the product (depending on the product)
- greater probability to earn superior profits (since many goods have not been marketed in Mexico in the past)
- cheaper factors of production (such as land and labor)
- possible exploitation of monopolistic advantages.

3. U.S. firms prefer to enter a country when the foreign country's currency is weak. In this way, the firms can get more out of the dollars they invest. U.S. firms normally would prefer that the foreign currency appreciates after they invest their dollars to develop the subsidiary. The executive's comment suggests that the Swiss franc is too strong, so any U.S. investment of dollars into Switzerland will not convert into enough Swiss francs to make the investment worthwhile.

4. U.S. firms may have difficulty in circumventing various barriers to direct foreign investment in China. However, it may be easier to engage in a joint venture with a Chinese firm, which is already well established in China.

5. The U.S. government could argue that the foreign competitors will retain some of the U.S. market share, even if they do not establish a production subsidiary in the U.S. If a production subsidiary is created, U.S. imports will decline and more jobs will be created in the U.S.

ANSWERS TO SELF-TEST FOR CHAPTER 17 _____

1. In addition to earnings generated in Jamaica, the NPV is based on some factors not controlled by the firm, such as the expected host government tax on profits, the withholding tax imposed by the host government, and the salvage value to be received when the project is terminated. Furthermore, the exchange rate projections will affect the estimates of dollar cash flows received by the parent as earnings are remitted.

2. The most obvious effect is on the cash flows that will be generated by the sales distribution center in Ireland. These cash flow estimates will likely be revised downward (due to lower sales estimates). It is also possible that the estimated salvage value could be reduced. Exchange rate estimates could be revised as a result of revised economic conditions. Estimated tax rates imposed on the center by the Irish government could also be affected by the revised economic conditions.

3. New Orleans Exporting Co. must account for the cash flows that will be forgone as a result of the plant, because some of the cash flows that used to be received by the parent through its exporting operation will be eliminated. The NPV estimate will be reduced after this factor is accounted for.

4. (a) An increase in the risk will cause an increase in the required rate of return on the subsidiary, which results in a lower discounted value of the subsidiary's salvage value.
   (b) If the escudo depreciates over time, the subsidiary's salvage value will be reduced, because the proceeds will convert to fewer dollars.

5. The dollar cash flows of Wilmette Co. would be affected more, because the periodic remitted earnings from Belgium to be converted to dollars would be larger. The dollar cash flows of Niles would not affected so much, because interest payments would be made on the Belgian loans before earnings could be remitted to the U.S. Thus, a smaller amount in earnings would be remitted.

6. The divestiture is now more feasible because the dollar cash flows to be received by the U.S. parent are reduced as a result of the revised projections of the krona's value.

7. The demand for the product in the foreign country may be very uncertain, causing the total revenue to be uncertain. The exchange rates can be very uncertain, creating uncertainty about the dollar cash flows received by the U.S. parent. The salvage value may be very uncertain; this will have a larger effect if the lifetime of the project is short (for projects with a very long life, the discounted value of the salvage value is small anyway).

ANSWERS TO SELF-TEST FOR CHAPTER 18 _____

1. Growth may have caused Goshen to require a large amount for financing that could not be completely provided by retained earnings. In addition, the interest rates may have been low in these foreign countries, to make debt financing an attractive alternative. Finally, the use of foreign debt can reduce the exchange rate risk, since the amount

in periodic remitted earnings is reduced when interest payments a[ ]
required on foreign debt.

2. If country risk has increased, Lynde can attempt to reduce its exposure
to that risk by removing its equity investment from the subsidiary.
When the subsidiary is financed with local funds, the local creditors
have more to lose than the parent if the host government imposes any
severe restrictions on the subsidiary.

3. Not necessarily. German and Japanese firms tend to have more support
from other firms or from the government if they experience cash flow
problems, and can therefore afford to use a higher degree of financial
leverage than firms from the same industry in the U.S.

4. Local debt financing is favorable because it can reduce the MNC's
exposure to country risk and exchange rate risk. However, the high
interest rates will make the local debt very expensive. If the parent
makes an equity investment in the subsidiary to avoid the high cost of
local debt, it will be more exposed to country risk and exchange rate
risk.

5. The answer to this question is dependent on whether you believe
unsystematic risk is relevant. If the CAPM is used as a framework for
measuring the risk of a project, the risk of the foreign project is
determined to be low, because the systematic risk is low. That is, the
risk is specific to the host country, and is not related to U.S. market
conditions. However, if the project's unsystematic risk is relevant, the
project is considered to have a high degree of risk. The project's cash
flows are very uncertain, even though the systematic risk is low.

ANSWERS TO SELF-TEST FOR CHAPTER 19

1. First, consumers on the islands could develop a philosophy of
purchasing homemade goods. Second, they could discontinue their
purchases of exports by Key West Co. as a form of protest against
specific U.S. government actions. Third, the host governments could
impose severe restrictions on the subsidiary shops owned by Key West
Co. (including the blockage of funds to be remitted to the U.S. parent).

2. First, the islands could experience poor economic conditions, which
would cause lower income for some residents. Second, residents could
be subject to higher inflation or higher interest rates, which would
reduce the income that they could allocate toward exports. Depreciation
of the local currencies could also raise the local prices to be paid for
goods exported from the U.S. All factors described here could reduce
the demand for goods exported by Key West Co.

3. Financial risk is probably a bigger concern. The political risk factors are
unlikely, based on the product produced by Key West Co., and the
absence of substitute products available in other countries. The financial
risk factors deserve serious consideration.

4. This event heightens the perceived country risk for any firms that have
offices in populated areas (especially next to government or military
offices). It also heightens the risk for firms whose employees commonly
travel to other countries, and for firms that provide office services or
travel services.

5. Rockford Co. could estimate the net present value (NPV) of the project under 3 scenarios: (1) include a special tax when estimating cash flows back to the parent (probability of scenario = 15%), (2) assume the project ends in 2 years and include a salvage value when estimating the NPV (probability of scenario = 15%), and (3) assume no Canadian government intervention (probability = 70%). This results in 3 estimates of NPV, one for each scenario. This method is less arbitrary than the one considered by Rockford's executives.

ANSWERS TO SELF-TEST FOR CHAPTER 20

1. A firm may be able to obtain a lower coupon rate by issuing bonds denominated in a different currency. The firm converts the proceeds from issuing the bond to its local currency to finance local operations. Yet, there is exchange rate risk, because the firm will need to make coupon payments and the principal payment in the currency denominating the bond. If that currency appreciates against the firm's local currency, the financing costs could become larger than anticipated.

2. The risk is that the franc would appreciate against the mark over time, since the German subsidiary will periodically convert some of its mark cash flows to francs to make the coupon payments.

   The risk here is less than it would be if the proceeds were used to finance U.S. operations. The franc's movement against the dollar is much more volatile than the franc's movement against the mark. Recall that the mark and the franc have historically moved in tandem against the dollar, which means that there is a somewhat stable exchange rate between the two currencies.

3. If these firms borrow U.S. dollars and convert them to finance local projects, they will need to use their own currencies to obtain dollars and make coupon payments. These firms would be highly exposed to exchange rate risk.

4. Paxson Co. is exposed to exchange rate risk. If the German mark appreciates, the number of dollars needed for conversion into marks will increase. To the extent that increased German interest rates cause the mark to strengthen, Paxson's cost of financing will increase.

5. The nominal interest rate incorporates expected inflation (according to the so-called Fisher effect). Therefore, the high interest rates reflect high expected inflation. Cash flows can be enhanced by inflation because a given profit margin converts into larger profits as a result of inflation, even if costs increase at the same rate as revenues.

ANSWERS TO SELF-TEST FOR CHAPTER 21

1. The withholding tax will reduce the cash flows that are remitted to the parent as a result of the foreign project. The higher the withholding tax, the lower is the present value of cash flows received by the parent. It should be mentioned that some tax treaties may allow for the MNC's home country to apply a tax credit on taxes imposed there, to offset part or all of the withholding tax.

2. Transfer pricing determines the price one subsidiary charges when selling goods or services to another subsidiary. The price affects the revenue received by the one subsidiary and the cost incurred by the other subsidiary. Thus, the profitability of each subsidiary is affected. MNCs prefer to set prices relatively high in low-tax countries and relatively low in high-tax countries to reduce their tax liabilities. Numerous restrictions and tax laws attempt to discourage such pricing strategies.

3. A foreign subsidiary in a high-tax country may use a debt-intensive capital structure to reduce its tax liability. A foreign subsidiary in a low-tax country may use an equity-intensive capital structure, since it cannot benefit much from tax-deductible interest payments.

4. Centralized management can recognize offsetting exchange rate exposures of different subsidiaries within the MNC. Since these offsetting effects do not need to be hedged, transaction costs are avoided.

5. This philosophy results in a waste of resources. It may also cause some subsidiaries to take positions opposite to those of others, because their forecasts are different. Yet, some of these positions will offset each other. Each subsidiary is essentially acting on its own without considering the MNC overall.

ANSWERS TO SELF-TEST FOR CHAPTER 22

1. If the pound depreciated against the dollar over time, the bank would convert pounds received from loan repayments into fewer dollars, which would reduce the bank's profits.

2. If short-term U.S. interest rates rose over time, the bank's spread between the rate received on its loans (which is fixed) and the rate paid on its deposits would be reduced, which would reduce the bank's profits.

3. The bank subsidiary's loan portfolio may be subject to a high degree of default risk, because the managers of East European firms are not <accustomed to operating in a competitive environment, and are not trained (in general) for a market-oriented system. Thus, there may be many mismanaged firms. The bank must take special care in assessing the loan requests.

   The bank will be subject to a high degree of exchange rate risk, because its assets (loans) will be demoniated in East European currencies, while its liabilities will be demoniated in dollars. If the East European currencies depreciate against the dollar, the subsidiary's profits will be reduced.

ANSWERS TO SELF-TEST FOR CHAPTER 23

1. There are numerous possible answers to this question. Perhaps the banks expected that the governments would raise taxes or issue securities to raise the necessary funds for loan repayment. In addition, banks overestimated the general financial conditions of the countries,

and perhaps did not realize how many of these countries could simultaneously experience severe financial problems. The worldwide recession in the early 1980s adversely affected all LDCs at the same time.

2. Additional regulation may not necessarily prevent a crisis, unless the regulators have better foresight than bank managers. It has been argued that banks should be required by regulators to maintain higher capital levels, to absorb possible losses that may occur. However, banks may argue that their capital levels are already adequate and any further boost in capital ratios would reduce their profitability. Furthermore, additional bank regulations must be financially supported by taxpayers or by a larger budget deficit. In general, the answer to this question depends on one's view as to whether the additional regulation could improve upon bank management. Students may have their own views, but should at least recognize the pros and cons of additional regulation.

3. As is true for corporate borrowers, a country's creditworthiness is primarily based on its ability to cover the debt payments. This is influenced by future cash inflows (tax revenues, etc.) relative to future cash outflows (forecasted debt payments, government expenditures etc.).

FUNDAMENTALS OF REGRESSION ANALYSIS

Businesses often use **regression analysis** to measure relationships between variables when establishing policies. For example, a firm may measure the historical relationship between its sales and its accounts receivable. It can then forecast the future level of accounts receivable based on a forecast of sales, using the relationship detected. Alternatively, it may measure the sensitivity of its sales to economic growth and interest rates so that it can assess how susceptible its sales are to future changes in these economic variables. In international financial management, regression analysis can be used to measure the sensitivity of a firm's performance (using sales or earnings or stock price as a proxy) to currency movements or economic growth of various countries.

Regression analysis can be applied to measure the sensitivity of exports to various economic variables. This example will be used to explain the fundamentals of regression analysis. The main steps involved in regression analysis are

1. Specifying the regression model
2. Compiling data
3. Estimating the regression coefficients
4. Interpreting the regression results.

SPECIFYING THE REGRESSION MODEL

Assume that your main goal is to determine the relationship between percentage changes in the U.S. exports to Germany (called *CEXP*) and percentage changes in the value of the German mark (called *CDM*). The percentage change in the exports sent to Germany is the **dependent variable,** since it is hypothesized to be influenced by another variable. While you are most concerned with how *CDM* affects *CEXP,* the regression model should include any other factors (or so-called **independent variables**) that could also affect *CEXP.* Assume that the percentage change in the German GNP (called *CGNP*) is also hypothesized to influence *CEXP.* This factor should also be included in the regression model. To simplify the example, assume that *CDM* and *CGNP* are the only factors expected to influence *CEXP.* Also assume that there is a lagged impact of one quarter. In this case, the regression model can be specified as

$$CEXP_t = b_0 + b_1(CDM_{t-1}) + b_2(CGNP_{t-1}) + u_t,$$

where

b_0 = a constant

b_1 = regression coefficient that measures the sensitivity of $CEXP_t$ to CDM_{t-1}

b_2 = regression coefficient that measures the sensitivity of $CEXP_t$ to $CGNP_{t-1}$

u_t = an error term.

The t subscript represents the time period. Some models, such as this one, specify a lagged impact of an independent variable on the dependent variable and therefore use a $t-1$ subscript.

COMPILING THE DATA

Now that the model has been specified, data on the variables must be compiled. Whether a mainframe or personal computer is used, the data are normally input into a data file as follows:

Period (t)	CEXP	CDM	CGNP
1	.03	−.01	.04
2	−.01	.02	−.01
3	−.04	.03	−.02
4	.00	.02	−.01
5	.01	−.02	.02
.	. . .	. . .	. . .
.	. . .	. . .	. . .
.	. . .	. . .	. . .

The column specifying the period is not necessary to run the regression model, but is normally included in the data set for convenience.

The difference between the number of observations (periods) and the regression coefficients (including the constant) represents the degrees of freedom. For our example, assume that the data covered 40 quarterly periods. The degrees of freedom for this example is 40 − 3 = 37. As a general rule, analysts usually try to have at least 30 degrees of freedom when using regression analysis.

Some regression models involve only a single period. For example, if you desired to determine whether there was a relationship between the firm's degree of international sales (as a percentage of total sales) and earnings per share of MNCs, last year's data on these two variables could be gathered for numerous MNCs, and regression analysis could be applied. This example is referred to as **cross-sectional analysis,** whereas our original example is referred to as a **time-series analysis.**

ESTIMATING THE REGRESSION COEFFICIENTS

Once the data have been input into a data file, a regression program can be applied to the data to estimate the **regression coefficients.** There are various packages that can be used on a mainframe computer system. Software packages with regression analysis capabilities are now also available for personal computers. For example, Version 2.01 of Lotus 1–2–3 contains a regression program that can easily be applied to a data file to run regression analysis.

The actual steps conducted to estimate regression coefficients are somewhat complex, which is why computer packages are commonly used. Computation time by the computer is usually a few seconds. For more details on how regression coefficients are estimated, see any econometrics textbook.

INTERPRETING THE REGRESSION RESULTS

Most regression programs provide estimates of the regression coefficients along with additional statistics. For our example, assume that the following information was provided by the regression program:

	Estimated Regression Coefficient	Standard Error of Regression Coefficient	t-statistic
Constant	.002		
CDM_{t-1}	.80	.32	2.50
$CGNP_{t-1}$	.36	.50	.72
Coefficient of determination (R^2) = .33			

The independent variable CDM_{t-1} has an estimated regression coefficient of .80, which suggests that a 1 percent increase in CDM is associated with a .8 percent increase in the dependent variable $CEXP$ in the following period. This implies a positive relationship between CDM_{t-1} and $CEXP_t$. The independent variable $CGNP_{t-1}$ has an estimated coefficient of .36, which suggests that a 1 percent increase in $CGNP$ is associated with a .36 percent increase in $CEXP$ one period later.

Many analysts attempt to determine whether a coefficient is statistically different from zero. Regression coefficients may be different from zero simply because of a coincidental relationship between the independent variable of concern and the dependent variable. One can have more confidence that a negative or positive relationship exists by testing the coefficient for significance. A t-test is commonly used for this purpose, as follows:

Test to determine whether CDM_{t-1} affects $CEXP_t$

$$\frac{\text{Calculated}}{t\text{-statistic}} = \frac{\text{Estimated regression coefficient for } CDM_{t-1}}{\text{Standard error of the regression coefficient}} = \frac{.80}{.32} = 2.50$$

Test to determine whether $CGNP_{t-1}$ affects $CEXP_t$

$$\frac{\text{Calculated}}{t\text{-statistic}} = \frac{\text{Estimated regression coefficient for } CGNP_{t-1}}{\text{Standard error of the regression coefficient}} = \frac{.36}{.50} = .72$$

The calculated t-statistic is sometimes provided within the regression results. It can be compared to the critical t-statistic to determine whether the coefficient is significant. The critical t-statistic is dependent on the degrees of freedom and confidence level chosen. For our example, assume that there are 37 degrees of freedom and that a 95 confidence level is desired. The critical t-statistic would be 2.02, which can be verified by using a t-table from any statistics book. Based on the regression results, the coefficient of CDM_{t-1} is significantly different from zero, while $CGNP_{t-1}$ is not. This implies that one can be confident of a positive relationship between CDM_{t-1} and $CEXP_t$, but the positive relationship between $CGNP_{t-1}$, and $CEXP_t$ may have occurred simply by chance.

In some particular cases, one may be interested in determining whether the regression coefficient differs significantly from some value other than zero. In these cases, the t-statistic reported in the regression results would not be appropriate. See an econometrics text for more information on this subject.

The regression results indicate the **coefficient of determination** (called R^2) of a regression model, which measures the percentage of variation in the dependent variable that can be explained by the regression model. R^2 can range from 0 to 100 percent. It is unusual for regression models to generate an R^2 of close to 100 percent, since the movement in a given dependent variable is partially random and not associated with movements in independent variables. In our example, R^2 is 33 percent, suggesting that one-third of the variation in $CEXP$ can be explained by movements in CDM_{t-1} and $CGNP_{t-1}$.

Some analysts use regression analysis to forecast. For our example, the regression results could be used along with data for CDM and $CGNP$ to forecast $CEXP$. Assume CDM was 5 percent in the most recent period, while $CGNP$ was −1 percent in the most recent period. The forecast of $CEXP$ in the following period is derived from inserting this information into the regression model as follows:

$$\begin{aligned}
CEXP_t &= b_0 + b_1(CDM_{t-1}) + b_2(CGNP_{t-1}) \\
&= .002 + (.80)(.05) + (.36)(-.01) \\
&= .002 + .0400 - .0036 \\
&= .0420 - .0036 \\
&= .0384
\end{aligned}$$

Thus, the $CEXP$ is forecasted to be 3.84 percent in the following period. Some analysts might eliminate $CGNP_{t-1}$ from the model because its regression coefficient was not significantly different from zero. This would alter the forecasted value of $CEXP$.

When there is not a lagged relationship between independent variables and the dependent variable, the independent variables must be forecasted in order to derive a forecast of the dependent variable. In this case, an analyst might derive a poor forecast of the dependent variable even when the regression model is properly specified, if the forecasts of the independent variables are inaccurate.

As with most statistical techniques, there are some limitations that should be recognized when using regression analysis. These limitations are described in most statistics and econometrics textbooks.

USING LOTUS TO CONDUCT REGRESSION ANALYSIS ____

Various software packages are available to run regression analysis. The LOTUS version 2.01 is recommended because of its simplicity. The following example illustrates the ease with which regression analysis can be run. Assume that a firm wants to assess the influence of changes in the value of the German mark on changes in its exports to Germany based on the following data:

Period	Value (in Thousands of Dollars) of Exports to Germany	Average Exchange Rate of German Mark Over That Period
1	110	$.50
2	125	.54
3	130	.57
4	142	.60
5	129	.55
6	113	.49
7	108	.46
8	103	.42
9	109	.43
10	118	.48
11	125	.49
12	130	.50
13	134	.52
14	138	.50
15	144	.53
16	149	.55
17	156	.58
18	160	.62
19	165	.66
20	170	.67
21	160	.62
22	158	.62
23	155	.61
24	167	.66

Assume the firm applies the following regression model to the data:

$$CEXP = b_0 + b_1 CDM + u,$$

where

$CEXP$ = percentage change in the firm's export value from one period to the next

CDM = percentage change in the average exchange rate from one period to the next

u = error term.

The first step is to input these three columns into a file using LOTUS. Then the data can be converted into percentage changes. This can be easily performed with a COMPUTE statement in the fourth column (Column D) to derive *CEXP*, and another COMPUTE statement in the fifth column (Column E) to derive *CDM*. These two columns will have a blank first row, since the percentage change cannot be computed without the previous period's data. Many students already know how to use LOTUS to do this. If you do not, ask a friend for a few minutes of help.

Once you have derived *CEXP* and *CDM* from the raw data, you can perform regression analysis as follows. On the main menu, select DATA. This leads to a new menu, in which you should select REGRESSION. Then, select X-RANGE, and identify the range of the independent variable (from D2 to D24 in our example). Then select Y-RANGE, and identify the range of the dependent variable (from E2 to E24 in our example). Then select OUTPUT, and identify the location on the screen where the output of the regression analysis should be displayed. In our example, F1 would be an appropriate location, representing the upper left section of the output. Then, select GO, and within a few seconds, the regression analysis will be complete. For our example, the output is listed below:

Regression Output:

Constant		0.00414
Std Err of Y Est		0.029699
R Squared		0.783608
No. of Observations		23
Degrees of Freedom		21
X Coefficient(s)	0.902989	
Std Err of Coef.	0.103549	

The estimate of the so-called slope coefficient is about .903, which suggests that every 1 percent change in the mark's exchange rate is associated with a .903 percent change (in the same direction) in the firm's exports to Germany. The *t*-statistic is not shown, but can be estimated to determine whether the slope coefficient is significantly different than zero. Since the standard error of the slope coefficient is about .10, the *t*-statistic is (.903/.10) = 9.03. This would imply that there is a significant relationship between *CDM* and *CEXP*. The R-Squared statistic suggests that about 78 percent of the variation in *CEXP* is explained by *CDM*. The correlation between *CEXP* and *CDM* can also be measured by the correlation coefficient, which is the square root of the R-Squared statistic.

If you have more than one independent variable (multiple regression), you should place the independent variables next to each other in the file. Then, for the X-RANGE, identify this block of data. The output for the regression model will display the coefficient and standard error for each of the independent variables. For multiple regression, the R-Squared statistic is interpreted as the percentage of variation in the dependent variable explained by the model as a whole.

Mean

The mean (or average) of a column can be estimated for any variables. In our example, the mean value of *CDM* can be computed by typing the following COMPUTE statement in a blank cell:

$$@AVG(E2..E24)$$

When you type this, the mean of .014 will be displayed.

Variability

The standard deviation of a column can be estimated for any variables. In our example, the standard deviation of *CDM* can be computed by typing the following COMPUTE statement in a blank cell:

$$@STD(E2..E24)$$

When you type this, the standard deviation of .0610 will be displayed. The variance of a column can be estimated by multiplying the cell described above by itself. In our example, the variance of *CDM* (from cell E2 to cell E24) is .0037.

Absolute Value

The absolute value of numbers in the columns can be determined by using @ABS.

Using the "COPY" Command

If you need to repeat a particular type of computation for several different cells, you can use the COPY command that is on the LOTUS menu. You must identify the particular cell in which the computation is performed, and instruct LOTUS to copy that computation over to whatever range of cells you desire. This particular function may take a few minutes of practice, but it is well worth the time.

GLOSSARY

Absolute form of purchasing power parity. Also called the law of one price, this theory suggests that prices of two products of different countries should be equal when measured by a common currency.

Accounts receivable financing. Indirect financing provided by an exporter for an importer by exporting goods and allowing for payment to be made at a later date.

Advisory bank. Corresponding bank in the beneficiary's country to which the issuing bank sends the letter of credit.

Agencies. Offices established by banks to provide loans in a particular area (agencies cannot accept deposits or provide trust services).

Agency problem. Conflict of goals between a firm's shareholders and its managers.

Airway bill. Receipt for a shipment by air, which includes freight charges and title to the merchandise.

All-in-rate. Rate used in charging customers for accepting banker's acceptances, consisting of the discount interest rate plus the commission.

American depository receipts (ADRs). Certificates representing ownership of foreign stocks, which are traded on stock exchanges in the United States.

Appreciation. Increase in the value of a currency.

Arbitrage. Action to capitalize on a discrepancy in quoted prices; in many cases, there is no investment of funds tied up for any length of time.

Asian dollar market. Market in Asia in which banks collect deposits and make loans denominated in U.S. dollars.

Ask price. Price at which a trader of foreign exchange (typically a bank) is willing to sell a particular currency.

Assignment of proceeds. Arrangement which allows the original beneficiary of a letter of credit to pledge or assign proceeds to an end supplier.

At-the-money. Descriptive term implying that the present exchange rate is equal to the strike price on a currency call (or put) option.

Balance of payments. Statement of inflow and outflow payments for a particular country.

Balance of trade. Difference between the value of merchandise exports and merchandise imports.

Balance on goods and services. Balance of trade, plus the net amount of payments of interest and dividends to foreign investors and from investment, as well as receipts and payments resulting from international tourism and other transactions.

Bank for International Settlements (BIS). Institution which facilitates cooperation among countries involved in international transactions and provides assistance to countries experiencing international payment problems.

Banker's acceptance. Bill of exchange drawn on and accepted by a banking institution; it is commonly used to guarantee exporters that they will receive payment on goods delivered to importers.

Bank letter of credit policy. Policy that enables banks to confirm letters of credit by foreign banks supporting the purchase of U.S. exports.

Barter. Exchange of goods between two parties without the use of any currency as a medium of exchange.

Basel Accord. Agreement among country representatives in 1988 to establish standardized risk-based capital requirements for banks across countries.

Bid price. Price that a trader of foreign exchange (typically a bank) is willing to pay for a particular currency.

Bid/ask spread. Difference between the price at which a bank is willing to buy a currency and the price at which it will sell that currency.

Bilateral netting system. Netting method used for transactions between two units.

Bill of exchange (draft). Promise drawn by one party (usually an exporter) to pay a specified amount to another party at a specified future date, or upon presentation of the draft.

Bill of lading. Document serving as a receipt for shipment and a summary of fright charges, and conveying title to the merchandise.

Blocked funds. Funds that cannot be remitted from the subsidiary to the parent due to host government restrictions.

Brady Plan. Bill intended to provide banks with the option of having some of their LDC debt replaced by the World Bank (and IMF), by trading it in at a discount.

Branch. Full-service banking office that can compete directly with other banks located in that area.

Break-even salvage value. Salvage value necessary to achieve a zero net present value for a particular project.

Bretton Woods agreement. Conference held in Bretton Woods, New Hampshire, in 1944, resulting in agreement to maintain exchange rates of currencies within very narrow boundaries; this agreement lasted until 1971.

Buyer credit policy. Policy permitting banks to extend loans to foreign borrowers to purchase U.S. goods.

Capital account. Account reflecting changes in country ownership of long-term and short-term financial assets.

Cash management. Optimization of cash flows and investment of excess cash.

Central exchange rate. Exchange rate established between two European currencies through the European Monetary System arrangement; the exchange rate between the two currencies is allowed to move within bands around that central exchange rate.

Centralized cash management. Policy that consolidates cash management decisions for all MNC units, usually at the parent's location.

Checklist approach. Method for evaluation involving a list of factors that are assigned ratings; used for various assessments (such as country risk assessment).

Chicago Mercantile Exchange (CME) Exchange. Exchange established to facilitate the trading of currency futures contracts.

Coefficient of determination. Measure of the percentage variation in the dependent variable that can be explained by the independent variables when using regression analysis.

Cofinancing agreements. Arrangement in which the World Bank participates along with other agencies or lenders in providing funds to developing countries.

Commercial invoice. Exporter's description of merchandise being sold to the buyer.

Commercial letters of credit. Trade-related letters of credit.

Comparative advantage. Theory suggesting that specialization by countries can increase worldwide production.

Compensation. Arrangement in which the delivery of goods to a party is compensated for by buying back a certain amount of the product from that same party.

Compensatory Financing Facility (CFF). Facility that attempts to reduce the impact of export instability on country economies.

Consignment. Arrangement in which the exporter ships goods to the importer while still retaining title to the merchandise.

Contingency graph. As applied to this text, graph depicting the profit per unit to be earned on a currency option for various possible exchange rate scenarios.

Counterpurchase. Exchange of goods between two parties under two distinct contracts expressed in monetary terms.

Countertrade. Sale of goods to one country which is linked to the purchase or exchange of goods from that same country

Country risk. Characteristics of the host country, including political and financial conditions, that can affect the MNC's cash flows.

Covered interest arbitrage. Investment in a foreign money market security with a simultaneous forward sale of the currency denominating that security.

Cross-border factoring. Factoring by a network of factors across borders. The exporter's factor can contact correspondent factors in other countries to handle the collections of accounts receivable.

Cross exchange rate. Exchange rate between currency A and currency B, given the values of currencies A and B with respect to a third currency.

Cross-hedging. Hedging an open position in one currency with a hedge on another currency that is highly correlated with the first currency. This occurs when for some reason the common hedging techniques cannot be applied to the first currency. A cross-hedge is not a perfect hedge, but can substantially reduce the exposure.

Cross-sectional analysis. Analysis of relationships among a cross-section of firms, countries, or some other variable at a given point in time.

Cumulative translation adjustment (CTA) account. Account used by FASB-52 for capturing translation gains and losses.

Currency call option. Contract that grants the right to purchase a specific currency at a specific price (exchange rate) within a specific period of time.

Currency cocktail bond. Bond denominated in a mixture (or cocktail) of currencies.

Currency correlation. Measurement of the relationship between movements of two currencies.

Currency futures contract. Contract specifying a standard volume of a particular currency to be exchanged on a specific settlement date.

Currency put option. Contract granting the right to sell a particular currency at a specified price (exchange rate) within a specified period of time.

Currency swap. Agreement to exchange one currency for another at a specified exchange rate and date. Banks commonly serve as intermediaries between two parties who wish to engage in a currency swap.

Current account. Broad measure of a country's international trade in goods and services.

Debt-equity swap. Exchange of a bank's debt (loans) held in return for an equity investment in the borrower's assets; this type of swap was used by commercial banks to reduce their amounts of debt owed by less developed countries.

Delphi technique. Collection of independent opinions without group discussion by the assessors who provide the opinions; used for various types of assessments (such as country risk assessment).

Dependent variable. Term used in regression analysis to represent the variable that is dependent on one or more other variables.

Depreciation. Decrease in the value of a currency.

Direct foreign investment (DFI). Investment in real assets (such as land, buildings, or even existing plants) in foreign countries.

Direct quotations. Exchange rate quotations representing the value measured by number of dollars per unit.

Direct Loan Program. Program in which the Eximbank offers fixed-rate loans directly to the foreign buyer to purchase U.S. capital equipment and services.

Dirty float. Exchange rate system in which exchange rates are allowed to fluctuate without set boundaries; yet, governments do intervene as they wish.

Documentary collections. Trade transactions handled on a draft basis.

Documents against acceptance. Situation in which the buyer's bank does not release shipping documents to the buyer until the buyer has paid the draft.

Documents against payment. Shipping documents that are released to the buyer once the buyer has paid for the draft.

Double-entry bookkeeping. Accounting method in which each transaction is recorded as both a credit and a debit.

Draft (bill of exchange). Unconditional promise drawn by one party (usually the exporter) instructing the buyer to pay the face amount of the draft upon presentation.

Dummy variables. Variables used in regression analysis that are classified as either a zero or a one, for qualitative variables.

Dumping. Selling products overseas at unfairly low prices (a practice perceived to result from subsidies provided to the firm by its government).

Dynamic hedging.   Strategy of hedging in those periods when existing currency positions are expected to be adversely affected, and remaining unhedged in other periods when currency positions are expected to be favorably affected.

Economic exposure.   Degree to which a firm's present value of future cash flows can be influenced by exchange rate fluctuations.

Economies of scale.   Achievement of lower average cost per unit by means of increased production.

Edge Act corporations.   Aid corporations that are involved in foreign trade; they are established by banks and can be set up across state borders.

Effective financing rate.   Cost of financing after considering exchange rate fluctuations; this term is commonly applied to financing with foreign currencies, since financing costs will be affected by exchange rate fluctuations.

Effective yield.   Yield or return to an MNC on a short-term investment after adjustment for the change in exchange rates over the period of concern.

Efficient frontier.   Set of points reflecting risk-return combinations achieved by particular portfolios (so-called efficient portfolios) of assets.

Efficient market.   Market in which prices reflect all available information, so that excess risk-adjusted returns are not possible.

Equilibrium exchange rate. Exchange rate at which demand for a currency is equal to the supply of the currency for sale.

Equity multiplier.   Assets divided by equity.

Eurobanks.   Commercial banks that participate as financial intermediaries in the Eurocurrency market.

Eurobond market.   Market in which bonds are underwritten by international syndicates and sold outside the country of the currency that denominated the bonds.

Eurobonds.   Bonds sold in countries other than the country represented by the currency denominating them.

Euro-clear.   Telecommunications network that informs all traders about outstanding issues of Eurobonds for sale.

Euro-commercial paper.   Debt securities issued by MNCs for short-term financing.

Eurocredit market.   Collection of banks that accept deposits and provide loans in large denominations and in a variety of currencies. The banks that comprise this market are the same banks that comprise the Eurocurrency market; the difference is that the Eurocredit loans are longer-term than so-called Eurocurrency loans.

Eurocredit loans.   Loans of one year or longer extended by Eurobanks.

Eurocurrency market.   Collection of banks that accept deposits and provide loans in large denominations and in a variety of currencies.

Eurodollars.   U.S. dollars deposited in European banks.

Euronotes.   Unsecured debt securities issued by MNCs for short-term financing.

European Currency Unit (ECU). Unit of account representing a weighted average of exchange rates of member countries within the European Monetary System.

European Monetary System (EMS) Group of nations whose exchange rates are held together within specified limits, and are also tied to a currency composite called the European Currency Unit (ECU).

Exchange rate. Value of one currency with respect to another.

Exercise price (strike price). Price (exchange rate) at which the owner of a currency call option is allowed to buy a specified currency; or the price (exchange rate) at which the owner of a currency put option is allowed to sell a specified currency.

Exposure to exchange rate. fluctuations Degree to which a firm can be affected by exchange rate fluctuations; three common types of exposure are (1) transaction exposure, (2) economic exposure, and (3) translation exposure.

Export-Import Bank. Bank that attempts to strengthen the competitiveness of U.S. industries involved in foreign trade.

Ex post real interest rate. Measurement of the interest rate after adjustment for inflation in a recent period.

Factor. Firm specializing in collection on accounts receivable; exporters sometimes sell their accounts receivable to a factor at a discount.

Factoring. Purchase of receivables of an exporter by a factor without recourse to the exporter.

Financial Accounting Standards Board No. 52. Consolidated accounting rules adopted in 1981.

Fisher effect. Theory that nominal interest rates are composed of a real interest rate and anticipated inflation.

Financial Institution Buyer Credit Policy. Policy that provides insurance coverage for loans by banks to foreign buyers of exports.

Fixed exchange rate system. Monetary system in which exchange rates are either held constant or allowed to fluctuate only within very narrow boundaries.

Floating rate notes (FRNs). Provision of some Eurobonds, in which the coupon rate is adjusted over time according to prevailing market rates.

Forecast bias. Consistent over- or underestimating in forecasting.

Foreign bond. Bond issued by a borrower foreign to the country where the bond is placed.

Foreign Credit Insurance Association (FCIA). Agency that insures firms against political and credit risk related to international trade.

Foreign exchange market. Market composed primarily of banks, serving firms and consumers who wish to buy or sell various currencies.

Foreign investment risk matrix (FIRM). Graph that displays financial and political risk by intervals, so that each country can be positioned according to its risk ratings.

Forfaiting. Method of financing international trade of capital goods.

Forward contract. Agreement between a commercial bank and a client about an exchange of two currencies to be made at a future point in time at a specified exchange rate.

Forward discount. Percentage by which the forward rate is less than the spot rate; typically quoted on an annualized basis.

Forward premium. Percentage by which the forward rate exceeds the spot rate; typically quoted on an annualized basis.

Forward rate. Rate at which a bank is willing to exchange one currency for another at some specified date in the future

Franchising. Agreement by which a firm provides a specialized sales or service strategy, support assistance, and possibly an initial investment in the franchise in exchange for periodic fees.

Freely floating exchange rate system. Monetary system in which exchange rates are allowed to move due to market forces without intervention by country governments.

Full compensation. An arrangement in which the delivery of goods to one party is fully compensated for by buying back more than 100 percent of the value that was originally sold.

Fundamental forecasting. Forecasting based on fundamental relationships between economic variables and exchange rates.

General Agreement on Tariffs and Trade (GATT). Agreement allowing for trade restrictions only in retaliation against illegal trade actions of other countries.

Gold standard. Era in which each currency was convertible into gold at a specified rate, allowing the exchange rate between two currencies to be determined by their relative convertibility rates per ounce of gold.

Hedging. Action taken to insulate a firm from exposure to exchange rate fluctuations.

Hostile takeovers. Acquisitions not desired by the target firms.

IMF Funding Bill. Bill passed by Congress in 1983 that called for funds to be sent from the U.S. government to the International Monetary Fund and then channelled to the LDCs.

Imperfect markets theory. Theory suggesting that because there are costs to the transfer of labor and other resources used for production, firms may attempt to use foreign factors of production when they are less costly than local factors.

Import-export letters of credit. Trade-related letters of credit in which a bank agrees to make payments on behalf of an importer.

Import/Export Letters of credit. Trade-related letters of credit.

Independent variable. Term used in regression analysis to represent the variable that is expected to influence another (so-called "dependent") variable.

Indirect quotations. Exchange rate quotations representing the value measured by number of units per dollar.

Interbank market. Market that facilitates the exchange of currencies between banks.

Interest Equalization Tax (IET). Tax imposed by the U.S. government in 1963 to discourage U.S. investors from investing in foreign securities.

Interest rate parity (IRP) line. Diagonal line depicting all points on a four-quadrant graph that represent a state of interest rate parity.

Interest rate parity theory. Theory suggesting that the forward rate differs from the spot rate by an amount that reflects the interest differential between two currencies.

Interest rate swap. Agreement to swap interest payments, whereby interest payments based on a fixed interest rate are exchanged for interest payments based on a floating interest rate.

Intermediary Loan Program. Program in which the Eximbank provides fixed-rate funding to commercial banks, which extends the funds to eligible foreign buyers of exports; the banks incur the default risk on the loans.

International Bank for Reconstruction and Development (IBRD). Bank established in 1944 to enhance economic development by providing loans to countries. Also referred to as the World Bank.

International Banking Act. Act passed in 1978 that restricted foreign-owned banks from accepting deposits across state lines.

International banking facilities (IBFs). Offices established as part of existing banks to allow for acceptance of deposits or loans to nonresidents of the U.S. Because IBFs are not subject to normal U.S. regulations, they are free from reserve requirements and interest rate ceilings.

International Development Association (IDA). Association established to stimulate country development; it was especially suited for less prosperous nations, since it provided loans at low interest rates.

International Financial Corporation (IFC). Firm established to promote private enterprise within countries; it can provide loans to and purchase stock of corporations.

International Fisher Effect (IFE) line. Diagonal line on a graph that reflects points at which the interest rate differential between two countries is equal to the percentage change in the exchange rate between their two respective currencies.

International Monetary Fund (IMF). Agency established in 1944 to promote and facilitate international trade and financing.

International mutual funds (IMFs). Mutual funds containing securities of foreign firms.

In-the-money. Descriptive term implying that the present exchange rate exceeds (is less than) the strike price on a currency call (put) option.

Intracompany trade. International trade between subsidiaries that are under the same ownership.

Irrevocable letter of credit. Letter of credit issued by a bank that cannot be cancelled or amended without the beneficiary's approval.

Issuing bank. Bank that issues a letter of credit.

J curve effect. Effect of a weaker dollar on the U.S. trade balance, in which the trade balance initially deteriorates; it only improves once U.S. and non-U.S. importers respond to the change in purchasing power that is caused by the weaker dollar.

Joint venture. Venture between two or more firms in which responsibilities and earnings are shared.

Lagging. Strategy used by a firm to stall payments, normally in response to exchange rate projections.

Law of one price. Also called the absolute form of purchasing power parity (PPP), theory suggesting that prices of two products of different countries should be equal when measured by a common currency.

Leading. Strategy used by a firm to accelerate payments, normally in response to exchange rate expectations.

Lease insurance policy. Policy that provides insurance coverage to banks and other firms that lease U.S.-manufactured equipment to foreign entities.

Letter of credit (L/C). Agreement by a bank to make payments on behalf of a specified party under specified conditions.

Licensing. Arrangement in which a local firm in the host country produces goods in accordance with another firm's (the licensing firm's) specifications; as the goods are sold, the local firm can retain part of the earnings.

Locational arbitrage. Action to capitalize on a discrepancy in quoted exchange rates between banks.

Lockbox. Post office box number to which customers are instructed to send payment.

London Interbank Offer Rate (LIBOR). Interest rate commonly charged for loans between Eurobanks.

Long forwards. Long-term forward contracts.

Long-term forward contracts. Contracts that state any exchange rate at which a specified amount of a specified currency can be exchanged at a future date (more than one year from today). Also called long forwards.

Louvre Accord. 1987 agreement between countries to attempt to stabilize the value of the U.S. dollar.

Macro-assessment. Overall risk assessment of a country without considering the MNC's business.

Mail float. Mailing time involved in sending payments by mail.

Managed float. Exchange rate system in which currencies have no explicit boundaries, but central banks may intervene to influence exchange rate movements.

Margin requirement. Deposit placed on a contract (such as a currency futures contract) to cover the fluctuations in the value of that contract; this minimizes the risk of the contract to the counter-party.

Market maker. Member firm that can serve as a buyer or seller.

Market-based forecasting. Use of a market-determined exchange rate (such as the spot rate or forward rate) to forecast the spot rate in the future.

Medium-Term Guarantee Program. Program conducted by the Eximbank in which commercial lenders are encouraged to finance the sale of U.S. capital equipment and services to approved foreign buyers; the Eximbank guarantees the loan's principal and interest on these loans.

Micro-assessment. The risk assessment of a country as related to the MNC's type of business.

Mixed forecasting. Development of forecasts based on a mixture of forecasting techniques.

Monetary/nonmonetary approach. System used for consolidated accounting rules before 1981, whereby current exchange rates were used to measure monetary assets and liabilities, while historic exchange rates were used to measure those of nonmonetary items.

Money market hedge. Use of international money markets to match future cash inflows and outflows in a given currency.

Multi-Buyer Policy. Policy administered by the Eximbank that provides credit risk insurance on export sales to many different buyers.

Multilateral Investment Guarantee Agency (MIGA).   Agency established by the World Bank that offers various forms of political risk insurance to corporations.

Multilateral netting system. Complex interchange for netting between a parent and several subsidiaries.

Negotiable bill of lading.   Contract that grants title of merchandise to the holder, which allows banks to use the merchandise as collateral.

Negotiating bank.   Bank that issues a letter of credit.

Net operating loss carrybacks. Practice of applying losses to offset earnings in previous years.

Net operating loss carryforwards. Practice of applying losses to offset earnings in future years.

Netting.   Combining of future cash receipts and payments to determine the net amount to be owed by one subsidiary to another.

Net transaction exposure. Consideration of inflows and outflows in a given currency to determine the exposure after offsetting inflows against outflows.

New-Export policy.   Policy administered by Eximbank that provides coverage on commercial risk defaults to new exporters.

Nonsterilized intervention. Intervention in the foreign exchange market without adjusting for the change in money supply.

Ocean bill of lading.   Receipt for a shipment by boat, which includes freight charges and title to the merchandise.

Open account transaction.   Sale in which the exporter ships the merchandise and expects the buyer to remit payment according to agreed-upon terms.

Options on futures contract. Contract that provides the right to purchase or sell the futures contract of a specified currency at a specified price by a specified expiration date.

Out-of-the-money.   Descriptive term implying that the present exchange rate is less than (exceeds) the strike price on a currency call (put) option.

Overhedging.   Hedging an amount in a currency larger than the actual transaction amount.

Parallel bonds.   Bonds placed in different countries and denominated in the respective currencies of the countries where they are placed.

Parallel loan.   Loan involving an exchange of currencies between two parties, with a promise to reexchange the currencies at a specified exchange rate and future date.

Partial compensation.   An arrangement in which the delivery of goods to one party is partially compensated for by buying back a certain amount of product from the same party.

Pegged exchange rate.   Exchange rate whose value is pegged to another currency's value or to a unit of account.

Perfect forecast line.   A 45 degree line on a graph that matches the forecast of an exchange rate with the actual exchange rate.

Petrodollars.   Deposits of dollars by countries which receive dollar revenues due to the sale of petroleum to other countries; the term commonly refers to OPEC deposits of dollars in the Eurocurrency market.

Planned divestment.   Act of phasing out a portion of business over time;

commonly used by MNCs to phase out their overseas investments.

Plaza Accord. Agreement among country representatives in 1985 to implement a coordinated program to weaken the dollar.

Political risk. Political actions taken by the host government or the public that affect the MNC's cash flows.

Preauthorized payment. Method of accelerating cash inflows by receiving authorization to charge a customer's bank account.

Prepayment. Method which exporter uses to receive payment before shipping goods.

Price-elastic. Sensitive to price changes.

Private Export Funding Corporation (PEFCO). Agency that provides medium- and long-term funds to importers of U.S. goods and services.

Privatization. Conversion of government-owned businesses to ownership by shareholders or individuals.

Product cycle theory. Theory suggesting that a firm initially establish itself locally and expand into foreign markets in response to foreign demand for its product; over time, the MNC will grow in foreign markets; after some point, its foreign business may decline unless it can differentiate its product from competitors.

Product differentiation. Development of a product that is unique, different from those produced by competitors, in order to maintain or improve market share.

Purchasing power parity (PPP) line. Diagonal line on a graph that reflects points at which the inflation differential between two countries is equal to the percentage change in the exchange rate between the two respective currencies.

Purchasing Power Parity (PPP) theory. Theory suggesting that exchange rates will adjust over time to reflect the differential in inflation rates in the two countries; in this way, the purchasing power of consumers when purchasing domestic goods will be the same as that when they purchase foreign goods.

Quota. Maximum limit imposed by the government on goods allowed to be imported into a country.

Real cost of hedging. The additional cost of hedging when compared to not hedging (a negative real cost would imply that hedging was more favorable than not hedging).

Real interest rate. Nominal (or quoted) interest rate minus the inflation rate.

Real net exports. Value of inflation-adjusted exports minus inflation-adjusted imports.

Regression analysis. Statistical technique used to measure the relationship between variables and the sensitivity of a variable to one or more other variables.

Regression coefficient. Term measured by regression analysis to estimate the sensitivity of the dependent variable to a particular independent variable.

Reinvoicing center. Facility that centralizes payments and changes subsidiaries fees for its function; this can effectively shift profits to subsidiaries where tax rates are low.

Relative form of purchasing power parity. Theory stating that the rate of change in the prices of products should be somewhat similar when measured in a common currency, as long as transportation costs and trade barriers are unchanged.

Revocable letter of credit. Letter of credit issued by a bank that can be cancelled at any time without prior notification to the beneficiary.

Rule 144a. Securities and Exchange Commission guideline that exempts issues of securities from some disclosure rules, when the securities are placed directly with private investors.

Semistrong-form efficient. Description of foreign exchange markets, implying that all relevant public information is already reflected in prevailing spot exchange rates.

Sensitivity analysis. Technique for assessing uncertainty whereby various possibilities are input to determine possible outcomes.

Simulation. Technique for assessing the degree of uncertainty. Probability distributions are developed for the input variables; simulation uses this information to generate possible outcomes.

Single-Buyer Policy. Policy administered by the Eximbank which allows the exporter to selectively insure certain transactions.

Single European Act. Act intended to remove numerous barriers imposed on trade and capital flows between European countries.

Smithsonian Agreement. Conference between nations in 1971 that resulted in a devaluation of the dollar against major currencies, and a widening of boundaries (2¼ percent in either direction) around the newly established exchange rates.

Snake. Arrangement established in 1972, whereby European currencies were tied to each other within specified limits.

Special Drawing Rights (SDRs). Reserves established by the International Monetary Fund; they are used only for intergovernment transactions; the SDR also serves as a unit of account (determined by the values of five major currencies) that is used to denominate some internationally traded goods and services, as well as some foreign bank deposits and loans.

Specialists. Firms designated by the exchange to maintain orderly trading and manage limit orders for each currency.

Spot rate. Current exchange rate of currency.

Standby letter of credit. Document used to guarantee invoice payments to a supplier; it promises to pay the beneficiary if the buyer fails to pay.

Sterilized intervention. Intervention in the foreign exchange market while retaining the existing money supply.

Straddle. Combination of a put option and a call option.

Strike price. *See* **Exercise price.**

Strong-form efficient. Description of foreign exchange markets, implying that all relevant public information and private information is already reflected in prevailing spot exchange rates.

Structural Adjustment Loan Facility. Facility established in 1980 by the World Bank to enhance a country's long-term economic growth through financing projects.

Supplier credit. Credit provided by the supplier to itself to fund its operations.

Syndicate. Group of banks that participate in loans.

Syndicated Eurocredit loans. Loans provided by a group (or syndicate) of banks in the Eurocredit market.

Systematic risk. Risk that cannot be diversified away and is common to all firms or countries.

Target zones. Implicit boundaries established by central banks on exchange rates.

Tariff. Tax imposed by a government on imported goods.

Technical forecasting. Development of forecasts using historical prices or trends.

Tenor. Time period of drafts.

Time-series analysis. Analysis of relationships between two or more variables over periods of time.

Time series models. Models that examine series of historical data; sometimes used as a means of technical forecasting, by examining moving averages.

Trade acceptance. Draft that allows the buyer to obtain merchandise prior to accepting it.

Transaction exposure. Degree to which the value of future cash transactions can be affected by exchange rate fluctuations.

Translation exposure. Exposure of the MNC's consolidated financial statements to exchange rate fluctuations.

Transferable letter of credit. Document that allows the first beneficiary on a standby letter of credit to transfer all or part of the original letter of credit to a third party.

Transfer pricing. Policy for pricing goods sent by either the parent or a subsidiary to a subsidiary of an MNC.

Translation exposure. Degree to which a firm's consolidated financial statements are exposed to fluctuations in exchange rates.

Triangular arbitrage. Action to capitalize on a discrepancy where the quoted cross exchange rate is not equal to the rate that should exist at equilibrium.

Umbrella policy. Policy issued to a bank or trading company to insure exports of an exporter and handle all administrative requirements.

Unilateral transfers. Accounting for government and private gifts and grants.

Weak-form efficient. Description of foreign exchange markets, implying that all historical and current exchange rate information is already reflected in prevailing spot exchange rates.

Withholding tax. Common name for a tax imposed by a host country on funds that are remitted from a subsidiary to its parent.

Working Capital Guarantee Program. Program conducted by the Eximbank which encourages commercial banks to extend short-term export financing to eligible exporters; the Eximbank provides a guarantee in the loan's principal and interest.

World Bank. Bank established in 1944 to enhance economic development by providing loans to countries.

Writer. Seller of an option.

Yankee stock offerings. Offerings of stock by non-U.S. firms in the U.S. markets.

Data Bank

Quarterly data is provided in this data bank for the following variables:

- Consumer Price Index
- Quarterly Inflation Rates
- Money Market Interest Rates
- Exports by Country
- Imports by Country
- Industrial Share Price Index
- Percentage Change in Industrial Share Prices
- Exchange Rates
- Exchange Rate Percentage Change
- Three-Month Forward Rates

The data were compiled from *International Financial Statistics,* which is published by the International Monetary Fund and is available at many university libraries.

Consumer price index (1980 = 100)

Year	Quarter	Canada	France	Germany	Japan	Netherlands	Sweden	Switzerland	U.K.	U.S.
1972	I	48.8	43.4	66.3	45.8	55.5	46.1	68.4	31.7	50.2
	II	49.2	44.1	67.0	46.7	56.9	46.9	69.2	32.2	50.5
	III	50.2	44.8	68.0	47.2	57.3	47.3	70.2	32.7	51.0
	IV	50.7	45.8	69.1	47.7	58.8	48.1	71.9	33.6	51.4
1973	I	51.7	46.2	70.6	49.1	59.8	49.0	73.7	34.1	52.2
	II	52.8	47.2	72.0	51.6	61.5	49.8	74.9	35.2	53.4
	III	54.3	48.3	72.5	53.2	62.0	50.6	76.0	35.8	54.5
	IV	55.3	49.6	74.0	55.6	63.4	53.1	79.6	36.9	55.8
1974	I	56.6	51.4	75.8	61.1	65.0	53.9	81.4	38.5	57.3
	II	58.5	53.6	77.0	64.0	66.9	54.4	82.0	40.8	58.9
	III	60.3	55.3	77.8	66.4	68.1	55.2	84.0	41.8	60.7
	IV	61.9	57.1	78.8	69.2	70.4	57.6	86.6	43.7	62.4
1975	I	63.2	58.6	80.3	70.6	71.9	58.4	87.9	46.3	63.6
	II	64.6	60.1	81.8	72.6	73.9	59.7	88.9	50.7	64.6
	III	66.9	61.4	82.5	73.2	75.3	61.5	89.5	52.9	66.0
	IV	68.2	62.7	83.2	75.1	77.0	63.0	90.1	54.7	67.1
1976	I	69.1	64.2	84.5	76.9	78.7	64.8	90.4	56.7	67.7
	II	70.2	65.7	85.5	79.4	80.9	66.4	90.3	58.8	68.6
	III	71.2	67.2	85.7	80.2	81.8	67.4	90.7	60.1	69.6
	IV	72.3	69.0	86.2	82.2	83.7	69.0	91.0	62.9	70.4
1977	I	73.8	70.0	87.7	84.0	84.4	70.9	91.4	66.1	71.6
	II	75.5	72.2	88.6	86.3	86.5	73.6	91.6	69.0	73.2
	III	77.2	73.9	88.9	86.6	87.1	76.1	92.0	70.1	74.3
	IV	78.8	75.3	89.3	87.3	88.0	77.9	92.2	71.1	75.1
1978	I	80.3	76.5	90.3	87.7	88.3	80.5	92.4	72.3	76.3
	II	82.2	78.7	91.1	89.4	89.6	81.6	92.8	74.3	78.4
	III	84.4	80.7	91.1	90.1	90.8	82.3	93.0	75.6	80.2
	IV	85.7	82.4	91.4	90.3	91.6	83.5	92.8	76.8	81.8
1979	I	87.6	84.3	93.0	90.0	92.1	85.1	94.2	79.3	83.9
	II	89.9	86.6	94.3	92.3	93.3	86.6	95.1	82.2	86.7
	III	91.7	89.4	95.5	93.2	94.3	88.6	97.0	87.7	89.6
	IV	93.8	91.9	96.3	94.8	95.8	91.3	97.5	90.2	92.2

Consumer price index (1980 = 100) (continued)

Year	Quarter	Canada	France	Germany	Japan	Netherlands	Sweden	Switzerland	U.K.	U.S.
1980	I	95.9	95.5	98.2	96.8	97.4	96.4	98.3	94.4	95.8
	II	98.5	99.1	99.9	100.0	99.5	98.2	99.5	99.8	99.3
	III	101.3	99.6	100.5	100.9	101.0	101.3	100.7	102.0	101.1
	IV	104.2	103.1	101.4	102.3	102.2	104.7	101.6	103.9	103.8
1981	I	107.6	107.3	103.8	103.2	103.9	108.8	104.0	106.3	106.5
	II	110.9	110.8	105.7	104.9	105.9	111.1	105.5	111.5	109.0
	III	114.2	115.2	107.2	105.2	107.6	113.5	107.9	113.4	112.1
	IV	117.0	118.9	108.6	106.4	109.6	115.1	108.6	116.2	113.7
1982	I	120.0	122.3	110.0	106.4	111.1	118.6	109.6	118.2	114.7
	II	123.7	126.1	111.3	107.5	112.6	120.6	111.7	121.9	116.4
	III	126.3	127.8	112.7	109.0	113.8	122.3	114.0	122.5	118.6
	IV	128.3	130.2	113.7	108.9	114.6	125.4	114.9	123.4	118.9
1983	I	129.1	133.6	114.4	108.6	114.7	129.1	114.9	124.0	118.8
	II	130.9	137.4	115.0	109.8	115.5	131.1	115.6	126.5	120.3
	III	133.0	140.3	116.2	109.5	116.6	133.6	116.0	128.2	121.7
	IV	134.2	143.0	116.7	110.7	117.8	136.5	117.0	129.6	122.8
1984	I	135.8	145.4	117.7	111.2	118.8	139.7	118.2	130.4	124.1
	II	137.0	148.1	118.3	112.1	119.8	142.3	119.0	133.1	125.5
	III	138.2	150.6	118.3	111.9	120.0	143.8	119.2	134.2	126.9
	IV	139.2	152.7	119.2	113.3	121.3	146.9	120.5	135.9	127.8
1985	I	140.8	154.8	120.5	113.7	121.6	150.9	122.8	137.6	128.6
	II	142.4	157.6	121.2	114.7	122.8	153.7	123.3	142.3	130.2
	III	143.7	159.1	120.9	114.9	122.8	154.0	123.1	142.7	131.1
	IV	145.0	160.1	121.3	115.3	123.4	156.4	124.3	143.4	132.3
1986	I	146.8	160.3	121.3	115.4	123.0	158.9	124.6	144.5	132.6
	II	147.9	161.4	121.0	115.7	123.3	159.7	124.4	146.3	132.3
	III	149.7	162.4	120.4	115.1	122.1	160.4	123.8	146.4	133.3
	IV	151.3	163.5	120.0	115.1	123.2	162.0	124.4	148.4	134.0
1987	I	152.7	165.5	120.7	114.1	121.5	164.5	125.7	150.2	135.5
	II	154.8	166.9	121.1	115.9	122.1	165.1	125.7	152.5	137.3
	III	156.6	167.9	121.1	115.6	122.3	168.0	126.1	152.8	138.8
	IV	157.7	168.7	121.2	115.9	123.1	170.5	126.9	154.5	140.0

Consumer price index (1980 = 100) *(continued)*

Year	Quarter	Canada	France	Germany	Japan	Netherlands	Sweden	Switzerland	U.K.	U.S.
1988	I	159.0	169.5	121.7	115.3	122.1	172.7	127.8	155.2	140.9
	II	161.0	171.2	122.3	116.1	123.0	175.8	128.2	158.9	142.6
	III	162.9	172.8	122.5	116.3	123.5	177.8	128.3	161.1	144.6
	IV	164.1	173.8	122.9	117.1	123.9	180.5	129.0	164.5	146.0
1989	I	166.1	175.3	124.7	116.6	123.2	183.9	130.6	167.1	147.7
	II	169.0	177.4	125.9	119.3	124.2	187.3	131.9	171.9	150.0
	III	171.4	178.7	125.9	119.4	124.9	189.0	132.4	173.5	151.3
	IV	170.2	180.1	126.8	119.6	124.5	188.9	134.4	172.6	152.8
1990	I	170.3	177.7	127.3	119.8	124.8	197.8	136.8	175.6	152.3
	II	172.5	179.4	128.0	121.5	125.9	202.2	138.1	183.8	153.8
	III	174.3	172.9	128.5	121.5	126.8	206.1	139.7	185.6	156.5
	IV	176.8	174.5	130.8	122.3	128.0	210.0	142.3	187.7	159.0
1991	I	181.8	175.4	131.9	122.4	128.2	219.3	144.9	188.8	160.3
	II	180.2	176.6	133.1	123.6	129.4	223.1	146.6	192.8	161.2
	III	181.1	178.1	135.0	123.6	132.1	223.7	148.2	193.7	162.5
	IV	181.0	179.6	136.0	125.2	133.4	226.5	149.8	195.5	163.8
1992	I	181.8	180.7	137.6	124.8	133.7	226.5	151.8	196.6	164.9
	II	182.6	182.1	139.0	126.4	128.8	227.8	153.1	200.8	166.2
	III	183.4	182.9	139.6	125.9	129.0	228.2	153.5	200.7	167.5
	IV	184.1	182.8	141.0	126.4	128.8	230.6	155.0	201.5	168.7
1993	I	185.5	184.3	143.5	126.4	129.5	237.4	157.1	200.1	170.2
	II	185.8	185.5	144.8	127.6	129.9	238.8	158.6	203.4	171.4
	III	186.6	185.9	145.4	128.1	129.8	238.6	158.9	203.9	172.1
	IV	187.6	186.6	146.3	127.8	129.7	240.6	159.3	204.6	173.3

Quarterly inflation rates (percentage change in consumer price index)

Year	Quarter	Canada	France	Germany	Japan	Netherlands	Sweden	Switzerland	U.K.	U.S.
1972	I	N/A	N/A	N/A	N/A	N/A	N/A	N/A	N/A	N/A
	II	.82	1.61	1.06	1.97	2.52	1.74	1.17	1.58	.60
	III	2.03	1.59	1.49	1.07	.70	.85	1.45	1.55	.99
	IV	1.00	2.23	1.62	1.06	2.62	1.69	2.42	2.75	.78
1973	I	1.97	.87	2.17	2.94	1.70	1.87	2.50	1.49	1.56
	II	2.13	2.16	1.98	5.09	2.84	1.63	1.63	3.23	2.30
	III	2.84	2.33	.69	3.10	.81	1.61	1.47	1.70	2.06
	IV	1.84	2.69	2.07	4.51	2.26	4.94	4.74	3.07	2.39
1974	I	2.35	3.63	2.43	9.89	2.52	1.51	2.26	4.34	2.69
	II	3.36	4.28	1.58	4.75	2.92	.93	.74	5.97	2.79
	III	3.08	3.17	1.04	3.75	1.79	1.47	2.44	2.45	3.06
	IV	2.65	3.25	1.29	4.22	3.38	4.35	3.10	4.55	2.80
1975	I	2.10	2.63	1.90	2.02	2.13	1.39	1.50	5.95	1.92
	II	2.22	2.56	1.87	2.83	2.78	2.23	1.14	9.50	1.57
	III	3.56	2.16	.86	.83	1.89	3.02	.67	4.34	2.17
	IV	1.94	2.12	.85	2.60	2.26	2.44	.67	3.40	1.67
1976	I	1.32	2.39	1.56	2.40	2.21	2.86	.33	3.66	.89
	II	1.59	2.34	1.18	3.25	2.80	2.47	-.11	3.70	1.33
	III	1.42	2.28	.23	1.01	1.11	1.51	.44	2.21	1.46
	IV	1.54	2.68	.58	2.49	2.32	2.37	.33	4.66	1.15
1977	I	2.07	1.45	1.74	2.19	.84	2.75	.44	5.09	1.70
	II	2.30	3.14	1.03	2.74	2.49	3.81	.22	4.39	2.23
	III	2.25	2.35	.34	.35	.69	3.40	.44	1.59	1.50
	IV	2.07	1.89	.45	.81	1.03	2.37	.22	1.43	1.08
1978	I	1.90	1.59	1.12	.46	.34	3.34	.22	1.69	1.60
	II	2.37	2.88	.89	1.94	1.47	1.37	.43	2.77	2.75
	III	2.68	2.54	.00	.78	1.34	.86	.22	1.75	2.30
	IV	1.54	2.11	.33	.22	.88	1.46	-.22	1.59	2.00
1979	I	2.22	2.31	1.75	-.33	.55	1.92	1.51	3.26	2.57
	II	2.63	2.73	1.40	2.56	1.30	1.76	.96	3.66	3.34
	III	2.00	3.23	1.27	.98	1.07	2.31	2.00	6.69	3.34
	IV	2.29	2.80	.84	1.72	1.59	3.05	.52	2.85	2.90

Quarterly inflation rates (percentage change in consumer price index) (*continued*)

Year	Quarter	Canada	France	Germany	Japan	Netherlands	Sweden	Switzerland	U.K.	U.S.
1980	I	2.24	3.92	1.97	2.11	1.67	5.59	.82	4.66	3.90
	II	2.71	3.77	1.73	3.31	2.16	1.87	1.22	5.72	3.65
	III	2.84	.50	.60	.90	1.51	3.16	1.21	2.20	1.81
	IV	2.86	3.51	.90	1.39	1.19	3.36	.89	1.86	2.67
1981	I	3.26	4.07	2.37	.88	1.66	3.92	2.36	2.31	2.60
	II	3.07	3.26	1.83	1.65	1.92	2.11	1.44	4.89	2.35
	III	2.98	3.97	1.42	.29	1.61	2.16	2.27	1.70	2.84
	IV	2.45	3.21	1.31	1.14	1.86	1.41	.65	2.47	1.43
1982	I	2.56	2.86	1.29	.00	1.37	3.04	.92	1.72	.88
	II	3.08	3.11	1.18	1.03	1.35	1.69	1.92	3.13	1.48
	III	2.10	1.35	1.26	1.40	1.07	1.41	2.06	.49	1.89
	IV	1.58	1.88	.89	-.09	.70	2.53	.79	.73	.25
1983	I	.62	2.61	.62	+.27	.09	2.95	.00	.49	-.08
	II	1.39	2.84	.52	1.10	.70	1.55	.61	2.02	1.26
	III	1.60	2.11	1.04	-.27	.95	1.91	.35	1.34	1.16
	IV	.90	1.92	.43	1.10	1.03	2.17	.86	1.09	.90
1984	I	1.19	1.68	.86	.45	.85	2.34	1.03	.62	1.06
	II	.88	1.86	.51	.81	.84	1.86	.68	2.07	1.13
	III	.88	1.69	.00	-.18	.17	1.05	.17	.83	1.12
	IV	.72	1.39	.76	1.25	1.08	2.16	1.09	1.27	.71
1985	I	1.15	1.38	1.09	.18	-.25	2.72	1.91	1.25	.63
	II	1.14	1.81	.58	.88	.99	1.86	.41	3.42	1.24
	III	.91	.95	-.25	.17	.00	.20	-.16	.28	.69
	IV	.91	.63	.33	.35	.49	1.56	.97	.49	.92
1986	I	1.24	.13	.00	.09	.09	1.60	.24	.77	.23
	II	.75	.69	-.25	.26	.26	.50	-.16	1.25	-.23
	III	1.22	.62	-.50	-.52	-1.78	.44	-.48	.07	.76
	IV	1.07	.67	-.33	.00	.90	.99	.48	1.37	.53
1987	I	.93	1.22	.58	-.87	-1.38	1.54	1.05	1.21	1.12
	II	1.38	.85	.33	1.58	.49	.36	.00	.67	1.33
	III	1.16	.60	.00	-.26	.16	1.76	.32	.20	1.09
	IV	.70	.48	.08	.26	.65	.89	.63	1.11	.86

Quarterly inflation rates (percentage change in consumer price index) (*continued*)

Year	Quarter	Canada	France	Germany	Japan	Netherlands	Sweden	Switzerland	U.K.	U.S.
1988	I	.82	.47	.41	-.52	-.81	1.29	.71	.45	.64
	II	1.26	1.03	.50	.70	.70	1.78	.29	2.37	1.20
	III	1.15	.92	.20	.20	.40	1.14	.10	1.42	1.37
	IV	.79	.55	.30	.69	.40	1.56	.58	2.11	.99
1989	I	1.22	.91	1.47	-.49	-.60	1.87	1.24	1.55	1.16
	II	1.72	1.17	.97	2.36	.80	1.84	.94	2.88	1.59
	III	1.44	.71	.00	.10	.59	.90	.37	.91	.87
	IV	-.70	.80	.67	.08	-.32	-.05	1.51	-.52	.95
1990	I	.06	-1.33	.39	.33	.24	4.71	1.78	1.74	-.33
	II	1.29	.96	.55	1.42	.88	2.22	.95	4.67	.98
	III	1.04	-3.62	.39	.00	.71	1.92	1.16	.98	1.76
	IV	1.43	.94	1.79	.66	.94	1.89	1.86	1.13	1.60
1991	I	2.82	.51	.83	.08	.15	4.42	1.82	.58	.82
	II	-0.91	.67	0.92	1.01	0.95	1.72	1.19	2.10	0.56
	III	0.53	.84	1.45	0.00	2.06	0.27	1.09	0.50	0.79
	IV	-0.08	.83	0.72	1.27	1.01	1.28	1.08	0.92	0.79
1992	I	0.45	0.66	1.16	-0.36	0.18	0.00	1.31	0.56	0.70
	II	0.45	0.74	1.06	1.35	0.91	0.53	0.89	2.15	0.78
	III	0.45	0.49	0.44	-0.44	0.19	0.20	0.24	-0.07	0.77
	IV	0.37	-0.08	0.95	0.45	-0.19	1.06	0.96	0.41	0.76
1993	I	0.75	0.81	1.80	0.00	0.57	2.95	1.35	-0.68	0.83
	II	0.15	0.64	0.93	0.89	0.28	0.57	0.94	1.64	0.75
	III	0.44	0.24	0.42	0.44	-0.09	-0.06	0.23	0.27	0.37
	IV	0.51	0.40	0.58	-0.26	-0.09	0.82	0.23	0.33	0.74

Money market interest rates*

Year	Quarter	Canada	France	Germany	Japan	Netherlands	Sweden	Switzerland	U.K.	U.S.
1972	I	3.46	5.11	4.08	5.12	2.84	5.00	5.50	4.36	3.43
	II	3.62	4.64	3.12	4.82	1.50	5.00	3.75	4.70	3.75
	III	3.53	3.80	3.85	4.46	.26	5.00	3.75	5.96	4.24
	IV	3.63	6.26	6.16	4.49	3.10	5.00	3.75	7.15	4.85
1973	I	4.12	7.49	6.38	5.19	1.48	5.00	3.75	8.13	5.64
	II	5.19	7.61	11.05	6.13	2.93	5.00	4.50	7.36	6.61
	III	6.14	9.26	12.06	7.88	9.04	5.00	4.50	10.24	8.39
	IV	6.44	11.27	11.25	9.44	12.29	5.00	4.50	11.50	7.46
1974	I	6.27	12.72	10.39	12.08	10.58	5.00	5.50	11.99	7.60
	II	8.34	12.77	7.49	12.17	9.81	6.00	5.50	11.36	8.27
	III	9.05	13.67	9.31	13.04	8.13	7.00	5.50	11.18	8.28
	IV	7.64	12.48	8.28	12.87	8.29	7.00	5.50	10.96	7.34
1975	I	6.33	10.18	5.60	12.86	7.17	7.00	5.00	10.01	5.87
	II	6.90	7.73	5.03	11.27	2.82	7.00	4.50	9.39	5.40
	III	7.91	7.13	3.44	10.45	1.86	6.00	3.50	10.17	6.33
	IV	8.44	6.62	3.60	8.10	4.83	6.00	3.00	11.13	5.68
1976	I	8.82	7.06	3.50	7.09	3.08	5.50	2.50	9.04	4.95
	II	8.97	7.57	3.60	6.80	4.33	6.00	2.00	10.19	5.17
	III	9.10	8.99	4.30	7.13	12.83	6.00	2.00	11.26	5.17
	IV	8.58	10.62	4.10	6.88	8.88	8.00	2.00	13.99	4.68
1977	I	7.74	9.83	4.50	6.90	6.17	8.00	2.00	11.20	4.62
	II	7.23	9.07	4.30	5.51	2.00	8.00	2.00	7.72	4.83
	III	7.13	8.50	4.10	5.46	2.20	8.00	1.50	6.55	5.47
	IV	7.22	8.88	3.70	4.85	4.82	8.00	1.50	5.26	6.14
1978	I	7.39	9.67	3.40	4.74	5.30	8.07	1.00	5.90	6.41
	II	8.19	8.11	3.50	4.10	4.40	7.47	1.00	8.11	6.48
	III	8.89	7.29	3.40	4.36	4.39	6.33	1.00	9.04	7.32
	IV	10.22	6.55	3.10	4.23	10.87	6.77	1.00	11.00	8.68
1979	I	10.84	6.70	3.70	4.43	7.84	5.67	1.00	11.94	9.36
	II	10.81	7.34	5.30	5.12	7.25	6.77	1.00	11.75	9.38
	III	11.45	10.26	6.20	6.43	8.92	9.43	1.00	13.34	9.63
	IV	13.63	11.86	8.30	7.46	12.12	10.90	2.00	14.87	11.80

Money market interest rates* *(continued)*

Year	Quarter	Canada	France	Germany	Japan	Netherlands	Sweden	Switzerland	U.K.	U.S.
1980	I	14.10	12.37	8.30	9.18	10.56	11.87	3.00	16.04	13.46
	II	12.37	12.48	9.60	12.47	10.86	12.10	3.00	16.02	10.05
	III	10.50	11.58	9.30	12.06	10.09	12.17	3.00	14.60	9.24
	IV	14.21	10.95	9.00	10.01	9.00	12.53	3.00	13.77	13.71
1981	I	16.71	11.98	11.20	8.59	9.32	15.20	4.00	12.16	14.37
	II	18.20	15.94	13.20	7.44	10.62	15.30	5.00	11.59	14.83
	III	20.15	17.44	12.80	7.50	12.30	13.43	6.00	13.55	15.09
	IV	15.81	15.69	11.20	7.24	11.81	13.48	6.00	14.82	12.02
1982	I	14.59	14.95	10.20	6.64	9.31	12.97	5.50	13.37	12.89
	II	15.50	16.14	9.30	7.27	8.48	13.93	5.50	12.57	12.36
	III	13.89	14.59	8.90	7.38	8.22	14.53	5.00	10.61	9.71
	IV	10.58	13.24	7.20	7.20	6.24	11.74	4.50	9.66	7.93
1983	I	9.33	12.85	5.70	6.92	4.82	9.77	4.00	11.00	8.08
	II	9.18	12.62	5.40	6.69	5.11	11.00	4.00	10.04	8.42
	III	9.27	12.56	5.70	6.79	5.50	10.81	4.00	9.53	9.19
	IV	9.44	12.50	6.30	6.48	5.70	11.84	4.00	9.04	8.79
1984	I	10.03	12.65	6.00	6.31	5.86	10.74	4.00	8.90	9.13
	II	11.33	12.47	6.00	6.26	5.70	10.83	4.00	8.69	9.84
	III	12.29	11.56	6.00	6.34	5.87	13.47	4.00	10.40	10.34
	IV	10.60	11.06	6.00	6.39	5.70	12.03	4.00	9.39	8.97
1985	I	10.39	10.75	6.10	6.41	6.38	12.53	4.00	10.96	8.18
	II	9.54	10.44	5.80	6.35	6.91	14.79	4.00	10.08	7.52
	III	8.92	9.94	4.90	6.40	6.11	15.13	4.00	11.25	7.10
	IV	8.87	9.19	4.80	7.64	5.82	12.94	4.00	10.83	7.13
1986	I	10.76	8.81	4.60	6.22	5.80	11.64	4.00	12.21	6.89
	II	8.55	7.46	4.60	4.75	6.09	10.94	4.00	9.42	6.13
	III	8.31	7.20	4.60	4.63	5.69	9.33	4.00	10.17	5.53
	IV	8.25	7.70	4.70	4.34	5.74	8.68	4.00	10.93	5.34
1987	I	7.11	8.33	4.20	4.15	5.62	10.95	3.22	10.47	5.53
	II	8.19	8.13	3.80	3.77	5.21	8.54	3.21	9.14	5.23
	III	9.09	7.92	3.90	3.68	4.97	8.55	3.09	9.81	6.03
	IV	8.19	8.51	4.10	3.91	4.85	8.61	3.19	9.22	6.00

Money market interest rates* (*continued*)

Year	Quarter	Canada	France	Germany	Japan	Netherlands	Sweden	Switzerland	U.K.	U.S.
1988	I	8.41	7.94	3.40	3.84	4.05	9.24	1.96	9.01	5.76
	II	8.99	7.75	3.60	3.90	3.70	10.28	2.35	8.39	6.23
	III	9.87	7.66	4.90	4.14	4.95	10.34	3.73	11.33	6.99
	IV	10.66	8.16	5.10	4.44	5.24	10.46	3.99	12.52	7.70
1989	I	11.64	8.97	6.20	4.57	6.02	10.61	5.55	13.06	8.53
	II	12.21	8.83	6.80	4.96	6.60	11.57	6.78	13.46	8.44
	III	12.17	9.15	7.10	5.45	7.12	12.11	6.71	13.93	7.85
	IV	12.20	10.40	8.10	6.52	8.23	11.79	7.38	15.07	7.63
1990	I	12.92	10.97	8.30	7.12	8.47	13.64	8.73	14.82	7.76
	II	13.60	9.83	8.30	7.38	8.10	12.83	8.38	14.79	7.77
	III	12.77	9.87	8.30	7.99	8.06	12.57	8.30	14.86	7.49
	IV	11.95	9.70	8.30	8.20	8.54	14.75	7.86	14.26	7.02
1991	I	9.96	9.58	9.10	8.11	8.95	12.93	7.74	13.57	6.05
	II	8.90	9.54	9.00	7.84	8.94	11.64	7.64	11.93	5.59
	III	8.51	9.29	9.20	7.10	8.90	10.40	7.66	10.95	5.41
	IV	7.54	9.56	9.40	6.18	9.24	12.27	7.94	10.53	4.58
1992	I	7.18	9.97	9.60	5.03	9.46	12.46	7.41	10.49	3.91
	II	6.13	9.91	9.70	4.68	9.37	11.91	8.80	9.96	3.72
	III	6.29	11.16	9.70	4.04	9.49	35.78	8.34	9.81	3.13
	IV	6.79	10.35	8.90	3.91	8.76	13.54	5.94	7.94	3.04
1993	I	4.79	11.49	8.60	3.47	8.25	10.41	5.40	6.10	3.04
	II	4.29	8.48	7.00	3.20	7.41	9.43	5.08	5.37	3.00
	III	4.36	8.19	7.00	3.08	6.65	8.47	4.78	5.42	3.06
	IV	3.79	6.83	6.50	2.48	6.08	8.02	4.49	5.50	2.99

*Discount rate used for Switzerland, and for Sweden up to the first quarter of 1978.

Exports by country*

Year	Quarter	Canada	France	Germany	Japan	Netherlands	Sweden	Switzerland	U.K.	U.S.
1972	I	4,610	31.25	35.19	1,896	13,053	9,618	6,110	2,320	11.89
	II	5,579	34.81	36.61	2,022	13,626	10,326	6,423	2,440	12.04
	III	4,713	29.69	35.11	2,315	12,864	9,742	6,177	2,050	11.57
	IV	6,047	37.74	42.01	2,574	14,356	12,063	7,304	2,852	13.70
1973	I	5,850	37.97	41.70	2,160	16,824	12,683	6,897	2,828	15.52
	II	6,920	41.54	43.58	2,288	16,751	13,047	7,276	3,075	17.45
	III	6,098	37.41	43.40	2,551	15,657	12,011	7,147	3,056	17.08
	IV	7,569	45.58	48.54	3,032	17,647	15,426	8,470	3,470	20.71
1974	I	7,335	51.98	54.58	3,009	20,420	15,592	8,460	3,583	22.73
	II	8,721	58.67	57.08	3,836	22,815	17,798	9,019	4,199	25.28
	III	8,329	52.69	57.39	4,422	22,071	17,459	8,419	4,216	23.37
	IV	9,078	59.79	61.02	4,953	22,622	19,582	9,094	4,496	27.13
1975	I	8,057	57.73	52.58	3,893	21,492	18,253	7,815	4,559	27.03
	II	9,163	59.25	55.67	3,989	22,487	18,521	8,415	4,915	26.55
	III	8,108	50.40	52.94	4,081	20,043	15,639	7,835	4,837	25.01
	IV	9,334	59.55	60.16	4,609	24,601	19,623	9,242	5,659	28.54
1976	I	9,189	63.35	60.59	4,359	25,356	19,176	8,559	5,848	27.31
	II	10,541	70.77	62.92	4,906	25,933	20,332	9,239	6,459	29.64
	III	9,793	62.91	63.74	5,102	25,387	19,340	8,614	6,309	27.31
	IV	10,409	76.22	69.40	5,564	29,341	21,347	10,603	7,405	30.55
1977	I	10,760	78.19	66.62	5,097	27,130	20,341	9,889	7,809	29.64
	II	12,081	82.84	68.02	5,430	26,788	21,614	10,389	8,463	31.78
	III	11,032	72.30	65.33	5,491	25,204	18,674	10,059	8,486	29.09
	IV	12,277	85.64	73.65	5,641	28,075	25,048	11,674	8,550	30.64
1978	I	12,139	88.04	67.29	5,239	27,398	23,026	10,030	8,756	30.95
	II	14,605	93.87	72.03	5,311	27,082	25,675	10,846	9,626	37.02
	III	13,129	80.04	68.17	4,956	25,603	21,436	9,901	9,031	35.26
	IV	15,365	95.64	77.08	5,062	28,121	28,054	11,031	9,998	40.34
1979	I	15,705	100.48	74.36	4,664	29,911	26,915	10,365	9,097	41.08
	II	16,770	108.88	78.12	5,376	31,716	30,053	11,004	11,068	44.45
	III	16,957	99.76	76.37	5,787	30,957	26,905	10,458	10,606	44.68
	IV	18,836	118.84	85.17	6,705	35,048	34,337	12,253	12,116	51.59

Exports by country* (continued)

Year	Quarter	Canada	France	Germany	Japan	Netherlands	Sweden	Switzerland	U.K.	U.S.
1980	I	19,402	121.70	88.80	6,618	38,412	34,368	12,333	12,682	53.02
	II	19,738	127.05	87.52	7,463	36,615	29,831	12,407	12,253	56.59
	III	18,519	110.32	82.91	7,384	33,691	30,448	11,573	11,878	52.99
	IV	21,343	131.48	91.10	7,921	38,042	35,423	13,332	12,698	58.11
1981	I	20,886	134.35	91.20	7,297	40,581	34,200	12,591	11,695	59.74
	II	23,312	148.96	97.18	8,335	42,444	35,600	13,167	12,192	60.76
	III	20,328	137.09	98.79	8,896	41,561	32,238	12,754	12,624	55.15
	IV	22,639	156.27	109.81	8,952	46,477	42,176	14,345	14,188	58.09
1982	I	21,607	154.96	107.62	81.84	46,484	40,582	13,045	13,368	55.31
	II	22,173	160.64	108.27	86.44	44,600	42,328	13,465	13,805	57.03
	III	21,721	143.79	101.34	87.55	40,402	36,810	11,903	13,427	50.24
	IV	21,399	173.69	110.51	88.50	45,365	48,412	14,274	14,940	49.69
1983	I	21,501	166.90	105.59	7,820	46,562	50,853	12,662	14,649	50.08
	II	24,612	184.27	106.12	8,586	46,191	58,503	13,302	14,731	50.51
	III	22,218	167.23	103.41	8,983	43,825	47,064	12,802	14,658	48.38
	IV	26,272	204.67	117.16	9,521	50,027	59,069	14,998	16,545	51.58
1984	I	27,259	206.01	120.06	9,042	53,897	62,538	14,412	16,847	53.79
	II	30,746	214.20	115.12	9,929	52,677	59,521	15,182	16,838	54.90
	III	28,910	197.55	117.97	10,343	47,999	53,056	14,339	16,686	53.28
	IV	30,271	233.18	135.05	11,023	55,807	66,900	16,697	20,140	55.92
1985	I	29,935	226.11	133.84	9,900	59,934	63,383	16,025	20,064	56.15
	II	32,630	236.77	134.01	11,027	57,264	66,679	17,057	20,262	54.32
	III	28,915	206.94	130.76	10,596	52,631	59,573	15,599	18,015	50.34
	IV	32,768	237.11	138.49	10,436	55,739	70,865	17,985	19,990	52.33
1986	I	30,337	218.44	130.28	8,674	54,246	64,482	16,040	17,669	53.66
	II	32,515	222.73	135.02	9,118	51,185	70,131	17,492	18,313	54.47
	III	29,551	199.28	125.94	8,633	45,067	59,617	15,978	16,772	52.83
	IV	32,907	223.90	135.13	8,866	46,479	70,874	17,465	20,263	56.36
1987	I	30,916	212.70	127.26	7,960	46,345	68,034	16,018	19,428	56.15
	II	32,834	219.70	129.33	8,154	46,407	70,966	16,832	19,256	61.69
	III	30,802	209.14	127.47	8,507	44,355	63,114	15,922	19,351	62.22
	IV	35,319	247.91	142.96	8,695	50,467	79,400	18,781	21,681	70.35

Exports by country* (continued)

Year	Quarter	Canada	France	Germany	Japan	Netherlands	Sweden	Switzerland	U.K.	U.S.
1988	I	35,284	239.31	128.21	7,714	48,785	72,420	17,648	19,181	74.86
	II	37,625	253.28	141.21	8,164	50,183	78,770	18,260	20,363	81.86
	III	33,352	234.08	138.86	8,917	49,996	67,600	17,714	20,127	79.08
	IV	38,542	270.99	159.46	9,133	54,765	85,400	20,331	21,806	85.80
1989	I	35,687	284.50	156.19	8,707	56,627	83,400	19,758	21,524	88.87
	II	37,130	293.73	165.25	9,290	58,333	87,600	21,763	22,962	93.80
	III	34,855	260.09	154.38	9,912	53,681	73,900	19,997	22,119	88.70
	IV	35,986	304.65	165.52	9,977	59,320	87,980	22,850	26,599	93.44
1990	I	37,354	308.11	168.88	9,768	60,017	88,090	22,577	25,158	97.37
	II	40,552	295.38	158.74	10,448	58,700	87,800	22,355	26,265	100.74
	III	36,602	265.66	151.90	10,652	56,598	74,100	20,591	24,155	93.88
	IV	39,114	306.75	163.14	10,592	63,606	90,240	22,737	28,054	101.91
1991	I	34,938	299.96	161.96	10,183	63,060	85,110	21,157	24,119	102.63
	II	38,377	308.39	162.28	10,225	61,815	87,950	22,317	26,503	107.82
	III	35,207	287.21	163.73	10,853	59,877	73,360	20,931	25,480	101.60
	IV	37,136	326.13	174.36	11,099	64,070	86,460	23,533	28,717	110.16
1992	I	38,199	325.23	168.66	10,522	63,837	86,010	23,288	25,657	110.21
	II	41,553	322.32	160.83	10,613	62,554	82,330	23,635	27,089	110.29
	III	39,219	286.94	161.10	11,000	58,140	73,710	20,345	25,233	107.63
	IV	43,530	314.19	167.89	10,942	61,119	83,940	22,114	30,311	116.32
1993	I	44,001	289.04	147.70	10,560	N/A	91,300	21,114	29,806	113.82
	II	48,525	300.37	143.71	9,840	N/A	94,810	21,833	29,250	117.74
	III	44,826	277.50	141.93	9,900	N/A	93,710	20,552	N/A	110.21
	IV	49,320	312.39	165.28	9,937	N/A	108,350	23,160	N/A	123.01

*The numbers for France, Germany, Japan, and the United States are expressed in billions of local currency units. The numbers for the remaining countries are expressed in millions of local currency units.

Imports by country*

Year	Quarter	Canada	France	Germany	Japan	Netherlands	Sweden	Switzerland	U.K.	U.S.
1972	I	4,512	33.58	30.56	1,667	13,767	9,492	7,772	2,717	14.09
	II	5,357	34.68	32.59	1,700	14,049	9,460	8,112	2,732	14.56
	III	4,650	30.15	30.39	1,808	13,273	8,883	7,840	2,550	14.33
	IV	5,428	37.60	34.60	2,055	15,150	10,783	8,593	3,156	15.89
1973	I	5,614	39.35	35.64	2,097	16,713	11,236	8,804	3,569	16.91
	II	6,467	41.79	36.39	2,488	16,591	10,800	8,811	3,723	18.32
	III	5,781	38.56	33.33	2,642	16,986	10,780	8,843	3,940	17.98
	IV	7,058	46.43	39.15	3,177	18,376	13,520	10,090	4,608	20.36
1974	I	7,300	59.89	40.89	4,061	21,209	16,200	10,815	5,332	22.65
	II	8,644	68.34	44.85	4,682	23,668	17,000	11,098	5,995	27.68
	III	8,389	61.58	45.44	4,565	23,067	18,850	10,564	5,762	28.49
	IV	9,471	64.36	46.80	4,758	23,168	19,804	10,434	6,028	29.18
1975	I	8,822	59.90	41.71	4,265	22,616	19,520	9,030	5,807	26.28
	II	9,879	57.30	46.24	4,171	22,073	19,002	8,735	5,813	24.73
	III	8,633	50.61	44.39	4,198	20,778	17,573	8,019	5,991	25.37
	IV	9,499	63.37	50.91	4,540	24,416	19,080	8,459	6,460	27.23
1976	I	9,689	70.29	51.96	4,488	24,771	20,000	8,560	6,847	29.34
	II	10,640	76.12	55.32	4,754	26,827	21,230	8,982	7,927	31.65
	III	9,273	73.45	55.28	4,894	25,487	20,010	9,131	7,874	33.73
	IV	10,124	88.25	59.61	5,093	30,157	24,060	10,201	8,923	34.84
1977	I	10,578	89.03	57.71	4,976	29,501	22,512	10,385	9,217	37.76
	II	12,153	88.94	58.56	4,921	28,868	22,221	10,828	9,766	39.73
	III	10,513	78.91	57.37	4,692	26,884	21,088	10,697	8,964	39.41
	IV	11,478	89.48	61.54	4,540	28,958	24,415	11,022	9,049	40.65
1978	I	11,276	93.96	58.60	4,349	28,640	22,043	10,517	9,791	43.14
	II	14,307	94.07	61.78	4,289	29,017	22,696	11,175	10,616	45.99
	III	12,330	82.02	58.58	3,898	27,870	21,319	9,896	9,995	46.02
1979	I	15,763	105.61	66.53	4,680	30,912	26,415	11,225	10,844	48.25
	II	16,743	111.85	71.66	5,579	33,545	29,750	11,698	12,136	53.23
	III	16,335	109.05	72.89	6,364	33,686	30,040	12,167	11,792	56.35
	IV	17,858	128.20	81.08	7,622	38,542	36,757	13,649	13,286	61.09

Imports by country* (continued)

Year	Quarter	Canada	France	Germany	Japan	Netherlands	Sweden	Switzerland	U.K.	U.S.
1980	I	18,067	144.89	86.06	8,043	40,073	36,801	15,590	14,257	65.17
	II	19,031	143.80	85.86	8,655	38,732	32,992	15,086	13,416	64.02
	III	16,678	120.52	81.42	7,588	36,164	34,633	14,691	12,042	59.99
	IV	19,281	150.78	88.04	7,708	40,211	36,210	15,516	11,934	63.82
1981	I	19,931	155.81	91.39	7,528	40,510	34,100	14,568	11,030	68.00
	II	23,170	161.42	90.64	7,904	43,783	34,000	15,081	12,073	69.82
	III	20,389	155.99	91.70	7,847	41,016	34,603	15,198	13,686	66.75
	IV	20,681	181.64	95.50	8,184	43,176	43,015	15,246	14,380	68.78
1982	I	18,693	183.43	96.46	8,307	41,612	40,037	14,160	14,207	64.40
	II	18,331	191.61	95.04	8,008	43,207	39,799	14,696	14,816	63.23
	III	18,481	179.47	89.69	8,021	41,633	40,245	13,943	13,699	65.70
	IV	16,483	203.84	95.28	8,321	45,096	53,851	15,316	14,236	61.55
1983	I	17,941	202.62	93.68	7,413	42,317	48,017	16,497	16,219	60.71
	II	20,245	201.52	95.91	7,213	42,656	47,102	15,471	16,636	66.36
	III	19,698	181.21	95.09	7,307	43,749	47,836	14,700	16,005	69.46
	IV	22,306	214.65	105.52	8,082	48,598	57,391	14,608	17,133	73.35
1984	I	24,194	231.02	108.74	7,999	50,088	53,152	17,318	18,458	82.92
	II	26,744	222.08	106.46	7,872	49,253	53,507	16,949	19,534	84.54
	III	25,354	203.84	105.85	8,211	48,074	50,578	16,778	19,044	90.77
	IV	25,259	243.17	113.16	8,231	52,188	60,400	18,105	21,511	82.95
1985	I	25,505	253.38	120.20	8,335	57,101	62,136	18,425	23,031	87.52
	II	28,804	246.80	115.53	8,097	53,851	62,032	19,277	21,868	92.22
	III	27,334	220.10	133.23	7,532	52,013	57,028	18,058	19,435	88.68
	IV	28,487	246.86	114.86	7,112	52,502	63,413	19,005	20,267	93.21
1986	I	28,450	231.54	108.05	6,335	49,342	55,444	18,339	20,476	97.13
	II	31,310	235.23	106.98	5,398	46,402	59,197	19,238	21,485	94.91
	III	28,876	204.79	96.55	4,758	42,627	54,181	17,812	21,020	96.75
	IV	29,549	224.34	102.63	5,060	46,420	63,661	18,150	23,194	98.29
1987	I	29,411	232.77	99.48	4,959	45,963	60,981	17,979	22,243	97.11
	II	31,314	238.08	101.58	5,207	44,295	62,823	18,769	23,051	105.12
	III	29,366	220.08	99.54	5,644	44,947	60,729	18,260	23,543	108.45
	IV	32,803	258.85	108.87	5,929	48,933	73,067	20,253	25,178	113.40

Imports by country* (continued)

Year	Quarter	Canada	France	Germany	Japan	Netherlands	Sweden	Switzerland	U.K.	U.S.
1988	I	37,304	258.96	103.02	5,688	46,969	67,310	19,378	24,814	110.00
	II	35,001	266.97	107.19	5,918	49,311	68,891	20,493	26,322	114.34
	III	32,054	248.45	107.21	6,280	48,318	65,400	20,572	26,752	114.39
	IV	33,796	288.78	122.34	6,121	51,751	77,660	22,162	28,525	120.55
1989	I	35,623	306.24	120.17	6,516	53,560	75,450	22,291	28,631	117.29
	II	38,352	319.52	130.97	6,969	57,133	80,000	25,082	30,868	124.22
	III	34,547	277.38	120.11	7,542	52,319	68,500	22,749	30,194	123.62
	IV	34,946	327.68	135.40	7,912	57,717	87,280	25,078	31,080	127.18
1990	I	36,637	328.45	132.01	7,941	57,721	81,730	25,390	32,115	124.89
	II	37,745	318.38	130.87	8,391	57,599	78,900	24,947	32,672	124.14
	III	33,078	293.34	132.76	8,364	54,937	73,400	22,640	29,940	129.92
	IV	38,597	333.38	154.93	9,158	58,767	87,320	23,635	30,451	137.20
1991	I	34,363	331.24	156.74	8,243	58,844	74,870	23,477	28,763	120.99
	II	36,888	328.54	164.07	7,775	59,363	75,830	24,672	30,083	124.38
	III	35,141	308.96	158.84	7,846	57,398	70,400	22,852	29,587	129.23
	IV	36,522	334.12	163.45	8,023	59,017	76,640	24,042	30,438	134.35
1992	I	37,798	334.68	163.05	7,312	60,131	74,740	23,871	30,275	127.47
	II	39,826	323.66	156.31	7,470	57,492	71,550	24,142	31,703	143.38
	III	38,049	293.40	149.19	7,386	56,298	67,210	20,638	30,480	142.88
	IV	40,446	316.73	159.65	7,308	58,035	74,980	20,990	33,387	147.38
1993	I	42,100	287.14	138.87	7,024	N/A	79,000	20,581	33,435	140.08
	II	45,982	290.11	131.53	6,698	N/A	80,860	21,260	34,438	150.09
	III	43,749	264.61	129.53	6,528	N/A	78,030	20,324	N/A	153.15
	IV	47,076	294.58	140.39	6,575	N/A	94,040	21,620	N/A	160.11

*The numbers for France, Germany, Japan, and the United States are expressed in billions of local currency units. The numbers for the remaining countries are expressed in millions of local currency units.

Industrial share price index (1980 = 100)

Year	Quarter	Canada	France	Germany	Japan	Netherlands	Sweden	Switzerland	U.K.	U.S.
1972	I	53.4	48.3	104.4	45.7	136.8	71.0	125.9	72.6	86.9
	II	55.4	54.5	114.3	54.3	157.7	74.0	131.1	76.4	89.8
	III	58.8	58.2	113.8	64.4	171.7	76.0	132.0	76.0	90.9
	IV	60.8	56.5	110.2	73.9	171.7	76.0	131.6	74.7	94.6
1973	I	64.7	64.5	116.6	83.2	189.8	77.0	131.6	69.1	95.8
	II	61.6	70.0	111.7	76.3	169.2	80.0	122.1	67.9	89.4
	III	64.4	65.7	99.1	77.5	173.1	78.0	115.7	63.3	87.7
	IV	65.0	62.5	93.8	68.9	152.2	76.0	112.8	58.6	85.4
1974	I	63.3	74.0	91.9	67.5	145.1	84.0	107.6	49.0	79.3
	II	56.9	62.9	92.7	70.1	136.1	85.0	97.0	43.9	76.0
	III	49.6	55.0	85.8	64.2	132.6	80.0	87.2	33.5	63.3
	IV	43.3	51.6	82.0	57.5	114.4	77.0	73.2	26.1	57.7
1975	I	48.2	68.5	94.3	62.5	150.4	82.0	81.2	37.1	65.3
	II	51.5	65.6	100.1	68.8	157.9	86.0	85.3	49.3	74.3
	III	52.0	65.7	98.5	65.5	148.9	89.0	79.3	48.5	73.1
	IV	47.7	68.6	104.3	66.1	141.4	93.0	81.7	55.5	74.2
1976	I	53.2	72.5	94.3	71.4	156.4	99.0	91.3	61.1	83.1
	II	54.8	68.1	100.1	72.3	150.4	109.0	90.0	61.1	85.0
	III	52.5	63.7	98.5	74.6	136.8	103.0	92.2	56.1	86.9
	IV	47.0	55.4	104.3	74.7	127.8	92.0	88.1	49.8	85.1
1977	I	48.4	53.9	112.7	79.9	129.3	96.0	93.2	63.1	84.0
	II	47.4	48.6	108.0	79.4	136.8	94.0	95.3	70.3	81.3
	III	46.3	51.8	103.2	80.4	127.8	83.0	96.2	77.7	80.1
	IV	43.7	54.1	97.5	78.1	121.8	78.0	95.8	81.4	76.8
1978	I	44.5	52.4	99.4	81.2	123.3	88.0	95.0	77.0	73.1
	II	47.8	65.7	105.4	86.6	127.8	93.0	92.0	80.0	78.7
	III	53.9	76.6	104.9	89.3	136.8	98.0	90.7	87.0	63.6
	IV	56.3	77.6	106.2	93.0	129.3	92.0	88.7	85.7	80.2
1979	I	63.1	76.7	111.3	95.6	126.3	96.0	104.6	89.1	82.1
	II	69.4	82.0	106.2	94.4	116.8	90.0	106.3	100.9	83.8
	III	77.8	93.8	103.9	94.8	116.2	90.0	106.4	94.3	87.6
	IV	82.7	92.7	100.9	94.9	107.7	90.0	104.8	90.2	87.7

Industrial share price index (1980 = 100) (continued)

Year	Quarter	Canada	France	Germany	Japan	Netherlands	Sweden	Switzerland	U.K.	U.S.
1980	I	100.4	98.2	100.2	97.7	100.6	96.0	104.4	93.3	92.7
	II	96.4	97.4	99.5	98.1	100.5	97.0	100.1	93.8	90.4
	III	103.6	99.0	101.4	100.2	100.6	97.0	97.1	104.0	103.8
	IV	99.6	105.4	99.0	103.9	98.2	109.0	98.4	109.1	112.9
1981	I	103.0	99.0	96.4	107.4	102.6	123.0	94.9	107.5	111.0
	II	104.4	84.3	103.0	117.4	111.9	139.0	93.2	117.7	111.5
	III	93.2	86.0	104.2	123.1	110.8	159.0	90.9	115.7	105.0
	IV	88.9	82.9	98.1	117.4	98.4	175.0	84.9	110.2	101.4
1982	I	78.6	75.6	99.0	118.1	106.4	173.0	86.2	119.3	94.5
	II	68.2	77.5	99.0	114.7	111.7	166.0	89.6	125.2	94.5
	III	71.9	72.0	96.2	111.5	106.2	179.0	87.4	131.0	94.6
	IV	88.3	74.2	101.6	118.9	119.8	222.0	95.5	147.2	113.5
1983	I	101.2	82.9	113.2	124.9	149.1	309.0	107.8	153.1	123.3
	II	114.9	96.5	133.9	133.3	164.5	346.0	113.7	166.2	135.9
	III	114.8	107.3	139.4	141.7	175.3	384.0	116.3	170.6	138.8
	IV	114.7	117.3	147.7	146.1	181.7	397.0	125.8	169.9	138.8
1984	I	111.8	131.8	152.6	164.9	210.0	430.0	131.9	187.6	134.4
	II	103.3	137.5	148.6	173.3	198.0	399.0	131.0	194.7	131.4
	III	106.6	134.7	144.5	168.4	200.8	386.0	131.5	190.7	135.4
	IV	114.5	141.5	155.8	181.7	219.0	355.0	136.1	211.8	137.7
1985	I	126.7	173.2	170.5	201.3	247.2	365	155.8	235.2	147.2
	II	129.6	188.5	185.9	208.6	266.4	350	162.9	239.9	152.2
	III	131.1	178.8	202.6	215.3	293.9	349	173.1	237.3	155.5
	IV	134.4	187.5	240.7	215.6	325.8	404	195.4	256.5	162.9
1986	I	140.8	234.1	273	229.5	383.9	483	218	280.4	180.5
	II	148.7	284.5	273.3	269.1	415.4	592	212.2	308.4	199.4
	III	140.6	294.5	261.7	309.0	453.6	643	197.3	304.5	198.2
	IV	145.3	309.3	273.5	309.4	437.9	678	209.8	308.8	201.3
1987	I	166.4	331.0	246.6	368.6	395.6	650	206.9	366.1	235.1
	II	174.8	344.8	257.1	447.3	401.3	740	211.5	415.1	253
	III	186.5	350.2	278.9	434.7	496.1	834	245.5	452.9	277.5
	IV	144.4	257.7	213.6	401.0	363.5	637	202.5	353	218.3

Industrial share price index (1980 = 100) (*continued*)

Year	Quarter	Canada	France	Germany	Japan	Netherlands	Sweden	Switzerland	U.K.	U.S.
1988	I	149.7	234.2	188.4	416.3	366.2	710.6	191.8	350.1	221.2
	II	156.8	266.1	199.0	458.4	393.9	776.9	197.5	357.4	226.9
	III	155.4	299.1	214.4	456.7	419.8	817.4	209.7	363.9	228.3
	IV	157.6	337.3	230.4	467.0	423.4	902.1	219.0	358.6	235.4
1989	I	168.3	384.3	244.4	514.9	465.7	1012.6	227.6	396.7	249.7
	II	173.5	407.4	257.6	524.6	499.2	1089.9	241.2	420.9	267.6
	III	186.4	432.5	280.0	546.9	537.0	1215.1	271.9	457.2	290.8
	IV	185.0	428.1	282.2	580.3	523.7	1119.4	258.9	433.2	293.2
1990	I	172.5	446.1	332.2	551.0	513.6	1093.2	250.6	438.0	288.3
	II	163.6	451.0	335.4	485.2	521.7	1148.4	257.1	428.3	303.1
	III	157.3	386.9	300.4	434.2	497.5	1041.7	231.7	416.0	294.7
	IV	148.3	346.8	254.2	368.0	448.5	806.1	206.4	393.0	276.4
1991	I	159.9	362.3	256.0	389.9	468.9	968.1	227.5	422.3	310.3
	II	163.8	396.8	283.2	410.7	529.3	1012.3	245.4	466.0	334.7
	III	163.3	403.7	281.6	376.0	525.6	990.2	246.4	480.3	340.9
	IV	163.7	406.0	265.6	377.1	513.5	890.8	235.6	470.1	339.5
1992	I	165.5	436.5	278.0	328.6	537.0	894.5	252.4	474.9	364.1
	II	158.4	459.1	288.0	279.0	558.9	890.8	260.5	498.1	361.1
	III	158.6	426.1	255.2	269.1	523.3	717.8	247.8	451.3	364.7
	IV	155.8	413.3	230.0	273.7	466.6	773.0	258.8	496.2	369.0
1993	I	161.9	437.1	247.6	276.5	500.5	890.8	284.1	532.2	379.3
	II	181.9	442.2	249.4	336.5	529.0	990.2	304.4	533.4	380.1
	III	189.0	478.8	274.2	347.7	574.3	1163.2	332.1	553.9	381.5
	IV	199.5	510.9	299.0	324.1	635.4	1273.6	378.5	585.3	396.5

Percentage change in industrial share prices

Year	Quarter	Canada	France	Germany	Japan	Netherlands	Sweden	Switzerland	U.K.	U.S.
1972	I	N/A	N/A	N/A	N/A	N/A	N/A	N/A	N/A	N/A
	II	3.75	12.84	9.48	18.82	15.28	4.23	4.13	5.23	3.34
	III	6.14	6.79	-.44	18.60	8.88	2.70	.69	-.52	1.22
	IV	3.40	-2.92	-3.16	14.75	.00	.00	-.30	-1.71	4.07
1973	I	6.41	14.16	5.81	12.58	10.54	1.32	.00	-7.50	1.27
	II	-4.79	8.53	-4.20	-8.29	-10.85	3.90	-7.22	-1.74	-6.68
	III	4.55	-6.14	-11.28	1.57	2.30	-2.50	-5.24	-6.77	-1.90
	IV	.93	-4.87	-5.35	-11.10	-12.07	-2.56	-2.51	-7.42	-2.62
1974	I	-2.62	18.40	-2.03	-2.03	-4.66	10.53	-4.61	-16.38	-7.14
	II	-10.11	-15.00	.87	3.85	-6.20	1.19	-9.85	-10.41	-4.16
	III	-12.83	-12.56	-7.44	-8.42	-2.57	-5.88	-10.10	-23.69	-16.71
	IV	-12.70	-6.18	-4.43	10.44	-13.73	-3.75	-16.06	-22.09	-8.85
1975	I	11.32	32.75	15.00	8.70	31.47	6.49	10.93	42.15	13.17
	II	6.85	-4.23	6.15	10.08	4.99	4.88	5.05	32.88	13.78
	III	.97	.15	-1.60	-4.80	-5.70	3.49	-7.03	-1.62	-1.62
	IV	-8.27	4.41	5.89	.92	-5.04	4.49	3.03	14.43	1.50
1976	I	11.53	5.69	-9.59	8.02	10.61	6.45	11.75	10.09	11.99
	II	3.01	-6.07	6.15	1.26	-3.84	10.10	-1.42	.00	2.29
	III	-4.20	-6.46	-1.60	3.18	-9.04	-5.50	2.44	-8.18	2.24
	IV	-10.48	-13.03	5.89	.13	-6.58	-10.68	-4.45	-11.23	-2.07
1977	I	2.98	-2.71	8.05	6.96	1.17	4.35	5.79	26.71	-1.29
	II	-2.07	-9.83	-4.17	-.63	5.80	-2.08	2.25	11.41	-3.21
	III	-2.32	6.58	-4.44	1.26	-6.58	-11.70	.94	10.53	-1.48
	IV	-5.62	4.44	-5.52	-2.86	-4.69	-6.02	-.42	4.76	-4.12
1978	I	1.83	-3.14	1.95	3.97	1.23	12.82	-.84	-5.41	-4.82
	II	7.42	25.38	6.04	6.65	3.65	5.68	-3.16	3.90	7.66
	III	12.76	16.59	-.47	3.12	7.04	5.38	-1.41	8.75	6.23
	IV	4.45	1.31	1.24	4.14	-5.48	-6.12	-2.21	-1.49	-4.07
1979	I	12.08	-1.16	4.80	2.80	-2.32	4.35	17.93	3.97	2.37
	II	9.98	6.91	-4.58	-1.26	-7.52	-6.25	1.63	13.24	2.07
	III	12.10	14.39	-2.17	.42	-.51	.00	.09	-6.54	4.53
	IV	6.30	-1.17	-2.89	.11	-7.31	.00	-1.50	-4.35	.11

Percentage change in industrial share prices (*continued*)

Year	Quarter	Canada	France	Germany	Japan	Netherlands	Sweden	Switzerland	U.K.	U.S.
1980	I	21.40	5.93	-.69	-2.95	-6.59	6.67	-.38	3.44	5.70
	II	-3.98	-.81	-.70	.41	-.10	1.04	-4.12	.54	-2.48
	III	7.47	1.64	1.91	2.14	.10	.00	-3.00	10.87	14.82
	IV	-3.86	6.46	-2.37	3.69	-2.39	12.37	1.34	4.90	8.77
1981	I	3.41	-6.07	-2.63	3.37	4.48	12.84	-3.56	-1.47	-1.68
	II	1.36	-14.85	6.85	9.31	9.06	13.01	-1.79	9.49	.45
	III	-10.37	2.02	1.17	4.86	-.98	14.39	-2.47	-1.70	-5.83
	IV	-4.61	-3.60	-5.85	-4.63	-11.19	10.06	-6.60	-4.75	-3.43
1982	I	-11.59	-8.81	.92	.60	8.13	-1.14	1.53	8.26	-6.80
	II	-13.23	2.51	.00	-2.88	4.98	-4.05	3.94	4.95	.00
	III	5.43	-7.10	-2.83	-2.79	-4.92	7.83	-2.46	4.63	.11
	IV	-22.81	3.06	5.61	6.64	12.81	24.02	9.27	12.37	19.98
1983	I	14.61	11.73	11.42	5.05	24.46	39.19	12.88	4.01	8.63
	II	13.54	16.41	18.29	6.73	10.33	11.97	5.47	8.56	10.22
	III	-.09	11.19	4.11	6.30	6.57	10.98	2.29	2.65	2.13
	IV	-.09	9.32	5.95	3.11	3.65	3.39	8.17	-.41	.00
1984	I	-2.53	12.36	3.32	12.87	15.58	8.31	4.85	10.42	-3.17
	II	-7.60	4.42	-2.62	5.09	-5.71	-7.21	-.68	3.78	-2.23
	III	3.19	-2.04	-2.76	-2.83	1.41	-3.26	.38	-2.05	3.04
	IV	7.41	5.05	7.82	7.60	9.06	-8.03	3.50	11.06	1.70
1985	I	10.66	22.40	9.44	10.79	12.88	2.53	14.48	11.05	6.90
	II	2.29	8.83	9.03	9.03	7.77	-4.11	4.56	1.99	3.40
	III	1.16	5.15	8.98	8.98	10.32	-.29	6.26	-1.08	2.17
	IV	2.52	4.87	18.81	.14	10.85	15.76	12.88	8.09	4.76
1986	I	4.76	24.85	13.42	6.45	17.83	19.56	11.77	9.32	10.80
	II	5.61	21.19	.11	17.26	8.21	22.57	-.26	9.99	10.80
	III	-5.76	3.51	-4.24	14.83	9.20	8.62	-.70	-1.27	-.60
	IV	3.34	5.03	4.51	.13	-3.46	5.44	6.34	1.41	1.56
1987	I	-14.52	7.02	-9.84	19.13	-9.66	-4.13	-1.38	18.56	16.79
	II	5.05	4.17	4.26	21.35	1.44	13.85	-2.19	13.38	7.61
	III	6.69	1.57	8.48	-2.82	23.62	12.70	16.08	9.11	9.68
	IV	-22.57	-26.41	-23.41	-7.75	-26.73	-23.62	-17.52	-22.06	-21.33

Percentage change in industrial share prices (*continued*)

Year	Quarter	Canada	France	Germany	Japan	Netherlands	Sweden	Switzerland	U.K.	U.S.
1988	I	3.67	-9.12	-11.80	3.82	0.74	11.55	-5.28	-0.82	1.33
	II	4.74	13.62	5.63	10.11	7.56	9.33	2.97	2.09	2.58
	III	-.89	12.40	7.74	-0.37	6.58	5.21	6.18	1.82	0.62
	IV	1.41	12.77	7.46	2.26	0.86	10.36	4.43	-1.46	3.11
1989	I	6.78	13.93	6.08	10.26	9.99	12.25	3.93	10.87	6.07
	II	3.09	6.01	5.40	1.88	7.19	7.63	5.98	10.61	7.17
	III	7.37	6.16	8.70	4.25	7.57	11.49	12.73	8.62	8.67
	IV	-.75	-1.02	0.79	6.11	-2.48	-7.88	-4.78	-5.24	0.83
1990	I	-6.75	4.20	18.07	-5.05	-1.92	-2.32	-3.20	1.11	-1.67
	II	-5.16	1.10	.96	-11.94	1.58	5.05	2.59	-2.21	5.13
	III	-3.85	-14.21	-10.43	-10.47	-4.63	-9.29	-9.88	-2.87	-2.77
	IV	-5.72	-10.36	-15.38	-15.20	-9.84	-22.62	-10.92	-5.52	-6.21
1991	I	7.82	4.47	0.71	5.95	4.55	20.10	10.21	7.44	12.26
	II	2.47	9.51	10.62	5.33	12.88	4.56	7.86	10.35	7.86
	III	-0.31	1.75	-0.56	-8.44	-0.70	-2.18	0.42	3.06	1.85
	IV	0.23	0.57	-5.68	0.28	-2.30	-10.04	-4.40	-2.11	-0.41
1992	I	1.09	7.52	4.6	-12.87	4.58	0.41	7.15	1.03	7.23
	II	-4.30	5.17	3.60	-15.09	4.06	-0.41	3.20	4.88	-0.81
	III	0.16	-7.20	-11.39	-3.54	-6.37	-19.42	-4.88	-9.41	0.98
	IV	-1.76	-3.00	-9.87	1.72	-10.84	7.69	4.44	9.96	1.19
1993	I	3.92	5.76	7.65	1.00	7.27	15.24	9.77	7.25	2.80
	II	12.33	1.18	0.73	21.73	5.70	11.16	7.14	0.23	0.20
	III	3.92	8.27	9.94	3.31	8.5	17.47	9.10	3.85	0.37
	IV	5.52	6.71	9.04	-6.77	10.64	9.49	13.98	5.67	3.93

Exchange rates* (end of period)

Year	Quarter	Canadian Dollar	French Franc	German Mark	Japanese Yen	Netherlands Guilder	Swedish Kronor	Swiss Franc	British Pound
1972	I	1.0031	.1920	.3157	.003287	.3131	.2094	.2604	2.6158
	II	1.0149	.1999	.3169	.003321	.3152	.2122	.2650	2.4440
	III	1.0169	.1995	.3123	.003321	.3090	.2108	.2631	2.4203
	IV	1.0044	.1951	.3123	.003311	.3100	.2108	.2650	2.3481
1973	I	1.0010	.2202	.3524	.003762	.3397	.2226	.3089	2.4777
	II	1.0016	.2436	.4124	.003769	.3817	.2445	.3378	2.5820
	III	.9942	.2353	.4132	.003764	.3945	.2380	.3309	2.4135
	IV	1.0046	.2124	.3700	.003571	.3541	.2180	.3083	2.3232
1974	I	1.0284	.2099	.3964	.003623	.3724	.2277	.3333	2.3940
	II	1.0286	.2073	.3914	.003520	.3771	.2283	.3336	2.3905
	III	1.0144	.2109	.3769	.003350	.3698	.2242	.3394	2.3323
	IV	1.0089	.2250	.4150	.003323	.3990	.2451	.3937	2.3485
1975	I	.9968	.2372	.4264	.003404	.4176	.2537	.3956	2.4090
	II	.9703	.2475	.4247	.003374	.4098	.2538	.3996	2.1980
	III	.9754	.2205	.3757	.003304	.3655	.2218	.3640	2.0409
	IV	.9839	.2229	.3813	.003277	.3720	.2280	.3817	2.0235
1976	I	1.0161	.2142	.3940	.003337	.3722	.2272	.3946	1.9157
	II	1.0324	.2110	.3885	.003362	.3656	.2247	.4044	1.7813
	III	1.0275	.2030	.4104	.003479	.3893	.2335	.4075	1.6775
	IV	.9909	.2012	.4233	.003415	.4070	.2423	.4081	1.7024
1977	I	.9463	.2012	.4186	.003604	.4013	.2382	.3933	1.7201
	II	.9435	.2033	.4277	.003736	.4044	.2274	.4064	1.7202
	III	.9316	.2039	.4334	.003767	.4071	.2069	.4276	1.7465
	IV	.9137	.2125	.4751	.004167	.4386	.2142	.5000	1.9060
1978	I	.8832	.2183	.4943	.004496	.4622	.2179	.5352	1.8563
	II	.8893	.2221	.4819	.004885	.4479	.2186	.5381	1.8602
	III	.8452	.2309	.5158	.005287	.4747	.2271	.6481	1.9721
	IV	.8432	.2392	.5470	.005139	.5079	.2328	.6173	2.0345
1979	I	.8616	.2327	.5354	.004778	.4965	.2288	.5914	2.0688
	II	.8563	.2334	.5411	.004608	.4926	.2337	.6020	2.1684
	III	.8616	.2439	.5739	.004478	.5177	.2422	.6521	2.1976
	IV	.8561	.2488	.5775	.004172	.5248	.2412	.6329	2.2240

Exchange rates* (end of period) (continued)

Year	Quarter	Canadian Dollar	French Franc	German Mark	Japanese Yen	Netherlands Guilder	Swedish Kronor	Swiss Franc	British Pound
1980	I	.8393	.2233	.5150	.004005	.4701	.2244	.5459	2.1668
	II	.8688	.2447	.5688	.004596	.5188	.2409	.6167	2.3620
	III	.8543	.2381	.5521	.004713	.5088	.2402	.6066	2.3883
	IV	.8370	.2214	.5105	.004926	.4696	.2287	.5679	2.3850
1981	I	.8426	.2017	.4758	.004739	.4296	.2177	.5229	2.2442
	II	.8330	.1749	.4183	.004429	.3757	.1967	.4927	1.9428
	III	.8286	.1796	.4306	.004297	.3873	.1786	.5072	1.8005
	IV	.8432	.1740	.4435	.004548	.4051	.1795	.5560	1.9080
1982	I	.8128	.1602	.4142	.004057	.3735	.1680	.5170	1.7817
	II	.7734	.1464	.4065	.003937	.3676	.1641	.4754	1.7383
	III	.8089	.1401	.3956	.003711	.3618	.1590	.4613	1.6927
	IV	.8134	.1487	.4208	.004255	.3810	.1371	.5014	1.6145
1983	I	.8104	.1376	.4121	.004177	.3658	.1332	.4804	1.4790
	II	.8148	.1309	.3934	.004172	.3511	.1308	.4752	1.5304
	III	.8115	.1249	.3789	.004235	.3390	.1278	.4695	1.4957
	IV	.8036	.1198	.3671	.004307	.3263	.1250	.4588	1.4506
1984	I	.7835	.1253	.3861	.004450	.3423	.1296	.4644	1.4426
	II	.7579	.1170	.3592	.004211	.3171	.1222	.4291	1.3527
	III	.7587	.1077	.3305	.004073	.2933	.1165	.4003	1.2480
	IV	.7568	.1043	.3177	.003982	.2817	.1112	.3868	1.1565
1985	I	.7315	.1061	.3233	.003960	.2872	.1125	.3820	1.2430
	II	.7360	.1073	.3267	.004017	.2902	.1136	.3904	1.2952
	III	.7294	.1227	.3746	.004608	.3315	.1240	.4585	1.4010
	IV	.7156	.1323	.4063	.004988	.3608	.1313	.4816	1.4445
1986	I	.7157	.1402	.4315	.005568	.3827	.1366	.5155	1.485
	II	.7211	.1426	.4548	.006061	.4040	.1405	.5569	1.5302
	III	.7202	.1510	.4949	.006510	.4377	.1449	.6104	1.4500
	IV	.7244	.1549	.5153	.006285	.4562	.1467	.6160	1.4745
1987	I	.7662	.1663	.5540	.006859	.4907	.1581	.6640	1.6049
	II	.7512	.1638	.5465	.006802	.4857	.1565	.6579	1.6101
	III	.7639	.1635	.5440	.006833	.4838	.1553	.6540	1.6297
	IV	.8131	.1873	.6309	.008097	.5626	.1709	.7825	1.8716

Exchange rates* (end of period) *(continued)*

Year	Quarter	Canadian Dollar	French Franc	German Mark	Japanese Yen	Netherlands Guilder	Swedish Kronor	Swiss Franc	British Pound
1988	I	.8103	.1778	.6027	.007970	.5368	.1701	.735	1.8798
	II	.8246	.1628	.5491	.007550	.4866	.1599	.6625	1.7093
	III	.8216	.1564	.5320	.007430	.4721	.1554	.6291	1.6855
	IV	.8384	.1650	.5617	.007950	.5001	.1624	.6649	1.8095
1989	I	.8381	.1564	.5283	.007570	.4684	.1557	.6024	1.6888
	II	.8345	.1507	.5122	.006940	.4541	.1504	.5977	1.5502
	III	.8487	.1578	.5352	.007180	.4739	.1560	.6180	1.6252
	IV	.8632	.1727	.5889	.006971	.5220	.1605	.6468	1.6055
1990	I	.8545	.1755	.5903	.006361	.5241	.1632	.6684	1.6428
	II	.8575	.1782	.5980	.006540	.5319	.1656	.7057	1.7418
	III	.8666	.1915	.6411	.007345	.5691	.1739	.7716	1.8812
	IV	.8625	.1962	.6685	.007417	.5937	.1772	.7832	1.9255
1991	I	.8635	.1759	.5951	.007153	.5283	.1641	.6967	1.7616
	II	.8763	.1645	.5584	.007237	.4958	.1540	.6519	1.6351
	III	0.8837	0.1765	0.6013	0.007527	0.5337	0.1648	0.6899	1.7525
	IV	0.8654	0.1931	0.6596	0.007987	0.5847	0.1808	0.7377	1.8707
1992	I	0.8404	0.1796	0.6088	0.007508	0.5409	0.1673	0.6673	1.7392
	II	0.8355	0.1948	0.6549	0.007968	0.5811	0.1814	0.7260	1.8980
	III	0.8013	0.2099	0.7096	0.008389	0.6296	0.1890	0.8133	1.7827
	IV	0.7867	0.1816	0.6196	0.008016	0.5512	0.1420	0.6868	1.5120
1993	I	0.7954	0.1825	0.6195	0.008595	0.5508	0.1291	0.6689	1.5035
	II	0.7798	0.1756	0.5923	0.009368	0.5281	0.1298	0.6625	1.5087
	III	0.7486	0.1766	0.6173	0.009510	0.5485	0.1244	0.7055	1.5107
	IV	0.7553	0.1696	0.5793	0.008941	0.5152	0.1204	0.6759	1.4812

*Value in U.S. dollars.

Exchange rate percentage change

Year	Quarter	Canadian Dollar	French Franc	German Mark	Japanese Yen	Netherlands Guilder	Swedish Kronor	Swiss Franc	British Pound
1972	I	N/A	N/A	N/A	N/A	N/A	N/A	N/A	N/A
	II	1.18	4.12	.38	1.03	.66	1.36	1.75	-6.57
	III	.19	-.20	-1.44	.00	-1.95	.67	-.71	-.97
	IV	-1.23	2.20	.00	-.30	.31	.03	.72	-2.98
1973	I	-.34	12.86	12.83	13.61	9.58	5.56	16.59	5.52
	II	.06	10.62	17.03	.20	12.37	9.86	9.36	4.21
	III	-.74	-3.41	.21	-.15	3.35	-2.67	-2.05	-6.53
	IV	1.04	-9.73	-10.47	-5.11	-10.23	-8.40	-6.84	-3.74
1974	I	2.37	-1.18	7.13	1.45	5.18	4.44	8.13	3.05
	II	.02	-1.22	-1.25	-2.85	1.24	.29	.07	-.15
	III	-1.38	1.73	-3.69	-4.82	-1.92	-1.79	1.77	-2.43
	IV	-.54	6.67	10.11	-.81	7.88	9.30	15.98	.69
1975	I	-1.20	5.43	2.75	2.43	4.68	3.51	.49	2.58
	II	-2.66	4.34	-.42	-.86	-1.86	.06	1.00	-8.76
	III	.53	-10.93	-11.52	-2.10	-10.02	-12.01	-8.92	-7.15
	IV	.87	1.12	1.49	-.80	1.77	2.79	4.87	-.85
1976	I	3.27	-3.93	3.31	1.82	.07	-.34	3.39	-5.33
	II	1.61	-1.50	-1.39	.77	-1.79	-1.14	2.47	-7.02
	III	-.47	-3.79	5.65	3.46	6.50	3.93	.77	-5.83
	IV	-3.57	-.86	3.13	-1.83	4.54	3.79	.15	1.48
1977	I	-4.50	.01	-1.10	5.51	-1.40	-1.70	-3.62	1.04
	II	-.29	1.02	2.17	3.66	.79	-4.56	3.32	.01
	III	-1.26	.33	1.33	.85	.65	-8.98	5.23	1.53
	IV	-1.92	4.21	9.62	10.60	7.74	3.50	16.92	9.13
1978	I	-3.34	2.72	4.05	7.91	5.38	1.76	7.04	-2.61
	II	.68	1.75	-2.52	8.65	-3.09	.29	.55	.21
	III	-4.95	3.94	7.05	8.22	5.98	3.89	20.43	6.02
	IV	-.24	3.61	6.05	-2.80	6.98	2.53	-4.75	3.16
1979	I	2.19	-2.72	-2.12	-7.02	-2.23	-1.74	-4.20	1.69
	II	-.62	.28	1.05	-3.55	-.79	2.15	1.79	4.81
	III	.62	4.50	6.07	-2.82	5.10	3.65	8.33	1.35
	IV	-.64	2.00	.64	-6.84	1.36	-.42	-2.94	1.20

Exchange rate percentage change (*continued*)

Year	Quarter	Canadian Dollar	French Franc	German Mark	Japanese Yen	Netherlands Guilder	Swedish Kronor	Swiss Franc	British Pound
1980	I	-1.96	-10.24	-10.83	-4.00	-10.41	-6.96	-13.76	-2.57
	II	3.51	9.58	10.45	14.75	10.35	7.39	12.98	9.01
	III	-1.67	-2.68	-2.93	2.54	-1.93	-.31	-1.64	1.11
	IV	-2.03	-7.01	-7.54	4.53	-7.70	-4.79	-6.39	-.14
1981	I	.67	-8.91	-6.79	-8.79	-8.53	-4.78	-7.92	-5.90
	II	-1.14	-13.28	-12.09	-6.55	-12.55	-9.69	-5.78	-13.43
	III	-.52	2.70	2.95	-2.97	3.10	-9.16	2.96	-7.32
	IV	1.76	-3.15	3.00	5.82	4.60	-.48	9.62	5.97
1982	I	-3.61	-7.91	-6.60	-10.79	-7.81	-6.39	-7.02	-6.62
	II	-4.85	-8.60	-1.85	-2.95	-1.56	-2.31	-8.05	-2.44
	III	4.59	-4.33	-2.68	-5.75	-1.59	-3.16	-2.96	-2.62
	IV	.56	6.14	6.35	14.68	5.32	-13.76	8.68	-4.62
1983	I	-.36	-7.49	-2.06	-1.84	-3.99	-2.86	-4.19	-8.39
	II	.54	-4.82	-4.54	-.13	-4.04	-1.75	-1.08	3.48
	III	-.41	-4.64	-3.68	1.52	-3.44	-2.29	-1.18	-2.27
	IV	-.97	-4.06	-3.11	1.68	-3.74	-2.24	-2.28	-3.02
1984	I	-2.51	4.61	5.17	3.34	4.91	3.69	1.22	-.55
	II	-3.26	-6.61	-6.98	-5.39	-7.37	-5.72	-7.60	-6.23
	III	.11	-7.97	-7.97	-3.26	-7.52	-4.65	-6.72	-7.74
	IV	-.26	-3.21	-3.90	-2.23	-3.93	-4.52	-3.37	-7.33
1985	I	-3.34	1.73	1.76	-.55	1.96	1.16	-1.24	7.47
	II	.90	1.31	1.05	1.43	1.04	.97	2.20	4.20
	III	-.89	14.35	14.66	14.71	15.42	9.15	17.44	8.17
	IV	-1.89	7.82	8.46	8.24	8.83	5.89	5.04	3.11
1986	I	.01	5.97	6.20	11.62	6.07	4.04	7.04	2.80
	II	.77	1.71	5.39	8.85	5.56	2.85	8.03	3.04
	III	-.12	5.89	8.82	7.40	8.34	3.14	9.61	-5.24
	IV	.58	2.58	4.12	-3.45	4.22	1.24	.91	1.69
1987	I	5.77	7.35	7.51	9.13	7.56	7.77	7.79	8.85
	II	-1.95	-1.50	-1.35	-.83	-1.01	-1.01	-.91	.32
	III	1.69	-.18	-.18	.45	-.39	-.76	-.59	1.21
	IV	6.44	14.55	15.97	18.49	16.28	10.04	18.74	14.84

Exchange rate percentage change (*continued*)

Year	Quarter	Canadian Dollar	French Franc	German Mark	Japanese Yen	Netherlands Guilder	Swedish Kronor	Swiss Franc	British Pound
1988	I	-.34	6.28	-4.47	-1.57	-4.59	-.47	-6.07	.44
	II	1.76	-8.44	-8.89	-5.27	-9.35	-6.00	-9.86	-9.07
	III	-.36	-3.93	-3.11	-1.59	-2.98	-2.81	-5.04	-1.39
	IV	2.04	5.50	5.58	7.00	5.93	4.50	5.69	7.36
1989	I	-.04	-5.21	-5.95	-4.78	-6.34	-4.13	-9.40	-6.67
	II	-.43	-3.64	-3.05	-8.32	-3.05	-3.40	-.78	-8.21
	III	1.70	4.71	4.49	3.46	4.36	3.72	3.40	4.84
	IV	1.70	9.44	10.00	-2.91	10.10	2.88	4.66	-1.21
1990	I	-1.00	1.62	.24	-8.75	.40	1.68	3.33	2.32
	II	.35	1.54	1.30	2.81	1.49	1.47	5.58	6.03
	III	1.06	7.46	7.19	12.31	6.99	5.01	9.34	8.00
	IV	-.47	2.45	4.27	.98	11.62	1.90	1.50	2.35
1991	I	.11	-10.34	-10.98	-3.56	-11.01	-7.39	-11.04	-8.51
	II	1.48	-6.48	-6.17	1.17	-6.15	-6.15	-6.43	-7.18
	III	.84	7.29	7.68	4.01	7.64	7.01	5.83	7.18
	IV	-2.07	9.41	9.70	6.11	9.56	9.71	6.93	6.74
1992	I	-2.89	-6.99	-7.70	-6.00	-7.49	-7.47	-9.54	-7.03
	II	-.58	8.46	7.57	6.13	7.43	8.43	8.80	9.13
	III	-4.09	7.75	8.35	5.28	8.35	4.19	12.02	-6.07
	IV	-1.82	-13.48	-12.69	-4.45	-12.45	-24.88	-15.55	-15.18
1993	I	1.11	0.50	-0.02	7.22	-0.08	-9.07	-2.61	-0.56
	II	-1.96	-3.79	-4.38	8.99	-4.13	0.50	-0.96	0.35
	III	-4.01	0.57	4.22	1.52	3.88	-4.16	6.49	0.13
	IV	0.89	-3.94	-6.16	-5.99	-6.07	-3.16	-4.19	-1.95

3-month forward rates* (End of period)

Year	Quarter	Canadian Dollar	French Franc	German Mark	Japanese Yen	Swiss Franc	British Pound
1974	I	1.02988	.20291	.38091	.00337	.32405	2.2882
	II	1.03664	.20220	.39952	.00354	.33662	2.3688
	III	1.01683	.20578	.37924	.00335	.33547	2.3039
	IV	1.01254	.21512	.40999	.00331	.38468	2.2931
1975	I	1.00114	.23667	.43365	.00348	.40639	2.3849
	II	.97177	.24794	.42918	.00341	.40363	2.2562
	III	.97099	.22339	.38559	.00332	.37337	2.0661
	IV	.97969	.22419	.38410	.00326	.38286	1.9982
1976	I	1.00352	.21290	.39296	.00333	.39390	1.9238
	II	1.01881	.20908	.39041	.00334	.41061	1.7348
	III	1.01535	.20081	.40249	.00348	.40861	1.6933
	IV	.97291	.19712	.41990	.00338	.41148	1.6368
1977	I	.94541	.19798	.41886	.00356	.39409	1.6896
	II	.94238	.20043	.42686	.00366	.40390	1.7015
	III	.93011	.20159	.43343	.03376	.42551	1.7431
	IV	.91073	.20548	.46913	.00419	.48834	1.8569
1978	I	.88793	.21054	.49697	.00439	.53703	1.9055
	II	.89181	.21751	.48608	.00474	.54011	1.8221
	III	.85806	.22938	.51453	.00535	.65022	1.9426
	IV	.84996	.23346	.54363	.00524	.61573	1.9792
1979	I	.85112	.23493	.54643	.00492	.61134	2.0311
	II	.85194	.22891	.53683	.00463	.60218	2.0976
	III	.85949	.23824	.56528	.00457	.63809	2.1847
	IV	.85643	.24650	.58508	.00423	.64019	2.1907
1980	I	.86201	.23467	.55399	.00407	.58561	2.2094
	II	.86379	.24152	.56619	.00457	.61884	2.2973
	III	.86166	.24050	.56375	.00467	.62060	2.3813
	IV	.84208	.22351	.52037	.00490	.57966	2.3747
1981	I	.83674	.20294	.47837	.00488	.52989	2.2487
	II	.82852	.17504	.42680	.00458	.49307	2.0028
	III	.82778	.17505	.43158	.00448	.50445	1.8312
	IV	.83812	.17347	.44612	.00465	.55650	1.8968

3-month forward rates* (End of period) (continued)

Year	Quarter	Canadian Dollar	French Franc	German Mark	Japanese Yen	Swiss Franc	British Pound
1982	I	.81767	.16110	.42652	.00424	.54191	1.8148
	II	.78203	.15012	.41891	.00407	.49445	1.7700
	III	.80595	.13902	.40368	.00385	.47716	1.7186
	IV	.80515	.14161	.41702	.00416	.49563	1.6159
1983	I	.81536	.13748	.41996	.00423	.49221	1.4865
	II	.81238	.12909	.39699	.00420	.47984	1.5505
	III	.81294	.12270	.37891	.00416	.46915	1.5001
	IV	.80312	.11848	.36761	.00431	.46242	1.4391
1984	I	.78811	.12360	.38998	.00449	.47411	1.4633
	II	.76721	.11855	.37068	.00434	.44697	1.3865
	III	.76019	.10783	.33556	.00413	.40664	1.2612
	IV	.75635	.10481	.32501	.00406	.39477	1.1851
1985	I	.73201	.10560	.32717	.00450	.38833	1.2653
	II	.73324	.10663	.32848	.00403	.39392	1.2874
	III	.72626	.12202	.37781	.00465	.46226	1.4046
	IV	.70451	.13197	.40932	.00499	.49611	1.4466
1986	I	.71103	.14321	.43439	.00560	.51861	1.4863
	II	.72033	.14515	.45720	.00613	.56026	1.5360
	III	.71615	.15369	.49655	.00656	.61345	1.4456
	IV	.70512	.15793	.51685	.00628	.61960	1.4715
1987	I	.76509	.16572	.55741	.00691	.66930	1.5981
	II	.74838	.16333	.55095	.00687	.66353	1.5982
	III	.75964	.16355	.54883	.00689	.66128	1.6200
	IV	.8082	.1867	.6365	.008256	.7912	1.8642
1988	I	.8062	.1778	.6081	.008121	.7438	1.8704
	II	.8209	.1629	.5538	.007633	.6709	1.7007
	III	.8179	.1567	.5365	.007514	.6356	1.6720
	IV	.8355	.1653	.5667	.008037	.6699	1.7932
1989	I	.8343	.1569	.5334	.007578	.6105	1.6787
	II	.8295	.1511	.5149	.007013	.6002	1.5531
	III	.8427	.1554	.5372	.007242	.6205	1.6041
	IV	.8548	.1702	.5933	.006954	.6454	1.5961

3-month forward rates* (End of period) (*continued*)

Year	Quarter	Canadian Dollar	French Franc	German Mark	Japanese Yen	Swiss Franc	British Pound
1990	I	.8451	.1745	.5917	.006329	.6661	1.6221
	II	.8443	.1789	.6026	.006583	.7052	1.7207
	III	.8562	.1915	.6409	.007244	.7735	1.8511
	IV	.8556	.1956	.6653	.007426	.7816	1.8975
1991	I	.8564	.1753	.5909	.007133	.6931	1.7362
	II	.8710	.1624	.5543	.007209	.6482	1.6153
	III	0.8776	0.17429	0.5937	0.007487	0.6824	1.7263
	IV	0.8628	0.18832	0.6446	0.007996	0.7249	1.8346
1992	I	0.8337	0.17594	0.5973	0.007427	0.6546	1.6972
	II	0.8276	0.19215	0.6475	0.007965	0.7206	1.8768
	III	0.7933	0.20303	0.6923	0.008334	0.7964	1.7083
	IV	0.7796	0.17723	0.6095	0.008003	0.6777	1.5013
1993	I	0.7906	0.17999	0.6145	0.008708	0.6684	1.5027
	II	0.7777	0.17214	0.5791	0.009335	0.6570	1.4817
	III	0.7468	0.17381	0.6072	0.009452	0.6694	1.4867
	IV	0.7546	0.16799	0.5723	0.008988	0.6722	1.4724
1994	I	0.7191	0.17418	0.5955	0.009792	0.7078	1.4797

*Value in U.S. dollars

INDEX

Movements of Major Currencies against the Dollar

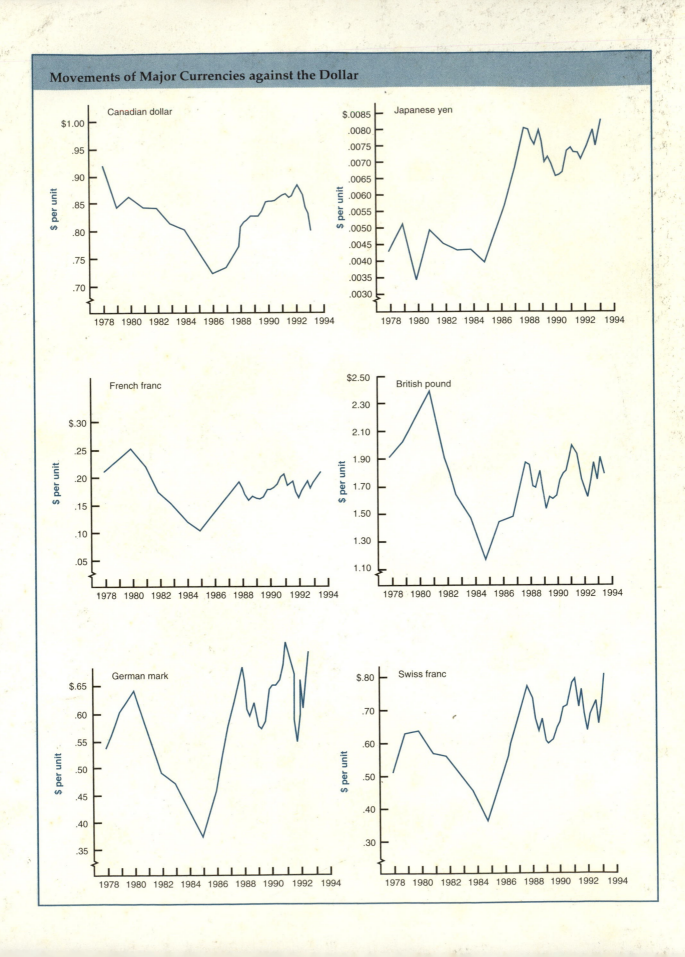